ENCYCLOPEDIA OF 20TH-CENTURY ARCHITECTURE

ENCYCLOPEDIA OF 20TH-CENTURY ARCHITECTURE

Volume 2
G–O

R. Stephen Sennott, Editor

Fitzroy Dearborn

New York   London

Editorial Staff
Sponsoring Editor: Marie-Claire Antoine
Development Editor: Lynn M. Somers-Davis
Editorial Assistant: Mary Funchion
Production Editor: Jeanne Shu

Published in 2004 by
Fitzroy Dearborn
An imprint of the Taylor & Francis Group
29 West 35th Street
New York, NY 10001

Published in Great Britain by
Fitzroy Dearborn
An imprint of the Taylor & Francis Group
11 New Fetter Lane
London EC4P 4EE

10 9 8 7 6 5 4 3 2 1

Library of Congress Cataloging-in-Publication Data

Encyclopedia of 20th-century architecture / R. Stephen Sennott, editor.
     p. cm.
Includes bibliographical references and index.
    ISBN 1-57958-243-5 (set : alk. paper) — ISBN 1-57958-433-0 (vol. 1 :
alk. paper) — ISBN 1-57958-434-9 (vol. 2 : alk. paper) — ISBN 1-57958-435-7
(vol. 3 : alk. paper)
    1. Architecture, Modern—20th century—Encyclopedias.   I. Title:
Encyclopedia of twentieth-century architecture. II. Sennott, Stephen.
    NA680.E495 2004
    724′.6′03—dc22

                                        2003015674

ISBN   1–57958–243–5 (Set)

Printed in the United States on acid-free paper.

CONTENTS

G

GABR, ALI LABIB 1898–1966

Architect, Egypt

Ali Labib Gabr belongs to the second generation of Egyptian architects, which was provided with significant professional opportunities by the Egyptianization policies adopted after Independence in 1922. Besides numerous residential buildings in Cairo and Alexandria (villas and blocks of flats), Gabr designed large scale housing schemes for industrial workers, together with several factories, hospitals, hotels and institutional buildings. In contrast with the earlier generation, Gabr was not concerned with the search for a distinctive "national style" for Egypt—although some of his buildings may recall the massiveness of Ancient Egypt architecture, e.g. the Lawyers' Syndicate in Cairo (1948). He rather worked at the diffusion of western contemporary forms in the country. His own inclination was towards a moderate modernism, or better a modern classicism, much in line with the bulk of inter-war architecture in Europe, particularly Great Britain and France; he was typically linked to members of the Réunions Internationaux d'Architectes, the rival organization of the CIAM (Congrès Internationaux d'Architecture moderne) that was to gave birth to the IUA (International Union of Architects). However Gabr was indeed much interested in Egyptian heritage, either pharaonic or Islamic, as his many sketches of details from Cairo's old quarters or monuments of Upper Egypt show. When preparing a project, he is also known to have paid acute attention to its function and future uses; his work is moreover characterized by remarkable execution, an exceptional achievement in the Egyptian context.

Educated at the Khedivial school, at the time one of the best public schools in Cairo, Gabr graduated in 1920 from the Architectural Department of the Cairo's Polytechnical School. The same year he was granted a governmental scholarship to complete his studies at the Liverpool University's School of Architecture, by then the leading one in Britain. Already a talented draughtsman, Gabr impressed much the teaching staff during his 4-years stay there: the working designs for a large "Repertory Theatre for Cairo" that he submitted for his thesis in 1924 were considered as "the best set ever submitted to the school," by Sir Charles-Herbert Reilly, with whom Gabr was to stay in contact. After a few months of practical training in the offices of the Nicholas and Dixon-Spain's firm in London, Gabr returned to Egypt, where he was appointed assistant-lecturer at the Architectural Department of the Polytechnical school in Cairo, then lecturer (1927), and professor (1930), acting subsequently as its Dean (1934–55). A committed teacher, Gabr did much to improve the architectural curriculum at the Polytechnical School; through his acute knowledge of architectural developments in Europe, where he regularly traveled, combined with his photographic skills (one of his hobbies, with music), he was moreover able to give his many students a solid culture on current international trends and ideas.

From 1928 onwards, Gabr was engaged in private practice. His first villas, in the typical Italianate manner of the time, reveal an early involvement with ornamental Art Deco—as in the Muhammad Rida Bey's mansion in Zamalek, Cairo (c.1930)—which did not lasted long as he soon moved towards simplified forms, made of horizontal lines and audacious semi-circular overhanging, as best exemplified by the restrained villa of the famous Egyptian singer 'Umm Kulthum (1935) in Cairo or the Makram Ebeid's villa in Alexandria (1936). His later works show more sensitivity to the cubism and plasticism of the Dutch School, and especially of Willem Dudok, of which he is known to have been a great admirer.

The opportunity to develop his conceptions into a large scale came in 1946, when he was commissioned by the Misr Spinning and Weaving Company with the design and execution of a workers' housing scheme in Mahalla al-Kubra, Lower Egypt, in collaboration with Ali al-Maligi Massa'ud, a member of the Royal Town Planning Institute in London, for the planning aspects of the project. The first of its kind in Egypt, the scheme was provided with the most up-to-date social, sporting and recreational facilities (stadium, gymnasium, swimming-pool, club, open-air cinema, public laundries equipped with washing machines . . .), besides row houses and blocks of flats for the 26,000 workers in the site; its layout was based on ample perspectives, with an emphasis on axiality and symmetry while horizontality predominate in the composition of the buildings, some with softly curved facades.

Other industrial complexes were subsequently entrusted to Gabr, such as the Misr Rayon Company Mills and workers' housing (1950) at Kafr al-Dawwar, near Alexandria, or the Misr

Silk Weaving Company Plants and workers' housing at Helwân, a Cairo suburb. Among his later most important works are the offices of the National Center for Scientific Research (1950) and the Government Press (1953) in Cairo, along two five-stars hotels, the New Cataract Hotel in Assuan, and the New Winter Palace in Louxor, both completed in the early 1960s.

Gabr was also much interested in painting and head for many years the Art Friends Society in Cairo. In 1962, he participated in the technical Committee set by UNESCO with the Egyptian Ministry of Culture for preparing the "Abu Simbel Salvage Operation" meant to rescue the ancient monuments of Nubia threatened by the building of a new dam at Assuan. Gabr was awarded the State Medal for Arts in 1964.

MERCEDES VOLAIT

See also **Cairo, Egypt**

Selected Publications

"L'architecture contemporaine en Egypte," *L'Art Vivant*, 16 (1930)
"Madîna al-'ummâl bi-Mahalla al-Kubra"[Workers' city at Mahalla al-Kubra], *Magalla al-muhandisin* (November 1948)

Selected Works

Muhammad Rida bey Mansion, Cairo, c. 1930
Mugib bey Fathy Villa at Giza, c. 1932
Abd al-Rahman Hamada Villa, Syriaqus, c. 1940
Cairo University Students Hospital, Giza
Workers City, Mahalla al-Kubra, 1946–48; Industrial complex, Kafr al-Dawwar, 1947–49; National Center for Scientific Research, Cairo, 1950; Gorge and Hilal Shama Apartment Building, Cairo, 1952; Government Press, Cairo, 1953

Further Reading

'Abd al-Mun'im Haykal, *'Alî Labîb Gabr wa fann al-'imâra* [Ali Labib Gabr and the Art of Architecture], Cairo: General Egyptian Book Organization, 1973
Tâhir al-Sâdiq, "Al-ustâz al-mi'mârî 'Alî Labîb Gabr," *Al-Mi'mâr* [The Architect], vol. 19 (1988).

GARDEN CITY MOVEMENT

In 1919, the Garden City and Town Planning Association adopted the following to define a garden city: "A town designed for healthy living and industry; of a size that makes possible a full measure of social life, but not larger; surrounded by a rural belt; the whole of the land being in public ownership or held in trust for the community."

The idea of the garden city is attributed generally to Ebenezer Howard, who in 1898 published his visionary essay, *To-morrow: A Peaceful Path to Real Reform* (republished in 1902 as *Garden Cities of To-morrow*), which projected a view of a new urban society. Howard was not an architect, surveyor, or town planner. Some elements of his proposals find precedent in utopian literature extending to the Renaissance and beyond; the ideas of utopian socialists, such as Robert Owen and Charles Fourier; and the pragmatism of 19th-century philanthropic industrialists, including Titus Salt, W.H. Lever, and the Cadbury Brothers. These ideas combined to form, in Howard's own words, a "unique combination of proposals."

Intended to be a self-sufficient community for fewer than 32,000 inhabitants on a site of less than 6000 acres, the ideal garden city was designed to encourage all types and conditions of people and to address the problems of squalor and social alienation in rapidly growing industrial cities as well as the deficiencies of rural life, characterized in Howard's "Three Magnets" diagram. The plan showed a concentric arrangement. The residential areas were to be subdivided into six wards or neighborhoods, surrounded by a greenbelt comprising cultivable land. Garden-surrounded houses, at a density of 12 to an acre, were laid out along well-planted streets, converging on the center, with civic buildings and a park designed for communal and recreational activities to be enclosed in a "crystal palace." Industry was to be on the periphery.

Howard's practical utopianism was perhaps the first to link social, economic, and political interests in what he termed a "social city." The combination of public ownership, private enterprise, and communal management appealed to a wide political spectrum. An active campaigner, Howard was instrumental in the formation of the Garden City Association in 1899, intended to promote his ideas. It comprised a unique combination of sponsors: social reformers, industrialists, philanthropists, politicians, literary figures, architects, and temperance campaigners, among others. The Garden City Pioneer Company Ltd. was formed after the first association conference at Port Sunlight, England, in 1902, with the intention of building Letchworth on a 3918-acre site in Hertfordshire, 35 miles north of London. Designed by Barry Parker and Raymond Unwin, the architecture drew its inspiration from English Domestic Revivalists, including Norman Shaw, C.F.A. Voysey, and E.J. May. Described by Nikolaus Pevsner as "the first garden city ever built," Letchworth differed in some respects from Howard's ideal conception but nevertheless reflected many of his ideas. The built-up area occupied only 1300 acres of the total site, the rest being reserved for an agricultural and recreational greenbelt. Houses were positioned propitiously to obtain the sunniest and most pleasant views and were set back at a minimum distance of 20 feet from the footpaths to ensure privacy.

By 1918, Letchworth had established an international reputation as a self-contained industrial town, but it had no imitators. Frederic Osborn and the Garden Cities and Town Planning Association (later the Town and Country Planning Association) were renewing their propaganda campaign for the garden city concept, but Howard believed that only a second practical demonstration would influence government policy. In 1919, he purchased nearly 1500 acres of land in Hertfordshire just north of Hatfield and formed the Welwyn Garden City Company in 1920. Similar in concept and general character to Letchworth, Welwyn is considered to be more compact and urban in layout and to exhibit a higher degree of overall architectural control. Louis de Soissons designed the plan and many of the neo-Georgian houses.

Although the superficial architectural and layout characteristics of Letchworth were to be copied in innumerable suburbs and speculative developments described erroneously as "on garden city lines," Howard's underlying principles and his promotion of decentralization nevertheless influenced the whole of suburban England and undoubtedly contributed to the success of the postwar New Towns policy. Often represented as a homogeneous, unchanging body of opinion, the Garden City movement was in fact more flexible, embracing a number of different interests and expressions. Its wider legacy was significant throughout the 20th century, finding powerful echoes in the United States and across Europe, particularly in Germany, France, and Belgium.

HILARY J. GRAINGER

See also **City Beautiful Movement; Parkways; Urban planning**

Further Reading

A great deal of literature exists on the subject of the Garden City movement. Although Creese suffers from some odd omissions, it is generally accepted as one of the most comprehensive views of the movement. It benefits from the fact that it was the first independent assessment, in architectural terms, of the movement's aims and objectives.

Abercrombie, Patrick, "A Comparative Review of Modern Town Planning and 'Garden City' Schemes in England," *The Town Planning Review* (1910)

Batchelor, Peter, "The Origin of the Garden City Concept of Urban Form," *Journal of the Society of Architectural Historians* (1969)

Creese, Walter L., *The Search for Environment: The Garden City Before and After*, New Haven, Connecticut: Yale University Press, 1966; expanded edition, Baltimore, Maryland: Johns Hopkins University Press, 1992

Howard, Ebenezer, *To-morrow: A Peaceful Path to Real Reform*, London: Swan Sonnenschein, 1898; 2nd edition, as *Garden Cities of To-morrow*, London: Sonnenschein, 1902; reprint, Cambridge, Massachusetts: MIT Press, 1965; revised edition, Eastbourne, East Sussex: Attic Books, 1985

Osborn, F.J., "The Garden City Movement: A Revaluation," *Journal of the Town Planning Institute* (1945)

Purdom, Charles B., *The Garden City*, New York: Dutton, and London: Dent, 1913; reprint, New York: Garland, 1985

Purdom, Charles B., *The Letchworth Achievement*, London: Dent, 1963

GARNIER, TONY 1869–1948

Architect and urban planner, France

Tony Garnier's famous publication, *Une Cité Industrielle* (1918, 1932), secured his position as an important precursor of modern architecture and urban planning according to the evolutionary schema drawn up by the architects, critics, and historians of the Modern movement. Only recently, however, has the real historical specificity of Garnier's particular amalgam of classicism and modernism been located in contemporary aspects of socialist utopianism and modern labor technologies and materials.

Garnier was born in Lyon, the major industrial city of France, during the 19th century. The son of a silk designer and a weaver, he spent his childhood in the working-class area of Croix-Rousse. At the age of 14, he enrolled in the École Technique de la Martinière in Lyon (1883–86), where he received his initial training as a draftsperson and painter. In 1886, he entered the École des Beaux-Arts in Lyon (1886–89) to study architecture under Elvin and Louvier. His success at the school, including the Prix Bellemain, enabled him to further his architectural studies in Paris.

In 1890, Garnier was admitted to the École des Beaux-Arts in Paris (1890–99), where he studied with Paul Blondel, Scellier

de Gisors, and the theorist Julien Gaudet. He won the prestigious Prix de Rome in 1899 for his design of a national bank headquarters. The entry demonstrated his abilities to formulate clear circulation routes, organize complex services, and allow for a building's future growth and expansion. Garnier's approach to planning—rooted in his mastery of Beaux-Arts principles of composition—would develop with the increasing industrial and urban scale of his work. The Prix de Rome earned him the right to reside as a *pensionnaire* at the Villa Medici in Rome for four years (1899–1904). During this period, he associated with other *pensionnaires*, such as Henri Prost, Léon Jaussely, and Ernest Hébrard, all of whom shared his interests and later became the first generation of urban planners in France.

Garnier contested the strict study of classical architecture required by the academy in the form of the annual submission of envois, or reconstructive drawings of ancient monuments. His first envoi (1901) was a rendering of the Tabularium, and across the drawings he wrote a provocative statement of faith: "Since all architecture is based on false principles, ancient architecture was a mistake. Only truth is beautiful." Yet Garnier hardly disavowed the classical tradition; rather, he critiqued the academicians' inability to link this tradition to modern social and urban needs. Addressing this problem, he supplemented the 1901 envoi with his first plan for an ideal, industrial city, called Une Cité Industrielle.

For his final envoi in 1904, Garnier explicitly linked the classical tradition with his interest in urban planning by submitting a reconstruction of the entire antique town of Tusculum. Again, he attached a supplementary project, a more elaborate version of his Cité Industrielle. Although his 1904 Cité Industrielle drawings were exhibited, the project was not published until 1918. The publication was a much enlarged and revised version of the initial plans. Garnier included many additional references, drawings, and photographs of his later work in Lyon, such as his industrial quarter for the silk-weaving industry, villas, a municipal stadium, and a market hall.

These plans describe an ideal city of 35,000 inhabitants located between a mountain and a riverbank to access hydroelectric power for local industry. The city was organized into a series of zones according to function: industrial, civic, residential, health related, and entertainment related. Garnier built flexibility into the plan by allowing free circulation within and between these zones as well as anticipating their future expansion and growth. Other components of the plan include the use of greenbelts throughout the city and the use of new materials—primarily reinforced concrete—for the architecture. These new materials enabled a standardized variation of building types and an aesthetic of simple geometric shapes that relied on plasticity rather than ornament for effect. The chief factor determining Garnier's design, however, was his emphasis on industrial labor. He was influenced by Emile Zola's great socialist utopian novel *Travail* (1901), which first appeared in serial form in 1900–01. Zola described a city strikingly close to the Cité Industrielle, and several passages from the novel are literally inscribed on the assembly hall of Garnier's Cité.

Because of favorable reviews in the Lyon press of his early conceptions of the Cité, Garnier returned there in 1904. His first major commissions were for a livestock market and slaughterhouse (1906–24) in the Mouche district and the Grange-Blanche Hospital (1910–27). Both designs allowed Garnier to elaborate on urban-planning issues only intimated in his Cité Industrielle. The market–slaughterhouse represented a complete study of the butchering process, from the transportation and classification of animals in the large-span market hall (built of steel and reinforced concrete), to the hygienic division of services in the reinforced-concrete pavilions, to the circulation of products via interior roadways linking the pavilions. (Significantly, the 1914 International Urban Exhibition, directed by Garnier, took place in the market hall of the slaughterhouse.) Likewise, in the Grange-Blanche Hospital, Garnier classified services, such as surgery and medicines, separated them into distinct pavilions, and linked them with underground passageways. The hospital's simple, reinforced-concrete pavilions with flat roofs are rhythmically aligned within a pastoral environment, characteristics that also echo the green spaces included in the Cité. These projects also began Garnier's career-long relationship with Lyon's new socialist mayor, Edouard Herriot, who was responsible for making him the city's chief architect. In 1913, Garnier was appointed a professor at Lyon's École des Beaux-Arts.

Garnier's work on low-cost housing projects further demonstrated his skill in meeting the aesthetic and technical challenges of modern urban planning. For the Foundation Rothschild housing competition in Paris (1905), Garnier submitted an innovative design for standardized apartment buildings angled at 45 degrees. This zigzag pattern maximized sunlight for each apartment, suppressed long corridors and enclosed courtyards, and created open green spaces around the buildings. Two other low-cost housing projects designed by Garnier for Lyon, an industrial quarter (1908, unbuilt) for the silk-weaving industry and the Quartier des Etats-Unis (1919–35), included the full range of domestic, industrial, and entertainment services necessary to support large working populations. Through these projects, Garnier came closest to achieving the large-scale ambitions of the Cité Industrielle.

The classicizing aspects of Garnier's work are particularly striking in his villas, built in Lyon (1911, 1913, 1921), Saint-Didier (1921), and Cassis (1930). All are reinforced-concrete structures, yet they evoke a Mediterranean classicism through their simple geometric forms, lack of ornamentation, terrace roofs, atriumlike spaces, pergolas, and intimate fusion of architecture and site. Many of these villas recall his first studies of pared-down domestic architecture that were depicted in the 1904 envoi of Tusculum and the Cité Industrielle. His Municipal Stadium in Lyon (1914–18)—the Stade de Gerland—is another study in abstract classicism on a monumental scale.

During the 1920s and 1930s, Garnier completed work on major projects that were conceived before the war, such as the Slaughterhouse, Grange-Blanche Hospital, Municipal Stadium, and the Quartier des Etats-Unis. He also began new projects, such as a sanatorium (1923) at Saint-Hilaire de Touvet, the Lyon–Saint-Etienne Pavilion (1925) for the Decorative Arts Exhibition in Paris, and a city hall (1928–34) for the new town of Boulogne-Billancourt. He produced little after 1937. In 1939, he left Lyon to live in Bédoule, where he died in 1948.

In 1920, Garnier published *Les grands travaux de la ville de Lyon*, an album containing his additional works planned and built in Lyon. The second edition of *Une Cité Industrielle* was published in 1932. With the exception of his brief preface to the *Cité*, Garnier wrote little. Drawing was his main vehicle of thinking and the principal means by which his work gained the

attention and admiration of modern architects and critics such as Le Corbusier and Sigfried Giedion.

ARON VINEGAR

Biography

Born in Lyon, France, 13 August 1869; son of architect Charles Garnier. Attended the École des Beaux-Arts, Lyon 1886–89; studied in the studio of Paul Blondel and Scellier de Gisors, École des Beaux-Arts, Paris 1889–99; Prix de Rome scholar 1899–1904. In private practice, Lyon from 1904. Died in La Bédoule, 19 January 1948.

Selected Works

Cité Industrielle (project), 1904
Rothschild Foundation Housing (competition entry), Paris, 1905
Housing Sector (unbuilt), Industrial Quarter, Lyon, 1908
Villa Tony Garnier, Saint-Rambert, Lyon, 1911
Municipal Stadium, Lyon, 1918
Villa Gros, Saint-Didier, 1921
Sanatorium, Saint-Hilaire de Touvet, 1923
Slaughterhouse and Stockyard, Lyon, 1924
Lyon and Saint-Etienne Pavilions, Exposition Internationale des Arts Decoratifs et Industriels Modernes, Paris, 1925
Grange-Blanche Hospital (now H. Edouard Herriot Hospital), Lyon, 1927
Hotel de Ville, Boulogne-Brillancourt (with J.H.E. Debat-Ponsan), 1934
Housing Sector, Quartier des Etats-Unis, Lyon, 1935

Selected Publications

Une Cité Industrielle: Etude pour la construction des villes, 1918
Les grands travaux de la ville de Lyon, 1920

Further Reading

A comprehensive catalog and chronology of Tony Garnier's work—and an excellent set of scholarly essays—appears in Guiheux and Cinqualbre. The March 1984 issue of the journal *Rassegna*, a monographic issue on Garnier, contains essays that remain essential reading on the topic.

Garnier, Tony, *Tony Garnier: L'oeuvre complète*, Paris: Centre Georges Pompidou, 1989
Giedion, Sigfried, *Space, Time, and Architecture*, Cambridge, Massachusetts: Harvard University Press, and London: Oxford University Press, 1941; 5th edition, revised and enlarged, Cambridge, Massachusetts: Harvard University Press, 1967
Guiheux, Alain, and Olivier Cinqualbre (editors), *Tony Garnier: L'oeuvre complète*, Paris: Editions du Centre Pompidou, 1989 (contains numerous essays by important scholars)
Le Corbusier, *Manière de penser l'urbanisme*, Paris: Édition de l'Architecture d'Aujourdhui, 1943; as *Looking at City Planning*, New York: Grossman, 1971; new edition, Paris: Donoël/Gonthier, 1977
Mariani, Riccardo (editor), *Tony Garnier: Une Cité Industrielle*, New York: Rizzoli, 1990
Pawlowski, Christophe, *Tony Garnier et les débuts de l'urbanisme fonctionnel en France*, Paris: Centre de Recherche d'Urbanisme, 1966
Pawlowski, Christophe, *Tony Garnier: pionnier de l'urbanisme du XXe siècle*, Lyon: Créations du Pélican, 1993
Piessat, Louis, *Tony Garnier, 1869–1948*, Lyon: Presses Universitaires de Lyon, 1988

Rassegna 17 (March 1984) (special issue entitled "Tony Garnier, da Roma a Lione; Tony Garnier from Rome to Lyon")

Roz, M., A. Lagier, and P. Rivet, *Tony Garnier*, Paris: Recherche CORDA, 1983

Siderakis, Kriti, "Introduction," in *Tony Garnier: Une Cité Industrielle: étude pour la construction des villes*, edited by Siderakis, New York: Princeton Architectural Press, 1989

"Utopian Aspects of Tony Garnier's Cité Industrielle," *Journal of the Society of Architectural Historians*, 19 (March 1960)

Vidler, Anthony, "The New World: The Reconstruction of Urban Utopia in Late 19th-Century France," *Perspecta*, 13/14 (1971)

Wiebenson, Dora, *Tony Garnier: The Cité Industrielle*, London: Studio Vista, 1969; New York: Braziller, 1970

GAS STATION

Gas stations are a 20th-century invention, born of necessity in the automobile age. Their ubiquitous presence symbolizes the way the automobile has fundamentally restructured American life and the built environment. The functional need that the gas station was invented to address—delivering gasoline to the automobile—has not changed since the days of the Model T. However, the manner of architecturally expressing and facilitating that function has evolved. In the process, the gas station has become a permanent presence in the urban and suburban landscape.

The first gas stations appeared in the early 1900s. They tended to be composed of gasoline pumps or above-ground tanks and simple wooden or tin sheds to store lubricating products. Prior to the advent of these structures, automobile owners bought their gasoline from curbside pumps in front of hardware or general stores. It appears that the American Gasoline Company of St. Louis built the first separate station away from the grounds of an oil company storage facility in 1909. The station consisted of a small tin shed and two makeshift gas tanks with attached garden hoses. A year later, the Central Oil Company built a prototypical station in Flint, Michigan: a hand-operated gas pump accessible from both sides and covered by a canopy. By the 1910s, the simple shed had been transformed into a recognizable building type. All the elements we associate with the gas station—driveways, canopies, gas pumps, and corporate signs—were commonplace by the decade's end. Even in these early days, the oil companies devised standardized architectural expressions for their stations; this was the first step in the development of a unique corporate identity. In 1914, Standard Oil of California created the first chain of 34 identical stations. Other companies soon developed their own architectural identity along the roadside.

Gas station styles varied widely in size, location, and design over the course of the century despite their rather unchanging function. In a systematic review of gas station architecture, John Jakle and Keith Sculle identified 11 distinct gas station types, including the "house," "house with canopy," "house with bays," "oblong box," and "small box." Different types have enjoyed fluctuating levels of popularity over time. For example, the early curbside pumps and rudimentary sheds disappeared by 1930, but a standard gas station form remained relatively consistent. Most stations had a building to store supplies and conduct transactions and one or more nearby gasoline pumps under a roof or canopy. In the 1920s, stations began to include a covered bay for car washing and lubricating services. These bays typically formed a prominent addition to the main building. Later, stations expanded the number of bays available for repair services, and by 1925 mechanical lifts were common in most service facilities.

Variations on the "gas station as house" type were popular in the 1920s and 1930s. Often located at street corners, many of these house stations, with gable roofs, mock chimneys, and flower gardens, were placed in residential neighborhoods, where their domestic appearance would attract customers while blending with the surroundings. During this time, the gas station truly became the "service station," offering repair and maintenance services, lubricating products, and restrooms along with gasoline. The most important impetus for the service station concept was the increasing competition between oil companies. When offering gasoline alone was no longer enough to attract motorists, the oil companies extended their services in an attempt to win public patronage, in much the same way that distinctive uniforms, logos, and slogans were developed to create a recognizable corporate identity. This identity often defined the design of the gas station in every detail. Because the average customer had no way of judging the quality of one gasoline over another, such extraneous advertising devices were necessary to instill brand loyalty in the consumer.

Alongside the increased standardization of the 1920s and 1930s was a parallel eclecticism. For every identical Standard Oil or Shell Oil houselike gas station, there was another station built to look like a Greek temple, a castle, a windmill, or a lighthouse. Regional identities were also expressed, such as Spanish Colonial in the Southwest and Georgian Revival in New England. These novelty stations tended to be dealer owned rather than company owned. The large oil companies found them expensive to replicate, which defeated the purpose of a nationwide corporate image. Some companies preferred prefabricated stations made with easy-to-maintain materials, such as brick, stucco, or steel. Because of their simple construction, if the intended location proved unprofitable, the building could be dismantled and transported to a new site.

As the modern design aesthetic of the post–World War II era spread to roadside building types, many oil companies preferred the oblong box form. Stations were built with flat roofs, glass walls, shiny clean surfaces, and streamlined curves, all emphasizing modernization and efficiency. Distinctive signage and color schemes were set against flat surfaces to serve as eye-catching advertisements. The gas station's increased prominence reflected the increasing role the automobile played in American life. Many oil companies hoped to augment their visibility by hiring famous industrial designers to create new corporate images. For example, Norman Bel Geddes' 1934 prototype for the Socony-Vacuum Oil Company proved too futuristic and was never built, but Walter Dorwin Teague's Texaco station of the same year was constructed in more than 10,000 locations across the country.

By the 1950s, the modern aesthetic became dominant. Eclectic or historic styles largely disappeared, being replaced by simple large or small boxes. Corporate logos became more important than particular building forms in courting the public. In the 1970s, the gasoline delivery system began to change with the increasing popularity of self-service stations and gasoline pumps at convenience stores. Toward the end of the century, traditional "service stations" with bays for repair and maintenance services rapidly declined. Gas stations have tended to merge with convenience stores to create a hybrid form that combines the oblong box with the small grocery store. Despite these formal changes, gas stations continue to be fixtures in our urban and rural landscapes, destined to remain a necessity as long as our society remains dependent on the automobile.

DALE ALLEN GYURE

See also **Roadside Architecture; Vernacular Architecture**

Further Reading

Jakle, John A., and Keith A. Sculle, *The Gas Station in America*, Baltimore, Maryland: Johns Hopkins University Press, 1994

Jennings, Jan (editor), *The Automobile in Design and Culture*, Ames: Iowa State University Press, 1990

Vieyra, Daniel I., *"Fill 'er Up": An Architectural History of America's Gas Stations*, New York: Macmillan, 1979

Witzel, Michael Karl, *The American Gas Station*, Osceola, Wisconsin: Motorbooks International, 1992

GATEWAY ARCH, ST. LOUIS, MISSOURI

Designed by Eero Saarinen, completed 1965

Gateway Arch, or the St. Louis Arch, is the main feature of the Jefferson National Expansion Memorial, a national park on the western bank of the Mississippi River in St. Louis, Missouri. The park commemorates the westward expansion following President Thomas Jefferson's Louisiana Purchase in 1803 from Napoleon. The arch's architect, Eero Saarinen, won the two-stage competition of 1947–48 in collaboration with J. Henderson Barr, Dan Kiley, Alexander Hayden Girard, and Lily Swann Saarinen. The construction had to wait for the end of Korean War, the appropriation of funding, and the removal of railroad tracks. The arch was completed in 1965, four years after Saarinen died of a brain tumor.

The arch is an inverted catenary curve, 630 feet tall, and finished with stainless steel. Its cross section is an equilateral triangle, with its side measuring 54 feet at the ground level and 17 feet at the top. The total of 142 triangular sections, made of double walls of steel, are welded one on top of another. The space between the double walls is filled with reinforced concrete up to 300 feet high and held by steel stiffeners above. A tram system of eight five-passenger capsules runs in the hollow core of the triangle on both sides, from the underground lobby to the observation room at the top. The Museum of Westward Expansion, which Saarinen envisioned as an independent structure on the site, is located beneath the arch.

Mayor Bernard F. Dickman and Luther Ely Smith, a St. Louis civic leader who had worked on the federal commission for the George Rogers Clark Memorial at the Wabash riverfront of Vincennes, Indiana, conceived the memorial on the riverfront in 1933. The nonprofit Jefferson National Expansion Memorial Association was formed in the same year, and Smith became its chairman. On 21 December 1935, President Franklin D. Roosevelt signed an executive order to allocate government funds that were to be matched by local contributions. Roosevelt also directed the National Park Service to acquire and develop the site. On 27 January 1938, the U.S. Court of Appeals legalized

the land clearing. The demolition of existing buildings on the site was completed in 1941; World War II, however, suspended further progress until after 1947.

George Howe, a fellow of the American Institute of Architects (AIA), was appointed by the association as the professional adviser and wrote the program of a two-stage competition. The AIA endorsed the competition, and a detailed announcement of the competition appeared on 26 March 1947. The competition was open to all U.S. citizens who considered themselves architects. The deadlines for each stage were 1 September 1947 and 3 February 1948, respectively.

The first-stage entries totaled 172, many of which were a collaboration of an architect, a sculptor, a painter, and a landscape architect, as the competition program recommended. The seven-member jury of S. Herbert Hare, Fiske Kimball, Louis LaBeaume, Charles Nagel, Jr., Richard J. Neutra, Roland Wank, and William W. Wurster met in St. Louis from 23 to 26 September 1947 and selected five teams for the second stage. Howe wrote the program addenda on the basis of the jury's comments as well as on those of the AIA and the National Park Service. When the jury members met one week after the second-stage deadline, the winner was decided unanimously.

This competition marked Eero Saarinen's professional coming of age. In 1936, after graduating from the School of Architecture at Yale University and traveling to Europe, he joined his father, Eliel, in the firm and the faculty at the Cranbrook Academy of Art in Bloomfield Hills, Michigan. This competition was one of the first projects that Eero undertook independent from his father.

During the postwar era, monumentality was a frequent topic of discussion and concern among architects and city planners. George Howe's article, "Memorials for Mankind," had appeared in *Architectural Forum* in May 1945, and Louis I. Kahn's "Monumentality" of 1944 included a sketch of steel sculpture, similar to the one that he included in his competition entry and to those that Kahn showed to Saarinen before the competition. Saarinen had been contemplating entering a competition for a great national monument, and for St. Louis he conceived of a dome, as found in John Russell Pope's Jefferson Memorial in Washington, D.C.

The dome conception did not last long, however. Examining the site model with Charles Eames, an old friend and a previous St. Louis resident, Saarinen found the dome too heavy in relation to the long stretch of the levee. The Saarinen team then constructed a more open dome, with three ribs that came together, out of pipe cleaners, and eventually experimented with the forms to settle on an arch that was neither too semicircular (thus appearing rainbowlike) or too pointed (associated with the ecclesiastical). The proportion of the arch was a persistent design issue. It was initially a parabola, as indicated by the mathematical equation on the first-stage entry. While preparing for the second-stage submission, Saarinen consulted Fred Severud, the structural engineer, to make it vertical, eventually arriving at a catenary curve, an upward-thrusting form.

After the winning design appeared in the national press, Gilmore D. Clarke, chairman of the National Commission on Fine Arts, criticized the arch as resembling the design for Benito Mussolini's fascist exhibition in Rome in 1942. Wurster, the chairman of the jury, replied in a newspaper article that so many arches existed in architecture that it was preposterous to associate

Gateway Arch of St. Louis, designed by Eero Saarinen
© Jeffereson National Expansion Memorial and National Park Service

such an impersonal, simple, and pure form with any political ideology and called Saarinen's arch a suitable symbol as a gateway to the West.

One of the most exciting moments in the construction of the arch was the placement of the keystone, which occurred in the morning of 28 October 1965. To avoid complications from the expansion of the steel by the sun's heat, fire engines sprayed cold water down the side of the south leg before the keystone was placed and welded. The arch was completed the following day.

RUMIKO HANDA

See also **Saarinen, Eero (Finland); Saarinen, Eliel (Finland)**

Further Reading

Arteaga, Robert, *Gateway to the West*, St. Louis: Arteaga, 1966; 3rd edition, as *Building of the Arch: a national monument on the St. Louis riverfront*, St. Louis: Jefferson National Expansion Memorial Association, 1967; 8th edition, as *The Building of the Arch*, 1998

Brown, Sharon, "Jefferson National Expansion Memorial: The 1947–48 Competition," *Gateway Heritage: Quarterly Journal of the Missouri Historical Society*, 1/3 (1980)

Gateway to the West, St. Louis: Jefferson National Expansion Memorial Association, 1980

Handa, Rumiko, "Design through Drawing: Eero Saarinen's Design for the Jefferson National Expansion Memorial Competition" (Ph.D. dissertation), University of Pennsylvania, 1992

Mehrhoff, W. Arthur, *The Gateway Arch: Fact and Symbol*, Bowling Green, Ohio: Bowling Green State University Popular Press, 1992

GAUDÍ, ANTONI 1852–1926

Architect, Spain

Antoni Gaudí i Cornet created a style of architecture so unique that it is difficult to imitate. In so doing, he brought attention not only to Spain but also to his native region of Catalonia. Most often described as blending Art Nouveau with neo-Gothic, the two main architectural movements of his day, his architecture is more accurately described as living sculpture. Using the parabola and motifs found in nature, Gaudí designed using scale models as well as architectural drawings and plans.

Gaudí incorporated elements of art—color, form, and texture—into his architecture. His work is known for its use of ornate ironwork, wide parabolic arches, and symmetrical designs emphasizing open interior space. His greatest achievement was the development of the "slanted" column to replace the flying buttresses used in Gothic and Romanesque cathedrals. His columns lean on a slight angle and branch at the top to further support the ceiling stresses of the tall and open buildings that he created.

Gaudí was born in Reus, Spain on 25 June 1852. He was plagued by rheumatic ailments from an early age. Unable to play with other children, he spent time observing the world around him and drawing what he saw. Perhaps it was during this time that he developed his keen observation of the elements in nature that would influence his architectural designs.

Gaudí first showed an interest in architecture and design while attending secondary school in 1867. With the help of two friends, he drew up plans and a proposal for the restoration of the monastery of Poblet, which at the time was abandoned and in ruins. César Martinell, in *Gaudí: His Life, His Theories, His Work*, describes the fascination that the ruins had on the youth and its lifelong influence on his vocation: "The crumbling vaults and arches revealed in skeletal form the mechanics of architectural structure which he had never seen so explicitly in well-preserved buildings."

In 1873, at the age of 17, Gaudí enrolled in the Provincial School of Architecture in Barcelona. To supplement the meager financial assistance that his family was able to offer, he worked as a draftsman for a number of architects in Barcelona. Perhaps it was this practical, hands-on learning that saved him, for his enthusiasm for his studies was erratic. His work for at least one project, that of a water depository, led to his passing his class in resistance materials. The professor, a friend of the architect, learned of the unique solution that Gaudí had suggested and allowed those results, along with a cursory exam, to provide Gaudí's grade for the class.

"He does not seem to have been a particularly good student, but good enough to acquire solid training in the fundamental principals of architecture," wrote Rainer Zerbst in *Gaudí—A Life Devoted to Architecture.* Zerbst describes how Gaudí was given the mark of "outstanding" on a draft for a cemetery gate: "In order to give his design-drawing more 'atmosphere,' he had started by drawing a hearse and, apparently, rendered a much more precise drawing of this carriage than of the subject matter at hand."

Although Gaudí completed his studies in the proper manner, acquiring the title of Architect in Madrid in March 1878, "he soon parted ways with the prevailing rules of architecture," according to Zerbst.

As a full-fledged architect, Gaudí was in his element. From his first commission, that of a decorative lamppost for the city of Barcelona, he demonstrated a zeal and precision that he never came close to as a student. He presented the municipal board with sketches, a watercolor rendering, and a detailed study for the project, which included a budget, the placement of the fixtures, and the details on their construction. Although never fully compensated for this project, "his professional dignity insisted that the first of his projects to be put on public view, small as it was, should be executed with the greatest possible perfection without regard for expenditure of effort or for personal profit," according to Martinell.

Gaudí had established the first of his "trademark" designs: ornate ironwork with motifs from nature. This design would be repeated and developed further throughout his career. He

Casa Batlló, facade, Barcelona (1907)
© Howard Davis/GreatBuildings.com

blended ornate ironwork with unplastered brick, patterned with brightly colored ceramic tile in two private homes that he designed during the 1880s. The result was reminiscent of Arabian architecture.

This mixture of materials continued with Casa Vicens (1883–85) for Don Manuel Vicens in Barcelona. The exterior included the trademark ornate ironwork. The interior of the building combined cheap stone, or rubble, with ornamental ceramic tiles. The result pointed to a Moorish influence on the young architect. "The costs nearly drove Gaudí's sponsor to the brink of bankruptcy," wrote Zerbst. "However, he was richly compensated in years to come: Gaudí's use of ceramic titles initiated a veritable wave of fashion in Catalonia, and Vicens manufactured large quantities of these tiles."

The use of two wide parabolic arches dominate the facade of the Palacio Güell (1885–89), a villa designed for Count Eusebi Güell, a textile manufacturer and leader in the Catalonian new industrial development. The rooftop formed a sculptural composition of chimney pots and ventilators. The main feature of the interior was the central domed hall, which rose to the top of the building. The hall was lit by the cupola, lined with hexagonal tiles and numerous small openings that punctuated the dome like stars. The design for the stables at Palacio Güell demonstrates Gaudí's structural independence. He used an elaborate vaulting system sectioned off with arches formed by mushroom columns. The horses descended into the stables using a spiral ramp that allowed an open, flowing space at the ground level.

As Gaudí took on new commissions, his style grew more expressive, combining design with recent influences on the architect—from art and the latest architectural fad to the books that he read in his leisure. He sought to create what he termed "Mediterranean Gothic" from the classic elements of Greek architecture, the engineering of Gothic cathedrals, and the decorative nature motifs of the Romantic movement. He worked to adapt architecture to the climate of the Mediterranean, allowing light and air a freer reign in the finished structure.

Each design also gave Gaudí an opportunity to find solutions for stress support problems that had impeded architects for centuries and that had intrigued him since his adolescence. He studied the angles and curves of natural structures, such as trees. "Instead of the geometry of rectangles and circles, he took his structures from nature, studying what forms allow trees and humans to grow and stay upright," said Joan Bassegoda, a Catalan professor, in the 28 January 1991 *Time* magazine article, "Heresy or Homage in Barcelona?" Using the helicoids, hyperbolas, and parabolas that he noted in nature, he experimented on scale models, performing calculations to properly engineer columns, vaults, and arches that would allow a taller ceiling height with a more open floor area.

In the Episcopal Palace (1887–94) at Astorga, Gaudí developed a symmetrical design emphasizing open interior space. The rooms of each floor surround a vertical central open space. In the College of Santa Teresa de Jesús (1889–94) in Barcelona, the exterior walls feature patterned rubble, brick, and terra-cotta. The interior demonstrates an exercise in structural precision—high, narrow parabolic arches of plaster on brick piers.

The Casa Batlló (1905–07) and the Casa Milá Apartment House (1905–07) exhibit free-form windows, curving balconies, and warped surfaces; further results of experimentation in structural design. Gaudí realized that warped surfaces were considerably more economical to build. The hyperboloids and paraboloids that he borrowed from nature "are ruled surfaces which can be easily reinforced by straight steel rods," according to Sweeney and Sert in *Antoni Gaudí*.

In Casa Milá the elevation appears to be in constant motion. Deep-cut, overlapping ledges bring to mind an influence of ocean waves and cliffs. The building is locally known as "La Pedrera" (the quarry). William J. R. Curtis describes the building in *Modern Architecture since 1900*: "The contrived textures of the ledges give the impression that these forms have come about over the years through a process of erosion."

Parc Güell, which Gaudí began in 1900, culminates his experimentation with the slanted column. In this 38-acre exercise in landscape architecture, he studied the topography and struggled to retain the original structure of the landscape. The concept was based on the English country garden suburb, and his original design called for homes to be built surrounding the park, which never came to fruition.

"The richness of Gaudí's art lies in the reconciliation of the fantastic and the practical, the subjective and the scientific, the spiritual and the material. His forms were never arbitrary, but rooted in structural principals and in an elaborate private world of social and emblematic meanings," according to Curtis.

To prevent destruction of the natural landscape, Gaudí carefully selected materials to blend in with the natural elements. Rough stone or warped surfaces built of brick were decorated with tile and broken-glass mosaics. Parc Güell creates a surrealistic atmosphere in an intricate system of roads, footpaths, and curving retaining walls. Road overpasses are supported with massive tilted columns, as are the covered areas and open-air theater stage, which doubles as the roof of the marketplace.

Gaudí's greatest architectural influence and most famous project is the Expiatory Temple of the Holy Family, better known as the Church of the Sagrada Familia. Gaudí took the commission in 1883, taking over from the original architect, Francisco de Paula del Villar, for whom he had worked while a student. This project shows the phases of Gaudí's continuing stylistic development. The mosaic decoration, elaborate finials of the spires, and ornamental nature-motif decorations suggest Art Nouveau influences, but neo-Gothic, Moorish, and primitive African influences are also evident in the design.

By 1908 Gaudí relied more on three-dimensional models for designing elements in the Church of the Sagrada Familia and less frequently on design drawings. He performed exact calculations to determine loads and stresses on the "tilted" columns that he was developing for the church and used models with weighted wires to verify his calculations. The columns slanted slightly and branched at the top like trees. Elaborating on the tilted columns used in Parc Güell, Gaudí achieved a height in the nave of the Sagrada Familia of 325 yards (300 meters). "He treated the piers as tree-trunks, tilting them inwards so as to counteract the thrust of the vault without recourse to any props or flying buttresses, which he dismissed as 'crutches'," describes David Watkin in *A History of Western Architecture*.

Sweeney and Sert explain Gaudí's theory: "Each branch of the 'tree-column' is directed towards the center of gravity of the section of the vault that it is supposed to carry. Each of these sections of the vaults is reinforced by steel rods, their shapes are hyperboloids and hyperbolic paraboloids."

Gaudí worked on this project intermittently for 31 years and exclusively for the last 12 years of his life. Even after 43 years of design and construction, the Sagrada Familia was not yet completed when Gaudí died in 1926. On 7 June 1926, he was hit by a trolley car while crossing the street. He died on 10 June 1926. The funeral procession stretched half a mile as it wound from the hospital to the crypt of the Sagrada Familia, the final resting place for Spain's most renowned architect.

LISA A. WROBLE

See also Art Nouveau (Jugendstil); Barcelona, Spain; Casa Milà, Barcelona; Spain; Expressionism

Further Reading

Gaudí's unique architectural style is referenced in many publications dealing with Modern Art and the history of architecture covering the Art Nouveau period. Biographies on the Catalan architect offer insights into how his nationalism and the rise of the Neo-Gothic influenced his style

Curtis, William J.R., *Modern Architecture since 1900*, 2nd edition, Englewood Cliffs, New Jersey: Prentice-Hall, 1987

Hornblower, Margot, "Heresy or Homage in Barcelona?" *Time* (28 January 1991)

Martinell, César, *Gaudí: His Life, His Theories, His Work*, translated by Judith Rohrer, Cambridge, Massachusetts: MIT Press, 1975

Solà-Morales, Ignasi de, *Gaudi*, Rizzoli: New York, 1983
Sweeney, James Johnson, and Josep Lluís Sert, *Antoni Gaudí*, New York: Frederick A. Praeger, 1960
Watkin, David, *A History of Western Architecture*, 2nd edition, London: Laurence King Publishing, 1996
Zerbst, Rainer, *Gaudí 1852–1926: Antoni Gaudí i Cornet—A Life Devoted to Architecture*, translated by Doris Jones and Jeremy Gaines, Cologne: Benedikt Taschen Verlag, 1988

GEHRY, FRANK OWEN 1929–

Architect, United States

Frank O. Gehry, an iconoclastic architect, has been alternately praised and maligned for exploring the boundaries between architecture and sculpture. The sheer joy in his exuberant forms was never contested, and even his critics credited the work for bringing popular attention to the profession. Architecture critic Paul Goldberger wrote that Gehry's "buildings are powerful essays in primal geometric form and . . . materials, and from an aesthetic standpoint they are among the most profound and brilliant works of architecture of our time" (Goldberger, 1989).

Gehry's small-scale work was marked by a skillful play of disparate volumes that were as carefully composed as a still-life arrangement. Among the strongest of these include his own house (1978) in Santa Monica, California, and the Winton Guest House (1981) in Wyzata, Minnesota, which complemented an austere glass house designed by Philip Johnson in 1952, almost 30 years before. At their most successful, Gehry's buildings create unusual spatial relationships. Gehry's ability to integrate his organic building forms into difficult urban sites was shown in many projects, most notably the Loyola Law School (first phase completed in 1982) in Los Angeles, California. Unafraid to use forms with metaphoric or figural associations, Gehry produced several whimsical buildings. In the headquarters (1991) for the Chiat/Day advertising firm in Venice, California, designed in collaboration with artists Claes Oldenburg and Coosje van Bruggen, a prominent pair of binoculars served as the entry below and conference rooms above. In the Nationale-Nederlanden Building (1996) in Prague, Czech Republic, nicknamed "Fred and Ginger," a glass tower and a concrete mass appear to be dancing together. The Fishdance Restaurant (1987) in Kobe, Japan, features a 60-foot-high fish sculpture. Gehry's museums have been appreciated for their manipulation of light and highly developed interior spaces. Among these are the Aerospace Museum (1984) in Los Angeles; the Vitra Furniture and Design Museum (1989) in Weil-am-Rhein, Germany; and the Frederick R. Weisman Art Museum (1994) in Minneapolis, Minnesota. The Guggenheim Museum Bilbao (1997) in Bilbao, Spain, is considered masterful for its magical, undulating forms.

Although known as a quintessentially American architect, Canadian-born Gehry had his most spectacular successes in Europe. It was only later in his career that he completed high-profile commissions in the United States, namely, the Walt Disney Concert Hall (construction begun in 1992, halted, and restarted in 1999) in Los Angeles, Millennium Park (2000) in Chicago, and the Experience Music Project (2000) in Seattle, Washington.

In the 1970s Gehry gained the reputation of using inexpensive materials in an irreverent manner that established in part what was called "California style." Loosely grouped under this heading were several younger architects, including Frank Isreal, Thom Mayne, Michael Rotundi, and Eric Owen Moss. Later, the dynamic collision of forms found in many Gehry buildings was sometimes mistakenly attributed to an affinity with the deconstructivist movement, although Gehry distanced himself from that school.

Gehry is more likely to cite visual artists as influences (such as Romanian sculptor Constantin Brancusi) than architects. He formed long-lasting collaborations with contemporaries Oldenburg, Coosje van Bruggen, and Richard Serra. Also important to him were friendships with artists, including Kenny Price, Ed Moses, and Ron Davis (the client for the Davis House and Studio, 1972, in Malibu, California).

The remodeling of Gehry's own house in Santa Monica brought him a great deal of attention and criticism for its formal and material originality. The house was a generic suburban bungalow that Gehry engulfed with a series of platonic and amorphous forms. Materials employed were a startling departure from "standard" residential language: chain-link fence became a scrimlike element to define volumes of space, wood framing was exposed, and galvanized metal and plywood were liberally used. The work was criticized for looking unfinished and arbitrary, but proponents pointed to the spatial sophistication and the reinvention of crude materials that produced undeniably elegant results.

Chain link was used as a screen element in large-scale projects as well. The 300-foot-long wall of a commercial project, Santa Monica Place (1980) in Santa Monica, California, was made from two layers of dense chain link with a supergraphic applied to the outer layer. The Cabrillo Marine Aquarium (1979) in San Pedro, California, utilized chain link as a means to lace various buildings together. Another lowly material, plywood, figured prominently in many of Gehry's interiors. Plywood was used for interior partitions, furniture, and large curved panels. A bold approach to these simple materials was shown in his design for the Temporary Contemporary (1983; later known as the Geffen Contemporary) in Los Angeles. Gehry renovated a vehicle warehouse building with a minimum of intervention and common materials to create a successful setting for contemporary art. Originally intended to be temporary, the building was so well received that it became a permanent venue for the Los Angeles Museum of Contemporary Art, even after its permanent building, designed by Arata Isozaki, was completed in 1986.

Less-common materials also found their way into Gehry's hands. In a later residential work, the Winton Guest House, Gehry used precious materials such as copper, lead-coated copper, and stone. Each function was contained in separate volumes with their own spatial identity. The Guggenheim Museum Bilbao was clad with limestone and sheets of titanium. This rare metal was chosen for its muted reflectivity and variable color. In all cases, the richness of the palette was generated by Gehry's interest in the sensual qualities of materials, regardless of their origin or price tag.

Gehry's reputation for creating skillfully integrated urban projects was established by the Loyola Law School campus. Given an eclectic neighborhood context, Gehry managed to form a coherent campus while maintaining the fabric of the community. Occupying an entire city block, the Acropolis-like complex was organized around a central plaza. A campanile and

Cabrillo Museum Aquarium, San Pedro, California (1979)
© Roger Ressmeyer/Corbis

grand stair contributed to a classical vocabulary that was suited to the image of a law school, and the colorful stucco and irregular planning fit well into a contemporary California setting. Known as a populist architect, Gehry was particularly concerned that people exist comfortably in the spaces that he created and that the buildings themselves contribute to the context and culture of their sites.

The sculptural and metaphoric nature of Gehry's work reached its height in his later buildings. The client for the Experience Music Project requested that the undulating forms be "swoopy," an apt description for the finished building. Four curvilinear volumes—blue, gold, red, and brushed stainless steel—were grouped around a simply curved purple building. Built as a high-tech museum dedicated to popular music, Gehry attributed his inspiration for the building form to the twisted shape of rock and roll's proverbial smashed guitar.

As Gehry's commissions became larger and more complex, it became clear that his forms could not be feasibly constructed without unreasonable costs. To solve this, Gehry became an unlikely pioneer in the high-tech realm of computer-aided design and manufacture. His partner, James Glymph, worked with the French aerospace company Dassault to adapt the firm's computer modeling software, called CATIA, for applications in building design. Using this and other software, Gehry's office

developed a methodology of working that used the computer in extremely effective ways. It is important to note that the introduction of the computer did nothing to change the essential nature of Gehry's design process, which was heavily based on sketches and models. Models were scanned, manipulations were made, and subsequently new models were made from the computer data. When the final computer model was established, it became the database for all dimensions and coordinates on the building, significantly altering the typical construction documentation and shop drawing process. All subcontractors and manufacturers could use these data and add to them. The process that Gehry developed used the computer as a tool to capture, check, and communicate his formal ideas, not to generate them. This unique use of the computer garnered Frank O. Gehry and Associates credit for reasserting the idea of the "master architect" after decades of erosion in the profession's scope of responsibilities. Widely praised for harnessing technology without being enslaved to it, Gehry's forms became ever more daring as data from the computer models were more commonly accepted by the building trades.

Gehry was one of the first architects to explore rapid prototyping in the construction of custom buildings. Experiments were made in both the Nationale-Nederlanden Building (1999) in Prague and Der Neue Zollhof (1999), a trio of waterfront towers in Dusseldorf, Germany. Computer-driven cutters were used to make foam shapes that could be inserted into formwork. Concrete panels could be precast in the forms, later to be mounted onto the structural frame. Gehry recognized the potential in using inexpensive automated processes to create highly individual forms.

Although theoreticians extensively cite him, Gehry remains more interested in the construction and inhabitation of his work than in its theoretical impact. Subsequent to the success of the Guggenheim Bilbao, attention by the popular press signaled Gehry as a celebrity architect whose name would bring brand recognition to a project. A flurry of large-scale projects followed the Guggenheim commission, ensuring his status as one of the most influential and prolific architects of the era.

RENEE CHENG

See also **Computers and Architecture; Deconstructivism; Guggenheim Museum, Bilbao, Spain; Museum; Postmodernism**

Biography

Born Ephraim Goldberg in Toronto, Ontario, Canada, 28 February 1929; family moved to Los Angeles 1947. Studied architecture, University of Southern California, Los Angeles 1949–51; bachelor's degree in architecture 1954; studied city planning, Graduate School of Design, Harvard University, Cambridge, Massachusetts 1956–57. Served, Special Services Division, United States Army 1955–56. Architectural designer, Victor Gruen Associates, Los Angeles 1953–54; planner and designer, Robert and Company Architects, Atlanta, Georgia 1955–56; designer and planner, Hideo Sasaki Associates, Boston, Massachusetts 1957; architectural designer, Pereira and Luckman, Los Angeles 1957–58; planner, designer, project director, Victor Gruen Associates, Los Angeles 1958–61; project designer and planner, André Remondet, Paris 1961. Principal, Frank O. Gehry and Associates, Los Angeles from 1962. Assistant professor, University of Southern California, Los Angeles 1972–73; visiting critic, University of California, Los Angeles 1977 and 1979; William Bishop Professor, Yale University, New Haven, Connecticut 1979; Charlotte Davenport Professor of Architecture, Yale University 1982; Eliot Noyes Professor, Harvard University, Cambridge, Massachusetts 1982, 1985, 1988, 1989. Fellow, American Institute of Architects 1974; fellow, American Academy of Arts and Letters 1987; trustee, American Academy, Rome 1989; fellow, American Academy of Arts and Sciences 1991. Pritzker Prize 1989.

Selected Works

Davis House and Studio, Malibu, California, 1972
Gehry House, Santa Monica, California, 1978
Cabrillo Marine Aquarium, San Pedro, California, 1979
Santa Monica Place, California, 1980
Winton Guest House, Wyzata, Minnesota, 1981
Loyola Law School (phase I), Los Angeles, 1982
Temporary Contemporary (later the Geffen Contemporary), Los Angeles, 1983
Aerospace Museum, Los Angeles, 1984
Fishdance Restaurant, Kobe, Japan, 1987
Vitra Furniture and Design Museum, Weil-am-Rhein, Germany, 1989

Chiat/Day Headquarters, Venice, California (with Claes Oldenburg and Coosje van Bruggen), 1991
Walt Disney Concert Hall, Los Angeles, construction begun in 1992, halted and restarted 1999
American Center, Paris, 1994
Frederick R. Weisman Art Museum, Minneapolis, 1994
Nationale-Nederlanden Building ("Fred and Ginger"), Prague, 1996
Guggenheim Museum, Bilbao, 1997
Der Neue Zollhof, Düsseldorf, 1999
Experience Music Project, Seattle, Washington, 2000

Further Reading

Arnell, Peter and Ted Bickford (editors), *Frank Gehry: Buildings and Projects*, New York: Rizzoli International, 1985
Bletter, Rosemarie Haag, et al., *The Architecture of Frank Gehry*, New York: Rizzoli International, 1986
"CATIA at Frank O. Gehry and Associates, Inc.," *IBM News: Engineering Technology Solutions* (October 1995)
Dal Co, Francesco and Kurt W. Forster, *Frank O. Gehry: The Complete Works*, New York: Monacelli Press, 1998
Friedman, Mildred S. (editor), *Gehry Talks: Architecture + Process*, New York: Rizzoli International, 1999
Futagawa, Yukio (editor), *Frank O. Gehry*, Tokyo: A.D.A. Editor, 1993
Levene, Richard C. and Fernando Márquez Cecilia, *Frank O. Gehry*, Madrid: El Croquis Editorial, 1990
Levene, Richard C. and Fernando Márquez Cecilia, *Frank O. Gehry: 1991–1995*, Madrid: El Croquis Editorial, 1995
Tomkins, Calvin, "The Maverick," *The New Yorker* (7 July 1997)

GERMAN PAVILION, BARCELONA

Designed by Ludwig Mies van der Rohe; completed 1929

Barcelona's Universal Exposition prompted one of modernism's most celebrated, if evanescent, buildings: Ludwig Mies van der Rohe's German Pavilion (1929). Following Mies' directorate of the 1927 Stuttgart Weissenhofsiedlung, the Weimar Republic commissioned him in mid-1928 to oversee exhibit installations of German manufacturing products in preexisting, multinational halls for the upcoming Barcelona fair. Mies asked his companion, Lilly Reich, an interior designer and exhibition specialist who had also collaborated at Stuttgart, to assist. Germany's hesitant decision to expand Mies' commission by erecting its own national pavilion followed later during 1928, after other nations had proceeded. Mere months remained for Mies to realize what would become a professional and aesthetic breakthrough. The Pavilion held many seminal innovations, particularly for his subsequent Weimar-era works, such as the Tugendhat (1930) and Berlin Building Exposition (1931) houses.

Prior to designing, Mies effected a change of site from a cramped position to a more prominent location terminating one arm of the exhibition's grand cross axis. The city of Barcelona's own boxy pavilion occupied the other, distantly opposite extremity of this concourse. A screen of immense neoclassical columns stood before each terminus, filtering views. The cross-axial route on Mies' side looped upward past his site to an amusement area, requiring him to fuse the roles of visual termination and functional gateway.

Mies provided no traditional facade behind the preexisting, triumphal columns. On a broad podium, he deployed an asymmetrically binuclear scheme composed of a larger reception zone and smaller office adjunct. These together partially enclosed a courtyard and reflecting pool. Through lateral, about-face turns up steps and into the entry, Mies deftly diffused the concourse's axis in preparation for the irregular climb up the hill beyond.

Mies' low podium, casually open courtyard, and asymmetrically congregating forms recalled examples of German Neoclassicism, especially Karl Friedrich Schinkel's Schloss Charlottenhof (1826) and Hofgärtnerei (1829) near Potsdam. Mies, however, having recourse to modern technology, achieved a spatial permeability beyond Schinkel's dreams. Enhanced by full-height glass partitions and removable glass doors, the interior and exterior experiences along the Pavilion's circuitous route interpenetrated to an unprecedented degree, dissolving in a reflective and refractive welter.

For the first time, Mies separated the functions of wall and support. Once distilled, he purposefully interlocked these in a tension of expression versus convention. Mies juxtaposed a romantically asymmetrical and orthogonally pinwheeling planar field (recalling his 1924 Brick Country House, De Stijl paintings, and Wrightian prototypes) against a cross-axial, classically composed belvedere of eight freestanding columns symmetrically supporting a roof. The columns' conventionally metrical order fragmented within a Piranesian labyrinth.

Mies' radical tectonic crafting of walls and columns further intertwined modernity and tradition. While his stone partitions' sides were made from enormous machine-polished, book-matched veneers only three centimeters thick (sandwiched onto metal studs), their ends culminated in massively traditionalized blocks. Likewise, his tautly cruciform, chromium-wrapped columns had reflective glimmers reminiscent of classical fluting but exhibited no traditional entasis, visible fixity, or differentiation of top and bottom. Mies' lifelong, pensively indeterminate dialectic of prospective/retrospective reached apogee at Barcelona.

The Pavilion's sumptuous roster of stones (blackish-green Alpine and Larissa marbles and creamy travertine) culminated with a centrally located, freestanding, pinkish-gold onyx *doré* veneered partition. The uncut block for this alone consumed 20 percent of the Pavilion's budget. Its golden hue, together with the nearby red shantung silk draperies and black woolen area rug, fulfilled the three colors of the German flag (flying on masts outside). A narrow, skylit, milky-glazed void stood to one side. Mies positioned his much admired Barcelona furniture (cross-legged, chrome-plated, and white-kid cushioned chairs and ottomans and smoked-glass tables) in this central zone for the Spanish monarchs' use.

Mies' exotic, almost kaleidoscopic palette—which distanced him from other, more abstractly formal modernists—doubtlessly

German Pavilion, Barcelona (exterior), with Georg Kolbe's *Dawn*, designed by Mies van der Rohe
© Photo courtesy Randall Ott

reflected Reich's luxurious taste. Reich also likely inspired the Pavilion's inclusion of Georg Kolbe's bronze *Dawn* figurative sculpture. This gestural, female nude, one of a series Mies placed in buildings immediately after initiating a personal relationship with Reich in 1926, stood untouchable in a second, smaller courtyard pool as the final objective of the most remote passage within Mies' Pavilion.

Despite many authors' claims, Mies used no rigorously modular system at Barcelona. The podium's grid incorporated slight dimensional irregularities suiting local conditions. Further, the walls did not center on grid lines, and only four of eight columns found grid nodes. Still, it is undeniable that Mies' subsequent penchant for modular reticulation gathered strength here. The grid, the freestanding veneered plane, and the sculptural figure all underwent clarification at the Pavilion and later populated his more austere 1930s Courthouse projects.

Without alternate use once the exposition closed in January 1930, the Pavilion was dismantled after eight-months; however the Pavilion's afterlife as a much eulogized modernist exemplar began with its inclusion in the aesthetically oriented International Style exhibition curated by Hitchcock and Johnson (1932) at the Museum of Modern Art—a befitting launching given the Pavilion's aesthetic rather than pragmatic conception. The apparent dearth of documentation gradually lent Mies' building near mythic status. For 50 years, it was published monotonously using only inaccurate plans and a singular set of *Berliner Bild-Bericht* black-and-white prints. Bonta (1979) dissected the Pavilion's literature to exemplify how scholars rigidly perpetuate canonic interpretations. Tegethoff (1985) finally brought copious amounts of ignored documentation forward. Simultaneously, de Solà-Morales (1993) and others launched a successful reconstruction campaign, ending decades of discussion. Between 1981 and 1986, a painstakingly researched facsimile (rendered complete with technical changes enhancing permanence) arose over the original foundation trenches.

Reconstruction has generated many fresh interpretations. Quetglas (1988) reorients critical attention to the Kolbe statue's role; Constant (1990) interprets the Pavilion as a picturesque landscape resembling the temporal flux of nature, and, most startlingly; Evans (1990) discovers a lateral axis of horizontal symmetry. The visitor's optical plane precisely halves the Pavilion's 3.10-meter clear height. The composition's nonisotropic, overwhelmingly horizontal bias and hovering, antigravitational impression result from Mies' dedication to this unprecedented device.

RANDALL OTT

See also **International Style; Mies van der Rohe, Ludwig (Germany); Tugendhat House, Brno, Czech Republic; Weissenhofsiedlung, Deutscher Werkbund, Stuttgart (1927)**

Further Reading

Having appeared in virtually every major work on 20th-century architecture since World War II and having already inspired several monographic studies, the German Pavilion possesses a vast and frustratingly multilingual literature. The sources are dispersed, fragmentary, and unusually riddled with unresolved contradiction, mythic supposition, and factual error. Published graphic documents are notoriously faulty. The most comprehensive written sources are Solà-Morales (which contains an extensive bibliography) and Tegethoff. What remains of Mies' original drawings are found in Drexler.

Bonta, Juan Pablo, *Architecture and Its Interpretation: A Study of Expressive Systems in Architecture*, New York: Rizzoli, and London: Lund Humphries, 1979

Constant, Caroline, "The Barcelona Pavilion As Landscape Garden: Modernity and the Picturesque," *AA Files*, 20 (Autumn 1990)

Drexler, Arthur (editor), *The Mies van der Rohe Archive*, New York: Garland, 1986–; see especially part 2, vols. 7–20, *1938–1967: The American Work*

Evans, Robin, "Mies van der Rohe's Paradoxical Symmetries," *AA Files*, 19 (Spring 1990)

Ford, Edward R., *The Details of Modern Architecture*, 2 vols., Cambridge, Massachusetts: MIT Press, 1990–96

Hitchcock, Henry-Russell, Jr. and Philip Johnson, *The International Style*, New York: Norton, 1932; reprint, with new foreword, New York and London: Norton, 1995

McQuaid, Matilda, *Lilly Reich, Designer and Architect* (exhib. cat.), New York: Museum of Modern Art, 1996

Quetglas, Jose, "Fear of Glass: The Barcelona Pavilion," in *Architectureproduction*, edited by Beatriz Colomina and Joan Ockman, New York: Princeton Architectural Press, 1988

Schulze, Franz, *Mies van der Rohe: Barcelona Pavilion and Furniture Design*, S.l.: s.n. 1979

Solà-Morales Rubió, Ignasi, Cristian Cirici, and Fernando Ramos, *Mies van der Rohe: El pabellón de Barcelona*, Barcelona: Gili, 1993; as *Mies van der Rohe: Barcelona Pavilion*, translated by Graham Thomson, Barcelona: Gili, 1993

Tegethoff, Wolf, *Mies van der Rohe: Die Villen und Landhausprojekte*, Essen, Germany: Bacht, 1981; as *Mies van der Rohe: The Villas and Country Houses*, edited by William Dyckes, translated by Russell M. Stockman, Cambridge, Massachusetts: MIT Press, 1985

Von Vegesack, Alexander and Matthias Kries (editors), *Mies van der Rohe: Architecture and Design in Stuttgart, Barcelona, Brno* (exhib. cat.), Milan: Skira, and Weil, Germany: Vitra Design Museum, 1998

GERMANY

German architecture in the 20th century was forged by the succession of political and social upheavals that swept through Europe during the century, so often with Germany at their epicenter. Conservative and progressive, as well as regional and international architectural tendencies battled for hegemony in trying to shape the German built environment, each in their own image. The result is a century of tremendously heterogeneous architecture with seemingly few continuities or unifying themes. Despite this diversity, a walk through many large German cities today gives the impression that German architecture, perhaps more than that of any other country in Europe, is an architecture of the 20th century. Indeed, many consider Germany to be one of the birthplaces, if not the home of modern architecture.

German architecture at the turn of the last century was characterized by a continuation of many trends from the prosperous decades immediately following German unification in 1871. In architectural design, the use of extravagant historical styles flourished amidst increasing modernization, particularly for the residences and commercial properties of the increasingly wealthy upper and middle class. Alfred Messel's Wertheim Department Store (1898–1908) in central Berlin, with it's mix of historicist exterior details and unprecedented use of steel and glass in a new building type celebrating the triumph of bourgeois, metropolitan consumer culture, epitomized this trend. The more nationalist and militarist tendencies of the German bourgeoisie were embodied in Bruno Schmitz's gargantuan *Völkerschlacht-denkmal* outside of Leipzig (1898–1913), celebrating the centenary of the Prussian victory over Napoleon.

The first sparks of a modern, non-historicist architecture came from the Secession and Art Nouveau inspired reforms against the conservative norm in Germany. The artist's colony on the *Mathildenhöhe* in Darmstadt patronized by the Grand Duke Ernst Ludwig of Hesse (1900–1908) and the Folkwang buildings and artist community in Hagen promoted by Karl Ernst Osthaus (1898–1912) both experimented with new forms. Houses and complete interior fittings in these communities by Peter Behrens, the Viennese Secession architect Joseph Maria Olbrich, and the Belgian designer Henri Van de Velde revealed to the public a fresh, anti-historicist sense of form and ornament. There was a desire to escape history and dry academicism in favor of a more realistic unification of art, design, life, and the everyday world.

Such brief forays into the Art Nouveau (Jugendstil) style at the turn of the century were soon subdued by a penchant for more reserved, monumental, and often neo-classically inspired forms that swept Germany in the years just before World War I. Olbrich's Tietz Department Store in Düsseldorf (1906–1909), Paul Bonatz's main train station in Stuttgart (1911–1928), and Hermann Billing's Art Museum in Mannheim (1906–1907) are typical of this often monumental trend in stone construction.

This general call for architectural order and regularity was promoted by several reform institutions founded in the first decade of the century. Among the most important were the preservation oriented German Heimatschutz Bund (Homeland Protection Association), founded in 1907, and the German Garden Cities Association, founded in 1902, to promote the establishment of traditionally planned towns or suburbs with a restrained, arts-and-crafts style architecture to contrast with the increasingly unlivable industrial metropolis. The most well-known reform organization, however, was the Deutscher Werkbund, founded in 1907, intent on promoting a greater cooperation of German artists and industrialists with the explicit intent of producing more modern consumer goods to increase German exports. Behrens' AEG Turbine Factory (1908–1909) and Walter Gropius' factories for the Fagus shoe last manufacturer (1911–1914) and for the Cologne Werkbund exhibition (1914) were typical Werkbund products as they expressed Germany's new industrial image with a reserved, classically inspired set of architectural forms.

World War I brought Germany's defeat in November 1918, and with it the end of empire, an unsuccessful communist revolution, the imposition of social democracy, as well as economically crippling war reparations payments imposed on Germany. Although there was little work for architects, culture and architecture took on increasing ideological power in the attempt to reform society in the new social democracy. In the wake of defeat, groups of young artists and architects such as the Arbeitsrat für Kunst (Working Council for Art) and the Novembergruppe, led by Gropius, Bruno Taut, Mies van der Rohe, and others, dreamed up Expressionist, utopian architectural fantasies that spoke of a revolution in architecture and a longing for a new architectures of glass and steel, color and purity. In 1919 state officials asked Gropius to unify Weimar's old art academy and applied arts schools and create a state-sponsored Bauhaus,

a school that unified all the arts under the leadership of architecture on the model of a medieval cathedral workshop. Although it produced very few buildings, the Bauhaus proved to be one of the most important forces in reforming and modernizing design and architectural thinking in Germany and throughout Europe.

In the years immediately after the war, shortages of building materials and spiraling inflation made most construction impossible. The overcrowded cites and poor housing conditions, a legacy of Germany's rapid industrialization, only grew worse. Some of the more successful attempts to create housing focused on do-it-yourself building technology such as rammed-earth construction and the small-scale *Volkswohnung* (People's House), similar to those advocated by the Garden Cities Association. Many of the important commissions that were built after the war, such as the *Grosses Schauspielhaus* (Large Theater) in Berlin by Hans Poelzig (1918–1919), the Einstein Tower in Potsdam by Erich Mendelsohn (1920–1921), and the *Chilehaus* by Fritz Höger in Hamburg (1922–1923), began to realize an architecture that was free of academic norms and focused on dynamic, expressive forms and a wide range of colorful materials. This Expressionism was a short-lived but very prevalent style that touched nearly all modern architects, but was rarely continued in the late 1920s. However, the organic functionalism of Hugo Häring and the ecclesiastical architecture of Domenikus Böhm are clearly related in spirit and form.

By the mid-1920s, through the help of American foreign aid, the German economy and building industry began to revive and came into one of the most vibrant and culturally avant-garde moments of 20th-century architecture, the so-called "Golden Twenties," when Berlin was the cultural capital of Europe. Although most construction in Germany continued regional traditions of the *Heimatstil* (homeland style) or the ornamental traditions of earlier decades, an unornamented, flat-roofed, technologically oriented modern architecture, or *Neues Bauen* (New Building) coalesced in urban centers such as Berlin, Frankfurt (Ernst May), and Dessau (Gropius, Hannes Meyer, and the Bauhaus), as well as Magdeburg (Bruno Taut), Celle (Otto Haesler), Hamburg (Karl Schneider), Munich (Robert Vorhoelzer), and Altona (Gustav Oelsner). Progressive architects increasingly associated with new left-leaning social democratic policies that sought technologically oriented renewal for the masses, while many conservative architects chose to associate with right-wing nationalist groups in favor of a pure German culture and architecture.

The most important endeavor which brought about the *Neues Bauen* were the vast public housing projects made possible by the Social Democratic municipal governments all over Germany: over 135,000 new housing units in Berlin, 65,000 units in Hamburg, and 15,000 in Frankfurt alone. Under the guidance of planners such as Martin Wagner and architects such as Taut, cities like Berlin taxed extant landowners steeply, purchased huge tracts of land, formed cooperative house-building associations that modernized the production of building materials, standardized building elements, and streamlined the construction industry. They produced government owned and subsidized housing of all types that allowed thousands of worker families to escape the infamous rental barracks and slums for small but efficiently planned apartment complexes with modern kitchens and other facilities. These innovative housing developments, most designed in a remarkably uniform style that would soon be dubbed the "International Style," drew almost universal international acclaim from architects such as Le Corbusier, J.J.P. Oud, and Philip Johnson. There was, however, increasingly harsh critique from within Germany, as the local press labeled the new architecture a "Bolshevik" or "Jewish" attack on German architectural traditions and inappropriate for the German climate and culture.

When Hitler and his National Socialist regime took over political control of Germany in January 1933, the modern styles associated with social democracy were halted in favor of a mix of conservative styles, including the pitched-roof cottage for domestic architecture, monumental classicism for the urban civic centers, and a highly technical modern architecture for transportation and industrial facilities. Many of the most esteemed modern architects were forced to leave Germany because of their Jewish heritage, while others such as May, Meyer, Taut, Gropius, Mies van der Rohe, Wagner, Ludwig Hilberseimer, and Marcel Breuer voluntarily left in search of more favorable political and architectural climates, especially in the United States.

Hitler took an intense personal interest in the development of a Nazi architecture; he chose Paul Ludwig Troost and later the young Albert Speer to oversee all major architectural production in the Third Reich. Speer and his teams of architects replanned and even started construction in seven major representative regional cities to serve as party headquarters, foremost among them Berlin. The severe, bombastic classical style, solid granite building ensembles they envisioned were to evoke the power, glory and longevity of the German Reich. World War II put a halt to most of these projects, although large ensembles remain in central Munich, namely the party grounds outside of Nuremberg by Speer (1934–1939), in the *Gauforum* in Weimar by Hermann Giesler (1936–1942), and in Berlin.

But the story of Nazi architecture was more insidious and pervasive than a few monumental projects. German architects designed the concentration and extermination camps of the Holocaust for maximum efficiency. Slave labor from the camps was used in quarries, brick furnaces, and many points of the building industry, especially for the most representative architectural projects. Architects also designed factories and entire industrial towns for the machinery of war such as the cities of Salzgitter for coal mining (Werner Hebebrand, 1937), and Wolfsburg for Volkswagen (Peter Koller, 1938), as well as transport facilities such as the Autobahn, and even vacation facilities for German workers and soldiers such as the great beach facilities on the island of Rügen (Clemens Klotz, 1935–1939). Thousands of German architects of all persuasions joined the Nazi party in order to keep their practices, and most continued their work after the war, despite their Nazi affiliations.

The victorious Western Allied powers (under the leadership of the United States' Marshall Plan) exercised strong control over the redevelopment of Germany's post-war economy, government, society, culture, and architecture. Throughout Germany, the immediate post-war years were dedicated to clearing and recycling literally mountains of building-rubble from bombed out cities—most of the work being done by women. This was followed by a rapid rebuilding of society's basic architectural needs, including hospitals, schools, temporary churches, and above all housing, with peak production reaching 600,000 units/year.

Under the sway of Communist Russia, in East Germany, an early "National Building Tradition" was officially dictated by Moscow in deliberate contrast to the "American" International Style architecture in West. The references to Schinkel's classicism in the signature project of the *Stalinallee* (1952–1958) by Hermann Henselmann in Berlin was an attempt to distilll references from history and region into the representational and monumentalizing goals of the regime intent on differentiating itself from both the Nazi past and the capitalist West. Over time, important historical monuments and historic city centers were restored with a care and expertise rarely seen in the West, as the best of architectural heritage was made available to the working class.

Following Stalin's death, Khrushchev ordered a complete about-face towards rationalization and standardization, both out of economic necessity as the cheapest way to build, but also to symbolize the modernity of the East. After 1955 the entire building industry was systematically reorganized to churn out factory prefabricated concrete apartment blocks both in and around every East German city. Housing developments in Berlin's Marzahn, Jena, and Hoyerswerda were technologically more primitive and less comfortable than similar developments in the West but represented a similar loss of urban and architectural quality and an exclusive orientation to function and economics.

In West Germany, the "Economic Miracle" brought on by reconstruction and the development of a capitalist, modern state radically reshaped the face of nearly every city and town by the 1950s. Minimalist, abstract modern architecture became pervasive, especially in the larger, representational projects that commenced after the primary needs of society had been met. Egon Eiermann's German Pavilion for the Brussels World's Fair of 1957 set the dominant tone for architecture that was to be transparent and simple, modest and modern. Increasingly successful German businesses chose to represent themselves with the image of American corporate modernism, such as Eiermann's designs for Neckermann (Frankfurt, 1958–1961), Olivetti (Frankfurt, 1968–1972), and IBM (Stuttgart, 1967–1972) and the refined glass slabs of the Thyssenhaus skyscraper in Düsseldorf (Hentrich & Petschnigg, 1957–1960). Entire new suburban business districts such as Hamburg's City Nord and Frankfurt's Niederrad were part of a general loosening of the traditionally dense core of German towns made possible by the emphasis on transportation and technology in planning and architecture.

A vast array of museums, theaters, and entire new university campuses built after the 1950s were visible symbols of the attempt by West German social democracy to rebuild German culture by heavily subsidizing arts and education. The Ruhr University in Bochum (Hentrich-Petschnigg, 1962–1967), and the Free University in Berlin by the English designers Candilis, Josic and Woods (1962–1973) were highly ordered megastructures built with purely functional and economic considerations. Mies van der Rohe's new National Gallery in West Berlin (1961–1968) and Philip Johnson's museum in Bielefeld (1963–1968) reinforced a trend towards a minimalist, highly technical and rectilinear, functionalist aesthetic.

As a counter-reaction to the strictures of this highly ordered, rational architecture inspired by Mies and American modernism, the Expressionist Hans Scharoun and others worked towards a more organic, anti-monumental planning and architecture. The freedom of the open spaces of Berlin's *Kulturforum*, as well as Scharoun's most well known architectural designs, the Berlin

Philharmonic and Chamber Music Halls (1956–1963, 1979–1984) and the State Library (1967–1976), each display a highly personal, expressive style based on curves and angled geometries. Located near the Berlin Wall at the heart of the Iron Curtain, they soon became symbols of Berlin's freedom, in opposition to the communist regime in the East. Some of the most evocative buildings by German architects after the war were churches and memorials such as those by Rudolf Schwarz, Gottfried Böhm, and Otto Bartning that provided simple but memorable spaces for worship and remembrance, often with organic plans and a hope in the future represented by modern architecture. The draped tensile structures by Frei Otto and Günther Behnisch for the Olympic Stadium in Munich (1972) continued this alternative trend in German modernism, a precursor to some of the fragmented shapes of more recent postmodernist and deconstructivist architecture.

Housing continued to be one of the most pressing issues facing German architects after World War II. Although Germans moved increasingly into single-family houses in the last five decades of the century, large-scale housing developments in the modern style such as those developed by the *Neue Heimat* housing agency still formed the dominant housing type. The Interbau Building Exhibition, built with the participation of 53 well-known architects from 13 nations in the Hansaviertel district of West Berlin in 1957, was prototypical, replacing a dense city section with a loose array of modern high-rise, low-rise, and single-family houses in a park-like setting. In its wake came a largely successful though often maligned and short-lived trend of developing mega-scale housing complexes such as the Neue Vahr Siedlung for 30,000 residents outside of Bremen (Ernst May, Bernhard Reichow, Alvar Aalto et al, 1957–1962), and the Märkisches Viertel for 60,000 in Berlin (Werner Düttmann, Georg Heinrichs, Oswald Matthias Ungers, et al., 1962–1972).

By the early 1970s there began to be an increasing reaction against the ascetic modernist planning ideas and architecture that had come to dominate the German landscape. Architects called for a more contextually sensitive and traditional approach to city building and architecture, and a wave of museum building throughout West Germany, including Hans Hollein's Abteiberg Municipal Museum in Mönchengladbach (1972–1978), James Stirling's Staatsgalerie in Stuttgart (1977–1982), and O.M. Ungers' German Architecture Museum in Frankfurt (1979–84), demonstrated an overt connection to the past, traditions, and postmodern variety. Rather than tearing down extant buildings, preservation, restoration, additions, and even reconstruction became increasingly popular alongside a more contextual approach to architecture that coincided with post-modernism. Berlin's International Building Exposition (IBA, 1979–1987) sought to reclaim some of the more run-down districts of West Berlin through a program of careful urban repair, while new infill housing projects, often with architectural references to history, tradition, and region, signaled a return to the traditional urban closed facade and block formation.

The collapse of the Soviet Union led to German unification and the dismantling of the Berlin Wall. The unified government invested heavily in the East and provided incentives for private industry to rebuild the infrastructure, renovate housing and cultural buildings, and set up branch offices and corporate headquarters throughout the Eastern states. The capitol was returned to Berlin, which soon became one of the biggest construction sites in Europe and the world. Department stores on the Friedrichsstrasse by I.M. Pei, Jean Nouvel, O.M. Ungers and others returned the street in the East to its former status as the most elegant shopping street in Germany.

Although Berlin continues to be Germany's dominant metropolis, the country's federal political structure gives large autonomy to the States, and helps reinforce regional identity, pride, and wealth distribution such that pockets of the newest, most innovative architecture appear all over the newly unified Germany. The new bank towers blossoming in Frankfurt, the expanding port and business centers in Hamburg, the new State Parliament in Dresden (Peter Kulka, 1991–94) and the innovative Leipzig Convention Center (Von Gerkan, Marg & Partners, 1995–98) all resulted from unification as well as the internationalization associated with Germany's powerful role in the new European Union and general globalization. Although German architects, with a few noteworthy exceptions, have received comparatively few opportunities to build abroad, the ubiquity of architectural competitions continues to make Germany more open than perhaps any other country to foreign and young architects, and new ideas. At the close of the 20th century bold experiments in theory and deconstructivism, in planning ideas, in environmental sustainability, as well as in all manner of technology and building performance in Germany continued to stimulate and inspire new developments all over the world that will help define the architecture of the succeeding century.

KAI K. GUTSCHOW

See also **Behrens, Peter (Germany); Deutscher Werkbund; Fagus Werk, Alfeld, Germany; Gropius, Walter (Germany); Hilberseimer, Ludwig (United States, Germany); Mendelsohn, Erich (Germany, United States); Mies van der Rohe, Ludwig (Germany); Poelzig, Hans (Germany); Scharoun, Hans (Germany); Taut, Bruno (Germany)**

Further Reading

Although the developments of German 20th-century architecture are summarized in every survey of modern architecture, and the literature on the subject is rich and growing rapidly, an authoritative comprehensive survey of this complex and often difficult century has yet to be written. Monographs exist on most of the major and minor architects, institutions and particular epochs, especially of the inter-war period. Guidebooks, including Nerdinger's, as well as studies on individual cities, especially Scheer's catalogue on Berlin, often provide the best overview of architecture across the century. The three catalogue volumes edited by Magnano Lampugnani (1992, 1994) and Schneider (1998) accompanied major retrospective exhibits at the German Architecture Museum and represent some of the best scholarship on German architecture, especially from 1900–1950. The best introductions in English to pre-WWII architecture are Lane, Pommer and Zukowsky, while the best surveys of the developments after the war in English are Marshall, De Bruyn, and Schwarz.

De Bruyn, Gerd, *Contemporary Architecture in Germany, 1970–1996: 50 Buildings*, edited by Inter Nationes, Berlin and Boston: Birkhäuser, 1997

Durth, Werner, *Deutsche Architekten: Biographische Verflechtungen, 1900–1970*, Brunswick, Germany: Vieweg, 1986, new edition 2001

Durth, Werner, and Niels Gutschow, *Architektur und Städtebau der Fünfziger Jahre*, Bonn, West Germany: Deutsches Nationalkomitee für Denkmalschutz, 1987

Durth, Werner, Jörn Düwel, and Niels Gutschow, *Städtebau und Architektur in der D.D.R.*, Frankfurt and New York: Campus, 1998

Feldmeyer, Gerhard G., *Die neue deutsche Architektur*, Stuttgart: Kohlhammer, 1993; as *The New German Architecture*, translated by Mark Wilch, New York: Rizzoli, 1993

Hoffmann, Hubert, Gerd Hatje, and Karl Kaspar, *Neue deutsche Architektur*, Stuttgart: Hatje, 1956; as *New German Architecture*, translated by H.J. Montague, New York: Praeger, and London: Architectural Press, 1956

Huse, Norbert, *Neues Bauen: 1918–1933: Moderne Architektur in der Weimarer Republik*, Munich: Moos, 1975; 2nd edition, Berlin: Ernst, 1985

James-Chakraborty, Kathleen, *German Architecture for a Mass Audience*, London and New York: Routledge, 2000

Jaskot, Paul B., *The Architecture of Oppression: The SS, Forced Labor, and the Nazi Monumental Building Economy*, London and New York: Routledge, 2000

Lane, Barbara Miller, *Architecture and Politics in Germany, 1918–1945*, Cambridge, Massachusetts: Harvard University Press, 1968; 2nd edition 1985

Magnano Lampugnani, Vittorio and Romana Schneider (editors), *Moderne Architektur in Deutschland 1900 bis 1950: Reform und Tradition*, Stuttgart: Hatje, 1992

Magnano Lampugnani, Vittorio and Romana Schneider (editors), *Moderne Architektur in Deutschland 1990 bis 1950: Expression und Neue Sachlichkeit*, Stuttgart: Hatje, 1994

Marschall, Werner and Ulrich Conrads, *Neue deutsche Architektur 2*, Stuttgart: Hatje, 1962; as *Modern Architecture in Germany*, translated by James Palmes, London: Architectural Press, and as *Contemporary Architecture in Germany*, New York: Praeger, 1962

Nerdinger, Winfried and Cornelius Tafel, *Guida all'architettura del Novecento, Germania*, Milan: Electa, 1996; as *Architectural Guide: Germany: 20th Century*, translated by Ingrid Taylor and Ralph Stern, Basel, Switzerland, and Boston: Birkhäuser, 1996

Pommer, Richard and Christian F. Otto, *Weissenhof 1927 and the Modern Movement in Architecture*, Chicago: University of Chicago Press, 1991

Posener, Julius, *Berlin auf dem Wege zu einer neuen Architektur: Das Zeitalter Wilhelms II*, Munich: Prestel, 1979

Schneider, Romana and Wilfried Wang (editors), *Moderne Architektur in Deutschland 1900 bis 2000: Macht und Monument*, Ostfildern-Ruit: Hatje, 1998

Schreiber, Mathias (editor), *Deutsche Architektur nach 1945: Vierzig Jahre Moderne in der Bundesrepublik*, Stuttgart: Deutsche Verlags-Anstalt, 1986

Steckeweh, Carl and Sabine Gülicher (editors), *Ideen, Orte, Entwürfe: Architektur und Städtebau in der Bundesrepublik Deutschland/Ideas, Places, Projects: Architecture and Urban Planning in the Federal Republic of Germany* (bilingual English and German text), translated by Larry Fisher, David Magee, and Renate Vogel Berlin: Ernst, 1990

Weiss, Klaus-Dieter, *Young German Architects/Junge deutsche Architekten und Architektinnen* (bilingual English and German text), Basel, Switzerland, and Boston: Birkhäuser, 1998

Zukowsky, John (editor), *The Many Faces of Modern Architecture: Building in Germany between the Wars*, Munich and New York: Prestel, 1994

GETTY CENTER

Designed by Richard Meier; completed 1997
Los Angeles, California

In 1982, the Getty Trust decided to build a facility to house its administrative offices and the staffs of its six cultural programs.

It purchased a 110-acre site at the base of the Santa Monica Mountains north of Los Angeles, California, and invited 80 architects to submit their responses to a program calling for soundly constructed buildings to serve and enhance the Getty's institutions in a scheme "appropriate to the site and responsive to its uniqueness." In addition, the Getty Trust emphasized the need to meet these objectives in a manner that would bring aesthetic pleasure to the building's occupants, visitors, and neighboring community. After interviewing the finalists, the selection committee chose the American architect Richard Meier (1934–) to formulate the design.

The rugged topography of the promontory and a strict conditional-use permit enacted by a powerful neighborhood coalition placed unusual constraints on the architect, especially the restriction limiting the height of the buildings to 65 feet above the 896-foot hilltop. To meet this restriction and reduce the scale and monumentality of the project, Meier located approximately half the built work below ground with passageways connecting many of the facilities at a level of 876 feet. Above ground, he planned a campus of low buildings instead of one dominant structure and added a five-acre propylaeum (vestibule or entrance) to furnish parking and provide access to the acropolis via an electric tram.

Meier's design for the Getty Center exhibits significant departures from his previous work. One example involves his decision to create an assemblage of buildings instead of a stand-alone structure. This decision forced him to consider urban-planning concerns, such as the relationship of buildings and the nature and sequencing of their interstitial spaces. His response is a 24-acre campus emphasizing freedom of movement between human-scaled edifices and through generous courtyards and gardens. His choice of materials represents another change. Local resident groups rejected both Meier's signature white-enameled exteriors and his alternate choice of metal panels but approved his later recommendation of rough-cleft Italian travertine for rectilinear surfaces and complementary colored enameled aluminum panels for the curvilinear areas. Cutting the fossilized stone into 30-inch blocks to conform to the grid used as the basis of the Getty design presented another challenge, requiring the invention of a guillotine-type apparatus. In addition, Meier devised a method of supporting the cladding on metal plates, leaving open seams between blocks and space between waterproofed interior surfaces and the travertine, diverting rainfall behind the stone to protect the rough exterior from erosion. Meier's suspension of the travertine panels denies the weight and massing of masonry, prompting some critics to describe the stone as having a fake appearance. The nontraditional handling of the material does produce insubstantiality and unfortunate results in some areas, particularly in the surface irregularity of the tall piers in the garden courtyard, but overall the effect of the travertine's variations in color and texture complements the tiled surfaces and contributes to the unified aesthetic of the complex.

Although the individual steel-frame and reinforced-concrete structures vary in form, they continue the uniform aesthetic by repeating Meier's characteristic 1920s vocabulary of ship railings, flat roofs, and extensive glazing. References to the work of Le Corbusier, Rudolph Schindler, Frank Lloyd Wright, and others provide the distinguishing features between the individual structures and the institutions they house. The design of the Research Institute and the Museum rotunda stand out as original and

Cantilevered canopy over the main entrance to the Getty Center, designed by Richard Meier (1997)
Photo © Mary Ann Sullivan

sensitive compositions, whereas the other buildings appear conservative and understated, achieving their greatest success in dramatic terraces and passages that carefully frame views of Los Angeles, the mountains, and the ocean.

Complexity is introduced in the magnitude of the scheme and the particularity of the plan. An assortment of buildings tailored to the identities and requirements of the Getty programs creates a diverse yet homogeneous campus. Further complexity is added with the division of the J. Paul Getty Museum into an orientation building plus five exhibition pavilions. Meier's decision to conform to the undulation of the topography for the placement of the buildings instead of creating a uniform base platform also adds variety and reduces the apparent scale of the complex. He arranges the buildings along two prominent natural ridges. Buildings located on the eastern ridge include the Museum cluster; a building for the Art History Information Program staff and the administrative offices of the Getty Trust; a building housing the employees of the Conservation Institute, the Grants Program, and the Center for Education; and a 450-seat Auditorium building. The Research Institute for the History of Art and the Humanities and a support facility containing a public restaurant and cafeteria, plus private dining rooms and meeting rooms for staff, occupy the western ridge. The ravine between the ridges accommodates the entrance plaza, a grand staircase leading to the Museum cluster, and outdoor terraces for dining, circulation, and relaxation.

The deflecting axes of the overall layout and the focus on central circular forms in both the Museum Entrance Hall and the plan of the Research Institute exhibit elements evident in Meier's late work. Inconsistent elements in the completed complex include the decoration of the Museum's interiors by the architect and interior designer Thierry Despont and the central garden design by the artist Robert Irwin. Although the decision to create formal interiors consistent with the items of the collection offers some justification, the installation of Irwin's self-important scheme for the Central Garden is most unfortunate. Irwin's flagrant excess ignores and mars the tranquility and importance of the place expressed in Meier's earlier plan for the garden.

Discounting Irwin's incompatible intrusion, Meier's scheme reaches its highest level in the equipoise attained between the luminous aesthetic of buildings bathed in golden California sunlight and the spectacular spaces and landscape to which they relate. Architectural historian and critic Charles Jencks has praised Meier's ability to create a sense of intoxicating disorientation through the combination of all-encompassing space and continuous surfaces that promote a sense of suspended time and transcendence. At the Getty, this aesthetic experience, which Jencks calls "liminal space," pervades the Getty complex and provides an uplifting experience for the visitor and a true work of art.

CAROL A. HRVOL FLORES

Interior, looking north toward main entrance of the Getty Center
Photo © Mary Ann Sullivan

See also **Los Angeles (CA), United States; Meier, Richard (United States)**

Further Reading

The following list includes both books and articles produced during the design and construction of the Getty Center and those written after its completion. Most include detailed plans and photographs taken during and after construction. The articles in particular present contrasting viewpoints about the success of the design.

Betsky, Aaron, "Faulty Towers," *Architecture*, 86/12 (December 1997)
Brawne, Michael, *The Getty Center: Richard Meier and Partners*, London: Phaidon, 1998
"The Getty Center in Los Angeles," *Baumeister*, 95/2 (February 1998)
Jodidio, Philip, *Richard Meier*, Cologne: Taschen, 1995
Meier, Richard, *Richard Meier*, London: Academy Editions, and New York: St. Martin's Press, 1990
Meier, Richard, *Richard Meier, Architect: 1985–1991*, New York: Rizzoli, 1991
Meier, Richard, *Building the Getty*, New York: Knopf, 1997
Meier, Richard, *Richard Meier*, edited by Yukio Futagawa, Tokyo: A.D.A. Edita, 1997
"Meier's Magic Mountain," *Architectural Review*, 203/1212 (February 1998)
Newhouse, Victoria, *Towards a New Museum*, New York: Monacelli Press, 1998
Reese, Thomas F. and Carol McMichael Reese, "Richard Meier's New Getty Center in Los Angeles," *A + U*, 328/1 (January 1998)
Sorkin, Michael, "Come and Getty: Archmodernist Meier's Work Takes an Unexpected Turn toward Kitsch," *Metropolis*, 17/9 (June 1998)
Steele, James (editor), *Museum Builders*, London: Academy Editions, 1994
Williams, Harold, *The Getty Center Design Process*, Los Angeles: Getty Trust, 1991
Williams, Harold, *Making Architecture: The Getty Center*, Los Angeles: Getty Trust, 1997

GIEDION, SIGFRIED 1888–1968

Architectural historian and critic, Switzerland

A Swiss national born in Prague and educated in Vienna, Sigfried Giedion turned from his early technical training as an engineer to art history, studying under Heinrich Wölfflin in Zurich during World War I. His formal education scarcely reveals the foundational role that he would play as architectural critic, social anthropologist, industrial archaeologist, and official historian and propagandist for the modern movement. In the latter role, Joseph Rykwert once called Giedion "the most important, indeed the only serious, historian of nineteenth- and twentieth-century architecture."

Under Wölfflin, he produced *Spätbarocker und Romantischer Klassizismus* (1922; [Late Baroque and Romantic Classicism]), a conventional study of architectural style. Giedion tentatively challenged typical categories of style as set down by his master, finding in neoclassicism not a style per se but a "coloring" that one could trace through baroque and other periods of architecture. Thus equipped, Giedion proceeded to explode the entire idea of style, dismissing the 19th-century obsession with it as a colossal squandering of energy. He substituted the experience of space for style, reading the history of architecture in terms of containing, framing, spanning, and shaping space.

Swept up by the political turbulence after World War I, Giedion turned to modern architecture as a means of achieving the cultural renewal that the rising generation sought. He met Walter Gropius at the 1923 Bauhaus Exhibition and Le Corbusier at the 1925 Esprit Nouveau Exhibition in Paris, becoming a colleague and intimate of both men. Out of the latter meeting was born the Congrès Internationaux d'Architecture Moderne (CIAM) in 1928, the organizational heart of modern architecture, for which Giedion served as secretary-general until 1954, when it dissolved. His house served as the group's headquarters and he as its chief apologist.

Also in 1928, Giedion published *Bauen in Frankreich, Bauen in Eisen, Bauen in Eisenbeton* (as *Building in France, Building in Iron, Building in Ferroconcrete*, 1995), in which he claimed a vast and forgotten patrimony for modern architecture in the ferrovitreous market halls, train sheds, and exhibition buildings of the 19th century. On Giedion, Spiro Kostof wrote, "the modern masters had gained an authoritative spokesman who would ease them into history." He would also turn that history into a weapon for their cause.

In the 1930s, Giedion wrote regular articles on modern design for two newspapers, built two model houses, organized an exhibition on the bathroom, tried his hand at film, and founded a company to foster connections between industry and interior architecture. He was more activist than academic until 1938–39, when with the help of Gropius he was invited to deliver the Charles Eliot Norton Lectures at Harvard.

The exposure to the United States allowed him to expand on the ideas first set down in *Bauen in Frankreich*, and in 1941 he published *Space, Time, and Architecture*. Here Giedion observed what he considered the disastrous rift between thought and feeling that arose in the 19th century, roughly parallel to the separation of structure from facade in 19th-century architecture. Giedion found in the simultaneous emergence of space-time theory, cubism, film, and a number of other phenomena at the beginning of the century the stirrings of the cultural regeneration that he sought. These parallel cultural ideas, he believed, would eventually reunite "the divided ego of man" through their apotheosis in modern architecture.

He thus rewrote the history of architecture, using the great works of 19th-century engineering as the heroic precursors to modern architecture, in the process culling out the bulk of historicist architecture as irrelevant. He isolated "constituent facts" ("those tendencies which, when they are suppressed, inevitably reappear") from "transitory" ones, which disappear after a time, a dubious method intended to reconstruct a more vital history. Giedion used history to press a set of contemporary concerns, and this widened his tome's relevance. For example, the ultimate object of Giedion's space-time theory was urban planning, the subject of the final three chapters of his book and arguably the most important issue of the early 1940s. Reprinted and expanded several times, *Space, Time, and Architecture* became the standard history of modern architecture for several generations of architecture and architectural history students who affectionately called it "Giedion's Bible."

However, the artifice of Giedion's method and history led Kostof to remark that in hindsight it was apparent "how often the advocate led the historian astray." Nikolaus Pevsner, although full of admiration, called his method "a sin in a historian." Giedion, however, believed passionately in a "presentist" history. He studied the past in order to engage with the issues of his day, and he did so without apology. This came with some radical methodological consequences. Chronology and periodicity meant less than correlation and connections between distant periods. He sacrificed exhaustive research of a topic to the broad survey of linked phenomena and scrapped dispassionate, objective inquiry for the passionate polemic. Great works yielded pride of place to fragments, anonymous objects, and a leveling of all artifacts to equal status as evidence. Even a spoon, he later wrote, reflects the sun. This led to a highly selective, one-sided history but one of immense rhetorical power, especially in an era in step with his polemic, ready to forgive his abuse of 19th-century historicism. With Lewis Mumford, he must be considered one of the pioneers of cultural history in its modern interdisciplinary form.

Giedion's next book, the classic *Mechanization Takes Command* (1948), left the field of architecture proper to survey what he called the "anonymous history" of industrialization and mechanization. The apocalyptic title announced the prevailing theme of the book: to assess how the increasing rationalization of our means of living had altered human consciousness, alienating humanity from nature and from its own nature. Nothing escaped Giedion's analysis, as nothing escaped mechanization, from birth, domestic work, and most famously the bath to the mechanization of death in Chicago's meat-packing industry. Of the last he wrote, with chilling implications (given that he wrote during the war years), "Has this neutrality to death had any further effect upon us? . . . It did not bare itself in large scale until the War, when whole populations, as defenseless as the animals hooked head downwards on the traveling chain, were obliterated with trained neutrality."

At about the same time that he wrote *Mechanization*, Giedion engaged in the important architectural debate on the "new monumentality," first addressed in his 1943 "Nine Points on Monumentality," written with Fernand Léger. On one level, Giedion recognized the limitations and sterility of functionalism as a representational idiom and sought to broaden modern architecture to express ceremonial and communal life. This is especially important in light of postwar reconstruction. As communities set out to rebuild the central institutions of society, Giedion keenly felt the need for a symbolic architecture in the absence of traditional forms. Already a contentious debate, given the uses to which fascism and communism had put monumental architecture, Giedion made it worse by proposing "great spectacles capable of fascinating the people." However, monumentality meant something even deeper: the search for enduring symbols and permanence in a society that was in a constant state of flux.

Herein lies both the continuity and the importance of Giedion's oeuvre. He was first and foremost a humanist. His study of society and its artifacts, whether architecture or the machine, was driven by a longing for a natural order, an organic history to counter the contingencies, ruptures, and ephemerality that characterizes so much of modernity and scholarship on modernity. In his work of the 1950s and 1960s, the search led him back to ancient and prehistoric art and architecture, surveying Rome, Greece, Mesopotamia, Egypt, and the cave paintings of Lascaux, where he squeezed out of the much earlier objects and images the same fundamental ideas about the human confrontation with its environment.

ANDREW M. SHANKEN

See also **Congrès Internationaux d'Architecture Moderne (CIAM, 1927–); Glass; Gropius, Walter (Germany); Mumford, Lewis (United States); Pevsner, Nikolaus (England)**

Biography

Born in Prague, 14 April 1888; son of a Swiss industrialist. Studied mechanical engineering in Vienna; studied art history in Zurich and in Munich under Heinrich Wölfflin 1913–22; visited the Bauhaus, Weimar 1923. Lecturer, Harvard University, Cambridge, Massachusetts 1938–39; professor, Technische Hochschule, Zurich from 1946. Founding member, CIAM 1928. Died in Zurich, 9 April 1968.

Selected Publications

Spätbarocker und romantischer Klassizismus, 1922
Bauen in Frankreich, Bauen in Eisen, Bauen in Eisenbeton, 1928; as *Building in France, Building in Iron, Building in Ferroconcrete*, edited by Georgiadis Sokratis, translated by Duncan Barry, 1995
Space, Time, and Architecture: The Growth of a New Tradition, 1941; 5th edition, revised and enlarged, 1967

Mechanization Takes Command: A Contribution to Anonymous History, 1948
Architecture, You, and Me: The Diary of a Development, 1958
The Eternal Present: A Contribution on Constancy and Change, 1962
The Beginnings of Architecture, 1964
Architecture and the Phenomenon of Transition: The Three Space Conceptions of Architecture, 1971

Further Reading

Sokratis has written the best recent work on Giedion, but much of the better scholarship comes from Giedion's contemporaries, including Pevsner, Rykwert, and, more recently, Kostof. See also Sokratis's excellent introduction to *Building in France* (see above).

Frampton, Kenneth, "Giedion in America: Reflections in a Mirror," *Architectural Design*, 51, no. 6/7 (1981)
Hofer, Paul (editor), *Hommage à Giedion, Profile seiner Persönlichkeit*, Basel, Switzerland, and Stuttgart, Germany: Birkhäuser, 1971
Kostof, Spiro, "Architecture, You, and Him: The Mark of Sigfried Giedion," *Daedalus* (winter 1976)
Pevsner, Nikolaus, "Judges VI, 34," *Architectural Review*, 106 (1949)
Rykwert, Joseph, "Siegfried Giedion and the Notion of Style," *Burlington Magazine*, 96 (1954)
Sokratis, Georgiadis, *Siegfried Giedion: eine intellektuelle Biographie*, Zürich: Amman, 1989; as *Siegfried Giedion: An Intellectual Biography*, translated by Colin Hall, Edinburgh: Edinburgh University Press, 1993

GILBERT, CASS 1859–1934

Architect, United States

Cass Gilbert belonged to a group of architects who advanced a distinctively American interpretation of the French Beaux-Arts academic tradition. Together with McKim, Mead and White, with whom he apprenticed as a young architect, Gilbert supported the American Academy in Rome and with Daniel Burnham contributed to the City Beautiful movement.

The two decades preceding World War I coincided with the emergence of the United States as a world power, the search for a national cultural identity, and the increasing dominance of corporate structure in American life. In this volatile context, Gilbert conceived his buildings, beginning with the Minnesota State Capitol (1895–1903) and culminating with the Woolworth Building (1910–13), as total works of art that carried rich symbolic meanings and enhanced their urban surroundings with beauty. As such, they served as persuasive communicators of emerging institutional identities and corporate power. Gilbert believed that architecture should affirm the existing social order, raise the general level of culture, and foster the mythology of America as heir to the great civilizations of the past.

Gilbert inclined toward the picturesque, resisting the efforts of his Beaux-Arts instructor at the Massachusetts Institute of Technology, Eugene Letàng, to discipline his designs with a French-inspired compositional rigor. Gilbert toured England, France, and Italy during 1880 to sketch significant historical buildings, an activity that inspired his design imagination throughout his career. His apprenticeship with Stanford White of McKim, Mead and White from 1880 to 1882 motivated his interests in classicism and encouraged his tendency to see buildings in a painterly way, as memorable compositions that

had scenographic potential within a broader urban or landscape setting.

Gilbert returned to St. Paul in 1882 and two years later formed a partnership with James Knox Taylor that was dissolved in 1891, when Gilbert began exploring the possibility of forming a partnership with Daniel Burnham in Chicago. Although Burnham chose Charles Atwood instead as the successor to John Wellborn Root, in 1895 Gilbert won the competition for the Minnesota State Capitol in St. Paul, which catapulted his name onto the national architectural scene. He moved east, and while working on his first steel-framed office building, the Brazer Building (1894) in Boston, he met Edward R. Andrews and in 1898 secured the commission for the Broadway Chambers Building in New York. Gilbert opened an office in the city the following year, in time to enter the United States Custom House competition of 1899. He tied with Carrère and Hastings for first place, and after a storm of controversy, he secured the commission.

Gilbert's emphasis on a Beaux-Arts composition's scenographic potential reached a climax following the World's Columbian Exposition of 1893 in Chicago with his designs for the Minnesota State Capitol and the United States Custom House (1899–1907) in New York. The Minnesota State Capitol had a classical composition inspired by McKim, Mead and White's Rhode Island State Capitol (1891–1903) and a dome modeled on St. Peter's in Rome. It had fine proportions, solid construction in white Georgia marble, and a profusion of sculptures and mural paintings, among them Daniel Chester French's gilded sculpture, *The Progress of the State*, and Edward Simmons' mural, *The Civilization of the Northwest*. These gave a powerful visual identity to the collectively held image of an ideal capitol. Similarly, Gilbert's United States Custom House had an opulent facade, graced with a giant Corinthian order and French Second Empire ornamental motifs.

Gilbert's involvement with the City Beautiful movement began with his plan for Washington, D.C. (1900), which presaged the later Senate Park Commission plan. For his Minnesota State Capitol, Gilbert designed three monumentally scaled approaches (1903–06, unexecuted), and for the center of New Haven, Connecticut, he designed two broad avenues connecting the historic green with a new, secondary civic center and railroad station (1907–10, unexecuted). Gilbert's campus plans, among them the University of Minnesota (1908) in St. Paul, the University of Texas (1909–14) in Austin, and Oberlin College (1912) in Ohio, had the compositional hierarchies, axial relationships, and terminal vistas typically featured in City Beautiful designs.

Like his Beaux-Arts contemporaries, Gilbert thought that designs for public buildings, inherently timeless, should respect the classical ideal of beauty. Skyscrapers, however, a modern building type, along with railroad stations and bridges, suggested more up-to-date solutions. Gilbert's West Street Building (1905–07) and Woolworth Building (1910–13), both in lower Manhattan, celebrated the skyscraper's lofty heights with verticals inspired by Louis Sullivan's skyscrapers. Seeking the proper composition for an office headquarters in the city, Gilbert studied the towered secular buildings—*hotels des villes*, cloth halls, and belfries—of medieval Flemish centers of trade, among them Bruges. These he associated with the intensely commercial, corporate, and competitive urban civilization then burgeoning in

United States Supreme Court Building (1935), Washington, D.C.
Photo © Mary Ann Sullivan

New York. The Woolworth Building, commissioned by Frank Woolworth as the headquarters for his five-and-ten-cent merchandising empire, had a tower that rose straight upward from the sidewalk to command the skyline like a cathedral spire. Gilbert's design reverberated with historical memories but also projected an adventuresome spirit of modernity by celebrating the energy and optimism of commercial New York.

Gilbert remained faithful to the distinction between the modern and the timeless according to building type, but by the late 1910s his finest works suggested a polarizing tension in his architectural designs that he never fully resolved. He designed the U.S. Army Supply Base (1918–19) for a 100-acre waterfront site in Brooklyn, New York, finding inspiration in the factories of Detroit architect Albert Kahn. The Supply Base's bold, abstract masses in concrete seemed to chart an increasingly modern direction for his practice. Gilbert's contemporary Detroit Public Library (1918–21), however, a finely proportioned, delicately detailed, and erudite Renaissance *palazzo*, showed that he continued to honor the classical past. The most convincing work of Gilbert's late career, the United States Supreme Court (1928–35) in Washington, D.C., had a composition that vividly proclaimed the majesty of the law, replete with allegorical sculpture and inscriptions symbolizing liberty and justice. It was among the last of such classical monuments erected near Washington's Mall.

GAIL FENSKE

See also **Burnham, Daniel H. (United States); Carrère, John Mervin, and Thomas Hastings (United States); City Beautiful Movement; Court House; Library; McKim, Mead and White (United States); Neoclassicism; Sullivan, Louis (United States); Woolworth Building, New York City**

Biography

Born 29 November 1859 in Zanesville, Ohio; attended Massachusetts Institute of Technology, Boston 1878–79. Moved to New York City to apprentice for McKim, Mead and White 1880–82; returned to St. Paul, Minnesota 1882. Formed partnership with James Knox Taylor in St. Paul 1884–91; won competition for the Minnesota State Capitol in St. Paul 1895; offers to design state capitols in West Virginia and Arkansas followed. President of American Institute of Architects (AIA) 1908, 1909; founder of the Architecture League of New York, served as president 1913–14. Chevalier of the Legion of Honor of France, received the order of King Albert of Belgium. Member of American Academy of Arts and Letters 1908; President of National Academy of Design, New York 1926–33; awarded Gold Medal, Society of Arts and Sciences 1931. Died 17 May 1934.

Selected Works

Brazer Building, Boston, Massachusetts, 1894
Minnesota State Capitol, St. Paul, Minnesota, 1903
United States Custom House, New York City, 1907
West Street Building, New York City, 1907
University of Minnesota Campus Plan, St. Paul, Minnesota, 1908
Woolworth Building, New York City, 1913
University of Texas Campus Plan, Austin, Texas, 1914
U.S. Army Supply Base, Brooklyn, New York, 1919
Detroit Public Library, Michigan, 1921
United States Supreme Court, Washington, D.C., 1935

Further Reading

Blodgett, Geoffrey, "Cass Gilbert, Architect: Conservative at Bay," *Journal of American History*, 72 (December 1985)
Christen, Barbara, "Cass Gilbert and the Ideal of the City Beautiful: City and Campus Plans, 1900–1916" (Ph.D. dissertation), Graduate Center, City University of New York, 1997
Fenske, Gail, "The 'Skyscraper Problem' and the City Beautiful: The Woolworth Building" (Ph.D. dissertation), M.I.T., 1988
Irish, Sharon, *Cass Gilbert, Architect: Modern Traditionalist*, New York: Monacelli Press, 1999
Irish, Sharon, "Cass Gilbert's Career in New York, 1899–1905" (Ph.D. dissertation), Northwestern University, 1985
Jones, Robert Allen, "Cass Gilbert, Midwestern Architect in New York" (Ph.D. dissertation), Case Western Reserve University, 1976; New York: Arno Press, 1982
Morgan, William Towner, "The Politics of Business in the Career of Cass Gilbert" (Ph.D. dissertation), University of Minnesota, 1972
Thompson, Neil, *Minnesota's State Capitol: The Art and Politics of a Public Building*, St. Paul: Minnesota Historical Society, 1974

GILL, IRVING JOHN 1870–1936

Architect, United States

Shortly after the turn of the 20th century in southern California, Irving Gill emerged from under the influence of various historical revivals and began to create a simple, straightforward architecture that looked to the future and not the past. Instead of highlighting traditional building methods (i.e., heavy frame construction) and materials (i.e., wood or stone) as most of his Californian Arts and Crafts contemporaries, such as the Greene Brothers, Ernest Coxhead, and Bernard Maybeck, were doing, Gill began to experiment with modern structural methods and materials as well as undecorated surfaces. The result was an architecture of aesthetic severity, technological breakthrough, and social inventiveness. As exemplified by his most famous building, the Walter Dodge House (1916), Gill created a sprawling reinforced-concrete frame of irregularly massed cubes organized around a raised patio and clad in nothing other than white stucco.

For the first 15 years of his career, which included a stint working in Louis Sullivan's Chicago office, Gill's buildings ranged over the terrain of 19th-century historicism. After 1906,

however, most of Gill's buildings began to be orchestrated by his own design method of straight lines and smooth plaster walls. Aside from arches, placed at entrance vestibules or covered passageways, or rustic columns, used around courtyards, Gill's buildings are soliloquies of the unornamented, crisp right angle. In the Russell Allen House (1907), Gill worked from a central box modulated by selected projections and perforations and relentless in its use of lean moldings around windows and the flat roof. The only ornament was a pair of columns at the entrance. In 1908, the rectangular Wilson Acton Hotel and Scripps Building, both in La Jolla, eschewed ornament altogether, relying only on a regular pattern of fenestration within quadratic white surfaces for their compositional effect.

Gill was among the first American architects to design principally from the fundamentals of geometry and modern construction. He envisioned a new aesthetic based on the visual revelation of structure and the banishment of cluttering ornament. As he wrote in his essay, "The Home of the Future" (1916), "There is something very restful and satisfying to my mind in the simple cube house with creamy walls, sheer and plain, rising boldly into the sky, unrelieved by cornices or overhang of roof, unornamented save for the vines that soften a line."

This stance on ornament is often compared to that of Adolf Loos. Yet, although the two architects shared an interest in blank surfaces as well as the savings of labor and materials brought about by eliminating ornament, Gill went further than Loos in his conception of inexpensive houses mass-produced for a democratic society of workers. The recently discovered technology of reinforced-concrete construction was the basis for Gill's new aesthetic of line and plane. Using either a concrete frame with hollow terra-cotta tile in-fill or poured-in-place concrete walls, Gill began to experiment with very thin walls, bringing down a building's mass to its utilitarian essentials and bringing down its cost to middle-class affordability. For the La Jolla Woman's Club (1913), Gill was one of the first architects to experiment with the new idea of tilt-up construction, which combines the permanence of concrete with the low costs of shortened construction schedules that come with the elimination of formwork.

Concrete appealed to Gill because of its strength, long-term cost savings, and permanence. He was opposed to the cheap, temporary wood-frame construction common to California home design, a method that encouraged senseless ornamental buildup. A concrete house expressed its interior arrangement on the exterior and derived its expressive power from concrete in both realms. It also provided the possibility for energy-efficient insulation and easy maintenance. In 1915, Gill published an article, "New Ideas about Concrete Floors," that promoted the idea of mixing color with the cement to produce polychrome tones in a floor, what he described as "an effect of old Spanish leather."

Given his interest in designing for the California landscape, Gill created a number of site plans that maximized the connectivity of indoor and outdoor spaces. The Bishop's School (1908) in La Jolla featured long arcades (influenced by California's Mission architecture) that created an expansive intermediate space between interiors and the central lawn as gathering space. At the Henry Timken House (1911), three loggias open onto a screened court that in turn faces onto a large garden and pool. The Paul Miltimore House (1911) is tied to its landscape by great project-

Walter Dodge House, Los Angeles, California (1916)
© Historic American Buildings Survey/Library of Congress

ing pergolas supported by rustic columns. However, perhaps Gill's most innovative planning took place in larger apartment complexes for workers, such as the Bella Vista Terrace (1910), a set of 12 cottages grouped around a central pergola. In contrast to typical workers' apartments, each cottage had a great deal of light and possessed private as well as shared community garden spaces. In 1912 Gill took these ideas further and designed several commercial and residential structures for the model city of Torrance, a Y-shaped plan oriented to give a view of Mount San Antonio in the San Gabriel Mountains.

In all, over the course of the first decades of the 20th century, Gill's architecture was one of the rare cases in which American scientific and practical approaches were embedded not only in building systems analysis or program efficiency but also in a forward-looking art of architectural composition and massing. By marrying aims of structural expression and geometric elementalism, Gill let architecture speak from the cubes and lines that emerge from the complexities of constructional actions and those that lead back to the most basic simplicities.

MITCHELL SCHWARZER

Biography

Born in Tully, New York (near Syracuse), 26 April 1870; son of a farmer, carpenter, and building contractor. No academic architectural training. Employed in architectural office of Ellis G. Hall, Syracuse 1889; employed in architectural office of Joseph Silsbee, Chicago 1890, who helped introduce the Shingle style into the Midwest; worked in architectural office of Dankmar Adler and Louis Sullivan, Chicago 1891–93, where Frank Lloyd Wright was chief draftsman. Arrived in San Diego 1893. Went into partnership with Joseph Falkenham, designer of Queen Anne homes, 1894–95; went into partnership with William Sterling Hebbard, former draftsman for firm of Burnham and Root, 1896–1907; established new partnership with Frank Mead 1907; independent architectural practice from 1907; took on Louis Gill, his nephew, as a partner, 1914. Elected secretary of San Diego Architectural Association 1910. Married Marion Waugh Brashears 1928. Died in Carlsbad, California, 7 October 1936.

Selected Works

All buildings are in California unless otherwise noted.

Birckhead House, Portsmouth, Rhode Island, 1902
Burnham House, San Diego, 1906
Laughlin House, Los Angeles, 1907
Russell Allen House, Bonita, 1907
Newell Webster House, San Diego, 1908
Scripps Building and Water Tower, La Jolla, 1908

Wilson Acton Hotel, La Jolla, 1908
Bishop's Day School, San Diego, 1908
G.W. Simmons House, San Diego, 1909
Christian Science Church, San Diego, 1909
Lewis Courts, Sierra Madre, 1910
Paul Miltimore House, South Pasadena, 1911
Henry Timken House, San Diego, 1911
Banning House, Los Angeles, 1912
Commercial and Residential Buildings, Torrance, 1912
Woman's Club, La Jolla, 1913
Walter Dodge House, Los Angeles, 1916
Ellen Scripps House, La Jolla, 1916
Gilman Hall, Bishop's Day School, San Diego, 1916
Horatio West Court, Santa Monica, 1919
First Church of Christ Scientist, Coronado, 1927
Master Plan, Oceanside Civic Center, 1929

Selected Publications

"New Ideas about Concrete Floors," *Sunset Magazine* (December 1915)
"The Home of the Future: The New Architecture of the West, Small Homes for a Great Country," *The Craftsman* (May 1916)

Further Reading

Gebhard, David, "Irving Gill," in *California Design, 1910*, edited by Timothy Andersen, Eudorah M. Moore, and Robert Winter, Pasadena, California: Design Publications, 1974
Gebhard, David, "Irving Gill," in *Toward a Simpler Way of Life: The Arts and Crafts Architects of California*, edited by Robert Winter, Berkeley: University of California Press, 1997
Hines, Thomas S., *Irving Gill and the Architecture of Reform: A Study in Modernist Architectural Culture*, New York: Monacelli Press, 1999
Jordy, William H., "Craftsmanship as Reductive Simplification: Irving Gill's Dodge House," in *Progressive and Academic Ideals at the Turn of the Twentieth Century*, by Jordy, Garden City, New York: Doubleday, 1972
Kamerling, Bruce, *Irving J. Gill: Architect*, San Diego, California: San Diego Historical Society, 1993
McCoy, Esther, *Five California Architects*, New York: Reinhold, 1960
Schaffer, Sarah, "A Significant Sentence upon the Earth: Irving J. Gill, Progressive Architect," parts 1 and 2, *Journal of San Diego History*, 43 and 44 (Fall 1997 and Winter 1998)

GINZBURG, MOISEI 1892–1946

Architect, USSR

Moisei Iakovlevich Ginzburg was the leading theoretician of Constructivism in architecture, a prolific designer, and a pioneer in the research and construction of collective housing. Ginzburg was born in Minsk, the capital of Belorussia, where his father was practicing architecture. On high school graduation, young Moisei departed for France to study. After a brief period in Paris at the École des Beaux-Arts and in Toulouse at the Art Academy, he enrolled in the architecture program of the Academia di Belle Arti in Milan, Italy, graduating in 1914. The outbreak of World War I forced him to return via the Balkans to Moscow, where he continued his education at the Riga Polytechnic (evacuated to Moscow during the war), earning a degree in architectural engineering in 1917.

A man of enormous energy and with a desire for continuous learning, Ginzburg departed for the Crimean peninsula to head the office for the preservation of cultural monuments and to investigate Tatar folk architecture. He returned to Moscow in 1921 and published a series of articles on Tatar art. He devoted the following years to pedagogical and scholarly work, teaching at the Moscow Institute for Civil Engineering (MIGI, later MVTI) and the Higher Artistic-Technical Studios (Vkhutemas). A member of the State Academy of Artistic Sciences, he headed an expedition to Bukhara, Uzbekistan in 1924 and during the following year traveled to Turkey. He published two theoretical works on architecture before becoming a founding member of the Society of Contemporary Architects (OSA) and editor (with Alexander Vesnin) of the society's journal, *Sovremennaia arkhitekture* (Contemporary Architecture) from 1926 to 1930.

During his student years, Ginzburg encountered French Art Nouveau, Italian futurism, and the work of Frank Lloyd Wright. Moscow in the early 1920s was the center of contending avant-garde factions, where European avant-garde periodicals were available. For example, the trilingual magazine *Vesch/Gegenstand/Object*, initiated in 1922 in Berlin by El Lissitzky (1890–1941) and Ilya Ehrenburg (1891–1967), related Soviet trends to their Western counterparts. Ginzburg's first building in Moscow, the Crimean Pavilion at the First Agricultural and Handicraft Exhibition (1923), was inspired by the picturesque asymmetry of traditional Tatar houses. He also aimed at abstracting the underlying principles that shaped folk architecture and defining the "distinct creative order" concealed behind its "picturesque spontaneity." He clarified this creative order in his theoretical work *Ritm v arkhitekture* [Rhythm in Architecture], published in 1923, and *Stil i epokha* (Style and Epoch), published the following year.

Vkhutemas was a testing ground for new aesthetic ideas. Ginzburg wrote his *Ritm v arkhitekture* as a pedagogical tool for his course on the theory of architectural composition. He analyzed the rhythm of architectural styles and the harmonious relationships between architectural forms. He defined harmony as "the mathematical essence of rhythm," supporting his claim with concepts from the physiology of visual perception. Ginzburg also compared proportional relationships in architecture to harmonious "chords consisting of melodious notes" in music. He began working on *Style and Epoch* while *Ritm v arkhitekture* was near publication, thus responding to the former to "express the rhythmical pulse of our time." Present dynamic trends are best manifested in new technologies, Ginzburg believed, and therefore he took the machine as a paradigm for modern functional design. He devised a system of vector diagrams to demonstrate "the dynamic content" of previous architectural styles compared with "a contemporary architectural concept" embedded in the 1923 Palace of Labor competition entry by the Vesnin brothers. Accordingly, the form and sense of dynamic movement is best captured in asymmetrical architectural compositions symbolizing "a previously unknown tension." Although Ginzburg did not elaborate his concept of rhythm and dynamism in subsequent publications, his concrete designs relied heavily on these constructs.

Ginzburg continued to clarify and develop the theoretical foundations of Constructivism through the pages of *Sovremennaia arkhitektura*. For him, the functional method integrated all possible aspects of architectural considerations into design solutions, including "the national uniqueness" of architecture. His 1926 project for the House of the Soviets in Makhach Kala, the capital of the Dagestan Autonomous Republic, accounted for the inferences of persistent climatic and biological conditions that sustain life and have defined the specific national aspect of each republic. Although Ginzburg did not win this competition, his design for the center of Alma-Ata, the new capital of Kazakhstan, placed first the following year. This urban public space was surrounded by the House of Government, the Turkestan-Siberian Railroad Administration (1899–1974, both designed by Ginzburg and his student Ignatii Milinis), and the House of Communications (1897–1972, designed by Georgi Gerasimov). Each building, a dynamic asymmetrical composition of several volumes, contained a semiprivate interior courtyard. Roof terraces provided magnificent views of the surrounding mountains.

After building an apartment and communal housing block (1927) in Moscow, Ginzburg was appointed in 1928 to organize and head the Standardization Section of the Construction Committee (Stroikom RSFSR). His group produced five types of housing units in several variations for prefabrication and speedy assembly all over Russia. The most economical type, yet novel in its spatial qualities, was immediately built in Moscow (1928–31), for the Commissariat of Finances (Narkomfin). This hous-

ing type was used by several OSA members in their subsequent projects and by Ginzburg in the workers' housing (1931) in Rostokino, near Moscow. It became fashionable among European intellectuals because of Le Corbusier's housing blocks based on similar apartment units.

Ginzburg also headed the Section for Socialist Resettlement and participated in the 1929 Green City Resort competition. His project, a model for transforming Moscow to a green city, consisted of ribbons of prefabricated housing units and transportation-commercial-cultural nodes forming community centers. Although several experimental units were built (1931), this project never materialized. None of his major competition projects—the Palace of Soviets in Moscow (1932), the Synthesizing Theater in Sverdlovsk (1932), and the Commissariat of Heavy Industry in Moscow (1934)—was realized. Yet they influenced modern architectural thought in Russia and Western Europe.

After all architectural organizations were disbanded and the official Union of Soviet Architects was formed in 1932, Ginzburg was elected to the board. From 1933 on, he headed a design studio to the Commissariat of Heavy Industry (Narkomtiazhprom), and when the Soviet Academy of Architecture was established in 1939, he was among its first academicians. Ginzburg

Apartment House (1931) for the People's Commissariat of Finance (Narkomfin), Moscow, by Moisei Ginzburg
© William C. Brumfield

became editor and contributor to the academy's multivolume *Vseobshchaia istoriia arkhitektury* (1940–45; *History of World Architecture*). In 1945, he headed the academy's team charged with the planning and restoration of Crimea. He died on 7 January 1946 as the work began.

MILKA BLIZNAKOV

Biography

Born in Minsk, Russia, 23 May 1892. Attended École des Beaux-Arts, Paris; attended École d'Architecture, Toulouse; studied under Gaetano Moretti, Academia di Belle Arti, Milan; graduated 1914; received an engineering degree from Rizhsky Polytechnic, Moscow 1914. Private practice, the Crimea 1918–21; editor, *Arkhitektura* 1923; founder and editor, with Aleksandr Vesnin, *Sovremennaia arkhitektura* 1926–30; head, Sector for Standardization and Industrialization of Construction 1941–45; founder, editor, contributor, *Vseobshchaya istoriya arkhitektury*. Professor, Vkhutemas, Moscow from 1923; instructor, Moscow Institute of Higher Technology from 1923. Member, Moscow Architectural Society; member, Russian Academy of Artistic Sciences; founding member, Association of Contemporary Architects (OSA) 1925; member, design studio, Heavy Industry Commissariat from 1933; member, First Congress of Soviet Architects 1937; academician, Soviet Academy of Architecture 1939. Died in Moscow, 7 January 1946.

Selected Works

Crimean Pavilion at the First Agricultural and Handicraft Exhibition, Moscow, 1923
Apartment and communal housing block for the State Insurance Bureau (Gostrakh), Moscow, 1927
House of Government, Alma-Ata, Kazakh Republic (with Ignatii Milinis), 1931
Experimental housing complex for the People's Commissariat of Finance (Narkomfin), Moscow (with Ignatii Milinis), 1931
Workers' housing in Rostokino, near Moscow (with Solomon Lisagor), 1931
Prefabricated individual housing units for the Green City competition, experimental models built near Moscow (with Mikhail Barshch), 1931
Experimental housing complex for Ural regional economic counsel (Uraloblsovnarkhos), Sverdlovsk (with Alexander Pasternak and S. Prokhorov), 1932
Turkestan-Siberian Railroad Administration, Alma-Ata, Kazakh Republic (with Ignatii Milinis), 1934
Ordjonikidze Sanatorium for the Ministry of Heavy Industry, Kislovodsk, 1937

Selected Publications

Ritm v arkhitekture, 1923
Stil i epokha, 1924; as *Style and Epoch*, translated by Anatole Senkevich, 1982 (includes substantial introduction by translator)
Zhilishche, 1934
Arkhitektura sanatoriia NKTP v Kislovodske, 1940
Ginzburg also published numerous articles in the journal *Sovremennaia arkhitektura* between 1926 and 1930.

Further Reading

Although Moisei Ginzburg is mentioned and/or quoted in every book on Constructivism, no book about him in English exists.

Bliznakov, Milka, "Rhythm as a Fundamental Concept of Architecture," *Experiment: A Journal of Russian Culture*, 2 (1996)
Bliznakov, Milka, "Soviet Housing during the Experimental Years, 1918–1933," in *Russian Housing in the Modern Age: Design and Social History*, edited by William Brumfield and Blair Ruble, Cambridge and New York: Cambridge University Press, 1993
Buchli, Victor, "Moisei Ginzburg's Narkomfin Communal House in Moscow: Contesting the Social and Material World," *Journal of the Society of Architectural Historians*, 57/2 (1998)
Cooke, Catherine, *Russian Avant-Garde: Theories of Art, Architecture, and the City*, London: Academy Editions, 1995 (includes translations of several articles by Ginzburg published in the journal *Sovremennaia arkhitektura*)
Khan-Magomedov, Selim O., "M.Y. Ginzburg," *Architectural Design*, 2 (1970)
Khan-Magomedov, Selim O., *Moisej Ginzburg*, Milan: Angeli, 1977; 2nd edition, 1983
Khan-Magomedov, Selim O., *Pioneers of Soviet Architecture: The Search for New Solutions in the 1920s and 1930s*, translated by Alexander Lieven, edited by Catherine Cooke, New York: Rizzoli, and London: Thames and Hudson, 1987
Kopp, Anatole, *L'architecture de la période stalinienne*, Grenoble, France: Presses Universitaires de Grenoble, 1978; as *Constructivist Architecture in the USSR*, London: Academy Editions, and New York: St. Martin's Press, 1985

GLACIER MUSEUM, FJÆRLAND, NORWAY

Designed by Sverre Fehn, completed 1991

The Glacier Museum (1989–91) in Fjærland, Norway, is the product of the Norwegian architect Sverre Fehn. A private entrepreneur commissioned Fehn to create a building that could serve as an educational center for schools, as a restaurant, and as an information center for tourists to explore Fjærland's two branches of the Jostedal Glacier. This glacier is the largest in Europe and attracts scientists and tourists alike to western Norway.

Fehn, born in 1924, is a key figure to emerge among the "progressive" Scandinavian architects organized by Arne Korsmo in 1950. The Progressives sought to create architecture that was void of any links with the nostalgic architecture of postwar nationalism in Scandinavia. Architects such as Fehn, along with Korsmo, Jørn Utzon, and Christian Norberg-Schultz, embraced the ideas of the Modern movement, especially Alvar Aalto's organic functionalist ideas. Fehn later was to exert the influence that Louis Kahn's architecture and phenomenological writings had on his work.

Fehn creates a regionalist architecture, using elements of traditional Nordic construction in innovative ways. His modernist materials include concrete, steel, glass, wood, and slate quarried in Norway. In his buildings, slate is used as it has been for more than a century in Norway: in large square shapes on floors and in various shapes as roofing. Fehn's architecture is usually devoid of additive color, although occasionally one color is used as an accent to the structure.

The Glacier Museum thus incorporates building traditions from Fehn's Nordic heritage that he translates into a modernist architectural language, giving the museum as well as his other works, by choice of materials as well as form, a distinct identity. Located in western Norway close to the end of the Fjærlandfjord is the long valley plain carved by the glacier, where the Glacier Museum, also known as the Norsk Bremuseum, resides. The museum lies on a delta formed by sediments dating back to a time when the glacier ran into the Fjærland Fjord. The site is created by deposits of sand and gravel that are loosened by the glacier's movement and melting. The sloping exterior walls consist of grayish-white concrete that repeats the forms of the steep mountain walls. The dark coloring of the slate and the weightiness of the concrete give the building its mass while the glass and wood evoke reflections of light in this dark but sometimes sunny region of the world.

The Glacier Museum, to Fehn, becomes a poetic temple for Norwegians and others to worship nature, especially the Jostedal Glacier. Norwegians, as Fehn notes, worship God in nature, and the building resembles a giant altar from which to worship nature. The walls become the mountains, the earth, while the roof, the platform, becomes the sky. It is difficult to exhibit the glacier, so the structure, the museum, becomes the object that is exhibited; that tells the narrative of the glacier. In the interior, the museum contains illustrations and models that help to make the invisible qualities of the glacier visible to the visitor.

The spatial quality and structure of the museum corresponds to its place. Fehn seldom uses explicit symbolism, yet in his writings he emphasizes the glacier and the surrounding mountains that it drapes as a metaphor for the form, materials, and spatial quality of the museum. The museum is an elongated, horizontal volume that has a smaller cylindrical volume comprising the auditorium, which lies to the left of the entrance portal. On the opposite side of the auditorium, facing the south, is the restaurant, which consists of a volume comprised of two wide-angled walls of glass that jut away from the main volume. To Fehn, this glass volume resembles the geometry of ice that comprises the glacier. As one approaches the museum, the entryway is flanked on each side by stairs leading to an observation deck on the roof. On the deck, which Fehn likens to a ship's deck, the visitor can view the Jostedal Glacier and view the landscape that has been created by the movement of the glacier. The long entryway, a slate-covered double-pitched roof with a narrow skylight, gives the illusion of narrowing as it meets the doors.

This journey of climbing the stairs and then descending them into the crevicelike portal, Fehn suggests, is similar to penetrating into the glacier to discover its mysteries. The interior, comprised of wood, slate, and concrete, is lit by a long, narrow skylight that runs down the center spine of the structure and is divided into space for visitor facilities and for educational exhibits with information on the geologic formation of the site. The interior roof of the main gallery gradually inclines upward with twin clerestory windows to its sides.

As in his earlier buildings, such as the Hedmark Cathedral Museum (1968–88) in Hamar, Norway, and the Villa Busk (1989) in Bamble, Norway, Fehn concentrates on the joint in the Glacier Museum. The joint is evident in this structure, especially in the traditional wooden cantilever entryway, where the meeting of wooden members with steel bolts and braces are left exposed. These later works all have movement in plan, making use of diagonals, and the use of natural lighting starts to become more articulated and the structures more defined.

In the late 1990s, Fehn's Glacier Museum was seen by the architectural theorist Francesco Dal Co, in the introduction to Christian Norberg-Schulz's book *Sverre Fehn: Works, Projects, Writings, 1949–1996* (1997), as disintegrating in its parts but having a clarity of plan and rigor of structure (12–13). Christian Norberg-Schulz, the architectural historian and architect, claims that the Glacier Museum is a "rural construction" that is composed of "figurative units" that aid in a dialogue with the land (28–29). During the early 1980s, the architectural historian and theorist Kenneth Frampton's remarks in his article "Prospects for a Critical Regionalism" (1983) helped to define Fehn's later works. Frampton emphasizes that Fehn's works are aligned phenomenologically to the site. Fehn's work, and his Glacier Museum especially, realizes a complicated understanding of place and tectonics.

REBECCA DALVESCO

See also **Aalto, Alvar (Finland); Fehn, Sverre (Norway); Frampton, Kenneth (United States); Norberg-Schulz, Christian (Norway); Utzon, Jørn (Denmark)**

Further Reading

Bay, Helle, "Braeen som Museum–Braeen på Museum," *Arkitektur DK*, 38 (1994)

Fehn, Sverre, "Norsk Bremuseum," *Byggekunst*, 74/2 (February1992)

Fehn, Sverre, "Spiriti del Nord," *Spazio I Società*, 60 (1992)

Fehn, Sverre, "The Norwegian Glacier Center," *Living Architecture*, 1 (1994)

Fehn, Sverre, *The Skin, the Cut, and the Bandage*, Cambridge, Massachusetts: MIT University Press, 1997

Fjeld, Per Olaf, "The Workings of Sverre Fehn," *Progressive Architecture*, 75 (February 1994)

Fjeld, Per Olaf, *Sverre Fehn: The Thought of Construction*, New York: Rizzoli, 1983

Grønvold, Ulf, "Fehn on Ice," *Architectural Review*, 187 (June 1990)

Grønvold, Ulf, "Gletsjermuseum door Sverre Fehn: Verleden als deel van het Heden," *Architect dossier* (July 1996)

Lavalou, A., "Musée Glaciaire à Fjærland," *L'architecture d'aujourd'hui*, 287 (1993)

Miles, Henry, "Cool Appraisal: Glacier Museum, Fjærland, Norway," *Architectural Review*, 193 (April 1993)

Norberg-Schulz, Christian, and Gennaro Postiglione, *Sverre Fehn: Works, Projects, Writings, 1949–1996*, New York: Monacelli, 1997

Norri, Marja-Riitta, "Registo Helado: Museo de los Glaciares, Fjærland," *Arquitectura viva*, 32 (September–October 1993)

GLASGOW SCHOOL

Although the term Glasgow School originally was applied to a group of painters (subsequently referred to as The Glasgow Boys) involved with the Glasgow School of Art (GSA), the term more definitively came to be used for a group of Glaswegians active in design and crafts between 1890 and 1920; recently the term Glasgow Style has replaced it. But Glasgow School remains the appropriate designation for "The Four," two couples who collaborated on interior design at the turn of the century: the sisters Margaret (1864–1933) and Frances (1873–1921) MacDonald and their future husbands, respectively, Charles Rennie Mackintosh (1868–1928) and James Herbert McNair (1868–1955). All had been students at the GSA: the MacDonalds in watercolor painting and decorative arts, the two men in architecture and design. Although their work and that of like-minded Glaswegian colleagues such as Talwin Morris (1865–1911), George Logan (1866–1939), George Walton (1867–1933), and E.A. Taylor (1874–1951) has affinities with Art Nouveau, it was indelibly and uniquely stamped by Glasgow, the bustling river port that was preeminent in industrialization and modernization in Scotland and that became in 1900 the "second city" of the British

Empire, with a population of 750,000. Clients of the Glasgow School, such as the tearoom proprietor Kate Cranston (1849–1934), the publisher Walter Blackie (1860–1953), and the merchant William Davidson (1861–1945), typified the new breed of progressive entrepreneurs who flourished in the blossoming conurbation on the Clyde River.

Critical to the development of the Glasgow School was Francis "Fra" Newbery (1853–1946), who headed the GSA from 1885 to 1917, and his wife, Jessie (1864–1948; she married Newbery in 1889), who elevated the hitherto disdained art of embroidery and taught classes in needlework that influenced all the design arts at the GSA. The couple worked to dissolve the separation between fine and useful arts, and they introduced design and technical arts studios into the curriculum. In keeping with parallel trends of the time in England and Europe, the credo of the GSA was that art should be a part of daily life and that through the applied arts, aesthetic choice should shape private in addition to public settings. Metalwork, mosaics, gesso, stencils, posters, appliquéd textiles, and ceramics joined watercolor drawing, book illustration, embroidery, and furniture as media emphasized at the GSA and practiced by the Glasgow School. An admirable characteristic is the preponderance of women in the design revolution that the Glasgow School signaled: Annie French (1872–1965), Jessie King (1875–1949), Ann MacBeth (1875–1948), and De Courcy Lewthwaite Dewar (1878–1959), in addition to Jessie Newbery and the MacDonald sisters, are among the most prominent.

The naturalistically based visual language of the Glasgow School is a rectilinear version of the more dominant curvilinear Art Nouveau of France, Belgium, and Spain. In the emphasis on geometry, symmetry, and abstraction, there is a resemblance to Dutch *nieuwe kunst* and the Austrian Secession, two movements with which the group had ties. Characteristic motifs of the Glasgow School are the square and such markedly conventionalized organic forms as the rose, the thistle, and the rose tree. Stylized allegorical figures are frequently present; the attenuated and often androgynous females found in early work by The Four briefly earned them the epithet the "Spook School." Color schemes evoked the pale palette of the Aesthetic Movement, but the pervasive pastel greens, pinks, and lavenders also echoed the countryside around Glasgow. Contrasts provided by wood—stained dark brown or occasionally black—and metal—usually pewter, silver, or copper—brought an urban reference into the harmoniously designed interiors.

The chief sources, assimilated and then integrated into an identifiable visual ensemble, of the Glasgow School were the English Arts and Crafts movement, as inspired by the writings of John Ruskin and manifested in the work of William Morris and Walter Crane; pre-Raphaelite imagery and style; aestheticism (notably the work of J.A.M. Whistler and Aubrey Beardsley); *Japonisme*; the Celtic Revival, promulgated by, among others, Patrick Geddes (1854–1932); and symbolism, especially as interpreted in the Netherlands and Belgium (Dutch artist Jan Toorop influenced the MacDonalds' drawings, and both the literary and visual representatives of Belgian symbolism—Maurice Maeterlinck, Jean Delville, and Carlos Schwobe—were well known in Glasgow).

The Glasgow School came to attention through the popular expositions that publicized new trends in the applied arts; in 1896 their work was shown at Arts and Crafts exhibitions in London and Liège, Belgium. Periodicals also introduced the Glasgow style to a wider public. *The Yellow Book* published reproductions in 1896, and in 1897 a four-part series titled "Some Glasgow Designers" appeared in *Studio* magazine. Gleeson White, the perspicacious editor of *Studio*, preceded other British journalists in recognizing that interior design had become a major art form, penetrating the communal consciousness and altering patterns of consumption, and that in the British Isles, at least, decorative arts surpassed in innovation all other visual media. In Glasgow, the ideal of the *Gesamtkunstwerk* (total work of art) received popular definition in the various interiors fashioned between 1897 and 1911 for Miss Cranston's tearooms, designed initially by Walton and then by Mackintosh, with accessories such as posters, menu cards, gesso panels, and stenciled wallpapers by the MacDonald sisters.

By the beginning of the 20th century, the Glasgow School had achieved international status. In 1900, The Four, together with Walton, Talwin Morris, and several other Glasgow designers, were invited to create a room and some furniture at the eighth Vienna Secession exhibition; the display caused a sensation, and affinities between the Glasgow School and that of the Wiener Werkstätte became discernible. In 1902, a special number of *Dekorative Kunst* dedicated to the MacDonald/Mackintosh entry for the Haus eines Kunst-Freundes (Art-Lover's House) was issued by Alexander Koch, the Darmstadt publisher who had sponsored the competition; the same magazine in March of that year had printed a sympathetic account of the work of the Mackintoshes by Hermann Muthesius. Also in 1902, the Scottish section, installed by Mackintosh, at the International Exhibition of Modern Decorative Art at Turin received critical acclaim. The McNairs furnished one of the rooms, the "Rose Boudoir" was by the Mackintosh/MacDonald partnership, and the Glasgow School dominated the other two Scottish rooms. Although the Turin exhibition marked the end of the Art Nouveau movement generally, the Glasgow School as a whole would remain viable until c. 1920. The Frances MacDonald and Herbert McNair collaboration, however, subsequently produced very little, and the Margaret MacDonald and Charles Mackintosh team suffered declining commissions after 1910. Recently, there has been a revival of interest in the Glasgow School, signaled by a notable impact of their formal strategies on contemporary interior design.

HELEN SEARING

See also **Arts and Crafts Movement; Glasgow School of Art**

Further Reading

The major items on the bibliography are very recent, fueled by the research of feminist scholars into a movement that had an extraordinarily high number of women among its adherents and by renewed appreciation for the social and aesthetic importance of the decorative arts. Previously, the literature concentrated almost exclusively on Mackintosh and virtually ignored the contributions of his wife and partner, Margaret MacDonald Mackintosh, as well as those by other designers associated with the Glasgow School.

Anscombe, Isabelle, *A Woman's Touch: Women in Design from 1860 to the Present Day*, London: Virago, and New York: Viking Penguin, 1984

Blench, Brian, et al., *The Glasgow Style, 1890–1920*, Glasgow: Glasgow Museums and Art Galleries, 1984

Burkhauser, Jude (editor), *"Glasgow Girls": Women in Art and Design 1880–1920*, Glasgow: Glasgow School of Art, 1988; revised edition, Edinburgh: Canongate, and Cape May, New Jersey: Red Ochre, 1993

Callen, Anthea, *Angel in the Studio: Women in the Arts and Crafts Movement 1870–1914*, London: Astragal, 1979; as *Women Artists of the Arts and Crafts Movement, 1870–1914*, New York: Pantheon, 1979

Eadie, William, *Movements of Modernity: The Case of Glasgow and Art Nouveau*, London and New York: Routledge, 1990

Groundwater, John, *The Glasgow School of Art through a Century*, Glasgow: Glasgow School of Art, 1940

Helland, Janice, *The Studios of Frances and Margaret MacDonald*, Manchester and New York: Manchester University Press, 1996

Kaplan, Wendy (editor), *Charles Rennie Mackintosh*, New York: Abbeville Press, and Glasgow: Glasgow Museums, 1996

Kinchin, Perilla, *Tea and Taste: The Glasgow Tea Room, 1875–1975*, Wendlebury: White Cockade, 1991

Kinchin, Perilla, and Juliet Kinchin, *Glasgow's Great Exhibitions: 1888, 1901, 1911, 1938, 1988*, Wendlebury: White Cockade, 1988

Larner, Gerald, and Celia Larner, *The Glasgow Style*, Edinburgh: Paul Harris, and New York: Taplinger, 1979

Muthesius, Hermann, "The Glasgow Art Movement," *Dekorative Kunst*, 9 (March 1902)

Muthesius, Hermann, *The English House*, edited by Dennis Sharp, translated by Janet Seligman, London: Crosby Lockwood Staples, and New York: Rizzoli, 1979 (translation of *Das Englische Haus*, 1904–05)

Neat, Timothy, *Part Seen, Part Imagined: Meaning and Symbolism in the Work of Charles Rennie Mackintosh and Margaret MacDonald*, Edinburgh: Canongate Press, 1994

Nuttgens, Patrick (editor), *Mackintosh and His Contemporaries in Europe and America*, London: John Murray, 1988

Reekie, Pamela, *The Mackintosh House, 1864–1933* (exhib. cat.), Glasgow: Hunterian Art Gallery, University of Glasgow, 1983

Reekie, Pamela, *Margaret MacDonald Mackintosh*, Glasgow: Hunterian Art Gallery, 1983

Taylor, James Russell, *The Art Nouveau Book in Britain*, London: Methuen, and Cambridge, Massachusetts: MIT Press, 1966

White, Gleeson, "Some Glasgow Designers and Their Work," *The Studio*, 11–13 (1897)

GLASGOW SCHOOL OF ART

Designed by Charles Rennie Mackintosh, completed 1908

The Glasgow School of Art (east wing, 1897–99; west wing and upper story, 1907–08), designed by Charles Rennie Mackintosh (1868–1928), is significant both as the culmination of the Arts and Crafts style and as a truly original interpretation of the Art Nouveau, the contemporary design movement in continental Europe.

The governors of the school, in setting the parameters for the 1896 limited competition for a new building, emphasized that their budget was small and that a plain building was all that was required. Funds were so limited, as it was determined somewhat later, that the building would have to be constructed in two phases. The school's board of governors selected the design put forth by Mackintosh, then an apprentice at Honeyman and Keppie. This project was the first significant building credited to Mackintosh, 28 years old at the time.

What clearly distinguished the design of the building was its innovative response to the constraints of a difficult site—long,

narrow, and steeply sloping with a drop of 30 feet from north to south. Mackintosh set back the northern entry wall from the property line at Renfrew Street to minimize the amount of cross section exposed to the severe angle of the slope, creating a light well that extends the entire 244-foot length of the site. This light well's glazed roofs illuminate the technical studios located in the building's lower level, bringing abundant natural light deep into the spaces.

The building's plan is relatively simple. The small vaulted entry leads to a stairway cloaked in a dark forest of simple wood tracery, suffused with light from the museum space above. A central corridor serves as an east-west spine with studios to the north and service spaces to the south. The school still functions well today, as the rooms are both well considered for their purpose and flexible.

Those studios, the primary expression on the north facade, reach a height of 26 feet with simple, gridded windows. Three huge studio windows on one side and four on the other side flank a carefully composed masonry form at the entry. The most striking feature of the front elevation is its asymmetry. The studio windows vary slightly in size, according to the spaces they light. Although Mackintosh placed the entrance at the physical center of the building, its treatment subverts this position, as justified again by the building's internal arrangement. Dynamic tension is created by the juxtaposition of the symmetrical front railings that flank the entrance stairway and declare its central position. The scalloped stone retaining walls, in-filled with sculptural wrought-iron railings, are a brilliantly creative solution to the problems presented by the site. The pedimented arched window, echoed by the wrought-iron archway at the street wall, and the balcony at the second floor are balanced by the bay windows and turret of the entry. The simple, relatively stark architrave contains the only sculpture on the face of the building; the stylized carved-stone keystone at the arched transom above the doorway symbolizes the function of the building. A simple unadorned cornice, like the brim of a cap over the austere studio windows, frames the facade and brings the prominence of the studio spaces into focus.

The cascading staircase that carries one from the street across the light well serves as a drawbridge across a moat. The building is a synthesis of comparable symbolism; the disparate influences include Scottish baronial castles, continental Art Nouveau, and the Arts and Crafts movement. Traditional Japanese decorative theme is evident not only in the wrought iron on the exterior but also in the wood framing and ornament in the interior. Contrasts and opposition can be found everywhere: the solidity of the masonry and the transparency of the glass, the delicacy of the iron ornament and the industrial scale of the windows. One of the most striking features on the front facade consists of the projecting iron stalks that serve to both brace the tall windows and provide mounting brackets for window washers' platforms. Those stalks terminate in delicate tracery finial clusters adjacent to the window. Within the studio spaces, the iron-work appears to be abstract iron flowers set in window boxes.

The south facade, strikingly plain and purposely functional, has been likened to a fortress; faced in a roughcast-concrete wash, the looming mass of the building is broken into three projecting wings with very sparse, deeply inset fenestration. The western half of the building, built several years after the initial portion was completed, was designed during a frenetic period in Mackin-

The Mackintosh Room, designed by Charles Rennie Mackintosh, Glasgow School of Art
Photograph by Eric Thorburn © The Glasgow Picture Library

tosh's professional growth. Still, the western wing complements and completes the first phase well while managing to establish an identity of its own.

The western facade, where the slope of the site along Scott Street is revealed, presented a particularly large challenge of composition. This wing contains the famous library space, a function unlike any other in the building. The narrow projecting oriel windows on the west facade are balanced in counterpoint with the recessed windows on the plain and completely unadorned south facade. The side entrance on the west facade also features a highly articulated mannerist doorway with layered motifs. The six bay windows that mark the first floor of this facade are set with deliberate care as delicate foils to the coursed and powerful stonework. The three southernmost bays grow to over 63 feet in height, encompassing the library's two-story windows. This modern composition emphasizes the verticality of the building at the low point of the site, further accentuating the effect.

No room in the building exhibits the full range of Mackintosh's mastery of space and detail more than the library, the most acclaimed interior space in the Glasgow School of Art. Like much of the tension that Mackintosh created on the building's exterior, this space is severe, yet serene and warm, much as contemplative spaces are in abbeys. The room's rugged dark-wood structure, complemented by the perimeter balcony's stylized and colorfully ornamented sculptural balustrade, is contrasted by the double-height bay windows and the cascading, modern metal chandelier.

Although the building was favored and appreciated by its users, it drew little adulation outside Glasgow other than the devoted followers of the Art Nouveau in Vienna. In the United Kingdom, this project was met with a deep critical apathy that lasted for many years, and Mackintosh quickly disappeared into relative obscurity. Unfortunately, it was not until after Mackintosh's death that a new generation of architects and critics came to appreciate his masterwork that is the Glasgow School of Art.

SCOTT J. KALNER

See also **Art Nouveau (Jugendstil); Arts and Crafts Movement; Glasgow, Scotland; Mackintosh, Charles Rennie (Scotland); Ornament**

Further Reading

Bliss, Douglas Percy, *Charles Rennie Mackintosh and the Glasgow School of Art*, Glasgow: Glasgow School of Art, 1961; 3rd edition, as *Charles Rennie Mackintosh and Glasgow School of Art*, edited and annotated by H. Jefferson Barnes, Glasgow: Glasgow School of Art, 1988–

Crawford, Alan, *Charles Rennie Mackintosh*, London: Thames and Hudson, 1995

GLASGOW, SCOTLAND

Glasgow, the largest city in Scotland, and the administrative center of the Strathclyde region, is situated on both banks of the River Clyde, 20 miles (32 km) from the river's estuary on the Atlantic coast. The Glasgow district, an administrative area slightly larger than the city proper, covers 76 sq. miles (198 sq. km) and had a population in 1995 of nearly 675,000. This represents a considerable decline from the 1961 figure of approximately 1,055,000. The dramatic rise of the city's population and industrial base during the 19th century and its equally precipitous decline during the 20th century form the underlying narrative of Glasgow's urban development and redevelopment.

Varying translations of the city's Celtic name, "Glas ghu" indicate an early history as a "green glen," or "dear green place." Nevertheless, centuries of development transformed it into a setting that was wholly urban. The 18th century grid, and its 19th century additions—unusually dramatic and extensive in the context of British cities—extended the crossroads of the medieval city to the west and south, across the River Clyde, providing the defining urban infrastructure for the city's growth. Into this grid have been fitted more than two centuries of housing, offices, shops and institutions, their architectural expressions including Georgian good manners, Victorian eclectic exuberance, and mostly mediocre modernism. Not until the last two decades of the 20th century has a new sense of robust contextualism and a re-appreciation of the city's urban heritage facilitated a revived "Glasgow style," evident in the work of several younger architectural firms in the city.

The gridded plan makes Glasgow's urban presence compelling. The rectilinear pattern of space stamps the city more deeply into the mind than any collection of individual buildings—including even Charles Rennie Mackintosh's masterwork of the Glasgow School of Art (1897–99; 1907–09). The urban quality of central Glasgow owes a great deal to the regulated street pattern, where heights of buildings in relation to street widths were more closely controlled than in other British cities during the 19th century. Overall, the architecture of neoclassical and Victorian buildings interrelates with the urban plan in a vibrant dialogue of figure and ground that have survived neglect and swathes of poor modern development. In substantial areas, Glasgow's character is maintained by the implacable integration of the grid and topography, a two dimensional arrangement full of potential drama brought into three dimensional life by the ubiquitous four story tenements.

The tenement as a building type, generally four stories of apartments, sometimes incorporating street level commercial uses, always accessed off communal stairs or "closes," and consistently arranged along street frontages, is a particularly Scottish typology, relating that country's pattern of city living more to continental Europe than to its English neighbor. Since the 1980s the tenement has enjoyed something of a revival, both in terms of preservation and new building. This is in stark contrast to most of the 20th century, when the building type bore the brunt of social and political distaste. Perceived as the symbol and cause of high-density urban squalor, the tenement had to be eradicated at all costs.

The tenement survived because it is inherently flexible; it responds to working-class and middle-class housing needs, and historically has been capable of various architectural expressions,

The Glasgow School of Art North Entrance
Photograph by Eric Thorburn © The Glasgow Picture Library

Fiell, Charlotte, and Peter Fiell, *Charles Rennie Mackintosh*, Cologne, London, and New York: Taschen, 1995

Harris, Nathaniel, *The Life and Works of Rennie Mackintosh*, New York: Smithmark, 1996

Jones, Anthony, *Charles Rennie Mackintosh*, London: Studio Editions, and Secaucus, New Jersey: Wellfleet, 1990

Kaplan, Wendy (editor), *Charles Rennie Mackintosh*, Glasgow: Glasgow Museums, and New York and London: Abbeville Press, 1996

Kimura, Hiroaki (editor), *Charles Rennie Mackintosh*, Tokyo: Process Architecture, 1984

Lowrey, John (editor), *The Age of Mackintosh*, Edinburgh: Edinburgh University Press, 1992

McKean, John, *Charles Rennie Mackintosh, Pocket Guide*, Grantown-on-Spey, Morayshire: Baxter, 1998

Macleod, Robert, *Charles Rennie Mackintosh: Architect and Artist*, New York: Dutton, 1983; revised edition, London: Collins, 1983

Pevsner, Nicholas, *Charles R. Mackintosh*, Milan: Il Balcone, 1950; as *Charles R. Mackintosh*, translated by Heather Roberts, Venice: Canal, 1998

Steele, James, *Charles Rennie Mackintosh: Synthesis in Form*, London: Academy Editions, 1994

Walker, Frank Arneil, *Glasgow*, London: Phaidon Press, 1992

Wilhide, Elizabeth, *The Mackintosh Style: Decor and Design*, London: Pavilion Books, 1995; as *The Mackintosh Style: Design and Decor*, San Francisco: Chronicle Books, 1995 from severe unornamented surfaces to eclectic and highly mod-eled facades. Postmodern versions generally substitute colored brick for the original red and yellow sandstone that created such pleasing cohesion in the Victorian city before pollution turned everything black. Recent manifestations of this building type respond in part to a new desire for urban living by younger professionals, reinhabiting the center city in sporadic new private developments very much in contrast to decades of government sponsored decentralization.

The first exodus from the city center was promulgated by local government action after the First World War. The working classes were decanted from overcrowded tenements in the city center—where densities climbed as high as 700 persons per acre—to English-style suburbs on the outskirts, built on cheap green-field land. Spurred by a genuine fear of a social(ist) revolu-tion bred from poor working and living conditions, the city government banned tenement-style development, and instead initiated low density developments based on garden city plan-ning ideals. However well intentioned, these new suburbs failed to live up to their model, as planning and construction were progressively simplified and cheapened in a desire to rehouse the greatest number of people for the minimum cost.

Cost was especially significant, as most new housing was pro-vided by public funds. This period of expansion occurred during the first years of Glasgow's industrial decline, when employment in heavy manufacturing, shipbuilding, and shipping fell dramati-cally. In 1932, an astonishing 75 percent of the city's working population was unemployed. In this context of private sector decline, the public authority took the lead in housing develop-ment, and by 1939, the city council was the main provider of new housing, mostly outside the old city boundaries. Between 1916 and 1944, the city built over 54,000 homes in this fashion, including, during the 1930s, a return to some modified tene-ment type buildings to meet the demand for rehousing within the available budget.

Public funding and rudimentary planning was also provided to attract new industries to offset the chronic unemployment. While heavy industries rotted on their sites within the old city, new employers located in rudimentary industrial parks around the periphery. This explosion of sprawl around the edges of the city during the 1920s and 30s was completed by private sector developments of small bungalows, sited, for marketing reasons, as far away from public housing as possible.

The 1950s and 60s extended the activist role of city govern-ment in urban development. The tenement was again mistakenly identified as the root of all urban evils, but this time the prescrip-tion for a new, modern city was based on more than decentraliza-tion. A three-pronged attack was launched on the city's urban environment, a program that was well intentioned, but with hindsight appears naive and needlessly destructive. First, whole-sale slum clearance and city center redevelopment were compre-hensively redeveloped, akin to American urban renewal projects, and all buildings within a defined area were demolished and a new urban pattern created, based, as elsewhere, on a modernist model of towers and slabs in open space. Allied to this wholesale demolition was the second strategy—a massive new urban high-way program that tore the heart out of many central neighbor-hoods in the name of improved transportation. The third strat-egy for a modern Glasgow involved mitigating the city's peripheral expansion by the creation of four New Towns, East

Kilbride (1947), Cumbernauld (1956), Livingston and Irvine (both 1962), separated from the city itself by a preserved green belt.

Glasgow City Council used the sweeping new powers of Comprehensive Development to pursue a vision of almost total rebuilding of the inner city in the 1950s and 1960s. While the center city was spared, vast areas of tenements to the east and south were replaced by a mix of low-rise terraces, medium-rise slabs, and high-rise towers. Tragically, this massive demolition and redevelopment of urban housing coincided with the final death throes of Glasgow's heavy industry, and this combination created huge areas of urban dereliction, many of which still ex-isted at the end of the 20th century.

Ironically, the main catalyst of this urban renaissance at the end of the 20th century was the rediscovery of the city's architec-tural heritage; the same building stock and urban pattern that had been under severe attack for the previous 60 years. A conser-vation boom beginning in the 1970s reeducated the public and professionals about their own city, switching emphasis from in-dividual buildings to whole neighborhoods. Simply cleaning sev-eral decades of soot from the grimy facades of tenements and older commercial and civic buildings revealed an attractive and robust urban environment, fashioned by architecture of surpris-ing sophistication.

Several civic initiatives during the 1980s and 90s enhanced this process of rediscovery and reinvention. An exquisitely de-tailed new building by Barry Gasson, to house the world-famous Burrell Art Collection, opened in 1983. Two years later, English urban designer Gordon Cullen produced a city center concept plan for the Scottish Development Agency that brilliantly re-vealed the huge potential in the urban core and adjacent river-side. This concept plan stimulated further proposals, for the city center and beyond, amongst which are exemplary new develop-ments like Ingram Square (1989) by Elder and Cannon, and The Italian Center (1991) by Page and Park. In 1989 the city was awarded the Europa Nostra Medal of Honour for its conser-vation work in the city center, and the following year Glasgow was appointed as the European City of Culture.

At the same time, the city set about remedying its mistakes of the Comprehensive Development program. In the late 1980s and continuing into the 1990s, the city embarked on an exten-sive program of demolition of the medium and high-rise blocks of flats that had proved such a failure during their short, 30 year life. In the infamous Gorbals area, a new urban fabric was created (based on a 1990 master plan by the London firm of CZWG) that brought back to life the traditional Glasgow typologies of the tenement, the perimeter block, the street and the grid. This initiative was followed in Page and Park's Gorbals East Renewal Project, and new buildings by Page and Park, Elder and Cannon, the Holmes Partnership and Cooper Cromar have created a high standard of new urban architecture.

Despite these successes, the city's declining population and an excessive supply of brown-field sites of little interest to private developers, have conspired to spread redevelopment too thinly in many areas, leading to the suburbanization of once urban districts. Additional problems also remain along the riverside. The major weakness of the 1985 Cullen plan was its failure to recognize the potential for the whole length of the River Clyde, as it dissects the city, to be the major form-giving spine for long term urban regeneration. A major garden festival in the derelict docklands in 1988 tried with limited success to redirect investment to those dilapidated areas, but the recession of the early 1990s allowed only piecemeal development along this riparian corridor—such as Sir Norman Foster's Clyde Auditorium (1997).

Glasgow's process of civic reinvention is a work in progress. But despite the significant physical and social problems that remain, the reformist spirit and urban energy that characterize the past three centuries of Glasgow's history provide the city with a powerful source of energy as it prepares to meet the next round of urban challenges.

DAVID WALTERS

See also **Glasgow School; Glasgow School of Art, Scotland; Mackintosh, Charles Rennie (Scotland)**

Further Reading

Gibb, Andrew, *Glasgow, the Making of a City*, London: Croom Helm, 1983
Gomme, Andor Harvey, and David Walker, *Architecture of Glasgow*, London: Lund Humphries, 1968; revised edition, Lund Humphries in association with the Glasgow Booksellers, J. Smith, 1987
Pacione, Michael, *Glasgow: The Socio-spatial Development of the City*, Chichester and New York: Wiley, 1995
Reed, Peter (editor), *Glasgow: The Forming of the City*, 2nd edition, Edinburgh: Edinburgh University Press, 1993; 2nd edition, 1999
Walker, Frank A., *Glasgow (Phaidon Architectural Guide)*, London: Phaidon, 1992
Walker, Frank A., "The Glasgow Grid," in *Order and Space in Society*, edited by Thomas A. Markus, Edinburgh: Mainstream, 1982

GLASS

With concrete and steel, glass is one of a triumvirate of materials that modern architects have invested with auratic properties and utopian possibilities. Consequently, the history of glass in 20th-century architecture is a history of exceptions, some of which by dint of aesthetic, technical, or practical merit found their way into common use. The result is that the canon does not always line up easily with what Sigfried Giedion might have called the "anonymous history" of glass.

The glazed vaults of the passenger concourse in McKim, Mead and White's Penn Station (1905–10) is the last of the ferrovitreous arcades of 19th-century train stations, market halls, and exhibition buildings. Attached to a proper Beaux-Arts building inspired by Roman baths, this was perhaps more an extension of the peculiarly 19th-century convention of separating the formal section of a train station from its functional sections, which were handled in entirely different manners. A more resolved contemporary use of glass can be found in Otto Wagner's Post Office Savings Bank (1905) in Vienna, with its glazed roof and floor, which borrowed from the Parisian arcades in anticipation of the modern atrium now seen so often in office buildings and hotels.

A more common launching point of the modernist canon, however, is Bruno Taut's Glass Pavilion at the 1914 Werkbund Exhibition in Cologne. With the bohemian novelist and proselytizer of glass architecture Paul Scheerbart as his collaborator,

Taut designed a faceted, multicolored bishop's hat of a glass dome raised on a drum of glass bricks. The novel exterior gave way on the inside to a circular staircase composed of glass treads and risers that led into a glazed prism, affording just a glimpse into the sort of all-glass architecture that Scheerbart anticipated, most prominently in his *Glasarchitektur* (1914). Despite the fact that the market halls, train sheds, and exhibition buildings of the 19th century were certainly the immediate models, Taut and Scheerbart reached back to the Gothic cathedral as a source, which Scheerbart called the "prelude to the glass architecture." As well as reveling in the pure delight of glass, Scheerbart ran through various practical considerations, but he is best known for mysticizing the material. He envisioned a world transformed by glass architecture, which he imbued with certain values and properties, from honesty and cleanliness to a new spirituality.

Scheerbart's writings and the Glass Pavilion inspired a short-lived correspondence in the late 1910s between a number of Berlin artists and architects, including Walter Gropius and Taut, called the Glass Chain Letters (*Die gläserne Kette*). These letters extended Scheerbart's glass mysticism through a series of complex crystal metaphors. Lyonel Feininger picked up on the Gothic connection in his well-known cubo-futurist woodcut for the frontispiece of the Bauhaus Manifesto of 1919, a soaring crystal cathedral that came to symbolize the new architecture. Taut went on to sketch a number of glass fantasies. In his *Alpine Architektur* (1919), he connected peaks of the Alps with dramatic and unbuildable glass cities that prefigured the megastructures of later decades.

Taut's pavilion is usually paired with Adolf Meyer and Gropius's model factory, also erected at the 1914 exhibition. Here the use of glass is much closer to later developments in the glass curtain wall. The architects subverted the conventional expectations of glass as a limited perforation in a solid masonry structure. Glass and masonry literally switched roles. Instead of solid side pavilions that would anchor the building visually—and hold the glass in place—Gropius and Meyer wrapped the elegant circular stairwells in a continuous, clear-glass wall. This was more than a game of solids and voids changing places. Glass, often a means of framing an external view or a way of permitting a limited exposure of the interior, here becomes a statement of honesty in architecture: the stairwells, a utilitarian architectural feature that is usually hidden behind masonry, are given pride of place. Glass provides the revelation of a new aesthetic, namely, that structure and construction possess beauty. Little thought was given to the fact that a glass stairwell was a liability in a fire.

To be fair, in the model factory, Gropius and Meyer worked within the generous strictures of exhibition architecture. In 1911–12, they had designed Fagus Werk in Alfeld-an-der-Leine, a factory in which they already had begun to play with the conventional roles of glass and masonry. The architects pushed the boxy grids of glass just beyond the masonry container of piers, projecting glass as the defining element of the wall. Not only did this have the advantage of letting in more light, an important consideration in a factory, but it also reinvented the idea of the wall, freeing it from the structure behind. It was this sort of maneuver that inspired Arthur Korn, a modern architect who was also one of the early apologists for the new glass architecture, to claim "the disappearance of the outside wall." The "wall is itself the window," he wrote in *Glas im Bau und als Gebrauchsgegenstand* (1926; *Glass in Modern Architecture*, 1968):

"It is the great membrane, full of mystery." Beyond the titillation of a glass surface, Korn found a new depth in the glass curtain wall. Its clarity yielded the workings of the building; he even hoped to dissolve the interior with glass partitions, matching the changeable realities of modern life and commerce with an equally protean material.

Although glass was slowly being improved in quality during the first two decades of the century, the dream of a glass architecture was decades beyond the state of manufactured glass. Most architects were not caught up in the utopian musings of the avant-garde, yet the period witnessed a wonderful variety of new uses of glass in everyday architecture and the stirrings of a professional dialogue on the modern uses of glass. Outside the modern movement, the needs of industry for ample light and of commerce for an arresting image inspired bold experiments with glass. The Hallidie Building (1917–18) in San Francisco by Willis Polk is an often cited example. Here a glass curtain wall extends more than three feet beyond the structural system of concrete columns and girders. At every third horizontal mullion, Polk cantilevered a structural member from the floor slabs in order to support the glass. An even earlier example that bears mention is Louis S. Curtis's Boley Building (1908–09) in Kansas City, featuring probably the first continuous, steel-mullioned strip windows, pre-dating Fagus by a few years.

The Boley and Hallidie Buildings are exemplars in a wave of commercial buildings that sprang up in cities across the United States. Yet they, too, are still exceptions. The first third of the 20th century was an age of eclectic design, of Beaux-Arts classicism in the United States, a "free classicism" in England, and a confident, if decadent, historicism throughout the West. Glass followed this historicism. Architects sought glass that would authenticate their designs, and manufacturers did well to supply architects with a range of glasses to suit their catholic range of projects. For example, warbled leaded glass flourished as the appropriate choice for the Collegiate Gothic. Some manufacturers went so far as to re-create historical glasses painstakingly, including ancient Roman glass that was found in archaeological sites. Revival architecture had long inspired the revival of older methods of manufacture. So it was with glass, giving rise to names such as "Colonial" and "Florentine" (two types of ribbed glasses) and "Etruscan" (a rippled glass). These were a world away from Taut's Glass Pavilion.

At the same time, the demands of new and changing building types stimulated the use of new forms of glass. Wired glass, first developed in the 1870s in Tacony, Pennsylvania, came into wider use in early 20th-century museums and other institutions that required a strong, shatterproof glass to thwart theft and bring in natural light, especially from above. Toughened (or "security") glass, made by rapidly cooling glass so that it compresses as it congeals, came into use in the late 1920s. It was up to 400 percent stronger than annealed glass and had the advantage of breaking into small pieces with rounded edges. It formed the basis for structural glazing and commercial glass doors and windows, in which strength was necessary.

Plate glass, a French invention of the 17th century, remained expensive and difficult to manufacture quickly. Before World War I, English plate glass was generally deemed the best, followed by French, German, and finally American, which was hampered more by the incredible rise in demand than by technical problems. The dream of a glass architecture, dependent on large expanses of clear glass, was still far ahead of its practical fulfillment. Drawn glass, a mechanical method of creating clear plate, was still in its infancy and undergoing almost constant improvement. In the years around the turn of the century, a number of glass manufacturers experimented with drawing sheets of molten glass evenly through a slit, or *débiteuse*, and slowly cooling it in an annealing chamber. In the first quarter of the century, various competing patents in Europe and the United States by Colburn, Fourcault, Libbey-Owens, Pittsburgh Plate Glass, and Pilkington slowly perfected this process. However, imperfect drawing and cooling methods—primarily involving glass touching rollers or a surface, or the corruption of the slit with devitrified glass—led to imperfections in the final product.

By 1911, about half of all American window glass was produced by machines, whether by drawing or by older methods. Yet at the same time it was widely believed that mechanically drawn glass would not displace hand-blown methods of creating plate, especially the cylinder method. In this method, a highly skilled glass blower would create a glass ball and, while it was still hot, elongate it by swinging it in circles, all the while keeping it hot enough to prevent devitrification, a feat that required great strength and knowledge of glass. The ends would then be cut away to form a cylinder, and the glass would be cut lengthwise with a diamond or hot iron and flattened in the oven. Naturally, a mechanical method of making plate was highly desirable.

In the 1920s, following Henry Ford's lead, the automobile industry dominated advances in the mechanization of plate glass. To meet the rising demand for clear plate glass for automobiles, Ford created a continuous mechanized process of drawing plate, grinding, and polishing. Manufacturers were slow to adopt the new methods, however. Only in the 1930s was the cylinder method displaced by sheet-drawing machines, making plate more affordable. As late as 1950, most of the sheet glass in the United States was still drawn through the older Fourcault and Colburn methods, but the process had been mechanized, reducing the cost of plate considerably. The consequences of affordable, high-quality plate glass for modern architecture were obvious, as generous spans of plate became less of a luxury. However, the influence might go much deeper. Standardization, especially of the metal-frame window, made the continuous horizontal band easier to achieve; just as important, it made such ribbon windows easier to imagine, the architectural effect in some sense deriving from the very means or image of the assembly line itself.

As early as the 1920s, architects began to explore the various possibilities of plate glass. As a supercooled liquid, whose viscous origins are manifested in the visual ambiguities of its solid form, glass tantalizes, pressing the metaphor of architecture as frozen music. Ludwig Mies van der Rohe is often considered the first modern architect to give this metaphor full sculptural expression. First in his project for an office building in Friedrichstrasse in Berlin (1919–21) and then in his glass-tower project of 1920, Mies emphasized the glass curtain wall. In the latter, he used an undulating, Expressionistic wall of glass—although he later disowned Expressionism—that captivated his contemporaries and inspired glass-clad skyscrapers half a century after he put his initial vision onto paper. Mies completely separated the glass curtain wall from the skeleton of the building, an independence that enabled a new level of abstraction and reinvigorated the facade with aesthetic possibilities. Erich Mendelsohn would exploit similar qualities in his designs for the Schocken department stores in the late 1920s.

In his later German Pavilion at the Barcelona World Exhibition (1929), Mies relied more on the play of surfaces. Here he combined highly polished glass, travertine, green marble and onyx, chromium-plated mullions, and a reflecting pool lined with black glass into a complex play of light reflection and transmission. Stone and water represent the polarities of this ambiguity, the one obdurate and impenetrable, the other malleable and translucent. Glass could be both, and by creating an abstract composition of all three in planar tension, Mies was able to execute one of the first essays in the elegant ambiguity of the glass wall as a surface. At his Tugendhat House (1930), Mies developed many of the ideas first executed in Barcelona, but here the continuous bands of plate came on vertical tracks, making it possible to slide the sections downward, opening the room to the outdoors.

Mies' experiments with glass tended to be abstract and aesthetic in concern. As projects or exhibition buildings, they could ignore many of the realities of glass. Architects in the 1930s began to study the advantages and drawbacks particular to the glass curtain wall, such as the disadvantage of excessive heat and light transmission. Turning this to his advantage, Le Corbusier realized that he could use the entire room as a light baffle of sorts, modifying light internally as required. In his flats in Geneva (c. 1932) with Pierre Jeanneret, he divided the space horizontally while still bringing the light and warmth of the large window to the entire room. At the same time, the horizontal division acted as a screen, blocking some portion of the heat and light. The basic idea subverted the conventional window. Where earlier architects punctured the wall to bring light or heat to a specific part of a space, Le Corbusier made the entire window a wall and organized the interior structure to suit the lighting and warming needs of the space. Interior space became light baffle.

Turning the exterior wall into window, as Korn had envisioned, brought with it a new flexibility—a term that would become key in modern architecture. Not only did it free the wall from following the dictates of the interior space, allowing for free experiment with the articulation of the glass, but it also engendered an architecture of immense malleability. In theory, the glass wall provided a neutral space that could be subdivided into infinite variations and changed as needed. In practice, this was never as neat as envisioned, and the "greenhouse effect" of the glass wall has only recently met serious solutions.

With flexibility came economy as well. As the thinnest architectural member necessary to shelter people, glass is a space saver. By decreasing the thickness of the wall even by mere inches, one is able to increase square footage significantly in a large building or skyscraper. Given that office space is rented by the square foot, the glass curtain wall increases potential earnings for developers. This idea, developed first in the 1930s, came into play heavily in the postwar period, especially in the United States, where hundreds of glass-clad buildings appeared on American skylines.

Many architects took up the application of the glass curtain wall to the house, most prominently at Mies' Farnsworth House (1951) and Philip Johnson's Glass House (1949), both of which are encased in glass curtains. In both houses, the glass wall is an accomplice to the open plan, reinforcing it visually and function-

ally. With the barest of internal walls, these houses left the flexibility of the neutral space intact in a tour de force of minimalist living. Much earlier, Harwell Hamilton Harris had created similar effects at his own Fellowship House (1935–37). From the inside, the house reads like a glass house, with the same sense of being able to throw open the walls to the outside that one finds at Tugendhat. However, the use of traditional materials such as wood and the grass matting (practically the only interior decoration) tempered the coldness often associated with glass houses. Despite the fact that it is essentially a glass pavilion floating on wooden piers, its gently sloping shingle roof and reclusive stance on a wooded hillside give it a far different countenance than the Mies and Johnson houses, which are extroverted objects of art floating in open space. However, all three are oddities, inspiring architectural historians more than imitations. The Mies and Johnson houses were also expensive, precluding adoption for the masses, who continued to choose Cape Cod and Colonial designs in which the main display of glass came in a picture window, usually framing the yard from the living room or breakfast room. Although the picture window is an early modern invention, with the availability of cheap plate glass it became a staple, a requisite component of suburban housing, the view itself adding value to the house by giving a sense of spaciousness to otherwise modest accommodations.

Problems with excessive heat transmission led Le Corbusier to attempt to double-glaze the walls, what he called the "*mur neutralisant*" in his Cité de Refuge (1929–33). The architect envisioned heated or cooled air flowing through the space between the glass, in theory neutralizing the air temperature outside. In reality, only one layer of glass was ever built, and the refrigeration plant was omitted, turning the building into a greenhouse. Cité revealed the disadvantages of a glass curtain wall, but the double-glass wall—a 19th-century idea elaborated by Scheerbart—pointed to what is today a standard solution in large glass-clad buildings. Placing two planes of glass together acts as sound insulation, reduces condensation, and is especially good for northern climes as a means of reducing heat loss.

Alvar Aalto's Paimio Sanatorium (1933) is a good example of double-glazing used for the purported health benefits of light. With fears of tuberculosis haunting much of urban Western society deep into the 20th century, a light and airy architecture held more than aesthetic value. It was deemed healthy, largely in opposition to Victorian architecture, which was thought to be dark and closed to nature. This healthful association with glass took on symbolic value as well: the openness of glass connected society to nature, reversing the process of alienation that many critics pinned on the industrial revolution and its concomitant urbanization. Along these lines, manufacturers developed heat-absorbing glasses to filter out the infrared rays and other glasses that allowed the penetration of ultraviolet rays, which were thought to be salubrious.

Also in the 1930s and 1940s, the development of air conditioning prompted many architects to forecast an architecture that could ignore climatic conditions. The thermal liabilities of glass, it was thought, would be made moot. This dream, which peaked in the 1940s and 1950s—especially in the United States, where energy was cheap—has never come to pass, although subsequent decades have witnessed the proliferation of buildings dependent on expensive and inadequate air cooling and heating systems.

The first in this line was the Lever House (1950–52) by Gordon Bunshaft of Skidmore, Owings and Merrill. It triggered a seemingly endless array of puristic, rectilinear, glass-clad buildings in the postwar decades. The pattern of green heat-absorbing glass (pale green windows and darker blue-green spandrels) created a complex, colorful grid. Lewis Mumford lauded the formal relationships of the cladding for its "sober elegance" but distrusted the building's reliance on air conditioning and the stubborn formalistic insistence on using the same glass on the southern exposure. However, Mumford also found a political symbolism in the Lever House that shows how glass could transcend mere function. He wrote, "Fragile, exquisite, undaunted by the threat of being melted into a puddle by an atomic bomb, this building is a laughing refutation of 'imperialist warmongering,' and so it becomes an implicit symbol of hope for a peaceful world." The same building could thus symbolize two of the defining elements of postwar American society: air conditioning and the threat of nuclear war.

Lever House, greeted as an exception, became the norm. It was joined a few years later by Mies' Seagram Building (1954–58), its de facto pendent and the archetype for the glass skyscraper in postwar America. Its iridescent selenium pink-gray-bronze glass varies in hue with the time of day and the position of the sun. Mies affixed slim I-beams to the facade as a means of creating scansion, but, depending on the light, the sheer dark glass and its bronze framing and paneling emphasize the mass rather than the skin of the building. The Lever House and the Seagram Building helped generate the fad in tinted glasses that continued through the 1970s. These glasses had the practical advantage of screening solar energy but proved impractical in colder climates and higher latitudes, where retaining the light and warmth of the sun is important. In northern Europe and the northeastern United States, tinted glass was little more than what Michael Wigginton has called "glamour wrap." In this tradition, one might include Pietro Belluschi's earlier Equitable Savings and Loan Building (1947–48) in Portland, Oregon; Eero Saarinen's elegant Bell Telephone Corporate Headquarters (1957–62) in Holmdel, New Jersey; and Roche and Dinkeloo's Federal Reserve Bank (1969) in New York City. The Bell Telephone Building is exceptional for extending the flexibility of the glass curtain wall, which Saarinen used as a container for what is essentially a series of discrete buildings within.

A technical advance in plate is partly to blame for ending the tinted-glass fashion. In the late 1950s, the English glass manufacturer Pilkington solved the last major problem with drawn plate glass, namely, that it had to be rolled on a surface or drawn through a slit, both of which caused inconsistencies in the glass. Pilkington used molten metal as a float for the molten glass, creating a firm, clean, even surface without grinding and polishing. Pilkington's method was cheaper and faster and yielded a higher-quality glass; and, although the glass it produced was not as brilliant as fired glass, it slowly displaced earlier methods of drawn plate glass. The one drawback to the method, which now plagues the plate-glass industry, is that it is cumbersome to create colored plate. The company produced a limited range of tinted glasses using its new technique, but not as many as had been the fashion before Pilkington's process was widely adopted in the 1960s and 1970s.

The reflectivity of glass has also been seen as a means of creating an architecture sensitive to context. I.M. Pei and Associates' Hancock Tower (1968, 1973) is often taken as an example of "mirror glass," which has a thin film applied to the finished plate glass. Situated in downtown Boston, the Hancock Tower joined a number of important 19th-century buildings, including H.H. Richardson's Trinity Church. On the ambiguity of its reflective glass, Keith Bell (1987–88) has written, "The building only appears to 'exist' up to about the seventh story, after which it becomes 'sky.' By this means, mass and volume are denied." However, this is a highly dubious claim, a case of the faith in glass outstripping its reality. The Hancock Tower, a massive glass high-rise, is not really invisible, and by reflecting Trinity Church it is no more sensitive to its context than a giant, faceted mirror. It does not help matters that some of the glass panels were improperly sealed and without warning popped out of their housing and crashed on the streets below.

Although most major cities can boast of their postmodernist reflective glass skyscrapers, Kohn Pederson Fox's green-glass tower in Chicago, at 333 East Wacker Drive (1979–83), exploits its riverbank site and uninterrupted vista with the use of a smooth mirrored glass facade that bends with the Chicago River. In Pittsburgh, Philip Johnson and John Burgee's PPG Place (1979–84) incorporates a 40-story tower and four other lower buildings around a public plaza that shimmers from the surface's mirror glass—silver PPG Solar Ban—produced by Pittsburgh Plate Glass, the largest producer of glass in the world when this complex was constructed.

Beginning in the 1970s, the modern glass atrium, a not-so-distant ancestor of the arcades, orangeries, train sheds, and great exhibition buildings of the 19th century, became an increasingly important typology for malls, hotels, and office buildings. In some cases, the arcade is used metaphorically, as in the "Court" at the King of Prussia Mall outside Philadelphia, where an entrance pavilion refers directly to Joseph Paxton's Great Exhibition Building (1851) in London. John Portman has made his livelihood exploiting the aesthetic, spatial, and symbolic potential of the glass atrium. In a long list of hotels beginning in the late 1960s, Portman employed the atrium's association with festive public spaces and places of commerce, most notably at the Hyatt Hotel (1967) in Atlanta. The idea has proliferated, and often to ill effect, in the more generic hotel atria of, say, Embassy Suites and the suburban malls (and increasingly urban malls) that spread throughout the United States in the 1980s and 1990s. Finally, Pei Cobb Freed and Partners' Louvre Pyramid (1983–89) in Paris, one of the most powerful architectural symbols in glass to be built near the end of the 20th century, exploits natural light in a way achievable only with vast glass surfaces.

The last quarter of the 20th century witnessed many improvements in glass manufacture. The desire to decrease the supporting structure such as mullions in order to make an even smoother surface has led to new systems of sealing and bolting glass. The strength-to-weight ratio of glass has been greatly improved as well, allowing architects to bolt glass much closer to its edge without structural compromise. Toughened glass and experiments with clips, brackets, knuckles, "patch" fittings, ceramic frits, glass fins, neoprene spacers, and other methods of holding glass in place have inched architects closer to a glazed architecture in which nonvitreous members have been reduced nearly to the magnitude of a staple on a page. For example, the glass curtain of the Willis Faber and Dumas Building (1973–75) in Ipswich, England, by Foster Associates uses toughened glass connected with glass fins and sliding patch fittings, with each pane hanging from the one above. The entire wall is thus in tension, bolted and hung from a mooring at the roofline. The glass curtain is reflective by day and lit up at night, transforming the building into a lantern for the street. The glass fin, a small piece of glass wedged perpendicularly between the plates as a connector, also becomes part of the facade's proportion and scansion, a staccato of metal and bolts puncturing and punctuating the surface.

With the patch, four panes of glass can be bolted together at their corners. The system has been developed and used without fins at "Les Serres," Cité des Sciences et de l'Industrie at the Parc de la Villette (1980–86) in Paris by Francis Ritchie with Adrian Fainsilber, the former being one of the premier glass-engineering firms. The bolt becomes the sole connector of the glass, the wall being supported by a complex cable-truss system within the building. These are so inconspicuous that the lines between the panels of glass disappear from a distance. For all of this, the glass pavilions at Les Serres give the sense of being tacked on, a high-tech stunt having little to do with the museum behind. Structural silicon glazing, usually sealed in the factory and delivered in frame to the site, is a relatively recent method for sealing glass. Although the method has not been perfected, such units promise to reduce mechanical attachments even further and to ease the handling of the glass and the erection of the building.

Whatever the advances in hardware, the glass curtain wall still suffers from excessive heat transmission, limiting its practicality. This hurdle has led architects and glass manufacturers to improve on the thermal qualities of glass with surface coatings and tints applied after the floating of the plate. These specialized coatings, applied through "sputtering" nanometer-thin layers of substrate onto the glass, have led to the idea of the "smart window," which variously blocks or absorbs light and heat. Low-emission glasses, which first appeared in 1983, block radiation emission and also allow internally heated spaces to hold their heat better. Increasingly thin coatings can produce glass that admits daylight while reducing solar heat gain. As coatings combine with double-glazing, which is rapidly being incorporated into the heating and cooling system of buildings as Le Corbusier had anticipated, the skin of the building is becoming more active. The primary problem with double-glazing, that dirt and moisture can build up on the inside, has been solved with factory-sealed units in which gasses such as argon and krypton have been trapped in order to block radiation. To this improvement one has to add glass laminates, in which various materials such as polyvinyl butyral have been sealed between layers of glass to create optical effects, to block radiation transmission, and for insulation. As the "smart window" takes shape, the architectural profession is again preoccupied with the utopian possibilities of glass, only this time technology has kept apace of the imagination.

ANDREW M. SHANKEN

See also **Aalto, Alvar (Finland); Bunshaft, Gordon (United States); Corbusier, Le (Jeanneret, Charles-Édouard) (France); Fagus Werk, Alfeld, Germany; Farnsworth House, Plano, Illinois; Giedion, Sigfried (Switzerland); Glass House, New Canaan, Connecticut; Glass Skyscraper (1920–21); German Pavilion, Barcelona (1929); Lever House, New York City; McKim, Mead and White (United States); Mendelsohn, Erich (Germany, United States); Mies van der Rohe, Ludwig (Germany); Pei, I.M. (United States); Seagram Building, New York City; Skidmore, Owings and Merrill (United States); Taut, Bruno (Germany); Tugendhat House, Brno, Czech Republic; Wagner, Otto (Austria); Werkbund Exhibition, Cologne (1914)**

Further Reading

Wigginton's excellent book is both a history and a technical guide. McGrath and Frost's much earlier work gives an architect's viewpoint from within the Modern movement. Bletter's contribution is the standard source for the Crystal Chain Letters.

Banham, Reyner, "The Glass Paradise," *Architectural Review*, 125 (1959)

Bell, Keith, "Glass in Architecture," *Structuralist*, 27/28 (1987–88)

Bletter, Rosemarie Haag, "The Interpretation of the Glass Dream," *Journal of the Society of Architectural Historians*, 40/3 (1981)

Bostock, Edgar H., "Glass: Its Adaptability in Building," *Architectural Record*, 27 (1910)

Eisenstadt, Sandy, "The Rise and Fall of the Picture Window," *Harvard Design Magazine* (October 1998)

Elliott, Cecil D., *Technics and Architecture: The Development of Materials and Systems for Building*, Cambridge, Massachusetts: MIT Press, 1992

Korn, Arthur, *Glas im Bau und als Gebrauchsgegenstand*, Berlin-Charlottenburg: Pollak, 1926; as *Glass in Modern Architecture of the Bauhaus Period*, New York: Braziller, and London: Barrie and Rockliff, 1968

McGrath, Raymond, and A.C. Frost, *Glass in Architecture and Decoration*, London: Architectural Press, 1937; new edition, 1961

Mumford, Lewis, "House of Glass," in *From the Ground Up: Observations on Contemporary Architecture, Housing, Highway, Building, and Civic Design*, New York: Harcourt Brace, 1956

Scheerbart, Paul, *Glasarchitektur*, Berlin: Verlag der Sturm, 1914; reprint, as *Glasarchitektur und Glashausbriefe*, Munich: Renner, 1986; as *Glass Architecture*, New York: Praeger, and London: November Books, 1972

Taut, Bruno, *Alpine Architektur*, Vienna: Hagen, 1919

"The Uses of Glass," *Progressive Architecture*, 70/3 (1989)

Whyte, Iain Boyd, *The Crystal Chain Letters: Architectural Fantasies by Bruno Taut and His Circle*, Cambridge, Massachusetts: MIT Press, 1985

Wigginton, Michael, *Glass in Architecture*, London: Phaidon, 1996

GLASS HOUSE

Designed by Philip Johnson; completed 1949
New Canaan, Connecticut

Designed by the architect Philip Johnson as a country retreat for himself, the Glass House was arguably the apotheosis of post–World War II modernism in American architecture. Its uncompromising expression of simplicity, prismatic form, and transparency elevated the building to the iconic status that it holds in the history of domestic designs. Through the bold juxtaposition of the technological image of the building with its lush, bucolic setting, the house is said to represent the archetypal landscape idea of the machine in the garden. Its innovative concepts include the virtual dissolution of the exterior wall; an open, seemingly unpartitioned interior floor plan; and the use of a steel structure with expansive glass panels.

Around 1945 or 1946, Johnson developed his earliest sketches for the house, and they indicated more discrete rooms. Learning in 1946 of the Edith Farnsworth House, commissioned from Ludwig Mies van der Rohe (1886–1969) by the physician for a site in the Fox River valley in Plano, Illinois, Johnson was indelibly impressed and influenced by the open floor plan for that house, which would be completed, ironically, approximately two years later than Johnson's house. Mies' idea for a glass and steel house had emerged in the previous decade in an unbuilt project for a house in the mountains of Wyoming. In the Farnsworth House, Mies sandwiched the space between two floating slabs that cantilever dramatically out beyond the glass enclosures to form a terrace; he also raised the house off the ground, thereby protecting it from periodic flood waters, with eight H-columns forming an exoskeleton. In contrast, the Glass House sits firmly on the ground, and its eight wide-flange H columns relate with more ambiguity to the sheets of glass. Its black-painted steel presents a more sober and recessive treatment of the frame than the highly burnished white frame of the Farnsworth House. Construction began in March 1948, and Johnson was able to occupy the house at the beginning of 1949.

Employing principles of ancient classical site planning, the house relates actively to its site—a meticulously manicured lawn amid mature deciduous and coniferous trees and beside a ravine that separates the house from a pond—and to the buildings that Johnson subsequently added to the compound. Walking toward the Glass House is not unlike the processional experience of the Parthenon (448–432 B.C.) on the Athenian Acropolis, which depends heavily on the angle of approach and the seemingly irregular spatial relationship of the temple to the other buildings on the hilltop. As one approaches the Glass House along an obliquely angled path, perceptions of the volume vary according to the proximity to the entrance, the particular angle from which the glass is viewed (generating either reflections of the foliage or a view through the house to the distant treetops), and the awareness of the other buildings on the compound: a guest house, a floating pavilion in the pond, a painting gallery, a sculpture gallery, and most recently a visitor center. The masonry accretion of the guest house serves, in addition to providing more private quarters, as an opaque complement to the open and diaphanous main house. With its almost uninterrupted Flemish-bond brick walls, it becomes a rural companion to the ground story of the emphatically urban Museum of Modern Art guest house (1950) in New York, designed also by Johnson.

Glass House (interior) New Caanan, Conecticut, designed by Philip Johnson
© Esto

Johnson, who later said that the architect "cannot not know history," incorporated other antecedents into the design, among them Andrea Palladio's Villa Capra (1566–70), popularly referred to as La Rotonda. Like La Rotonda, the Glass House is a suburban villa, with a symmetrical enclosure; a highly rational disposition of spaces, although physically abstract; and a prominent circular element, the brick cylinder containing the bathroom and fireplace, at its core. Having been impressed also by the vestigial quality of the brick foundation and chimney that were the sole remains of a burned wooden village he once saw, Johnson thus incorporated an accident of history into the plan with his emphatic representation of the brick podium and service core.

Resting on a brick plinth four courses high in Flemish bond, the enclosure of the 56- by 32-foot unitary space exhibits axial symmetry, with floor-to-ceiling glass between floor and roof slabs. Running uninterrupted between the ground and the underside of the roof slab, the four corner wide-flange H columns are exposed on both exterior and interior, separating the plinth at its corners and revealing the complex intersection of the long sides with the short sides of the enclosure. Four additional columns divide the long walls into approximately thirds and sit within the glass. An elongated door bisects each of the four walls and runs from floor to roof, and two stone steps, triple the width of the door, mark the main entrance at the conclusion of the obliquely angled walkway. Four gooseneck lamps on each long side bathe the walls in light after sundown.

Perhaps the ultimate expression of the dematerialized building element, the glass window in Johnson's house becomes the wall, and the wall has evolved into a screen or the lightest of building membranes, separating indoor space from outdoor space. By means of steel mullions, there is a subdivision of the glass wall: a horizontal dado or chair rail runs continuously, except within the four doors, which provide cross ventilation. Between columns, vertical muntins further subdivide lower sections of glass.

All service components of the house sit well within the interior, away from the enclosure. Extending the brick of the podium inward, the floor of the interior is herringbone-patterned brick. Positioned asymmetrically to the right of the main entrance, a brick cylinder containing a fireplace and the bathroom pierces the roof. On the side away from the entry, the cylinder contains the bathroom, and on the side facing the center of the space, it encloses a shallow concave hearth. Opposite the entry there is a white carpet, on which a grouping of Mies-designed furniture sits: two chrome-plated and leather Barcelona chairs (designed originally for the inauguration of the German Pavilion of the Barcelona International Exposition of 1929), a chrome-plated and leather chaise longue and matching stool, and a chrome-plated and glass X table. A four-legged lamp with a shallow conical shade, designed by the architect himself, completes the ensemble along with the freestanding *Funeral of Phocion*, attributed to Nicolas Poussin (1593/94–1665), and a bronze sculpture of two female figures by Elie Nadelman (1882–1946). A row of wood closets divides this area from the sleeping area. In the left rear corner there is a marble-topped dining table and four Mies-designed Brno chairs of 1930, and in the left near corner waist-high cabinets contain the kitchen appliances. Silk panels, installed on the main entry side, can be slid to filter strong light.

Johnson's reductive experiment for himself demonstrated his unique talent for appropriating and interpreting the ideas of others. The Glass House epitomizes the idea of uninterrupted, universal space adapted to a specific place and translated into a modern symbol of an aesthete's discriminating country life.

PAUL GLASSMAN

See also **Farnsworth House, Plano, Illinois; German Pavilion, Barcelona (1929); Mies van der Rohe, Ludwig (Germany)**

Further Reading

Drexler, Arthur, "Architecture Opaque and Transparent: Johnson's Glass and Brick Houses," *Interiors*, 109 (October 1949)

Frampton, Kenneth (editor), *Philip Johnson, Processes: The Glass House, 1949, and the AT&T Corporate Headquarters, 1978* (exhib. cat.), New York: Institute for Architecture and Urban Studies, 1978

"Glass House Permits Its Owner to Live in a Room in Nature," *Architectural Forum*, 91 (November 1949)

"House at New Canaan, Connecticut," *Architectural Review* (September 1950)

Johnson, Philip, *Johnson House, New Canaan, Connecticut, 1949–*, edited by Yukio Futagawa, Tokyo: A.D.A. Edita, 1972

Johnson, Philip, *Philip Johnson*, New York: Simon and Schuster, and London: Thames and Hudson, 1972

"Le Pavillon de Verre, Maison de Week-End," *L'architecture d'aujourd'hui*, 20 (July 1950)

Schulze, Franz, *Philip Johnson: Life and Work*, New York: Knopf, 1994

Scully, Vincent, "Philip Johnson: The Glass House Revisited," *Architectural Digest* (November 1986)

Stern, Robert A.M., "The Evolution of Philip Johnson's Glass House, 1947–1948," *Oppositions*, 9 (Fall 1997)

Whitney, David, and Jeffrey Kipnis (editors), *Philip Johnson: The Glass House*, New York: Pantheon Books, 1993

GLASS SKYSCRAPER

Designed by Ludwig Mies van der Rohe

Wartime, by denying architects actual opportunities to build, offers them instead the time to indulge in theoretical activity. Taking advantage of Berlin's slowed economy following World War I, Ludwig Mies van der Rohe completed a number of projects that, in their technological content and aesthetic expression, contrast dramatically with the more historically-oriented projects he built in the early 1920s such as the Eichstädt House (Berlin, 1921–23) and the German Pavilion at Barcelona (1928). Early plans and unbuilt projects such as the Concrete Country House Project (1923) and the Brick Country House Project (1924) forecast the hovering volumes of the Farnsworth House (1946–51, Plano, Illinois) for example. The prismatic towers he would build in Chicago and New York in the years around 1950 are first suggested in his skyscraper projects of the early 1920s.

Departing from his generally conservative design, Mies' entry to the Friedrichstrasse Skyscraper Competition of 1921 wholly ignored the technical limits of 1920s tall building construction with impossibly thin floor slab dimensions and unfeasible cladding details. Likewise, the massing of the building broke dramatically from German traditions of office building design. Its jagged clover of a plan consumed a triangular site with three sharply articulated and notched leaves gathered around a central core. Each of the sections provided retail and office space while sharing a communal service element: elevator, stairs, and lavatories.

A majority of the 145 submissions to the competition adopted prismatic characteristics for the triangular site. However, Mies' skyscraper was especially evocative, as seen in his perspective sketches and photomontages of the project that emphasize its sharp edges and faceted massing. In an exaggerated perspective view, the building's blade-like silhouette looms as a shimmering prism over a rough cobblestone street and the grim, load-bearing masonry buildings that lay in its shadow. Distinctly unlike these vernacular buildings, glass falls from the top of Mies' building as a continuous curtain wall, this sheer scrim obscuring the wafer-like floor slabs only where light dazzles in long vertical slashes from the building's surface.

Such images illustrate the theoretical content of the project, emphasizing the means by which different building materials modulate light. In essence, masonry bearing walls absorb light and cast shadows, while glass allows light its free play through reflective activity. These perceptive qualities place the project in the context of German Expressionism, one of the many revolutionary movements circulating in self-consciously progressive artistic circles in postwar Berlin. Expressionist manifestos expounded upon prismatic socialist utopias housed in a shimmering architecture of glass. Paul Scheerbart's prophetic book *Glas Architektur* (1914) encouraged the construction of whole crystalline cities to rejuvenate European civilization; in *Alpine Architektur* (1919) Bruno Taut similarly suggested that social listlessness and apathy was a product of masonry architecture: man would be spiritually and physically awakened by living in glass architecture open to the sun and stars.

Although Mies' crystalline tower fulfills the Expressionists' call for fully-glazed and multi-faceted architecture, the architect seemed never to have wholly embraced the emotional content of the movement. His intent was to study the manner in which different materials respond to light, rather than to consider the emotive appeal of such illumination. Intentionally or not, in the lively interplay of light and transparent surfaces, matched with the building's spiky plan, Mies amplified the skyscraper's expressionistic nature. At the same time, the logic so clearly expressed in his later grid-ordered planning is already present in the competition entry which otherwise makes clear formal overtures to Expressionism. Writing on the project, Mies failed to achieve the emotional tenor of Scheerbart or Taut in his measured language. In a rational explanation of the seemingly willful and emotive forms he explained "The building site was triangular; I tried to make full use of it. The depth of the site compelled me to split the fronts, so that the inner core received light" (Riley, 180). Thus it was no desire for a new expression of architecture or celebration of the regenerative potential of modern materials but the simple desire for economical use of the site and wish for well-illuminated interiors that guided Mies.

In the following year, for another theoretical skyscraper project Mies explained in similarly rational terms the genesis of this second glass-enclosed shaft. The curving edge of its plan filled a highly irregular, five-sided site with three unevenly balanced lobed elements meeting at two common circular elevator cores. This scalloped plan provided a supple, layered frame over which glass hung like a gently undulating curtain, suggesting a means to harness the plastic potential of the material unlike the rigid, shard-like character of his first skyscraper design. Mies insisted that this building's design was similarly rational; its curves were not "arbitrary," but rather they "were determined by three factors: sufficient illumination of the interior, the massing of the building viewed from the street, and lastly the play of reflection" (Riley, 186). Thus Mies revealed neither revolutionary affectations in the building's shimmering transparencies nor romance for its thin, cantilevered floor slabs. Although this skyscraper too would never be constructed, the cool logic and rationality behind it traveled with Mies as he emigrated to America. The photographed presentation of the model expresses horizontal layers within a glass scrim in a manner which is closer to the clear expressions of structure in such later skyscrapers of his as the Lake Shore Drive Apartments (1948–51) and Seagram Building (1954–58); in its slenderness it also anticipated their proportions and was a clear, cogent forecast of those later curtain-walled towers.

JHENNIFER A. AMUNDSON

See also **Glass; Mies van der Rohe, Ludwig (Germany); Skyscraper**

Further Reading

Cohen, Jean-Louis, *Mies van der Rohe*, Paris: Hazan, 1994; as *Mies van der Rohe*, translated by Maggie Rosengarten, London and New York: E and FN Spon, 1996

Riley, Terence, and Barry Bergdoll (editors), *Mies in Berlin*, New York: Museum of Modern Art, 2001

Scheerbart, Paul, *Glasarchitektur*, Berlin: Sturm, 1914; and Taut, Bruno, *Alpine Architektur*, Vienna: Hagen, 1919; both as *Glass Architecture, by Paul Scheerbart, and Alpine Architecture, by Bruno Taut*, edited by Dennis Sharp, *Glass Architecture* translated by James Palmes and *Alpine Architecture* translated by Shirley Palmer, edited by Dennis Sharp, New York: Praeger, 1972

Schulze, Franz, *Mies van der Rohe: A Critical Biography*, Chicago: University of Chicago Press, 1985

GOFF, BRUCE ALONZO 1904–82

Architect, United States

The idiosyncratic designs of Bruce Goff, one of America's most important but also most misunderstood architects, take a unique position in Western architecture. Although Goff was undeniably influenced by Louis Sullivan, Frank Lloyd Wright, and Antoni Gaudí, he worked well beyond contemporary architectural tradition. His exotic taste, paired with an enormous variety of design and a preference for unusual materials, divided critics over his work, leading to such memorable judgments as the "Michelangelo of Kitsch" or a "poet of the unredeemable," as suggested by Charles Jencks (1978). However, behind the unusual if not fantastic shapes of his buildings lie qualities that are important contributions to modern architecture. These include the spatial organizations of his houses and his use of recycled materials. From 1916 until 1982, Goff designed around 500 buildings, of which at least 147 were built in 14 states of the United States.

Although most of the commissions were residential, he also designed some commercial and civic buildings, such as the Riverside Studio (1928) in Tulsa, Oklahoma; the Redeemer Lutheran Building (1959) in Bartlesville, Oklahoma; and the Mercedes Benz Agency (1967) in Atlanta, Georgia. Goff's early projects resemble buildings by Frank Lloyd Wright; Goff certainly worshiped similar geometric principles in his architecture, yet he was even more tempted to free himself from the right angle. Considering himself both an architect and a composer until the age of 30, Goff took considerable inspiration from music, especially the compositions of Claude Debussy. In several experiments, he sought parallels between music and architecture, an obsession that also played an important part in his teachings.

Although Goff's designs might appear to be floating, he usually adhered to proportional systems to lend coherence to his buildings. He also followed certain (usually symmetrical) plan typologies, one, for instance, being a central, vertically emphasized volume encircled by compartmented spaces, another being a continuous band of interlocking spaces surrounding a central service core. Despite his link to the organic or Expressionist tradition, Goff's buildings are usually detached from the surrounding landscape, a quality that separates him from Wright's preference to integrate a building with nature.

At the age of 12, Goff became an apprentice in the architectural office of Rush, Endacott, and Rush in Tulsa. By the age of 22, he had already built a major design, the Boston Avenue Church in Tulsa. After a short correspondence with Wright and Sullivan, he decided not to pursue formal architectural training. In 1929, he passed the Oklahoma licence examination as a registered architect without a degree in architecture. In 1934, he moved to Chicago, where he opened his own office. For seven years, Goff taught architecture at the Chicago Academy of Fine Arts. From 1947 to his resignation in 1956, he served as chair of the School of Architecture at the University of Oklahoma, Norman. During this productive time as a teacher, Goff built 17 of 41 commissions, including the Ford House (1947) in Aurora, Illinois; the Hopewell Baptist Church (1948) in Edmond, Oklahoma; and perhaps his most famous design, the Bavinger House (1950) in Norman. Typically, his single-family houses feature a large central room designed to serve different functions. The interior of the Bavinger House is divided by plants, carpets, and fishnet as opposed to regular doors. The steel cables supporting the roof structure are biplane braces hung from a central mast used by the oil-drilling industry. Walls in Goff's houses sometimes included waste used as rustication or discarded glass reused as decorative crystal-like forms. Similar

Los Angeles County Museum of Art, Pavilion for Japanese Art (Shin'en Kan Museum, 1988)
Photo © Mary Ann Sullivan

elements appear in the circular-plan Ford House, another significant example of Goff's adoption of war materials. Here, for instance, Quonset hut elements are put to residential use. Stylistically, Goff's designs defy any traditional classification, varying between the Prairie style of his early buildings to organic forms showing Japanese influence (e.g., the Al Dewlen House Project, Amarillo, Texas, 1956).

During the years in Oklahoma, Goff was discovered by Joe Price, who was to become Goff's most important client. In 1956, Goff started designing and building a house for Price and a studio, Shin'enKan, in Bartlesville. The designs followed one of Goff's typologies, the crystalline building consisting of a central volume that is partly surrounded by smaller screened spaces. The composition of irregular pentagons, however, does not seem to refer to any precedent. Whereas the plan might be reminiscent of Wright's experiments with hexagonal modules, the spatial solution and the unusual materials identify it as a unique Goff design.

From 1956 to 1964, Goff stayed in Bartlesville and maintained his own office in Frank Lloyd Wright's Price Tower. Supported by Joe Price, in the following years he was able to travel to Japan, where he gave several lectures. Later on, a Japanese influence became very evident in the Harder House (1970) in Mountain Lake, Minnesota, and in the Shin'enKan Museum (1988) at the Los Angeles County Museum of Art, commissioned by Price to house his collection of Japanese art.

Despite the fact that Goff spent several years teaching at the University of Oklahoma, few students followed his footsteps. The most famous of them are Herb Greene, who built his own house (1959) in Norman, Oklahoma in the shape of a buffalo, close to the Bavinger House, and Bart Prince, who completed the Shin'enKan Museum in Los Angeles after Goff's death.

DORTE KUHLMANN

See also **Los Angeles (California), United States; Prairie School; Wright, Frank Lloyd (United States)**

Biography

Born in Alton, Kansas, 8 June 1904. Apprenticed at the age of twelve to Rush, Endacott and Rush of Tulsa, Oklahoma, Goff became a partner with the firm in 1928 and a registered architect without a university education. In 1934 he moved to Chicago to work for Alfonso Iannelli and started teaching at the Academy of Fine Arts. Joining the armed forces as a Seabee in World War II allowed him travelling to California, Alaska, and the Aleutian Islands. Professor of architecture at the University of Oklahoma 1947–1955, professional office in Price Tower at Bartlesville, Oklahoma until 1964 when he moved to Kansas City where he stayed to 1969. Goff died in Tyler, Texas on 4 August 1982. In 1987 the Bavinger House was awarded the prestigious 25 Year Award from the American Institute of Architects.

Selected Works

Boston Avenue Methodist Church, Tulsa, Oklahoma, 1926–1927
Riverside Studio, Tulsa, Oklahoma, 1928
Colmorgan House, Glenview, Illinois, 1937
Ford House, Aurora, Illinois, 1948
Hopewell Baptist Church, Edmond, Oklahoma, 1948

House for Eugene and Nancy Bavinger, Norman, Oklahoma, 1955
Al Dewlen House, Project, Amarillo, Texas, 1956
Joe Price House, Bartlesville, Oklahoma, 1976
Redeemer Lutheran Building, Bartlesville, Oklahoma, 1959
Mercedes Benz Agency, Atlanta, Georgia, 1967
Glen and Luetta Harder House, Mountain Lake, Minnesota, 1971
Barby II Residence, Tucson, Arizona, 1976
Al Struckus House, Woodland Hills, California, 1987
Shin'en Kan Museum, Pavillion for Japanese Art at Los Angeles County Museum of Art, Los Angeles, 1988

Further Reading

Cook, Jeffrey, *The Architecture of Bruce Goff*, New York and London: Harper and Row, 1978
De Long, David G., *The Architecture of Bruce Goff—Buildings and Projects*, New York: Garland Publishing, 1977
De Long, David G. *Bruce Goff: Toward Asolute Architecture*, Boston: MIT Press, 1988
Jencks, Charles, "Bruce Goff: The Michelangelo of Kitsch," *Architectural Design*, 48/10 (1978)
Saliga, Pauline and Mary Woolever (editors), *The Architecture of Bruce Goff* (exhib. cat.), Chicago: Art Institute of Chicago, 1995
Sergeant, John and Stephen Mooring (editors), "Bruce Goff," *A.D. Profiles* 48 (1978)
Welch, Philip B. and Arthur Dyson (editors), *Goff on Goff: Conversations and Lectures*, Norman: University of Oklahoma Press 1996

GOLDBERG, BERTRAND 1913–97

Architect, United States

Bertrand Goldberg was an American architect and designer whose work reflected his commitment to rationalism, economy, environmental psychosociology, and industrial production. Born and raised in Chicago, he studied architecture at the Cambridge School of Landscape Architecture (now Harvard University's Graduate School of Design) while an undergraduate at Harvard College from 1929 to 1931. He left Harvard to attend the Bauhaus in Berlin under Mies van der Rohe from 1932 to 1933 and, upon his return to Chicago, attended some classes at the Armour Institute of Technology (now the Illinois Institute of Technology [IIT]). He opened his own office, Bertrand Goldberg Associates, in Chicago in 1937.

From the beginning of his career, Goldberg embraced industrial design as much as architecture. In 1939 he founded the Standard Houses Corporation as a venue for researching and producing prefabricated architecture. These designs included a bathroom unit that was distributed nationally in 1946 as well as a plastic refrigerator and freight car for the Pressed Steel Car Company, which was produced between 1949 and 1952, when steel was in short supply. His work on the railroad car led to his design for a prefabricated housing unit called the Unishelter. Although Goldberg had designed and built prefabricated housing as early as 1937 (first in Lafayette, Indiana, and then in Suitland, Maryland), the prefabricated origins of these early panel-system schemes were not made manifest; they were simple homes with pitched roofs. The Unishelter, in contrast, adopted a streamlined, industrial look. Initially manufactured for the U.S. Army, the Unishelter, which was constructed of stress-skin plywood, could be used as a shipping container while it was being transported. Unishelter units could be combined in the field to form large, flexible, economical houses. The Pressed Steel Car Company manufactured about 2,000 Unishelters between 1948 and 1950 for use by the army, but, despite Goldberg's efforts to expand the unit's market, the design never went into civilian production.

Two other designs that reveal Goldberg's desire to blur the line between industrial production and architectural design include the North Pole Mobile Ice Cream Store and the Clark/Maple Gasoline Service Station, both constructed in Chicago in 1938. These two projects used tension-cable structural systems, presaging the high-tech design movements of the 1960s and 1970s. The ice cream store in particular illustrates Goldberg's interest in flexible pragmatism. It was designed in such a way that three units could fit onto a flatbed truck. The intention was that the stores would be dropped off in urban parking lots; as the weather cooled, the truck would move the units to cities farther and farther south.

Goldberg studied under Mies van der Rohe at the Bauhaus and also at the Armour Institute (IIT), where he often acted as a translator for Mies. Although the technological and structural innovations of his industrial designs suggest Mies's influence, Mies's impact is more directly evident in Goldberg's early house projects of the 1930s. These employed such Miesian strategies as slipped axes and freestanding screens to maximize the flow of space through the interiors. According to an unpublished lecture that Goldberg gave at IIT in 1997 ("The Ghost Walks"), he practiced under his mentor's influence until the mid-1950s, when he grew skeptical of the rationality and geometry of the grid. Turning to Expressionists, such as the Viennese artist Friedensreich Hundertwasser, who asserted that "we live today in a chaos of straight lines," Goldberg abandoned rectilinearity. At this point, he broke off definitively with Miesian design.

Goldberg's first large-scale departure from the grid is his most famous building: his innovative—and decidedly nonrectilinear—Marina City complex, nicknamed "Chicago's Corncobs" (1964). This mixed-use project, sited on a three-and-a-half-acre site along the Chicago River, combines housing, office space, parking, and commercial and recreational programs. Marina City was the first central city multiuse project to include housing as well as the first FHA (Federal Housing Authority) project to be located in an urban downtown rather than in the suburbs. In order to qualify for FHA funding within the central city, Goldberg went to Washington, D.C., and successfully lobbied to change the wording of FHA Title 207 from "an intent to build for families with children" to building "for family living," thereby broadening the legal definition of "family." At 635 dwellings per acre, Marina City remains today one of the densest modern residential projects in the world. Recreational components included a marina in the river, a bowling alley located on the fourth floor of the office block, an ice-skating rink at the ground level, and a theater complex containing one television theater and three movie theaters.

Although the combination of so many programs is certainly innovative, particularly for a building dating from the early 1960s, the project is most notable for its formal and structural novelty. At the time of its construction, Marina City's two 65-story towers were the tallest concrete buildings in the world. Built for only ten dollars per square foot, the cylindrical towers

Marina City, Chicago (1964)
© Corbis

provide a striking contrast to the orthogonal buildings that form their context. Central, tubular, concrete cores—containing elevators, stairs, cold water, telephone, and electrical service—brace the post-and-beam structure of the apartments, which branch out from the core like flower petals or corn kernels. The nonparallel walls fanning outward from the core created what Goldberg termed a "kinetic, geocentric space" in the apartments. To convince his client—International Union of Janitors—of the viability as well as the kinetic effect of this atypical formal strategy, Goldberg leased space in a Chicago loft building where he constructed a full-size mockup of two adjacent apartments, complete with an 80-foot-long photographic cyclorama backdrop. The mockup convincingly revealed that the combination of the form and the generous balconies—each habitable room in the towers had its own balcony—made the building's FHA-sized apartments appear to be more generous than their standard, rectilinear counterparts.

Goldberg's other prominent Chicago projects—Astor Tower (a luxury hotel and apartment tower, completed in 1963), the Raymond Hilliard Center (public housing for the elderly and for families, completed in 1966), and River City (another mixed-use project, with middle- and upper-income housing, completed in 1985)—continued his research into nonorthogonal form and concrete construction. His interest in the psychological effects of form on a building's inhabitants as well as his desire to promote community life in these structures, either through shared spaces or shared uses, led Goldberg in the direction of health care design.

Goldberg's best-known hospital project was his first, his longest running, and his biggest: the Health Sciences Center (1968–81) for the State University of New York at Stony Brook. The 250-acre medical campus complex was designed as a megastructure: a seven-story, one-million-square-foot environmental envelope containing academic, research, and clinical facilities, which served as a base for more specialized buildings, such as the clinical science tower, the hospital bed tower, and a basic science tower.

Other medical facilities designed by Goldberg include St. Joseph Hospital (1974) in Tacoma, Washington; Northwestern University's Prentice Women's Hospital (1975) in Chicago; and the Good Samaritan Hospital (1982) in Phoenix, Arizona, all of which employed concrete structural shell construction with undulating exterior walls enclosing centripetally oriented rooms. Additional hospital projects included the Dana Cancer Center (1974) in Boston; St. Mary's Hospital (1976) in Milwaukee, Wisconsin; and Providence Hospital (1982) in Mobile, Alabama.

SARAH WHITING

See also **Apartment Building; Hospital; Illinois Institute of Technology, Chicago; Mies van der Rohe, Ludwig (Germany)**

Biography

Born in Chicago, 17 June 1913. Attended, Harvard University, Cambridge, Massachusetts 1930–32; studied at the Bauhaus, Berlin 1932–33; worked in the office of Mies van der Rohe, Berlin 1932; attended, Armour Institute of Technology (now IIT), Chicago 1933–34. Principal, Bertrand Goldberg Associates, architects and engineers, Chicago from 1937; branch office, Boston 1964; director, subsidiary companies in Chicago: Computer Service Incorporated from 1969, Environmental Engineering Corporation from 1974, Copy Corporation from 1975. Fellow, American Institute of Architects 1966. Died 9 October 1997, Chicago, Illinois.

Selected Works

Clark/Maple Gasoline Service Station, Chicago, 1938
North Pole Mobile Ice Cream Store, Chicago, 1938
Unicel (stress-skin plywood freight car, 1950–51
Unishelter (prefabricated housing unit), 1952
Astor Tower (hotel and apartment tower), Chicago, 1963
Marina City (housing complex), Chicago, 1964
Raymond Hilliard Center (public housing), Chicago, 1966
Health Sciences Center, State University of New York at Stony Brook, 1968–81
Dana Cancer Center (hospital), Boston, 1974
St. Joseph Hospital, Tacoma, Washington, 1974
Northwestern University's Prentice Women's Hospital, Chicago, 1975
St. Mary's Hospital, Milwaukee, Wisconsin, 1976
Good Samaritan Hospital, Phoenix, Arizona, 1982
Providence Hospital, Mobile, Alabama, 1982
River City (housing complex), Chicago, 1985

Selected Publications

"Rich Is Right," *Inland Architect*, 26/1 (1982)
"The Critical Mass of Urbanism," *Inland Architect*, 28/2 (1984)
"Kindergarten Plauderei (Kindergarten Chats)," *Inland Architect*, 30/2 (1986)

Further Reading

A + U, 55 (1975) (special issue on Goldberg)
Cook, John W., and Heinrich Klotz, *Conversations with Architects*, New York: Praeger, and London: Lund Humphries, 1973
Klotz, Heinrich, "Bertrand Goldberg," *Perspecta*, 13–14 (1971)
Legner, Linda, "The New Architecture of Bertrand Goldberg," *Inland Architect* 18 (1974)
"Marina City, Chicago," *Architectural Record*, 134 (1963)
Miller, Ross, "Chicago Architecture after Mies," *Critical Inquiry*, 6 (1979)
"A Portfolio of Work," *The Architectural Forum*, 84 (1946)
Ragon, Michel, *Goldberg, dans la Ville; Goldberg, on the City* (bilingual French-English edition), Paris: Paris Art Center, 1985

GOLOSOV, ILYA 1883–1945

Architect, Russia

Among the leading early Soviet architects, Ilya Golosov was perhaps the most successful in adapting the rigorous, unadorned geometric volumes of Constructivism to the social goals of the new regime through a series of workers' clubs that have become landmarks of Russian architecture. In Golosov's best work, the apparent austerity of 1920s modernism acquired a dramatic—indeed, romantic—cast. In this regard, it is telling that during the early 1920s, Golosov led a theoretical movement known as "symbolic romanticism."

Born in Moscow, Golosov entered Moscow's Stroganov School of the Arts in 1898, where he completed the full eight-year course. He continued his professional training at the Moscow School of Painting, Sculpture, and Architecture in 1907–12 and then moved to St. Petersburg, where he studied at the Academy of Arts until 1915. This extended academic education grounded Golosov in the principles of Neoclassicism, and at the beginning of his career he came under the influence of the leading neoclassical revivalist, Ivan Zholtovskii. Even as Golosov accepted modernist architectural concepts, the order system retained its underlying importance in his understanding of form.

In the early 1920s, Golosov taught with Melnikov at VKhUTEMAS-VKhUTEIN, and, like Melnikov, he built or projected a number of wooden exhibition pavilions. At the same time, he produced rather eclectic, "romantic" sketches for competitions on a grand scale, such as the Moscow Palace of Labor project (1922–23), with the arched roof of its central auditorium suggesting the shape of a dynamo. By 1925 Golosov's acceptance of Constructivist principles became markedly evident in a number of large office building designs, streamlined and reduced to a carefully considered balance of rectilinear elements. Golosov's articulation of form centered on the concept of "lines of gravity" that created a logical, organic frame on which structure took shape. Like other modernist theoreticians, Golosov also explored the innate properties of basic geometric forms, such as the square and circle.

Zuev Workers' Club (1927–29), Moscow, designed by Ilya Golosov
© William C. Brumfield

The juxtaposition of square and circle is developed in depth by Golosov in his Zuev Workers' Club (1927–29). Many such clubs were built in the late 1920s and 1930s, and in the most pragmatic sense they were intended to provide a meeting and recreational space for both workers and professionals (whose alternative might have been the tavern). On the level of ideology, the workers' clubs provided an opportunity for the integration of architecture and social politics in the creation of communal structures, and they firmly announced the leading role of the Communist Party in the creation of a new society. It is not surprising, therefore, that the club concept (or "palace of labor") stimulated some of the most interesting designs of the period.

The Zuev Club has deteriorated over time, like most Constructivist buildings, but the vigor of Golosov's concept has not diminished. The large corner cylinder, containing a stairwell enclosed in glass, is clenched with a rectangular extension of one of the upper floors. The resulting contrast of shapes epitomizes Constructivist architecture both in its display of unadorned steel, glass, and concrete and in its massing of sharply defined volumes. A new industrial aesthetic created a building that resembles a machine, symbolizing the machine age. Yet the bold modeling of its forms recalls the work of architects such as Bazhenov, whose neoclassical designs display a similar volumetric approach. (The closest example is Bazhenov's Iushkov mansion, which also

turns on a corner cylinder and, by fitting coincidence, served as the main location of VKhUTEMAS.)

The organization of interior space at the Zuev Club also devolves on the staircase cylinder, whose wall of glass not only illuminates with a brilliance unusual in Moscow architecture but also highlights the radial construction of the reinforced-concrete beams beneath the upper landing. The dynamism of this machine-like space, which served to concentrate motion within the building, is both functional and lyrical in its relation to the urban landscape beyond the walls. Like Shekhtel, Konstantin Melnikov, and Le Corbusier, Golosov was particularly attuned to the properties of the glass membrane in defining the relation between interior and exterior space, but he went beyond them in his use of glazed components to endow the structure with the sense of a living organism whose interior workings—people moving from one level to another within the building—were exposed to view. Unfortunately, in the few of Golosov's projects that were realized (primarily apartment buildings), the divergence between the crisp lines of his drawings and the realities of Soviet construction methods is all too evident.

By 1933 Golosov, like many of his contemporaries, had abandoned the idealistic view of transparent structure in favor of a massive, opaque neoclassicism. One of the most obvious and best preserved examples of this later phase is the large apartment house (1934–36) on Yauza Boulevard. In this and other administrative buildings of the late 1930s, Golosov melded the neoclassical principles of his early career with the formal restraint of his modernist period.

Throughout the prewar decades, Golosov's architectural work was complemented by that of his older brother, Panteleimon Golosov (1882–1945). Although the two did not collaborate as closely as the Vesnin brothers (Alexander, Leonid, and Viktor), their careers followed similar paths, from early study at the Stroganov School and the Moscow School of Painting, Sculpture, and Architecture to teaching positions at VKhUTEMAS-VKhUTEIN and the Moscow Architectural Institute. Panteleimon Golosov's most successful modernist structure was also one of the last: the Pravda Building, designed for the publishing empire of the same name and still very much in use. The building combined a nine-story office block, fronted by the lower printing plant, with its streamlined, horizontal window lines.

The parallel paths of the two Golosov brothers continued with the turn of Panteleimon Golosov to the design of classically articulated apartment buildings at the end of the 1930s. Although their careers can be seen as a successful example of the transition from modernist, functional architecture to the more conservative political and cultural environment of the 1930s, it seems evident that the pressures of the prewar and war years led both to a premature death in the same year, 1945.

WILLIAM C. BRUMFIELD

See also **Constructivism; Melnikov, Konstantin (Russia); Moscow, Russia; Neoclassicism; Russia and Soviet Union; Shekhtel, Fedor (Russia); St. Petersburg, Russia; Vesnin, Alexander, Leonid, and Viktor (Russia)**

Biography

Born in Moscow, 31 July 1883. Brother of architect Panteleimon Golosov. Studied at Stroganov School, Moscow 1898–

1907; attended School of Painting, Sculpture, and Architecture, Moscow 1907–12. Engineer, Russian Army 1914–17. Worked with Ivan Zholtovskii 1918–21. Professor, architecture faculty, Moscow Polytechnical Institute from 1921; professor and head of a workshop, with Konstantin Melnikov, VKhUTEMAS, Moscow from 1921. Member, Union of Contemporary Architects (OSA). Died in Moscow, 29 January 1945.

Selected Works

Design for Palace of Labor (competition entry; unexecuted), Moscow, 1923
Far East Pavilion, All Russian Agricultural Exhibition, Moscow, 1923
Palace of Culture, Stalingrad, 1928
Zuev Workers' Club, Moscow, 1929
House of Soviets, Khabarovsk, Russia (with B.Y. Ulinich), 1929
Government Building of Kalmykiya, Elista, Russia (with B.Y. Mittelman), 1932
Zhilkombinat (Residential and Service Complex), Ivanovo-Voznesensk, Russia, 1932
House of Soviets, Rostov-on-Don, Russia, 1934
Housing Complex, Yauza Boulevard, Moscow, 1936
Trade Union School, Moscow, 1938

Selected Publications

"My Creative Path," *Arkhit. SSSR* 1 (1933)
"On Large Architectural Forms," *Arkhit. SSSR* 5 (1933)
"New Trends in Architecture," paper given at the Moscow Architectural Society, 13 December 1922

Further Reading

The standard monograph, richly illustrated, on Golosov's life and work is Khan-Magomedov 1988. A good selection of contemporary documents on workers' clubs is contained in Afanasev.

Afanasev, K.N. (editor), *Iz istorii sovetskoi arkhitektury, 1926–1932 gg.: Dokumenty i materialy: Robochie kluby i dvortsy kultury* (From the History of Soviet Architecture, 1926–32: Documents and Materials: Workers' Clubs and Palaces of Culture), Moscow: Nauka, 1984
Barkhin, M.G., et al. (editors), *Mastera sovetskoi arkhitektury ob arkhitekture* (Masters of Soviet Architecture on Architecture), 2 vols., Moscow: Iskusstvo, 1975
Brumfield, William C., *A History of Russian Architecture*, Cambridge and New York: Cambridge University Press, 1993
Cooke, Catherine, *Russian Avant-Garde: Theories of Art, Architecture, and the City*, London: Academy Editions, 1995
Khan-Magomedov, Selim O., *Pioneers of Soviet Architecture: The Search for New Solutions in the 1920s and 1930s*, translated by Alexander Lieven, edited by Catherine Cooke, New York: Rizzoli, and London: Thames and Hudson, 1987
Khan-Magomedov, S.O., *Ilia Golosov*, Moscow: Stroiizdat, 1988
Khazanova, V.E., *Sovetskaia arkhitektura pervykh let Oktiabria, 1917–1925 gg.* (Soviet Architecture of the First Years of October, 1917–1925), Moscow: Nauka, 1970

GONZÁLEZ DE LEÓN, TEODORO 1926– AND ABRAHAM ZABLUDOVSKY 1924–

Architects, Mexico

The collaboration of Teodoro González de León (1926–) and Abraham Zabludovsky (1924–) has been a highly significant development in the evolution of contemporary Mexican architecture. As classmates in the Escuela Nacional de Arquitectura in Mexico City, both men absorbed the functionalist approaches of professors such as José Villagrán García. Through distinct paths, both rejected certain premises of the doctrine after beginning their own private practices. After further study in France in the studio of Le Corbusier from 1947 to 1948, González de León attempted to construct prefabricated housing in the capital city to meet pressing demand for such; eventually realizing that his designs should harmonize with the existing urban fabric, he was determined to find solutions in native materials, techniques, and design. Zabludovsky, too, had cause to reconsider the central tenets of Mexican functionalism. Functionalism had appealed to idealistic Mexican architects of the late 1920s and 1930s as they were faced with the imperative of designing new facilities for the social services promised by revolutionary governments. Simply stated, they perceived the answer to complex social and economic problems to be structural—that through better design, centuries-old inequalities might disappear. Yet, as Zabludovsky witnessed, in practice this approach could not serve the nation. As he recalled later, "We now know that architecture cannot alter a society's economic conditions . . . we, as architects, cannot direct society with the tools of our trade: our work has only a specific area of influence. Although we may be able to play a part in the process of social transformation from within this field, it is not the result of any inherent quality of architecture" (Zabludovsky, 1993).

As González de León and Zabludovsky realized the failure of functionalism to construct a new, more just nation, they developed a more flexible architectural vocabulary that would permit the government and private sector to pursue goals of social justice and economic development. Their collaboration began in 1968, after each architect had experienced almost a decade of successful private practice. Their first works were a series of master plans commissioned by PEMEX (Petróleos Mexicanos) for Poza Rica and Minatitlan, in the state of Veracruz, where growth was rapid and uncontrolled because of dramatic growth in the oil industry. Zabludovsky and González de León studied the existing natural environment to determine which areas were unsuitable for urbanization, surveyed land usage, and developed planning forecasts, determining demand for housing, health and social services, and commercial enterprises. Their subsequent work, spanning two decades, would be in the areas of low-income housing, apartment buildings and private residences, and public-sector works.

In 1968 and 1970, they proposed ambitious solutions to the chronic shortage of low-income housing in Mexico City. In the Torres de Mixcoac (1971) and La Patera (1973) housing developments, the architects sited approximately 4000 brick-faced units around tranquil, open public space, allowing for a variety of informal, recreational uses and integrating sculpture by Mathias Goeritz with their overall design. Later works, among them González de León's development of the Ex-Hacienda de Enmedio (1978), further refined these principles. In projects for upper-income residents, such as the Torre Manhattan (1975) and La Herradura (1982) apartment buildings, Zabludovsky and González de León demonstrated similar care concerning the site and the Mexican climate. In treating the wall as a mass, drawing on the Mexican vernacular, they rejected large expanses of plate glass in favor of protected, smaller windows.

These elements are also present in their designs for government-sponsored projects, among them the Delegación Cuauhtémoc (1972–73), a building to house the administrative units overseeing the central area of the city, offices for the workers' housing fund INFONAVIT (1973–75), the Mexican Embassy in Brasilia (1973–75), educational facilities such as the Colegio de México (1974–75) and the Universidad Pedagógica Nacional (1979–82), and the Rufino Tamayo International Museum of Contemporary Art (1981). Constructed over a period of 12 years, these structures manifest the evolution and refinement of Zabludovsky's and González de León's unique approach to architecture. Common to these works is a singular attention to Mexican culture and national identity. The architects have drawn from the preconquest and colonial eras in emphasizing horizontality, centering these massive structures around patios and courtyards, and protecting entrances through gracefully executed porticos. Both interior open spaces and entrances have frequently achieved unanticipated utility as meeting places and landmarks, as in the case of the INFONAVIT and Colegio de México structures. Further, the architects' frequent use of berms and sloping terraces, derived from preconquest design, serves to join these structures to the urban landscapes. Notable also is their innovative use of concrete. Zabludovsky and González de León chose to mix concrete with marble aggregate. The concrete was then chiseled, resulting in a rough surface that reflects light, creating a warm cast to building exteriors. In recent works, such as the Capuchinas-Banamex Building (1988–89), adjacent to the Palacio de San Mateo de Valparaíso in the oldest section of the city, the architects employed rose-hued *tezontle* sand in the concrete, creating a medium that complements rather than intrudes on viceregal structures.

Together, these elements have come to constitute a prominent trend in contemporary Mexican architecture, "integrated functionalism." The architects' use of massive, sculptural volumes, whether in the Cultural and Tourist Services Unit (1984) at Chichén Itzá or in the award-winning Banamex Financial Centers (1986–88), employ logical aspects of functionalism, combined with a sensitivity to current socioeconomic and cultural needs, to yield an authentically Mexican architecture.

Both architects have also pursued dynamic private practices. González de León's later works include the Fondo de Cultura Económica Building (1992) and Federal Palace of Justice (1993). Recent publications, among them *Architecture as Art*, reveal his commitment to excellence in design. Zabludovsky's recent work includes libraries, theaters, civic centers, apartment buildings, and office buildings, most notably his restoration of La Ciudadela (1988) and the Celaya Multipurpose Auditorium (1990), which received the Gold Medal at the Sofia, Bulgaria, Bienal. In sum, their work consistently provides numerous examples of the complexity and dynamism of postrevolutionary Mexican architecture.

PATRICE E. OLSEN

Biography

Teodoro González de León

Born in Mexico City, 29 May 1926. Attended the Universidad Nacional Autonoma de México, School of Architecture 1942–47; degree in architecture 1947. Worked in the architectural studio of Le Corbusier, Paris 1948–49. In private practice, Mexico City from 1949; director of Rural Housing, National Housing Institute 1956–58; technical director, Council of Economic and Social Planning, Mexico City 1958; advisor, operating and banking discount fund for housing, Mexico City 1966–70; advisor, P.W. Department, Mexico City 1970–76; advisor, Ministry of Public Education, Mexico City 1970–76. Visiting professor, Pratt Institute, New York 1982 and 1983. Member, Colegio de Arquitectos de México 1966; emeritus member, Sociedad de Arquitectos Mexicanos 1978; honorary fellow, American Institute of Architects 1983; member, Academia de Artes 1984.

Abraham Zabludovsky

Born in Bialystok, Poland, 14 June 1924; emigrated to Mexico 1927; naturalized 1941. Attended the Universidad Nacional Autonoma de México, School of Architecture 1943–49; degree in architecture 1949. In private practice, Mexico City from 1949; director, INURBASA, Mexico City from 1973; advisor to the director, CODEUR, Mexico City from 1978. Teacher of composition 1965–67, lecturer and advisor, Universidad Nacional Autonoma de México; lecturer and advisor, Museum of Modern Art, Mexico City. Fellow, Academy of Architecture, Mexico; honorary fellow, American Institute of Architects 1982; honorary fellow, International Academy of Architecture 1991.

Teodoro González de León and Abraham Zabludovsky

Partnership established in Mexico City 1968; have received awards for their work in Mexico and South America.

Selected Works

Cuevas House, San Ángel, Mexico City, 1968

Mixcoac-Lomas de Plateros Housing Complex, Mexico City (with sculpture by Mathias Goeritz), 1968

Office building, Nuevo León and Campeche streets, Mexico City, 1970

Office building, Campos Elíseos 165, Mexico City, 1970

Office building, Presidente Mazaryk 191, Mexico City, 1970

Vallejo-La Patera Housing Complex, Mexico City, 1970

Sports Complex, Tlalnepantla, State of Mexico, 1972

Delegación Cuauhtémoc building, Mexico City (with Jaime Ortiz Monaterio and Luis Antonio Zapiain), 1973

Mexican Embassy, Brasilia (with J. Francisco Serrano), 1975

Headquarters, Instituto del Fondo Nacional de la Vivienda para los Trabajadores, INFONAVIT, Barranca del Muerto 280, Mexico City, 1975

El Colegio de México, Camino al Ajusco, Mexico City, 1975

Torre Manhattan apartments, Tecamachalco, State of Mexico (with sculpture by Mathias Goeritz), 1975

Rufino Tamayo International Museum of Contemporary Art, Paseo de la Reforma y Gandhi, Bosque de Chapultepec, Mexico City, 1981

Torre Palmas office building, Paseo de las Palmas, Mexico City, 1981

Universidad Pedagógica Nacional, Camino al Ajusco, Mexico City, 1982

La Herradura apartment building, Mexico City, 1982

Banamex Cuadra Complex, enlargement and remodeling, Mexico City, 1984

Cultural and Tourist Services Unit, Chichén Itzá, Yucatán, 1984

Banamex Insurgentes Encanto Financial Center, Av. Insurgentes y Encanto La Florida, Mexico City, 1988

Banamex Revolución Financial Center, Av. Revolución y
Altamirano, Mexico City, 1988
Banamex Lomas Financial Center, Lomas de Chapultepec, Mexico
City, 1988
Capuchinas Building—Banamex, Av. Venustiano Carranza y Palma,
Mexico City, 1989
National Auditorium, enlargement and remodeling, Paseo de la
Reforma y Parque Lira, Mexico City, 1990

Selected Publications

Teodoro González de León

Barra de Navidad, Estudio de un Área, 1958
Investigaciones de Vivienda en Once Ciudades del País, 3 vols., 1966
Catálogo de Cartogramas, 1969
"Diseño y praxis en la enseñanza del concreto," *Arquitectura y
Sociedad 3* (1980)
"La Piedra del Siglo XX," *IMCYC*, 142 (February 1983)
La Voluntad del Creador, 1994
Retrato de Arquitecto con Ciudad, 1996
Architecture as Art, 1998

Abraham Zabludovsky

"El Centro Cívico Cinco de Mayo," *Arquitectura/México*, 79
(September 1962)
"Unidad de Habitación Terrazas Satélite," *Arquitectura/México*, 91
(September 1965)
*Arquitectura Contemporánea Mexicana: Obras de Teodoro González de
León y Abraham Zabludovsky*, 1969
"Dos Edificios de Departamentos," *Arquitectura/México*, 68
(December 1969)
"Central de Abasto de la Ciudad de México," *Obras* (Mexico)
(March 1983)
La Ciudadela, Biblioteca Mexicana, 1991
"Arquidiálogo del Arq. Zabludovsky: El Museo Rufino Tamayo,"
Excélsior (8 August 1992)
Abraham Zabludovsky, architect, 1993
Abraham Zabludovsky: Cinquenta Años de Arquitectura, 1995
Abraham Zabludovsky, Arquitecto, 1998

Further Reading

Bienal de arquitectura mexicana, Mexico City: Federación de
Colegios de Arquitectos de la República Mexicana, 1990–
Bullrich, Francisco, *New Directions in Latin American Architecture*,
New York: Braziller, and London: Studio Vista, 1969
Drexler, Arthur, *Transformations in Modern Architecture*, New York:
Museum of Modern Art, 1979; London: Secker and Warburg,
1980
"Edificio Municipal de Delegación Cuauhtémoc," "El
INFONAVIT," and "Museo Tamayo," in *Modern Mexican
Architecture*, edited by Makoto Suzuki, Tokyo: Process
Architecture, 1983
Garay Arellano, Graciela de (editor), *Historia oral de la ciudad de
Mexico: testimonios de sus arquitectos (1940–1990), Abraham
Zabludovsky*, Mexico City: Lotería Nacional para la Asistencia
Pública, Instituto Mora, 1995
Glusberg, Jorge, *Seis arquitectos mexicanos*, Buenos Aires: Ediciones
de Arte Gaglianone, 1983
Heyer, Paul, *Mexican Architecture: The Work of Abraham
Zabludovsky and Teodoro González de León*, New York: Walker,
1978
Heyer, Paul, *Abraham Zabludovsky, Architect, 1979–1993*, New
York: Princeton Architectural Press, 1993
"Museo Rufino Tamayo," *Arquitectura y Sociedad*, 9 (1981)
Neuvillate Ortiz, Alfonso de, *Diez arquitectos mexicanos*, Mexico
City: Ediciones Galería de Arte Misrachí, 1977
Noelle, Louise, "Mexican Contemporary Architecture: An
Approximation," in *Modern Mexican Architecture*, edited by
Makoto Suzuki, Tokyo: Process Architecture, 1983
Noelle, Louise, "Arquitectura mexicana: 1952–1985," in *México, 75
años de revolución*, edited by Otto Granados Roldán, Mexico
City: Fondo de Cultura Economica, 1988
Noelle, Louise, *Arquitectos contemporáneos de México*, Mexico City:
Editorial Trillas, 1989; 2nd edition, 1993
Noelle, Louise, *Crónicas de arquitectura*, Mexico City: Academie
Nacional de Arquitectura, Universidad Autónoma Metropolitana,
1993
*Ocho conjuntos de Habitación: arquitectura contemporánea mexicana;
Mexican Contemporary Architecture* (bilingual Spanish-English
edition), Mexico City: Arquitectura y Sociedad, 1976
Sondereguer, Pedro Conrado, *Memoria y utopia en la arquitectura
mexicana*, Mexico City: Universidad Autónoma Metropolitana,
1990
Toca, Antonio, and Aníbal Figueroa Castrejón, *México: nueva
arquitectura*, Mexico City: Gili, 1991; 5th edition, 1995
Yáñez, Enrique, *Del funcionalismo al post-racionalismo*, Mexico City:
Universidad Autónoma Metropolitana-Limusa, 1990

GOODHUE, BERTRAM GROSVENOR
1869–1924

Architect, United States

Born in the small New England town of Pomfret, Connecticut,
on 28 April 1869, Bertram Grosvenor Goodhue lacked the financial support from his family to follow the route pursued by
many aspiring American architects to the École des Beaux-Arts
in Paris. Accordingly, he followed the other conventional path
to the architectural profession, going to work at the age of 15
as an office boy–apprentice in the New York City office of Renwick, Aspinwall and Russell, headed by James Renwick, the architect of both the elegant Grace Church on lower Broadway
and the grandiloquent St. Patrick's Cathedral on Fifth Avenue.

Having won a competition on his own in 1891 for a church
in Dallas, and needing help in carrying it out, Goodhue formed
an association with the Boston architects Ralph Adams Cram
and Charles Francis Wentworth and became a partner in Cram,
Wentworth and Goodhue in 1892. The name of the firm was
changed in 1898 to Cram, Goodhue and Ferguson when Frank
William Ferguson was brought on following the death of Wentworth.

In addition to his architectural work, Goodhue was involved
from the beginning of his career in other aspects of design, especially publications; he was, for example, the originator of the
Cheltenham typeface, designed in 1904 and, with Cram, published an avant-garde arts quarterly, *The Knight-Errant*.

Although the firm of Cram, Goodhue and Ferguson produced an impressive range of buildings in their early years, the
commission that established their reputation was for the rehabilitation and expansion of the U.S. Military Academy (1903–10)
at West Point. One of the finest elements of the extensive project
was the austere Cadet Chapel (1910), in which Goodhue had
an especially strong hand.

Whereas the design collaboration between Cram and
Goodhue seemed to exploit their individual strengths—Cram's
in the development of the overall plan, Goodhue's in the refinement and ornamentation of it—the personal relationship be-

New Nebraska State Capitol, Lincoln, Nebraska
Photo © Mary Ann Sullivan

tween the two men became increasingly competitive. Cram continued to work out of the Boston headquarters, but Goodhue in 1903 established a separate New York office. When the commission for St. Thomas Episcopal Church in New York was announced, each man submitted his own design. Cram's was selected, but Goodhue insisted that major credit for the finished building go to him for his role in the execution of it. In any case, St. Thomas remains a high point in American Gothic architecture, the quality of its exterior massing matched by that of the elegant nave and the enormous altar screen, done by the German-born sculptor Lee Lawrie under Goodhue's direction.

Not surprisingly, St. Thomas proved to be the last collaboration between Cram and Goodhue, and in 1914 the junior partner set out on his own.

The vigor of Goodhue's search for his own aesthetic—one free of Cram's personal and religiously doctrinal commitment to the Gothic—is evident in the combination of Romanesque and Byzantine that Goodhue applied to the design of St. Bartholomew's Episcopal Church on New York's Park Avenue (begun in 1914 and finished four years later). At the same time, Goodhue embarked on an experiment in town planning, with the design of a new community (1914) for a copper-mining concern in Tyrone, New Mexico.

Goodhue's stylistic investigation continued with his "Churrigueresque" buildings for the Panama–California Exposition (1911–15) in San Diego, an invocation of traditional Spanish motifs that helped fuel the local enthusiasm for a Spanish revival.

The rather bloodless Rockefeller Chapel at the University of Chicago (begun in 1918 but not finished until 1927) shows a lingering willingness on Goodhue's part to work in the Gothic, but his heart had clearly gone out of it.

The building that resolved much of Goodhue's apparent indecision over styles was one that abandoned all of them while embracing some vintage Beaux-Arts planning principals. It was the Nebraska State Capitol (1920–32), the commission for which Goodhue won over a host of competitors wedded to conventional Roman domes and colonnades.

An essentially classical cross-axial composition centered on a 400-foot tower, the Capitol broke new ground in its stripped geometry while retaining a sensitivity to the tradition of figurative ornamentation. What makes the complex so effective is the combination of abstract form with enough pictorial narrative to create a personal connection with the building's program of public service. Much of the credit must go to Lee Lawrie, whose heroic sculptures embodying assorted virtues and historical figures emerge from the plane surfaces of the building to give this austere structure a welcome plasticity. Although some critics have associated the building with the chilling classicism of the contemporaneous work in Italy and Germany, a glance at the celebration of the role of law and the importance of the individual citizen expressed in the Capitol's ornament makes its different motivation abundantly clear.

Goodhue did not live to enjoy all of the accolades that greeted the Capitol, among them the American Institute of Architects

Balboa Park, California Tower, San Diego County, California
© Library of Congress

Selected Works

Gillespie House, Montecito, California, 1902
United States Military Academy, West Point, New York (with Ralph Adams Cram and Frank W. Ferguson), 1910
St. Thomas Church, Fifth Avenue, New York (with Cram and Ferguson), 1913
Panama–California Exposition Buildings, San Diego, 1915
All Saints' Church, Ashmont, Boston (with Cram and Ferguson), 1913, completed 1941
Tyrone, New Mexico, 1914
St. Bartholomew's Church, Park Avenue, New York, 1918
Rockefeller Chapel, University of Chicago, 1927
National Academy of Sciences Building, Washington, D.C., 1924
State Capitol (First prize, competition), Lincoln, Nebraska, 1932
Central Public Library, Los Angeles, 1926

Selected Publications

A Book of Architectural and Decorative Drawings, 1914
Book Decorations by Bertram Grosvenor Goodhue, 1931

Further Reading

Brown, Elinor L., *Architectural Wonder of the World: Nebraska's State Capitol Building*, Ceresco, Nebraska: Midwest, 1965
Kidney, Walter C., *The Architecture of Choice: Eclecticism in America, 1830–1930*, New York: Braziller, 1974
Oliver, Richard, *Bertram Grosvenor Goodhue*, New York: Architectural History Foundation, 1983
Roth, Leland, *A Concise History of American Architecture*, New York: Harper and Row, 1979
Shand-Tucci, Douglass, *Ralph Adams Cram: Life and Architecture*, Amherst: University of Massachusetts Press, 1995
Whiffen, Marcus, and Frederick Koeper, *American Architecture, 1607–1976*, Cambridge, Massachusetts: MIT Press, and London: Routledge and Kegan Paul, 1981
Wiseman, Carter, *Shaping a Nation: Twentieth-Century American Architecture and Its Makers*, New York: Norton, 1998

(AIA) Gold Medal in 1925, a year after his death at age 55. A poll of 500 architects taken by the AIA in 1948 ranked the Capitol fourth among the 25 greatest works of architecture in the world (and ahead of the Parthenon and Chartres Cathedral).

By the time of its completion in 1932, however, the Capitol had already been condemned by the advocates of the modernist avant-garde as a retrograde work. But in light of the sensitive innovations evident in this building—and the closely related design for the Los Angeles Public Library (begun in 1922 and completed in 1926)—one can only speculate about where Goodhue's independent pursuit of an architecture of evolution rather than revolution might have led.

CARTER WISEMAN

Biography

Born in Pomfret, Connecticut, 28 April 1869. Attended Russell's College, New Haven, Connecticut. Office boy to James Renwick, Renwick, Aspinwall and Russell, New York 1884; chief draftsman, Cram and Wentworth, Boston 1891; partner, Cram, Wentworth and Goodhue, Boston 1892; partner, Cram, Goodhue and Ferguson, Boston 1898. Private practice, New York from 1914. Gold Medal, American Institute of Architects 1925. Died in New York, 23 April 1924.

GOODY, JOAN EDELMAN 1935–

Architect, United States

In a century when architecture has been overwhelmingly dominated by male practitioners, Joan Goody, a Fellow of the American Institute of Architects and since 1969 a principal in Goody, Clancy and Associates, provides the welcome exception not only for the quality of her work but for its range as well. It is exceedingly rare for an American woman of Goody's generation to have realized buildings of such programmatic variety and consequential scale.

Goody's path to prominence as partner in what would become one of Boston's premier architectural firms was steady, sure, and swift. In 1960, she entered the office of Marvin E. Goody and John M. Clancy. (Goody had established the practice in 1955 with Richard Hamilton, who died before Joan's arrival; one notable achievement was the Monsanto Plastics "House of the Future," 1956, at Disneyland.) By the 1970s the firm had grown from five to 50 persons and was receiving major commissions for housing, offices, and research and teaching facilities and began to focus more on actual construction. The partnership of Goody, Clancy and Associates was continued after Marvin's death in 1980 and today employs more than 100 people.

One key to Goody's success is her willingness to collaborate not only with her partners and employees but also with her clients. This process includes the users no less than those who provide the finances, which typically are public or institutional bodies. In particular, the firm has welcomed the challenge offered by housing, one of the most urgent and difficult tasks set by 20th-century economic and political conditions. Whether for families, the elderly, a temporary student population, or the affluent, the lower-income occupant, or the disempowered, Goody has provided highly regarded dwellings and places of community for people of diverse resources and needs. Another distinguishing trait of the partnership is the deferral to the context no less than the practical requirements.

The technical sophistication of Goody's buildings, constructed with the most current materials and methods, never belittle the neighborhoods with which they mingle. Rather, her designs update, enliven, and repair the surroundings without diminishing viable existing structures. Such sensitive awareness has been expedited by the firm's decision to concentrate the practice in New England, especially the Boston area, the incremental character of which delights Goody, who sees her work as contributing to the historical progression of the city's built environment. Her experience with the climate has inspired her to apply energy-saving strategies, such as solar panels and recycling heat pumps (State Transportation Building, Boston), which are especially popular with the government agencies that frequently favor her firm. Not surprisingly, Goody, Clancy and Associates has eagerly embraced jobs that encompass historic preservation, such as the 17th-century Faneuil Hall/Old State House, Charles Bulfinch's late 18th-century Massachusetts State House, and Henry Hobson Richardson's 19th-century Trinity Church, all in Boston. In the last decade of the 20th century, Goody has extended the geographic reach of the practice by accepting commissions in Pittsburgh (a mixed-income community, Allequippa Terrace), Chicago (master plan for 5000 units of housing on the near north side, cited by the *Wall Street Journal* as one of the six most important projects of the year 2000), and West Virginia (Federal Courthouse).

One of Goody's most lauded projects, which illustrates the originality and mastery with which she approaches complex urban problems, is the redevelopment of Harbor Point, Boston (constructed 1987–90; Goody was involved in various capacities from 1978), which won the Rudy Bruner Award for Excellence in Urban Design in 1993. Forged from the remains of the ill-started 1504-unit Columbia Point housing project, dilapidated and only 20 percent occupied in 1979 and a sad example of the failure of 1950s public housing policies, Goody's then-radical vision of a mixed-income, multiracial enclave at first was met with skepticism. However, her tenacity prevailed, and today the 1300 dwellings, some subsidized and others rented at market rates, designed to accommodate a range of households and distributed among 46 new townhouses and five- to seven-story apartment buildings, have been transformed into a beguiling prospect. There are views of the harbor, a waterfront park, a landscaped mall based on Boston's late 19th-century Commonwealth Avenue, public greens as well as private patios, communal facilities (meeting hall, centers for day care and for the elderly, clubhouse with pool, and so on), and shops. The alienating abstraction and monotony of the Le Corbusian tower-in-the-park idea that had shaped the former Columbia Point has been replaced by references to traditional neighborhoods in terms of street patterns, rooflines, materials (including clapboard and red brick), and details (dormer and bay windows and gables).

The highly praised Tent City (1988; named for an earlier protest against further commercialization of the site), with 271 mixed-rental units, was a rehearsal on a smaller scale. Situated in the heart of Boston in the shadow of the sleek, looming John Hancock Tower, Tent City provides contrast not only in its residential program of 12-story apartment blocks and low-rise row houses but also in its polychromatic brick facades and domestic detailing, which humanize the mainly commercial area.

Goody also excels in the very different assignments offered by colleges and universities, for which she has designed an assortment of new and renovated structures and extensions that are integrated into existing campuses and urban settings. Here, too, the disparate requirements of the occupants—faculty, staff, students, and visitors—are harmonized through aesthetic and practical choices. The many laboratories built by the firm offer both the flexibility necessary in the rapidly changing world of scientific and technical research and the sense of specific place indispensable for comfortable engagement with the institution. At the Whitehead Institute for Biomedical Research (1994) in Cambridge, the sleek brick, stone, and glass facade encloses both gleaming, well-equipped, businesslike laboratories and warm and intimate curved spaces that encourage more personal interaction.

HELEN SEARING

Biography

Born in New York, 1 December 1935. Attended, University of Paris 1954–55; studied architecture, Cornell University, Ithaca, New York; bachelor's degree in architecture 1956; studied architecture, Harvard Graduate School of Design, Cambridge, Massachusetts 1960. Married 1) architect Marvin E. Goody 1960 (died 1980); 2) Peter Davison 1984. Principal, with husband, Goody, Clancy and Associates, Boston from 1961. Instructor, 1961–64, board member 1975–80, Boston Architectural Center; assistant professor 1973–76, design critic 1976–80, Eliot Noyes Visiting Critic 1985, Harvard Graduate School of Design. Member, Boston Landmarks Commission 1976–87; honorary member, Boston Architectural Center 1982; chair, Boston Civic Design Commission from 1992.

Selected Works

Jewish Family and Children's Service Building, Boston, 1970
Faculty Club, Massachusetts Institute of Technology, Cambridge, 1974
Heritage Gardens Housing for the Elderly, Winthrop, Massachusetts, 1977
Latin Way and Hillside Housing, Tufts University, Medford, Massachusetts, 1981
Village at Fawcett's Pond, Hyannis, Massachusetts, 1983
Massachusetts Department of Transportation Building, Boston, 1984
Paine Webber Office Building, Boston, 1984
Austin Hall (restoration), Harvard University, Cambridge, 1986
Sports Center, Simmons College, Boston, 1987
Tent City Housing, Boston, 1988

Salomon Center for Teaching, Brown University, Providence, Rhode
    Island, 1989
Harbor City, Columbia Point, Boston, 1992
Faneuil Hall/Old State House (preservation and rehabilitation),
    Boston, 1992
Whitehead Institute for Biomedical Research, Cambridge, 1994
Olin Hall, Babson College, Babson Park, Massachusetts, 1996
Barker Center for the Humanities, Harvard University, Cambridge,
    1997
Linsly-Chittenden Hall (renovation), Yale University, New Haven,
    1998

Selected Publications

New Architecture in Boston, 1965
"A Rare and Rich Response to Context: Keio University Library,
    Tokyo, Japan, Maki and Associates," *Architectural Record*, 171/5
    (May 1983)
"Essays on Social Housing," *Progressive Architecture*, 65/7 (July
    1984)
"Do You See New Directions?" *Architecture*, 74/5 (May 1985)
"Ethics in Design and Practice," *GSD News* (Fall 1995)

Further Reading

Anderson, Grace, "From Tents to Town Houses: Mixed Income
    Housing, Tent City, Boston," *Architectural Record*, 176/13
    (November 1988)
Anderson, Grace, "A Proper Dignity," *Architectural Record*, 178/9
    (August 1990)
"Austin Hall Regains Its Character," *Design Solutions*, 6/1 (Spring
    1986)
Berkeley, Ellen Perry, and Matilda McQuaid (editors), *Architecture:
    A Place for Women*, Washington, D.C.: Smithsonian Institution
    Press, 1989
"Celebrating Pluralism," *Architecture*, 82 (May 1993)
Davis, Sam, *The Architecture of Affordable Housing*, Berkeley:
    University of California Press, 1995
Diamonstein, Barbaralee, *American Architecture Now II*, New York:
    Rizzoli, 1985
"Housing for the Future," *Progressive Architecture*, 69/10 (October
    1988) *Places* 8 (Summer 1993) (special issue on Harbor City,
    Columbia Point)
"Waste Not, Want Not: The Transportation Building, Boston,"
    Progressive Architecture, 66/4 (April 1985)

GRAHAM, ANDERSON, PROBST AND WHITE

Architectural firm, United States

Before forming the largest architectural firm of the great American building period of the early 20th century, the principals of Graham, Anderson, Probst and White all worked for Daniel Burnham (1846–1912). Their subsequent work covered the full spectrum of urban building—public and cultural institutions, railroad stations, skyscrapers, banks, department stores, warehouses, power stations, lofts, and some private commissions. With few exceptions, their well-designed buildings are still in use today, continuing to nourish public pride and civic spirit. The firm was neither avant-garde nor conservative but solidly in the mainstream of the architecture of its day. Solving new problems for such new building types as the railroad station, the architects creatively adapted the time-honored principles of the Beaux-Arts tradition to meet changing needs and to take advantage of new technology. Over the years, the firm used many different styles—classical, Art Deco, art moderne, modernist and postmodern—but until the death of Graham, the planning principles were always Beaux-Arts.

Ernest R. Graham (1866–1936) founded a new firm shortly after Burnham's death. As two of Burnham's sons were still in the office, the new firm was called Graham, Burnham and Company. In 1917, by mutual agreement, this firm was dissolved, and William Pierce Anderson (1870–1924), Edward Probst (1870–1942), and Howard Judson White (1870–1936) formed with Graham the firm that is still in existence today.

The United States Post Office in Washington, D.C. (1914) completed part of the urban scheme for the city, which also included Union Station (designed by Anderson in the Burnham era) and the semicircular plaza in front. An arriving visitor passed through the triumphal arches of the station to see the sparkling white of the Capitol beyond the green foreground of the park plaza. The building group then takes its place among the great architectural glories of the nation's capital. As in many of their other urban ensembles, the firm's work exemplified the classical principle of each part being an end in itself yet subordinate to the larger whole.

The Cleveland Terminal Group (1930), an ensemble of office buildings grouped around a railroad station, also exemplifies the guiding principles of the firm's work. The soaring tower above the station marked a new emphasis on height for this building type. However, the planning followed the time-tested principles of the Beaux-Arts: symmetrical massing, spaces organized along axes for the most efficient use with the exterior composition reflecting the interior disposition of the rooms, and traditional ornament adapted to express the function of the building. In addition, buildings had to be carefully sited to take advantage of the topography or to relate to surrounding structures. The broad expanses of windows and the airy colonnades of Chicago's Union Station (1925), together with its efficient traffic layout and the grandeur of its waiting room, are other examples of the renowned railroad design of the firm, as is the Thirtieth Street Station (1934) in Philadelphia.

Cultural institutions were also designed according to Beaux-Arts principles, but despite the shared characteristics, each building was unique. The distinctive qualities emanated from the specific problems involved in the design. No two buildings were alike because each had a different site, context, client, and program. The Field Museum of Natural History (1919) and the Shedd Aquarium (1930), both in Chicago, illustrate the point. Both are sited to take advantage of the sublime union of Lake Michigan and the Chicago skyline and to relate to each other with their classical temple fronts, yet in the interior the plan and the ornament reflect different purposes. The visitors walk in a grid pattern through the light-filled corridors of the Field Museum, whereas they seem to float around through the darker passages of the Shedd. Together, the two buildings are subordinated to the larger whole—the city itself. In this role, they work jointly as a cohesive link in the urban scheme. Recently, this relationship has been underscored and improved by relocating South Lake Shore Drive to the west, allowing the two institutions to share a campus.

Of the firm's many office buildings, three are outstanding, but for different reasons. The Wrigley Building (1924) in Chi-

Wrigley Building, Chicago, Illinois (1924) by Graham, Anderson, Probst and White
© Greatbuildings.com

cago applies Spanish renaissance ornament to a soaring skyscraper, making the most of its prominent site where Michigan Avenue bends at its junction with the Chicago River. Structurally, the building is like older Chicago models, and its exterior is articulated in the same tripartite manner, but the cladding is in dazzling white terra-cotta. A special, painterly attention to the glazing called for six different shades of white, varying from gray to pale cream and getting progressively lighter toward the top so that the Wrigley seems to "soar from mists and fog to clear skies." Add to this the effects of dramatic nighttime illumination, and the continued dominance of the Wrigley Building in the hearts of Chicagoans seems assured.

The Koppers Building (1929) in Pittsburgh is a brilliant adaptation of Beaux-Arts planning with the new Art Deco styling. The uninterrupted verticals of the facade suggest the soaring speed of the new machine age, but the spaces within are traditionally disposed.

In the 1920s, office buildings were often combined with other building types. Banks, colleges, and even churches were hybridized with skyscrapers, and the Civic Opera Building (1929) remains a stellar example of this tendency. The majestic office tower gives monumental grandeur to the broad auditorium of the opera house below and expresses the original intention (no longer viable) that the income from rentals would subsidize the production of operas. The musical motifs of the ornament in the lobby and the interior of the theater are original and were designed by Jules Guerin.

Department stores were another specialty of the firm. Wm. Filene's Sons (1912) in Boston, Gimbel Brothers (1927) in Philadelphia, and Marshall Field's (1914) in Chicago were all like multileveled marketplaces full of specialty shops. Inspired by the great world's fairs of the period, all were microcities, but they were microcities for women where customers could lunch with friends, listen to music, buy steamship or theater tickets, send a telegram, and shop for household goods, furniture, or clothing for the whole family. Filenes' was essentially a loft building, with one floor stacked atop another, but for Marshall Field's, Anderson had a new conception of the disposition of the interior spaces. Instead of simply using horizontal loft spaces, he inserted three large vertical spaces in the steel-cage support system: a six-story urban square, a 12-story arcade, and a four-story restaurant, the Walnut Room. Gimbels' incorporated a new version of the 19th-century galleria on its ground floor, luring in customers by combining the advantages of a street with the advantages of a covered roof. Each store was endowed with a central space so that the subsidiary spaces could be organized in a meaningful relationship. As in an ideal city, destinations could be reached in a logical manner; once there were waiting rooms and first-aid stations, and to this day the ensembles still seem to lend themselves to courtesy, safety, art, entertainment, diversity, and an inexhaustible supply of goods from all over the world.

The high architectural standards of the firm were also used for the design of light manufactories, lofts, and other industrial buildings, such as Western Union Telegraph Company (1919) or the Butler Brothers Warehouses (1913, 1922), both in Chicago. Less-expensive building materials were used, and ornament was simplified or ordered ready-made from a catalog. Well-proportioned, well-made, and workmanlike in their strong simplicity, these buildings still have the dignified air of a carpenter in well-pressed coveralls. Exceptions to the rule for utilitarian structures were the firm's power stations. The Crawford Avenue Generating Station (1925) in Chicago is a palace of industry, distinguished by rhythmic massing, textured brick cladding, and terra-cotta architectural detail. Machinery dictates the dimensions, proportions, and arrangements of a power station, but the architects used every device at their command to endow the building envelopes with imposing character. The State Line Generating Station (1929) in Hammond, Indiana, for example, has a triumphal arch entryway, implying, as their client Samuel Insull no doubt believed, that victory and electricity were synonymous and using imagery befitting an emperor of industry.

Throughout his career, founder Ernest R. Graham and his partners tried to preserve what was valuable in the architectural traditions that they had inherited while embracing the best that new discoveries (e.g. high-speed elevators and better fireproofing) had to offer. Constantly, they had to respond to pressures from clients and to an ever-changing economy. They were successful partly because Graham (like Burnham before him) had grasped the importance of operating an architectural office as a big business. Few firms were able to handle the large, complex, multifunctional structures that required a specialized staff of more than 200. In 1970, Edward Probst's two sons, Marvin and Edward, Jr., sold the firm to William Surman. Still using the traditional name, today the firm operates on a smaller scale under the direction of his son, Robert E. Surman (1967–).

SALLY A. KITT CHAPPELL

Biography

Ernest Graham

Born in Lowell, Michigan, 22 August 1866; son of a general carpenter. Learned carpentry and masonry from father. Worked, Holabird and Roche, Chicago 1886; assistant chief of construction, with D.H. Burnham, World's Columbian Exposition 1893, Chicago. Partner, D.H. Burnham and Company, Chicago 1894–1912; partner, with Burnham's sons Hubert and Daniel Jr., Graham, Burnham and Company, Chicago 1912–17; partner, Graham, Anderson, Probst and White, Chicago from 1917. Died in Chicago, 22 November 1936.

William Pierce Anderson

Born in Oswego, New York 1870. Bachelor of arts from Harvard University 1892; studied electrical engineering, Johns Hopkins University, Baltimore, Maryland; master's degree in engineering; degree from the École des Beaux-Arts, Paris 1899; Grand Tour 1899. Chief designer, D.H. Burnham and Company, Chicago 1900; partner, D.H. Burnham and Company, Chicago 1908–12; partner, Graham, Burnham and Company, Chicago 1912–17; partner, Graham, Anderson, Probst and White, Chicago from 1917. Died in Chicago, 1924.

Edward Probst

Born in Chicago 1870. Son was architect Marvin G. Probst. Worked for Peter B. Wright. Supervisor, working drawings, D.H. Burnham and Company, Chicago 1893–1912; partner, Graham, Burnham and Company, Chicago 1912–17; partner, Graham, Anderson, Probst and White, Chicago from 1917; became head of firm after Graham's death in 1936. Died in Chicago 1942.

Howard Judson White

Born in Chicago, 21 February 1870. Draftsman, D.H. Burnham and Company, Chicago 1898–1905; Graham's assistant, in charge of letting contracts and supervising construction, D.H. Burnham and Company, Chicago 1905–1912; partner, Graham, Burnham and Company, Chicago 1912–17; partner, Graham, Anderson, Probst and White, Chicago from 1917. Died in Chicago, 18 December 1936.

Graham, Anderson, Probst and White

Started as D.H. Burnham and Company, Chicago; became Graham, Burnham and Company, Chicago after the death of D.H. Burnham 1912; became Graham, Anderson, Probst and White, Chicago after Hubert Burnham and Daniel Burnham, Jr. left to found Burnham Brothers 1917; lasted until Graham's death in 1936, when Anderson became head of firm.

Selected Works

Union Station (Anderson), Washington, D.C., 1907
William Filene's Sons Department Store, Boston, 1912
Butler Brothers Warehouses, Chicago, 1913
United States Post Office, Washington, D.C., 1914
Marshall Field's Department Store, Chicago, 1914
Western Union Telegraph Company, Chicago, 1919
Field Museum, Chicago, 1919
Butler Brothers Warehouses, Chicago, 1922
Wrigley Building, Chicago, 1924
Crawford Avenue Generating Station, Chicago, 1925
Union Station, Chicago, 1925
Gimbel Brothers Department Store, Philadelphia, 1927
Koppers Building, Pittsburgh, 1929
State Line Generating Station, Hammond, Indiana, 1929
Civic Opera Building, Chicago, 1929
Shedd Aquarium, Chicago, 1930
Cleveland Terminal Group, 1930
30th Street Station, Philadelphia, 1934

Selected Publication

The Architectural Work of Graham, Anderson, Probst, and White, Chicago, 2 vols., 1933

Further Reading

Chappell, Sally A., "Beaux Arts Architecture in Chicago," *Inland Architect*, 24 (October 1980)
Chappell, Sally A., "As If the Lights Were Always Shining: The Wrigley Building at the Boulevard Link," in *Chicago Architecture: 1872–1922*, edited by John Zukowsky, Chicago: Art Institute of Chicago, 1987; London: Prestel, 2000

Chappell, Sally A., "Urban Ideals and the Design of Railroad Stations," *Technology and Culture*, 30 (April 1989)

Chappell, Sally A., "The Equitable Building in New York Reconsidered," *Journal of the Society of Architectural Historians*, 49 (March 1990)

Chappell, Sally A., *Architecture and Planning of Graham, Anderson, Probst, and White, 1912–1936: Transforming Tradition*, Chicago: University of Chicago Press, 1992

GRAIN ELEVATOR

A grain elevator is a granary set on end or elevated in such a way that requires a lifting apparatus or leg to fill it. Granaries date to antiquity, but the grain elevator is a modern invention. It appeared first in Buffalo, New York, in 1843, and shortly after throughout the upper Midwest of North America. The earliest were built on the edges of rivers, canals, and the Great Lakes, and with the advent of the railroad they became ubiquitous. The cylindrical, reinforced-concrete grain elevator was an innovation that appeared at the end of the 19th century, and its type is still being constructed. Grain elevators can now be found throughout the grain-producing regions of the world, but until the early decades of the 20th century, the larger of these were exclusive to the United States and Canada. Images of tall cylindrical bins, usually seen in tandem with dozens more equally utilitarian, captured the imagination of early modernists, such as Le Corbusier and Walter Gropius, who marveled at their size, function, and geometry, all rendered in concrete. To them, these anonymous geometric forms suggested a lasting sense of beauty and monumentality.

A distinction should be made between terminal elevators and country elevators. The earliest and largest were terminal elevators, so named because they were located at the receiving end of waterways or railroad lines from which they gathered grain sent directly from farms or country elevators. Buffalo was the easternmost terminal of the Great Lakes and connected to the industrial Northeast by means of the Erie Canal. As such, it became a point of transshipment for freighters and canal boats. The volume of grain passing through Buffalo in the early 1800s increased each decade, and the grain elevator was invented as a structure to alleviate the bottleneck of supply and demand confronting grain dealers. By the middle of the 19th century, Cleveland, Chicago, and Milwaukee, among others, became grain terminals as well.

From the outset, grain elevators were large because of the economies and profit of bulk purchase and storage. Terminal elevators of 100,000-bushel capacity would grow to 1,000,000

J. Harrington and Co., Grain Elevator and Office, La Salle County, Illinois, c. 1892
Photo © Historic American Engineering Record/Library of Congress

bushels or more before 1900. The earliest were constructed of heavy timber set on masonry piers. The tremendous weight exerted on the piers was spread to a foundation supported by timber pilings driven below grade into the spongy soil of waterfront locations. The heavy timber above the piers supported wooden bins of square cross section, the bottoms of which were like inverted pyramids. These bins were laid up in crib construction: dimensioned lumber laid flat, one piece on top of another, and spiked through. Above the bins were shed roofs and usually a clerestory with gable roof containing a headhouse or distribution floor. In profile, these early elevators were rather like attenuated Christian basilicas, where grain bins filled the nave and side aisles.

The leg used to lift the grain from the holds of freighters was an external structure, the upper portion of which was enclosed. The lower part of the leg, which could be 50 feet in length, could be raised and lowered. The leg was simply a large conveyer belt with buckets attached and operated at first by a steam engine. The buckets would lift the grain from the boat and carry it to the headhouse, where it was distributed by chutes to one of the many bins. Chutes attached to the bottoms of the bins and projecting from the external wall above the slip or shoreline conveyed the grain to smaller canal boats or railroad cars. Country elevators differed from terminal elevators in size and organization but otherwise were similar in appearance. The principal difference resulted from operation. The leg of these smaller elevators was internal, rising from a basement or boot where grain was dumped from farm wagons and then lifted to the headhouse and distributed to bins as earlier described. None of the early timber terminal elevators survive, but the timber-constructed country elevators, which are usually clad in galvanized sheet iron, continue to be seen in small towns and railroad crossings as symbols of agricultural dominance.

Cylindrical bins associated with 20th-century elevators and captured in the industrial landscapes of artists such as Charles Demuth and Charles Sheeler are constructed largely of reinforced concrete. Cylinders better accommodated the fluid behavior of bulk grain and created fewer structural eccentricities. Moreover, a cylinder requires less material per volume than a parallelogram. However, before concrete was employed, iron plate was rolled into curved sections and riveted together. The earliest instances appear to borrow from the design of standpipes, which predate the construction of steel water towers. Among the more famous of these iron-bin elevators were the Great Northern Railway's elevators in Duluth, Minnesota; West Superior, Wisconsin; and Buffalo, the latter of which was built in 1897–98 and continued in use until the 1980s. The problem with iron bins was manifold. Condensation easily formed affecting grain on the inside and causing corrosion on the outside; metal conducts electricity, and grain dust is highly explosive; and the expense of fabricated components of such large scale and number discouraged its use. To mitigate these drawbacks, the Great Northern's bins were enclosed in a masonry shell. Masonry, and particularly tile, became an alternative to iron in the construction of cylindrical bins, and the earliest tile-constructed elevators appear in the 1890s as well.

An experiment in Minneapolis, Minnesota, in 1899 would transform the appearance of grain elevators. Frank H. Peavey, a grain dealer, and architect Charles F. Haglin designed a cylindrical concrete elevator using a slip form to pour the concrete.

The cylinder was reinforced with wrought-iron hoops, bedded into the material during the pour. Similar hoops had been used as an external reinforcement in stave-constructed wooden supply tanks used to replenish steam locomotives. After 1900 the exposed reinforced-concrete elevator dominated. Despite difficulty in supplying sufficient quantities of concrete to job sites dependent on rail and then elevating the mix by crane as slip forms reached 100 feet or higher, the new system of construction quickly became dominant. Concrete provided greater thermal insulation to protect the grain and was less expensive when employed in large-scale construction.

JOHN S. GARNER

Further Reading

Banham, Reyner, *A Concrete Atlantis: U.S. Industrial Building and European Modern Architecture, 1900–1925*, Cambridge, Massachusetts: MIT Press, 1986

Dart, Joseph, "The Grain Elevators of Buffalo," *Proceedings of the Buffalo Historical Society*, 1–2 (1879–80)

Mahar-Keplinger, Lisa, *Grain Elevators*, New York: Princeton Architectural Press, 1993

Wiley, D.A., "Operation of a Modern Grain Elevator," *Engineering Magazine*, 23 (May 1902)

GRAND CENTRAL TERMINAL, NEW YORK

New York, New York
Engineered by William J. Wilgus; designed by Charles A. Reed, Allen H. Stem, Whitney Warren, and William Wetmore; completed 1913

Built at the beginning of the 20th century, Grand Central Terminal (1909–13) at 42nd Street between Madison and Lexington Avenues in New York City straddles two epochs. It is one of the greatest examples of Beaux-Arts architectural planning in North America. At the same time, it is technologically one of the most advanced works of early 20th-century architecture and a powerful influence on early modernism in Europe. Antonio Sant'Elia, for example, used Grand Central Terminal as the model for his railway station design (1914); the design of the transportation node at Slussen (1931–35) in Stockholm, Sweden, might also have been influenced by it. As late as 1935, the architect Le Corbusier could still call it "a marvel."

The present station is the third on the site. In 1867, the railway magnate Cornelius Vanderbilt consolidated the Harlem Line (covering southern New York State) with the New York Central Railroad (with tracks to Chicago) under the name New York Central and Hudson River Railroad and built a unified terminal, Grand Central Terminal. Its architect was John B. Snook (1815–1901). As rail traffic increased, the building ceased to be adequate, and in 1897–98 a new train shed was built by Samuel J. Huckel, Jr. (1858–1917), with artificial stone stucco work designed by Bradford Gilbert (1853–1911). Yet the renovations did not address urgent functional problems. The Park Avenue train yards were unsightly and dirty; crosstown traffic was hindered by sprays of smoke and ash that erupted onto the street from just below the street level. Following a railway accident early in 1902 in which 17 people were killed, the State of New York passed legislation banning steam engines on the entire island of Manhattan: electrification became the driving force for a bold new Grand Central Terminal.

The key figure in this transformation was the engineer William J. Wilgus (1865–1949). Already in 1899, he had proposed partial electrification and in 1901 had argued that the whole line should be electrified. After the accident, he prepared a "portfolio of suggested preliminary plans." The most important innovation was electrification, which would allow trains to make an underground approach and discharge and receive passengers in an underground train shed. To save lateral space, trains would arrive and depart on two vertical levels: a suburban station below and a national station above; through trains would be accommodated on a double-level continuous loop of track that encircled the station. Wilgus foresaw a multicomplex of station and train yard, hotel, offices, restaurants, and stores standing over the old train yards and underground tracks that would give "a distinctive and monumental appearance to the entire project that will probably make it the most attractive locality in New York." Other parts of his plan included an elevated roadway to surround the station, connected on the north to Park Avenue over the depressed yard and on the south by a bridge across 42nd Street. Inside, he planned ramps "on easy gradients . . . down to the train platforms . . . Elevators and . . . easy stairways . . . up to the carriage concourse where vehicles are in plain view of the passengers and under cover." Wilgus's visionary plans formed the basis for the new Grand Central Terminal.

A limited competition was held in 1903 based on the Wilgus plans. Entries were invited from Stanford White (1853–1906) for McKim, Mead and White; Daniel H. Burnham (1846–1912); Huckel; and Charles A. Reed (1857–1911) and Allen H. Stem (1856–1931), who were declared the winners. Like so many competitions of its era, however, this one was tainted by favoritism: Huckel was Wilgus's associate on the earlier Grand Central project, and Charles Reed was his brother-in-law, but to confound the results completely, William K. Vanderbilt, grandson of Cornelius and the chairman of the board of the New York Central, decided that his cousin Whitney Warren (1864–1943), in partnership with William Wetmore (1866–1941), who had not even entered the competition, should receive the commission. In the end, Reed and Stem and Warren and Wetmore were appointed associated architects and, with some difficulty, collaborated on the project. Construction began in 1909. There were two major aboveground elements to the plan as built.

The central ticketing hall is known as the main concourse. Its design was based on the forms of an ancient Roman bath. Although the floor was marble, the walls were sheathed with Caen stone, an artificial stone. At the west end of the concourse,

Grand Central Terminal, perspective drawing by H. M. Pettit of original plan, New York City
© Museum of the City of New York Print Archives

leading up to Vanderbilt Avenue and the taxi stand, was a grand staircase; a staircase to the east was not built (although it has been added in the restoration by Beyer Blinder Belle of 1999), but clearly marked exits led to south, west, and east. To the south side were the ticket windows, and along 42nd Street was a large waiting room. Between ticket windows and waiting room were ramps that led to the suburban level below. The ceiling was decorated with the constellations of the autumn night sky (October to March); by accident, the constellations were painted backward. The main concourse remains the greatest indoor secular space in New York City.

For early modernists, however, the most exciting part of early Grand Central Terminal was the integration of the various levels of transportation into one building. Not only were there subway service and two vertical lines of train traffic, but a flying upper level roadway encircled the station.

For all its modernity, Grand Central Terminal has many of the virtues of a solid piece of late Victorian industrial design: ruggedly practical, as in the cranking system that opens and closes the windows in the east and west double-glazed walls. It is characteristic of Grand Central that its architects made extensive use of fireproof tiles by the Guastavino Company with their rough-edged textured surfaces. Early plans for Grand Central Terminal show an art gallery and an art school in the upper-level towers on the south side.

Grand Central Terminal was also an advertisement for the New York Central Railroad. Contemporary newspaper reports make it clear that the interior ramps were one sign of modern efficiency as well as a way to make the building friendly to women and their long skirts. The *Evening Sun* (1 February 1913) noted, "In the building of the new Grand Central Terminal woman played a highly important part—not in the actual work, however, but in the influence she exerted over the architects and engineers. They had her constantly in mind as they planned every important and minor item whose purpose was the convenience of the New York Central's passengers. It was she who was responsible for the elimination of steps; man made steps, and ever since woman has had to climb them except at the Grand Central, where she has caused them to be abolished."

It was the peculiar gift of the early 20th century to combine, at times, modernity and tradition so deliberately and so fearlessly. Working in a universal style like Beaux-Arts classicism provided a certain confidence; its principles really can be adapted to the most advanced problems of the times (mass transport) and incorporate the most advanced ideas (electrified rail service).

Today, Grand Central Terminal can be seen in a form close to the original plans. As rail traffic lessened following World War II, the main concourse became littered with advertising, and the great east window was blocked. Following the demolition of Pennsylvania Station in 1962, only heroic efforts saved Grand Central from the wrecker's ball. All this changed in 1995, when the Metropolitan Transportation Authority and Metro-North, the suburban rail company that operates the building, undertook a brilliant restoration (completed in 1999) directed by the architectural firm of Beyer Blinder Belle.

NICHOLAS ADAMS

See also **Railroad Station**

Further Reading

Adams, Nicholas, "Rinascità del Grand Central Terminal, New York: Il restauro della 'moderna elettrica,'" *Casabella*, 661 (November 1998)

Belle, John and Maxine Leighton, *Grand Central: Gateway to a Million Lives*, New York: Norton, 2000

Condit, Carl, *The Port of New York: A History of the Rail and Terminal System from the Grand Central Electrification to the Present*, Chicago: University of Chicago Press, 1981

Powell, Kenneth, *Grand Central Terminal: Warren and Wetmore*, London: Phaidon Press, 1996

Schlichting, Kurt C. *Grand Central Terminal: Railroads, Engineering, and Architecture in New York City*, Baltimore, Maryland: Johns Hopkins University Press, 2001.

GRANDE ARCHE DE LA DÉFENSE

Designed by Johann Otto von Spreckelsen; completed 1989
Paris, France

The Grande Arche de La Défense, designed by Johann Otto von Spreckelsen (1929–87), was completed just in time for the second centennial of the French Revolution. It forms the western termination (known as "Tête Défense") and the third triumphal arch of Paris' so-called Royal Axis, which stretches eight kilometers from the Grande Louvre to the business district of La Défense. Von Spreckelsen chose to incorporate this complex historical and urban program into a design that is at once evocative of a historical past and respectful of the aesthetic and technological ambitions of then-President François Mitterrand's program of the *grands projets*, or important projects meant to embody the civic and economic achievements of contemporary France.

Johann Otto von Spreckelsen was virtually unknown outside his native Denmark at the time he won the competition for La Défense in 1983. His selection was even more surprising given his relatively modest architectural production: his own house just outside Copenhagen (1958) and a handful of modernist churches. A well-respected academic, von Spreckelsen directed the architecture department of the Royal Academy of Fine Arts in Copenhagen. However, it was von Spreckelsen's demeanor rather than his résumé that won him the respect of Mitterrand and the popular press. It was hoped that the architect's sincerity and modesty would translate into a sense of Nordic humanism in the context of the concrete plazas and glass towers of La Défense. Midway through construction, however, in July 1986, von Spreckelsen tendered his resignation because of constant and controversial budget and program modifications that effectively transformed the Grande Arche from a major public work into a speculative office building. Although he visited the site several times after this date, the architect's death in 1987 prevented him from seeing the completion of his Paris monument.

In accordance with the guidelines of the commission, von Spreckelsen selected a French associate, Paul Andreu, a graduate of the Polytechnique known for his designs of airports. This arrangement proved convenient for von Spreckelsen, who thereafter acted as the auteur of the project, working from Denmark and forwarding his conceptual drawings to the technically adept Andreu. After von Spreckelsen's resignation from the project, Andreu saw the design to completion.

The Grande Arche is a massive 110-meter-high steel and reinforced-concrete cube. Because of practical considerations, the cube is offset six degrees relative to the historic axis. The "posts" of the structure contain offices, and the "lintel," or *le toit*, houses the main public spaces for exhibitions and shops.

The raised ground level of the cube is a public plaza—the monumental centerpiece of the project. From this plaza, a gleaming, freestanding elevator shaft ascends toward the top platform, and a synthetic canvas "cloud," suspended by steel cables and inlaid with glass disks, covers the plaza and serves to humanize the scale of the looming cube. This suspension structure was a modification to von Spreckelsen's original plan, which called for a structure made purely of glass and steel.

Von Spreckelsen met the historical and aesthetic challenges of Tête Défense with a void, or what he preferred to call a "window to the world." At the time his visionary design was taking shape, this optimistic symbolism seemed entirely appropriate, for the building was intended to house not only the Ministry of Town Planning and Housing as well as the Ministry of the Environment but also a new International Carrefour of Communication—a kind of modern agora for the exchange of progressive ideas in industry and technology. The latter organization was never formed, and thus the civic aspect of the space was greatly compromised. The hollow frame was also meant to open, both literally and metaphorically, the possibility of further urban development beyond La Défense to the west.

The Grande Arche forms the third and by far the largest of the triumphal, or commemorative, arches along the Royal Axis, the others being Charles Percier and Pierre Francois Leónard Fontaine's Arc du Carousel (1807) and Chalgrin's Jean-François magisterial Arc de Triomphe (1806). Perceived as a cube, the structure is symbolic, forming as it does the last link in an urban chain of simple geometric volumes along the Royal Axis, beginning with I.M. Pei's Louvre Pyramid (another *grand projet* being constructed simultaneously with the Grande Arche) and including the obelisk in the Place de la Concorde. More allusively, perhaps, the evocation of the Phileban solids connects the Grande Arche with a French rationalist tradition stretching from the 17th-century philosopher René Descartes to Le Corbusier. Symbolism of a cosmological significance is included in the design in the form of astrological symbols inlaid into the marble on the top platform of the cube, to the design of Jean-Pierre Raynaud.

Stylistically, the arch manages to transcend the polemics of postmodern historicism versus late modern functionalism (presumably one key to its success in the competition). The design fulfills its symbolic duty as described previously and simultaneously forms a harmonious component of the postwar functionalist buildings constituting La Défense via its frank exposure of concrete and clean geometries free of applied ornamentation. Of equal importance is the privileging of the monumental aspects of the site; the arch both creates a public space at its base and frames striking urban vistas.

The district of La Défense has long been in the political and urban consciousness of French officials. The historical importance of the site, as well as the political aspects of development within Paris more generally, ensured that completing a project

View looking upward from the plaza, Grande Arche de La Défense, Paris (1989), by Johann Otto von Spreckelsen
© Esto

on the Royal Axis would not be easy. Another consideration since the 1960s, was the graceful recontextualization of La Défense itself—a business district built during the 1950s and 1960s, to the designs of Bernard Zehrfuss that includes Pier Luigi Nervi's Exhibition Hall (1955). Since the time of an invitational competition held in 1970, the ideological debate regarding the Tête Défense site revolved around opening the axis to the west for further possible development or terminating the axis with a more closed composition. For better or worse, it was Mitterrand's determination to open the axis and the resources that he devoted to the *grands projets* that resulted in von Spreckelsen's visionary, albeit compromised, design.

LARRY D. BUSBEA

See also **Nervi, Pier Luigi (Italy); Pei, I.M. (United States)**

Further Reading

Camino de Broadbent, Gloria, "Johan Otto von Spreckelsen: La Grande Arche, La Défense," *Architectural Design*, 62/1–2 (1992)
"Canopy Structure: Tête Défense Cube," *Architect's Journal*, 190/2 (1989)
Chaslin, François and Virginie Picon-Lefebvre, *La Grande Arche de La Défense*, Paris: Electa Moniteur, 1989
Courtiau, Jean-Pierre, *La Grande Arche: Otto von Spreckelsen, Paul Andreu*, Paris: Editions de Demi-Cercle, 1994
Mangin, David and Gerard Monnier, "La Grande Arche de La Défense," *L'Architecture d'Aujourd'hui*, 252 (1987)
Tête Défense: 1983, Concours International d'Architecture, Paris: Electa Moniteur, 1984

Humana Building (1985), Louisville, Kentucky
© Pashall/Taylor Photo. Courtesy of Michael Graves and Associates

GRAVES, MICHAEL 1934–

Architect, United States

Michael Graves is a leading twentieth century architect and designer whose drawings, buildings and products are notable for their manipulation of archetypal form into highly abstract, figurative compositions. He is especially interested in responding to the scenes and practice of everyday life with designs that can be universally understood while responding to site, program and context with a degree of sensitivity that has often eluded his peers.

One of the so-called "New York Five" (along with Peter Eisenman, Charles Gwathmey, John Hejduk, and Richard Meier) Graves gained recognition in his career at a relatively early age through a meeting of the Conference of Architects for the Study of the Environment (CASE) held at the Museum of Modern Art, New York, in 1969. The work exhibited by these five architects at this meeting led to the publication of a seminal book, *Five Architects* (1972). Immortalized as the progeny of "The White Gods" (Le Corbusier, Walter Gropius, Ludwig Mies van der Rohe) in Tom Wolfe's *From Bauhaus to Our House* (1981), these five were linked by a common interest in both reviving and reinterpreting the forms, typically painted white, of the modernist architects, Le Corbusier and Guiseppe Terragni. This deliberate focus on form constituted a radical break from the contemporary preoccupation with technology as the guiding force behind modern architecture. Graves, however, is the one member of the group whose work introduced figural

form and color to this monochromy: a wavy shape painted blue made reference to the sky while a terra-cotta rail suggested a closeness to the earth.

Along with his penchant for using color to refer to the natural environment, an interest in Cubist painting led Graves to concentrate on the design of surfaces and elevations, an approach that had all but disappeared with the Modernist movement. Introducing classical motifs in an abstract, collage-like manner, with a variable palette, Graves established a new identity for himself that was much more painterly, based on the history of architecture and strongly concerned with the relationship between building and nature.

While in Italy in 1978, Graves became increasingly preoccupied with the rustic simplicity of the Mediterranean landscape—its topography and colors, vernacular barns and farmhouses. It was during this second stay in Italy that Graves developed an even keener appreciation of Classical and Renaissance architecture that he would apply to his own work in highly original ways.

In 1980 Graves achieved instant international fame with his winning entry for the competition to design a new civic building for the city of Portland, Oregon (Portland Public Services Building). Forsaking the neutral glass curtain wall of late modernism in favor of a colorful cloak of cladding that reintroduced the hierarchical composition of classical buildings, he brought a new and unexpected image to the otherwise ubiquitous glass box of the American city.

Following this tour-de-force, an avalanche of highly visible commissions poured into the Graves atelier including the Humana Corporate Headquarters in Louisville, Kentucky (1982), the highly controversial unbuilt schemes for an extension to the Whitney Museum of American Art in New York (1985–87), the Dolphin and Swan Hotels at Disney World in Orlando, Florida (1987), and the Disney Corporate Headquarters in Burbank, California (1986). All of these projects employed a similar colossal scale in their design while addressing the salient features of their locations. The Humana Building defines the Louisville skyline with an enormous bow-front sky porch overlooking the city and the Mississippi River while its base responds to its mid-rise neighbors. The Whitney proposals made Marcel Breuer's 1966 building just one element of a much bigger three-part composition. The Denver Central Library in Colorado (1990) has enjoyed a great deal of visibility and success as well, marking the skyline of the city with a giant crown of copper-clad truss work.

More recently, Graves' design for the scaffolding of the Washington Monument Restoration in Washington, D.C. (1999) afforded him the opportunity to distill his ideas into a single iconic gesture: revealing the essence of the building through a magnification of scale and representation so that it can be read from a great distance for what it is—simple and powerful stone coursing.

Graves continues to test his own knowledge of architecture and design through teaching and working closely with his associates, many of whom are former students. By adroitly synthesizing the programmatic logic and figuration of historically-based architecture with the compositional devices of abstraction and scale variation associated with modernism, Graves has established himself as a major figure in twentieth century architecture.

CHRISTIAN ZAPATKA

See also **Disney Theme Parks; Eisenman, Peter (United States); Gwathmey, Charles, and Robert Siegel (United States); Museum of Modern Art, New York City; Portland Public Services Building, Portland, Oregon; Postmodernism; Stern, Robert A.M. (United States)**

Biography

Born 9 July 1934, Indianapolis; educated at the University of Cincinnati and Harvard University before winning the Rome Prize in architecture 1960; subsequently studied at the American Academy in Rome 1960–62; began teaching at Princeton University 1962, New Jersey (currently Schirmer Professor of Architecture). Established practice 1964, in Princeton, New Jersey with satellite office in New York City. Architect-In-Residence, American Academy in Rome 1978. Recipient of numerous awards and honorary degrees including the Gold Medal from the American Institute of Architects, the Brunner Prize in Architecture from the American Academy of Arts and Letters, the National Medal of the Arts from the National Endowment for the Arts as well as numerous state and national awards from the American Institute of Architects. Fellow, American Institute

of Architects, a member of the American Academy of Arts and Letters and serves on the Board of the American Academy in Rome, of which he is a Fellow.

Selected Works

Hanselmann House, Fort Wayne, Indiana, 1967
The Portland Building, Portland, Oregon, 1980
The Humana Building, Louisville, Kentucky, 1981
Clos Pegase Winery and Residence, Napa Valley, California, 1984
Sotheby's Apartment Tower, New York City, 1985
The Disney Company Corporate Headquarters, Burbank, California, 1986
Walt Disney World Dolphin Hotel & Walt Disney World Swan Hotel, Orlando, Florida, 1987
Federal Triangle Development Site Competition, Washington, D.C. 1989
Denver Central Library, Denver, Colorado, 1990

Selected Publications

"The Necessity of Drawing: Tangible Speculation," *Architectural Design* (June 1977)
"A Case for Figurative Architecture," in *Michael Graves Buildings and Projects 1966–1981*, edited by Karen Vogel Wheeler, Peter Arnell and Ted Bickford, New York: Rizzoli, 1981

Further Reading

Bletter, Rosemarie Haag, "About Graves," *Skyline* (Summer 1979)
Carl, Peter, "Towards a Pluralist Architecture," *Progressive Architecture* (February 1973)
Colquhoun, Alan, "From Bricolage to Myth: Or How to Put Humpty Dumpty Together Again," *Oppositions 12* (Spring 1978)
Eisenman, Peter, "The Graves of Modernism," *Oppositions 12* (Spring 1978)
Five Architects: Eisenman, Graves, Gwathmey, Hejduk, Meier, New York: Wittenborn, 1972; new edition, New York: Oxford University Press, 1975
Frampton, Kenneth, "Five Architects," *Lotus International* (February 1975)
Gandelsonas, Mario, "On Reading Architecture," *Progressive Architecture* (March 1972)
Goldberger, Paul, "And Now, an Architectural Kingdom," *The New York Times Magazine* (10 October 1982)
Goldberger, Paul, "Architecture of a Different Color," *The New York Times Magazine* (10 October 1982)
Graves, Michael, "The Necessity of Drawing: Tangible Speculation," *Architectural Design* (June 1977)
Graves, Michael, *Michael Graves*, edited by David Dunster, London: Academy Editions, and New York: Rizzoli, 1979
Graves, Michael, *Michael Graves: Buildings and Projects 1966–1981*, edited by Karen Vogel Wheeler, Peter Arnell, and Ted Bickford, New York: Rizzoli, and London: Architectural, 1982
Graves, Michael, *Michael Graves: Buildings and Projects 1982–1989*, edited by Karen Vogel Nichols, Patrick J. Burke, and Caroline Hancock, New York: Princeton Architectural Press, and London: Architecture Design and Technology Press, 1990
Graves, Michael, *Michael Graves: Buildings and Projects 1990–94*, edited by Karen Nichols, Lisa Burke, and Patrick Burke, New York: Rizzoli, 1995
Huxtable, Ada Louise, "A Unified New Language of Design," *The New York Times* (27 May 1979)
Jencks, Charles, *The Language of Post-Modern Architecture*, London: Academy Editions, and New York: Rizzoli, 1977; 6th edition, 1991

Jencks, Charles, "Abstract Representation," *Architectural Design*, 53/ 7–8 (1983)

Jencks, Charles, *Kings of Infinite Space: Michael Graves and Frank Lloyd Wright*, London: Academy Editions, and New York: St. Martin's Press, 1983; revised and enlarged edition, 1985

Jordy, William H., "Aedicular Modern 6: The Architecture of Michael Graves," *The New Criterion* (October 1983)

Papademetriou, Peter, "Four Not-So-Easy-Pieces," *Progressive Architecture* (March 1990)

Stern, Robert A.M., *New Directions in American Architecture*, London: Studio Vista, and New York: Braziller, 1969; revised edition, New York: Braziller, 1977

Stevens, Suzanne, "Semantic Distinctions," *Progressive Architecture* (April 1975)

Tafuri, Manfredo, "Five X Five-Twenty-Five," *Oppositions 5* (Summer 1976)

Viladas, Pilar, "Full Circle," *Progressive Architecture* (September 1985)

Zapatka, Christian, "Michael Graves, the Media and the Making of Metonymic Architecture," in *Michael Graves, Selected and Current Work*, by Michael Graves, Mulgrave, Victoria: Images, 1999

GRAY, EILEEN 1878–1976

Architect and furniture designer, England and Ireland

Eileen Gray directed her remarkable integration of architecture, furnishings, and textiles to address the modern individual's need for physical and psychological comfort, qualities that were frequently neglected in the early 20th-century quest for innovative forms. Through a relatively small number of buildings and conjectural projects, Gray offered a significant challenge to heroic ideals of the modern movement. Because her architecture drew on the ideas of her avant-garde contemporaries, it was both admired by her peers and forgotten in historical accounts of the modern movement.

Born into a wealthy family in Enniscorthy, Ireland, Gray studied drawing at the Slade School in London and the École Colarossi and Académie Julian in Paris. She settled definitively in Paris in 1906 after training in Asian lacquer techniques with a London firm specializing in antique restoration. After establishing her reputation as the first European designer to adapt traditional lacquer techniques to modern Western taste, Gray opened her own decorating shop, Jean Désert (1922), where she displayed her furniture and carpet designs. The simplicity of her forms and her interest in exploiting the sensual impact of materials brought Gray's textiles and lacquer furnishings to the attention of the Parisian avant-garde. Her approach was both unprecedented among decorative artists and influential for her subsequent pursuit of architecture.

In 1926, Gray began a six-year collaboration with Romanian architect Jean Badovici (1893–1956) that led to her independent involvement in architecture. As editor of the influential periodical *L'architecture vivante* (1923–33), Badovici was an enthusiastic agent for the modern movement. He encouraged Gray to take up architecture, introduced her to the works of the major European designers, and collaborated with her on several buildings in Vézelay that have been attributed inaccurately to him alone. The early issues of *L'architecture vivante* were Gray's textbooks, providing fertile territory for her initial architectural speculations. Whereas her lacquer interiors were motivated by the sensual luxury associated with the French decorative arts, Gray derived her subsequent architecture from a critical engagement with contemporary approaches to the modern dwelling in which she distilled ideas from Le Corbusier, Adolf Loos, and the advocates of De Stijl, among others. Rather than begin her designs from a set of theoretical precepts declared in a manifesto—an approach adopted by her more polemical counterparts—Gray challenged the all-encompassing claims of such examples of contemporary theorizing by adapting a selective combination of modern movement tenets to address the occupants' physical, psychological, and spiritual needs. This reliance on certain leaders of the architectural avant-garde was a necessary corollary to her creative work, however. By working within the framework of certain modern-movement spatial devices, such as Le Corbusier's "Five Points of a New Architecture," in her early buildings and projects, Gray sought to overcome the dehumanizing qualities frequently associated with abstraction by engaging the subjective qualities of experience. After initiating this approach in her independent House for an Engineer (1926), she exploited it more fully in the small vacation house that she built both for and with Badovici on a remote site directly on the Mediterranean in Roquebrune-Cap Martin (1929). She named the villa "E.1027"—a cipher for the authors' intertwined initials (E.J.B.G.)—reflecting the collaborative nature of the undertaking. Gray exhibited the models of the house and its furnishings at both the 1929 Salon d'Automne and the Union des Artistes Modernes, the latter a dissident group of designers of which she was a founding member. She articulated her intentions in a dialogue with Badovici that he published in a special issue of *L'architecture vivante* devoted to the E.1027 villa.

Gray's focus on the kinesthetic, tactile, and sensual potential of architecture and furniture in both E.1027 and the Paris apartment that she renovated for Badovici (1931) was unprecedented in modern-movement discourse. It derived from her interest in merging an aspiration for luxury emanating from the French decorative arts tradition with the liberal social aims of the architectural avant-garde. With her own vacation house near Castellar (1934), Gray abandoned overt references to the work of her contemporaries while absorbing certain modernist design principles into her own values and expression. She named the house Tempe à Pailla, citing a local proverb to allude to the maturation of her ideas over time. In comparison with E.1027, Tempe à Pailla is less of a showpiece; it is more compact and introverted, tailored both to Gray's tendency toward intimate and minimalist forms and to her solitary way of life. The Castellar house also had a more explicit social agenda; its minimal dimensions and spartan material qualities impart a degree of reality that is not evident in her previous work.

During the 1930s, Gray began to address the broader social implications of this approach in a series of hypothetical proposals for public leisure facilities, including her Vacation and Leisure Center (1937) and Cultural and Social Center (1947). Whereas her private vacation houses provided bodily comfort and served as temporary respites from the complexities of urban life, in her conjectural civic projects Gray transformed this interest in the modern individual's physical and psychological well-being into a more general concern for public welfare. Rather than starting from broad social or political assumptions, she proposed options that would encourage the occupants to make choices about en-

Living Room, Tempe à Pailla, Castellar, France (1932)
© Photograph by Eileen Gray reproduced with permission by Peter Adam

gaging her forms. This quality accounts for ideological consistencies between Gray's built work and her hypothetical designs.

Le Corbusier was a fervent admirer of Gray's architecture; he displayed her Vacation and Leisure Center alongside the work of his fellow Congrès Internationaux d'Architecture Moderne (CIAM) delegates in his Pavillon des Temps Nouveaux at the Parisian International Exposition "Art et Technique" of 1937. After this brief flurry of attention, Gray's work was largely ignored until Joseph Rykwert initiated a reappraisal in a series of articles dating from 1968. Late in her life, Gray received a number of honors; she was named a Royal Designer for Industry by the British Royal Society of Arts (1972) and an Honorary Fellow of the Royal Institute of the Architects of Ireland (1973). When she died in Paris in 1976, Gray was 98 years old and still producing furniture.

CAROLINE CONSTANT

Biography

Born in Enniscorthy, County Wexford, Ireland, 9 August 1878. Attended Slade School of Art, London 1898–1902; studied lacquerwork at D. Charles furniture workshops, Soho, London 1900–02; studied drawing at École Colarossi and Académie Julian, Paris 1902–05; studied furniture making and lacquerwork with Sugawara, Paris 1907–14. Ambulance driver, French Army 1914–15. Proprietor, with Sugawara, lacquerwork and furniture studio and workshop, London 1915–17; proprietor, Galerie Jean Désert, Paris 1922–30. First architectural projects, with Jean Badovici, Roquebrune, France 1926; worked in Castellar, France 1939–45; worked in Paris from 1945. Honorary Royal Designer for Industry, Royal Society of Arts, London 1972; fellow, Royal Institute of Irish Architects, Dublin 1973; member, Union des Artistes Modernes. Died in Paris, 28 November 1976.

Selected Works

Most of Gray's extant architectural drawings and photographs are in the Archive of Art and Design, Victoria and Albert Museum, London; additional drawings and models are in the Royal Institute of British Architects, London; numerous examples of her furniture from E.1027 are in the Centre Georges Pompidou, Paris.

Apartment for Mme Mathieu-Lévy, Paris (no longer extant), 1924
Jean Désert, Paris (no longer extant), 1922
Boudoir de Monte Carlo, Salon des Artistes Décorateurs, Paris (no longer extant), 1923

E.1027, Roquebrune-Cap Martin (with Jean Badovici), 1929
Badovici House, Vézelay (with Jean Badovici; extensively modified), 1931
Badovici Apartment, Paris (no longer extant), 1931
Tempe à Pailla, Castellar, 1934
Vacation and Leisure Center (project), 1937
Cultural and Social Center (project), 1947
Lou Pérou, Chapelle-Ste-Anne (Saint-Tropez; extensively modified), 1961

Selected Publications

"Maison en Bord de Mer," *L'architecture vivante* (Winter 1929) (issue on E.1027, with Jean Badovici; includes dialogue "De l'eclecticisme au doute")
"La maison minimum," *L'architecture d'aujourd'hui*, 1/1 (November 1930), inset following page 64, with Jean Badovici
"Projet pour un Centre Culturel," *L'architecture d'aujourd'hui* 82 (February/March 1959)

Further Reading

Adam, Peter, *Eileen Gray, Architect/Designer*, New York: Abrams, and London: Thames and Hudson, 1987; revised edition, New York: Thames and Hudson, 2000 (includes list of exhibitions, catalogue raisonné of furniture designs, and extensive bibliography)
Constant, Caroline, *A Non-Heroic Modernism: The Architecture of Eileen Gray*, New York and London: Phaidon Press, 2000 (includes catalogue raisonné of architecture and translation of dialogue "From Eclecticism to Doubt" by Gray and Badovici)
Constant, Caroline, and Wilfried Wang (editors), *Eileen Gray: An Architecture for All Senses*, Cambridge, Massachusetts: Harvard University Graduate School of Design, and Frankfurt: Deutsches Architektur-Museum, 1996
Johnson, J. Stewart, *Eileen Gray: Designer, 1879–1976*, New York: Museum of Modern Art, 1970; London: Debrett's Peerage, 1979
Rykwert, Joseph, "Eileen Gray: Pioneer of Design," *Architectural Review*, 152/910 (December 1972)
Rykwert, Joseph, "Eileen Gray: Two Houses and an Interior, 1926–1933," *Perspecta*, 13/14 (1972)

GREAT MOSQUE OF NIONO, MALI

Designed by Lassiné Minta and others; completed 1983

The Great Mosque of Niono (1948–83) in Mali in western Africa was built without drawings and without an architect. It thus provides a wonderful opportunity to question some of architectural history's basic tenets, such as the primacy of the architect and the drawn plan. A work firmly entrenched in a local building tradition, this huge mud-brick structure also calls into question the description of vernacular architecture as average and typical: the Great Mosque of Niono is clearly a stunning monument.

Work started in 1948 when an existing mosque was deemed too small. Largely designed by master mason Lassiné Minta, his son and other members of the community assisted in building this new mosque. The most notable feature is the dynamic facade that fronts the marketplace, with its piers, crenellated parapet, and towers from which palm-wood beams poke into the air.

Several terms are used to identify the style of the Niono Mosque: Djenné, Sudanese, or Dyula. "Djenné" refers to the most famous example of this type of architecture: the Great Mosque at Djenné. "Sudanese" refers more broadly to the traditional mud-brick architecture of the western Sudan. (Sudan, in this case, means the lands at the southern edge of the Sahara. This strip stretches across Africa, from the Atlantic to the Red Sea. The modern nation of Sudan occupies but the easternmost portion of the geographic area also called Sudan.) Labelle Prussin prefers the term "Dyula," which emphasizes that Islamized Mande speakers initially created this kind of architecture.

Regarding both form and style, the Great Mosque of Niono relies heavily on the Great Mosque of Djenné. In fact, the Niono Mosque is at once homage to Djenné and its modern architectural rival. The famous Djenné Mosque itself could be considered a 20th-century masterpiece if there were not such confusion regarding its date of construction. The Djenné Mosque dates primarily to 1909, and although it is certain that it was built using an existing architectural vocabulary, it is uncertain how much of the design existed prior to its reconstruction in 1909. That is, it is unclear the extent to which the Djenné Mosque followed trends or created them. According to Raoul Snelder, the technique of mud-dried bricks dates to approximately A.D. 400, although the original Djenné Mosque was probably constructed during the period 1180–1330. Djenné, on the Niger River, was a major ancient Saharan trading center. Written sources by travelers and traders confirm that the historic Djenné Mosque had many of the features that Minta incorporated into the Niono Mosque: galleries, colonnades, buttresses, and pillars.

Different scholars have detected different cultural origins for this West African architectural style. Some see an Egyptian influence, and at the most basic level, the forest of columns, the hypostyle hall, does date back to the ancient Egyptian pylon temples. Prussin argues, however, that North African Maghreb influence, chiefly Moroccan, was more influential. However, she also emphasizes the importance of the local architectural and artistic traditions from which this Dyula style arose.

If the exact stylistic origins of the earlier Djenné Mosque are uncertain, there is no doubt that in the 20th century the Djenné building is considered the prototypical mosque for the region. Mosques, ancient and modern, with which Niono shares similar characteristics, are found in Agades, Bamako, Gao, Kong, Mopti, Segú, and Timbuktu.

Although a small local rural settlement preceded Niono, the present city of 5000 is largely a French colonial construction, built in 1937. The desire to build a central religious monument in a centuries-old local architectural style affirms the people's ties to the region's more distant past. The Great Mosque is a monument that stylistically dates to a period when the present village did not exist.

A doctor from Timbuktu and the local imam initiated the project to replace a small wooden mosque. A site was acquired, bordered by open streets on three sides and houses on one side. The Niono Mosque was built primarily in three stages: the initial structure dating to 1948, the first enlargements in 1955, and the completion of the project, the last phase of construction, from 1969 to 1983. The initial mosque was a small rectangular prayer hall built as a hypostyle hall. Fourteen columns created a structure of three bays by eight bays. In 1955 side wings were added, greatly increasing the width of the mosque and more than doubling the size of the prayer hall. In this type of mosque

Facade of the long *qibla* wall, Great Mosque of Niono
Photo by Kamran Adle © Aga Khan Award for Architecture

architecture, the buildings extend in their width and not their length, so that the rows of worshipers facing Mecca extend as far as possible. In the last wave of construction at Niono, between 1969 and 1973, the prayer hall grew to 7800 square feet, and an area was built for women worshipers. A storeroom and a guardian's house were added, and a separate ablutions building was built. The ablutions building is for the ceremonial washing that precedes prayer. In 1983 the guardian's house was turned into a tomb for the first imam of the mosque. Tombs are one of the elements that can be a part of a mosque complex. During the last phase of construction, the entire site was surrounded by a wall, in effect placing the mosque within a courtyard of a larger layout. The open space between the mosque and the outer wall acts as an overflow area for prayers. Although the mosque essentially was finished by 1983, its outer mud layer is periodically renewed.

The most notable feature is the highly dynamic *qibla* facade (*qibla* denotes the direction toward Mecca). A worshiper inside the mosque faces the interior side of this wall and thus prays in the direction of the Islamic holy city. The three towers that dominate the *qibla* facade received their final form during the final expansion. The center tower has four tiers, and two shorter three-tiered towers flank it. Projecting palm-wood beams give

this type of mosque its distinctive profile. These act as scaffolding during the building's construction, and they remain for workers to use for the building's annual resurfacing. The top of the facade features low pyramid-shaped pinnacles that add to the building's dynamic profile. The highly articulated and lively external form contrasts with the forest of columns of the prayer hall.

This facade makes an urban gesture, for it defines the space in front of the mosque. Frequently with mosques such as Niono, the *qibla* facade is the main, not the entry, facade. At Niono the central tower is the tallest, and this gives an external expression to the mihrab, the prayer niche in which the imam leads prayers. It is located toward the center of the *qibla* wall. An entrance tower, a fourth tower, is Minta's bold innovation, for it strengthens the east-west axis, which runs perpendicular to the all-important *qibla* axis. A prominent entrance tower is not a typical element of mosque architecture, and in this case it may derive from Minta's familiarity with colonial Christian churches.

The towers and pinnacles relate to several pre-Islamic architectural forms, such as granaries and ancestral pillars, and symbols, such as phalluses and animal horns. This Djenné style is the result of a web of cultural influences, a complicated process whose exact origins are unclear but that includes indigenous practices, Islamic practices, and, most recently, French colonial architecture. Reflecting these diverse influences, the building's materials include sun-dried clay bricks, precast concrete, metal door frames, and steel tubing.

An example of how Niono inhabits a liminal space between tradition and modernity is its incorporation of amplified speakers at the top of its central mud-brick tower (something that it has in common with many mosques today). Although this might seem a discordant move by architectural purists, to community members it was a logical response to the issue at hand: the need to call worshipers to prayer.

Although there is no doubt that the Great Mosque of Niono was built in the 20th century, it demonstrates the continued usefulness of centuries-old building techniques. Mediating the demands of tradition and modernity, a local congregation and a global Islam, Niono is doubtless a striking addition to the West African architectural landscape. It was honored with an Aga Khan Award in 1983.

MARK HINCHMAN

See also **Africa: Western Africa; Egyptian Revival; Mosque**

Further Reading

Elleh, Nnamdi, *African Architecture: Evolution and Transformation*, New York: McGraw-Hill, 1997

"The Great Mosque of Niono, Mali," *Architectural Review*, 174 (October 1983)

Holod, Renata, and Hasan-Uddin Khan, *The Contemporary Mosque: Architects, Clients, and Designs since the 1950's*, New York: Rizzoli, 1997; as *The Mosque and the Modern World*, London: Thames and Hudson, 1997

"A Major Source of Continuing Inspiration: The Great Mosque of Niono, Niono, Mali," *Architectural Record*, 171 (September 1983)

Prussin, Labelle, *Hatumere: Islamic Design in West Africa*, Berkeley: University of California Press, 1986

Snelder, Raoul, "The Great Mosque at Djenné: Its Impact Today as a Model," *Mimar*, 12 (April–June 1984)

GREECE

In the 20th century, Greek architecture has vacillated between a desire to follow closely the international avant-garde and an effort to spring up autonomously from its own earth and its own traditions. This divided quest, which crosses the international with the Greek—as if they were two separate systems—is, of course, a feature shared with other countries and other periods. Nevertheless, the very constitution of the new Greek state in the early 19th century went hand in hand with a revival of antiquity, which had precisely this double significance: it ensured, through the architectural forms themselves, the continuation of the autochthonous classical tradition and a place in the vanguard of international Neoclassicism. This was, in any event, the chief reason why Greek Neoclassicism, transmuted by the historical influences of the late 19th century, went on into the 20th as an official and as a vernacular architecture until the interwar years. Evidence of this is supplied by the works of Ernst Ziller (1837–1923), Anastasios Metaxas (1862–1937), and other architects that still adorn Athens and the great variety of ornamental and typological features of Neoclassicism that have been imprinted on anonymous buildings throughout Greece. Under the weight of this long duration, there was very little room left for quests for renewal, which in other places developed Art Nouveau buildings.

For Greece, World War I effectively began in 1912 with the great Balkan conflict and ended in 1922 with the Asia Minor disaster. The wide-ranging restructuring of the country at the end of a decade of war was accompanied by social and ideological changes, all of which had a direct effect on architecture. Modernization was in the air, and this did not confine itself to morphological explorations with models borrowed for the European avant-garde or to the mechanical equivalent of innovation in construction. Beyond or alongside these, an almost programmatic wish was cultivated for a public architecture that would faithfully reflect the organization of a social state orientated toward education, health, and welfare. There was a parallel quest in the middle and upper strata of society for a metropolitan and, therefore, modern way of life. This pursuit found expression in the mechanization of everyday routines and the vocabulary of modern architecture. However, at the very time that this turn toward the more glittering centers of Western culture was taking place, another "domestic" avant-garde identified the absolutely modern with an undefiled Greekness that had existed before the classical and had continued without interruption until the third and fourth decades of the 20th century in the work of anonymous builders and painters and unlettered writers and composers.

In the early years of the 1930s, some 3000 schools were built all over Greece. For the design and execution of this large project, the Ministry of Education recruited the younger generation, living within the vibrancy of the Modern movement. By the end of the decade, a large number of hospital and social welfare buildings were constructed; these generally followed a strict rationalism that was both functional, constructional, and aesthetic. The systematic spread of these buildings throughout Greek territory did not merely implement the intentions of a modern social state; it also disseminated its image—condensed into simple rectangular prisms with a simple geometric layout, large apertures, and more rarely curves and free-standing columns—into the tradition-bound environment of small towns or the peripheral quarters of Athens, Piraeus, and Thessaloniki.

The primary school (1932) on the pine-covered slope of Lycabettus, in the center of Athens, was designed by Dimitris Pikionis (1887–1968). Its clean-cut prismatic masses, with their large rectangular plate-glass windows, follow the incline of the terrain and draw attention to the natural landscape through the paved pathways and the fact that the classrooms extend to the flat roofs. This diffused rationalism nevertheless has grafted on to it typological features from ancient Greek tradition, such as the colonnade on the southeastern side, and eloquent references to the art of building of anonymous Greek architecture. Two primary schools (1933) in Athens by Kyriakoulis Panayotakos (1902–82), both built with imposing geometry and austere masses with selected features on cantilever or *pilotis* with large plate-glass windows and a rational organization of the spaces, were a striking intervention in simple working-class neighborhoods of limited development that gave the measure of the modernization aimed at with the strictest character of Greek interwar architecture. A large number of important schools were also built by Patroklos Karantinos (1903–76) and Nikos Mitsakis (1899–1941).

The sanatoriums and hospitals of Ioannis Despotopoulos (1903–92), who spent some of his time as a student at the Bauhaus, are developed with flexible articulations and an elaboration of the syntax that is reminiscent of Alvar Aalto. In the case of the "Sotiria" Sanatorium (1932) in Athens, he gave particular emphasis to the simultaneously aesthetic and functional layout of the various needs and demands in a composition that had all the basic characteristics of the Modern movement. The central kitchen and laundry building of the same "Sotiria" hospital complex (1939) in Athens by the architect Periklis Georgakopoulos (1903–58) manifests the richest elaboration of design up to then in Greece, on the basis of the principles of the Modern movement, in a state of total liberation from any morphological and typological memories of the past. Also of importance were the social welfare buildings of Panos Tzelepis (1894–1978).

Similar features are recognizable in a number of residences and, above all, in apartment blocks in the center and suburbs of Athens, most built by Stamos Papadakis (1906–91), Patroklos Karantinos, Panos Tzelepis, Thoukididis Valentis (1908–82), and other lesser-known architects. Many of these architects acted as channels of communication with the European avant-garde, and some of them had studied in Paris. It is no accident that the fourth congress of CIAM (Congrès Internationaux d'Architecture Moderne) in 1933 chose Athens as its symbolic point of reference. Many of the modern buildings of Athens attracted the attention of the delegates and were published in the better-known German, French, British, and Italian architectural periodicals, and Le Corbusier signed his *compliments* on the walls of at least two of these. The reverse is also important: that the attraction and influence that the radical ideas and the physical presence of the distinguished delegates exerted on students and the youngest architects—for example, Georges Candilis (1913–95) and Constantinos Doxiadis (1913–75)—was considerable.

The parallel interest in Greekness and the unsullied anonymous architecture of the islands or the mountain regions of Greece and in the effectively modern revival of the ancient found fertile ground at precisely the same period and often through the work of the same people, including Dimitris Pikionis and Panos Tzelepis. They saw no contradiction in the double dimension of their quest. Nor was this, of course, exclusively a question of architecture, as similar cross-fertilizations can be seen in the dance of Isadora Duncan and the critical work of Christian Zervos and in contemporary painters, writers, and musicians.

World War II was a determining event for the Greeks: they had fought from the very first moment and had endured a harsh occupation. The end of the war proved the starting point for a civil war that lasted until 1949 and gave an altered meaning to the 1950s and 1960s. Greek identity, as a field for architectural explorations and constructs, lost a great part of the aesthetic dimension of the prewar period and gave expression to a will

Byzantine Museum (1978–1993), Thessaloniki by Kyriakos Krokos
Photo by B. Louizidis © K. Krokos archive

for self-determination in comparative isolation from the ideas of international modernism. Pikionis emerged as the ideological leader of the young architects who recognized in the landscaping of the hills of the Acropolis and of Philopappus in Athens (1957) the best version of the modern Greek vision. Genuine fragments from the passage through time of Greek architecture are poetically composed into a network of pathways that culminate in a little chapel and a pavilion with a view of the Parthenon. At the same period, but on a different wavelength, Aris Konstantinidis (1913–93) cultivated a structural and, above all, rational interpretation of the Greek earth and the simple buildings that had sprung up on it, which he transcribed into an architectural idiom with extensive influence down to the end of the century. Under the notion of genuine modern architecture, he gave a new interpretation to the aesthetic and moral truth of materials and architectural forms, combining in a creative manner international reinforced concrete and hewn stone from the site of the building itself. The holiday homes and the series of Xenia state hotels that he designed in the period 1958–67, the leading examples being the Xenia of Mykonos (1960) and the houses at Anavyssos (1962) and Spetses (1967), are model constructions of an architecture of the summer sun and the sea.

However, the Greek attention to a regional tradition represented only one direction. The gaze of many architects was turned to the West or sought a forward vista liberated from the burden of tradition. In the 1950s and early 1960s, optimism returned with a new prosperity. The houses of California met up with utopian quests of Central Europe and brought forth daring villas and similar experimentations. For example, the designs of Nikos Valsamakis (1924–) and Takis Zenetos (1926–77) show their interest in new materials and forms. Valsamakis designed two typical weekend villas (1963), both in Anavyssos, that virtually take off from the rocks at the sea's edge; three apartment blocks (1953, 1954, 1955) that gave new meaning to the commonest type of housing in Athens; and a hotel (1963) in Delphi that treated in a rational manner a very sensitive relationship with history and site. Zenetos designed villas (1967) that were technologically, functionally, and aesthetically weightless in the best suburbs of Athens, Kavouri, and Glyfada; a striking circular school of raw reinforced concrete that incorporates the logic of the ancient theater (1976) in Athens; factories in which their industrial aesthetic was emphasized; and a series of unexecuted or utopian proposals, the most outstanding of which was the constantly evolving project "Town Planning and Electronics: City of the Future" (1952–74).

In the 1960s, another generation collectively looked on modern architecture with admiration and doubt; showed interest in rugged architectural forms, vital functions, and simple elaborations of materials; and cultivated a relationship with the country's cultural and building values. In Greek history, these were difficult years, as the seven-year dictatorship (1967–74) changed the direction of society. At the same time, however, these problems served as the catalyst that turned the eyes of many from the international avant-garde to the social aims of architecture. Greece of the 1970s and 1980s did not experience the essence of postmodernist architecture, but it did incorporate a large part of the postmodernist critique into simple and almost understated but solid revisions. The most important presence of Greek architecture in the examples of the 20th century, after the interwar years, were built in these two decades under the heading of "critical regionalism," as formulated by Alexander Tzonis and Kenneth Frampton.

The most important expression of this critical spirit is bound up with the work of Dimitris (1933–) and Suzana Antonakakis (1935–) within the context of Atelier 66. What is effectively a reinterpretation of Greek traditional architecture in their work passed through the filters of Le Corbusier of the 1950s and of Dutch revisionist architects of the 1960s. Simple materials and the art of the anonymous craftsman served to hold together the visible concrete. The three-dimensional and clearly expressed function and geometry defined by light retain the feeling of the modern on a scale and with an atmosphere that is entirely Greek in identity. The residence (1981) near the Acropolis, the apartment block (1975) in the center of Athens, and the painter's studio (1993) on Aegina are among their most characteristic works.

Another person in this era is Kyriakos Krokos (1941–98), an architect and a painter who took delight in the Greek Neoclassicism of the 19th century, especially in its simplest, almost anonymous forms of expression. Nevertheless, his cultural poetics bear the marks of modern logic. The structure of his buildings is a skeleton of entirely visible reinforced concrete, but the most important feature is the plastic elaboration of their surface. The composition is enhanced with typological or stylistic memories from centuries of architectural tradition in Greece. The result is an architecture of place, more as a form and a message than as a structure and an essence. The Museum of Byzantine Civilisation (1993) in Thessaloniki and a series of residences in the suburbs of Athens (1991, Philotheian, and 1996, Ekali) bring out the logic and the truth of the contemporary construction, on the edge of a mannerism, while they forget nothing of the diachronic presence of the past.

In the late 20th century, the conscious participation of Greek architects in the global community represents just a small reflection of broader quests that emphasize localism as a point of intersection between Greece and the rest of the world. These two poles define the contemporary identity of a country defined proudly by its difference from and its identification with the most characteristic meanings of Western civilization.

PANAYOTIS TOURNIKIOTIS

Further Reading

The greater part of the bibliography dealing with the Greek architecture of the 20th century is written in Greek; however, the most important architects and exhibition catalogues have been published in English. The most important of these exhibitions was held in 1999 by the Hellenic Institute of Architecture and the Deutsches Architektur-Museum. In the international and Greek bibliographies, many articles have appeared, but the most important sources are the two bilingual annual reviews—*Architektonika themata; Architecture in Greece* and *Themata chorou + technon; Design + Art in Greece*—and the older bimonthly *Architektonikē*.

Aesopos, Yannis, and Yorgos Simeoforidis (editors), *Landscapes of Modernisation: Greek Architecture, 1960s and 1990s*, Athens: Metapolis Press, 1999

Architektonika themata; Architecture in Greece (1967–)

Architektonikē Architecture (1957–67) (with summaries in English)

Atelier 66: The Architecture of Dimitris and Suzana Antonakakis, New York: Rizzoli, 1985

Condaratos, Savas, and Wilfried Wang (editors), *Greece*, Munich and New York: Prestel, 1999

Constantopoulos, Eliasdf (editor), *Nicos Valsamakis, 1950–83*, London: 9H, 1984

Ferlenga, Alberto, *Pikionis, 1887–1968*, Milan: Electa, 1999

Konstantinidis, Aris, *Meletes + kataskeues; Projects + Buildings* (bilingual Greek-English edition), Athens: Agra Editions, 1981

Philippides, Demetres, *Neoellenikē architektonikē: Architektonike theoria kai praxe, 1830–1980, san antanaklase ton ideologikon epilogon tes neoellenikes koultouras* [Modern Greek Architecture: Theory and Practice, 1830–1980, as a Reflexion of Ideological Currents in Greek culture], Athens: Melissa, 1984

Philippides, Demetres (editor), *Spitia tou '30: Monterna architektonike Athena; Urban Housing of the '30s* (bilingual Greek-English edition), Athens: Nereas, 1998

Pikionis, Dimitris, *Dimitris Pikionis, Architect, 1887–1968: A Sentimental Topography*, London: Architectural Association, 1989

Takis Ch. Zenetos, 1926–1977, Athens: Architecture in Greece Press, 1978

Themata chorou + technon; Design + Art in Greece (1972–)

GREENBELTS AND GREENBELT TOWNS

The Greenbelt movement was an American depression-era outgrowth of the older Garden City movement. Like their predecessors, the greenbelt planners sought to decentralize congested cities all across the United States and to create new communities with a higher quality of life. The Greenbelt movement was institutionalized within President Franklin Roosevelt's New Deal as the Greenbelt Town Program, spearheaded by Rexford Guy Tugwell (1891–1979), and administered by the Resettlement Administration (RA).

The Garden City ideas that inspired Tugwell were largely developed by Ebenezer Howard (1850–1928), a social reformer in Britain who had also lived in the United States. Howard's garden cities were new settlements located some distance away from the central city, separated from it by a 5000-acre "greenbelt" containing farmlands and linked to it by train. Howard's idea was to re-create all of the residential, social, commercial and industrial facilities of the central city in the new communities while avoiding urban squalor and related ills. This would be accomplished partly by limiting them to a manageable size (32,000 people on 1000 acres) and partly by the inclusion of many gardens, parkways and public greens. Howard's garden cities were funded as cooperative ventures, with the residents receiving a share of the returns from increased property values. Among the more successful and famous examples are Letchworth and Welwyn, both outside London.

At the same time, the United States already had a number of "garden suburbs"—planned communities such as Riverside, Illinois that were built near existing industry, where workers could live in a community with ample open space. The more self-contained approach advocated by Howard was first tried in America by the Regional Planning Association of America (RPAA), headed by Lewis Mumford, with their plan for Radburn, New Jersey. Architects Stein and Wright laid out three villages in 1928, dividing each into superblocks, with houses facing away from the street and into a park. The pedestrian and vehicular traffic were completely separated and peripheral roads terminated in cul-de-sacs. Unlike the original English garden cities, property in Radburn was privately held. As a result, the village remained mostly beyond the reach of the urban working class even though it was originally planned for a mixed income group.

Rexford Tugwell, a Columbia University economist and advisor to Roosevelt, was impressed by these ideas and convinced the president that the Federal Government should be involved in this process of making livable communities outside the urban core. The communities Tugwell imagined were similar in philosophy to the earlier garden cities, with one major exception: virtually every step of the process, from building design and construction to tenant selection, was to be conducted by the federal government, who would own all of the property. Tugwell saw himself as organizing an inevitable migration out of the urban core; once this process had proceeded far enough, the abandoned slums could be torn down and redeveloped.

Tugwell ultimately envisioned 3000 or so greenbelt towns across the country; for the initial project he identified 25 cities and received approval from Congress for only five. Three of these were ultimately developed: Greenbelt, Maryland (outside Washington, DC), Greenhills, Ohio (outside Cincinnati), and Greendale, Wisconsin (outside Milwaukee). The RA was unable to purchase any suitable land for a project outside St. Louis, Missouri, and another in New Jersey was blocked by legal action brought by the township in which it was to be located, who feared the loss of property tax revenues (the federal government is exempt from property taxes). In physical layout, the three greenbelt towns generally followed the Radburn model, with superblocks, separation of pedestrians and automobiles, open spaces, and small, local commercial centers; to this approach they added space for local industry. The three communities were completed and opened to residents in 1937 and 1938. Federal policies allowed the towns to remain inclusive of a wider income spectrum than previous attempts, although the RA openly excluded blacks from the towns.

The Greenbelt towns faced difficulties from the outset. Their construction ran far over budget. Industry was more difficult to attract than expected. Disagreements about community management began early, as residents began to resent the top-down control over so many aspects of their lives. Rising national sentiment against the "socialism" of the New Deal caused the end of the Resettlement Administration in 1938, within a year of the communities' opening. Ownership and management of the towns was transferred to the Federal Republic Housing Agency (FRHA), then transferred again four years later to the Federal Public Housing Authority (FPHA). The rapid economic growth of the post-war years rapid and the resulting rise of suburbanization and automobile ownership sealed the fate of the communities; by the mid-1950's they were little different from the surrounding sea of commuter suburbs.

The federal government in the 1950s sold off the towns. Greenbelt, the largest of the communities, was sold to a cooperative housing association that is still in existence and that has kept much of the original plan intact. The original settlement was placed on the National Register of Historic Places in 1980 and rehabilitated with federal funds; in 1997 it was named a National Historic Landmark. Greenhills was also sold to a cooperative housing association and later to private owners; they have managed to maintain some of the green space around the original village, and this village was also placed on the National Register in 1989. Greendale, however, was sold to private investors immediately and has lost most of its original green space.

Few of the original families remain in any of the three, and the villages now have no more in-town jobs or community facilities than other suburbs of comparable size.

The importance of the greenbelt movement comes not from the success of the three towns, but from the inspiration the movement provided to future projects. Among these are the postwar British New Towns, which took their physical plans more directly from Howard, but adopted the centralized federal approach that only the Greenbelt towns had taken thus far. New generations of new town planning in the United States, from Columbia, Maryland to the present New Urbanism movement, rely on the Greenbelt experience to understand what aspects of design or policy may or may not be successful. These new movements generally turn to the private sector for development, unlike the greenbelt towns, but do adopt other elements such as pedestrian orientation, community facilities and spaces, and socioeconomic integration as their cornerstones.

MANISH CHALANA

See also **Garden City Movement; New Urbanism**

Further Reading

Arnold, Joseph L., *The New Deal in the Suburbs: A History of the Greenbelt Town Program 1935–1954*, Columbus: Ohio State University Press, 1971

Buder, Stanley, *Visionaries and Planners: The Garden City Movement and the Modern Community*, New York: Oxford University Press, 1990

Christensen, Carol Ann, *The American Garden City and the New Towns Movement*, Ann Arbor, Michigan: UMI Research Press, 1986

Hall, Peter Geoffrey, *Cities of Tomorrow: An Intellectual History of Urban Planning and Design in the Twentieth Century*, Oxford and Cambridge, Massachusetts: Blackwell, 1996

Osborn, Frederic James, *Green–Belt Cities*, New York: Schocken, 1969

GREENE AND GREENE

Architectural firm, United States

Charles Sumner Greene (1868–1957) and Henry Mather Greene (1870–1954) are appreciated today as seminal architects of the American Arts and Crafts movement in the early 20th century. For a fortunate few, they combined their fraternal symbiosis with formal training to create houses and complementary furnishings of artistic beauty and meticulous craftsmanship. Their secondary education at the Manual Training School of Washington University (1884–88) taught them the fundamentals of machine-tool making and woodworking. They studied architecture at the Massachusetts Institute of Technology from 1888 to 1891 and later apprenticed in some of the finest Boston firms in practice at the time. Beginning their practice in 1894, their first house designs were uninspired, but within a few years Greene and Greene were known for dwellings that harmonized with the topography and climate of southern California. The Greenes believed that success as classically trained architects in a remote corner of the country meant rejecting classicism. The warm climate, relaxed lifestyle, and rugged landscape of the re-

sort town of Pasadena demanded it, as did their own creative impulses. As students and apprentices, they had witnessed a mix of academic and progressive architecture that had posed meaningful theoretical questions but that did not necessarily offer appropriate answers for building in California. They realized, too, from their younger days at the Manual Training School of Washington University in St. Louis, that their work should be done with care and precision. Adhering to these simple tenets—looking beyond the dictates of history, profiting from the best examples of contemporary architecture, and executing work to the highest standards—successfully sustained the Greene and Greene firm for more than 20 years. Ultimately, however, it was the brothers' strong familial bond that sustained their collaborative genius and made possible the creation of exceptional works of art and craft.

Charles and Henry Greene were well matched yet utterly different. Charles tended toward a critical, artistic, and searching intellect, whereas Henry's approach to life was methodical, precise, and more dependable in a traditional sense. These tendencies were their strengths, and so it is not surprising that during their professional years together, Henry was depended on to run the office while his elder brother primarily exercised his prodigious design creativity on the jobs at hand. Charles processed daily stimuli into a particular artistic vision—rocks in a streambed, trees on the landscape, and images in books of faraway temples and cliffside castles—that contributed to the firm's unique aesthetic. Henry organized and transformed his brother's visions into practical form, allowing Charles to respond to his muse undistracted. As their success in architecture grew, they became more free to choose clients who were willing to take risks and spend large sums of money to create houses of spectacular beauty and perfect craft. Artistic expression of structure was the basis of the Greenes' design philosophy, and beautifully grained wood was their favored medium. Numerous species, including Honduras mahogany, Burma teak, California redwood, and Oregon pine, were shaped and smoothed to create houses with a sensuous, sculptural quality. Their designs boldly drew attention to structure by prominently articulating timbers and joinery. They did not abandon applied ornament, but neither did they allow it to overtake the expression of rationality and structure. The contractors and craftsmen who worked with the Greenes, most notably Peter and John Hall, were held to the same high standards to which the architects held themselves. Nothing was spared in the quest to make whole their vision of beauty.

Best known among the Greenes' houses (all of which, save one, were built in California) are the Robert R. Blacker house (1907) in Pasadena, the David B. Gamble house (1908) in Pasadena, the Charles M. Pratt house (1909) in Ojai, and the William R. Thorsen house (1909) in Berkeley. Each is formally distinct, yet fully characteristic of the classic Greene and Greene style. The Blacker house is the largest of these, its vast interior spaces meant to reflect and complement the more than five acres of grounds (now subdivided). The Gamble house was given somewhat more modest proportions, but its extensive use of exotic hardwoods and leaded art glass put it in the same rarified class as the Blacker house. The elegant rusticity of the Pratt house speaks more of a Japanese country inn or an elegant version of

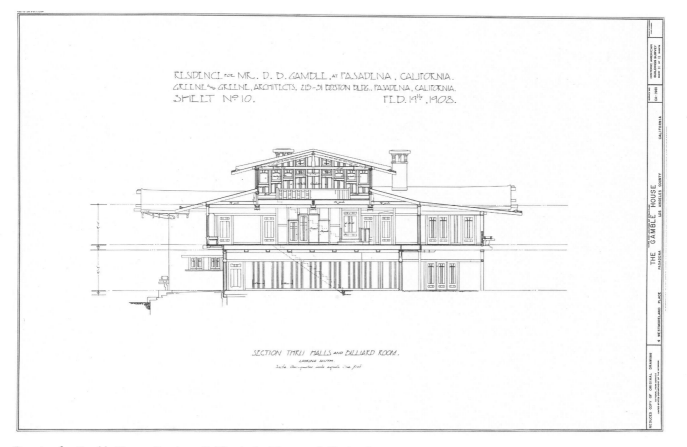

RESIDENCE for MR. D. B. GAMBLE, at PASADENA, CALIFORNIA.
GREENE & GREENE, ARCHITECTS, 215-21 BOSTON BLDG., PASADENA, CALIFORNIA.
SHEET N° 10.   FEB. 19th, 1908.

SECTION THRU HALLS and BILLIARD ROOM.

Drawing for Gamble House, Pasadena, California, by Henry and Charles Greene
© Historic American Buildings Survey/Library of Congress

the Adirondack "camp," transported to the idyllic Ojai valley. The Thorsen house followed a different typology, being one of the Greenes' few dwellings that reflected pedestrian-oriented patterns of life in an urban setting. Sometimes misleadingly referred to as "ultimate bungalows," these four houses stand as the most eloquent expressions of the Greenes' careers together and mark excellence in the American Arts and Crafts movement. They were known also for beautiful and finely crafted furniture that was designed to complement their houses. The Greenes' furniture was praised by the English Arts and Crafts architect and designer C.R. Ashbee as being "quite up to [the] best English craftsmanship."

After moving with his family to the bohemian enclave of Carmel-by-the-Sea in 1916, Charles Greene began a radically different phase of his life that ultimately served to reprove him spectacularly as an artist/architect in a clifftop dwelling in stone (1918–22) for D.L. James in Carmel Highlands. Its romantic site, massing, and use of materials make it more of a sculpture than a work of progressive domestic architecture. After Charles' departure from Pasadena, Henry was more able to explore his own design talent, even as he upheld the expected legacy of the firm's earlier work. The adobe ranch house (1929) in Porterville that he designed for Walter L. Richardson remains Henry's great late-career expression of his essentially self-effacing character and his personal, antimodernist interpretation of "less is more." Yet, however compelling their separate works are, the brothers were at their best working together, and it was their collective creativity that brought the greatest architectural and artistic value to their clients.

Although the Greenes' influence on other architects was not particularly widespread, their influence on developers and builders was. The ubiquitous California bungalow of the 1910s and 1920s was often modeled after images of the Greenes' work published in *Craftsman* magazine, *Ladies Home Journal,* and other national journals. Professional recognition of their work came from the American Institute of Architects in 1952, long after they had set aside their drafting tools. Today, the Gamble house, operated by the University of Southern California School of Architecture, is the only house designed by the Greenes that is open to the public and the only one to contain nearly all its original, architect-designed furnishings. In an era of mass marketing, machine-driven production, and instantaneous global communication, the Gamble house offers echoes of a slower-paced society wherein craft and art held equal status.

EDWARD R. BOSLEY

See also **Arts and Crafts Movement**

Biography

Charles Sumner Greene

Born in Cincinnati, Ohio, 12 October 1868. Attended the Manual Training School, Washington University, St. Louis, Missouri 1883–88; studied at the Department of Architecture, Massachusetts Institute of Technology, Boston 1888–91. Worked for H. Langford Warren and Winslow and Wetherell, among other firms, Boston 1891–93. Partnership with brother, Henry Mather Greene, Pasadena, California 1894–03; practice moved to Los Angeles 1903–06; practice moved to Pasadena 1906–22. Independent practice, Carmel, California from 1922. Died in Carmel, 11 June 1957.

Henry Mather Greene

Born in Cincinnati, Ohio, 23 January 1870. Attended the Manual Training School, Washington University, St. Louis, Missouri 1884–88; studied at the Department of Architecture, Massachusetts Institute of Technology, Boston 1888–91. Worked for Chamberlin and Austin, Boston 1891–93 then for Shepley, Rutan and Coolidge, Boston 1893. Partnership with brother, Charles Sumner Greene, Pasadena, California 1894–03; practice moved to Los Angeles 1903–06; practice moved to Pasadena 1906–22. Independent practice, Pasadena from 1922. Died in Pasadena, California, 2 October 1954.

Greene and Greene

Founded in Pasadena, California, by brothers Charles Sumner Greene and Henry Mather Greene 1894; moved to Los Angeles 1903–06; returned to Pasadena 1906–22; dissolved in 1922, when the brothers pursued independent practices.

Selected Works

Robert R. Blacker House, Pasadena, 1907
Arturo Bandini House (El Hogar; destroyed), Pasadena, 1903
Adelaide M. Tichenor House, Long Beach, 1904
Charles W. Hollister House (destroyed), Hollywood, 1904
David B. Gamble House, Pasadena, 1908
Charles M. Pratt House, Ojai, California, 1909
William R. Thorsen House, Berkeley, 1909
D.L. James House, Carmel Highlands, California, 1918–22
Walter L. Richardson House, Porterville, California, 1929

Further Reading

Bosley, Edward R., *Gamble House: Greene and Greene,* London: Phaidon Press, 1992
Bosley, Edward R., *Greene and Greene,* London: Phaidon Press, 2000
Current, William R., and Karen Current, *Greene and Greene: Architects in the Residential Style,* Fort Worth, Texas: Amon Carter Museum of Western Art, 1974
Makinson, Randell L., *Greene and Greene,* 2 vols., Salt Lake City, Utah: Peregrine Smith, 1977–79; volume 1, 2nd edition, 1982
Makinson, Randell L., *Greene and Greene: The Passion and the Legacy,* Salt Lake City, Utah: Gibbs Smith, 1998
Smith, Bruce, *Greene and Greene: Masterworks,* San Francisco: Chronicle Books, 1998
Strand, Janann, *A Greene and Greene Guide,* Pasadena, California: Dahlstrom, 1974
Winter, Robert (editor), *Toward a Simpler Way of Life: The Arts and Crafts Architects of California,* Berkeley: University of California Press, 1997

GREGOTTI, VITTORIO 1927–

Architect, Italy

Born in Novara, Italy in 1927, Vittorio Gregotti graduated from the architecture faculty of Milan Polytechnic in 1952 and worked on the editorial board of *Casabella* magazine from 1953 to 1955. He was chief editor from 1955 to 1960, with Aldo Rossi and Gae Aulenti among the editors, and was managing editor from 1982 to 1995. Gregotti also worked for Ernesto Rogers at BBPR (Belgioioso, Banfi, Peressutti, Rogers). Like Gae Aulenti, Gregotti began his career in a professional environment in Milan that combined architecture with industrial design and other design arts. Gregotti's early work included designs for exhibition posters, book covers, showrooms, offices, and boutiques, but he is best known for hundreds of significant architectural projects, including housing complexes, supermarkets, department stores, and college campuses.

The 1950s and 1960s were a period of economic boom in Milan, with the large influx of workers providing a need for new residential housing projects. Gregotti met this demand for housing. During the 1970s, his work expanded to projects for factories and research centers. Later, in the 1980s, he also designed large stadium complexes. During the 1990s, his office designed everything from cruise ships to city plans. During the 1970s and 1980s, Gregotti became one of Italy's leading architects and most influential theorists, participating with great influence in two important institutions, the Venice Biennale and the Milan Triennale. He has written several books on architecture throughout his career, including *Il territorio dell'architettura* (1966; The Territory of Architecture), *L'architettura dell'espressionismo* (1967; The Architecture of Expressionism), *New Directions in Italian Architecture* (1968), *Questioni di architettura* (1986), *Cinque dialoghi necessari* (1990; Five Necessary Dialogues), *Dentro l'Architettura* (1991; Inside Architecture, translated into English in 1996), and *La città visibile* (1993; The Visible City). Kenneth Frampton called *Inside Architecture* "the most important book by the most important architect, critic and intellectual writing today."

As an important educator, Gregotti has been professor of architectural composition at the University Institute of Architecture in Venice, professor at the University of Palermo, and visiting professor in the United States at Harvard University, Princeton University, the Massachusetts Institute of Technology, and the University of Pennsylvania. He influenced architectural education and theory in Italy during the 1970s and 1980s. His work has been the subject of important essays by Joseph Rykwert, Kenneth Frampton, and Manfredo Tafuri. It was also the subject of a monograph published in Italy by Manfredo Tafuri in 1982 and of one published in the United States by Joseph Rykwert in 1995.

Gregotti's earliest projects included the Room of the Kaleidoscope (1963) at the XIII Triennale in Milan and cooperative housing projects on Via Montegani and Via Palmanova. The exhibition and showroom designs, such as those of Gae Aulenti, reflected the times in complex and experimental compositions "Decorative and Industrial Arts" with underlying geometric bases. For Gregotti, as he describes in his essay in Joseph Rykwert's *Vittorio Gregotti and Associates,* geometry "plays a role in restoring meaning to the original and fundamental gesture of placing, arranging . . .". His large-scale housing projects combined an inventive use of materials in formal, geometric compositional exercises. The materials included glass, iron, brick, stone, terra-cotta, and ceramic tiles. The same combination was applied to projects for office buildings in Novara and Milan from the 1960s through the 1980s.

Throughout northern Italy and other European countries in the 1970s and 1980s, Gregotti designed office and factory complexes and research centers. The construction of the buildings follows the nature of the materials, the interior of the buildings creates a dialogue with the exterior, and the design takes into account the history of the site. As Gregotti writes, "Materials come from a context." However, the form of the buildings always marks a clear distinction with its surroundings: there is a professed distinction between the natural and artificial in the architecture. Such a distinction is maintained throughout Gregotti's career, beginning with the showroom and industrial designs.

Gregotti also makes a clear distinction between what he calls "instrumentality" and "meaning," which constitutes his definition of "post-social hyper-modernity." The form and function of the building as they are realized in 20th-century social and economic conditions are divorced from "any narrative concept of the human experience." Gregotti professes to practice a kind of pure avant-garde formalism that is removed from "sociopolitical and scientific progress."

Inside Architecture, Gregotti's first book to be translated into English, examines theories of modernism in the wake of the deterioration of the natural and built environment caused by mass culture and public institutions. During the 1980s, Gregotti's office designed sports complexes such as the Olympic Stadium in Barcelona, the Luigi Ferraris Stadium in Genoa, and the Sports Complex in Nîmes, and developed town-planning projects for Florence, Arezzo, Brescia, Turin, Milan, Novara, and Vicenza. Gregotti said of the stadium that it is "a cult place for mass society and at the same time the space where imitations of its personal and collective conflicts are played out," (Rykwert 1995). In the end, his buildings are structures of profound communication, servicing the needs of the 20th century and after.

JOHN HENDRIX

Biography

Born in Novara, Italy, 10 August 1927. Attended Milan Polytechnic, School of Architecture 1948–52; degree in architecture 1952. Partner, with Lodovico Meneghetti and Giotto Stoppino, Architetti Associati, Milan 1952–67; associate editor, *Casabella*, Milan 1952–60; editor, Edilizia Moderna monographs, Milan 1962–64; architectural editor, *Il Verri*, Milan 1963–65. In private practice, Milan 1968–74; architectural consultant, La Rinascente Stores Group, Milan 1968–71; partner, with Pierluigi Cerri and Augusto Cagnardi, Gregotti Associati, Milan 1974–present; director, visual arts section, *Biennale di Venezia*, Venice 1974–76; coeditor, *Lotus*, Venice 1974–present; director, *Rassegna*, Milan 1979–present; director, *Casabella*, Milan 1982–95; professor of architectural composition, University Institute of Architecture, Venice 1978–present.

Selected Works

Case d'affitto, Novara, 1957
Room of the Kaleidoscope, XIII Triennale, Milan, 1963
Cooperative Housing in Milan, 1964
L'Università degli Studi di Palermo, Dipartimenti di Scienze, 1969–90
Residential Buildings, Palermo, 1969–73 with Amoroso, Bisogni and Matsui.
Offices and Factory, Bossi Textile, Novara, 1980
Offices and Factory, Gabel Textile, Como, 1980
Residential Housing in Lützowstrasse, Berlin, 1981
Sports Complex, Nîmes, 1986
Luigi Ferraris Stadium, Genoa, 1986
Olympic Stadium, Barcelona, 1988
Heating Power Station, Genoa, 1988
Costa Line Cruise Ships, 1990–94
Fila Store on Madison Avenue, New York City, 1991
Lisbon Cultural Center, 1993
Residential Development in Cannaregio, Venice, 1994
Brera Picture Gallery, Milan, 1994

Selected Publications

Il territorio dell'architettura, 1966
L'architettura dell'espressionismo, 1967
New Directions in Italian Architecture, translated by Giuseppina Salvadori, 1968
Il disegno del prodotto industriale, Italia 1860–1980, 1982
Questioni di architettura, 1986
Cinque dialoghi necessari; Five Necessary Dialogues (bilingual Italian-English edition), translated by C. Evans, 1990
Dentro l'architettura, 1991; as *Inside Architecture*, translated by Peter Wong and Francesca Zaccheo, 1996
La città visibile, 1993

Further Reading

Colao, Paolo, and Giovanni Vragnaz (editors), *Gregotti Associati, 1973–1988*, Milan: Electa, 1990
Crotti, Sergio, *Vittorio Gregotti*, Bologna: Zanichelli, 1986
Frampton, Kenneth, "Città senza baudiere," in *Domus*, no. 609, 1980.
Matsui, Hiromichi (editor), *Gregotti Associates*, New York: Van Nostrand Reinhold, 1984
Rota, Italo (editor), *The Project for Calabria University and Other Architectural Works by Vittorio Gregotti; Il Progetto per L'Universita delle Calabrie e altre Architetture* (bilingual English-Italian edition), Milan: Electa, 1979
Rykwert, Joseph, *Vittorio Gregotti and Associates*, New York: Rizzoli, 1995
Tafuri, Manfredo, *Vittorio Gregotti, "Architectural Narratives." progetti e architetture*, Milan: Electa, 1982; as *Vittorio Gregotti, "Adventures of the object" Buildings and Projects*, New York: Rizzoli, 1982

GRIFFIN, WALTER BURLEY 1876–1937 AND MARION (LUCY) MAHONY GRIFFIN 1871–1961

Architects, United States

Young followers of Louis Sullivan, Marion Lucy Mahony, and Walter Burley Griffin were major participants in the Prairie School, who in the main practiced from the attic of the Steinway Hall office block in Chicago. Steinway Hall's designer, Dwight Heald Perkins, Mahony's cousin, was their first employer, she in 1894 and he in 1899. By January 1901, both were working

Frederick B. Carter Jr. House Evanston, Illinois (1911)
© Historic American Buildings Survey, Library of Congress, Washington, D.C.

with Frank Lloyd Wright in his Oak Park Studio until March 1906, when Griffin established his own practice. Walter and Marion Griffin then entered the 1911–12 international competition for the city of Canberra, the new federal capital of Australia. Inspired by the City Beautiful movement, their winning design consisted of a central triangle of avenues spanning a man-made lake nestled within a majestic hilly landscape and river valley, with dispersed subcenters radiating boulevards like snow-flake structures. They established Melbourne and Sydney offices in 1914 and continued to create an idiosyncratic organic architecture in the United States, Australia, and Lucknow, India.

Mahony designed Frank Lloyd Wright's fancifully abstract yet pragmatic interiors, according to Arts and Crafts taste. Combining characteristics of Vienna Secession drawings and Japanese prints, she pioneered the rendering style made famous by Wright's two Wasmuth volumes (Berlin, 1910–11). Mahony designed the Unitarian Church of All Souls (1903) in Evanston, Illinois, a sparse hall with strongly textured stone walls beneath a steeply pitched gable roof. The street elevation featured a huge Gothic window. Smooth plaster interior walls contrasted with radiant ceiling lights in colored glass and a delicately joined wooden ventilation grille. The ordinary timber house (1906) for her mother was plainly Craftsman. Between 1909 and 1911,

Mahony was commissioned as architect (Griffin as landscape architect) to finish projects abandoned by Wright when he went to Europe with Mamah Cheney. Mahony designed and built Prairie School houses for the brothers Adolph and Robert Mueller (1910, Decatur, Illinois) and for David Amberg (1910, Grand Rapids, Michigan) as well as a long, low mansion designed in concrete and rusticated stone for Henry Ford but never built.

While at the University of Illinois, Urbana, Griffin studied the writings of Berlin-trained Professor Nathan Clifford Ricker, who had translated French and German texts on building construction and architectonic aesthetics. During Griffin's time at the Champaign campus (1895–99), Ricker also translated Otto Wagner's *Moderne Architektur* (1895), which expected that vital modern architecture would engage with new construction techniques. Louis Sullivan's observation that "form follows function," as it does in nature, also appealed to Griffin.

In Wright's Oak Park Studio, Griffin occasionally designed Wright's buildings but typically provided residential landscape designs. He supervised site construction, controlled costs and the selection of materials, and directed the practice during Wright's absences. Only then were certain new architectural elements and architectonic themes to appear in Wright's projects, which recurred in Griffin's independent practice. Griffin repeated the flat roof and timber trelliswork for the Lamp House (1903) in Madison, Wisconsin, in "Solid Rock" (1911) in Winnetka, Illinois, a theme shared with the Vienna Secession. Griffin's house (1903) for a neighbor and fellow Congregationalist, W.H. Emery, in Elmhurst, Illinois, showed massive, capped corner piers between which were white plaster walls patterned with vertical frame members. A square plan type from late 19th-century architect-designed American houses was used for the Peters house (1906) in West Chicago, featuring a central fireplace surrounded by open living and dining rooms in an L shape, with a closed kitchen in the fourth quarter.

In the Rock Crest–Rock Glen estate in Mason City, Iowa, during 1912–13, the Griffins created diverse forms for large houses in concrete, terra-cotta block and stucco, or rough stone-work finish. A similar variety in materials appeared at Beverly (1910–14) near Chicago for modest houses in stained timber and stucco. The stained-timber window joinery for each Griffin house in America or Australia was given its own distinct signature pattern of vertical, horizontal, and sometimes diagonal lines; each fireplace opening had a distinct signature lintel, corbel, or arch. Griffin interiors were characterized by ocher-tinted plaster surfaces and exposed stained-timber beams and strapwork, by split-floor levels and intriguing picturesque staircase routes, and by concealed electric-lighting troughs. The architectonic elements of battered base, random-rubble coursed stonework, and chunky concrete frame occurred variously in the Stinson Memorial Library (1912–14) in Anna, Illinois; in Newman College, University of Melbourne (1915–18); and in houses on the Castlecrag Estate (1921–35) in Sydney. At Castlecrag, the Griffins demonstrated their desire for organic integration: contour-hugging roadways and rugged flat-roofed slab buildings blended with the natural horizontal rock escarpments and plateaus on which the Griffins restored the denuded native bush. Some of these houses were not rough textured but constructed of flat-surfaced "Knitlock," a vertically ribbed concrete tile system with a double skin and cavity, patented by Griffin in Melbourne in 1917. This system predated Wright's California blockwork by six years. Knitlock tile-making machines were designed for leasing so that landholders could build their own houses.

Standing eight stories, Capitol House (1922–24) in Melbourne was constructed of smooth-shuttered reinforced concrete. The adjoining Capitol Theatre cinema was spanned in concrete lattice girders. The ceiling was hung with multifaceted Alhambra-inspired plasterwork projections, with concealed colored electric light globes behind; the hues of the spectrum were cycled through so that various crystal formations appeared to emerge and recede from view. A glazed curtain-wall system was used for the Leonard House offices (1922–24) in Melbourne.

Demolition has also recently befallen the Griffins' brick-and-stucco Pioneer Press buildings (1936) in Lucknow. Ornamental geometries were invented for each of the bamboo, burlap, and plaster pavilions for the temporary United Provinces Industrial and Agricultural Exhibition (1936). Only a brick-and-stucco pumping station block beside the Gumti River survives. Repetitive overlapping cubes were used in the breathtaking perspective drawing of the Raja Mahmudabad Library Project (1937). Although the foundation stone of the Griffins' Lucknow University Library was laid during January 1937, this building was completed posthumously.

After his return from Europe in 1911, Wright successfully belittled the contributions to Prairie School architecture by his colleagues, including Perkins, Robert C. Spencer, Jr., William Drummond, Henry Webster Tomlinson, and the Griffins. Walter Burley Griffin and Marion Lucy Mahony had been directly involved in seminal Prairie School works, such as the Darwin D. Martin and Ward Willetts houses, the Larkin Building, and the Unity Temple. The Griffins' competition design for Canberra was widely published and exhibited but was never fully implemented.

JEFF TURNBULL

See also **Prairie School; Sullivan, Louis (United States); Wright, Frank Lloyd (United States)**

Biography

Walter Burley Griffin

Born in Maywood, Illinois, 24 November 1876. Attended University of Illinois, Urbana 1895–99; bachelor's degree in architecture 1899. Married architect Marion Mahony 1911. Worked for several Chicago architects 1899–1901; worked for Frank Lloyd Wright, Chicago 1901–06. Private practice, Chicago 1906–11; partnership with wife from 1911; associated with Barry Byrne 1913–14. Moved to Australia; director of design and construction for new federal capital, Canberra 1913–20; partnership with J. Burcham Clamp, Sydney, Australia 1914–15. Private practice, Australia 1915–35; designed and patented the Knitlock system of construction 1917; Eric Nicholls became a partner 1925–39; worked in Lucknow India, from 1935. Died in Lucknow, 11 February 1937.

Marion Mahony Griffin

Born in Chicago, 14 February 1871. Graduated with a degree in architecture, Massachusetts Institute of Technology, Cambridge 1894. Married architect Walter Burley Griffin 1911. Worked with cousin, architect Dwight Heald Perkins, Chicago; worked for Frank Lloyd Wright, Chicago 1895–1909; worked for Hermann von Holst, Chicago 1909–11. Partnership with husband from 1911–37; associated with Barry Byrne 1913–14. Moved to Australia; partnership with J. Burcham Clamp, Sydney, Australia 1914–15. Private practice, Australia 1915–35; Eric Nicholls became a partner 1925–39; worked in Lucknow, India, from 1935. Worked in Chicago from 1938. Died in Chicago, 10 August 1961.

Walter Burley Griffin and Marion Mahony Griffin

Partnership founded in Chicago 1911; moved to Australia 1915–35; moved to Lucknow, India 1935–37; dissolved upon Walter Burley Griffin's death 1937.

Selected Works

Emery House, Elmhurst, Illinois, 1903
Lamp House, Madison, 1903
Northern Illinois State Normal School Landscape Plan, DeKalb, 1906
Peters House, Chicago, 1906
Cooley House, Monroe, Louisiana, 1908 (built 1926)
Ralph Griffin House and Grounds, Edwardsville, Illinois, 1909

Carter House, Evanston, Illinois, 1911.
Tempel House ("Solid Rock"), Winnetka, Illinois, 1911
Rock Crest–Rock Glen Community and Landscape Plan, Mason City, Iowa, 1913
Model Brick Cottage, Chicago Coliseum Exhibition, (rebuilt at 5632 S. Maplewood), Chicago, 1913
Stinson Memorial Library and Grounds, Anna, Illinois, 1914
Blount Houses, Beverly, Chicago, 1914
Summit Estate, Mount Eagle Estate, Eaglemont, Melbourne, 1914
Campus Plan, University of New Mexico, Albuquerque, 1915
Lippincott House, Glenard Estate, Melbourne, 1917
Newman College, University of Melbourne, 1918
City Plan, Canberra, Australian Capital Territory, 1920
Castlecrag Estate, Middle Harbor, Sydney, 1921
Croydon Hills Estate, Melbourne, 1921
Liberty Hall, Melbourne, 1921
Palais de Danse and the Palais Picture Theatre Cinema, St Kilda, Melbourne, 1922
Fishwick House and Wilson House, Castlecrag, Sydney, 1929
Flats, Benares University Workers (now Varanasi Hindu University), Uttar Pradesh, 1935
Lucknow University Extension Plan, 1935
Lucknow University Library, 1935
Zenana Palace, near Lucknow, 1936
Capitol Theatre Cinema, Lucknow, 1936
Pioneer Press Offices and Works, Lucknow, 1936
United Provinces Industrial and Agricultural Exhibition Pavilions and Victoria Park, 1936
Lucknow University Student Union (project), 1937
Raja of Mahmudabad Library (project), 1937

Selected Publications

The Federal Capital, 1913
The U.P. Industrial and Agricultural Exhibition, Lucknow, 1936

Further Reading

Birrell, James, *Walter Burley Griffin*, St. Lucia: University of Queensland Press, 1964
Brooks, H. Allen, *The Prairie School: Frank Lloyd Wright and His Midwest Contemporaries*, Toronto, Ontario: University of Toronto Press, 1972
Harrison, Peter, *Walter Burley Griffin: Landscape Architect*, edited by Robert Freestone, Canberra: National Library of Australia, 1995
Johnson, Donald Leslie, *The Architecture of Walter Burley Griffin*, South Melbourne, Victoria: Macmillan, 1977
Maldre, Mati, and Kruty, Paul, *Walter Burley Griffin in America*, Urbana: University of Illinois Press, 1996
Peisch, Mark L., *The Chicago School of Architecture: Early Followers of Sullivan and Wright*, New York: Random House, 1964
Sprague, Paul E., "Griffin's Beverly Buildings, a Catalog," *Prairie School Review*, 10/1 (1973)
Turnbull, Jeff, and Peter Y. Navaretti (editors), *The Griffins in Australia and India: The Complete Works of Walter Burley Griffin and Marion Mahony Griffin*, Melbourne: Melbourne University Press, 1998
Van Zanten, David (editor), *Walter Burley Griffin, Selected Designs*, Palos Park, Illinois: Prairie School Press, 1970
Vernon, Christopher, "Walter Burley Griffin, Landscape Architect," in *The Midwest in American Architecture*, edited by John S. Garner, Urbana: University of Illinois Press, 1991
Walker, Meredith, Adrienne Kabos, and James Weirick, *Building for Nature: Walter Burley Griffin and Castlecrag*, Castlecrag, New South Wales: Walter Burley Griffin Society, 1994
Walter Burley Griffin: A Re-View (exhib. cat.), Clayton, Victoria: Monash University Gallery, 1988
Watson, Anne (editor), *Beyond Architecture: Marion Mahony and Walter Burley Griffin: America, Australia, India*, Sydney: Powerhouse, 1998

GRIMSHAW, NICHOLAS, AND PARTNERS

Architects, England

Together with Richard Rogers and Norman Foster, Nicholas Grimshaw is credited with pioneering High-Tech modernism in Britain in the early 1970s. Grimshaw's buildings demonstrate the fusion of well-tempered, functional engineering and the fundamental principles of architecture. Always understandable spatially and organizationally, Grimshaw's buildings employ high-quality materials and detailing and show his interest in engineering.

Born in London in 1939, the son of an aircraft engineer and great grandson of Victorian civil engineer Sir George Alderson, Grimshaw claims Victorian subject painter Atkinson Grimshaw as an ancestor. After studying architecture at Edinburgh University, he transferred to the third year at the Architectural Association in 1962. Tutored by Cedric Price, he was subsequently influenced by Peter Cook and Archigram. He admired engineering structures such as the Dome of Discovery and the Skylon at the Festival of Britain in 1951 as well as the Crystal Palace of 1851. Grimshaw's work shares Paxton's clarity of concept, supported by detailed and thorough development. Concept sketches invariably embody the complete essence of the final design.

His first project, the Sussex Gardens Service Tower (1967) in London, provided sanitary facilities for student accommodation. Its helical form, illustrating Grimshaw's interest in geometry, was innovative, predating computer-assisted design (CAD) and involving the coordination of 35 specialist subcontractors. Apartments on Park Road (1968) in London, built of lightweight materials the same year as Ronan Point was constructed in heavy precast concrete, reveal Grimshaw's developing interest in "technology transfer."

The expanding towns of the 1970s and the advent of the business park led to the construction of acres of humdrum storage buildings. Grimshaw soon proved that the simple industrial building could assume the form of a shell, capable of being altered to suit the changing needs of users and the processes inside. The Citroën Warehouse (1972), commissioned to be unobtrusive, with maximum size at minimum cost, was the first to show a sensitivity to landscape, occupying a riverside site at Runnymeade. The Furniture Factory for Vitra (1981) at Weil am Rhein, Germany, and the Headquarters for Editions Van der Velde (1979) continue this theme. The green fiberglass panels of the low-lying building for Van der Velde, in the Loire valley, were designed to imitate the green glass of Vouvray bottles.

Grimshaw's belief that people should be able to manipulate their surroundings was developed in the Herman Miller Distribution Centre (1982) at Chippenham, Wiltshire, which he described as "the ultimate long-life loose-fit building." At the Advanced Factory Units (1978) at Winwick Quay, Warrington, carefully detailed cladding systems were employed. The potency of the clear expression that structure can give to a building is

Grand Union Walk Housing, London (1988)
© Don Barker/GreatBuildings.com

first seen at the Sports Hall for IBM Winchester, 1980 that echoes the branches of the surrounding trees. This effect reaches a climax at the Oxford Ice Rink, where the structure, with its spine beam running the length of the building, hung dramatically between two masts, signals the thrill and excitement of the activity inside. The Financial Times Printing Works (London, 1988) is a building with a more formal and disciplined approach, where the support for the roof and for the cleaning gantries is combined in one clear system. This apparently simple move allows the all-glass facade and reveals the printing activity within. In the Sainsbury Supermarket Development (1989) in Camden Town, Grimshaw's designs come to terms with the urban context. Here, scale, grain, and color point the way to his more recent, high-profile projects. The British Pavilion at Expo '92 in Seville, constructed from glass, with canvas sides and a water cascade down one side, secured international fame.

The International Terminal addition to Waterloo Station (1990–93) has become an architectural landmark. This complex structure, conceived to evoke the feats of the great Victorian engineers, heralds the "Gateway to Europe." The building comprises four main components—a car park, which forms the foundation for the terminal; a two-story viaduct, which supports the platforms; the brick arches of the original station that house

services; and a flattened, sweeping roof, 400 feet in length. The structure moves away from surface articulation toward a more profound interest in light and space. The 1990s have brought a new dimension of meaning—the technically superlative Stock Exchange in Berlin (1996), the RAC Headquarters in Bristol (1995), and the Western Morning News Building (1998), all demonstrating evolution and refinement. The Eden Project in Cornwall (2000), the Ludwig Erhard Haus in Berlin (1998), the Mabeg Office in Germany (1999), Zurich Airport, and the restoration of Brunel's Paddington Station in London represent Grimshaw's most recent, ambitious, and diverse work.

HILARY J. GRAINGER

See also **London, England; Rogers, Richard (England); Supermodernism**

Selected Publications

Product & Process, London: 1988
"The Future of Industrial Building," *Journal of the Royal Society of Arts* (December 1984)

Further Reading

Amery, Colin, *Architecture, Industry and Innovation: The Early Works of Nicholas Grimshaw and Partners*, London: Phaidon, 1995

Davies, Colin, *High-Tech Architecture*, New York: Rizzoli, 1988

Glancey, Jonathan, *New British Architecture*, New York: Thames and Hudson, 1990

Lyall, Sutherland, *The State of British Architecture*, London: Architectural Press, 1980

Moore, Rowan (editor), *Structure, Space and Skin: The Work of Nicholas Grimshaw and Partners*, London: Phaidon, 1993

GROPIUS HOUSE

Designed by Walter Gropius; completed 1938
Lincoln, Massachusetts

The home that Walter Gropius designed for himself in 1937–38 even today seems strikingly modern. With its flat roof; clean, boxlike silhouette; ribbon windows; and interacting, seemingly weightless planes, the design has an affinity with Picasso's faceted analytic Cubist paintings. Gropius intended for his house to exemplify humankind's spirit, creativity, and industry. Perfectly situated within the context of the Massachusetts landscape and climate, it is also deferential to local building traditions. It has been hailed as the first widely accepted modern house in conservative New England.

The history of the Gropius House begins when the German pioneer architect and creator of the Bauhaus arrived in 1937 in the United States to teach at Harvard University, where he was to redesign and modernize architectural education. In search of a house in the rural surroundings of Boston, Gropius and his wife, Ise, ended up renting a colonial house in the small town of Lincoln, half an hour's drive from the university. On trips in the area, Gropius became impressed with the local domestic architecture in adapting to the New England climate and resources. He began to see a basic kinship between their practical approach and clean unpretentious design and his own modern architecture. He later stated, "I made it a point to absorb those features of the New England architectural tradition that I found still alive and adequate."

Gropius's first commission in the United States was to be the modest house for his own family. Because Gropius lacked the funds to build the project, Henry Shepley, an architect on the Harvard Board of Overseers, persuaded a wealthy Lincoln landowner, Mrs. James Storrow, to commission what Gropius's TAC (The Architects Collaborative) partner, Norman Fletcher, later dubbed the first unequivocally modern house in New England. She allowed Gropius to select a site on her extensive property and provided the $18,000 for the construction of the house with the understanding that Gropius could first rent and later

Gropius House, Lincoln, Massachusetts, by Walter Gropius
© Roger Straus/Esto

Gropius House, Lincoln, Massachusetts, by Walter Gropius
© Wayne Andrews/Esto

buy the dwelling with its four acres of land from her over the years.

Gropius was eminently prepared to accept the offer. For a long time, certainly since 1925, when he designed the Bauhaus faculty houses and began planning the housing development Dessau-Törten in Germany, Gropius had thought much about domestic architecture, as evidenced in his essay, "The Small House of To-Day," published in *Architectural Forum* in March 1931. In this text he advanced his conception of a modern single dwelling, that it be of "light construction, full of bright daylight and sunlight, alterable, time-saving, economical" and that it be of the utmost use to its occupants. He also pointed to the availability of new materials and construction methods that would allow large expanses of glass. At great length, he enumerated the advantages of a flat roof.

His two-story house (2300 square feet) in the shape of a rectangle, with its broad sides north and south, sits on the crest of a small hill with a view to Mount Wachusett. Screened from the main road by a large apple orchard, it is carefully positioned to catch maximum sunlight in winter.

In 1938, the flat roof of the Gropius House caused one neighbor to derogatorily liken it to a chicken coop. Actually, it slants slightly toward the center (one-quarter inch per foot) for runoff of rain and melted snow into a drain that, running through

the house to prevent freezing, leads into a dry well. The most unconventional side of the house is its north facade. Coming from the driveway, the diagonal of a long marquee leads to the front entrance, which is protected from weather and street view by a large glass-block wall. The animated juxtaposition of contrasting materials is countered on the facade's other side with the sculptural twisting of a large spiral staircase. This leads to the second-floor roof terrace, where one finds a private entrance to a second-story bedroom area.

For the layout of the interior, Gropius had advocated in his 1931 article "no artificial symmetry, but free functional succession of room . . . clear separation living, sleeping and housekeeping parts of the house." The plan of the first floor generally conforms to this ideal. A large area (21 by 28 feet) is divided into a living room and dining room separated by a glass-block wall from the study.

On the south side, two large plate-glass windows (each 6 by 11.5 feet) and a tall, glass door provide glorious light for the dining and living rooms. The latter even has an additional plate-glass window on the west side; these large expanses of glass generate a constant awareness of the beautiful outside with its indigenous birds and other wildlife. From May to September, the south side is shaded with a large wooden screen that projects from the roof and is placed three feet away from the house to allow the rising hot air to escape.

The large west-side window deflects the sun by means of a heavy exterior aluminum blind that is operated from inside. The entrance hall leads straight through a pantry to the screened patio (11.5 by 23 feet and 9 feet high), which unconventionally juts out at right angles from the rear of the house.

Although the design of the house stands in sharp contrast to that of its colonial neighbors, its fieldstone foundation, retaining walls, most of its building materials, and basic structure are the same: light wood frame, sheathed with white-painted redwood siding, and a west-side fireplace wall of gray-painted bricks. Gropius used clapboards, the ubiquitous exterior siding in New England, vertically as inside wall cover in the hallways.

All the structural items and indoor features, such as doors, lighting fixtures, shelves, glass bricks, and even the exterior spiral staircase, were ordered from stock catalogs. According to his wife, Gropius "wanted to prove that the mass-produced output of American industry was quite capable of producing a sophisticated house of contemporary design" (see Gropius, 1989).

The use of these materials proved a useful object lesson for students of architecture. The builder recalled that almost every afternoon students from Harvard came out to look at the progress of the house, watching and listening to the architect discuss his reasons for using the materials that were inexpensive without sacrificing quality.

In 1974, the Society for the Preservation of New England Antiquities took over the governance the Gropius House and its furniture, a large portion of which was constructed in the Bauhaus, as its first modern historic artifact. In 1982, the building was depicted on a 20-cent U.S. postage stamp as part of the American Architecture series, which included Frank Lloyd Wright's Fallingwater.

ANNELIESE HARDING

Further Reading

Buck, Susan, "A Material Evaluation of the Gropius House: Planning to Preserve a Modern Masterpiece," *Association for Preservation Technology Bulletin*, 28/4 (1997)

Gittleman, Peter, "The Gropius House: Conception, Construction, and Commentary" (Master's thesis), Boston University, 1996

Gropius, Ise, "History of the Gropius House in Lincoln, Massachusetts," 1977; reprint, as "Trip to Epoch-Making Walter Gropius House, Lincoln, Massachusetts" *GA Houses*, 25 (March 1989)

Gropius, Walter, "The Small House of To-Day," *Architectural Forum*, 54 (March 1931)

"Gropius House," in *SPNEA Annual Report 1987*, Boston: Society for the Preservation of New England Antiquities, 1988

Summers, Nevin, "Analyzing the Gropius House as Energy-Conscious Design," *AIA Journal*, 66/2 (February 1977)

GROPIUS, WALTER 1883–1969

Architect, Germany and United States

Walter Gropius, émigré architect, whose International Style and social insight helped to define the aesthetics of the 20th century, would certainly grasp and give vital form to the 21st century were he alive to see it today. The strength of Gropius's vision was his humanistic ability to comprehend the essentials of the world in which he lived and to design the basic forms and metaphors that would give meaning to those essentials.

In the prewar Germany that Gropius inhabited for the first half of his life, Sigmund Freud, fellow intellectual émigré, had defined the essentials of human life as "work" and "love." In the contemporary milieu of Gropius's Bauhaus, one might make the analogy of Freud's theories of "work" to Gropius's theories of the machine and of Freud's "love" to Gropius' concepts of the house and housing. These essential elements of life were given architectural expression by Gropius in the factory and in the housing projects for workers, respectively. Gropius modeled the total environment for the common man, from the public place in which he toiled to the private place that he came home to. Thus, in the utopian new world of the decent factory environment and the humane housing for its workers, Gropius, too, expressed modern man's search for work and love.

Gropius has developed an almost mythic, monolithic reputation as founder of the German Bauhaus and functionalist architect of American high modernism, but in many ways he was a complex, contradictory man. For whereas he worked passionately for the causes of the proletariat, he conversely represented the dispassionate ideal of *die Neue Sachlichkeit* (The New Objectivity). Although he developed conceptual repetitive type forms for architecture, the quality of his own work was highly variable. Even Gropius had to have been cognizant that his early creativity was unmatched in his later life. He was a true believer moving through turbulent times, forced from his homeland and relentlessly driven by politics and war, and yet Gropius prevailed where others would have fallen to despondency. When the Bauhaus was closed by the Nazis, Gropius moved as a refugee from Germany, through Britain, and on to the United States, leaving buildings and theory behind as his legacy.

Although Gropius had been born in Berlin to a prominent intellectual and artistic family, he chose early to identify not with the privileged but with the common man, believing that he could build a better world through architecture. He was a visionary but also a clear thinker. Unlike many German architects of the early 20th century, Gropius was not seduced for long by impractical theories such as postwar Expressionism; he sought a concrete way to integrate his humanism and his art. If disillusionment with the old world of art, architecture, and societal inequity brought Gropius pain, he used this discontent as an impetus toward a new pragmatic idealism.

Gropius found his salvation in the machine. As he moved theoretically from the early utopianism of the 1910s into the realms of the practicable and buildable by the 1920s, his interests in factories and mass housing were already dominating his work. Gropius joined the Deutscher Werkbund and began his architectural career in the office of Germany's leading proponent of total industrial design, architect Peter Behrens, in whose office design objects ranged from typography to factory buildings. Gropius, too, would soon articulate the gospel of total design within the Bauhaus, the "building house," that was at once a school, a style, and a way of life.

The Bauhaus, originally established at the confluence of fine art and craft, under Gropius was refocused toward the synthesis of artistic design with machine production. For Gropius was a synthetic thinker, a multidisplinary agent, who felt that all the arts must be united under architecture. The world was changing with industrialization, and as Gropius understood that man might be either degraded or uplifted by mechanization, he chose to see man as master of the machine. Machine production, not *Handwerk*, was the way of the future to ensure that good design would reach the proletariat. The role of the architect, as the avant-garde of a new civilization, was to design the prototypes for the machine, and thus models of metal furniture, of light fixtures and tea sets, and of industrialized housing were drawn at the Bauhaus workshops. As director of the Bauhaus, Gropius's intention was to assemble artists and craftsmen under one roof, to end the class struggle of artist over craftsman. Together, this unified design school, expressing Gropius's tenet of "unity in diversity," worked toward the common goal of the creation of type forms, or models, for the modern world, for the machine was manufacturing the future.

Many of the masters whom Gropius appointed to direct the Bauhaus workshops themselves achieved major reputations in their fields, and quite of few of them followed Gropius's path to the United States: Marcel Breuer and Mies van der Rohe continue to be famous for furniture and architecture, Herbert Bayer for typography, Laszlo Moholy-Nagy for photography, and Wassily Kandinsky and Paul Klee for painting. As much a dynamic group leader as an architect, Gropius always surrounded himself by an artistic circle through which he simultaneously helped to advance and then relied on the creativity of a wide variety of colleagues. This creative group effort he called "work and teamwork." Later in his career, Gropius sought to continue this pattern of cooperative work in his architectural partnerships, in Britain with Maxwell Fry (1930s) and in the United States with Breuer (late 1930s to 1940s), later with TAC (The Architects Collaborative; late 1940s to 1960s), and at the Harvard University School of Design, where he was named director and professor of architecture after his immigration to America in 1937.

Had Gropius's Bauhaus career not been interrupted by the Nazi interference that forced his resignation in 1928, had he been able to carry on the work of the Bauhaus, one can only speculate on the heightened state that modern design would have reached. Had Gropius done no other work than the years he spent at the Bauhaus, had his oeuvre contained no other works than his designs for factories and the Dessau Bauhaus, he would be a famous architect even today. He did, however, push on, dedicating the latter half of his career to the design of housing and schools, working at the scales of architecture and urban planning. The early years of Gropius's career were spent coming to grips with the architecture of work, through factory and prototype design, and were highly charged symbolically and aesthetically. In later years, Gropius's aim was toward finding solutions to social problems and standardized housing, and thus aesthetics were deemphasized.

Certainly, Gropius's greatest period of architectural creativity and symbolism was his early factory aesthetic. He had foreseen man and machine in synergy, through a utopian vision of a mechanized world. Our contemporary interpretation of the machine has changed since Gropius's time, for the machine has since been put to devastating use in two world wars; however, there are those who today apply metaphors to the computer that were earlier reserved for the mechanical machine. Gropius went further than simple rhetoric in his time, inventing symbolic form

for the machine world through design prototypes and a series of factory designs.

The first and one of the most significant of these factories was Gropius's Fagus Werk (1911) at Alfeld-an-der-Leine. Here, Gropius designed the glass curtain wall that was to become so influential a theme throughout his career. In this building, glass is used in opposition to masonry, the glass wall at once dissolving and ever present, confirmed and reconfirmed via its gridded iron structure in a taut design. Thus, very early on Gropius was exploiting and refining the crude elements of the factory into an aesthetic comment on itself. The beauty of the factory and the machine was understood to be inherent within their own elemental forms.

The Model Factory for the Werkbund Exhibition (Cologne, 1914) shows Gropius exploring his vision of the factory, here in a theoretical setting. In this context, the factory is allowed to be expansive, to be divided into its functional parts, each function in a separate form, the array of interconnected parts influenced by Constructivism. Some of these buildings are glass, some are masonry, and some combine elements of both. The Model Factory is memorable for the variation in elegant geometric forms in a complex functional plan in which each part is a complete architectural composition in itself. Most outstanding are the powerful shapes of the triangular roof line of the machine hall and the cylindrical extruded-glass staircase.

Following the expansive design for the Werkbund Model Factory, Gropius designed an even looser Cubist, Constructivist composition for the defining work of his life, the Bauhaus (1925–26) in Dessau. Here, Gropius's glass curtain wall attains its greatest mastery in the workshop building, a giant crystalline vision of architecture, a worthy last link of the German theoretical *glässerne Kette*, the glass chain of architecture. In the Bauhaus, Gropius played the aesthetics of glass—its transparency, reflectivity, and dissolution—against architectural oppositions, no longer against masonry but now against the white stucco cube of high modernism. The Bauhaus in plan is dynamic, an asymmetrically counterbalanced composition. What makes the Bauhaus complex so endlessly fascinating is not only that it is one of the progenitors of the International Style but also that it is a many-layered symbolic form in itself. Formally, it is a machined building, functionally, a factory for design of machine prototypes; thus, the facade is a self-referential metaphor for the work that goes on within the structure.

With the Dessau Bauhaus complex, Gropius at last had the opportunity to design not only the working buildings but also the housing in a unified ensemble. He constructed living quarters for students, Bauhaus masters, and for himself, and these dwellings can be read as early models of his theories of mass housing in microcosm. In the Bauhaus complex, he was able to test the architectural theory that he was developing. Gropius was committed to designing the *Typisierung*, or type forms for a modern society: the *Wohnungstype*, or standardized apartment type, for the *Siedlung*, or mass housing project, based on his research into *Existenzminimum*, or minimum living standards.

Throughout his long career, Gropius applied his theoretical type forms, ranging from factories to housing to schools, in Germany, Britain, and the United States. In buildings for education, Gropius's influence continues to be felt in his type forms for modern school design in England and the United States: at Impington Village School (1936) in Cambridgeshire; in the

Harvard Graduate Center (1949) in Cambridge, Massachusetts; and in the numerous TAC (The Architects Collaborative) schools of the 1950s to 1960s throughout suburban New England. In housing, he is remembered internationally for major works, including the German Siemensstadt Siedlung (1929) in Berlin and Weissenhofsiedlung (1927) in Stuttgart, for his British project for Windsor Hill Flats (1935, unbuilt plans) in Windsor, and much later, while living in the United States, for Gropiusstadt (1955) at the Interbau Exhibition in Berlin, for which he was able to return to his homeland to see his early housing concepts again constructed and justified by time.

In Europe and in the United States, Gropius designed not only public housing but personal residences as well, and these works may be read as highly individual statements and memories of his emigration. The Director's House (1925) at the Dessau Bauhaus and the Gropius House (1937) in the Woods End Colony in Lincoln, Massachusetts, are important works for understanding Gropius. The houses that Gropius built for himself and his family show both a continuity of design and a contrast of meaning. In design, both are white, asymmetrical, volumetric boxes in which the ornament is inherent in the design: glass voids against flat, white, geometric facades articulated with factory elements. The German house, however, is a cool Cubist, abstract stucco, very polemical design, whereas the American house is a much quieter synthesis of the International Style white box with the America white wooden vernacular house. The houses, intensely personal statements, beckon us to interpret the man as well as the architecture. The first is a confrontation with modernism, the second more a reflective refuge. These two houses stand, with his Bauhaus and his factories, as Gropius's testament to a lifelong search for work and love.

LESLIE HUMM CORMIER

See also Bauhaus; Bauhaus, Dessau; Behrens, Peter (Germany); Breuer, Marcel (United States); Constructivism; Cubism; Deutscher Werkbund; Fagus Werk, Alfeld, Germany; Glass; Gropius House; International Style; International Style Exhibition, New York (1932); Mies van der Rohe, Ludwig (Germany); Werkbund Exhibition, Cologne (1914)

Biography

Born in Berlin, 18 May 1883; immigrated to England 1934; immigrated to the United States 1937; father Walter and great-uncle Martin were architects. Attended the Humanistisches Gymnasium, Berlin; studied at Technische Hochschule, Munich 1903–04; apprentice, Solf and Wichards, Berlin 1903–04; studied at Technische Hochschule, Charlottenburg, Berlin 1905–07; traveled Europe 1906–07. Married 1) Alma Schindler Mahler (widow of composer) 1916 (divorced): 1 child; married 2) Ise Frank 1923: 1 child. Served in German Army 1904–05, 1914–18. Chief assistant to Peter Behrens, Berlin 1907–10. Private practice, Berlin 1910–14; private practice, Berlin 1928–33; partnership with E. Maxwell Fry, London 1934–36; partnership with Marcel Breuer, Cambridge, Massachusetts 1937–41; founder and partner, TAC (The Architects' Collaborative), Cambridge from 1945. Director, Grand Ducal Academy of Arts and Grand Ducal Saxon School of Applied Arts, Weimar, Germany 1915–19 (schools merged in 1919 to become Das Staatliche Bauhaus); director, Bauhaus, Weimar 1919–25; director, with Ludwig Mies van der Rohe, Marcel Breur et al., Dessau 1925–28; professor of architecture 1937–52, chairman of Department of Architecture 1938–52, professor emeritus from 1952, Graduate School of Design, Harvard University, Cambridge. Founder, member, president 1928, vice president 1929–57, CIAM; vice president, Institute of Sociology, London 1937; honorary member, Royal Institute of British Architects, London 1937; honorary member, Royal Society of Arts, London 1946; fellow, Society of Industrial Artists and Designers, London 1950; fellow, American Institute of Architects 1954; honorary senator, Hochschule für Bildenden Künste, Berlin 1962; Honorary Royal Academician, London 1967; associate, National Academy of Design 1967; member, National Institute of Arts and Letters. Royal Gold Medal, Royal Institute of British Architects, London 1956; Grand Cross of Merit with Star, West Germany 1958; Gold Medal, American Institute of Architects 1959. Died in Boston, 5 July 1969.

Selected Works

Fagus Werk, Alfeld-an-der-Leine, Germany (with Adolf Meyer), 1911
Model Factory, Werkbund Exhibition, Cologne (with Meyer), 1914
Director's House, Bauhaus, Dessau, 1925
Bauhaus, Dessau, 1926
Weissenhofseidlung (two), Stuttgart, 1927
Dammerstock Housing, near Karlsruhe, Germany, 1928
Siemensstadt Siedlung, Berlin, 1929
Siemensstadt District, Berlin (supervising architect with Bartning, Fabat, Häring, Henning, and Scharoun), 1930
Apartments (unbuilt), St. Leonard's Hill, Windsor, Berkshire (with E. Maxwell Fry), 1935
Impington Village School, Cambridgeshire (with Fry), 1936
Gropius House, Lincoln, Massachusetts (with Marcel Breuer), 1937
Housing Development, New Kingston, Pennsylvania (with Breuer), 1941
Harvard University Graduate Center, Cambridge, Massachusetts (with TAC), 1949
Interbau Apartment, Berlin (with TAC), 1955

Selected Publications

Programm des staatlichen Bauhauses, 1919
Idee and Aufbau des staatlichen Bauhauses, 1923
Neue Arbeiten in Bauhauswekstätten (editor), 1925
Internationale Architektur, 1925
Bauhaus-bauten, 1928
The New Architecture and the Bauhaus, 1935
Bauhaus, 1919–1928 (with Herbert Bayer and Ise Gropius), 1938
Rebuilding Our Communities, 1945
Architecture and Design in the Age of Science, 1952
The Scope of the Total Architecture, 1955
Architektur: Wege zur optischen Kultur, 1956
Katsura: Tradition and Creation in Japanese Architecture (with Kenzo Tange and Y. Ishimoto), 1960
The Architects' Collaborative, 1945–1965 (editor), 1966
Vertical City, 1968
Apollo in the Democracy: The Cultural Obligation of the Architect, 1968

Further Reading

Cormier, Leslie Humm, "Walter Gropius, Emigré Architect: The Persistence of Typeforms," *Arris: Journal of the Southeast Society of Architectural Historians*, 4 (1993)

Nerdinger, Winfried (editor), *The Walter Gropius Archive: An Illustrated Catalogue of the Drawings, Prints, and Photographs in the Walter Gropius Archive at the Busch-Reisinger Museum, Harvard University*, 4 vols., New York: Garland, 1990

Wingler, Hans Maria, *Das Bauhaus, 1919–1933: Weimar, Dessau, Berlin*, Bramsche: Gebr. Rasch, 1962; 2nd revised edition, as *Das Bauhaus, 1919–1933: Weimar, Dessau, Berlin, und die Nachfolge in Chicago seit 1937*, Cologne: DuMont Schauberg, 1968; 2nd edition translated as *The Bauhaus: Weimar, Dessau, Berlin, Chicago*, translated by Wolfgang Jabs and Basil Gilbert, edited by Joseph Stein, Cambridge, Massachusetts: MIT Press, and London: Cambridge Press, 1969; 3rd revised edition, Cambridge, Massachusetts: MIT Press, 1976

GRUEN, VICTOR DAVID 1903–80

Architect, United States

Victor Gruen is best known for his large-scale enclosed shopping centers built in the 1950s, such as Northland Center (1954) in Detroit, Michigan. Although a number of other architects participated in the development of the modern shopping mall, notably John Graham, I. M. Pei, Welton Becket, and William Wurster, Gruen espoused a particularly compelling vision of the shopping center.

Instead of serving merely as a place to shop, Gruen proposed that the shopping center serve a new community center for suburban America, with places for recreation, commerce, and civic activity. Architecturally, his designs favored a slick commercial modernism, with asymmetrical plans, multiuse spaces, screen walls, and enlarged attic stories for signage. More significant than his career as a shopping center designer and developer was his lifelong interest in environmental planning and urban renewal. Gruen was deeply interested in creating new strategies for economic and social renewal for America's decaying urban centers. His strategy involved knocking down much of the existing urban fabric and building new, mall-like commercial and civic centers, such as Midtown Plaza (1962) in Rochester, New York. Extremely popular in the 1960s and 1970s, this approach to urban renewal, as practiced by Gruen and a number of other architects and planners, resulted in the destruction of countless historic city blocks, the displacement of innumerable residents, and in all too many cases a failure to produce the promised financial windfall for the host city. Regardless of the ultimate negative connotations of the rampant commercialism of the modern shopping mall or the failed social experiment of urban renewal, Gruen had a lasting effect on American architecture in the 20th century.

Born in Vienna, Austria, in 1903, Gruen attended the Architectural School and Academy of Fine Arts in Vienna. Following his formal education, he worked in the offices of architect and industrial designer Peter Behrens, whose office functioned through the 1920s as a training ground for architects and designers interested in modernism. Behrens was an early proponent of modernist design, and his work ranged from architecture to industrial designs for mass production. It is likely that Gruen's interest in total, environmental design (along with his long-standing commitment to modernist forms) was developed during this period. By 1933 Gruen had opened his own office in Vienna, where he worked as an architect and urban planner.

This phase of his career was brought to a halt by the advance of Adolf Hitler in 1938, an event that prompted Gruen to immigrate to the United States. Gruen worked in the office of industrial designer Norman Bel Geddes, who was responsible for the very popular Futurama pavilion at the 1939 World's Fair in New York City. In 1939 Gruen received his first architectural commission in the United States with the modernist storefront and interior of the Lederer Shop (1939) in New York City. In 1940, Gruen formed a partnership with Elsie Krummeck that lasted until 1948. By 1951, Gruen had settled in Los Angeles and opened his own practice as Victor Gruen Associates. From 1951 to 1980, Victor Gruen Associates was responsible for many commissions, ranging from shopping malls to large-scale urban-renewal projects. During this time, a number of architects worked in Gruen's office, most notably Cesar Pelli, whose Courthouse and Commons (1976) in Columbus, Indiana represents the logical extension of Gruen's earlier ideas of blending commercial space and civic activities. By the time of his death in 1980, Gruen's ideas had transformed the commercial and social landscape of America's cities and suburbs.

In the 1950s, Gruen recognized that people were unhappy with the increased traffic and decentralization that accompanied commercial strip development in the United States. In fleeing to the suburbs, Americans had left behind far more than congestion and crime—they had lost a sense of civic and social focus. Aware of the historic importance of public space, Gruen proposed that the modern shopping center could fulfill all the functions of the city centers of the past by creating a place for the inhabitants of suburbia to work, learn, socialize, and shop. Along with the economist Larry Smith, Gruen outlined this idea of the shopping center as town in his 1960 book *Shopping Towns USA: The Planning of Shopping Centers*. In it, Gruen recaps the work of shopping center designers in the 1950s by focusing on how he designed several of his own projects to function as a new suburban town center. He also offers advice to the shopping center developer, from financial issues to site planning and administration. All the examples rely on modernist forms with open airy plazas, atriums, and courts surrounded by ample spaces for parking and shopping. These projects underscore the importance of providing the visitor with an interesting environment that might include pedestrian streets, fountains, and public art. Although architecture figures prominently, the book also provides a backdrop for signs or a container for public spaces. The authors pay far more attention to the financial and practical concerns of building and operating a shopping center, echoing Gruen's interest in architecture and planning as an interdisciplinary and collaborative process among economists, investors, designers, and developers.

Among Gruen's many enclosed shopping centers, Detroit's Eastland Mall (1957) illustrates many of these concepts. Surrounded by a huge parking lot, the mall turns inward, isolating the pedestrian from the outside world. The visitor is met with a sprawling collection of horizontal blocks marked by enlarged attics and prominent signage. On entering the complex, screen walls protect the visitor from the outside world, and fountains and public sculpture (he convinced the developers of Eastland Mall to spend over $200,000 on public art) provide points of focus for the indoor streets and squares. In all, his shopping center designs took on the trappings of pedestrian cities, a theme

The Commons shopping center, Columbus, Indiana, designed by Victor Gruen
© Patrick Bennett/CORBIS

that he would take up in urban-planning projects of the 1960s and 1970s.

In looking back at his work from the end of the 20th century, it is all to easy to find fault with the large shopping centers that contributed to the paving of suburbia and the windswept remnants of vast urban-renewal schemes that failed to rejuvenate their urban sites. All too often, these grand renewal projects resulted in the demolition of entire city blocks and the creation of cold, sterile urban cores. However, it is important to realize that Gruen sincerely believed in the potential of pedestrian malls and modern architecture to rejuvenate America's cities and towns. He also practiced at a time when many architects, planners, economists, and designers actively sought a new vision of the city that swept aside the problems of the past. It has now become the challenge of architects and planners to explore other ways of reinvigorating the civic, social, and commercial vitality of cities and towns across the United States.

MATTHEW S. ROBINSON

See also **Pelli, Cesar (Argentina); Shopping Center; Wurster, William (United States)**

Selected Works

Lederer Shop, New York, New York, 1939
Northland Shopping Center, Detroit, Michigan, 1954

Southdale Shopping Center, Minneapolis, Minnesota, 1960
Midtown Plaza, Rochester, New York, 1962
The Commons, Columbus, Indiana, 1976 (Cesar Pelli with Gruen Associates)

Further Reading

The biography on Gruen is surprisingly thin, considering his relative importance to American architecture and urbanism in the later 20th century. He published three books, the first on shopping centers, the latter two on urban planning. His ideas held considerable currency in the 1960s and 1970s, and Gruen was an active commentator on major events in cities throughout the United States, writing a number of letters in the *New York Times*, among others.

"Architecture, sculpture; the Northland regional shopping center [Detroit, Michigan]," *Arts and Architecture*, 72 (May 1955)
"Northland; a new yardstick for shopping center planning," *Architectural Forum*, 100 (June 1954)
"Piazza, American Style: Courthouse Center and The Commons, Columbus, Indiana," *Progressive Architecture*, 57 (June 1976)
Gruen, Victor, *The Heart of Our Cities: The Urban Crisis: Diagnosis and Cure*, New York: Simon and Schuster, 1964
Gruen, Victor, *Centers for the Urban Environment*, New York: Simon and Schuster, 1964
Gruen, Victor, and Larry Smith, *Shopping Towns USA: The Planning of Shopping Centers*, New York: Reinhold Publishing Company (Progressive Architecture Library), 1960

GRUNDTVIG CHURCH, COPENHAGEN

Designed by Peder Vilhelm Jensen-Klint; completed 1940

The Grundtvig Church, one of Denmark's most impressive and monumental buildings, may be said to fulfill a number of roles as a sacred space, a memorial monument, and a national symbol. The church is one of the three largest in Denmark; it lies on a hillock in a small suburb of Copenhagen called Bispebjerg, surrounded by low tenement buildings planned to conform to the church and built largely in conjunction with it. Some of the architects designing the tenement houses had also been involved with the building of the church.

When designing Grundtvig Church, architect Peder Vilhelm Jensen-Klint (1853–1930) was inspired mainly by medieval Danish churches, such as Marie Kirke in Helsingör and Sankt Peder in Naestved. However, the inspiration resulted in something totally unique: a building that unites Danish formal tradition with an expressionistically dramatic flair. The church, built of light-yellow bricks, is broadly rectangular with three naves, side chapels, a chancel with a crypt, and a huge tower. The middle nave is slightly higher than the side ones, but not enough to provide a proper windowed clerestory. From the outside, only a low wall interrupts the roofing of the naves. Interior cross-ribbed vaults made external buttresses necessary, but they are of a slender and austere type without ornamentation. Narrow and rectangular windows end in slightly pointed arches.

Gables with vertical recesses provide the church with its main decorative motifs both on the side facades and on the tower. The latter is considered to be the most dramatic feature of the church, especially when viewed from the west. Striving energetically upward, the tower offers a severe stepped silhouette divided into three parts corresponding to the interior naves and with gable surfaces striated by recesses. The narrow, vertical recessing and the stepped gable are repeated in the low, shallow porch below. The slim recesses, partially whitewashed, emphasize the upward movement, as does the broad and relatively low portals. Seen from a distance, the western aspect of the tower brings a gigantic organ facade to mind. Within, the yellow brick appears again, used not only in the walls but also for some of the fixtures (e.g. in the pulpit designed by Jensen-Klint's son). The interior is otherwise ascetically bare, with no paintings, sculpture or ornamentation. Thus, aesthetically it makes an impression mainly through the effect of its building material and its proportions. The color was initially disliked by the public, but today this decision has not been regretted, as the nature of the material enhances the detached, severe character of the building.

The Grundtvig Church was built in 1921–40 by public subscription as a memorial to Nikolai Frederik Severin Grundtvig (1783–1872), a clergyman and politician whose influence on modern Danish mentality and society has been overwhelming. Grundtvig wrote songs and psalms that are still popular, and he was a champion for democracy. An important tool for this was the Danish folk high school movement initiated by Grundtvig to ensure that the general population would be given a chance to acquire the learning necessary for public rule. His patriotism influenced many of these establishments.

Jensen-Klint, the architect of the Grundtvig Church, shared Grundtvig's patriotic ideals and was an eager advocate for the study of traditional, national architecture. Jensen-Klint graduated as a building engineer in 1877, but he also attended the Royal Academy of Arts in Copenhagen where he studied painting. He was employed full time with the city engineering office in Copenhagen from 1890. At age 43, he received his first architectural commission for a town villa in Hellerup. From then on he intermittently worked as an architect, drawing mainly villas but eventually also five churches, following the ideals of the National Romantic movement. He was much troubled by the crisis in architecture, which he ascribed to the rift between contemporary and old traditional Danish architecture, where the former was inspired by foreign models. His patriotic take on architecture became an important inspiration to younger Danish architects in the beginning of the 20th century.

The issue of a monument over Grundtvig was introduced to the public when the sculptor Rasmus Bögebjerg exhibited a plaster statue of the bishop in Copenhagen in 1905. It was suggested that it should be cast in bronze and placed in a public location. A majority of Copenhagen's intellectuals rejected his work. Although the statue project was discarded, the idea of a monument had become rooted. Thus, an open competition was announced in 1912 and it received 32 projects, ranging from sculpture to architecture. Jensen-Klint, together with a friend, Ivar Bentsen, suggested a small memory hall with a square plan and a vault open to the skies.

The committee could not decide on a winner, so it ran the contest a second time in 1913. Jensen-Klint and Bentsen reworked and enlarged their original project, but Jensen-Klint also submitted a suggestion of his own: a huge tower. The sculptor Hansen-Jacobsen was awarded first prize and Jensen-Klint and Niel Bentsen second prize for the memorial hall. The statue was never realized, and a number of influential people had become enamored with Jensen-Klint's unrewarded majestic tower, and a committee was elected to promote and organize the building of the Grundtvig Memorial Church. It was decided that the tower would be erected first and that the rest of the church would be built as the economy allowed. A large fund-raising campaign was launched not only in Denmark but also in the United States, where there was much interest in the project. Eventually enough money was secured, but it took more than 20 years to complete the project because of a temporary lack of funding and because the building materials were handcrafted.

BRITT-INGER JOHANSSON

Further Reading

Hansen, Hanne, *Grundtvigskirkens bygmester* [The Building Master of the Grundtvig Church], Copenhagen: 1991

Jelsbak, Jens (editor), *Grundtvigs Kirke* [The Grundtvig Church], Copenhagen: 1977

Marstrand, Jacob, *Grundtviks Mindekirke paa Bispebjerg* [The Grundtvig Memorial Church at Bispebjerg], Copenhagen: 1932

Steen Petersen, Anne-Marie, *Som i ét stof: en fortaelling om Grundtvigskirken og dens bygmester* [As if Made of One Fabric: A Story about the Grundtvig Church and its Building Master], Copenhagen: Gyldendal, 1997

GUADET, JULIEN 1834–1908

Architect, France

Julien Guadet was admitted in 1853 to the Paris École des Beaux-Arts as a student in the atelier of Henri Labrouste and then in 1856 in that of Jules André. At the same time as he followed his studies, he entered in 1861 the *Agence des travaux* of the Paris Opera (the office supervising the construction of the Paris Opera) under the supervision of Charles Garnier. He was one of the principal leaders of the student revolt against the reform of the teaching at the Beaux-Arts provoked by E.E. Viollet-le-Duc in 1863. The following year, after winning the First Grand Prix, he left for Rome. On his return, he devoted almost all the rest of his life to his teaching and to the defense of the architectural profession, building very little: his two memorable achievements were the construction of the Central Post Office (1880–86) of Paris and the reconstruction of the Theatre Français (1900). He was named in 1871 head of the official atelier of Simon-Claude Constant-Dufeux, a position that he gave up in 1894, when the *Conseil supérieur* (managing council) of the École appointed him professor of theory of architecture, a position he held until his death. In this post, he was in charge of drawing up the programs for the school's competitive examinations, programs for which he endeavored to vary the themes, and to carefully draft them while at the same time remaining up to date. In addition, he was in charge of giving a weekly course.

It was the content of this course that Guadet wrote up in four volumes and published from 1901 to 1904, titled *Elements et Theorie de l'Architecture*. Stemming from the academic tradition (an institution that he defended all his life), Guadet was the first teacher holding the chair of architectural theory to have tried to give a theoretical presentation on the workings of the project and to have fixed in writing and theorized the system of eclecticism. We can thus look at the *Elements* as the eclectic reply of the writings of Viollet-le-Duc. Guadet's premise in the introduction to his course would not in fact have been denied by his renowned predecessor of 40 years earlier: "The object of this course is the study of the structure of edifices, their elements and as a whole, from the double point of view of art and of the adaptation to defined programs, to material necessities." He removed himself radically from this premise when, instead of a doctrine of principle, he begins from the hypothesis that there exists an open corpus of classic edifices that constitute the patrimony to be taught. He invited each person to draw freely, with common sense and intelligence, the models that would permit him to put together his proper program.

Guadet rejected the historicist approach, these "archeological styles" that he considered a servile copy, criticizing with the same contempt the Roman imitations of the first half of the 19th century as well as the Gothic imitations of Viollet-le-Duc and his followers. On the contrary, he rejoiced at the necessary adaptation of architecture to his programs always more varied and complex, leading to realizations that, in this upward and continuous movement constituting the essence of history, would become the classics of tomorrow. "Classic" to Guadet was that which is consecrated by custom, recapturing quite seriously a joke of his former patron Charles Garnier: "the classic is, to the architect, everything which is built."

This intuitive and experimental method of composition was acquired in the atelier, "the perfect instrument of artistic teaching," where the patron lavished counsel on his pupil. For Guadet, the atelier was the backbone of Beaux-Arts teaching, the school itself being content to teach "indisputable" subjects, such as construction, history, or legislation, teaching that the student could in the end do without.

Unfortunately, the demonstration is a little spoiled by the ambiguity of the approach, which oscillated endlessly between tradition and rupture, functionalism and classicism, symmetry and picturesque, and construction and decoration. Furthermore, the examples chosen convey a heavy classical culture, a lack of interest for the medieval, and finally, for the contemporary examples, mainly ethnocentric choices—Guadet was intimately convinced, like his contemporaries, that the only good architecture was French—and a relative lack of curiosity vis-à-vis new materials: iron was a utilitarian element, to be used inside to permit vast supporting structures, and concrete was simply not yet on the agenda.

Thus, the writings of Guadet are far from being revolutionary, as had been those in their time of Viollet-le-Duc. However, it is to his credit that he tried to instill the functionalist thought in the academic stronghold. He had considerable influence in his time, as much on French students as on foreigners. This influence may be translated in two fashions: either directly through the students who came in Paris (American students, principally from the East Coast, constituted at the turn of the 20th century a tenth of the contingent of the architectural section of the school) or indirectly through teaching put in place in the United States late in the 19th and early 20th centuries using the model of the École des Beaux-Arts. Thus, Louis I. Kahn learned these teaching methods through his professor, the Frenchman Paul Philippe Cret, who went to Philadelphia to teach architecture.

However, after World War I, the school resumed its courses, without the generation of students killed in the war, and no professor was capable of resuming the corpus of Guadet to bring it up to date. The Americans turned their back little by little on the French teaching system, increasingly formal and disconnected from architectural production, and the Beaux-Arts influence would be supplanted in the United States by that of the Bauhaus. One proof is that the translation of *Elements* that had been prepared by the architect Nathan Clifford Ricker (1843–1924), a teacher at the University of Illinois who was in fact formed by the German school of architecture, was never published. At the same time, Guadet's compilation, republished for the sixth time in 1929–30, was still read in France by students in the 1950s, by which time it had become a purely theoretical book.

MARIE-LAURE CROSNIER LECONTE

See also **Classicism**

Selected Publications

Éléments et théorie de l'architecture, cours professé à l'École nationale et spéciale des Beaux-arts, 1901–04
"Société centrale des architectes français, devoirs professionnels des architectes, rapport de la Commission des devoirs professionnels," *L'architecture* (27 April 1895)
"Étude sur la disposition et la construction du Colisée", *Moniteur architects*, 7–9/1 (1879)
"A l'École des beaux-arts, souvenirs de 1863," *Recueil du millième de la société des architects par le gouvernement* (1911)

Further Reading

Drexler, Arthur (editor), *The Architecture of the École des Beaux-Arts*, London: Secker and Warburg, 1977

Epron, Jean-Pierre, *Comprendre l'éclectisme*, Paris: Norma, 1997

Lucan, Jacques, "Da Guadet a Kahn: Il tema della stanza," *Casabella*, 50/520–521 (January/February 1986)

Lucan, Jacques, "Kahn et Guadet: La question de la pièce," *Moniteur d'architecture, AMC*, 30 (April 1992)

Middleton, Robin (editor), *The Beaux-Arts and Nineteeth-Century French Architecture*, London: Thames and Hudson, and Cambridge, Massachutes: MIT Press, 1982

O'Donnell, Thomas Edward, "The Ricker Manuscript Translations, I–IV: Guadet's 'Elements and Theory of Architecture,' vols. 1–4," *Pencil Points*, 7 (November 1926) and 8 (March 1927, May 1927, August 1927)

Vigato, Jean-Claude, *Histoire des architectoniques modernes, France, 1900–1940: Notes interrompues pour 6 quinze premières années (Decembre 1985)*, Villers-lès-Nancy, France: École d'Architecture de Nancy, 1986

GUEDES, JOAQUIM 1932–

Architect, Brazil

Joaquim Guedes's work is fundamental for understanding Brazilian architecture in the second half of the 20th century. Departing from the rationalism, or Brutalism, of the so-called *Escola Paulista* (São Paulo's school) in the 1950s, Guedes developed a unique response to the challenges of Brazilian modern architecture, one that is much closer to the local demands and tectonic responses. Guedes understands "architectural design as the art of building" (Camargo, 2000).

Born in 1932, the first of 15 siblings, Guedes graduated in 1954 from the university of São Paulo, where he was influenced by Le Corbusier's method (but not its formal solutions) and Aalto's materiality. Aalto would continue to be a strong reference in Guedes's works, as were his professors—pioneers of the *Escola Paulista*—Vilanova Artigas, Oswaldo Bratke, and Eduardo Knesse de Mello. With them, Guedes shares the belief in tectonics as a base for a coherent architecture.

Having the opportunity to work on all scales, from objects to renovations to hospitals to entire cities, Guedes is striking in his objectivity and rationality. Opposed to anything superfluous, Guedes has always criticized Brazilian modern architecture of the 1950s and 1960s for its exaggerated formalism. For him, the submission to social programs, technology, economy, and human activities is most important and comes before expressionism and personal creation.

Guedes's work is also outstanding for the rigorous detailing (not a stronghold of Brazilian Modernism), which pushes his work to a higher level. Rigor and detailing have been trademarks of Guedes as a professor also. Teaching at the School of Architecture of the University of São Paulo since 1958, Guedes has been a strong influence throughout the last 30 years. He also taught in Strasbourg (France) between 1970 and 1973. His incisive rational process can be summarized in his own words: "the more I doubt, inquire and criticize, the more I feel closer to knowledge and truth" (Camargo, 2000).

Working with his wife, Liliana, from 1954 to 1978, Guedes's architectural talent manifested itself very early on. He was only 24 years old when, in 1956, his entry for the Brasilia Plan competition broke up with the Charter of Athens. Still debated and studied today, his proposal for Brasilia presented a city based on quotidian experiences, able to grow and expand with the pace of Brazilian modernization and consequent urbanization.

In 1957 he designed the J. Guedes house (for his father) in a difficult site (30 by 150 ft) for a large family. In this house, the principles of his later work—rationality and tectonics—are already laid out. Shortly after the J. Guedes house (1958), he designed the Cunha Lima house, which made him famous and won the prize at the VII São Paulo Bienal. At the Cunha Lima house, the exposed reinforced concrete structure that was the trademark of the Paulista School is reinterpreted with emphasis on economy of means and maximization of spaces for social life. For Guedes, architecture has always been a rational and economic way to materialize spaces for the needs of society. In the Cunha Lima house, as is common in all his buildings, the structural solution is very important and the economy of columns increases the flexibility of interior spaces.

The same structural emphasis would occur in his own house (Liliana and Joaquim Guedes house, 1968), where the fantastic slabs continue outside the plan and work as a shading device. In this house, the outstanding detailing is fully harmonized with the overall plan, and the exposed reinforced concrete slabs are humanized by the wooden fenestration subordinated to the structure.

In the 1970s Guedes had the opportunity to design and build entire cities in the Brazilian backlands and the Amazon jungle. The cities of Carajás (1973), Marabá (1973), and Barcarena (1980) in the Amazonian state of Pará were designed as part of a major mining project for which Guedes worked from the beginning, influencing even the path of the railway that connects the project to the port, 400 miles away. Many hundreds of miles from the major cities of Belém and Brasília, the design of the new city plans included complex logistics of transportation and labor—a task for Guedes's rationality.

In the design and construction of the city of Caraíba (1976) in Bahia's backland, Guedes faced a completely different task. Caraíba is located in a very dry region of the Brazilian *sertão* (dry savana), where the challenge was to shade and protect it from the hot winds. Guedes solved this problem with little shaded spaces instead of large plazas, and a high respect for the traditional local way of building guided him toward very simple facades whose elegance adds a delicate touch to the hard life of the *sertanejos*.

Guedes's focus on economy instead of aesthetic expressionism guides him to think of the Brazilian slums, for instance, not as a problem but as a solution, because it reveals the amazing capacity that people have to build and overcome daily problems.

Structure, economy, rationality, and emphasis on quotidian life might be the major forces behind Guedes's architecture, but they are not enough to explain the strength of his major works. To those qualities we need to add the extremely developed sensibility of a humanist.

FERNANDO LARA

Selected Works

Guedes House, São Paulo, 1957
Cunha Lima house, São Paulo, 1958
Architect's own house, São Paulo, 1968
Plan of Carajás, Pará, 1973
Plan of Caraíba, Bahia, 1976
Plan of Barcarena, Pará, 1980

Further Reading

Bruand, Yves, *Arquitetura Contemporânea no Brasil*, São Paulo: Perspectiva, 1981

Camargo, Mônica J., *Joaquim Guedes*, São Paulo: Cosac e Naify, 2000

Lemos, Carlos A.C., *Arquitetura Brasileira*, Sao Paulo: Melhoramentos, 1979

Segawa, Hugo, "The Essentials of Brazilian Modernism," *Design Book Review*, 32/33 (1994)

GUGGENHEIM MUSEUM, BILBAO, SPAIN

Designed by Frank Gehry; completed 1997

Designed by Frank O. Gehry and Associates and completed in 1997, the Guggenheim Museum Bilbao in Bilbao, Spain was the fourth in the constellation of spaces that constituted the institution known as the Guggenheim Museum. The exuberantly curved titanium and limestone building is considered to be the finest of Gehry's career, an achievement to which all his subsequent work was compared.

The success of the Guggenheim Museum Bilbao established the reputation of the Solomon R. Guggenheim Foundation's director Thomas Krens as a visionary who redefined the relationship between a museum's collection and its public. By the late 1990s, Krens had extended the museum well beyond the spiraling ramp of its other signature building by Frank Lloyd Wright (Solomon R. Guggenheim Museum, 1959, New York, expanded in 1992 by Gwathmey Siegel and Associates). At the time it was built, the Bilbao Guggenheim was the most ambitious of the museum's new spaces. Other Guggenheim satellites included the Peggy Guggenheim Collection (built in the 18th century, renovated and expanded in 1995 by Leila and Massimo Vignelli) in Venice, the Deutsche Guggenheim Berlin (1997, Richard Gluckman) in Germany and the Guggenheim Hermitage in Las Vegas (Rem Koolhaas and the office for Metropolitan Architecture).

The Basque administration had originated the partnership with the Guggenheim as part of a commitment to revitalizing the industrial center of Bilbao, the fourth-largest city in Spain. The autonomous northern region of Spain was seeking to remake its public identity and the Guggenheim was intended to function as one of the means by which to redefine the physical space and remake the cultural economy of Bilbao. After considering and rejecting an idea to renovate a historic warehouse building, the Basque group held an invited competition for a waterfront site. Gehry, Coop Himmelb(l)au (Wolf Prix and Helmut Swiczinsky), and Isozaki were selected by Krens and asked to submit designs. Gehry's scheme was chosen for its strong iconic identity and sensitivity toward the site.

The museum joined a series of large-scale design projects that were intended to transform the city into an international cultural and financial hub. Other projects under construction in 2000

Guggenheim Museum Bilbao, by Frank Gehry, at Bilbao, Spain (1997)
© Johnson Architectural Images/GreatBuildings.com

Skycourt of the Guggenheim, Bilbao
© Dan Delgado *d2 Arch*

included an airport terminal and control tower by Santiago Calatrava, a subway system by Norman Foster, and a master plan for a waterfront by Cesar Pelli. The museum was financed and owned by the Basque administration and managed by a foundation comprised of members of the Guggenheim Foundation and the Basque administration.

The Guggenheim Museum Bilbao became a symbol of what could be architecturally accomplished with the intelligent application of computer modeling. The curved forms were made economically feasible through optimization of the forms and the use of computer data for calculating, manufacturing, and assembling all building elements, from structural steel to cladding. The use of titanium for exterior cladding material was one of the first such applications on a large building. The material was chosen for the mercurial liveliness of the finish, which would alternately take on the color of the river or the sky. Its durability and strength allowed the panels to be just 0.38 millimeters thick, thin enough for a slight pillowing effect to soften the appearance of the building.

The design of the building was acclaimed for its sensitive response to an urbanistically vital site. The 24,000-square-meter building sits 16 meters below the level of the city streets, a design move that served several purposes. The lowered entry level provided a powerful sequence, beginning with a public

plaza at street level on the south side of the building and descending a funnel-like stair to the entry. The sectional shift also reduced the overall massing of the building without sacrificing the high vertical space of the atrium. The Puente de La Salve, a major artery into the city, cuts through the site and is integrated into the massing of the building. The banks of the Nervion River define the northern limit of the site, developed as a waterfront plaza.

There was a powerfully moving quality of the museum's exterior presence and interior spaces. Gehry organized the building around an extremely vertical atrium rising 50 meters above the level of the river. It is crowned with a sculptural skylight whose whirling forms are variously compared to the image of Marilyn Monroe's billowing skirt (from the film *The Seven Year Itch*), an artichoke, or an opening flower (the architect's own description). Three levels of galleries connect to the atrium with catwalks and vertical circulation. A total of 11,000 square meters of exhibition space is distributed among 19 galleries. Limestone volumes contain traditional orthogonal exhibition rooms, and titanium-clad volumes define highly organic spaces that offer unusual proportions and dynamic lighting effects. The most spectacular of the galleries is "the boat," a temporary exhibition area with a clear span 30 meters wide and 130 meters long. Its volume stretches under the La Salve Bridge, connecting to the tower element on the other side of the bridge. Since its opening the Guggenheim has commissioned many pieces customized for the site, including *Snake* (1994–96, Richard Serra), *Installation for Bilbao* (1997, Jenny Holzer), and *Wall Drawing #831* (1997, Sol LeWitt).

The intense media attention focused on Bilbao has been unusually united in its praise of the building. Herbert Muschamp, chief architecture critic of the *New York Times*, called it "a miracle," and Ada Louise Huxtable, critic and architecture writer for the *Wall Street Journal*, called it "one of the most significant, as well as *the most beautiful, museums* in the world."

The highly sculptural forms of the Bilbao Guggenheim are not unique in Gehry's work. The skillful resolution of multiple forms can be found in small-scale work, such as Gehry's private house (1978) in Santa Monica, California, and the Winton Guest House (1987) in Wyzata Minnesota. Bilbao's sinuous curves were related to the office building Nationale-Nederlanden Building (1996) in Prague, Czech Republic, and the many fish-inspired forms that Gehry has executed, such as the Walker Art Center installation (1986). The museum also contained the experimental seeds for several large-scale Gehry buildings completed in the years after it: the Experience Music Project (2000) in Seattle, Washington; the Walt Disney Concert Hall (construction began in 1992, halted and restarted in 2000) in Los Angeles, California; and Millennium Park (2000) in Chicago.

RENEE CHANG

See also **Gehry, Frank (United States); Guggenheim Museum, New York**

Further Reading

Bruggen, Coosje van, *Frank O. Gehry: Guggenheim Museum Bilbao*, New York: Guggenheim Museum, 1998
Forster, Kurt Walter and Ralph Richter, *Frank O. Gehry: Guggenheim Bilbao Museoa*, Stuttgart and London: Edition Axel Menges, 1998

GUGGENHEIM MUSEUM, NEW YORK

Designed by Frank Lloyd Wright, completed 1959
New York, New York

The only museum designed by Frank Lloyd Wright, the Guggenheim was also his most time consuming commission. Formed in 1937, the Solomon R. Guggenheim Foundation was the source of the Museum of Non-Objective Painting, the original name of the institution. Located at 1070 Fifth Avenue, between East 88th and 89th Streets, Wright's museum is alternately viewed as his most kinetic structure, his most egregious expression of hubris, or as his magnum opus.

In 1927 Solomon Guggenheim met Baroness Hilla Rebay von Ehrenwiesen, a tireless advocate of abstraction in the visual arts, and in 1943, as his curator, she wrote the architect, asking whether he might be interested in creating "the dome of spirit," thus conceiving, at least in words, of the central idea of the building. Disagreement about location delayed the project from the start: Wright, unsympathetic as always to dense, urban sites, advocated a location in Riverdale, the Bronx, near the Spuyten Duyvil and overlooking the Hudson River. Guggenheim, however, persisted in his preference for a more central location, making the primary purchase of land on Fifth Avenue in 1944, although not until 1951 were the requisite parcels of land on Fifth Avenue assembled.

In response to the constrained site, Wright designed a vertical rather than horizontal form and by building upward created almost the antithesis to the Prairie style of his early career. The most plastic of his designs, the museum is a spiral, ballooning outward as it ascends and encloses a unitary space. Echoing this rotunda is a smaller volume, which he called the "monitor." Poured into curvilinear forms, the steel-reinforced concrete made possible the plasticity of the form and marked Wright's ultimate abandonment of post-and-lintel structure.

Not the sole instance of Wright's use of the spiral, the Guggenheim owes its form to numerous antecedents: its central rotunda is heir to the great domed central spaces in the ancient and early medieval worlds, such as the Pantheon (A.D. 128) in Rome, to which Wright himself compared the museum, and Santa Costanza (c. A.D. 350), also in Rome. Le Corbusier had developed an unbuilt scheme for a spiraled vertical museum. In 1924, Wright designed a domed planetarium for Gordon Strong in Sugarloaf Mountain, Maryland, in which a double helix of ramps, one for automobiles and a second, narrower, inner ring for pedestrians, wraps around the exterior of the form. Completed before the museum, the V.C. Morris Gift Shop (1950) in San Francisco exhibits a central coiled ramp. Similarly introverted schemes preceded the museum as well: the Larkin Building (1903, demolished) in Buffalo, New York; Unity Church (1908) in Oak Park, Illinois; and the S.C. Johnson and Son Administration Building (1936) in Racine, Wisconsin.

Earlier in his career, Wright had relied on the vertical core as an anchoring device, as in the fireplace and chimney core of the Frederick C. Robie House (1909) in Chicago and the vertical fieldstone core of the Edgar S. Kaufmann Sr., House (Fallingwater, 1936) in Bear Run, Pennsylvania. Wright's central and radical concept relied on the continuity of the spiral in combination with the service of an elevator. By claiming that the museum visitor would no longer need to retrace steps,

Wright further justified the form, which evolved through four versions. The first approximately eight-story volume, developed in 1943, comprised hexagonal tiers with level floors and a subordinate spiral for moving between levels. Clerestory windows with glass tubing as in the S.C. Johnson Administration Building would provide natural light. The next version derived, in Wright's own words, from the ancient Near Eastern ziggurat, with perpendicular outer walls clad in red marble. By the end of 1943 and early 1944, he inverted the ziggurat, thus creating the expanding spiral, and in the final phase of the development he inflated the volume somewhat and tilted the walls outward. Perhaps the most controversial aspect of the design, the tilted walls—deemed an appropriate form for the display of art by the architect, who felt that they would approximate salon easels—vexed museum curators and directors who adapted the eccentric conditions with a system of metal rods to hold the canvases vertically.

The position of the larger rotunda in relation to the smaller monitor varied, and in 1948 Wright reversed them, placing the rotunda at the south end of the block. By 1952 he developed a proposal for an annex, in which the patterned facade facing Fifth Avenue, in contrast to the smooth expanses of concrete of the gallery spaces, consisted of small squares further divided into smaller squares. Surrounding the monitor, a concrete balustrade, originally circular but executed as a contrasting rectangle, derived from those seen earlier in Fallingwater, and circular patterns, seen in the windows of the Avery Coonley Playhouse (1912) in Riverside, Illinois, define the mullion arcs of the monitor windows and the brass strips of the terrazzo flooring. As a secondary geometric element, the lozenge form of the fountain at the base of the spiral repeats most notably in the cornice of the monitor, grouped in pairs within semicircular arcs. Modified between 1954 and 1956, the skylight was originally pictured as a series of tangent concrete or stainless steel rings with an inner shell of coffering. Cost constraints, however, resulted in the subtraction of the inner shell and the addition of more prominent hairpin-shaped ribs supporting the glass. Although Wright wanted a fluid, continuous structure, structural vertical fin-like piers support the ramps.

In 1952 the building was renamed the Solomon R. Guggenheim Museum, and in the summer of 1956 construction began, supervised by William Short in collaboration with David Wheatley and Morton Delson. Jaroslav Joseph Polivka served as engineering consultant for the structural design, and Wright hoped in vain that he would be able to make the vertical fins that support the ramps unnecessary. John Ottenheimer designed the distinctive embossed exterior lettering, and the builder was George N. Cohen of the Euclid Construction Company.

Opened in 1959, Wright's last and posthumous work received several alterations, including the enclosure in 1974 of the driveway between the rotunda and monitor to contain the bookstore and cafe and the addition in 1978 by Richard Meier of the Aye Simon reading room off the rotunda. Envisioned as a second atrium with balconies and a skylight, the monitor had been closed to accommodate administrative offices. In 1992 the firm of Gwathmey Siegel and Associates began a comprehensive restoration of the building and the realization of an annex east of the monitor. Relating approximately in scale and pattern to the annex visible in a pencil-and-ink perspective by Wright from 1951, Gwathmey Siegel's ten-story tower, clad in gridded lime-

Guggenheim Museum, New York
© The Frank Lloyd Wright Foundation

stone, includes, in addition to offices, one single-height and three double-height galleries. Reopened as a gallery, the monitor contains a second spiraled ramp. Also accomplished were the installation of ultraviolet-filtering glass in the dome, the return of the café to East 88th Street, and restoration of the below-grade-level auditorium to contain its original seating configuration, balcony, and loft.

Whether viewed as among the noblest or as the most impositional of Wright's public spaces, the Solomon R. Guggenheim remains, like an uninvited but determined guest at a staid and exclusive dinner, Fifth Avenue's most defiant denizen.

PAUL GLASSMAN

See also **Corbusier, Le (Jeanneret, Charles-Édouard) (France); Fallingwater, Bear Run, Pennsylvania; Gwathmey, Charles, and Robert Siegel (United States); Meier, Richard (United States); Museum; Robie House, Chicago; Unity Temple, Oak Park, Illinois; Wright, Frank Lloyd (United States)**

Further Reading

Although there is a vast number of sources on the building, Neil Levine's analysis is perhaps the most thorough in addressing its formal, spatial, and structural aspects.

Gill, Brendan, *Many Masks: A Life of Frank Lloyd Wright*, New York: Putnam, 1987; London: Heinemann, 1988
Jordy, William H., *The Impact of European Modernism in the Mid–Twentieth Century*, Garden City, New York: Doubleday, 1972
Levine, Neil, *The Architecture of Frank Lloyd Wright*, Princeton, New Jersey: Princeton University Press, 1996
McCarter, Robert, *Frank Lloyd Wright*, London: Phaidon, 1997
Scully, Vincent, *Frank Lloyd Wright*, New York: Braziller, and London: Mayflower, 1960
Stern, Robert A.M., Thomas Mellins, and David Fishman, *New York 1960: Architecture and Urbanism between the Second World War and the Bicentennial*, New York: Monacelli Press, 1995; 2nd edition, 1997
Wright, Frank Lloyd, *Frank Lloyd Wright, the Guggenheim Correspondence*, compiled by Bruce Brooks Pfeiffer, Fresno: Press at California State University, 1986

GULLICHSEN, KRISTIAN 1932–

Architect, Finland

Practicing for over 40 years, Kristian Gullichsen is one of a few surviving second-generation modernists in Finland today. As a student in the 1950s, he worked as an intern in the offices of

Alvar Aalto and Heikki and Kaija Siren. These two firms were the most significant players on the Finnish architecture scene at that time, winning between them most of the architectural competitions.

Gullichsen's designs demonstrate his interest in the work of Le Corbusier and range from a mass-produced vacation house prototype of minimalist elegance and simplicity (Module 225, designed with Pallasmaa, 1969) to a singular, primitive stone house at Grasse, France for his mother (1972). In the case of the Module 225, the debt is to Le Corbusier's modular steel system, and in the latter, to the French architect's filtering of Mediterranean building themes such as masonry walls, vaults, and cylindrical towers. The Module 225 system is a brilliant prefabricated wood column-and-beam structure, approximately eight-foot square, with infilling panels, designed for assembly on any site. It is also evidence of structural discipline, an important ethical theme in Finnish architecture of the 1960s. The house at Grasse, on the other hand, is site specific, built into a hill of stone terraces with olive trees. Composed of repetitive bays like the Module 225, the stone house opens and closes itself to the sun with sliding barn doors.

Other housing designed by the firm—Gullichsen Kairamo Vormala—explores remarkably different themes of lightness, transparency, and wall as light membrane. This appears to be the influence of Erkki Kairamo, whose semidetached houses and apartment blocks in the suburb of Espoo, built from 1971–90, reveal De Stijl–inspired planar compositions. Sliding screens, circular stairs, glass skins, and tiled surfaces enliven and give scale to the facades.

Linking the two types of housing production is an interest in proportion and number, likely passed on to them by the revered Helsinki University of Technology teacher Aulis Blomstedt. These and other design themes emerge in the buildings done for industry. One finds in such works as the Varkaus Paper Mill (1985) and Marimekko Textile Factory (Helsinki, 1978) a celebration of structure, function (smoke stacks, ducts, and fire escapes), and durable industrial materials.

The firm's exquisitely proportioned and detailed industrial complexes find parallel in an urbane project for Helsinki's shopping district: an addition to the Stockmann Department Store (1989). Together Gullichsen, Kairamo, and Vormala reinterpreted two significant features of Aalto's nearby downtown work: the internal atrium of Aalto's Academic Bookstore and the repetitive square-bay facade of his Enso-Gutzeit Office Building (1962). The focal point of the Stockmann addition is an irregularly shaped atrium topped with a domed skylight. Externally, taut glass block screens supported by stainless steel frames stretch between stone columns, creating a rich, layered facade for the lower floors.

When approaching religious or civic architecture, Gullichsen returns to the theme of the wall. It is a hallmark of three fine works, characterizing his brick Malmi Church (Helsinki, 1980), reminiscent of Scandinavian medieval churches with walled courtyards, and of the late churches of Sigurd Lewerentz), the Kauniainen Parish Center (Kauniainen, Finland, 1983), and Pieksamaki Civic Center (Pieksamaki, Finland, 1989). Gullichsen's skill as a site designer emerges in his response to an urban condition, a hillside, and a lakefront park respectively. In each case, an entry court establishes the procession into the building, adjusting the scale of the experience from the outside to the inside. The moves are those of a skilled planner, well versed in both Aalto and Le Corbusier, in the free plan and the enclosed room. References to ancient and modern ways of inhabiting the landscape comfortably coexist in these buildings. The grounded hearth and the light-studded ceiling are both present. It is also the fusion of the vernacular and international in Gullichsen's work that gives it, and the best of Scandinavian architecture, resonance beyond the Nordic countries.

KATE NESBITT

See also **Aalto, Alvar (Finland); Blomstedt, Aulis (Finland); Corbusier, Le (Jeanneret, Charles-Édouard) (France); Lewerentz, Sigurd (Sweden); Pallasmaa, Juhani (Finland); Siren, Heikki and Kaija (Finland)**

Biography

Born 29 September 1932 in Helsinki; studied architecture at Helsinki University of Technology (1951–60). Upon graduation worked briefly with Alvar Aalto, then opened his own practice in Helsinki, 1961. Mentors included, in addition to Aalto, such major mid-century Finnish architects and theorists as Aulis Blomstedt and Reima Pietilä. Head of the Exhibitions Office of the Museum of Finnish Architecture, Helsinki, (1965–67); later became State Artist Professor of Finland (1988–93). Taught at Helsinki University of Technology, 1961–69; founded a partnership with two younger architects from HUT, Erkki Kairamo (1936–1994) and Timo Vormala (b.1942) in 1973. Recipient of the State Award for Architecture (1978), honorary doctorate (1986), the State Chair in the Arts (1988–93), the Urban Environment Award (1989), and the Concrete Construction Award (1990). Gullichsen continues to practice with Vormala in Helsinki.

Selected Works

Module 225, designed with Pallasmaa, 1969
Stone house, Grasse France, 1972
Marimekko Textile Factory, Helsinki, 1978
Varkaus Paper Mill, Helsinki, 1985
Stockmann Department Store addition, Helsinki, 1989
Malmi Church, Helsinki, 1980
Kauniainen Parish Center, Kauniainen, Finland, 1983
Pieksamaki Civic Center, Pieksamaki, Finland, 1989

Selected Publications

"Villa Mairea: private residence for the Gullichsen family, Finland," *Living Architecture*, 15, 1997
Gullichsen/Kairamo/Vormala (Current Architecture Catalogues) Barcelona: Editorial Gustavo Gili, S.A., 1990. (Spanish and English; translation: Santiago Castan)

Further Reading

There are two monographs on Gullichsen and his partners, one of which recently appeared. The Gili monograph on Gullichsen and his partners is comprehensive and well illustrated, fully translated, and includes descriptive texts by Gullichsen and an introduction by Colin St. John Wilson. The other books on Finnish architecture also include some of his work. Issues of the Finnish journal *Arkkitehti* too numerous to mention feature his work and/or the work of the firm, sometimes with texts by Gullichsen. Gullichsen has written several articles on Alvar

Aalto, of which one is mentioned below. All works are in English except as noted.

Brandolini, Sebastiano, *Kristian Gullichsen, Erkki Kairamo, Timo Vormala: Architecture, 1969–2000*, Milan: Skira, 2000

Brandolini, Sebastiano, Kristian Gullichsen, and Silvia Milesi, "Opere recenti in Finlandia di Gullichsen Kairamo Vormala," *Casabella*, 53/562 (November 1989)

Gullichsen, Kristian, *Gullichsen/Kairamo/Vormala* (bilingual English-Spanish edition), Barcelona: Gili, 1990

Gullichsen, Kristian, "Villa Mairea: Private Residence for the Gullichsen Family, Finland," *Living Architecture*, 15 (1997)

Korvenmaa, Pekka (editor), *Arkkitehdin Työ: Suomen arkkitehtiliitto, 1892–1992: Finlands Arkitektförbund Arkitektens Arbete*, Helsinki: Suomane Arkkitehtiliitto, and Rakennustieto Oy, 1992; as *The Work of Architects: The Finnish Association of Architects, 1892–1992*, translated by Jüri Kokkonen, Helsinki: Finnish Association of Architects, and the Finnish Building Center, 1992

Norri, Marja-Riitta, and Peter Davey, *Arkkitehtuurin Nykyhetki: 7 Näkökulmaa; An Architectural Present: 7 Approaches* (exhib. cat.); (bilingual English-Finnish edition), Helsinki: Museum of Finnish Architecture, 1990 (includes an interview with the architect)

Poole, Scott, *The New Finnish Architecture*, New York: Rizzoli, 1992

"Profile: Works of Kristian Gullichsen," *Architecture and Urbanism*, 2/209 (February 1988)

Quantrill, Malcolm, *Finnish Architecture and the Modernist Tradition*, London and New York: E and FN Spon, 1995

GÜREL FAMILY SUMMER RESIDENCE, ÇANAKKALE, TURKEY

Designed by Sedat Gürel; completed 1971

The Çanakkale region on the southwestern Aegean coast of Turkey has a mild climate with abundant sunshine, making it attractive to tourists. Its traditional architecture is akin to other Mediterranean styles and consists of cubic, whitewashed stone buildings with flat roofs, usually clustered together in the landscape. Most houses retain the same design characteristics but today are usually constructed of brick with a wooden roof structure covered with terra-cotta tiles. The room sizes and structural spaces are usually modest, with several rooms joined around more public spaces. Turkish houses have many built-in elements, such as alcoves (*eyvan*), shelves, and niches, and *sofas*, or raised seating platforms, are often placed in the living rooms. Screened windows help modulate the bright sunlight, as do vine-covered trellises in shaded courtyards. The functional vernacular architecture reflects both the climatic and the social environment.

The summer residence of the Gürel family was completed in 1971. The late Sedat Gürel and his wife, Guzin, had spent many vacations in the region and wanted a house of their own to which they could invite family and friends. They appreciated the climate, the area (which hosts several historic and archaeological places), and the site, which overlooks the sea. Sedat Gürel, a professor of architecture at the University of Istanbul, studied the climate, ecology, and construction techniques of the area before embarking on the design in 1968 and commencing the construction a year later. The house had to accommodate the extended family, providing spaces for interaction yet privacy for individuals.

The site covers an area of about 1000 square meters, sloping down to the beach, and lies along a road parallel to the water.

The house, more accurately described as a complex of seven single-story units consisting of living and sleeping spaces, is strung along different courtyards resembling a small village. The units relate spatially to the boundary stone wall running roughly north to south with the water's edge to the west.

A clearing to the north marks the entrance and car parking area. Along the edge of the parking area, perpendicular to the wall, is a narrow building that houses storage areas and a small bedroom and bathroom used by staff. Adjacent to it on the other side is the family courtyard, flanked by two units built for Guzim Gürel's sister and family. The one to the west has four bedrooms, and the one to the south contains the common living areas. The courtyard, which does not have a view to the sea, becomes a secluded and shaded family living and cooking area—an outdoor room. A fourth unit to the south of this grouping consists of a double bedroom and bathroom intended for Sedat Gürel's parents. Placing the parents in this central position was seen as the spiritual and physical bond of the complex as well as a sign of respect for the elder generation. (Since the death of the parents, it has become the guest room.) A grouping of another three buildings for the Gürel family itself surrounds another east-facing courtyard adjacent to the boundary wall. Two of the units contain sleeping quarters, and the third has the living, dining, and kitchen functions. A south-facing deck of the living area overlooks the water, which can be reached by a meandering paved pathway.

The elegant placement of the buildings in the landscape, leaving free the seashore and using the stone boundary wall as a datum, gives the almost random arrangement a structural order that is evident in both plan and elevation. The high wall with its row of planted trees also insulates the compound from noise and street traffic. The juxtaposition of units successfully gives the inhabitants privacy yet provides several communal areas, courtyards, and patios that enable the family members and guests to gather. The arrangement allows people to come and go as they like without disturbing the others and works remarkably well.

The sea, sky, trees, and rocky earth have been incorporated into the design, and the architect left the natural rocky landscape with its pine, olive, and oak trees in its undisturbed state. The relationship between built form and the earth's texture is exemplary. The arrangement of the buildings with their balconies, courtyards, and patios help funnel breezes through the site, and stone stairways built into the rocks lead down to the sea through the trees.

The buildings are constructed on strip foundations and floors of local brick with load-bearing in-fill plastered brick walls. Roughly applied whitewash covers the exteriors. The wood beams and gently sloping roofs are covered with handmade tiles, as are the floors. A local carpenter made the timber ceilings and shuttered windows as well as the simple furniture. A number of niches, storage areas, and seats of concrete and brick form an integral part of the rooms and courtyard spaces.

The cost of the 126-square-meter residence, excluding land, was around TL 103,000 (U.S. $7,250), or TL 816 (U.S. $57) per square meter on completion in 1971, a figure that was lower than for other traditional buildings in the area. Maintenance costs are very low as well, and because the residence is used only in the summer, there are no heating costs, although there are

Exterior of Gürel Family Summer Residence, by Sedat Gürel
Photo by Reha Gunay © Aga Khan Trust for Culture

fireplaces if needed. The lime whitewash has to be reapplied every two to three years.

All the family members and guests seem to be very satisfied with this retreat. In 1989, the residence was brought to national and international attention when it won an Aga Khan Award for Architecture. In awarding the prize, the master jury noted that the project was "sensitive, competent, intelligent, and unpretentious . . . where landscape and building are of equal importance. It has desegregated the functions of living . . . with humane and calm decision."

The building complex has a spiritual dimension that has little to do with either religion or regionalism but rather with the fundamental relationship of human beings to the earth and to the deep structures of human consciousness. The essence of such buildings, also seen in the work of Hassan Fathy and Geoffrey Bawa, lies in their poetic quality and their ability to allow the users to commune between the physical experience of nature and leaps of imagination. The Gürel summer residence remains in harmony with nature around it. Its timeless simplicity continues to demonstrate its importance as an exemplary work of contemporary vernacular architecture.

HASAN-UDDIN KHAN

Further Reading

"The Aga Khan Award for Architecture 1989 Winners," *Mimar*, 33 (December 1989)

al-Radi, Selma, "Gürel Summer Residence," in *Architecture for Islamic Societies Today*, edited by James Steele, London and New York: Academy Editions, 1994

GWATHMEY, CHARLES 1938– AND ROBERT SIEGEL 1939–

Architects, United States

Many critics see the architecture of Charles Gwathmey and Robert Siegel as a continuation of the modernist aesthetic developed in the 1920s and 1930s. Gwathmey's architecture belies the influence of Louis Kahn, who taught Gwathmey at the University of Pennsylvania. Siegel's work was influenced by William Breger, Sibyl Moholy-Nagy, and Aldo van Eyck. Their work compares favorably to the early ideas of Le Corbusier, especially that of the free plan and the free facade.

One of Gwathmey's early works represents a model of his mature architecture, the Robert Gwathmey Residence and Studio (1965). Sited in Amagansett on Long Island, New York, the house and associated studio are clad in tongue-and-groove cedar plank. The choice of materials reflects the context of the house on the beach and recalls the shingle-style architecture of the 1890s. The house is designed on a modular grid. Gwathmey manipulated the system to create curved spaces and volumes that are contrary to the cube's rigid geometry. Staircases are indicated on the exterior by curved walls. A portion of the roof is sloped to give added complexity to the building's form. The house reveals Gwathmey's ability to sculpt space, either adding or subtracting volume from the cube.

Gwathmey Siegel used the grid in their early residential work as a design tool for the articulation of form. The building's site (access, orientation, and topography) determines aspect of form as well. Gwathmey Siegel selected a range of materials both modern and vernacular. For example, the cedar siding on the Gwathmey Residence has modern planar qualities, but it is also a traditional building material on Long Island.

In 1970 the architects designed Whig Hall at Princeton University, which had been gutted by fire. The university wanted to preserve the remaining walls of the building and also desired 10,000 square feet of programmed space in a building that originally held 7,000 square feet. Gwathmey Siegel developed free-form interior volumes masked by the original Classical Revival facade. Major program elements included a conference room, a debating area, a 250-seat multipurpose space, and work areas. Blank interior walls were used to create discrete and private spaces. The curved exterior wall gave the building its sense of space.

Gwathmey Siegel's new thoughts about space and walls were evident after the completion of the Dunaway Apartment (1970;

New York City). Here the architects used curved walls and color to create their signature volumes of space within a renovated space. A heavy column was used in the center of the apartment to make the modular system evident to the casual observer.

According to Philip Johnson, the Elia Bash House (1973) in Clifton, New Jersey, is the prototypical Gwathmey Siegel house. The building differs from the Le Corbusian modern idiom in that it is slab-on-ground construction; there are no *pilotis*, and the form is based on an exact cube rather than a horizontal orientation. The decorative elements are cuts and flourishes to the cube, and the cube itself is gouged. The composition focuses on the grid anchored by a singular, defined column.

In the Cogan Residence (1972; Easthampton, New York), scale is used as an ordering device primarily to relate the interior and exterior masses. Cabinetwork and color are used to articulate the interior space. The grid structures and defines their design through the repetition of elements, most notably columns. Relying on a stylistic reference to the work of Le Corbusier, the architects employed a ramp as the major vertical transportation element.

Gwathmey's house on Amagansett was important in gaining critical recognition for his architecture and the work he would later complete with Siegel. In 1969, the Conference of Architects for the Study of the Environment (CASE) held a meeting at the Museum of Modern Art in New York City. The conference

Wick Alumni Center, University of Nebraska (1985)
Photo © Mary Ann Sullivan

ultimately led to the selection of five architects to exhibit at the Museum as a New York school. Charles Gwathmey was one of the group know as the New York Five.

Gwathmey Siegel has also completed many major public works, including the addition to the Solomon R. Guggenheim Museum in Manhattan; the Museum of Contemporary Art in North Miami, Florida; the Science, Industry and Business Library of the New York Public Library in New York City, and university commissions from Princeton, Cornell, and Columbia University.

The work of Gwathmey and Siegel has not seen a school of followers. However, sensitivity to site and materials is consistent with other practitioners of late 20th-century design. An attempt to work within the modernist aesthetic divorced from its socialist agenda is important in the legacy of these two architects.

JILL MARIE LORD

Biographies

Charles Gwathmey

Born June 1938, Charlotte, North Carolina. Attended University of Pennsylvania School of Architecture, 1956–1959, B. Arch; Yale University, 1962, M.Arch. Received The William Wirt Winchester Fellowship as the outstanding graduate from Yale University and a Fulbright Grant. Awarded Brunner Prize from the American Academy of Arts and Letters 1970; Yale Alumni Arts Award from the Yale School of Architecture 1985; Lifetime Achievement Medal in Visual Arts from Guild Hall Academy of Arts in 1988. Elected to the American Academy of Arts and Letters 1976. Served as President of the Board of Trustees for The Institute of Architecture and Urban Studies 1981. Elected as a Fellow of the American Institute of Architects in 1981. Taught at Pratt Institute, Cooper Union for the Advancement of Science and Art, Princeton University, Columbia University, the University of Texas, and the University of California at Los Angeles 1965–1991. He was Davenport professor and Bishop Professor (1991) at Yale, and the Eliot Noyes Visiting Professor at Harvard University (1985).

Robert Siegel

Born New York City 1939. Awarded B. Arch from Pratt Institute, 1962; M.Arch from Harvard University 1963. Organized the Pratt Institute Student Intern Program with the Gwathmey Siegel office 1963. Awarded Pratt Institute Centennial Alumni

Award in Architecture 1988. Elected Fellow of the American Institute of Architects 1991. In 1983 The New York Chapter of the American Institute of Architects awarded the firm, Gwathmey Siegel Associates, the Medal of Honor. In 1990 Charles Gwathmey and Robert Siegel won a Lifetime Achievement Award from the New York Society of Architects.

Selected Works

Gwathmey Residence and Studio, Long Island, New York, 1965
Whig Hall (renovation), Princeton University, New Jersey, 1970
Dunaway Apartment (interior), New York, 1970
Elia Bash House, Clifton, New Jersey, 1973
Cogan House, East Hampton, New York, 1972
State University of New York, College at Purchase, Dormitory, Dining, and Student Union, Purchase, New York, 1972
State University of New York, College at Purchase, Service Building and Heating Plant, Purchase, New York, 1972
Cornell University, College of Agricultural and Life Sciences, Ithaca, New York, 1981
De Menil Residence, Easthampton, New York, 1983
Wick Alumni Center, University of Nebraska, Lincoln, 1985
American Museum of the Moving Image, Astoria, New York, 1988
Solomon R. Guggenheim Museum (addition), New York City, 1992
New York Public Library (Science, Industry and Business Library), New York City, 1996
The City University of New York, Graduate Center, New York City, 1999
David Geffen Foundation Building, Beverly Hills, California, 2000
International Center of Photography, New York City, 2001

Selected Publications

"Gwathmey Siegel and Associates, Architects 1987–1991," (with Charles K. Gandee), special issue, *Architecture + Urbanism* (April 1989)

Further Reading

Abercrombie, Stanley, *Gwathmey Siegel*, New York: Whitney Library of Design, and London: Granada, 1981
Arnell, Peter, and Ted Bickford (editors), *Charles Gwathmey and Robert Siegel: Buildings and Projects, 1964–1984*, New York: Harper and Row, 1984
Breslow, Kay, and Paul Breslow, *Charles Gwathmey and Robert Siegel: Residential Works, 1966–1977*, New York: Architectural Book, 1977
Collins, Brad, and Diane Kasprowicz (editors), *Gwathmey Siegel: Buildings and Projects, 1982–1992*, New York: Rizzoli, 1993
Five Architects: Eisenman, Graves, Gwathmey, Hejduk, Meier, New York: Wittenborn, 1972
Mulgrave, Victoria, *Gwathmey Siegel and Associates Architects: Selected and Current Works*, Images, The Master Architec Series III 1998

H

HABITAT 1967, MONTREAL

Designed by Moshe Safdie; completed 1967

Constructed of an assemblage of prefabricated modular units, Habitat '67 was an experimental, single-family housing prototype built in conjunction with the 1967 World Exhibition in Montreal. One of the most publicized and controversial buildings of Expo '67, Habitat immediately attracted the attention of both the local and international public and the architectural profession.

Israeli-born architect Moshe Safdie first developed the concept in his fifth-year graduate thesis, "A Three-Dimensional Modular Building System," at McGill University's School of Architecture in 1960–61. The project was intended as a model of inexpensive, high-density housing in urban centers to accommodate escalating postwar populations. To counter urban sprawl and provide an alternative to apartment blocks, Safdie proposed three prototype building systems that utilized cellular, prefabricated components produced by mechanization to reduce materials and labor costs. Inspired by Le Corbusier's sketches for "Immeubles Villas" (1922), in which dwellings were vertically stacked in a checkerboard pattern with gardens in the voids, Safdie's "houses in the sky" combined various terraced permutations to ideally create a complete community environment. The vertical structure was designed to incorporate commercial, cultural, and educational facilities for up to 5,000 residents.

After graduation, Safdie apprenticed with Van Ginkel and Associates in Montreal (1961–62) and then worked with architect Louis Kahn in Philadelphia (1962–63). In 1963, Sandy Van Ginkel, then director of planning for the World Exhibition slated for Canada's 1967 centennial, asked Safdie to return to Montreal to assist on Expo's master plan. Safdie agreed with a condition that he be given the chance to realize his housing project. Named "Habitat '67," the visionary concept for universal housing aptly suited the exhibition's theme, "Man and His World." In 1964, Safdie resigned from the planning of Expo to work exclusively on Habitat for the Canadian Corporation for the 1967 World Exhibition as client. To design the project, he gathered a team of mostly young McGill architecture graduates, with two of the most important contributors coming from

Kahn's office: architect Dave Rinehart and structural consultant August Komendant. Peter Barott represented the associated firm of David, Barott, Boulva, Architects.

Funding the construction of Habitat '67 proved difficult until the federal government's Central Mortgage and Housing Corporation (CMHC) agreed to provide $11.5 million for a dramatically scaled-down version of the complex. The estimated $42 million original Phase 1 scheme called for a 22-story complex housing up to 1,200 units, supported on giant inclined A-frames containing stairs and elevators. The as-built project consisted of a structurally revised 12-story building of 158 units, without a planned community school or the commercial and office facilities.

Overlooking the Saint Lawrence River and the Expo islands, Habitat '67 was built on Mackay Pier in Montreal's port area, about a mile from the downtown area. The 354 reinforced-concrete components for the rectangular apartment "boxes" and primary structural elements were manufactured at the site and then finished on an assembly-line basis. Although elements such as fiberglass bathrooms and assembled kitchens were separately prefabricated as well, other decorative functional and structural elements had to be executed in the traditional manner. Weighing 70 to 90 tons, the completed units were hoisted into place by crane and stacked into three irregular ziggurats. The resulting clustered design generated by the construction process resembled ancient European and Middle Eastern hillside towns.

On the recommendation of Komendant, the concrete modular boxes became load bearing as well as space enclosing and formed an integrated three-dimensional structural grid with horizontal pedestrian corridor units and vertical service cores containing elevator and stair shafts. By assembling the modules in various combinations, 15 dwelling types were created, producing one- to four-bedroom apartments of one to two levels that ranged in size from 600 to 1,700 square feet. The varied and projecting arrangement of the completed complex offered apartments with privacy, vistas of the river and city, ample sunlight, and a garden balcony formed by the roof of the unit below. The interior pedestrian streets held common spaces, including children's play areas on the fifth and ninth floors. Outside the building, pedestrian circulation was kept separate from vehicle access roads and underground parking.

Habitat 1967, Montreal Expo, designed by Moshe Safdie
© GreatBuildings.com

Yet Habitat '67 turned out to be an expensive proposition as an alternative model to factory-produced housing and fell short in several of its primary objectives. The openness of its staggered box forms reduced the building's resident-to-land-area ratio from high to medium density. Even if Habitat had been built as a 22-story complex as intended, it is still debatable whether it would have been economically feasible as low-cost, affordable housing. After Expo '67, the rents charged by the CMHC to recoup costs put Habitat into the luxury housing range, and no private developers came forward as was hoped to construct additional phases of the complex.

After the completion of Habitat '67, Safdie continued to experiment into the 1970s with similar housing systems using geometric forms for the modules other than rectangular. These uncompleted projects include a student union housing complex in San Francisco (1968) and multiple housing in Washington, D.C. (1968), New York City (1969), Jerusalem (1970), Rochester, New York (1971), San Juan, Puerto Rico (1972), and Tehran, Iran (1978). One of the major problems hindering the general acceptance of these housing prototypes, according to Safdie, was the inability of the building industry to develop the extensive mass-production capabilities needed to refine the system and make it affordable.

Despite its inherent shortcomings, Habitat '67 is still internationally known and greatly admired as a landmark housing complex. By creatively combining prefabricated factory-produced components with a historic vernacular housing type of hillside villages, Habitat embodied a utopian vision of designing a humanistic, universal housing alternative to standardized slab apartment towers. Since the 1970s, the occupancy rate of Habitat has remained very high, and the relatively intact building underwent a $1.6 million upgrade in 1988–91 paid by its current tenant cooperative owners.

MICHÈLE PICARD

See also **Corbusier, Le (Jeanneret, Charles-Édouard) (France); Expo 1967, Montreal; Kahn, Louis (United States); Safdie, Moshe (Canada, Israel)**

Further Reading

Komendant, August E., "Post-Mortem on Habitat," *Progressive Architecture* 49 (1968)

Murray, Irena Zantovska (editor), *Moshe Safdie: Buildings and Projects, 1967–1992*, Montreal and Buffalo, New York: McGill-Queen's University Press, 1996

Newman, Oscar, "Habitat '67: A Critique," *The Canadian Architect* 9, no. 10 (1964)

Interior of Habitat 1967, Montreal Expo
© GreatBuildings.com

Safdie, Moshe, *Beyond Habitat*, Cambridge, Massachusetts: MIT Press, 1970.
Safdie, Moshe, "Habitat at 25," *Architectural Record* 180, no. 7 (1992)

HADID, ZAHA M. 1950–

Architect, Iraq

Zaha M. Hadid was transformed from an unknown architect into an international presence when she won the prestigious competition for the Hong Kong Peak Club in 1983. In addition, this victory helped to establish deconstruction as a viable style of architecture. Although the project was canceled for financial reasons, Hadid used the momentum generated by her unexpected triumph to build a strong reputation and remain in the international arena. This was quite a feat for the Iraqi architect, as her first building, Vitra Fire Station (Weil-am-Rheim, Germany), was not completed until 1993. The power and quality of the deconstructive designs produced throughout her career are impressive, and they have brought her international renown.

Hadid's success was demonstrated early when she was awarded the Architectural Association (AA) in London Diploma Prize in 1977. Her deconstructivist designs, composed of dynamic forms and presented in elaborate renderings, are critically acclaimed and influential. For example, her paintings of the Peak Club project have become icons for architectural students. However, by 1999, after more than 20 years of professional practice, Hadid had entered numerous competitions, completed many projects, designed some furniture and a few decorative objects, and realized fewer than ten buildings.

Quality, not quantity, is the foundation of Hadid's reputation. Her fourth-year student project, Malevich's Tektonik (1976–77), and her fifth-year student design thesis, "Museums of the Nineteenth Century" (1977–78), are composed of the regular geometric forms of modernism that are arranged like Suprematist and Constructivist compositions. Although Hadid has maintained this method of composition, in her deconstructivist designs she combines orthogonal forms with curves, rhomboids, and parallelograms. This was a slow change that was evidenced first in her Dutch Parliament Extension (1978–79) for Rem Koolhaas's Office of Metropolitan Architecture and firmly established in her project for 59 Eaton Place (1981–82); it has since become her signature style.

Hadid produces innovative, aesthetic, and functional buildings, whether they remain on paper (Al Wahda Sports Center, 1988, Abu Dhabi) or are constructed (IBA Housing, 1986–93, Berlin). She has won important international competitions, such as those for the Cardiff Bay Opera House (1994–96) in Cardiff and the Contemporary Arts Center (1998–) in Cincinnati.

The Contemporary Arts Center is Hadid's first building in the United States, and it serves as an excellent example of architectural design at the end of the 20th century. On the other hand, Hadid's design for the Cardiff Bay Opera House will not be realized, and it stands for much that is wrong with the state of the profession. Despite having won two separate competitions for the Opera House commission, one open and one invitational, the project has been taken away from Hadid. Although perhaps disputed, the official explanation is that her design was unfavorably received. Hadid believes that the general public and the Opera House Trust officials, who were laypersons and not architects, reacted negatively to her design because they could not read her drawings. In her presentation drawings, Hadid depicts a structure at different angles and in different stages instead of the traditional method of giving a single view, such as an elevation. It is true that they can be difficult to read, but challenging drawings do not automatically represent bad buildings, as Hadid's designs for the Opera House and the Contemporary Arts Center illustrate.

Throughout her career, Hadid has produced high-caliber, innovative work. At the beginning of her career, she helped to establish deconstruction as a credible style of architecture. Unlike many other deconstructivist architects, such as Daniel Libeskind and Peter Eisenman, Hadid is interested in an architecture that is primarily formal rather than theoretical. At the dawn of the 21st century, Hadid embodies what facets of the profession should be left in the past and what facets offer potential in the future.

LORETTA LORANCE

Vitra Fire Station, Weil-am-Rheim, Germany (1993)
© Dan Delgado *d2 Arch*

Vitra Fire Station, Weil-am-Rheim, Germany (1993), detail
© Dan Delgado *d2 Arch*

See also **Deconstructivism; Eisenman, Peter (United States); Koolhaas, Rem (Netherlands)**

Biography

Born in Baghdad, Iraq, 31 October 1950. Attended the American University, Beirut. Studied under Rem Koolhaas, Architectural Association, London 1972–77. Unit master, Architectural Association, London 1977–87; worked in the Office of Metropolitan Architecture, founded by Rem Koolhaas, London; private practice, London from 1979. Professor, Architectural Association, London 1980–87; visiting professor, Harvard University, Cambridge, Massachusetts, and Columbia University, New York 1986, 1987; Kenzo Tange Chair, Graduate School of Design, Harvard University; Sullivan Chair, School of Architecture, University of Illinois, Chicago 1997; guest professor, Hochschule für Bildenden Künste, Hamburg 1997. Member, School Council, Architectural Association, London; member, Master Jury, Aga Khan Awards for Architecture 1998.

Selected Works

Dutch Parliament Buildings (additions), The Hague, 1979
Irish Ambassador's Residence, Eaton Place, London, 1981
Peak Club (first prize, competition; unbuilt), Kowloon, Hong Kong, 1983
Office Building (first prize, competition), Kurfürstendamm, Berlin, 1983
Al Wahda Sports Center (unbuilt), Abu Dhabi, 1988
Vitra Fire Station, Weil-am-Rhein, Germany (with Patrik Schumacher), 1993
IBA Social Housing, Berlin, 1993

Cardiff Bay Opera House (first prize, competition), Cardiff, 1996
Contemporary Arts Center (first prize, competition), Cincinnati,
    1998–

Selected Publications

"The Dead Zone," *Architectural Design* (July/August 1991)

HAJ TERMINAL, JEDDAH AIRPORT, SAUDI ARABIA

Designed by Skidmore, Owings and Merrill; completed
1981

The Haj Terminal, opened in 1981 at King Abdul Aziz Airport,
12 miles north of Jeddah, Saudi Arabia, is among the most
spectacular airport terminals in the world. The name of the
terminal refers to its use by Muslim pilgrims who come to
Mecca, 45 miles distant. Architects and engineers working for
Skidmore, Owings and Merrill's offices in New York and Chicago conceived it in 1976 after taking into account technical and
material considerations, wedded to those of climate, suitability to
an unusual variety of users, and exceptional traffic patterns. It
adapts modern architectural principles of monochromatic simplicity, relationship to engineering, and temperature control to
the specific site and culture without adding details evocative of
ancient times.

Mecca, Mohammed's birthplace, is the focus of a vast annual
Muslim pilgrimage, the Haj, during a roughly six-week period
including the month of Dul-i-hija. Pilgrims arrive from all over
the world to worship at the mosque surrounding the Ka'aba
shrine. Each pious Muslim hopes to make this journey at least
once, and more than a million individuals come by air for this
purpose each year. The time limits of the designated season cause
a rapid influx of passengers at the airport and rapid departure.
The normally used terminal spaces designed in the 1960s by the
firm of Edward Durell Stone could not accommodate this traffic,
making a separate terminal necessary. Worshipers of every climatic and cultural origin must be able to use the same terminal
space, whether they be robed, lightly clad, or dressed in business
suits. Many have never experienced air conditioning. The building had to be flexible enough to accommodate the pilgrims'
different cultural and personal habits.

Consequently, the arrangements at the Haj Terminal are unlike those at Western airports, which are designed to hold passengers for brief periods and are outfitted with shops, fast-food
restaurants, club and conference rooms, and bars. The usual
international traveler tolerates artificial climate control and never

Each tent unit consists of a double-curvature tensile surface that rises conically to a tension ring
Photo by Reha Gunay © Aga Khan Award for Architecture

Haj terminal, designed by Gordon Bunshaft of Skidmore, Owings and Merrill (1971)
© Photo courtesy Skidmore, Owings and Merrill

sees merchandise displayed on the floor or hung from an informal apparatus, as is done at the Haj Terminal.

The designers at Skidmore, Owings and Merrill avoided air conditioning, lest people unaccustomed to it become uncomfortable or ill. Nevertheless, the building had to be habitable despite the hot, dry climate in which the temperature reaches 130 degrees Fahrenheit. They proposed a set of ten modular spaces, expandable by ten more identical modules. Raul de Armas, a design partner, suggested concrete umbrellas to cover the modules, but an anticipated shortage of concrete and potential interference with ground-level facilities prompted a change of material to fabric structure, an idea proposed by design partner Roy O. Allen. Noncombustible glass fiber coated with fluorocarbon resin (Teflon) had become commercially available by 1973. The engineering firm of Geiger-Berger, which had built the United States Pavilion at the Osaka World's Fair of 1970, made computer analyses of the structural design of the Haj Terminal. Fazlur Khan—Skidmore, Owings and Merrill's chief structural engineer and partner in the Chicago office—directed the engineering of the Haj Terminal, while Gordon Bunshaft, design partner in the New York office, supervised the design.

Familiar with cable-hung tent construction, Khan understood that the innovative coated fabric reflects sunlight back into the air instead of allowing it to heat the area below the tent.

Using this material kept the temperature in the pilgrims' waiting area at a tolerable level in the mid-80s. Warm air under the tents rises to the exterior through a vent at the top center of each tent, where the tent pole penetrates the fabric. The movement of hot air upward from the reflective roof also creates air currents around the construction.

The tents are constructed on modules of 150 by 150 feet. Each of the ten units is 450 by 1,050 feet, dimensions related to the length of the Immigration Procedures building. Only that two-story building (that houses customs and passport controllers) is artificially cooled; its length is a multiple of the length of bays needed to accommodate Boeing 747 airplanes and the buses parked beside the aircraft that transport pilgrims to Mecca. Under each tent, kiosks and toilet modules provide for the passengers' needs. The tent-covered terminal is flexible and the structure unobtrusive because fabric-covered tents require less massive support than do many other roofing materials. Here, the supports are slender cylinders of epoxy-painted steel columns rising about 150 feet from concrete footings underneath the terminal's floor. The columns taper from over eight feet in diameter at the base to just over three feet at the top and contain roof drains and lighting equipment. The tents' reflective underside bounces illumination from up-lights used at night; they are mounted on four pylons in each bay. Each tent is stretched and formed in a semiconical form by 32 radial steel cables attached to a steel tension ring about 13 feet in diameter. Corrosion-preventive material covers the cables, making the large roof units possible. The raised tension ring rises about 40 feet higher than the base of the tent cloth, creating a semiconical shape. The fabric is not straight sided as a cone would be but has a double curvature that ensures stability under varied wind loads. Double-pylon portal frames separate the tents and guard against collapse of the whole if one fails. Satisfactory air quality is ensured by mechanical fan towers in the pylons and elsewhere.

The building is not overtly Islamic or Saudi in its aesthetic references. It is an example of the modernist marriage of aesthetics with function that, although ostensibly superseded by Postmodern reminiscent design at the time, nevertheless responds sensitively to local climatic and religious needs. Universally admired, it has won the Aga Khan Award for innovative modern Islamic architecture.

CAROL HERSELLE KRINSKY

See also **Airport and Aviation Building; Bunshaft, Gordon (United States); Jeddah, Saudi Arabia; Skidmore, Owings and Merrill (United States)**

Further Reading

Chadirji, Rifat, *Concepts and Influences: Towards a Regionalized International Architecture*, London: KPI, 1986

Expressions of Islam in Buildings: Exploiting Architecture in Islamic Cultures, Geneva: Aga Khan Trust for Culture, 1991

Krinsky, Carol Herselle, *Gordon Bunshaft of Skidmore, Owings and Merrill*, New York: Architectural History Foundation, and Cambridge, Massachusetts: MIT Press, 1988

Nanji, Azim A. (editor), *Building for Tomorrow: The Aga Khan Award for Architecture*, London: Academy Editions, 1994

Steele, James, *Architecture for a Changing World: The Aga Kahn Award for Architecture*, London: Academy Editions, 1992

HAMLIN, TALBOT FAULKNER 1889–1956

Architect and architectural historian, United States

Trained as an architect, Talbot Hamlin became an important critic and architectural historian during the first half of the 20th century. Hamlin thought of architecture as an "art for all men" and wrote numerous books about the history and practice of American architecture from this point of view. He also left a legacy for architectural scholars through his creation of the Avery Index to Architectural Periodicals.

Hamlin wanted both the American public and architectural professionals to appreciate and develop an understanding of American architecture. In this vein, he wrote several books that are accessible to both the seasoned professional and the novice. For example, *The American Spirit of Architecture* (1926) is a heavily illustrated text that is organized chronologically with the United States divided into regions and periods. The chapters each have a brief introduction, usually consisting of a page or two of text, followed by a series of illustrations with lengthy, descriptive captions placing the architecture in its appropriate historical context. The concern in this text is to allow the reader to see the visual history of American architecture.

In *Forms and Functions of Twentieth Century Architecture* (1952), Hamlin attempted to write a "theory book" that incorporated the knowledge of structural methods and new problems and their solutions that had developed during the 1930s, 1940s, and 1950s. The four-volume series is divided into three categories: elements of architecture, principles of architecture, and building types. The book was intended to provide architects with examples of modern architecture but did not prescribe or advocate a particular style.

Greek Revival Architecture in America (1944) and *Benjamin Henry Latrobe* (1956) are Hamlin's most scholarly books. They are thoroughly researched and include footnotes and bibliographic references. *Greek Revival Architecture in America* argues that the Greek and associated classical revivals are not merely stylistic revivals but rather a distinct representation of the newly formed United States. His biography of Benjamin Henry Latrobe, considered by many to be the first professional architect practicing in the United States, is his most important book and remains the only major work on this seminal figure. The biography includes selected letters written by Latrobe and is a well-researched text. Hamlin won the Pulitzer Prize for biography in 1956 for *Benjamin Henry Latrobe*.

During his lifetime, Hamlin's works were well received; today, however, most of his books are out of print. His accessible approach to architecture has been rendered out of date by the successive developments in architectural scholarship during the second half of the 20th century.

In addition to his many books, Hamlin developed the Avery Index to Architectural Periodicals. During his tenure as librarian of the Avery Architectural Library at Columbia University, Hamlin began to index the architectural periodicals received by the library. He began the systematic indexing that became the Avery Index to Architectural Periodicals. Maintained originally as a card file, this standard bibliographic tool has been published in two editions (1963 and 1973) with 13 annual supplements published through 1993. In 1979, the Avery Index became the first special database in the Research Libraries Information Network (RLIN) and through this network has been available to scholars internationally. The Avery Index is considered the best resource for architectural articles and is used by historians and researchers all over the world.

Hamlin graduated from Horace Mann School and received a bachelor of arts degree from Amherst College in 1910. He received a bachelor of architecture from Columbia University in 1914 and was hired as an instructor and lecturer on the history and theory of architecture at Columbia University's School of Architecture from 1916 to 1947. He became a professor in 1947 and professor emeritus in 1954. While an instructor at Columbia, Hamlin served as librarian of the Avery Architectural Library from 1935 to 1945. He also served as the librarian of the Fine Arts Library during the same time period. He was the first librarian at Columbia to solicit drawings from active architectural firms.

JILL MARIE LORD

Biography

Born in New York, 16 June 1889; son of A.D.F. Hamlin, architectural historian. Attended Columbia University School of Architecture, New York 1910–14; traveled Europe 1914. Worked for Murphy and McGill, New York 1915–21; partner, Murphy and McGill 1921–34. Avery Architecture Librarian, Columbia University from 1934; began the *Avery Index to Architectural Periodicals;* full professor of architecture, Columbia University 1946–56. Fellow of the American Institute of Architects and an honorary associate of the New York Historical Society. Served on the architectural committee of the Museum of Modern Art, New York. Died in Beaufort, South Carolina, 16 August 1956.

Selected Publications

The Enjoyment of Architecture, 1916; revised edition, as *Architecture, an Art for All Men*, 1947
The American Spirit in Architecture, 1926
House Plan Books Prior to 1890 in the Avery Library, 1938
Some European Architectural Libraries, 1939
Architecture through the Ages, 1940; revised edition, 1953
Greek Revival Architecture in America, 1944
Forms and Functions of Twentieth Century Architecture (editor), 4 vols., 1952
Benjamin Henry Latrobe, 1955

HÄRING, HUGO 1882–1958

Architect, Germany

A significant contributor to the discourse surrounding modern architecture, Hugo Häring built relatively few of his designs over the course of his architectural career. This was due to several factors, chief among them the context in which he found himself—Germany during the years prior to, during, and following World War I. Although the buildings that Häring realized are key examples of a significant, if somewhat marginalized, strain of Modern architecture, it is his writings and theoretical pronouncements that constitute his greatest legacy.

Becoming a key member of Germany's art and architectural avant-garde immediately following World War I, Häring and his contemporaries—a generation of architects that included, among others, the Taut brothers, Erich Mendelsohn, Hans Scharoun, Hans Poelzig, Ludwig Mies van der Rohe, Hermann Finsterlin, Walter Gropius, and Le Corbusier—articulated the manifold aspirations of modern architecture. Häring's vision, what Peter Blundell-Jones refers to as "constructed organicism," sought a spiritual dimension in architecture, asserting the dual significance of *Gestalt* and *Geist*. *Gestalt*, a term that denotes "form imbued with meaning or significance" (Blundell-Jones), and *Geist* (Spirit in the sense of "the organizing force of mind") are concepts he emphasized repeatedly in his writings. Häring's ideas and focus on program as the generator of architectural form were distinct from the *Typsierung* (standardization, normative form) advocated by many of his peers (Hannes Meyer, Walter Gropius, and Ludwig Hi(l)berseimer among them). Two essays in particular, "Strukturprob(l)eme des Bauens" (Structural Problems of Buildings) of 1931 (rev. 1946), a tract that looks at the underlying orders of building, and "Über des Geheimnis der Gestalt" (Concerning the Secret or Mystery of *Gestalt*), his last complete essay, frame his essential thoughts on architecture. However, these essays are supplemented by his building designs and collected writings, all of which are critical in comprehending

the nuances of his ideas. Shared by many of the architects collected around the *Arbeitsrat, Novembergruppe,* and *Der Ring,* Häring's ideas trace their origins to the early writings of Goethe, writings that stand as the seminal works of German Romanticism. Also embedded in Häring's conceptual apparatus are ideas closely associated with German nature mysticism, a theological perspective that undergirds German Romanticism. The embrace of these ideas—formulated through repeated attempts to clarify and distinguish his positions from his contemporaries—became more apparent as Häring's architectural career progressed.

Häring was born in Biberach, a town south of Stuttgart, on 22 May 1882. Like most of his colleagues, who would come of age immediately after World War I, Häring was born into a world that was becoming more open and more standardized. Germany, a country that had lagged economically behind much of Western Europe, experienced an infusion of new ideas and new influences immediately following Bismarck's successful unification of the northern and southern halves of the German state. Häring's father was a highly respected cabinetmaker who maintained a workshop on the premises of his family home. Not accidentally, Häring exhibited a decided preference for the use of wood and handcraft detail throughout the course of his career.

After completing high school, Häring enrolled in a formal course of study, entering the architectural program at the Technische Hochschule in Stuttgart in 1899. At the time, design studies were very conservative, with various historical styles (Gothic, Classical, and early Renaissance) representing the range of architectural styles permitted within the academy. For many of Germany's architects at the time, *Baukunst* (the art of building) reigned as the ideal, and students were subsequently taught the mechanics of building in construction courses, statics and structures, and geometry. Freehand drawing was also taught, although the use of individual artistic expression was restricted. Häring evidently reacted to the insistent pedantry and limitations imposed by his faculty, disdaining from using the word *Architektur* throughout his career. Yet the impact of the terms associated with *Baukunst*, as distinct from the academically burdened *Architektur*, cannot be underestimated, either; *Baukunst*, with its emphasis on structural systems, new technologies and materials, and vernacular building, provided the foundation for departure from academic rules and principles. Open-minded architects, Häring among them, used the term to signal their departure from academic tradition.

After a brief foray to Dresden just after the turn of the century, Häring returned to Stuttgart and began to study under one of Germany's earliest advocates of Modern architecture, the German architect Theodor Fischer. Although Fischer's progressive curriculum encouraged students to study the accepted classical idiom, it was from a critical perspective. Embracing the concept of *Baukunst*, he also suggested that his students endeavor to look at vernacular precedents, such as farms and industrial buildings. Along with his students, Fischer's research into vernacular architecture enabled him to formulate a concern for the circumstances of context, organization, and function, an approach that would have a profound impact on the development of "the organic Modernist tradition" (Blundell-Jones). Fischer's promotion of alternatives to the academic tradition in turn suggested that architects probe technological development and social change in their search for the meaning and significance of architecture.

During the early years of his architectural practice, from roughly 1904 to 1914, Häring, like many progressively minded architects of his generation, struggled to obtain work. Neoclassicism remained the accepted mode in both the academy and professional practice, and the persistent resort to tradition by most of Europe's established architects and their clients, however derivative and tired, was broken only by the catastrophe of World War I. For most young architects, the war served to sideline the activities of practice, which up to that time had been taken up by failed competition submissions and limited professional exposure. Although already in his 30s, Häring was called to duty, serving as a soldier for a year before finally being tapped for service as an architect in East Prussia. Situated within a contested and heavily damaged area of Germany caught between Russian, Polish, and German claims, large parts of East Prussia (now in northern Poland) were in need of rebuilding, if only to further Germany's assertion of ownership.

Completing his tour of duty in 1918, Häring remained in the Balkans until 1921, executing significant private commissions in Gross Plauen and Neu-Ulm. With his marriage to the German actress Emilia Unda, Häring moved to Berlin, where he developed an interest in theater and film—both significant aspects of Weimar culture—while also becoming acquainted with the energies and ideas of Berlin's cultural elite throughout the 1920s. Häring's association with members of Germany's architectural avant-garde, many of them relocated to Berlin after the war, developed quickly. Of particular note is Häring's friendship with Mies van der Rohe, who by then had established his own office that he offered to share with Häring. The arrangement, which lasted from 1923 to 1926, was beneficial to both architects, who traded ideas and worked on projects together. During these years, Mies and Häring's atelier became the "nerve center" of *Der Ring*, an association of artists and architects who shared a progressive, utopist vision of architecture. Members were drawn from both the *Arbeitsrat für Kunst* and the more radical *Novembergruppe* (an international organization that included Russians, Hungarians, and members of the Dutch De Stijl); an abbreviated list of participants included Bruno and Max Taut, Walter Gropius, Wassily Luckhardt, Hans Poelzig, Hans Sharoun, Häring, Paul Scheerbart, and Mies van der Rohe.

Although both Mies and Häring continued to share a vital and mutually beneficial friendship during these crucial years of development, it was at this time that Mies began to clarify his ideas about architecture, ideas that progressively distinguished themselves from Häring and other members of the architectural avant-garde who sought to develop an "organic functionalism." This splitting of Modern architecture into two strains, one "geometric" and the other "organic," reinforced Häring's earlier thoughts on the foundational premises of architecture's two worldviews. In later years, Häring commented on the situation with carefully chosen words: "[When working together] we [Mies and Häring] saw . . . that each must go his own way, Mies that of architecture, and I that of building." As Blundell-Jones remarks, whereas Mies came to assume the "normative Classicism of Behrens," Häring strove to further the "responsive Regionalism" of his mentor, Theodor Fischer. Despite the fact that both lines of argument emphasized functionalism as the primary

aim, this distinction, reflected in the arguments of other groups at the time (both the Deutscher Werkbund and the early years of the Bauhaus are prime examples), suggests that there are in fact two principal theoretical venues for the practice of modern architecture. On the one hand, there is the universal and typical, a point of view that consciously extends Neoclassicism's high regard for rules, principles, and order. On the other hand, there is the equally compelling argument for specificity and individual difference, where irregularity and the specific response to a set of programmatic and site considerations govern each project. For various reasons, the former vision for modern architecture, represented by, among others, Walter Gropius, the French-Swiss Le Corbusier, Mies, and modern architecture's preeminent historian and propagandist, Sigfried Giedion, eventually became the standard for Modern architecture, culminating in Hitchcock and Johnson's limiting and exclusionary International Style Exhibition of 1936.

The repression of Häring's voice—along with that of his fellow "organic functionalists," such as Hans Scharoun and Erich Mendelsohn—furthered the misinterpretation of Modern architecture as a distilled style, producing assumptions that continue to resonate to this day. It did not help that Häring, with Hans Scharoun, his fellow German architect with whom he had his most important association, chose internal exile over immigration during the years of fascist rule. Häring's choice to remain in Germany led to severe limitations and choices; although he did not cooperate with the Nazis, he all but lost his battle for the soul of Modern architecture. After the war, it became obvious that standardization and scientific positivism would drive architectural discourse, with the *sachlich* architects Gropius, Mies, and Meyer representing the horizon of Modern architecture against the traditionalists. Despite his best attempts to reframe the debate on Modern architecture according to its original terms, Häring's words were lost to the pace and demands of Europe's redevelopment and the entrenchment of scientific objectivity as the touchstone of Modern architecture. His resistance to factions that dominated architectural debate are best chronicled by the proceedings of CIAM (Congrès Internationaux d'Architecture Moderne), events that led his eventual withdrawal from membership due to the excessive control exerted by Le Corbusier and Giedion, the preeminent modern historian and Le Corbusier's principal champion. Häring was not alone in his resistance to Giedion's exclusive version of Modern architecture. Berlin's *Ring*, the group he cofounded and for which he served as secretary, had come to effectively represent Germany's burgeoning architectural avant-garde. Yet the positions set forth by the *Ring* went unrecognized by CIAM (Häring accused Gropius of facilitating this turn of events) so that a more unified, positivist approach to Modern architecture might be realized. This approach, based on standardization and "formalist functionalism," was eventually ratified, a circumstance that correlated with the dispersal and eventual demise of the Modern movement in Germany in 1933. What began as a general and open debate on the direction of Modern architecture degenerated into a one-sided monument to historical progress and "rational building methods." The most significant alternative to Giedion's vision, espoused by members of the *Ring*, was effectively suppressed, and history's turn of events only increased its marginalization.

For contemporary debates on architecture, Häring's ideas have begun to receive their due, with organicism and functionalism resurfacing as viable modes of thought. This is due to several factors, including architecture's current concern for nature (sustainability, organic form, and green architecture), technological thinking, space, and materials. Häring's preoccupation with nature (*Natur*), organic form, *Gestalt* (unified form), and *Raum und Geist* (space and spirit) support a view that architecture, the "art of building," is anything but a standardized, efficient, and abstract practice beholden to a set of objective, quantifiable requirements. Rather, the embrace of both qualitative substance and circumstance—particularly the sensitivity to context and specificity—supports Häring's view that architecture is organized in similar manner to all forms of life *(Lebensformen)*.

Häring's buildings, although few and far between, remain important as well, providing necessary material for revisionist histories of Modern architecture. This is particularly true of his masterpiece, Gut Garkau, a highly detailed yet simple building representative of the "new functionalism" that Häring represented. The structure, a compound of buildings devoted to agricultural work, was built between 1922 and 1928. Its program, pieces of which include a barn and cowshed (both built in 1925) and various other unbuilt components (pigsty, stable loft, and farmhouse), reflected the architect's preoccupation with the vernacular, Fischer's "responsive regionalism." This project was followed by a sausage factory in Neustadt, a building that, although reflecting similar concerns with Gut Garkau, was constructed hurriedly and of poor materials.

Häring also built several private homes over the course of his career, but his most important contributions to housing were part of the general program for social housing during the 1920s, the years of the Weimar Republic and, in retrospect, Modern architecture's "golden years" in Germany. These included a housing project in Berlin-Wedding and his contributions to the large housing project Siemensstadt for the German company Siemens, a 1920s planning and housing development in Berlin that provided many architects the latitude to develop their ideas. Only a very few of Häring's projects were constructed during the 1930s, 1940s, and 1950s (he succumbed on 17 May 1958 after a long illness), although these, alongside his unbuilt designs, betray a continuation of his earlier ideas and their developing sophistication.

Although never ceasing to draw projects with the intention of realizing them, Häring himself understood that his major impact was as a theoretician of architecture. To this end, he elaborated his ideas at length, producing essays and notes and giving lectures until it became impossible for him to do so. Even then, he gave interviews, many of which further refine his writings and statements. Although Gut Garkau remains a seminal event in the development of modern architecture, Häring's most significant contributions to architecture reside in his impact on others who managed to realize their work—particularly the German architect Hans Scharoun—and in his importance to a vital strain of Modern architecture that resonates today.

ELIZABETH BURNS GAMARD

See also **Deutscher Werkbund; Germany; Mies van der Rohe, Ludwig (Germany); Scharoun, Hans (Germany); Taut, Bruno (Germany)**

Further Reading

Blundell-Jones, Peter, *Hans Scharoun*, London: Phaidon Press, 1995
Blundell-Jones, Peter, *Hugo Häring: The Organic versus the Geometric*, Stuttgart, Germany: Edition Axel Menges, 1999
Kaes, Anton, Martin Jay, and Edward Dimendberg (editors), *The Weimar Republic Sourcebook*, Berkeley: University of California Press, 1994
Lauterbach, Heinrich, and Jürgen Joedicke (editors), *Hugo Häring: Schriften, Entwürfe, Bauten*, Stuttgart, Germany: Krämer Verlag, 1965
Mumford, Eric, *CIAM Discourse on Urbanism, 1920–1960*, Cambridge, Massachusetts: MIT Press, 2000

HARRISON, WALLACE K. 1885–1981 AND MAX ABRAMOVITZ 1908–

Architects, United States

Wallace Kirkman Harrison (b. 1895 in Worcester, Massachusetts, d. 1981 in New York City) and Max Abramovitz (b. 1908 in Chicago, Illinois) belong to the generation of architects marking the transition between Beaux-Arts and modernism in American practice. From large-scale collaborative design and planning projects for government agencies and universities to corporate office buildings and private residences, much of their work melds forms introduced by leading modernists, such as Mies van der Rohe, Alvar Aalto, Pier Luigi Nervi, and Le Corbusier. Yet, when free of the restraints of collaboration and client demands, both produced original and imaginative work, often inspired by engineering in their innovative techniques and uses of material.

Harrison received his training as a draftsman for architectural and construction firms, supplemented by part-time study at Worcester Polytechnic Institute, the Boston Architectural Center, and the École des Beaux-Arts (1920–21). A Rotch Traveling Scholarship (1922) supported two years in Europe and the Middle East. After 1916, Harrison worked for several New York architects: McKim, Mead and White; Bertram Goodhue; Raymond Hood; and Harvey Wiley Corbett, with whom he studied and later taught at Columbia University (1925–26). In 1927, he became a partner in Helmle and Corbett. Their Roerich Museum and Master Apartments (1929) in New York and collaborative work on Rockefeller Center featured masonry-clad slab towers that had setbacks characteristic of New York office buildings between the wars and that prefigured Harrison's mature work.

Abramovitz received degrees in architecture from the University of Illinois (B.S., 1929) and Columbia University (M.S., 1931), where he also taught design. He became a student of Harrison's in a housing study group at the New School for Social Research, New York City, in 1931. A postgraduate scholarship from Columbia afforded two years at the École des Beaux-Arts (1932–34). In 1934, Abramovitz joined Corbett, Harrison and MacMurray (1929–35; later Harrison and Fouilhoux). Abramovitz became a full partner in 1941. Following Fouilhoux's 1945 death, the firm became Harrison and Abramovitz.

Harrison and Abramovitz ran a progressive office resembling the ateliers and design studios of their youth. Despite conventional educations, both became committed modernists by the late 1930s. At Yale University (1939–42), they helped rejuvenate

Empire State Complex—Mall, Albany, New York (1965–79)
Photo © Mary Ann Sullivan

the design and planning curricula. Their design studios hosted such visiting artists, planners, and architects as Le Corbusier, José Lluis Sert, Lewis Mumford, Robert Moses, Amedée Ozenfant, Ferdinand Léger, Alexander Calder, Oscar Nitzchke, and R. Buckminster Fuller. Their firm soon became a magnet for talented young designers.

A consummate diplomat, Harrison's ease in handling the complex demands of multiple clients for business, institutions, or government secured a broad client base, resulting in many high-profile commissions. His genius for forming key liaisons with powerful, well-placed individuals extended the scope of the firm's business both locally and internationally. Harrison's friendships with Robert Moses and members of the Rockefeller family helped him execute important buildings at the United Nations (1946–52), Lincoln Center (1956–66), and the Empire State Plaza (1961–77) in Albany. These jobs led to other commissions, especially politically sensitive ones, such as the U.S. Embassy buildings, designed by Abramovitz, in Havana (1951) and Rio de Janeiro (1952), and the CIA Headquarters (1961) in Langley, Virginia. Abramovitz attained multiple commissions for educational institutions: the Law School at Columbia University, 16 buildings (1951–70) at Brandeis University, a library and student residence (1966–70) for Radcliffe College, and the Krannert Performing Arts Center (1969) and the Assembly Hall (1963) at the University of Illinois.

For Harrison, collaboration was a typical and successful working method, but in his work for Nelson Rockefeller at Albany, it proved a liability. From 1961 to 1977, he was involved almost exclusively in the design of the Empire State Plaza. Dubbed "Halicarnassus on the Hudson" by one critic, its angled slab office towers, egg-shaped performing arts center, and monumental cultural education center betrayed a loss of artistic control typical of bureaucratic design. Inspired by Le Corbusier's Monastery of La Tourette and Oscar Niemeyer's work in Brasilia, the ensemble lacks subtlety of detail and the originals' sureness of form.

Under more favorable circumstances, the firm produced such highly original structures as the Trylon and Perisphere at the New York World's Fair (1939–40) and Harrison's fish-form First Presbyterian Church (1958) in Stamford, Connecticut. Harrison felt freest to explore new ideas in domestic architecture. His fascination with circular forms emerged in designs such as his Milton House (1936) in Bermuda, where rooms radiate out from a circular core. For Nelson Rockefeller's International Basic Economy Corporation, Harrison designed 1,500 experimental low-cost reinforced-concrete houses (1953) for Las Lomas, Puerto Rico.

Both architects contributed novel solutions to the design and planning of tall office buildings, often adapting industrial materials in remarkable ways to relieve the monotony of the slab form.

Two such postwar office towers in Pittsburgh also displayed to advantage the products of their clients. At Alcoa (1952), Harrison designed luxurious modular aluminum cladding for the exterior. At U.S. Steel (1971), Abramovitz supported the triangular tower with hollow external members providing uninterrupted office space on all floors. These Cor-ten steel members, filled with antifreeze and water, created structurally stable fireproofing at significantly reduced costs. At the United Nations Secretariat (1950), Abramovitz transformed the Le Corbusian slab into an Americanized curtain wall heat-reducing glass by Libbey-Owens-Ford. The firm's work for Corning Glass over two decades, beginning in 1949, included a Visitors' Center and several office buildings with lavish expanses of glass. Links with producers of key building materials contributed to their role as one of the leading corporate design firms of the postwar period.

From the mid-1960s, with Harrison occupied nearly exclusively by his work in Albany, Abramovitz produced the majority of the firm's other designs. This long separation eventuated in the dissolution of the partnership in 1976. Abramovitz retained the firm as Abramovitz, Kingsland, Schiff while Harrison practiced independently.

LINDA S. PHIPPS

See also **Corbusier, Le (Jeanneret, Charles-Édouard) (France); Lincoln Center, New York City; United Nations Headquarters, New York City**

Selected Works

U.S. Embassy, Havana, Cuba, 1951
United Nations Plaza, New York City, 1952
U.S. Embassy, Rio de Janeiro, 1952
Alcoa Headquarters, Pittsburgh, Pennsylvania, 1952
CIA Headquarters, Langley, Virginia, 1961
Assembly Hall, University of Illinois, Chicago, 1963
Lincoln Center, New York City, 1966
Krannert Performing Arts Center, University of Illinois, Chicago, 1969
Library and student residence, Radcliffe College, Cambridge, Massachusetts, 1970
U.S. Steel Headquarters, Pittsburgh, Pennsylvania, 1971
Empire State Plaza, Albany, New York, 1979

Selected Publications

"Drafting Room Practice," *Architectural Forum*, 56/1 (January 1932), 81–84.
New Living Space for New York: "Battery Park City": A Proposal for Creating a Site for Residential and Business Facilities in Lower Manhattan, New York: privately published.
"Office Buildings," in *Forms and Functions of Twentieth-Century Architecture*, vol. 4 (of 4), *Building Types*, edited by Talbot Hamlin, New York: Columbia University Press, 1952
Harrison, Wallace K., and C.E. Dobbin, *School Buildings of Today and Tomorrow*, New York: Architectural Book Publishing Company, 1931
Harrison, Wallace K., Harvey Wiley Corbett, Robert Moses, Eliel Saarinen, and Hugh Ferriss, "New York in 1999—Five Predictions. Architects and City Planners Look into the Crystal Ball and Tell What They See," *New York Times Magazine* (February 6, 1949), 18–19, 51, 53

Further Reading

The Architecture of Max Abramovitz (exhib. cat.), Urbana: s.n., 1963
"Art: Cheops' Architect," *Time Magazine* (22 September 1952)
Bleecker, Samuel E., *The Politics of Architecture: A Perspective on Nelson A. Rockefeller*, New York: Rutledge Press, 1981
Doumato, Lamia, *Wallace K. Harrison: A Bibliography*, Monticello, Illinois: Vance Bibliographies, 1989
Dudley, George A., *A Workshop for Peace: Designing the United Nations Headquarters*, New York: Architectural History Foundation, and Cambridge, Massachusetts: MIT Press, 1994
Max Abramovitz and University Architecture: An Introductory Bibliography, Monticello, Illinois: Vance Bibliographies, 1983
Newhouse, Victoria, *Wallace K. Harrison, Architect*, New York: Rizzoli, 1989
Pippin, Paul W.T., *A Design Assignment: Preliminary Design Study Models for the Facade of the United Nations Secretariat Building, N.Y.C.*, Bethel, Connecticut: Rutledge Books, 1996
"U.S. Steel Headquarters Building," *Civil Engineering ASCE* (April 1970)
Wind, Herbert, "Profiles: Architect," *The New Yorker* (20 November 1954, 27 November 1954, 4 December 1954) (on Wallace K. Harrison)

HASEGAWA, ITSUKO 1941–

Architect, Japan

Itsuko Hasegawa stands virtually alone among Japanese architects in her attempts to develop a critical practice. From her earliest work, Hasegawa addressed the manner in which public buildings are designed and programmed, eschewing bureaucratic directives in favor of a public process. As she matured, other themes also emerged, especially a concern for the environment and for the disenfranchised: women, children, the elderly, the disabled, and the homeless. Although some of these issues remain incompletely realized in her work, their introduction into professional discourse in Japan is significant.

Ironically, Hasegawa was educated by one of the nation's leading formalists, Kazuo Shinohara. In 1969, she entered his graduate studio at the Tokyo Institute of Technology, and she remained with him as his assistant until 1978. Many of Japan's critics note today that their understanding of the master prevented them from initially understanding Hasegawa's approach.

Furthermore, Hasegawa often used building materials as a tool to achieve her agenda, drawing attention to the materials rather than their purpose. This is most apparent in her debut project, the widely acclaimed Shonandai Culture Center, won by competition in 1986 and built just outside Tokyo. Hasegawa's earlier projects were almost exclusively residential, and she brought to Shonandai the same concern for client input and attention to detail. The 14,315-square-meter complex (which includes a children's museum) remains highly accessible through the use of tiles embedded with animals' footprints, constellations of mirrored fragments implanted in walls, and marbles scattered across punched-metal ceilings.

Punched metal was also significant in framing her initial reputation. She first used it in the House at Kuwahara (1980), designed for a metals supplier, and the commodity quickly became ubiquitous in the arsenal of Tokyo's trendiest designers. She followed this with explorations of various transparent and translucent surfaces in the late 1980s, anticipating trends that would emerge internationally ten years later by stretching fabric into bulbous shapes, projecting light onto frosted glass, layering polycarbonate skins, and choreographing reflected light.

Hasegawa's position as an iconoclast may be rooted in difference. She was one of only a handful of women architects in Japan and stood virtually alone in her international acclaim and her alliance with the small cadre of architects shaping the profession. Although she exploited this status, using her position as a bully pulpit, a heavy schedule of lecturing and teaching abroad has also prevented her from engaging fully with the opportunities of Japan's construction process. As a result, her buildings lack the refinement and attention to detail found in much of the work from Japan. Although it may be that Hasegawa felt liberated by the deliberately rough detailing found in Shinohara's architecture from the late 1980s, her own approach is less clearly committed to one position or the other, having areas of refinement and delicacy juxtaposed with roughly executed components.

Hasegawa calls the materials and form of architecture "hardware" and feels that this side has been overemphasized to the detriment of architectural "software." In particular, her efforts lie in developing a richly rendered set of sensory experiences, apprehended by moving along multiple pathways. In publications, her descriptions often attempt to deliver something that photography cannot, calling attention to rising tides and flickering light or to the sound of the wind, the cool touch of water, and the emergence of a view along a rising path.

For Hasegawa, architecture essentially acts as a constructed form of landscape or, in her words, "a new nature." With Toyo Ito, a close friend, Hasegawa reinterpreted the dense Japanese cityscape as a form of nature, to be celebrated. She often refers to her buildings as hills, and in her most recent large-scale work, the Niigata City Performing Arts Center (1998), she established the roof as a city park. At a smaller scale, Hasegawa introduces the texture of landscape in her work by mixing soil into mortar finishes or setting stones and shells in the surfaces of walkways and pools.

This is not done arbitrarily. Hasegawa strives to awaken what she sees as the latent memories of nature possessed by each site, embracing accidental or dormant qualities over rational exposition. Botond Bognar quotes Hasegawa as saying that she wants to "accept those things that had been rejected by the spirit of rationalism—the translucent world of emotions and the supple and comfortable space woven by nature—and to create a landscape filled with a new form of nature where devices enable one to hear the strange music of the universe" (Bognar, 157). This gives her work an instinctual character that is particularly uncommon in public works, the bulk of her output.

Since completing the Shonandai Culture Center in 1990, Hasegawa's office also produced the Sumida Culture Factory (1994), the Oshima Machi Picture Book Museum in Imizu (1994), the Museum of Fruit (1995) in Yamanashi, the Himi Seaside Botanical Garden (1996), and the previously mentioned Niigata City Performing Arts Center—extraordinary output for her tiny office. Hasegawa has also taken on several underfunded typologies, designing public housing—the Takuma Housing Project (1992), the Namekawa Housing Project (1998), and Imai Newtown Housing (1998)—and two small, rural elementary schools—Busshouji Elementary (1994) and Kaiho Elementary (1996).

In her most recent discussions, it is clear that Hasegawa feels frustrated in her attempts to reshape the character of Japan's public architecture. In particular, she has begun to question the scale and underutilization of museums, performing arts centers, and other large-scale facilities intended by government authorities as chic urban outposts, attempts to staunch population losses from small communities to the more dynamic Tokyo. Hasegawa has come to believe that these structures are rarely embraced by the local community despite her best efforts to reshape the buildings' programming. Instead, she has begun to call for integrated efforts drawn from local traditions and the rhythm of the community. If she is able to cajole local governments into considering this approach, she will have considerable effect on the life and texture of Japan's smaller cities.

DANA BUNTROCK

Biography

Born Shizuoka Prefecture, Japan, 1941. Graduated from Kanto Gakuin architecture program with a bachelor's in 1964 and studied in the Shinohara lab at Tokyo Institute of Technology from 1969 to 1971, afterward becoming Shinohara's assistant in the lab. Hasegawa worked for the Metabolist Kiyonori Kikutake from 1964 to 1969, between her graduate and undergraduate studies. Established Itsuko Hasegawa Atelier in 1979. She teaches regularly at Waseda University and Tokyo Institute of Technology and has been a visiting professor at Harvard's Graduate School of Design. Selected awards include the Building Constructors Society Award for Shonandai Culture Center in 1992, a design award from the Architectural Institute of Japan for Bizan Hall in 1986, the Japan Cultural Design Award in 1986, and the Japan Art Academy Prize in 2000.

Selected Works

Stationery Shop, Yaizu, Shizuoka Prefecture, 1978
Tokumaru Children's Clinic, Matsuyama, Ehime Prefecture, 1979
House in Kuwahara, Matsuyama, Ehime Prefecture, 1980 (destroyed)
NC House, Nakano-ku, Tokyo, 1983
House in Ikebukuro, Tokyo, 1984
Bizan Hall, Shizuoka City, 1984 (destroyed)
House in Nerima, Tokyo, 1986
Silk Road Exposition Pavilions, Nara, 1988
Shonandai Culture Center, Fujisawa, Kanagawa, 1990
STM House, Shibuya Ward, Tokyo, 1991
Takuma Housing Project, Kumamoto City, 1992
Footwork Computer Center, Katou, Hyogo Prefecture, 1992
Sumida Culture Factory, Sumida Ward, Tokyo, 1994
Oshima Machi Picture Book Museum, Imizu, Toyama Prefecture, 1994
Museum of Fruit, Yamanashi City, 1995
Gymnasium for the University of Shiga Prefecture, Hione, 1995
Himi Seaside Botanical Garden, Himi City, 1995
Niigata Performing Arts Center, Niigata City, 1998

Further Reading

Hasegawa's unique position as a woman practicing architecture in Japan has drawn significant attention to her work, and there are several good monographs available on her in English. Most include essays that draw attention to the theoretic positions she has taken. Like many of Japan's practitioners, however, Hasegawa writes little beyond simple descriptive statements, reserving discussions of the reasons behind the work for lectures. Botond Bognar and Koji Taki are two of Hasegawa's most sympathetic critics.

Architectural Monographs No. 31: Itsuko Hasegawa. London: Academy Group, 1993 (Sometimes Hasegawa is listed as author.)

Bognor, Botond, *The New Japanese Architecture*, New York: Rizzoli, 1990

The Complete Work of Itsuko Hasegawa, Tokyo: *Space Design*, Kajima Institute of Publishing, 1985

Dobney, Stephen (editor), *The Master Architect Series II: Itsuko Hasegawa, Selected and Current Works*. Mulgrave, Victoria: The Images Publishing Company, 1997

Hasegawa, Itsuko, "A Search for New Concepts through Filtering My Life in Tokyo" and "Sumida Metaphorical Townscape, Tokyo," *Architectural Design No. 99—Japanese Architecture 2*. London: Academy Group, 1992

Itsuko Hasegawa, 1985–1995, Space Design, 11 (374), Tokyo: Kajima Institute of Publishing, 1995

Itsuko Hasegawa: Recent Buildings and Projects, Basel: Birkhäuser/ Institut Fraçais d'Architecture, 1997

"Opening up a New Architecture Scene through Communication," *Kenchiku Bunka*, special issue on Hasegawa (January 1993); includes an essay by Koji Taki

HASSAN II MOSQUE

Designed by Michel Pinseau; completed 1993
Casablanca, Morocco

King Hassan II, who claimed that he was inspired by the Koranic verse "The throne of God is on the waters," raised this vast monument in his own honor. The verse inspired the site of the mosque, a reclaimed parcel from the Atlantic shore, giving the edifice the moniker "The Floating Mosque." Standing as the tallest religious building in the world, the Hassan II Mosque was designed to celebrate the 60th birthday of King Hassan II of Morocco. Built between 1980 and 1993, this mosque is also the largest of its type in the world, with space for 25,000 people, including space set off for 5,000 women in keeping with customs. Situated boldly along the Atlantic coast and pointing toward Mecca, the mosque was designed by French architect Michel Pinseau. Beyond its enormous scale and monumental urban presence, the mosque is astounding for its abundance of luxurious decoration, crafted from a wide range of exquisite decorative materials. The mosque, visible from great distances, rests at the endpoint of many important roadways.

As it stands today, the approach to the Hassan II Mosque accidentally recaptures the mysteries and auras of the labyrinthine medieval city. Even though Casablanca is carefully laid out in the baroque style by the French, this city does not reveal the locations of objects easily. Unless one is in one of the newly built high-rise structures in the town, the location of the mosque does not allow any warning that the individual is about to arrive at the tallest religious building of the 20th century. As a pedestrian, the only way one can have a view of the minaret of the structure from a distance is if the person approaches the complex on the roads that border the Atlantic Ocean. From the west, it would be the beautiful meandering Boulevard Corniche, which becomes Boulevard Sidi Mohammed Ben Abdellah and terminates at the Round About, which abuts the southern terminus of the complex. From the northeast, it would be along Boulevard Des Almohads, which begins at the junction of the Port of Casablanca and Boulevard Félix Houphouët-Boigny and ends at the Round About at the northern terminus of the complex. The coastal road between Boulevard Sidi Mohammed Ben Abdellah and Boulevard Des Almohads is subterranean in order to direct the traffic to and from the parking structures below the complex and also to enable the continuous flow of traffic along the coast. However, neither of these two pleasant approaches gets one into the complex through the main entrance. The main entrance is on Rue de Tiznit, and it is flanked on the west by the Bibliothèque (Library) and on the east by the Musée (Museum).

As one proceeds to the main entrance from Rue Tiznit, the L-shaped structures of the Library and Museum form a gate and frame the person's view of the expansive esplanade, focusing it directly on the mosque. Besides, neither the finish of the Library nor that of the Museum can hold the individual's attention for long, and they suggest very little about the level of finish of the edifice, so that one is naturally curious to explore what lies beyond the expansive esplanade, which covers an area of 30,000 square meters and can hold up to 80,000 people during prayers. The first part of the entrance at Rue Tiznit is in the form of a C-shaped colonnade, whose back acts as the starting point for an immense U-shaped arcade that is divided into multiple courtyard screens in front of the Library and the Museum structures. The U-shaped arcade also helps to frame one's views along the expansive esplanade and gives the sense of multiple transitions from one space to another as one moves from the Rue Tiznit into the esplanade. The configuration of the arcades into double cloisters of columns gives one a sense of contained volumes of space as one proceeds farther into the esplanade. However, the esplanade expands into a void once the individual goes beyond the arcades in front of the Library and the Museum and proceeds farther toward the mosque.

It is at a much closer proximity that one begins to interact with the monumental scale of the mosque. The scale of the human figure becomes very small compared to the scale of the columns of the arcade, and it is about the last moments that one can look up and have a glimpse at the top of the minaret. Moreover, looking up at the minaret also shows how its two facades to the south elevation are tilted almost at 45-degree angles from Rue Tiznit, thereby determining the orientations of the wings of the peristyle. However, more impressive is the glow of the marbles and the granites on the esplanade paving, the marbles and *zellij* ornaments on the walls, the columns, and the ornate square bastions of the peristyle of the courtyard. On a bright sunny day, the giant green roof and the marbles are showered by the sunlight, forming sculptured interlocking volumes and surfaces of a massive golden and green gem. The moment of transition from the vast esplanade into the courtyard of the mosque also reveals the fact that the peristyle that encloses the courtyard of the mosque is maneuvering several angles to maintain the essentially symmetrical design of the structure.

The minaret rises to a total height of 200 meters (650 feet) from its base, including *jamour*, on which the 15-meter (49-foot) copper finial is mounted. The finial is equipped with a laser beam with a range of 30 kilometers (20 miles), and it points to the direction of the *qibla*, which always indicates the direction of Mecca, but the 30-kilometer-range laser beam also serves as a lighthouse for vessels coming into the Casablanca harbor. The copper finial at the top of the minaret reads very brightly on a sunny day, so that one sees three major colors as one looks at the minaret: the white marble, the green *zellij*, and the shiny yellow finial. Although the white marble and its intricately carved diamond-shaped laces make up the primary cladding over the heavily reinforced concrete minaret, the two friezes on the tower are also quite visible.

The ultimate space of the mosque is the prayer hall with a capacity of 25,000 worshipers in a 200-by-100-square-meter (650-by-325-square-foot) space. The plan is essentially basilical: a rectangle with three arched naves that are delineated by 10 giant pairs of piers. The two side naves are further subdivided by 10 smaller piers that are near to the southern and northern walls. The piers that flank the central nave and the ones that are near the walls of the southern and northern facades are connected by a series of huge, serrated, high-arched walls. Each pier, the ones on the sides and the ones that define the central nave,

is lavishly decorated with polished granite, marbles, plasters, and stuccos that drop into stalactites (*mouqarnas*) that are made up of numerous lobes and arches. The *mourqarnas* are well defined by the additions of tiny columns along their edges and by the intensity of the colored stones in the multiple lobes. The serrated arches that flank the central nave and connect the piers are also lavishly decorated with *mourqarnas*. The two side naves contain the galleries, mezzanine for women, who can access them from the ablution rooms in the basement. The fine woodwork that clads the mezzanines on either side of the naves is further embellished with stuccos that radiate green, yellow, and white colors. The floor glows with the shine of a mixture of polished granite and marble. The giant retractable roof that covers the prayer hall is 65 meters (210 feet) above the floor, but the height of the ceiling then drops to 38 meters (125 feet) and finally to 27 meters (90 feet) above the floor at its lowest point. The mobile ceiling is lavishly decorated with ciders that are embossed with gold, but its function is primarily to bring natural light into the huge space when it is open. Even then, the depth of the building from the sides and from the length still does not allow natural light into all parts of the building. Rather, it alters the whole atmosphere in a dramatic way that is quite different from the light provided by the stained glasses. By the time one leaves the prayer hall and descends to the ablution rooms and the *hammams*

Hassan II Mosque: Casablanca, Morocco (1993)
© Nnamdi Elleh

(large heated pools or Turkish baths) in the basement, all the resistance one has for rejecting or celebrating an artwork is gone.

NNAMDI ELLEH

Further Reading

Basri, Driss, *Hassan II Mosque: A Spiritual and Architectural Work*, Rabat, Morocco: Ministry of Information, 1994

Combs-Schilling, M.E., *Sacred Performances: Islam, Sexuality, and Sacrifice*, New York: Columbia University Press, 1989

Holod, Renata, and Hasan-Uddin Khan, *The Mosque and the Modern World: Architects, Patrons, and Designers since the 1950s*, London: Thames and Hudson, 1997

Ploquin, Philippe, Francoise Peuriot, and Mohammed-Allal Sinaceur, *La Mosquée Hassan II*, Dremil-Lafage, France: Éditions Daniel Briand, 1993

HEATING, VENTILATION, AND AIR CONDITIONING (HVAC)

The 20th-century proliferation of HVAC systems for conditioning the interior environment played a seminal role in the development of modernism. "Manufactured weather," which Willis Carrier described in 1919 as cleaner and purer than what nature could provide, freed the building envelope from its role as the environmental mediator between inside and outside. Interior spaces no longer needed to be adjacent to the perimeter to receive ventilation or natural lighting, and materials and construction details were no longer subject to regionally specific conditions, resulting in a design universality that divorced building from site. Planar surfaces, constructed of unprecedented cladding materials and stretched as thin skins across the building exterior, retained only one nonaesthetic function: the prevention of water penetration. The 19th-century permeable masonry building, with its high perimeter-to-core-area ratio, was steadily supplanted by the 20th century's impermeable curtain-wall building with its deep floor plate. The deterministic relationship between the building and its exterior environment abruptly shifted to one between the building and its HVAC systems.

During the 20th century, the rapid dissemination of HVAC systems, particularly in the United States, established the American systems as the standard to which all other systems and technologies were to be compared. The Arab oil embargo of 1973–74 provoked the first scrutiny of the relationship between the building and its systems since before World War I, but many of the subsequent investigations tended to reinforce the hegemony of the technology rather than dismantle it. Many of these investigations, ranging from vernacular revivals and passive solar designs to systems integration theory and high-tech buildings, found a natural home in the architecture academy, as most were based on a formal determinism. The resulting strategies were unable to replicate the conditions produced by the standard HVAC system, which emerged preeminently from this nexus of activity; furthermore, its implementation is beginning to surge again, particularly in Europe, where new HVAC installations are increasing by 30 percent annually. Paradoxically, the HVAC technology itself was little investigated during this period, undergoing only minor revisions in its control strategy, with the result that the HVAC system of the late 20th century was conceptually and operationally the same as the system in place at the beginning of the century.

The roots of the relationship between 20th-century architecture and HVAC systems can be found in 19th-century experiments in heating and ventilation. Indeed, the formal determinism was in place even before air conditioning was well established. This determinism was not, however, a product of the technology; rather, both the technology and the architecture were driven by the social, cultural, and scientific milieus of the 19th century that, although no longer relevant, have maintained their influence on architectural form and HVAC systems.

The development of modern chemistry during the 17th and 18th centuries led to widespread concern in the 19th century about the human contamination of air through respiration and bodily processes. Ranging from carbonic acid gas to "crowd poison," human bioeffluents were considered to be the source of deadly diseases. Ventilation with outside air of any quality, even from a highly polluted urban environment, was seen as the only solution to preventing dullness, dementia, and perhaps death from human-contaminated interior air. Although steam-driven fans had long been used for ventilating mines, they could not be practically deployed in small and nonindustrial buildings that did not manufacture their own steam. Instead, other schemes for moving air were used, particularly convection shafts that contained heat sources to "induce" air movement. These shafts were inserted into the interstices of buildings and were meant to carry away the "respired" air before it could contaminate the occupied spaces. This approach, although having little success, was still considered more desirable than cross ventilation, as there was also a persistent fear that drafts caused many epidemic diseases. Foul-air shafts were a common design element during the 19th century and established the formal precedent of building infrastructure ceded to air distribution.

When district steam service brought low-pressure steam to urban areas during the 1880s, many buildings used the steam primarily in heating systems and secondarily in convection shafts, but few took advantage of the widely available steam-driven fans. The germ theory of contagion had begun to overtake the theory that disease was spread by air, and the belief that human respiration produced a poisonous gas was on the wane. The added expense of ventilation, particularly in the winter, convinced many building owners to shut down their ventilation systems. Many of the manufacturers of steam-heating systems also produced fans, and in the 1890s, combination fan/heating systems began to be marketed. These "blowers" were advertised as providing "free" ventilation: one steam supply drove the fan, and the spent steam, or condensate, was then circulated through the heating coils. These small systems combining heating and ventilation rapidly gained in popularity and became so well established that when the steam supplying the fan was replaced with an electrical drive, the components stayed packaged together. The mechanical integration of heating and ventilation, although originally a marketing scheme, became an unquestioned precedent during the 20th century.

The early decades of the 20th century witnessed enormous opposition to mechanical systems. Many opponents believed that the use of mechanical systems encouraged employers to relocate to spaces that normally would have been unsuitable, such as basements, turning workers into "cave dwellers" in monotonously heated, artificially lit environments. Other opponents were again raising the issue of cost, as the electrically driven fan was no longer a free byproduct of the steam-heating coils.

The most vociferous opposition, which was nearly successful in dismantling the integrated system, came from the public health arena. Fresh, mountain air had long been the desired environment for tuberculosis patients, but the demographic shift of the disease during the 19th century from the general populace to the urban poor and immigrants precluded their treatment in an alpine-like sanitarium. Urban tuberculosis patients were encouraged to sleep on their roofs and balconies, and schools for tubercular children were established in which the windows were kept open year-round. Eventually, open windows were recommended as a prophylactic measure for the healthy as well, and mechanical systems were shut down in many urban schools. In 1913, a major study was funded in New York evaluating the performance of 5,500 children over a four-year period with the conclusion that open windows were as effective as mechanical ventilation in providing the necessary interior environment. Mechanical systems may well have been eliminated from many public buildings had not the conclusion of the report coincided with the 1918 influenza epidemic, during which more people died than had in World War I. The popular belief that the flu was spread through air encouraged many people to close their windows, and mechanical systems suddenly became a very desirable means of isolating occupants from the germs of others. Hygiene replaced tuberculosis as the public's focus, particularly as increasing class consciousness in the United States was propelling the rich to separate themselves further from the poor and the American born to differentiate themselves from the foreign born. Manufacturers of mechanical systems were quick to capitalize on this emerging concern with hygiene and cleanliness, and air washers were incorporated into mechanical heating and ventilation systems, giving rise to the air handler. The air handler became so well established as the standard system that the inclusion of cooling coils, forming the last component of the HVAC system, was almost incidental. The air-handler–based system, having originated from the 19th-century desire to bring outside air into a building, had been subverted into a system for isolating the inside from the outside.

These three precedents—the concept that fresh air and foul air must be separately maintained in an infrastructure-intensive distribution system, the integration of different functions into the same system, and the development of the hermetically sealed "manufactured" environment—formed the basis of the prevailing architectural incorporation of HVAC systems. Unquestionably, the advent of HVAC technology facilitated the spread of new functions, such as movie theaters; the development of new forms, such as high-rise office towers; and the proliferation of new materials, such as glazed curtain walls. Nevertheless, the incorporation of the technology into the architecture remains rooted in the 19th-century precedents, and this determinism was accepted as a given for much of the 20th century.

The networks of ducts that typify most large-building HVAC systems are little different from the distribution systems intended to purge "crowd poison" in the 19th century. Although there were examples of direct ventilation through the exterior envelope as well as the use of corridors and occupied spaces for air distribution, they were overshadowed by the use of ducts or infrastructural elements, such as plenums, as only "contained" systems could isolate the "foul" air from the "fresh." In 1929, the Philadelphia Savings Fund Society building became the second office tower to be fully air-conditioned, with a service floor inserted

at the 20th floor for the intake of uncontaminated fresh air, and part of the elevator shaft space was dedicated to vertical ducts rising multiple stories. Louis Kahn's design of the Richards Medical Laboratories (1957–64) carried the foul/fresh shafts beyond the interstices of the building and replaced them with service towers flanking the laboratory spaces. Although Kahn claimed to have hated ducts, his assignation of air distribution to separate towers simply reinforced the 19th-century desire to isolate foul air in vertical shafts. By the time of the Pompidou Center (1972–76), designed by Richard Rogers and Renzo Piano, the language of the air-distribution system overshadowed its purpose, and gratuitous ducts and intakes found an aesthetic expression that signified them as the hallmark of "high technology."

The integration of different functions within a single system may have originated from the clever marketing strategies of 19th-century manufacturers and engineers, but in the 20th century, integration was given an immaculate conception as the fundamental attribute of an organic structure analogous to the human body. HVAC distribution systems were likened to the body's circulatory system, and Le Corbusier once described the air handler as the lungs of the building. This organicist undercurrent may have prevented the decoupling of functions as other technologies changed, particularly during the switch from steam power to electricity, and 20th-century architects have looked instead to expand the integration. The use of infrastructure as air-distribution space seemed to logically extend to integrating the air-distribution system with the structural system, even though these systems are operationally incompatible. In the Yale Art Gallery (1950–53), Louis Kahn's space frame was designed with tetrahedral elements so that multitudes of small ducts could be threaded through the triangular voids. In Marco Zanuso's Olivetti factory (1964), integration went a step further, as the girders supporting the roof plane were hollow tubular elements that also served as the air supply ducts. During the 1970s and 1980s, after integration of HVAC and structural systems had become fairly standard, architects and engineers turned their attention toward extending the functionality of the HVAC system, although it already integrated several very different types of functions: cooling, heating, ventilation, humidity control, odor control, and filtration. Distribution loops were added to circulate through luminaires for directly relieving their heat generation, and in buildings exemplified by Lloyd's of London (1979–84), circulation loops were inserted between the layers of double glazing to control the mean radiant temperature. This extension of HVAC functionality into the building envelope led to the current trend of vented double-skin buildings, in which air circulates through the entire facade of the building, adding mostly operational complexity and additional construction and maintenance cost in exchange for a more organic integration of building systems.

The isolation of the building interior from the exterior environment was common when pre-Enlightenment theories of contagion presumed that air was the carrier of pestilence and that only the conscientious sealing of buildings could protect one from contracting epidemic diseases such as cholera, consumption, and the plague. Although developments in 19th-century chemistry and medicine dismantled the theory of "miasmic" contamination, equipment manufacturers and engineers capitalized on the general public's fear of invisible germs and resurrected the latent belief that air was dangerous. The air-handler–

based system came to fruition when urban air pollution was peaking in the 20th century and when tenement dwelling immigrants were perceived to be the source of tuberculosis. The 1906 Larkin Building in Buffalo, New York, incorporating one of the first air washers, was described later by Frank Lloyd Wright as being hermetically sealed to keep out the poisonous gases produced by nearby trains. Willis Carrier boasted in 1919 that his HVAC system was able to manufacture an interior environment that was "completely free" from bacteria. As air conditioning proliferated, high-rise buildings in particular began to eliminate operable windows, and the Lever House (1951), by Skidmore, Owings and Merrill, sealed the entire facade, including the floor slabs, behind a curtain wall that read as a single hermetic skin. Even in buildings designed as "sustainable" responses to the energy crisis, the belief remains that the hermetic seal protects the interior. The Audubon House, renovated in 1991 by Croxton Collaborative, has operable windows that the architects have suggested be kept closed so that the HVAC system can properly clean and filter the air.

The technology for conditioning the interior environments of buildings has changed little during the course of the 20th century, and the nature of the deterministic relationship between buildings and conditioning systems is even older, dating back to the 19th-century precedents of the HVAC system. There is a good reason why the technology has not been substantially challenged. Unlike most other problems in fluid mechanics and heat transfer, building air behavior is a true mixing pot of phenomena: wide-ranging velocities; temperature/density stratifications; conductive, convective, and radiant transfer; laminar and turbulent flows; and randomly moving (and randomly heat-generating) objects. The air-handler–based HVAC system has maintained its hegemony for nearly a century because of its ability to provide reasonably homogeneous conditions among this cacophony of behaviors. Since the energy crisis, however, the disadvantages of the single integrated system have begun to outweigh its advantages. Control systems have become much more expensive and complex while air quality and thermal comfort have degraded. In addition, efforts to improve energy efficiency in HVAC systems are producing diminishing returns, and sustainability initiatives have just begun to renew the focus toward reducing energy consumption further. Many architects have looked to return to passive and natural convection strategies but have not been much more successful than their 19th-century predecessors, particularly in regard to application of their methods to urban buildings in variable climates. Other architects are attempting to circumvent the sustainability concerns by searching for alternatives to fossil fuel conversion for building systems. These alternatives, including solar power and geothermal energy, may provide long-term benefits with regard to greenhouse gas emissions but do not address the more immediate weaknesses of the HVAC system or the direct architectural contribution to energy consumption.

D. MICHELLE ADDINGTON

Further Reading

The new field of technology and culture has recently begun to address the implications of environmental control, and books such as Cooper's and Tomes's clarify the cultural and social contexts surrounding the emergence of HVAC systems. A comprehensive overview and discussion of the development of 19th- and early 20th-century HVAC technology occurs in Donaldson.

Banham, Reyner, *The Architecture of the Well-Tempered Environment*, Chicago: University of Chicago Press, and London: Architectural Press, 1969; 2nd edition, Chicago: University of Chicago Press, and London: Architectural Press, 1984

Billings, John Shaw, *The Principles of Ventilation and Heating and Their Practical Application*, New York: Sanitary Engineer, and London: Trübner, 1884; 2nd edition, New York: Sanitary Engineer, 1886

Carrier Engineering Corporation, *The Story of Manufactured Weather, by the Mechanical Weather Man*, New York: Carrier Engineering, 1919

Cooper, Gail, *Air-Conditioning America: Engineers and the Controlled Environment, 1900–1960*, Baltimore, Maryland: Johns Hopkins University Press, 1998

Corbin, Alain, *Le miasme et la jonquille: l'odorat et l'imaginaire social, XVIIIe–XIXe siècles*, Paris: Aubier Montaigne, 1982; as *The Foul and the Fragrant: Odor and the French Social Imagination*, Cambridge, Massachusetts: Harvard University Press, and Leamington Spa, Warwickshire: Berg, 1986

Donaldson, Barry, and Bernard Nagengast, *Heat and Cold: Mastering the Great Indoors: A Selective History of Heating, Ventilation, Air-Conditioning, and Refrigeration from the Ancients to the 1930s*, Atlanta, Georgia: American Society of Heating, Refrigerating, and Air-Conditioning Engineers, 1994

Elliott, Cecil D., *Technics and Architecture: The Development of Materials and Systems for Buildings*, Cambridge, Massachusetts: MIT Press, 1992

New York (State) Commission on Ventilation, *Report of the New York State Commission on Ventilation*, New York: Dutton, 1923

Reid, David Boswell, *Illustrations of the Theory and Practice of Ventilation, with Remarks on Warming, Exclusive Lighting, and the Communication of Sound*, London: Longman, Brown, Green, and Longmans, 1844

Tomes, Nancy, *The Gospel of Germs: Men, Women, and the Microbe in American Life*, Cambridge, Massachusetts: Harvard University Press, 1998

HEGEMANN, WERNER 1881–1936

Architect, Germany

Werner Hegemann achieved early renown and international prominence. After his death in exile, he became shrouded in obscurity. Only recently has his involvement with the emergence of city planning and modern architecture regained attention, yet he remains less known than other "invisible planners" whose impact on the perception of modern architecture and urbanism derived from their ideas rather than visible, built examples. Hegemann's intellectual inquiry focused on the evolving totality of the city, aspiring to a grasp of the city as a cultural phenomenon resulting from collective action over time. This quest for a comprehensive overview energized his academic and theoretical trajectory. The inclusion of political and cultural history as significant factors for present and future city planning distanced Hegemann from the salient architects of the 1920s. It also contributed to the repudiation and eventual rediscovery of his position, which assigned pride of place to city planning and considered architecture as but one element within the dynamics of the evolving metropolis.

Although Hegemann never acquired architectural training, he studied philosophy, history, and economics at the University of Berlin, eventually earned his doctorate in political science from the University of Munich.

His return to Philadelphia in 1908 to work as a municipal housing inspector led to a sequence of events crucial for Hegemann's career and to city planning. It brought him to Boston, where he participated in the civic improvement movement "Boston 1915" and its promotional activities and exhibition of 1909. Otto March, a main proponent of the Greater Berlin Competition for a master plan and contemplating a future exhibition, urged his nephew to study and report on the "Boston 1915" exhibition (1909) and the so-called Congestion Show in New York (1909). These American exhibitions on city planning and related subjects are noteworthy precedents of the major Universal City Planning Exhibition in Berlin and its sequel, the International City Planning Exhibition in Düsseldorf (both 1910). Beyond the expectations of the organizers in Berlin that he would contribute experience and material from across the Atlantic, Hegemann structured the major conceptual content of the exhibitions in Berlin and Düsseldorf. They are considered landmarks within a cluster of city-planning high points in the years from 1909 to 1913.

American Progressivism had shaped Hegemann's interpretation of exhibitions as vehicles for stimulating public awareness of urban issues, deeming this essential for advancing urbanism for the benefit of society. City planning required social action to be carried forward. In Berlin, the winning competition entries were shown together with a wide selection of European and American plans and models. The historic past, the present, and schemes for the future metropolis were displayed together with explanatory texts and statistical charts. This orchestration facilitated comparison and enhanced the concept of city planning as a concern that bridged national boundaries.

In the wake of the city planning exhibitions, Hegemann became engrossed in the action group "Für Gross-Berlin," which crusaded against the dismal housing conditions in the rental barracks (*Mietskasernen*), agitating for better housing and open space, especially playgrounds.

An invitation to lecture and consult in the United States brought Hegemann's activities in Berlin to a halt. Following an invitation by The People's Institute (dedicated to progressive adult education), he arrived in New York in March 1913 to visit more than 40 towns and cities across the country. In his lectures, amply reported in the local newspapers, Hegemann gave as much attention to the value of the "experience," not "example," of Europe to American planning as he did to the reverse. His journey ended in California, where he remained until March 1914 and composed *Report on a City Plan for the Municipalities of Oakland and Berkeley* (1915). Rather than a summary of recommendations, this work is an exposition of the author's ideal of reconciling a rational, scientific approach with responsiveness toward the historical and cultural uniqueness of a given city.

Hegemann departed for Japan, China, and Australia, anticipating that he would be back in Europe by the end of 1914. He did not reach this destination until 1921. At the outbreak of World War I, his German ship was detained off the coast of East Africa. Eventually, regretfully abandoning his copious notes and photographs, Hegemann jumped ship and made his way back to the United States.

From 1916 until 1921, Hegemann pursued a career as a consultant, setting up an office in Milwaukee, Wisconsin. When the United States declared war in 1917, he was considered an enemy alien but was allowed to work. Forming a partnership with the landscape architect Elbert Peets (1886–1968) proved auspicious. Their projects, mostly residential developments, are preserved in promotional brochures illustrated by Peets's drawings. The layouts reflect the influence of the English garden cities, adapted to an American landscape and melded into the adjacent street grid. Significant among them are Washington Highlands, Wauwatosa, Wisconsin, and Wyomissing Park, Reading, Pennsylvania. Working on the latter, they opened an office with Joseph Hudnut in New York. Described as a "residential park," the design preserves the scenic beauty of the large tract. An architecture using the local red brick and gray limestone was recommended.

Few of the projects by the partnership Hegemann and Peets were realized, although their *The American Vitruvius: An Architects' Handbook of Civic Art* (1922), a compendium of over 1,000 illustrations of historic and contemporary ensembles of buildings, emphasized a sense of place and the primacy of the urban fabric. The text abdicates chronological time and architectural styles in favor of space and the relationship of buildings that frame it, achieving a synthesis of volume and void. The text has since become an important contribution to the literature of urban planning.

Hegemann's opinion (as editor of the *Wasmuths Monatshefte für Baukunst*, 1924–33) regarding the architecture by the heroic figures of the Modern movement tended to be critical, but to consider him anti-Modern is simplistic. He wrote perceptively on Erich Mendelsohn, J.J.P. Oud, and Adolf Loos. His architectural criticism was conditioned by his belief in the primacy of city planning over architecture, his profound socialist leanings, and enduring commitment to housing. Historians of the International Style have often dismissed Hegemann as reactionary, questioning his defense of traditional architecture and individuals later tainted by Nazism, such as Paul Bonatz, Paul Schmitthenner, and Paul Schultze-Naumburg, whom he eventually repudiated. Adverse reactions to Hegemann's position were fanned by his attack on the Weissenhofsiedlung, Deutscher Werkbund, Stuttgart (1927), a project that became recognized as exemplary for Modern building. Hegemann saw a degeneration of functionalism into superficial stylistic formalism in most of the Weissenhofsiedlung projects; his outlook was probably tinged by the affront to his self-esteem as a city-planning and housing expert when he was shunned by those involved with Weissenhof.

Professional and increasing political tensions made the year 1928 a watershed for Hegemann. His attention shifted from architectural matters and his dedication to the editorial work at Wasmuth to political activism and urban history. He published *Das steinerne Berlin: Geschichte der grössten Mietskasernenstadt der Welt* (Berlin, 1930) in which he attributed the tragedy of this metropolis to a sequence of missed opportunities and erroneous decisions by those in power, primarily the Prussian state, which caused the city's failure to achieve the status of a major capital.

His book *Entlarvte Geschichte* (History Debunked), bearing the ironically misleading dedication "Den Führern der Deutschen, Paul Hindenburg und Adolf Hitler in erwartungsvoller Verehrung gewidmet," was published in February 1933 by

Jakob Hegner, Leipzig. He urged the author to leave Germany immediately, fearing for his arrest or worse. Initially, the dedication deluded the Nazis, but soon all copies of this first edition were confiscated. At the notorious book burning of 10 May 1933, Hegemann's historical publications, *Entlarvte Geschichte* among them, were condemned to the flames.

A proposal to lecture at the New School of Social Research in New York and assistance from the Emergency Committee in Aid of Displaced German Scholars enabled the family to leave Europe in late October 1933. Alvin Johnson, president of the New School of Social Research, offered Hegemann a teaching position, but not in the prestigious "University in Exile," which would have entitled him to a higher salary. This self-governing research institute had been established only recently by socialist and Jewish scholars. Its faculty voted against accepting Hegemann, claiming that city planning and housing—the topics of his courses—were architecture and not social science.

In 1935, Hegemann embarked on writing a major work on housing as an integral component of city planning that may be considered a possible sequel to *The American Vitruvius: Civic Art. City Planning: Housing* comprises three volumes: volume 1, *Historical and Sociological* (1936); volume 2, *Political Economy and Civic Art* (1937); and volume 3, *A Graphic Review of Civic Art, 1922–1937* (1938). Hegemann did the groundwork for all volumes and completed the text for volumes 1 and 2, which demonstrate his impressive knowledge of American history and contemporary concepts and conditions. Volume 3 entailed the selection and obtaining more than 1,000 illustrations from all over the world and was carried to completion by two dedicated friends: William W. Forster and Robert C. Weinberg. Considering that it was brought forth under the adversities of exile, Hegemann's last published work is noteworthy, being imbued with his pragmatic idealism and faith in the city as the highest cultural attainment.

CRISTIANE CRASEMANN COLLINS

See also **Urban Planning**

Biography

Born in Mannheim, Germany, 15 June 1881. Graduated from Gymnasium Ploen 1901; enrolled at Königliche Friedrich-Wilhelms-Universität, Berlin 1901 and 1905; studied at the Faculté de Droit de L'Université de Paris 1903–04; studied at University of Pennsylvania 1904–05; earned doctorate in political science from University of Munich 1908. Organized planning exhibitions in Boston 1909 and Berlin 1910; published *Report on a City Plan for Oakland and Berkeley* 1915; traveled to Japan, China, Australia 1914–15; formed partnership Hegemann and Peets (Elbert Peets), City Planning and Landscape Architects, Milwaukee, Wisconsin 1916–21; returned to Europe 1921; edited *Wasmuths Monatshefte für Baukunst* 1924–33. Actively opposed Nazism; published *Entlarvte Geschichte* 1933, burned by Nazis; departed from Germany 1933 to New York; taught at The New School for Social Research, Columbia University (professor of urban planning) 1933–36. Died in New York 12 April 1936.

Selected Publications

Amerikanische Parkanlagen: Zierparks, Nutzparks, Aussen- und Innenparks, Nationalparks, Park-Zweckverbände, 1911
Der Städtebau nach den Ergebnissen der allgemeinen Städtebau-Ausstellung in Berlin nebst einem Anhang: Die Internationale Städtebau-Ausstellung in Düsseldorf, 2 vols., 1911–13
The American Vitruvius: An Architect's Handbook of Civic Art (with Elbert Peets), 1922
International Cities and Town Planning Exhibition, Jubilee Exhibition (editor), 1923
Amerikanische Architektur und Stadtbaukunst: Ein Überblick über den heutigen Stand der amerikanischen Baukunst in ihrer Beziehung zum Städtebau, 1925; revised edition, 1927
Facades of Buildings: Fronts of Old and Modern Business and Dwelling Houses, 1929
City Planning, Housing, 3 vols., vol. 3 edited by William W. Forster and Robert C. Weinberg, 1936–38

Further Reading

Kohtz, Otto, *Mit einer Einleitung von Werner Hegemann*, Berlin: J.E. Hübsch, 1930

HEIKKINEN, MIKKU 1949– AND MARKKU KOMONEN 1945–

Architects, Finland

Heikkinen-Komonen Architects, a Helsinki, Finland, office founded by principals Mikku Heikkinen (1949–) and Markku Komonen (1945–) in 1974. Both were trained at the Helsinki University of Technology's Otaniemi campus (designed by Alvar Aalto, 1949–69) and influenced by the 1960s interest in standardization of building components and harmonic modular design systems, particularly those devised by Aulis Blomstedt. Heikkinen and Komonen's work draws on influences ranging from midcentury California modernism and Jean Prouvé to American minimalist sculpture of Donald Judd and James Turrell. Their built work is mostly institutional, set in a wide variety of rural or semiurban settings. Generally simplified, abstracted massing schemes give many of their buildings a sculptural quality.

The firm first attracted attention outside Finland with its competition-winning entry, "Heureka," for the Finnish Science Center (1988), constructed in Vantaa outside Helsinki. Heikkinen and Komonen's design houses a collection of disparate programs in discrete platonic forms, appearing both in plan and elevation as a collage of minimalist elements. Sited at the junction of a commuter railway and a river, its free-form plan is integrated into both the natural and man-made landscape—a monolithic tunnel under the railway connects the Center to a parking lot, whereas a suspension bridge over the river provides pedestrian access. Building materials vary widely, with the architects deploying steel frames, concrete, and timber in structural schemes suitable for shaping each separate portion. Contrasting volumes and surfaces—in the building and out into the site—demonstrate the architects' preoccupation for specific forms to be matched to appropriate materials. Other, scientific demonstrations are integrated into the building fabric, as with a facade of mirrored glass and steel armature set against the railway line, where it doubles as both a demonstration of the color spectrum and an acoustical shield.

Heureka's varied materials and colliding masses avoided the pitfalls of Postmodern pastiche by being experiments with archetypes—sphere, cylinder, bar, grid—rather than literal historical elements. Similarly, the firm's construction palette has not been limited to contemporary High-Tech or pure modernist; modified indigenous construction techniques and materials appear in variety, especially in the projects for West African school buildings (Guinea, 1994) or a pair of Karelian interpretation centers (Kuhmo, Finland, and Kostamus, Russia, 1993). Nonetheless, a formal emphasis on simple geometries and proportions remains the stylistic locus.

Komonen, editor of the leading Finnish architectural review, *Arkkitehti*, between 1978–80, noted that "Postmodern eclecticism" never gained much ground in Finland because historical quotation was seen as best left metaphorical, and modernist experimentation, especially in materials, standards or assemblies, was a strategy not yet exhausted.

The emphasis on sweeping facades and archetypal forms reappears with the Rovaniemi Airport Terminal (1992). The terminal functions are housed in a steel box with a cable-stayed roof. In turn, the box is fronted by a long arc of a canopy, also cable-stayed, and other site improvements that inscribe larger arcs out into the landscape. This specific reference to Rovaniemi's location on the Arctic Circle is continued on the interior, where a skylight documents the Arctic's subtle year-to-year shifts and an art installation traces evidence of the Earth's orbit onto the terminal's floor.

The Emergency Services College in Kuopio, Finland (1995) creates a precisely ordered landscape around separate buildings. A long bar with a double-loaded corridor houses the teaching college. Surmounting the corridor is sloped glazing and exposed steel frame for cable stays, typical in Heikkinen and Komonen's work, creating a rhythmic roofscape. Students are housed in a dormitory shaped as a gentle arc set back from the college, an arrangement that articulates the college's entrance. This *parti* of a curved dormitory shape, in contrast to a rectilinear instruction space was reworked for the European Film College at Ebeltoft in Denmark (1993). But instead of the courtyard-style grouping of elements at the Emergency Services College, the film college's bar and arc are deployed in contrast to its sloping site. The dormitory's access stairs have been dramatically pulled out of the arc and grouped to make five pavilions crowning the higher portion of the school's site. Opposite, the instructional building cuts the site in half, rakishly perpendicular to a depression in front, which facilitates a dramatic suspended main entrance to the second floor of the embedded bar.

Heikkinen and Komonen's international work continued with the commission for the Finnish Embassy in Washington, D.C. (1994). The embassy is a box fronted by a mesh facade, juxtaposed by green granite facades, and sited against a steep ravine to the north. The south mesh facade is fitted with a bronze trellis to allow creepers to shade the interior, whereas the north facade's extensive glazing visually brings the great trees of the ravine into the building. Inside the box a light well through the center of the building provides illumination for the lower level. Elements of the building entwine the site figuratively: at the front, lights set into the drive mark the embassy's construction

module, whereas at the back, lights set on the tips of poles continue the main floor datum out among the trees.

The recently completed Lume Media Center (2000) in Helsinki's Arabia neighborhood is a part of the expansion of the Helsinki University of Art and Design and continues the experimentation with the vocabulary of metal facades fronting boxes, exposed steel frames, cables, and glazed walkways, but now works within a context of old factory buildings. Also recently completed is a molecular biological research center for the Max Planck Institute of Molecular Cell Biology and Genetics in Dresden, Germany (2000).

TIMO LINDMAN

See also **Aalto, Alvar (Finland); Blomstedt, Aulis (Finland); Helsinki, Finland**

Selected Publications

Heikkinen, Mikko, "Architecture Beyond Philosophical Ideas," *OZ* 18 (1996)
Komonen, Markku, "Heroic Tales and Everyday Building," *Process Architecture* 37 (1983)

Further Reading

Davey, Peter (editor), *Heikkinen and Komonen*, by Heikkinen and Komonen, Barcelona: Gili, 1994
Morgan, William (editor), *Heikkinen and Komonen*, New York: Monacelli Press, 1998
Quantrill, Malcolm, *Finnish Architecture and the Modernist Tradition*, London and New York: E and FN Spon, 1995

HEJDUK, JOHN 1929–2000

Architect, United States

Throughout his career John Hejduk's speculative designs examined the limits and potentials of architectural representation. Transforming the dominant 20th-century tenets of functionalism, Hejduk's work interrogates the origins of architectural making and meaning located within personal desire and memory (informed by literature, painting, and other parallel forms of representation). Generative pragmatic and programmatic issues were infused with this poetic intention, resulting in works of extreme spatial plasticity. Hejduk's research initially explored architecture in speculative axonometric design, then moved toward built works, and finally toward pure poetic impulse.

As a link between what has been built and what could be built, all of Hejduk's proposals were inherently constructable, although few were realized. As the dean of the architecture program at the Cooper Union for the Advancement of Science and Art (1965–2000), Hejduk decisively influenced many generations of designers with this unique vision of the vocation of architecture.

The beginning of this research began in the mid-1950s while he was teaching at the University of Texas at Austin (along with American architect Colin Rowe). Later named the "The Texas Rangers," their revisionist investigations of modern architecture strongly shaped the theory and practice of architecture after modernism. Hejduk's earliest design work interrogated and extended a strict Le Corbusian vocabulary of forms, frames, and gridded spaces with a degree of precision and control drawn more from De Stijl painter Piet Mondrian's paintings than from the Cubist precursors. This first series, the Texas Houses (1957–63), examined the mutability of space composed within idealized structural frames where the precision of modern space and its discrete systems are fused into an autonomous apparatus. These formalist works, precisely inscribed in axonometric sketches and drawings, extended the void of modern space into a hermetic negation of site and context.

In the houses of the Diamond Series (1963–67), the influence of Mondrian's paintings is more explicit. Using both orthogonal grids and a fundamental 45-degree rotation of plan, the resultant structure, enclosure, space, and objects are compressed into a dialogue that strains at the limits of axonometric representation.

The exploration of the elemental relations of form, function, and planes was transformed and liberated from determinist grids in the next phase of research, the Wall Houses (1968–74). The Wall Houses represented a search for a symbolic order governing the forms of functional program where individual spaces are encoded as extremely primary volumes (circle, square, triangle, and oval). In the Wall Houses, Hejduk also questioned the historical status of the wall in architecture as a space-defining element. In these projects, the walls, often separated from and extending beyond functional volumes, became significant metaphorical representations of passage, boundary, and mass. The "1/4 House C" used Miesian planes of the brick villa to extend into hypothetical landscape. In the "1/4 House D," these planes disappeared, and in the "3/4 House," the differentiated spaces were distributed by elongated circulation paths. In the "Wall House 2/Bye House," (designed in 1973 but only built in 2001, in Groningen, the Netherlands) the diagrammatic distillation of function is distributed across both sides of a metaphoric wall. The "Wall House 3" used the wall as a plan or plane for compositionally arranging purist volumes of space, appearing to be turned inside out, and achieving the fluidity of space that the earlier series resisted.

Among the significant examples of his built work are the Berlin Tower and Garden Apartments (1998) and a civic center (2000, with Antonio San Martin G. de Azcon) in Santiago de Compostela, Spain.

Hejduk was later recognized in the publication *Five Architects* as a significant figure in the emergence of a new American modernist style, along with Charles Gwathmey, Peter Eisenman, Richard Meier, and Michael Graves (known as the "New York Five"). These architects drew on the legacy of Le Corbusier modernism at the scale in the design of the domestic house to develop a theory of architectural construction that remained relevant to modernism.

Throughout the 1970s and early 1980s, Hejduk worked through a new series of proposals that led to the radical fragmentation of space into freestanding object-buildings. These "masques" (1979–83) manifest as structures that defy categorization, blending architecture, scenography, sculpture, and poetry. The term "masque" (*máscara*) reflects the masking of function by form and recalls fetes, festivals, and even death masks, rejecting the functionalism of architecture for metaphor. The Berlin *Máscara*, built in 1981 at the IBA in Berlin, Germany, reveals Hejduk's interest in the pastische of rhetoric with architectural form. Situated in a site ravaged during World War II, the Berlin *Máscara* contradicted the dominant urban logic of reconstructing the shattered perimeter-block urbanism with in-fill buildings.

In 1998 Hejduk staged the *La Máscara de la Medusa* (the Mask of Medusa) in Buenos Aires. Constructed of wood and metal and painted black, *La Máscara de la Medusa* is sited within an historical neighborhood called "La Boca" whose houses are made of primary color–painted metal and wood sheets. Erected at the doorstep of Fundación Proa, alongside a riverbank, the *Medusa* project is visible from several entrances to Buenos Aires. It was designed to be a collaborative space where urban-artistic projects including performances, poetry readings, plays, and even a disco would flourish. Other *Máscara* projects were done in Vladivostok, Russia, Riga, Latvia, and elsewhere.

THOMAS MICAL

See also **Le Corbusier (Jeanneret, Charles-Édouard) (France)**

Biography

Born 9 July 1929 in New York. Studied at the Cooper Union for the Advancement of Science and Art (New York City) and the University of Cincinnati, Ohio; earned master's degree in architecture, Harvard University, 1953. Traveled to Rome, Italy, on a Fulbright grant the following year; taught at University of Texas, Austin (1954–56). Worked for I. M. Pei and Partners (New York,) and A. M. Kinney and Associates (New York,). Assistant professor, Cornell University, Ithaca, New York (1958–60); Yale University (1964); professor, Cooper Union, New York (1964–2000); dean of architecture program, Cooper Union (1975–2000). Fellow, American Institute of Architects (1979). Died 3 July 2000 in New York.

Selected Works

Atelierturm Charlottenstrasse, Berlin, Germany, 1988
Mask of the Medusa, Buenos Aires, 1998
Bye House (or Wall House), Groningen, Netherlands, designed in 1973; built posthumously in 2001

Selected Publications

Adjusting Foundations, New York: Monacelli Press, 1995
Education of an Architect, New York: Rizzoli, 1988
Pewter Wings, Golden Horns, Stone Veils, New York: Monacelli Press, 1997
Soundings, New York: Rizzoli, 1993
Vladivostok, New York: Rizzoli, 1989
Mask of Medusa: Works 1947–1983, New York: Rizzoli, 1985

HELSINKI, FINLAND

Architecture in Helsinki is above all young, the vast majority having been built in the 20th century. Through such an abrupt transformation of urban environment, Finnish architecture has formed a worldwide heritage. A certain unmistakably Finnish quality in architecture is created out of the blending of Finnish traditions, climate, and nature with cosmopolitan modernity. The architecture of Alvar Aalto, for example, who dominated Finnish architecture from 1927 until his death in 1976 at the age of 78, is regarded as distinctively Finnish in character.

The National Romantic movement was the first style to be inspired by Finnish building heritage. The firm of Eliel Saarinen,

Herman Gesellius, and Armas Lindgren took the lead in the creation of new architecture. International influences ranged from the architecture of American H.H. Richardson to German and Viennese Art Nouveau (Jugendstil). Imaginative and picturesque, this movement sought to fuse architecture with decorative motifs. Authentic Finnish building materials such as wood, natural stone, and granite were favored. Lars Sonck's Telephone Building (1905) in Helsinki recalls the Finnish medieval tradition. Sonck's Stock Exchange (1911), a neoclassical monumental building, features a grandiose interior of alternating white and red colors.

In the decade preceding World War I, Finnish architecture achieved greater simplicity, as seen in Selim A. Lindqvist's work. Eliel Saarinen's monumental Helsinki Railway Station (1919) features a high tower and regulated cubic pavilions. Another notable building is Sigurd Frosterus' residential and office building "Taos" (1912). Saarinen's mostly unrealized Munkkiniemi-Haaga plan (1915) and the Greater Helsinki plans (1918) expressed the ideal of the city as a work of art. Although this tradition was broken by the next generation of architects, architects such as Erik Bryggman and Aalto were able to integrate new buildings into old surroundings.

After the declaration of Finland's independence in 1917 from Russia, Nordic classicism became the leading style, enriched by Finnish classical architectural heritage and new international models. The Parliament House (1931), designed by J.S. Siren, was the greatest classical project. Oiva Kallio produced a plan for the reorganization of central Helsinki based on Siren's Parliament Building. However, the greatest achievements were in residential buildings and social housing. The garden suburb Käpylä (1925), designed by Birger Brunila and Otto-I Meurman, embodied the social ideals of the period. The architect Martti Välikangas freely interpreted wooden classical style to create intimate domestic architecture with standardized elements. An important model was Finnish wooden farmhouses in the ironworks communities.

During the period of transition to functionalism, a new generation of classically trained architects, such as Hilding Ekelund, Bryggman, and Aalto, created architecture that is natural, light, humane, and delicate, as seen in Ekelund's Helsinki Art Hall (1929). Bryggman's works range from functionalist designs to those of the 1940s and 1950s that emphasize the assimilation of tradition as well as the role of the landscape. Märta Blomstedt's Union Bank (1926) in Helsinki, in Romantic Classicism, also pointed toward functionalism.

White functionalism was in full force by the 1930s. During the functionalist phase, from 1927 until 1939, Finnish architects gradually assimilated international influences, such as the work of Le Corbusier, modern Dutch industrial buildings, Soviet architecture, and the work of the Swedish architect Gunnar Asplund. Functionalism led to a radical reform of architecture and aimed at resolving real problems and creating interconnected, well-lit spaces. One of the first functionalist building was Glass Palace (1935) by Viljo Revell, Niilo Kokko, and Heimo Riihimäki. The Olympic Village (1940) by Ekelund and Martti Välikangas was the first significant project built by a Finnish public utility housing company. Uno Ullberg's Bensow Office Building (1940) exhibits a mature command of the modernist vocabulary.

In the 1930s, a larger variety of materials, such as wood, natural stone, clinker, and brick, was used in functionalist architecture, which was becoming more practical and more regionalist. Combinations of building parts and room forms that opened onto outdoor spaces achieved flexible spatial arrangements. The wooden structures and joint forms developed by Aalto would become a source of inspiration for decades to come. Aalto made a significant contribution in the creation of a living and working environment that is close to nature. Aalto's house and studio (1936) in Helsinki reflect this ideal. Its simple L-shaped plan integrates a much more complex form. The purity of Aalto's earlier functionalism is replaced by a unique blend of the romantic tradition, classicism, and functionalism that would be expressed in his mature work. Through his design for standardized wood furniture, Aalto achieved a cohesion between interior spaces and the furnishing that refer to Saarinen's work and to Frank Lloyd Wright's concept of organic architecture.

The central aim of postwar reconstruction was the creation of cost-efficient and well-functioning housing. Standardization, initiated by the Finnish Association of Architects, became important. Cubelike houses in wood—the only available material—came to epitomize Finnish housing. Aalto initiated the "AA system" of industrially produced expandable wooden house types. His aim in the 1940s was the development of "flexible standardization," which pointed far into the future. An important source of inspiration for Aalto was the Karelian house, a flexibly evolving group of buildings with a variety of forms.

The 1950s are often seen as the golden age of modern Finnish architecture. The period saw a fundamental change in building because of widespread urbanization. In 20 years, over a million new dwellings—two-thirds of the entire number in Finland—would be built. Some of the finest achievements are the early parts of Tapiola Garden City, in the suburbs of Helsinki, which showcase the integration of the landscape and the application of industrial construction techniques. Aarne Ervi, who designed the master plan, also designed the apartment complex at Myllytie 3 (1961) in Helsinki. Ervi's finest building is Töölö Library (1970) in Helsinki. The Palace Hotel and Industrial Center (1952) at the harbor, designed by Revell (a former assistant of Aalto) and Keijo Petäjä, marked the trend toward rational, clear-cut forms. The plan of Revell's Kärjensivu Terrace Houses (1955) near Helsinki has variations that are well adapted to the topography. This project resonates with Yrjö Lindegren's celebrated Snake House flats (1951), which gave diverse forms and sheltered yards to 190 municipal apartment blocks. The annex to the Helsinki Workers' Institute (1950) by Aulis Blomstedt remains one of the finest examples of an extension to an old building. A landmark competition, held in 1954 for the Otaniemi Chapel (1957) on the campus of Helsinki Technical University, led to the creation of one of the most celebrated modern Finnish buildings. The groundbreaking design by Heikki and Kaija Siren combined the classicism of Mies van der Rohe and Aalto's organic forest imagery. The intensive, spiritual interior space features a glass wall through which nature can be seen beyond the altarpiece.

In the 1960s, architects shifted attention to the issues of fast growth, technological development, and global problems. One trend, marked by structuralism, Constructivism, minimalism, and purism, was toward the design of universal and flexible systems and structures, especially those that were disposable and

Helsinki Parliament House, by J.S. Siren (1931)
© Chris Lisle/CORBIS

variable. The Enso-Gutzeit Headquarters (1962) by Aalto and the Marimekko Factory (1974) by Erkki Kairamo and Reijo Lahtinen are notable industrial and business projects. Aalto also focused on cultural buildings. The copper-clad Academic Bookshop (1969) contains an atrium *parti* inspired by Sonck's Stock Exchange. The atrium, decorated with vertically striped balustrades of white marble, is lit by sculptural roof lights and prism-shaped skylights. Aalto's dream cultural project was the creation of a new center of Helsinki that was to give a new image to Helsinki based on completely new symbols. Of his designs, only one, the massive Finlandia Concert Hall (1971), was built on the western shoreline of Töölö Bay. Clad in white marble, the building dominates the townscape. Aalto's perennial sensitivity to light can be seen in the light-filled hall with wooden louvering in indigo.

The most influential Finnish architect after Aalto is a disciple of Blomstedt, Reima Pietilä, whose work spans from the 1960s to his death in 1993. His ecologically balanced designs are powerfully individual. Finnish local expression is blended with references to the experimental European architecture of the 1920s. Pietilä's winning design for the President's Residence (1993), with a form of a mermaid washed up on a shore, is based on natural metaphors, such as the crystalline structure of ice. Tree motifs decorate the doors. Another influential figure, Aarno Ru-

usuvuori, a master of pure, modern, minimalist architecture, created buildings that are cool, stripped, and self-contained. Significant projects include the restoration and extension of the Helsinki City Hall (1988). One of Timo Penttilä's outstanding designs for power stations is the Hanasaari Power Plant (1976) for Helsinki. In the Helsinki Municipal Theater (1967), Penttilä achieved a lively dialogue between the natural terrain outside and its constructed counterpart inside. An important representative of classical modernism in Finland is Juha Leiviskä. Myyrmäki Church (1985) illustrates Leiviskä's highly recognizable aesthetic and exemplifies his sculptural use of light.

The 1980s and 1990s saw the manifestation of a diversity of style, often inspired by old buildings with varied surface treatments. Gullichsen, Kairamo, and Vormala's Stockmann Department Store extension (1989) is one of the rare recent urban interventions in the center of Helsinki. The refined and simple glass-and-steel facade successfully defers to the neoclassical landmark. The works of Juhani Pallasmaa, the firm of Heikkinen and Komonen, and MONARK, which represent three generations of contemporary practice, are uncompromisingly modernist with an emphasis on precision, purity, and meditation. The Itäkeskus Tower (1987) of Erkki Kairamo used repetition, rhythm, and emphasis on the vertical. One of the new landmarks by Mikko Heikkinen and Markku Komonen, whose work emphasizes precise, clean, and taut lines, is the perforated metal lighting columns (1998) lining the road to Vuosaari. The Center for Changing Exhibitions (mid-1990s) by Pekka Helin and Tuomo Siitonen has a luminous glass entry hall that takes advantage of the darkness of Finnish winter and fall.

The unique quality of Finnish architecture is often represented by the concept of the "architecture of silence," which points to a philosophical, internalized process that generates a wide range of architectural expressions. The urban tradition is young, and the greatest achievements in Finnish architecture tend to be the buildings that are placed in untamed nature or a landscaped park. The archetypal simplicity that is inspired by the landscape has been the source of the astonishing tradition of asceticism, restraint, measure, rationality, and above all silence. The tendency toward "natural architecture" has manifested itself in the ways in which Aalto sought repeatedly to liberate architecture; Pietilä integrated warm, organic forms into modernism; and modernist architects sought to carve away excess and create singular organic forms and volumes, a universe of solitude.

HAZEL HAHN

See also **Aalto, Alvar (Finland); Heikkinen and Komonen (Finland); Helsinki Railway Station, Finland; Pietilä, Reima and Raili (Finland); Saarinen, Eero (Finland); Saarinen, Eliel (Finland); Siren, Heikki and Kaija (Finland)**

Further Reading

The majority of English-language works on Finnish architecture focuses on the work of Alvar Aalto. In the last decade several comprehensive works on modern Finnish architecture have appeared, and significant works on the romantic national movement also came out.

Connah, Roger, *Writing Architecture: Fantômas Fragments Fictions: An Architectural Journey through the Twentieth Century*, Cambridge, Massachusetts: MIT Press, 1989

Connah, Roger, *The End of Finnish Architecture, or, Ciao, Potemkin!* Helsinki: Finnish Building Centre, 1994

Hausen, Marika, et al., *Eliel Saarinen: Projects, 1896–1923*, Cambridge, Massachusetts: MIT Press, 1990

Helander, Vilhelm, and Simo Rista, *Suomalainen rakennustaide*, Helsinki: Kirjayhtymä, 1987; as *Modern Architecture in Finland*, Helsinki: Kirjayhtymä, 1987

Koho, Timo, *Alvar Aalto: Urban Finland*, Helsinki: Finnish Building Centre, 1995

Korvenmaa, Pekka (editor), *The Work of Architects: The Finnish Association of Architects, 1892–1992*, Helsinki: Finnish Association of Architects, Finnish Building Centre, 1992

Mikkola, Kirmo, "Alvar Aalto and Town Planning," in *Genius Loci: Otto-I. Meurmanin 90-vuotisjuhlakirja; In Commemoration of the 90th Birthday of Otto-I. Meurman. 4/6/1980*, Helsinki: Rajennuskirja, 1980

Moorhead, Gerald, "Finland after Aalto," *Architectural Record* 178, no. 10 (1990)

Moorhouse, Jonathan, Michael Carapetian, and Leena Ahtola-Moorhouse, *Helsinki Jugendstil Architecture, 1895–1915*, Helsinki: Otava, 1987

Nerdinger, Winfried (editor), *Alvar Aalto: Toward a Human Modernism*, Munich and New York: Prestel, 1999

Nikula, Riitta, *Architecture and Landscape: The Building of Finland*, Helsinki: Otava, 1993

Norri, Marja-Riitta, Elina Standertskjöld, and Wilfried Wang (editors), *Finland*, Munich and New York: Prestel, 2000

Poole, Scott, "Foreign Brief: Finland (The Emergence of Contemporary Finnish Architecture)," *Progressive Architecture* 73, no. 5 (1992)

Poole, Scott, *The New Finnish Architecture*, New York: Rizzoli, 1992

Quantrill, Malcolm, *Alvar Aalto, a Critical Study*, New York: Schocken Books, 1983

Quantrill, Malcolm, *Reima Pietilä: Architecture, Context, and Modernism*, New York: Rizzoli, 1985

Quantrill, Malcolm, *Finnish Architecture and the Modernist Tradition*, London and New York: Spon, 1995

Quantrill, Malcolm, and Bruce Webb (editors), *The Culture of Silence: Architecture's Fifth Dimension*, College Station: Texas A and M University Press, 1998

Reed, Peter (editor), *Alvar Aalto: Between Humanism and Materialism*, New York: Museum of Modern Art, 1998

Richards, James Maude, *A Guide to Finnish Architecture*, New York: Praeger, 1967

Richards, James Maude, *800 Years of Finnish Architecture*, London: David and Charles, 1978

Salokorpi, Asko, *Modern Architecture in Finland*, New York: Praeger, 1970

Schildt, Göran, *Alvar Aalto: The Complete Catalogue of Architecture, Design, and Art*, New York: Rizzoli, and London: Academy Editions, 1994

Schildt, Göran, *Alvar Aalto: The Decisive Years*, New York: Rizzoli, 1986

Schildt, Göran, *Alvar Aalto: The Mature Years*, New York: Rizzoli, 1991

Tempel, Egon, *Neue finnische Architektur*, Teufen, Switzerland: Niggli, 1968; as *New Finnish Architecture*, translated by James C. Palmes, New York: Praeger, 1968

Trencher, Michael, *The Alvar Aalto Guide*, New York: Princeton Architectural Press, 1996

Tuomi, Timo, Kristiina Paatero, and Eija Rauske (editors), *Alvar Aalto in Seven Buildings: Interpretations of an Architect's Work; Alvar Aalto in Sieben Bauwerken: Interpretationen des Lebenswerks eines Architekten* (bilingual English-German edition), Helsinki: Museum of Finnish Architecture, 1998

HELSINKI RAILWAY STATION, FINLAND

Designed by Eliel Saarinen; completed 1914–

The Helsinki Central Railway Station is one of the earliest celebrated landmarks of post-Art Nouveau architecture. It was built in response to Finland's increasing turn-of-the-century demand for railway services that could link domestic and international cities. Designed in 1904 by Finnish architect Gottlieb Eliel Saarinen (1873–1950), the winning entrant in the competition held by the State Railway Administration, its phased construction commenced in 1905. The first phase was completed in 1909, the second phase, however, comprising the station proper itself, was only substantially completed in 1914.

The work on the interiors continued for several years. The inauguration was delayed until March 5, 1919, because of its conversion to a military medical facility in 1914 and its use as such by the Russians until the end of World War I. After the war, when Finland reclaimed its national independence, additional modifications were necessary. The elaborate waiting area for example, that was previously designated for the czar of Russia had to be redesigned and reconstructed for the president of the new

Helsinki Railway Station, designed by Eliel Saarinen (1914–)
© Esto

republic. Although these unforeseen circumstances compromised the design development of the building's interior and delayed its intended civic use as a gateway to the capital, they never detracted from the Station's farsighted role in Helsinki becoming a modern 20th-century metropolis.

The Central Station's design that was intended to resonate the spirit of the emerging Romantic Nationalistic movement in Finland instead sparked extensive public debates in the volatile climate of public opinion about Romantic Nationalism versus Romantic Classicism. Whereas the former was driven by a search for a Finnish national style, the latter was associated with nostalgia and the imperialist Russian mannerism apparent in building designs in Helsinki. Protracted criticisms and an equally important fusion of progressive design influences led to several major revisions, which were informed by American architecture and new developmental trends in German and British railway station design. The station's arch, for example, with input from Herman Gesellius, was characterized as a simplified interpretation of the Transportation Building designed by the American architect Louis Sullivan for the 1893 World's Columbian Exposition in Chicago, Illinois. Similarly, the side elevations were linked to Sullivan's other well-known building, the National Farmers Bank (1908) in Owatonna, Minnesota. The station tower's affinity to that of the Palais Stoclet (1911) by Austrian architect Josef Hoffmann has also been extensively noted. The most frequent association, however, was made with a prominent example of Jugendstil, the Secession Exhibition Building in Vienna, Austria (1899), designed by Austrian architect Josef Olbrich.

Although a tectonic correspondence between the station and its sources of inspiration is evident, it has been filtered by an unpretentious and logical Nordic design strategy that has abstracted the classical and the Finnish vernacular influences to achieve architectural clarity. Saarinen's final design emerges as rational and without referencing any romanticism typically evident in architecture of the post-Art Nouveau era.

The station complex creates an overall impression of a meticulously detailed Expressionistic Modern form, even though it was spatially configured as an angular U-shaped terminus in compliance with a predetermined plan prepared by Board of Railways staff architect, Bruno Granholm. The boldly scaled and geometrically defined heraldic single-arched granite elevation of the main entrance is dominated by a barrel-vaulted and copper-trimmed roof. The arched window with reeded frames is horizontally divided by a massive flat copper-trimmed canopy to emphasize the entrance. The geometric force of the flanking piers is relieved by a pair of stylized sculptures of masculine Nordic figures by Emil Wilstrom on both sides of the entrance, each extending a spherical lantern as they emerge from the walls. Asymmetrically planned, the mass of the terminus is punctuated by a 49-meter high clock tower with a copper-cladded dome that mediates the vertical upward thrust of its shafts from an octagonal plan. The synergy of these forms with their clean-lined geometry is a potent introduction to a building, within which formal design issues dealing with modern functions have been successfully addressed as evidenced by the relationship between internal functions and external form.

The station, a remarkably advanced building for the period, also represents a celebration of new construction technologies and redefined collaborative relationships between architect and engineer, in this case Jalmari Castren. Although conventional materials, such as brick, concrete, smooth hewn granite, and plaster for wall surfaces were used routinely, the arches in the waiting area were constructed with dimensional concrete, which at the time was a relatively new procedure in Europe and unfamiliar to the Finnish construction trades.

The Central Station drew international critical acclaim not only to its design and the architecture of Finland in general, but also to its architect, who until 1907 was only regionally known as a founding member of the Gesellius, Lindgren, Saarinen Partnership. The timely convergence of the winning entree's design approach tempered by an empirical understanding of Helsinki's inner city and environs and how planned transportation systems would affect these as a coherent metropolis established Saarinen's international stature.

The Central Station not only provided Helsinki with a monumental focal point and a picturesque landmark, but also made material contribution to the definition of the historical dimensions of Modern architecture. This is significant when considering that Finnish architecture was previously hindered by the culture's geographic isolation from mainstream Western cultures and a language unfamiliar to outsiders. Acclaimed by the passage of time, the Central Station continues to represent the virtues of architectural clarity and the courage to creatively confront them.

ATTILA LAWRENCE

See also **National Farmers' Bank, Owatonna, Minnesota; Palais Stoclet, Brussels; Saarinen, Eliel (Finland); Vienna Secession**

Further Reading

Christ-Janer, Albert, *Eliel Saarinen*, Chicago: University of Chicago Press, 1948; revised edition, as *Eliel Saarinen: Finnish-American Architect and Educator*, 1979

Hausen, Marika, "The Helsinki Railway Station in Eliel Saarinen's First Versions, 1904," in *Taidehistoriallisia tutkimuksia: Konsthistoriska studier*, vol. 3, Helsinki: Taidehistorian Seura, 1974

Hausen, Marika, *Eliel Saarinen: Soumen-aika*, Keuruu, Finland: Kustannusosakeyhtiö, 1990; as *Eliel Saarinen: Projects, 1896–1923*, translated by Desmond O'Rourke and Michael Wynne-Ellis, Cambridge, Massachusetts: MIT Press, and Helsinki: Otava, 1990

Higuchi, Kiyoshi, "Railway Station, Helsinki, Finland, 1910–1914," *A + U* 153, no. 6 (June 1983)

Meeks, Carroll Louis Vanderslice, *The Railroad Station: An Architectural History*, New Haven, Connecticut: Yale University Press, 1956

Muto, Akira, and Keibun Sano, "Railway Station, Helsinki, Finland, 1914–1919," *Space Design*, 218 (November 1982)

Norri, Marja-Riitta, "Ideas above Their Station," *Architectural Review*, 198/1183 (September 1995)

Parissien, Steven, *Station to Station*, London: Phaidon Press, 1997

Saarinen, Eliel, *Search for Form: A Fundamental Approach to Art*, New York: Reinhold, 1948

Wodehouse, Lawrence, *The Roots of International Style Architecture*, West Cornwall, Connecticut: Locust Hill Press, 1991

HERTZBERGER, HERMAN 1932–
Architect, the Netherlands

The enduring Dutch legacy of a socially committed architecture tempered by strong functionalist beliefs found in Herman Hertzberger one of its most eloquent practitioners. Admired as much for his pedagogy as for his built work and theoretical writings, Hertzberger has maintained active participation in all three disciplines. He has taken the term *codetermination* as a sort of creed, one that speaks of the duality of structure and in-fill as well as of the need for inhabitants to participate in some meaningful way in the construction of their individual habitats. As for the latter, Hertzberger has written, "The architect's task is above all to apply more than cut-to-fit, readymade solutions and as much as possible to free in the users themselves whatever they think they need, by evoking images in them which can lead to their own personally valid solutions."

Hertzberger began his career as a follower of Aldo van Eyck during the latter's early days with the Team X (10) group. The two architects, along with Jaap Bakema, shared editorship of the prominent Dutch architectural journal *Forum* from 1959 to 1963, four fertile years in which a new approach to architecture, one promulgated most publicly by the Team X group, was detailed and comprehensively theorized. Characterized by a nonhierarchical design layout and fiercely polemical writings (many by the editors themselves), the *Forum* of these years emerged as one of the most important and singular voices in opposition to the instrumentalized functionalism of prewar architecture as characterized by Walter Gropius, Ludwig Mies van der Rohe, and Le Corbusier.

Hertzberger's experience at *Forum* played a pivotal role in the creation of the Dutch School of structuralism, of which he was to become the principal proponent. Following Team X's attempt to triumph over the functionalist divisions of CIAM (Congrès Internationaux d'Architecture Moderne), structuralism proposed an integrative approach to a building's functions, emphasizing a multiplicity of elements in a loose, complex pattern, with the whole subordinated to a single, homogeneous structural principle. The legibility that results would exist within the discrete units as well as throughout the entirety of the building. Patterns of relations between the user and the built environment, allowing for an interweaving of functions, also characterize the structuralist paradigm. Despite concerns that structuralism's infinite flexibility served to blur the programmatic distinctions between buildings of different functions, architects such as Hertzberger were able to subvert the deterministic ideals of functionalism by positing notions of an archetypal human and his or her community while still acknowledging the inexorable press of history on the effects of human interaction with built form.

Hertzberger's Centraal Beheer Insurance offices (1972) in Appeldoorn offer a textbook example for the democratic organization of building components. A regularized grid of floors, supporting columns, and service ducts provides a framework for the irregular clustering of offices and conference rooms. The modularity of the interior allows for infinite reconfigurations through the deployment of furniture and cabinets; the interior atrium recalls Frank Lloyd Wright's Larkin Building (1904) in its interwoven fabric of tectonic elements, yet it opens up the latter's more regulated symmetry through Hertzberger's deliberate attempt to infuse the space with the needs of the inhabitants to individually modify their own work spaces. Workers are thus provided with personal areas whose participation in a collective environment avoids any sense of psychological alienation; interpenetrating top-lit voids from both natural and electric sources enhance the drama of the interior and tie together the cellular workstations.

The Central Beheer offices also represent the ways in which Hertzberger's practice maintained the humanistic investigations of van Eyck with more structurally rational forms handed down from the Dutch architects Hendrik Berlage and Johannes Duiker. This insistence on corporeality and human scale while maintaining structural integrity is at the heart of this enterprise; Hertzberger has written, "Structure is the minimal order necessary to make possible the maximum liberty and even stimulate this effect."

The Diagoon Houses (1971) in Delft, a set of eight prototype houses originally designed in a larger formation for the city of Vaassen, aptly embody the aspect of self-determination that Hertzberger considered so crucial to the development of meaningful living conditions. Referred to as "half-works," the details of each dwelling unit are left deliberately ambiguous: window openings that can receive glazing or in-fill, depending on the needs of the inhabitant; carports on the lowest level to be either used as garages or converted into additional work space; and roof terraces that can become greenhouses, children's play areas, or additional penthouse space.

Hertzberger's Chassé Theatre (1995) in Breda showcases the more Expressionistic side of Hertzberger's neohumanism. Reversing the orthogonal ordering of his earlier work, the undulating roofline of the theater announces itself over the rooftops of surrounding houses, a gesture echoing the parabolic arch from which is suspended the roof of his project for the Bibliothèque de France (1989), and the curved ramps and balustrades of the foyer carve out interior space much like in the central hall of his Ministry of Social Welfare and Employment (1979–90) in The Hague. This latter work, spanning almost a decade of effort, embodies both the modular and the Expressionistic, where curvilinear staircases and elevator shafts meet the strict orthogonals of the Centraal Beheer's offices.

The exterior pays homage both to Le Corbusier's Plan Voisin with its cluster of cruciform towers and to Gropius's Fagus Werk with its glazed corner stair towers, but the interpenetration of masses and volumes, the oblique positioning at the site, and the hinged capitals that seem to allow each block to pivot against its adjoining member recall such forms as are often affiliated with Hans Scharoun, especially his Philharmonic Concert Hall (1963) in Berlin. Such varied elements of influence, integrated with the utmost integrity and conjoined with the ability to balance the necessary realms of structure and freedom, are the hallmarks of Hertzberger's style.

NOAH CHASIN

See also **Van Eyck, Aldo (Netherlands)**

Biography

Born in Amsterdam, 6 July 1932. Attended the Technische Hogeschule, Delft, Netherlands; graduated 1958. Private practice, Amsterdam from 1958; editor, *Forum*, Amsterdam 1959–63; town planning consultant, Deventer, Netherlands 1969. Instructor, Academy of Architecture, Amsterdam 1965–70; professor, University of Delft from 1970; visiting professor, Massachusetts Institute of Technology, Cambridge 1966–67, 1970, 1977, 1980; visiting professor, Columbia University, New York 1968; visiting professor, University of Toronto 1969–71, 1974; visiting professor, Tulane University, New Orleans, Louisiana 1978; visiting professor, Harvard University, Cambridge, Massachusetts 1979; visiting professor, University of Pennsylvania 1981; visiting professor, University of Geneva 1982–86; professor, University of Geneva from 1986. Honorary member, Académie Royale de Belgique 1975; chairman, Berlage Institute, Amsterdam from 1990; honorary fellow, Royal Institute of British Architects 1991.

Selected Works

Eight Experimental Houses (Diagoon), Delft, 1971
Centraal Beheer Office Building, Apeldoorn, Netherlands (with Lucas and Niemeijer), 1972
De Drie Hoven Home for the Elderly, Amsterdam-Slotervaart, 1974
Vredenburg Music Center, Utrecht, 1978
Bibliothèque Nationale (first prize, competition), Paris, 1989
Ministry of Social Welfare and Employment Office Building, The Hague, 1990
Chassé Theater, Breda, 1995

Selected Publications

Herman Hertzberger: Buildings and Projects 1959–1986 (with Arnülf Lüchinger), 1987
Herman Hertzberger: Lessons for Students in Architecture, 1991

Further Reading

Bergeijk, Herman Van, and Deborah Hauptmann, *Notations of Herman Hertzberger*, Rotterdam and New York: NAi Publishers, 1998
Lüchinger, Arnülf, *Herman Hertzberger: Bauten und Projekte 1959–86*, The Hague: Arch-Edition, 1987
Lüchinger, Arnülf, et al., "Dutch Structuralism—Contribution to a Present-Day Architecture," *Architecture + Urbanism*, 75 (1977) (special issue)
Nakamura, Toshio (editor), "Herman Hertzberger, 1959–1990," *Architecture + Urbanism*, 4/247 (1991)
Reinink, Adriaan Wessel, *Herman Hertzberger, Architect*, Rotterdam: Uitgevrij 010, 1990
Van Dijk, Hans, "Herman Hertzberger: Architectural Principles in the Age of Humanism," *Dutch Art and Architecture Today*, 6 (1979)
Vidotto, Andrea, "The Chassé Theatre in Breda," *Domus*, 776 (1995)

HERZOG AND DE MEURON

Architecture firm, Switzerland

Jacques Herzog (1950–) and Pierre de Meuron (1950–) were born in Basel, Switzerland. They attended university together at the Eidgenössische Technische Hochschule Zurich (ETH, or Swiss Federal Institute of Technology) in Zurich and were awarded their architecture degrees in 1975. Both served as assistants to Professor Wolf Schnebli at ETH in 1977. They formed their partnership, Herzog and de Meuron, in Basel in 1978. The firm has two additional partners, Harry Gugger (1956–) and Christine Binswanger (1964–), both of whom received their architecture degrees from ETH in 1990. Friends since kindergarten, Herzog and de Meuron developed a very natural collaboration in their early careers that they extended in the creation of their firm.

The firm first gained notice through a series of exhibitions that they mounted and treated as architectural projects at STAMPA Galerie in Basel in 1979, 1981, 1983, and 1988. By 1995 their work was the subject of larger exhibitions at both the Center Pompidou in Paris and the Museum of Modern Art in New York. A strong connection with the art world has been constant through the history of the firm, a natural phenomenon given their location in an art center such as Basel. Herzog has said, "We prefer art to architecture, and for that matter, artists to architects." They have been influenced by the formalism and minimalism of artists such as Donald Judd, Sol LeWitt, James Turrell, and Richard Serra and share with those innovators an interest in perception and in the relationship between object and the social, geographic, and physical context. Herzog and de Meuron collaborated early on with artist Helmut Federle on color studies for a facade design and have had several fruitful collaborations with French artist Rémy Zaugg, whom Herzog has referred to as fifth partner. The studio that they designed in 1996 for and with Rémy Zaugg in Mulhouse-Pfastatt, France, is one of several buildings that the firm has created for the production or display of art.

The project that attracted the greatest early international interest in Herzog and de Meuron was the Goetz Gallery (1992) in Munich, designed to house a private contemporary art collection on the grounds of the owners' home. Building restrictions limiting the height and footprint of the structure in a residential neighborhood required construction of a basement level to provide the stipulated amount of exhibition space. This restriction provoked an ingenious section for the building wherein both basement and upper-level galleries have equivalent spatial qualities and lighting from a high horizontal band of matte-glazed windows. The exterior of the simple rectangular pavilion appears to be a wooden volume hovering between two milky glass strips. The project is inextricably tied to art, from its cleanly detailed galleries where controlled, glare-free light falls from technically sophisticated clerestories to its elegantly skinned volume that rests like a huge piece of minimalist sculpture in the garden.

The largest art-related work of Herzog and de Meuron is the Tate Gallery of Modern Art (2000) at Bankside in London. The project renovates and extends a historic power station on the Thames River directly across from St. Paul's Cathedral. This ambitious architecture and urban design undertaking creates not just a building but a whole urban district for viewing art. Grand public spaces dedicated to display of sculpture are linked to existing walkways along the river. The neighborhood to the south is enlivened by a new public square with shops and kiosks joining the museum to its environs. The Tate Bankside, according to Herzog and de Meuron, is about looking, perception, and communication. Its six suites of galleries, along with the spectacular renovated Turbine Hall, offer a wide variety of spaces and contexts in which to experience modern and contemporary art and interact with other visitors.

Herzog and de Meuron have dealt with a wide range of building types, including offices, housing, university buildings, and industrial projects. The firm approached each of these with the same refined sensibilities that they have brought to their art-related work. In a series of railway projects in the Auf dem Wolf industrial area of Basel, Herzog and de Meuron have demonstrated their ability to transform ordinary building programs and nondescript sites into significant works of architecture. The large Railway Engine Depot (1999) gives clarity and order to a wasteland of railway tracks, warehouses, sheds, and weeds. Nearby, Signal Box 4 (1995) is a six-story district landmark that, in its treatment as a single monolithic block, becomes a powerful sculptural object. The Central Signal Box (2000) creates a visual dialogue with its earlier counterpart but also functions as a part of the rest of the city in its close relationship to the street and existing solitary buildings around it. Both signal boxes are clad in eight-inch-wide copper strips that are twisted in the midsection of some walls to admit daylight. The copper cladding not only provides durability in a corrosive industrial environment but also becomes a Faraday cage, protecting electronic equipment inside from electromagnetic fields on the site.

The Dominus Winery (1998) in Napa Valley, California, similarly elevates a building of modest purposes to high art. Its long, thin volume parallels the rows of vines that surround it as well as a ridge of hills in the distance, creating an impressive

Tate Modern extension (2000) at Bankside, London, by Herzog and de Meuron
© Christian Richters/Esto

symbiosis of structure and site. The building's skin is constructed of gabions (wire cages filled with rocks) employing a local basalt that further links the agriculture structure to the land. Elegantly and poetically detailed, the winery combines, like wine making itself, technical proficiency and sensory delight.

This combination characterizes much of Herzog and de Meuron's work in which experiments with wood, copper, stone, concrete, and glass have produced dazzling and innovative visual effects. Patterns created by varied concrete textures or by silk-screened printing on glass, for example, have gone through several generations of refinement, from the Pafaffenholz Sports Center (1993) in France to the Technical School Library (1999) in Eberswalde, Germany.

LAWRENCE W. SPECK

See also **Ricola Storage Building, Laufen, Switzerland; Switzerland**

Biography

Jacques Herzog

Born in Basel, Switzerland 19 April 1950. Studied architecture under Aldo Rossi and Dolf Schnebli, ETH–Zurich; degree in architecture 1975. Assistant to Dolf Schnebli, ETH–Zurich 1977. Partner, with Pierre de Meuron, Herzog and de Meuron Architecture Studio, Basel from 1978. Arthur Rotch Design Critic in Architecture, Graduate School of Design, Harvard University, Cambridge, Massachusetts.

Pierre de Meuron

Born in Basel, Switzerland 5 May 1950. Studied architecture under Aldo Rossi and Dolf Schnebli, ETH–Zurich; degree in architecture 1975. Assistant to Dolf Schnebli, ETH–Zurich 1977. Partner, with Pierre de Meuron, Herzog and de Meuron Architecture Studio, Basel from 1978.

Herzog and de Meuron Architecture Studio

Formed in 1978 in Basel, Switzerland by Jacques Herzog and Pierre de Meuron.

Selected Works

Goetz Gallery, Munich, 1992
Pafaffenholz Sports Center, France, 1993
Signal Box Four, Auf dem Wolf, Basel, Switzerland, 1995
Rémy Zaugg Studio, Mulhouse-Pfastatt, France, 1996
Dominus Winery, Napa Valley, California, 1998
Railway Engine Depot, Auf dem Wolf, Basel, Switzerland, 1999
Technical School Library, Eberswalde, Germany, 1999
Tate Gallery of Modern Art at Bankside (renovation and extention), London, 2000
Central Signal Box, Auf dem Wolf, Basel, Switzerland, 2000
Ricola Storage Building, Laufen, Switzerland, 1986–87

Selected Publication

Herzog and de Meuron–Sammlung Goetz, 1998

Further Reading

Gilber, Mark, and Kevin Alter (editors), *Construction, Intention, Detail: Five Projects from Five Swiss Architects; Funf projekte von funf Schweizer architekten* (bilingual English-German edition), Zurich: Artemis, 1994
Herzog and de Meuron, 1983–1993, Madrid: Croquis, 1993
Levene, Richard C. (editor), *Herzog and de Meuron, 1993–1997*, Madrid: El Croquis, 1997
Lucan, Jacques (editor), *Herzog and de Meuron: Six Works, 1987– 1995*, Tokyo: A + U, 1995
Mack, Gerhard, *Herzog and de Meuron: das Gesamtwerk: The Complete Works* (bilingual German-English edition), 2 vols., Basel and Boston: Birkhäuser, 1996–97
Ruff, Thomas, and Steven Holl (editors), *Architectures of Herzog and de Meuron*, New York: Blum, 1994; 2nd edition, 1995
Wang, Wilfried, *Herzog and de Meuron: Projects and Buildings, 1982–1990*, New York: Rizzoli, 1990
Wang, Wilfried, *Herzog and de Meuron* (bilingual English-German edition), Zurich: Artemis, 1992; 3rd enlarged edition, Boston: Birkhäuser, 1998

HIGH MUSEUM OF ART

Designed by Richard Meier, completed 1983
Atlanta, Georgia

The High Museum of Art in Atlanta has been cited as one of the ten best works of American architecture of the 1980s by the American Institute of Architects. Situated in midtown, this white porcelain–clad museum sits on a corner site facing Peachtree

High Museum of Art, interior, designed by Richard Meier (1983)
© Brad Wrisley. Photo courtesy the High Museum of Art

High Museum of Art, exterior, designed by Richard Meier
© Brad Wrisley. Photo courtesy the High Museum of Art

Street, the main north–south artery of the city. It houses a significant collection of 19th- and 20th-century American art and American folk art.

The plan has four quadrants with one square displaced and pivoted at an angle of 60 degrees, creating a separate auditorium. The space created by this displacement becomes the focal atrium space. Externally, this is reflected in the piano-shaped entrance and the curved facade of the atrium. The remaining three squares are the galleries that wrap around the atrium in an L shape. A diagonal ramp takes visitors from the street, through a gateway, past a two-story 250-seat auditorium, and into a low entrance foyer, culminating in the 67-foot skylit atrium flooded with light. This procession is further continued up the superimposed series of ramps situated on the curving external side of the atrium connecting the galleries at various levels. Ramps and the galleries are designed to create multiple perspectives. The windows of the curved facade along the ramp open the museum toward the city, enlivening the social area of the museum.

Processional movement from the entrance to its interior creates a variety of spatial experiences. Critics suggest that the museum has a theatrical quality that places visitors in a multiplicity of frames, turning them into spectators and performers. The ramp becomes a central compositional device that organizes and manipulates horizontal and vertical surfaces. Its regular pendulum-like movement induces visitors to appreciate the building's geometry and to celebrate the circumference by not passing through the galleries but receiving glimpses into them. The three large square galleries that anchor the corners have walls with inset display cases that allow views through creating new interrelationships from a variety of vantage points. Yet architect Richard Meier creates the domestic feeling of the early museums (situated in grand residences and palaces) from which he derives inspiration. The interplay of display cases, walls with windows, and ceiling grids all create a sense of nested scales throughout the galleries. In addition, the column grid interacts with the pattern of subdivision so that the columns choreograph movement. Along the ramp, they mark the direction of bound movement, and at the center of the galleries, they slow down movement in addition to defining and breaking up space. Light is also used to further enhance movement, drawing visitors into galleries through the use of floor-to-ceiling windows and glass-block slits at the cross axes. Within the galleries are spotlights for the exhibits while daylight floods the atrium delineating the geometry of the quarter circle.

The program was originally developed by Gudmund Vigtel, the first director of the High Museum. He felt that architecture of the highest quality was important to the success of the museum in order to place it on the cultural map and thereby draw support from key institutions and individuals. The program also contributed to making this museum unique in that, unlike others, it originally allocated two-thirds of the plan space for service functions. Initially, the granite-paneled two lower floors of the building had an education department with its own gallery, resource center, screening room, and major service areas, including storage. Today, they house a cafe, offices of curators and assistants, and meeting rooms. The lowest floor has carpenter shops and other utilities. The main entrance level has a gallery with an interactive introduction to the fundamental elements of art for visitors of all ages, a gift shop, and the main atrium, occupying 5000 square feet, which is the social and public space of the building and is available for special events. Originally, the galleries were arranged chronologically on three floors above this level with the display of decorative arts designed by Meier. In 1996, when a special exhibition was organized to celebrate the Olympics in the city, the internal layout of gallery spaces was changed, walls were removed, and the organization since then has been thematic rather than chronological. As a result, the original experience of the galleries has not been retained. In 1993, for the tenth-anniversary celebration, a 64-foot-high wall drawing was commissioned by the museum from the minimalist artist Sol LeWitt for the atrium.

Comparisons have often been made between this building and Meier's earlier works. Although very different in its design approach, the basic parti of four quadrants is much like a reinterpretation of his Frankfurt Museum (1979–85), the design of which was completed just before receiving the commission for the High Museum. The ramp is a key element in the earlier Athenaeum (New Harmong, Indiana, 1979) which incidentally also extends out to the street and the city and is similarly used to intensify the architectural experience but internally is organized in a very different manner. The external appearance of the building features porcelain enameled square panels, pipe railings, and mullion windows—Meier's signature marks.

Although organized in a different manner, the use of the ramp within an atrium is compared by critics, and by Meier himself, to Frank Lloyd Wright's Guggenheim. The spatial sequences and the play of masses in light can be compared to some of Le Corbusier's works. Classical references from the four-quadrant plan and the idea of center and symmetry seen in both the Frankfurt Museum and the High are important features in Karl F. Schinkel's work, who also uses central skylit atrium spaces that are surrounded by exhibition galleries. The High has also been seen as reflecting more of the rational sensibilities of the 18th century and deriving in essence much more from the first European museums of the Enlightenment. Compared to the work of Charles Nicholas Ledoux, Meier's building is seen as allowing the contemplating of forms as abstract entities that can be appreciated for their poetic qualities alone. In this museum and in much of Meier's other work, one can observe a concern for visual order that desires reason over function.

AARATI KANEKAR

Further Reading

A publication was prepared by the High Museum of Art on 6 October 1983 on the occasion of the dedication of the new building. It is a chronicle of the building's planning, design, and construction and includes a statement by the architect together with the Ames essay listed following.

Ames, Anthony, "A Modern Synthesis," in *High Museum of Art*, Atlanta, Georgia: High Museum of Art, 1983

Blaser, Werner (editor), *Building for Art*, Basel and Boston: Birkhäuser Verlag, 1990

Balfour, Alan, "Atlanta High: High Museum, Atlanta, Georgia," *Architectural Review*, 175/1044 (1984)

Campbell, Robert, " 'Forms Exploding' from a Drum: High Museum, Atlanta," *Architecture: The AIA Journal*, 73/5 (1984)

Fox, Catherine, "A New High for Atlanta," *Art News*, 82/9 (1983)

Freeman, Allen. "Demanding Showcase," *Architecture: The AIA Journal*, 78/12 (1989)

Maxwell, Robert, "The High Museum, Atlanta, Georgia," *AA Files*, 7 (1984)

Meier, Richard, *Richard Meier, Architect*, 3 vols., New York: Rizzoli, 1984, 1991, 1999

Meier, Richard, *Richard Meier*, London: Academy Editions, 1990

HIGHPOINT I APARTMENT BLOCK, LONDON

Designed by Lubetkin and Tecton, completed 1935

Situated on a hill in the Highgate area of north London and offering expansive views of the city, Highpoint I—an apartment block designed by the Russian architect Berthold Lubetkin and his firm, Tecton—was completed in 1935. The building is Lubetkin's personal synthesis of the social aspects of housing and urban planning that were the concern of so many modern architects during the 1920s and 1930s, a knowledge of the conceptual ideals and visual forms of modern art and architecture, and an understanding of his client's (and London's) needs. Highpoint I reflects the sophisticated, often unacknowledged state of modern British architecture in the 1930s.

The project was launched when a wealthy industrialist, Sigmund Gestetner, commissioned Lubetkin to design communal worker housing. When the only appropriate site that Gestetner could find was located in affluent Highgate, he altered the original program and asked Lubetkin to design flats to rent to middle- and upper-class tenants on the open housing market. Although Lubetkin agreed to the change as well as to Gestetner's precisely calculated profit margin for developing the site, the actual building reveals that the architect never quite renounced a commitment to collective ideals.

The garden site chosen was accompanied by a set of zoning regulations, including a height limit on the street facade and a restriction on developing the land to the building's rear, and Lubetkin's design also had to maximize the privacy, sunlight, views, and cross ventilation accorded each flat. Highpoint I consists of a symmetrical double-cruciform plan, rising seven stories on the street front and eight stories on the rear, garden-view side. The building is raised on reinforced-concrete *pilotis* (stilts), and each residential floor contains four two-bedroom flats and four three-bedroom flats. The rooftop is a communal sundeck, and the ground floor also contains a series of public spaces encountered sequentially, in essence offering a passageway from the front entrance to the garden. One enters the building from the columned *porte-cochère* (carriage entrance) that faces the street and is led on a *promenade architecturale* into an off-axis entrance hall, a semicircular winter garden and lounge, a large windowed hallway, a tearoom, and a ramp that curves down

Highpoint 1 Apartments, Highgate, London, designed by Lubetkin and Tecton (1935)
© Angelo Hornak/CORBIS

into the garden. Along the way, one passes the elevators that provide upper-floor access.

Highpoint I's ribbon windows, roof terrace, and *pilotis* clearly reflect an awareness of Le Corbusier's "five points," and, as at Le Corbusier's Villa Savoye (1929), Lubetkin's *pilotis* enable cars to pull directly up to the entranceway. The *plan libre* (free plan), however, exists only on the ground floor, and there is little flexibility within each flat. Structurally, the building diverges from Le Corbusier's notion of a free facade; the walls, made of solid concrete, are weight bearing, although they are part of an innovative structural system engineered by Ove Arup. Despite the overall simplicity of the relatively unadorned white exterior and the rigid ordering of the residential floors, Lubetkin inserted many sculptural elements into his design, similar to Le Corbusier's interpenetration of curves and diagonals into the modernist cube of Villa Savoye. At Highpoint I, for example, curved, internal towers house stairs and elevators. In plan, the distinctly round forms of the stairwells amidst the overall grid of the upper floors not only add visual complexity but also reveal a Beaux-Arts–inspired sensibility by clearly separating the so-called served and servant spaces. Sculptural forms also appear on the exterior: the balconies are curvilinear, and the now altered radio antennae on the roof (at the time, the roof of the building was the highest point in London) were modeled after the Vesnin brothers' 1923 design for the Palace of Labor. The curved ramp that descends

to thegarden from the ground floor calls to mind Constructivist sculpture and theater design and also appears in Lubetkin's 1934 design for the Penguin Pool at Regent's Park Zoo in London.

Although Highpoint I can be linked by its formal, visual language to larger understandings of modern art and architecture, Lubetkin's interest in the social role of architecture cannot be ignored. Lubetkin had been in Russia during the revolution, and he always remained connected to art and politics in his native country. Highpoint I, with its private flats and many communal spaces, invites comparisons to the Soviet social condensers and collective housing blocks of the 1920s that were so important to Le Corbusier as well, such as Moisei Ginzburg's Narkomfin apartments (1928) in Moscow. Even though Highpoint I had been intended for fairly well off tenants—the ground floor included small flats for maids and porters—Lubetkin's pared-down, modernist forms and collectivist ideals suggest a progressive, social vision for mass housing that was unusual for England at the time and offer an example of the way in which his plea to architects to "build socialistically" was modified for England's class hierarchies.

In 1936 Le Corbusier visited Highpoint I and praised its modernity, declaring it the "vertical garden city" that he had imagined but not yet built. He saw Lubetkin's apartment block as the perfect prototype for modern urban housing, one that exemplified his own ideal of a tower-in-a-park by optimizing standardization, offering clear pedestrian routes away from automobile traffic (often via *pilotis*), and providing ample communal space. By building vertically instead of horizontally, the urban structure of the future would release the surrounding land for recreational purposes. Lubetkin's Highpoint I—with its gardens, its *pilotis*, its pedestrian walkway through the ground floor, its careful attention to light and air, its use of modern materials, and its cruciform plan akin to the towers in Le Corbusier's own Contemporary City for Three Million Inhabitants (1922)—was precisely the type of building that Le Corbusier envisioned as the solution to global urban ills.

Lubetkin designed a second apartment block adjacent to Highpoint I three years later. Highpoint II (1938), as it has come to be known, failed to generate the enthusiastic response that had met Highpoint I. Lubetkin was criticized for having abandoned his rationalist principles in favor of a more mannered facade, replete with classical caryatids, and the architectural community looked nostalgically to Highpoint I for having more fully embodied the ideals of modern architecture.

DEBORAH LEWITTES

See also **Apartment Building; Arup, Ove (England); Contemporary City for Three Million Inhabitants; Corbusier, Le (Jeanneret, Charles-Édouard) (France); Ginzburg, Moisei (Russia); London, England; Lubetkin and Tecton (England)**

Further Reading

The article "Flats at Highgate" in *Architectural Review* includes two separate smaller articles that are contemporary responses to Highpoint I: "The Vertical Garden City" by Le Corbusier and "The Building" by J.M. Richards.

Allan, John, *Berthold Lubetkin: Architecture and the Tradition of Progress*, London: RIBA Publications, 1992

Curtis, William J.R., *English Architecture, 1930s: The Modern Movement in England, 1930–1939: Thoughts on the Political Content of the International Style*, Milton Keynes, Buckinghamshire: Open University Press, 1975

Diehl, Thomas, "Theory and Principle: Berthold Lubetkin's Highpoint One and Highpoint Two," *Journal of Architectural Education* 52, no. 4 (May 1999)

"Flats at Highgate," *Architectural Review* 79 (January 1936)

Hitchcock, Henry Russell, and Catherine Bauer Wurster, *Modern Architecture in England*, New York: Museum of Modern Art, 1937

Reading, Malcolm, "Tall Order," *The Architects' Journal* 23, no. 181 (5 June 1985)

Reading, Malcolm, and Peter Coe, *Lubetkin and Tecton: An Architectural Study*, London: Triangle Architectural, 1992

HILBERSEIMER, LUDWIG KARL 1885–1967

Theorist and urban planner, Germany and United States

Better known as a prolific theoretician than practicing planner, Ludwig Karl Hilberseimer left his legacy in several volumes of writing rather than in built projects or even a substantial appointment as city planner. A graduate of the Technische Hochschule's (Karlsruhe) architecture program in 1911, within

a decade Hilberseimer had turned to writing, first as art critic for many European journals and later as the author of a dozen books and more than 50 articles on city planning, architecture, and related issues.

Hilberseimer published his first theoretical work, *Hochhausstadt* [High Rise City], in 1924. This vertically zoned, centralized organization of resident–workers housed in tall, unornamented skyscrapers placed in a rectilinear grid defined by automobile traffic was well within general contemporary European city-planning tendencies (the project in many ways resembles Le Corbusier's Contemporary City for Three Million Inhabitants of two years earlier) and drew the attention of many leading European architects. Hilberseimer was invited to show these plans in the Novembergruppe Exposition of 1925; in 1927 he exhibited a centralized "Welfare City" and also collaborated with Mies van der Rohe in the Weissenhof Exposition in Stuttgart. The following year, Hannes Meyer appointed him to develop the urban-planning curriculum at the Bauhaus, where he taught until its close in 1933. Since 1931, he had been the director of the German Werkbund, another group that emphasized the machine as a tool for everyday life. In these short years, in lieu of pursuing an architectural practice, Hilberseimer produced four books that explained his utopian, modernist planning ideas. In 1938 he left Europe, accepting Mies' invitation to teach urban planning at the Armour (later Illinois) Institute of Technology.

In 1944 Hilberseimer published his first work in English, *The New City: Principles of Planning*, which codified his earlier work and revealed some new values: the potential of such natural factors as prevailing winds and solar orientation as design generators, the idea of choice among a variety of housing types, and decentralization. These ideas formed the core of his teaching at the Illinois Institute of Technology from 1938 to his death in 1967.

The "New City" attempted to accommodate modern industrial life in a more appropriate and effective manner than the "Historic City." Spanning from ancient Miletus to Penn's Philadelphia, Hilberseimer studied a variety of cultures' technologies as generators of different built environments. Modern man had failed by trying to fit his technology into extant, outmoded development patterns.

Natural forces, industrial smoke and fumes, and the burdensome reality of automobile traffic were givens and Hilberseimer's starting point. Automobiles and telephones allowed people to move into the cleaner countryside, with administrative focal points that would link country and city as one "organism." Residents could choose to live in freestanding, single-family houses as well as apartment blocks, all of which would be mixed together. Like others before him, Hilberseimer practiced exclusionary zoning, separating industrial, commercial, residential, and recreational areas. However, his was not a graphic exercise (like Le Corbusier, who endeavored to avoid "all special cases" in his "City of Tomorrow"); Hilberseimer's New City responded to specific characteristics of site: prevailing winds, solar orientation, natural resources, and topography, which would determine the shape of the settlement, allowing wind to naturally sweep industrial pollution away from residential, academic, and commercially zoned areas. To reduce pollution within these zones, Hilberseimer called for "Superblocks," which combined several regular blocks without through streets to increase green space and reduce paving and conflicts between automobile and pedestrian traffic. Limited growth would allow residents to walk to work and school. His conservative approach to the historical city included its incremental transformation, illustrated by such examples as London and Chicago. Their decrepit city centers would be vacated in waves to the cleaner, better-planned outskirts, allowing eventual replanning of old city centers.

As wind patterns organized the settlement unit, solar orientation established housing design. The placement of every room in a house was to be determined by the time of day that each was occupied. Solar rays also dictated the density of housing structures, none of which would cast shadows on another. Hilberseimer believed that this natural approach would also alleviate social problems that were thought to be caused in part by density.

Thus, nature dictated a kind of template for Hilberseimer, from the scale of the city to the individual dwelling. Once these primary considerations were made, Hilberseimer granted the architect "absolute creative freedom" (*The New City*) to articulate the individual buildings. Beyond this rhetoric—unusually accommodating to such a modernist—Hilberseimer still proposed Bauhaus ideals of mass production: like an automobile, a house should be mass-produced from industrial materials and thus made cheaply available to all. Certainly, Hilberseimer's own architectural designs show little of the creativity that his occasional statements about artistic license seem to imply.

Like other modern architects, Hilberseimer thought that the profession had a moral obligation and power to correct social ills through architecture and city planning. He emphasized the potential of new industrial materials and methods to allow freedom of housing choice for people. Placing his own work in a historical continuum, he judged his plans against such investigators whose ideas he incorporated into his own work, such as Wright (decentralization and the single family home), Le Corbusier (towers in a garden), Howard (garden space), Soria y Mata (ribbon systems), and others.

Neglected in Hilberseimer's theory were virtually any other building type but the residential unit—a marked contrast to others who designed all buildings to house modern life (e.g., Sant'Elia's power stations and Wright's office towers). Furthermore, Hilberseimer's confidence in the environment's ability to absorb limitless pollution, his indifference toward any downwind regions, and his willingness to condemn historical city centers that once provided models for his study left his theories, on the whole, impossible to implement. Still, his Superblock and his insistence on the importance of solar orientation saw application through the second half of the 20th century. Furthermore, he predicted the traffic and health problems that the suburbs would come to suffer in their lack of planning. His calls for variety of housing type to suit different human needs and consent to allow choice in architectural style were innovative. No manifesto on style, *The New City* was unusual in allowing personal intervention and individuality within the planner's overall scheme, a welcome alternative to his own inhumane and unexpressive designs.

JHENNIFER A. AMUNDSON

Biography

Born in Karlsruhe, Germany, 14 September 1885; immigrated to the United States 1938; naturalized 1944. Studied under Friedrich Ostendorf and Hermann Billing, Technische Hochschule, Karlsruhe 1906–11. Architect and planner in various European cities, especially Berlin 1918–38; during WWI designed aircraft hangars and workshops; European architectural correspondent, *Chicago Tribune* 1925. Private practice, town planner, Chicago from 1938. Founder and director, City Planning Department, Bauhaus, Dessau, Germany 1929–32; professor, director of Department of City and Regional Planning 1938–57, professor emeritus, from 1957, Illinois Institute of Technology, Chicago. Member, Novembergruppe, Berlin 1919; member, Arbeitsrat fr Kunst, Berlin 1919; member, Der Ring, Berlin 1924; member, Der Sturm artists' group, Berlin 1925; member, CIAM from 1928; director, Deutsche Werkbund from 1931; member, Advisory Board, Burnham Library, Art Institute of Chicago 1938–60; fellow, American Institute of Architects; member, Academie der K nste, Berlin. Died in Chicago, 6 May 1967.

Selected Works

Opera House, Berlin, 1911
Housing Estates: Adlergestellstrasse, Adlershofstrasse, Dörpfeldstrasse, Berlin, 1927
Rheinlandhaus, Berlin, 1926
Werkbund Exhibition Hall, Weissenhof Estate, Stuttgart, 1927
City Development Plan, Dessau, 1932
Rupendom Housing Estate, Berlin, 1935
Lafayette Park Development Plan, Detroit, 1963
Hyde Park Development Plan, Chicago, 1956

Selected Publications

Hochhausstadt, 1924
Grosstadtbauten, 1925
Groszstadt Architektur, 1927
Internationale neue Baukunst, 1927
Beton als Gestalter (with Julius Vischer), 1928
Hallen-bauten, 1931
The New City: Principles of Planning, 1944
The New Regional Pattern: Industries and Gardens, Workshops and Farms, 1949
The Nature of Cities, 1955
Mies van der Rohe, 1956
Contemporary Architecture: Its Roots and Trends, 1964
Entfaltung einer Planungsidee, 1963
Berliner Architektur der 20er Jahre, 1967

Further Reading

Banham and Curtis provide sound background for Hilberseimer's period and peers as well as commentary on the planner himself. Pommer remains the most complete single source on Hilberseimer's life and work, whereas Spaeth provides a brief overview of his life as well as a fine summary of the dozens of books and articles written by Hilberseimer.

Banham, Reyner, *Theory and Design in the First Machine Age*, New York: Praeger, and London: Architectural Press, 1960
Curtis, William J.R., *Modern Architecture since 1900*, Englewood Cliffs, New Jersey: Prentice Hall, and Oxford: Phaidon Press, 1982; 3rd edition, Upper Saddle River, New Jersey: Prentice Hall, and London: Phaidon, 1996
Dearstyne, Howard, *Inside the Bauhaus*, New York: Rizzoli, 1986
Pommer, Richard, David Spaeth, and Kevin Harrington, *In the Shadow of Mies: Ludwig Hilberseimer, Architect, Educator, and Urban Planner*, New York: Rizzoli, 1988
Spaeth, David, *Ludwig Karl Hilberseimer: An Annotated Bibliography and Chronology*, New York: Garland, 1981

HILVERSUM TOWN HALL, NETHERLANDS

Designed by Willem Marinus Dudok, completed 1931
Hilversum, the Netherlands

Hilversum Town Hall, in Hilversum, the Netherlands, was constructed between 1924 and 1931 by Willem Marinus Dudok (1884–1974). Known internationally as one of the most influential buildings of its date, the design is reminiscent of early Frank Lloyd Wright (1867–1959) design, specifically the Larkin Building (1903) in Buffalo, New York, and Unity Temple (1904) in Oak Park, Illinois.

Located approximately 15 miles southeast of Amsterdam, Hilversum is a small modern town with tree-shaded, brick-paved roads and well-kept properties and is well known to have had one of the Netherlands' premier 20th-century architects. Willem Marinus Dudok, an Amsterdam-born Dutch military engineer, became one of the most influential architects working in the Netherlands between the two world wars and was credited with more than 240 buildings. In 1915, he became the director of public works for Hilversum, where he produced a town development plan based on the English Garden City movement promoted by Briton Ebenezer Howard (1850–1928). For nearly 40 years, Dudok was in the service of the municipality.

Heavily influenced by the work of Wright, as depicted in the Amsterdam School publication *Wendingen* (Trends), Dudok is also thought to have garnered some minor influence from Amsterdam School expressionism, De Stijl functionalism, Delft School traditionalism, Cubism, and simply the Dutch vernacular. This enigmatic way of nonconformity has caused some critics to erroneously refer to his "style" as a hybrid of some or all of these rather than as a creation of an independent character of apparent individualism. One self-proclaimed influence was the music of his childhood. Born to musicians, he felt that the great composers influenced him more than all the great architects. He believed that the rhythm, mood, and character of music were easily transferred to architecture through the use of their commonality: proportions.

Dudok's oeuvre, known colloquially as "going Dudokey," formed the model for many later architects. International examples emerged throughout Europe and the United States. The 1935 Brussels Exhibition and the 1937 Paris Exhibition contained many buildings that reflected Dudok's existing work, specifically Hilversum Town Hall, which also inspired clones in Cachan, France, and Lausanne, Switzerland. The irony was that as his once personal style was mimicked ad nauseam and as the fluidity of his design style developed, taking further cues from the modernist, its earlier individuality was eroded into apparent anonymity. As a result, Hilversum Town Hall has been hailed

Hilversum Town Hall, the Netherlands (1931)

Hilversum Town Hall clock tower
© Elisabeth A. Bakker-Johnson

a seminal building that set an architectural tone and marked a pinnacle in Dudok's career.

Surrounded by a neighborhood of semidense, medium- to dark-colored brick and stucco residences, the imposing buff-colored Hilversum Town Hall rises up from the water in the midst of a wide-open space, bounded by large trees. Dudok's use of cantilevered eaves, an unusual feature for the Netherlands, and a simple asymmetrical three-dimensional geometry arranged around a square inner courtyard provides a modern structure while still reflecting the historicism of the medieval town halls by use of a large hall and a tower. The verticality of the looming tower breaks up the Wright-inspired horizontality, producing a sense of balance and harmony between the two axes. Also, a hierarchical use of light through varied fenestration adds yet another dimension of equilibrium. Dudok's euphonic design seems to reconcile the apparent discordant use of solids and voids, the horizontal and vertical, and light and dark.

Slightly askew of the tower, the main entrance is defined by a hovering canopy that extends toward the lake. Instead of an axial approach, one enters along a low wing or covered colonnade perpendicular to the main entrance into a low vestibule with a contrasting large marble staircase that leads up to a space more than 20 meters high. The overall cubic volumetric massing of advancing solids and retreating voids held together by the unifying glazed yellow-brick skin enfolds the components to a whole body. Bands of glass, subdivided into small panes, running parallel between the clean, flat roofline and the horizontal ground plane, are juxtaposed to similar panes that rise as a group from the entry colonnade parallel to the clock tower mass and its elongated windows.

The sequence of spaces within produces a series of interlocking solids and voids that the functional hierarchy of fenestration augments. For example, natural light enters from clerestory windows; reflects on the ceiling; is filtered by way of translucent, decorated glass panels; and then glows through the glass canopy high above the public main stairs. The private council chamber, however, is naturally lit by only three high, narrow, vertical slits of windows. Horizontal windows above the galleries and bright light accented with chromatic variations in the reception hall round out the diverse styles of illumination.

When finished in 1931, the public embraced this example of modern architecture because of its balance of form and function and because it still seemed traditional through its composition, fine craftsmanship, and high-quality materials. Most of all, it was praised for its monumentality. As Dudok once stated, "Monumentality is the most pure expression of the human sense of harmony and order" (Holzbauer 1981). Some critics, however, felt that the building was a nonstructural, proportionally irresponsible arrangement of its shapes and accused Dudok of diluting modernist forms or of being a middle-of-the-road modernist who produced yet another contemporary style rather than creating a formal language of his own. By insisting that his architecture be of a specific stylistic mode, critics suggested that his designs lacked fluidity, thereby confining it to a strict formula that must be applied to all architecture. Nevertheless, the final product becomes a sculptural expression of a compositional theme. It is a testimony of the harmonious consonance of form, function, art, and human necessity. Hilversum Town Hall is not only the magnum opus in the work of Dudok but also one of the most successful buildings in the history of the Modern movement.

ELISABETH A. BAKKER-JOHNSON

See also **Amsterdam School; City Hall; Cubism; De Stijl; Dudok, Willem Marinus (the Netherlands); Garden City Movement; Larkin Building, Buffalo, New York; Unity Temple, Oak Park, Illinois; Wright, Frank Lloyd (United States)**

Further Reading

An exhaustive list of available material can be found in Langmead 1996.

Groenendijk, Paul, and Piet Vollaard, *Gids Voor Moderne Architectuur in Nederland (Guide to Modern Architecture in the Netherlands)* Rotterdam, the Netherlands: Uitgeverij 010 Publishers, 1987; 4th edition, 1992

Holzbauer, Wilhelm, "Willem Marinus Dudok. Town Hall, Hilversum, the Netherlands. 1928–31," *Global Architecture: An Encyclopedia of Modern Architecture*, 58 (1981)

Langmead, Donald, *Willem Marinus Dudok, A Dutch Modernist: A Bio-Bibliography*, Westport, Connecticut: Greenwood Press, 1996

Whittick, Arnold, *European Architecture in the Twentieth Century*, 2 vols., New York: Philosophical Library, and London: Crosby Lockwood, 1950

Wit, Wim de (editor), *The Amsterdam School: Dutch Expressionist Architecture, 1915–1930*, New York: Cooper-Hewitt Museum, and Cambridge, Massachusetts: MIT Press, 1983

HISTORIC PRESERVATION

Historic preservation is one of the most significant popular and professional movements of the 20th century to influence architecture and urban redevelopment in the United States. By its impact on policy and the design, finance, and review of programs and projects in thousands of communities, the preservation movement continues to make a lasting impact on the development of the built environment, including associated landscapes. The examples abound.

Beginning as a pietistic initiative and nativist reaction, concern for archaeological sites in the Southwest led to the Antiquities Act of 1906 and the establishment of the National Park Service in 1916. Regional efforts by the American Scenic and Historic Preservation Society, based in New York City, and the Society for the Preservation of New England Antiquities, based in Boston, provided the earliest sustained preservation activities. The first forward-looking documentation program dedicated to aboveground buildings began during the Great Depression. The Historic American Building Survey, begun in 1933, was a joint effort of the National Park Service in cooperation with the American Institute of Architects and the Library of Congress. Although Colonial Williamsburg remained an important popular influence and critical training ground for early professionals, the nationwide zoning and planning models promoted during the 1920s inspired the shift away from only the restoration and reconstruction of sites and toward the designation and protection of existing historic neighborhoods. The early efforts in Charleston and New Orleans set the tone, with San Antonio joining them before World War II, and Alexandria, Williamsburg, Winston-Salem, Georgetown, Natchez, and Annapolis all passing local landmarks district legislation by 1951.

From these and other local efforts, the void of national leadership became apparent. The need for advocacy in saving sites led to the establishment of the National Trust for Historic Preservation in 1949. The organization's purposes were to further the policies of the Historic Sites Act of 1935, that is, the preservation of sites, buildings, and objects of national significance, and to encourage public participation in preservation efforts. The National Trust claimed 235 members the first year, but membership had swelled to about 8,000 by the mid-1960s.

The growing interest in preservation was largely in response to the expansion of the federal housing and transportation programs during the 1950s, which caused considerable demolition of inner-city areas in the name of civic improvement. Congress passed several housing acts, the most notable in 1954 calling for widespread urban renewal, and supplied millions of dollars for clearance. It also approved the Federal Aid Highway Act of 1956, which authorized the largest joint federal-state domestic public works venture ever: $31 billion to be spent over 13 years to provide a 41,000-mile "National System of Interstate and Defense Highways." The rise of environmental conservation, underscored by Rachel Carson's *Silent Spring* (1962) and Stewart L. Udall's *The Quiet Crisis* (1963), was mirrored by Jane Jacobs's *Death and Life of Great American Cities* (1962). Jacobs's attack on then-current rebuilding claimed that the housing complexes being built were worse than the slums they replaced. Although the country generally enjoyed considerable prosperity, the accelerated "white flight" to the suburbs left many people who remained behind frustrated by lack of economic opportunity and the political isolation. The riots that plagued several communities during the late 1960s underscored the problems.

During the Johnson administration, the federal government took the first positive steps to stop the wholesale destruction of urban neighborhoods. In 1965, the Task Force on the Preservation of Natural Beauty called for a joint federal-state program in historic preservation and cited the work of the National Trust for Historic Preservation. Additional efforts to accelerate historic preservation came from the U.S. Conference of Mayors, which sponsored a report later that year. It recommended (1) a comprehensive statement of national policy regarding the activities of all federal agencies; (2) an advisory council on historic preservation to provide leadership and guidance in interagency actions and a liaison to state and local governments; (3) a formal National Register of Historic Places based on a systematic inventory of the districts, structures, and objects significant at the national, state, and local levels; (4) added authority and funding for federal acquisition of threatened buildings; and (5) provision of federal loans and other financial aid for historic preservation. These recommendations guided the framing of the National Historic Preservation Act of 1966 (P.L. 89–665), signed by President Lyndon Johnson on 15 October 1966 (Glass, 1987).

Two other laws in 1966 reflected a growing consciousness of historic preservation. The Transportation Act stipulated, in Section 4f, that any program or project that required land from a public park, recreation area, wildlife or waterfowl refuge, or historic site would not be approved "unless there is no prudent and feasible alternative," arguably the strongest restriction to demolition to date. The provision was almost immediately tested in New Orleans, where a six-lane, 108-foot-wide, 40-foot-high elevated interstate expressway along the waterfront was challenged, and the project halted (Borah, 1981). The Demonstration Cites and Metropolitan Development Act marked a shift from urban renewal to providing money for "model cities." It declared "a need for timely action to preserve and restore areas, sites and structures of historic or architectural value . . . in our Nation's urban areas" (Friedan and Kaplan, 1975). The Demonstration Act amended the Housing Act of 1954 to make urban-renewal demonstration grants available to municipalities and towns of fewer than 50,000 people, required the recognition of historic and architectural preservation in urban-renewal plans, allowed the planning for these projects to be included as eligible costs, provided grants covering up to 50 percent of the preservation project's costs to the state and local governments, and allowed for the acquisition of an interest in historic properties and restoring them for public use. Listing on the National Register of Historic Places was a prerequisite. The passage of the National Environmental Policy Act of 1969, with its required environmental impact analysis and public hearing process, also underscored the concern for historic properties.

These broad federal mandates accelerated the shift away from the recognition of single historic sites and toward the designation and protection of historic districts. In addition, neighborhood conservation became local public policy with the Housing and Community Development Act of 1974, signed by President Gerald Ford. Categorical grants of a number of different kinds were replaced by "lump sum" revenue payments, termed "community development block grants," and the local planning community determined the priorities through a series of public hearings. Projects included a wide range of infrastructure improvements, public facilities, assisted housing, mortgage credit assistance, and urban homesteading and rehabilitation loans. Revolving loan funds for housing rehabilitation played an essential role in communities such as Savannah and Charleston.

By the early 1970s, major projects, such as Ghiradelli Square in San Francisco, the Fanueil Hall/Quincy Market renovations in Boston, and Pike Place Market in Seattle, became models for dozens of subsequent waterfront revitalization schemes (Friedan and Sagalyn, 1989). Bringing the mall to the inner city has met with marked success in some locations and with abject failure in other places. However, largely by virtue of the initiatives of James Rouse, a suburban developer turned inner-city visionary, the festival marketplace became a permanent fixture in several downtowns, including South Street Seaport in New York and Harbor Place in Baltimore. In the 1990s, many city councils increasingly looked to heritage tourism as at least one portion of the public entertainment venue that should be offered by former downtown central business districts.

Meanwhile, in academia, schools of architecture were the first to take an interest in teaching preservation, with seminars and classes at the University of Virginia (1957), Cornell University (1962), and Columbia University (1964), the latter becoming the first to institute a graduate degree program in 1973. Both graduate and undergraduate programs blossomed in the advent of the U.S. Bicentennial, embracing a broad range of disciplines. Focused at first on the need to staff the 50 state historic preservation offices across the country, the graduates soon found the private sector offering considerably more opportunities. In part, this was due to historical celebrations associated with the U.S. Bicentennial itself. The history of the country was being redefined from a story of cultural unity to an alternative narrative of cultural pluralism. Although the principal restoration campaign centered on the Statue of Liberty, an early all-metal skeleton with sheet-metal skin, the sensitivity of the country to its social evolution was accelerated by the enormous popularity of Alex Haley's *Roots* (1976).

New challenges also came with the introduction of the Tax Reform Act of 1976, which spurred billions of dollars in privately financed "certified rehabilitation" of historic properties during the early 1980s. Projects such the revitalization of the mammoth Union Station in St. Louis gave enormous hope to inner-city enthusiasts. Unfortunately, a general tax reform in 1986 reduced the incentives and cooled this kind of investment activity. A gradual resurgence with smaller projects occurred during the 1990s (Thatcher, 1995). Especially when coupled with the low-income housing tax credit program, federal incentives remain reasonably lucrative for interested investors (Sullivan, 1998). As with the federal historic preservation and environmental legislation during the 1960s that spurred similar state-level initiatives during the 1970s, the more important long-term impact of the federal tax credit programs is that they have continued to serve as models for more recently adopted state and local tax credit programs.

The significant effect that this private-sector activity has had on the historic preservation movement cannot be underestimated. Corollary commercial enterprises specializing in finance and providing skills and historical reproductions grew markedly, in part by tapping the do-it-yourself approach in home renovation. A number of private, nonprofit advocacy organizations were established—such as the Association for Preservation Technology (1968), providing technical information, and Preservation Action (1974), a nationwide lobbying organization—and contributed to strengthening general understanding through their publications and educational programs. The number and role of regional and citywide groups also increased substantially, with "friends" groups, such as that involved in the restoration of Central Park, taking the lead in fund-raising. In the case of at least one statewide nonprofit advocacy organization, the Historic Landmarks Foundation of Indiana, regional offices were established in historic sites throughout the state. Widespread recognition of the legitimate role of local historic district designation and review power came in 1978 with the U.S. Supreme Court opinion in the landmark case *Penn Central Transportation Co v. New York City*. Subsequent challenges in state courts have repeatedly relied on this decision.

During the last two decades of the 20th century, however, the trend in government sponsorship of historic preservation projects followed the overall shift from federal and state-funded programs to a near-complete reliance on local resources. From the late 1970s, during the Carter administration, federal and state housing programs, once a staple for neighborhood revitalization, have seen relatively little growth. Housing rehabilitation has fallen to community development corporations, some of which are faith-based groups that have often acquired formerly publicly owned properties in poor repair.

With the end of the Cold War, "defederalization" was most apparent in the sale of defense facilities. Perhaps the best example is the Presidio, one of the most valuable pieces of real estate in the Bay Area, which occupied much of San Francisco's attention. The opportunity to reuse elements of a number of largely self-contained former military bases was the most obvious deliberate preservation planning effort of the last decade of the 20th century.

State-sponsored environmental bond initiatives have offered some direct funding in cases such as Vermont, New Jersey, and New York, but they are comparatively rare. The only significant federal domestic public improvement program is that devoted to transportation, beginning with the Intermodal Surface Transportation Act of 1986 and the Transportation Equity Act for the 21st Century. Both pump billions of dollars into highway building, public transit, and bridge building and offer millions for various enhancements, including transportation-related historic preservation projects. Saving historic roads themselves has become a concern. Perhaps the most obvious side effect of this work is that it has brought contract archaeologists, under the rubric of cultural resource management, into closer working relationship with the preservationists in site planning, interpretation, and treatment.

The role of the National Park Service (NPS), the steward of the nation's cultural resources, was reframed during the Clinton administration to focus on accommodating more public access to and improvement in the parks. The NPS has promoted the belief that guidance, coupled with economic incentives, is better than outright grants-in-aid and that partnerships are preferable to outright acquisition and long-term management responsibility. In architecture projects, for example, the need for guidance in housing rehabilitation led to the creation of the Secretary of the Interior's Standards for Rehabilitation in 1977 (Morton, 1994). These were used by the NPS and state historic preservation offices as performance standards for the evaluation of projects whose sponsors sought federal preservation tax credits and have been increasingly used in project review at all levels of government. The most obvious examples of the partnerships with state and local agencies include the various Heritage Corridor initiatives that followed the establishment of the Lowell Urban Cultural Park, such as the Gateway National Recreation Area, the Cuyahoga Valley National Recreation Area, the Illinois-Michigan Canal Heritage Corridor, and the Blackstone River National Heritage Corridor (Thorson, 1998). In terms of direct funding for NPS programs, outside the national parks and the federal support for all the 50 state historic preservation offices and the 1,200 local certified governments serving historic districts, it has not increased in more than 20 years. It remains at a little over $30 million so that, in real terms, given even relatively modest inflation, funding has actually declined.

The National Trust for Historic Preservation, having gradually lost its federal funding during the 1990s, became more self-supporting by attempting to expand its membership and curtailed its broader public advocacy and education programs. A notable exception of a local preservation controversy that rose to the attention of the National Trust during the 1990s was the plan for the Disney Corporation to build a theme park near Manassas, Virginia. Congressional hearings on this problem led many leading preservationists in the mid-Atlantic states to focus their attention on sprawl, characteristic of their expanding regional economy. The National Trust's most successful program, the National Main Street initiative, launched with three small midwestern towns in 1977, spread through a network of statewide programs to embrace 1,500 communities. Experimentation with urban demonstration projects, beginning in 1985, prepared the way for the citywide program launched in Boston in 1995, a model that other cities are attempting to follow.

Postmodern design, introduced in architecture in the late 1970s, has generally become widely embraced by the historic preservation community, for it is generally understood to allow for more sensitivity to the context. Designers also continue to link the popular acceptance of historic materials and neotraditional schemes to the increasing recognition given them in the historic preservation process. During the 1980s, for example, urban and suburban designers interested in traditional layout and design used the historic preservation movement to usher in "New Urbanism." New Urbanists have recently gained recognition by the Department of Housing and Urban Development.

Meanwhile, many icons of the Modern movement are threatened. The Los Angeles Conservancy's initiative to promote the "case study houses" that introduced the Modern movement to the Southwest was one of the earliest efforts to gain public support for endangered properties of the recent past. Meanwhile, federal housing projects of the postwar era, such as Pruit-Igoe in St. Louis, have suffered demolition, largely because of the memories associated with the failure of the social service programs. Other houses, such as Frank Lloyd Wright's Fallingwater near Pittsburgh and the Darwin Martin House in Buffalo, have become the subject of major restoration campaigns. The notable effort to recognize the importance of the McDonald's in Downey, California, saved it from the wrecking ball as well.

Hence, the character of what is felt worthy of saving continues to change as our society changes and as 20th-century culture enters history. The concerns for wood, brick, and stone are supplemented and sometimes supplanted by the need to conserve fiberboard, glue-laminated timber, plywood, ceramic veneer, concrete, glass curtain wall, and a variety of specialized metals. The investigative techniques have also broadened. Supplementing measured drawing and microscopic analysis are several nondestructive techniques, including X-ray analysis, ground-penetrating radar, impact echo modeling, various forms of three-dimensional visualization, and computer-aided design. Regional preservation issues are also more obvious. For example, California preservation organizations and agencies became much more conscious of disaster preparedness, particularly after the Northridge earthquake. Seismic retrofit projects on the West Coast and some mountain states generally centered on the importance of providing base isolation, influencing design in other parts of the country and the world. Hurricanes in Charleston and flooding in the upper Mississippi River Valley have also focused attention on the special problems of retrofitting historic properties and their contents to natural disasters. During the 1990s, an era of relative worldwide peace, this expanded to include the problem of protecting cultural sites from terrorist attacks.

The United States entered the 20th century theoretically and practically behind most European countries in historic preservation, and Americans were fortunate enough never to have suffered the ravages of a world war on their own soil that would have necessitated rebuilding its urban cores on the same scale. During the second half of the century, however, the country has gained considerable experience in rehabilitation owing to tremendous private-sector initiative and the ability to marshal considerable financial resources. At the dawn of the new century, it frequently serves to provide models for other countries to follow.

MICHAEL A. TOMLAN

Further Reading

Borah, William E., *The Second Battle of New Orleans. A History of the Vieux Carre Riverfront Expressway Controversy*, Tuscaloosa, Alabama: University of Alabama Press, 1981

Burns, John (editor), *Recording Historic Buildings*, Washington, D.C.: The American Institute of Architects Press, 1989

Frieden Bernard J. and Marshall Kaplan, *The Politics of Neglect: Urban Aid from Model Cities to Revenue Sharing*, Cambridge, Massachusetts: MIT Press, 1975

Frieden, Bernard J. and Lynne B. Sagalyn, *Downtown, Inc. How America Rebuilds Cities*, Cambridge, Massachusetts: MIT Press, 1989

Glass, James Arthur, "The National Historic Preservation Act," Ph.D. diss, Cornell University, 1987

"Historic American Engineering Record: Thirty Years of Documenting America's Technological History, *CRM* 23, 4 (2000)

Hosmer, Jr., Charles B., *Presence of the Past: A History of the Preservation Movement in the United States before Williamsburg*, New York: Putnam, 1965

Hosmer, Jr., Charles B., *Preservation Comes of Age: From Williamsburg to the National Trust, 1926–1949*, Charlottesville, Virginia: University Press of Virginia, 1981

Howard, J. Myrick, "Where the Action Is," in *The American Mosaic*, edited by Robert E. Stipe and Antoinette J. Lee, Washington, D.C.: US/ICOMOS, 1987

Judd, Dennis R. and Susan S. Fainstein (editors), *The Tourist City*, New Haven, Connecticut: Yale University Press, 1999

Lindgren, James M., *Preserving the Old Dominion: Historic Preservation and Virginia Traditionalism*, Charlottesville, Virginia: University Press of Virginia, 1993

Marriott, Paul Daniel, *Saving Historic Roads*, New York: Wiley, 1997

Morton, W. Brown III, "The Secretary of the Interior's Standards for Historic Preservation Projects: Ethics in Action," *Ethics in Historic Preservation*, Ithaca, New York and Washington, D.C.: National Council for Preservation Education, 1994

Mulloy, Elizabeth D., *The History of the National Trust for Historic Preservation, 1963–1973*, Washington, D.C.: The Preservation Press, 1976

Scarpino, Philip V., "Planning for Preservation: A Look at the Federal-State Historic Preservation Program, 1966–1986," *Public Historian*, 14, no. 2 (spring 1992)

Sullivan, Aleca, *Affordable Housing. Combining the Tax Credits: A Symposium*, Washington, D.C.: National Park Service and Historic Preservation Education Foundation, 1998

Thatcher, James, "Historic Rehabilitation Tax Credits: An Effective Policy in Perspective," Masters of Public Administration, Cornell University, 1995

Thorson, Julia Taylor "Evaluating the Implementation of the Blackstone River Valley National Heritage Corridor: The Museum of Work and Culture and Visitor Center, Woonsocket, Rhode Island," Ithaca, New York: M.A. thesis in historic preservation planning, January, 1998

Tomlan, Michael A., "Preservation Practice Comes of Age," *When Past Meets Future: Historic Preservation in the Next 25 Years*, Washington, D.C.: National Trust for Historic Preservation, 1992

U.S. Conference of Mayors, *With Heritage So Rich*, Washington, D.C.: National Trust for Historic Preservation, 1965

HISTORICISM

Generally defined, historicism is a system of thought in which the past is understood as a series of periods or epochs, each distinct from each other and the present. These various periods are characterized by a number of prevailing philosophies, social structures, and technologies—the Zeitgeist—which are the inevitable results of the conditions present within the subject time and place. These characteristics are considered independent of those that came before or those that might follow, so that the values and social mores understood and respected in one period may hold no currency in a succeeding time or place. Historicism is both relativist, in that the actions of an individual in a specific temporal or locative context should not be judged by the standards of another and progressive, in that the present condition is held to be superior to the past, while being at the same time the result of all that has come before.

A hallmark of the post-Enlightenment West, historicism has been the prevailing attitude toward the past since its formulation in the mid-18th century. Under the historicist paradigm, the act of recording history became the placement of events within the prevailing context. As professional historians began to particularize the Western experience into discrete periods, further subdivided by ethnic or national cultural components (for example, the English Late Middle Ages, the French High Renaissance), this same pseudo-scientific mania for classification was extended to the history of architecture, with the result that history became regarded by many as the ability to describe each of dozens of historic styles, identified by time and place, and to categorize correctly a given building into one or more of these styles. Within the design community, the application of this history in practice meant the ability to detail correctly a building in any appropriate style as the client, program, or principal designer demanded. Yet this application of historicist history violated the very intellectual framework from which it was derived, for if the art of every time and place is an expression of its unique context—its Zeitgeist—then the modern industrial age must have its own set of national styles and should be loathe to embellish its buildings with the vestments of another time or place. It was thus incumbent on the artists of the day to develop the "style of the age"; indeed, many self-conscious attempts were made in the late 19th century to develop an ahistorical architecture that expressed the ambitions of the emerging industrial culture.

Most practicing architects of the early 20th century did not sense a conflict between historicist architecture and their present context, nor were they overly concerned with producing wholly unprecedented architectural form. Writers of the next generation, such as Nikolaus Pevsner and Henry-Russell Hitchcock, would view this insouciance as a near betrayal to the profession, and they often sought to exclude traditional designers from the historical record of the first half of the century. In the formative years of the Modern movement, they contemptuously branded as historicist any designer who chose to emulate too closely forms or elements from the past. Yet, these architects did not view themselves as somehow apart from their time, and they certainly were not involved in a cabal to destroy architecture from within. Rather, they simply adhered closely to a second tenet of historicism: that historical change not only is the result of a change in the Zeitgeist but also is evolutionary. From this viewpoint, it was entirely reasonable to continue the use of past architectural forms where the program, client, and public expectation required it. It also was reasonable to assume that a "style of the age" would emerge out of the innumerable variations the architectural community generated while reconciling these forms to modern requirements, materials, and techniques of construction.

Several justifications for the continuation of historicist architecture into the 20th century were advanced within the profession and the schools. The first and most popularly understood was that in an age of rapid technological and social change, traditional architectural forms emphasized continuity and stability. Those with a stake in society as it was naturally wished to reinforce the connection between the past and the present and perhaps to assume some of the authority expressed by older forms. Governmental buildings, such as the large administrative complexes constructed around the Capitol and along the National Mall in Washington, D.C., or at Whitehall in London, appropriated neoclassical and neobaroque forms to emphasize the longevity and authority of the governmental institutions they housed. A second justification for historicist design, the doctrine of associationalism, held that each historical building form triggered within the mind of the viewer a set of qualities, characteristics, and emotions that could be transferred to new construction and by extension to the occupant. By the late 19th century, this principle was melded with the systematic study of building typology to become the academic theory of *caractère*, in which the designer carefully chose an architectural vocabulary that communicated the purpose and qualities of the institution, keeping within design parameters accepted for the building type. The theory of *caractère* was most clearly promulgated at the French École des Beaux-Arts in Paris, where, under the tutelage of Professor of Theory Julien Guadet, students were challenged to apply their developing understanding of history to a wide variety of contemporary architectural problems, from workers' housing to hydroelectric dams. The strength of the study of *caractère* was in its emphasis on the public understanding of the structure's purpose, status, and organization, based as it was on buildings and patterns knowable to the laity as well as the profession.

The use of analogy also extended to new structural systems. Eugene-Emanuel Viollet-le-Duc's demand in the mid-19th century for an architecture of iron was predicated on parallels between the skeletal nature of Gothic structure and iron construction. At the end of the century, Louis Sullivan put forward the analogy of the tall building as a classical column. Twenty years later, the construction of Cass Gilbert's Woolworth Building (1913) in New York City initiated a series of Gothic skyscrapers, all of which proposed that the stacked piers within the steel frame be equated to the great compound piers of the Gothic cathedrals of Europe, leading to the inevitable references to "cathedrals of commerce." In concrete construction as well, the analogy to past forms proved essential to understanding the nature of the material. Anatole de Baudot's Church of Saint-Jean de Montmartre (1902) in Paris exploited the tensile and compressive capabilities of reinforced concrete construction within a stylized Gothic Revival format. The frank expression of the concrete frame usually is credited to Auguste Perret, a student of Guadet's at the École des Beaux-Arts; in Perret's institutional work, however, such as the Théâtre des Champs-Elysées (1913) or Nôtre Dame de Raincy (1923), Perret makes allusions to historic forms while demonstrating the potential of concrete as a surface material capable of receiving an ornamental finish. Halfway across the world, in California, the plastic nature of concrete and its ornamental potential were being explored by protégés of Ernest Ransome, including Arthur Brown Jr., whose city hall for Pasadena (1927) presents a 205-foot high domed tower accented with sinuous neo-baroque ornament executed in cast and poured high-test concrete. In the best Beaux-Arts tradition, Pasadena City Hall recalls many buildings in Mediterranean Europe, but these references are fused together in a unified composition immediately identified with southern California.

The development of modernist architectural culture in the 1920s challenged established justifications for historicist design. Advocates for the Modern movement demanded a complete repudiation of the historical past, largely in order to weaken the hold of traditionalist doctrine in the schools, professional societies, and the press. Even those who sought a compromise position, such as those who designed in the stylized modern classicism now known as Art Deco, were deemed not to go far enough in the Modern movement's campaign to eradicate all vestiges of historicist practice. This rejection of the past was persuasive to many in the profession, but in the 1930s, work in historicist, modernist, and hybrid modes coexisted, each form finding an audience and a set of typologies appropriate to it. Yet the adoption of Neoclassicism as the officially sanctioned style of both Nazi Germany and the Stalinist Soviet Union associated modern classicism with these totalitarian regimes in Europe and precluded the use of all historical forms in the rebuilding of Europe's cities at the conclusion of World War II, except

Humana Building, designed by Michael Graves, Louisville, Kentucky (1985), interior
Photo © Paschall/Taylor Photo

in the reconstruction of prominent landmarks destroyed during the war.

Although hardly a force in high-style architectural practice from World War II on, historicism remained the *bête noir* of architectural theory throughout the middle decades of the 20th century. In 1960 the Canadian theorist Peter Collins was moved to write an essay for the London-based *Architectural Review*, in which he termed the practice "the curse of the 19th century," the one construct that could prevent architecture from developing to its full potential. The following year, Nikolaus Pevsner sounded the alarm that some architects were again looking at the past too closely but now were raiding the history of the Modern movement itself for design ideas (that this was a complement to his own *Pioneers of the Modern Movement* Pevsner was reluctant to acknowledge). To Pevsner the work of designers such as Edward Durell Stone was indicative of willful rebellion among those in active practice against the strict functionalism of the International Style; by example, Pevsner identified Stone's use of concrete screens, such as at the American Embassy at New Delhi (1954), as derivative of Perret's use of the same device at Raincy. Other late-Modern architects infused their work with traditional elements and composition. New York's Lincoln Center (1966), a collaborative effort headed by Harrison and Abramovitz with considerable design input from Philip Johnson, recalled Michelangelo's Piazza del Campidoglio in its urban form and the abstracted neoclassicism of its principle buildings. Although this complex was extraordinarily well received by the general public, many architecture critics decried its overt historicist character as a retreat from truly principled modern design.

The debate over historicism, once limited to a select segment of the architectural profession, gained a wider audience in the 1970s and 1980s as a number of prominent practitioners and theorists publicly advocated a reexamination of the use of past forms in contemporary architecture. Robert Venturi and Denise Scott-Brown's call for a renaissance of meaning in architecture met a receptive audience in a public that found both functionalism and late-Modern expressionism austere and incomprehensible. By the end of the 1970s, architects were aware that ignorance of the past was no longer a sign of creative strength but of cultural impoverishment. Architects previously identified with the Modern movement, such as Robert A.M. Stern and Charles Moore, produced work that acknowledged both the modern and traditional heritage. No building signaled the new attitude toward the past more than Johnson and Burgee's AT&T Building (1984) in midtown Manhattan. Johnson's modestly scaled tower revived the Sullivanian formula for the skyscraper and presented a well proportioned if somewhat flatly modeled base and body. The building's crown, an enormous broken pediment, was controversial for both its form and its intent. Johnson's flamboyant design statement, located just blocks from both the Seagram Building and Lincoln Center, demonstrated to many not only his uncanny ability to identify and exploit trends in American architecture but also that the profession had indeed arrived at what Stern denoted "the edge of Modernism."

The careful reevaluation of history promised by the beginnings of the Postmodern movement failed to materialize as many theorists had wished. The license to examine and interpret historical sources was quickly abused in the name of irony. While Postmodern architects were free to utilize historical motifs to communicate a building's structure or program to the masses, they were expected to do so tongue-in-cheek, lest their intentions be misinterpreted as a genuine interest in revivalism. At times this ironic posture was perhaps appropriate, such as with Michael Graves's headquarters building for the Disney Corporation at Burbank, California (1990), in which a heavy Tuscan pediment is carried by atlantes modeled on six of Snow White's seven dwarves (Dopey holds up the raking cornices with good-natured resignation). Here Graves not only remarked on the tradition of the figural column and made a wry substitution of Disney's dwarves for Herculean Atlases, but he also referenced the origins of the Disney entertainment empire.

Usually, however, postmodern historicism lacked specific meaning, a deeply felt connection to the past, or the carefully crafted detail of pre-Modern traditional building. Quotations from the past frequently were slapped onto otherwise unremarkable buildings, often at a ridiculously inflated scale. Graves's Portland Building (1982) was hailed by some at its completion as a monument that would reinvigorate architectural rhetoric and often is cited as the first postmodern building; his Humana building (Louisville, Kentucky) followed in 1985. Most Portlanders today, however, think of Raymond Kaskey's statue *Portlandia* as the building's true representational device—not the technicolor award ribbons or the four-story-high keystones. In Europe postmodern historicism was both disdained and embraced. While many still associated classicism with the fascist appropriation of the classical language in the 1930s, other,

younger architects reveled in the opportunity to be working in the mannerist vein of Michelangelo or Giuliano Romano. The large public-housing complexes Ricardo Bofill and his Taller de Arquitectura constructed outside of Paris and Barcelona became known as near-parodies of the Postmodern movement, as the outsized columns, arches, and pediments affixed to their facades took on a cartoon-like quality that looked more ephemeral than eternal.

Most architects of the 1990s who were interested in the historical heritage approached the past with a more circumspect attitude than Bofill. Three approaches to the past seem to be particularly relevant to the question of historicism. The critical regionalists, represented best by Mario Botta or Antoine Predock, examined the building traditions of the site and interpreted these traditions while employing an abstracted modern vocabulary. A second group, the revivalists, employed historical styles in their most literal form, believing that these enduring forms continue to retain their validity. Allied at times with the New Urbanism movement, the revivalists have received much public attention in the United Kingdom, where designers such as Demetri Porphyrios and Quinlan Terry challenged leading figures within the nation's planning establishment and the Royal Institute of British Architects (RIBA) with regard to urban form and the design of several prominent public projects.

The third stream of history-conscious architects might be termed the contextualists. These designers use historical forms where the status of the project and the strong urban form of the surroundings demand it, but they integrate these contextual gestures into what are essentially modernist buildings. This design strategy is proving quite successful in the reconstruction of Berlin and also has become an important means of resolving the numerous aesthetic forces at work within the monumental core of Washington, D.C. A leading practitioner of this approach is James Ingo Freed, whose United States Holocaust Memorial Museum (1994) south of the National Mall integrated a number of existing structures into a complex that at once deferred to the nearby Jefferson Memorial and that recalled the architectural apparatus of the Nazi regime. Across the mall, Freed again integrated traditional and modern in his design for the Ronald Reagan Building (1998), which completed the massive Federal Triangle complex and gave Washington one of its few large modern spaces in the building's light-flooded rotunda. As architects around the world reinvigorate the 21st-century city with structures that advance the art and science of building while maintaining a continuity of meaning and form with the past, they may well find that it is this contextual approach that will finally reconcile the historicist tradition with the Modern movement.

JEFFREY THOMAS TILMAN

See also **Art Deco; AT&T Building, New York City; Bofill, Ricardo (Spain); Botta, Mario (Switzerland); Disney Theme Parks; Graves, Michael (United States); Harrison, Wallace K. and Max Abramovitz (United States); Hitchcock, Henry-Russell (United States); Holocaust Memorial Museum, Washington, D.C.; Johnson, Philip (United States); Lincoln Center, New York City; Moore, Charles (United States); New Urbanism; Notre Dame, Le Raincy; Pevsner, Nikolaus (England); Postmodernism; Scott Brown, Denise (United States); Stern, Robert A.M. (United States); Stone, Edward Durell**

(United States); Venturi, Robert (United States); Woolworth Building, New York City

Further Reading

A monograph-length study of the problem of historicism has yet to be written, although many prominent theorists and historians have considered the use of the past in architectural practice. The definition of historicism used here is based on Van Pelt and Westfall's *Architectural Principles in the Age of Historicism*. This bibliography lists the most important works of theory that explained historicist practice and several seminal histories of the Modern movement that countered them. Finally, a number of books and articles from the near past illustrate the many points of view practitioners now have with regard to historicism.

Banham, Reyner, *Theory and Design in the First Machine Age*, London: Architectural Press, and New York: Praeger, 1960; 2nd edition, New York: Praeger, 1967

Choisy, Auguste, *Histoire de l'architecture*, 2 vols., Paris: Gauthier-Villars, 1899; reprint, Paris: Bibliotheque de l'Image, 1996

Collins, Peter, "Historicism," *The Architectural Review* 127, no. 762 (1960)

Curtis, William, "Modern Transformations of Classicism" and "Principles and Pastiche," *The Architectural Review* 176, no. 1050 (1984)

Drexler, Arthur, editor, *The Architecture of the École des Beaux-Arts*, New York: Museum of Modern Art, and London: Secker and Warburg, 1977

Giedion, Sigfried, *Space, Time, and Architecture*, Cambridge, Massachusetts: Harvard University Press, and London: Oxford University Press, 1941; 5th edition, Cambridge, Massachusetts: Harvard University Press, 1967

Guadet, Julien, *Eléments et Theories de l'Architecture*, 4 vols., Paris: Librarie de la Construction Moderne, 1902–04; 6th edition, 1929; reprint, 1979; as *Elements and Theory of Architecture*, 3rd edition, Urbana: University of Illinois Press, 1916; reprint, 1980

Hamlin, Talbot, *Forms and Functions of Twentieth-Century Architecture*, 4 vols., New York: Columbia University Press, 1952

Hitchcock, Henry-Russell Jr., and Philip Johnson, *The International Style: Architecture Since 1922*, New York: Norton, 1932; reprint, London: Norton, 1995; New York: Norton, 1996

Jencks, Charles, *The Language of Post-Modern Architecture*, London: Academy Editions, 1972; New York: Rizzoli, 1977; 6th edition, 1991

Jencks, Charles, "Post-Modernism and Discontinuity," *AD Profile* 65 (1987)

Pevsner, Nikolaus, *Pioneers of the Modern Movement from William Morris to Walter Gropius*, London: Faber and Faber, 1936; New York: Stokes, 1937; revised edition, as *Pioneers of Modern Design: From William Morris to Walter Gropius*, London and New York: Penguin, 1991

Pevsner, Nikolaus, "Modern Architecture and the Historian, or The Return of Historicism," *RIBA Journal* 68, no. 6 (1961)

Pevsner, Nikolaus, *The Sources of Modern Architecture and Design*, New York: Oxford University Press, and London: Thames and Hudson, 1968

Porphyrios, Demetri, *Classical Architecture*, London: Academy Editions, 1991; New York: McGraw-Hill, 1992

Van Pelt, Robert Jan, and Carroll William Westfall, *Architectural Principles in the Age of Historicism*, New Haven, Connecticut: Yale University Press, 1991

Venturi, Robert, *Complexity and Contradiction in Architecture*, New York: Museum of Modern Art, 1966; 2nd edition, New York: Museum of Modern Art, and London: Architectural Press, 1977

HISTORIOGRAPHY

The *New Oxford Dictionary of English* defines historiography as both the writing of history and the study of the writing of history. There is a fundamental ambivalence present in the word's meaning when it refers to both the writing of history—as the activity of the historian—and the self-conscious study of historical method and research. A twofold meaning is already present in the Latin and Greek roots of the word: *historio-graphia*, history and the writing of history. As Panayotis Tournikiotis points out, in the 19th century, an important third meaning was added; the historiographer was now the historian employed to write the history of a group or public institution, and subsequently, the study of history assumed the character of the study of a completed corpus of written history. An example of such a "completed" set of histories about a chronological period can be found in the historiography of modern architecture, although its corpus is far from homogeneous.

The Dutch historian Franklin Rudolf Ankersmit gives an indication of the place of historiography within the broader horizons of theory and history. On the one hand, there is the activity of the historian as the producer of history; on the other hand, there is the field of the philosophy of history, of which historiography might or might not be a part. Historiography occupies a position on the border between history and the philosophy of history because its task is mainly factual and descriptive, describing the work of historians in the past or the evolution of the representation of the past through the ages. As such, historiography may be seen as a part of history itself, especially of the specific branch called intellectual history. However, when historiography assumes a critical task as an inquiry after the methods used by historians and the justification of their representation of the past, historiography may be seen as a part of the philosophy of history (see Ankersmit, 1984).

The Italian theorist Giorgio Pigafetta concentrates on the specific discourse of the historiography of modern architecture and emphasizes, in contrast to Ankersmit, the unbreakable unity between history and historiography. Both discourses share, according to Pigafetta, the fact that through their historistic character they function mainly as the developmental instruments for Reason and Necessity; both discourses are therefore centered around questions of meaning: a story that has a *senso* intended as a direction and a destiny toward which the story develops and through which it becomes (see Pigafetta, 1993).

Within the tradition of the historiography of modern architecture, two moments can be discerned. First, we can speak of the historiography of the Modern movement as the construction of a corpus of written histories about modern architecture. This tradition had a starting point in 1927 when Gustav Adolf Platz published the book *Die Baukunst der Neuesten Zeit* (1927; The Art of Building of the Newest Time) and could be said to have an end point in the year 1965, when Peter Collins published his *Changing Ideals in Modern Architecture 1750–1950*. This last book already marked the emergence of a second tradition in which the word historiography denotes a critical reflection on what was by now a substantial corpus of histories about modern architecture. Within this second tradition of historiography, an important subdivision can be identified. First, there are those histories in which the idea of the Modern movement is fundamentally problematized but that still use the formula of a history of modern architecture; Kenneth Frampton's *Modern Architecture: A Critical History* (1980) or Manfredo Tafuri and Francesco Dal Co's *Architettura contemporanea* (1976; Modern Architecture) are examples of this category. Second, there is an even more recent category of study that departs from the idea that the narrative structures of the historical genre have been "consumed" and that a profound study of those narratives is necessary to define fresh interpretative instruments for analyzing contemporary architecture and its history. For example, Tournikiotis's research is motivated not as much from an interest in the machinery of history as from a commitment with contemporary architecture.

The engagement of Tournikiotis also vaguely calls to mind the strategies of the so-called pioneers: the first historians to take up contemporary architecture as an object of history writing. These pioneer historians are characterized by their commitment to the discipline and a direct and personal concern with the protagonists of its histories. The relationship between the architecture historian and critic Sigfried Giedion and the architect Walter Gropius may be called exemplary for this commitment. Another example is constituted in the relationship between the historian Henry Russell Hitchcock and the architect Frank Lloyd Wright. It is important to realize that many of the pioneer historians of modern architecture were art historians and received their formative training from the German tradition of *Kunstgeschichte* (art history) that dominated universities in Europe and America. The methods of historicism are fully elaborated in the German tradition of art history, in which historicism can be said to constitute the very eco of art history. Wilhelm Worringer (1881–1965), Heinrich Wöfflin, and Alois Riegl (1858–1905) among other critical German historians recognized that knowledge about art objects in the past could be achieved by placing them in the narrative context of history writing. Also, as an important second component, it was now agreed on that such historical knowledge about art could bear on the final interpretation and judgment of the art object. Historicism also provided the possibility of conceiving the representational values of art in a historical context: if art was regarded as a visual and material embodiment of ethical and ideological instances, then history could locate those instances within the broader historical narrative. Art and history were now mutually enhancing and coconstitutive: whereas art clarified the ethical dimensions of history, history acknowledged the normative identity of art. The classical model of historicism in art history was provided by Johann Joachim Winckelmann (1717–1768) in the publication *Geschichte der Kunst des Altertums* (1764; The History of Ancient Art). Winckelmann idealized the Greek world and its art by organizing particular (now canonical) art objects into a systematic account of stylization with terms retained today, including classical, Romanesque, Gothic, Renaissance, and baroque. Central in Winckelmann's account was a development or progression going from simple and insecure beginnings to a full bloom of beauty or the high point of artistic achievement. Importantly, Winckelmann also considered historical knowledge about the past to be applicable to a present appreciation of ancient art; furthermore, his history was teleological and marked by a predictability of past events (Soussloff, 1998).

Although Platz was not an art historian—he worked as an architect for the city of Mannheim and as an assistant for the technical university of Berlin-Charlottenburg—in his publication *Die Baukunst der neuesten Zeit* (1927), it becomes clear how the historistic method of the art-historical discourse also shapes the first outlines of a new discipline. In his attempt to provide a historical framework for "the art of building" of modern times, Platz adopts a historical proceeding that is dialectical of nature: epoch B is configured as the contrast and as a reaction to epoch A. The historical dynamic proceeds through absolute ruptures; these revolutions find their legitimization in the idea of Zeitgeist; that is, the idea that all artistic results should be a faithful translation of the spirit of the age. Adopting this motive meant that the historical proceeding could, as a consequence, only be teleological: as each epoch had to live up to its own spirit, history could only culminate in the leading role of modern architecture. The history of modern architecture assumed both a constituting and a regulating value: it constituted knowledge about the architectural past and confirmed the moral authority of contemporary architecture.

In the work of the German-English art historian Nikolaus Pevsner, the art-historical method strongly contributed to the crystallization of a canonical image of the history of modern architecture. With the publication of Pevsner's *Pioneers of the Modern Movement from Morris to Gropius* in 1936, an important instrument was provided for the formation of an ideology of modern architecture. Important is the treatment of the architecture of his time as morphology, a complex system of *forms*—as a succession of horizontal or vertical planes, geometric shapes, surfaces, flat roofs, bay windows, and so on. This method goes back to Johann Wolfgang von Goethe, who, as a reaction to the current materialistic philosophy of his time, developed the morphological method. For Goethe, the world could not be reduced to a materialistic system of parts, a complex interaction of atoms or physical particles as was elaborated, for example, in the theory of Isaac Newton. Contrary to a vision of the world as a cohesive pattern of parts, what was needed, according to Goethe, was an encompassing framework to "wrap" the parts, a whole that was necessary to first understand the parts. Goethe saw this whole present in the agent of the form and envisioned the world accordingly as a complex interplay of forms. In the writing of Pevsner, we see how the form is discerned as the privileged agent. It is in the form that modern architecture manifests because it is here that the crucial combination of aesthetics and value judgments becomes apparent. Lines, shapes, and forms are judged by Pevsner as "honest," "sound," or "sober." Both historians and architects have the possibility to almost intuitively perceive of this crucial combination of form and value; therefore, they are important partners in contributing—from the point of view of form—to the broader process of social evolution.

After World War II, the crisis of modern architecture necessarily resulted in an associated awareness of the problematic content of its history. An important contribution to this debate is now given by Italian historians, specifically in the work of historians and architects Bruno Zevi (1918–2000) and Leonard Benevolo (1923–). The ethical questions accompanying modern architecture now forge novel relevance. In the book *Storia dell'architettura moderna* (1950; History of Modern Architecture), Zevi advocated an operative use of history. Influenced by the philosophy of Benedetto Croce (1866–1952), he sees actuality not only as determined by history but also as present only in history; therefore, his goal is not to provide a historical narrative for the most recent expressions of architecture but to distill out of historical knowledge a guide for the actions of present and future architects. In *Storia dell'architettura moderna* (1960; History of Modern Architecture), Benevolo confronted the questions and hesitations about the ideals of the Modern movement. Benevolo believed in the need to revise Modernism's history to ensure its continuing relevance. To this end, he integrated the historical narrative into a broader sociological context, demonstrating how modern architecture is narrowly intertwined with the lives of modern peoples and cultures. From this derives the justification of modern architecture as the only protagonist of contemporary architectural history.

Finally, in the 1970s and 1980s, the historiography of modern architecture developed in myriad contradictory ways. Whereas on the one hand we see an objectivation of the method of a modern architectural history in what by now has become a "manual," on the other hand we see a deepening of the crisis, leading to radical questions about the legitimization of the historical genre of a history of modern architecture per se.

RIXT HOEKSTRA

See also **Benevolo, Leonardo (Italy); Frampton, Kenneth (United States); Gropius, Walter (Germany); Pevsner, Nikolaus (England); Tafuri, Manfredo (Italy); Zevi, Bruno (Italy)**

Further Reading

A very usable introduction to the historiography of modern architecture is written by Panayotis Tournikiotis (1999). The book is clearly Postmodern in character: inspired by French deconstructive philosopher Jacques Derrida, Tournikiotis treats historiography as a number of written texts, diverse in character, whose narrative and discursive structures require analysis. On the other end of the spectrum, texts by Maria Luisa Scalvini and Maria Grazia Sandri (1984) focus on the early phase of historiographic production between 1927 and 1941; in contrast to Tournikiotis's approach, an historical method is followed, emphasizing the process by which the authors derived their view of history. A particularly strong tradition in historiographical study is present in Italy; because of this, many books are written in Italian.

Ankersmit, Franklin Rudolf, *Denken over geschiedenis: een overzicht van moderne geschiedfilosofische opvattingen*, Groningen: Wolters Noordhoff, 1984

Benevolo, Leonardo, *Storia dell'architettura moderna*, 2 vols., Bari: Laterza, 1960; new edition, Rome: Laterza, 1999; as *History of Modern Architecture*, translated by H.J. Landry, 2 vols., London: Routledge and Paul, and Cambridge, Massachusetts: MIT Press, 1971

Frampton, Kenneth, *Modern Architecture: A Critical History*, London: Thames and Hudson, and New York: Oxford University Press, 1980; 3rd edition, London: Thames and Hudson, 1992; New York: Thames and Hudson, 1997

Pevsner, Nikolaus, *Pioneers of the Modern Movement from William Horri's to Walter Groupius*, London: Faber and Faber, 1936

Pigafetta, Giorgio, *Architettura moderna e ragione storica: la storiografia italiana sull' architettura moderna: 1928–1976*, Milan: Guerini Studio, 1993

Platz, Gustav Adolf, *Die Baukunst der neuesten Zeit*, Berlin: Propylaen Verlag, 1927; 2nd edition, 1930

Porphyrios, Demetri (editor), *On the Methodology of Architectural History*, New York: St. Martin's Press, and London: Architectural Design, 1981

Scalvini, Maria Luisa, and Maria Grazia Sandri, *L'immagine storiografica dell'architettura contemporanea da Platz a Giedion*, Rome: Officina Edizioni, 1984

Sousloff, Catherine, "Historicism in Art History," in *Encyclopedia of Aesthetics*, edited by Michael Kelly, New York: University Press, 1998

Tafuri, Manfredo, and Francesco Dal Co, *Architettura contemporanea*, Milan: Electa, 1976; as *Modern Architecture*, translated by Robert Erich Wolf, 2 vols., New York: Abrams, 1979; London: Academy Editions, 1980

Tournikiotis, Panayotis, *The Historiography of Modern Architecture*, Cambridge, Massachusetts: MIT Press, 1999

Watkin, David, *The Rise of Architectural History*, London: Architectural Press, and Westfield, New Jersey: Eastview Editions, 1980

Winckelmann, Johann Joachim, *The History of Ancient Art*, translated by G. Henry Lodge, 4 vols., Boston: Osgood, 1849–73; reprint, New York: Ungar, 1969 (translation of *Geschichte de Kunst des Altertums*, 1764)

Zevi, Bruno, *Il linguaggio moderno dell'architettura*, Torino: Einaudi, 1973; as *The Modern Language of Architecture*, Seattle: University of Washington Press, 1978

HITCHCOCK, HENRY-RUSSELL, JR. 1903–87

Architecture critic and historian, United States

Henry-Russell Hitchcock Jr., was one of the small number of nonarchitects (which include historian and cultural critic Lewis Mumford and, somewhat later, the architectural historian Vincent Scully) who exercised a crucial influence on modern architectural practice in the United States. As a chronicler of then-recent currents in European architecture, Hitchcock defined the historical and formal frameworks through which Americans in the 1930s and 1940s understood the new phenomenon of the Modern movement. Beginning as an unabashed partisan supporter of what he and his circle dubbed the International Style, Hitchcock went on as an influential architectural historian to offer an exhaustive, magisterial overview of more than two centuries of European and U.S. architecture.

As a student of architectural history in the 1920s at Harvard, he was shaped equally by the holistic vision of architecture and cultural history of his mentor, medievalist Kingsley Porter, and by the enthusiasm for avant-garde art and literature of a cadre of undergraduates with whom Hitchcock founded the arts journal *Hound and Horn* in 1927. From Porter, Hitchcock took an all-inclusive stance toward architecture that included construction as well as the history of widely differing forms. Hitchcock shared with his young pro-Modernist friends a preoccupation with the role of creative artists as living parts of their culture. The latter concern drove him to explore the roots and potentialities of contemporary architecture in a wide variety of essays and monographs, climaxing with *Modern Architecture* (1929).

Modern Architecture recounts the major trends and talents of the 19th and 20th centuries, from the collapse of rococo to the emergence of Le Corbusier, to prove the thesis Hitchcock laid out in his first *Hound and Horn* essay, "The Decline of Architecture," in 1927. Mainstream, revivalist practice, Hitchcock stated, was merely scenographic, without integral relationship to building technology and thus was dead. Hitchcock viewed with sympathy and respect the work of those architects around 1900, chief among them Frank Lloyd Wright, who worked to strip traditional forms of their most dishonest and obsolete features. A new, living approach to architectural style, however, would have to limit itself to engineering's new forms and methods of construction—but with primarily aesthetic, not functionalist, motivations. Accordingly, Hitchcock argued that despite the achievements of Wright and the "New Tradition," the direction of the "New Pioneers"—J.J.P. Oud, Le Corbusier, and Ludwig Mies van der Rohe—had formal creativity, structural logic, and the force of history on its side. Hitchcock thus staked out a position in favor of the most extreme modernism but without the antiaesthetic stance that dominated defenses of it in Europe at that time.

Hitchcock's ideas achieved nationwide influence through his connections with the Museum of Modern Art in New York. Hitchcock's Harvard friend Alfred Barr, the museum's founding director, persuaded Hitchcock to turn a planned revision of *Modern Architecture* aimed at a European readership into an exhibition and short book for a U.S. audience. Barr, Hitchcock, and Barr's young acolyte Philip Johnson, the millionaire volunteer director of the architecture show, replaced Hitchcock's term *New Pioneers* with the label *International Style*. In 1932, the year of Johnson's exhibition at the museum, Hitchcock and Johnson published a pithy, well-illustrated synopsis of Hitchcock's earlier book under the title *The International Style*. Hitchcock reduced the formal devices of the radical European modernists and some of their polemics, especially Le Corbusier's, into a short list of stylistic features: non-load-bearing walls, thin-walled spatial volumes, regular proportions and finish, asymmetry, acknowledgement of industrial building methods, and lack of ornament. This list both described the style as it had evolved historically and prescribed its application in various building types. Although the book and exhibition were criticized widely for being both dogmatic and apathetic toward modernism's social message, they did much to focus the confused understanding and eclectic adoption of nonacademic architecture in the United States at the beginning of the Depression. *The International Style*, remaining in print throughout the next two decades, came to be accepted in the 1940s as the primary text on modernism's genesis and, as a generation of young reformist architects entered the profession, a rulebook for its styles and terms.

In 1936 Hitchcock published *The Architecture of H.H. Richardson and His Times*, the first full-length study of Richardson's career since 1888 and still an invaluable, sympathetic guide. (Hitchcock's appreciation of U.S. Victorian architecture, unexpected in the author of *The International Style*, was lifelong; in the 1930s he and photographer Berenice Abbott launched a project to document Victorian design in New England.) His later publications vary widely, from Victorian Gothic to Dutch modernism to the German Renaissance, but his most lasting achievement is likely to be his classic survey for the Pelican History of Art series, *Architecture: Nineteenth and Twentieth Centuries* (1958, with later revised editions). This work evinces Hitchcock's sheer enthusiasm for looking at buildings of all kinds, in combination with his encyclopedic range and gift for the convincing overview that confirmed him a major contributor to the acceptance of modernism as well as to the writing of architectural history in the United States.

MILES DAVID SAMSON

See also **Corbusier, Le (Jeanneret, Charles-Édouard) (France); Gaudí, Antoni (Spain); International Style; International Style Exhibition, New York (1932); Johnson, Philip (United States); Mies van der Rohe, Ludwig (Germany); Mumford, Lewis (United States); Museum of Modern Art, New York City; Oud, J.J.P. (Netherlands); Scully, Vincent (United States)**

Biography

Born in Boston, 3 June 1903; raised in Plymouth, Massachusetts, the son of a doctor. Studied architecture at Harvard University, Cambridge, Massachusetts 1923–24; received a master's degree in art history from Harvard University 1927; toured Europe 1930. Helped organize *Modern Architecture: International Exhibition* at the Museum of Modern Art, New York 1932. Professor, Vassar College, Poughkeepsie, New York 1927–28; professor, Wesleyan University, Middletown, Connecticut 1929–41; professor, Smith College, Northampton, Massachusetts 1941–68. Died in New York, 19 February 1987.

Selected Publications

Modern Architecture, 1929
The International Style (with Philip Johnson), 1932
The Architecture of H.H. Richardson and His Times, 1936
In the Nature of Materials, 1940
Architecture: Nineteenth and Twentieth Centuries, 1958

Further Reading

Recent attention to Hitchcock has focused on his motivations for the selective account of modernism he offered American readers in the 1930s; the most exhaustive account on the topic is Riley. However, he has also received attention as a member of New York's arts avant-garde in the same period; Watson discusses Hitchcock's activities in the musical and art worlds of New York, Cambridge, and Hartford between 1929 and 1935. A brief but authoritative account of Hitchcock's career as a whole is Searing.

Riley, Terence, *The International Style: Exhibition 15 and the Museum of Modern Art*, New York: Rizzoli, 1992
Searing, Helen, "Henry-Russell Hitchcock: The Architectural Historian As Critic and Connoisseur," in *The Architectural Historian in America*, edited by Elisabeth Blair MacDougall, Washington, D.C.: National Gallery of Art, 1990
Watson, Steven, *Prepare for Saints: Gertrude Stein, Virgil Thomson, and the Mainstreaming of American Modernism*, New York: Random House, 1998

HODGETTS AND FUNG

Architects and designers, United States

Hodgetts and Fung Design Associates in Santa Monica, California, is distinctly unlike the typical American architecture office, for their production includes not only buildings and their surroundings, but also exhibition design, performance art, installations, film set design, interactive game environments, and visionary urban design proposals at all scales. They are perhaps the only firm to carry forward the legacy of the office of Charles and Ray Eames, who also successfully combined architecture with other design media, notably that of film.

Hodgetts and Fung buildings are known as progressively modernist; clarity of form and spatial organizations inherited from the Modern movement often serve as an organizational basis. Within these armatures, elements are added and manipulated at a smaller scale, overlaying both artistic and engineering logic to achieve flexibility, choice, dynamism, a humanist assimilation of technology, and a concern for context. Each building tends to have an individual character arising out of its unique solution, giving the work an iconoclastic and antimonumental stance that appears almost like an anonymous modern vernacular, lacking as it does the recognizable hallmarks of personal style favored by the traditional design firm.

This approach was first evidenced in the Southside Settlement Community Center in Columbus, Ohio (1980), where the young architects successfully integrated such diverse influences as James Stirling's Flats at Ham Common (1955), Alvar Aalto's Sanyatsalo Town Hall (1959), Herman Hertzberger's Student Union in Amsterdam (1966), providing the villagelike building with an eclectic and exuberant vocabulary of archetypal Modern forms interwoven with idiosyncratic popular idioms derived from the surrounding urban context. Later buildings that embody this approach include the Click and Flick Agency in West Hollywood, California (1992), the Towell Library at University of California, Los Angeles (1992), and the Sinclair Pavilion at the Art Center School of Design in Pasadena (2001).

Hodgetts and Fung have produced a great number of exhibition designs, including the well-known "Blueprints for Modern Living: History and Legacy of the Case Study Houses" in the Temporary Contemporary, Los Angeles, which included full-size replicas of two of the Eames Case Study Houses (1989). Other exhibition design projects have included the Experience Music Project in Seattle, Washington (1995), a series of cyber-environments for Microsoft at the Electronic Entertainment Exposition in Los Angeles (1996) and Atlanta (1997), an urban theme park in Beijing for Universal Studios (1997), and an interactive game environment for Disney in Orlando, Florida (1997).

Hodgetts and Fung's work is distinguished by an integration of technologies into their projects that is, unlike most architecture labeled as High-Tech, neither glorified nor romanticized. Instead, advanced materials and products throughout their buildings ergonomically and aesthetically enhance the environment. Their work seeks to avoid the overwhelming sense that people have of being dominated by technology; it is, instead, comfortable and accessible as it enters the realm of the vernacular.

Because of the nature of these projects, Hodgetts and Fung operate in a collaborative manner that is quite different from a typical architecture office, where the architect is given the lead role in the design process with other team members as merely supportive. They expand and blur the boundaries of the archi-

Southside Settlement Community Center, Columbus, Ohio (1980)
Photo © Mary Ann Sullivan

tect's role by a seamless and sometimes even anonymous integration into a substantial range of creative environments.

JOHN M. CAVA

Biography

Craig Hodgetts

Born in Cincinnati, Ohio, 9 September 1937. Attended General Motors Institute, Flint, Michigan 1955–57, earned bachelor's degree, Oberlin College, Oberlin, Ohio 1960. Attended San Francisco State University, California 1961–62, and University of California at Berkeley 1962–64, earned master's degree 1966 in architecture at Yale University, New Haven, Connecticut. Principal and cofounder, New York and Venice, California offices of Studio Works 1968–83; principal and cofounder, Hodgetts + Fung Design Associates, Santa Monica, California 1984–present; principal and cofounder, Harmonica Inc., Santa Monica, California 1989–present. Member, California Council on Design Education 1975; member, NEA Design Advancement Panel 1984, 1986, 1987; member, NEA Panel on Architect/Artist Collaborations 1984; member, NEA USA Fellowship Policy Panel 1986; speaker, International Design Conference, Aspen, Colorado 1995. Associate Dean, California Institute of the Arts 1969–72; visiting professor, Rice University, Houston, Texas 1984; adjunct professor, University of Pennsylvania 1982–90; professor, University of California at San Diego 1990–93; Eero Saarinen visiting professor, Yale University, New Haven, Connecticut 1995; professor, University of California at Los Angeles, Los Angeles, California 1993–present; Architecture Award, American Academy of Arts and Letter 1994; Chrysler Award for Innovation in Design 1996, Architectural Foundation of Los Angeles 1997.

Hsin-Ming Fung

Born in Hanoi, China 29 May 1953. Attended Oxford College, Oxford, Ohio 1971–72, Miami University, Oxford, Ohio 1973–74, earned bachelor's degree 1977, California State University, Dominguez Hills, California; master's in architecture at the University of California at Los Angeles 1980. Principal and cofounder, Hodgetts + Fung Design Associates, Santa Monica, California 1984–present; principal and cofounder, Harmonica Inc., Santa Monica, California 1989–present. Board member, Museum of Contemporary Art, Los Angeles 1992–present; president, Los Angeles Forum for Architecture and Urban Design 1994–95; Association of Collegiate Schools of Architecture 1994–present; fellow, International Design Conference, Aspen, Colorado 1995. Visiting professor, Southern California Institute of Architecture 1993–present; associate professor, California State Polytechnic University, Pomona, California 1985–present; Eero Saarinen visiting professor, Yale University, New Haven, Connecticut 1995; Architecture Award, American Academy of Arts and Letter 1994; Chrysler Award for Innovation in Design 1996, Architectural Foundation of Los Angeles 1997.

Selected Works

Gagosian Gallery, Venice, California, 1979
Southside Settlement Community Center, Columbus, Ohio, 1980
Venice Interarts Center, Venice, California, 1983
"Blueprints for Modern Living: History and Legacy of the Case Study Houses," (exhibition design), The Temporary Contemporary, The Museum of Contemporary Art, Los Angeles, California, 1989
Visionary San Francisco, San Francisco Museum of Modern Art, 1991
Click and Flick Agency, West Hollywood, California, 1992
Tokyo Disneyland Gate II Main Street, Tokyo, Japan, 1992
Five Shrines, Installation, World Financial Center, New York, 1992
Towell Library, University of California at Los Angeles, 1992
Occidental College Sculpture Studio, Los Angeles, California, 1997
Score Zone, Disney Quest, Orlando, Florida, 1997
American Cinematheque, Hollywood, California, 1998

Further Reading

Architecture + Urbanism, Tokyo: A + U Publishing, March 1991
Constantinopoulos, Vivian (editor), *10 × 10: 10 Critics, 100 Architects*, London: Phaidon Press, 2000
Forster, Kurt, *New West Coast Architecture 1982*, New York: Institute for Architecture and Urban Studies, 1982
Forster, Kurt, *Hodgetts + Fung: Scenarios and Spaces*, New York: Rizzoli, 1997
International Architecture Yearbook, Mulgrave, Australia: Images Publishing, 2000
Jodidio, Philip, *Contemporary California Architects*, Cologne, Germany: Benedikt Taschen Verlag, 1995
Jodidio, Philip, *Architecture in the 1990's*, Cologne, Germany: Benedikt Taschen Verlag, 1997
Polledri, Paolo, *Visionary San Francisco*, Munich: Prestel-Verlag, 1990

HOFFMANN, JOSEF (FRANZ MARIA) 1870–1956

Architect, Austria

Today, Josef Hoffmann's historic significance is firmly established; together with Otto Wagner and Adolf Loos, he is one of the three internationally best-known Viennese architects from the period around 1900. His international renown had been equally strong during the first three decades of the 20th century, but by the middle of the century much of Hoffmann's oeuvre was practically forgotten or at least deemed irrelevant. The reasons for this were partly intrinsic to the subculture of architecture with its built-in alterations of attitude and partly consequences of the dramatic changes of external conditions that accompanied his practice.

When Hoffmann was born in the small Moravian town of Brtnice (then Pirnitz), Moravia was an integral part of the Austro-Hungarian monarchy, and when he arrived in Vienna to study at the Academy of Fine Arts under Carl von Hasenauer, he entered the thriving capital of an empire inhabited by some 24 million people. At the time of his death, the same city was the capital of a very small, impoverished central European state, and the economic and social framework of architectural practice in it had changed in many ways.

Hoffmann's strength lay in a never-flagging wealth of creative imagination paired with a strong talent as form giver and graphic artist. He trusted his intuition and, with a dream walker's assurance, on sheets of squared paper made freehand designs for anything that came his way, from surface patterns and small objects to furniture, exhibitions, houses, and palaces. Today, his drawings and the objects carried out after them are highly priced collector's items, but for decades they were the butt of attacks by those of his contemporaries who, like Adolf Loos, were trying to rid the world of ornament.

What Hoffmann brought to his profession as natural endowment was supplemented by the effects of several strong educational experiences. He was fortunate to complete his studies under Otto Wagner, Hasenauer's successor at the Academy, and to win the Rome prize for a stay in Italy. The Mediterranean impressions received there became as formative for him as in Vienna Wagner's buildings and clearly formulated teachings about an architecture appropriate for "modern man." In addition, he became imbued with the teachings of John Ruskin, William Morris, and Alfred Lichtwark. At the same time, his association with artists of the Vienna Secession, such as Gustav Klimt and Koloman Moser, and his appointment as professor at the Vienna School of Applied Arts, where he taught from 1899 to 1936, became important factors in his career.

A crucial development occurred in 1903, when, together with Koloman Moser and the wealthy art-loving businessman Fritz Wärndorfer, Hoffmann founded the Wiener Werkstätte. Inspired by the English Arts and Crafts movement and encouraged by Charles Rennie Mackintosh, the Viennese firm employed highly skilled artisans to execute designs by Hoffmann and

Moser. For several years, it provided the interiors for buildings by Hoffmann, who also directed its architecture department.

Hoffmann's best-known surviving buildings from the early 20th century are the Sanatorium Purkersdorf (1904) near Vienna and the Stoclet House (1911) in Brussels. Before he received these commissions, however, he had securely established his reputation in Vienna by a number of successful works, including a shop, interiors, stunning exhibitions, and a group of four houses in the suburb of Hohe Warte.

After the exterior of the Purkersdorf building had been thoroughly restored in the recent past, it became possible to experience again what a powerful pioneering statement it made by the superb interplay of simply proportioned white cubic and slablike forms that, like all window openings, were clearly delimited at the edges by borders of small blue-white ceramic elements. The building, which invites comparisons with contemporaneous works by Mackintosh and Wright, was constructed in brick and stucco with reinforced-concrete ceilings and stairs. Recent research has related the architectural treatment of the building to the advances in psychiatric medicine made in Vienna at the time (see Topp, 1997).

At the Stoclet house, the device of formally framing all surfaces of the facades also became a main design feature, only here

Moser House, Vienna (1903), designed by Josef Hoffmann
© GreatBuildings.com

it was a matter of enclosing cladding slabs of white marble with chased-metal moldings. It is highly likely that Hoffmann, inspired by Otto Wagner, here gave his version of interpreting Gottfried Semper's theory about the role of cladding in architecture.

The Stoclet commission, by a rare chance, brought Hoffmann together with a congenial art-loving client of almost unlimited means. The result was one of perfect harmony of program, design, and execution for the building, its garden, and its interiors. Several artist friends of Hoffmann helped in carrying out his intentions at Brussels, none of them more brilliantly than Gustav Klimt with his by now world-famous, but at present generally inaccessible, mosaics for the Stoclet dining room. When after six years the building was finished, architects and artists from all over Europe came to marvel at the owner's precious art collections and their architectural frame. A performance in the theater/concert hall of the Stoclet house must have come as close to being a *Gesamtkunstwerk* (total work of art) as was possible at the time.

As at Purkersdorf, the carefully proportioned plan was laid out along two main axes, and on the upper floor it reveals a perfect symmetry. On the ground floor, however, the solution is more complex because of the asymmetrical elements of entrance, staircase tower, and service wing. Seen from the street, the building looks vaguely ecclesiastical because of the apsidal termination of the ground floor at one end and the staircase tower at the other. The tower's decorative and sculptural treatment seems intended to symbolize a fusion of power and beauty.

The Stoclet house is but the largest and most monumental representative of its type—the well-appointed private garden residence that was considered one of Hoffmann's specialties. In Vienna, he created a number of these, not all of which survived. Among the best preserved and most impressive are the Villa Ast (1911) at Steinfeldgasse 2; the large, sumptuous Villa Primavesi (1915) at Gloriettegasse 18; and the Villa Sonja Knips (1925) at Nusswaldgasse 22.

Ever since his beginnings at the Vienna Secession, with the 14th exhibition of Klinger's Beethoven (1902) as the artistic climax, exhibitions were considered Hoffmann's true bailiwick. His Vienna *Kunstschau* (1908), the Austrian pavilion for the international art exhibition in Rome (1911), and above all the Austrian pavilion for the Werkbund exhibition in Cologne (1914) were considered genuine masterworks by contemporaneous critics. However, only his Austrian pavilion for the Venice Biennale (1934) has survived as testimony to his skill. At the Austrian pavilion for the 1925 International Exhibition of Decorative Arts in Paris, a single molding, taken out of context and given new meaning at a different scale, became the generating element of the building's entire facade treatment. With such highly original and effective inventions and a sophisticated way of giving the formal language of classicism new, often atectonic and ambiguous interpretations, Hoffmann became one of the unacknowledged progenitors of Art Deco.

Hoffmann had come a long way from the world of late 19th-century historic eclecticism to that of the Modern movement, when, in opposition to Victor Horta, he voted for Le Corbusier's entry at the international competition for the League of Nations palace. His oeuvre is rich in changes of direction, but in every case he ended up with something unmistakably his own, something that had undergone a subtle transformation in keeping with his ideal to "advance from the correct to the noble conception" (Sekler, 1985). His influence was widespread and explicitly acknowledged by such 20th-century masters as Alvar Aalto, Gio Ponti, and Carlo Scarpa, and some of his favorite motifs, such as the multiple recessing of edges, are still parts of current architectural language.

EDUARD F. SEKLER

See also **Art Deco; Arts and Crafts Movement; International Exhibition of Decorative Arts, Paris (1925); Loos, Adolf (Austria); Palais Stoclet, Brussels; Vienna, Austria; Vienna Secession; Wagner, Otto (Austria); Werkbund Exhibition, Cologne (1914)**

Biography

Born in Pirnitz, Moravia (now Brtnice, Czech Republic), 15 December 1870. Studied in the Department of Building, Staatsgewerbeschule, Brünn, Moravia (now Brno, Czech Republic); studied architecture under Carl von Hasenauer and Otto Wagner, Akademie der Bildenden Künste, Vienna 1892–95; Rome Prize, traveled Italy 1895. Private practice, Würzburg, Germany 1891–92; worked in the studio of Otto Wagner, Vienna 1896–97. Private practice, Vienna from 1898; founding member of Vienna Secession 1897. Professor, Kunstgewer-beschule, Vienna 1899–1936. Founder, with Kolomon Moser and Fritz Wärndorfer, Wiener Werkstätte 1903; director, with Gustav Klimt, Kunstschau, Vienna 1908–09; cofounder and director, Austrian Werkbund, Vienna 1910; director, Künstler-werkstätte, Vienna from 1943. Died in Vienna, 15 May 1956.

Selected Works

Moser House, Vienna, 1903
Sanatorium, Purkersdorf, Austria, 1904
Austrian Pavilion, Rome, 1911 (destroyed)
Palais Stoclet, Brussels, 1911
Villa Ast, Vienna, 1911
Austrian Pavilion, Werkbund Exhibition, Cologne, 1914 (destroyed)
Villa Primavesi, Vienna, 1915
Villa Sonja Knips, Vienna, 1925
Austrian Pavilion, Exposition des Arts Décoratifs, Paris, 1925 (destroyed)
Austrian Pavilion, Biennale, Venice, 1934

Selected Publications

"Einfache Möbel," *Das Interieur* II, 1901
"Wiens Zukunft," *Der Merker*, December 1919

Further Reading

The most comprehensive treatment including a catalog of works is Sekler; its full bibliography is updated in the Italian edition of the book (1991). Muntoni on the Stoclet House contains plans that were inaccessible before. For many illustrations of designs by Hoffmann, see Noever.

Gresleri, Giuliano (editor), *Josef Hoffmann,* Bologna: Zanichelli, 1981; as *Josef Hoffmann,* New York: Rizzoli, 1985
Muntoni, Alessandra, *Il palazzo Stoclet di Josef Hoffmann, 1905–1911,* Rome: Multigrafica, 1989
Noever, Peter (editor), *Josef Hoffmann, 1870–1956: Ornament zwischen Hoffnung und Verbrechen,* Vienna: Österreichisches

Museum für Angewandte Kunst, 1987; revised and expanded, as *Josef Hoffmann Designs,* Munich: Prestel, 1992

Sekler, Eduard F., *Josef Hoffmann: das architektonische Werk: Monographie und Werkverzeichnis,* Salzburg: Residenz Verlag, 1982; 2nd edition, 1986; as *Josef Hoffmann: The Architectural Work,* Princeton, New Jersey: Princeton University Press, 1985

Topp, Leslie, "An Architecture for Modern Nerves: Josef Hoffmann's Purkersdorf Sanatorium," *Journal of the Society of Architectural Historians* 56/4 (December 1997)

Vergo, Peter, "Fritz Wärndorfer and Josef Hoffmann," *Burlington Magazine* 125 (1983)

HOLABIRD, WILLIAM 1854–1923 AND JOHN WELLBORN ROOT 1887–1963

Architecture firm, United States

One of Chicago's most venerable architectural firms, Holabird and Root is also one of the oldest in continuous practice in the United States. Founded in 1880 by William Holabird and Martin Roche, Holabird and Roche became Holabird and Root in 1928 on the succession of John Holabird (1886–1945) and John Wellborn Root, Jr. With the change of name came a shift in design method. Although both men had trained in Paris in the Beaux-Arts tradition, they concluded that historicism was inappropriate for modern buildings. While nurturing the Chicago tradition of the skeletal frame, the firm achieved national acclaim by supplanting classicism and devising a distinctive architectural expression with their powerful, vertical, streamlined skyscrapers of the late 1920s. Some critics, such as Carl Condit, contend that Holabird and Root might have pioneered a new American architecture had the Great Depression not intervened.

Holabird and Root's assertive new style was first proclaimed in two Michigan Avenue office towers in Chicago, 333 Michigan Avenue (1928) and the Palmolive Building (1929). These simplified skyscrapers, which comply with the 1916 zoning law that increased the cubic volume of buildings and required setbacks, replace the bulk and mass characteristic of earlier large buildings. As its sheer vertical walls soar over the city and the Chicago River, 333's pared-down silhouette and complex massing adhere to the skeletal principle of the Chicago School while simultaneously anticipating modernism's preferences for slab design. Root, the firm's chief designer (Holabird's expertise was engineering and management), acknowledged the lasting influence of Eliel Saarinen's second-place entry for the Chicago Tribune Tower competition (1922), which inspired 333's tower and long, narrow design. The 37-story machine-age Palmolive Building contains an unprecedented number of setback volumes (six) that create a pattern of receding masses and define the building's sculptural disposition. Deep window channels set in the wall plane accentuate its pronounced verticality. The Chicago Daily News Building (1929; now Riverside Plaza), for which the firm was awarded the coveted gold medal from the Architectural League of New York in 1930, paved the way for development along the Chicago River. It was the first building constructed on air rights over railroad facilities; its foundation is cantilevered over Union Station's tracks, and ventilation shafts are incorporated into the design. As commuters shuffle through the 26-story

building and gather in the city's first public plaza, the vertical surge and horizontal span are in equilibrium.

Arguably, the most successful commission for Holabird and Root was the Chicago Board of Trade (1930). The country's foremost agricultural trading center required offices, an exchange floor, trading pits, and retail space. The building's nine-story base fills an entire city block while the lean, symmetrically arranged setbacks bound toward a pyramidal hipped roof capped by a cast aluminum sculpture of Ceres, Roman goddess of the harvest, by John Storrs. At 45 stories, it was once the city's tallest structure. Its streamlined massing and refined detail epitomize the modernistic, Art Deco skyscraper. Prior to the Depression, these modern, rational office towers, enlivened by complicated massing, striking verticality, and dramatic lighting, generated much enthusiasm, causing some to regard Holabird and Root as successors to Louis Sullivan and Frank Lloyd Wright. Critic Earl Reed, Jr., maintained "nothing so significant has happened here since the pre-Columbian Exposition days which witnessed the coming to our streets of the epochmaking works of that mighty band which surrounded Sullivan" (Reed, 1930, 1).

Ornament was not antithetical to Holabird and Root's early towers. Low reliefs and stylized carving, at times rectilinear, as in the Board of Trade, and at times narrative, as in the frieze at 333 Michigan Avenue commemorating Chicago's pioneer days, frequently appear above windows, along cornice lines, and at entryways. While decorative elements nod at tradition, they do not interrupt the broad expanse of the curtain wall. The fully unadorned structural frame did not gain prominence until the late 1930s, with the arrival of Mies van der Rohe, whom Holabird was influential in bringing to Chicago's Armour Institute (now the Illinois Institute of Technology). Modern detail was prominent in Holabird and Root's interiors as well. Materials such as walnut, marble, glass, and nickel, as well as murals, sculpture, exotic motifs, and polychromatic patterning, signify the firm's response to the eclecticism of Art Deco. Diana Court, in the Michigan Square Building (1930; demolished 1973), was one of the most resplendent interiors of the period with its kaleidoscopic semicircular rotunda of polished metalwork and marble. Design was undertaken by the firm's in-house sculpture and interior design departments and by several fine artists, such as Carl Milles and John Norton. As a collaborative practice, Holabird and Root created complete environments in their signature buildings.

The firm reached its pinnacle in 1930 with its lofty, modern office towers that glorified American commercialism, yet Holabird and Root has mastered many building types, including theaters, capital buildings (North Dakota), courthouses (Birmingham, Alabama; Racine, Wisconsin; and St. Paul, Minnesota), railroad cars, hotels, public and private housing, exhibition buildings for Chicago's 1933–34 Century of Progress Exposition, and research-and-development buildings, such as the innovative A.O. Smith Laboratory (1929) with its aluminum and glass facade and free-span interior spaces. Illinois Bell and Monsanto have relied on Holabird and Root's utilitarianism and adaptability for more than 75 and 40 years, respectively. The hegemony of international modernism and an emphasis on engineering rather than design typified the firm's post–World War II production; however, from the early 1970s to the present,

Riverside Plaza, Chicago, Illinois (1929), William Holabird and John Wellborn Root
© GreatBuildings.com

inventive design practices have once again solidified its reputation. In educational, institutional, and corporate schemes, modernist principles regarding detail and structural refinement are employed.

Holabird and Root can be characterized as a rational and pragmatic team whose focus is on collaboration and innovation. With attention to client needs and the ability to carry a project through from design to production, the firm has made substantial contributions, from its authoritative role in the development of the skyscraper to the shaping of the urban and suburban environment. Despite its pursuit of a modernist typology, it has never been an avant-garde practice. Instead, progressivism, adaptability, and sound design and construction characterize Holabird and Root's most celebrated buildings of the late 1920s as well as many of their other buildings. The centenarian firm reflects the nature of architectural practice in the United States throughout much of the 20th century and, quite possibly, in the present century.

ANDREA FOGGLE PLOTKIN

See also **Chicago (IL), United States; Chicago School; Holabird, William, and Martin Roche (United States); Illinois Institute of Technology, Chicago; Mies van der Rohe, Lud-**

wig (Germany); **Tribune Tower International Competition (1922), Chicago**

Biography

William Holabird

Born in Union, New York, 11 September 1854. Studied engineering as a cadet at the United States Military Academy, West Point, Virginia 1871–73. Married; son was John Holabird, architect. Draftsman, office of William Le Baron Jenney, Chicago 1873–80. Partner, with Ossian Simonds, Chicago 1880; partner, with Simonds and Martin Roche, Chicago 1881–83; partner, Holabird and Roche, Chicago from 1883. Member, Western Association of Architects; fellow, American Institute of Architects 1889. Died in Evanston, Illinois, 19 July 1923.

Martin Roche

Born in Cleveland, 1 August 1853. Studied at the Art Institute of Chicago; apprenticed to a cabinetmaker, Chicago 1867–72; draftsman, office of William Le Baron Jenney, Chicago 1872–81. Partner, with Ossian Simonds and Martin Roche, Chicago

1881–83; partner, Holabird and Roche, Chicago from 1883. Member, Western Association of Architects; fellow, American Institute of Architects 1889. Died in Chicago, 6 June 1927.

Selected Works

333 Michigan Avenue, Chicago, 1928
A.O. Smith Laboratory, 1929
Palmolive Building (now Playboy), Chicago, 1929
Chicago Daily News Building (now Riverside Plaza), Chicago, 1929
Chicago Board of Trade, 1930
Diana Court, Michigan Square Building (destroyed), Chicago, 1930
Exhibition Buildings, Chicago's Century of Progress Exposition, 1934

Further Reading

Prior to Bruegmann's landmark, three-volume catalogue (1991), no book on Holabird and Root had been written since the 1920s, when the firm published its own collection of photographs. Both Blaser and Condit contend that the firm elaborated on the fundamental principles of the Chicago School. Bruegmann (1980), Stamper, and Zukowsky analyze the firm's principal buildings and pioneering role in the 1920s, and Wilson examines Holabird and Root's significance from its inception up to the present day.

Blaser, Werner (editor), *Chicago Architecture: Holabird and Root, 1880–1992*, Basel and Boston: Birkhäuser Verlag, 1992
Bruegmann, Robert, "Holabird and Roche and Holabird and Root: The First Two Generations," *Chicago History*, 9/3 (Fall 1980)
Bruegmann, Robert, *Holabird and Roche, Holabird and Root: An Illustrated Catalog of Works*, 3 vols., New York: Garland, 1991
Condit, Carl W., *Chicago: Building, Planning, and Urban Technology*, Chicago: University of Chicago Press, 1973
Reed, Earl H., Jr., "Some Recent Work of Holabird and Root, Architects," *Architecture*, 61 (January 1930)
Stamper, John W., *Chicago's North Michigan Avenue: Planning and Development, 1900–1930*, Chicago: University of Chicago Press, 1991
Wilson, Richard Guy, "Holabird and Root: Century of (Intermittent) Progress," *AIA Journal*, 72/2 (February 1983)
Zukowsky, John (editor), *Chicago Architecture and Design, 1923–1993: Reconfiguration of an American Metropolis*, Munich: Prestel, and Chicago: Art Institute of Chicago, 1993

HOLABIRD, WILLIAM 1854–1923 AND MARTIN ROCHE 1853–1927

Architecture firm, United States

William Holabird and Martin Roche, together with William Le Baron Jenney, Burnham and Root, and Adler and Sullivan, belonged to the Chicago School style of architecture. Founded in the 1830s, Chicago gradually emerged as the commercial center of the United States, and it was here that the first skyscraper appeared. After the great fire of 1871, architects from all over the country were attracted by the unparalleled opportunities offered by reconstruction. They slowly evolved solutions to the aesthetic problem of the high office building by allowing the new structural techniques not only to admit the building structure but also to express it.

Holabird arrived in 1875, after two years at West Point, and took an engineering job in the office of Jenney, where he met Roche, with whom he formed a partnership in 1880. Regard

for economy and utility, demanded by Chicago investors, is reflected consistently in their work. They never resorted to historicism, and the objective clarity of their designs witnessed a drastic reduction of piers and spandrels, allowing vast expanses of glass. They pioneered the "Chicago window," involving a large center pane flanked by a narrower operating sash.

Their 12-story Tacoma Building (1889), with its generous employment of glass, followed Jenney's Home Insurance Building (1884) in establishing steel-skeleton frames and curtain walling for skyscrapers. The well-proportioned Marquette Building (1894) shows an alternative to the Tacoma design, which had involved cantilevering tiered bay windows over the property line to obtain more space. The Marquette Building is similar to Jenney's Sears, Roebuck and Company (second Leiter) Building (1890) in its threefold division, but its shortcoming results from enlarged and rusticated corner piers, which invoke masonry rather than steel-frame construction. Horizontal windows and crisp, unenriched moldings herald the 20th century.

The McClurg Building (1900) shows a clarification of this design. The piers and mullions, reduced to mere lines, combine with the wider spandrels to make a cellular pattern that both balances and expresses the horizontal and vertical nature of the steel frame. The vast expanse of glass also testifies to the internal steel frame. Holabird and Roche designed two structures adjoining Sullivan's intimately scaled Gage Building (1899). Also a part of the Gage group, their economic lines contrast with Sullivan's and exemplify the more objective and programmatic designs that characterized the Chicago School. Three commissions for State Street stores, in the strategic Loop location, were all under way by 1911. Holabird and Roche designed a 15-story structure for Mandel Brothers, for whom they had already designed an annex, with characteristic wide bays and large glass windows, at the corner of Wabash Avenue and Madison Street. Featuring huge granite pilasters along the base and an arcade of Corinthian columns at the top, it replaced a smaller building and created one of the largest Chicago department stores, incorporating 6,500 square feet of plate glass for display, essential for commercial success. The ten-story Rothschild Store (1912), faced with enameled terra-cotta, boasted 38 elevators, seven miles of aisles, a specially designed ventilation system, and an advanced fireproof construction. The projecting cornice, arcaded lower floors, and delicate detailing distinguish it from its neighbors.

The first of a series of buildings for the Boston Store was described on completion in 1912 as "the architectural embodiment of the 'Chicago Idea' in commercial architecture." Plain in design, the building was flooded with light. The Netcher Building, which followed in 1917, at 17 stories, became the second-tallest building in the city. This flat, cellular structure incorporated three basements, housing small workshops for making candy, cigars, and ice cream; a full-size tennis court on the roof; and a branch of the Chicago Public Library. A magnificent multistory colonnade ran across the upper stories, echoing the neighboring Marshall Field's complex (1892) by Burnham. The architecture of the boom years after World War I and before the Great Depression of the 1930s included new hotels notable for their size and efficiency. Palmer House (1927) covered more than half a city block, with its three basements and 25 stories accommodating 2,268 guest rooms. With facades of brick above a limestone base, its gracious second-floor reception lobby and

Auditorium Annex, Michigan Avenue, Chicago, designed by Holabird and Roche
© Historic American Buildings Survey/Library of Congress. Photo by Cervin Robinson

connecting banquet room and ballroom were among the city's most elegant interiors. This was followed by the Stevens Hotel (1927), where 25 stories stretched along an entire block, enjoying a magnificent view of Lake Michigan.

Holabird and Roche continued to produce straightforward, imposing designs, very much in accord with the Chicago School, until Roche's death in 1927.

HILARY J. GRAINGER

See also **Burnham, Daniel (United States); Chicago, Illinois; Chicago School; Holabird, William and John Wellborn Root (United States)**

Further Reading

The fullest account of the work of Holabird and Roche is in Bruegmann (1977).

Bach, Ira J. (editor), *Chicago's Famous Buildings*, 3rd edition, Chicago, 1980
Bruegmann, R., *Holabird and Roche and Root*, Garland, 1991
Bruegmann, R., *The Architects and the City: Holabird and Roche of Chicago 1880–1918*, Chicago, 1997
Condit, Carl W., *The Rise of the Skyscraper*, Chicago, 1952
Condit, Carl W., *The Chicago School of Architecture: A History of Commercial and Public Buildings in the Chicago Area, 1875–1925*, Chicago, 1964
Jordy, William H., *American Buildings and Their Architects: Volume 4: Progressive and Academic Ideals at the Turn of the Century*, New York and Oxford, 1972
Kunz, Fritz, *Der Hotelbau von heute im In- und Ausland*, Stuttgart, 1930
Wight, Peter, B., "Additions to Chicago's Skyline: A Few Recent Skyscrapers," *Architectural Record*, 28 (July 1910)
Zukowsky, John (editor), *Chicago Architecture 1872–1922, Birth of a Metropolis*, Munich, London and New York, 1988

HOLL, STEVEN 1947–

Architect, United States

Steven Holl, architect, theorist, and teacher, has been considered a leader in late 20th- and early 21st-century architecture, his work distinguished by a subtle abstract rhythm that defies both modernist and postmodernist sensibilities. Known for developing diagrams that define the design of each project, the essence of Holl's work lies in the quality of space, light, materiality, and ultimately, the overall guiding concept. As founder and principal of Steven Holl Architects, he has maintained an office in New York City since 1976, and his projects have been built worldwide.

Holl's significant projects include the Museum of Contemporary Art Kiasma (1998) in Helsinki, Finland; Knut Hamsun Museum (1999) in Hamarey, Norway; and the Bellevue Art Museum (1999) in Bellevue, Washington. Some of his residential work includes the Pool House and Sculpture Garden (1981) in Scarsdale, New York; Stretto House (1992) in Dallas, Texas; the "Y" House (1998) in Catskill Mountains, New York, and the Berkowitz-Odgis House (1988) on Martha's Vineyard, Massachusetts. He has gained recognition through large residential projects, including the Seaside Hybrid Housing project (1987) in Seaside, Florida; Makahari Housing (1996) in Chiba, Japan; and Void Space/Hinged Space Housing (1991) in Fukuoka, Japan. Other works include the Sarphatistraat Offices (2000) in Amsterdam, the Netherlands; the Chapel of St. Ignatius (1999) in Seattle, Washington; and the addition to Cranbrook Institute of Science (1998) in Bloomfield Hills, Michigan, as well as a collaborative project for a Storefront for Art and Architecture (1993) with conceptual artist Vito Acconci in New York City.

Encouraged by an influential professor at the University of Washington, Hermann Pundt, Holl left Seattle and studied abroad his junior year in Rome, Italy. It was here that Holl made frequent visits to the Pantheon to study structure and light and was exposed to the urban layers of the city, both of which had a great influence on his later perceptions in architecture and theory. In 1976 he did postgraduate work at the Architectural Association in London, where he came in contact with architects such as Rem Koolhaas, Leon Krier, Charles Jenks, Elia Zenghelis, Zaha Hadid, and Bernard Tschumi. After traveling through Europe for several months, Holl returned to San Francisco and soon after moved to New York, where he established his office in 1976.

Nearly bypassing architecture for a career in painting in the 1970s, Holl still relies on two-dimensional media as a means to develop studies and diagrams that facilitate his search for the "elusive essence of architecture." Holl's buildings are described as aural as well as visual, and he has earned a reputation for creating designs that evolve from conceptual meaning rather than from a specific stylistic form. Although it is hard to distinguish one architect or style as a guiding influence, much of his work shows reflections of Louis Kahn, for whom Holl had been planning on working until the architect's sudden death, and Le Corbusier, both for their attention to structure and sense of materiality.

Although projects such as the D.E. Shaw and Co. offices (New York City, 1992), the Cohen Apartment (New York City, 1983), and the Void Space/Hinged Space Housing (1991), reflect early modernist qualities of clean lines and reductive materials such as concrete, glass, and metal, Holl experiments with a new three-dimensional language of planes and volumes that moves beyond the pure modernist influence. In the Stretto House, inspired by the overlapping stretto between heavy percussion and light strings in a musical piece by Béla Bartók, light metal roofs float between four heavy face-ground concrete pavil-

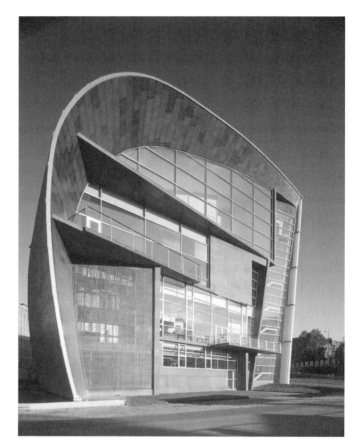

Museum of Contemporary Art Kiasma (1998), Helsinki, Finland, by Steven Holl
© Frederick Busam Esto

ions, echoing the musical score and illustrating a shift between Holl's early and later work.

In the mid-1990s Holl's work shifted from the rectilinear to abstract, curvilinear forms with strong expressions of light and color. In the St. Ignatius Chapel, Holl constructed a precast-concrete box of colored tilt-up slabs that framed six skylights, each reflecting the incoming light off colored interior baffles. At the Museum for Contemporary Art Kiasma in Helsinki, the patinated zinc, hand-polished aluminum, and sand-blasted glass exterior intertwines the building's mass with the geometry of the city and landscape.

KATHRYN ROGERS MERLINO

See also **Corbusier, Le (Jeanneret, Charles-Édouard) (France); Kahn, Louis (United States); Museum**

Biography

Born in Bremerton, Washington, 9 January 1947. Earned a bachelor's degree 1971 at University of Washington; moved to San Francisco for internships with Howard Bracken and Lawrence Halprin; graduate work at the Architectural Association in

London 1976–77. Moved to New York City and established office in 1976. Associate professor, Columbia University, New York City, since 1989. Selected for the Palazzo del Cinema Competition (Venice, 1990) and the Museum of Modern Art Expansion Competition (New York City, 1989). Married Janet Olmsted Cross 1992, divorced 1997. (Also an architect, Cross worked in the office from 1990–1997 and worked closely with Holl on projects.) Married Solange Sabiao, 1999. Awards include the 1990 Arnold W. Brunner Prize for Achievement in Architecture as an Art—American Academy and Institute of Arts and Letters; 1997 New York AIA Medal of Honor; 1998 National AIA Design Award, Chapel of St. Ignatius; 1998 Alvar Aalto Medal; 1998 Chrysler Award for Innovation in Design; 1999 National AIA Design Award, Kiasma.

Selected Works

Pool House and Sculpture Garden, Scarsdale, New York, 1981
Seaside Hybrid Housing project, Seaside, Florida, 1987
Berkowitz-Odgis House, Martha's Vineyard, Massachusetts, 1988
Metropolitan Tower Apartment, New York City, 1988
Void Space/Hinged Space Housing, Fukuoka, Japan, 1991
Stretto House, Dallas, Texas, 1992
Makahari Housing, Chiba, Japan, 1996
"Y" House, Catskill Mountains, New York, 1998
Museum of Contemporary Art Kiasma, Helsinki, Finland, 1998
Cranbrook Institute of Science, Bloomfield Hills, Michigan, 1998
Knut Hamsun Museum, Hamarey, Norway, 1999
Bellevue Art Museum, Bellevue, Washington, 1999
Chapel of St. Ignatius, Seattle, Washington, 1999
Sarphatistraat Offices, Amsterdam, the Netherlands, 2000

Selected Publications

Anchoring: Selected Projects 1975–1991, New Jersey: Princeton Architectural Press, 1996.
Parallax, New Jersey: Princeton Architectural Press, 2000.
Pamphlet Architecture (1–10), New Jersey, Princeton Architectural Press, 1998.
The Chapel of St. Ignatius, New Jersey: Princeton Architectural Press, 1999.
The Stretto House, New Jersey: Princeton Architectural Press, 1996.

Further Reading

Betsky, Aaron, "Steven Holl," *Metropolitan Home*, 30/6 (1998)
Futagawa, Yukio (editor), *Steven Holl* (bilingual English-Japanese edition), Tokyo: ADA Edita, 1993
Pamphlet Architecture, 1–10, New York, Princeton Architectural Press, 1998
Stein, Karen, "Project Diary: Steven Holl's Makahari Housing Complex," *Architectural Record*, 185/1 (1997)
The Stretto House: Steven Holl Architects, New York: Monacelli Press, 1996

HOLLEIN, HANS 1934–

Architect, Austria

Hans Hollein is an architect, artist, teacher, exhibition designer, curator, and a designer of furniture and silverware. After graduating from the Vienna Art Academy in 1956, he traveled in the United States on a scholarship and continued his studies at the Illinois Institute of Technology (IIT) in Chicago, receiving a master of architecture degree from Berkeley in 1960. During these years he was able to study with Ludwig Mies van der Rohe, Frank Lloyd Wright, Richard Neutra, and other famous architects. After working in Australia, South America, Sweden, and Germany, he returned to Vienna and established a practice in 1964.

Together with Walter Pichler, Hollein issued a manifesto of "absolute architecture" in 1963, declaring that "architecture is not the satisfaction of the needs of the mediocre or the environment for the petty happiness of the masses. . . . Architecture is an affair of the elite." (Burkhardt and Manker, 2002, 35). Despite such grand aspirations, Hollein's first commission in 1965 was rather modest, the design of the Retti Candleshop in the center of Vienna. Though the project was small, he received the $25,000 Reynolds Memorial Award and achieved international fame.

In the 1960s Hollein was a prominent figure in the lively Viennese scene, which also included Friedrich St. Florian, Raimund Abraham, Coop Himme(l)blau, and the theorist Günter Feuerstein. In his two-dimensional collages, Hollein developed a paper architecture in line with pop art, transforming banal objects, such as spark plugs or airplane carriers, into architecture through scale changes and incongruent combinations. Declaring that everything is architecture, he suggested in 1967 that a perception-altering drug would also be architecture; in the same year, Ron Herron of the Archigram announced the same idea as the "Enviro-Pill."

In 1970 Hollein won praise for his first commission in New York, the Richard Feigen Gallery. Other commissions for elite shops followed, including two jewelry stores for Schullin (1974 and 1982) in Vienna. These designs represent a mannerist version of late modern architecture. With the intention of creating a facade with a strong image, Hollein used marble and chromed steel in sensuous shapes that carried anthropomorphic, often sexual, connotations and occasionally contained veiled allusions to death.

By the mid–1970s Hollein emerged as a leading Postmodern architect in Europe. The interior he designed for the Austrian Tourist Office in Vienna (1978, demolished) features all the crucial aspects of Postmodern architecture, as defined by Charles Jencks in his seminal book in 1975, in particular the principles of metaphor and multiple coding. For a layman, the birds hanging from the ceiling would function as a metaphor for airplane travel, the Rolls-Royce radiator grills of the ticket counters as a clear sign for money and the peculiar metal palm trees in the interior as a promise of exotic beaches. A connoisseur, however, would recognize the palm trees as a reference to John Nash's Royal Pavilion in Brighton (1815–22), just as he would trace the origins of a small metal pavilion in the Tourist Office back to the Mughal pavilions in Fathpur Sikri and the glass ceiling of the Office to the Postal Savings Bank (1912) in Vienna by Otto Wagner.

Even more significant an achievement was Hollein's design for the Abteiberg Municipal Museum Mönchengladbach, Germany (competition in 1976, completed in 1982). Like the interior of the Tourist Office, the exterior of the museum is a collage of classical and Modern styles and building types: a miniature skyscraper, industrial sheds, a steel bridge, two symmetrical classical pavilions. Like in James Stirling's Staatsgalerie in Stuttgart, the different codes of architecture are not resolved to any syn-

Haas House (1985–90), view of the interior, designed by Hans Hollein
Photo © Mary Ann Sullivan

thetic totality but they coexist in tension, underscoring the heterogeneity of contemporary society. In the interior of the museum, however, the pop attitude to collage and assemblage is no longer in evidence. Rather, the interiors are designed with modest restraint and a sensitive use of light to provide the best possible exhibition spaces for the works of art.

In Hollein's Museum of Modern Art in Frankfurt (1983–91), the gallery spaces are even more precisely determined according to the needs of each individual work in the permanent collection, with the consequence that the museum may be less ideal to present other works. Because of the tight urban setting, also the facades are more restrained and less heterogeneous than in Mönchengladbach.

In 1985, Hollein received the Pritzker Prize, establishing his reputation as one of the foremost architects in the world. The same year, he started designing the Haas Haus, a small shopping center in the most precious location in Vienna, opposite St. Stephen's Cathedral. The design is a summary of Hollein's most successful designs over the years, a cornucopia of chromed facades, curved mirror glass, fountains, bridges, staircases, all tied together by an architectural promenade that recreates the mountain hikes loved by Austrians. In the nineties, Hollein had achieved the goals of his first manifesto, becoming the architect of the elite.

Like his fellow Pritzker Prize winner, Frank Gehry, Hollein has also made designs for spectacular new Guggenheim museums, one in Vienna and another in Salzburg. Especially the Salzburg project (1990) could well function in the same way as Gehry's Bilbao, as a spectacular mass attraction by a star architect. The design realizes some of the promises of Hollein's first manifesto: though not soaring in the heights, the museum penetrates deep into the mountain next to the Salzburg castle, creating an intriguing multilevel cave. Stylistically, Hollein has not changed dramatically. More recently, Hollein has reduced the ornament and began to experiment with complex curved surfaces, as in his design for the Austrian embassy in Berlin.

DÖRTE KUHLMANN

See also **Abteiberg Municipal Museum, Mönchengladbach, Germany; Gehry, Frank (United States); Museum of Modern Art, Frankfurt; Museum; Neue Staatsgalerie, Stuttgart; Postmodernism**

Biography

Born in Vienna, Austria, 30 March 1934. Studied at the Academy of Fine Arts (Akademie der bildenden Künste) in Vienna under Clemens Holzmeister where he graduated in 1956. Toured and studied in the United States on a Harkness Fellowship. Graduate studies at the Illinois Institute of Technology in Chicago, Master of Architecture degree at the University of California, Berkeley in 1960. 1978–90 Austrian state commissioner, Architecture Biennale Venice, Italy 1991, 1996 and 2000; director of architecture section, Architecture Biennale Venice, Italy 1994–1996; curator exhibition "Contemporary Art, Architecture and Design" Shanghai Art Museum, 2001. Visiting professor, Washington University 1963/64 and 1966; professor, Acadamy of Fine Arts, Düsseldorf, Germany 1967–76; 1976–2002 professor at the University of Applied Arts, Vienna, Austria. Awarded Reynolds Memorial Award 1966, Grand Austrian State Prize 1983, Pritzker Prize 1985.

Further Reading

Burkhardt, François, and Paulus Manker (editors), *Hans Hollein: Schriften and Manifeste*, Vienna: Universität für Angewandte Kunst, 2002

Cable, Carol, *Hans Hollein: A Bibliography of Books and Articles*, Monticello, Illinois: Vance Bibliographies, 1983

Feuerstein, Günther, *Visionäre Architektur: Vienna 1958/1988*, Berlin: Ernst, 1988

Fritsch, Herbert (editor), *Architekten: Hans Hollein*, 4th edition, Stuttgart: IRB Verlag, 1995

Hans Hollein Museum in Monchengladbach: Architektur Als Collage, Monchengladbach, Germany: Stadtisches Museum Abteiberg Monchengladbach, 1986

HOLOCAUST MEMORIAL MUSEUM, WASHINGTON, D.C.

Designed by James Ingo Freed; completed 1994

Initiated by President Carter and confirmed by a unanimous act of Congress in 1980, the program for the Holocaust Memorial Museum was to construct "a permanent living memorial museum to the victims of the Holocaust" on the National Mall. After a series of controversies involving the building's design, the Holocaust Memorial Council asked James Ingo Freed (b. 1930 in Essen, Germany), a partner of the New York architectural firm Pei, Cobb, Freed and Partners, to amend a previous scheme thought to be too "fascistic" by the committee, and following a number of interviews, Freed agreed to rework the museum's design. Built on a 1.7-acre site between the Victorian-era Auditor's Building and the neoclassical Bureau of Engraving and Printing, the Holocaust Memorial Museum has 258,000 square feet of space dedicated to exhibits, program spaces, offices, and archives. It is conceived, as its name and program suggests, as both a public memorial and a private museum.

With certain exceptions, the events that the Holocaust Memorial Museum commemorates are unlike most of the public monuments and celebrations of culture along the Mall. Even outside this particular context, there are few building programs dedicated to such a complex set of issues: A historical fact, a collective memory, and a failed humanity are only a few of the difficult and complex issues that underlie the building program. In accepting the project, Freed acknowledged these and other considerations: the political nature of the commission, the repre-

sentational limitations of architecture, and the inability of any art or cultural enterprise to give form or words to the inarticulable. To this end, Freed's research began not in archives or books but with the attempt to ascertain the material dimensions—the experiences and places that spoke to the need for such a memorial museum. Thus, the architect, returning to the region where he was born, traveled to the sites of the Holocaust—camps, ghettos, factories, and urban areas—hoping to find a way to conceptualize and shape the material and experience of unimaginable human tragedy into architectural form and space.

The architect's oblique siting of the museum relative to the relatively straight line of buildings located on the National Mall—its front facade is positioned slightly off the projected line of its peer buildings—gives the first indication of Freed's intention to subvert the conformance of the whole. The building incorporates the materials—brick and limestone—of the buildings immediately adjacent, and the museum's scale, also at variance from either structure, suggests both discontinuity and compression; the building literally appears to be slightly out of place, its language at once commensurate and at odds with its surroundings.

The building contains numerous formal references to the material, technology, and structures that aided and abetted the Holocaust. Freed's use of the traditional form of the synagogue for the Hall of Remembrance—here windowless, solid, and remote despite its prominent position on the Mall—is coupled with a line of looming and anonymous brick towers, positioned as sentinels. The towers suggest, among other things, the camp guard towers, the rigid and anonymous subscription to collective order, the vernacular factorylike buildings of the death and work camps, and the chimneys from which the ashes of victims spewed into the sky. In delineating such dissonance (the building is full of references to the technological rigidity, instrumental chaos, and disorder of the Holocaust), the architect's pointed use of symbolic form creates a condition where any number of references, like memories exposed by dreams (*Traumen*), become both proximate and disjunctive figures in space and time.

Another example of this is found when approaching or leaving either of the building's two faces. The entrance sequences, from either 14th Street or 15th Street, although distinct, are both expressive of a sense of pervasive lack or perhaps undermined expectations. Entering from 14th Street, one is struck by the aggressively symmetrical, neoclassical entrance—a formal mechanism reminiscent of the reductivist monuments of modern imperialist states. From the 15th Street side, the entry, inverse in magnitude and references, stands in direct contrast: It is inappropriately modest. Like the scaleless and mute brick facade standing prominently and anonymously within the Hall of Witness, the entry from 15th Street expresses the underlying, anonymous horror codified in the vernacular architecture of the Fascist state.

Approaching the museum's main space, the Hall of Witness, from either entrance, the sequence of spaces also appears to lack direction. Visitors become confused, disoriented by the almost casual, even arbitrary lack of directional cues. This moment marks the beginning of the architect's conceptual program, where the visitor is no longer directed to view objects in the museum, but instead becomes a participant in a set of events.

The form, space, material, and temporal orchestration of architecture are arrayed in a manner that will maintain heightened awareness. Materials are used diachronically; black granite reflec-

U.S. Holocaust Memorial Museum, Washington, D.C., rear facade overlooking the Tidal Basin (1994)
Photo © Mary Ann Sullivan

tive surfaces, mirroring the outlines of the indistinct figures passing by, stand in response, albeit obliquely, to dense, white marble surfaces suggestive of purity, impenetrable veils, the harsh winter snow, or simply nothingness. Freed's details expose the mechanistic, precise thinking of the German bureaucracy as well as the compulsive recording of quantities, names, and dates. Railway schedules are juxtaposed to a daily death tally, both recorded in the strict anonymity of an unknown hand: all evidence is equal, whether it be disposal procedures, personnel needs, eyeglasses, deaths, transport arrival and departures, shoes, brushes, or hair. The qualitative—that which grants a face to humanity—is hidden behind a highly efficient array of quantities, locations, and requests. In this sense, the educational component of the program is not solely didactic but immersive. The spaces and their confused, disorienting choreography; formal manipulations; scale; and material work to undermine a visitor's looking at by inducing a sense of being there. For Freed, wholesale immersion dispenses with the screening, objectifying effects of language and pictures: only experience compels empathy.

Freed's promiscuous use of technology and detail suggests a deliberate mining of metaphor. Bridges, gates, mesh fences, brick, light, steel, and cable—all practical effects of the Holocaust terror—become condensed metaphors as well, just beyond the reach of definitive articulation. In his use of the various forms

of technological enterprise, Freed came to understand what Elie Weisel calls "the banality of evil," one located not in higher ideals but in the baseness of an anonymous, self-evident vernacular tradition. In the awkward assemblage of the various parts, Freed also understood that it was important to maintain the friction, the difficulty in arriving at a conclusion, and the profound inadequacies of any symbolism afforded the memorial's historic context.

The architect's concentration on the interrelationships produces an inclusive, albeit unsettled, edifice where the whole exceeds the sum of individual experiences. Nonetheless, the reality that the Holocaust Memorial Museum attempts to expose, the meaning of its particular historic fact, continues to resist, as Freed and others have acknowledged, attempts to articulate it wholly or fully: The staging of artifacts, the collections that reside within (seemingly banal refuse), transcends the mechanisms provided by linguistic and symbolic metaphors, however capably rendered.

ELIZABETH GAMARD

See also **Jewish Museum, Berlin; Memorial; Museum**

Further Reading

Dannatt, Adrian, *United States Holocaust Memorial Museum: James Ingo Freed*, London: Phaidon, 1995

U.S. Holocaust Memorial Museum, Washington, D.C., Hall of Witness
Photo © Mary Ann Sullivan

Hass, Matthais, " 'Political Memory': Studien zur Planung und Realisierung des Holocaust Memorials in Washington," Ph.D. diss., Freie Universität Berlin, 1995
Linenthal, Edward Tabor, *Preserving Memory: The Struggle to Create America's Holocaust Museum*, New York: Viking, 1995
Miller, Judith, *One, by One, by One: Facing the Holocaust*, New York: Simon and Schuster, 1990
Weinberg, Jeshajahu, and Rina Elieli, *The Holocaust Museum in Washington*, New York: Rizzoli International, 1995

HONG KONG, CHINA

At the start of the 20th century, Hong Kong was a colony of the British Empire, an impoverished port of minor importance, one of several outposts on the coast of the China from which the British conducted and protected their trading activities in the region. By the end of the century, Hong Kong rose to surpass most countries of the world in terms of wealth, trading volume, and financial stature. Limited by land and sea borders, with largely hilly terrain, Hong Kong has from the start relied on reclamation to create buildable land; through the century, reclamation created more than 10,000 acres (4,000 hectares) for buildings and infrastructure, most of it around the harbor. Be-

cause reclamation is an expensive process, high-density solutions have been the assumed strategies for accommodating the expanding population and economy. It is in the realm of high-density designs that Hong Kong has contributed notably in the 20th century.

Noteworthy architectural structures in the colony in 1900 were the Hong Kong Club (1897, demolished 1981) and the governor's summer residence, Mountain Lodge (1902, demolished 1946), both designed by a local architectural and engineering practice, Palmer Turner. The other significant local practice of the time was Leigh and Orange, designers of Prince's Building (1901), Queen's Building (1902), and the University of Hong Kong (1912). These architecturally hybrid buildings were created in the colonial image using architectural vocabulary current in London, although perhaps more liberally combined than Home County taste may have permitted. Other important buildings of that time include the granite Supreme Court (1912, Aston Webb and E. Ingress Bell as consultants to the Colonial Office), demonstrating in architectural form the British legal dominion, and the General Post Office (1911, Denison, Ram and Gibbs) in polychromatic Amoy red brick and local granite.

High densities existed in the urban situation from early on, leading to typical problems in sanitation and public health. After a plague in 1894, authorities looked to urban improvements to prevent a recurrence and enacted the Public Health and Buildings Ordinance of 1903 (not amended until 1932). From this arose a typical building form of a three to five-story apartment building, ornamented on the street facades in engaged columns, perhaps with deep-shading verandas or street-level arcades to provide relief from the summer sun; a fine extant example is Lui Seng Chun (1934, architect unknown). These tight urban blocks surrounded by narrow streets, captured in movies such as *Love Is a Many-Splendored Thing* (1955) and *The World of Suzie Wong* (1961), typified the streetscape of urban Hong Kong until the 1960s. Although largely demolished in the third quarter of the century, one example of a commercial building that survived to the end of the century is Pedder Building (1932, Palmer Turner).

The first headquarters for the Hong Kong and Shanghai Bank (1886, Palmer Turner) was replaced in 1935, again designed by Palmer Turner. Satisfying instructions from the chief manager of the bank to "build the best possible building regardless of cost," it was the tallest building between Cairo and San Francisco. An Art Deco tower (220 feet tall) flanked by two lower wings, the building was a leading example of technological applications in building. The stone-clad building was the first outside North America to use high-tensile (Chromador) steel throughout, achieving a comparatively lightweight structure. The tower was serviced by high-speed electric elevators, and the building was fully air-conditioned using a seawater cooling system and heating delivered internally in concealed-panel systems. Several buildings from the same practice followed in this vein (Bank of China, 1950; Chartered Bank, 1959). The building was replaced in 1985 by Norman Foster's design, likewise a technologically significant building of its time. By the time this latest headquarters was completed, it represented the most expensive building in the world and became an icon for Hong Kong. In distinction to the massive concrete construction that typifies Hong Kong, Foster employed a highly articulated steel exoskeleton. The structure consists of five suspended-floor sections, each consisting of a central atrium dominated by escalators serving the floors in that section. A thin raised floor system serves all spaces with air conditioning, cabling, and power, providing for extreme flexibility in configuration. Reassembled restrooms and stair elements plugged in to the building, and a computer-controlled sun scoop was designed to reflect light into the depths of the banking hall atrium.

In addition to the bank construction, the 1930s contributed other notable architecture, including the Royal Hong Kong Jockey Club Grandstand with clock tower and nearby mechanically ventilated stables (1932, both Palmer Turner, demolished), municipal market buildings in Wanchai (1936, Public Works Department) and Central (1937, Public Works Department) in the modernist style, and the circular Royal Hong Kong Yacht Club (1939, Leigh and Orange) with its Art Deco interior. Although little of note was erected in Hong Kong between 1940 and 1960, a number of International Style explorations were erected in the 1960s. A new City Hall (1962, Ron Phillips and Alan Fitch of the Public Works Department) was erected on the reclaimed waterfront consisting of a walled garden flanked by a tall tower of offices and library and a lower block to the north containing concert halls, exhibition spaces, and restaurants. The Hilton Hotel (1962, Palmer Turner), located on a busy corner of Garden Road and Queens Road Central, placed

an L-shaped tower on a curved podium with cabanas around a swimming pool. This form spoke much about the start of the shift from a colonial outpost to a minor city in the international circuit. St. George's Building (1969, F. Wong and W. Chu and Associates) is an elegant aluminum-clad building owing much to the Chicago School, and the HK Electric Company headquarters (1971, Palmer Turner, demolished 1998) presented as a bridge in reinforced concrete spanning a stream in a deep valley above Central District.

Hong Kong's place on the architectural map was marked in 1983 with the design by Zaha Hadid for the Peak Club. Although never realized, the building initiated a remarkable career for Hadid and demonstrated that there was interest in Hong Kong for architecture of international repute. This change was emphasized by the construction of the Hong Kong Club replacement (1984, Harry Seidler) with its prestressed T beams to create clear-span spaces within and expressed externally to present a structurally articulated facade to the central business district.

Although municipal and institutional buildings have set the standards for much of architecture in Hong Kong, it is in the realm of housing that remarkable achievements were also made. Subjected to successive waves of refugees, housing became one of the defining issues in Hong Kong. Initially, the government's only intervention in housing was through ordinances to attempt to keep disease and safety in hand, defining a standard of 3.25 square meters of floor space and 9.34 cubic meters of volume per person. Private enterprise responded by erecting very dense tenements. The influx of refugees as a result of the civil wars in China following World War II led to large squatter settlements. It was a fire through one of these in December 1953 that led the government to initiate a massive building program for subsidized housing, resulting in the government itself becoming the largest residential developer in the world with annual production reaching a peak of 32,000 units in 1967. Most of these units were designed by the Hong Kong Housing Authority itself, although some were designed by private practitioners, as was Choi Hung Estate (1965, Palmer Turner). Starting with the Mark I H blocks in Shek Kip Mei in 1954, units were designed to 2.23 square meters per person. The Mark VI type in 1969 increased this allowance increased back to 3.25 square meters. Although remarkable in its achievements for housing so many in so short a time frame, the program was pressed by the urgency to maximize output and lapsed into brutal forms and simplistic site plans.

In addition to housing estates providing subsidized housing, population growth was absorbed by the establishment of new towns to divert pressure away from the urban concentration around the harbor. Influenced by the British Garden City movement, development started with three towns—Tsuen Wan (1950s) for 720,000 residents, Sha Tin (1970s) for 600,000 residents, and Tuen Mun (1970s) for 540,000 residents—and continued with six more in the last two decades, each coming to maturity in less than ten years. The typical typology is a substantial podium-focused design topped by tall point blocks, leaving urban spaces poorly resolved between the tall structures. Where they have succeeded is due to good high-capacity public transportation connections to existing urban centers. In later developments, we find the issues of high-density development being addressed more carefully. For example, Verbena Heights (1997, Anthony Ng) in the new town of Tseung Kwan O and Tung Chung Crescent (1999, Anthony Ng) on Lantau near

Hong Kong Club (1984), designed by Harry Seidler
© Thomas Kvan

Peak Tram Station (1996), designed by Terry Farrell
© Thomas Kvan

the new airport offer examples of environmentally conscious high-density designs for medium- to lower-cost units. Varied building heights capture prevailing winds and control solar angles to permit better natural ventilation and lighting, reducing energy consumption and improving microclimates in the tower blocks while also resolving very tall residential structures to the human scale at the ground level.

The harbor dominates Hong Kong both economically and physically. Throughout most of its history in the century, Hong Kong had no permeable land border—all contact was by air or sea. It is appropriate, therefore, that transportation-related architecture has found manifestation in two successful structures, both designed by partners of Spence Robinson, an expatriate firm founded in Shanghai that moved to Hong Kong in the 1930s. The first is Ocean Terminal (1966, Spence, Robinson, Prescott and Thornburrow, fatally marred by a renovation in the late 1980s), a three-level cruise ship pier and shopping center of elegant simplicity and detailing. The second interchange is the Shun Tak Centre and Macau Ferry Terminal (1986, Spence Robinson), a twin-tower transportation interchange that brings together high-speed ferries, buses, helicopters, and a connection to the underground train with hotel, residential, and office spaces standing on a commercial podium with two piers beyond, realizing proposals from the beginning of the century for the integra-

tion of transportation systems and building form (for example, *La Città Nuova*, 1914, Sant'Elia).

With the center of Hong Kong crowded around the harbor, the shortage of land has dictated ever-taller structures, an "architecture of density," in which all manner of activities are accommodated. Legislation has enabled mixed-use zoning such that commercial, residential, and manufacturing can be found within single structures. Examples include some unusual combinations of uses: multiuse markets and community centers, as in the Tsing Yi Complex (1999, Anthony Ng) with a wet market, library, and games hall organized around an internal street under a tensile roof; cemeteries and memorial halls, as in the Tsuen Wan Columbarium (1987, Dennis Lau and Ng Chun Man); and warehouses, as in the Hong Kong International Distribution Centre (1992, LPT Architects and Planners), which offers storage space on seven levels and where vehicles can enter the building at mezzanine level and drive up a 3.5-kilometer internal ramp to a rooftop waiting area for 400 trucks. Common throughout Hong Kong are podium structures with the lower three floors given over to commercial uses, often connected by sky bridges to a neighboring podium, creating layered urban space and highly segregated traffic flows. Steep slopes often demand ingenious solutions. Educational buildings that have succeeded are the University of Science and Technology (1992,

Simon Kwan and Associates/Percy Thomas Associates), which resolves a complex program for a tertiary institution on a steep hillside, and the French International School (1984, Design Consultants Ltd) and the Hong Kong International School (1989, Design Consultants Ltd), which resolve primary and secondary school programs elegantly on tight, sloping sites.

By the end of the century, the skyline of the harbor of Hong Kong was flanked on the south (island) side by ever-taller office buildings against a backdrop of tall residential buildings working their way up to the Peak Club. Structures in Kowloon remained constrained in height by the needs of Kai Tak Airport. In 1970, the waterfront was again reclaimed from the harbor in Central, opening land for new construction, including Jardine House, formerly Connaught Centre (1973, Palmer Turner), with its distinctive circular portholes; at 52 stories, it was the tallest building in Asia for many years. More land was made available for construction to the east of Central District when the British armed forces withdrew as part of the agreement in the run-up to the handover of Hong Kong to China in 1997. This land soon became a new financial and commercial center known as Admiralty with several notable buildings. The twin octagonal towers of Lippo Centre, formerly Bond Centre (1988, Paul Rudolph), with alternating cantilevered bays, form a distinctive centerpiece. Nearby, the Bank of China erected its local headquarters (1989, I.M. Pei), employing the geometry of a diagonally bisected cube to achieve a lightweight building of considerable height and a column-free interior. Also on this released land is Pacific Place (1988–91, Wong and Ouyang), a major shopping complex with three hotels and one office tower standing on a podium of four levels of shopping with parking below. To the south of the Bank of China is Citibank Plaza (1992, Rocco Yim), an intelligent building with centralized building management and raised floors throughout. With its stepped twin towers, it forms an urban forecourt to the Bank of China building. The major part of the barracks land was converted into Hong Kong Park, in which can be found the Aviary (1991, Ove Arup and Partners with Wong Tung and Partners). The British Consulate and British Council (1996, Terry Farrell) were given a significant location adjacent to both the park and Pacific Place for consular and cultural representation after the handover.

As the Central District expanded eastward across the released military land, it connected to Wanchai and Causeway Bay districts beyond. Coupled with the construction of the underground rail system (the Mass Transit Railway), commercial facilities began to be erected along more of the waterfront. Central Plaza (1992, Dennis Lau and Ng Chun Man), a Postmodernist interpretation of a 1930s Manhattan skyscraper, presents its 374-meter-tall brightly lit facade, the tallest reinforced-concrete structure in the world, topped by a neon-light timepiece that marks the quarter hours throughout the night by presenting various combinations of colors. As the airport was moved from its harbor location at Kai Tak to the remote northwestern location on Lantau Island in 1997, building regulations were relaxed in Kowloon to permit buildings of greater height (e.g., the Peninsula Hotel extension, 1995, Rocco Yim) as well as an increased application of architectural lighting. Although brightly festooned with neon previously, this relaxation rapidly changed the look for Hong Kong at night (e.g., The Centre, 1999, Dennis Lau and Ng Chun Man) with its use of computer-controlled lights across its 73-story facade.

By the last decade, changing economics led to a greater demand for office space. The Hilton Hotel was replaced by the Cheung Kong Centre (1999, Cesar Pelli with Leo A. Daly) when property prices rendered office space more profitable than hotel use. A desire to establish an iconic image of the harbor led to the construction of the Hong Kong Convention and Exhibition Center (1997, Wong and Ouyang in association with Skidmore, Owings and Merrill), a multilevel rectilinear assemblage of exhibition spaces topped by massive sweeping roofs. The move of the airport led to substantial associated infrastructure construction and also set a new standard for architecture. The clarity of design and structural elegance of the Hong Kong International Airport Terminal (1997, Foster) could not be ignored. Hong Kong Station (1998, Rocco Yim in association with Arup Associates), the terminus of the airport railway, reflects the clarity of organization found at the airport terminal, with large voids connecting the upper-level shopping levels with the ticket hall, in-town check-in facilities, and the subterranean train platforms, covered by a sweeping roof coated in titanium. This terminus is flanked by One International Finance Centre (1998, Rocco Yim in association with Cesar Pelli), in which a circular podium resolves a complex pedestrian connection, topped by a faceted tower above. Across the harbor, a complex brief for commercial, residential, and transportation functions was resolved in the Kowloon Station (1998, Terry Farrell). The increased interest in technological solutions to architectural problems is also demonstrated in the Kadoorie Biological Sciences Building, University of Hong Kong (1999, Leigh and Orange), in which a double skin is employed to accommodate servicing needs and reduce energy consumption.

The century also saw the city move from a colonial British outpost to a world city within China. In order to make this change, the people of Hong Kong faced difficult questions of political and social identity. The architecture of Hong Kong reflected this struggle for identity and recognition. At the beginning of the century, colonial power was reflected in the classical language of all public and most major private buildings. Yet Hong Kong is a city in China, and its architecture has striven to express this reality. Although indigenous construction has continued (e.g., the walled village of Hakka Wai, 1904), Chinese architectural vocabulary was also used to place official and privately developed buildings into the local context (Tai Po Market Railway Station, 1913). Sometimes Chinese plan forms were adapted to Western elevations (St. Stephen's Girls College, 1929). The Chinese Methodist Church (1936, Mehlert) was a successful melding of vocabularies (replaced with a less-successful church and office tower, 1997, Kwan and Associates Architects Ltd). Government House (1855, Charles St George Cleverly) morphed, starting the century as a Victorian residence and later being hybridized with Japanese forms to become the Japanese military governor's residence (1944, Seichi Fujimura). Some architects tried to engage Chinese architectural language more directly; Tao Fung Shan (1934, Prip-Møller), a Lutheran religious study center, was designed after an extensive study of Buddhist monasteries throughout China but implemented a site layout owing much to the architect's Danish heritage. Although the architectural language was largely international by the end of the century, architects continued to interpret Chinese vocabulary into international form; for example, the Hong Kong Arts Centre (1977, Tao Ho) integrates Chinese philosophies with modern functions using Metabolist principles. The Peak Tram station, with its prominent location on the saddle on the ridge overlooking Central District, has been home to two interpretations of a Chinese gate. In 1972, Chung Wah Nan designed a heavy oval plan block on twin pillars, said to be a watchtower. This was replaced in 1996 by the upswept-dish form by Terry Farrell, in which the vocabulary of a temple (podium, columns, and sweeping roof) is used. Abandoning interpretation, a technically accurate replica of Tang-dynasty wooden construction was erected at the Chi Lin Nunnery (1998, Don Pan and Associates).

THOMAS KVAN

See also **Bank of China Tower, Hong Kong; Città Nuova (1914); Hong Kong International Airport, Hong Kong; Hongkong are Shanghai Bank, Shanghai; Shanghai**

Further Reading

Bristow, M.R., *Hong Kong's New Towns*, New York and Hong Kong: Oxford University Press, 1989

Chung, Wah Nan (compiler), *Contemporary Architecture in Hong Kong*, Hong Kong: Joint (HK), 1989

Hong Kong Housing Authority, *The First Two Million*, Hong Kong: Hong Kong Housing Authority, 1980

"Hong Kong," in *Presente y futuros: Arquitectura en las ciudades* (exhib. cat.), edited by Ignasi de Solà-Morales and Xavier Costa, Barcelona: Centre de Cultura Contemporània de Barcelona, 1996; as *Present and Futures: Architecture in Cities* (exhib. cat.), translated by Mark Waudby, Barcelona: Centre de Cultura Contemporània de Barcelona, 1996

Lampugnani, Vittorio Magnago (editor), *Hong Kong Architecture: The Aesthetics of Density*, New York and Munich: Prestel, 1993

Pryor, Edward G., *Housing in Hong Kong*, New York and Hong Kong: Oxford University Press, 1973; 2nd edition, New York: Oxford University Press, 1983

HONG KONG INTERNATIONAL AIRPORT

Designed by Foster and Partners, completed 1997
Chek Lap Kok, Hong Kong

Located on the north shore of Lantau, the largest of the islands in Hong Kong, Hong Kong International Airport is built on the radically enlarged 1,248-hectare island of Chek Lap Kok. The passenger terminal building is set at the east end of the island between two runways lying east to west. When opened in 1997, the terminal consisted of 39 wide-body aircraft stands (for 35 million passengers annually) laid around the perimeter of a Y with the arms opening west and crossed on the east by a processing terminal in which are sited the check-in and ground facilities. By 2000 there were 47 aircraft stands in operation; the airport master plan includes expansion to more than 70 stands with the addition of an X-shaped satellite to the west to symmetrically complement the westward arms of the first terminal building and a second terminal building to the east to handle 87 million passengers annually.

The airport was designed by a joint-venture consortium of Foster and Partners, Mott Connell Ltd, and BAA PLC, although the latter subsequently withdrew as a partner in the venture for risk management reasons. The phase 1 terminal is 1.2 kilometers

Hong Kong International Airport (Chek Lap Kok), interior (1997)
Photo © Dennis Gilbert/VIEW

Aerial view, Hong Kong International Airport
Photo © Dennis Gilbert/VIEW

from front door to the farthest gate and covers an area of 550,000 square meters, with up to eight levels in the building enclosed, capped by distinctive undulating barrel vaults spanning east to west along the long central axis. The architectural clarity of the building is exemplified by this singular roof, creating as it does the soaring and uninterrupted views internally and the billowing lateral forms externally. Tall glass walls enclose the building below these barrel vaults, revealing the green hills of Lantau and the waters of the Pearl River delta to the passengers within. The immense building is rendered comprehensible by the long sight lines from almost any vantage point. The visual experience of those waiting for their flights is one of freedom, lightness, and expanse, a far cry from the segmented boxes that typify terminal buildings in other major airports of the world.

Prequalification of project teams for the competition for the airport terminal was completed in September 1991; the competition started in October 1991, and submissions were due on 24 December 1991. The design contract was awarded in March 1992, with only 26 months allowed for detailed design and construction documents, a very short period for such a complex building. Foster and Partners were able to accommodate this compressed schedule by drawing on the many operational and technical lessons learned at the recently completed Stansted Airport project in Essex, England. That project was initiated in 1981, entailing five years of technical study and functional analysis before construction started, finally opening in March 1991. In this decade, Foster's team examined every aspect of airport terminal design, from groundbreaking ideas for building services to specific operational requirements for all users. An extensive database was evolved of design and spatial methods to coordinate the many complexities. Key members of the Stansted team led the Hong Kong project from competition to completion; with this knowledge and background, the team was well placed to combine the advanced technical understanding and the required design signature and to develop strategies for coordinating the design and construction information to allow the project to be completed in a compressed schedule.

The concept of an open and expansive terminal experience was first explored by Foster in Stansted. There, the flat roof hovers over the 35,000 square meters of departure-and-arrival hall on a single level, held aloft by branched columns within which services and lighting are integrated. The supershed form continued ideas explored by Saarinen at Dulles Airport, Chantilly, Virginia (1962), reestablishing the romance and excitement of air travel by exposing waiting passengers to views of the sky and the aircraft, framed by soaring roofs and columns, marking the airport terminal as the quintessential building type for the 20th century. These examples demonstrate a typology for an airport terminal—the large shed roof under which passengers and activities are organized in a clear diagram of process flow to handle passengers, aircraft, and baggage, uncluttered by services and structure.

In order to achieve the desired openness of the interior, the design team solved several difficult technical problems without sacrificing the clarity of the design concept. This was achieved only through a tight integration of the multidisciplinary design team, including the quantity surveyors WT Partnership, who controlled costs as design alternatives were explored. Among the critical technical issues resolved in remarkable ways are the integration of structure, fire safety, ventilation, and lighting. For example, the roof is a thin (650 millimeters thick) composite roof of PVC sheeting over insulation and plywood on aluminum structural decking, lying on an undulating 36-meter steel-lattice barrel vault, supported by columns at 36-meter centers. The one-to-six barrel vault structure was created in units in Singapore and the United Kingdom and assembled on site in 129 modules. Drainage of the large roof area is achieved through small-bore downpipes within the concrete columns, made possible by employing a siphonic drainage system that removes the need for large and unsightly downpipes and deep gutters. Similarly, the cool air that keeps the passenger at a comfortable temperature is delivered from vents just above head height built in to binnacles that double as flight or passenger information systems. Air lamination maintains warm air above the lowest 4.5 meters within the departure hall like a blanket over the cool air, achieving high energy efficiency despite the terminal's large volume. All these ideas were first explored in the Stansted project (for which Ove Arup and Partners were also consulting engineers) but were refined in Hong Kong to achieve an even more dramatic interior in a very much larger building. These results were achieved only within a tightly monitored budget and the demanding 26-month design schedule through very close working relationships in the design team and extensive coordination of all elements from the initial design stages, a discipline learned and rehearsed by both Foster and Arup at Stansted. The building has won awards from the Hong Kong Institute of Architects, British Construction Industries, and the International Association of Lighting Designers and was identified as one of the ten most important construction achievements of the 20th century.

THOMAS KVAN

See also **Airport and Aviation Building; Arup, Ove (England); Dulles International Airport, Chantilly, Virginia; Foster, Norman (England); Hong Kong; Saarinen, Eero (Finland)**

Further Reading

Davey, Peter, "Plane Sailing," *The Architectural Review*, 204/1219 (September 1998)

Graham, Mark, *Chek Lap Kok: Touchdown in Hong Kong* Hong Kong, Asia Magazines Ltd., 1998.

Green, Glynis, *Vision to Reality in Total Harmony*, Hong Kong: Airport Authority, 1998

Pawley, Martin, *Norman Foster: A Global Architecture*, New York: Universe, 1999

Robbins, Jack, "How did they do that? The team behind Chek Lap Kok," *World Architecture*, 68 (July–August 1998)

HONGKONG AND SHANGHAI BANK

Designed by George Leopold Wilson and others;
completed 1923
Shanghai, China

Since its completion in 1923, the former Shanghai headquarters of the Hongkong and Shanghai Banking Corporation (HSBC) has been the keystone of the Shanghai Bund, a roughly 1.5-kilometer-long stretch of land along the Huangpu River where approximately 35 commercial structures, most dating from between 1911 and 1937, mark an earlier period of intense capitalistic activity in Shanghai. The Bund (*waitan*), as well as Zhongshan Number One Road East, is now shadowed by a forest of high-rise towers, especially in Pudong, a former warehouse and industrial area that has become the paragon of Shanghai's 21st-century expansion. The bank's significant role stems partially from its imposing stance: its dome rises 180 feet above ground and its facade spans 300 feet wide. When completed, it was reputedly the second-largest bank building in the world (see Johnston, 1993). The structure has also carried enormous symbolic weight, in Shanghai and beyond, as the anchor of foreign capitalists' investments in pre-1949 China. The building now occupying the site, on the corner of Fuzhou Road, is the third that the bank occupied on the Bund. Beginning in 1865, the bank's Shanghai branch was in a modest building by comparison, but in 1875 the bank erected a larger structure, which it outgrew by World War I, but then waited until 1919 to decide to erect "a building which would dominate the Bund and make a positive statement about the Bank's importance and confidence" (see Lambot, 1986). After 1949 the Communist Party's municipal government located its headquarters in the bank and placed a prominent red star on the dome's finial. It was only in 1993 that the municipal government vacated the building. In the context of attracting new investors to a booming Shanghai, city officials urged HSBC to renovate, lease, and relocate to its former premises. However, the corporation decided against that option, and instead, after an extensive rehabilitation program, the Pudong Development Bank leased the building beginning in December 1996.

The main architect of the former bank was George Leopold "Tug" Wilson (1880–?), a Londoner who immigrated to Hong Kong in 1907 and became a partner in the firm of Palmer and Turner, the most influential of all foreign architectural offices operating in Shanghai during the Republican period (1911–49). The firm was based in Hong Kong, where it still prospers under the name P and T Architects, Ltd. The British architect William Salway established the firm in 1868, 26 years after Hong Kong became a British colony. In 1870 Salway took on a partner, Wilberforce Wilson (no relation), and eight years later the firm was known as Wilson and Bird. In 1883 the HSBC selected the firm as one of three to submit designs for the expanding company's new Hong Kong office at One Queen's Road Central. To assist them, Wilson and Bird hired a young British architect, Clement Palmer (1857–c.1952), whose skill helped them win the competition. Before the domed neoclassical-style bank was completed in 1888, Palmer replaced Wilson as a partner, and three years later Arthur Turner, a structural engineer, replaced Bird. Palmer and Turner was established, and the company prospered in commercially vibrant Hong Kong. In 1908 the Union

Insurance Company of Canton hired Palmer and Turner to design the Union Building, Shanghai's first steel-frame office building, on the corner of Guangdong Road and the Shanghai Bund. "Tug" Wilson was dispatched to Shanghai to work with M.H. Logan, head of the firm's operations there. Completed in 1912, the Union Building was where Palmer and Turner located its branch office, from which in the succeeding quarter century the company designed a dozen other hallmark structures along the Bund for thriving companies, among them the Hongkong and Shanghai Bank.

Wilson characterized his design for the bank as neo-Grecian and "to achieve the dignity with simplicity which that name implies the architects have eschewed the use of carving or sculpture almost entirely and relied upon proportion and line" (HSBC, 1923). Wilson also relied on several neoclassical precedents for British banks, such as John Soane's Bank of England (1788–1823). He was doubtlessly aware of projects in contemporary London, such as Sir Reginald Blomfield's refacing of the Carlton Club in Pall Mall (1921), which reflected a predilection for arcaded, rusticated bases and prominent attic stories (see Zheng, 1999). Wilson also echoed certain stylistic motifs from the Hong Kong headquarters, such as paired granite columns *in antis* on the main elevation and a colossal dome.

However, Wilson and the larger construction team with whom he collaborated surpassed mere imitation in three notable ways. One of those concerned the structural nature of the building. Rather than relying on local engineers and contractors to erect this massive edifice, Palmer and Turner joined forces with the eminent London and Liverpool engineering firm of Trollope and Colls. Mr. Faber of this company designed an innovative, concrete raft foundation (instead of employing Shanghai's conventional but less-secure deeply driven wooden piles) and utilized steel from the reliable British company Dorman and Long to fabricate a frame to which cladding materials such as Hong Kong granite were attached. The success of both the foundation and the frame set a significant precedent in Shanghai, where Palmer and Turner (and other firms) subsequently felt more secure in convincing clients to utilize the more innovative materials of concrete and steel that were becoming so popular elsewhere by the 1920s.

A second innovation concerned what might be termed the advertisement of pre-Depression financial globalization, especially reflected in the bank's large octagonal entrance hall surmounted by a dome whose conception was related to aspiration (see HSBC, 1923). The London artist George Murray created cartoons for eight richly colored mosaic panels above the cornice

Hongkong and Shanghai Bank, Shanghai, China (1923)
Photo © Jeffrey Cody

that depicted eight of the bank's most prominent locations: Hong Kong, Shanghai, London, New York, Paris, Tokyo, Bangkok, and Calcutta. Customers would have passed under the panels and dome on their way to a vast barrel-vaulted skylit space accented with soft-toned gray Italian marble.

The third innovation was to set a higher architectural standard for commercial property in Shanghai. Because of the bank's success, Palmer and Turner was hired by at least four other banks to design offices on the Bund (for example, the Bank of Taiwan, the Chartered Bank, the Bank of China, and the Yokohama Specie Bank). Other companies followed suit (for instance, Sassoon House, Cathay [Peace] Hotel, Palace Hotel, Jardine Matheson Building, Glen Line Building, Yangtsze Insurance Building, and Broadway Mansions [Purvis, 1985]). The foundation and steel solutions employed for the Hongkong and Shanghai Bank building were then refined in later designs. Furthermore, the dramatic visual appeal created by the bank's presence within central Shanghai inspired clients and their architects to try to meet that higher standard.

Therefore, the Hongkong and Shanghai Bank is of fundamental significance to 20th-century commercial architecture. More than just a palpable link to Hong Kong, the bank connects Shanghai with contemporary European building technology, places Shanghai within a global commercial context, and epitomizes Shanghai's capitalistic activities in the early 20th century.

JEFFREY W. CODY

See also **Hong Kong, China; Shanghai, China**

Further Reading

A detailed description of the bank is found in the extensive inaugural booklet printed for the bank's opening on 23 June 1923. The most comprehensive journalistic treatment of the bank's construction is in *The Far Eastern Review.* The most informed history of Palmer and Turner is by Purvis. For congruencies with the bank's Hong Kong branch, see Wong.

Cody, Jeffrey W., "Remnants of Power behind the Bund: Shanghai's IBC and Robert Dollar Buildings, 1920–1922," *Architectural Research Quarterly* 3, no. 4 (1999)

Hongkong and Shanghai Banking Corporation, *The Official Opening of the New Building at Shanghai, 23 June 1923,* Shanghai: Kelly and Walsh, 1923

Huebner, Jon, "Architecture on the Shanghai Bund," *Papers in Far Eastern History* 39, 65 (1989)

Johnston, Tess, and Erh, Tung-ch'iang, *A Last Look: Western Architecture in Old Shanghai,* Hong Kong: Old China Hand Press, 1993

Lambot, Ian, and Gillian Chambers, *One Queen's Road Central: The Headquarters of Hongkong Bank since* 1864, Hong Kong: Lambot, 1986

Lu, Xiao-mo (editor), *Shanghai jianzhu zhinan; A Guide to Shanghai Architecture* (bilingual Chinese-English edition), Shanghai: Shanghai Renmin Meishu Chubanshe, 1996

Purvis, Malcolm, *Tall Storeys: Palmer and Turner, Architects and Engineers—The First 100 Years,* Hong Kong: Palmer and Turner, 1985

Wilson, G.L., "Architecture, Interior Decoration, and Building in Shanghai Twenty Years Ago and To-day," *China Journal* 12, no. 5 (May 1930)

Wong, Shirley S.W., "The Hongkong and Shanghai Bank Headquarters Buildings (1886, 1935, 1986): A Historical Analysis of Colonialism and Architecture," Ph.D. diss., Bartlett School of Graduate Studies, University College London, University of London, 1997

Wu, Chiang, *Shang-hai pai nien chien ch'u shih, 1840–1949; The History of Shanghai Architecture,* 1840–1949 (bilingual Chinese-English edition), Shanghai: T'ung Chi ta Hsüeh Ch'u Pan She, 1997

Zheng, Shilin (editor), *Shanghai jindai jianzhu fengliu* [The Evolution of Shanghai Architecture in Modern Times], Shanghai: Shanghai Jiaoyu Chubanshe, 1999

HOOD, RAYMOND 1881–1934

Architect, United States

Raymond Mathewson Hood is remembered as a major figure in American architecture who was known not only for his irreverence but also for his commitment to the development of a particularly American modernist language of forms.

Hood was born in Pawtucket, Rhode Island, on 21 March 1881. He began his education at Brown University but transferred to the Massachusetts Institute of Technology. He then went to work for the firm of Cram, Goodhue and Ferguson, which was renowned for both its neo-Gothic designs and its skill at formal massing.

Hood left the United States in 1904 for the École des Beaux-Arts in Paris but failed the examinations in draftsmanship and came back to Cram, Goodhue and Ferguson in 1906. He then spent a brief period with the architect Henry Hornbostel in Pittsburgh but returned to Paris in 1908 and completed his École studies in 1911. After rejoining Hornbostel's office for another brief period, Hood set out on his own in 1914. Fortune smiled on him in 1922 when John Mead Howells, who had decided to enter the competition for an office building for the *Chicago Tribune,* called on Hood to assist him.

The 1922 Tribune Competition attracted 263 architects from the United States and abroad, among them some of the most avant-garde. Hood and Howells took no risks with their entry, which was a sturdy Gothic tower crowned with flying buttresses. Despite his training with Cram and Goodhue, Hood was not a Gothic Revivalist at heart, but he evidently knew what would please the jurors, and the design he and his collaborator submitted was just traditional enough to overcome the bolder Europeans, including Eliel Saarinen, who finished second, Adolf Loos, and Walter Gropius.

The success of the Tribune Building lay less with its stylistic treatment than with its fundamentally sound formal organization. Hood followed this with the American Radiator Building (1924) in New York City, a slender tower with a gilded top that retained Gothic touches but relied more heavily on sculptural simplicity and a sense of vertical thrust. This effect was amplified by Hood's decision to clad the building in black brick. He argued that window glass tends to appear dark against a light cladding and that by using a dark one instead he could create a more unified visual impression.

Hood carried this concern for simplicity yet further in his building (1930) for the *New York Daily News.* The stepped-back form, this time clad in white brick that was distributed along slender piers of equal width, was dictated largely by the city's 1916 zoning ordinance, but the architect amplified it by giving up enough of the site on one side to provide for a corridor

American Radiator Building at night, New York City
© Gottscho-Schleisner Collection/Library of Congress

through the block. The result was a freestanding tower that otherwise would have been crowded at some future date by another building on the adjacent lot.

Hood's steady refinement of the tower form proceeded with New York's Rockefeller Center (1933), a complex of several buildings centered on a 70-story slab. Hood, working with the French engineer J. Andre Fouilhoux, was part of a team calling itself the Associated Architects and made up of two other firms: Reinhard and Hofmeister and Corbett, Harrison, and McMurray. However, Hood became the primary influence on the overall design. The result was arguably the finest modern urban complex in the world. The central tower seems to gather the lower buildings to itself while opening up to the city through an internal street and a generous pedestrian corridor: the Channel Gardens.

Moving back to the single-shaft form, Hood completed the McGraw-Hill Building in 1931. In contrast to his earlier, strongly vertical towers, this one was distinguished by the use of strong horizontals and was clad in an innovative skin of green-blue terra-cotta bricks. The industrial look of the design won Hood inclusion as the only American architect in the influential show and subsequent book by Henry-Russell Hitchcock and Philip Johnson, International Style Exhibition, New York (1932).

That selection depended heavily on the superficial similarity between Hood's work and that of the avant-garde Europeans, but whatever the influence, Hood always insisted that he was foremost a practical architect in the service of his clients and that he fully supported their goal of making money. Indeed, Hood was quite capable of putting an oversize replica of a refrigerator on the roof of a building for a client who owned a chain of General Electric showrooms.

In an article written for the 7 December 1929 issue of *Liberty* magazine titled "What Is Beauty in Architecture?" Hood answered the question himself by saying that it "is utility, developed in a manner to which the eye is accustomed by habit, insofar as this development does not detract from its quality of usefulness."

CARTER WISEMAN

See also **International Style Exhibition, New York (1932); Rockefeller Center, New York City; Tribune Tower International Competition (1922), Chicago**

Biography

Born in Pawtucket, Rhode Island, 21 March 1881. Degree from Brown University, Providence, Rhode Island 1899; studied architecture, Massachusetts Institute of Technology, Cambridge 1899–1903; trained in the offices of Cram, Goodhue, and Ferguson, Boston 1901–04 and the offices of Palmer and Hornbostel, Pittsburgh 1906–08; attended the École des Beaux-Arts, Paris 1904–06, 1908–11. Set up office with Henry Hornbostel, Pittsburgh 1911–14. Private practice, New York from 1914; partner with J. André Fouilhoux 1920; member, Board of Design, Century of Progress Exposition, Chicago 1933. President, Architectural League of New York 1929–31; fellow, American Institute of Architects 1934. Died in Stamford, Connecticut, 15 August 1934.

Selected Works

American Radiator Building, New York, 1924
Chicago Tribune Tower (first prize, competition; with John Mead Howells), Chicago, 1925
National Broadcasting Company Studios, New York, 1927
Ideal House, London, 1929
Masonic Temple and Scottish Rite Cathedral, Scranton, Pennsylvania (with Frederick Godley, J. André Fouilhoux, and H.V.K. Henderson), 1929
Daily News Building, New York (with Howells), 1930
McGraw-Hill Building, New York (with Godley and Fouilhoux), 1931
Rex Cole Showroom, Bay Ridge, New York, 1931
Rex Cole Showroom, Flushing, New York, 1931
Rockefeller Center, New York (with others), 1933

Selected Publications

"The Chicago Tribune Competition," *Architectural Record* (February 1923)
"Exterior Architecture of Office Buildings," *Architectural Forum*, 41 (September 1924)
"The American Radiator Company Building, New York," *American Architect*, 126 (19 November 1924)

"The National Broadcasting Studios, New York," *Architectural Record* (July 1928)
"The Spirit of Modern Art," *Architectural Forum* (November 1929)
"Beauty in Architecture," *Architectural Forum* (November 1930)
"The News Building," *Architectural Forum* (November 1930)
"The Design of the Rockefeller Center," *Architectural Forum* (January–June 1932)

Further Reading

Kilham, Walter Harrington, *Raymond Hood, Architect: Form through Function in the American Skyscraper*, New York: Architectural Book, 1973
Stern, Robert A.M., and Thomas P. Catalano, *Raymond Hood*, New York: Institute for Architecture and Urban Studies, 1982
Thorndike, Joseph J. (editor), *Three Centuries of Notable American Architects*, New York: American Heritage, and London: Orbis, 1981
Wiseman, Carter, *Shaping a Nation: Twentieth-Century American Architecture and Its Makers*, New York: Norton, 1998

HOPKINS, MICHAEL 1935– AND PATTY HOPKINS 1942–

Architects, England

Sir Michael and Lady Hopkins, principals and founding partners of the London-based architectural practice Hopkins Architects Ltd., established in 1976, are responsible for some of the most spectacular and influential buildings from the British High-Tech movement of the late 20th century. Their work is characterized by its materiality and attention to detail, from the early buildings in steel and glass to the later contextual projects using traditional materials, such as brick, stone, and lead. Coupled with a boldness and simplicity of form, this flexibility allows a constructional economy of repetitive systems—enriched in recent years as the scale and complexity of the Hopkins' work has steadily increased.

The practice built its early reputation on a series of industrial commissions, mainly for stand-alone buildings on green-field sites, such as the Greene King Beer Warehouse (Manchester, England, 1980) and the Schlumberger Cambridge Research Centre (Cambridge, England, 1985), both of which clearly express function through the dramatic display of technology. The Patera Building System (1982), a factory-produced kit of parts for light-industrial buildings, also shares with Schlumberger the use of an external, or exoskeletal, structure. One of the prototypes of this system was eventually recycled for use as the Hopkins' offices in north London. The Schlumberger building included a Teflon-coated fabric roof structure, the first of what has since become a trademark element in Hopkins' architecture, appearing in a series of more recent public projects, such as the Mound Stand (1991) at Lord's Cricket Ground in London, the temporary ticket office (1994) for Buckingham Palace, and the Dynamic Earth exhibition building (1999) in Edinburgh.

The shift toward a contextual and site-responsive approach, marked by the Mound Stand, resulted in a series of projects in sensitive surroundings, including Bracken House (1992) near St. Paul's Cathedral in London; Glyndebourne Opera House (1994), built on the grounds of a Sussex country house; and, more recently, Portcullis House (2000), providing new government offices adjacent to the Westminster Houses of Parliament. The latter building also manifests a concern with energy effi-

ciency and environmental issues; these were first explored in two earlier projects, both for institutional clients: the Inland Revenue Headquarters (1994) in Nottingham, which again included a fabric roof structure, and the Jubilee Campus (1999) for the University of Nottingham. Other major projects under way at the time of writing include several cultural buildings funded by the Millennium Lottery Commission, such as the Norfolk and Norwich Library (1996–2001) and the Manchester City Art Gallery (1994–2001).

Michael Hopkins is the son of a builder from Dorset, and his early architectural experience is marked by a fascination with construction. Beginning with small-scale building projects undertaken as a child to the restoration with Patty Hopkins of a 400-year-old house in Suffolk, this interest also led to his dropping out of art school at an early stage in favor of practical experience in an architect's office. After working as an assistant to Frederick Gibberd and then Sir Basil Spence, he returned to study at the Architectural Association (AA) in London and there encountered an influential group of young designers and architectural theorists. Chief among these were Cedric Price and Peter Smithson, both now seen as exerting a significant early influence on the development of high-tech architecture in Britain. Four years after Michael, in 1967, Patty also completed her studies

Canopy roof of the Glyndebourne Opera House, Sussex, England (1994)
© Grant Smith/CORBIS

at the AA, with a thesis project inspired by the Charles and Ray Eames House (1949) in California and its use of factory-produced components. In 1968, they were offered a commission by Hopkins' father, then a director of a national construction company, and for this they teamed up with the young Norman Foster (who they had also met at the AA) and his practice Team 4, which also included Richard Rogers. Although this first project fell through, they worked on another of Foster's groundbreaking buildings, the Willis Faber Dumas offices (1975), a cantilevered concrete structure with a frameless full-height glass curtain wall. The minimalism of the Foster buildings and the domestic scale of the Eames House came together in the Hopkins' own family house (1976) built in north London—the firm's inaugural project. This two-story steel-and-glass pavilion also became an icon for the burgeoning High-Tech movement; with its lightweight lattice roof trusses, corrugated-metal side walls, full-height sliding windows, and metallic venetian blinds, it contained most of the basic ingredients of the practice's early larger projects, particularly the Green King Warehouse as well as the offices at Schlumberger and the later Solid State Logic (1988).

In the Hopkins' later work, these materials were augmented according to context, particularly where existing buildings are involved, as a contrast is created with materials that heighten the distinction between old and new. For instance, at the Mound Stand an existing brick arcade is dramatically offset by the new white fabric canopies cantilevered out above the street. At the Bracken House office building, the monumental brick wings of the old printing works frame a delicate assembly of bronze-and-glass bay windows that screen the newly inserted structure.

This rediscovery of traditional materials through the adaptation to historic contexts has also found another function in the practice's later experiments in ecologically oriented, or "green architecture." The property of thermal mass that is missing in many lightweight high-tech buildings has been exploited for environmental comfort and to help improve energy efficiency. At the Inland Revenue headquarters, this was used to help ventilate the buildings naturally, together with glass stair towers to generate air movement and exposed-concrete ceilings to absorb heat. More successful from an environmental point of view has been the Nottingham University Jubilee Campus, where a combination of natural and mechanical ventilation provides substantial energy savings. The expressive rotating wind towers and photovoltaic solar panel arrays, together with the cedar-clad elevations and grass-covered roofs, have also proved influential in dramatizing ecological factors in architecture. This new direction in the practice's work is also visible at Portcullis House but is less successful from a compositional viewpoint, perhaps because of the constraints of fitting in with some rather undistinguished neighboring buildings.

The Hopkins practice has received numerous awards, including the Royal Gold Medal from the Royal Institute of British Architects (1994). In 1995, Michael received a knighthood in recognition of his contribution to architecture. A modest and practical couple with a clear focus on creating enduring buildings rather than the transient realm of theoretical debate, they have inspired many of their collaborators to embark on similar ventures of their own.

JONATHAN A. HALE

See also **Contextualism; Foster, Norman (England); Post-structuralism; Schlumberger Cambridge Research Centre, Cambridge; Smithson, Peter and Alison (England)**

Selected Works

Hopkins House, London, 1976
Greene King Draught Beer Cellars, Manchester, 1980
Patera Building System, 1982
Schlumberger Research Centre, Cambridge, 1985
Solid State Logic, Oxford, 1988
Mound Stand, Lord's Cricket Ground, London, 1991
Bracken House, London, 1992
Temporary Ticket Office, Buckingham Palace, London, 1994
Opera House, Glyndebourne, Sussex, 1994
Inland Revenue Headquarters, Nottingham, 1994
City Art Gallery, Manchester, 1994–2001
Library, Norfolk, 1996–2001
Library, Norwich, 1996–2001
Dynamic Earth Exhibition Building, Edinburgh, 1999
Jubilee Campus, University of Nottingham, 1999
Portcullis House, Westminster, 2000

Further Reading

Davies, Colin, *Hopkins: The Work of Michael Hopkins and Partners*, London: Phaidon, 1993
Davies, Colin, *Hopkins 2: The Work of Michael Hopkins and Partners*, London: Phaidon, 2001

HORTA, VICTOR 1861–1947

Architect, Belgium

Victor Horta was the leading European architect of the movement to create a modern architecture in the 1890s. His work blended a structural rationalism influenced by the writings of E.E. Viollet-le-Duc with a personal, curvilinear decoration derived from abstracted botanic form as proposed by V.-M.-C. Ruprich-Robert to produce works of astounding internal spatial complexity and organic completeness. Horta's buildings were complete works of art for which, when given the opportunity, he designed every object, from furniture and table linens to doorknobs and andirons. Often remembered as one of the practitioners of the Art Nouveau style, Horta was in fact the chief inventor of that style. More than that, his ability to use iron and glass in place of load-bearing masonry remained unsurpassed among turn-of-the-century architects.

Born in Ghent in 1861, Horta briefly studied music at the local conservatory before enrolling in the architecture course at the Academy of Fine Arts in Ghent. In 1878, he traveled to Paris to work for an interior decorator, returning to Ghent on his father's death in 1880. The following year, he married, moved to Brussels, undertook the study of architecture at the Brussels academy, and began drafting for Alphonse Balat, the royal architect to King Leopold II, whose work reflected a rational, if classical, approach to architecture. Horta work intermittently for Balat until 1891.

In Paris in the late 1870s, Horta discovered the power of Beaux-Arts design, as exemplified by both the urban planning of Baron Haussmann's boulevards and the architecture of Charles Garnier's opera house. Returning in 1889 for the world's fair, he was similarly drawn to the Galerie des Machines, an iron-

Tassel House (1892–93), Brussels, Belgium
© GreatBuildings.com

and-glass building whose trusses spanned almost 400 feet. He was amazed not only by the possibilities of Victor Contamin's engineering but also by the curvilinear decoration created by the architect Charles Dutert.

Horta's pavilion for Jef Lambeaux's "Passions Humaines," begun in 1889, reveals a search for a new expression within the vocabulary of classicism. In the Autriche house (1893), Horta first explored a more original decorative vocabulary based on abstracted botanic forms and simple geometry. Yet neither prepares us for the extraordinary accomplishment of his next building, the Tassel house (1893). Within the parameters of the standard Brussels townhouse—party walls with its neighbors to the sides, built to the street, and with an open yard behind—Horta began an architectural revolution. He split the building into two parts and connected them with a metal-and-glass circulation zone that brought natural light into the whole building. He set the whole composition in motion by melding his new curvilinear decoration to the structural systems. Horta developed this solution into its most elaborate form in the Solvay house (1894) and into its most perfect form in the Van Eetvelde house (1895).

Horta brought this approach to nondomestic architecture in 1895 at la Maison du Peuple, the Brussels headquarters of the Belgian Workers Party, which contained large and small lecture halls, meeting rooms, a coffee house, and commercial shops. He combined structural iron freely exposed in a "rational" manner with sinuous curves of iron, wood, and masonry to produce a work of great expressive power that is clearly organized.

Horta's mature style was perfectly tuned to the values of the *haute bourgeoisie* of the 1890s throughout Europe. His architecture strongly influenced emerging architects, such as Hector Guimard, whereas the superficial aspects of his decorative forms were easily copied by lesser designers. Horta's very popularity contributed to a rapid change of taste in the middle of the first decade that left him without sufficient clients to continue investigating the problems posed in the 1890s. His work gradually became simpler in form and reflected a return to classicism.

Horta was deeply affected by the German occupation of Belgium. In February 1915 he traveled to London to meet with British architects and Belgians in exile to plan the rebuilding of Belgium after the war. In December he continued to New York to enlist the support of American architects. The proposed lecture tour became a three-year exile. Returning home in 1919, Horta was overwhelmed by the devastation.

Respected in Belgium as both master architect and teacher, Horta in the 1920s was involved in a number of civic projects, including a new gallery and concert hall, the central train station, a major public hospital, and the Belgian Pavilion at the 1925 Paris World's Fair. All these were expressed in an abstracted classical manner. The rebuke of this work by early historians of the Modern movement has been reversed by a recent generation of historians, who find a continuity in approach despite a change of style. The concert hall le Palais des Beaux-Arts (1920), built of reinforced concrete, has come to be regarded as Horta's most accomplished work. Although the massing of rectilinear solids that characterizes this building has more in common with Art Deco than with the emerging International Style, the design exhibits the same expressive rationalism of Horta's earlier work.

Horta's work stands as an early expression of the possibility of incorporating the cataclysmic changes brought about by the industrial revolution into a system of design that, like the great historic styles of past, reflects contemporary values and possibilities.

PAUL KRUTY

See also **Art Deco; Art Nouveau (Jugendstil); Brussels, Belgium**

Further Reading

Aubry, Françoise and Jos Vandenbreeden (editors), *Horta: Naissance et dépassement de l'Art Nouveau*, Ghent, Belgium: Ludion, and Paris: Flammarion, 1996; as *Horta: Art Nouveau to Modernism*, Ghent, Belgium: Ludion Press, 1996

Borsi, Franco and Paolo Portoghesi, *Victor Horta* Rome: Edzioni del Tritone, 1969; as *Victor Horta*, translated by Marie-Hélène Agüeros, London: Academy Editions, and New York: Rizzoli, 1991

Delhaye, Jean and Françoise Aubry, *La Maison du Peuple de Victor Horta*, Brussels: Atelier Vokaer, 1987

Dernie, David and Alastair Carew-Cox, *Victor Horta*, London: Academy Editions, 1995

Hanser, David, "Victor Horta, Art Nouveau, and Freemasonry" in *Belgium, the Golden Decades, 1880–1914*, edited by Jane Block, New York: Peter Lang, 1997

Hustache, Anne, Steven Jacobs, and Frans Boenders, *Victor Horta: Le Palais des Beaux-Arts de Bruxelles*, Brussels: Snoeck-Ducaju, and Crédit Communal, 1996

Loyer, Françoise and Jean Delhaye, *Victor Horta: Hotel Tassel, 1893–1895* (bilingual English and French edition), Brussels: Archives d'Architecture Moderne, 1986

Oostens-Wittamer, Yolande, *Victor Horta: L'Hôtel Solvay; The Solvay House* (bilingual English-French edition), 2 vols., Louvain-la-Neuve, Belgium: Institut Supérieur d'Archéologie et d'Histoire de l'Art, Collège Erasme, 1980

HOSPITAL

The hospital is among the most complex and reinvented buildings of the 20th century. Whereas hospitals in 1900 were charitable institutions for the sick poor, resembling other benevolent establishments such as schools, prisons, convents, and workhouses, by 2000 the hospital had become a complicated architectural project that housed areas dedicated to health care, research, teaching, and new medical technologies.

Four distinct types of hospitals evolved during this period; in many ways, each of these hospital types developed as a reaction to the form that preceded it while adapting its program to rapid new developments in the delivery of health care. At the beginning of the century, new hospitals were typically constructed according to the highly developed pavilion-plan model. After World War I, new hospitals were more compact (although some-times larger), multistory buildings with conservatively styled exteriors, accommodating patients in smaller rooms along double-loaded corridors. The post-World War II hospital was often an isolated tower, with minimal decoration and neutral colors. Since the 1970s hospitals have become "health care facilities," with a renewed emphasis on flexibility, patient-focused care, access, and an architectural form and language that reflects concerns for inviting and comfortable spaces.

These four types were also the result of complex and competing social, economic, medical, and professional concerns. The main issues that influenced hospital architecture in the 20th century were the evolving nature of medical theory and practice, expanding patient populations, the drive toward hospital standardization, changing notions of privacy, and increasing specialization among hospital architects.

Continuing from accepted hospital plans developed during the 19th century, the basic form of the pavilion-plan hospital was well established by 1900 and continued to be constructed into the 1930s. The type had become an international standard in the 19th century, with major examples in India, Persia, Russia, Australia, the United States, and Europe. Based originally on the ideas of Florence Nightingale and other midcentury reformers, the concept of separate or minimally connected pavilions and the open plan of the wards was believed to discourage the spread of infection by maximizing ventilation. The hallmark of the pavilion-plan type was the open ward, in which 30 to 40 beds were arranged against a regular rhythm of large windows. The presumption was that the copious amounts of fresh air circulating between patients would mitigate the chances of contagion, even following the development of the germ theory in the 1870s.

The premier example of an American pavilion-plan hospital is the Johns Hopkins Hospital (1885, John Billings and John Niernsee) in Baltimore. An illustration of the persistence of this type at the turn of the century is University College Hospital (1897–1905, Alfred Waterhouse) in London. An innovation on the pavilion plan was made at the Rigshospital (1911) in Copenhagen, where the beds were turned parallel to the window. Here the ward of 26 beds was divided by screens into sections of three or four patients. This afforded the patients more privacy without sacrificing accessibility or ventilation and foreshadowed the eventual eclipse of the open ward by the semiprivate and private room.

Hospitals in the interwar period were much more compact than those constructed around 1900. Although these buildings were planned according to Tayloristic principles of efficiency and employed modern materials, such as reinforced concrete, hospitals constructed between the wars were likely to resemble Georgian mansions or Scottish castles, employing a series of revival styles. Typical of this period is the work of Boston- and Toronto-based architects Edward Fletcher Stevens and Frederick Lee, who designed hundreds of hospitals in North America, such as the Ottawa Civic Hospital (1924).

A constellation of other hospital design experts appeared in the interwar period, contributing to the architectural development of the hospital. Sigismund Schulz Goldwater, a physician and commissioner of New York City's hospitals from 1934 to 1940, acted as "advisory construction expert" for 156 hospitals. Goldwater was an outspoken advocate of the "vertical" hospital,

Postcard of Ottawa Civic Hospital, Ottawa, Ontario; designed by Stevens and Lee (1922–1924)
Photo courtesy Annmarie Adams

ideas that were published posthumously in his *On Hospitals* (1947).

A number of social and medical factors also influenced the design of the interwar hospital, such as the increasing significance of surgery, the arrival of middle-class and paying patients, and the establishment of hospitals for special patients, such as women and children. Whereas the pre-World War I surgeon had likely performed in an amphitheater with tiered seating, surgery in the 1920s commonly took place in a suite of smaller specialized rooms. Surgery was one of the means by which middle-class patients were convinced that the hospital was a better place for healing than home. To this end, hospitals constructed luxurious pavilions for paying patients in the 1920s that were frequently compared to hotels. Like other building types, new hospitals in the 1920s accommodated large numbers of automobiles for the first time, offering both parking and patient drop-off by car.

Interwar hospitals were also often much larger than those constructed before World War I, especially in the United States. The Columbian Presbyterian Medical Center (1928, James Gamble Rogers) in New York and the Cornell Medical Center of New York Hospital (1933, Coolidge, Shepley, Bulfinch and Abbott) are illustrations of this jump in scale.

In the name of economy, the post-World War II hospital was most likely a multistory tower, resembling an office building

more than any domestic model, often surrounded by huge parking facilities. Hallmarks of the post-World War II hospital were standardized floor plans, undecorated facades, flat roofs, vertical circulation, and controlled ventilation. The image of these hospitals, with their sleek, hard-surfaced interiors, was detached and neutral, whereas the interwar institution had been romantic and highly decorative.

Postwar hospital architects also experimented with the hospital's section. In Europe, a number of huge urban replacement hospitals were built in the 1960s following a "matchbox on a muffin plan," whereby patient towers were constructed atop a podium of high-tech services. Examples of this type include the Free University Hospital Center (1969, Arthur Q. Davis and Franz Mocken) in Berlin. A system of interstitial space, where flexible service floors were located between patient levels, was first used in a health-related building in the Salk Institute of Biological Studies (1960–62, Louis Kahn) in La Jolla, California. It subsequently (until about 1980) became a popular model for acute-care hospitals in England, Canada, and the United States. Among the first hospitals to employ the system was the Health Sciences Centre (1966–72, Craig, Zeidler, and Strong) at McMaster University in Hamilton, Ontario, Canada.

Since the 1970s, hospitals constructed after World War II have been sharply criticized for their impersonal scale, urban isolation, visual sterility, and confusing circulation. The hospice movement, the rise of patient-driven (as opposed to provider-driven) care, and increased consumer awareness about health care matters have encouraged alternatives to these machinelike forms. A new focus on patient-centered facilities, which embraced homelike spaces and furniture, regional symbolism, increased access, and humanly scaled buildings, characterized hospitals of the final three decades of the 20th century.

In terms of hospital planning, architects also looked to three significant models in the design of hospitals since the 1970s: the shopping mall, the village, and the home. The Dartmouth-Hitchcock Medical Center (1991, Shepley Bulfinch Richardson and Abbott) in Hanover, New Hampshire, resembles a mall in its skylit rotunda and three-story galleria. "Health villages," comprised of low-rise interconnected buildings, are a conscious critique of the megahospital of the immediate postwar period in their use of brick (and other materials that express human scale), sloping roofs, and enclosed walkways. The inclusion of domestic imagery, as an attempt to infuse intimacy and meaning into the institution, has sometimes meant a confusion of contexts. For example, the Hijirigaoka Hospital (1990, ARS Design Associates) in Tokyo boasts red-brick cladding, colonial detailing, and classical porticoes, as found on the eastern seaboard of the United States.

The end of the 20th century was marked by unprecedented hospital mergers and the closure of many historic hospital buildings. Whereas some of these have been preserved as administrative adjuncts to new health care facilities or transformed to completely new uses, many historic hospitals have been simply abandoned and/or demolished—costly reminders of the swift pace of medical progress.

ANNMARIE ADAMS

See also **Salk Institute, La Jolla, California**

Further Reading

Adams, Annmarie, "Modernism and Medicine: The Hospitals of Stevens and Lee, 1916–1932," *Journal of the Society of Architectural Historians* 58, no. 1 (March 1999)

Forty, Adrian, "The Modern Hospital in England and France: The Social and Medical Uses of Architecture," in *Buildings and Society: Essays on the Social Development of the Built Environment*, edited by Anthony D. King, London and Boston: Routledge and Kegan Paul, 1990

Goldin, Grace, *Work of Mercy: A Picture History of Hospitals*, Toronto, Ontario: Boston Mills Press, 1994

Goldwater, Sigismund Schulz, *On Hospitals*, edited and compiled by Clara Aub Goldwater, New York: Macmillan, 1947

Ochsner, Albert John and Meyer J. Sturm, *The Organization, Construction, and Management of Hospitals, with Numerous Plans and Details*, Chicago: Cleveland Press, 1907; 2nd edition, 1909

Risse, Guenter B., *Mending Bodies, Saving Souls: A History of Hospitals*, New York: Oxford University Press, 1999

Sloane, David Charles, "Scientific Paragon to Hospital Mall: The Evolution of the Hospital, 1885–1994," *Journal of Architectural Education* 48, no. 2 (November 1994)

Stevens, Edward Fletcher, *The American Hospital of the Twentieth Century*, New York: Architectural Record, 1918; 2nd revised edition, New York: Dodge, 1928

Stevenson, Christine, "Medicine and Architecture" in *Companion Encyclopedia of the History of Medicine*, edited by William F. Bynum and Roy Porter, London and New York: Routledge, 1993

Taylor, Jeremy and Reginald Buckley, *The Architect and the Pavilion Hospital: Dialogue and Design Creativity in England, 1850–1914*, Leicester: Leicester University Press, 1997

Thompson, John and Grace Goldin, *The Hospital: A Social and Architectural History*, New Haven, Connecticut: Yale University Press, 1975

Verderber, Stephen and David J. Fine, *Healthcare Architecture in an Era of Radical Transformation*, New Haven, Connecticut: Yale University Press, 2000

HOTEL

At the most basic level, a hotel provides temporary shelter for travelers, a function that the 20th-century hotel shares with its predecessors extending back to the ancient inn. As a modern building type, the hotel integrates a complex variety of uses, including lodging, food service, and retail, into a specialized building program. After the office building, the hotel is the most important building type to embrace the skyscraper form, thus addressing the architectural challenge of efficiently arranging codependent yet distinct public, private, and service spaces. Hotels generally have major public spaces on the lower- and uppermost floors, largely identical floors of guest rooms between, and related service areas carefully woven throughout the plan. This basic program appeared in the 19th century and was associated with large railway hotels located in cities around the world. However, the scale and complexity of the 20th-century hotel make it a distinctive building type and an important focal point in the urban landscape. By virtue of its location, the resort hotel caters to tourists and merits its own analysis.

The hotel is a building type intimately linked to the socioeconomic changes of the 20th century. The rise of a consumer culture, especially in the United States, spurs urban growth and directly benefits service-sector businesses such as the hotel industry. Increased tourism, widely accessible commercial travel, and annual conventions provide an expanded clientele for the commercial hotel. Since the early decades of the 20th century, competition to attract conventions has especially shaped the planning of new hotels. Major exhibit halls, meeting rooms, and auditoriums require a large percentage of space on the public floors of the hotel to be devoted to convention-related facilities.

These trends first peaked in the 1920s, making that decade the heyday of the development of the hotel as a 20th-century building type. New hotels, such as the Roosevelt (1924, George B. Post and Sons) in New York, Hotel Statler (1927, George B. Post and Sons) in Boston, and the Los Angeles Biltmore (1923, Schultze and Weaver), are just a few of the massive hotels from that period with around 1,000 guest rooms. The Stevens Hotel (Holabird and Roche), the largest hotel in the world, opened on South Michigan Avenue in Chicago in 1927. With 3,000 guest rooms, 3,000 baths, and a huge array of public spaces, dining rooms, and convention facilities, the Stevens epitomizes the early 20th-century architectural development of the hotel.

The balance between the commercial purpose of the hotel and the need to create a domestic atmosphere often led hotels to embrace historically inspired architectural styles and interior design. Multitowered, Beaux-Arts–influenced skyscraper forms with eclectic decorative programs were common during the early

20th century. After World War II, hotels followed the shift to modernism in commercial architecture. The resulting aesthetic change to ahistoric minimalism was dramatic, but hotels largely retained the same basic functional arrangement and preference for mainstream architectural styles.

Hotels often feature a combination of conservative architectural design and innovative systems and technology. Among the most significant hotels in the 19th century, Adler and Sullivan's Auditorium Building (1889) in Chicago combined a theater, modern hotel, and office space. Using the latest in modern conveniences has been vital to a hotel's success since the 19th century, and 20th-century hotels quickly incorporated any important new technology. The most significant improvements were plumbing and air conditioning and their subsequent influence on the form and use of the hotel. Although indoor plumbing was available in 19th-century hotels, private baths were relatively rare. The basic standard for hotels changed rapidly in the early 20th century, and by the 1920s nearly all new hotels provided a private bathroom for each guest room. Arranging and servicing the bathrooms is a problem specific to the 20th-century hotel. The architectural firm of George B. Post and Sons developed an efficient layout to provide private bathrooms in an affordable commercial hotel with its designs for the important early chain Hotels Statler. Bathrooms arranged in pairs along the interior wall create mirror-image room plans that allow two bathrooms to share one plumbing shaft. Standardized hotel architecture did not emerge until the postwar period, but this plan was an important first step.

Ventilation creates another challenge for the 20th-century hotel. The multiple towers of the large pre–World War II hotel provide exterior light and air to all the guest rooms. Mechanical air conditioning was first introduced in the public rooms of some major urban hotels in the 1920s. Starting in the 1950s, new hotels provided air-conditioned guest rooms, eliminating dependence on exterior ventilation. The new possibilities that air conditioning brings to the hotel form are perhaps best utilized by the Hyatt Regency Hotels of John Portman and Associates. Portman's Hyatt Regency Atlanta (1967), Hyatt Regency O'Hare (1971), and Hyatt Regency San Francisco (1973) feature a dramatic new form focused inward on the atrium lobby. Portman and his imitators use a modernist vocabulary to create the grand public space of the atrium, but the functional program of the hotel remains essentially the same.

External forces, such as urban development and transportation patterns, also help reconfigure the fundamental relationship between hotel and location. The shift in the United States from railroad to automobile travel transforms the shape, scale, and location of hotels. The downtown skyscraper hotel usually lacks parking facilities, and motels emerge along highways to serve the interstate traveler. In the post–World War II period, hotel development moves beyond downtown, especially with construction around outlying airports. However, the form and program of the hotel building type remain essentially urban.

The American hotel defines the building type throughout the 20th century, especially in the postwar period with the growing international dominance of a few large hotel chains. The standardized Hilton, Sheraton, or Marriott hotel, more than any other building, symbolizes American commercial culture throughout the world. Standardized commercial hotels sell a self-contained vision of urban order and prosperity closely tied to the emergence of a deindustrialized global economy. Throughout the 20th century, hotels reflect the impact of economic change in the urban landscape and the social demands that shape a complex commercial building type.

LISA PFUELLER DAVIDSON

See also **Holabird, William and Martin Roche (United States); Imperial Hotel, Tokyo; Park Hotel, Shanghai; Portman, John C. (United States); Resort Hotel**

Further Reading

A comprehensive architectural history of the hotel has yet to be written, and many of the available secondary sources are general or anecdotal in nature. Hotel trade journals such as *Hotel Monthly* and *Hotel World* are useful for tracing this building type's development.

Bruegmann, Robert, "Palaces of Democracy: The Business Hotel," in *The Architects and the City: Holabird and Roche of Chicago, 1880–1918*, Chicago: University of Chicago Press, 1997

Denby, Elaine, *Grand Hotels: Reality and Illusion: An Architectural and Social History*, London: Reaktion Books, 1998

Donzel, Catherine, Alexis Gregory, and Marc Walter, *Palaces et grands hotels d'Amerique du Nord*, Paris: Flammarion, 1989; as *Grand American Hotels*, New York: Vendome Press, and London: Thames and Hudson, 1989; as *Grand Hotels of North America*, Toronto: McClelland and Stewart, 1989

Jakle, John A., Keith A. Sculle, and Jefferson S. Rogers, *The Motel in America*, Baltimore, Maryland: Johns Hopkins University Press, 1996

Lapidus, Morris, and Alan Lapidus, "Commercial Hotels," in *Time-Saver Standards for Building Types*, edited by Joseph De Chiara and John Hancock Callender, New York: McGraw-Hill, 1973; 3rd edition, 1990

Pevsner, Nikolaus, *A History of Building Types*, Princeton, New Jersey: Princeton University Press, and London: Thames and Hudson, 1976

Raitz, Karl B., and John Paul Jones, III, "The City Hotel as Landscape Artifact and Community Symbol," *Journal of Cultural Geography* (1988)

Root, John Wellborn, "Hotels and Apartment Hotels," in *Forms and Functions of Twentieth-Century Architecture*, vol. 3: *Building Types: Buildings for Residence, for Popular Gatherings, for Education, and for Government*, edited by Talbot Hamlin, New York: Columbia University Press, 1952

Williamson, Jefferson, *The American Hotel: An Anecdotal History*, New York and London: Knopf, 1930; reprint, as *The American Hotel*, New York: Arno Press, 1975

HOUSE

Given its special place in the life and development of human beings, the house is an important architectural type. It protects us from external influences, both from nature and, by creating places for privacy, from the full and immediate absorption into social and public life. Thus, because of its social and psychological significance, the house is the most universally desired form of habitation. For these same reasons, the house is also considered by some to be the most useful architectural type for explorations into questions of culture and life.

Similarly, the house in the 20th century attracted the attention of architects, clients, developers, and historians and theorists because the house as a type and expressive architectural form often synthesized the aspirations of individual architects and leading architectural movements or schools as well as home owners who wanted to choose the most up-to-date architectural style for their house. Whether large or small, houses were built in various forms and materials around the world, thus attesting to the enormous variety of meanings for dwelling and shelter. Dwellings in developing countries, for example, are often made from locally available natural materials that adhere to long-standing vernacular forms and ornament, sometimes centuries old.

In house societies of South America, Southeast Asia, and elsewhere, for example, the house serves to express social hierarchies and kinship or to provide a ritual site, thus functioning less as a practical dwelling for daily activities, as is customary in Western industrial societies. Wherever the house serves to express social and institutional values of a culture, the analytic methods of Claude Levi-Strauss and other leading anthropologists and ethnographers provide significant ways of learning about the house in single- and multihouse societies as representations of culture. Yet this article addresses the house as the prominent and architect-designed type associated with the architectural profession and wealthy, developed societies.

One of the most important aspects of the house in the 20th century is its emergence as a primary medium for architectural experimentation. The house, including those built by architects for their own use, has proven to be a remarkable laboratory for new ideas. In the architectural avant-garde, the house became an important instrument for the transformation of society in urban, suburban, and rural environments. Such changes were possible, according to architects and theorists, through the invention of new forms of domestic settings that were more responsive to and appropriate for the new, modern era.

According to most modernists, proper attention to the new way of life in the house would lead to new forms and spaces and a new aesthetic, all of which were facilitated by the introduction of new materials and technologies as well as radically new ideas about the arrangement of interior domestic spaces. In the Robie House (1908), for example, Frank Lloyd Wright used long-span construction materials to create open and flowing spaces for the democratic individual whom he envisioned as the proper subject of his work. He achieved this by eliminating walls between rooms and introducing continuous bands of glass windows and doors to create a new freedom of movement and vision. Wright's development of an organic architecture and the Prairie-style house during the first 15 to 20 years of his practice left a broad and lasting effect on 20th-century house forms far beyond Chicago and the Midwest. His many writings about the house provide a detailed philosophy for giving form and meaning to family life in the 20th-century home. In his "Five Points Towards a New Architecture" (1926)—based on his earlier invention of the Dom-ino House (1914–15)—Le Corbusier presented a system of columns and slabs that formed the basis for his interpretation of the free plan. This framework made it possible for him to use the house as a means of presenting, according to the critic Colin Rowe, the disparities as well as the concurrences between the past (as manifested in the classical arrangement of structural columns) and the present (the practical and thus asymmetrical arrangement of rooms and functions) in his 1920s villas and maisons (Villa Stein, 1926–27; Villa Savoye, 1929–31).

Through the influences of new materials, inventive conceptions of interior spaces, and economic and practical concerns, a widespread interest in an aesthetic of abstraction emerged that was considered consistent with modern, analytical thought and thus appropriate to the modern house. Josef Hoffmann reduced walls to thin planes as surfaces enclosing interior volumes in the Palais Stoclet (1905). In one of his most important essays, "Ornament and Crime," Adolph Loos argued that the true style of the times would be found only when ornament was eliminated; this meant a reduction to the essential underlying qualities of form and proportion, a concept that he applied in his house designs (Steiner House, 1910; Tristan Tzara House, 1926–27). Gerrit Rietveld's Schröder-Schräder House (1923–24) exemplified a dynamic architecture liberated from the constraints of gravity with its rectangular, smooth shapes and open, pinwheel, "transformable plan." This was another version of the "free plan," each of which carried a symbolic message of liberation that promoted a new way of life.

In the second half of the century, late modernism continued the interest in abstraction. In its extreme cases, in which architects sought greater refinement, this preference led to an interest in the experience of the sublime. Ludwig Mies van der Rohe, for example, pushed the abstract to its architectural limits in his minimal presentation of space, as in the Farnsworth House (1946–50); in this now canonic building, a series of glass planes is held in space by thin, drafted vertical and horizontal steel members. Philip Johnson's Glass House (1949–51) is one of the finest examples of this propensity to suggest an otherwise invisible volume of space.

The dedication to abstraction was one of the reasons that many began to question modernism in architecture in the second half of the century. Strong public criticism began in the 1950s and was widespread a decade later. The relevancy of abstraction was questioned by architectural and cultural critics alike, particularly as it applied to domestic environments. Several buildings in Minori Yamasaki's Pruitt-Igoe Housing Project (1958) in St. Louis, Missouri, were razed in 1972 in an effort to reduce the vandalism and crime that had plagued the project for 14 years; it was an event that some referred to as the end of modernism. Studies such as those of Philip Boudon's examination of Le Corbusier's Pessac Housing (1926) in Bordeaux, in which a modernist aesthetic was replaced by its residents with conventional images of local domestic architecture, alerted everyone to the fact that modernism had not been successful in its grander aspirations to transform life.

While these interests did not disappear, other interpretations of the house filled the void left behind in the retreat of modernism. Aldo Rossi and Venturi, Scott Brown and Associates (VSBA), for example, turned to vernacular buildings as a common housing stock that guaranteed cultural relevance. While Rossi eliminated all evidence of ornament and historical change in his analysis of types (Pavilion, 1973), however, VSBA embraced ornament and signs, claiming that these were the source for Zeitgeist relevance (Vanna Venturi House, 1964). VSBA took it as a responsibility to represent the age through signs applied to "sheds"—simple, straightforward, economical boxes. While the architectural critic and theorist Alan Colquhoun found the separation between the sign and the "substance" disquieting, VSBA's Postmodernist ideas were highly influential in the work of Michael Graves (Plocek House, 1980) and Robert Stern (House for an Academical Couple, 1974–76).

In the last quarter of the century, others used the house as a means for deconstructing architectural assumptions concerning domestic life. In his own house (1976) in Santa Monica, for example, Frank Gehry took a California bungalow apart, literally and figuratively, and wrapped it with a volume of rooms enclosed by chain-link fence and corrugated metal siding; he used this as a means to explore relationships between inside and outside, surface and structure, and forms and materials. Other architects used the house to question the way architecture is conceived: Peter Eisenman (House VI) and Bernard Tschumi (Project for a Villa, 1992) explored the relationships between form and function and between spaces and events, respectively. One of the most influential houses in the latter part of the 20th century was Coop Himme(l)blau "Open House" (1981), a proposed house that reversed the relationship between form and function, one of the central tenets of modernism.

The configuration of the house and the domestic life it sheltered were affected throughout the century by changes outside architectural circles as well. Among the most important of these influences came from manufacturing, legislation, and financing. The manufacturing industry generated new products throughout the century that would have far-reaching effects on the house. The single most important of these consumer products in the West was the automobile; its introduction and widespread acceptance contributed powerfully to the development of the suburbs and the distribution of single-family houses across vast expanses of land (Levittown). Commuter rail lines and vast highway networks permitted home owners to locate their houses in communities far from the city. With increased wealth and an expanding middle class, houses were designed in a wide range of styles and scales to suit the tastes of new owners. Large mansions and country houses, for example, were designed during the early 20th century in the United States by Howard Van Doren Shaw; David Adler; McKim, Mead and White; and others in a wide variety of revival, historicist, and modernist styles, including the Chateauesque, Tudor, Romanesque, and Italian Renaissance as well as the Craftsman, Prairie, and International styles.

However, house life changed also because of new appliances and household equipment. The transformation of the kitchen, for example, can be followed from its origins in the open stone hearth as the sole source of heat for cooking and warmth. The hearth was central to the Cape Cod type and became the conceptual and symbolic focus of Wright's houses throughout his entire career. Running water was introduced in most major cities in the West by the late 19th century and hot water in the early 20th. The typical compact residential bathroom was standardized around 1930. Heating and cooling, in concert with the automobile, made it possible to live in regions of the world that were formerly questionable environments for domestic life. Over the course of the century, typical suburban houses were equipped with dishwashers, clothes washers and dryers, vacuum cleaners and other appliances, radios, televisions, telephones, and computers. Some of these required that new rooms be added to the program for the typical house; all had significant impacts on daily domestic life.

Manufacturing also affected the construction and supply industries, eventually leading to the standardization of materials (dimensioned lumber, plywood, and drywall) and the invention of new elements and materials (compressed wood elements, box beams, plastics, and polycarbonates), most of which found their way into residential construction. Standardized parts could be assembled with a minimum level of expertise, making it possible for many to build their own homes, often from kits or mail-order plans. Some architects explored the use of standardized, "ready-made" parts in their houses as well (Eames House, 1949). The appetite for self-help home construction was fed by magazines in the beginning of the century (*Ladies Home Journal* and *House and Garden*) and by television programs at the end (*This Old House*) that gave home owners endless advice about how to improve their residential environments. The local lumberyard and hardware store grew into large wholesale supply companies, such as Home Depot.

For others interested in houses of their own, manufactured and prefabricated houses were available through catalog stores such as Sears, Roebuck and Company; Montgomery Ward; and others during the early 20th century. By 1934, 100,000 of these houses had been sold. In 1927, Buckminster Fuller designed a mass-produced hexagonal house (Dymaxion House) that was suspended from a central mast and that could be transported to almost any site and rapidly set in place. Continued interest in economic, industrial housing eventually led to the mobile home, a housing type that became relatively popular in post–World War II society. The demand for manufactured homes created a new form of residential landscape, the trailer park. Although important primarily in the United States, popular house forms, including the ranch house and split-level, townhouses, apartment complexes, and another generation of revivalist styles (including the neo-Tudor, neo-Colonial, Midwest vernacular, and Postmodern or Deconstructivist), were designed to accommodate the lifestyles and changing tastes of suburban families and builders.

Changes to the financing of home construction and government legislation made it possible for more people to own their own homes and thus transformed the housing market in may parts of the world. The Housing and Town Planning Act (1919) in England and the Federal Housing Act (1934) in the United States, for example, committed both nations to housing issues. The United States created the Federal Housing Authority and a mortgage guaranty program to increase home ownership. After World War II, the Department of Veterans' Affairs operated a similar program for those who served in the military. The federal commitment to housing also led to greater commitment in the banking community. Mortgage credit played a vital role in the growth of home ownership in the United States, from 33 percent in 1891 to 65 percent in 1998. England had a similar increase.

After World War II, other countries undertook similar plans for legislation and changes to financial practices with modest success in increased home ownership. While in the first half of the century affluent households lived in mansions that generally repeated the local traditions or the architecture that was imported from colonial Western authorities, with the spread of modernism in the 1950s houses in these countries began to reflect the aesthetic practices of abstraction and the commitment to economy that were associated with the style. In the last part of the century, modernism was coupled with contextualist convictions about integrating architecture with local contexts. This perspective was practiced in most of the countries in the world.

The works of Luis Barragán (Las Arboledas, 1958–61), Hassan Fathy (house near Luxor, n.d.), Tadao Ando (Kidosaki House, 1982–86), and Herzog and De Meuron (Villa E.M., 1988–93) represent skillful examples of this integration.

Although the detached house continues to be an important and pervasive building type, by the end of the 20th century it received criticism from various perspectives. For phenomenologists, the transformation of the house in the 20th century has serious consequences for the human sense of well-being and the development of public life. Many critics raised concerns about the influences of technology—from the television to the Internet—on typical, everyday life in houses. Feminists argued that individual home ownership in low-density suburbs helped oppress women: it constrained their mobility and defined the social spaces granted to them. Others have argued that low-density suburban development has a significantly negative effect on the environment. Marxists have criticized the growth of home ownership because it has relied on rapid and excessive extension of consumer credit. Studies have also raised questions about the cultural appropriateness of modernist intentions and the vernacular alternative, which can perpetuate social inequities, status differentials, and economic disparities.

JEAN LA MARCHE

See also **Ando, Tadao (Japan); Barragán, Luis (Mexico); Deconstructivism; Dom-ino Houses (1914–15); Farnsworth House, Plano, Illinois; Fathy, Hassan (Egypt); Feminist Theory; Glass House, New Canaan, Connecticut; Hoffmann, Josef (Austria); Postmodernism; Pruitt Igoe Housing, St. Louis, Missouri; Robie House, Chicago; Rossi, Aldo (Italy); Schröder-Schräder House, Utrecht, Netherlands; Steiner House, Vienna; Vanna Venturi House, Philadelphia; Villa Savoye, Poissy, France**

Further Reading

Coleman, Debra, Elizabeth Danze, and Carol Henderson (editors), *Architecture and Feminism*, New York: Princeton Architectural Press, 1996

Gardiner, Stephen, *Evolution of the House*, New York: Macmillan, 1974; London: Constable, 1975

Marcus, Clare Cooper, *House As a Mirror of Self: Exploring the Deeper Meaning of Home*, Berkeley, California: Conari Press, 1995

Moore, Charles Willard, Gerald Allen, and Donlyn Lyndon, *The Place of Houses*, New York: Holt Rinehart and Winston, 1974

Oliver, Paul (editor), *Encyclopedia of Vernacular Architecture of the World*, Cambridge and New York: Cambridge University Press, 1997

Rapoport, Amos, *House Form and Culture*, Englewood Cliffs, New Jersey: Prentice-Hall, 1969

Riley, Terence, *The Un-Private House*, New York: Museum of Modern Art, 1999

Rybczynski, Witold, *Home: A Short History of an Idea*, New York: Viking, 1986

Rykwert, Joseph, *On Adam's House in Paradise: The Idea of the Primitive Hut in Architectural History*, New York: Museum of Modern Art, 1972; 2nd edition, Cambridge, Massachusetts: MIT Press, 1981

Van Vliet, Willem (editor), *The Encyclopedia of Housing*, Thousand Oaks, California: Sage, 1998

HOUSTON, TEXAS

In the mid-1970s, an article in *The New York Times* exulted, "Houston is *the* city of the second half of the twentieth century." Author Ada Louise Huxtable proclaimed it "the place that scholars flock to for the purpose of seeing what modern civilization has wrought" and "the city that has supplanted Los Angeles in current mythology as the city of the future." Currently the fourth-largest city in the United States, Houston has been among the fastest growing urban regions in the country for most of the postwar period. In the act of transforming itself from backwater to boomtown, its development has covered the featureless Gulf coast landscape, replacing pastures with skyscrapers at a mind-boggling pace. Sometimes called Instant City, Freeway City, Space City, or even a noncity, Houston has redefined urbanity in a way that is both tantalizing and deeply disturbing.

Three factors help explain the raw vitality of Houston's architectural and urban form. First, the blank-slate neutrality of both its populace and its site has provoked a kind of "anything goes" permissiveness for much of its history. The largest demographic group in the city seems always to be newcomers, and the flux of population is constant. Houston is a melting pot in the truest sense, neutralizing the history and character of the diverse people that come and go in favor of a new conglomeration. The similarly undifferentiated coastal prairie where the city resides is flat and featureless with no major rivers or other natural bodies of water. Even the port of Houston was made, not found. The effect of this blank-slate quality on architecture was well described by Ralph Adams Cram, who, when he began his work for the Rice University campus in 1909, found "a level and stupid site—no historic or stylistic precedent." He concluded, "Manifestly, the only thing to do was to invent something approaching a new style." Architects throughout the century felt a similar, unfettered release from the constraints of culture, geography, history, and precedent. In the right hands, the result has been buildings that are fresh, adventuresome, and full of derring-do. In the wrong hands, the results have ranged from banal to self-indulgent.

A second factor that has figured strongly in Houston's character is its long-standing commitment to individualism, personal freedom, and a resistance to controls. Houston is the only American city with no zoning laws. The city's transportation system (a primary urban form determinant) is based on optimizing individual choice, which means heavy reliance on the personal automobile. This factor, combined with almost complete dependence on the individual single-family home for housing stock, has created vast sprawl with endless freeway systems, strip developments, and big-box retail clusters. As Joel Garreau noted in his influential 1991 book *Edge City*, "Yes, Houston is nuts. But it's so much fun. There is so much individualism. You have so much freedom."

A third factor crucial in the shaping of Houston's architectural and urban form is money, specifically real estate profits. Founded by the Allen brothers as an entrepreneurial venture in 1836, the city has been called "an act of real estate, rather than an act of God or man." The doctrine of "highest and best use" is gospel. In Houston, the correct shape of the city has been deemed to be whatever someone thinks the marketplace will make most profitable on a lot-by-lot basis. Because the marketplace is notoriously unstable and unpredictable, the result is urban chaos—a cacophony of bonanzas and bankruptcies played out in the form of strip shopping centers, cul-de-sac subdivisions, office parks, fast-food joints, car lots, and malls.

The urban fabric that money, individualism, and the city's blank-slate neutrality have produced is both frightening and surprisingly livable. The jarring contrasts, visual blight, cultural emptiness, and sheer ugliness of much of the city are daunting to visitors. Yet Houstonians often find the city's freedom of expression and diversity of opportunity more than compensatory. Aside from the inevitable traffic problems, Houston works surprisingly well both socially and physically, belying much of what planners and urban designers have preached over the last half of the 20th century. People find places to live, work, and raise their families in amiable if somewhat stretched-out and circuitous patterns. A strong sense of community often occurs, although not in the traditional sense of a physical neighborhood.

The architecture of Houston evokes similarly conflicting reactions. The city's permissiveness has generated a generally low quality of architecture. More significant, however, the city's openness and freedom of expression has produced some isolated objects and enclaves of very great architectural distinction. Three Houston buildings of the latter part of the century have garnered significant international renown. Pennzoil Place (1976) by John-

Pennzoil Place Building, by Philip Johnson and John Burgee at Houston, Texas (1976)
© Mary Ann Sullivan

son/Burgee Architects and S.I. Morris Associates is the most striking pedigreed architectural object in the city. Composed of two 36-story towers, each with a trapezoidal plan and an angled top, the downtown office complex offers radically different perspectives when viewed from various parts of the city. A kind of minimalist freeway sculpture, Pennzoil's dark color, shifting geometries, and dramatic 10-foot slot between the towers confirmed again Philip Johnson as a prominent high-rise designer and brought developer Gerald Hines international recognition as a savvy client who knew how to combine high design and profitability.

If Pennzoil is the favored architectural emblem of Houston among the subculture of architecture, the Astrodome by Herman Lloyd and W.B. Morgan and Wilson, Morris, Crain and Anderson (1965) is its counterpart in popular culture. The first permanent air-conditioned sports facility built for football and baseball games, the Harris County Domed Stadium was the brainchild of larger-than-life politician and promoter, Judge Roy Hofheinz. It broke new ground for a generation of lavish sports palaces all over the United States that followed in the last decades of the 20th century. The 53 skyboxes, ostentatious club facilities, and lighted scoreboard (almost 500 feet long and four stories high) predicted the hallmarks of future stadium and arena design.

A third signature building of the city, The Menil Collection by Renzo Piano and Richard Fitzgerald and Partners (1987), contrasts sharply with Pennzoil Place and the Astrodome. The Menil draws its strength from subtlety and understatement. It is hidden away in an unprepossessing neighborhood to which it demurs graciously. The collaboration of client Dominique de Menil, architect Renzo Piano, and engineers Ove Arup and Partners has produced a quiet rectilinear structure with a white steel frame and an in-fill of gray cypress siding. The graceful S-shaped concrete "leaves" that top exterior porches and soften interior light quality are the tour de force of The Menil—refined, elegant, and particularly effective in creating a luminous environment ideal for viewing art.

Many significant architectural objects by well-known designers grace the city's skyline and isolated urban sites, including Republic Bank Center (1983) by Johnson/Burgee and Kendall/Heaton Associates, Texas Commerce Tower (1981) by I.M. Pei and 3D/International, and the Museum of Fine Arts Houston with contributions by Ralph Adams Cram (1924, 1926), Ludwig Mies van der Rohe (1958, 1974), and most recently, Rafael Moneo (2000). Several enclaves of great design distinction have also been influenced by renowned designers. The Rice University campus was originally planned by Cram, Goodhue and Ferguson in the early part of the century and now has buildings designed by Cesar Pelli, James Stirling, Antoine Predock, Ricardo Bofill, Tom Beeby, and other notable architects. The nearby St. Thomas campus boasts buildings designed by Philip Johnson from the 1950s to the 1990s. The Galleria/Post Oak district is a virtual beauty pageant of glittery architectural objects with works by I.M. Pei; Cesar Pelli; Philip Johnson; Skidmore, Owings and Merrill; and Hellmuth, Obata and Kassabaum.

Houston has produced many notable architects as well. William Ward Watkins, Alfred C. Finn, Kenneth Franzheim, Joseph Finger, John Staub, and Birdsall Briscoe, among others, made great contributions early in the century. Karl Kamrath, Howard Barnstone, Eugene Aubrey, Anderson Todd, William Cannady, Charles Tapley, and John Chase were among the leading practitioners in the postwar period. Firms such as Caudill Rowlett Scott, Neuhaus and Taylor; Golemon and Rolfe; Lloyd Jones Brewer and Associates; Pierce Goodwin Alexander; and Wilson, Morris, Crain and Anderson made architecture into big business. More recently, design-oriented practitioners, such as TAFT Architects and Carlos Jiménez, have made a significant mark as well.

LAWRENCE W. SPECK

Further Reading

In addition to the following books, a continuing Houston architecture and design review journal published by the Rice Design Alliance, *Cite* (3/year), is an excellent source of information on the city's development.

Barna, Joel Warren, *The See-Through Years: Creation and Destruction in Texas Architecture and Real Estate, 1981–1991*, Houston: Rice University Press, 1992

Barnstone, Howard, *The Architecture of John F. Staub: Houston and the South*, Austin: University of Texas Press, 1979

Feagin, Joe R., *Free Enterprise City: Houston in Political-Economical Perspective*, New Brunswick, New Jersey: Rutgers University Press, 1988

Fox, Stephen, and Gerald Moorhead, *Houston Architectural Guide*, Houston: American Institute of Architects, Houston Chapter, and Herring Press, 1990; 2nd edition, 1999

Garreau, Joel, *Edge City: Life on the New Frontier*, New York: Doubleday, 1991

Jiménez, Carlos, *Carlos Jiménez* (bilingual English-Spanish edition), Barcelona: Gustafo Gili, 1991

McComb, David G., *Houston, the Bayou City*, Austin: University of Texas Press, 1969; revised edition, as *Houston, a History*, 1981

Rowe, Peter G., *Making a Middle Landscape*, Cambridge, Massachusetts: MIT Press, 1991

HOWE, GEORGE 1886–1955 AND WILLIAM LESCAZE 1896–1969

Architects, United States

Although their partnership was short-lived, George Howe and William Lescaze were among the leaders of modernist architecture in the United States in the 1930s. Notwithstanding counterclaims by admirers of the work of Richard Neutra, Rudolf M. Schindler, and Frank Lloyd Wright, the significance of Howe and Lescaze's East Coast work in the International Style is at times overlooked, perhaps because of the limited duration of the partnership (1929–34), the small scale of most of the commissions, or the unbuilt status of some of the projects.

Early in his career, Howe designed a romantic villa ("High Hollow") for his family in Chestnut Hill, Philadelphia. It incorporated the spatial principles of his Beaux-Arts training, observations from travels in Italy, and the regional characteristics of Pennsylvania. In 1916, he entered the firm of Mellor and Meigs in Philadelphia and became a partner in the firm of Mellor, Meigs and Howe, where he remained through 1928. During the years 1921–24, Howe's major design activity centered on the Arthur E. Newbold, Jr., Estate in Laverock, Pennsylvania, a romantic country house based on the vernacular forms of French architecture in Normandy. Perhaps his first true exposure to

European modernism occurred in 1925, when he visited the Exposition Internationale des Arts Décoratifs in Paris.

In 1923, Lescaze opened a practice in New York, acquiring mostly small commissions and demonstrating throughout a natural inclination toward the International Style, which would become the dominant architectural force in the second quarter of the 20th century. It treats architectural form as volume rather than mass and seeks to liberate those forms from references to architectural history. Favoring asymmetry in plan as well as in elevation, the style features smooth, planar surfaces; the elimination of applied ornament; steel or concrete framing; and large expanses of glass. Lescaze's small-scale designs from this period include the Capital Bus Terminal (1927, now demolished) in New York, his first attempt to introduce the International Style to the eastern seaboard of the United States. In addition to some innovative interior design projects, he produced prototypical residential designs in the style, having been commissioned by both *Architectural Forum* and *Architectural Record*. Lescaze's 1928 unbuilt projects, an apartment house and garage at Broadway between 50th and 51st Streets and another apartment house at Park Avenue and 72nd Street, represent his experiments with a modernist vocabulary on a larger scale.

Lescaze was introduced to Howe in 1929, by which time Howe had already acquired the commission for what would be their most important work together, an office tower for the Philadelphia Saving Fund Society (PSFS), on a site at Market and 12th Streets near the Reading Terminal and Wanamaker's Department Store. Their partnership began in the same year and was characterized by a division of work not unlike that of Burnham and Root in Chicago 50 years earlier. Howe cultivated and developed business contacts, monitored agreements, and put forth concepts, whereas Lescaze was the chief designer, working on the development of architectural content and details.

In 1926, Howe had already developed a scheme, his first attempt at skyscraper design, for the president of the bank, James M. Willcox. It was a hybrid of Beaux-Arts emphasis on the masonry enclosure and Secessionist or Art Nouveau forms. The bank reconsidered its plans for an office tower, constructing in its place a small and temporary branch bank to Howe's design in 1927. By 1929, however, the society was ready to realize the more ambitious plan, and with their recent partnership, Howe and Lescaze were poised to introduce the International Style to the United States in a large-scale building, resulting in the pioneering form of the truly modern skyscraper.

Antecedents to the design are Howe's own scheme from 1926, in which he included spaces for retail shops at the street level, raising the banking floor up one level, and Knud Lönberg-Holm's entry to the 1922 Chicago Tribune Tower competition. Lescaze's sketches from December 1929 introduce the sweeping polished green granite and glass curtain wall base, with its rounded corner prefigured perhaps by the unitary broad curve of Erich Mendelsohn's Schocken store (1928–30) in Chemnitz, Germany, in addition to uninterrupted horizontal bands of glass, alternating with opaque spandrels, in the office tower above. The bank reserved three stories above its main public space for offices, and above those, the 32 speculative office floors are subtly cantilevered. The top was reserved for a penthouse suite and observatory, and the T-shaped plan allowed for the separation

PSFS Building, designed by Howe and Lescaze
(1932)
© GreatBuildings.com

of services (stairwells, elevators, and restrooms) from the offices. Distinct materials indicate different functions on the exterior: polished granite for the banking floor, sand-colored limestone for exterior columns on the east and west sides, gray brick for office-floor spandrels, and glazed and unglazed brick for the service tower. Set originally at a slight angle, a 27-foot-high sign with neon letters identifying the PSFS initials for the bank is visible for 20 miles. Although PSFS's expression of verticality, with its continuous externalized columns at the office floors, derives from the principles of the Sullivanesque tall office building, with its articulated wall, it also anticipates icons of skyscraper design of the 1950s: Lever House (1952, Skidmore, Owings and Merrill) in New York, with its cantilevered tower floating over an elevated horizontal pavilion, and Inland Steel (1954–58, Skidmore, Owings and Merrill) in Chicago, with its exoskeleton and fully discrete service tower. In 2000, PSFS became Loews Philadelphia Hotel, adapted by Bower Lewis Thrower Architects and Daroff Design.

Other notable works by the firm include Oak Lane County Day School (1929, demolished) in Oak Lane, Pennsylvania; high-rise projects for the Museum of Modern Art (1930–31), to conform to a typical Manhattan city lot, 60 feet wide and 100 feet deep; Hessian Hills School (1931–32) in Croton-on-Hudson, New York; and the Charles Edwin Wilbour Memorial Library (1933–34) at the Brooklyn Museum of Art.

After the dissolution of the partnership in 1935, Howe combined modernist forms with local materials. He worked with Louis I. Kahn (1901–74) and Oscar Storonov (1905–70), forming the firm of Howe, Storonov and Kahn, and later with Robert Montgomery (fl. 1946–58). From 1950 to 1954, Howe was chair of the Department of Architecture at Yale University. Lescaze's work independent of Howe included three painted stucco and glass-block houses on Manhattan's east side, one for himself (1932–33) at 211 East 48th Street, the first fully modern townhouse in the United States; a second for Raymond Kramer (1934) at 32 East 74th Street; and a third for Edward Norman (1941) at 124 East 70th Street. Comparing Lescaze's own house on East 48th Street with Howe's remodeled townhouse for Maurice J. Speiser in Philadelphia (1935) reveals the essential natures of two architectural personalities: the Lescaze House replaces an earlier row house, employing white-painted stucco and expanses of glass block and royal blue freestanding columns, and the Speiser House is fully contextual, employing conforming window heights, blending masonry, and retaining a mansard roof and dormer windows. During World War II, Lescaze worked with experimental materials and prefabrication, and by the end of his career he favored a Miesian idiom for office buildings in Manhattan.

Despite important careers independently and as the firm of Howe and Lescaze, the two architects will occupy a place in architectural history as the creative forces behind one building, the PSFS Building, a landmark in the evolution of the skyscraper, paradigmatic for its machinelike clarity.

PAUL GLASSMAN

See also **International Style; Lever House, New York City; Skidmore, Owings, and Merrill (United States); Skyscraper; Tribune Tower International Competition (1922), Chicago**

Biography

George Howe

Born on 17 June 1886 in Worcester, Massachusetts, George Howe studied architecture at Harvard University, graduating in 1907, and received a diploma from the École des Beaux-Arts in Paris in 1912, having joined the atelier of Victor Laloux. Returning to the United States, he joined the firm of Furness and Evans in 1913, shortly after the death of Frank Furness. He died in Philadelphia on 16 April 1955.

William Lescaze

Born in Onex (near Geneva), Switzerland, on 27 March 1896, William Lescaze attended the Eidgenossische Technische Hochschule in Zurich (1915–1919), studying with Karl Moser. Before arriving in the United States in 1920, he worked in the Paris office of Henri Sauvage. After a position in the firm of Walter R. MacCormack in Cleveland, Ohio, he opened a practice in New York in 1923. He died in New York on 9 February 1969.

Selected Publication

Lescaze, William, *On Being an Architect*, New York: Putnam, 1942

Selected Works

Designed by George Howe
High Hollow, Philadelphia, 1917
Arthur E. Newbold, Jr., Estate, Laverock, Pennsylvania, 1924
Philadelphia Saving Fund Society branch (demolished), Philadelphia, 1927
Maurice J. Speiser House (remodeling), Philadelphia, 1935

Designed by William Lescaze
Capital Bus Terminal (demolished), New York, 1927
Apartment house and garage (unbuilt), Broadway between West 50th and 51st Streets, New York, 1928
Apartment house (unbuilt), Park Avenue and East 72nd Street, New York, 1928
William Lescaze House and Office, New York, 1933
Raymond Kramer House, New York, 1934
Edward Norman House, New York, 1941

Designed by Howe and Lescaze
Oak Lane Country Day School (demolished), Philadelphia, 1929
High-rise projects for the Museum of Modern Art, New York, 1931
Hessian Hills School (now Temple Israel of Northern Westchester), Croton-on-Hudson, New York, 1932
Philadelphia Saving Fund Society (now Loews Philadelphia Hotel), Philadelphia, 1932
Charles Edwin Wilbour Memorial Library, Brooklyn Museum of Art, Brooklyn, New York, 1934

Further Reading

Hitchcock, Henry-Russell, Jr. and Philip Johnson, *The International Style*, New York: Norton, 1932; reprint, with a new foreword, New York and London: Norton, 1995
Hubert, Christian and Lindsay Stamm Shapiro, *William Lescaze*, New York: Rizzoli, 1982
Jordy, William H. and Robert A.M. Stern, "The Philadelphia Saving Fund Society," *Journal of the Society of Architectural Historians* 21 (May 1962)
Lanmon, Lorraine Welling, *William Lescaze, Architect*, Philadelphia, Pennsylvania: Art Alliance Press, and London: Associated University Presses, 1987
"A New Shelter for Savings: George Howe and William Lescaze, Architects," *Architectural Forum* 57 (December 1932)
"The Philadelphia Saving Fund Society Building," *Architectural Review* 73 (March 1933)
The PSFS Building, Twelve South Twelfth Street, Philadelphia, Pennsylvania: Philadelphia Saving Fund Society, 1976
Stephens, Suzanne, "Project Diary: The Landmark PSFS Building by Bower Lewis Thrower Architects and Daroff Design Is Reincarnated as a Loews Hotel," *Architectural Record* 188 (October 2000)
Stern, Robert A.M., *George Howe: Toward a Modern American Architecture*, New Haven, Connecticut: Yale University Press, 1975

HUNGARY

The history of Hungarian architecture in the 20th century developed between the opposite poles of traditionalism and modernity, or the search for national identity and international validity. Between 1876 and 1919, Hungary constituted one of the two states of the multinational Habsburg Empire, the Austro-Hungarian monarchy. The first two decades of the century were a period of the pluralism of styles. Beside the neostyles, such as Gothic Revival, neo-Renaissance, and their idiosyncratic variations, the most important tendencies were Art Nouveau, early modernism, and National Romanticism. The key monument of monumental historicism is the Parliament Building (1885–1904) on the Danube riverfront in Budapest by Imre Steindl. In Hungary, Art Nouveau architects developed forms that are still rooted in historicism but used floral ornaments and allegorical sculptural details. The major representative of this widespread and popular style was the Budapest office of Aladár Kármán and Gyula Ullmann (apartment house, 1899–1901, on Perczel Mór Street in Budapest). The biomorphism of French Art Nouveau was very rare in Hungary; its main example is the Reök Palace (1906–07, Ede Magyar) in Szeged. Ödön Lechner, the most discussed and most influential figure of the Hungarian "national style" at the turn of the century, was known for his highly individual ornamental language using the lessons of Oriental, primarily Indian, architecture. His most important works in Budapest are the Museum of Applied Art (1892–96), the Geological Institute (1899), and the Postal Savings Bank (1899–1901). Lechner's colorful facades, clad with glazed terra-cotta (known as Pyrogranite), attracted many followers who erected large public buildings in other Hungarian towns, such as the City Hall (1907) in Szabadka (present-day Subotica, Yugoslavia) and the Palace of Culture (1910) in Marosvásárhely (present-day Tirgu Mureş, Romania), both by Marcell Komor and Dezső Jakab, and the County Hall (1913) in Debrecen by Zoltán Bálint and Lajos Jámbor. József Vágó worked for Lechner early in his career, but he soon became influenced by the efforts of early modernism in Vienna by the architecture of Otto Wagner and Josef Hoffmann (toy store "Árkád Bazár," 1909, in Budapest).

Around 1908, a group of young architects pursuing the issue of a national style rejected Lechner's ornamentalism and urged architects to study the vernacular art and architecture of the Hungarian village. Known as the "Young Ones," they initiated National Romanticism in Hungary in close connection with similar tendencies in Scandinavia, first of all in Finland. They were also influenced by the goals of the English Arts and Crafts movement, the writings of John Ruskin, and the designs of William Morris. An interest for picturesque massing and for richer connections with the surrounding landscape or urban environment as well as the use of natural materials such as natural stone and wood characterize their buildings (Church, 1908–09, in Zebegény, Károly Kós and Béla Jánszky; Wekerle Colony, 1912–13, in Budapest, Károly Kós, Béla Eberling, and others; apartment building of the Reformed Church, 1911, in Kecskemét, Valér Mende; Elementary School, 1912, in Kiskunhalas, Dénes Györgyi; Protestant Church, 1913, in Kolozsvár (today Cluj, Romania) Károly Kós.

István Medgyaszay attempted to synthesize efforts of the national style with the aesthetics of Vienna modernism. He studied in the school of Otto Wagner but also participated in the fieldwork documenting the art of Transylvanian villages in the region of Kalotaszeg. His intention was to develop a modern aesthetic for reinforced-concrete structures based on the instinctive logic of vernacular wooden constructions. The main results of this search are the theaters in Veszprém (1908) and Sopron (1909) and the Catholic Church (1911) in Rárósmulyad (present-day Mul'a, Slovakia).

The buildings of Béla Lajta and Béla Málnai that were executed around 1910 represent a major achievement of early modernism in Hungary. Preferring durable materials such as brick and stone and using ornament sparingly, their buildings were esteemed by representatives of the avant-garde after the war (Commercial School, 1912, and Rózsavölgyi Store, 1911–13, both in Budapest, Béla Lajta; apartment house, 1911, on Eötvös Street in Budapest, Béla Málnai). Around 1910, classical references start to appear in the work of both offices (apartment block, 1910, on Visegrádi Street, Béla Málnai and Gyula Haász).

Building activity radically decreased during World War I (1914–18). The Austro-Hungarian monarchy lost the war and broke up into smaller national states. With the peace treaty of Trianon (1920), Hungary lost two-thirds of its historic territory to the surrounding countries. In a very difficult situation, Hungary's conservative government managed to restore the economy by the 1930s. After a failed attempt to introduce a Soviet-style "Republic of Councils" in 1919, the political restoration forced left-wing intellectuals such as László Moholy-Nagy, Marcel Breuer, and Farkas Molnár out of the country; they became important figures of the international avant-garde. In Hungary during the 1920s, a conservative neobaroque style dominated (Déry Museum, 1926, in Debrecen, Dénes Györgyi and Aladár Münnich; Franciscan Monastery, 1927, in Zalaegerszeg, Iván Kotsis). In the interwar period, new universities were built using an eclectic language of form in Szeged, Debrecen, and Pécs to replace lost centers of higher education. Some of the most attrac-

tive ensembles were created by architects who studied the Nordic Romanticism of Scandinavian countries, such as the Cathedral Square (1930) in Szeged by Béla Rerrich. In 1928, the cities of Pécs and Györ organized urban competitions for their master plans of future development. The artistic reconstruction of the baroque city center (1938) of Székesfehérvár by Iván Kotsis was a very successful urban intervention. Kotsis strengthened the historic image of the city by transforming buildings and public squares by careful interventions. The cultural and political connections with Italy were intensive. Novecento architecture influenced not only ecclesiastical architecture but also office buildings, such as the Hungarian Credit Bank (1938) in Debrecen by Jenő Padányi Gulyás.

After 1925, as the political climate became more liberal, some representatives of the avant-garde, such as Farkas Molnár and Fred Forbát, returned to Hungary. Joining forces with other followers of modernism, such as Pál Ligeti and József Fischer, they erected a number of villas and smaller apartment buildings for open-minded intellectuals (Schwarcz House, 1932, in Szeged and villa, 1932, on Lejtő Street in Budapest, Farkas Molnár; villa on Csatárka Street in Budapest, József Fischer). The social utopia of modernism was represented by the Hungarian CIAM (Congrès Internationaux d'Architecture Moderne) group with Farkas Molnár as its leader. The group organized exhibitions to demonstrate the connections between architecture, housing conditions, and social inequality. As by the mid-1930s modernism had abandoned its political goals, the style became increasingly popular in larger Hungarian cities. The office of Béla Hofstätter and Ferenc Domány realized large apartment blocks using innovative technology and new materials to provide luxurious dwellings (Dunapark apartment building, 1937, in Budapest). The airport (1936) in Budaörs by Virgil Bierbauer and László Králik also shows a freer application of modernist aesthetic principles than before. Many summerhouses and hotels in natural environment were built using regional materials, especially natural stone (Mecsek Hotel, 1936, in Pécs, László Lauber and István Nyíri; Summerhouse, 1936, in Mecsek at Pécs, Fred Forbát).

During World War II, many Hungarian cities suffered serious damage. After the war, great efforts were made to restore infrastructure, buildings, and factories. In the first years after the war, the influence of Le Corbusier was obvious in many new structures (Trade Union Headquarters, 1949, in Budapest, Lajos Gádoros, Gábor Preisich, and others). However, Hungary was situated within the zone of Soviet interest, and this helped the Communist Party assume political power in 1948. The party made radical changes in political and economic structure and abandoned a market economy (1948–89). The centralized plan economy forced the development of industry. During the 1950s, large-scale centers of heavy industry were built next to small, traditional settlements, such as Kazincbarcika, Ajka, Várpalota, Komló, Tatabánya, Ózd, and Pécs in coal-mining, metallurgical, and steel production areas. Sztálinváros (present-day Dunaújváros), a "socialist city" (master plan, 1950, Tibor Weiner), and the University of Heavy Industry in Miskolc (1952, István Janáky, György Jánossy, and others) were newly founded. Design and construction, like the whole economy, were nationalized and organized in large offices. In 1951, the Communist Party declared functionalist modern architecture cosmopolitan and decadent; Hungarian architecture now had the task to express the values of socialism. Architects studied the tradition of Hungarian classicism and used the lessons of the Scandinavian neoclassicism of Gunnar Asplund and Sigurd Lewerentz to avoid the imitation of more monumental Russian models. The most convincing examples of this tendency are the Cultural Center (1952) in Tolna by Béla Pintér, the County Hall (1952) in Debrecen by Péter Molnár, the Mining School (1953) in Várpalota by Gyula Rimanóczy, the Institute building "R" (1955) of the Technical University in Budapest by Gyula Rimanóczy, and the County Hall (1953) in Salgótarján by Pál Németh.

Modern architecture had slowly returned, already before the failed revolution against Communism in 1956. A process of liberalization started, and a productivist approach to modernism dominated Hungarian architecture from the 1960s on. Industrial architecture achieved international recognition; engineers and architects of the planning office IPARTERV designed industrial plants for the whole country, such as the heating plant (1959) in Pécsújhely by Gyula Mátrai, the cold-storage warehouse (1960) in Miskolc by László Csaba, and the Debrecen Cannery (1969) by Lajos Földesi. The construction of public health and higher education, cultural centers, trade union holiday hotels, and kindergartens and schools started on a larger scale, mostly using standardized plans and prefabrication. The spread of the International Style is represented by the Tátika Restaurant (1961) in Badacsony by Ferenc Callmeyer, the Hotel (1962) in Kecskemét by István Janáky, the University of Agriculture (1963) in Debrecen by Tibor Mikolás, the Hospital (1964) in Dunaújváros by Zoltán Farkasdy, hotels (1964) in Siófok by Endre Czigler, and the City Center (1965) in Salgótarján by Géza Magyar and György Szrogh. Regionalism was present in projects such as the Observatory (1964) on Piszkéstető mountain by György Szrogh and the Cultural Center (1969) in Orgovány by Károly Jurcsik. In 1968, a reform program was introduced to liberalize the economy. The monotony of prefabricated-concrete housing estates all over the country triggered increasing criticism. György Csete emphasized the role of ornament in humanizing large-scale housing construction in Pécs. The organic movement of Imre Makovecz, which soon gained international recognition, was also the result of the dissatisfaction with bureaucratic design methods. Makovecz and his young followers, Dezső Ekler, Sándor Dévényi, Tamás Nagy, and others, studied the anthroposophy of Rudolf Steiner and created a biomorphic architecture. The dominance of spectacular, shingle-covered roofs over circular or free-shaped plans is a significant characteristic of their architecture (Town-Center, 1984, in Zalaszentlászló and Catholic Church, 1987, in Paks, both by Imre Makovecz). The Bull's Head House (1988) in Pécs by Sándor Dévényi shows how Makovecz's growing success and the rise of Postmodernism in the West could result in an excessive use of ornamental forms. The regionalists were seeking at the same time more modest means of expression using stone, brick, or wood (Greek-Catholic Church, 1983, in Edelény, Ferenc Török; Schaár Museum, 1986, in Pécs, István Janáky, Jr.; Forest School, 1996, in Visegrád, Gábor Turányi). The VIDEOTON Cultural Center (1884) in Székesfehérvár by Péter Reimholz is a significant work of structuralism.

After the political change in 1989, the introduction of a free-market economy and a democratic government changed the organization of architectural design and building construction. The large state-owned planning offices disappeared, and private ones emerged. Multinational firms started to build headquarters or remodeled existing structures. Although the organic architecture of Imre Makovecz and his followers is still alive, the latest examples of American and Western European architecture are carefully studied; deconstructivism and High-Tech have their followers (VIDEOTON Compact Discs Workshop, 1989, in Székesfehérvár, János Dobai; Glaxo Wellcome Building, 1997, in Törökbálint, László Szász). Ecclesiastic architecture has also produced remarkable results (Catholic Church and School Center, 1995, in Miskolc, István Ferencz; Lutheran Church, 1996, in Dunaújváros, Tamás Nagy; Catholic High School and Dormitory, 1998, in Szeged, János Golda and Attila Madzin). Modern aesthetics and traditional craftsmanship characterize the small-scale buildings of the Farm for Disabled Children and Adolescents (1999) in Perbál by Péter Janesch and Tamás Karácsony.

KATALIN MORAVÁNSZKY-GYÖNGY AND ÁKOS MORAVÁNSZKY

Further Reading

Ferkai, András, "Hungarian Architecture Between the Wars" and "Hungarian Architecture in the Postwar Years," in *The Architecture of Historic Hungary*, edited by Dora Wiebenson and József Sisa, Cambridge, Massachusetts: MIT Press, 1998
Lesnikowski, Wojciech (editor), *East European Modernism: Architecture in Czechoslovakia, Hungary, and Poland between the Wars, 1919–1939*, New York: Rizzoli, 1996
Moravánszky, Ákos, *Competing Visions: Aesthetic Invention and Social Imagination in Central European Architecture, 1867–1918*, Cambridge, Massachusetts: MIT Press, 1998

HUXTABLE, ADA LOUISE
Architecture critic, United States

Ada Louise Huxtable is considered one of the leading architecture critics of the modern era. Over a period of 25 years, from 1963 to 1982, she wrote more than 800 articles commenting on contemporary buildings for the *New York Times*. Focusing exclusively on architecture, Huxtable's weekly, and sometimes biweekly, missives on local architectural projects became a fixture within the *New York Times*. Her concern with the quality of design and its impact on the urban fabric of New York raised awareness of the importance of architecture among New Yorkers.

Born and raised in New York, Huxtable studied art history at Hunter College and embarked on a career in interior design after graduation. While working at Bloomingdale's on a modern furniture design competition, she was introduced to Philip Johnson, who was then a curator at the Museum of Modern Art. Johnson hired Huxtable as assistant curator at the museum, where she worked with Johnson to produce several shows on modern architecture, including the work of Mies van der Rohe. After completing her graduate work at the New York University Institute of Fine Arts in 1950, she received a Fulbright grant to Italy, which she used to study modern Italian architecture of the 1920s and 1930s. On her return, she began to write on a freelance basis for *Art News* and *Progressive Architecture*. Her articles focused on local projects that demonstrated innovation in structure or design, and they were published regularly in a column titled "Progressive Architecture in America." By the late 1950s, Huxtable had applied for and received a Guggenheim grant to further her investigations into the contemporary architecture of New York. During this time, she published a guide to New York's classical architecture and, for the Municipal Art Society of New York, created several walking tours of New York architecture.

In 1963, Huxtable began working as an architecture critic for the *New York Times*. Ultimately, her position at the *New York Times* allowed her not only to raise public interest in architecture but also to extend the influence of the critic over the processes of architectural and urban design. Her writing focused on projects that the everyday reader found accessible rather than on high style or foreign designers. She believed that architecture should account for and respond to its urban context and that architecture must be not only functional but creative and pleasing as well. Her articles made architecture relevant to New Yorkers through a palpable emphasis on their own home, and in doing so she created popular demand for good design.

As an ardent conservationist, many of Huxtable's articles emphasized the importance of preserving the urban fabric of the city. While her humorous criticisms of new architecture resonated with her audience, her concern over and protection of the spaces that contributed to the character of New York created enthusiasm for maintaining old New York buildings. Huxtable promoted stronger zoning laws to preserve local spaces and to prevent modernist projects from obliterating viable neighborhoods with insensitive designs. She spoke out against projects that were disrespectful to the urban scale and scene, such as the demolition of Pennsylvania Station and the construction of the Olympic Tower, promoting the idea that social factors of design were equally important to artistic concerns.

A champion of modernism, Huxtable believed in the creative power and innovation of Modern architecture. For Huxtable, Modern architecture's social content, where the problems of society would be solved through good design, appropriately considered the functional and personal needs of the user, a fact that she argued superseded the artistic concerns. For Huxtable, it was more important that a building work for the human being, and she believed that Modern architecture contained the suitable creative properties to address this concern. In her later articles, she recognized that modernism had failed to measure up to its promise and had yielded to a new style, that of Postmodernism, the latter of which she defined as the reintegration of context into architecture, embodying it with a human meaning and scale.

Huxtable's work ultimately shaped the role of the critic, to the extent that she was awarded a Pulitzer prize in 1970, the first awarded for distinguished criticism. Her ideas were common sense rather than theoretical and appealed to a broad audience through a matter-of-fact, humorous tone. At their heart was a greater concern for the social context of a structure and how architecture would affect the general reader to whom Huxtable wrote. She carefully researched the economic, political, and legal issues involved in a project and injected a concern for preserving the urban fabric and generating a human scale for a design. Her ability to clarify the present architectural situation for her audience helped to bridge the gap between academy and practice.

CATHERINE W. ZIPF

See also **Johnson, Philip (United States); New York, New York; Postmodernism**

Selected Publications

The Architecture of New York: A History and Guide, Garden City, New York: Anchor Books, 1964

Architecture, Anyone? New York: Random House, 1986

Goodbye History, Hello Hamburger: An Anthology of Architectural Delights and Disasters, Washington, D.C.: Preservation Press, 1986

"The Ideal City," *Preservation*, 49/2 (March/April 1997)

Kicked a Building Lately? New York: Quadrangle/New York Times Book Co., 1976

"Is Modern Architecture Dead?" *Architectural Record*, 169/3 (October 1981)

Pier Luigi Nervi, New York: G. Braziller, 1960

"A Question of Quality," *AIA Journal*, 71/1 (January 1982)

"The Tall Building Artistically Reconsidered: The Search for a Skyscraper Style," *Architectural Record*, 192/1 (January 1984), 63–79

The Tall Building Artistically Reconsidered: The Search for a Skyscraper Style, New York: Pantheon, 1984

"The Troubled State of Modern Architecture," *Architectural Record*, 169/1 (January 1981)

The Unreal America: Architecture and Illusion, New York: New Press, 1997

Will They Ever Finish the Bruckner Boulevard? New York: Macmillan, 1970

Further Reading

Most of the best biographical and critical information on Huxtable is written by the critic herself (Huxtable [1982] above). An annotated bibliography of Huxtable's work, listing her articles in an easy-to-read format, can be found in Wodehouse. Wodehouse also includes articles written about Huxtable, dating to 1979. For a summary of Huxtable's impact on the architectural profession, see Stephens (1982). Stephens (1977) includes an analysis of Huxtable's contribution to women in the field of architecture.

"Architectural Criticism: Four Women," *Progressive Architecture*, 58 (March 1977)

Campbell, Robert, "A Conversation with Ada Louise Huxtable," *Architectural Record*, 181/4 (April 1993)

Pevsner, Nikolaus, "Books: The Modern Movement: Theory and Criticism," *Journal of the Society of Architectural Historians*, 38 (March 1979)

Richardson, Margaret, "Women Theorists," *Architectural Design*, 45 (August 1975)

Stephens, Suzanne, "Ada Louise Huxtable," in *Women in American Architecture: A History and Contemporary Perspective*, edited by Susanna Torre, New York: Whitney Library of Design, 1977

Stephens, Suzanne, "Times without Huxtable: Ada Louise Huxtable in Perspective," *Skyline* (March 1982)

Wodehouse, Lawrence, *Ada Louise Huxtable: An Annotated Bibliography*, New York: Garland, 1981

I

ILLINOIS INSTITUTE OF TECHNOLOGY

Designed by Ludwig Mies van der Rohe,
completed 1956
Chicago, Illinois

The first work executed by Ludwig Mies van der Rohe (1886–1969) in the United States, the campus of the Illinois Institute of Technology (IIT) in Chicago represents the fullest embodiment of modernist planning principles applied to the renovation of the city at midcentury. The campus is also notable as a site for Mies' development of industrial building techniques in the service of modernist spatial principles. Ultimately, IIT's most enduring significance is as a site for the direct architectural expression of steel-frame construction applied across scales from the individual structural member to the overall urban plan. The resulting campus and the 22 original structures completed by Mies between 1939 and 1956 remain among the seminal works of 20th-century architecture and planning in the Western Hemisphere.

After the rise of Fascism in his native Germany, Mies resigned as director of the Bauhaus on its closure by the Nazis. Already an architect and educator of international stature, Mies accepted the directorship of the School of Architecture at the Armour Institute of Technology and immigrated to Chicago in 1938. With this appointment, Mies also accepted the commission to prepare plans for the institute's rapidly expanding campus.

Developed as a regional technical institute with funding from the eponymous meatpacking fortune, the Armour Institute of Technology was housed on Chicago's near south side. On its merger with the Lewis Institute in 1940, the institution was renamed the Illinois Institute of Technology, and its mission grew to include the creation of a world-class technical institute for the American Midwest comparable with those on the East and West Coasts.

Mies' preliminary scheme for the smaller campus (1939) exhibits a set of principles that would continue to inform all work done on the site. First was the erasure of the existing Chicago grid and its building fabric, leaving a blank slate for development. Second was the organization of a series of prismatic rectangular volumes sliding past one another in a series of local cross-axial compositions, resulting in a continuous flow of exterior space. Third was the use of industrialized building components,

including steel framing and large glass panels on a monumental scale. Fourth was the introduction of a thin carpet of landscape dotted with occasional plantings as a compensatory residue from the process of urban erasure.

Mies' final plans for the larger campus as partially implemented (1940) employ a 24-by-24-foot planning module as an organizing element for the entire site. The 24-foot dimension was selected for its economy and utility as a structural spanning dimension in steel-frame construction as well as its flexibility as an interior-planning dimension for classrooms, offices, and labs. This modular dimension system related interior and exterior spaces and ensured the integration of individual building components, such as columns and beams, with the overall planning strategy of the campus.

The first building completed on the campus, the Minerals and Metals Research Building (1942–43), revealed Mies' interest in the articulation of a language of building construction based on the expression of the structural steel frame. The precise relation of steel column, fireproofing, representational steel mullion, brick panels, and glass curtain wall posed a series of architectonic and technical questions that Mies and architects of the Second Chicago School would work to articulate and solve for three decades. Subsequent work for the unrealized Library and Administration Building Project (1944) extended this research to Mies' ongoing interest in long-span spaces. These first two projects developed the palette of regularly dimensioned steel-frame buildings that would inform the Institute Buildings (1945) as well as the exceptionally dimensioned long-span structures that would be consummated with the completion of Mies' masterpiece, Crown Hall (1950–56), designated a National Historic Landmark in 2001.

Crown Hall was conceived as a single interior volume completely enclosed by glass and devoid of any interior structural members. As an expression of direct construction, the clarity of its spatial volume and subtlety of its structural system reinforce each other to produce the site's single most powerful architectonic statement and one of Mies' most important works. In a series of significant deviations from the majority of buildings on the campus, Crown Hall was developed as a hierarchically important exception to, as well as an ultimate reinforcement of, Mies' overall strategy for the campus and has been considered his most valued commission at IIT.

Crown Hall (1956), Illinois Institute of Technology
© GreatBuildings.com

Intended as both an architectural and a pedagogical act, the clear-span space of Crown Hall served as both a site for and a subject of Mies' educational program at IIT. Ultimately, the IIT curriculum itself became canonical as a reductive and systemic application of Miesian principles of the building art applied within a rigorous system of architectural education. This educational model would become world renowned as generations of architects were trained under Miesian principles and disseminated those beliefs through their buildings, writings, and teachings.

One of two Bauhaus faculty members to emigrate with Mies to form the initial faculty at IIT, Ludwig Hilberseimer (1885–1967) was an influential modernist planner and theoretician in his own right before coming to the United States. Hilberseimer's earlier urban projects and writings reveal his commitment to modernist principles of urban planning that can also be found in Mies' work at the IIT campus. The influence of Mies' associate can be seen in a number of planning decisions taken on the campus, including the reliance on decreasing the density of building fabric and the use of landscape elements as a continuous horizontal carpet of urban ground. Although Hilberseimer had no formal role in the planning of IIT, his proximity to the process is best evidenced by the resonance of the IIT campus plan with the results of his subsequent collaboration with Mies for Lafayette Park (1956) in Detroit and other later works.

An important contributor to the IIT campus, Alfred Caldwell (1903–98) was responsible for the design and planting of the campus landscape. Caldwell's thin carpet of horizontal vegetation, although only partially implemented, constructed the site's ground plane as an element of spatial and material continuity. Caldwell, also an early member of the IIT faculty, employed a regional palette of landscape plantings as a counterpoint to the essentially placeless abstraction of Miesian space and industrialized building construction at the IIT campus.

CHARLES WALDHEIM

See also **Chicago (IL), United States; Hilberseimer, Ludwig (United States, Germany); Mies van der Rohe, Ludwig (Germany)**

Further Reading

Domer, Denis, *Alfred Caldwell: The Life and Work of a Prairie School Landscape Architect*, Baltimore, Maryland: Johns Hopkins University Press, 1997
Frampton, Kenneth, *Modern Architecture: A Critical History*, London: Thames and Hudson, and New York: Oxford

University Press, 1980; 3rd edition, London: Thames and Hudson, 1992

Hays, K. Michael, *Modernism and the Post Humanist Subject: The Architecture of Hannes Meyer and Ludwig Hilberseimer*, Cambridge, Massachusetts: MIT Press, 1992

Lambert, Phyllis (editor), *Mies in America*, Montreal: Canadian Centre for Architecture, 2001

Mertins, Detlef (editor), *The Presence of Mies*, New York: Princeton Architectural Press, 1994

Neumeyer, Fritz, *Mies van der Rohe: Das kunstlose Wort*, Berlin: Siedler, 1986; as *The Artless Word: Mies van der Rohe on the Building Art*, Cambridge, Massachusetts: MIT Press, 1991;

Pommer, Richard, David Spaeth, and Kevin Harrington, *In the Shadow of Mies: Ludwig Hilberseimer, Architect, Educator, and Urban Planner*, Chicago: Art Institute of Chicago, 1988

Schulze, Franz, *Mies van der Rohe: A Critical Biography*, Chicago: University of Chicago Press, 1985

Schulze, Franz (editor), *Mies van der Rohe: Critical Essays*, New York: Museum of Modern Art, 1989

Spaeth, David, *Mies van der Rohe*, New York: Rizzoli, and London: Architectural Press, 1985

IMPERIAL HOTEL

Designed by Frank Lloyd Wright, completed 1922
Tokyo, Japan

The Imperial Hotel, located in Tokyo, Japan, was designed by Frank Lloyd Wright between 1916 and 1922. Wright's interest in Asian arts is generally traced to the 1890s, when he saw an authentic Japanese pavilion on display at the World's Columbian Exposition of 1893 in Chicago. In 1905 Wright made the first of several trips to Japan to collect Japanese woodcut prints and study Japanese architecture. On his return to the United States, he displayed his collection and used his experience with Japanese architecture to obtain commissions in the Far East. Although the events surrounding Wright's receipt of the Imperial Hotel commission are unclear, his background and his interest in Japanese art made him a highly suitable candidate for the job. The Imperial Hotel readily displays Japanese principles of architecture, and it serves as one of the more prominent examples of Wright's work abroad.

On receiving the commission from a governing board of directors, Wright was instructed to replace the old, dilapidated, traditional, wood-framed Imperial Hotel with a new, larger structure made of brick and stone. In plan, Wright's structure formed an H with two crossbars in which he placed the public facilities. These facilities included the lobby, dining room, theater, banquet rooms, garden, tea balcony, lounge, shops, post office, and the Peacock Room, which was the centerpiece of the design. Along the sides of the H, Wright designed three levels of individual rooms, each containing built-in furniture and a balcony. On the exterior, the balconies created a dynamic yet rhythmic facade to hide the building's full seven-story height. Wright intended the facade to be low in profile but grand in decoration, which he believed fit with traditional principles of Japanese architecture. In terms of decoration, Wright contrasted brick, his primary building material, with a lava stone called *oya*, a highly porous and easily carved material. *Oya* was native to Japan, and Wright's use of the material tied the design of the hotel to its natural context. The stone's color, ranging from gray-green to a light umber, also created a polychromatic effect

on both the exterior and the interior of the structure and helped to energize the design.

Because Wright was acutely aware of the frequency of earthquakes in Japan, he accounted for this possibility in his structural scheme. Traditionally, Japanese architecture was timber framed and therefore easily reparable after a natural disaster. Wright, however, intended to work in stone, and he supported the additional weight of the stone by placing his building on a series of preformed-concrete slabs. Underneath, the slabs rested on thin concrete piles that were driven to a depth of eight feet through a layer of mud and placed at two-foot intervals throughout the foundation area. Wright reasoned that the piles would permit the slabs to float on the mud, allowing the mud to cushion the building during an earthquake. The frequency of the pins and the flexibility of the slabs would help the building absorb earthquake tremors in a tensile manner instead of breaking against competing forces.

Although this unique structural system accounted for the difference in weight between stone and timber, it also necessitated that Wright design a lighter-than-average masonry building to rest on the piles. To this end, he carved away at the solidity of his stone walls, creating an interior of interpenetrating voids where different ceiling heights and wall placements defined each room. This idea appeared best in the public rooms, where space flowed from room to room in all three dimensions. Although each room was a separate area, it was easy to walk from the lounge to the dining room to the tea balcony. In total, Wright's design embodied what he termed "organic architecture," which meant not only that space continued from part to part but that the design embodied natural principles and was not rigid or forced in any manner. This fluidity in the spatial organization recalled the writings of Chinese philosopher Lao-Tzu, who argued that the reality of the building was the space within. Ultimately, the experience of the design made the building seem even more Asian in its conception.

Following his well-established principle of a totally designed environment, Wright included patterns for the decorations, furniture, sculpture, and landscape space in his architectural scheme. His decorative motifs were linear and recalled earlier Japanese designs through their common emphasis on simplicity. Wright wrote extensively on the Asian principles of balance in design, and he praised the Japanese for knowing how to use simple forms to convey a basic theme without too much detail. As Wright argued, Japanese design encouraged each line to work toward the whole but did not include any line that was extraneous. His decorative motifs for the Imperial Hotel were therefore simple, without overwrought detail, and were generally based on pure geometric forms. The dining room chairs, for example, used hexagons for the primary motif, whereas the ceilings and walls were decorated with inset squares. Wright used geometric cutouts for his light fixtures to create a play of shadows over repetitive but moving forms. In the Peacock Room, his ceiling had multiple planes that intersected according to an easily visible geometric pattern. He even designed railings, frames, and floors according to these themes such that the entire environment was subjected to his overall design scheme.

In 1923, shortly after the completion of the Imperial Hotel, Tokyo experienced an earthquake of epic proportions. Although the Kanto quake leveled most of Tokyo's buildings, the Imperial Hotel sustained only minor damage, a substantial feat that pro-

Imperial Hotel, Tokyo (1922)
© The Frank Lloyd Wright Foundation

pelled it to legendary status. Wright took immense pride in the success of his design, and his accomplishment brought him back to the forefront of the architectural profession. In subsequent years, the Imperial Hotel received several additions, all of which ignored the character of the building, and new plumbing and electrical mechanics sliced through Wright's original scheme. By the 1960s, the Imperial Hotel had been further damaged by the industrial atmosphere of Tokyo and by a structural imbalance caused by the installation of Tokyo's subway system. In 1967, when skyrocketing land values and a decreasing clientele made the area occupied by the Imperial Hotel extremely valuable, the hotel was demolished, despite massive protest. Perhaps partly because of Wright's fame, the Imperial Hotel still occupies an important place in the architectural history of Japan, and its survival of the Kanto earthquake will not soon be forgotten.

CATHERINE W. ZIPF

See also **Hotel; Toyko, Japan; Wright, Frank Lloyd (United States)**

Further Reading

For a good history of Wright's work in Japan, see Kostka. Wright's version of the history of the Imperial Hotel can be found in Wright and Futagawa. Two concise and informative biographies of Wright are Gill, a more accessible version, and Twombly, which presents an academic approach to Wright's life. An analysis of the design can be found in Alofsin.

Alofsin, Anthony, *Frank Lloyd Wright: The Lost Years, 1910–1922*, Chicago: University of Chicago Press, 1993

Birk, Melanie (editor), *Frank Lloyd Wright's Fifty Views of Japan: The 1905 Photo Album*, San Francisco: Pomegranate Artbooks, 1966

Burns, Ken, and Lynn Novick, *Frank Lloyd Wright: A Film by Ken Burns and Lynn Novick* (videorecording), Washington, D.C.: PBS, 1998

Futagawa, Yukio (editor), *The Imperial Hotel, Tokyo, Japan, 1915–22*, Tokyo: A.D.A. Edita, 1980

Gill, Brendan, *Many Masks: A Life of Frank Lloyd Wright*, New York: Putnam, 1987; London: Heinemann, 1988

James, Cary, *The Imperial Hotel: Frank Lloyd Wright and the Architecture of Unity*, Rutland, Vermont: Tuttle, 1968; as *Frank Lloyd Wright's Imperial Hotel*, New York and London: Dover, 1988

Kostka, Robert, *Frank Lloyd Wright in Japan*, Park Forest, Illinois: Prairie School Press, 1966

Levine, Neil, *The Architecture of Frank Lloyd Wright*, Princeton, New Jersey: Princeton University Press, 1996

Lind, Carla, *The Lost Buildings of Frank Lloyd Wright: Vanished Masterpieces*, London: Thames and Hudson, 1996

Nute, Kevin, *Frank Lloyd Wright and Japan: The Role of Traditional Japanese Art and Architecture in the Work of Frank Lloyd Wright,*

London: Chapman and Hall, and New York: Van Nostrand Reinhold, 1993

Twombly, Robert C., *Frank Lloyd Wright: His Life and His Architecture*, New York: Wiley, 1979

Wright, Frank Lloyd, *An Autobiography*, New York and London: Longman's Green, 1932

INDIA

Twentieth-century architecture in India is a product of diverse regional practices and historical precedents, the country's colonial legacy, and the policies adopted by the independent state. Individual aspirations as well as visions of the collective—nation, class, and religious affiliation—have also left their imprints on this matrix. The proliferation of stylistic labels in recent discussions of 20th-century architecture in India—Indo-Deco, Anglo-Indian modern, neovernacular, and Bania-Gothic—some invoked more humorously than others, indicate not only the multiple agencies at work but also a problem of description. More specifically, this is a conceptual problem of situating Indian architecture in the matrix of a global culture and the century-long effort to tease out what is "Indian."

Far from being a monolithic construct, the multifarious notions of Indian identity shifted numerous times during the century. Certain assumptions, however, underlay all discussions of architecture: that modernity had no originary roots in India and was of European import, implying that Modern architecture in India was derivative; that any notion of Indian architecture must retain connection to the traditional architecture of the country, in contrast to Euro-American modernism, which claimed a break with the past; and finally that the task of Indian architects was to develop a regional vocabulary. The first assumption was based on a British colonial discourse that viewed Indian culture as static and maintained that any change must be due to foreign influence. Although Indian nationalists argued that change could be home wrought, most viewed groundedness in a pre-British tradition a necessary condition for a modern Indian identity. Those, such as Jawaharlal Nehru, India's first prime minister, who deviated from this norm, ensured that Le Corbusier's modernist design of Chandigarh would be treated as a watershed in Indian architecture. The changing ideology of state patronage in independent India from a modern international outlook after independence to a modern valorization of Indian tradition since the 1980s has invited a narrative of Indian architecture that constructs the latter as a sign of independence and originary acts. A small coterie of Indian architects who are central to this late-20th-century development have ensured through writings and interviews that their work is understood within frames of reference set by themselves, most important, that these acts of tradition are read back as universal gestures (and not simply as application of universal principles to a local vocabulary creating variation on a modernist theme). In a larger perspective, this ability to determine the narrative of contemporary architecture is a significant change from the beginning of the century, when Indian architects operated with limited power under colonial rule.

Preindependence Architecture

At the beginning of the century, the major cities showcased the work of the reigning Anglo-Indian firms, such as Martin and Co. in Calcutta, William A. Chambers and Co., Hall and Batley in Mumbai (then Bombay), and Jackson and Barker in Chennai (then Madras). The establishment of architectural education programs (the J.J. School of Arts in Mumbai augmented its five-year diploma in 1913) as well as the formation of the Indian Institute of Architects in 1929 increasingly formalized professional practice. By the 1920s, more and more Indian architects were securing commissions, and architectural firms, such as Master, Sathe, Bhuta, and Maherwanjee Bana and Co. in Mumbai, enjoyed the patronage of wealthy Indian industrialists.

In terms of architectural design, some important changes were taking place. Designers in urban areas were responding to new technology, such as electrical lighting, elevators, and the widespread use of indoor plumbing and to changing conceptions of privacy and gender structure in both European and Indian residences. The three-bay bungalow plans with a hall in the center and two rows of rooms on either side and its counterpart, the urban courtyard house, were being replaced by a larger variety of house plans that used bay windows, oblong rooms, and rounded verandas. Designers clearly intended to distinguish between the use of rooms and used corridors for separating functions and people. The practice of aggregating spaces in terms of use and incorporating an elaborate network of passages had already transformed the plans of institutions and office buildings. Now a classical treatment of the exterior, the hallmark of respectability in the early 19th century, and the official neo-Gothic and Indo-Saracenic were supplemented with a number of stylistic variations inspired by Art Deco and inquiry into Indian architectural vocabulary. The New India Assurance Building (1935) in Mumbai, a reinforced-concrete structure by Master, Sathe, Bhuta, was a symbol of modern outlook in business adopted by the Tata Company, a leading Indian industrial house. It was meant to be distinguished from its contemporaries, such as the Statesman House (1931) in Calcutta by Sudlow, Ballardie, and Thomas and the late 1920s projects for the Indian Tobacco Company on Chowringhee Road by Martin and Co. The latter had conventional *partis* and attempted to fit into the colonial neoclassical surroundings. In contrast, the Assurance Building had an open plan, then synonymous with business efficiency, and a forced-air cooling system that was complemented by adequate natural ventilation as a contingency plan.

The bold vertical elements of this six-story facade competed with a new building type, the movie theater, which also used this Art Deco treatment to emphasize a novel identity. Buildings such as the Eros Cinema in Mumbai, designed by Sohrabji K. Bhedwar in the 1930s, also cropped up in Calcutta, Chennai, Patna, and other cities. Located at prominent street locations with highly illuminated facades, theaters were designed to convey the fantasy world of movies. The entrance foyer, bar and lounge, and sweeping staircases were dressed in marble and adorned with murals, etched glass, and chandeliers. These public spaces were one of the few places the middle class could celebrate elegant life. For a section of the growing middle class, at least, there was a domestic counterpart to the Modern approach to design exemplified by the Assurance Building and the cinemas. The architects of numerous residential projects between the 1930s and 1950s resorted to fluid lines in designing the building envelope. This aesthetic agreed with the need to provide continuous shade over windows and with the building codes that stipulated uniform setbacks to render coherence to the street view and yet allowed individual residences to project modern aspirations of the nuclear families for which they were designed. Apartments in the Back Bay in Mumbai and detached residences in Ballygunge in Calcutta are classic examples of this era.

Although this kind of domestic architecture has become inseparable from Indian middle-class respectability, to contemporary architects, such as Sris Chandra Chatterjee (1873–1966), their looks did not denote Indianness. He advocated "an internal arrangement suitable for modern life" but a decorative program directly derived from ancient Indian architecture. Pattern books, such as A.V.T. Iyer's *The Indian Architecture* (1926), recommended "a proper national style" by adapting colonial building types to reflect classical Indian notions of beauty. This was contrary to 19th-century residential designs for the Indian middle class in which a traditional *parti* was augmented by a "modern" neoclassical facade. If in the 19th century the inner space of domestic life was considered the repository of Indian values, that identity was now to be translated in a clearly recognizable vocabulary on the public face. Of course, Chatterjee's ideas were not restricted to residential design alone; his suggestions for banks and educational institutions demonstrated the attempt to define a "Greater Indian Order" by assimilating elements from different regions and eras of India's ancient architecture. Chat-

Indira Gandhi Institute for Development, designed by Uttam Jain (1987)
Photo courtesy Uttam Jain © Aga Khan Award for Architecture

terjee's vision documented in the "Draft Manifesto for the Proposed All-India League of Indian Architecture" found a number of prominent supporters but was not persuasive enough to determine the narrative of Indian architecture.

The desire to define a national language of architecture appropriate for the 20th century came out of the *swadeshi* movement. *Swadeshi* (national), a response to British economic and cultural domination, meant the rejection of foreign goods and support for native industries. This *swadeshi* quest in the arts was grounded in a "new Orientalism" that found enduring aesthetic merit in India's ancient (mainly "Hindu") tradition and believed in a revival of that tradition as the necessary basis for a modern Indian art as opposed to its 19th-century British Orientalist view that belittled this tradition. The *swadeshi* spirit in architecture, however, took various forms, from a championing of the local vernacular to pan-Asianism. The Japanese victory in the Russian-Japanese War (1905) injected a confidence in Asian power and a desire for a pan-Asian solidarity in the arts. A remarkable celebration of such a pan-Asian aesthetic was the resident of Nobel laureate poet and novelist Rabindranath Tagore in Santiniketan, Bengal.

Tagore established a school (later to become Viswa Bharati University) at Santiniketan with the objective of providing an education that would be nurtured in an idyllic natural surrounding reminiscent of the ancient forests (*tapavan*) where the sages of the Vedas were said to have resided. He rejected the unimaginative regimen of the British school system and its urban moorings in Calcutta. Of the many residences that were designed for Tagore by Surendranath Kar with the aid of Nandalal Bose and the poet's son Rathindranath Tagore, the largest was named "Udayan" (facing the rising sun). The multilevel design of the building (1919–28) was developed in several phases, and its unusual qualities resided in the attempt to break out of the confines of the room as a unit of habitation. Its staggered terraces reached out to "connect with nature" from various vantage points, and its eclectic decorative program was intended to create different moods in different spaces and owed much to Japanese wood interiors. The richness of the decoration was also hierarchically layered, with decorative features disappearing at the topmost level, where the empty form alone would provide repose. The ideas embedded in the house plan appear to have stepped out of the gender hierarchies of the 19th-century Calcutta mansion that he grew up in (with its separation between the inner apartments for women and outer apartments for men), but the necessity of a laboring population to serve the master house had not disappeared. A substantial single-story building, housing kitchen, storage, and servants' quarters, was constructed as a separate attached structure. Although not conventionally "revivalist," Udayan was as much a symbol of the poet's personality as it was of the emergent nations.

The use of Indian referents in such well-known buildings was invariably perceived as a political statement in light of the planning process of New Delhi (1911–31). The neobaroque plan of New Delhi and the design of the capitol buildings by Edwin Lutyens and Herbert Baker were meant to impress British resolution to rule India despite Indian nationalist agitation. The new capital, with its insistent differentiation along lines of race, class, and occupation, was to enshrine in stone the relation between the rulers and the ruled.

Postindependence Practices

The independent state inherited the impressive monuments of New Delhi as well as an inadequate physical infrastructure, a weak economic and industrial base, and a massive housing shortage. The latter was exacerbated by the influx of refugees from Pakistan following the bloody partition of the country as the cost of independence. Primary industries, power generation, self-sufficiency in food grains, and housing were national priorities. As a socialist democracy, the state shouldered the responsibility of much of the building activity that took place in the formal sector. The state's intervention had a profound influence over architectural expression throughout the rest of the century.

Instead of making Indian motifs secondary to the building program, as in the case of Lutyens's design, architects after independence, at the behest of politicians, made them central to their scheme. If the overscaled entrance to the Vigyan Bhavan (1955) in New Delhi by R.I. Gehlote demonstrated the possibility of manipulating ancient formal elements while keeping the cord of historical association intact, the abundant decorations in the Vidhana Soudha (1952–57) in Bangalore strove to assert the viability of the traditional building craft in India. The architects of Mysore's Public Works Department sought out experts in the decorative arts of the South and constructed a building shunning new materials, such as glass and steel. The latter stood opposite the neoclassical High Court (1865) and replicated its plan and section in spirit. A decorative program paying tribute to Kannada culture adorned the building's profile and structural members. The proud originator of this idea, Kengal Hanumanthiah, the chief minister of Mysore (present-day Karnataka), is memorialized in front of the building, standing with a model of the building in the palm of his hand. The building program, the siting, and the sculpture were telling of identity and power at stake in the newly formed nation-state. Viewed from one angle, Hanumanthiah's conception of the building offered less resistance to the British colonial legacy than it did to the modernist architectural vision that was unfolding contemporaneously in Chandigarh. From another perspective, it demonstrated that the formal conception was often not the most important platform for expressing independence; rather, it was the question of who had the power to make decisions regarding major financial and cultural investments.

The most celebrated example of state-sponsored construction was the planning of Chandigarh (1951–57), the capital of the new states of Punjab and Haryana. At the invitation of Jawaharlal Nehru, the Department of Public Works appointed Le Corbusier and a team of consultants—Pierre Jeanneret, Jane Drew, and Maxwell Fry—to design the city and several important buildings. The largest commission of Le Corbusier's life became an opportunity to explore his notions of a modern city and modern monuments. The spacious 1200-by-800-meter city grid with its low-density built form was designed with an affluent car-owning citizen in mind and ignored lessons from contemporary Indian urbanism. Taken together, the Assembly Building, the Secretariat, and the High Court presented an array of formal possibilities of reinforced concrete in a context that offered brilliant sunshine and manual labor. Considered individually, their objectlike presence, the pragmatic concerns of users, and the weatherworn concrete expose the lapses in design consideration. Nehru had supposedly intended Chandigarh as shock therapy

for the nation—an expensive way for exorcising the ghost of colonialism that continued to haunt the policies and politics in the region for years to come. Formal experiments in modernism, however, were not new in India. The Dining Hall (1947) of the Institute of Science in Bangalore by Otto Koenigsberger, the New Secretariat (1944–47) in Calcutta by Habib Rahman, the Shodhan House (1939, now demolished) in Ahmedabad by Atmaram Gajjar, and the Golconda (1936–48) in the Aurobindo Ashram in Pondicherry by Antonin Raymond predated Chandigarh, as did many others. Chandigarh differed from these examples in the objectives and the scale of undertaking and in the charisma of the architect himself but most of all in the explicit ideology that accompanied it. Nehru had supported other approaches to architecture as well, many of which were conspicuous in their "traditional" referents. However, it was not traditional forms but the social premise and cultural baggage that accompanied the forms that he found problematic. He was contemporaneously fighting legislative battles to keep in place his vision of a secular democracy that did not discriminate on the basis of caste, class, gender, or religion with the excuse of tradition. Although he did not determine (nor did any one individual) all the aspects of city plan or building design, Nehru envisioned Chandigarh as his political legacy—the daring to experiment with new ideas and his belief that a new democracy deserved a novel architectural form.

The architectural imaging of Nehru's vision of a modern, industrial nation found several subscribers and continued well into the 1970s. Achyut P. Kanvinde's design for the Milk Processing Plant (1974) at Mehsana relied on a heroic gesture of turning the ordinary and mechanical functions of a factory into a theatrical interplay of form and light. Few examples, however, were more telling of national architectural aspirations and limitations than the commission for the Permanent Exhibition Complex for the 1972 Trades Fair in New Delhi. The building designs by Mahendra Raj, an architect turned structural engineer, and Raj Rewal were contemplated as steel space frames to span 78- and 44-meter modules unencumbered by supports, but ultimately it was constructed of reinforced concrete when the cost of steel construction proved prohibitive.

The more mundane cult of the concrete—a brick-filled reinforced-concrete frame with a concrete flat-slab roof and concrete ledges and shades—used en masse in government housing projects and institutions became the most common language of architecture across the country. Invariably distinguished into income groups—higher, middle, and lower income—hundreds of housing projects for government employees and for sale at subsidized rates were laid down on gridded plans. Some of the privately sponsored residential projects, such as the Tara Group Housing (1978) in New Delhi, deviated from the previously mentioned mechanistic schemes. Designed by Charles Correa, Jasbir Sawhney, and Ravindra Bhan, the project consisted of 160 double-story row house units (varying from 84 to 130 square meters) built on 3-by-15-meter modules. The residential units were staggered in both plan and section along an internal landscaped "street." The street acted as a "humidifying zone" convivial for social interaction. High-density low-rise housing and the vocabulary of courtyards, *chowks* (streets), and *mohallas* (pedestrian alleys) became the mainstays of housing design in the 1980s. Raj Rewal's design for the Asiad Village (1982) in New Delhi took this vocabulary to its extreme. The Village, built for the 1982 Asian Games, consisted of 700 units that later became apartments for high-income tenants. The units were clustered in groups of 12 to 36 units around a common space, with terraces for outdoor living and sleeping, and gateways were formed by overhanging residential units that attempted to render variety to the repetitive pattern.

At the other end of the socioeconomic scale, housing solutions met with glaring limitations. To meet the demand for housing the poor, government development agencies promoted user-initiative programs in "sites-and-services" projects. The cost of infrastructure—roads, water supply, wastewater drainage, and a small toilet—were borne by the agency, and the construction of the individual dwelling was left to the individual owner. The Integrated Urban Development project (1975) in Ahmedabad by Kirtee Shah, designed for flood refugees, attempted to provide dwelling units as well as opportunities for education and supplementary employment. The design, developed on the basis of architect-owner participation, consisted of two-room units made of exposed brick and roofed with asbestos cement sheets. The veranda and a shared courtyard worked as outdoor living/work space. The viability of these projects was circumvented by their location away from cities and employment opportunities, and two-thirds of the targeted economically disadvantaged population could not even afford these subsidized projects. Consequently, migrants to the cities continued to swell the population of squatter settlements and slums.

Most architects recognized that the housing shortage was not a design problem but required a drastic reconsideration of basic issues of resource, employment, and social equity. Nonetheless, the problem of low-cost housing continued to be addressed by most architects as a design challenge—discovering low-cost forms and low-cost technology that necessitated an inquiry into vernacular building practices. In the ashrams at Sabarmati (1918) in Ahmedabad and at Sevagram (1930s) in Maharashtra, Mahatma Gandhi had used traditional construction to demonstrate its viability, and these became touchstones for a generation of postindependence architects. The simple rectangular buildings at Sevagram were mud-on-timber-frame constructions on stone foundation. Pitched timber roofs with tiles, a few bamboo columns, spacious verandah, and small fenestration covered with slatted bamboo screens completed the ensemble.

Laurie Baker, an English emigrant to India, inspired by Gandhi's vision, built a large repertoire of buildings that eschewed contemporary design fads and were rooted in an appreciation of the resourceful vernacular architecture of Kerala. His design for the Center for Development Studies (1975) in Thiruvanathapuram, Kerala, was developed to demonstrate responsible building practices. A vocabulary of exposed local bricks for walls and screens, wood and concrete for structural members, and ceramic tiles for roofs was rendered in simple but elegant details. Concrete was used economically, substituted with reject clay tiles in the lower tension portion of slabs. The most lavishly detailed building was the guesthouse, where the brick *jali* (lattice) screens were accompanied by carefully crafted woodwork.

Considerations of climate and local building practices led Uttam Jain to explore a completely different vocabulary in Rajasthan that was shaped in large measure by an allegiance to modernist principles. In the buildings of the Jodhpur University campus (1971), Jain used dressed yellow sandstone in lime mortar to give the buildings a rugged feel. In the Faculty of Arts

and Sciences, stair-towers and voids for cross lighting punctuated the double-loaded corridors of a conventional U-shaped plan. The load-bearing, glazed inner wall was shaded by an outer wall to reduce heat load and render the building a sculptural quality. Jain's Indira Gandhi Institute for Development in Mumbai (1987) asserts a similar relationship between building and site; this research complex with residences for staff and scholars coalesces around open courtyards and green space.

It was the space-structure relationship of vernacular traditions that most architects found useful for their modern buildings. Charles Correa's design for the Gandhi Smarak Sangrahalaya (1957) in Ahmedabad exploited the versatility of the courtyard typology and included a concern for climate, human scale, and history. By the 1980s the critical acclaim of Correa's designs, the design of the Indian Institute of Management (1972) at Ahmedabad by Louis Kahn, and the campus designs that followed (such as the Indian Statistical Institute, 1981, in New Delhi by Anant Raje and the Indian Institute of Management, 1983, at Bangalore by Balkrishna Doshi) ensured not only a significant change in the design of the institutional campus (compared to the Institute of Technology campuses in Kharagpur, Kanpur, and New Delhi and scores of that ilk) but also the establishment of an Indian modern vocabulary. Academic facilities around a spacious courtyard or amphitheater, shaded networks of "streets," diagonal axes of movement, broken symmetries, and the bold geometry of locally quarried stones or bricks on a reinforced-concrete structural system were the leitmotifs of these institutional designs. The austere aesthetics and the monumentality of these projects were softened in the experiments with typology in smaller academic complexes. The preference for a more intimate scale in designing institutional projects was related to the establishment in the 1980s of a number of agencies to study and conserve physical and cultural resources. These were small semiautonomous academic and research institutes that desired an architectural image in harmony with changing concerns about sustainability. The Center for Development Studies (1987) in Pune by Christopher Beninger; the Inter-University Center of Astronomy and Astrophysics Center (1998) by Charles Correa; the Entrepreneurship Development Institute (1987) by Bimal Patel and the Center for Environmental Education (1990) by Neelkanth Chhaya and Kallol Joshi, both projects located in Ahmedabad; and the Visitors Hostel (1990) at the Nehru Science Center in Bangalore by Chandravarkar and Thacker adapted a domestic scale that was integrated with the landscape.

Repositioning Indian Identity

One of the most innovative precedents that integrated landscape and architecture was Balkrishna Doshi's studio and architectural foundation Sangath (1980). The building consisted of two sets of parallel barrel-vaulted structures, partly subterranean and the totality integrated with a carefully designed landscape. The vaults were made of cylindrical terra-cotta tiles sandwiched between thin ferro-cement shells. The external surface of the vaults was animated by a heat-reflecting waterproof covering of china mosaic. Water channels between vaults carried rainwater to reflecting pools and the garden. Although the cooling effect of the form and materials was limited in the Ahmedabad summers, the design and ideas presented through lyrical drawings and thumb sketches signaled a departure from the modernist vocabulary of Indian architects: here a concern for typology, material, climate, and form was squarely located in the realm of India's architectural tradition.

The centrality of "tradition" in a newly emerging narrative was evident in two architectural exhibitions in 1986. The first, titled "Vistara" (vistas/openings), was exhibited in Mumbai and was designed for the Festival of India tour abroad; the second, titled "Kham" (space/pause), was organized by the Indira Gandhi National Center for the Arts (IGNCA) in New Delhi. Whereas the first attempted to locate contemporary architecture in the continuum of India's architectural history, the second suggested multisensorial "acts" of space and commonalties between India's preindustrial architecture with those around the world. Both emphasized the role of myths in architecture and everyday life (including myths of modernity and industrialization) and claimed an aesthetic universality that was simultaneously grounded in regional practices and tradition. These were professional designers' attempts to designate acceptable sources and practices and to craft an Indian Modern style that claimed to have come to terms with the past.

The political climate that supported these ideas wrestled with the reemergence of tradition as a political problem. Although tradition in the revival of Indian crafts and advertising tourist destinations was profitable and found an eager audience among international tourists and the Indian bourgeoisie, the logic of tradition in the religious nationalisms that were attempting to tear apart the secular democracy needed to be confronted. In demonstrating links between the great architecture of different eras and emphasizing their metaphysical dimensions, one could pass over the political difficulties facing the architect when dealing with troubled historical legacies (e.g. the recent ones of British colonialism) and overlook sociopolitical fractures in the contemporary fabric of the country. Not surprisingly, in the brief of the international design competition for the IGNCA complex (1986) in New Delhi, the overwhelming theme was one of assimilation. The Center, a cultural complex of museums, performance, and education facilities, was intended to be a memorial to Indira Gandhi, who was assassinated in 1984 by Sikh militants demanding a separate homeland. The Center was to articulate a unique all-encompassing "Indian worldview" (which in the brief passed as a "Hindu" worldview) to launch Gandhi as one of the canonical figures of Indian nationalism equated with some of the mainstays of the nationalist movement in British India. Situated in the heart of Lutyens's New Delhi, this complex was to harmonize with the colonial surroundings. Ralph Lerner's winning entry, a Lutyenesque response to the brief, was commended for maintaining "a necessary connection with history." Here historical connections necessarily resided on the surface.

Similarly, an investigation of folk architecture central to the new interest in tradition could only include questions of form and beauty. In such a view, the "typical" Indian village and the historical architecture of the country were seen as the repository of a universal good, notwithstanding the caste, class, and gender dynamics that inhabit(ed) and influenc(ed) these forms. Revathi and Vasanth Kamath's design for the Tourist Village at Mandawa (1986) in Rajasthan was conceived as sun-dried mud-brick-and-thatch structures replicating the anthropomorphic village forms of the Shekhawati region. The client, the rajah of Mandawa, was hard to convince—he wanted a *pucca* (masonry) construction for his investment, preferably one that looked like a Canadian resort. The architects convinced him to adopt a regional vocabulary of mud architecture—"not only cheap but also the most appropriate way, both climatically and aesthetically." It was a place for the international tourist looking for the Indian village experience without the squalor and inconvenience and one in which folk artisans and performers could market their traditional skills. The architect here is not only the arbiter of taste, but also is responsible for decoding and interpreting cultural memories and reviving traditional building practices forgotten by the Dubai-returned local masons. The client's and the architect's aspirations were not that different—both borrowing distant images to produce an object, an experience for consumption, each in their own way crafting a contemporary Indian identity with their imaginings of a good life.

Creating an architecture rooted in tradition when images from across the world are easily accessible through television and the Internet is a difficult proposition at best. In a country in which most buildings are not designed by design professionals, many Indian architects have resorted to myths to distinguish their work from that of the contractor-builder and the truant middle-class consumers who apply architectural forms to residences and commercial complexes as objects of desire culled from a global economy. For example, in narrating the meaning literally underlying the design concept for the Bharat Diamond Bourse (1998) in Mumbai, Balkrishna Doshi spoke of spiritual rather than corporate revelations. The three-million-square-foot megacomplex consists of nine towers clad in mirrored glass located on a landscaped base of granite outcrop. The tightly secured walled-in complex was constructed with the aspiration to compete in the lucrative global diamond market. Doshi, however, imagined the rocky site as having mythical origins and claimed that the complex is now the "most sacred site in India" and a "true sanctuary." This sort of mythmaking romanticizes what was otherwise a blatantly commercial project and might well forebode a very different landscape in the 21st century.

SWATI CHATTOPADHYAY

See also **Ahmedabad, India; Chandigarh, India; Correa, Charles Mark (India); Doshi, Balkrishna (India); Entrepreneurship Development Institute, Ahmedabad, India; Indian Institute of Management, Ahmedabad; New Delhi, India; Rewal, Raj (India)**

Further Reading

Ashraf, Kazi Khaleed, and James Belluardo (editors), *An Architecture of Independence: The Making of Modern South Asia*, New York: Architectural League of New York, 1998

Bhatia, Gautam, *Punjabi Baroque and Other Memories of Architecture*, New Delhi and New York: Penguin, 1994

Bhatt, Vikram, and Peter Scriver, *After the Masters*, Ahmedabad, India: Mapin, 1990

Chatterjee, Malay, "The Evolution of Contemporary Indian Architecture," in *Architectures en Inde*, edited by Jean-Louis Véret, Paris: Electa Moniteur, 1985

Evenson, Norma, *Chandigarh*, Berkeley: University of California Press, 1966

Evenson, Norma, *The Indian Metropolis: A View towards the West*, New Haven, Connecticut: Yale University Press, 1989

Grover, Satish, *Building beyond Borders: Story of Contemporary Indian Architecture*, New Delhi: National Book Trust India, 1995

Guha-Thakurta, Tapati, *The Making of a New "Indian" Art: Artists, Aesthetics, and Nationalism in Bengal, c. 1850–1920*, Cambridge and New York: Cambridge University Press, 1992

King, Anthony, "India's Past in India's Present: Cultural Policy and Cultural Practice in Architecture and Urban Design, 1960–1990," in *Perceptions of South Asia's Visual Past*, edited by Catherine Ella Blanshard Asher and Thomas R. Metcalf, New Delhi: American Institute of Indian Studies, 1994

Lang, Jon T., Madhavi Desai, and Miki Desai, *Architecture and Independence: The Search for Identity—India, 1880 to 1980*, Delhi and New York: Oxford University Press, 1997

Tillotson, Giles Henry Rupert, *The Tradition of Indian Architecture: Continuity, Controversy, and Change since 1850*, New Haven, Connecticut: Yale University Press, 1989

INDIAN INSTITUTE OF MANAGEMENT

Designed by Louis Kahn, completed 1974
Ahmedabad, India

The Indian Institute of Management (IIM) (1962–74) at Ahmedabad, India, remains among the major building complexes designed by Louis Kahn in the latter part of his career. This institute took a number of years to complete, and Kahn's drawings show a considerable change in design during construction. It is a significant project primarily because it brings into focus many issues that were of concern to the architect throughout his career, such as the use of light and shadow, solids and voids, geometry and composition, formal juxtapositions, integrity of building materials, monumentality, and a fascination with ruins.

At the time it was designed, this 65-acre campus was situated at the outskirts of the city. The institute compensated for this lack of an urban setting and context through its own monumentality. The main school building forms the focus of the composition and was inspired by medieval monasteries. As one enters the tree-lined parking area, there is not one entry but a number of entries. Yet the visitor is immediately drawn to the diagonal staircase of the main school building that leads into the central courtyard, which is now called the Louis Kahn Plaza and which forms the main quadrangle of the building. The institute comprises this U-shaped main building, which houses the classrooms and lecture halls in one wing, the administrative offices in the other, and the library connecting the two sides. The six classrooms or lecture rooms on one side of the court are perfect cubes, but in contrast to the exterior, the interior is an amphitheater-like diagonal arrangement. Each classroom and administrative block is a distinct entity and connected on one side through a corridor that has openings onto the central courtyard. In between the classrooms are spaces that open to the outside, thus continuously shifting the view between outside and inside. Both wings of the U-shaped main building are unified through the use of arcades with thick brick walls and arched openings. The wings are linked by the library building, which dominates the structural composition. The play of light and shadow in the arcades, the use of thick brick walls, and the perfect geometry of forms all contribute to a sense of serenity.

The second part of the IIM campus comprises a cluster of triangular buildings, which are the student dormitories that stand in close proximity to the main building. Each block is four stories high with 20 individual rooms and triangular common rooms that open to the outside through huge circular openings. Kitchens and toilets are in the square tower attached to the long face of the right-angled triangle. This block, then, completes the square. The voids between the dormitories are exactly the same size as the dormitories themselves, and one sees an exploration of reversibility of solids and voids in this project along with that of light and matter. The lower floors serve as meeting places in keeping with Kahn's idea of unchoreographed yet interactive spaces that are present throughout the campus and that in his opinion shape where education occurs. The dormitories are in fact interspersed with a series of courtyards, partially enclosed ground floors, and walkways, which are read on the plan as essentially a grid. It is the diagonal movement that changes continuously from closed to semiclosed to open and the rapid transitions from light to shade that make this place especially compelling as a living and learning environment.

The main school building and the dormitories were completed first; A.D. Raje, an architect who worked in Kahn's Philadelphia office initially and who was left in charge of the project, designed the faculty housing on the basis of Kahn's drawings. The faculty housing possesses a simplicity that is articulated by Kahn's "composite order," a system of shallow brick arches and

Indian Institute of Management, Ahmedabad, India, (1974)
© GreatBuildings.com

concrete tie beams that he had specially designed for this project. Raje, who had gone on to complete the project, independently designed several other buildings on the campus: the dining halls, the Management Development Center, the Mathai Center for Innovative Education, and the married students' housing; some of these were later additions to the program. These all follow the vocabulary set forward by Kahn.

Much has been written about the compositional aspect of the IIM, which was laid out with respect to the wind direction, in particular the southwesterly breezes. Apparently, the architect, B.V. Doshi, played an important role in convincing Kahn to utilize such an arrangement, and this choice is reflected in the changes in Kahn's design seen in the early and later drawings. In addition, an artificial lake, regarded as important by Kahn, was not implemented. The dormitories were supposed to be surrounded on both sides by a shallow lake with bridgelike walks that would connect them. This lake was also meant to separate the faculty housing from the student housing, but malarial mosquitoes prompted worry. Nonetheless, the viewer can imagine the successful effect of the forms, especially the curved, sail-like walls with huge circular openings. Although geometrically each part of the complex is quite distinct, the use of brick creates a sense of unity and integration. Similarly, the repetition of certain formal elements, such as arcades, unifies the parts. The repetitive character of the spatial framework enhances the diversity of functions and geometry further. Arcades form the transient spaces and create the play of light and shadow. The connections between various buildings define much of Kahn's architecture. At the same time, the individual expression of various buildings is maintained in strong formal terms.

Although Kahn drew references here to the classical European medieval tradition of the monastery, one can also see reflections of formal ideas, especially the sense of scale, composition, and geometry from the 12th-century royal tombs and palaces of Mandu and some Islamic monuments of Ahmedabad such as the Sarkhej complex and mosques.

AARATI KANEKAR

See also **Ahmedabad, India; Doshi, Balkrishna (India); India; Kahn, Louis (United States)**

Further Reading

Anderson, Stanford, "Public Institutions: Louis I. Kahn's Readings of Volume Zero," *Journal of Architectural Education*, 49/1 (September 1995)

Bathia, Gautam, "Anant Raje, dopo Kahn; After Kahn: The Indian Institute of Management," *Spazio e società*, 17/66 (April–June 1994)

Brownlee, David B., and David G. De Long, *Louis I. Kahn: In the Realm of Architecture*, New York: Rizzoli, 1991

Devillers, Christian, "L'Indian Institute of Management ad Ahmedabad, 1962–1974, di Louis I. Kahn," *Casabella*, 54/571 (September 1990)

Futagawa, Yukio (editor), *Indian Institute of Management, Ahmedabad, India, 1963–; Exeter Library, Phillips Exeter Academy, Exeter, New Hampshire, U.S.A., 1972*, Tokyo: A.D.A. Edita, 1975; revised edition, 1978

Giurgola, Romaldo, and Jaimini Mehta, *Louis I. Kahn*, Boulder, Colorado: Westview Press, 1975

James, Kathleen, "Louis Kahn's Indian Institute of Management's Courtyard: Form versus Function," *Journal of Architectural Education*, 49/1 (September 1995)

Kahn, Louis I., *The Louis I. Kahn Archive: Personal Drawings*, 7 vols., New York: Garland, 1987

Rassegna, 7/21 (March 1985) (special issue titled "Louis I. Kahn, 1901/1974")

Ronner, Heinz, Sharad Jhaveri, and Alessandro Vasella, *Louis I. Kahn: Complete Works, 1935–74*, Boulder, Colorado: Westview Press, 1977

Sekler, Eduard F., "Formalism and the Polemical Use of History: Thoughts on the Recent Rediscovery of Revolutionary Classicism," *The Harvard Architecture Review*, 1 (Spring 1980)

INSTITUTE FOR ARCHITECTURE AND URBAN STUDIES

New York, New York

Peter Eisenman founded and directed the Institute for Architecture and Urban Studies (IAUS) as an intellectual and cultural hub in 1967, at a time of social unrest and an increase in monies for urban projects from governmental and private sources. As stated in its charter, the institute sought to bridge the university, the museum, and architectural practice. It combined highly learned research with exhibitions and intensely felt design. The urban direction of the institute predominated from the beginning until 1975, when financial sponsorship considerably slowed.

Eisenman established an office in New York City that was to last for two years with very few participants. The first endeavor was a study of the Kingsbridge Heights section of the Bronx. Colin Rowe, the renowned theorist and practitioner of design who had been Eisenman's mentor at Cambridge University, brought three of his graduate students from Cornell University: Stephen Potters, Michael Schwarting, and Jonathan Stouman. Rowe also recruited William Ellis, another one of his students from the University of Texas, to work with him at the IAUS. The students conducted many studies from on-site surveys of the topography, infrastructure, and building conditions in the Kingsbridge vicinity before marrying these observations with Rowe's figure and ground ideas. Rowe gave lectures and supervision every fortnight, traveling from Cornell. Nothing was implemented by the city planning authorities, but the study was part of the New York City Master Plan, and the exercise was worthy for its site investigations and design variations.

The major urban project to come out of the institute was a book, *On Streets* (1978), edited by Stanford Anderson, a professor at the Massachusetts Institute of Technology (MIT) and a fellow at the institute. Anderson and Ellis codirected the initial research and assembled materials from the analytic phase of the study, which was supported by the Department of Housing and Urban Development (HUD). The street had become the microcosmic element of public space. Much of the public life in preindustrial days had become interiorized, and Anderson, Ellis, and the rest of the institute explained this transition and the processes of communication before and at the time of publication of *On Streets*. Anderson and Ellis's contribution was as leaders and participants in many of the studies in *On Streets*; Anderson also assumed editorial responsibility for authors' production of their committed essays. Three of the essays to come out of this project included Anderson's explorations of use types and their locations in cities such as Paris, Savannah, Georgia, and north Boston;

Anthony Vidler's account of utopian communities and the defensive urbanism of revolutionary Paris in the 19th century; and Kenneth Frampton's study of generic streets that defined, described, and critically analyzed building complexes (mainly residential) and their communicative potentials for public and private activities.

Another notable essay was a demonstration project—a study of Binghamton, New York, by a team of architects: Eisenman, Victor Calliandro, Thomas Schumacher, Judith Magel, Peter Wolf, and Vincent Moore. They closed off a residential street of townhouses with slightly taller buildings and made it a park street, with trees lining the way to a preexisting park. This was similar to the surrogate street that the institute had planned with HUD in 1970, but by 1971 the federal agency withdrew its support, and the projected street design remained on paper in the *On Streets*. The book reflects the broad, multidisciplinary scope of the study; it was translated into five languages and has been used as a primer for architecture and planning schools.

Architectural education was a major endeavor for the institute. A program for undergraduates began in 1974. There were institute lecture series with many burgeoning and established architects from Europe and the United States speaking, which was very inspirational to the student body. Before the inception of the education program, the institute found a new home on 40th Street with ample room for lectures and exhibitions in a grand space in addition to offices and studios. At any given time there could have been 12 to more than 100 people in this office space.

According to Kenneth Frampton, the most important education program was called "Open Plan." This was a nighttime extension school attended by adults as well as undergraduates. Awarded with a $350,000 National Endowment for the Humanities grant obtained by Frederieke Taylor, this series addressed a mixed audience who would tirelessly come to the institute after the workday. Joan Copjec, who entered the institute in 1977, took over from Andrew MacNair and Anthony Vidler, organizing the program and selecting speakers. Another part of the education program was the high school program run by Deborah Berke and Lawrence Kutnicki, in which youths were encouraged to enjoy the art of architecture.

The institute also made a valuable contribution with its publications, *Oppositions* and *Skyline* (the latter was a design newspaper edited by MacNair and then by Suzanne Stephens), and the catalogue series. Each of these publications retained a critical integrity and independence, more or less free of political or personal alignments. Although the more astute at the institute carried forth—with critical hindsight—the lineage of their modernist forerunners, there were historicists, such as Robert A.M. Stern.

Oppositions attracted the best talents around, and as its name declares, it featured divergent views and divergent topics. The contradictory nature of the material was managed by leading figures at the institute, including Eisenman, Frampton, Mario Gandelsonas, Vidler, Kurt Forster, Julia Bloomfield as managing editor, Joan Ockman as executive editor, and Diana Agrest as a silent partner. Agrest was one of the few women who, from the institute's inception, was recognized in the male-dominated organization. She was active in the education program and design tutorials and also joined her partner, Gandelsonas, in leading semiotics research. Frampton and Silvia Kolbowski, a con-

ceptual artist, coedited the catalog series, which not only accompanied exhibitions but, as in the catalog on the AT&T building by Philip Johnson, wrote biting critiques.

The last serious project to emanate from the institute was ReVisions. Funded by Walter Chatham and organized by Joan Ockman, the group at first hosted public events. In its second phase, an intense reading group met regularly and studied many of the great thinkers of their day. They revered Manfredo Tafuri, the Italian Communist who had come to prominence with his *Architecture and Utopia,* in which he exposed the true underpinnings of modern architecture as a capitalist pursuit. He opposed the operative criticism of Kenneth Frampton as Frampton opposed his hardline Marxism.

The disintegration of the institute began around 1983, although it managed to eke out an existence for a few more years under the leadership of Steven Peterson, a follower of Rowe, and Ed Saxe, a former corporate CEO. The demise of the institute followed in the wake of Eisenman's departure in order to build. Although he had designed buildings while at the institute, he wanted to open an office. It must be said that most of the institute leaders and some students have stuck to the serious sociocultural values that emerged from the institute in the 1970s.

SUZANNE FRANK

See also **Agrest, Diana, and Mario Gandelsonas (United States); AT&T Building, New York City; Eisenman, Peter (United States); Frampton, Kenneth (United States); Tafuri, Manfredo (Italy)**

Further Reading

Anderson, Stanford (editor), *On Streets*, Cambridge, Massachusetts: MIT Press, 1978

Eisenman, Peter, et al., "The City as an Artifact," *Casabella*, 35 (1971)

Frampton, Kenneth, *Modern Architecture: A Critical History*, London: Thames and Hudson, and New York: Oxford University Press, 1980; 3rd edition, London: Thames and Hudson, 1992; New York: Thames and Hudson, 1997

Frampton, Kenneth (editor), *Philip Johnson, Processes: The Glass House, 1949, and the AT&T Corporate Headquarters, 1978*, New York: Institute for Architecture and Urban Studies, 1978

Hays, Michael (editor), *Oppositions Reader: Selected Readings from a Journal for Ideas and Criticism in Architecture, 1973–1984*, New York: Princeton Architectural Press, 1998

Institute for Architecture and Urban Studies, *New Urban Settlements*, New York: Institute for Architecture and Urban Studies, 1971

Institute for Architecture and Urban Studies and New York State Urban Development Corporation, *Another Chance for Housing: Low-Rise Alternatives, Brownsville, Brooklyn, Fox Hills, Staten Island*, New York: Museum of Modern Art, 1973

Museum of Modern Art, *The New City: Architecture and Urban Renewal*, New York: Museum of Modern Art, 1967

Ockman, Joan, "Resurrecting the Avant-Garde: The History and Program of Oppositions," in *Architectureproduction*, edited by Beatriz Colomina, New York: Princeton Architectural Press, 1988

Risselada, Max, and Kenneth Frampton, *Art and Architecture, USSR, 1917–32*, New York: Wittenborn, 1971

INSTITUTES AND ASSOCIATIONS

Architectural institutes and associations played a fundamental role throughout the 20th century in legitimizing architecture as a specialized practice and defining it as a profession. Formed as national and, secondarily, as regional or urban organizations, architectural institutes and associations provided an arena for dialogue and information exchange by their members through the venues of meetings, conferences, competitions, exhibitions, and journals. Although the priorities differed somewhat among countries, the general goals were to establish regulations for the protection of architects and their clients, particularly through a uniform fee structure; to gain public recognition and consolidate a market for their services; and to improve and standardize architectural training. Professional associations validated the credentials of their members and provided them with collegial support.

The professionalization of many occupations initially occurred during the 19th century in Western Europe as a feature of the division of labor in industrial capitalism. By the beginning of the 20th century, distinctions between the activities of architects, engineers, quantity surveyors, and contractors had been established, and each group had formed separate professional or trade organizations. The divisions became more firmly adhered to over the course of the century as universities and technical schools developed distinct programs, further differentiating the practices and identities of the various groups. With the increased separation of professional fields characteristic of democratic governance, institutes became instrumental in negotiating legislation and contracts with the governing bodies of the political region in which they operated. In defining specific practices and values that constituted a professional identity, institutes and associations supported the process by which architects were recognized as the producers of specialized services, and the market for this expertise was both formulated and controlled.

Architectural organizations such as the Royal Institute of British Architects (RIBA) and the American Institute of Architects (AIA) have been influential worldwide and have greatly contributed to the standardization and respectability of architectural practice. In countries that were under current or former colonial rule, the architectural profession was, not surprisingly, dominated by practitioners and ideas from the ruling state. For example, both the Royal Architectural Institute of Canada (RAIC) and the Indian Institute of Architects (IIA) were modeled on the practices and policies of the RIBA. In both instances, there were subsequent attempts within the profession to construct a definitive national architectural identity, and the institutes were instrumental in negotiating these issues. In late 19th-century Japan, British architects were favored over traditional Japanese builders for major public commissions because of their expertise in modern building practices. As a result, the British architectural profession had a significant impact on the formation and ideas of the Architectural Institute of Japan (AIJ). Here again, efforts to create a distinctly national (Japanese) modern architecture in the first half of the 20th century produced a professional culture that attempted to adapt new building techniques and some British stylistic attributes into Japanese institutions and culture.

Architectural institutes and associations concerned themselves with the education of prospective members of their profession throughout the 20th century. The Architects' Registration Act of 1931 granted the RIBA control over architectural training and entry into the profession in Britain, where the system of articled pupilage was the conventional means of obtaining architectural education until the focus on office training in the 1950s.

The *Strategic Study of the Profession*, commissioned by the RIBA in 1995, determined that the most important task for the future was in the realm of education—specifically, in developing the knowledge and skills of architects by linking education and practice and encouraging increased specialization.

Prizes awarded by architectural institutes, such as the gold medals of the RIBA, the AIA, and the Paris-based Union Internationale des Architectes (UIA), exemplify the ideals of the profession. Providing public recognition for both the individual winner and the profession as a whole, the awards establish national and international standards. The institutes offering these prestigious awards have a significant effect on which architects become world renowned and highly influential.

The early architectural institutes and associations were similar in form to gentlemen's clubs. Women, ethnic minorities, and the lower classes were implicitly excluded from the training necessary to gain acceptance into the profession, and the professional organizations were formed by and for cultured gentlemen architects. Public universities were influential in opening the profession to women and ethnic minorities, particularly in North America, as the formal training and accreditation helped individuals overcome the initial discrimination and obstacles to working in mainstream offices and become accepted into the profession. Organizations such as the Finnish Architectura Association and the Union Internationale des Femmes Architectes (UIFA) have increased the visibility of women in particular countries while protecting their interests within the profession. Since the 1970s, some women's architectural organizations have been involved in compiling revisionist histories, seeking to include gender issues in the history of architecture.

As the responsibilities of architects have changed, so too have the mandates of professional associations. In their early years, architectural institutes represented a small number of practitioners working in the field. With the growth of large-scale corporate architectural firms and an increase in the authority of professional organizations, institutes enjoyed a broad-based membership. However, substantial differences remain among various countries in terms of the role of architects and in their professional associations. Although the UIA currently represents 98 countries that have some form of professional organization for architects, the issues that these associations are dealing with are often vastly dissimilar. At the 1986 International Seminar of the Aga Khan Award for Architecture, which focused on architectural education in the Islamic world, the strengthening of professional associations, along with the separation of architects and planners from engineers, was suggested as one part of a solution to the problems of the architectural profession in Muslim societies. In contrast, the administration of the AIA has recently attempted to restructure the conservative, well-established institute into a flexible, democratic one that is responsive to the interests of the young and minority architects for whom it has previously had little relevance. The challenge for architectural institutes in modernizing countries is to adapt the goals of professional practice to traditional cultural values, whereas in postindustrial economies the difficulty for associations will be to maintain their significance in an increasingly specialized profession with a diverse range of practitioners.

SARAH BASSNET

See also **Aga Khan Award (1977–); Education and Schools; Royal Institute of British Architects**

Further Reading

The source material dealing with architectural institutes and associations in the 20th century is for the most part found in histories of particular institutes or associations and in association reports. More of the publications are oriented towards the formation and beginnings of professional organizations, and British and American institutes are the most widely discussed in secondary sources. Brief mention of the status of the architectural profession and the formation of organizations can often be found in histories of architecture for individual countries, and there are several fairly recent publications that address the presence of women in the profession.

Adams, Annmarie, and Peta Tancred, *Designing Women: Gender and the Architectural Profession*, Toronto: University of Toronto Press, 2000

Aga Khan Award for Architecture, *Architecture Education in the Islamic World*, Singapore: Concept Media, 1986

Gotch, J. Alfred (editor), *The Growth and Work of the Royal Institute of British Architects, 1834–1934*, London: Simson, 1934

Hawthorne, Christopher, "Meet the New AIA (Same As the Old AIA?)," *Architecture*, 89/4 (2000)

Kaye, Barrington, *The Development of the Architectural Profession in Britain: A Sociological Study*, London: Allen and Unwin, 1960

Kostof, Spiro (editor), *The Architect: Chapters in the History of the Profession*, New York: Oxford University Press, 1977

Simmins, Geoffrey, *Ontario Association of Architects: A Centennial History, 1889–1989*, Toronto: Ontario Association of Architects, 1989

Summerson, John Newenham, *The Architectural Association, 1847–1947*, London: Pleiades Books, 1947

Suominen-Kokkonen, Renja, *The Fringe of a Profession: Women As Architects in Finland from the 1890s to the 1950s*, Helsinki: Muinaismuistoyhdistyksen Aikakauskirja, 1992

Woods, Mary N., *From Craft to Profession: The Practice of Architecture in Nineteenth-Century America*, Berkeley: University of California Press, 1999

(EXPOSITION INTERNATIONALE DES ARTS DÉCORATIFS) INTERNATIONAL EXHIBITION OF DECORATIVE ARTS, PARIS (1925)

Le Corbusier, whose Pavillon de l'Esprit Nouveau was a *succes de scandale* at the International Exhibition of Decorative Arts, an important exhibition held from April through October 1925, dubbed it "the international 'Marathon' of the arts of the home [arts des maisons]." There the modernistic was pitted against the modern, luxury goods against mass-produced commodities, hand-craftsmanship against the machine, the singular against the typical. The exposition gave its name to the Art Deco style, a popular blend of motifs from Fauvism, Cubism, Futurism, the Ballets Russes, and African, Melanesian, and pre-Columbia art rendered decorative through the lens of a schematized classicism. Although that style characterized the Pavillons des Prestige, gates, and gardens by such Beaux Arts architects as Louis Bonnier (1856–1946), Charles Plumet (1861–1928), and Pierre Patout (1879–1965), the exhibition also played host to some buildings that were truly new departures.

The organizers had directed that all displays be "confined to articles of modern inspiration and real originality" and threatened to ban any work of a traditional nature. Here they frankly acknowledged the example of the 1902 Exposition held in Turin, which had been the showcase for the style that preceded Art Deco—Art Nouveau. Another principle that guided the sponsors was the need to encourage artists and craftspersons to collaborate with manufacturers as a means to make French decorative art commercially competitive; here, they were taking up the challenge of the Deutscher Werkbund. However, the corollary of this principle—that the "arts of the home" would thereby be made accessible to people other than the wealthy—was not very much in evidence. Thus the Ambassade Française, the contribution of members of the Société des Artistes Décorateurs, one of the original sponsors of the exhibition, had interiors of sumptuous elegance furnished with unique pieces. Three of the rooms epitomized the Art Deco style, and even the others, by the more orthodox modern Pierre Chareau (1883–1950) and Frantz Jourdain (1847–1935), demonstrate the French disdain for the mechanistic visions of the Werkbund and the Bauhaus, neither of which participated in the exhibition.

Only a trio of French architects resisted the prevailing Art Deco extravagance. Robert Mallet-Stevens (1885–1945) used unadorned reinforced concrete for his engagingly cubistic Pavilion of Tourism; cantilevered horizontal planes and a strip window emphasized its modernity. The two elder masters of the technical possibilities of concrete also employed it for their contributions. August Perret (1874–1954) reworked the successful formula of Notre Dame du Raincy for his brilliantly conceived theater, and Tony Garnier (1869–1948) provided for his native city of Lyons a pavilion that, except for an emblematic plaque over the entrance, is reminiscent of the austere buildings he designed for the Cité Industrielle.

The most innovative structures, however, were to be found among the 21 foreign pavilions located along the banks of the Seine. If the majority were conservative and historicizing despite the putative requirement of modernity—thus Armando Brasini (1879–1965) and Victor Horta (1861–1947) used classical motifs in an unusual, quasi-Mannerist way for the Italian and Belgian kiosks—there nevertheless were a few striking examples by members of a younger generation of the diverse currents swirling through progressive circles in 1925. The Austrian pavilion was multivalent, not surprisingly, as its chief designer, Josef Hoffmann (1870–1956), enlisted several architects prominent in Vienna, including the German Peter Behrens (1868–1940), at that time professor at the Viennese Academy, who provided a faceted glazed winter garden that reflected his post–World War I flirtation with crystalline Expressionism. Hoffmann, in contrast, erected a low wooden building clad with bulbous stucco moldings that made this section of the Austrian Pavilion resemble its French Art Deco neighbors. Similarly diverse in its formal vocabulary, though representing very different contemporary stylistic currents, was the Dutch Pavilion by J. F. Staal (1879–1940), a member of the Amsterdam School. Constructed of brick, favored in the Netherlands though an anomaly at this exposition, one facade displayed the irregular curves, nautical iconography, and Indonesian references characteristic of Amsterdam School practice, and the other showed the willingness of that group to assimilate some of the formal inventions of its rival, De Stijl. The Danish Pavilion, by Kay Fisker (1893–1965), was also of brick, but its prismatic simplicity looked ahead to Scandinavia's pragmatic interpretation of modernism.

The most avant-garde of the foreign pavilions was by Konstantin Melnikov (1890–1974), who specifically emphasized the ephemeral and didactic nature of such a building type. Erected in timber by local carpenters, his pavilion's red and white frame supported large glass walls and created a latticework tower of Constructivist origin that bore large Russian characters that spelled "USSR." An external stair, open to the sky under sloping intersecting beams that carried the hammer and sickle, sliced diagonally through the enclosed spaces; the parallelogram of the plan with its dynamic lines and planes approximated a Suprematist painting by Kasimir Malevich (1878–1935). Inside was a replica of a workers' club, with a folding display unit and speakers rostrum of metal and a reading table and semicircular wooden chairs by Aleksandr Rodchenko (1891–1956).

Comparable in its daring contemporaneity was the Pavillon de l'Esprit Nouveau, which so offended the authorities that originally it was hidden behind a tall fence. Named after Le Corbusier's polemical journal, it was a full-scale mockup of one unit of the *immeuble-villas* that formed part of the City for Three Million Inhabitants (1922) and represented the ideal maisonette that continued to be the basis for most of his housing projects. Attached was a curved enclosure where such Utopian projects as the Voisin Plan for Paris were displayed. In the context of the exhibition, Le Corbusier's most provocative challenge came in the area of the fittings, the *objets utiles* or the *equipement* of the dwelling. For instead of specially designed, costly furnishings, he included factory-produced and readily affordable items like Thonet chairs and a series of interchangeable storage units that he called *casiers standards*.

During its brief existence, the exhibition functioned as a boutique of rival artistic and technical manifestations. Its effect on the decorative arts was far-reaching, and although most of the items on display were available only to those with large incomes, the Art Deco style did eventually influence the design of mass-produced objects. As for architecture, the many meticulous photographs taken at the time document the divergent and often brilliant possibilities on offer in 1925 before these movements were consolidated into an International Style.

HELEN SEARING

See also **Amsterdam School; Bauhaus; Behrens, Peter (Germany); Chareau, Pierre (France); Une Cité Industrielle; Contemporary City for Three Million Inhabitants; Corbusier, Le (Jeanneret, Charles-Édouard) (France); De Stijl; Deutscher Werkbund; Fisker, Kay (Denmark); Garnier, Tony (France); Hoffmann, Josef (Austria); Horta, Victor (Belgium); Mallet-Stevens, Robert (France); Melnikov, Konstantin (Russia); Notre Dame, Le Raincy; Perret, Auguste (France); Russia and Soviet Union; Voisin Plan for Paris**

Further Reading

Brunhammer, Yvonne, *1925*, Paris: Les Presses de la Connaissance, 1976

Brunhammer, Yvonne, and Suzanne Tise, *The Decorative Arts in France, 1900–1942: La Société des Artistes-Décorateurs*, New York: Rizzoli, 1990

Encyclopédie des arts décoratifs et industries modernes au XXe siècle, 12 vols. Paris: Office Centrale d'Editions et de Librairie, 1925; New York: Garland 1977

Greenhalgh, Paul, *Ephemeral Vistas: The Expositions Universelles, Great Expositions and World's Fairs*, Manchester: Manchester University Press 1988

Janneau, Guillaume, *L'Art décoratif moderne, formes nouvelles et programmes nouveau*, Paris: n.p., 1925

Magne, H.-M., *Les Enseignements de l'exposition internationale des arts décoratifs et industriels modernes*, Paris: L. Eyrolles, 1926

Magne, H.-M., *Rapport général: Expositions des art décoratifs et industriels modernes*, 12 vols. Paris, 1925–31

Troy, Nancy, *Modernism and the Decorative Arts in France: Art Nouveau to Le Corbusier*, New Haven, Connecticut, and London: Yale University Press, 1991

INTERNATIONAL STYLE

The International Style is defined aesthetically by a series of design rules emphasizing volume rather than mass, regularity rather than symmetry, surface continuity, and the absence of applied ornament. Often buildings of this group shared the additional characteristics of the articulation of structure, the commonality of the white cube or the gridded glass box, and the use of the modern materials of the 20th century: glass and steel.

The aesthetic characteristics and the name were codified and popularized by the catalog of a museum exhibition, *The International Style, Architecture since 1922*, held in New York City in 1932 at the Museum of Modern Art, curated by Henry-Russell Hitchcock and Philip Johnson; *Bauhausbuch, Internationale Architektur*, by Walter Gropius, had previously commented on the developing pan-European phenomenon. During the decade that separated the books, the International Style underwent transformations in its theoretical basis as well as its locus. The movement that had begun so optimistically, however, as a social/political/ aesthetic synthesis evolved over time toward pure aesthetics. Although the proletariat, for whom the early modernists toiled, had never fully accepted the International Style, ironically, capitalist corporate America embraced it. *Internationale architektur* became the International Style. Though the theoretical meaning of the International Style changed over time, it maintained throughout its history an aesthetic consistency rarely seen in artistic movements of the 20th century. Thus, the International Style is readily identifiable today as one of the primary architectural movements and motifs of the 20th century.

Early International Style, 1920s

The early didacticism and proselytizing of the International Style meant that many of the finest examples of the style were often found in design expositions and schools. These demonstration buildings were intended to drive home the message of the new architecture from the avant-garde to the proletariat throughout Europe. Many of these European exhibitions of the new architecture had prefigured the International Style exhibition in New York. Among the most successful demonstrations of the new architecture were the Weissenhofsiedlung (1927; Stuttgart), the Bauhaus (1925–26; Dessau), the German Pavilion at the Barcelona Exposition (1929), and the Pavillon de l'Esprit Nouveau at the International Exhibition of Decorative Arts, Paris (1925).

The Weissenhofsiedlung was the first great demonstration of the theme that would define the existence of a developing International Style. Under the sponsorship of the Deutscher

Werkbund, Ludwig Mies van der Rohe created the overall design of a *siedlung*, or housing project, and many architects from European nations contributed houses, almost all white, flat-roofed functionalist boxes. It is astounding today, but must have been even more so then, that so many architects were thinking and creating simultaneously within the same genre: simplicity, whiteness, and geometry. This aesthetic seemed to arise spontaneously on drawing boards as architects sought the "Holy Grail" of a new architecture, for the white cube has the universal appeal of a tabula rasa, just the metaphor on which to build a new world.

By inviting European neighbors not only to view their exhibition but also to participate actively in it, the Werkbund extended itself beyond political barriers, even to countries that technically had been enemies, for a common social cause: housing for the proletariat. Architects participated from Germany, France, and Holland. By the time of the International Style Exhibition in New York, multiple countries were represented by architects whose names are still familiar: Mies, Gropius, Breuer, and Mendelsohn from Germany; Le Corbusier and Pierre Jeanneret from France; Oud from Holland; Emberton from England; Alto from Finland; and George Howe and William Lescaze from the United States, to name but a few. Even one non-Western architect from Japan was presented. The International Style, therefore, may be thought of as a farsighted movement, a watershed in the progress toward European unity or, in contemporary terminology, as globalization or as the creation of an architectural global village.

Many European architects who had made the pilgrimage to Germany to view the Weissenhofsiedlung traveled to Dessau to see the most significant modern design school of its time, the Bauhaus, which even from its inception was a recognized landmark. The International Style architecture of the building complex was a metaphor for the creation of the modern prototypes, or type forms, that were designed within. In this complex of studios and school buildings, Gropius not only explored the white, cubic aesthetic of the most prevalent International Style, but made another daring leap as well in his juxtaposition of the glass curtain wall of the atelier building with the cubic buildings. The glass curtain wall first celebrated at the Bauhaus would eventually become the major metaphor of the high International Style.

In the German Pavilion, Barcelona (1929), Mies contributed another major step to the aesthetics of the developing International Style. His volumetric spatial composition was contained by a series of flat planes of polished travertine, chrome, glass, and water—the sparely elegant planes intersecting planes and planes intersecting space. Using a reductivist aesthetic previously restricted to Modern art, Mies created International Style architecture that was as close as possible to his dream of a zero-degree architecture.

An early composition by Le Corbusier, the Pavillon de l'Esprit Nouveau (1925) became significant not only stylistically for the International Style but also for the clearly stated utopian faith of its name, "the new spirit," about which Le Corbusier expounded in his seminal commentary, *Vers une architecture* (Towards a New Architecture) (1923). The pavilion, a double-height, cubic box with gridded windows, is a study of life lived within geometry, showing that all the necessities of the modern home can be contained in a tight Le Corbusian universe, stripped of historical associations, and furnished in *objets-types*. Within

the geometric Le Corbusian universe, nature too is juxtaposed in the form of a tree growing bravely through a circle cut through the roof of the pavilion.

International Style and Émigré Architects, 1930s

Despite the expositions and pavilions, despite the artistic visions and humane intentions of the early International Style, architecture could not deny reality, which intervened in the form of Nazi interference and World War II. Utopian European architects were silenced, and the thrust of modern design was abruptly truncated. The floodlights of the expositions went out all over Europe. Under such great duress, many refugee architects fled to England or to the United States, where the International Style would later reemerge triumphantly in the American postwar building boom.

In the devastating wake of World War II, Le Corbusier, unlike many other architects, remained in Europe. Even he, however, was not untouched, for he had to reinvent his style, building in cast concrete in a weighty, sculptural style that, though highly influential to late modernism, could no longer be called mainstream International Style. As émigrés, Mies and Gropius, with their compatriots such as Marcel Breuer, carried the tenets of the original International Style to American soil in Chicago, Boston, and New York. Here they reinvigorated the style and their careers with it, Mies as prime mover of corporate modernism, Gropius as professor of architecture.

In America, Gropius functioned primarily as theoretician and teacher of architecture, but he created one significant monument to his European International Style roots: the house he designed for himself in a country setting (1937; Lincoln, Massachusetts) outside Cambridge, where he directed Harvard University's Graduate School of Design. This house is a landmark in the transfer of modernism and the subsequent integration of European aesthetics with American vernacular architecture. Its novel synthetic approach made this work a kind of visual textbook of the transfer of European aesthetics, pointing toward the assimilation of the International Style into midcentury American domestic architecture. Other German émigré architects, Marcel Breuer and Richard Neutra in particular, spread the International Style along the East Coast and California, bringing it into the contemporary home, in the guise of their simplified, informal compositions in wood and glass, as modern American domestic design.

High International Style, 1940s to 1950s

Mies concentrated on large-scale American corporate modernism. His high-rise commercial headquarters spoke symbolically of a new, upwardly mobile world where economy and aesthetics were fused. Mies' restrained reductivism, his use of the new materials of steel and glass, and his insistence on the articulation of structure made his International Style buildings the defining monuments of postwar America. The greatest of Mies' works of the high International Style were 860 Lake Shore Drive (1950) in Chicago, the Seagram Building (1957) in New York, and the Farnsworth House (1946) in Plano, Illinois. The first two structures are studies in simplicity, yet they are metaphorically complex. They are high-rise towers of gridded steel and glass, arranged in perfect prisms, reaching ever upward, full of

John Hancock building (1970) Chicago, Illinois,
designed by Skidmore, Owings and Merrill
© Esto Photographics

self-referential comments on architecture, speaking not only of
their own structure but also of the very essence of architecture.
Mies' insistence on the articulation of the simplest possible form,
the post and lintel of trabeated architecture, reminds us of his
roots in classical architecture.

As Mies bridged the antique to the modern, he created an
International Style with intimations of the eternal. To comprehend Mies' obsession with the classical values of architecture
within the modern, note in particular the Farnsworth House,
which is a Greek temple reformulated in white enameled steel
and glass. As International Style architecture, it is entirely volumetric and denies mass; it is subtly asymmetrical, white, structural, and wholly unornamented. If the Gropius House can be
read as a study in the assimilation of European International
Style into the American environment, Mies' Farnsworth House
can be understood as the purest example of unadulterated, classical International Style in America.

The International Style was broad and sufficiently flexible to
encompass variations on its themes created by Mies, Gropius,
Le Corbusier, and many other architects. The myriad creative
responses of architects, all within the International Style, seem
to point to the ongoing relationship of modern architecture with
modern art. In Mies, we find the suave passages of planes intersecting planes, planes parallel to and perpendicular to one another, forming an open structure that seems to be coming
together and pulling apart simultaneously. Thus, Mies' International Style, particularly seen in plan, recalls Dutch De Stijl

design and the late paintings of Piet Mondrian. In Gropius and
the Bauhaus, we find the International Style to be composed
of an opaque box and its opposition in the transparency and
reflectivity of glass, the elements asymmetrically arranged within
a tightly spinning plan. The Bauhaus composition, therefore,
may be thought of as analogous to both Cubism and Russian
Constructivism. In Le Corbusier, we find the configuration of
the white box in all its starkness, the cube being understood
metaphorically as the essence of architectural object within space,
reduced to its simplest possible form. Le Corbusier certainly was
inspired in his International Style aesthetics by French Cubism.

Late International Style, 1960s to 1990s

From the Seagram and the Farnsworth, Philip Johnson absorbed
the Miesian style, producing his own International Style high-
rises and his own house (1951) in New Canaan, Connecticut,
which comments on and extrapolates from Mies' Farnsworth
House. Other Philip Johnson works continued in the classical
International Style, until Johnson's work began to raise visual
and theoretical challenges to the credo of "almost nothing." His
early work for Lincoln Center in New York City (New York
State Theater, 1964) played with Neoclassicism, while in his
later ornamental and mass-implying AT&T Building (1978) in
New York, within blocks of the master's Seagram, Johnson directly challenged and even repudiated the very style for which he

had helped write the credo. Through these challenges, Johnson created the first cracks in the International Style, opening the field to variants of Postmodernism and deconstructivism. Rebellion against the International Style found theoretical support in the seminal text of architect Robert Venturi, *Complexity and Contradiction in Architecture* (1966), which, in an inversion of Mies' much-quoted "Less is more," answered "Less is a bore."

Other architects who, unlike Johnson, had not been so closely associated with a master were freer to follow the course of the International Style to its natural conclusions rather than rebel against it. These were the second-generation modernists, architects free of the constriction of the early orthodox tenets and postwar boom mentality who could study the expressive qualities of the International Style. Among the most astute and creative of those currently working is I.M. Pei, who took all that was elegant about the International Style and within its constraints created prismatic forms. Pei's Hancock Tower (1969) in Boston is one of the most powerful expressions of the International Style and a wholly new interpretation of Mies' reductivism. The building is a blue, reflective prism that literally chooses to disappear and reappear with the changing sky. The uninterrupted surface so perfectly reflects the floating clouds that, Zenlike, it becomes one with the sky and therefore, metaphorically at least, achieves a sense of "nothingness."

Other later exemplar International Style buildings include Lever House by Gordon Bunshaft (1951; New York City), an unprecedented blue-green glass Constructivist statement that has remained for half a century one of the central images of the International Style. Contrasting with the Seagram's tightly unified slab form, Lever House is a composite composition, annealing two slabs perpendicular to each other, one plane floating above the other. Lever House, after half a century, was justifiably named one of the first International Style historic landmarks, initiating the start of a public appreciation after the fact of the beauty of mid-20th-century design.

Later interpretations of the International Style have been variations on the gridded glass box or the slab. In midtown Manhattan, the Citicorp Center (1978, Hugh Stubbins and Associates), in which the simplified glass box is sliced diagonally at the roofline, creates a sophisticated silhouette against the skyline. Chicago holds claim to the tallest International Style building on the American skyline, the Sears Tower (1974, Skidmore, Owings and Merrill), a combination of the International Style with the setback skyscraper, though this is not a building to be celebrated for anything but size and surely does not compare to the firm's classic Lever House. One of the latest and most adventurous variations on the International Style slab is the Atlantis (1982, Arquitectonica) in Miami, where the basic gridded glass box is punched through with a giant void, allowing views of the clouds and sunrise over Biscayne Bay through to the city.

Current proponents of the International Style, architects who truly understand its aesthetics include Gwathmey Siegel Associates and Richard Meier. Gwathmey Siegel's Whig Hall (renovations, 1972) at Princeton University and the Busch-Reisinger Museum (1989) at Harvard University speak to a contemporary continuity of design with classical early International Style. Meier's very late International Style J. Paul Getty Museum (1998) in Malibu, with its modern, antique, and Le Corbusian imagery, can be read as a kind of millennial summation of the form and meaning of the style.

Critiques of the International Style

The most powerful ensemble of International Style buildings in America remains the great triumvirate of Park Avenue in Manhattan. Standing on one corner of the avenue, one may look east to the Seagram Building, west to Lever House, and south to the Pan Am Building. Although two of the buildings give the viewer the perfect new world vision of the International Style, one, the Pan Am (1957, Gropius and Belluschi), offers a cautionary tale of modernism. Where good architects make bad buildings, we find all the mistakes that have given the International Style its latter-day bad reputation: the aggressiveness of the building's stance, the overall repetition and boredom of the facade, and most of all the intrusive, callous placement of the building in its urban space. Bizarrely sited above and across Park Avenue rather than along the street, the Pan Am blocks the elongated processional of the Manhattan street plan, nearly devouring its landmark predecessor, Grand Central Station (thankfully now fully restored though still supporting the Pan Am).

International Style ought to be studied and understand theoretically and visually, and judged chronologically. It is blatantly unfair to the pioneer architects of the International Style to be judged by the worst architects and developers who copied them. For each of the excellent examples here presented, there are hundreds of hideous glass boxes purporting to be International Style that line United States' strip streets, fill our malls and industrial parks, mar our university campuses, and worst of all scar our city skylines. It is the bad fortune of the International Style that the meaning of architectural simplicity has been corrupted repeatedly and ignorantly to mean cheapness. A clear example of this contrast may be observed along the Boston skyline, where Pei's Hancock Tower is often paired with its artistic opposition, the Prudential Center, an ill-proportioned glass box nearby.

Influence of the International Style

Certainly, International Style was a cleansing aesthetic, purging the architectural world of ornamental decadence and sentiment. It substituted an aesthetic of truthfulness and structure, clarifying architecture through its rigorous reductivism. Draped only in curtains of glass, it spoke honestly of skeletal structure. Recalling the significance of structure, proportion, simplicity, and geometry to architecture, it insisted on the elemental forms of architecture, reminding us of the continuity of the modern with the antique. Most significant, the International Style created the models, prototypes, or type forms for a modern world. First for a new Europe and then for a new America, both of which were becoming mass societies, the International Style invented the forms for the housing, the schools, and the institutions of the new proletariat, the rising middle class. The International Style thus remains a monumental aesthetic and social experiment in architecture.

LESLIE HUMM CORMIER

See also **Bauhaus, Dessau; Breuer, Marcel (United States); Corbusier, Le (Jeanneret, Charles-Édouard) (France); Farnsworth House, Plano, Illinois; German Pavilion, Barcelona (1929); Glass; Glass Skyscraper; Gropius, Walter (Germany);**

Gropius House, Lincoln, Massachusetts; Gwathmey, Charles, and Robert Siegel (United States); International Style Exhibition, New York (1932); Johnson, Philip (United States); Lever House, New York City; Lincoln Center, New York City; Meier, Richard (United States); Mies van der Rohe, Ludwig (Germany); Pei, I.M. (United States); Seagram Building, New York City; Skidmore, Owings and Merrill (United States); Skyscraper; Weissenhofsiedlung, Deutscher Werkbund, Stuttgart (1927)

Further Reading

Frampton, Kenneth, *Modern Architecture: A Critical History*, New York: Oxford University Press, and London: Thames and Hudson, 1980

Gropius, Walter (editor), *Internationale Architektur*, Munich: Langen, 1925; reprint, Berlin: Florian Kupferberg, 1981; English translation included in *Images*, edited by Charlotte and Tim Benton and Milton Keynes, Buckinghamshire: Open University Press, 1975

Hitchcock, Henry-Russell, Jr., and Philip Johnson, *The International Style: Architecture since 1922*, New York: Norton, 1932; 3rd edition, as *The International Style*, New York and London: Norton, 1995

Pierson, William Hardy, *American Buildings and Their Architects*, 5 vols., Garden City, New York: Doubleday, 1970–; see especially vol. 5, *The Impact of Modernism in the Mid-Twentieth Century*, by William H. Jordy, 1976

Khan, Hassan-Uddin, *International Style: Modernist Architecture from 1925 to 1965*, London, New York, and Cologne, Germany: Taschen, 1998

INTERNATIONAL STYLE EXHIBITION

New York, New York, 1932

"Modern Architecture: International Exhibition," shown at the Museum of Modern Art in New York (MoMA) in the late winter and early spring of 1932, has become part of the mythology of modern architecture in the United States. It was mounted at a time when Art Deco, the nascent streamlined Moderne style (a more horizontal, less ornamented version of Deco), the stripped Classicism of Josef Frank in Austria, the vernacular Classicism of Ragnar Östberg and E. G. Asplund in Scandinavia, and more radical design tendencies seemed equally possible and equally confusing to Americans. MoMA's display of advanced European architecture offered a decisive alternative to the prevailing eclecticism. It is because of this show and its accompanying book, *The International Style: Architecture since 1922*, that a generation of architects adopted the formal language of Le Corbusier, Walter Gropius, and Mies van der Rohe and thought of themselves as working in a technically, artistically, and socially mandated International Style. The exhibition's impact on the American architectural profession is all the more remarkable because it attracted a limited audience and a generally critical press reception. Moreover, the worsening Great Depression made the show's chiefly formalist concerns seem irrelevant and also ensured that next to no building was done in the "International" or any other style. However, the striking and logical manner in which book and exhibition presented the Gropius-Mies-Le Corbusier direction in architecture made MoMA an authorita-

tive guide to it, as faith in revivalist and Art Deco design modes faded during the Depression and as practitioners in the manner advocated by MoMA (chief among them Gropius and Mies) emigrated to the United States.

The impetus for the show came from Alfred H. Barr, Jr., the Museum of Modern Art's young founding director. Barr's intention on assuming the directorship of the new museum in 1929 was to educate the American public—especially its patrons of art—on the evolution and forms of radical art since post-impressionism. Barr generally presented modern painting and sculpture in pluralistic and inclusive terms. However, he was sharply critical of trends in American architecture, especially the Gothic and Classical Revival architecture that dominated such college campuses as Princeton, Harvard, and Wellesley, where Barr was educated and began his scholarly career. He contrasted the shallow eclecticism of American design with the purity and unity of direction he saw at the Dessau Bauhaus in 1927. It was Barr's ambition to make his museum present modern forms in all the visual arts, just as the Bauhaus gave all forms of art and design equal importance. Accordingly, architecture and applied design were important parts of Barr's exhibition plans for MoMA. However, he intended MoMA shows on such topics to be explicitly didactic. Unlike his generally catholic displays of post-1880 painting, Barr intended to feature in architecture only the style of Walter Gropius and like-minded designers to counter what he saw as the inauthenticity of Deco and revivalist architecture. Barr especially wanted to counter the pernicious influence of such skyscraper architects as Raymond Hood, whom Barr saw offering a false, cynical, profit-driven corruption of such concepts as "modernity" and "functionalism."

Barr's intention to mount an architecture show at MoMA was made possible by the help of two associates. Henry-Russell Hitchcock, Jr., was a young Harvard-educated architectural historian who had broken out of a training in revivalist design and joined forces with undergraduate enthusiasts for avant-garde art. His writings made a strong case for Gropius's and Le Corbusier's modernism as the only constructive direction for architectural history. Hitchcock and Barr became friends when they were graduate students in the Fine Arts Department at Harvard. Either there or at Wellesley College, where Barr taught before joining MoMA, Barr and Hitchcock met and befriended a wealthy Harvard undergraduate named Philip Johnson, who had just discovered architecture as a life's calling. Under Hitchcock's and Barr's tutelage, Johnson became not a student of architecture but a writer, investigator, historian, and financial patron in the cause of modern architecture. With Barr's encouragement, Hitchcock's plans to write a book on modernist aesthetics became a plan to mount an exhibition at MoMA of key modernist works, stressing formal elements of the new "style" over social and technical concerns. Johnson assumed chief responsibility for collecting material and mounting the show.

From the beginning, the two historians and their exhibition director had several circumstances limiting them. They wanted to make as strong a case as possible for the work represented by the Dessau Bauhaus and the villas of Le Corbusier. They wished to present this approach as an artistic direction—a program for the creation not merely of functional spaces but of monuments in a genuinely modern style. To bolster their case, they needed to show executed work, not hypothetical projects; too many Americans knew of European modernism solely in terms of utopian projects. To show executed work, however, meant showing municipal housing estates and other projects whose purpose was practical, not artistic. From the other direction, Barr, Hitchcock, and Johnson wanted to make clear that radical European work was necessary to cleanse architecture of the extreme individualism of pre-World War I radical designers. Only pure, simple work, executed in a uniform way with uniform assumptions, could prove the worldwide existence of a single new direction for architecture, yet this work had to be demonstrably aesthetic in conception, not (as the MoMA historians thought of it) uncreatively technical and practical. Finally, the show's planners wanted to convince American patrons of architecture that the new approach would suit their specific needs.

The manner in which Johnson, Hitchcock, and Barr turned varied radical experiments into a single aesthetic entity is demonstrated by their creation of a label for the work they exhibited: "International Style." As Hitchcock and Barr knew, many leaders of the new European architecture, especially Gropius, had labeled their approach "international"; the term connoted an antinationalist, egalitarian view of modernity and design in which a global architecture culture and, eventually, a new global society would be created on the basis of the machine. The MoMA historians were uneasy about the political and antimonumental implications of the term, less because of any political qualms (although Johnson despised the political left) than because of their training as art historians. To Barr and Hitchcock in particular, the idea of a universal formal language whose proponents rejected formal concerns and who refused to believe architectural decisions could be formal at all was an oxymoron in the visual arts. While discussing the need for an art-historical style label for the work they were to show, Barr and his colleagues adopted the term International Style. "International" meant for them simply that the new approach to architectural form, whether arrived at through aesthetic or functionalist choices, was pretty much identical in its results wherever it appeared. The label "International Style"—left in lowercase by Johnson and Hitchcock but capitalized by Barr—had more in common with habits of art-historical terminology—for example, the label given the so-called International Gothic style of 1400—than with politics and technology.

Hitchcock and Barr decided that the most genuinely "international" architecture was that which resembled the reductivist formal language of Le Corbusier. These formal elements—thin, non-load-bearing walls; assertive use of new building technologies; expansive interior spaces; dynamic asymmetry; geometric and Cubist-derived composition; and eschewal of applied ornament—were presented in show and book as the art historian's matter-of-fact catalog of features. The "style" was for them, in fact, the climax of architectural history: It had the geometric purity of classicism and the structural expressiveness of the Gothic, without the ornament that had reduced both styles to mere scenography in the hands of later revivalists.

The format of the show that Johnson mounted in 1932 was in some respects a severe compromising of his original vision. Johnson planned at various times to have leading modernists design models of representative "modern" building types (for example, factories and prisons) and to bring Mies van der Rohe over from Germany to design a more artistically ambitious installation. Museum trustees' qualms and the worsening Depression scaled back these schemes. As it opened in February 1932,

"Modern Architecture: International Exhibition" had three sections. One section displayed photographs of "international style" work from all over the world. Designed to underline the style's ubiquity and inevitability, the section featured much German and French work, a body of generally mediocre American designs, and an entry from as far off as Japan. Modern architecture from socialist countries was shown very sparingly, with the most ambitious Soviet projects not shown at all. The emphasis on executed work, although wise as far as attracting American supporters was concerned, was misleading in its omission of the hypothetical projects through which the modern movement had largely defined itself. It was also ironic, as MoMA, like many leading modernists of the preceding decade, had decided to propagandize for modernism through a temporary show and not a permanent project.

A section called "Housing" was an admission by MoMA of the social agenda of many leading modernists. It was curated by the architectural and social critic Lewis Mumford and documented the conditions that made mass-housing projects necessary in the United States, paying little attention to issues of aesthetics (in contrast, Hitchcock and Johnson argued in *The International Style* that housing projects should follow the formal vocabulary of the International Style). The centerpiece of the show was the section called "Modern Architects." It featured the work (photographs of buildings, models of built and unbuilt designs, and a few unexecuted drawings) of the masters of the new style. These were Le Corbusier, Mies, Gropius, J.J.P. Oud from Holland, Frank Lloyd Wright, and four other American architects or partnerships. This section, demonstrating the similarities and differences between, for example, the Dessau Bauhaus and Mies' Tugendhat House (both displayed in elaborate models), was offered as proof that individual artistry was still possible within the narrow range of the "style." However, a glance at the section called "The Extent of the International Style" reconfirms the narrowness of that range as defined by MoMA, with Expressionist currents in Holland and Germany omitted altogether. Only a very few entries in the show deviated from the canonical Le Corbusian forms. Ironically, these were mostly works by Le Corbusier himself, such as the rubble wall of the just-designed Pavillon Suisse in Paris. Hitchcock seems to have decided that Le Corbusier's great stature as an artist entitled him to liberties that no other designer should dare.

The criteria for including American designers in the "Modern Architects" section seem in retrospect to have been the most compromised and shortsighted aspects of the show. The MoMA historians felt that Wright had to be included as the greatest living master, indeed the founder, of modern architecture, even though he had been vocally contemptuous of new European work. The show and the book, especially the latter, cautioned that Wright's individualism was no longer a constructive attitude in architectural reform. Wright designed a striking "House on the Mesa" for the show, but later demanded that his work be omitted from the traveling version of the exhibition created by MoMA's education department.

After Wright, the best-known modernists in Johnson's show were the revivalist-turned-modernist George Howe and his Swiss-born partner, William Lescaze. Howe and Lescaze's public housing proposal for the Chrystie-Forsyth site in lower Manhattan garnered much press attention. Both Howe and Lescaze's work and that of the Vienna-born Californian Richard Neutra were programmatically "international" in form. Johnson regarded Neutra as the best modern architect in the United States, and the museum's decision to feature Neutra and exclude another Viennese modernist in California, the more Expressionist-oriented Rudolph Schindler, has become notorious as an example of Johnson's narrow vision. Surprisingly, among the other Americans featured in this section was Barr's bête noire, Raymond Hood, who contributed a model of a complex of ribbon-windowed towers in an open field, the fruit of his interest in Le Corbusier's work. Hitchcock's essay on Hood in the show's catalog came close to calling Hood an opportunist but claimed that the skyscraper stylist's use of "international" mannerisms proved how inevitable the style must be. A final American firm, Bowman Brothers of Chicago, was included because of Johnson's enthusiasm for its striking drawings. Embarrassingly, it turned out that the firm had built nothing.

"Modern Architecture: International Exhibition" ran for a month and a half, until late March 1932. Critical reaction was generally positive toward the work shown, especially the New York media's response to the Chrystie-Forsyth project. However, the museum—and Hitchcock and Johnson as authors of *The International Style*—were taken to task for their formalism and the obvious narrowness of their criteria. The book, however, remained in print, and a smaller version of the show circulated to Cleveland, Los Angeles, and other cities. The show aroused heated and generally hostile debate within the New York architectural community. As the Great Depression deepened, respect grew for the point of view set forth in the show's designs, if not for the viewpoint of the MoMA historians. The museum itself established a permanent Department of Architecture and Design in the wake of the show, with Johnson as director; even after Johnson left in 1934 for an abortive career in fringe politics, the department kept alive the crusading spirit and didactic program that Johnson had established in his first show.

The term "International Style" itself went almost unused except in a few decorating magazines that were under Johnson's influence. It was not until the architecture profession revived after World War II, with Gropius, Mies, and other émigré modernists remaking design education and practice, that Hitchcock's and Johnson's assertion of an International Style became useful. By the time MoMA held a symposium on directions in modernism in 1948, its participants were using International Style freely as a name for modern architecture at its purest. For the next two decades after that, debate on modernism centered in large part on whether any design innovation could be fit into the guidelines of the "Style."

The International Style show of 1932 was both a failure and a success. Critics noted immediately that the show, catalog, and book proscribed the technical and aesthetic possibilities of modernism in unacceptably arbitrary ways. At the same time, the MoMA historians' hopes that the show would regroup American architects around a unified style went unanswered during the Depression. As responses to the changing nature of architecture, both the show and *The International Style* seem shallow in their antitheoretical biases and their old-fashioned definition of architecture as monument. However, it was just these qualities—Hitchcock's, Barr's, and Johnson's evasion of intellectual and ideological pitfalls—that made MoMA's vision of modernism indispensable to the corporate and university patrons of modernism after 1945. While the show and book's protagonists, especially Johnson, emphasized the avant-garde nature of the forms they showed, they managed to give them a European and art-historical pedigree (and a short, simple set of formal rules) that was comforting to patrons and designers weaned on a Beaux-Arts approach. Finally, whatever distortion of the European modern movement the International Style exhibition perpetrated, its eventual success linked architects, patrons, and academic art historians in ways that had profound effects on future architectural change.

MILES DAVID SAMSON

See also **Bauhaus, Dessau; Corbusier, Le (Jeanneret, Charles-Édouard) (France); Gropius, Walter (Germany); Hitchcock, Henry-Russell (United States); International Style; Johnson, Philip (United States); Mies van der Rohe, Ludwig (Germany); Mumford, Lewis (United States); Museum of Modern Art, New York; Neutra, Richard (Austria); Oud, J.J.P. (the Netherlands); Tugendhat House, Brno, Czech Republic**

Further Reading

Scholarship on the International Style show and book has benefited greatly in recent years from access to previously unseen documentation, especially at MoMA. However, the museum's own scholars have been the main beneficiaries. In other scholarship in the field, the long-running argument that Hitchcock, Barr, and Johnson had a private agenda or agendas for misrepresenting European modernism has been redefined—but not dismissed—as these protagonists receive greater scholarly study.

Hitchcock, Henry-Russell, Jr., and Philip Johnson, *The International Style: Architecture since 1922*, New York: Norton, 1932; reprint, with new foreword, New York and London: Norton, 1995
Riley, Terence, *The International Style: Exhibition 15 and the Museum of Modern Art*, New York: Rizzoli, 1992
Schulze, Franz, *Philip Johnson: Life and Work*, New York: Knopf, 1994

IRAN

The contemporary architecture of Iran is predicated on the impact of Europe in the late 19th century and of modernism in the 20th. Since 1980, the expression of Islam in building has played a major role.

The Qajar dynasty (1794–1925) maintained cohesion by emphasizing the Persian values of Shiite Islam. The dominant public buildings were religious—mausoleums, shrines, and most important, mosques. They formed the foci of the *mahalla,* or residential neighborhoods, determined the city fabric, and continued long-standing building traditions. Around 1850, the Persian elite who traveled to the West introduced European-style Palladian villas into the urban landscape. They began to make spatial changes by eliminating traditional elements, such as the *hashti* (the octagonal transitional space) and by installing indoor bathrooms and mechanical heating (using kerosene). New materials, such as steel and concrete, changed the architecture, and new housing forms, such as row houses, appeared. Persia also became a focus of study in the West, known through publications such as the American Arthur Upham Pope's eight-volume *Survey of Persian Art* (1938).

Discontent with Iran's rulers erupted in the early years of the 20th century, leading to the "constitutional revolution" of

1905–11, supported by the British and the Russians. After a bloodless coup d'état in 1921, Reza Shah formed a republic and launched the country's reconstruction and modernization. He established a strong centralized government and, like Atatürk of Turkey, moved toward secularization, regarding religion as a force that hindered progress. The traditional Islamic and metaphysical thought of the late 19th-century Qajar dynasty gave way to the introduction of Western scientific and rationalist ideas coupled with new economic and political considerations. However, unlike Atatürk, Reza Shah not only maintained a monarchy (he was crowned in the Citadel in 1925) but also used history for his own ends. In architecture, he revived a consciousness of ancient Achaemenid glory in an interpretation of the newly rediscovered sites of Susa and Persepolis. He also initiated grand urban projects while demolishing in the 1930s symbols of the Islamic past, such as the wall and 12 gateways to Tehran. Many of the buildings of the Citadel (Arq) were replaced with new public structures, such as ministry buildings.

The capital city of Tehran well illustrates nationalist and secularist aspirations. The plan imposed a grid of streets on the dense existing city patterns and provided separation of vehicles from pedestrians. It changed the scale, accommodating new modes of transport and multistory apartment buildings. The planners used the new *maidans,* or squares, as focal points of axial layouts and as symbols of modernity instead of as centers of activity for the neighborhood's inhabitants.

From 1921, the state was the most active patron of architecture, which changed with the influx of foreign architects. Among the first were the Frenchmen André Godard (1881–1965) and Maxime Siroux (1907–75), who arrived as archaeologists but soon started to design buildings. Siroux restored historic buildings and designed a number of schools that displayed sensitivity to climate, materials, and local customs. Godard became the first director of the Iran e-Bastan (Archaeological) Museum (1929–36) and its architect. He also planned Tehran University in 1934—the first in the country based on a Western model— and Siroux designed its Medical School. Other works in the rationalist modern mode followed, including the School of Fine Arts by Roland Dubrelle and Mohsen Foroughi. Another pioneering architect was Nikolai Marcoff (1882–1957) from St. Petersburg, who introduced the use of plate-glass-and-steel-frame construction. He designed, among other buildings, several churches and the Bank Melli (c. 1928) in Tehran. The building uses the crenellated roof derived from traditional palaces as well as Zoroastrian symbols, such as the Eagle of Ahura. Marcoff referred to Achaemenid building again in his monumental Triumphal Arch (c. 1930).

The mid-1930s marked the beginning of modernism in Iran with its cubic forms, new materials, and buildings raised on *pilotis* (stilts). The Viennese architect Gabriel Guevrekian (1900–70) came to work in Iran in the mid-1930s, having been the secretary-general at the first congress of CIAM (Congrès Internationaux d'Architecture Moderne) in 1928. Guevrekian's buildings for the ministries of foreign affairs, justice, and industry and new building types, such as the Tehran Theatre, were built between 1934 and 1937. Among the local architects trained either abroad or in the recently established School of Architecture, Vartan Avanessian (1896–1982), an Armenian from Tabriz, was perhaps the most prolific. His designs include Reza Shah's palace at Sadabad and apartment buildings and cinemas in Tehran. On his return from France in 1936, Mohsen Foroughi (1907–82) worked on a series of buildings for Tehran University. Other significant architects were Keyghobad Zafar (1910–), who studied at the Architectural Association in London, and Hoshang Seyhoun, who graduated from the École des Beaux-Arts in Paris in 1948. The latter designed modern

Al-Ghadir Mosque, 1988, Tehran, designed by Djahanguir Mazloum
© Aga Khan Awards for Architecture

Brickwork frames a pedestrian street in Shustar New Town, designed by Kamran Diba (D.A.Z. Architects, Planners and Engineers)
Photo by Kamran Adle © Aga Khan Award for Architecture

buildings that also referred to Persian vernacular architecture, as in the Mausoleum of Nader Shah in Mashad.

After Reza Shah's abdication in 1941, his son Mohammed Reza, the self-styled shah of Iran, furthered the cause of secular modernism during his reign, which lasted until 1979. Architecture as a profession finally came fully into being. The journal *Architecte,* founded by the architect Iradj Moshiri, appeared around 1937; a decade later, the Society of Iranian Architects was chartered.

Under the Pahlavi reign (1925–79), Iran experienced a growing commercialization of agriculture and crafts, especially carpets. The most important economic sector, oil, was nationalized during the 1951–53 prime-ministership of Mosaddeq, making available a tremendous source of income for state projects. The shah's "White Revolution" of 1962 inaugurated a program for the establishment of new towns and buildings. In 1971, the Borj-e Azadi, the inverted Y-shaped Freedom Monument close to Tehran Airport, was built, commemorating the 2,500th anniversary of the Persian Empire along with lavish celebrations at Persepolis. Other religions besides Islam also constructed religious edifices, the most impressive of which is the modernist Armenian Cathedral (1964–70) in Tehran by Mirza Koutchek.

The modernizing nation-state, boosted by oil money, embraced modern architecture with its cubic forms, large windows, lightweight-steel structures, flat roofs, and thin walls. Small builders, the *besaz-o-befaroush* (build-and-sell), flourished, as did major architectural practices, such as that of Abdolaziz Farman-Farmian and Associates. The number of architects who built architecturally significant buildings remained small, and many of them were trained abroad. Among these, the most distinguished are Kamran Diba (1937–) and Nader Ardalan (1939–).

Diba's work in Iran, under the name DAZ Architects, consists entirely of institutional works in concrete and brick. Jondishapour University (1968–76) in Ahwaz, the Garden of Niavaran (1970–78), and the Museum of Contemporary Art (1967–76) in Tehran illustrate well his concerns. Arguably, Diba's finest work was that of Shushtar New Town (1974–80) in Kuzestan, a remarkably designed settlement that is spatially and architecturally elegant and focuses on intensifying human interaction.

From 1972 to 1979, Ardalan's Mandala Collaborative produced a number of important works. These include the Iran Center for Management Studies (1970–73), now Imam Sadegh University in Tehran, designed when Ardalan was working for Farman-Farmian, and the Master Plan for Bu Ali Sina University

(1975) in Hamadan with Georges Candilis. Ardalan also wrote about Iranian architecture, geometric order, and Islam in an influential publication, *The Sense of Unity,* coauthored in 1973 with Laleh Bakhtiar. Both Diba and Ardalan have worked outside the country since 1979.

Other prominent architects working in the shah's Iran were Djhanguir Darvich, who designed the Farahabad Sports Center in Tehran; the Aratta Collaborative of Farroukh Essalat, the University of Mashad; Cyrus Hessamian, an elementary school in Shiraz; Ali Amanat, the Cultural Heritage Office (1980) in Tehran; and Mehdi Kowsar, several Brutalist buildings. At the same time, many foreign architects, such as Roche and Dinkeloo, Maxwell Fry, and Jane Drew, realized works all over the country.

In the 1970s, building was spurred even further by the success of OPEC (the Organization of Petroleum Exporting Countries), which was able to reconstruct the vital oil market in its favor. This caused a worldwide oil crisis, and as building production slowed in the West, it boomed in the Middle East, attracting architects from all over the world into the region. Many influential architects from the West cannibalized preconceived images of Islamic architecture, sometimes an easier way to satisfy clients. An increase of rural-to-urban migration and the decrease in oil income in Iran due to pressure placed on OPEC by the West aggravated the economic situation, and a major cutback in construction around 1977 brought massive unemployment, adversely affecting the population and architectural production.

The notion of expressing an Islamic identity through architecture for states with majority Muslim populations spread in popularity around the same period, becoming a political and cultural rallying cry to distinguish Islam. This usually meant the secular West. Islamic and regional modernist styles vied with each other for recognition as the "authentic" expression for architecture in several countries, including Iran and Saudi Arabia. Equating the country with the religion reinforced the notion of Islam as a cultural force as well, intertwining the realms of the religious with the secular.

Opposition to the shah's regime by Ayatollah Khomeini's followers, beginning in 1977 with the slogan "Independence, Freedom, Islamic Republic," led to the Islamic Revolution of 1978–79. The grievances behind the revolution were as much socioeconomic as cultural. The social historian Nikki Keddie wrote in the *American Historical Review* (no. 88), 1983, "Far more than the Qajars, the Pahlavis were perceived as tools of Western or Westernized powers, chiefly the United States and Israel . . . there developed amongst the alienated a search for roots and a return to 'authentic' Iranian or Islamic values." The Iran-Iraq war that lasted several years, beginning in 1980, reinforced patriotic/Islamic ideas but adversely affected the building industry.

Iran questioned the symbols of modernism, denigrating everything from the shah's time and promoting "Islamic" architecture. In the mid-1980s, this unfortunately led to a pastiche of badly interpreted elements, such as the dome, the arch, the enclosed courtyard, and even stained-glass windows. The school of architecture in Tehran that had promoted modern architecture succumbed to the stylistic modes of Postmodernism, high-tech design, and traditionalism and became the purveyor of an eclectic design approach. Architecture for new buildings paid lip service to historical Islamic building in formalistic terms and use of materials but without any real interpretation of its intrinsic principles. Architects and teachers alike discussed at length issues of identity and culture but built very little of note despite the explosive growth of the cities.

Tehran's population reached 10 million by the mid-1990s. New major infrastructure works were undertaken: expressways, a subway, and a sewage system. The old *maidans* were redesigned, and myriad small urban plots turned into gardens with curious fountains and murals depicting revolutionary themes. In the late 1980s and 1990s, the architecture seemed to convey a sense of celebration and populism. The mausoleum dedicated to Imam Khomeini and built on his death in 1989, with its iron structures and onion-shaped domes covered with glazed tiles, is the most obvious expression of this Postmodern atmosphere. A design competition for Farhangistan, the Academies of the Islamic Republic (science, medicine, and language), drew on stereotypical Islamic architectural elements, especially the *chahrbagh* (the quadripartite garden) in the winning project by the Naqsh-i Jehan/Pars Consulting Group, headed by Seyyed Hadi Mirmeian. Another competition project for the Great Historical Museum of Khorasan, Mashad, by Dariush Mirfenderski, refers to Kalat-i Nadiri, a palace-fortress built by Nadir Shah at the end of the 18th century.

Reflecting a different aspect of contemporary architecture in Iran, Ali Saremi, a modernist of Tajeer Architects, abstracts past elements and archetypes to produce modern buildings. The Afshar Residence (1976) and the Jolfa Residential Complex (1985), using both concrete and brick, illustrate his approach. The Bavand Consulting Group, headed by Iradj Kalantari and Hossein Sheikh Zeyneddin, one of the largest architectural practices in the country, designed in the same vein the Faculty of Engineering (1984–90) at Imam Khomeini University in Qazvin. Faryar Javaherian used a similar approach in an apartment building at Farmaniyya. The Al-Ghadir Mosque (1988) in Tehran by Djahanguir Mazloum is among the most successful syntheses of tradition and modernity.

The architectural profession has very little influence on decisions in building and operates in an atmosphere of uncertainty. The struggle continues between a symbolic "Islamic architecture" referring to some notion of the past and the desire to be "modern." The social and religious aspects of architecture and urbanism dominate the rhetoric of the politicians and the professionals. The production of high-quality architecture is impeded by the complexity of procedures, by speculation, and by outdated technology applied to new building types. In general, the architecture in Iran remains in a state of great flux, although a few struggle to do interesting work, and a sense of idealism exists.

HASAN-UDDIN KHAN

See also **Ardalan, Nader (Iran); Mosque**

Further Reading

Adle, Chahryar, and Bernard Hourcade (editors), *Téhéran: Capitale Bicentenaire,* Paris: Institut Français de Recherche en Iran, 1992

Diba, Darab, "Iran and Contemporary Architecture," *Mimar,* 38 (March 1991)

Frampton, Kenneth (series editor), *World Architecture, 1900–2000: A Critical Mosaic,* 10 vols., Vienna and New York: Springer, 1999–2002 (see especially volume 5, Hasan-Uddin Khan, *The Middle East,* 2000).

Keddie, Nikki R., "Iranian Revolutions in Comparative Prespective," *American Historical Review,* 88 (1983)

Khan, Hasan-Uddin, *Contemporary Asian Architects,* Cologne and New York: Taschen, 1995

Marefat, Mina, "Building to Power: Architecture of Tehran, 1921–1941" (Ph.D. dissertation), Massachusetts Institute of Technology, 1988

"Recent Buildings in Iran," *The Architectural Review,* 162/695 (July 1977)

Saremi, Ali, *Perennial Values in Iranian Architecture,* Tehran, 1997

Saremi, Ali, "The Status of Iranian Architecture in Today's World," *Abadi* (1998)

Seyhoun, Houchang, *Regards sur l'Iran,* Paris: La Déesse, 1974

Tihran dar yik nigah; Tehran at a Glance (bilingual Persian-English edition), Tehran: Public Relations Office and International Affairs Department of the Tehran Municipality, 1992

ISLAM, MUZHARUL 1923–

Architect, Bangladesh

Muzharul Islam has been active since the early 1950s in defining the scope and form of a modern architectural culture, first in Pakistan and after 1971 in Bangladesh. Beginning in the early 1950s as the only formally trained architect working in Dhaka, Bangladesh, Islam started with the enormous task of creating a modern yet Bengali paradigm for architecture. His steadfast commitment to a modernist ideology stems from an optimistic vision for transforming society. For Islam, modernism is more than an architectural vocabulary; it is above all an alternative ethical and rational approach for addressing what he perceives as social inequities and deprivation of the region. Consequently, his commitment for establishing a strong design culture in Bangladesh is paralleled by an equally deep engagement with the political and ethical dimension of society.

Islam's contribution to creating a vibrant architectural culture depended on establishing the architectural profession of a new nation in the face of strong opposition from bureaucratic and engineering circles. To this end he introduced an international and national dialogue in Bangladesh by inviting Louis Kahn, Stanley Tigerman, and Paul Rudolph to work there. As teacher, mentor, and organizer, Islam influenced the development of vigorous architectural activities; the most notable was the founding of Chetana Architectural Research Group in 1983.

Islam was the Senior Architect of the Government of East Pakistan (1958–64) before opening his own practice in Dhaka. His architectural repertoire is wide; he has designed and built universities, large-scale housing, government buildings and institutions, and numerous residences. His architectural production, from his earlier skeletal approach expressing the pavilion para-

Jahangirnagar University Student Dormitories (1973)
© Aga Khan Trust for Culture

digm of the hot, humid Bengal delta, as in the N.I.P.A. Building at Dhaka University (1964) and his own house (1969), to his later stereotomic, earth-hugging idiom, best shown in the National Library (1980), has sought to derive a place-oriented architecture from modern tectonic and constructional methods, from environmentally sensitive responses, and from abstract cultural typologies overlaid with geometric order. The buildings respond to the nature of dwelling in the hot, humid delta as receptacles of "light, green, and air."

In Islam's large-scale projects, especially Jahangirnagar University (1967–70) and Joypurhat Housing (1978), the order of the plan is determined by a geometric web of tilted squares, triangles, and diagonals. The projects are situated in nonurban areas where the natural landscape is transformed into a scene of deep-green foliage and clustered masses of red brick. These projects address alternative ideas of urbanity by moving away from the conventional morphology of either city or country. In the Polytechnique Institutes, designed with Stanley Tigerman for five sites (1966–78), the project became an occasion to produce rational and methodological principles of design for Bangladesh where none really existed in a contemporary sense. The initial study by the architects resulted in an extraordinary meticulous research on form determinates in relation to tectonics, ecology, climatology, and materials and traditional building techniques.

During the time when Islam was establishing his practice—the 1950s and 1960s—Pakistan was in political turmoil. The dominant political consciousness in then East Pakistan, roused by the issue of economic disparities between the two provinces of Pakistan, and the manipulative use of religion by the central government, polarized most Bengali intellectuals such as Islam toward secular, socialist thinking. Islam has always insisted on architecture's link to larger social and political issues, especially within the South Asian context. His continued commitment to a rationalist and materialist philosophy has led to his vehement antipathy to the manipulation of architecture and culture within highly politicized religious situations. In this context, his work, remaining distanced from exclusivist symbolization and what he sees as architectural fashion, has approximated a kind of ascetic architecture. Since his direct participation in the Bangladesh War of Liberation in 1971, he has received fewer commissions from various governments.

Islam holds the view that architecture is not only a reflection of society but also a medium for social critique and transformation. In his increasing political engagement he has argued for a broadening of the role of architects in South Asia in order to confront and transform existing social conditions, including the vast rural areas that mostly lie outside the pale of formal architectural activities.

KAZI KHALEED ASHRAF

See also **Dhaka, Bangladesh; Kahn, Louis (United States); Rudolph, Paul (United States)**

Biography

Born 25 December 1923, Bangladesh; earned bachelor's degree in civil engineering, 1946 at Calcutta University; bachelor's of Architecture, 1952, at Oregon University, and master's degree, 1961 at Yale University, New Haven, Connecticut (trained under Paul Rudolph). Received Rockefeller Fellowship 1961 and toured Europe. Junior Architect to the Government of East Pakistan 1953–58, and Senior Architect 1958–64; began private practice 1964; consultant to the Government of Pakistan for the Pakistan Embassy in Peking, 1965. President, Institute of Architects, Pakistan 1968–69; President, Institute of Architects, Bangladesh 1972–75, and 1978–80. Member, International Jury, for selection of Best Design for the competition for the Grand Mosque in Islamabad 1968; Chairman, Committee for review and finalization of the Fourth Five Year Plan containing the sector "Physical Planning, Housing and Architecture," Islamabad 1970; Member, Master Jury, of the first Aga Khan Award in Architecture 1980; Member, International Jury, for the competition for the Ministry of Foreign Affairs Building in Riyadh, Saudi Arabia 1982. Initiated with group of architects Chetana Study Group (later to become Chetana Architecture Research Center) 1983. Special Award, Institute of Indian Architects (West Bengal Chapter) 1991; Great Master's Award for lifetime contribution to the architecture profession from AYA (Architects of the Year Awards) India 1997; and Fellow of the American Institute of Architects 1999.

Selected Works

Art and Crafts College, Dhaka, 1953
Dhaka University Library, Dhaka, 1953
Town Plan for Rangamati, 1958
Government Housing, Azimpur, 1960
Science Laboratory, Dhaka, 1964
Krishi Bhaban, Dhaka, 1965
National Institute of Public Administration Building, Dhaka University, 1964
Polytechnique Institutes, 1970 (with Stanley Tigerman)
Chittagong University, 1971
Atomic Energy Commission Housing, Roopur, 1971
Jahangirnagar University, 1971
Roads and Highways Laboratory Housing, Mirpur; Bangladesh Pavilion, New Delhi, 1973
Limestone Factory Housing, Joypurhat, 1979
National Library and Archives, Dhaka, 1980.

Further Reading

Ashraf, Kazi Khaleed, "Muzharul Islam, Kahn and Architecture in Bangladesh," *MIMAR*, 38 (1989)
Ashraf, Kazi Khaleed, and James Belluardo, *An Architecture of Independence: The Making of Modern South Asia*, New York: The Architectural League of New York, 1997
Banerji, Anupam, "Conversation with Muzharul Islam," *Environments: Journal of Interdisciplinary Studies*, University of Waterloo, Ontario, Vol. 2, 1988
Husain, Rabiul, "Bangladesher Sthapatya O Sthapati Muzharul Islam" (in Bangla), *Architect Muzharul Islam: 70th Birthday Souvenir*, Dhaka, 1993
Lifchez, Raymond, "Master Plan Study Gives East Pakistan New Approaches for Tropical Architecture," *Architectural Record* (September 1968)

ISOZAKI, ARATA 1931–

Architect and theorist, Japan

Arata Isozaki is one of the most influential architects and theorists of the Postmodern era in Japan. He studied architecture at the University of Tokyo under Professor Kenzo Tange. After graduating in 1954, Isozaki worked on several important projects at Kenzo Tange and Urtec up until 1963, including the Tokyo plan (1960) and the main pavilion for Expo '70 in Osaka. Later, he was regarded as Tange's successor in the international architectural scene. Although he started his practice in Tokyo, most of his early works were commissioned and built in Oita, his native town in the southern part of Japan. He went into architectural practice with a sense of absence. His parents had died, and his hometown was burned down during the war. These experiences made him a typical lost-generation architect in Japan. In 1962 he made a drawing titled *City of Ruins*, which depicted a future city on the columns of ancient ruins. This became his manifesto as an architect. The juxtapositions of past and future, of destruction and construction, are key motifs of his architecture.

The Oita Medical Hall (1960, demolished in 1999) was Isozaki's first built work. His work from the late 1960s shows the influence of the Metabolism School. In Oita he designed such early works as Iwata High School and the Nakayama Residence (1964), Oita Prefectural Library (1960), and the Oita branch of Fukuoka City Bank (1967). Years later in the same area, he designed Yufuin Station (1990), the new Oita Prefectural Library (1995), and B-con Plaza (1995). In 1968 he experienced

the worldwide student revolution. He considered that revolution symptomatic of the end of the early modern era. Since then, his attitude toward architecture has changed. Through his writing, he revealed his preference for Western architectural history. The Tsukuba Center building (1983) was the embodiment of his writings and consisted of accumulated fragments of the products of Western architectural history from the Renaissance to Neo-classicism. In the center of the building, he placed a copy of the plan of the capital city, Rome, as it was laid out by Michelangelo. The original piazza was lowered, and the central statue of Marcus Aurelius was removed. He assembled the historical elements, but without a recognizable essence. As a result, Isozaki's treatment produced a sense of absence. In 1986 he designed the Contemporary Museum of Art in Los Angeles, his first work abroad. With its dominating pyramidal shape set above an Asian sandstone building, Richard Meier described this museum as "a beacon in the land of the lost."

After the Tsukuba Center building (1983), Isozaki tried to draw his identity from a Japanese sense of place. The Mito Art Tower (1990) shows the results of his quest for identity. He put a double helix-shaped tower among Western motifs in this building complex. At the center of the court, he designed a compelling cascade. In the center of this cascade, a huge stone was suspended with chains and showered with water, an allegori-

Palau Sant Jordi Sports Hall, Barcelona (1990).
Photo © Mary Ann Sullivan

cal reference to the battles between students and riot police in the late 1960s. In 1990, he was nominated to design the Sant Jordi Sports Hall in Spain for the Olympics, a project that brought him international recognition. The next year, in Orlando, Florida, he completed the Team Disney Building, in which he inserted a replica of the sacred site of Ise shrine as a central sundial court for the building.

Although Isozaki began his career as a modernist architect, he gradually assumed a critical position toward modernism. He does not believe in a reductive functionalism, and his forms have been described as stylized, eclectic and mannerist in keeping with a Postmodernist visual paradigm. Throughout his career, Isozaki has constantly changed his method of design from one standpoint to another. Most of his friends are not architects but, rather, artists, composers, and novelists. As early as 1966, he took curves from the body lines of Marilyn Monroe to design furniture and architecture. This technique of anthropomorphic projection was drawn from the works of Marcel Duchamp and pop art. His monument (1977) of Otomo Sorin, a Christian feudal lord in the 17th century; his monument (1993) to architect-poet Michizo Tachihara; and the gravestone (1993) of Italian composer Luigi Nono in Venice are products of his friendship with artists and scholars. In this respect, he is quite exceptional among Japanese architectural professionals. He has written many articles and edited several series of books on art and architecture.

In the 1990s Isozaki's style became more free and dynamic. Oval, hyperbolic, and parabolic shapes dominated his architecture. Historical references gradually faded away from his design, coinciding with rise and fall of Postmodern architecture. The Nara Convention Hall (1998) and the Shizuoka Prefectural Convention and Art Center (1998) show his interest in abstract composition. Isozaki inherited enthusiasm for mechanical devices from Kenzo Tange and the Metabolists. He was also influenced by the legacies of Western architecture and contemporary art. Nevertheless, he preferred to treat them with irony. In this respect, Isozaki's architecture can be seen as an opposition to the "will to construct" evident in modernism.

HIROYUKI SUZUKI

See also **Metabolists; Tange, Kenzo (Japan); Tokyo, Japan**

Biography

Born in Oita City, Japan, 23 July 1931. Studied at the University of Tokyo, Faculty of Architecture, under Kenzo Tange; degree in architecture 1954. Married sculptor Aiko Miyawaki 1971. Worked for Kenzo Tange and Urtec, Tokyo 1954–63. Director, Arata Isozaki and Associates, Tokyo from 1963. Visiting professor, University of California, Los Angeles 1969; visiting professor, University of Hawaii, Honolulu 1974; visiting professor, Rhode Island School of Design, Providence 1976; visiting professor, Columbia University, New York 1976, 1979; visiting professor, Harvard University, Cambridge, Massachusetts 1981; visiting professor, Yale University, New Haven, Connecticut 1982. Member, Accademia Tiberina, Italy 1978; honorary fellow, American Institute of Architects 1983; honorary member, Bund Deutscher Architekten, West Germany 1983. Gold Medal, Royal Institute of British Architects 1986.

Selected Works

Oita Medical Hall, Oita (demolished 1999), 1960
Tokyo Plan (project with the Kenzo Tange Team), 1960
Cities in the Air (project), 1960
Oita Medical Hall, Oita, 1960
Oita Prefectural Library, Oita, 1960
City of Ruins (project), 1962
Nakayama Residence, Oita, 1964
Oita Branch, Fukuoka City Bank, Oita, 1967
Electric Labyrinth (photo collage), 1968
Main pavilion for Expo '70, Osaka (demolished), 1970
Kitakyushu City Museum, Kitakyushu City, 1974
Gunma Prefectural Museum of Fine Art, 1974
Kamioka Town Hall, Gifu, 1978
Tsukuba Center Building, Ibaragi, 1983
The Museum of Contemporary Art, Los Angeles, 1986
Sant Jordi Sports Hall, Barcelona, 1990
Yufuin Station, Oita, 1990
Mito Art Tower, Ibaragi, 1990
Team Disney Building, Orlando, 1991
Luigi Nono's Gravestone, Venice, 1993
Kyoto Concert Hall, 1995
Oita Prefectural Library, 1995
B-con Plaza, Oita, 1995
Nara Convention Hall, Nara, 1998
Shizuoka Prefectural Convention and Art Center, Shizuoka, 1998
Gunma Prefectural Observatory, Gunma, 1999

Selected Publications

Kenchiku no kaitai [Deconstruction of Architecture], 1975
Shuho ga [On Maniera], 1979
Kukan e [Towards Space], 1984
Anywhere, 1992
Anyway, 1995
Shigen no Modoki: Japanesukizeshon [Reproduction of Origin], 1996
Anyplace, 1997
Anyone, 1998
Anywise, 1999

Further Reading

Arata Isozaki, Inax Report 140, Tokyo: Inax, 1999
Drew, Philip, *The Architecture of Arata Isozaki*, New York and London: Granada, 1982
Frampton, Kenneth (editor), *A New Wave of Japanese Architecture*, New York: Institute for Architecture and Urban Studies, 1978
Futagawa, Yukio (editor), *Arata Isozaki*, volume 1: *1959–1978*, Tokyo: A.D.A. Edita, 1991
Futagawa, Yukio (editor), *Arata Isozaki*, Tokyo: A.D.A. Edita, 1996
GA Document 57 (1999)
Stewart, David (editor), *Arata Isozaki: Architecture, 1960–1990*, Los Angeles: Museum of Contemporary Art, and New York: Rizzoli, 1991
Stewart, David, and Richard Meier (editors), *Arata Isozaki: 1960/1990 Architecture*, Tokyo: Imex, 1991

ISRAEL

Although the state of Israel was officially founded on 15 May 1948, its architecture dates from the turn of the 20th century, when waves of Jewish immigrants arrived in Palestine. Over the century, architecture was fashioned under a number of successive political and geographic changes, wars, riots, economic fluctuations, waves of immigration, and demographic changes that forced it to adapt and respond to constantly shifting pressures and conditions.

The architecture of the Jewish settlers, who arrived in the 1880s, was limited essentially to residential structures and tended to follow the style that was in fashion at the time in Palestine, the Southern Mediterranean, mixed to various degrees with local Arab idioms. Buildings had stone or stucco exteriors, red tile roofs, and shuttered windows.

The need for public buildings that would constitute and express the new identity and aspirations of the settlers and symbolize the new, yet old, Hebrew culture emerged at the beginning of the 20th century. Unlike other colonists in other parts of the world who were able to draw on the architectural heritage of the mother country when building their new settlements, the Jewish pioneers had no architectural tradition to call their own. Not even the architecture of synagogues, which served as centres of Jewish religious, cultural, and communal life in the diaspora, could be used as inspiration, as they reflected the styles and fashions prevalent in their surrounding societies.

The "Oriental" movement that formed during this period influenced painting, literature, theatre, dance, and music. The new settlers saw their return to Zion as the establishment of a direct link with their Biblical ancestors, and the eclectic aspect of the Oriental movement enabled architects to incorporate Biblical and local Arabic elements within the contours of monumental European buildings. This is evident in the Gimnasia Herzeliah, Tel Aviv (1910), designed by Yosef Barski, and the Technion, Haifa (1914), by Alexander Berwald. However, the movement was not restricted to public buildings, as exemplified by the Bialik Residence (1920) by Yosef Minor and the Palm House (1920s) by Y. Tabachnick, both in Tel Aviv.

By the end of the 1920s, as reflected elsewhere in Western Europe, eclectic architecture that borrowed motifs from the previous century slowly gave way to a modern architecture; that is, one based on a unique formal language. This is best demonstrated by the school on Kibbutz Degania (1928) by Richard Kauffmann and the dining hall at Kibbutz Tel Yosef (1931) by Leopold Krakauer. Both structures were designed to fit the new conditions, and their forms explore solutions to the existing climatic problems.

In the 1930s, the rise to power of the Nazis in Europe led to new waves of immigrants who brought with them architects schooled in the new theories of Le Corbusier, Walter Gropius, and the Bauhaus. At the same time, a number of young architects returned to Palestine after a period of studies in places such as Paris, Berlin, and Ghent (the Netherlands). The common opposition of these two groups to the prevailing eclecticism and their acceptance of the contemporary concept of building within the local context in turn led to the demise of historical architecture and marked the beginning of the pursuit of purely abstract functionalism.

However, although the European newcomers unequivocally proclaimed the superiority of the International Style, the returning architects, having knowledge of the local milieu and familiarity with the way of life of the established community, were in favor of a more gradual adaptation of European concepts to Israeli conditions. Among this group were Zeev Rachter, Arieh Sharon, Dov Karmi, and Joseph Neufeld, who were to become leaders of Israeli architecture.

The restrictions on land use imposed by the British Mandate resulted in a decline in the construction of private residences and an increase in cooperatively owned apartment buildings. Structures such as the Kiryati House, Tel Aviv (1941), by Shmuel Mestiechkin, the Cooperative Workers Residences, D, E, and F, Tel Aviv (1935), by Arieh Sharon, and others of the period reflect the Spartan Bauhaus philosophy. Flat-roofed, monochromatic monoliths of stuccoed concrete, with surfaces broken only by cubist protrusions or slotted recesses of balconies, these Bauhaus-inspired structures eschewed any articulation of nature, ornamentation, or relief work.

Erich Mendelsohn, renowned for his idiosyncratic style, came to Palestine from England to design the residence for Chaim Weizman near Tel Aviv in 1934. Influenced by the Palestinian environment, he abandoned his usual plasticity in favor of a restrained and somber style and designed buildings such as the Hadassah University Medical Centre on Mount Scopus, Jerusalem (1938). World War II and the decline in construction ended Mendlesohn's activities in Palestine.

In his search for novel, enlightened, hygienic, and efficient architectural forms, Le Corbusier discovered the "white cities" on the Mediterranean, with their flat roofs and white walls broken into small units. Whereas Le Corbusier brought the Mediterranean style to Paris, those influenced by him brought back his "modern" Mediterranean style to the streets of Tel Aviv. Buildings such as the Idelson Street Apartment House, Tel Aviv (1930s), by Dov Karmi; Engle House, Tel Aviv (1933), by Zeev Rechter; and Villa, Tel Benjamin, Ramat Gan (1936), by Nahum Salkind reflect a typical Mediterranean expression infused with the local climate and atmosphere.

During wartime in the 1940s, construction was limited, and architectural development was confined to refinement of previous trends. The declaration of Israel as a sovereign state in 1948 brought the promise of a renaissance in all phases of activity in the country, including architecture. The departure of the British and their building codes and land restrictions provided the opportunity to develop new building ordinances that were seen as more fitting to the condition of the new state of Israel. New energies that had heretofore been directed toward political and armed struggles were freed for architecture and construction.

However, a sudden influx of thousands of immigrants created an urgent need for mass housing. Because of time and budget constraints, quality of design and construction gave way to haste, uniformity, and low cost. By the mid 1950s Israel had a great number of poorly planned and constructed housing projects that were designed with little if any regard to regional concerns such as climate and landscape.

In response, a new wave of Israeli architecture began, and the Israeli architects turned to the Western world for inspiration. Europe's resources were devastated by World War II, and European architects, engineers, and designers, therefore, had little to offer in terms of architectural development. Within Brazil, however—a county unaffected by the war—a group of young architects who were stimulated by Le Corbusier and led by Oscar Niemeyer emerged. Their work demonstrated, among other things, how solar control could be achieved by *brise-soleil*, a device both functional and decorative, and how concrete could be translated into both elegant and playful forms. Israel architects borrowed elements of the Brazilian modernism, incorporating these structures and techniques into buildings such as the Ad-

The Knesset (Parliament Building), Jerusalem, designed by Yosef Klarwein, c.1960
© Michael Nicholson/CORBIS

ministration Building (1960s) by D. Karmi and Z. Metzer and the Hebrew National and University Library (1960), designed by a large group of leading architects both at the Hebrew University in Jerusalem.

The gradual recovery of European and American architecture in the postwar years created a number of significant buildings that generated additional influence on Israeli architects. The Royal Festival Hall, London (1951), by Robert H. Matthew and the Lever House, New York (1952), by Gordon Bunshaft of Skidmore, Owings and Merrill found their echoes in buildings such as the Rederic R. Mann Auditorium, Tel Aviv (1950s), by Zeev Rechter and Karmi and the Supersol high rise, Tel Aviv (1959), by Nachum Zolotov.

However, the greatest impact was made by Le Corbusier's Unité d'Habitation (apartment building) near Marseilles (1952), as exemplified by the Beit Altchul Immigrants' Hostel, Beersheva (1957) by Avraham Yaski and Amnon Alexandroni. The Unité d'Habitation provided an answer to the problem of mass housing as well a new way of using concrete—the primary construction material in Israel. The discovery that concrete need not be plastered proved to be a windfall to Israeli architects, as the deterioration of plaster under the hot sun and high humidity was a perpetual problem.

Experimentations with new materials and technology emerged in the 1960s. One of the most interesting attempts was the "space packing" theory, introduced at the Technion, which was the only recognized architecture school in Israel. Alfred Neumann, together with Zvi Hecker and Eldan Sharon, created a series of buildings composed of repetitive geometrical forms and dominated by strong three-dimensional qualities, such as the Mechanical Engineering Buildings, Technion, Haifa (1960s, Neumann, Hecker, and Sharon) and the desert synagogue at an army base in the Negev (1968) by Neumann and Hecker.

One of the most interesting buildings to come out of the Technion aesthetic is the Town Hall, Bat Yam (1963, Neumann, Hecker, and Sharon). A three-story inverted ziggurat, this building is modern in concept, yet at the same time is evocative of regional architecture. Although Neumann, Hecker, and Sharon's designs did not become mainstream, their formal influence can be found in the work of follower Moshe Safdie.

More typical of the time were projects such as the Knesset (Parliament Building), Jerusalem (1960s), by Yosef Klarwein, consulting architect Dov Karmi; Yad Vashem Memorial Shrine, Jerusalem (1960), by Arieh Elhanani; the El Al Building, Tel Aviv (1960s), by Dov Karmi and Ram Karmi; and the Shalom Mayer Tower, Tel Aviv (1960s), by Y. Perlstein. It is interesting to note that these Jerusalem buildings are not stone-faced, as are most others in Jerusalem, following the ordinance imposed by the British Mandate of 1918 and continuing until the present time.

The architecture of the buildings constructed in the 1970s attempted to establish a link with the country's past. The Town Hall in Beersheva (1972) by Nadler, Nadler, and Bixon and the Beit Ariella Library in Tel Aviv (1977) by Lofenfeld and Gamerman, like many other buildings from the same period, were influenced by Crusader structures and by European and American Brutalism. They are characterized by an aggressive, fortress-like appearance, with narrow windows and large areas of exposed rough concrete.

The search for a regional architecture and a dialogue with the past continued in the 1980s and the 1990s. Moshe Safdie incorporated Arab-Moslem elements in Beit Shmuel, Hebrew Union College, Jerusalem (1986). However, the most serious attempt at dialogue was made by Ram Karmi and Ada Karmi in the Supreme Court Building in Jerusalem (1992). This edifice makes reference to a wide range of structures built in Israel over the centuries, starting with the Herodian period, through the Hellenistic, Crusader, and Greek Orthodox monastery periods and up to the British Mandate period.

Architects in Israel had the rare opportunity to participate in the formation of a new society, and it would seem that in the course of their century-long search for a national identity, they have come full circle. Israeli architecture started with and returned to historical eclecticism. It is clear that what did emerge as a national Israeli style is very much indebted to changing fashions and styles in the world. Although Israeli architects did not merely copy international examples but, instead, adapted them to local conditions and traditions, the styles of the buildings that were created remain conscious of their foreign qualities and ties to European and American architecture.

HAGIT HADAYA

See also **Bauhaus; Concrete; Corbusier, Le (Jeanneret, Charles-Édouard) (France); Niemeyer, Oscar (Brazil); Safdie, Moshe (Canada, Israel); Unité d'Habitation, Marseilles**

Further Reading

Harlap provides a comprehensive history of architecture Israel in the 20th century, and Levin takes an in-depth look at the architecture in Tel Aviv in the early part of the century and the styles and movements that influenced it. Best and Shechori provide a more concise version of Israeli architecture up to the time the articles were written. The additional sources provide further general information on more specific aspects of Israeli architecture and on the ideology that created the state.

Architettura contemporanea in Israele, Rome: Officina Edizioni Roma, 1969

Best, David, "Architecture in Israel," *RIBA Journal*, 79 (November 1972)

Harlap, Amiram, *New Israeli Architecture*, Rutherford, New Jersey: Fairleigh Dickinson University Press, 1982

Herzl, Theodor, *Der Judenstaat: Versuch einer modernen Lösung der Judenfrage*, Leipzig and Vienna: Breitenstein, 1896; as *A Jewish State: An Attempt at a Modern Solution of the Jewish Question*, translated by Sylvie d'Avigdor, London: Nutt, 1896; 6th edition, as *The Jewish State: An Attempt at a Modern Solution of the Jewish Question*, London: Pordes, 1972

Kiriaty, Josef (editor), *Contemporary Israeli Architecture*, Tokyo: Process Architecture, 1984

Levin, Michael D., *White City: International Style Architecture in Israel: A Portrait of an Era*, Tel Aviv: Tel Aviv Museum, 1984

Shechori, Ran, "The State of the Arts in Israel, 1998: Architecture," *ARIEL: The Israel Review of Arts and Letters* 1998 (special issue on Jerusalem)

ISTANBUL, TURKEY

Twentieth-century Istanbul rises on an area that was formerly occupied by the capitals of the Byzantine and Ottoman Empires. That manifold past had culminated in the classical Ottoman city of wooden houses and religious and civic monuments in masonry that were lining winding streets and cul-de-sacs. However, the traditional city of Byzantine and Ottoman tour de forces such as Hagia Sophia and the Süleymaniye Mosque, which had already been spreading beyond city walls, began to change in the 19th century. Then, the sporadic regularization attempts of the street pattern were facilitated largely by frequent fires that often left whole neighborhoods desolate. Some other contemporaneous developments were the construction of huge military barracks, bringing a much larger scale and a regular geometry to the traditional organic city, and the flourishing of new building types and materials, as in the case of masonry palaces and apartment buildings where European architectural styles, such as Neoclassicism, were employed. All these were the consequences of the Ottoman reform attempts initiated in the 18th century with the gradual weakening of the empire. By the 18th century, the Ottomans had started to appropriate European models in military, legislative, and social matters. Those attempts ratified the unique position of Istanbul as a city between "East" and "West" by exposing it to powerful Western influences. Accordingly, an oscillation between the universal (that meant European) and the local shaped the architecture of Istanbul in the first half of the 20th century.

At the turn of the century, Istanbul was a cosmopolitan city of about one million people, with Greek, Armenian, Jewish, Bulgarian, and European inhabitants in addition to the Muslim population. Among the diverse, eclectic, and historicist examples in which foreign and non-Muslim Ottoman architects combined pseudo-Islamic and Ottoman facade features with Beaux-Art plans and new building types, one imported architectural style actually fit with local building traditions. Until the 1960s, when they were beginning to be demolished, Istanbul had the largest number of Art Nouveau buildings of any city in the world.

Italian architect Raimondo D'Aronco had arrived in the city in 1893 to design the pavilions for the Ottoman Agricultural and Industrial Fair, which was later canceled because of the disastrous earthquake in 1894. D'Aronco, instead, worked as the architect in charge of the imperial palaces and directly in the service of the sultan until 1909. During his sojourn, besides many government buildings and annexes to the sultan's residence at Yildiz, he designed numerous villas, fountains, apartment buildings, and even a small mosque. In many of these projects, such as the Seyh Zafir Tomb (1903–04), he achieved a refined reinterpretation of Ottoman architecture that he combined with a modernizing Art Nouveau sensibility. Both the apartment buildings he designed for the Pera district, where inhabitants were mainly European and Levantine, and his *yalis* (wooden, waterfront mansions) along the coasts of the Bosphorus were part of the fin-de-siècle Art Nouveau frenzy in Istanbul.

Many non-Muslim Ottoman architects contributed to the spreading of Art Nouveau with their apartment and office buildings and particularly with villas and *yalis* on Büyükada (one of the nine Princes' Isles on the Marmara Sea) and the Bosphorus until the 1920s. The latter were singular syntheses of Ottoman wooden house types and techniques with Art Nouveau details that, since then, became part of the image of Istanbul.

That period coincided with the emergence of a nationalist reaction to the European architects working in a historicist, eclectic language, as in the case of the pseudo-Oriental Sirkeci Train Station (1890) by A. Jachmund and the Frenchified, neo-Renaissance Haydarpasa Train Station (1909) by Otto Ritter and Helmuth Cuno. Probably under the influence of the ideas of the Young Turks movement, two Turkish architects, Vedat Tek and Kemaleddin, started to employ Seljukid and classical Ottoman features in their architecture to achieve a stylistic unity vis-à-vis the eclecticism of the foreign architects, who randomly combined different so-called Islamic styles. Tek and Kemaleddin thus became the harbingers of a historicist architecture that has come to be known as the First National Style.

Particularly in the examples where they tried to bring together new building types and materials with historical features, the "Turkishness" of their architecture remained at the level of the surface treatment. Nonetheless, in the projects where the preoccupation with the past was relatively suspended, as in Tek's own residence (1914) and Kemaleddin's Harikzedegân Apartment Complex (1922), built for the victims of the 1918 fire, they produced examples of a sophisticated architecture. The former is an elaborate synthesis of Ottoman residential architecture and an almost Wrightian modernism, whereas the latter is one of the first reinforced-concrete apartment complexes in the historic peninsula with communal service facilities, courtyards, open staircases, and stores introducing a new type vis-à-vis the inward-looking Turkish house.

The Harikzedegân Apartment Complex was built during the Allied occupation of Istanbul while the War of Independence was being fought after the defeat of the Ottoman Empire, alongside Germany, in World War I. The victory in the War of Independence led to the abolition of the surviving institutions of the empire and the proclamation of the Turkish Republic. That change in the regime brought the change of the capital as well: in 1923, after 1600 years, Istanbul lost its status as a capital to the central Anatolian town of Ankara. The aim was to dissociate the new state founded on Turkish nationalism from the cosmo-

Gön Leather Product Factory, designed by Nevzat Sayin (1995)
Photo courtesy Nevzat Sayin © Aga Khan Award for Architecture

politan, imperial heritage of Istanbul. Accordingly, during the first decades of the republic, a vast building program was undertaken in Ankara while the construction activity in Istanbul stayed meager. In accord with the republican elites' preference of an international architectural language, however, some modernist projects were realized also in Istanbul. These include the purist Presidential Summer Residence (1935) by Seyfettin Nasih Arkan, a pupil of Vedat Tek, who has also worked with Hans Poelzig, and the Observatory of the Istanbul University (1936), which combines a horizontal, modern exterior with the traditional Ottoman cruciform plan, by Hikmet Holtay.

In the first decades of the republic, the demand for great numbers of architects was tried to be met by both sending Turkish students to Europe for training, mostly to Germany because of the cultural pacts signed with this country, and inviting European architects, again mostly Germans, to teach at the two architecture schools in Istanbul. From the 1930s to the end of the 1950s, Ernst Egli, Bruno Taut, Clemens Holzmeister, and Paul Bonatz, among others, taught either at the Academy of Fine Arts, the first architecture school of the country founded in the 19th century, or at Istanbul Technical University, the Engineering School, which in the 1920s started to give the degree of architecture as well. Although the teaching activities of these architects deeply affected Turkish architectural discourse and education, the majority of their architectural activities remained confined to Ankara. Taut's Istanbul residence (1936) is one of the exceptions: it displays both Turkish and Japanese influences in a building set on a cliff overlooking the Bosphorus and is daringly carried by four pillars, two of which are 10 meters high.

Both Taut and his predecessor, Egli, while teaching modern, rational principles of design at the Academy of Fine Arts, also gave support to a seminar on national architecture founded to study the characteristics of Turkish architecture. In the 1940s that course, also in accord with the resurgence of nationalism in Europe, fueled the second spate of National Style, the major proponents of which were Sedad Hakki Eldem and Emin Onat. This time, the main source of inspiration was Anatolian vernacular architecture, particularly the Turkish house, on which typological studies were undertaken under the supervision of Eldem at the Academy. Eldem, who contributed extensively to 20th-century Istanbul through his numerous projects, is one of the shapers of Turkish architecture of the century. Although his Taslik Coffee House (1948) is a typical example of the Second National Style, his collaborative project (1952–84) for the Hilton hotel chain together with the American firm Skidmore, Owings and Merrill disclosed the shift in trends: International Style was becoming the dominant architectural paradigm together with the rampant American influence in the cultural sphere.

In the 1950s, with the change from an ascetic etatism to a populist liberalism, political authorities' interest in Istanbul was renewed. Extensive demolitions were undertaken to make space for boulevards, which could only partially be justified by the pressing needs of a growing metropolis leading to Istanbul's nascent (now uncontainable) internal migration problem. The immense rate at which the city, whose population as of 2002 was about 10 million, grew resulted in the squatters and rather stale apartment blocks that wrap the city today. That, on the other hand, does not mean that attempts to solve the housing problem were not made, as in the case of the Levent settlement (begun in 1947) and the Ataköy satellite town (begun in 1957),

both architecturally fine examples that nevertheless could not live up to the ideal of providing housing for low-income families.

After the waning of the International Style and the pluralistic architecture of the 1960s and 1970s—exemplified in the organic apartment building of the 1960s by Nezih Eldem; the Brutalist Retail Shop Complex (1959) by Tekeli, Sisa, and Hepgüler; and the contextualist Social Security Complex (1970) by Sedad Hakki Eldem—Istanbul, since the 1980s, has been characterized by a new type of international architecture: that of the faceless shopping malls, high-rise office buildings, and international hotel chains. On the other hand, the newly awakened interest in the Ottoman past, while helping to develop a consciousness for the protection of the historical heritage, reveals itself also in the rather superficial trappings of luxurious housing. At the end of the 20th century, Istanbul is a world city, displaying all the problems of megalopolises: environmental pollution, heavy traffic, shortage of quality housing, and spreading squatters. Among all these, it still retains remnants of its age-old beauty to which projects by both old and young generations of architects, such as Turgut Cansever (with his *yali* restorations and Anadolu Club Building [1951] on Büyükada) and Nevzat Sayin (with his Gön Leather Factory [1995]), have been and are still contributing.

BELGIN TURAN

Further Reading

There is no single scholarly source devoted to the architecture of 20th-century Istanbul. The architectural guide by Beck and Forsting is the first attempt to compile a list of 20th-century buildings in the city.

Barillari, Diana, and Ezio Godoli, *Istanbul, 1900: Architettura e interni Art Nouveau*, Florence: Octavo, 1996; as *Istanbul, 1900: Art-Nouveau Architecture and Interiors*, New York: Rizzoli, 1996

Beck, Christa, and Christiane Forsting, *Istanbul: An Architectural Guide*, London: Ellipsis, and Cologne: Könemann, 1997

Bozdogan, Sibel, Suha Özkan, and Engin Yenal, *Sedad Eldem: Architect in Turkey*, Singapore: Concept Media, and New York: Aperture, 1987

Holod, Renata, and Ahmet Evin (editors), *Modern Turkish Architecture*, Philadelphia: University of Pennsylvania Press, 1984

Kuban, Dogan, *Istanbul, an Urban History: Byzantion, Constantinopolis, Istanbul*, Istanbul: Economic and Social History Foundation of Turkey, 1996

Sey, Yildiz (editor), *75 yilda degisen kent ve mimarlik*, Istanbul: Türkiye Ekonomik ve Toplumsal Tarih Vakfi, 1998

Tekeli, Ilhan (editor), *Dünden bugüne Istanbul ansiklopedisi*, 8 Vols., Istanbul: Kültür Bakanligi, Tarih Vakfi, 1993–95

Yücel, Atilla, "Contemporary Turkish Architecture," *Mimar*, 10 (October–December 1983)

ITO, TOYO 1941–

Architect, Japan

At first glance, it is possible to mistake Toyo Ito's work as high tech or perhaps late modernist. Early on, he was heavily influenced by Metabolism (especially as it was defined by his mentor, Kiyonori Kikutake) and its English correspondent, Archigram, even going so far as to initially name his firm "Urban Robot." However, Ito came to see that to celebrate the machine in the latter half of the 20th century represented a position that was fallacious in its nostalgia. The shift in his thinking is marked by White U, a building he designed in 1976 for his recently widowed sister; this project catalyzed Ito to embrace immateriality over form.

Although White U is often treated as an anomaly because it is heavy concrete construction (most of Ito's work strives to be paper thin), he established goals for the project that remain the basis for much of his designs over the subsequent 25 years. Ito used the building to shape light, both to evoke beauty and to create a constantly changing space, either fluid and continuous or set off by light and shadow. The lack of formal room divisions encouraged free movement, and the flow of both people and energy became the heart of Ito's architecture. Ito also extended this sense of spatial continuity into the central courtyard of White U, foreshadowing later efforts to unify architecture and landscape, as seen at the Shimosuwa Municipal Museum (1992) and the Nagaoka Lyric Hall (1996).

In later work, Ito explores materials such as glass and corrugated aluminum as well as the effects of natural light, most evident in his 1990 T Building. Ito also studied the implications of changing translucency in glass materials, especially in the 1989 Guest House for Sapporo Brewery and in a 1990 proposal for La Maison de la Culture de Japon. Ito extended these investigations to artificial light with the competition entry for the Tower of Winds (1986; Yokohama), where wind speed and direction, sound, and the time of day activate electrical lighting in varying overlapping patterns. More important was the 1991 installation Ito designed for "Visions of Japan." In this space, multiple scenes of everyday life in Tokyo flashed across every surface of a room, creating a filmic effect Ito is only beginning to approach in his built work.

In addition to light, Ito has attempted to embody the flow of other forms of energy in his work. Wind shaped the appearance not only of the Tower of Winds, but also his 1984 house for his family, Silver Hut in Tokyo. The flow of economic demand during the volatile "Bubble" period made Ito conscious of the relatively short life spans of many postwar buildings, and his designs for Nomad Restaurant (1986) and the temporary Noh Theater (1987), intended from the start to be used for only short periods, allowed him to explicitly explore the impermanence of architecture. Ito proved himself a keen observer of actual conditions in a changing society, recognizing that the rapid economic expansion of Japan's postwar period signaled an ephemeral and superficial role for buildings and attempting to discover the relevance of architecture under these new circumstances. It was at this time that Ito deliberately began to position his architecture as antiheroic or nonmonumental, and his interior spaces became increasingly important.

His prescient designs for the "Tokyo Nomad Woman," Pao I (1981) and Pao II (1985), were immediately understood to recognize the new social freedoms young Japanese women enjoyed in the 1980s, but also stood as a criticism of the otherwise staid expectations that held true for much of Japanese society. Although it was not recognized until recently, these designs also anticipated the placeless portable networks that have become common at the end of the century. (Perhaps it is not coincidental that the I-mode, a system for receiving and sending e-mail or downloading Web pages and other data through a cellular phone, was developed by the wife of another Japanese architect whose work is clearly influenced by Ito.) In response to the emergence of rootless communities, in the 1990 T Building and the 1993 ITM Building, Ito began to concentrate his efforts on creating "communication locations," natural eddies in people's movement through a building that would enhance meeting and exchanging information—thus refuting the dystopian isolation many perceived in the Pao designs.

Ironically, as Ito attempted to create an architecture of the electronic age, he was increasingly driven to readdress the themes of machine-age architecture. More importantly, Ito has been one of Japan's most technologically sophisticated architects, applying the collaborative opportunities in Japan's construction community to introduce new construction materials and develop ambitious structural approaches. His applications of technology, however, differ. In Nagaoka Lyric Hall (1997; Nigata), he erodes the organizing power of structure with an apparently random organization of columns, whereas in projects such as the Ota-ku Resort Complex (1998; Nagano), Ito's structural planes achieve new levels of improbable thinness. In 2000, Ito revived a longstanding interest in aluminum by using it in the delicate structure for a small Tokyo residence, and he has projects on the boards that explore the implications of aluminum as a structural skin.

Ito's competition-winning proposal for Sendai Mediatheque (2001; Miyagi-Senadai) is a summation of many of these themes and a landmark in his career. The structure is composed of 13 latticed tubes, intended to frame vertical movement through horizontal layers of the building that are barely divided by extremely thin, beam-free steel floor plates. The tubes encase elevators, stairs, pipes, ducts, and other building systems. Daylight is directed through several tubes by means of a motorized set of vertical louvers and electrical lighting seeping between floors is made apparent by the use of different colors of high-intensity lighting. To ride the elevators up one tube, while other elevators and elevator weights slip soundlessly up and down the adjacent tubes, is to understand the sense of fluidity that Ito has long intended in his work.

DANA BUNTROCK

See also **Metabolists**

Biography

Born 1 June 1941 in Seoul, South Korea, under Japanese occupation. Graduated from Tokyo University, bachelor's degree 1965; worked for Kiyonori Kikutake Architect and Associates 1965–69. Established his own office, Urban Robot (URBOT), Tokyo 1971 (office was renamed Toyo Ito and Associates, Architects in 1979). Selected awards include the Architectural Institute of Japan Award for Silver Hut 1986, Togo Murano Award for the Sapporo Brewery Guest House 1990, Mainichi Art Award for Yatsushiro Municipal Museum 1992, Building Constructors' Society Award for Yatsushiro Municipal Museum 1993, Japanese Education Minister's Art Encouragement Award (for Odate Dome, 1998), and Building Constructors' Society Award and the Japan Art Academy Prize 1999. Exhibitions dedicated to Ito's work include "Pao I, Exhibition Project for Pao: A Dwelling for Tokyo Nomad Woman" (Seibu Department Store, 1985), "Architecture in the City of Winds" (Gallery Ma, Tokyo, 1986), "Anemorphosis: Transformations by Wind" (Tokyo,

1986), "Pao II, Exhibition Project for Pao: A Dwelling for Tokyo Nomad Woman" (Brussels, Belgium, 1989), "Toyo Ito, Architecture Fluctuante" (Institut Francais d' Architecture, Paris, 1991), "Toyo Ito" (Tokyo, 1992), "Blurring Architecture" (Suermondt-Ludwig-Museum, Aachen, 1999), and "Al chitecture [sic] 2000" proposals for aluminum structural systems (GA Gallery, Tokyo, 2000).

Selected Works

Aluminum House, Tsujido, Kanagawa Prefecture, Japan, 1971
White U, Nakano, Tokyo, Japan, 1976
PMT Building, Nagoya, Aichi, 1978
Silver Hut, Nakano-ku, Tokyo, Japan, 1984
Nomad Restaurant, Roppongi, Tokyo, Japan, 1986
Tower of Winds, Yokohama-shi, Kanagawa prefecture, Japan, 1986
M Building in Kanda, Tokyo, Japan, 1987
Guest House for Sapporo Brewery, Eniwa-shi, Hokkaido, 1989
I Building, Asakusabashi, Tokyo, Japan, 1989
T Building, Nakameguro, Tokyo, Japan, 1990
Yatsushiro Municipal Museum, Yatsushiro-shi, Kumamoto prefecture, Japan, 1991
Egg of Winds (Okawabata River City 21 Town Gate B), Chuo-ku, Tokyo, Japan, 1991
Shimosuwa Municipal Museum, Shimosuwa-cho, Nagano prefecture, Japan, 1992
Kindergarten in Eckenheim, Frankfurt, Germany, 1992
ITM Building, Matsuyama-shi, Ehime, Japan, 1993
Old People's Home, Yatsushiro, Kumamoto prefecture, Japan, 1994
Yatsushiro Fire Station, Yatsushiro, Kumamoto prefecture, Japan, 1995
Nagaoka Lyric Hall, Nagaoka, Niigata prefecture, 1997
Dome in Odate, Odate, Akita prefecture, Japan, 1997
Ota-ku Resort Complex in Nagano, Chi'isagata-gun, Nagano prefecture, Japan, 1998
Notsuharu Town Hall, Notsuharu-machi, Oita prefecture, Japan, 1999
Taisha-cho Bunka Palace, Taisha-cho, Shimane prefecture, Japan, 2000
Sendai Mediatheque, Sendai, Miyagi prefecture, Japan, 2001

Selected Publications

Toyo Ito—Kaze no Hen'yotai [Transfiguration of Winds] English title: *Toyo Ito – Semi-permeable Architecture*, Tokyo: SD Henshubu/Kajima Publishing, 1986. Second edition by Seidosha, 1989 (Originally *SD* no. 8609, special issue on Ito.)
Tousou Suru Kenchiku, Tokyo: Aoshi Sha, 2000

Further Reading

Goto, Nobuko, Sachiko Goto, and Fumiko Goto, *Nakano Honmachi no Ie* (House in Nakanohonmachi), Tokyo: Sumai no Toshokan Shuppankyoku, 1998
Shannon, Kelly, "Into the City of Replicants," *World Architecture*, 43 (February 1996)
Stanishev, Georgi, "Avant Space: The Architectural Experiments of Toyo Ito," *World Architecture*, 34 (1995)

J

JACOBS, JANE 1916–

Architecture critic, United States

Jane Jacobs has been an important and controversial observer and critic of the American city since the 1961 publication of her most important book, *The Death and Life of Great American Cities*.

Jacobs's work at *Architectural Forum* trained her to become an articulate critic of the patterns of development and urban planning that she observed from mid- and downtown Manhattan and her own home in Greenwich Village. In particular, she became at first suspicious of, and then increasingly hostile to, urban renewal, the growth of housing projects, the highways that radiated from center cities to the ever-growing suburbs, the need for more and bigger parking lots in the city, and the removal of small neighborhoods to accommodate all the new infrastructure. She decried the loss of the diverse elements that made for community: residences, commerce, culture, street life, and recreation that she felt worked best when found in manageable proportions in a local neighborhood.

Jacobs's dissatisfaction with the kind of planning that was represented in her mind by the plans and projects of Robert Moses finally coalesced into her influential book that made her the champion of all who opposed what they saw as the cause of sterility of contemporary life. There is much debate as to whether Jacobs was attacking urban planners or only misguided bureaucrats in her 1961 volume, *The Death and Life of Great American Cities*, but there is no doubt that she struck a sympathetic cord in reformers, community organizers, and those who saw planning and urban renewal as the cause of neighborhood disinvestment, suburban sprawl, and endless commuter traffic jams. Some also extended the critique to blaming the work of planners for racial separation, growing estrangement of people from their neighbors, and an increase in crime. In addition, although Jacobs might not have taken the argument as far as some who cited her writings in support of their own social agendas, there is no doubt that her book presented a strong critique of such pioneers of modern planning as Ebenezer Howard and Daniel Burnham. Perhaps a romantic Jacobs presented the neighborhood as the place where people would live, shop, educate their children, and keep a careful eye out for those threatening their community.

In that regard, she emphasized the same values as others saw in the ideal American small town. In contrast, she spoke of the sterility of planned communities, in which carefully tended parks remained empty because of their lack of conveniences and their ability to protect criminals who might prey on those who ventured to these inconvenient settings far from the watchful eyes of their neighbors.

Jacobs's later books covered a variety of related subjects as she moved to both historical analysis and an overview of how societies operate. *The Economy of Cities* (1969) attacked the notion that cities arose in response to patterns of agriculture and the tendency for people to congregate together. Instead, she posited that the needs of trade were what created the earliest major concentrations of people. In *Cities and the Wealth of Nations* (1984), Jacobs carried that point further, making the case that the growth of powerful commercial centers created the country's wealth, rather than seeing the growth of cities as an outgrowth of wealth in the Jeffersonian sense. Her book, *Systems of Survival* (1992), examined the impact of both commerce and government in contemporary urban life and explored the changes in the relationship between the public and private sectors that have evolved with changes in urban life.

Jacobs's detractors have pointed out that she generalized from too few examples of "cities that worked," that the cities themselves were only selected neighborhoods in the city, and that her arguments ignored economic and political realities. She could also be accused of seeing only the positive side of the traditional community, whether urban or small town, and ignoring the demands for conformity, invasion of privacy, and hostility to outsiders that often accompany the intimacy of the community. However, she wrote as a journalist and activist reformer, not as a scientist, and has had an influence on both public figures and an entire generation of advocates for the New Urbanism

DAVID M. SOKOL

See also **New Urbanism; Urban Planning; Urban Renewal**

Biography

Born Jane Butzner in Scranton, Pennsylvania, on 4 May 1916; had an uninspired high school career and then, to gain some experience in the middle of the Great Depression, worked one year without a salary as a reporter for the women's page editor for the *Scranton Tribune*. Moved to New York, surviving in part-time positions as a stenographer and freelance writer for newspapers, magazines, and trade publications. As the nation moved from the Depression to a wartime economy, obtained a position with the Office of War Information and married a fellow employee, a young architect. Continued her peripatetic career while having three children and finally took a position as an associate editor and writer for *Architectural Forum*. After 30 years in New York City, and with substantial visibility as the author of her widely discussed first book, moved to Toronto with her family where she still resides.

Selected Publications

The Death and Life of Great American Cities, 1961
The Economy of Cities, 1969
Cities and the Wealth of Nations, 1984
Systems of Survival, 1992

Further Reading

Writings about Jane Jacobs are divided between reviews of her books, journalistic accounts of her ideas, and some scholarly appraisals of her contributions. The latter are often submerged in broader discussions of the issues she tackled and do not appear on a general bibliography.

Atkinson, Brooks, "Critic at Large: Jane Jacobs, Author of Book on Cities, Makes the Most of Living in One," *New York Times* (10 November 1961)
Cook, James, "Cities and the Wealth of Nations," *Forbes* (30 July 1984)
Duany, Andreas, and Elizabeth Plater-Zyberk, "The Second Coming of the American Small Town," *Wilson Quarterly*, 16/2 (1992)
Hoppenfeld, Morton, "Review: The Death and Life of Great American Cities," *Journal of the American Institute of Planners*, 28/2 (1962)
Montgomery, Roger, "Is There Still Life in the Death and Life?" *American Planning Association Journal* (Summer 1998)
Sewell, John, "Golden Report Misreads Urban Guru Jane Jacobs," *NOW* (8 February 1996)
Warren, David, "Two Ways to Live: Jane Jacobs Speaks with David Warren," *The Idler*, 38 (Summer 1993)
Zotti, Ed, "Eyes on Jane Jacobs," *Planning* (September 1986)

JACOBSEN, ARNE EMIL 1902–71

Architect, Denmark

In his contributions to Danish modern architecture, industrial design, exhibition design, and urban design, Scandinavian architect Arne Jacobsen demonstrated a broad understanding of the role of good design in life, from the scale of kitchen implements to the scale of the housing estate. He had the opportunity to work on a tremendous range of building types, from the mundane to the honorific, and he endowed all with a sense of the sublime: factories, laboratories, offices, schools, sports facilities, housing, and town halls.

Jacobsen completed the typical course of study for an architect in Denmark, beginning with academic high school, technical college, and finally the Kunstakademiets Arkitektskole (Royal Danish Academy of Fine Arts School of Architecture) in Copen-

hagen. This path included an apprenticeship to a bricklayer and study tours to France, Italy, and Germany. Jacobsen received his professional degree in 1927 and was awarded the 1928 Lille Guldmedalje (Small Gold Medal) for the design of a National Museum in Klampenborg, north of Copenhagen.

At the Kunstakademie, Jacobsen was taught by leading practitioners of the Scandinavian Doricist (Neoclassical, 1910–30) movement, including Ivar Bentsen, Kay Fisker, and Edvard Thomsen. The influence of these professors is evident in Jacobsen's disciplined use of proportion and material. His characteristic austerity of means, which today might be labeled minimalist, is in fact an aspect of continuity in Danish architecture since the 1700s. Restraint and elegance mark Jacobsen's development as the most significant modern architect in Denmark, a stature recognized in his selection to design the Royal Danish Embassy in London. (This 1969 proposal was executed after his death in 1971 by Dissing and Weitling, a firm founded by two of his associates.) Jacobsen's work had admirers abroad, as evidenced by the many international awards, honors, and commissions bestowed on him.

Jacobsen worked only briefly for other architects (Fisker, Niels Rosenkjaer, and Paul Holsøe) before setting up his own practice. Winning the Bellevue Beach competition (1932) was his breakthrough, initiating a series of projects along the shore in Klampenborg. He designed beach club facilities (1932), a theater and restaurant (1935), and three housing complexes: Bellavista (1934), Søholm I and II (1951), Søholm III (1955), and Ved Bellevue Bugt (1961).

By no means the only modern architect in Denmark, Jacobsen was probably influenced in the late 1930s and 1940s by Vilhelm Lauritzen's Kastrup Airport (1936) and Radio House (1937–45). During these years, another influence can be detected in the Stellings House (1937), Aarhus Town Hall (1942), and Søllerød Town Hall (1942). Jacobsen had a friendly relationship with the Swedish architect Erik Gunnar Asplund from the 1920s to 1940, during which time the latter was working on the Gothenberg Law Courts Addition (1913–36). Jacobsen might have derived his contextual design approach from this model.

Jacobsen's reputation and many contacts in Sweden helped smooth the way for him during his flight from the occupying Nazis in 1943. During a two-year exile in Stockholm, he worked primarily as a textile designer, using his extraordinary skills in drawing and watercolor painting to create patterns for fabric and wallpaper.

In the postwar period, shortages of material and labor forced architects to employ alternative means of construction, new technologies, and new materials. Jacobsen was an important figure introducing these in Denmark. He explored the possibilities that industrialization (such as curtain wall construction and prefabricated elements) offered in such projects as the Jespersen Office Building (1955). In fact, the poetics of construction is a major theme in his work. Jacobsen's structural solutions are innovative, pushing materials to their limits, for example, the concrete in the Gas Station (1937) and the Belvedere Restaurant project (1964). Furthermore, his details are exquisite and refined, reflecting the admiration that he held for Ludwig Mies van der Rohe. This influence is most apparent in the Rødovre Town Hall (1955) and Library (1969). In general, structure and detail provide the ornament in Jacobsen's buildings.

The second theme is beauty, which Jacobsen felt was misunderstood in modern architecture. He said that simply resolving functional problems did not constitute a beautiful solution. Instead, the architect needed to provide an aesthetic dimension, which in his case consisted of elemental massing, reduction of detail, and elegant proportions to organize the whole. Jacobsen recognized that because the modern architect works with standardized elements, proportion is the way to express his individuality. Simplicity of form and detail contributes to a sense of the sublime, akin to Mies' "almost nothing." In time, Jacobsen designed buildings, such as St. Catherine's College at Oxford University (1963), as total works of art, encompassing landscape, interior design, furniture, lighting, hardware, and fittings.

The third theme is site design. One of Jacobsen's strengths is the integration of a building with its site. It is likely that his studies at the Kunstakademi included the new garden design courses. He also collaborated with the celebrated landscape architect C.Th. Sørensen on two early projects.

Jacobsen's mature works of the 1950s show mastery of building type, proportion, material, and detail. This period saw realized important public commissions, including town halls, the Munkegård's School (1955), and commercial works, such as the Massey Harris Showroom (1953), the Carl Christensen Factory (1956), and the SAS Royal Hotel (1959).

Jacobsen maintained ongoing relationships with manufacturers and clients through the four decades of his career. For example, Novo Industries retained him for three separate laboratory designs in 1935, 1959, and 1969. Similarly, Fritz Hansen has produced Jacobsen furniture designs since 1952. Five chairs are still in production, including his most famous designs, the Ant chair (1952) and the 3107 (1955), which have sold five million copies, and the Grand Prix (1957), the Egg (1958), and the Swan (1958).

Standardized construction and the single-family house type were current interests in the 1950s and 1960s. Jacobsen developed a series of villas influenced by the American Case Study houses of Charles Eames, Pierre Koenig, and Richard Neutra as well as Mies' houses. Although the availability of materials and cost required that Danish architects transform these models, another factor in the synthesis was traditional Japanese architecture with its panelized systems of construction and proportional order. Jacobsen's Siesby House (1957) is a clear example of the genre, and the Jürgensen House (1956) with its courtyard plan and rooms *enfillade* is a stunning variation.

In 1961, Jacobsen won the limited competition for one of his most important Danish buildings, the National Bank (and mint), which was built in Copenhagen in three stages beginning in 1965. The 1960s brought him expanded opportunities abroad, including competitions and commissions in England, Germany, the Netherlands, Switzerland, Pakistan, and Kuwait.

Some of Jacobsen's most experimental work was done in 1970, when he developed three different system houses: Kubeflex for summer cottages, Kvadratflex for a housing exhibition, and Møllehuset. Similarly, two of his most successful industrial designs are from late in life: the Cylinda line of stainless-steel tableware for Stelton A/S (1967) and the Vola plumbing fittings for I.P. Lunds (1969). These timeless designs, along with light fixtures for Louis Poulsen (1957) and cutlery for A. Michelsen's (1957; now made by Georg Jensen), are still in production.

Jacobsen's work ethic is legendary: he tirelessly sketched, studied, and modeled a design problem until a good solution was found. He imparted this and the need to simplify form to his students at the Kunstakademi (1956–65) and to his employees. Gehrdt Bornebusch, Knud Holscher, and Henning Larsen are three of Jacobsen's former employees who became leading second-generation modernists.

Jacobsen's influence on contemporary architecture and design continues. His work remains fresh; the simple and organic shapes remain vital, colors soothing, and details inspiring. Jacobsen spoke of the importance of beauty in distinguishing architecture from building. It is his achievement to have created beauty while working across a spectrum of building types, scales, and locales. He has improved the fields of modern architecture and industrial design with the clarity of his vision.

KATE NESBITT

See also **Asplund, Erik Gunnar (Sweden); Denmark; Eames, Charles and Ray (United States); Fisker, Kay (Denmark); Larsen, Henning (Denmark); Mies van der Rohe, Ludwig (Germany)**

Biography

Born in Copenhagen, Denmark, 11 February 1902. Attended the School of Architecture, Academy of Arts, Copenhagen; degree in architecture 1928. Married: 2 children. Worked in the office of architects Paul Holsoe, Copenhagen 1927–30. Private practice, Copenhagen from 1930; designed textiles and furniture from 1943. Professor of architecture, Academy of Arts, Copenhagen from 1956. Honorary corresponding member, Royal Institute of British Architects; honorary fellow, American Institute of Architects. Died in Copenhagen, 24 March 1971.

Selected Buildings

Bellevue Seaside Development (First prize, competition), Copenhagen, 1932
Bellavista Housing Estate, Klampenborg, Denmark, 1933
Stelling House, Gammel Torv, Copenhagen, 1937
Bellevue Theater and Gammel Bellevue Restaurant, Copenhagen, 1937
Town Hall (First prize, competition; with Erik Møller), Aarhus, 1942
Town Hall (First prize, competition; with Flemming Lassen), Søllerød, 1942
Søholm Terraced Housing, Klampenborg, 1950
Massey-Harris Showroom and Spare Department, Roskilde Landevej, Copenhagen, 1952
Jespersin and Son Office Building, Copenhagen, 1955
Town Hall, Rødovre, 1955
Ruthwen Jurgensen House, Vedbaek, Denmark, 1956
Munkegaard School, Vangedevej, Gentofte, Denmark, 1956
Carl Christensen Factory, Aalborg, 1957
SAS Royal Hotel and Air Terminal, Vesterbrogade, Copenhagen, 1959
Erik Siesby House (project), Prinsessestien, Lyngby School, Rødovre, 1959
Bellevue Bay Housing Estate, Klampenborg, 1961
St. Catherine's College, Oxford University, 1963
Library, Rødovre, 1969
Danish Embassy, London (with Dissing and Weitling), 1971

Danish National Bank, Copenhagen (with Dissing and Weitling), 1971

Further Reading

Most of the books on Jacobsen have appeared in Danish, Spanish, or Italian, with English translations, except as noted. By far the most comprehensive and lavishly illustrated book is Thau and Vindum's 1998 work, which is entirely in Danish. The Centre d'Estudis de Disseny monograph (Jacobsen 1991) is excellent, fully translated, and includes texts by the architect.

2G: Revista Internacional de Arquitectura: International Architecture Review 4 (1997) (special issue entitled "Arne Jacobsen Edificios Públicos; Public Buildings")

Faber, Tobias, *Arne Jacobsen*, Stuttgart, Germany: Verlag Gerd Hatje, London: Tiranti, and New York: Praeger, 1964

Jacobsen, Arne, *Arkitekten Arne Jacobsen, 1902–71* (exhib. cat.), Copenhagen: Dansk Arkitektur og Byggeeksport Center, 1991

Jacobsen, Arne, *Arne Jacobsen*, Barcelona: Centre d'Estudis de Disseny and Santa and Cole Ediciones de Desino, 1991

Møller, Erik, *Aarhus Raadhus*, Copenhagen: Arkitektens Forlag, 1991

Pedersen, Johan, *Arkitekten Arne Jacobsen* (with English summary), Copenhagen: Arkitektens Forlag, 1954

Rubino, Luciano, *Arne Jacobsen: opera completa, 1909–1971*, Rome: Kappa, 1980

Solaguren-Beascoa de Corral, Félix, *Arne Jacobsen*, Barcelona: Gili, 1989; 2nd edition, 1991

Thau, Carsten, and Kjeld Vindum, *Arne Jacobsen*, Copenhagen: Arkitektens Forlag, 1998

Tøjner, Poul Erik, and Kjeld Vindum, *Arne Jacobsen: Architect and Designer*, Copenhagen: Dansk Design Center, 1994

JAHN, HELMUT 1940–

Architect and designer, United States

The design work of Helmut Jahn has always engaged technology at the center of architectural activity. His flamboyant personality is duplicated in his later architectural design works, which have shifted from a late-Miesian vocabulary to a Postmodern phase characterized by high-tech stylizations. His rapid climb within C.F. Murphy and Associates (founded 1937) put him in an influential position to redefine the established firm's exclusive position in Chicago into a firm of international significance. The most recent work incorporates the transparency of glass, futuristic systems, and advanced ecological concerns that can be traced to the technological imperative of his earliest works and education.

After Jahn studied in Munich and at the Illinois Institute of Technology (IIT), his work privileged the expression of the mechanics of construction within the formalist idiom. Working with Gene Summers, his first design work included the McCormick Place Convention Center in Chicago (1970), a project influenced by the detailing and structured space of Ludwig Mies van der Rohe's Neue Nationalgalerie (1965–68) in Berlin and his unbuilt project for a convention hall (1953) in Chicago. Situated between Lake Michigan and Lake Shore Drive, the gridded interior space is defined by a large-scale space frame overhead, spanning the open plan of 150 feet with additional 75-foot cantilevers projecting over the exterior space. In 1973–74, Jahn designed the Kemper Arena in Kansas City, Missouri.

This project utilized three steel trusses to hang a roof over a large oval-shaped athletic arena space and seating for 18,000 spectators. Suspended over a solid exterior cladding of insulated metal panels and rounded corners, the project expresses a faith in space-age technology. After this, he directed the design of many large urban projects, including courthouses, libraries, convention centers, and corporate office towers across the midwestern United States, experimenting with this emergent style. The works of the period 1974–78 exhibited a growing confidence in the expressive use of primary colors and exposed technological devices, in sympathy with the Archigram group in England.

Jahn was a member of the informal group of nascent voices who called themselves the Chicago 7 since 1977. During this period he began to participate in a larger discourse on the direction of architecture informed by the communicative and symbolic functions of architecture. The work of Murphy/Jahn turned from a strict interpretation of the technologically driven design of the Miesian tradition and aligned itself with a rising trend defined by critic Charles Jencks as Postmodernism. Jahn acknowledged this perceptible shift in his work's meaning as a new attitude allowing the firm to "free our skills to practice architecture beyond a mere problem solving, functionalist methodology, resulting in a pluralism, which is multi-directional, less restrictive and less dogmatic, characterized by a loss of conviction as to exclusivist principles and more communicative and user-oriented." This new emphasis on populism and pluralism informed his subsequent urban projects as a directed search for a "variable, wide-ranging architectural language." The towers proposed for the Xerox Center (Chicago, designed 1977, built 1980), the Chicago Board of Trade Addition (designed 1978, built 1982), the unbuilt Chicago Tribune Tower Late Entry Competition (1979), the Northwestern Terminal (Chicago, designed 1979, completed 1986), and One South Wacker (Chicago, designed 1979, built 1981–82), utilized exterior curtain walls of glass, reflective and selectively colored for ornamentation distinctly different than the exhausted Miesian prototype of somber discipline. The lobbies of these tall buildings express this concern with populism and ornamentation in their simplified echoes of Art Deco and art moderne precedents. Physically and structurally dependent on earlier technology, these projects participated in a larger cultural shift toward forms that recall the past and break overall volume into subordinate masses. The influence of the early pioneering phase of tall-building design is recalled in a distinctly reductivist execution, achieving the Postmodern goal of reconciling modernism to its historical past. It is during this time that the preliminary design sketches and representations of projects become self-conscious tools in the development of style, where the explorations of "paper architecture" appear transferred to the skins of the buildings.

This process is evident in the project submitted for the competition for a tall building in Houston—the Bank of the Southwest Tower (1982). Here, the submitted drawings and design-process sketches for an 82-story building reveal a search for an appropriate style for the tall building in a city with much fewer built precedents as context. The multiple studies range across high-tech mechanical volumes to historically reminiscent stacked and tiered forms following the base-shaft-top typology of the early 20th century. The resulting submission utilizes masonry cladding at the ground level, a clear prismatic solid shaft (with Jahn's frequent use of multicolored glass-curtain walls as decora-

First Source Center, South Bend, Indiana (1982)
Photo © Mary Ann Sullivan

tion), and a schematic top that mimics the Chrysler Building (1930) in New York.

The most prominent commission of this period was for the State of Illinois Center, later renamed the James R. Thompson Center. Designed in 1979, it was finally constructed in May 1995. The program for the square site adjacent to City Hall included over a million square feet of office and administrative spaces for various branches of the State of Illinois government, stations for subway and elevated trains, and retail at the plaza level. The building's form has a large cylindrical rotunda 160 feet across rising all 17 floors to an inclined glass roof. It is an internalized public space, animated by the flow of people and sounds than the mannered exterior space. The vertical circulation of elevators, escalators, and stairs move up through this futuristic space that performs a valuable energy-conserving function. The overall building form is a quarter circle in plan, with three faces built to the street lines, but the curved face that faces the exterior plaza is inclined with three setbacks. The ground level contains exterior cladding of pink and gray granite forming a continuous arcade. The red, white, and blue glazing and metal panels are a glib reference to its government function and employ details from Jahn's other tall buildings in Chicago. The Thompson Center has received near-constant public criticism for its expense, execution, and appearance.

Contemporaneous with these projects for tall buildings, a significant series of commissions for the growing O'Hare International Airport allowed Jahn to explore his vocabulary in a radically different building type. Projects at O'Hare included the Rapid Transit Station (designed 1979, built 1983) and the award-winning United Airlines Terminal and Satellite Building (built 1985–87) arising from the successful proposal for the overall development of O'Hare in 1982. The airport's growth continues, and Murphy/Jahn remains the primary architect of one of the world's largest airports. Accommodating over 40 new gates and over a million square feet of circulation and supporting facilities, this project was designed as two parallel linear systems composed of a repetitive series of steel structural bays. The structural system is expressed in curved-steel arches and cross bracing that incorporate mechanical modernist strategies from Victorian influences. The successes of the project are its legibility, clarity, and ease of movement through the vaulted space. Folded trusses and four-post structural columns create human-scaled modules of space in a vast project. Subterranean connections are designed as moving walkways surrounded by kinetic light and sound sculptures, an overt populist treatment of a potentially gloomy space.

In 1985 three projects were designed for New York City: the unbuilt tower for the New York City Coliseum at Columbus

Circle, the unbuilt Times Square redevelopment project, and the City Spire Project (designed 1985, built 1985–89). The recession of the late 1980s put an end to most large construction in Chicago and other large American cities, and the office of Murphy/Jahn responded by pursuing more international work. Projects and competitions for Jahn's native Germany and works in Asia formed the basis of the late phase of 20th-century design work for the firm. Two variations of the United Airlines Terminal were proposed for the Consolidated Terminal for American Airlines and Northwest Airlines (1988) at JFK International Airport in New York. A vast Second Bangkok International Airport (designed 1995) was stopped because of public criticism over cost and the absence of "Thai elements" in the design.

Jahn's Messeturm (1988–91) in Frankfurt am Main, Germany, was one of Europe's tallest buildings, towering over the sprawling city. Its design follows the logic of the earlier tall buildings, with a historically informed silhouette. An adjoining market hall for the Frankfurt fairgrounds (one of ten designed by multiple architects) formally anticipates the later unsuccessful Richard H. Driehaus Foundation Design Competition (1997) for a new student center at the campus of Illinois Institute of Technology (IIT). Across State Street from Mies' S.R. Crown Hall, Jahn designed State Street Village (2003), a set of residence halls that face off with the Miesian legacy. These forms span large blocks of programmatic space with a gracefully curved but monolithic metal roof, a softening of the orthodoxy of the earliest works.

The most prominent and anticipated work of Murphy/Jahn in the 1990s was the vast Sony Center (1995–2000) in Potsdamer Platz, Berlin. This project, like many others, was initiated on the collapse of the Berlin Wall and a deliberate attempt by the federal government of Germany to rebuild a totalizing urban fabric across the barren areas created by the Cold War division of the city. Potsdamer Platz received special attention, as its prewar status as a vibrant urban center gave way in the 1950s and 1960s to a vague territory of emptiness in the middle of the city, desolate in comparison to the adjoining Tiergarten. The overall master plan for the sites was won previously in a competition by architect Renzo Piano, who was responsible for overseeing all the new construction. Contemporaneous design projects near Potsdamer Platz were done by established international architects, including Rafael Moneo, Richard Meier, and Daniel Libeskind.

Within the Sony complex, the ruins of the Grand-Hotel Esplanade (1908–12, Otto Rehnig) were incorporated with some difficulty: the "Emperor's Hall," weighing 1300 tons, was raised 2.5 meters and transported 75 meters on rails to its final location within the ensemble. The large office tower for Sony, executed in a neomodern technique of technology, signifies the movement away from the flagrant populism of earlier work and is remarkably restrained and serious, in contrast with Jahn's slender office tower on Ku'damm. The concrete-frame construction of the diverse program is clad in smooth glass skins to emphasize the transparency of the volumes and the public space between them.

Major elements of the project pursue the historical function of the site and the technology of the client as a public overture—although now as useful themed functional space, not as privatized icons. The Sony Center entertainment facilities include an eight-screen multiplex cinema and an IMAX three-dimensional theater. In accordance with the cinematic programming, the Berlin Filmmuseum and the German Mediathek are joined with an education facility, the Film and Television Academy Berlin, the Filmlibrary, the Film Distribution House, and the programs of the German Kinematheck. Restaurants and shops at ground level, below-grade parking facilities, and a significant amount of housing above ring the difficult triangular site. The project follows the Berlin model of perimeter block housing defining large interior public spaces (here gardens and a formal paved plaza). The most visible component of this mixed-use urban block is the elliptical tensile construction echoing the tent forms of a pre-cinematic form of popular entertainment: the circus.

The Hotel Kempinski (1993–94) near the Munich Airport places hotel space aside a vast atrium with a thin overhead canopy and all-glass entry facade designed to deflect up to one meter with changing climatic conditions. The increasing reliance on glass skins and exposed mechanical systems overtakes the earlier strategies without stepping entirely away from the earliest formalism. Transparency is not pursued as an allegory of a transparent or democratic society but as a citation of the earliest experiments in the potential of glass as a signifier of modernism, as in the unbuilt office towers proposed by Mies in the 1920s or the socialist expressionism of Paul Scheerbart and Bruno Taut. The literal transparency of glass in his last 20th-century work shows a fusion of history and technology. As Wener Blaser has stated, "Helmut Jahn has given the use of steel and glass in architecture an exceptional technical and aesthetic articulation that is inseparably associated with the concept of transparency. Standing squarely in the tradition of the 19th century and yet interested in the continued development of innovative facade technologies, Jahn places the supporting steel structure of his buildings on the outside. At the same time, he wraps his glass skins around a light and weightless interior that acquires a special force through effects of light and color." (see Blaser, 1996) A reliance on sophisticated technology, "high-tech" signature pieces, "passive/active systems," technical innovation, and an emphasis on the image of technology are all manifest in the later works, although they are implied in the imagery of the earliest.

THOMAS MICAL

See also **Historicism; Mies van der Rohe, Ludwig (Germany); Postmodernism**

Biography

Born in Nuremberg, Germany, 4 January 1940; moved to the United States in 1966. Attended the *Technische Hochschule*, Munich 1960–65; degrees in architecture and engineering 1965; studied under Myron Goldsmith and Fazlur Khan at the Illinois Institute of Technology, Chicago 1966–67. Married Deborah Ann Lampe 1970: 1 child. Worked with P.C. von Seidlein, Munich 1965–66. Joined C.F. Murphy Associates, Chicago 1967; assistant to Gene Summers 1967–73; partner, director in charge of planning and design, executive vice president 1973–81. Principal, from 1981, president, from 1982, chief executive officer, from 1983, Murphy/Jahn Associates, Chicago. Lecturer, University of Illinois, Chicago 1981; Eliot Noyes Visiting Design Critic, Harvard University, Cambridge, Massachusetts 1981; Davenport Visiting Professor of Architectural Design, Yale University, New Haven, Connecticut 1983; Thesis Professor, Illinois Institute of Technology 1989–92. Member, Chicago 7 from 1977; corporate member, American Institute of Architects 1975. Chevalier, Ordre des Arts et Lettres 1988.

Selected Works

Kemper Arena, Kansas City, Missouri, 1974
Tribune Tower Late Entry Competition (unbuilt), Chicago, 1979
Xerox Center, Chicago, 1980
Board of Trade (addition), Chicago, 1982
First Source Center, South Bend, Indiana, 1982
One South Wacker Office Building, Chicago, 1982
O'Hare Rapid Transit Station, Chicago, 1983
New York City Coliseum (unbuilt), Columbus Circle, 1985
Times Square Redevelopment, New York, 1985
Northwestern Rail Terminal, Chicago, 1986
United Airlines Terminal, O'Hare International Airport, Chicago, 1987
City Spire, New York, 1989
Messe Frankfurt Convention Center, 1989
Messe Tower, Frankfurt-am-Main, 1991
Hotel Kempinski, Munich, 1994
State of Illinois (James R. Thompson) Center, Chicago, 1995
Sony Center, Postdamer Platz, Berlin, 2000

Selected Publications

"Architectural Form" (with James Gottsch), *Bauen und Wohnen* (December 1975)
"Romantic Hi-Tech" (interview), *Planning and Building Developments* (March/April 1983)
"The First 20 Years," *A + U* (1986)

Further Reading

A + U Extra Edition (June 1986) (special issue edited by Toshio Nakamura and titled "Buildings in Progress")
A + U Extra Edition (September 1992) (special issue titled "Helmut Jahn")
Blaser, Werner, *Helmut Jahn: Transparency; Helmut Jahn: Transparenz* (bilingual English-German edition), Basel and Boston: Birkhäuser, 1996
Jahn, Helmut, *Airports*, edited by Werner Blaser, Basel and Boston: Birkhäuser, 1991
Joedicke, Joachim Andreas, *Helmut Jahn: Design einer neuen Architektur*, Stuttgart, Germany: Krämer, 1986; as *Helmut Jahn: Design of a New Architecture*, translated by Peter Green, New York: Nichols, 1987
Miller, Nory, *Helmut Jahn*, New York: Rizzoli, 1986

JEDDAH, SAUDI ARABIA

What began over 3000 years ago as a fishing settlement in a bay situated halfway on the east coast of the Red Sea is now Jeddah, a thriving metropolitan area and the second-largest city in the kingdom of Saudi Arabia. The name Jeddah, meaning "Grandmother" in Arabic, refers to Eve, who is reputed to have descended from heaven in Jeddah to look for her mate Adam. Today a tomb for Eve exists in a burial ground bearing her name, Our Mother Eve's Cemetery, in the Al Baghdadiya district just to the north of the old city. The significance of the geographic location of Jeddah at the time was the existence of rich fishing waters with three major lines of coral reefs off the shore of the Red Sea and the "Fatima" valley that links it inland to the holy city of Makkah. Throughout its existence, the city experienced shifts in its prominent role because of regional and international power changes and continued to evolve into its current major international seaport status.

The opening of the Suez Canal in 1869 proved to be a huge opportunity for city merchants to trade with international ports in India, Africa, and even Liverpool and Marseilles. Thus, Jeddah's later significance in the 20th century was started by means of this access.

In 1925 the city surrendered to King Abdul Aziz Ibn Saud, and its modern history continued when, in 1933, the king's finance minister, Al Sulaiman, signed in Jeddah a lucrative oil concession with the Standard Oil Company of California. In 1938 oil began flowing in the eastern province of Saudi Arabia, and life for all cities in Arabia, including Jeddah, was never again the same.

The wall of old Jeddah came down in 1947, and the city began sprawling to the north. Up until 1947, the population of Jeddah was about 25,000. Within the span of the last 53 years, this population has jumped to a staggering two million inhabitants, requiring vast numbers of architecture and infrastructure projects.

Before the 1960s Jeddah's architectural designs were influenced by cultural/religious and environmental factors. The selection of construction materials was controlled by local availability of raw building supplies. Located at 21°33′ north latitude and 39°10′ east longitude, Jeddah's annual environmental factors include an average temperature of 28.1°C (82.6°F), a relative humidity of about 50 percent, and a total of about two weeks of rainfall. Cultural and religious factors centered on the issue of privacy. Those influences could be seen in the simplest yet most visible feature of a building, the bay window. Known as *Rawashin*, bay windows are striking features of the architecture of old Jeddah. Displaying lavish woodworkings and engravings on imported teakwoods, which are highly resistant to insect attacks and relative high humidity; these *Rawashin* provided fresh cooling air and preserved the privacy of the occupants. A similar arrangement existed in small balconies with lattice screens (*Seesh*) and wood casements (*Mushrabiyah*), fulfilling the combined requirement of natural ventilation and privacy in Jeddah's typical home. The main construction material of old houses was selected out of relatively stiff materials of the available Red Sea reefs. Limestone blocks were cut from those corals and mortared together using date pulp-based compounds. This combination allowed builders to construct one-, two-, three-, or even four-story buildings. Elaborate and original handcrafted designs ornamented the exterior limestone stucco, which was either white or colored mainly with pastel shades.

The most famous house in the city featuring such traditional methods and materials is a 50-room stone house called Beit Nassif (Nassif House) on Al Alawi Street. Designed by Egyptian architect Hassan Fathy and completed in 1973, it was home of the Nassif family for over a century and is currently part of tremendous government efforts to preserve 550 such structures scattered around old Jeddah's quarters.

After the oil boom of the mid-1970s, almost all construction used concrete, steel, and glass as materials, and the traditional Jeddah style of building was abandoned.

The city is also remarkable for its monuments created by prominent and international architects, including the Jeddah

Abdul Raouf Hasan Khalil Museum (1975–85)
Photo courtesy Zouheir A. Hashem

Sports Hall (by Frei Otto, 1981); Jeddah Royal Palace and Royal State Palace (by Kenzo Tange, 1980); King Saud Mosque (1987) and Aziziyyah Mosque (1988), both by Abdel-Wahed El-Wakil; and National Commercial Bank (Gordon Bunshaft and Skidmore, Owings and Merrill, 1983). Award-winning buildings in Jeddah include the Haj Terminal at King Abdul Aziz International Airport (designed by Skidmore, Owings and Merrill, 1981). The project is considered to be the world's largest roofed structure, covering 1.5 square kilometers (370 acres) and designed to accommodate the one million pilgrims who make their way to Mecca each year. The Haj Terminal consists of 210 conical Teflon-coated fiberglass roof units divided into ten rectangular sections, each with 21 (3-by-7) of those conical roof units. The project received the Aga Khan Award for Architecture in 1983. Gordon Bunshaft's National Commercial Bank Headquarters building reflects the importation of International Style modernism and features dramatic 100-foot-wide facade openings and recessed windows. Above the first-floor level, a small triangular core draws up warm air and vents it through the center of the roof.

At about every kilometer, a mosque has been erected for the convenience of praying crowds of tourists and locals alike. The most famous of all these mosques on this Red Sea strip is the Corniche Mosque, which received the Aga Khan Award for Ar-

chitecture in 1989. Built in 1986, the mosque was designed by the Egyptian architect Abdel-Wahid El-Wakil. Recognized by its simple dome and minaret construction, the mosque's interior provides praying men and women with a serene atmosphere overlooking the blue waters of the Red Sea.

El-Wakil also designed the King Saud Mosque (1987) on El-Medina Road. The largest domed mosque in the city, it features an open central courtyard with properly oriented shading devices that allow warm air from the entire structure to vent naturally through the rooftop. The main feature of the King Saud Mosque is its segmental central dome, which has a height of 40 meters. This type of dome construction was never realized before this project's completion. For weight consideration, the dome was constructed using hollow, yet load-bearing, bricks. Starting with the square, the construction allowed for going through the remaining multisided layers of the dome in a much slower rate than was typically done and, as such, permitted the dome to be significantly higher than typical domes.

If history offers us any lessons, it would teach us that Jeddah will continue to survive and prosper. Given government support, the resourcefulness of its population, and the tourism prospects in Saudi Arabia (religious, internal, and external), the city will face a potentially tremendous growth dilemma. Infrastructure rejuvenation and expansion will be a must for the city to take on anticipated challenges. Architecturally, the city still has the potential to witness the creation of many more salient building achievements in both the private and the public sector.

ZOUHEIR A. HASHEM

See also **Fathy, Hassan (Egypt); Haj Terminal, Jeddah Airport; Saudi Arabia**

Further Reading

Buchan, James (editor), *Jeddah Old and New*, London: Stacey International, 1980; revised edition, 1991

Schofield, Daniel (editor), with an essay by Sir Norman Anderson, *The Kingdom of Saudi Arabia*, London: Stacey International, 1977; 9th edition, 1993

THE JEWISH MUSEUM, BERLIN

Designed by Daniel Libeskind; completed 1999

The Jewish Museum in Berlin is a building that is rooted in the history of its site, the city, and its Jewish residents in the 20th century. Its collections and exhibitions include cultural and historical objects of art and artifacts of Jewish people from the 4th century to the present. Begun by the American architect Daniel Libeskind in 1989 and completed in 1999, the museum was designed to physically and emotionally challenge its community and visitors alike through interpretation and perception.

Born in Lodz, Poland, and raised in Israel before becoming an American citizen in 1965, Libeskind has become recognized for his engagement with the critical theory that surrounds much contemporary architecture. He has developed a distinct aesthetic with a specialization in museum design. The Jewish Museum, Berlin (also titled, as if a work of art itself, *Between the Lines*) represents the first of many similar projects including the Danish Jewish Museum, Copenhagen (*Mitzvah*, 2003), the San Francisco Holocaust Museum, California (*L'Chai'm: To Life*, 1998–2005), and extensions for the Denver Museum of Art (*The Eye and the Wing*, 2000–2005) and the Victoria and Albert Museum, London (*The Spiral*, 1996–2006).

In 1988 Libeskind was invited by the Berlin Senate to submit a proposal to the architectural competition for the design of the Jewish Museum (before the fall of the Berlin Wall in 1989), a project and institution that would come to represent one of the first steps toward establishing dialogue in a city shrouded by its history of Nazism and destruction.

The design concept for the Jewish Museum reflects and relates to its physical and historical place within the city of Berlin. Built on a prominent and visible site in the old section of the

Jewish Museum, Berlin, designed by Daniel Libeskind (1999)
© Bitter Bredt, Berlin

"Memory Void," interior of the Jewish Museum (1999)
© Bitter Bredt, Berlin

from one time and space into another is suggestive of the kind of expected and unexpected experience to be encountered by the visitor inside the 10,000 square meters of interior space. A descending stairway leads visitors into a dramatic void that runs below the foundations of the old building into the new. The new building arises from the void as an independent structure, tied to the old only by time and space. Three underground "roads" lead visitors to other areas of exploration from where they can symbolically reach different conclusions and perceptions. The longest "road" or hallway directs one to the main staircase and to future exhibition spaces. Symbolically, this path represents the continued history of Berlin. A second "road" heads off toward a garden, the E. T. A. Hoffmann Garden. The unique design for this space, described by Libeskind as "a kind of upside down garden," places green foliage above the heads of the visitors, atop 17 concrete columns who stand on a slope. Also referred to as the "Garden of Exile," the space is intended to represent and reflect the experiences of the exile and emigration of Jews from Germany and their imprisonment in concentration camps. The third "road," several hundred yards in length, leads to dead-end that starkly represents the void of the Holocaust.

Central to the organization and design of the interior space is a large void, 90 feet in height, which cuts through the form of the building, creating a spine around which exhibitions are to be organized. To cross from one side of this void to the other, visitors pass across 60 connecting bridges that further highlight the intentional contrast of void and space and draw attentions to elements that are both present and absent. Libeskind's dynamic building has been subject to a common criticism of museum architecture; that is, that the structure upstages the art and artifacts that it was designed to house.

As expressed by Libeskind, the Jewish Museum, Berlin, is meant to be understood as "an emblem of hope" that reflects the heritage of the past, expresses the sentiments of the present, and projects a future of greater understanding.

EVIE T. JOSELOW

See also **Deconstructivism; Libeskind, Daniel (United States); Museum**

Further Reading

Binet, Helene, *A Passage Through Silence and Light*, London: Black Dog Press, 1997
Libeskind, Daniel, *Countersign*, London: Academy Editions, 1991 and New York: Rizzoli, 1992
Libeskind, Daniel, and Helene Binet, *Jewish Museum Berlin*, [Amsterdam?]: Gordon and Breach Publishing Group, 1999
Schneider, Bernhard, *Jewish Museum: Between the Lines*, foreword by Daniel Libeskind, Munich and New York; Prestel, 1999

city, and adjacent to the Kollegienhaus, a Prussian Baroque courthouse, the Museum contrasts with its surroundings. However, according to Libeskind there exist invisible counterparts to the site and the design of the building that are in constant play, in the exterior and the interior. Metaphorically, the contrasts and contradictions that are built into the structure represent relations between Germans and Jews and underscore the primary aspects of the building: to define the Jews of Berlin and to remember the names of persons deported from Berlin during the Holocaust, specifically those listed in two massive official volumes known as the *Gedenkbuch*, or remembrance book.

The distorted Star of David, inscribed upon the facade of the building and facing the courtyard, represents the architect's efforts to use plastic form as a visible means of creating links between Jewish traditions (the history inside the building) and German culture (the exterior that is the city of Berlin). The seemingly irrational arrangement of points creates a compressed and distorted star that functions as an emblem of religious faith, but also of oppression: Berlin Jews were forced to wear yellow stars on the very site where the building now stands.

Emphasizing the sharp contrasts between old and new, visible and invisible, visitors enter the Jewish Museum through the Baroque doors of the adjacent Kollegienhaus. The movement

JIRICNA, EVA 1939–

Architect, England

Eva Jiricna is one of few women with an international reputation in architecture, design, and engineering. Born in 1939, she trained in her homeland of Czechoslovakia with a strong emphasis on science and engineering. In 1968 she moved to Britain, where she remained, becoming a British citizen in 1976. She worked for ten years on the mammoth Brighton Marina project while with the firm Louis de Soissons Partnership, where she learned about high-tech materials such as steel, aluminum, neoprene, and glass fiber, among others.

During the period 1982–84, Jiricna worked as team leader for the interior design packages for the Lloyds headquarters building at the Richard Rogers Partnership. Having her own London office since 1984, she is often recognized as an architect of interiors. She has designed retail spaces for Harrods in London and for Joan and David and Esprit shops in Britain and the United States (1985–87). Her versatile designs make maximum use of industrial materials in limited spaces and often incorporate sculptural staircases as dramatic focal points.

Each commission is unique to Jiricna, and the parameters and conditions are the starting point for the search for the solution. The actual design is preceded by dozens of analyses that look not only at the functional requirements to be fulfilled but also at possible materials and structural, and spatial solutions. She employs a minimal number of materials, thus allowing the nature and characteristics of each to be declared in a clear and often surprising way.

In 1989 one of Jiricna's first signature staircases was designed for the Joseph store on Sloane Street in London. The new staircase was located in the center of the store and used to organize the space while creating a visual focal point of activity. The risers are glass, and the entire structure is suspended using a system of steel rods. Each detail is carefully calculated and precisely crafted, and its transparency formally unites the different levels of the shop. Although the initial impression of the staircase is one of fragility, the principles of engineering are unwavering, and as the customer ascends or descends the staircase, sensations of security and surprise are experienced.

The design of a new system for exhibitions was the task the architect faced at the Sir John Soane Museum in London in 1993. The house-museum needed freestanding elements to allow for the display of drawings, sketchbooks, models, and other architectural documents. However, the new supports could not interfere or modify the existing buildings, designed by Sir John Soane in the late 18th and early 19th centuries. A series of freestanding glass cases were designed that solve multiple problems. The cases, made of clear toughened glass, move on rails controlled by pistons. The interior of the case is a glass panel with a mild steel sheet in a glass frame for the exhibition of two- and three-dimensional objects. Drawings are held in place by magnetic strips. Three-dimensional objects rest on glass shelves. Easy access to the drawings is made possible by opening an end of the case and sliding out the inner glass panel. A mixture of florescent and tungsten halogen sources is incorporated within the case design and provides both direct and indirect lighting to minimize possible reflections inside the case.

In 1993 President Havel of the new Czech Republic invited Jiricna to become a member of the Prague Presidential Council in an advisory capacity as an architectural consultant. In 1998 Jiricna was asked to create a greenhouse for the Royal Garden. The first Orangery at the Prague Castle was established in the 15th century. The new commission called for a proposal that would maintain the historical function of the site while using 20th-century architectural language. The solution again looked to a stainless steel structure, which supports a suspended glass shell. A constant in her work, structural efficiency has produced clear volumes and expanses of delicate shell while never relinquishing the functional concerns of the building. It is sited in a striking way, and visitors along the new path from Klarov to Powder bridge can appreciate a truly this modern building, which fits gracefully in a historic setting.

Recent projects also include adapting the interior of the Frank Gehry building in Prague for the offices of Andersen Consulting, a pedestrian bridge for the Docklands, and a bus station in London. Jiricna's office designed the Faith Pavilion within the Millennium Dome, designed by the firm of Richard Rogers and Partners.

MARTHA THORNE

See also **Rogers, Richard (England)**

Biography

Born 3 March 1939 in Czechoslovakia. Studied engineering and architecture at the University of Prague; received a Master of Arts degree, Academy of Fine Arts in Prague, 1967. Travelled to London in 1968, just weeks before the Soviet invasion of Czechoslovakia. She stayed in London permanently, and worked for the Greater London Council (1968–9); partner with De Soissons (1969–80); and with David Hodge (1980–82). Established Eva Jiricna Architects in London, 1987. Jiricna is an Honorary Fellow of the Royal College of Art and of the Royal Incorporation of Architects of Scotland. She was elected to the British Royal Academy of Arts. She frequently lectures at universities in Europe and the United States, including Harvard University, the University of Pennsylvania, and Illinois Institute of Technology.

Selected Works

Joseph shop design, London, 1989
Alex Boutique, Florence, Italy, 1989
Koliste Footbridge, Brno, Czech Republic, 1991
Gallery designs, Sir John Soane Museum, London, 1993
Extension and Conversion, Ove Arup House, Highgate, London, 1994
Orangery, Prague Castle, Czech Republic, 1998
Faith Zone, Millennium Dome, Greenwich, England, 1999
Hotel Josef, Prague, Czechoslovakia, 2002

Further Reading

Almaas, Ingerid Helsing "Galleri I Sir John Soane Museet," *Byggekunst: The Norwegian Review of Architecture*, 76 (1996)
Davey, Peter, "Jiricna Bravura," *Architectural Review*, 185 (January 1989)
Etteggui, Joseph, *Eva Jiricna Designs*, London: Architectural Association, 1987
Hughes, Elmer, "In Person: Eva Jiricna" (interview), *Plan: Architecture, Building, Interior Design*, 7 (July 1992)
Manser, Jose, *Joseph Shops: Eva Jiricna*, London: Architecture Design and Technology Press; and New York: Van Nostrand Reinhold, 1991
McQuire, Penny, "Drawing Inspiration," *Architectural Review*, 197 (June 1997)
McQuiston, Liz, *Women in Design: A Contemporary View*, New York: Rizzoli, 1988

Richardson, Sara, *Jiricna Kerr and Associates, a bibliography* (no. A2212), Monticello, Illinois: Vance Bibliographies, 1989

Pauley, Martin, *Eva Jiricna: Design in Exile*, New York: Rizzoli, 1990

Powell, Kenneth, "Back to the Future," *Architects' Journal*, 206 (July 31–August 7 1997)

Stungo, Naomi, "Station to Station. Canada Water Interchange," *RIBA Journal*, 106 (September 1999)

JOHNSON, PHILIP 1906–

Architect, United States

Philip Johnson has been a crucial figure in introducing conservative American clients to avant-garde architectural forms and publicizing these forms in striking ways. He began as an early and important advocate of the architecture of the European Modern movement in the United States through exhibitions, lectures, and juries, in addition to his own built structures. He lived long enough to become one of the best-known and most prolific Postmodern designers of the 1980s. Throughout his career, Johnson emphasized the formal values of architecture above all others, far more so than adherence to any one style or approach. More paradoxically, he has maintained a posture of permanent avant-gardism, attacking the architectural certainties of the moment—admitting all the while that his aim has been to influence the wielders of power as they choose architectural expressions of that power.

Under the influence of young Harvard-trained art historians Henry-Russell Hitchcock, Jr., and Alfred H. Barr, Jr., Johnson quickly became a formidable authority on Western architecture. However, Hitchcock and Barr, as well as Johnson's brilliant Harvard circle of future Modern-art patrons, persuaded Johnson to put his energies and considerable wealth into education and propaganda for modern architecture.

In 1930, shortly after the 1929 founding of the Museum of Modern Art (MoMA) in New York under Barr's directorship, Johnson began acting as the museum's de facto, unpaid curator of architecture. His 1932 exhibition, "Modern Architecture: International Exhibition," is generally known as the "International Style" show, after the title of the accompanying book by Johnson and Hitchcock. The exhibition followed Barr's lead in presenting the most extreme and accomplished modernists—Le Corbusier, Ludwig Mies van der Rohe, Walter Gropius, and J.J.P. Oud— as masters of a unified, teachable, inevitable style, for which the MoMA historians invented the label "International." The exhibition and book were criticized for their frankly formalist stance, but the thoroughness with which Johnson documented and publicized this branch of modernism made MoMA the authority on it for the next 30 years.

Through his MoMA contacts and presence on the Berlin art scene, Johnson became a major figure among the avant-garde's elite patrons on two continents while still in his 20s. Johnson's most important Berlin acquaintance was Mies van der Rohe, whose presence in American design began under Johnson's patronage. After the exhibition, Johnson was hired (paying his own salary) as MoMA's curator of architecture and design. However, the mercurial and impetuous Johnson became attracted to the Hitler movement in Germany and in 1934 left architecture to serve as activist and publicist for several fascist and radical-right causes.

In 1940 Johnson enrolled in Harvard's Graduate School of Design, then run by Gropius. His first executed building was a Cambridge house that he built for himself using Mies' "court house" concept; it was offered as his senior thesis in architecture in 1942. In 1947, Johnson curated a seminal eponymous retrospective of Mies' work, accompanied by a monograph that was the first extended discussion of Mies' career in any language. The show and book made Mies a major figure in American architecture almost overnight and returned Johnson to the place of influence in architecture that he had occupied before 1934.

In 1949 Johnson erected his first important work: a single-room, steel-framed, glass-walled house for himself on property in New Canaan, Connecticut. The concept derives from Mies' Farnsworth House in Plano, Illinois, that was in the planning stages at the time. However, Johnson's Glass House departs crucially, if subtly, from its prototype. The Farnsworth project is asymmetrical and seems to float above a floodplain on its white-painted I beams. Johnson's Glass House is symmetrical, rests on a low brick platform, and is anchored to its hilltop by a chimney cylinder of brick. The black finish and heavy corners of the steel frame imbue the house with a weighty, classical air that works in striking dialogue with the building's radical transparency. The Glass House is regarded as among the best, possibly the very best, of Johnson's buildings and is an important monument of the International Style's acceptance in the United States.

In the early 1950s, Johnson achieved some eminence as a designer of suburban houses in Mies' manner as well as of the beautiful MoMA Sculpture Garden (1953) in New York, inspired by Mies' 1929 German Pavilion at Barcelona. He was Mies' partner in the design of the Seagram Building (1959) in New York, a commission that he had obtained for Mies as a MoMA consultant to Seagram heiress Phyllis Lambert. The building's elegant Four Seasons Restaurant is Johnson's chief contribution. However, beginning in 1953 with a domed bedroom in his Guest House, Johnson began experimenting with non–International Style elements such as curves, vaults, pilasters, and axes. His approach was to adopt avant-garde forms in more accessible, elegant, or recognizably honorific ways. Johnson often added cerebral, rather stagy references to earlier architecture, ranging from the work of Claude-Nicolas Ledoux to that of obscure German modernists, but he always paid careful attention to materials (frequently luxurious) and details. Johnson's buildings share a pronounced concern for the plan in both making useful spaces and considering their aesthetic effect on the pedestrian.

In the late 1950s Johnson began to assert that the verities of the International Style were dead and that change was now architecture's only constant. He soon became identified with the quasi-classical manner with which architects such as Edward Durell Stone and Minoru Yamasaki tried to temper modernist austerity; his New York State Theater (1964) at Lincoln Center is such an example. However, Johnson also played with compositional schemes based on circles and cylinders (for example, the exquisite domed pavilions of the Museum of Pre-Columbian Art, Dumbarton Oaks, Washington, D.C., 1963). The Roofless Church (1960) in New Harmony, Indiana, and several urban parks in Texas show Johnson's gift for siting abstract forms in open spaces. His most breathtaking exercise in abstract form is

Fagus Werk (1911–14), Alfeld an der Leine, Germany
Designed by Adolf Meyer and Walter Gropius (Germany)
© Peter Aaron / ESTO. All rights reserved.

Glass House (1949), New Canaan, Connecticut
Designed by Philip Johnson (United States)
© Ezra Stoller / ESTO. All rights reserved.

Grundtvig Church (1940), Copenhagen, Denmark
Designed by Peder Vilhelm Jensen-Klimt (Denmark)
© MIT Collection/CORBIS

Sunila Pulp Mill (1936–38, 1951–54), Kotka, Finland
Designed by Alvar Aalto (Finland)
© Adam Woolfitt / CORBIS

Sahat al-Kindi Plaza (1986), Riyadh, Saudi Arabia
Designed by Beeah Group Consultants (Ali Shuaibi and Abdul-Rahman Hussaini, Saudi Arabia)
© Saleh Al-Hathloul

Cultural Centre Jean Marie Tjibaro-Noumia (1998), New Caledonia
Designed by Renzo Piano (Italy)
© Tim Griffith / ESTO. All rights reserved.

Jewish Museum (1988–98), Berlin, Germany
Designed by Daniel Libeskind (Poland and United States)
© Bitter + Bredt, Berlin

Managua Cathedral (1993), Managua, Nicaragua
Designed by Ricardo V. Legorreta (Mexico)

Grande Arche de La Défense (1982–89), Paris, France
Designed by Johan Otto von Spreckelsen (Denmark)
© Alex Bartel / ESTO. All rights reserved.

Lovell Health House Interior (1929),
Los Angeles, California
Designed by Richard Neutra (Austria and
United States)
© Roberto Schezen / ESTO. All rights reserved.

Bank of America Corporate Center (formerly Nations Bank Corporate Center) 1992, Charlotte, North Carolina
Designed by Cesar A. Pelli (United States)
Photo © Cesar Pelli and Associates

Parliament Building (1952–62), Chandigarh, India
Designed by Le Corbusier (Charles-Édouard Jeanneret, France)
© Chris Hellier / CORBIS

Habib Gorgy Sculpture Museum Interior
Ramses Wissa Wassef Arts Centre (1974), Harrania, near Giza, Egypt
Designed by Ramses Wissa Wassef (Egypt)
Photo by Chant Avedissian © Aga Khan Trust for Culture

Casa Amatller (detail) (1898–1900), Barcelona, Spain
Designed by Josep Puig i Cadafalch (Catalonia)
© Mary Ann Sullivan

Sheldon Memorial Art Gallery, University of Nebraska, Lincoln, Nebraska (1962)
Photo © Mary Ann Sullivan

the all-glass Crystal Cathedral (1980) in Garden Grove, California.

During this period, Johnson's career as an architect was almost secondary to his status as a pundit. He took an interest in the reform of urban planning and became a hero to the nascent preservation movement by protesting the 1963 demolition of New York's Pennsylvania Station. At the same time, with the guidance of art consultant David Whitney, his companion, Johnson became an important collector and patron of pop art. Johnson was awarded the American Institute of Architects Gold Medal in 1978 and the Pritzker Prize in 1979.

In 1967 Johnson took Chicago architect John Burgee into his firm, making him a partner in 1969. Burgee's experience with skyscraper design made it possible for Johnson to enter the high-rise market. The firm experimented with variations on the standard glass-slab skyscraper, such as the IDS Center (1973) in Minneapolis, with its faceted corners, and the slant-top adjoining trapezoids of Pennzoil Place (1976) in Houston. The publication in 1978 of the firm's famous scheme for the AT&T headquarters in New York marked a controversial new direction. Essentially a modernist slab in layout, AT&T (constructed 1979–84, now the Sony Building) featured a 60-foot-high neo-Renaissance loggia with a 116-foot central arch, a granite-clad shaft, and a roofline in the form of a classical broken pediment. The vast "Chippendale" top reflected Johnson's admiration for

Robert Venturi, whose writings mixed calls for readable symbolism with a pop sense of irony and contradiction. (AT&T's pediment also recalls the split-top "gable" front of Venturi's 1964 house for his mother.) The skyscraper's granite casing and classical details showed the influence of more earnestly historicist Postmodernists, such as Robert Stern. AT&T's monumental elements and its stripped-down classicism are in keeping with Johnson's earlier predilections, but never before had he repudiated the International Style so completely. Nor had a Postmodern design on such a large scale been accepted in the United States by such a conservative client. The commission made Johnson the leader of the best-publicized and most lucrative architectural trend of the following decade.

Between 1980 and 1985, Johnson and Burgee dominated the market for Postmodernist skyscrapers and other high-budget projects. In addition to works in countless historical styles, from French classical to German Renaissance to Art Deco, Johnson designed several buildings, such as PPG Corporate Headquarters (1984) in Pittsburgh and International Place (two stages, 1988 and 1992) in Boston, that collage and distort familiar forms in provocative ways. These were the fruit of his interest in pop art and were not always respectful of his clients' desire for clear architectural representation. However, Johnson's restless design sensibility often kept him from mastering either straight revivalist forms or these pop appropriations to critics' satisfaction. Despite the excellence of works such as the Transco Tower (1983) in Houston, less-accomplished designs, such as the Times Square redevelopment (1983; unbuilt), with its overpowering scale, seemed to be cynical insults to Postmodernism's representational and urbanistic concerns.

In 1988 Johnson dropped historicist Postmodernism and involved himself with MoMA's exhibition, "Deconstructivist Architecture." This move reinforced Johnson's reputation for cynical power brokering, yet Johnson was correct in noting that stylistic revivalism had begun to wane as a major force in architecture. The use of signature architectural styles (historicist or avant-garde) as high-class commodities is a more lasting legacy from the Postmodern period, which Johnson's career as an architectural impresario did much to encourage.

MILES DAVID SAMSON

See also **AT&T Building, New York; Church: Corbusier, Le (Jeanneret, Charles-Édouard) (France); Farnsworth House, Plano, Illinois; Glass House, New Canaan, Connecticut; Gropius, Walter (Germany); Historicism; Hitchcock, Henry-Russell (United States); International Style; International Style Exhibition, New York (1932); Mies van der Rohe, Ludwig (Germany); Museum of Modern Art, New York; Oud, J.J.P. (the Netherlands); Stern, Robert A.M. (United States); Postmodernism; Seagram Building, New York; Venturi, Robert (United States)**

Biography

Born in Cleveland, Ohio, 8 July 1906, the son of a lawyer. Entered Harvard College in 1923 with class of 1927; graduated 1930 with a B.A. in classical Greek. Volunteer advisor and curator at Museum of Modern Art, New York 1930–32; curator of architecture and design 1932–34. Co-cofounder and director of right-wing National Party 1934; offered services to Louisiana Senator Huey Long's national political efforts 1934–35; affiliated himself with Father Charles Coughlin's National Union for Social Justice 1936; co-organized "Youth and the Nation" political movement (later Young Nationalists) 1936–37; lecturer for American Fellowship Forum 1939–40. Studied at Graduate School of Design, Harvard University 1940–43, earning B.Arch. degree. Served in U.S. Army 1943–44. Architectural practice with Landis Gores 1945–51; director of department of architecture, Museum of Modern Art 1946–54; trustee of museum from 1958; visiting critic, Yale School of Architecture, from 1950 until early 1960s. Partnership with Ludwig Mies van der Rohe, New York 1954–59, on Seagram Building exclusively; partnership with Richard Foster from mid-1950s to 1962 and 1964–69; partnership with John Burgee 1969–86; consultant to John Burgee Architects 1986–91; participated in and contributed financially to Institute for Architecture and Urban Studies from about 1970 until the early 1980s. Awarded Gold Medal of the American Institute of Architects 1978; awarded Pritzker Prize for Architecture 1979; awarded honorary degrees from Yale University, Pratt Institute, Ohio State University, University of Houston, and University of Nebraska.

Selected Works

Philip Johnson House (Glass House), New Canaan, CT, 1949. Other significant works on the New Canaan property include Guest House (1949; bedroom remodeling 1953), Pavilion at Pond (1962), Sculpture Gallery (1970) and Gate House (1995).
Abby Aldrich Rockefeller Sculpture Garden, Museum of Modern Art, New York City (in collaboration with James Fanning, landscape architect), 1953
Boissonnas House, New Canaan, CT, 1956
Four Seasons Restaurant, Seagram Building, New York City, 1959
Roofless Church, New Harmony, IN, 1960
Sheldon Memorial Art Gallery, University of Nebraska, Lincoln, 1962
Museum for Pre-Columbian Art at Dumbarton Oaks, Washington, D.C., 1963
New York State Theater at Lincoln Center, New York, 1964
Kline Biology Tower, Yale University, New Haven, CT, 1966
IDS Center, Minneapolis, MN, 1973
Pennzoil Place, Houston, TX, 1976
Thanksgiving Square, Houston, TX, 1976
Transco Tower, Houston, TX, 1979–83
PPG Headquarters, Pittsburgh, PA, 1979–84
AT&T Building (now Sony Building), New York City, 1979–84
Republic Bank Center, Houston, TX, 1981–84
Fifty-Third at Third, New York City, 1984
St. Basil Chapel, University of St. Thomas, Houston, TX (project), 1987

Selected Publications

Hitchcock, Henry-Russell, Jr. and Philip Johnson, *The International Style: Architecture since 1922,* New York: Norton: 1932; 2nd edition, 1966
Machine Art, New York: Museum of Modern Art, 1934
Mies van der Rohe, New York: Museum of Modern Art, 1947; 2nd, revised edition, 1953; 3rd, revised edition, 1978
Architecture 1949–1965, introduction by Henry-Russell Hitchcock, Jr., New York: Holt Rinehart and Winston, 1966
Writings, introduction by Peter Eisenman, New York: Oxford University Press, 1979
Johnson, Philip and Mark Wigley, *Deconstructivist Architecture* (exhib. cat.), New York: Modern Museum of Art, and Boston: Little Brown, 1988
Modern Architecture: International Exhibition, New York: Museum of Modern Art, 1932 (with Alfred H. Barr, Jr., Henry-Russell Hitchcock, Jr., and Lewis Mumford, exhib. cat.)

Further Reading

Blake, Peter, *Philip Johnson*, Basel and Boston: Birkhäuser Verlag, 1996
Frampton, Kenneth (editor), *Philip Johnson, Processes; The Glass House, 1949 and the AT&T Corporate Headquarters, 1978* (exhib. cat.), New York: Institute for Architecture and Urban Studies, 1978
Jacobus, John M., *Philip Johnson*, New York: Braziller, 1962
Johnson, Philip, Hilary Lewis, and John O'Connor, *Philip Johnson: The Architect in His Own Words*, New York: Rizzoli, 1994
Kipnis, Jeffrey, *Philip Johnson: Recent Work*, London: Academy Editions, 1996
Riley, Terence, *The International Style: Exhibition 15 and the Museum of Modern Art*, New York: Rizzoli, 1992
Schulze, Franz, *Philip Johnson: Life and Work*, New York: Knopf, 1994
Whitney, David and Jeffrey Kipnis, *Philip Johnson: The Glass House*, New York: Pantheon, 1993

JOHNSON WAX ADMINISTRATION BUILDING

Designed by Frank Lloyd Wright; completed 1939
Racine, Wisconsin

By the 1930s the brilliance of Frank Lloyd Wright's early career seemed eclipsed by the new and innovative architecture in Europe. In the years since the Robie House, he had left the city of Chicago for the exploration of an architecture based on an organic merger of program and site as the vehicle for the direct experience of a transcendental Nature. In his scheme for Broadacre City, first developed during the late 1920s, Wright had extended the scope of this investigation to recommend the full-scale dispersal of urban and industrial elements throughout the countryside, overcoming traditional dichotomies of city and nature. Following this, it was with Fallingwater (Pennsylvania, 1934–37) and the Johnson Wax Administration Building (1936–39) that Wright signaled his return to international prominence.

Located in Racine, Wisconsin, the building is a two-part mass composed of a large clerical work floor connected to an adjoining parking garage by a bridge of services and executive offices. The building's design incorporated innovative technical details, in-cluding floor heat, steel-mesh reinforcing for the concrete, and glass tubing for skylights. The larger problem that Wright faced in the design lay in tying the corporate work environment to an experience of the natural world while remaining on the industrial urban site, in this case an entire city block. He accomplished this by relating the exterior of the building to the motion of the automobile on the surrounding streets rather than to the existing buildings of the city and by turning the design inward, enveloping workers in an unexpectedly remote interior environment.

When first seen, the building appears as a low streamline brick mass with softly rounded edges. The size of the building is obscured by a lack of ornamental detail and the use of diagonal or nonhierarchical massing on its third floor. As is characteristic of so many of Wright's buildings, the entry does not announce itself but must be sought out. Planes of brick and muted glass move into one another, creating a fluid arrangement that stands apart from the abrupt verticality and singular massing of the more traditional office buildings of the surrounding city.

Rather than deny the automobile as an intrusion into the entry experience, Wright incorporated it, pulling vehicles into the composition at the point of entry. The covered entry drive, nestled beneath the bridging executive offices, is a low, sheltered area. As one steps inside, light floods down from a three-story lobby, providing an immediate contrast to the darker, com-

Johnson Wax Building (interior), Racine, Wisconsin, by Frank Lloyd Wright
© Historic American Buildings Survey/Library of Congress

pressed entry area and acting as a screen between that and the singular, unprecedented work space beyond.

The "great workroom," as Wright called it, was designed as a communal workspace where each of the many clerical workers and managers could draw inspiration from participation in the shared corporate endeavor. Its spatial strategy inverts much of what we are accustomed to in our expectations of enclosure. Four walls meeting a ceiling with doors and windows clearly marked by molding as interruptions in the enclosure is not the way the character of this space is determined. A sweeping brick wall envelops an orchard of tall, flowering columns. A continuous band of glass tubes at the traditional juncture of wall and ceiling disengages expectations of an orthogonal space limited by such definitions of enclosure. This is not so much a room built simply as a device to exclude the outside as it is the creation of a unique experience on its own terms. To work in this building, Wright said, would be like "[being] among the pine trees breathing fresh air and sunlight."

Noted for structural innovation, the concrete columns stand out as the dominant element of the space. A careful reversal of classical entasis in the columns creates a gentle spreading sense of space, made indistinct by an illusive relation of column grid to ceiling plane and load. These rise into large circular caps that do not touch one another as they spread out to establish a ceiling plane. These circles do not reinforce the orthogonality of the overall frame of the building as given by the enclosing brick wall. Rather, one's most determinate reading of the room is given by the columns, each standing with a presence of its own yet still as a member of the group, much like the effect of trees in a forest. Their shape is carefully crafted to pull one's attention above the clutter of the working floor to the shared pool of light above. Their connection to the ground is obscured by the rounded furniture that Wright designed for the building.

Wright had experimented with many of these elements before in the Larkin Building (1904). He is explicit about the connection between these two. This great workroom "[is] the daughter of the Larkin Building," he wrote, "born . . . on provincial American soil." The Johnson Wax Administration Building resembles the Larkin in plan, with an entry sequence sliding between two masses to engage the short axis of a large interior volume. However, the differences between these two buildings are more important than the similarities. At Larkin, Wright opened an atrium in a three-dimensional structural grid. The resultant space was appointed with decorative elements and finishes in line with programmatic objectives. In the Johnson Wax Administration Building, the order of design is more powerful. Not only are the decorative elements incorporated into the architectural forms, but these forms, and the concept of structure that

they develop, are reshaped—one might say reconceived—in service of the design idea. No preconceived structural or typological form was allowed to intervene between the spatial conception and its execution. It is architectural invention at its very best.

Life magazine opened its 8 May 1939 issue with a tribute to the building, saying, "It is genuine American architecture, owing nothing to foreign inspiration, different from anything ever built in the world." Comparing the building to the recently opened New York World's Fair, it added, "[The] Fair, sprawling its gigantic mass of freak and futuristic buildings is undeniably a great show. But future historians may well decide that a truer glimpse of the shape of things to come was given last week by a single structure, built strictly for business, which opened in a drab section of Racine, Wisconsin."

In this era of rapidly changing society, Wright sought to emphasize the role of the industrial establishment, the corporation, in bringing people together in "peaceful and productive collaboration." The values of loyalty, participation, and membership enshrined in the prairie house dining rooms emerge in the quiet formality of the great workroom. Wright himself called it "simply and sincerely an interpretation of modern business conditions . . . designed to be as inspiring a place to live and work as any cathedral ever was to worship in."

In the Johnson Wax Administration Building, Wright has identified the significance of work as a social bond and the potential of the workplace to act as a binding agent. The adaptation and transformation of the ancient form of top-lit hypostyle hall, invoking a sense of community based on the participation of the workers, is among his most significant architectural inventions. Architectural historian Kenneth Frampton has called the Johnson Wax Building "possibly the most profound work of art America has yet produced." It ranks among America's most ambitious statements of the possibilities of corporate capitalism.

J. MICHAEL DESMOND

See also **Broadacre City (1934–35); Fallingwater, Bear Run, Pennsylvania; Wright, Frank Lloyd (United States)**

Further Reading

Architectural Forum, 68/1 (January 1938)

Egbert, Donald Drew, "The Idea of Organic Expression and American Architecture," in *Evolutionary Thought in America*, edited by Stow Persons, New Haven, Connecticut: Yale University Press, 1950

Lipman, Jonathan, *Frank Lloyd Wright and the Johnson Wax Buildings*, New York: Rizzoli, and London: Architectural Press, 1986

Wright, Frank Lloyd, *An Autobiography*, New York and London: Longman Green, 1932

K

KADA, KLAUS 1940–

Architect, Austria

Klaus Kada is one of the leading figures in contemporary Austrian architecture. His work and contribution are to be understood in the context of the regional architecture culture that developed around the city of Graz, the second-largest city in Austria, from the early 1970s onward and that gained international attention in the mid-1980s. Other members of the group, all of whom share a passion for formal and material experimentation, include Günther Domenig, Volker Giencke, and the husband-and-wife team of Michael Szyszkowitz and Karla Kowalski. Nourished by active government building programs, expansive competition systems, and vivid public debate about architecture, these Graz architects have recently challenged the hegemony of Vienna as the center of Austrian architecture.

Kada was born in the small city of Leibnitz, about 20 miles south of Graz near the Slovenian border, where his parents owned a department store. As the eldest son, he was expected to take over the family business, but instead he chose to study building construction at a technical college. In 1961, Kada entered the Technical University of Graz to study architecture and earned a diploma at a relatively mature age in 1971.

In 1976, Kada opened his own office after a five-year training period in various architectural offices in Germany and Austria. Such training is required of Austrian architects prior to taking the licensing examination. Since then, Kada has built a very successful practice designing private, public, and institutional buildings, mostly around the Graz region. The office has a broad scope of building types to its credit: private houses, mass-housing projects, a dormitory, a museum, laboratory buildings, office buildings, hospitals, and auditoriums.

Kada's strength lies in his commitment to the practice of building rather than in theoretical pronouncements. His architecture is known for precision of detail and experimentation with new building technologies, most recently with glass construction. He is also known for intelligent site strategies, his ability to combine old and new, and his ability to respond to a variety of programmatic needs. Formerly known for exuberant forms, Kada's mature work has settled into restrained geometric formal language with clear structural and material articulation.

One of his first commissions was to design a new facility for the family business. The Kada Department Store (1971–73), with its prefabricated-concrete skeleton and paneling systems, manifests Kada's early interest in new technologies and construction methods as it pays tribute to his early affinity to the megastructural projects of the 1960s. Kada also cites Pier Luigi Nervi and Louis Kahn, both known for their highly articulated and systematic approach to structure, as early influences.

As common to Austrian architectural practices, Kada has gained most of his larger commissions through design competitions. In recent years, he has completed major public and institutional projects, including a dormitory (1988–92) in Graz, a glass museum (1987–88) in Bärnbach, the Institute for Plant Physiology (1993–97) for the University of Graz, a nursing home (1993–95) in Leibnitz, and a concert hall (1993–95) in St. Pölten.

The dormitory building in Graz and the glass museum in Bärnbach are perhaps the most celebrated Kada buildings to date. In the student housing project, Kada shows his mastery of a difficult urban site and his passion for communal housing. The dormitory is located along Wiener Strasse in a slightly dilapidated part of town. The building is pushed into the interior of the block with a narrow axial entrance to the road. From the street, between old houses, one can catch a glimpse of the slightly curving south-facing facade of the main building mass, which is articulated with red balconies, longitudinal access galleries, and vertical glazed staircases reminiscent of Ralph Erskine's Byker Wall (1969–81) in Newcastle-upon-Tyne, England. On warm days, students occupy these spaces, making the building appear as a large wall of life and movement. The communal student life is centered around an auditorium (also red) and a cafe on the ground-floor level.

The glass museum is located in the existing glassworks in Bärnbach, near Graz. Like the dormitory, the glass museum manifests Kada's mastery of a difficult site condition and his ability to mediate between old and new. Unlike other competitors, Kada chose to preserve the old generator house and to use it as the core of the new museum. The new elements wrap and form spaces around what came to be reduced to a concrete skeleton. Appropriate to the function, the building bears witness to Kada's passion for experimenting with glass and its new structural possibilities. The composition is dominated by two high walls that use glass in an inventive and spectacular way: the 30-foot-high freestanding glass entrance wall, one of the first of its kind in the world, and a slightly higher diagonal wall, made of shimmering glass tiles, that marks the edge of the site. Kada's glass museum belongs to the group of projects built in Austria and France during the late 1980s and early 1990s that celebrate glass as the ultimate modern building material.

In addition to his building activities, Kada is a professor in the Aachen Reinisch-Westfälische Technische Hochschule in Germany, where he has held the chair of building construction and design since 1996. Kada was also a founding member of EUROPAN, a housing and urbanism competition program for young European architects. His work has been published widely in the Austrian and the international architectural press, and he has won numerous national and international prizes for design excellence.

EEVA-LIISA PELKONEN

See also **Austria**

Biography

Born in Leibnitz, Austria, 1940. Graduated from the Technical University of Graz, Austria, with a degree in architecture 1971. Five-year mandatory training period with firms in Germany and Austria 1971–75. Set up private practice in Graz, 1976. Professor, chair of building construction and design since 1996, Aachen Reinisch-Westfälische Technische Hochschule. Founding member, EUROPAN.

Selected Works

Kada Department Store, Leibnitz, Austria, 1973
Glass Museum, Bärnbach, Austria, 1988
Dormitory, University of Graz, Austria, 1992
Nursing Home, Leibnitz, Austria, 1995
Concert Hall, St. Pölten, Austria, 1995
Institute for Plant Physiology, University of Graz, Austria, 1997

Selected Publication

Klaus Kada, edited by Otto Kapfinger and the Austrian Institute for Architecture, Vienna: Springer Verlag, 2000

Further Reading

Becker, Annette, Dietmar Steiner, and Wilfried Wang (editors), *Architektur im 20. Jahrhundert*, Munich and New York: Prestel, 1995
Blundell-Jones, Peter, *Dialogues in Time: New Graz Architecture*, Graz, Austria: Haus der Architektur, 1998
Giselbrecht, Ernst (editor), *Architektur-Investitionen: Grazer "Schule," 13 Standpunkte*, 2nd edition, Graz, Austria: Akademische Druck-und Verlagsanstalt, and Forum Stadtpark, 1984
Hellmayr, Nikolaus, and Peter Zinganel (editors), *Architektur als Engagement: Architektur aus der Steiermark, 1986–1992; Architecture as Commitment: Styrian Architecture, 1986–1992*, Graz, Austria: Haus der Architektur, 1993
Pelkonen, Eeva-Liisa, *Achtung Architektur! Image and Phantasm in Contemporary Austrian Architecture*, Cambridge, Massachusetts: MIT Press, 1996
Zinganel, Peter (editor), *Standpunkte '94*, Graz, Austria: Forum Stadtpark, 1994

KAHN, ALBERT 1869–1942

Architect, Germany and United States

The son of Rabbi Joseph Kahn, Albert Kahn was born in the town of Rhaunen, Germany (near Frankfurt), on 21 March 1869. Difficult economic conditions led to the family's immigration to the United States (by way of the grand duchy of Luxembourg), and in 1881 the Kahn family settled in Detroit, a major industrial center in the upper Midwest.

For various reasons—his family's economic difficulties being perhaps the most significant—Kahn was not able to follow a normal course of education leading to a university degree. Instead, his design abilities, developed through a series of free private lessons given to him by the sculptor Julius Mechers, enabled him to begin his architectural apprenticeship with the Detroit firm Mason and Rice at the age of 15. Quickly finding success as a draftsman in the firm, Kahn focused on the practical aspects of architecture and made excellent use of the firm's library. The combination of Kahn's intellectual interests and practical experience enabled him to win a scholarship from the journal *American Architect* for a year's study abroad. Kahn's year of travel through Italy, France, Belgium, and Germany—roughly the same as the traditional European tour undertaken by more privileged students of architecture—allowed Kahn to develop new, significant friendships (including with Henry Bacon, architect of the Lincoln Memorial in Washington) while deepening his knowledge of architecture through site visits and the sketching of buildings and their details. Returning to Mason and Rice, Kahn's sketches of notable works, while significant from an educational perspective, had a direct bearing on his architectural work for the office. In 1896 Kahn, along with two other architects from Mason and Rice, formed a new firm, Nettleton, Kahn and Trowbridge. After Trowbridge left to become dean of the Cornell School of Architecture in 1897, the firm became Nettleton and Kahn until finally, on the death of Nettleton in 1900, Kahn reassociated with George Mason, his original employer, for a brief period before finally opening an office under his own name.

In the course of his early career, Kahn worked with numerous historical styles, the Italian Renaissance being perhaps the most prominent. Nonetheless, the architect's stylistic predilections did not preclude an interest in the development of new materials and methods—an interest that foreshadowed his understanding of industrial and technological enterprise. This tendency was further facilitated by his firm's development in the early part of the 20th century; having facilitated his brother Julius's engineering education, the two brothers were able to create a professional association in 1903, with Julius working with Albert as the architect's chief engineer. Julius Kahn, an expert in the use of reinforced concrete, was also something of an entrepreneur, founding a company (Trussed Concrete Steel Company in Youngstown, Ohio) in order to develop and manufacture what became known as the "Kahn bar" or "Kahn system" of reinforced concrete. This turn of events was to prove essential to the development of Kahn's own architectural practice, culminating in Albert Kahn Incorporated Architects and Engineers.

Kahn's commissions during the early years of the 20th century included prominent civic, institutional, and residential buildings in the Detroit metropolitan area, lower Michigan, upstate New York, and Ohio. These works included Temple Beth

Ford Plant Offices (1909), Highland Park, Michigan, by Albert Kahn
© Esto

El; the Belle Isle Conservatory and Casino; the Belle Isle Aquarium; several classroom, auditorium, and library buildings for the University of Michigan in Ann Arbor; and numerous large private residences in the Grosse Pointe, Bloomfield Hills, and Windsor, Ontario, suburbs of Detroit. In addition, Kahn began to design industrial buildings—the type of structures for which he is best known—as early as 1901. These industrial buildings, most of which were for various automobile manufacturers headquartered in Detroit, were not limited to automobile assembly plants but included office buildings, showrooms, and materials processing plants (mills, stamping plants) as well. During the same period, Kahn was also involved with the design of buildings for the military; many of them affiliated with the development of airpower.

Although usually overlooked given the significance of his industrial buildings, Kahn's civic, institutional, and corporate architecture, along with the numerous residences, were of very high quality, adhering to architecture's traditional aesthetic and building principles. Scripps Library and Gallery in Detroit (1898, Nettleton and Kahn), the Belle Isle recreational buildings (1903–08), the William L. Clements Library (1922) at the University of Michigan, the Detroit Athletic Club (1915), and the Grosse Pointe residences, among other works, are elegantly proportioned, well-constructed works that bespeak Kahn's attention

to the civic nature of architecture—in the case of the institutional building—and the highly specific aspects of formal and informal private life.

Over the course of his career, there was little stylistic unity between the different categories of building projects. For Kahn, every architectural program type required a different set of criteria; thus, he saw no inherent contradiction in designing a residence in Tudor style, a library building in the manner of the Italian Renaissance, and an office building according to the principles inherent in tall-building architecture. In this sense, Kahn distanced himself from the modernist promotion of universal, internationalist principles. Working in a region outside the "epicenters" of modern American architecture (Chicago and New York) over the course of his career enabled Kahn to continue to develop a mode of architectural production that many would judge to be inconsistent.

Unlike many architects of his day, who often delegated industrial-design projects to junior members of the firm, Kahn did not consider the design of industrial buildings to be beneath him. For Kahn, these projects represented an untapped opportunity for architecture, a view primed by the firm's embrace of the engineering aspects of building design. Kahn's early work with the automobile industry (the Packard Motor Car Company buildings [1903–10], the Grabowsky Power Wagon Company

Plant [1907], and the Chalmers Motor Car Company [1907]) was noticed by Henry Ford, founder of Ford Motor Company. Ford, known for his persistent search for improvements in the efficiency of production techniques, contacted Kahn for the design of a new production facility in Highland Park, Michigan, just outside Detroit. With Ford, Kahn not only designed an industrial edifice but also facilitated a new program for production. Kahn's work with Ford established the view that the architect was no longer simply the recipient of an organized set of programmatic needs but an agent in the development of the program itself—a critical member of a team that engaged the functional aspects of industrial processes. In his work with Ford and in later projects for commercial and military assembly plants, airport terminals and hangars, hospitals, office buildings, laboratory buildings, and libraries, Kahn exemplified the notion that architecture is a matter of both form and function and that every building type exerts specific functional needs that can be facilitated through building form, and, vice versa, that form is able not only to support but also to enable functional requirements.

Kahn's work was notable for its embrace of modern technological enterprise, including new materials, structural assemblies, and means of production. Accordingly, the architect was not relegated to being a "form giver" but rather could also participate in the development of systems that underpin modern technological enterprise and, hence, modern life.

ELIZABETH BURNS GAMARD

See also **Automobile; Lincoln Memorial, Washington, D.C.**

Biography

Born in Rhaunen, Germany, 21 March 1869; immigrated to the United States 1880. Received no formal education in architecture; apprentice, and later chief designer, office of Mason and Rice, Detroit, Michigan 1884–95. Private practice, Detroit from 1902; architect, Packard Motor Car Company, Detroit 1903; architect, George N. Pierce Company, Buffalo, New York 1906; architect, General Motors, Chrysler Corporation, and Glenn Martin Aircraft; practiced in Moscow 1929–32. Gold Medal, International Expo of Arts and Sciences, Paris 1927; Chevalier, Legion of Honor, France. Died in Detroit, 8 December 1942.

Selected Works

Grand Hotel, Mackinaw Island, Michigan, 1888
Scripps Library and Gallery, Detroit (with Nettleton), 1898
Conservatory and Aquarium, Belle Isle, Michigan, 1903
Packard Motor Car Company Plant, Detroit, 1903–10
Chalmers Motor Car Company Plant, Detroit, 1907
George C. Booth House (now Cranbrook House), Bloomfield Hills, Michigan, 1907
Casino, Belle Isle, 1908
Ford Motor Car Company Main Building and Machine Shop, Highland Park, Michigan, 1909
Detroit Athletic Club, 1915
William L. Clements Library, University of Michigan, Ann Arbor, 1922
Chrysler Half-Ton Truck Plant, Detroit, 1937

Selected Publication

Architecture (with others), 1948

Further Reading

Bucci, Federico, *Albert Kahn: Architect of Ford*, New York: Princeton Architectural Press, 1993
Doumato, Lamia, *Albert Kahn, 1869–1942: A Bibliography*, Monticello, Illinois: Vance Bibliographies, 1988
Hildebrand, Grant, *Designing for Industry: The Architecture of Albert Kahn*, Cambridge, Massachusetts, and London: MIT Press, 1974
King, Sol, *Creative-Responsive-Pragmatic: 75 Years of Professional Practice, Albert Kahn and Associates, Architects-Engineers*, New York: Newcomen Society in North America, 1970
The Legacy of Albert Kahn (exhib. cat.), Detroit, Michigan: Detroit Institute of Arts, 1970

KAHN, LOUIS I. 1901–74

Architect, United States

The works of Louis I. Kahn were among the greatest influences on world architecture during the second half of the 20th century. Trained in the classical tradition of the Beaux-Arts by Paul Philipe Cret at the University of Pennsylvania, Kahn nevertheless embraced the Modern movement in his early practice experience with various housing authorities and in partnership with Oscar Stonorov and George Howe. Kahn was slow in developing as an architect, and the works of the first 50 years of his life, mostly derived from International Style precedents, did not receive significant notice.

Yet by World War II, Kahn had begun to question the capacity of the International Style to embody contemporary cultural meanings and social institutions. In 1944, Kahn published an essay wherein he defined monumentality in architecture as a spiritual quality conveying a sense of eternity, of timelessness, and of unchanging perfection. He felt that modern society had failed to give full architectural expression to the institutions of human community, and he pointed to the great monuments of the past, which, although not possible to literally duplicate, embodied the qualities by which all new buildings should be measured. Finally, he indicated the critically important part played by structural perfection and material character in the creation of historical monumental form, calling for a reexamination of contemporary norms of construction. Although he had yet to find their appropriate expression in his architectural designs, Kahn had established what would be the key themes of his career.

Kahn first gained notice not as an architect but as a professor of design at Yale University, starting in 1947. His inspired teaching led to his appointment in 1950 as the architect-in-residence at the American Academy in Rome. Kahn spent much of this time traveling in Italy, Greece, and Egypt, and this period of historical rediscovery would prove to be pivotal in his development as the most important modern architect of his time. The eternal quality of heavy construction and the spaces shaped by massive masonry made a lasting impression on Kahn. Although the building he had completed just prior to leaving for Rome was of steel construction, after this year abroad Kahn never again made use of lightweight steel structures, building only with reinforced concrete and masonry.

On his return from Rome, Kahn was commissioned to design the Yale University Art Gallery (1951–53) in New Haven, Connecticut. The first modern building on the Yale campus, its primary street facade was a massive brick wall marked only by concrete stringcourses at the floor lines. The plan was divided into three primary spaces: two column-free galleries flanking a central service zone where the main stairs, triangular in plan, were housed in a reinforced-concrete cylinder that rose through the four floors to a clerestory light at its top. Kahn's floor structure was likely inspired by the geodesic domes of Buckminster Fuller, yet the triangular grid of poured-in-place concrete, exposed in the ceilings below, was a powerful and heavy presence quite unlike the lightness idealized by Fuller. Incorporating the mechanical and lighting services within their dark pyramidal depths, Kahn's floor structure was also the exact opposite of the structurally and spatially neutral slab heretofore typical of International Style buildings.

The Bath House for the Trenton Jewish Community Center (1954–58) was the project where, as he said, Kahn found himself as an architect. Four pavilions formed a cruciform plan with a court in the center, open to the sky, each pavilion composed of four concrete-block U-shaped hollow piers at the corners, on which sat a pyramidal roof of wood that floated above the heavy earthbound masonry walls enclosing the open-air spaces. For contemporary architects, the Bath House was a revelation—at once modern, built of the most typical of materials, and ancient, a place where earth and sky meet, signified by the unfinished stone circle in its central court.

Although the larger Community Center was never built, the grid of individually roofed volumes was the first design in which Kahn made each space within the complex program into a separate building with its own structure and light. In direct opposition to the undifferentiated free-plan space-in-extension typical of International Style modernism, Kahn now conceived of each function as requiring its own room-as-place, and the plan was now to be understood as "a society of rooms," their spatial relationship articulating their collective purpose.

In 1957, Kahn was appointed to teach at the University of Pennsylvania in Philadelphia, and he began a long and productive association with two remarkable engineers at the university, Robert Le Ricolais, a visionary poet of structure, and at the office, August Komendant, an expert on concrete construction. At this time, he also received the commission for the A. N. Richards Medical Research Building (1955–64) at the University of Pennsylvania and was able to fully develop his concepts of expressive construction and articulate function. Each of the five laboratory towers, a square in plan, was constructed with an elegant precast-concrete cantilevered structure, the columns placed at third points and the structurally independent, load-bearing masonry service shafts located at the midpoints of each side. Exemplifying Kahn's distinction between the "served spaces" (primary function) and the "servant spaces" (services), the floors of each tower were entirely free of structure or services. In what Kahn held to be an ethical imperative, the materials of construction were left exposed, showing how the building was made and becoming the only ornament appropriate to modern building.

The Tribune Review Publishing Company Building (1955–61) in Greensburg, Pennsylvania, was Kahn's first design to demonstrate his emerging understanding of the relationship between structure and light. The main space was spanned by precast-concrete beams, bearing on brick piers, and on the east and west elevations Kahn revealed the concrete-block walls between these piers to be non–load-bearing by placing glazing between the tops of the walls and the roof structure above, within the depth of the beams. Under these horizontal windows, the in-fill walls were split at their centers by tall, narrow windows, and together these windows produced a T-shaped opening, large at the top to bring in maximum light and narrow at eye level to allow views but to minimize glare.

The First Unitarian Church (1959–69) in Rochester, New York, is directly related to Frank Lloyd Wright's Unity Temple of 1905, indicative of the important influence of Wright's early work on Kahn. Like Wright's design, Kahn's sanctuary is a central, top-lit space enclosed by solid walls, offering no eye-level views out and accessed by a surrounding ambulatory. Yet in the relation of the school to the sanctuary, Kahn took a different approach, ringing the sanctuary with the classrooms. The walls of the sanctuary are made of nonbearing concrete block, the hollow spaces within allowing the return of ventilation air. The roof of the sanctuary is a gently folded plane of cast concrete, lifting to clerestory lights at the corners to form a huge cross shape overhead, and is supported at its center points by columns that stand in each of four doorways from the surrounding ambulatory. The classrooms, also entered from the ambulatory, form a thick protective layer around the sanctuary, their brick exterior walls folded to produce a deeply shadowed edge into which large windows are recessed and small window seats projected.

This concept of surrounding primary spaces with shadow-giving walls, which Kahn described as "wrapping ruins around buildings," emerged fully developed in his design for the Salk Institute (1959–65) in La Jolla, California. This is unquestionably Kahn's greatest design, yet its most important component, the Meeting House, remained unbuilt. The Meeting House plan was also Kahn's first fully developed "society of spaces" plan, a series of independent-room buildings, each with its own geometry and structure, surrounding a central cubic hall. The outer range of rooms facing the ocean assumed the form of hollow cylindrical concrete shells wrapped around and shading cubic glazed rooms within (and vice versa), giving the whole an unparalleled monumentality.

The Salk Institute Laboratories, which were realized, consist of column-free laboratory floors alternating with service floors containing the reinforced-concrete truss structure, the whole constructed of meticulously detailed cast-in-place concrete. Between the two laboratory buildings, where the scientists' wood-clad studies were placed in towers, Kahn envisioned a garden but was convinced by Luis Barragán to make instead a paved plaza, open to the sky and the ocean. Today this plaza, without any formal program of use, remains one of the most powerful and deeply moving spaces ever built.

The Indian Institute of Management (1962–74) in Ahmedabad, India, and the capital of Bangladesh (1962–74) in Dhaka were Kahn's greatest built examples of his "plan as a society of rooms" concept. In both buildings, the secondary spaces, such as corridors, arcades, stair landings, and vestibules, became as important to the overall experience of the building as the primary spaces of program. Kahn understood that learning and decision making happen not only in the classroom and assembly hall but in the passageways, cafes, and courtyards as

Yale Center for British Art, New Haven, Connecticut (1969–77), designed by Louis Kahn
© Jeff Goldberg/Esto

well. As Kahn said, he acted as the philosopher for his clients, interpreting their program of uses in ways both culturally resonant and socially suggestive.

The Exeter Academy Library (1965–72) in Exeter, New Hampshire, was Kahn's most subtle and yet revolutionary work in that he turned the traditional program of library (central reading room surrounded by book stacks) inside out. The design again involved a building-within-a-building, this time a brick load-bearing outer shell, containing the reading spaces, surrounding the inner reinforced-concrete book stacks. In this way, as Kahn said, one could take the book from the protective darkness of the inner stacks to the natural light of the outer reading rooms. At the center of the building, Kahn placed the entry hall, a space that went from ground to sky, with giant circular concrete openings revealing the books, celebrating the purpose of the building.

The Kimbell Art Museum (1966–72) in Fort Worth, Texas, is rightly considered Kahn's greatest built work. The space was composed of a series of concrete vaulted roof forms, each spanning 100 feet, split at their center to allow light to flow in, bouncing off aluminum deflectors to spray the underside of the vaults with an ethereal silver light. Without question Kahn's most beautiful space, the Kimbell was also the most rigorously resolved example of Kahn's concept of the relation between light and structure, the interior spaces receiving natural light in ways that precisely articulated the structural elements. Finally, the Kimbell was Kahn's most elegant built example of landscape planning, its entry sequence taking us past sunken sculpture gardens, under a vaulted loggia, past sheets of cascading water, through a gravel-floored courtyard filled with a grid of trees, and then quietly into the very heart of the gallery itself.

Many of Kahn's greatest designs were never built, including the Salk Institute Meeting House (1959), the U.S. Angolan Embassy (1959), the Mikveh Israel Synagogue (1961), the Dominican Motherhouse (1965), the Memorial to the Six Million Jewish Martyrs (1966), the Palazzo dei Congressi (1968), and the sublime Hurva Synagogue (1967) in Jerusalem—a group of works that, considered alone, would constitute one of the most significant contributions to 20th-century architecture. Yet even without realizing these astonishing designs, Kahn's importance to the development of modern architecture in the second half of the 20th century cannot be overestimated.

Kahn's work redefined modern architecture in two primary ways. First, by reestablishing the relevance of historical architecture for the design of contemporary buildings, Kahn's work was crucial to the emergence of both the American Postmodern and the European neorational critiques of International Style modernism. Second, by reestablishing the primacy of the art of construction in the design of contemporary buildings, Kahn was critical to the emergence of a "tectonic" interpretation of architectural history and practice. By midcentury, Kahn was one of many who felt that modern architecture had lost its direction and sense of purpose. Yet Kahn stands virtually alone in having opened a way out of this impasse, a way he achieved by reconnecting construction to its ethical imperatives and space making to its ancient origins.

ROBERT MCCARTER

See also **Barragán, Luis (Mexico); Fuller, Richard Buckminster (United States); Indian Institute of Management, Ahmedabad; International Style; Kimbell Art Museum, Fort Worth, Texas; Salk Institute, La Jolla, California; Wright, Frank Lloyd (United States)**

Biography

Born on Ösel Island, Russia (now Saaremaa Island, Estonia), 20 February 1901; immigrated to the United States 1906; naturalized 1915. Educated at Central High School and the Pennsylvania Academy of Fine Arts, Philadelphia 1912–20; member of the Graphic Sketch Club, Fleisher Memorial Art School, and student at the Public Industrial Art School, Philadelphia 1916–20; Studied at the University of Pennsylvania, Philadelphia, under Paul Cret 1920–24; bachelor's degree in architecture 1924; studied and traveled in Europe 1928–29. Married Esther Virginia Israeli 1930: one child. Draftsman, the firm of Hofman and Henan, Philadelphia 1921; draftsman, the office of Hewitt and Ash, Philadelphia 1922; senior draftsman, City Architects' Department, Philadelphia 1924–27; chief of design, Sesquicentennial Exhibition, Philadelphia 1925–26; designer, office of Paul Cret, Philadelphia 1929–30; designer, the firm of Zantziger, Borie, and Medary, Philadelphia 1930–32; squad head in charge of housing studies, City Planning Commission, WPA (Works Progress Administration), Philadelphia 1933–35; associate principal architect, office of Alfred Kastner and Partner, Philadelphia 1935–37. Private practice, Philadelphia from 1937; consultant architect, Philadelphia Housing Authority 1937; consultant architect, United States Housing Authority 1938; associated with George Howe 1941–42; associated with Howe and Oscar Stonorov 1942–43; associated with Stonorov 1943–48; consultant architect, Philadelphia City Planning Commission 1946–52 and 1961–62; consultant architect, Philadelphia Redevelopment Authority 1951–54. Teaching assistant, University of Pennsylvania, Philadelphia 1923–24; critic in architectural design and professor of architecture, Yale University, New Haven, Connecticut 1947–50, chief critic in design, 1950–57; resident architect, American Academy, Rome 1950–51; Albert Farnwell Bemis Professor, School of Architecture and Planning, Massachusetts Institute of Technology, Cambridge 1956; professor of architecture, 1957–66, Paul Cret Professor, 1966–71, emeritus professor, 1971–74, University of Pennsylvania, Philadelphia. Organizer and director, Architectural Research Group, Philadelphia 1932–33; fellow, American Institute of Architects 1953; member, National Institute of Arts and Letters 1964; honorary member, Royal Swedish Academy of Fine Arts 1966; member, American Academy of Arts and Sciences 1968; fellow, Royal Society of Arts, London 1970; member, American Academy of Arts and Letters 1973; honorary member, College of Architects of Peru. Centennial Gold Medal, American Institute of Architects, Philadelphia Chapter 1969; Gold Medal of Honor, American Institute of Architects, New York Chapter 1970; Gold Medal, American Institute of Architects 1971; Royal Gold Medal, Royal Institute of British Architects 1972. Died in New York, 17 March 1974.

Selected Works

Yale Art Gallery, Yale University, New Haven, Connecticut, 1953
Bath House and Master Plan, Jewish Community Center, Trenton, New Jersey, 1954–58
Salk Institute Meeting House (unbuilt), 1959
United States Angolan Embassy (unbuilt), 1959
Tribune Review Building, Greensburg, Pennsylvania, 1959–61
Mikveh Israel Synagogue (unbuilt), 1961–73
Richards Medical Research Building, University of Pennsylvania, Philadelphia, 1957–64
Salk Institute Laboratory Buildings, La Jolla, California, 1959–65
Dominican Motherhouse (unbuilt), 1965
Jewish Martyrs' Memorial (unbuilt), 1966
First Unitarian Church, Rochester, New York, 1959–69
Hurva Synagogue (unbuilt), 1967–73
Palazzo dei Congressi (unbuilt), 1968–72
Library and Dining Hall, Phillips Exeter Academy, Exeter, New Hampshire, 1965–72
Kimbell Art Museum, Fort Worth, Texas, 1966–72
Institute of Management, Ahmedabad, India, 1962–74
New National Capital, Dhaka, Bangladesh, 1962–74

Selected Publications

Why City Planning Is Your Responsibility (with Oscar Stonorov), 1942
You and Your Neighborhood (with Stonorov), 1944
Louis I. Kahn: Talks with Students, 1969
The Notebooks and Drawings of Louis I. Kahn, edited by Richard Saul Wurman and Eugene Feldman, 1973

Further Reading

Two books written with Kahn's approval and involvement were in final preparation at the time of his death: Ronner and Jhaveri documents Kahn's complete works with many design drawings and models from the Kahn Archives (at the University of Pennsylvania), and Giurgola and Mehta, a monograph covering Kahn's complete career, lucidly presents Kahn's poetic ideas and illustrates how they structure his architectural designs. Scully is a prescient early study, written before many of the buildings for which Kahn is today most famous were designed, yet correctly foreseeing Kahn's importance. Wurman and Latour are catalogs of Kahn's writings and talks—excellent sources for understanding one of the very few great architects to attempt to articulate the mysteries of the design process. Hochstim documents Kahn's travel sketches, allowing insight into the importance of historical architecture for Kahn's design process. Brownlee and De Long is the most comprehensive recent assessment and includes brief building "biographies" of all Kahn's major works. Büttiker and Gast analyze Kahn's larger ordering principles and how they shaped his buildings. McCarter is the first comprehensive monography to be published since Kahn's death.

Brownlee, David Bruce, and David Gilson De Long, *Louis I. Kahn: In the Realm of Architecture,* New York: Rizzoli, and Los Angeles: Museum of Contemporary Art, 1991; condensed edition, New York: Universe, 1997
Büttiker, Urs, *Louis I. Kahn: Light and Space; Licht und Raum* (bilingual English-German edition), Basel and Boston: Birkhäuser, 1993

Gast, Klaus-Peter, *Louis I. Kahn: The Idea of Order*, Basel and
    Boston: Birkhäuser, 1998

Giurgola, Romaldo and Jaimini Mehta, *Louis I. Kahn*, Boulder,
    Colorado: Westview Press, 1975

Goldhagen, Sarah, *Louis I. Kahn's Situated Modernism*, New Haven,
    Connecticut: Yale University Press, 2001

Hochstim, Jan, *The Paintings and Sketches of Louis I. Kahn*, New
    York: Rizzoli, 1991

Latour, Alessandra (editor), *Louis I. Kahn: Writings, Lectures,
    Interviews*, New York: Rizzoli, 1991

McCarter, Robert, *Louis I. Kahn*, London: Phaidon Press, 2003

Ronner, Heinz and Sharad Jhaveri, *Louis I. Kahn: Complete Work,
    1935–1974*, Basel: Birkhäuser, and Boulder, Colorado: Westview
    Press, 1977; 2nd revised and enlarged edition, Basel and Boston:
    Birkhäuser, 1987

Scully, Vincent Joseph, *Louis I. Kahn*, New York: Braziller, 1962

Wurman, Richard (editor), *What Will Be Has Always Been: The
    Words of Louis I. Kahn*, New York: Rizzoli, 1986

KALACH, ALBERTO 1960–

Architect, Mexico

Alberto Kalach was born in Mexico City in 1960. He studied architecture at the Iberoamericana University, graduating in 1981. He later attended Cornell University (1983–85). From 1991 to 1997, he worked in partnership with Daniel Alvarez.

Kalach is interested primarily in weaving his architecture into the urban landscape and context of the city. He belongs to a generation of contemporary architects whose works reflect an international modernist language that subtly alludes to traditional form. His references include Le Corbusier, Ludwig Mies van der Rohe, Luis Barragán, Louis Kahn, and the work of the Spanish and Italian rationalists. Although small in scale, his buildings carefully relate to the urban context and the landscape and spatially express structure and materials.

The development of the patio and garden as gathering places in Mexican architecture is a principal recurring theme in Kalach's residential design. Adapted well to climate and form, the patio is used in several of his early works. His three cubelike houses (1990) in Fuente Mercurio, Tecamachalco, Mexico City, are similar in scheme and are arranged to articulate the entrance and generate a common patio. The geometric relationship between the patios and gardens offers different perspective views while varying planes of light enrich the spatial relationships between the interior and exterior.

The significance of landscape, site, and memory is explored in several of Kalach's houses built in the 1990s. These works interpret the topographical elements of landform and existing vegetation and recognize ephemeral components, such as natural light and regional landscape character. In the house (1994) in Palmira, Cuernavaca, all rooms are surrounded by gardens, and the core of the house is focused on the patio. Long walls echo Barragán's aesthetic while two concrete towers evoke Louis Kahn's interest in expressing bold architectural elements.

The House and Garden (1994) in Valle del Bravo, Mexico, consists of four simple platforms that are related topographically to the site. The platforms offer the opportunity to view the forest from different perspectives. The house utilizes a small room as a connecting link to the outside world of the street. The site's organizational structure creates a journey from the road, through the gate, and into the house itself. The journey orchestrates leisure garden activities, such as dining or sitting on a swing. Exposed brick, concrete, and wood are organized into precise geometric grids to interact with the existing organic forms of the landscape.

Kalach further explored these concepts in the Negro House (1997) in Contadero, Mexico City. This project is designed as a series of five structures built into a steep slope. The structures sit on platforms that seem to float in a ravine of *tepozan* trees. The structure is anchored into the ground to minimize tree root damage and to avoid site disturbance. Rainwater is channeled from the patios and the roof to the foundations, where it is collected and stored in cisterns. Materials such as concrete, glass, and steel are combined with an on-site stone called *tepetate*. This house emphasizes the transformative role that occurs when architecture interacts with a site and exemplifies Kalach's interest in creating a sustainable intervention between nature and everyday human activity.

Kalach designed and built several apartment projects throughout Mexico City, including the Holbein Building (1991) in Mixoac, the Rodin Apartment Complex (1993) in Mexico City, and the Fresas Building (1993) and the Adolf Building (1996) in Colonia del Valle. All these projects unify permanent and ephemeral components of the urban fabric and refer to a modernist or Le Corbusian use of materials and typologies.

Kalach's design for a hardware store (1991), built 50 kilometers from Mexico City in the industrial city of Toleca, represents his use of simple everyday materials to create sophisticated elements and details. The scheme, which is a small warehouse intended to store and sell iron products, consists of one building inside another. A centralized office, designed in the form of a ship, is contained within an external envelope of concrete panels that have been covered with iron sheets. The roof structure is a light barrel vault constructed of galvanized sheet iron. The roof is separated from the concrete-and-brick walls, giving to the whole structure a sense an exquisite lightness and beauty.

Kalach's geometric rigor is exemplified in the Monte Sinai Kindergarten (1992) in Tecamachalco State, Mexico. The project's program called for increasing the number of classrooms. The project was conceived as a series of austere pavilions connected to the existing school by a bridge. The strict geometry is accentuated by terraced gardens and patios that are enclosed by stone walls, ramps, and stairs.

The importance of topography to Kalach is exemplified in project for the Maguen David Jewish Community Center (1996) in Cuajimalpa State, Mexico, located at the edge of a dramatic ravine on the outskirts of Mexico City. Its pure forms, constructed of reinforced concrete, create an introspective and contemplative atmosphere. The scheme is unified by a distinct physical and spiritual gathering center that connects the synagogue, via a hall of slender columns, to other areas in the complex.

In the design of the Alexander Von Humboldt German School (1996) in Cholula, Puebla State, Mexico, Kalach proposed a completely artificial landscape that is organized on a circular embankment. The powerful scheme is surrounded by dense vegetation that separates the school from the immediate surrounding yet preserves the magnificent view of the distant mountains. Classrooms occupy the center of the circular scheme.

Earth that has been removed from the foundation is used to form an undulating landscape of smooth hills.

Since 1997, Kalach has been a member of the Taller Ciudad de México (City of Mexico Studio). This team proposed a feasibility study to determine how to reverse the desiccation of Texcoco Lake in Mexico City. The study, in collaboration with Gonzalez de León, proposes the use of waste and rainwater to increase the size of the lakes in the metropolitan area of the Mexican capital. The plan will expand the surfaces of lakes in the city from 1000 hectares in 1998 to 13,800 by 2008. By proposing a low-density plan for development within the area, the plan is intended to benefit the environment and attract tourism. The proposal reflects the political and social nature of architectural practice in Latin America. It suggests a strong relationship between urban renewal and environmental mutations and strongly reflects current architectural trends in Mexico.

Kalach's work has received significant critical attention as a result of his delicate detailing, subtle referencing to older cultures, and interest in the relationship between landscape and architecture.

JOSE BERNARDI

See also **Barragán, Luis (Mexico); Mexico City, Mexico**

Biography

Born in Mexico 1960. Attended the Universidad Iberoamericana 1977–1981; degree in architecture; postgraduate studies in architecture at Cornell University, Ithaca, New York, 1983–1985. In private practice, Mexico City; partnership with Daniel Alvarez 1991–97. Eliot Noyes Visiting Design Critic, Harvard University Graduate School of Design, Cambridge, Massachusetts, 1998–99. Member, Team X (10) from 1991; member, Taller Ciudad de México from 1997.

Selected Works

Three Houses, Avenida de las Fuentes, Mexico City, 1990
Holbein Building, Mixoac, Mexico City, 1991
Hardware Store, Tolteca, 1991
Monte Sinai Kindergarten, Tecamachalco State, 1992
Rodin Apartment Complex, Mexico City, 1993
Fresas Building, Colonia del Valle, Mexico City, 1993
House, Palmira, Cuernavaca, 1994
House and Garden, Valle del Bravo, Mexico, 1994
Adolf Building, Colonia del Valle, Mexico City, 1996
Maguen David Jewish Community Center, Cuajimalpa State, 1996
Alexander von Humboldt German School, Cholula, 1996
Negro House, Contadero, Mexico City, 1997

Further Reading

"Alberto Kalach, Daniel Alvarez, Negro House, Contadero, Mexico City," *GA Houses* 57 (August 1998) (contains photos, plan, section, elevations; in English and Japanese)
"Alberto Kalach: House and Garden in Valle del Bravo, Mexico," *GA Houses* 46 (1995) (contains plans, site plans, sections, elevations, details, photos)
"Alberto Kalach: Houses and Gardens, Palmira, Cuernavaca, Morelos, Mexico," *GA Houses* 46 (June 1995) (contains photos, plans, site plans, sections)
León, Adriana, *Kalach and Alvarez*, Gloucester, Massachusetts: Rockport, 1998 (the only book in English devoted to the production of the studio)
"Mexico: Five Architectural Teams in a Country in Full Renewal," *L'architecture d'aujourd'hui* 288 (September 1993)

KANSAI INTERNATIONAL AIRPORT TERMINAL

Designed by Renzo Piano, completed 1994
Osaka, Japan

The Kansai International Airport Terminal (1988–94) is a major achievement with regard to location, concept, and architecture. Designed under the leadership of the Renzo Piano Building Workshop Japan (in collaboration with Ove Arup and Partners [Peter Rice] and Nikken Sekkei), it consists of a main rectangular block with wing-shaped linear extensions and a total span of 1.7 kilometers. The wing buildings contain the circulation spine for the 41 gates. The central building houses the check-in for domestic and international flights, immigration control, customs, and baggage handling and is characterized by its vertical separation of functions: access from and to the building occurs on three levels. The international departure area is situated on the upper deck and the international arrival area on the ground floor. The domestic arrivals and departures are located in between and connect to the regional train station. All three functions are visually and physically integrated in the so-called canyon. This vertical cut through the building functions as the main entrance hall and demonstrates the concept of the building as a flowing landscape: under a single roof, a wide-open space is created, with trees and bamboo on the bottom and colorful bridges, elevators, escalators, and transparent staircases openly connecting the different levels.

The long, curved roof features the aerodynamic form of a landing jet and functions as the building's main facade, giving the terminal its identity. It refers to early constructions by Piano, such as the Bercy shopping center (1987–90) at Charenton le Pont in Paris, as well as to the large roofs of traditional Japanese buildings. The form was designed in response to the needs of air-conditioning: cold air is drawn from the canyon and blown from air nozzles that are directed toward cloudlike smooth-surfaced Teflon sheets stretched out between the structural elements. These "open-air ducts" outline the shape in which air diffuses when blown free of obstruction from the air nozzles. This form does not force the flow of air but merely guides it from landside to airside. The whole building functions as a macroclimate for air control, and the spaces where people move are adjusted as microclimates. These sheets simultaneously reflect indirect light, further reducing the number of objects hanging from the roof and allowing for the roof's very light construction. The shape of the roof determined the form of the structure, which consists in the center building of inverted triangular section trusses that span 82.8 meters, have a total length of 150 meters, and are supported by inclining columns. Painted gray, they call to mind a dinosaur skeleton.

The boarding wings are conceived as part of an imaginary ring 16.4 kilometers in diameter that extends into the earth at an angle of 68.2 degrees to the ground surface. The ribs of the building become slanted toward the end as they correspond to this overall concept. This program allows the use of identical panels (1,800 to 600 millimeters) for the whole 90,000-square-meter roof. The highly weather-resistant stainless-steel panels have been treated with a dull finish to reduce light reflection. On the airside, the wings feature an elegant curve with large glass panels that allow observation of the planes from the lobbies. The design produces close links among form, structure, and geometry, giving the building unity despite the huge dimensions of a centralized airport.

The concept of a single-unit terminal had been chosen by Aéroports de Paris in negotiation with Japan Airport Consultants in the earlier phases of planning. This design has won favor in recent years, following the threat of terrorism and the need for greater security, although it often requires patrons to walk fairly long distances and makes terminals difficult to expand. In contrast, decentralized terminals, with individual airport buildings linked by a corridor, allow easy expansion and make connecting between different traffic forms more convenient for travelers. They are, however, increasingly difficult to manage as the distance between terminals grows over the years.

The Kansai Airport Terminal is an important architectural and technical achievement and a milestone in the opening of Japan to the world. The development of the Kansai region, Japan's second largest urban concentration, which includes Osaka, Kobe, and Kyoto, has been promoted to counteract the over-concentration of development in Tokyo. The existing Itami Airport in Osaka is located in a densely populated urban area and thus did not allow for extension or 24-hour usage. As a result, a new international gateway was required, and several sites were discussed. The lack of flat and buildable areas of land, together with difficulties relating to expropriation, environmental and noise reduction issues, and the problem of future expansion, led to the construction of an airport (1987–91) on 511 hectares of landfill, five kilometers into Osaka Bay. The airport could thus be designed independent of the constraints of an existing urban environment. Special solutions had to be found, however, to prevent differential settlement of the building on the recent landfill.

Selection of a concept for the new airport began in 1986 and involved a consortium of Japanese companies. The decision was made to invite overseas participation in the construction of the enormous Kansai Airport, since the project's estimated total cost would be 1.5 trillion yen. This led to the inclusion of Aéroport de Paris and especially its vice president, Paul Andreu, and the decision to hold an international design competition. Following an open registration, 15 groups—including world-renowned architects such as Sir Norman Foster, Cesar Pelli, and Bernard Tschumi—were invited to participate in a two-stage competition held in 1988. Renzo Piano was the eventual winner. In contrast to many of the competing designs, Piano's project was elaborated independent of Japanese construction firms. Not surprisingly,

Kansai International Airport Terminal, Osaka (1994)
© Yoshio Hata

the plan was criticized for not complying with UIA (International Association of Architects) regulations and for the close relationship between the architects and construction companies involved in the project. Nevertheless, the holding of a competition and its realization may be seen as indicators of a new attitude in Japan, where competitions are rare. The inclusion of foreign companies in the construction process further signaled an opening of the Japanese market.

The Kansai Airport Terminal is an outstanding example of airport design. At century's end, it is also an important piece of the puzzle of global architecture, represented by a limited number of star architects designing prestigious buildings for large and small cities around the world.

CAROLA HEIN

See also **Airport and Aviation Building; Japan; Piano, Renzo (Italy)**

Further Reading

The architectural and technical design of the Kansai International Airport Terminal has been presented in architectural magazines such as *Japan Architect* and *Process Architecture*. Miyake focuses his comments on the competition process that led to the winning design (asking whether it is a positive precedent for future competitions in Japan). Information on design concepts can be found in Piano's work catalog. The history and functions of airports in Europe and the United States are analyzed in Zukowsky, which also provides much background information.

Kansai International Airport Passenger Terminal Building, Tokyo: Process Architecture, 1994
Kansai International Airport Passenger Terminal Building, Tokyo: Shinkenchiku-sha, 1994
Miyake, Riichi, *Toshi to kenchiku Competition*, Tokyo: V + K Publishing Laren, 1991
Piano, Renzo, *Renzo Piano progetti e architecture, 1987–1994*, Milan: Electa, 1994; as *Renzo Piano, 1987–1994*, translated by David Kerr, Basel, Switzerland, and Boston: Birkhäuser Verlag, 1995
Zukowsky, John (editor), *Building for Air Travel: Architecture and Design for Commercial Aviation*, Munich and New York: Prestel, and Chicago: The Art Institute of Chicago, 1996

KARL MARXHOF

Designed by Karl Ehn; completed 1930
Vienna, Austria

Of the various housing projects built by the city of Vienna in the 1920s, the Karl Marxhof is the most remarkable. Not only the name but also the size and architecture of this project emphatically express the social-democratic aspirations of the city government.

The Karl Marxhof was built in the framework of a long-term residential building program that was started in 1919 and eventually came to an end during the civil war of 1934. The building program was part of the socioeconomic policies of Austrian social democracy, also known as Austromarxism. The central focus of their political outlook, in stark contrast to the violent Russian Revolution of October 1918, was an evolutionary path to a socialist society, as a result of citizen participation and a strong directing role of the state. From 1920 their political programs were focused on the capital city of Vienna, where the Social Democrats held a comfortable majority.

Like other metropolitan cities in Europe, Vienna had struggled with problems of rapid population growth since the second half of the 19th century. The population of Vienna had almost tripled since 1870 to a total of 2,380,000 in 1918. Losing the war exacerbated the urban situation. Before the war, Vienna was the capital of an empire of 52 million. At the end of 1918, it was the center of a small country with six million citizens. The most important industries and natural resources now lay beyond its borders, the destruction of capital was overwhelming, and the social situation was unstable. There was a tremendous housing shortage, and the quality of existing housing was very poor.

The Vienna city government tackled the housing shortage, financing the effort with a municipal tax structure targeting privately owned housing and businesses. New housing was built on land bought by the city, and rents were low. The motivation for this rent policy was not exclusively social in nature. Because rents were low, wages were kept down as well, making businesses more competitive. The building program was centrally managed out of the *Stadtbauamt* (city building office), and a share of the commissions went to local construction companies. Market pressures were entirely evaded in the program.

At the beginning of 1919, the residential building program was based on two concepts: that of the *Siedlungen*, a continuation of the garden city approach, and that of residential blocks, a compact urban multistory building form laid out around courtyards. Governing Social Democrats preferred the latter because of political considerations. In 1923 the municipal government launched a five-year plan for the construction of 25,000 housing units. Most of the funding went to the building of residential blocks.

The residential blocks were built on empty lots between existing buildings and on the outskirts of Vienna. The city aimed for considerable density, striving to build up 50 to 60 percent of the lots. Later, these percentages were lowered. The number and size of the housing units in the blocks varied per location, but the majority of them were one-room flats with an area of 38 square meters. From 1926 several "superblocks" were built with more than 1,000 units each. The Karl Marxhof is the second largest, with 1,382 units and an area of 15.6 hectares (about 38.5 acres).

The choice of location for the Karl Marxhof was a narrow garden strip, only 1.2 kilometers wide, between the local tramway station and a soccer stadium in the Heiligenstadt quarter. The first plans, designed by the architect Clemens Holzmeister (1886–1983) in 1926, were rejected by the *Stadtbauamt*. Holzmeister's design, nowhere rising higher than four stories and in long, partially freestanding blocks, was thought uninspired, and the commission went to city architect Karl Ehn (1884–1957), who presented an early concept in October 1926.

Ehn's plan was much more compact and conveyed its political status and importance more effectively. He grouped units in two long, closed courtyard blocks of uneven size, with a higher block and a large square at the center. This higher block has six large arches at the base to facilitate pedestrian traffic and towers with flagpoles. Together with the square, it forms the central focus of the complex and of its sociopolitical statement. The central block, between the stadium and the station, lies on the route by which soccer fans reached the stadium for Sunday games and

Karl Marxhof, Vienna (1930)
© Howard Davis/GreatBuildings.com

arches, gives the building a monumental allure. Both scale and degree of abstraction are reminiscent of the neoclassical work of Boullée and Ledoux. Ehn had studied, like several of his colleagues, with Otto Wagner, and this might explain the combination of a classical idiom and his modern, functional approach.

The typological background of the Karl Marxhof—the courtyard block form itself—comes out of a Central European tradition. The line originated in convents and the baroque palaces of the nobility and evolved in the 19th century into residential complexes and tenements. The preference of the city's social-democratic government for the residential block form was not innocent of conscious references to the palaces in which the form originated. The city government's concern with solving the housing shortage was to be clearly visible in the "social palace" of the residential block. The Karl Marxhof furnishes a particularly clear example of this trend. An analogy with the USSR's "palaces of the people" of the 1930s might also be present, except that the cultural and political doctrine of Soviet socialist realism found an exclusive inspiration in the neoclassical past.

The similarities to palace architecture of the Karl Marxhof and other residential blocks came in for criticism also, among others by Josef Frank (1885–1967), who took aim at the dissonance between older architectural types and the new social aspirations as early as 1926. Even functionalist architects failed to appreciate Vienna's social housing construction, as it diverged too far from the principles formulated by CIAM (Congrès Internationaux d'Architecture Moderne). For these reasons, architectural history barely paid attention to the Viennese residential blocks after World War II. Only during the past two decades has this exceptional phenomenon of a people's housing program received more detailed attention. Although the Karl Marxhof became a battleground during the civil war of 1934, the complex remained inhabited.

OTAKAR MÁCEL

See also **Congrès Internationaux d'Architecture Moderne (CIAM, 1927–); Frank, Josef (Austria); Palace of the Soviets Competition (1931); Vienna, Austria; Wagner, Otto (Austria)**

Further Reading

General studies on politics and the housing program include Gruber, Gulick, and Hardy. Blau, Öhlinger, Tafuri, and Weihsmann discuss architecture in the context of housing policy.

Blau, Eve, *The Architecture of Red Vienna, 1919–1934*, Cambridge, Massachusetts: MIT Press, 1999
Gruber, Helmut, *Red Vienna: Experiment in Working-Class Culture, 1919–1934*, New York: Oxford University Press, 1991
Gulick, Charles A., *Austria from Habsburg to Hitler*, 2 vols., Berkeley: University of California Press, 1948
Hardy, Charles O., and Robert R. Kuczynski, *The Housing Program of the City of Vienna*, Washington, D.C.: The Brookings Institution, 1934
Öhlinger, Walter (editor), *Das Rote Wien, 1918–1934*, Vienna: Museen der Stadt Wien, 1993
Tafuri, Manfredo, *Vienna Rossa: la politica residenziale nella Vienna socialista, 1919–1933*, Milan: Electa, 1980; 2nd edition, 1995

serves to remind them of the city's building efforts. In contrast to earlier residential blocks built in Vienna, only 18.4 percent of the total area was built up. Most of the gardens that take up the remaining space lie within the courtyards of the blocks.

Because of its scale and the closed form of the blocks, the Karl Marxhof formed an independent element in its environment. It was self-sufficient also in the sense that its 5,000 to 6,000 tenants could rely on their own facilities: 25 stores, a post office, a pharmacy, a dental practice, a pediatric practice, two bathhouses with showers and tubs, a preschool, and two central laundry areas. The units themselves were relatively small: 54 percent of them consisted of a kitchen, a living room, and one additional room, with a hallway and toilet, taking up 41 square meters.

In comparison to the earlier residential blocks, which were designed with building volumes of different sizes and decorated with arcades, bay windows, and expressive detail, the Karl Marxhof presents a severe design. To further the unity of this complex, such severity was almost inevitable. Moreover, Ehn's earlier work also distinguished itself in its sober approach from the work of most of his colleagues (see Lindenhof, 1924; Bebel-Hof, 1925). The principal building volumes of the Karl Marxhof are straight blocks, enlivened here and there with balconies and setback corners. Most remarkable is the plastic articulation of the gable of the central block, which, in combination with the six large

Weihsmann, Helmut, *Das Rote Wien: sozialdemokratische Architektur und Kommunalpolitik*, Vienna: Promedia, 1985

KIMBELL ART MUSEUM, FORT WORTH, TEXAS

Designed by Louis I. Kahn; completed 1972

Often cited as one of the finest museum buildings in the world, the Kimbell Art Museum in Fort Worth, Texas, demonstrates the power of a fruitful collaboration between a strong, knowledgeable client and one of the most probing and creative architects of the 20th century. Dr. Richard F. Brown, who spoke for the Kimbell trustees on design issues, and architect Louis I. Kahn were joined by a talented group of consultants and experts, including engineer August E. Komandant and lighting designer Richard Kelly, in the conceptualization and development of this tour de force of sophistication and refinement. Preston M. Geron's firm in Fort Worth as associate architects (in particular, Frank Sherwood) and Thomas S. Byrne, Contractors (in particular, A.T. Seymour), were essential in ensuring the quality execution of the beautifully made structure. Marshall D. Meyers, one of Kahn's most capable assistants, played a particularly important

role throughout what was a tumultuous design and construction process.

On his death, industrialist Kay Kimbell bequeathed a collection of 350 art objects along with the capital funds for a building to establish a new museum near downtown Fort Worth. In 1965 Richard F. Brown was hired as director, having previously served at the Los Angeles County Museum during a period when it had built a new building. Disappointed in his previous role in the design process, Brown stipulated to the Kimbell trustees, before accepting the position, that he should have full control over architect selection and client input. He then began a meticulous process of researching the work of leading designers and preparing a lengthy pre-architectural program that documented very specifically his vision for what kind of building the museum required.

Brown initially thought that Ludwig Mies van der Rohe, the architect whom he had supported unsuccessfully for the Los Angeles County Museum project, should receive the commission. However, further research inclined him to favor the maverick Louis Kahn, whose Yale University Art Gallery (1953) had taken Mies' work (and modernism in general) in a somewhat different direction. When Kahn began the Kimbell Museum project in 1966, he was at a turning point in his career. Having just completed the Salk Institute (1965) in California and a

Kimbell Museum of Art, Fort Worth, Texas, designed by Louis Kahn (1972)
© GreatBuildings.com

dormitory complex (1965) for Bryn Mawr College in Pennsylvania, the late-blooming architect was moving into a period during which he would produce a series of timeless public buildings imbued with a powerful architectural order and clarity.

Both Brown and Kahn were strong individuals with personal, but compatible, goals for the new building. Brown wanted a beautiful, inviting museum with intimate spaces more like a gracious home or villa. He wrote in his pre-architectural program, "The overwhelming percentage of people whom this building is intended to serve will not be art historians, other architects or progressive artists with a sophisticated background in architectural form. Their total experience of a visit to a museum should be one of warmth, mellowness, and even elegance. ... A visitor to an art museum ought to be *charmed*." Kahn sought the architectural forms that were fundamental to the museum, its program, and its locale. He said that his mind was "filled with Roman greatness" and that the vault was etched in his consciousness—"the vault, rising not high, not in an august manner, but somehow appropriate to the size of the individual, and its feeling of being at home and safe came to mind."

From his first sketches, Kahn conceived the museum as a series of long, narrow galleries topped by shells or vaults. As was his habit, however, the design took many different configurations before the final scheme emerged. In early stages, the museum had a very large square footprint with a dozen or so courtyards of various sizes captured within. In later stages, an H-shaped configuration was developed with separate auditorium and gallery wings joined by a generous passageway. The final scheme emerged as a C-shaped plan around an entry plaza with only three small light courts penetrating the vaulted portion of the building.

Appropriate natural light was a priority for both the client and the architect. Brown desired "a psychological effect through which the museum visitor feels that both he and the art are still a part of the real, rotating, changeable world." Kahn also believed that a structure designed to house painting and sculpture ought, by nature, to echo the art's sensitivity to different aspects of mood, light, and color. Working with Richard Kelly, Kahn and Meyer developed a system of lighting that ran the length of the vaults at their peak. The intense Texas sun was softened, bounced, and cooled as it washed across perforated stainless-steel screens and the concrete underside of the vaults before finally reaching the rooms below.

Brown admired the fact that Kahn was "willing to let the specific situation posed by the creation of a building guide him and tell him what the structure, engineering and aesthetic ought to be." The building that emerged from their joint efforts certainly exemplifies that responsiveness. The Kimbell Museum embodies not only the director's well-defined program but also particular parameters of site, climate, and regional character. Its flatness, toughness, and tawny natural surfaces, along with the way in which it withstands the sometimes brutal sun, make it part and parcel of the northern Texas landscape.

Stylistically, the Kimbell Museum is distinct among Kahn's work. It shares an affinity for order, a constructional logic, and an expressive use of materials with other mature works, but its forms and spatial qualities are unique. The Kimbell Museum has become a pilgrimage point for visitors from all over the world who can witness Kahn's magnificent marriage of modernity and romance, logic, and sensuality. The building speaks the language

of human experience—pocked satin of travertine against the "liquid stone" of concrete, silvery stainless steel against honey-colored oak paneling, and everywhere the glow of light borrowed from the sun.

LAWRENCE W. SPECK

See also **Kahn, Louis (United States); Museum; Salk Institute, La Jolla, California**

Further Reading

In addition to the readings below, almost any compilation of the works of Louis I. Kahn will include information on the Kimbell Art Museum.

Bellinelli, Luca, *Louis I. Kahn: The Construction of the Kimbell Art Museum*, Milan: Skira, 1999

Benedikt, Michael, *Deconstructing the Kimbell: An Essay on Meaning and Architecture*, New York: SITES Books, 1991

Gattamorta, Gioia, and Luca Rivalta, *Louis I. Kahn: Kimbell Art Museum*, Florence: Alinea, 1991

Giurgola, Romaldo, and Jaimini Mehta, *Louis I. Kahn*, Boulder, Colorado: Westview Press: Artemis, 1975

Heinz, Ronner, Alessandro Vasella, and Sharad Jhaveri, *Louis I. Kahn: Complete Works, 1935–1974*, Basel: Birkhäuser, and Boulder, Colorado: Westview Press, 1977; 2nd edition, Basel and Boston: Birkhäuser, 1987

Johnson, Nella E., *Light Is the Theme: Louis I. Kahn and the Kimbell Art Museum: Comments on Architecture*, Fort Worth, Texas: Kimbell Art Foundation, 1975

Komendant, August E., *18 Years with Architect Louis I. Kahn*, Englewood, New Jersey: Aloray, 1975

Lobell, John, *Between Silence and Light: Spirit in the Architecture of Louis I. Kahn*, Boulder, Colorado: Shambhala, 1979

Speck, Lawrence, *Landmarks of Texas Architecture*, Austin: University of Texas Press, 1986

KOHN PEDERSEN FOX

Architecture firm, United States

In 1976 A. Eugene Kohn, William Pedersen, and Sheldon Fox formed one of the late 20th century's most commercially and critically successful firms, Kohn Pedersen Fox (KPF). Although KPF is best known for its high-profile commercial skyscrapers, each of its diverse projects reveals the firm's commitment to structures not only of unique importance to the individual client but also with an overriding contextual focus. Frequently responsive to the nearby environment, the firm's designs demonstrate an assimilation of modernist and Postmodern ideals, epitomized by a varied and adaptable architectural vocabulary and a healthy appreciation for luxurious materials and clarity of form. Finding strength in this flexibility, the firm quickly gained a reputation for design excellence. In 1990 the American Institute of Architects (AIA) awarded KPF with its Architectural Firm Award, the youngest firm ever to receive such high recognition.

To no small degree, KPF's success is due to the specialized role that each founding partner has played in the firm, very much like the symbiosis that existed within another highly successful firm at the beginning of the century, McKim, Mead and White. A. Eugene Kohn (1930–) energetically marketed the firm and Sheldon Fox (1930–) functioned as the manager and William Pedersen (1938–) as the chief designer. A fourth principal, Patricia Conway (1937–), specialized in planning and interiors and in 1984 became president of KPF's splinter interiors firm, Kohn Pedersen Fox Conway Associates, All four met while employed by John Carl Warnecke and Associates directly prior to KPF's founding.

Both Eugene Kohn and Sheldon Fox received their architectural degrees from the University of Pennsylvania. Kohn worked as a designer for Vincent G. Kling Associates from 1960 to 1965 and as New York design director for Welton Becket Associates until 1967, when he became president and partner at John Carl Warnecke and Associates. By 1976 Fox had risen to senior vice president at Warnecke, following employment with Kahn Jacobs (1955–72). After receiving his bachelor's degree in architecture from the University of Minnesota, William Pedersen attended the Massachusetts Institute of Technology (MIT), where after graduation he worked for Pietro Belluschi, MIT's dean of architecture and planning. In 1965 he won the Rome Prize, spent two years of study at the American Academy in Rome, and worked with Italian architect Eduardo Catalino. In 1967 he joined I.M. Pei and Associates until he was lured away in 1971 to become vice president of John Carl Warnecke and Associates. Columbia University graduate Patricia Conway was associate director of planning for Warnecke from 1972 to 1976.

After several well-executed but hardly memorable designs, the firm's first widely acclaimed building was 333 Wacker Drive (1983) in Chicago, a 36-story green-reflective-glass office tower

333 Wacker Drive (1983), view from elevated train tracks
Designed by Kohn Pedersen and Fox
Chicago, Illinois
© Barbara Karant. Photo courtesy Kohn Pedersen and Fox

whose lustrous sculptural curtain wall imitated the bending Chicago River along its triangular site. The structure exploited the sheer reflective mass of the curtain wall by minimizing individual windows through tinting gray-green the vertical aluminum window mullions. Green marble and gray granite octagonal columns at the base level made a subtle reference to the Merchandise Mart's octagonal towers across the river. Additional methods employed in reaction to the building's environment included beginning the office floors above the track level of the nearby elevated train, thus permitting a large four-floor masonry-block base that better integrated the structure with neighboring buildings. The sides of the building facing the city are set at right angles, responding there to the urban grid. The AIA rewarded this design with its National Honors Award in 1984, validating KPF's coming of age as a major player in skyscraper design.

The Postmodernist manner in which lush materials such as colored marble and forms reminiscent of classical architecture were employed by KPF became a hallmark of the firm's buildings in the 1980s, many of which were corporate commissions. Some of the best examples include the Hercules Incorporated Headquarters (1983) in Wilmington, Delaware; the Third National Bank (1985) in Nashville; and CNG Tower (1987) in Pittsburgh. Its second AIA National Honor Award came in 1987 for the Procter and Gamble General Offices Complex (1985) in Cincinnati, an 836,000-square-foot expansion to the company's existing 11-story headquarters. The multivolume solution consisted of two 17-story octagonal towers with pyramidal roofs that formed a visual gateway to the city from Interstate 71 and a six-story L-shaped base that embraced new public space and that connected to the older structure. The prevailing concern for humanizing both the scale and the siting of the complex typified KPF's best work during this period.

Responding to new global economic conditions, KPF increasingly produced speculative structures abroad for international clients in the 1990s. It opened offices in London (1989) and Tokyo (1995) and added a number of new principals to the firm. In all, KPF has built in more than 30 countries. The political unification and economic revitalization of Germany, as well as the establishment of the European Union, presented unique building opportunities in Central Europe particularly. One of KPF's first significant overseas commissions was the Westendstrasse 1/DG Bank Headquarters Building (1993) in Frankfurt. As a 915,000-square-foot mixed-use complex that includes a 52-story office tower, residential apartments, and a winter garden, the design sought to link the commercial Mainzer Landstrasse corridor with the nearby Westend residential area. In characteristic KPF fashion, the complex reveals a multitude of interlocking geometric forms, each responding to yet another aspect of the surrounding micro- and macroenvironment. In 1994 KPF received its third AIA Honors Award for the Westendstrasse 1 design.

A booming Asian economic market led KPF to a large number of commissions on the Pacific Rim, particularly in China's provincial city of Shanghai. Begun in 1997 and scheduled for completion early in the 21st century, the Shanghai World Financial Center will be one of the tallest buildings in the world at 1,509 feet. As with most KPF designs, the Shanghai World Financial Center not only physically references its surroundings through its form and materials but also suggests cultural integration with its emblematic use of a "moon gate" cut through the top of the tower. Lightly mirrored glass and horizontally banded stainless steel form a reflective membrane for the square prism shaft that serves as both office tower and hotel, with retail space at the base. Difficulty with soft soil resulted in piles being driven over 260 feet into the soil to anchor the three-million-square-foot building, yet the sheer size of the structure is visually negated by the wind pressure–relieving 164-foot-diameter cylindrical void. Although a daring use of form sometimes trivializes KPF's designs, the firm's adroitness at adapting to clients' needs and to changing world economic realities leaves KPF one of the top ten architectural firms at the end of the century and poised to continue making significant contributions well into the 21st century.

VALERIE S. GRASH

See also **McKim, Mead and White (United States); Shanghai World Financial Center, Shanghai**

Biographies

A. Eugene Kohn
Born in Philadelphia, Pennsylvania, 1930. Educated at the University of Pennsylvania, Philadelphia.

William Pedersen
Born in St. Paul, Minnesota, 1938. Studied at the University of Minnesota, Minneapolis, and at the Massachusetts Institute of Technology, Cambridge.

Sheldon Fox
Born in New York City, 1930. Educated at the University of Pennsylvania, Philadelphia.

Kohn Pedersen Fox
Partners met while working in the office of John Carl Warnecke in the early 1970s; Kohn Pedersen Fox established in New York 1976. Specialized in corporate offices and office towers. A branch office, headed by partner Patricia Conway, specialized in corporate office interiors.

Selected Works

ABC Television Studio Building, New York, 1979
333 Wacker Drive Office Building, Chicago, 1983
Hercules Incorporated Headquarters, Wilmington, Delaware, 1983
Third National Bank, Nashville, Tennessee, 1985
Proctor and Gamble General Offices Complex, Cincinnati, Ohio, 1985
CNG Tower, Pittsburgh, Pennsylvania, 1987
Westendstrasse 1/DG Bank Headquarters, Frankfurt, 1993
Shanghai World Financial Center, 1994 (Still under construction)
IBM World Headquarters, Armonk, New York, 1997

Further Reading

Documentation in the form of photographs, building and site layouts, and details regarding the roles of the firm's principals in each work are found in two *catalogues raisonné*: Cháo and Abramson, and James.

Anderson, Grace, "Five by KPF," *The Architectural Record* 175, no. 2 (1987)
Boles, Daralice Donkervoet, and Jim Murphy, "Cincinnati Centerpiece," *Progressive Architecture* 66, no. 10 (1985)
Cháo, Sonia R., and Trevor D. Abramson, editors, *Kohn Pedersen Fox: Buildings and Projects, 1976–1986*, New York: Rizzoli, 1987
James, Warren A., editor, *Kohn Pedersen Fox: Architecture and Urbanism, 1986–1992*, New York: Rizzoli, 1993; revised edition, 1994
"Kohn Pedersen Fox: Profile," *Progressive Architecture* 64, no. 10 (1983)
McQuade, Walter, "The High Rise of Kohn Pedersen Fox," *Architecture: The AIA Journal* 78, no. 5 (1989)

KOOLHAAS, REM 1944–
Architect, designer, Netherlands

Rem Koolhaas is an internationally known architect, urbanist, and writer. He gained initial recognition in 1978 with the publication of his first book, *Delirious New York*, in which he analyzed the exuberant, complex, and popular modernism of New York City of the 1920s and 1930s. His interpretations of New York were presented as a critique of canonical European modernism and as a platform for designing architecture in the contemporary city. Koolhaas's writing, building, and teaching are all instruments for research into the architectural possibilities for the contemporary city.

In 1975, Koolhaas founded OMA with Madelon Vriesendorp and Elia and Zoe Zenghelis and produced theoretical projects, such as the City of the Captive Globe (1978), published as a postscript to *Delirious New York*. The young firm also began entering competitions. After winning a preliminary competition for the addition to the Parliament Buildings in The Hague, OMA opened its office in Rotterdam in 1981, where they continued preparing competition entries (Parc de la Villette, Paris, 1982; Ville Nouvelle Melun-Senart, 1987) while carrying out awarded commissions including the IJ-Plein Urban Housing Project in Amsterdam (completed 1986) and the Netherlands Dance Theater (completed 1987).

In the early 1990s Koolhaas and OMA's activities expanded to include the publication of *OMA: S,M,L,XL* (1995). Koolhaas and OMA were awarded significant commissions, including Nexus Housing, Fukuoka, Japan (1991); Villa dall'Ava, Paris (1991); the Kunsthal, Rotterdam (1992); Euralille Masterplan (1994), and Grand Palais, Lille (1994); Netherlands Embassy, Berlin (1996); Educatorium, University of Utrecht (1997); Illinois Institute of Technology (IIT) McCormick Tribune Campus Center, Chicago (1997); Maison a' Bordeaux (1998); and Seattle Public Library (1999). OMA's projects—built and unbuilt—have been published widely in international journals and have been the subject of numerous exhibitions, including *Rem Koolhaas and the Place of Public Architecture* at the Museum of Modern Art in New York (1994).

Like other architects who emerged as part of the postwar generation, Koolhaas's work both breaks with modernism and reformulates it as he reconfigures relationships among architectural forms, contemporary building programs, and the Postmodern city. His essays, projects, and built work reject certain aspects of first-generation Postmodernism, including the contextualism of Colin Rowe (United States), the typological propositions of Aldo Rossi (Italy), and in the Netherlands, the Structuralism of Herman Hertzberger. Because Koolhaas's architecture is conducted as research, not as the outcome of any fixed theoretical

Lille Grand Palais, Lille, France (1994), designed by Rem Koolhaas and OMA
© Dan Delgado *d2 Arch*

position, his architecture cannot be labeled stylistically or associated with specific movements. For Koolhaas, the mélange of projects and places for his research produces an alchemical environment: Atlanta, Tokyo, Lagos, Shanghai, Paris, Amsterdam, and New York; highways, airports, transportation tunnels, and shopping malls in addition to libraries, private villas, and museums.

Koolhaas and OMA's projects operate with two major design strategies; the first emerged from *Delirious New York* and embraced the city as an infinite grid of streets, blocks, and skyscrapers and the penultimate sign of modernity. Here Koolhaas cites the Downtown Athletic Club (1930) as architectural design that fulfills the promise of alternative modernism within a "culture of congestion" (see Koolhaas, 1978). This design strategy organizes urban territory—gridiron or otherwise—into increments that set radically different programs side by side and that are joined or separated with the boundary of the floor, the exterior skin of the building, or the city grid. Projects of Koolhaas's that exploit this paradigm include the urban and landscape competitions entries for the Parc de la Villette in Paris (1992), the new town of Melun-Senart outside of Paris (1987), and later architectural projects, especially the competition entries for the Jussieu Libraries (Paris, 1992) and the Bibliotheque de France (Paris, 1989). The second strategy emerged not from conventional research but from experimentation, especially within the Kunsthal (Rotterdam, 1992), Euralille master plan (Lille, 1995), and Educatorium (Utrecht, 1996), and later elaborated in Koolhaas's essays "Bigness: The problem of Large" and "The Generic City." In these texts, he calls for the accommodation of the global spaces of flows, instead of just the local spaces of place, as the basis for design within the contemporary city. These projects wrap and fold spaces, programs, and the landscape in and around a neutral structural frame. Although OMA's current work resists classification, several recent experimental projects continue these explorations of congestion and flow, such as the Urban Design Forum master plan (Yokohama, Japan, 1991), Nexus World Housing (Fukuoka, Japan, 1991), and Almere City Center (expected completion 2005).

In addition to being an influential international figure in architecture and urbanism, Koolhaas has stimulated an emerging generation of young architects, especially in the Netherlands. These architects are not following stylistic canons but, rather, carrying forward an attitude that focuses on architecture's place in the contemporary city, on the programs of everyday life, and on the research and creative invention that Koolhaas has kept alive as a challenge to a new generation.

RICHARD DAGENHART

See also **Hertzberger, Herman (Netherlands); Netherlands; Rotterdam, Netherlands**

Biography

Born in Rotterdam, Netherlands, 1944. Lived in Indonesia 1952–56. Journalist with the *Haagse Post* in The Hague, screenwriter in the Netherlands and in Hollywood. Graduated from Architecture Association, London, 1968–72; went to Cornell University on a Harkness Fellowship to study with O. M. Ungers, 1973. Visiting fellow, Institute for Architecture and Urban Studies, New York, 1974; cofounded the Office of Metropolitan Architecture, London 1975; opened OMA office in Rotterdam 1981. Taught at the Institute for Architecture and Urban Studies, New York, 1975; Architectural Association, London, 1976; Technical University, Delft, 1988–89; Rice University, Houston, 1991–92, Visiting scholar, J. Paul Getty Center, Los Angeles, 1993, and Harvard University, Cambridge, Massachusetts, 1995–present. Numerous awards for architecture and urban projects, including the 2000 Laureate of the Pritzker Architectural Prize.

Selected Works

Parc de la Villette (competition), Paris, France, 1982
World Exhibition 1989 (study), Paris, France, 1983
Ville Nouvelle Melun-Senart (competition), Melun-Senart, France, 1987
Nexus Housing, Fukuoka, Japan, 1991
Villa dall'Ava, Paris, France, 1991
Kunsthal, Rotterdam, Netherlands, 1992
Euralille Masterplan, Lille, France, 1994
Lille Grand Palais, Lille, France, 1994
Netherlands Embassy, Berlin, 1996
MCA Universal Studios, Los Angeles, 1996
Educatorium, University of Utrecht, Utrecht, Netherlands, 1997
Illinois Institute of Technology Student Center, Chicago, 1997
Maison a' Bordeaux, Bordeaux, France, 1998
Public Library, Seattle, Washington, 1999

Selected Publications

Delirious New York: A Retroactive Manifesto for Manhattan, New York: Oxford, 1978; Rotterdam: 010 Publishers, 1994; New York: Monicelli, 1995
OMA: S,M,L,XL, Rotterdam: 010 Publishers, and New York: Monicelli, 1995

Further Reading

Lucan, Jacques, *OMA. Rem Koolhaas*, Munich and Zurich: Artemis Verlag für Architektur, 1999
Sinning, Heike, *More Is More: OMA/Rem Koolhaas, Theorie und Architektur*, Berlin: Wasmuth Verlag, 2000
Verwijnen, Jan, "Rem Koolhaas ja office for Metropolitan Architerture," *Arkkitehti*, 5 (1988)

NIHON KOSAKU BUNKA RENMEI (JAPANESE WERKBUND)

The Japanese Werkbund, under the official name of *Nihon* (Japanese for "Japan") *Kosaku* (making) *Bunka* (culture) *Renmei* (assembly), was an organization of Japanese architects and industrial designers who came together with a common regard for

the European Modern movements. The German Werkbund (1907) was the model from which the organization's name was drawn. The Japanese group was formed on 6 December 1936.

Between the two world wars, Japan's most important institutional building designs were characterized by a pluralism vaguely borrowed from the European tradition. A number of organizations had already been formed by progressive Japanese architects who were inspired by European modernist ideologies. For example, the *Nihon Bunriha Kyokai*, or the Japan Secession (1920), modeled itself on the Austrian (Vienna) Secession, and *Nihon Kokusai Kenchiku-kai* [the Japan International Architectural Association (1927)] echoed ideals of the CIAM (Congrès Internationaux d'Architecture Moderne) formed the same year. The mainstream debates tended to focus on establishing a proper style for Japanese architecture. The Japanese Werkbund attempted to find a way to capture the essence of Japanese culture in modern and rationalistic expressions that were compatible with international European predecessors.

The 1936 conference held by the Japanese Academy of Architecture prompted the formation of the Japanese Werkbund. The conference was organized to discuss appropriate styles for modern Japanese architecture. Many of the future members of the Werkbund attended this conference. Ken Ichiura published an article afterward that represented the group's position regarding an appropriate style for Japanese architecture. Ichiura considered it false to replicate the details of the Buddhist temples and Shinto shrines in modern construction and instead urged architects to look for the essence of the Japanese expressions from Katsura Detached Palace, Ise Shinto Shrine, and folk houses. This statement was directed against a number of institutional buildings that had been completed only several years earlier. The identification of Katsura, Ise, and Japanese folk houses as the sources of the cultural identity was in accordance with Bruno Taut's observations of Japanese traditional architecture. Already an internationally well-known architect, Taut had fled Nazi Germany and arrived in Japan three years earlier. After visiting a number of traditional buildings, Taut claimed to have rediscovered Japanese beauty in the simple forms of straight lines, sober colors of materials, and direct expressions of construction in Katsura, Ise, and folk houses. Predictably, Taut denounced ornate and colorful treatments, such as those seen in Buddhist halls. Taut's lecture, titled "Fundamentals of Japanese Architecture," was held in Tokyo in October 1935. With its enthusiastic reception in Japan, Taut's lecture had a strong influence on future Japanese architecture in general. His statement that the functionality and rationality of these buildings were equivalent to the principles of European modern architecture was particularly well received by members of the Japanese Werkbund.

Like its model German organization, the Japanese Werkbund shared the idea that architecture would create a unity among other allied arts. Architects and artists were encouraged to collaborate. The group proclaimed its objectives by setting up the three sets of opposites: architecture for living, not of styles; crafts with purpose, not for leisure; and products with value, not lacking taste. The group saw its activities categorized into the following three areas: collaborative research, the training of craftsmen and workers at the production sites, and the education of the general public. The group organized exhibitions, site trips, and workshops held in support of the Japanese Ministry of Commerce and Industry. The group's journal, *Gendai Kenchiku* (Contemporary Architecture), was published between 1939 and

1940. Although short-lived, this publication laid the foundation for Japan's architectural journalism that developed after World War II.

The Japanese Werkbund shared some nationalistic and military ideas. In their proclamation, the group urged Japan to take the leading role in the construction of an Asian alliance. They foresaw an opportunity in the near future in which architecture and other allied disciplines would face many challenges and difficulties. The group's charge was to endow a great force to culture that would bring true success to the building of a great Asian alliance. In addition, the group had the intention of becoming the major contributor to the Japan Exposition, which had been planned to celebrate the 2,600th year of the Japanese Imperial calendar (1940). This, then, was yet another aspect of the Japanese Werkbund, one that showed the group's reflexive acceptance of the nationalistic movements in the country at that time. The group terminated its journal publication and dissolved its other activities when the exposition was canceled. It would, however, be putting too much emphasis on the group's interests in this exposition to consider the event's cancellation as the direct cause of the group's termination. Other newspapers and journals were terminated under the military government as well. The political and social climate of the time under the newly formed military alliance with Fascist Germany and Italy did not allow the group's activities.

Although the Japan International Architectural Association included international members such as Bruno Taut, Erich Mendelsohn, Gerrit Rietveld, Josef Hoffmann, J.J.P. Oud, Peter Behrens, Walter Gropius, and Richard Neutra, all the members of the Japanese Werkbund were Japanese. These included influential modernist architects, such as Hideto Kishida, Sutemi Horiguchi, Junzo Sakakura, Yoshiro Taniguchi, and Kunio Maekawa. The works of the membership include Wakasa House (1937) by Sutemi Horiguchi, the Japan Pavilion (1937) at the Paris Exposition by Junzo Sakakura, and the Dormitories (1938) at Keio Preparatory College by Yoshiro Taniguchi.

RUMIKO HANDA

Further Reading

"The Horiguchi legacy: Centennial of Sutemi Horiguchi's birth," *Kenchiku-bunka*, 50/582 (April 1995)

Taut, Bruno, *Grundlinien der Architektur Japans*, Tokyo: Kokusai Bunka Shinkokai, 1936; as *Fundamentals of Japanese Architecture*, translated by Glenn Baker and H. E. Pringsheim, Tokyo: Kokusai Bunka Shinkokai, 1936

30 People Who Moved Modernism: Rethinking the Modernists: The Japanese Perspective, special issue of *Kenchiku-bunka*, 55/634 (January 2000)

KUROKAWA, KISHO 1934–

Architect, urban planner, and theorist
Japan

Kisho Kurokawa is one of Japan's leading designers known for his theory of symbiosis. According to Kurokawa, "symbiosis" is an alternative conceptual model for Japanese architecture that simultaneously embodies seemingly conflicting ideas, such as universal principles and regional differences, Western and Eastern sensibilities, history and future, small and large scales, or

cultural identity and modern technology. His large-scale architectural projects, both built and unbuilt, parallel his theoretical writing regarding architecture in the Postmodern era and reflect his attempt to define an essential character of Japanese architecture.

Kurokawa's early career was shaped largely by his experiences as one of the founders of the so-called Metabolist movement during the early 1960s, whose members included other well-known Japanese architects, such as Fumihiko Maki and Kiyonori Kikutake. Rejecting modernism's functionalist approach, the Metabolists proposed large-scale urban projects that used biological concepts and structures as models for ways in which architecture could address practical and sociological issues, such as population increase and the need for structures that could adapt to the changing demands of their inhabitants. Kurokawa first gained recognition outside Japan in 1962 for his design of the Agricultural City Plan, exhibited in the "Visionary Architecture" show at the Museum of Modern Art in New York. During the same period, he was invited by Peter Smithson and Aldo van Eyck to participate in Team X meetings, the largely Netherlandish group of young architects who rejected strict functionalism in order to promote individual concepts of architectural and social identity. However, although the urban agendas of Team X and the Metabolists were similar, the Metabolist experiments with biological metaphors gave them a distinct identity.

For example, Kurokawa's urban proposals were formally based on structures that incorporated the possibility for constant growth and change. The Helix City Plan for Tokyo (1961) was literally derived from the double-helix structure of the DNA molecule. This abstract model expressed the concept of both vertical and horizontal urban expansion, potentially infinite. Building projects such as the Nagakin Capsule Tower (Tokyo, Japan, 1972) embodied Kurokawa's urban concepts of mutable, modular forms and references to cellular structure. Built between 1970 and 1972, the tower consists of prefabricated living units that were lifted into place by a crane. The modules provided what Kurokawa referred to as "spatial equipment" that could be operated by its inhabitants. In addition, by providing hotel-like amenities in the most efficient way possible, he attempted to encourage the development of residential buildings for commuters within the city center during a time when many city dwellers were moving to the outlying suburbs.

Kurokawa's interests in modular form and possibilities for three-dimensional expansion were explored at the scale of the structural component in the Toshiba IHI Pavilion at Expo 1970 in Osaka. The circular, domed, 500-seat theater provided Kurokawa with the opportunity to experiment with a metal space frame of tetrahedral units that could be expanded in 14 different ways. "The first aim," stated Kurokawa, "was to introduce this regenerating process into architecture and city planning, the name being expressive of the conviction that a work of architecture should not be frozen once it is completed, but should be apprehended instead as a thing—or as a process—that evolves from past to present and from present to future."

Metabolism could be seen as a reaction to the practical concerns about the growing population crisis in Japan's cities and as a challenge to the so-called machine age that operates without consideration of human history. Kurokawa and the Metabolists shared similarities with, and may have been influenced by, other architectural styles, such as Team X and the British Archigram group, but Kurokawa was also motivated by his strong reaction against the rigid International Style, which had been an influential force in Japanese architecture during the first half of the century. The perceived Eurocentrism and homogeneity of International Style buildings was heavily criticized by Kurokawa as a form of colonialism. In particular, he objected to the notion devised by European architects Bruno Taut and Walter Gropius during their visit to the Katsura Palace in Japan that the simple, spare forms of the building anticipated modernist principles and represented Japanese architecture a whole; rather, Kurokawa believed that the Katsura Palace represented only part of the country's architectural tradition.

From his early work as a Metabolist, exploring the tension between technology and culture and between global and local architecture, Kurokawa developed his cultural theory of symbiosis. He has written extensively on his theories of symbiosis, and his writings, including the 1992 publication *From Metabolism to Symbiosis*, are virtually manifestos. Writing in a manner that recalls the work of French literary critics such as Roland Barthes, Gilles Deleuze, and Felix Guattari among others, Kurokawa draws inspiration from local tradition and culture to inform a new paradigm for Japanese architecture that continues the multicultural dynamic characteristic of Japanese culture, for ex-

The Colisée Buildings, designed by Kisho Kurokawa, Nimes, France
© Chris Bland; Eye Ubiquitous/CORBIS

ample, the incorporation of Chinese elements into Japanese culture.

Beginning in the 1970s and continuing with his contemporary work, Kurokawa has explored the ways in which contemporary architecture can draw on the past and present to express regional identity. Most, if not all, of his projects contain references to the centuries-old *sukiya* style of Japanese architecture. Literally translated as an aesthetic of "artlessness," the *sukiya* style was employed in the design of teahouses, most notably during the Edo period of the early 17th through the mid-19th centuries. The Nagakin Capsule Tower employs cutting-edge technology and materials, is constructed of mass-produced units, uses high-tension connections to a central core, and addresses contemporary urban population issues; at the same time, however, the individual rooms within the tower contain references to the traditional *sukiya* style: 8- by-13-foot dimensions are based on the plan of the tearoom; molded plastic interiors express the simplicity, orderliness, and economy evident in the spare design of the tearoom; and passage from the street up to individual quarters could be described as conveying the sense of isolation and escape expressed by traditional tearoom design.

Many of Kurokawa's buildings are museums, a building type well suited to the exploration of culture, history, and the notion of symbiosis. For example, the Ehime Prefectural Museum of General Science (Ehime, Japan, 1995) is a complex of several buildings, each with its own program and discrete form: the conical entrance, the rectangular exhibition hall, the spherical planetarium, the crescent-shaped restaurant, and the triangular parking garage. The noncentralized arrangement of the buildings, which includes a shallow pool within which the planetarium is situated, recalls the asymmetry and nonhierarchical layouts of traditional Japanese forms, from the random placement of stepping-stones in a garden to the rambling plan of the Katsura palace and gardens, another prime example of *sukiya* style. Through his use of pure geometry in many of these buildings, Kurokawa aims to evoke "past cosmologies and symbols of *topos*," an approach that he refers to as abstract symbolism. For example, in traditional Chinese architecture, the earth was often represented as square and the heavens as round, references that were incorporated by Kurokawa in his spherical planetarium and rectangular exhibition hall. However, the crescent-shaped buildings and slightly tilted walls of the rectangle are examples of how pure geometry, while referring to the past, may be distorted to create new forms. The cone, frequently used in many of his projects, contains multiple references, including the European tower and the roof the traditional Chinese palace. In the Ehime Prefectural Museum of General Science, references to traditional forms are juxtaposed with contemporary construction materials of aluminum, glass, and concrete to create a synthesis of past and present.

CATHERINE MOY

See also **Archigram; Maki, Fumihiko (Japan); Metabolists; Tange, Kenzo (Japan); Team X (Netherlands); Tokyo, Japan**

Biography

Born in Nagoya, Japan, 8 April 1934. Attended Kyoto University, Department of Architecture; bachelor's degree in architecture 1957; studied under Kenzo Tange, Tokyo University, Department of Architecture; master's degree in architecture 1964. Married Sumie Tsuchiya in 1959, had children; divorced; married Ayako Wakao in 1984. Founder, Kisho Kurokawa and Associates, Tokyo 1962–68; president, K.K. Architect and Associates, Tokyo from 1968; principal, Institute for Social Engineering, Tokyo from 1969; adviser to the Japanese National Railways from 1970; analyst for the Japan Broadcasting Corporation from 1974; adviser to the International Design Conference, Aspen, Colorado, from 1974; general overseer, 1998 World Architecture Exposition Triennale. Honorary fellow, American Institute of Architects 1982; honorary member, Union of Architects of Bulgaria 1982; life fellow, Royal Society of Art, London.

Selected Works

Helix City Plan, Tokyo, Japan, 1961
Toshiba IHI Pavilion, Expo 1970, Osaka, Japan, 1970
Nagakin Capsule Tower, Tokyo, Japan, 1972
Fukuoka Bank, Fukuoka, Japan, 1975
Sony Tower, Osaka, Japan, 1976
National Ethnological Museum, Osaka, Japan, 1977
Saitama Prefectural Museum of Modern Art, Urawa, Japan, 1982
National Banraku Theater, Osaka, Japan, 1983
Wacoal Kojimachi Building, Tokyo, Japan, 1984
Nagoya City Museum of Contemporary Art, Nagoya, Japan, 1987
Hiroshima City Museum of Modern Art, Hiroshima, Japan, 1988
Japanese-German Center of Berlin, Berlin, Germany, 1988
Victoria Central, Australia, 1988
Japanese-Chinese Youth Center, Beijing, China, 1990
Shirase Memorial Hall, 1990
Sporting Club at the Illinois Center, Chicago, Illinois, 1990
Pacific Tower, Paris, France, 1991
Ishibashi Junior Highs School, Tochigi, Japan, 1994
Ehime Prefectural Museum of General Science, Ehime, Japan, 1995

Selected Publications

Metabolism in Architecture, 1977
Kisho Kurokawa: The Architecture of Symbiosis, introduction by Francois Chaslin, 1988
Intercultural Architecture: The Philosophy of Symbiosis, 1991
From Metabolism to Symbiosis, 1992
The Philosophy of Symbiosis, 1994

Further Reading

Blackwood, Michael, director and producer, *Kisho Kurokawa from Metabolism to Symbiosis* (videorecording), New York: Michael Blackwood Productions, 1993
Dobney, Stephen (editor), *Kisho Kurokawa: Selected and Current Works*, Mulgrave, Victoria: Images, 1995
Guiheux, Alain, *Kisho Kurokawa: Architecte: Le Métabolisme, 1960–1975*, Paris: Centre Georges Pompidou, 1997
Kisho Kurokawa (exhib. cat.), Paris: Moniteur, 1995

KYOTO, JAPAN

Kyoto, the former capital of Japan and its center of traditional culture, is situated in the country's heartland; its larger metropolitan area is interwoven with two other major centers in the Kansai region: Osaka and Kobe. One of the few Japanese cities not to have been bombed during the Second World War, Kyoto houses numerous ancient buildings. Major socioeconomic changes transformed most Japanese cities since the mid-19th

century and did not bypass Kyoto; nonetheless, these historic structures form the backdrop and reference for contemporary architecture.

Kyoto was established in 794 as capital city on a site surrounded on three sides by mountains and crossed by two main rivers, the Kamogawa and the Katsuragawa. It is one of the few Japanese cities laid out on a grid following the design of imperial Chinese cities. Inspired in particular by the T'ang dynasty city of Ch'ang-an, its regular layout contrasts with the maze of Tokyo's urban landscape and the organic design of most other Japanese cities.

European and American architecture, introduced to Japan after the Meiji restoration of 1868, was considered a status symbol in efforts to modernize Japan. It was particularly well suited to the outward-looking new national center, Tokyo, but it also entered the architectural world of Kyoto, when the city was struggling to redefine its role after the loss of the capital city function. The Ryukoku University Main Building (1879), the Daiichi Kangyo Bank (1906) by Kingo Tatsuno, or the Kyoto Prefectural Library (1909) by Goichi Takeda are examples of Western influences. All did not accept the new forms. The French Second Empire style, such as Kyoto National Museum (1895), and particularly its predecessor, the Nara Imperial Museum (1894), by Tokuma Katayama, provoked debate at the time of construction.

In reaction to these Western-style buildings, the new Nara prefectural office (1895) by Uheiji Nagano combined the size and layout of a contemporary building with an overall Japanese look in the design of the roofs and the entrance space. Conceived as a modern "Japanese-style" architecture (kindai wafu-kenchiku), and not an imitation of traditional forms, the new Japanese style quickly spread to other building types and places in Japan. Examples in Kyoto are the Nijo station (1904) and the Minamiza Kabuki theater (1929), the latter featuring reinforced concrete in combination with traditional forms. The traditional Kyoto landscape was particularly suited for the Kitamura house (1963) by Isoya Yoshida, a Japanese architect convinced that Japanese could not rival European buildings and who focused on reinterpreting and modernizing traditional Japanese forms.

In the 1920s and 1930s, Kyoto also saw the construction of several modernist buildings, such as the Toba High School Main Hall (1931), the Kyoto Institute of Technology University Main Building (1931), and the Kansaidenryoku Kyoto Branch (1937), the latter by Goichi Takeda. Their number, however, is significantly smaller than in Tokyo. The few modern buildings in Kyoto that received international attention were conceived in the postwar period. Nonetheless, even these buildings responded to the historic environment. Kunio Maekawa's Kyoto Hall (1960) preceded the Tokyo Metropolitan Festival Hall by a year; while displaying many similar features, the forms and materials used in Kyoto are restrained compared to Tokyo so as not to compete with the nearby Heian shrine. Contemporary architects largely respected the horizontal Kyoto skyline; the only vertical landmark introduced was the Kyoto Tower by Mamoru Yamada (1964). The most surprising building in the subdued Kyoto environment is the Kyoto International Conference Hall (1966, addition 1973) by Sachio Ohtani, a member of the Metabolist group. Based on a hexagonal structural system practically without vertical columns or walls, the building pays homage to the roofs of traditional Japanese buildings and particularly the Ise shrine using modernist forms. The particular spirit of the city and its narrow paths inspired even a foreigner, David Chipperfield. His Toyota Auto Kyoto building (1991) reflects the old city in its interweaving of different functions and relates to the mountains surrounding Kyoto.

Whereas few foreigners built in Kyoto, Tokyo-based architects who adapted their formal language to the particular context designed numerous major contemporary buildings. Fumihiko Maki's Kyoto National Museum of Modern Art (1986) is limited in height in accordance with the historic/scenic zone where it is built, and the gridiron pattern of the facade reflects the grid plan of the city. Arata Isozaki's Kyoto Symphony Hall (1995) is associated with Kyoto's commemoration in 1994 of the 1200th anniversary of the city's founding. The three geometric-form volumes—a rectangular box, a cylinder, and a cubic lattice—are arranged on three urban axes hidden in ancient Kyoto.

The largest and most important urban change is the construction of the new Kyoto Station building (1997). Conceived during the bubble period as part of a larger regional development project focused on the Kansai airport, it reflects Kyoto's attempts at attracting tourists. Following on the privatization of the Japanese national railway JR, the new owner, JR Nishi Nihon, conceived a redevelopment plan in cooperation with the city of Kyoto. Aimed at revitalizing the station area, it integrates numerous functions usually found in the vicinity of a station such as hotels, department stores, theaters, shops, and restaurants. The new building, designed by the Tokyo architect Hiroshi Hara, resulted from a 1990 competition. Hara proposed a high-density, low-rise structure to conform with the horizontal landscape of Kyoto but consciously opted against assimilation with traditional architecture. Instead, he conceived the 230,000-square-meter building in the spirit of the great railway stations of the 19th century. Transportation functions take up only 15 percent of the ground floor, and the great glass roof covers primarily the commercial functions. The entrance hall takes the form of a valley between two mountains, the Western "slope" being designed as a huge staircase. A "skywalk," featured previously in Hara's Umeda Sky Building (1993) in Osaka, provides a promenade inside the roof structure and links both wings of the building to allow a wide view over the city. The commercial function took precedence over an additional link across the rails. For the time being, only one underpass and one overpass connect the 470-meter (1,540 feet) building with the south of the city.

The traditional urban landscape of Kyoto is the backdrop to numerous contemporary small-scale buildings, many of which are designed by architects of the Kansai region. Tadao Ando's minimalist architecture and the exotic, mechanical structures of Shin Takamatsu have become particularly famous. Ando has created one of his best urban projects in Kyoto: the Time's I (1984) and Time's II (1991) building complex. Located in a popular neighborhood close to the Sanjo-Ohashi Bridge, the building faces a busy street while extending alongside a river, the Takasegawa. Ando used this location to create a layered system of interwoven interior and exterior spaces accessible through various staircases as well as a curving deck at the water level that functions as an oasis of calmness in the bustling city. This area is also home to several buildings by Takamatsu, the Pontocho-no-Ochaya (Yoshida House) (1982), Cella (1991), and Maruto Building 4 (1987).

The fantastic architecture of Takamatsu, reminiscent of 1920s Expressionist sketches, is based on mechanical references and High-Tech forms. The Ark Building (Nishina Dental Clinic) (1983) is one of Takamatsu's most powerful images of machinery, a horizontal silvery cylinder laid over a rectangular concrete volume crowned by lanterns reminiscent of smoke stacks. His buildings feature strong contrasts in materials such as the combination of highly polished granite and copper rivets in Origin 1 (1981). The building has been extended as Origin 2 (1982) and Origin 3 (1986), the latter displaying an aggressive look more typical of Takamatsu's design. On Kitayama Street in the north of Kyoto, Takamatsu designed the Week Building (1986) and the Kitayama Ining '23 (1987), as well as the noted Syntax Building (1990). The latter, a four-story construction with two basement levels houses shops and restaurants. Its most astonishing characteristic is two cantilevering features on the rooftop stretching their arms over neighboring houses seemingly searching for future connections. Tadao Ando's B-Lock Kitayama (1990) and his Garden of Fine Arts (1994), a peaceful oasis in the bustle of the city, are also located on this street.

Other notable examples of small-scale architecture in Kyoto are the Maruto Buildings n 15 (1990) and n 17 (1991) in Kyoto's Gion district by Hiroyuki Wakabayashi, who uses a language similar to that of Takamatsu. Wakabayashi, known for his avant-garde buildings, has also responded to the historic environment by transforming a traditional building for his office: the Studio Arch Wakabayashi (1990). Closer to Ando's formal language are Waro Kishi's houses in Kamigyo (1990), Nakagyo (1993), and Shimogamo (1995) that demonstrate his capacity to use simple elements to make complex forms and his desire to translate Japanese elements into modern design.

Many recent buildings have been erected on the outskirts of the city or even in the larger metropolitan area. Jun Tamaki's Tofu (1997) house for an elderly couple is built on a housing estate on the western side of Kyoto. This white building suggests a block or lump, filled with some homogenous material, floating above the ground surface. It is organized around a central area that functions as reception, dining, living, and bedroom and gives access to the other service rooms. Large deep windows underline the lumplike character of the building. Another site for contemporary construction is the Kansai Science City in the hills of the Kyoto-Osaka-Nara area, where the Kyoto-Kagaku Research Institute by Waro Kishi is located.

Traditional forms continue to influence contemporary construction in Kyoto. The importance given to the city's history is reflected in the recent discussion to build a replica of the Paris Pont des Arts as a pedestrian bridge over the Kamogawa to celebrate the Year of France in Japan. The proposal, seen as an opportunity to show public art in Kyoto, was abandoned in 1998 after heavy criticism for borrowing from the West in the context of traditional Kyoto.

CAROLA HEIN

See also **Ando, Tadao (Japan); Isozaki, Arata (Japan); Kurokawa, Kisho (Japan); Maki, Fumihiko (Japan); Metabolists; Shinohara, Kazuo (Japan); Tange, Kenzo (Japan)**

Further Reading

Few books discuss solely the architectural history of Kyoto. Most publications on Japanese architecture, however, include issues of the city's urban and architectural development. Finn discusses some Kyoto buildings in the context of Meiji-time architecture. Hatsuda, Ookawa, and Fujita concentrate on modern Japanese-style architecture, including buildings in Kyoto. Books on modern architecture, such as Suzuki, Banham, and Kobayashi; Kultermann; Tempel; or Ross mention only a few constructions in Kyoto. The buildings of Maki, Isozaki, Ando and Takamatsu in Kyoto are discussed in monographs on these architects (see other entries). A monograph on Waro Kishi, who is slightly less known, is included. *The Japan Architect* 1993 issue on Kyoto and Osaka features architecture primarily from the early 1990s.

Bognár, Botond, *The Japan Guide*, New York: Princeton Architectural Press, 1995

Finn, Dallas, *Meiji Revisited: The Sites of Victorian Japan*, New York: Weatherhill, 1995

Gallery Ma, *The Architectural Map of Kyoto*, Toto Shuppan 1998 (in Japanese)

Hatsuda, Tohru, Mitsuo Ookawa, and Yoetsu Fujiya, *Kindai wafū kenchiku*, 2 vols, (A Modern Japanese-Style Architecture), Kenchiku Chishiki, Tokyo: Kajima Shuppankai Shōwa, 1988 (in Japanese)

Kultermann, Udo, *New Japanese Architecture*, New York: Praeger, 1960

"Kyoto Osaka," *The Japan Architect*, 11 (1993)

"Kyoto Station," *Extra Issue of Designers' Workshop*, 14/93 (1997)

Montagnana, Francesco, *Guida all'architettura del Novecento Giappone*, Milano, Electa, 1995; as *Birkhäuser Architectural Guide, Japan: 20th Century*, Basel, Berlin, and Boston: Birkhäuser, 1997

Ookawa, Mitsuo, Masato Kawamukai, Tohru Hatsuda, and Koichi Yoshida, *Kindai kenchiku no keifu* (A Genealogy of Modern Architecture), Shokokusha, 1998

Ross, Michael Franklin, *Beyond Metabolism: The New Japanese Architecture*, New York: Architectural Record Books, 1978

Stewart, David B., *The Making of a Modern Japanese Architecture: 1868 to the Present*, Tokyo and New York: Kodansha International, 1987

Suzuki, Hiroyuki, Reyner Banham, and Katsuhiro Kobayashi, *Nihon no gendai kenchiku*, New York: Rizzoli, 1985; as *Contemporary Architecture of Japan, 1958–1884*, New York: Rizzoli, 1985

Tempel, Egon, *Neue Japanische Architektur*, Stuttgart, Germany: Verlag Gerd Hatje, 1969; as *New Japanese Architecture*, translated by E. Rockwell, London: Thames and Hudson, 1969

Waro Kishi: Buildings and Projects, introduction by Hiroshi Watanabe, Stuttgart: Edition Axel Menges, 2000

L

LAPIDUS, MORRIS 1902–2001

Architect, United States

Morris Lapidus is best known for 1950s resort hotels that combined International Style modernism with a decorative formal vocabulary. Born in Odessa, Russia, in 1902, Lapidus came to the United States in 1903 with his parents, who were fleeing the pogroms. Like most Jewish immigrants in this period, they settled on the lower east side of New York. An early love of the theater led Lapidus to study drama in college. In 1923 he gave up acting and entered the School of Architecture at Columbia University to become a set designer. Though Lapidus abandoned this goal, his work retained an essential theatricality.

Trained in the Beaux-Arts method, Lapidus's schoolwork focused on monumental and idealized projects and classical revival styles. Contemporary architectural developments were rarely discussed at Columbia, though Lapidus did become familiar with some modern design, principally Art Deco, while still a student. After school, Lapidus worked for Warren and Wetmore, designing ornamental details for the New York Central Building on Park Avenue. In 1928 he joined Ross-Frankel, a firm specializing in store design and construction.

Despite the Great Depression, the 1930s were a professionally productive period for Lapidus. His stores for prominent chain retailers appeared in New York City and across the United States. By the time he left Ross-Frankel in 1943, Lapidus was an established store designer whose work was published in the architectural press and was critically well received.

Lapidus continued to absorb architectural ideas from Europe, namely the work of Ludwig Mies van der Rohe and Erich Mendelsohn. His stores were also influenced by modern German graphic journals such as *Gebrauchsgraphik*. With asymmetry, transparency, flowing spaces, and bold graphics, Lapidus's stores brought modernism to American commercial architecture. But even as Lapidus came to terms with the International Style, he developed a highly personal vocabulary—his so-called "cheese holes," "woggles," and "bean poles"—which gave his architecture visual exuberance. Though critics deemed this manner appropriate in a small-scale retail context, as Lapidus's commissions increased in size after his move to independent practice in 1943, Lapidus came under fire for his architectural flamboyance.

In his first years as an independent designer, retail remained Lapidus's primary focus, and despite material restrictions during World War II, his firm thrived. Notwithstanding this success, Lapidus was unsatisfied because he did not consider store design as real architecture because it so often involved the renovation of existing buildings rather than new construction. The opportunity to broaden his practice arrived in 1949 when hotel developer Ben Novack hired Lapidus as associate architect for a new resort he was building in Miami Beach, Florida. After designing the interiors and facade details for the San Souci, Lapidus received numerous commissions to alter and improve the design of other Miami Beach hotels already under construction. In these projects, for the Delano and the Algiers among others, Lapidus employed many of the same techniques and signature forms that he had used in his retail work, reasoning that hotels, like stores, had something to sell—be it leisure, pleasure, or luxury.

In 1952 Lapidus received what would be the most celebrated and notorious commission of his career when Ben Novak hired him to design the Fountainbleau Hotel, Miami Beach, providing the architect with his first opportunity to plan a building from start to finish. Dominated by a sweeping curve embracing the ocean, the Fountainbleau was an essay in International Style mannerism, which strongly recalled Erich Mendelsohn's work of the late 1920s, as well as the work of Brazilian modernist Oscar Niemeyer, whom the architect met in 1949. Though the hotel's 440-foot curve had dramatic visual flair, it was also a strategy intended to minimize the monotony of the endless corridors needed to accommodate 565 rooms. The interiors, extravagantly decorated with marble, crystal, and mirrored glass, were influenced by Hollywood movie sets and designed in a style Lapidus dubbed "modern luxury." Upon its completion in 1954, the Fountainbleau became synonymous with the swank and glamour of the star-studded Miami Beach social scene and established Lapidus as a leading hotel designer.

In the mid-1950s Lapidus opened an office in Miami Beach to handle the large hotel commissions his firm was now receiving. These included the Eden Roc (1955) in Miami Beach; the Americana (1956) in Bal Harbour; and the Sheraton (1960), Summit (1961), and Americana (1962), all in New York City. Lapidus also designed several resorts in the Caribbean including

Fountainbleau Hotel, Miami Beach (1954), designed by Morris Lapidus
© John Margolies/Esto

the Aruba Caribbean (1956) in the Dutch West Indies, the Arawak in Jamaica (1957), and the El Conquistador in Puerto Rico (1965). In 1960 Lapidus completed an urban renewal scheme for the Lincoln Road commercial strip in Miami Beach, transforming five run-down blocks into an early example of a car-free pedestrian mall with fountains, canopies, and pavilions. In addition, he designed numerous apartment buildings and shopping centers in the eastern United States.

Despite the enormous popular success of Lapidus's work, it was regarded as a critical failure by members of the modernist architectural establishment of the 1950s and 1960s, who viewed the hotels in particular as a capitulation to kitsch, or mass taste. By the late 1960s and early 1970s, however, his work was being defended by a new generation of architects who, in revolt from high modernism, were drawn to its populist content and formal excess. By the 1980s Lapidus had been critically rehabilitated and was regarded by his supporters as a progenitor of Postmodernism.

Lapidus closed his New York office in the early 1970s, having moved permanently to Miami Beach in the previous decade. He continued to practice in Florida until 1984. Following a resurgence of interest in his work, Lapidus came out of retirement in the late 1990s and began to consult on projects in the Miami Beach area, including the design of several restaurants

and bars and the restoration of his own Eden Roc Hotel completed in 2000.

GABRIELLE ESPERDY

See also **Mendelsohn, Erich (Germany); Resort Hotel**

Biography

Born in Odessa, Russia, on 25 November 1902; immigrated to New York in 1903; raised in Brooklyn, New York. Attended architecture school at Columbia University graduating in 1927. Worked as store designer during 1930s; established independent office in 1943. Achieved prominence and notoriety in 1950s as designer of resort hotels in a flamboyant modern style. Mature worked dismissed by modernist architectural establishment but Lapidus was critically rehabilitated with rise of pop art and Postmodernism. Retired from practice in 1984; died on 19 January 2001.

Selected Works

Fountainbleau Hotel, Miami Beach, Florida, 1954
Eden Roc Hotel, Miami Beach, Florida, 1955
Americana Hotel, Bal Harbour, Florida, 1956

Lincoln Road Outdoor Mall, Miami Beach, Florida, 1960
Summit Hotel, New York City, 1961
Americana of New York Hotel, New York City, 1962

Selected Publications

Too Much Is Never Enough, New York: Rizzoli, 1996

Further Reading

Cook, John Wesley, and Heinrich Klotz, *Conversations with Architects*, New York: Praeger, 1973
Düttmann, Martina, and Friederike Schneider (editors), *Morris Lapidus: Architect of the American Dream*, Basel: Birkhäuser Verlag, 1992
Friedman, Alice T., "The Luxury of Lapidus," *Harvard Design Magazine* (summer 2000)

LARKIN ADMINISTRATION BUILDING

Designed by Frank Lloyd Wright; completed 1906
Buffalo, New York

Frank Lloyd Wright's Larkin Building was designed and constructed between 1903 and 1906 for the Larkin Company, a soap and mail order concern based in Buffalo, New York. The firm had begun as a soap manufactory in the 1870s, but a series of clever marketing innovations involving the inclusion of premium items with the bulk purchase of soap increased sales dramatically in the 1890s and transformed the business into a mail-order operation. These conditions gave rise to the need for a new office building wherein the company's ever-increasing customer correspondence could be efficiently handled. Frank Lloyd Wright was chosen as architect on the strength of his growing national reputation and his five years' experience with Adler and Sullivan, a leading tall office building firm in Chicago. The commission was especially important to Wright because he was then known primarily as a domestic architect and his work was confined to Illinois and the adjoining midwestern states.

The site for the Larkin Building was in a mixed industrial and residential neighborhood one mile east of downtown Buffalo, immediately across the street from the Larkin factory and warehouse buildings and nearby the main New York Central railroad trunk lines. The program called for a building that would house about 1,800 secretaries and their supervisors, as well as the Larkin Company executives, in an environment that would be clean, brightly illuminated, fireproof, and attractive. Wright's design consisted of a steel-framed, brick-clad structure approximately 100 feet wide, 100 feet tall, and 200 feet long. Its principal feature was an internal light court surrounded by five stories of balconies and topped with a skylight. Beneath the main floor

Larkin Administration Building, Buffalo, New York (1906)
Photo © Buffalo & Erie County Historical Society

was an above-grade basement for receiving mail trucks. On the north side of the building, Wright designed an annex—a diminished version of the main structure that contained an entrance lobby—and three more floors for restrooms, lounges, and classrooms. Wright would use versions of this binuclear plan subsequently in his Unity Temple (Oak Park, Illinois, 1906), the Johnson Wax Building (Racine, Wisconsin, 1937), and Guggenheim Museum (New York City, 1959).

In the original design, stairways were located at either end of the light court as in Burnham and Roots's Rookery Building (1888) in Chicago, but during the design process Wright was inspired to relocate these features on the four outer corners of the building and the two corners of the annex, in brick towers, thereby more than doubling the number of fire escape routes. This change led him also to transform the intake and exhaust units into pseudotowers of the same proportions, thereby transforming the two principal facades of the building into monumental pylons, evocative of ancient Egypt yet modern in the expression of the building's mechanical functions. However, this was only one of a number of innovations in the building.

The building was designed to accommodate the Larkin Company's system of organizing customer accounts in divisions based on states (for example, Pennsylvania A and B, Florida, and Canada). Each group of states had its assigned position among the tiers of balconies. The mail was delivered by elevator from the basement to sorters on the third floor and, once sorted, to each state group by messengers on roller skates. The main floor was devoted to the leading executives and department heads and the fifth floor to a restaurant open to all, including visitors. Wright designed metal chairs and desks throughout the building and built metal file cabinets into all the exterior walls as a fireproofing measure. The furniture was constructed with magnesite panels, and each floor was of magnesite, a resilient, lightweight concrete that dampened sound. Light poured in from the central skylight and from windows high in the outer walls that channeled light across the balconies. The quality of light was enhanced by Nerst glowers and by a uniform use of a semivitreous cream-colored brick in the interior.

In an effort to seal the interior of the office building from the infiltration of soot from the passing trains, Wright was quick to capitalize on Willis Carrier's experiments with air conditioning made only a few years earlier. Two plenum air-conditioning units were installed below grade in the base of two of the stair towers. Air drawn down by fans from above the building was washed in a sheetlike spray of water and then cooled by a Kroeschell refrigeration unit to lower its temperature and thus precipitate out moisture. The cooled air was circulated throughout the building through a system of ducts under the basement floor that carried up to each floor within the structural piers that formed the light court. Returns were located high on the outer walls. By doing this, Wright enabled the Larkin secretaries to correspond with customers comfortably and neatly, as is appropriate to a soap company.

Many of Wright's innovations were intended to promote work efficiency and safety, but the building's historical prominence lies as well in its beauty and inspirational nature. The light court was not large in plan, but its piers soared upward toward the skylit top, where they burst into abstract exfoliations. To enhance this effect, Wright shifted the fifth-floor balcony frontward, back from the plane established by the four lower balconies so as to open the uppermost portion of the space fur-

ther to the light. All the fifth-floor balcony fronts were inscribed with gilded inspirational words and passages from Scripture. Just above the fifth floor at the short ends of the building, Wright provided a partial sixth floor containing a conservatory filled with palms and ivies that spilled their tendrils just into view at the edges of the gridded skylight—a hint of something serene and wonderful high above the hum of the workplace.

Although the Larkin Building was criticized by Russell Sturgis for "ugliness" that he perceived in the rectilinear purity of its forms, the building does exhibit traces of the Beaux-Arts classicism that dominated in the United States at the turn of the 20th century. Its massing conforms to the symmetry, the three-part organization, and, along its flanks, a temple-like columniation reminiscent of the classical, all of which add a certain familiarity and authority.

The Larkin Building was designed so specifically to suit the needs of the Larkin mail-order business as it functioned in 1903 that it resisted changes within the business and did not lend itself to new uses in the late 1940s, after the Larkin Company abandoned it. Following an extended period of vacancy and attempts to make some use of it, the Larkin Administration Building was demolished in 1950.

The impact of the Larkin Administration Building on the modern movement in Europe and in the United States is substantial both in terms of individual works that are inspired by its forms (such as Jan Wils, project for a pension, 1921; William Drummond, First Congregational Church, Austin, Illinois, 1908) and as an agent of encouraging younger architects, such as Ludwig Mies van der Rohe, Erich Mendelsohn, Walter Gropius, and others to the possibilities of a greater abstractness of form and to the expressive potential of mechanical functions.

JACK QUINAN

See also **Chicago School; Guggenheim Museum, New York City; Johnson Wax Building, Racine, Wisconsin; Mies van der Rohe, Ludwig (Germany); Sullivan, Louis (United States); Unity Temple, Oak Park, Illinois; Wright, Frank Lloyd (United States)**

Further Reading

Hitchcock, Henry-Russell, *In the Nature of Materials, 1887–1941: The Buildings of Frank Lloyd Wright*, New York: Duell, Sloan, and Pierce, 1942; with new foreword and bibliography, New York: Da Capo Press, 1973

Quinan, Jack, *Frank Lloyd Wright's Larkin Building: Myth and Fact*, New York: Architectural History Foundation, and Cambridge, Massachusetts: MIT Press, 1987

Wright, Frank Lloyd, *Frank Lloyd Wright Collected Writings*, edited by Bruce Brooks Pfeiffer, 5 vols., New York: Rizzoli, 1992–95

Wright, Frank Lloyd, *Frank Lloyd Wright, Architect*, edited by Terrance Riley, New York: Museum of Modern Art, 1994

LARSEN, HENNING 1925–

Architect, Denmark

During his almost five decades of practice, Henning Larsen has had the chance to design a wide range of buildings, ranging from newspaper offices to churches, housing to embassies, colleges to museums, and factories to theaters. Although his work is occasionally marred by a misfit in scale, Larsen carries on the excellent traditions of Danish architecture: elegant detailing, beautiful use of materials, and massing of geometric forms. Larsen's work is inventive and deliberate. The body of work has changed over time as themes and references shifted, and several major periods can be established within his oeuvre, roughly as represented by work between 1960–79, 1980–89, and 1990 to the present.

Larsen was born in Brejning, in Jutland, Denmark, in 1925, and studied at the Technical College in Copenhagen before entering the Kunstakademie in 1949. He spent a year of his professional studies at the Architectural Association in London. A graduation scholarship allowed him to take courses at Massachusetts Institute of Technology, tour the United States, and work for a Milwaukee firm. After returning to Copenhagen, he opened his own drawing office, and worked briefly for the State Building Research Institute.

In the late 1950s Larsen collaborated with three contemporaries: Gehrdt Bornebusch, Max Brüel, and Jørgen Selchau. The foursome entered and placed in several competitions, and produced the austere Crematorium Chapel (1960) in Glostrup, an essay in brick and light similar to Sigurd Lewerentz's St. Mark's Church (1960). Henceforth, Larsen worked on his own; one of his first works to be built was another funeral chapel, this time in Århus (1967).

In the 1960s Larsen was a guest professor at Yale and Princeton universities, where he would have encountered American architects Louis Kahn, Robert Venturi, and Michael Graves. Quite likely, it was there he gained exposure to and developed an interest in literary theory, which he has since claimed as a preoccupation. Architecturally, this took the form of structuralist designs that dealt with issues of flexibility, growth, and legibility of form. The clearest examples of Larsen's structuralist thinking are two school projects: Høje Tåstrup Grammar School (Denmark, 1981) and Trondheim University (1978). In 1970 Larsen won the Nordic competition for the design of Trondheim University in Norway, but only a portion of this megascaled campus plan was realized. One of his finest works, it explores the use of industrialized building elements (prefabricated concrete, steel, and glass), and accommodates growth by extending its gridded modules and glazed street. Resemblances to Vittorio Gregotti's University of Calabria design (1974) of the same period are manifest.

In the 1980s a more whimsical side of Larsen's work emerged, comparable to the historicist Postmodern work of Venturi, Graves, and British archtitect James Stirling. His designs from this period, such as the Nation Center in Nairobi, Africa (1993), and Dalgas Have housing Frederiksburg, Denmark (1991), are characterized by figural and ornamental experimentation. They

Ministry of Foreign Affairs, Riyadh, Saudi Arabia; sloped ramp-stair leads to the ministry's entrance (1984)
© Aga Khan Trust for Culture

are frequently charming and possess a storybook quality akin to Aldo Rossi's work, but without the melancholic side. Larsen realized one of his most important works in the immense Ministry of Foreign Affairs (1984) in Riyadh, Saudi Arabia, which fuses a Danish sensibility with a deferential interpretation of Islamic culture.

In the 1990s Larsen returned to an emphasis on the tectonic expressiveness of material and form. As a result, recent work has been some of his most vital, and includes the addition to the Ny Carlsberg Glyptotek (1996) Copenhagen, the Enghøj Church, (Nordby, 1994), and the BT Building (Copenhagen, 1994).

Spatial themes unify Larsen's diverse oeuvre, which includes the use of elemental forms such as the cone and cylinder, as the rotunda and hinge, the monolithic treatment of the exterior, siting on a plinth, and organization along a glazed interior street. By utilizing daylight, Larsen at times initiates a processional sequence through the building: an ascent toward the light.

The tone of Larsen's buildings is usually monumental, harkening back to ancient and Enlightenment sources (such as 18th-century architects Charles Nicholas Ledoux and Etienne-Louis Boullée). The expression of weight is manifested through battered walls and exaggerated cornices, and is a theme found in Scandinavian Doricist architecture, which is an evident reference for Larsen. For example, he reinterprets the spatial and decorative ideas (drum and block) of Erik Gunnar Asplund's Stockholm Library (1927) in his Malmö Library (1997) in Sweden.

On a similar note, Larsen's Gentofte Library (1985) refers to Alvar Aalto's library at Viipuri. In both cases, a mezzanine wraps around an atrium that contains book stacks. Larsen repeats this arrangement in smaller scale to make an exhibition space. The ubiquitous half vault and circular skylights, as well as the reading room tables and chairs designed by Aalto, reflect the Finnish architect's influence on Larsen. The Gentofte exterior makes use of traditional Danish construction techniques that Aalto appropriated as his own: brick walls rendered with a thin layer of white stucco.

Larsen's buildings are usually white, with occasional splashes of blue for interest. Much like the rendered walls, material texture and geometric pattern are part of his decorative palette. The buildings manage to connect to the primitive traditions inhabiting the Nordic landscape, and suggest new possibilities.

KATE NESBITT

See also **Aalto, Alvar (Finland); Asplund, Erik Gunnar (Sweden); Graves, Michael (United States); Jacobsen, Arne (Denmark); Stirling, James (Scotland and England); Structuralism; Venturi, Robert (United States)**

Biography

Born in Brejning, Denmark, 20 August 1925. Educated at the Technical College, Copenhagen; attended the School of Architecture, Royal Academy of Fine Arts, Copenhagen; studied under Eduardo Catalano, Architectural Association School, London 1950–51; studied under Pietro Belluschi, Massachusetts Institute of Technology, Cambridge 1952; private practice, Copenhagen from 1952; director, Skala Gallery, Copenhagen; editor, *Skala* magazine, Copenhagen. Associate lecturer, 1959–68, professor of architecture, 1968–95, Royal Academy of Fine Arts, Copenhagen. Honorary fellow, American Institute of Architects 1991; honorary fellow, Royal Institute of British Architects 1991. Aga Khan Award for Architecture 1989.

Selected Works

Crematorium Chapel, Glostrup, Denmark (with Gehrdt Bornebusch, Max Brüel, and Jørgen Selchau), 1960
Funeral Chapel, Århus, 1967
University of Trondheim Campus (first prize, 1970 competition; partially built), 1978
Høje Tåstrup County Grammar School, Denmark, 1981
Ministry of Foreign Affairs, Riyadh, Saudi Arabia, 1984
Gentofte Library, Gentofte, Denmark, 1985
Dalgas Have Housing Complex, Frederiksburg, Denmark, 1991
Nation Communications Center, Nairobi, Africa, 21993
Enghøj Church, Randers Nordby, Denmark, 1994
BT Building, Copenhagen, 1994
Ny Carlsberg Glyptotek (addition), Copenhagen, 1996
Kolonihavehus, Kolonihaven Architecture Park, Denmark, 1996
Malmö Library (addition), Malmö, Sweden, 1997

Selected Publications

"Lessons from the Orient," *Daidalos* (15 December 1983)
"Henning Larsen on Architecture," *Living Architecture* 4 (1984)

Further Reading

Articles on Larsen have appeared in more than a dozen journals in different languages. The special issue of *Arkitektur DK* devoted to Larsen's work provides a good overview of 15 recent projects and is fully translated. The articles in *Living Architecture* offer thorough coverage of projects in English. Lund's comprehensive monograph is well illustrated but is written entirely in Danish.

Abel, Chris, "Modernism in the Danish Manner," *Architectural Record* 6 (1990)
Arkitektur DK 40, no. 6A (1996)
Davey, Peter, "Sculptural Street," *The Architectural Review* 200, no. 1198 (December 1996)
"Henning Larsen/Henning Larsens Tegnestue: Malmö City Library," *A + U* 335 (August 1998)
"Henning Larsen: University of Trondheim, High School in Høje Tastrup," *A + U* 148 (January 1983)
"Henning Larsen's Tegnestue A/S, University of Trondheim," *GA Document* 4 (1981)
Khan, Hasan-Uddin, "Nation Center, Nairobi," *Mimar* 30 (December 1988)
Lund, Nils-Ole, *Arkitekt Henning Larsen*, Copenhagen: Gyldendal, 1996
Morton, David, "P/A Portfolio: Desert Buildings," *Progressive Architecture* (May 1987)
Petersen, Steen Estvad, "The Ministry of Foreign Affairs, Riyadh," *Living Architecture* 4 (1984)
Præstegaard, Ida, "The B.T. Newspaper Building in Copenhagen," *Living Architecture* 14 (1995)

LAS VEGAS, NEVADA, UNITED STATES

Las Vegas, Nevada, began the 20th century as a speck on the map and ended the century as the United States' fastest-growing city. From an Old West outpost to a resort town to the most improbable of Sunbelt metropolises, Las Vegas has become a celebration of unrestrained entrepenurism and unashamed individualism to some and a dystopia dedicated to the exploitation of human frailty to others. At its extremes, Las Vegas is both these things, but it is much more, and its history is far more complex and rich than is usually expected.

The city has always been a road town. Las Vegas (the name means "the meadows" in Spanish) started as a supply stop along a wagon road between Salt Lake City and Los Angeles. Originally settled by the Mormons in 1855, attempts to make the village an agricultural center failed, but its location at the division point of a stage route and later the San Pedro, Los Angeles, and Salt Lake Railroad ensured the town a commercial life long after the Mormons headed back north to Utah. The railroad, under the directorship of William Clark, inaugurated the town's modern existence, for, after locating its repair shops and yards in the valley, it subdivided its excess holdings at Las Vegas into a grid of parcels sold at public auction. The purchasers of these lots incorporated the town in 1905 and constructed the first city, a brick and wood-frame western town similar to hundreds of others built all over the West between the end of the Civil War and World War I.

This sleepy town gradually improved its physical infrastructure throughout the 1910s and 1920s and made a few overtures toward capturing a share of the tourist trade that was developing in the Southwest following the adoption of the automobile. The underlying economic structure of the town did not change until the late 1920s, when the site of Hoover Dam was fixed at 30 miles outside of the city limits. Although dam workers and their families were required to live at Boulder City, the Bureau of Reclamation's straight-laced planned community near the work site, the project's many single, male workers sought entertainment in Las Vegas. Prophetically, just as the dam's workforce was assembled in 1931, the Nevada state legislature legalized gambling throughout the state; that same year, a half-dozen bars and gentlemen's clubs obtained gambling licenses along Fremont Street in Las Vegas.

These first gambling establishments were not large structures, and they represented themselves as an extension of the city's Southwestern heritage rather than something new or apart; in fact, many of them were remodelings of preexisting saloons or commercial buildings. The exteriors were predominantly Mission Revival or Western ranch in feeling, although the interiors often attempted a sophisticated moderne, in imitation of the latest in elegant European gaming locales. These institutions were strictly entertainment venues, and although they might contain a supper club or a restaurant on the premises, patrons spent the night (or the following morning) elsewhere downtown. After 1940, these patrons were more often then not defense workers or uniformed personnel as Las Vegas became host to a number of defense industries and several important military bases north of town.

Not all of the early entertainment development was downtown. With a series of reform governments in the late 1930s, gaming establishments sprang up outside the city limits on the Los Angeles highway, beginning the transformation of the highway into the Strip, or more formally, Las Vegas Boulevard. The first significant venue, Los Angeles hotelier Thomas Hull's El Rancho Vegas, established as early as 1941 the type of the hotel-casino in its Las Vegas incarnation. Hull's architect, Wayne McAllister, cast the sprawling motel and casino in the image of a oversized dude ranch. The buildings themselves were low-slung arcaded stucco ranges situated around the Spanish Revival main building, which contained the dining room, showroom, and all-important casino. The structure was further distinguished from the rooms by a windmill tower, which proclaimed the name of the complex high above the street in brilliant neon. Inside, the El Rancho reinforced the Old West theme with heavy wooden furniture, wrought iron fixtures, open timber trusses, and murals; the impression was that of a 19th-century hacienda that had somehow sprouted craps tables and roulette wheels.

After the war, the development of the hotel-casino accelerated with the arrival of Eastern syndicate money. While Bugsy Siegel extended Capone-Luciano interests into Las Vegas in 1941, his development of the Flamingo in 1947 cemented organized crime's commitment to the Strip. Architecturally, the Flamingo announced a new sensibility—the Old West imagery of the El Rancho or Fremont Street was traded in for a highly chromatic interpretation of International Style modernism, as practiced in Los Angeles. Architects George Vernon Russell and Richard Stadelman set two- to four-story room wings around a lush, landscaped courtyard that gave pride of place to the swimming pool. At the head of the composition was the casino and restaurant. Sleek and contemporary, the main building set off stone masses against a sea of crystalline glass and dramatic cantilevers. Above the low roof soared a neon sign nearly three times the height of the building, which marked the site with a sophisticated authority.

The Flamingo was the first of five establishments along the Strip that established the hotel-casino typology. The Thunderbird, Desert Inn, Sahara, and Sands each expanded on the Flamingo's prototype. Guests located each property from the highway by means of a sign-tower that was often integrated into the main structure; many of these were designed and executed by the Young Electric Sign Company (YESCO). They drove under a sweeping porte-cochere, left their car with an attendant, and entered a themed lobby. To one side, one usually found the bar and restaurant, to the other the casino proper. A new feature, the showroom, was located on the far side of the casino, ensuring that patrons would linger at the tables after their intimate encounter with Dean Martin or Nat King Cole. As competition along the Strip grew more fierce, getting noticed along the highway became ever more important, as postcard views of the period suggest. The Thunderbird incorporated a stylized sculpture on its sign, starting a trend toward three-dimensional signs that would eventually engulf the building. The design of these new hotel-casinos became so startling that by 1953 the Flamingo was out of date; Perriera and Luckman designed a new colonnade and sign for the building, as well as the famous champagne tower, a cylinder of neon. Sadly, this new Flamingo would be superceded in its turn by the mid-1960s.

The architectural innovations found in the casino buildings were not extended to the rooms in these early properties. Until the mid-1960s, the rooms were simply arrayed in low two- or three-story motel ranges, often completely detached from the casino building. Towers began to pop up on Fremont Street, where building sites were compact and casino floor space at a premium. Few towers were built on the Strip, but the nine-story Riviera, designed by Roy France and Son in 1955, was an exception. The master of the Las Vegas tower hotel was Martin Stern Jr., who created crisp International Style complexes for the Sahara (1959), the Sands (1967), the International (1969), and

Hotel Flamingo Patio, Las Vegas, Nevada, designed by George Vernon Russell (1946)
© Bettmann/CORBIS

the first MGM Grand, now Bally's Las Vegas (1973). The International (later the Hilton Las Vegas) heralded the corporate future of the Las Vegas casino, in that it was 1500 rooms big, featured an impressive porte-cochere, and had an extensive landscape surrounding it. The MGM Grand was even larger and greeted guests with an eight-lane porte-cochere and an Aztec pyramid (all of which was consumed in a disastrous fire in November 1980). Although the International and the Grand were successful convention hotels, they were not the Las Vegas resorts most tourists came to town to experience.

One property of the 1960s led the way back to the themed future of the Strip—Caesars Palace. Opened in 1966 and expanded throughout the following decade, Caesars fused historical and modern architectural and artistic imagery to create an entire environment. The architecture was not strictly Roman, Baroque, Beaux-Arts, or Mussolini Modern, but a fusion all of this and the classically minded modernism of Edward Durrell Stone, Minoru Yamasaki, and Philip Johnson as well. Developer Jay Sarno and architect Melvin Grossman attempted to exceed the expectations and fantasies of the middle-class tourist, who might muse that this was what Rome might have been like if Hadrian had precast concrete and air conditioning and if the Vestal Virgins had taken up employment as keno runners. The project announced its presence with an enormous temple-front

sign designed by YESCO; visitors were hailed as honored citizens of Rome by overscaled centurions as the pulled into the property. Arrival was monumentalized by the quatrefoil pools and soaring fountains of the entry court, which was further punctuated by faux-Roman statuary. Visitors entered the hotel-casino on axis under a long, sweeping elliptical porte-cochere that provided counterpoint to the circular 14-story hotel block beyond. The saucer-domed lobby was trimmed in electric light and defined by stylized Ionic columns. One ventured beyond to the gaming pits and Cleopatra's Barge, an Egyptian-themed cocktail lounge calculated to make would-be Richard Burtons and Elizabeth Taylors swoon.

It was to the post-Caesars Palace Las Vegas that Robert Venturi, Denise Scott Brown, and Stephen Izenour and their students traveled in 1968. Their study of the structure of the Strip and its implications for late-20th-century American development became the landmark book *Learning from Las Vegas*. The Yale-based team of academics, practitioners, and students came to Las Vegas to analyze the Strip's then-novel spatial distribution. They found that the Strip represented a new automobile-based scale of building, in which architectural imagery had to deliver its message at 40 miles an hour. Buildings were widely spaced to gain an identity in the highway blur, but given the architectural standardization of the hotel-casino type, it was the elaboration of the sign that provided each property with its identity and introduced the traveler to the fantasy environment to be found beyond the porte-cochere. Thus, the sign at Caesars Palace not only conveyed the textual facts of the property's name and the lounge acts of the week, but its Ionic columns (with a Doric entablature) set the theme, and its centurions beckoned the driver to share the wholesome decadence of the empire as promised by the property's costumed staff and advertising campaign.

The book's most lasting concepts are that of the "duck" and the "decorated shed." A "duck" is a building that embodies in form that which it represents, such as duck-shaped egg store on Long Island that gave the type its name. A "decorated shed" is a building that announces its contents on its exterior surfaces, a melding of signifier and structure. The casinos of Las Vegas were seen to be mostly decorated sheds, some becoming more sign than building, such as the Golden Nugget, the Mint, or the Stardust. Others became veritable "ducks," such as Harrah's "riverboat" casino on the Strip or the then-new Circus-Circus, which literally contained a circus under its steel big top. Both types illustrated a then-nearly forgotten function of architecture—that architecture describes through form the people and activities housed within it and signifies the relative place of these contents within the political, social, and cosmological structure of the society that creates it. Although the Modern movement discounted the continuing validity of this function, at Las Vegas this traditional function was democratized; with wedding chapels, gas stations, and hotel-casinos all cheek-by-jowl on the Strip, it was the system of signage and architectural imagery that gave it order and that was to be celebrated.

The Las Vegas the Yale explorers experienced in the late 1960s was undergoing great social stress. The development of Las Vegas as the nation's premier resort city was threatened by its segregationist housing patterns and the resorts' past discriminatory patronage and employment practices. A statewide civil-rights law passed in 1965 mandated equal access to accommodations throughout Nevada, which eased the obvious discrimination on the public side of the Strip but did not extend to fair housing or to fair employment practices. It was not until after a series of riots in 1969 and 1970 that open housing laws were achieved, that all of the area's public schools were integrated, and that agreements were reached between the NAACP and the hotel operators and employees' unions to promote nonwhites to nonmenial positions in the bars, restaurants, and gaming rooms.

This lifting of barriers in the 1970s came at a time when Las Vegas was beginning to see competition from other resort cities seeking gaming revenue. Once Atlantic City permitted legalized gambling in 1978, it became clear that the city's hotels would need to cater to an expanded demographic to remain viable. The corporate owners of the hotel-casinos understood that Las Vegas would have to become a year-round family-friendly resort whose bread-and-butter would be the trade show and the convention. The Vegas of Sinatra and Liberace would give way to that of the Cirque du Soleil and Siegfried and Roy. The driving force behind these changes may very well have been Steve Wynn, who launched a number of new hotel-casinos in the 1980s and 1990s. The first of these, the Mirage, located just north of Caesars Palace, was completed in 1988, the first major property to be built on the Strip in 15 years. At the Mirage, Wynn catered both to high-rollers with million-dollar accounts and to families attracted to the lobby's 20,000-gallon saltwater marine tank and Siegfried and Roy's tigers. Although the Mirage's architecture is not heavily themed, the grounds evoke a Polynesian paradise where guests can snuggle up to dolphins and watch a lava-spewing volcano erupt every 30 minutes. Next door, Wynn built Treasure Island, a Caribbean-themed property that is even more kid friendly and whose primary draw is a mock pirate battle right on the Strip. Kirk Kerkorian also competed for the family market in 1993 with the opening of his second MGM Grand Hotel, which takes its imagery from the Emerald City of the Wizard of Oz and that boasts a small theme park in its back lot along Tropicana Boulevard.

By the mid-1990s, the casinos downtown were feeling squeezed by the new development and the declining quality of the urban fabric around them. In 1995 they roofed over Fremont Street with a glass-and-steel arcade designed by Jon Jerde. The "Fremont Street Experience," as it is termed, is best seen at night, when a light show plays across the ceiling, intensifying the visual density of the place. Jerde also lent his design talents to Wynn's Bellagio, an upscale hotel-casino modeled on the town of the same name on Lake Como. Here Jerde and his team integrated a series of exclusive restaurants and shops along a fountain-studded lakefront that sought to create a distinctive and exclusive ambiance to the property. The theming of hotel properties continued throughout the latter 1990s, with particular attention to the recreation of cities. The best of these have carried the theme beyond the "decorated shed" and into the realm of the three-dimensional "duck." At the New York New York, the city's skyline is compressed into an almost cartoonish forest of towers, scaled down and painted up like a Red Grooms sculptural ensemble. The whimsical mood is punctuated by the property's roller coaster, which darts among the towers and copies of the Statue of Liberty and Ellis Island. At the Venetian, the juxtaposition of that city's landmarks is perhaps more troubling, because a veneer of ersatz "authenticity" pervades the work—the monuments are not scaled down, and they take on the form and materials of the original, but their relationship to one another is jumbled.

Whatever the theme, the purpose of all of this architectural simulation is to promote a mood of escapism. This sensibility also pervades much of the Las Vegas valley's recent residential development. Enormous master-planned communities such as Summa Corporation's Summerlin offer controlled-access neighborhoods that are carefully edited to present a marketable lifestyle distinct from older urban places. Summerlin attempts to create a "total community" in which residential, commercial, and recreational uses are balanced against each other and against open space reserves according to the developer's certified land use plan. Eventually the project will contain some two dozen "villages" of about 600–800 acres each grouped around a town center. The architecture of the housing is developer Mediterranean and not particularly distinguished, although a variety of housing types and target income groups is accommodated. The public community amenities, such as Robert Fielden's Library and Performing Arts Center (1993), evoke an emerging Southwest regional modernism and give the town center a greater sense of locality.

If Las Vegas is to have a civic identity apart from the Strip, it will likely come from the city's aggressive campaign to hire name architects for its public buildings. The Las Vegas-Clark County Library District was certainly the most progressive architectural patron in the valley in the 1990s and secured excellent facilities from Antoine Predock, Michael Graves, and other lesser-known practitioners, such as HSA Architects and Welles-Pugsley Architects. The city, county, and state governments also became design-minded in the 1990s and commissioned several interesting civic buildings. Perhaps the most significant of these is the Clark County Government Center (1995) by C. W. Fentress, J. H. Bradburn and Associates. Fentress reinterpreted nearly the entire history of desert architecture in this sprawling 38-acre campus, evoking forms as disparate as the pyramid, the amphitheatre, and the kiva in its red sandstone elements. The building is both serious and theatrical, mediating between the visual artifice of the Strip and the genuine natural beauty of the valley and its encircling mountains.

Few cities better illustrate the state of late-20th-century city building in the United States than Las Vegas. The town serves as the chief exemplar of the modern capitalist settlement—its urban structure is shaped by the circulation of money. Funds that fly into town at McCarron Airport are dropped at the gaming tables northward along the Strip and spent by the hotels' employees in the suburban districts at the periphery. Yet most in the Las Vegas Valley feel a commitment to making the city work as a whole and well-integrated community apart from the gaming industry. To its people, Las Vegas is no Far West boomtown, no life-size Monopoly board, but a real community with a rightful place in the story of the development of the human city.

JEFF TILMAN

See also **Resort Hotel; Scott Brown, Denise (United States); Venturi, Robert (United States)**

Further Reading

Betsky, Aaron, "Vegas, Seriously: Mark Mack Brings Substance to Las Vegas' Skin Deep Suburbs," *Architecture* 88, no. 8 (August 1999)

Curtis, Wayne, "Belle Epoxy: Las Vegas, Nevada," *Preservation* 52, no. 3 (May–June 2000)

Fitch, James Marston, "Highway to Las Vegas," *Art in America* 60, no. 1 (January–Febuary 1972)

Hess, Alan, *Viva Las Vegas: After-Hours Architecture*, San Francisco: Chronicle Books, 1993

Kaplan, Sam Hall, "Summerlin," *Urban Land* 53, no. 9 (September 1994)

Kroloff, Reed, "The Other Las Vegas," *Architecture* 85 no. 4 (April 1996)

Land, Barbara, and Myrick Land, *A Short History of Las Vegas*, Reno: University of Nevada Press, 1990

Moehring, Eugene P., *Resort City in the Sunbelt: Las Vegas, 1930–1970*, Reno: University of Nevada Press, 1989

Porter, Douglas R., "Betting on Growth," *Urban Land* 57, no. 6 (June 1998)

Stern, Julie D., "Fremont Street Experience: Reviving Downtown Las Vegas," *Urban Land* 55, no. 8 (August 1996)

Venturi, Robert, Denise Scott Brown, and Steven Izenour, *Learning from Las Vegas*, Cambridge, Massachusetts: MIT Press, 1972

Villiani, John, "On a Roll: In Las Vegas, the Casino-Resort Concept Is Reaching New Heights," *Urban Land* 59, no. 3 (March 2000)

Wright, Lance, "Robert Venturi and Anti-Architecture," *Architectural Review* 153, no. 4 (April 1973)

LASDUN, (SIR) DENYS 1914–2001

Architect, England

Denys Lasdun, former president of the Royal Institute of British Architects (RIBA) and a recipient of its Gold Medal, occupies a unique place in the history of British Modern architecture. By virtue of his birth date, his career brackets the introduction and subsequent (in the 1960s) transformation (but not repudiation) of Modern architecture in his country. Trained at the Architecture Association from 1931 to 1934, Lasdun immediately allied himself with the small number of progressive designers in conservative Britain who, in the 1930s, sought to plant on English soil the principles of functionalism, which Lasdun calls "a purifying agent in the architectural process . . . demand[ing] that design be underpinned by reason and research to produce a sane and purposeful architecture" (1984).

Already in the 1930s, Lasdun was strongly influenced by Le Corbusier, who was, despite the arrival in that decade of German exiles such as Walter Gropius, the major continental master for British architects. This admiration continued after World War II, when Lasdun exchanged the purist geometries of the International Style he had briefly embraced (residence in Paddington, 1938, which resembled Le Corbusier's Maison Cook) for the sculptural massing and weathered concrete surfaces associated with Brutalism, also inspired to some extent by Le Corbusier's late work. However, Lasdun did reject the Swiss master's ideas on urbanism, which he felt were flawed by the refusal to acknowledge a sense of place and to forge necessary links with tradition, a critique that was complemented by his concept of the urban landscape, which held that a building's fluid and layered interiors should connect with the space of the city, often through platforms or "strata."

On prestigious and less economically stringent institutional and private commissions, such as the Royal College of Physicians (1964) and the luxury duplexes on St. James' Place (1960), Lasdun incorporated lush granite, travertine, terrazzo, mosaic, and richly tinted engineering brick along with the textured concrete to add color and sensuality to the palette of materials. What binds together all his postwar work is the forceful articulation of program to create asymmetrical compositions of great complexity in plan, section, and elevation that extend assertively into the surroundings, whether urban or rural.

His first significant postwar work, the large primary school in Paddington, was completed in 1955, when it was named "Britain's most modern school." The commission originally had come to the British architectural firm Tecton and was done in collaboration with Lindsey Drake, another former partner of the firm. The varied spaces that comprise classrooms, administrative offices, and the auditorium receive vigorous differentiation in height, shape, materials, and fenestration.

By 1957 Lasdun's vocabulary had shifted to the boldly massed, dynamic, and faceted shapes that visually and conceptually link his work not only with general postwar developments in European architecture but also with the English baroque tradition he explicitly cherished, embodied especially in the work of Nicholas Hawksmoor.

Lasdun continued his commitment to socially oriented projects, at that time energetically sponsored by the government to redress a dramatic housing crisis due to wartime damage. His

Royal National Theatre (1976), London, England
© Michael Nicholson/CORBIS

14-story "cluster" blocks (1955–59) in Bethnal Green, London, were considered very innovative and user-friendly; regrettably, poor maintenance has threatened their continued existence. On each double-height level, four separate sets of two-story apartments are connected by bridges to a central service core. The varied orientation of each of the maisonettes affords unusual privacy to the tenants, and the setbacks of individual facades from the concrete frame identify the spatial system while providing balconies and sun relief. The term *cluster* derives from Kevin Lynch's writings; Lasdun in turn popularized the concept in Britain, where it was used to combat the rigidity of CIAM (Congrès Internationaux d'Architecture Moderne) planning and Le Corbusier's *Ville Radieuse* and to emphasize the importance of context.

One of Lasdun's most admired buildings is the Royal College of Physicians in Regent's Park (1964), which won him the Trustees Medal of the RIBA (1992) and has received Grade 1 listing from English Heritage, a signal honor for a 20th-century work. The need for distinctive public and private rooms, some serving ceremonial and others professional purposes, was the ideal challenge for this architect, who revels in clarifying while expressing intricate multipurpose institutional programs. At the same time, he took pains to respect the scale and color of John Nash's neighboring terraces and to maintain the interplay of nature

and architecture that George IV's brilliant town planner had achieved. His faith that the design could be expanded if necessary without doing damage to the formal coherence of the initial building was proved justified when he seamlessly added a chapter house and lecture theater in 1995.

The Royal National Theatre (1963–76) is another triumph of sophisticated circulation through areas that serve varied functions, although all were intended to enhance the theatrical encounter. If its unremittingly severe gray surfaces have been criticized, its bold concrete cantilevers and lively silhouette eloquently communicate the National Theatre's purpose and cultural prominence. Lasdun created an impressive theatrical mecca that knits together without confusion three auditoriums of diverse sizes and characters, box offices, bookstores, restaurants, cafes, and waiting areas where musical performances and readings take place. In addition, it is an important element in the cityscape of the South Bank; even those who do not enter make use of the multilevel walkways that offer enticing river views and connect pedestrians with Waterloo Bridge. Lasdun sought through the "strata inside and outside . . . to capture the fundamental sense of the theatre as a place of gathering and a framework for the experience of visiting the [National Theatre] which takes the city itself as a backdrop" (1984).

In a postwar Britain that was dramatically expanding traditional universities and establishing new ones, Lasdun also played a highly visible role. For the tabula rasa that was East Anglia University (1962–72) outside Norwich, he designed a complex that encompassed housing for students and staff, the library, lecture theaters, and the University and Senate House, conceiving the building as "hills and valleys." He developed his principle of interlocking spaces and stratified terraces further in the residences at Christ's College, Cambridge (1966). For the University of London in Bloomsbury (1965–79), Lasdun prepared a major extension scheme that includes the Institute of Education and the School of Oriental and African Studies; its aggressive massing, bold play of light and shadow, and creation of an academic square within the embrace of the new buildings make the work a quintessential expression of Lasdun's aesthetic.

HELEN SEARING

See also **Brutalism; Corbusier, Le (Jeanneret, Charles-Édouard) (France); Ville Radieuse (ca.1930)**

Biography

Born 8 September 1914, London; trained at the Architectural Association in London (1931–34), and with Wells Coates, the leading English Modernist (1935–37). Joined the architectural group Tecton (1937) until its dissolution in 1939. Worked in conjunction with Lindsey Drake (1949–59); served as a major in the Royal Engineers, in charge of building the first airfield used in the Allied invasion on D-Day; served as chairman of the MARS (Modern Architectural Research) Group. Won the Trustees Medal of the RIBA (1992) for Royal College of Physicians in Regent's Park; died 11 January 2001.

Selected Works

House, 32 Newton Road, Paddington, London, 1938
Hallfield School (with Lindsey Drake), Paddington, London, 1955
Cluster Tower blocks, Bethnal Green, London, 1959
Duplexes, St. James's Place, Green Park, London, 1960
Fitzwilliam College, Cambridge University, Cambridge, 1961
Royal College of Physicians, London, 1964
University of East Anglia, Norwich, 1972
Royal National Theatre, London, 1976
Extensions, University of London, Bloomsbury, 1979
Extension, Royal College of Physicians, London, 1995

Selected Publications

"Mars Group, 1953–57," *Architect's Year Book* 8 (1957)
Architecture in an Age of Skepticism: A Practitioners' Anthology, New York: Oxford University Press, 1984
A Language and a Theme: The Architecture of Denys Lasdun and Partners, London: RIBA, 1976

Further Reading

Banham, Reyner, *Design by Choice*, edited by Penny Sparke, New York: Rizzoli, and London: Academy Editions, 1981
Curtis, William J.R., *Denys Lasdun: Architecture, City, Landscape*, London: Phaidon, 1994
Curtis, William J.R., *Modern Architecture since 1900*, Oxford: Phaidon, 1982; Englewood Cliffs, New Jersey: Prentice Hall, 1983; 3rd edition, Englewood Cliffs, New Jersey: Prentice-Hall, 1996

Jackson, Anthony, *The Politics of Architecture: A History of Modern Architecture in Britain*, Toronto: University of Toronto Press, and London: Architectural Press, 1970
Peto, James and Donna Loveday (editors), *Modern Britain, 1929–1939*, London: Design Museum, 1999

LE HAVRE, FRANCE

Le Havre was a great seaport town until World War II, when it was besieged by the German forces on 2 September 1944 and occupied until 13 September. The old Le Havre was planned in 1541 on a gridiron principle by Italian engineer Girolamo Bellarmarto, then in political exile in France. With the end of the battle of Normandy and the liberation of Paris, Le Havre was left as one of Europe's worst-damaged port cities. Virtually wiped out, it suffered 146 raids and more than 4,000 deaths, and 9,935 dwellings were totally destroyed and 9,710 damaged. After two years of help from the Allies to clear the destruction, reconstruction began in 1946.

In France, the plan of modernization and reconstruction after the war was conceived on a national scale, although the relation between political and architectural intentions remained vague. Rationalist and neovernacular solutions were largely discredited on account of their associations with Pétainist conservatism, and different towns were assigned to individual modern architects in the late 1940s: Maubeuge to André Lurcat, the heart of St-Dié to Le Corbusier (eventually canceled), and Le Havre (1954) to Auguste Perret, aged 70 when the war ended. The pioneer of reinforced-concrete construction had designed buildings as diverse as Notre Dame du Raincy (1923) and the Théâtre des Champs Elysées (1913), both in Paris. He envisaged a new town that, although keeping the principle of Bellarmato's plan, would achieve a suitable balance between space and volume and between horizontals and verticals and incorporate monuments worthy of a town with a noble history. Perret's original concept involved a vast pedestrian precinct, with all the traffic going underground. The postwar climate of austerity could accommodate neither the cost nor the volume of concrete required. Perret's plan was modified accordingly and realized with the cooperation of his many pupils and disciples.

Le Havre represents Perret's most important postwar work and has served as a model example of 20th-century neoclassical urban planning. The buildings rely on his characteristic simplified classical rationalist vocabulary of frame and panel, which did at least permit a degree of civic rhetoric in the handling of institutions and urban spaces, but the results were considered disappointing by many critics, who saw in the blocks of flats and offices, a drab repetition of an outmoded design aesthetic. One French writer considered it to be "one of the most dismal urban landscapes to be found anywhere in France." In favoring vehicular over pedestrian access, the human scale of Le Havre is somewhat unsympathetic. Furthermore, the concrete has weathered ungracefully.

The Place de l'Hôtel de Ville is one of the largest squares of Europe and does achieve a remarkable architectural unity. It offers wide perspectives made possible by the three-story housing and commercial units whose horizontal roofs are broken by six ten-story towers blocks. The town hall includes a theater and exhibition hall and forms the fourth side of the square. Designed in raw concrete with curtain walls, it has long, low, pleasing lines; a flat roof; and a rectangular tower. A public garden occupies the center of the square, in which a monument to the Resistance has been erected in the center. The Rue de Paris, Le Havre's finest street in the 18th century, leads off the square opposite the town hall and is lined by arcades of luxury shops. The impressive Avenue Foch, Le Havre's Champs-Elysées, opens up to the west, offering a fine perspective toward the Porte Océane. It is a heroic gesture that symbolizes the important part the sea has always played in the life and development of the town.

The Bassin du Commerce, now reserved for pleasure craft, has been made the focal point of the new quarter accessible by the Pont de la Bourse, a footbridge. Overlooking the north side of the dock is the Chamber of Commerce, which houses the Stock Exchange; at the end stands the International Centre of Commerce.

The Church of Saint-Joseph (1959), serving as a memorial to the victims of the 1944 bombing as well as a place of worship, was Perret's last work. Although less successful in many ways than Notre Dame at Le Raincy in Paris, its 109-meter octagonal tower, piercing the skyline of the Boulevard Francois I, was considered by Perret to be not only a hieratic symbol but also a pivotal accent in the design of the town. Rising from the square church, the tower, with its hard reticulated surfaces, has been compared with a rocket on a launching pad. The interior structure is strikingly monumental, designed on a square plan, with four groups of four towers supporting the base of the bell tower, which forms an 84-meter lantern tower. The brute concrete of the interior is exposed, but the walls of the church and tower alike are a mosaic of light streaming in through the stained-glass windows, their colors carefully graduated on all four sides of the tower.

At the end of the Boulevard Francois I is one of the unquestionable successes of the new Le Havre. The culture of construction, wedded to technological exploration and to a mechanistic imagery that had emerged in French postwar architecture, is expressed clearly in the Maison de la Culture (1952–61) by Lagneau and Weill. It sought a balance between formal rhetoric and the desire to treat a civic building as a flexible social instrument in glass, steel, and aluminum. The lightness of materials provides a welcome contrast to the inert mass of so many of the other buildings in the town. The roof, designed to provide the best possible light to the galleries inside, is highly original, consisting of six sheets of glass covered by a horizontal slatted aluminum sun blind through which natural light passes, together with electric light, which is subsequently filtered through a series of clear and opaque panels above the glass of the ceiling. The galleries are linked on different levels by gangways, similar to those on the outside of the building and reminiscent of those on board a ship. The building faces the sea through a monumental concrete sculpture, known locally as the "Eye." When opened in 1961, it was the most modern museum in Europe. The interior is planned on the principle of manipulating rather than enclosing space, and screens and partitions can be adjusted to the needs of changing exhibitions. Somewhat appropriately, the museum's fame rests on the work of Eugène-Louis Boudin and Raoul Dufy, 19th-century painters who were born in Honfleur and Le Havre, respectively.

Ste-Adresse extends Le Havre to Cape Hève. The resort and old town has garden-surrounded mansions that form a succession of terraces up to Cape Hève. Le Havre now consists of three maritime terminals, one for cruising ships and the other two for cross-channel ferries, which allowed in 1981 for the movement of more than a million passengers. The opening of the Tancerville suspension bridge (1981) and more recently the Pont de Normandie (1992), connecting the commercial and industrial firms of the Le Havre region with the left bank, has brought additional traffic to the city. Furthermore, the alluvial land along the north bank, extending to Tancerville, affords excellent opportunities for extending the port in the future.

HILARY J. GRAINGER

See also **Notre Dame, Le Raincy; Perret, Auguste (France)**

Further Reading

Ache, Jean-Baptiste (editor), *Perret* (exhib. cat.), Paris, 1959

Champigneulle, Bernard, *Perret*, Paris: Arts et Métiers Graphiques, 1959

Collins, Peter, *Concrete: The Vision of a New Architecture: A Study of Auguste Perret and His Precursors*, London: Faber and Faber, and New York: Horizon Press, 1959

Curtis, William J.R., *Modern Architecture since 1900*, Oxford: Phaidon, and Englewood Cliffs, New Jersey: Prentice Hall, 1982; 3rd edition, London: Phaidon, and Upper Saddle River, New Jersey: Prentice Hall, 1996

Jamot, Paul, *A.-G. Perret et l'Architecture du béton armé*, Paris and Brussels: Vanoest, 1927

Roberts, Nesta, *The Companion Guide to Normandy*, London: Collins, 1980; Englewood Cliffs, New Jersey: Prentice Hall, 1983

Rogers, Ernesto Nathan, *Auguste Perret*, Milan: Il Balcone, 1955

LEGORRETA, RICARDO 1931–

Architect, Mexico

Over the past 40 years, Ricardo Legorreta has created innovative solutions to contemporary building challenges. His work combines architecture, landscape architecture, and interior design, with a respect for the regional climate and the diverse heritage of Mexican society. In projects ranging from private residences to factories, libraries, hotels and resorts, and museums, Legorreta's work stands out for his use of color, water, proportion, light, and planes.

For all its references to a European-derived modernism, Legorreta's work profoundly reflects the images of indigenous Mexico. His designs remain rooted in an understanding of Mexico's pre-Columbian and colonial past. Legorreta studied at the Escuela Nacional de Arquitectura of the Universidad Nacional Autónoma de México, under architect José Villagrán García. Villagrán García, part of the vanguard of the first generation of postrevolutionary Mexican architects, instilled in his students a sense of social responsibility, as well as the moral dimension of architecture. Upon completion of his studies in 1952, Legoretta worked in Villagrán García's studio, becoming a partner in 1955; the results of this collaboration are seen in the functionalist/rationalist Hotel María Isabel (1961).

Legoratta was aware of the limitations of functionalism as practiced in Mexico, particularly what he perceived as its rigidity, universality, and lack of warmth. He sought a new architectural identity that expressed a Mexican sensibility, and one that recognized the nation's diverse, regional components–something that the rationalist.

In his private practice begun in 1959, Legoratta was able to develop his own vocabulary. Among the first buildings completed by his new firm were the Smith Kline and French Laboratories (1964; Mexico City) and factories for Chrysler (1964; Toluca) and Nissan Motors (1966; Cuernavaca). These structures drew on his academic training gained in Villagrán García's studio, as evidenced in their balance, efficiency, and functionality. Further, these buildings contain the first indications of what would become a constant theme in Legorreta's industrial architecture: a concern for those who labor within the buildings. To that end, assembly lines are designed to human scale and work and office space is blended seamlessly.

The Chrysler factory also represents a watershed in Legorreta's development of design solutions that are relevant to Mexican social and physical climates. It was at this point that Legorreta met Luis Barragán, who advised him to invest more attention into the landscape. This led to further refinement of what became known as an emotional or empathic architecture.

Subsequent works in collaboration with Barragán, such as the Camino Real Hotel (1968) in Mexico City, represent a fusion of tradition and modernity. One sees the architect's awareness of

Managua Cathedral, Nicaragua (1993), designed by Ricardo Legorreta
© Peter Aaron/Esto

the central propositions of functionalism imbued with his admiration for the vernacular. In the Hotel Camino Real, Legorreta departed from convention, which dictated high-rise construction. Instead, with pre-Hispanic and colonial forms in mind, he emphasized horizontality. The resulting form blends public spaces effortlessly: the horizontal emphasis allows for lavish gardens, patios, pools, and fountains, all accentuated by a brilliant use of color, which commences with a startling magenta screen at the hotel entrance. The interior is an intimate refuge, given his attention to interior light, to details in the design of furnishings, and in the placement of artworks (including murals by Rufino Tamayo and Mathias Goeritz, and sculpture by Alexander Calder.) Together these elements infuse this work with a sense of mystery and of warmth, elements that characterize Legorreta's style.

These elements are also prominent in later hotels executed by Legorreta's firm, notably the Hotel Camino Real Cancún (1975) and the Hotel Camino Real Ixtapa (1981). These hotels are graceful adaptations to their sites, whether placed between the sea and a lagoon, as at Cancún, or following the slope of the face of a cliff, as in Ixtapa. The results harmonize with the environment, mediating interior and exterior spaces. The Ixtapa site features expansive, welcoming, open public areas, as well as terraces and walkways to the beach, and pools that invite exploration and contemplation of the dramatic setting.

A similar integration of building and site is apparent in Legorreta's industrial architecture of the 1970s and 1980s. Projects such as the IBM factory (1975) in Guadalajara, Kodak Laboratories (1975) in Mexico City, and the Renault factory (1984) in Durango, manifest this tendency in diverse environments. In the Renault factory, Legorreta drew inspiration from the desert site; the final form is a striking composition of massive red and ochre walls, whose mass complements the limitless desert horizon, providing protection from harsh elements as well as an affirmation of the desert itself. The cobblestone landscape continues the desert hues and textures, joining building to site in a manner that would be impossible to achieve solely with vegetation.

In 1985 Legorreta Arquitectos began one of their most extensive works: the master plan for Solana in Dallas, Texas, and the design of the Solana Village Center and the IBM National Marketing and Technical Support Center. Legorreta's master plan was intended to evoke traditions of the Hispanic southwest, avoiding the anonymity, sterility, and boredom, often evident in office and mixed-use complexes. The result, created on a site measuring some seven million square feet, succeeds in linking modern construction techniques with a sense of timelessness. The Solana Village Center, reminiscent of Mexican colonial-era plazas, presents a hotel with clusters of office and retail buildings, where brown and white stucco exteriors harmonize with the colors and textures of the prairie landscape.

In Legorreta's residential work a personal, contemplative side emerges, illustrating the extensive talent of this architect. To this point, the Molinas (1973), Montalban (1985; Los Angeles), and Greenberg (1991; Los Angeles) residences demonstrate his fluidity in designing for distinctive physical environments and cultures. Massive walls preserve privacy and offer scant clues as to the function of a particular segment, in keeping with the Mexican vernacular traditions. Light and color create warmth; walls are often perforated by lattices, balanced further by the gentle flow of water into pools. As in his large scale works, the result is an organic composition, ably blending art and architecture, exterior and interior, light and shadow.

PATRICE OLSEN

See also **Barragán, Luis (Mexico); Mexico; Mexico City, Mexico**

Biography

Born in Mexico City, 7 May 1931. Educated at the Universidad Nacional Autónoma de México, Mexico City 1948–52; degree in architecture 1952. Married Maria Luisa Hernandez 1956: 6 children. Draftsman, 1948–52, project manager, 1953–55, for José Villagrán García, Mexico City; partnership with Villagrán 1955–60. Freelance architect, Mexico City 1961–63; principal, Legorreta Arquitectos, Mexico City from 1963; principal, Legorreta Arquitectos Diseños, Mexico City from 1977; Los Angeles office established 1985. Design professor, 1959–62, chief of the experimental architecture group, 1962–64, Universidad Nacional Autónoma de México, Mexico City; visiting professor at numerous universities in North America and Spain. Distinguished honorary fellow, Mexican Society of Architects 1978; honorary fellow, American Institute of Architects 1979; juror, Pritzker Prize from 1983; member, consultant committee, J. Paul Getty Museum, Los Angeles 1986; member, Urban Development Council of the Miguel Hidalgo Delegation, Mexico City 1989; member, International Jerusalem Committee 1989; adviser to the president of CNCA, Mexico City 1992; honorary member, Academy of Arts, Mexico. Awarded the AIA Gold Medal in 2000.

Selected Works

Hotel María Isabel, Mexico City (with Villagrán García), 1961
Chrysler Factory, Toluca, Mexico, 1964
Smith Kline and French Laboratories, Mexico City, 1964
Nissan Mexicana Office and Manufacturing Building, Cuernavaca, Mexico, 1966
Camino Real Hotel, Mexico City (with Luis Barragán), 1968
Molinas House, Mexico City, 1973
IBM Factory, Guadalajara, 1975
Kodak Laboratories, Mexico City, 1975
Camino Real Hotel, Cancún, 1975
Camino Real Hotel, Ixtapa, 1981
Renault Factory, Gomez Palacio, Durango, Mexico, 1984
Montalban House, Los Angeles, 1985
Westlake Park Master Plan, Texas (with others), 1985
IBM Offices, Solana, Westlake-Southlake, 1988
Solana Village Center, Westlake-Southlake, 1988
Contemporary Art Museum, Paloma, Mexico, 1991
Greenberg House, Los Angeles, 1991
El Papalote Children's Museum, Mexico City, 1992
Managua Cathedral, Nicaragua, 1993
Max Palevsky Residential Commons, University of Chicago, 2001

Selected Publications

"Legoretta Remembers Barragán," *Progressive Architecture* 70/2 (February 1989)
"The Wall in Mexico," *Architecture and Urbanism* 265 (October 1992)

Further Reading

Amtmann, Gloria, "Hacer una arquitectura congruente con el país," *Razones*, 62 (May 1982)
Antoniades, Anthony, "Ricardo Legorreta: una arquitectura mexicana," *Summa*, 235 (March 1987)
Bayón, Damián, and Paolo Gasparini, *Panorámica de la arquitectura latino-americana*, Barcelona: Blume, 1977; as *The Changing Shape of Latin American Architecture: Conversations with Ten Leading Architects*, translated by Galen D. Greaser, New York and Chichester, West Sussex: Wiley, 1979
Burian, Edward R. (editor), *Modernity and the Architecture of Mexico*, Austin: University of Texas Press, 1997
Díaz de Ovando, Clementina, "El Palacio de Iturbide," *Artes de México*, 21 (1972)
"Entrevista al Arq. Legorreta y al Arq. Castro," *Arquitectos de México*, 28 (August 1967)
Gasparini, Graziano, *Muros de México*, Mexico City: San Ángel Ediciones, 1978
"IBM Guadalajara," *Obras*, 55 (July 1977)
Legorreta Vilchis, Ricardo, *The Architecture of Ricardo Legorreta*, edited by Wayne Attoe and Sydney H. Brisker, Austin: University of Texas Press, and Berlin: Ernst, 1990
Mutlow, John V. (editor), *Legorreta arquitectos*, Naucalpan, Mexico: Gili, 1997; as *Ricardo Legorreta, Architects*, New York: Rizzoli, 1997; as *The Architecture of Ricardo Legorreta*, London: Thames and Hudson, 1997
Noelle, Louise, *Ricardo Legorreta, tradición y modernidad*, Mexico City: Universidad Nacional Autónoma de México, 1989
Smith, C. Ray, "The Mexican Minimalism of Ricardo Legorreta," *The Architectural Record*, 160 (October 1976)
Smith, Clive Bamford, *Builders in the Sun: Five Mexican Architects*, New York: Architectural Book, 1967
Toca Fernández, Antonio, "Ricardo Legorreta," *La arquitectura mexicana del siglo, XX*, edited by Fernando González Gortázar, Mexico City: Consejo Nacional para la Cultura y las Artes, 1996

LEONIDOV, IVAN ILICH 1902–59

Architect and urban designer, Russia

Ivan Leonidov began his formal art studies in the *Svomas* (free art studios) in Tver and continued his education from 1921 until 1927, at the VKhUTEMAS (Russian acronym for Higher State Art and Technical Studios or workshops) in Moscow. It was there, in the studio of Aleksandr Vesnin, that his interests shifted from painting to architecture.

Leonidov's diploma project for the Lenin Institute and Library (1927) captured widespread attention and brought him public prominence. Featured at the 1927 Exhibition of Contemporary Architecture in Moscow, the precocious scheme received further recognition after its publication in the Constructivists' architectural journal, *Sovremennaia arkhitektura* (Contemporary Architecture).

Leonidov's design for the Lenin Institute, situated in the Lenin Hills near Moscow, envisioned a centrifugal arrangement of buildings connected to the slender and centrally placed book-stack tower of the library. An elevated monorail connected the institute to the city below and communicated with it by using the best telephone systems of the time. His proposal also included a science theater with a planetarium, various laboratories and offices for the research personnel, and a spherical glass auditorium, audaciously supported by an inverted conical structure.

From 1927 to 1930 Leonidov taught at the VKhUTEMAS and was one of the editors of *Sovremennaia arkhitektura*. During this period he produced unexecuted designs for a variety of building types: the Sov-Kino Film Production Complex (1927), the Tsentrosoyuiz Headquarters (1928) in Moscow, and the Government Center in Alma-Ata (1928), projects for the Christopher Columbus Monument in Santo Domingo (1929), and the House of Industry in Moscow (1929). His design for Moscow's extensive Proletarsky district provided a full range of recreational facilities for workers living in a comprehensively planned environment.

As an active member of the Constructivist Objedinenie sovremennykh arkhitektorov (OSA; Society of Contemporary Architects), Leonidov's designs were a species apart. While the other Constructivists tended to conceive of buildings as dynamic combinations of functionally and geometrically distinct spaces, Leonidov isolated the programmatic elements into simplified, freestanding figures. The Constructivists generally articulated the structure, and differentiated the cladding of their dynamicbuildings. Leonidov, however, preferred to neutralize the surfaces of his buildings, creating visual interest by vigorously contrasting the scale, geometric form, and orientation of the buildings themselves.

Leonidov's notable urban designs include a project for a Palace of Culture in Moscow and plans for the city of Magnitogorsk; both were designed in 1930 but remained unexecuted. Located in the Urals, a new industrial center was conceived as a linear city, extending from an industrial core out into the countryside. It featured a broad residential spine that was placed between two parallel zones reserved for parks, athletic facilities, community service buildings, and the main highway. Streets were placed perpendicular to this highway, and divided the city into sectors, with each superblock defined by its zoning. The scheme allowed for linear, incremental growth by the addition of new sectors as the need arose.

In the early 1930s, Leonidov's projects became embroiled in the debate between the "urbanists," representing traditional planning ideas, and the "disurbanists," who were supporters of new urban paradigms. When the Soviet government began withdrawing support for modernism, Leonidov's proposals drew increasing criticism. In the official press, "Leonidovism" became a derogatory term usually applied to projects deemed idealistic, financially naive, utopian, or formalistic.

Leonidov responded to the critics by submitting a project of striking originality for a 1934 design competition. The competition was for the headquarters of the Ministry of Heavy Industry (Dom Narkomtiazhprom), sited in Red Square, Moscow's most important and sensitive site. For this project, Leonidov drew inspiration from the vernacular buildings of medieval Russia, and sought to engage the Kremlin, Lenin's Mausoleum, and the Church of St. Basil in a compositional dialogue. The new ministry—a keystone of Stalin's plans for rebuilding central Moscow—also was intended as a counterpoint to the Palace of the Soviets (1931), sited to the Kremlin's southwest. Had these two projects been built, they would have bracketed the medieval Kremlin between them, and created a symbolically charged juxtaposition celebrating Stalin's regime.

Leonidov's proposal for the Ministry of Heavy Industry consisted of three skyscrapers, each one asserting its particular identity through its distinctive form, structure, and materials. Bridges interconnected the three towers, which rose above an elongated tribune of stepped terraces, created to better view the parades in Red Square. The foremost and tallest tower, built from an exposed skeleton frame, crowned its topmost stories with trusses and radio antennas. Behind it stood an elegantly elongated rotational hyperboloid, its surface completely veneered with bricks of black glass and punctuated by boldly projecting balconies. The third tower, Y-shaped in plan, alternated concave curtain walls of glass against flat end walls of concrete. North of this tower, Leonidov placed an auditorium—a multicolored and modestly scaled rotational hyperboloid—that responded in modern terms to the neighboring Neoclassical Bolshoi Theatre.

From the mid-1930s to the start of World War II, Leonidov worked for Moisei Ginzburg, producing various projects for coastal sites in the Crimea. Of these projects, only the amphitheater and ornamental staircase were built in 1937, for the park of the Ordzhonikidze Sanatorium in Kislovodsk. During this period Leonidov also designed the House for Young Pioneers (1935), built in Kalinin (Tver).

After World War II, Leonidov developed his urban and architectural ideas in a series of sketches titled "City of the Sun," a utopian vision that remained unfinished at his death. As his work became better known in the 1970s, Leonidov's significance in modern architecture became internationally recognized.

K. PAUL ZYGAS

See also **Constructivism; Palace of the Soviets Competition (1931); Russia and Soviet Union; Vesnin, Alexander, Leonid, and Viktor (Russia)**

Biography

Born in Vlasikh, Russia, 9 February 1902. Apprenticed to an icon painter in Tver, Russia; studied art at the *Svomas*, Tver; studied under Aleksandr Vesnin, VKhUTEMAS, Moscow 1921–27. Editor, *Sovremennaia arkhitektura* 1927–30. Instructor, VKhUTEMAS 1927–30. Member, Union of Contemporary Architects (OSA). Died in Moscow, 6 November 1959.

Selected Works

Model Peasant Cottage (competition entry), 1925
Apartment Building (competition entry), Ivanovo-Voznesnsk, USSR, 1926
Belorussian State University Buildings (competition entry), Minsk, 1926
Prototypes for Workers' Clubs, 1927
Lenin Institute and Library (unbuilt), 1927
Sov-Kino Film Production Complex (unbuilt), 1927
Tsentrosoyuiz Headquarters (unbuilt), Moscow, 1928
Government Center (unbuilt), Alma-Ata, USSR, 1928
Christopher Columbus Monument (unbuilt), Santo Domingo, Dominican Republic, 1929
House of Industry (unbuilt), Moscow, 1929
Palace of Culture (unbuilt), Moscow, 1930
Master Plan (unexecuted), Magnitogorsk, 1930
Ministry of Heavy Industry (competition entry, unbuilt), Moscow, 1934
House for Young Pioneers, Kalinin (now Tver), 1935

Selected Publications

"The Ministry of Heavy Industry in Moscow: The Project of Ivan Illich Leonidov: Explanatory Notes about the Project," *Arkhit. SSSR* 10 (1934)

"The Architect's Palette," *Arkhit. SSSR* 4 (1934)

Further Reading

Gozak provides the most comprehensive coverage, including an extensive bibliography of primary sources and secondary literature in Russian.

Cooke, Catherine, "Ivan Leonidov: Vision and Historicism," *Architectural Design* 56 (June 1986)

Gozak, Andrei, and Andrei Leonidov, *Ivan Leonidov: The Complete Works*, New York: Rizzoli, and London: Academy Editions, 1988

Ivan Leonidov, New York: Institute for Architecture and Urban Studies, 1981

Koolhaas, Rem, "A Foundation of Amnesia," *Design Quarterly* 125 (1984)

Latour, Alessandra, "Ivan Leonidov: An Exhibition in New York and Naples," *A + U* 227 (August 1989)

Sik, Miroslav, "The Kremlin's Constructivist Cathedral: Ivan Leonidov's Design for the Steel Industry's Commissariat, 1934," *Lotus International* 45, no. 1 (1985)

LEVER HOUSE, NEW YORK CITY
1949–51

Designed by Skidmore, Owings and Merrill; completed 1951

New York, New York

Lever House, at Park Avenue between 53rd and 54th Streets in Manhattan, was built as the American headquarters of Lever Brothers, a British firm of soap manufacturers that became, by the mid-20th century, a company offering various cleaning products. This building established the fashion for glass-walled office towers in the United States. Designed and erected between 1949 and 1951, it is contemporaneous with the United Nations Secretariat, which has two broad glazed surfaces, but while the latter is an institutional and international monument, Lever House is a corporate headquarters constrained by zoning and budgetary rules, and thus the more specific model for many glass-and-steel commercial buildings that followed these pioneers.

Lever House established the reputation of its architects — the firm of Skidmore, Owings and Merrill, and especially of its New York City office where Gordon Bunshaft was the partner in charge of design; William S. Brown was administrative partner for this structure. They worked closely with Lever's American president, Charles Luckman, who had been trained as an architect shortly before the Depression. All three had been young when European modernism was of intense interest to progressive architects, and the client was therefore willing to risk commissioning an unconventional building.

Lever House garnered exceptional publicity for the owners in part because of the unusual surface materials. Greenish glass and stainless steel cover the tower and a low extension, intended for the era's huge computers, that encompasses the perimeter of the site at second story level. The owners publicized the use of their detergents for the continuous program of window washing, for which a worker's "gondola" apparatus anchored to the roof was invented.

Another reason for the unusual attention paid to Lever House was that the building left open space, primarily to the south of the office tower. Inside the rectangle formed by the elevated computer corridor is a small garden bed open to the sky. While meager by standards of famous urban plazas, and while offering no amenities such as seats or tables, the small plaza was nevertheless virtually unheard-of in commercial premises, the open space at Rockefeller Center being the only other example.

Lever House became famous, too, because of its limited size. Lever Brothers did not want to build more than was required for an exclusive corporate headquarters. Because the owners requested no speculative office floor space for rental, the resulting building could be low compared to most postwar structures in midtown Manhattan, where high land costs usually dictate maximal exploitation of the lot. Nevertheless, the interior was spacious enough so that employees at interior desks were located five feet closer to the perimeter windows than was common at the time. A service core at the west occupies the most confined end of the building.

At both Rockefeller Center (Raymond Hood, New York, 1940) and Lever House, the open space was partly a consequence of zoning regulations. Following rules established in 1916, a

Lever House, New York City (1951)
Photo © Skidmore, Owings and Merrill

tower might be built to any height if it covered no more than a quarter of the site; that determined what Lever's tower and the supports for the computer extension do. Other rules required a setback from the building line, hence the widened sidewalk along 54th Street. By contrast, earlier office buildings such as the Chrysler (Van Alen, 1930) and Empire State Buildings (Shreve and Lamb, 1931) fill the lot before setting back gradually to the one-quarter limit. Younger modernists like Luckman, Bunshaft, and Brown preferred the avant-garde geometric slabs inspired by Le Corbusier and Ludwig Mies van der Rohe to commercially conservative setback designs.

Many architects of the period, including some on the Skidmore, Owings and Merrill staff, produced designs combining vertical slabs rising above horizontal extensions, all made of glass and metal. Like Bunshaft, they based these on Le Corbusier's glazed surface at a Salvation Army hostel in Paris, his slab on stilts with a horizontal extension at a Swiss students' dormitory in Paris, and on the glass and metal walls at Mies van der Rohe's Lake Shore Drive Apartments in Chicago.

The proportions eventually chosen for Lever House, and the finesse of the surface—especially given the limited choice of materials at the time—aroused the admiration of critics and the public. The architects were proud of having produced a thin exterior wall, a much-admired achievement of the time, and of having made a sealed building comfortable, thanks to the combination of air conditioning and relatively cool fluorescent lighting that was then available. While a sealed building reduces the interior noise level and penetration of dust, Lever House was sealed for aesthetic reasons. Framed by thin aluminum mullions, the blue-green glass, the only color then available for heat-absorbing glass, made the tower seem ethereal as compared to buildings covered in stone or brick. Some of the original effect is now lost, as much of the glass has had to be replaced because of cracking due to expansion and contraction in sun and shade; some replacements are inharmoniously colored. Glazed spandrels below the windows made the outer surface consistent. Inside the building, the effect of sleek and efficient modernity was enhanced by a sound-absorptive suspended ceiling custom-designed by its manufacturer. Metal flashings to keep water from penetrating the surface, and a nickel-copper alloy to prevent water seepage from the roof showed that the planners were aware of risks to the structure resulting from their unfamiliar design and materials.

While response to Lever House was overwhelmingly positive, dissenters criticized sealed buildings as the consequence of focusing on an idea instead of on the natural needs of human beings. Some lamented the absence of the more abundant plants and sculpture seen in early plans. Others have criticized the detailing as brittle and the color as gaudy as compared to the nearby Seagram Building by Mies van der Rohe, where there is also more generous plaza space. Nevertheless, Lever House was designated an official city landmark in 1982. Repairs are to be made by Skidmore, Owings and Merrill for the present owners, RFR Holding L.L.C., Lever Brothers having vacated all but four floors of the building following a corporate merger with Unilever Home and Personal Care U.S.A.

CAROL HERSELLE KRINSKY

See also **Bunshaft, Gordon (United States); Corbusier, Le (Jeanneret, Charles-Édouard) (France); Mies van der Rohe,** **Ludwig (Germany); Rockefeller Center, New York City; Seagram Building, New York City; Skidmore, Owings and Merrill (United States)**

Further Reading

Barnstone, Howard, "Are Our Buildings Livable?" *Buildings* 54 (1954)

Danz, Ernst, *Architecture of Skidmore, Owings, and Merrill, 1950–1962,* translated by Ernst van Haagen, New York: Praeger, 1962; London: Architectural Press, 1963

"Glass-Walled Skyscraper," *Engineering News-Record* 147 (1 May 1952)

Krinsky, Carol Herselle, *Gordon Bunshaft of Skidmore, Owings, and Merrill,* New York: Architectural History Foundation, and Cambridge, Massachusetts: MIT Press, 1988

Mumford, Lewis, "The Sky Line," *The New Yorker* 28 (9 August 1952)

New York (NY) Landmarks Preservation Commission, *Lever House, 390 Park Avenue, Borough of Manhattan,* New York: New York Landmarks Preservation Commission, 1982

LEVI, RINO 1901–65

Architect, Brazil

Rino Levi was one of the pioneers of modern architecture in Brazil. His career spanned more than 40 years, and has made a definitive contribution to the diffusion of modernist ideas within the country.

A son of Italian parents, Levi was born in 1901 in São Paulo, where he studied at the Colégio Dante Alighieri before traveling to Italy to continue his studies. While in Italy, he studied at the Polytechnic School of Milan before moving to the superior School of Architecture in Rome. This was the first unified school of architecture in Italy, founded with the objective to unite the academic teaching tradition with a rigorous technical-scientific framework. Levi studied under Marcello Piacentini and graduated in 1926. That same year, he returned to São Paulo, and he remained there for the rest of his life, contributing to the architectural configuration of that metropolis.

In the years following 1926, he, along with Russian emigrant Gregori Warchavchik, was one of the few defenders of the renewal of formal and technical architecture in Brazil. However, Levi differed from Warchavchik and did not devote himself to the diffusion of ideals through manifestos but concerned himself with building a solid professional career. The influence of the Italian architectural culture is notable in Levi's works, and although his ideas refute the imitation of classicism, he did not deny it as a source of inspiration. Another important inheritance from the Italian tradition was his conception of architecture as volume; it is identified as "weight," which combines with the characteristic "lightness" of Brazilian architecture.

Breaking with the local tradition, Levi was the first architect in São Paulo to devote himself exclusively to the architectural project, separating it from the construction process. Throughout his career, he encouraged the recognition of architecture as a profession. This goal is best represented in the technical elaboration of his projects, and the manner in which he always researched new materials and different construction techniques. He did not attempt to dissociate himself however, from formal questions, and insisted on constant experimentation with many forms, materials, and construction systems. He searched for the most appropriate combinations for each project, and never lapsed into formulaic patterns.

In 1932, Levi designed one of the first skyscrapers in São Paulo—the 10-story Columbus Building (Edifício Columbus) which not only provided structural challenges but also led to careful consideration regarding planning, and comfortable accommodations for the residents. In referencing Italian rationalism, the building can be viewed as formally robed, with flat walls, curved counters, and discrete ornamental details. In this project, we see some of the traits that would mark many of Levi's skyscrapers; these buildings break with the scale of the city, but at the same time they value the urban streetscape, with careful treatment of corners, ground floors, and entrance halls. Among Levi's numerous buildings, the office of the Institute of Brazilian Architects (1947), the Prudência e Capitalização Building (1947), the Trussardi Building (1947), and the Plavinil-Elclor Building (1961) were all situated in São Paulo. In these projects, Levi emphasized concerns relating to the climate, whenever possible, avoiding large expanses of glass, which he saw as inadequate for a tropical climate. Instead, he frequently returned to the use of balconies and *brises-soleil.*

This attention to detail also marks his residential projects and his careful treatment of natural lighting. The residences were usually organized around internal patios and were characterized by their introspective nature; in a sense they denied the existence of the city. The architect integrated interior environment, articulating living space with gardens. His interest in tropical vegetation brought about his long collaboration with Brazilian landscape architect Roberto Burle Marx. Among his residential projects, the architect's own residence (1944), the Milton Gruper residence (1951), and the house of Clemente Gomes (1963–64) represent his best domestic architecture.

Levi was commissioned to design several movie theaters between 1936 and 1941 and turned his attention to acoustics. Some of his most notable cinema projects include the Art-Palácio (1936), the Cinema Universo (1939), and the Cine Ipiranga (1941), which offer perfect audio and visual environments.

The same care and technical concern assisted Levi in becoming a specialist in complex architectural typologies, such as hospitals and factories. In these projects, he developed detailed flow and sectorization studies. This can clearly be seen in his project for the Maternity Building (1945) of the University of São Paulo, which he developed following detailed collaboration with a team of hospital doctors. This building marks a series of similar commissions, including the Cancer Hospital (Hospital do Câncer) (1947) and the Hospital Albert Einstein (1958). His hospital architecture culminated in reviews in several international publications, and led to an invitation by the Venezuelan government to organize the country's system of hospital buildings (1959–60). Among his industrial projects, it is fitting to mention the offices and roasting houses of Café Jardim (1943) and the Laboratório Paulista de Biología (pharmaceutical industry, 1956–59), in which he adopted a fragmented solution with isolated buildings for each function.

In his response to Italian design, Levi always considered architecture within the context of the city. For example, his project for Brasília (1957) won third place in the competition. His design explored the theme of a city with many centers and proposed residential sectors as mega-structures (300 m high, 400 m wide, and 18 m deep) that incorporated a sophisticated system of vertical circulation intended to provide for three street levels. His final project was the Civic Center for the city of Santo André, and resembled the Brasília project in its arrangement of the executive, legislative, and judiciary buildings.

Levi actively participated in the Institute of Brazilian Architects and served as president for two consecutive administrations (1952–53, and 1953–54).

Levi died in 1965 during an exploratory trip to the interior of Bahia. His professional life included more than 230 completed projects. His office continues today under the control of his partners.

LEONARDO B. CASTRIOTA

See also **Brasília, Brazil; Brazil; São Paulo, Brazil**

Biography

Born in São Paulo, Brazil, 31 December 1901. Attended the Academy of Fine Arts, Milan 1921–22; studied at the School of Architecture, Rome; degree in architecture 1926. Established office in São Paulo 1927; partnership with Roberto Cerqueira Cesar 1941; partnership with Luiz Roberto Caravalho Franco

Facade of Institute Sapientiae headquarters (1942), São Paulo, Brazil
© G.E. Kidder Smith/CORBIS

1951. Taught at the University of São Paulo 1954–59; taught at the University of Caracas 1959. Founder and president, Institute of Architects of Brazil; member, Congrès Internationaux d'Architecture Moderne (CIAM). Died in São Paulo, 29 September 1965.

Selected Works

(All buildings in São Paulo)

Columbus Building, 1932
Art-Palácio, 1936
Cinema Universo, 1939
Cine Ipiranga, 1941
Institute Sapientiae Headquarters, 1942
Offices and Manufacturing Plant, Café Jardim, 1943
Rino Levi House, 1944
Maternity Hospital (unexecuted), University of São Paulo, 1945
Institute of Brazilian Architects Office, 1947
Prudência e Capitalização Building, 1947
Trussardi Building, 1947
Central Cancer Hospital, 1947
Milton Gruper House, 1951
Albert Einstein General Hospital, 1958
Laboratório Paulista de Biología, 1959
Plavinil-Elclor Building, 1961
Clemente Gomes House, 1964

Selected Publications

"A arquitetura e a estética das cidades," *O estado de São Paulo* (15 November 1925); also published in *Arquitetura moderna Brasileira: depoimentos de uma geração*, compiled by Alberto Xavier, 1987
"O que há na arquitetura," in *Revista anual do terceiro salão de maio*, 1939
Obras 1928–1940, 1940
"Situação da arte e do artista no mundo," *Colégio* 4 (1948)
Planejamento de hospitais (with Jarbas Karman and Amador Cunha do Prado), 1954
"Justificação arquitetônica," *Revista projeto* 111 (1988)

Further Reading

Many of Levi's works elicited coverage in important architectural journals such as *Architectural Forum, The Architectural Record, Progressive Architecture, L'architecture d'aujourd'hui, Domus, Zodiac, Architettura, Architectural Review, Architectural Design*, and *Die Kunst*. For a detailed inventory of his projects, see Levi.

Anelli, Renato, "Arquitetura e cidade na obra de Rino Levi," *Espaço and Debate* 40 (1997)
Bruand, Yves, *L'architecture contemporaine au Brésil*, Paris: Université de Paris IV, 1971
Corona, Eduardo, Carlos Lemos, and Alberto Xavier, *Arquitetura moderna paulistana*, São Paulo: Editora Pini, 1983
Debenedetti, Emma, and Anita Salmoni, *Architettura Italiana a San Paolo*, São Paulo: Instituto Cultural Italo-Brasileiro, 1953
Goodwin, Philip, *Brazil Builds: Architecture New and Old, 1652–1942*, New York: Museum of Modern Art, 1943; 4th edition, 1946
Levi, Rino, *Rino Levi*, Milan: Edizioni di Comunità, 1974
Mindlin, Henrique, *L'architecture moderne au Brésil*, Rio de Janeiro: Colibris, 1956; as *Modern Architecture in Brazil*, Rio de Janeiro: Colibris, New York: Reinhold, and London: Architectural Press, 1956
Santos, Paulo, *Quatro séculos de arquitetura*, Rio de Janeiro: IAB, 1981
Segawa, Hugo, *Arquiteturas no Brasil, 1900–1990*, São Paulo: Editora da Universidade de São Paulo, 1998; 2nd edition, 1999

LEVITTOWN

New York (1947), Pennsylvania (1951), and New Jersey (1958)

The architecture and planning of the 20th-century American suburb invariably returns to the model communities known as Levittown. In 1947 the first Levittown began to emerge from the potato fields of Hicksville, Long Island. The Island Trees development provided some 17,000 homes for 60,000 residents and included nine swimming pools, numerous "village greens," seven shopping centers, five public schools, a professional-size baseball field, and a town hall. Levitt and Sons moved on to build Levittown, Pennsylvania (1951), and Levittown (now Willingboro), New Jersey (1958). The firm was composed of father Abraham Levitt and sons William and Alfred. All told, the company built some 140,000 houses, mainly in the eastern United States.

Levittown, Long Island, began a trend toward mass-produced suburban developments. In his authoritative history of suburban development, *Crabgrass Frontier*, Kenneth Jackson (1985) argues that "Levittown was the largest housing development ever put up by a single builder, and it served the American dream-house market at close to the lowest prices the industry could attain." The developments were built rapidly; at peak production, Levitt and Sons was able to complete 36 houses per day.

The Levittowns were made possible by a constellation of factors. These included the post–World War II housing crisis, cost-reducing innovations in mass production and building materials, the increasing impact of the automobile and its attendant legislation, a host of new federal legislation designed to resuscitate the housing industry, and a gradual increase in postwar affluence as more Americans joined the middle class. The Levittowns drew somewhat on the planning innovations of 19th-century developments, such as Glendale, Ohio (1851, designer Robert C. Phillips), Riverside, Illinois (1868, designer F.L. Olmsted), and Radburn, New Jersey (1928, designers Clarence Stein and Henry Wright). Radburn, New Jersey, for example, pioneered the concept of the "superblock" and grouped homes in villages with internal parks. In addition, Ebenezer Howard's garden city movement and its preference for open green spaces was a likely influence on Alfred Levitt's later community plans. These early suburban developments, which Spiro Kostof classifies as "planned picturesque," created the appearance of houses in a park (1991).

Unlike most other postwar developers, the Levitts planned their communities with many parks and recreational amenities. Although Levitt and Sons frequently used the term "planned" to hearken back to earlier, more lush and upper-class communities, characteristics of the late 19th-century planned communities, such as curvilinear roadways, staggered house setbacks, landscaped plots, and clubhouses, were only weakly imitated (or absent) in Levittown.

Levittown planning improved over time. Construction in Levittown, Long Island, for example, was initially so rapid that streets were often laid out "as needed." In the Pennsylvania and

Levittown house, Mrs. Dorothy Aiskelly residence at 44 Sparrow Lane, Levittown, NY
© Gottscho-Schlesisner Collection (Library of Congress, United States)

New Jersey developments, community and street planning was much more comprehensive and informed. Levitt and Sons had originally planned to build a model community called "Landia" in Jericho, Long Island. With the building moratorium that accompanied the Korean War, the project was permanently postponed. However, the planning concepts that Alfred Levitt developed for Landia came to inform the firm's future developments in Pennsylvania and New Jersey. The Landia plan divided the community into residential neighborhoods, separated the industrial area from the rest of the community with a "wooded shelter belt," utilized one through street in the interior of the community along with circumferential drives surrounding each neighborhood, provided parks as a separation device between neighborhoods by locating them at the ends of major streets, and included sites for public schools within walking distance of every home (Levitt, 1951).

Following the Landia planning concept, Levittown, Pennsylvania, provided for four high schools and 21 primary and middle schools spaced throughout the community. Recreational areas in the community were placed in locations roughly central to the "neighborhoods," or subsections, of which they were a part. Levittown, Pennsylvania, incorporated parklike "buffer zones" between neighborhoods in the development to enhance the rural

feel of the community and provide additional recreation space. The addition of these natural elements heightened the perceived similarities between Levittown and more upscale housing developments and country suburbs. Community landscaping, orchestrated by Abraham Levitt, was a significant factor in the design of the Levittowns. Furthermore, each house was surrounded by an ample lawn complete with four fruit trees. Levittown, New Jersey, also followed the planning concepts evident in the Pennsylvania development: the master block, residential neighborhoods, park buffer zones, and the provision of school sites.

The lot size available in the Levittown developments was a source of pride for Levitt and Sons. In Levittown, Long Island, houses were built in the center of 60- by 100-foot lots with uniform setbacks from the street. In later developments, such as Pennsylvania and New Jersey, lot sizes varied because of the adoption of a curvilinear street pattern but were still roughly 70 by 100 feet in size. Because property-line fencing was prohibited in Levittown, the generous lots served to provide a sense of privacy for residents and made expansion of the house possible.

Levittown, Long Island, was frequently criticized for the monotony of its home designs and streets. Over time, however, Levitt and Sons offered more exterior variety in its home designs and used circumferential drives to make navigating the development easier. Although Levittown, Long Island, initially provided nearly identical Cape Cod cottages, the 1949 and 1950 ranch houses were built with several exterior elevations involving small variations in the roofline. Different exterior color combinations also contributed to the perception of variety, even though the homes were identical inside. In Levittown, Pennsylvania, despite the fact that houses within neighborhoods were of the same type, the precise external color and shape of a home varied so that "a house of the same shape and color occurs only once in every twenty-eight houses" (Popenoe, 1977).

Another Levittown planning innovation was the integration of different house types on each street. Previous developments typically grouped home types by neighborhood or street. This combination of housing types was the primary innovation of Levittown, New Jersey. Although post–World War II suburbs have been ridiculed for decades, recent scholarship by Barbara Kelly and others suggests that such suburbs provided a strong sense of community and civic awareness.

CYNTHIA DUQUETTE SMITH

See also **Suburban Planning**

Further Reading

The most comprehensive discussion of Levittown is provided by Kelly; this work also includes a detailed bibliography of primary and secondary sources. Gans provides a sociological account of Levittown, New Jersey. A thorough discussion of the Landia planning concept is provided in Levitt.

Gans, Herbert J., *The Levittowners*, New York: Pantheon, 1967
Jackson, Kenneth T., *Crabgrass Frontier: The Suburbanization of the United States*, New York: Oxford University Press, 1985
Kelly, Barbara M., *Expanding the American Dream: Building and Rebuilding Levittown*, Albany: State University of New York Press, 1993
Kostof, Spiro, *The City Shaped: Urban Patterns and Meanings through History*, Boston: Little Brown, and London: Thames and Hudson, 1991
Levitt, Alfred, "A Community Builder Looks at Community Planning," *Journal of the American Institute of Planners*, 17 (spring 1951)
Popenoe, David, *The Suburban Environment: Sweden and the United States*, Chicago: University of Chicago Press, 1977

LEWERENTZ, SIGURD 1885–1975

Architect, Sweden

The work of Sigurd Lewerentz encompasses two of the strongest architectural currents of the 20th century; the first is classicism in its Nordic version, and the second is modernism. It is only recently that Lewerentz has been recognized internationally, and it is only in the final two decades of the 20th century that scholars in regions other than Germany and the Scandinavian countries have paid attention to Lewerentz's prolific work, which is located solely in Sweden.

Lewerentz's sensitivity to materials is a feature that characterized his lifelong work; it undoubtedly was first developed in Sandö, his native town located in the *Vasternorrlands* region of central Sweden. Lewerentz learned the craft of forging at his father's glass factory during the summers of 1905 and 1906. He also, during this time, studied at the Chalmers Technical Insti-

tute in Göteborg, from which he graduated in 1908. While at Chalmers, Lewerentz became very interested in the ideas of the emerging Deutscher Werkbund in Germany. Between 1908–09, he was an apprentice in Munich under Richard Riemerschmid and Theodor Fischer, who were members of the famous group.

In 1910 Lewerentz returned to Sweden and entered the School of Architecture of the Royal Academy of Arts in Stockholm. After one year of classical training, Lewerentz's disagreement with the established classical precepts taught at that institution became evident. He and some of his classmates abandoned the academy and founded the Klara School. There, Lewerentz had the opportunity to explore some of the interests that had been elicited by the Deutscher Werkbund, as well as to share in the ideas from the Klara School movement, which included such figures as Ragnar Östberg, Carl Bergsten, and Ivar J. Tengbom. Among the principal concerns of these architects was the search for regionalism and authenticity through the use of indigenous materials and forms. One of Lewerentz's classmates and contemporaries was Erik Gunnar Asplund (1885–1940), who would become the best-known figure in the development of modern Swedish architecture and played an important role in Lewerentz's career.

In 1915 Lewerentz formed an architectural partnership with Torsten Stubelius. This lasted only two years but produced a significant number of designs, ranging from industrial objects—such as lighting fixtures and glass products—to churches, housing, and landscape interventions. Lewerentz's interests and fascination with industrial design resonated throughout his entire professional career. In the 1920s he developed the IDESTA window system with engineer Cläes Kreuger, and directed its manufacture during the following two decades, at his own factory in Eskilstuna.

During this initial period with Stubelius an important aspect of Lewerentz's practice took shape specifically, his use of drawings to investigate and reveal the possibilities of site, architecture, and object. Thus, drawings became the tool he used to rigorously scrutinize all of the scales of a project, ranging from the topography to the minutest details.

In 1915 Lewerentz, in association with his contemporary Gunnar Asplund, won a competition for the Woodland Cemetery in Enskede, Stockholm. This joint venture produced one of the most significant monumental sacred landscapes of the 20th century and became a locus of intervention by both architects for the next 20 years. Here, Lewerentz built his famous Neoclassical Resurrection Chapel (1926), and he remained responsible for the landscape design of the complex until 1935, when the Cemetery Authority excluded him from the design of the Chapel of the Holy Cross, and two additional minor chapels that were executed by Asplund alone. This unfortunate incident affected Lewerentz deeply, and he never reconciled with either his former friend and partner Asplund, or with the Cemetery Authority.

During the decade of the 1910s as a result of overcrowded cemeteries, traditional burial practices in Sweden were often ignored in favor of cremation. Lewerentz and his partner were responsible for the design of several new cemeteries, crematoriums, and churches. Among these, the Eastern Cemetery (1920–69) in Malmö became his main focus until his death. This cemetery includes neoclassical buildings executed prior to Lewerentz's switch to a modernist vocabulary in the early 1930s.

Despite the fact that the furnishings, architecture, and landscape of Malmö's Eastern Cemetery were designed over a span of half a century, they still speak in unison.

During the 1930s, Lewerentz explored rationalist and functionalist ideas in a variety of projects. They included architectural, industrial, and graphic designs for the 1930 Stockholm Exhibition, architectural projects such as the Malmö Theater (1933–44) with David Helldén and Erik Lallerstedt, the Villa Edstrand (1938–45) in Falsterbo; and large complexes and urban projects, such as the one for Lower Norrmalm, Stockholm (1932). In the early 1940s, Lewerentz's chapels of St. Knut and St. Gertrude (1943) became, as critic Colin St. John Wilson pointed out, the markings of a definitive shift from the neoclassical form to the vigorous and original work that characterized his later output.

Following this commission, Lewerentz withdrew from architecture, emerging again only during the late 1950s. This final energetic and more mature period corresponds with three of his most important works: the Church of St. Mark (1960) in Björkhagen, Stockholm; St. Petri's Church (1966) in Klippan; and his final project, the Flower Kiosk (1969) in Malmö's Eastern Cemetery.

It is undoubtedly St. Petri's Church that is the culmination Lewerentz's career, and it became an emblem of his long years of practice. The building can be considered a repository of sacred and secular memories that the architect used to emphasize the Lutheran rite and liturgy, and was achieved by exploring the experiential aspect of architecture. His primary strategy was the skillful manipulation of details and forms: conventional materials such as brick, mortar, and glass are treated in unorthodox ways, and light and water play an important role in creating an interior atmosphere for procession, introspection, and meditation.

The Flower Kiosk in Malmö's Eastern Cemetery, which unfortunately has been altered now, is Lewerentz's final statement and deals with the possibility of creating maximum sensory impact with minimal repertory of architectural forms and devices. It was executed with a limited vocabulary of materials: concrete, copper, glass, laminated wood, and ceramics. Nevertheless, the Flower Kiosk speaks eloquently—as pointed out by Alison and Peter Smithson—of the broad-mindedness of a man who was one of the silent architects of the 20th century.

RICARDO L. CASTRO

See also **Asplund, Erik Gunnar (Sweden); Deutscher Werkbund; Sweden**

Biography

Born in Sandö, Bjärtrå, Sweden, 29 July 1885. Educated at the School of Building, Chalmers Technical College, Gothenburg, Sweden 1905–08; attended the Academy of Arts, Stockholm 1910; founded and attended the Free School of Architecture, Stockholm under Carl Westman, Ragnar Östberg, Ivar Tengbom, and Carl Bergsten 1910–11. Married Edit Engblad 1911: three children. Worked for Bruno Möhring, Berlin 1907–08; employed by Theodor Fischer, Munich 1909; worked for Richard Riemerschmid, Munich 1910; partnership with Torsten Stubelius, Stockholm 1915–17. Private practice, Stockholm 1917–43; moved practice to Eskilstuna, Sweden 1943–58; moved practiceto Skanör, Sweden 1958–70; private practice,

Lund, Sweden from 1970; founder, director, with Claës Kreüger (1928–35), Idesta Metal Window Company, Stockholm 1928–40 and Eskilstuna 1940–75. Died in Lund, 29 December 1975.

Selected Works

Woodland Cemetery (first prize, competition; with Erik Gunnar Asplund), Stockholm, 1915–35
Eastern Cemetery, Malmö, Sweden, 1920–69
Chapel of the Resurrection, Woodland Cemetery, Stockholm, 1926
Lower Norrmalm, Stockholm, 1932
Villa Edstrand, Falsterbo, Sweden, 1935
Chapels of St. Knut and St. Gertrude, Malmö Cemetery, 1943
Municipal Theater, Malmö (with D. Helldén and E. Lallerstedt), 1944
St. Mark's Church, Stockholm, 1960
St. Petri Church, Klippan, Sweden, 1966
Flower Kiosk, Eastern Cemetery, Malmö, 1969

Further Reading

For a comprehensive view of Lewerentz, see Dymling. This two-volume publication includes essays on the architect as well as photographs of Lewerentz's works with corresponding reproductions of his drawings.

Ahlin, Janne, *Sigurd Lewerentz, arkitekt*, Stockholm: Byggförlaget, 1985; as *Sigurd Lewerentz, Architect, 1885–1975*, Cambridge, Massachusetts: MIT Press, 1987
Codrington, James, "Sigurd Lewerentz, 1885–1975," *The Architectural Review* 159, no. 950
Dymling, Claes (editor), *Architect Sigurd Lewerentz*, 2 vols., Stockholm: Byggförlaget, 1997
Mansilla, Luis Moreno, "Parrahasius' Veil: Lewerentz' Journey to Italy," *9H* 9 (1995)
St. John Wilson, Colin, "Sigurd Lewerentz and the Dilemma of the Classical," *Perspecta* 24 (1988)
Sigurd Lewerentz, 1885–1975: The Dilemma of Classicism, London: Architectural Association Press, 1989

LIANG SICHENG 1901–72

Architect and architectural historian, China

Liang Sicheng has been considered the founder of the modern study of Chinese architecture, including architectural history. Trained in the United States in the practice of architecture before such an option existed in China, Liang was involved in the establishment of China's first architectural schools. He was the teacher of China's first generation of architects, and the only 20th-century Chinese of his generation to achieve significant recognition outside of China, culminating in his involvement in the planning of the United Nations headquarters. Moreover, he was a central figure in the movement to find and identify premodern Chinese buildings and bring them into the global study of architecture. Liang saw some of his goals for China's buildings—and for China as defined by her buildings—come to pass, but others were thwarted by the political chaos that plagued every decade of his life.

Liang Sicheng was born into China's privileged, educated elite. His father, Liang Qichao, was a central figure in China's reform movement. Liang's decision to become an architect was inspired by his future wife, Lin Huiyin (Whei-yin; Phyllis [1904–55]).

In 1927 Liang and Lin met at the University of Pennsylvania while pursuing the same course of studies. She became his chief collaborator, usually executing the architectural drawings for their projects. Liang, Lin, and at least 16 other Chinese students, had chosen the Pennsylvania School of Architecture because of the reputation of Paul Cret (1876–1945). Prior to their return in 1928 to China, Liang and Lin worked in Cret's Philadelphia office, and he spent a year at the Harvard School of Design.

Once home, Liang was charged with founding a department of architecture at Northeast University in Shenyang (Mukden), Manchuria. The curriculum was based on Cret's Beaux-Arts model.

Liang and three other architects who had also trained at the University of Pennsylvania established a firm that immediately received a commission to design a campus for another university in Manchuria. It was during this time, that Liang, first carefully looked at historic Chinese buildings, and he became a local advocate for the preservation of premodern architecture at a time when most of it was being demolished. All this came to an end in 1931, when the Japanese took Manchuria.

That same year, Liang accepted the charge of a Chinese scholar-official in Beijing to form a society for research in Chinese architecture, initiating his career as an architectural historian. With war raging on several sides of Beijing, Liang launched field trips into China's most remote villages, questioning locals about old structures and seeking buildings whose names he had found in historical documents. The work was especially grueling for Liang, who had never fully regained use of a leg he had injured in a motorcycle accident in 1923. No one has tallied how many buildings were recovered during this period, but at least 10 of the pre-12th-century wooden buildings that he measured, drew, and photographed were lost before the end of the war in 1945. Much of the research of this group was published in seven of the volumes of the *Bulletin of the Society for Research in Chinese Architecture*. The last volume was written by hand, during their years in Kunming or Chongqing when the major cities of North China were under occupation or siege. Those articles are still utilized and form the basis for education in the history of Chinese architecture in China and abroad.

Liang's continuous research and writing under wartime conditions did not go unnoticed. During the war Liang was appointed vice chairman of the Chinese Commission for Preservation of Cultural Relics in War Areas. In 1949 he returned to Beijing, and was appointed by the Ministry of Education to head a new department of architecture at Qinghua University, where he developed a curriculum in urban design. Shortly thereafter, he was invited to teach at Yale University. One of his projects was the completion of a history of Chinese architecture, in English. While he was there (academic year 1946–47), he served as the appointed Chinese member on the Board of Design Consultants for UN Headquarters. In 1947 some of his drawings and photographs were exhibited at Princeton University, where he received an honorary degree.

The establishment of the People's Republic of China brought changes that proved more severe than any Liang had experienced during the war. Initially, he was named vice director of the Beijing City Planning Commission his five-point plan was rejected, with the exception of the plan to save the Forbidden City from destruction. Liang had to contend with Soviet advisers at every stage, and he continued to conflict with the party leaders and their antihistorical reform position, but because of his international reputation he was often sent abroad, to the USSR, eastern Europe, Cuba, and South America.

Although Liang Sicheng produced no architectural masterpiece, his legacy is a vision that China would take its rightful place in the contemporary world. The place he envisioned included buildings and urban designs that utilized the most sophisticated technology but did not lose the attachment to China's architectural past. A movement to restore Liang to a place of honor in Chinese history was begun in the 1980s and peaked in 1986, when, in commemoration of the 85th year following his birth, the fourth volume of his collected writings was published. Students and colleagues at Qinghua University issued a set of essays in his honor, and a postage stamp featuring his picture was issued in 1982.

NANCY STEINHARDT

See also **China**

Biography

Born in Tokyo, 20 April 1901. Attended the School of Architecture, University of Pennsylvania 1924–27; master's degree in architecture 1927. Married architect Lin Huiyin 1928 (died 1955). Collaborated with wife 1928–55. Professor of architecture, University of Mukden (Shenyang), Manchuria 192?–31; professor of architecture, Qinghua University, Beijing, from 1949. Married architect Lin Zhu in 1962. Director, the Society for Research in Chinese Architecture, Beijing. Spent the last six years of his life as target of antireactionary, antiacademic attacks at Qinghua University during the Cultural Revolution. Liang's library of writings subsequently destroyed. Died in 1972.

Selected Publications

Song Yingzhao fashi tuzhu (Drawings for the Yingzhao fashi of the Song) *Qingshi yingzhao suanli ji zeli* (Building Regulations of the Qing Dynasty), 1934
Yingzhao fashi zhushi, juan shang (Commentaries to the Yingzhao fashi), 1980

Further Reading

Chen, Mingda, "In Memory of Professor Liang Ssu-ch'eng," *Building in China* 4 (1986)
Fairbank, Wilma, *Liang and Lin: Partners in Exploring China's Architectural Past*, Philadelphia: University of Pennsylvania Press, 1994
Liang, Cong Jie, "Liang Sicheng: Architect with a Dream," *China Reconstructs* 2 (1986)
Liang, Ssu-ch'eng, *Liang Ssu-ch'eng wen chi* (Collected Essays of Liang Sicheng), 4 vols., Beijing: Wenwu Press, 1982–86
———, *A Pictorial History of Chinese Architecture*, edited by Wilma Fairbank, translated by Lian Cong Jie, Cambridge, Massachusetts: MIT Press, 1984
———, *Liang Ssu-ch'eng hsien sheng tan ch'en pa shih wu chou nien chie nien wen chi, 1901–1986* (Collected Essays on the Occasion of the Eighty-Fifth Birthday of Liang Sicheng), Beijing: Qinghua University Press, 1986
Lin, Zhu, "Wo yu Liang Sicheng (Liang Sicheng and I)," *Renmin Ribao* (30-article series, 30 October 1990–98 December 1990)
Luo, Zhewen, "Huainian Liang Sicheng Xiansheng (In Memory of Liang Sicheng)," part 1, *Wenwu tiandi* 4 (1991); part 2, *Wenwu tiandi* 5 (1991)
Wang, Zhuo, "Liang Sicheng nianpu dawang (Biographical Profile of Liang Sicheng)," in *He Chenci Jiaoshou qiqiu shouqing lunwen ji* (Festschrift for the 70th Birthday of Professor He Chenci), Taizhong: Tunghai University, 1990

LIBERA, ADALBERTO 1903–63

Architect, Italy

Adalberto Libera is representative of a whole generation of young Italian architects, artists, and urban designers whose participation in the building culture of the 20th century was significantly marked by the tumultuous sociopolitical events of the first half of the century. His buildings, paintings, exhibit designs, poster designs, competition entries, and polemical writings attest to the material and philosophical challenges posed by two world wars and numerous years of reconstruction. In addition, like many of his Italian colleagues, Libera's actions as an architect were directly contingent on his actions as a political being.

During the interwar years (1927–42), Libera sought the support of the Italian Fascist state. He participated in state-sponsored design competitions, built a number of iconic exhibition pavilions, and promoted a language of architectural figuration highly effective in the dissemination of fascist rhetoric. As codesigner of the principal facade for the Tenth Anniversary Exhibition of the Fascist Revolution (Rome, 1932), the Italian Pavilions for both Chicago's World Fair (Chicago, 1933), Brussels' International Exposition (Belgium, 1935), and the Reception and Congress Hall for the E'42 Universal Exposition (Rome, 1942), Libera's designs were instrumental in creating an exportable image of Italian military power.

Nevertheless, in the years following the war, Libera participated in extensive rebuilding efforts aimed at ameliorating the lives of those most devastated by the fighting. He administered the planning efforts of INA Casa (1947–54), a postwar agency that oversaw the implementation of building standards for the construction of worker housing units. In this capacity, Libera developed technical specifications for all aspects of a building's performance including key ergonomic measures for kitchen, bathroom, and work desk layouts. Via Galilei (Trento, 1949) was built precisely in this manner, adopting the physical measures that Libera had meticulously studied and codified in his manuscript *La tecnica funzionale dell'abitazione* (1943–46).

However, Libera's legacy in the annals of 20th-century architecture is, most notably, the result of his unequivocal commitment to the development of an Italian language of Modern architecture. Throughout his career, Libera advocated the radical transformation of Italian building practices. In 1927, while still a student at the School of Architecture in Rome, he joined the ranks of Gruppo 7 and helped champion the tenets of Italian Rationalism. With Milanese collaborators Giuseppe Terragni, Gino Pollini, and Luigi Figini, Libera promoted the emergence of an entirely new culture of architectural making. Aware of transformations in the material, social, and programmatic conditions of daily life throughout Western Europe, Libera called for the development of a contemporary language of architectural figuration expressive of such transformations. The appearance of new building technologies such as reinforced concrete, steel, and glass necessitated a parallel invention in the nature of architectural forms. As such, the Rationalist credo was centered on the absolute rejection of all forms of Neoclassicism, including those of the *Novecento* Movement: a post–World War I movement that promoted a renewal of Italian architecture via the stylized representation of select architectural motifs.

Within months of joining Gruppo 7, Libera traveled to Germany, where he was introduced to Europe's most innovative building practices. He visited the Weissenhofseidlung Exhibition in Stuttgart, seeing firsthand projects built by Ludwig Mies van de Rohe, Walter Gropius, and Le Corbusier. On his return to Rome, in 1928 Libera co-organized with Gaetano Minucci the First Exhibition of Rationalist Architecture, which showcased projects by burgeoning modernists such as Alberto Sartoris and Matte Trucco; the latter having completed in 1925 the highly popular Fiat Factory in Turin. Libera's own contribution included two designs for low-income housing devised using the Rationalist principles of standardization and mass production.

By 1930, Libera had become a founding member of *Movimento Italiano per l'Architettura Razionale* (MIAR), a national organization seeking to promote Italian Rationalism. It's first and most audacious event was the launching of the Second Exhibition of Rationalist Architecture. Held in Rome in 1932, the exhibition's organizers openly sought, in their struggle for modernism on Italian soil, the support of the Fascist leader Benito Mussolini. To this end, they mounted a series of polemical exhibits that challenged and ridiculed examples of architecture they deemed retrograde. Although the exhibit's argumentative stance eventually resulted in the demise of MIAR, the course had been set for a series of collaborative ventures between Rationalists and Fascists. Libera designed and built some of the most emblematic buildings of this collaboration.

Post Office and Telecommunications Building (1933), Rome, designed by Adalberto Libera
© Andrea Jemolo/CORBIS

The first such project was the resurfacing of the 19th-century neoclassical Exhibition Building on Via Nazionale destined to house the Tenth Anniversary Exhibition of the Fascist Revolution (Rome, 1932). Libera, along with Mario De Renzi, employed large-scale columnar steel fasces to inaugurate a figural language of mass rhetorical appeal. Framing the building's triumphal arch entry, these oversized and stylized emblems of imperial power convincingly portrayed the emerging influence of Italian Fascism. In a similar manner, the success of Libera's design for the Exhibition's Sanctuary of the Martyrs, the final room in the ritual procession through the building's layout, was once again assured by his use of over-scaled geometries and iconic figures.

Libera's mastery in the design of exhibitions was repeated in 1937 with his project for the National Exhibition of Summer Camps and Youth Programs. Sponsored by the Fascist Party and built on the grounds of the ancient Circus Maximus, Libera, Renzi, and the painter Giovanni Guerrini ushered in a language of horizontal extension and expansive parterres. Albeit a temporary structure, the simplicity of its construction and the singular power of its porticoed pavilions made of this project an easily imitated symbol of Italian Modernism.

In 1933, Libera built the first of his winning competition entries: the Aventino Post Office and Telecommunications Building (Rome). The clarity of its commitment to Rationalism was clearly evident in the building's C-shaped plan and in its cubic volumetric proportions. A year later, in 1934, such allegiance to elemental and primary forms was again in evidence with Libera's completion of the Elementary School in Piazza Raffaello Sanzio, Trento, and the four apartment buildings for the Tirrena Corporation in Ostia, Rome. Libera's reputation continued to grow as a result of his competition entries for the Palazzo del Littorio of 1934 and for its second stage entry of 1937. Also, like many architects of the period, Libera participated in the design of new urban centers; the most notable of which being his 1936 Master Plan for Aprilia.

However, on the eve of World War II, his career was focused on the completion of his most publicized commission to date: the design and construction of the Reception and Congress Hall for the Universal Exposition, E'42. This most grandiose of building projects initiated by the Fascist regime aspired to advertise to the world Italy's most acclaimed new works of architecture and urban design. Planned for a site of 400 hectares and seven years in the making, Mussolini launched the construction of well over 50 monuments to Italy's industrial successes, cultural history, and artistic riches. Libera's Reception and Congress Hall was one such building and, contrary to most, whose fate was never to be built, Libera's Congress Hall was constructed.

The project of the interwar years that continues to garner the most animated discussion is that of Casa Malaparte (Capri, 1940). Sited on the exceptional cliffs of Punta Massullo, the house designed for the writer Curzio Malaparte still elicits admiration for its highly articulated Modernism. The manner in which its principal volume forcefully delineates its profile against the existing landscape makes Casa Malaparte the most lyrical and transcendental of Libera's projects.

During the final years of the war and the German occupation of Italy, Libera returned to Trento to work on his ergonomic studies for the optimization of residential living. It was only with his involvement in postwar reconstruction that Libera returned to Rome to design numerous housing projects, including the highly innovative complex at Tuscolano (Rome, 1954). As well, following the war, Libera oversaw the construction of his winning entry for the Trentino-Alto Adige Regional Governmental Headquarters for well over a decade (1953–1963). Finally, Libera's most successful and acclaimed postwar project was the construction of the residential village for the Olympic Games held in Rome in 1960. This highly publicized project returned once again both Libera and Italian building to international prominence.

Teaching subsequent generations of Italian architects was of importance to Libera, and in his final years, from 1954 until his death, he taught both in Florence and in Rome. In March of 1963, at the age of 60, Libera passed away, leaving a much-contested legacy.

FRANCA TRUBINO

See also **Casa Malaparte, Capri; Fascist Architecture; Terragni, Giuseppe (Italy)**

Biography

Born 1903 in Trento, Italy; studied at the School of Architecture in Rome (1925–27); earned his diploma in 1928. Joined Gruppo 7 in 1927 whereby he championed Italian Rationalism, founding member, MIAR group (*Movimento Italiano per l'Archittetura Razionale*), 1930. Participated in designs for the Tenth Anniversary Exhibition of the Fascist Revolution (Rome, 1932); administered rebuilding projects for INA Casa post–World War II (1947–54). Taught in Florence and Rome, 1954–63. Died in Rome, 1963.

Selected Works

Italian Pavilion, Chicago World's Fair, 1933
Italian Pavilion, Brussels International Exposition, 1935
Reception and Congress Hall, Universal Exposition, Rome, 1942
Aventino Post Office and Telecommunications Building, Rome, 1933
Casa Malaparte, Capri, 1940

Further Reading

Ciucci, Giorgio, "Lo Stile Libera; The Style of Libera," *Casabella* 53, no. 555 (1989)
Doordan, Dennis P., *Building Modern Italy: Italian Architecture, 1914–1936*, New York: Princeton Architectural Press, 1988
Etlin, Richard, "Italian Nationalism," *Progressive Architecture* 64, no. 7 (1983)
Garofalo, Francesco, and Luca Veresani (editors), *Adalberto Libera*, Bologne: Zanichelli, 1989; as *Adalberto Libera*, New York: Princeton Architectural Press, 1992
Ghirardo, Diane Yvonne, "Italian Architects and Fascist Politics: An Evaluation of the Rationalist's Role in Regime Building," *Journal of the Society of Architectural Historians* 39, no. 2 (1980)
Mariani, Riccardo, "The Planning of the E42: The First Phase," *Lotus International* 67 (1990)
Quilici, Vieri, "Adalberto Libera: Roman Rationalism between Wars," *Lotus International* 16 (1977)
Talamona, Marida, *Casa Malaparte*, Milan: CLUP, 1990; as *Casa Malaparte*, New York: Princeton Architectural Press, 1992

LIBESKIND, DANIEL 1946–

Architect, United States

Daniel Libeskind gained recognition as one of the world's foremost deconstructivist architects through his participation in the New York Museum of Modern Art's "Deconstructivist Architecture" exhibition (1988), which included like-minded architects Peter Eisenman, Rem Koolhaas, Frank O. Gehry, and Coop Himmelb(l)au. In 1989 Libeskind won an international competition for the Jewish Museum extension to the Berlin History Museum (1999). This project was his first major commission and proved to be pivotal for his subsequent architectural career.

Libeskind first attracted attention with his architectural drawings titled *Micromegas* that were devoid of perspective, context, and narrative. They were produced in 1979 and exhibited in Helsinki (1980), London (1980), and Zurich (1981). One of his most prestigious early awards was the first prize in the Leone di Pietra at the Venice Biennale (1985) for his "Three Lessons in Architecture" or the "three machines" for reading, writing, and memory.

Libeskind's proposal for the Jewish Museum extension in Berlin (1989) achieved international acclaim and criticism for its unique and unconventional forms and intentions. The building is designed in the form of two bars of spaces, one called the void (the space of loss and disenfranchisement), which is built in a straight line, and the other the space of the observer (the space of the collections and the rest of the museum's functions), which is a broken, folded bar that crosses and recrosses the void. The angles and lines that generate the form of the museum inflect and refer to places in the city of Berlin in which the history of ideas emerged. The void suggests the loss of this history, as well as of the individuals who contributed to it, in the Holocaust. These external references are coupled with the stark and claustrophobic character of the building that evokes the anxiety and angst associated with the loss of human life and intellectual history in the Holocaust. The project, therefore, is a profoundly exegetical work that evokes both emotional and imaginary interests in a complex mapping of the nature of human existence today generally and of Berlin and Jewish history specifically.

Libeskind's writings on architecture and architectural theory have been translated into most major languages. He has criticized what he sees as a problem in modern human culture and the architecture that it produces, constantly challenging the architectural community to create a different kind of architecture, one that is not determined or valued from a purely utilitarian, economic, and visual point of view. Instead, his work, as he describes it, is meant to evoke experiences and engage the spirit. His architecture lies at the nexus of painting, mathematics, and music. This aggregate of interests testifies to his avid exploration of these subjects, to a broad education in literature, music, art and philosophy. Moreover, Libeskind's extensive teaching career testifies to his interest in alternative architecture.

His other projects include, among many, a master plan and elements of a "City Boundaries" urban design scheme for Groningen (with Fokko van der Veen, 1988) in the Netherlands; a winning competition entry for the UNY Corporation Pavilion (1990) in Nagoya; an urban design competition for the Potsdamerplatz area (1991) in Berlin; the dramatic spiral-shaped extension to the Victoria and Albert Museum in London (begun in 1996, expected to be completed in 2006); the Bremen Philharmonic Hall (1995–98) in Bremen, Germany; and a garden for the Polderlands (1995) in the Netherlands.

In September of 2002 the Lower Manhattan Development Corporation, in conjunction with the city and state of New York, established an international design competition for a memorial for the World Trade Center site that was devastated by terrorist attacks on 11 September 2001. In February 2003, a project titled *Memory Foundations* by Libeskind was honored as the winner. Libeskind designed a museum with an entrance at the Ground Zero Memorial Site that leads viewers down into a quiet, meditative space of reflection. "To commemorate those lost lives, I created two large public places, the Park of Heroes and the Wedge of Light," Libeskind stated. "Each year on September 11th between the hours of 8:46 a.m., when the first airplane hit and 10:28 a.m., when the second tower collapsed, the sun will shine without shadow, in perpetual tribute to altruism and courage." A dramatic, glass encased 1,776 foot tall spire will create a powerful new skyline for Lower Manhattan, while a new rail station with a concourse linking the trains and subways, will coalesce in a bustling urban space including a performing arts center, office towers, hotels, street level shops, and restaurants that reaffirm life in the aftermath of tragedy.

JEAN LA MARCHE

See also **Deconstructivism; Eisenman, Peter (United States); Jewish Museum, Berlin; Gehry, Frank (United States); Koolhaas, Rem (Netherlands); Memorial**

Biography

Born in Lodz, Poland, 12 May 1946; immigrated to the United States 1960; naturalized 1965. Studied music in Lodz, Poland, and Israel before 1960; attended The Cooper Union for the Advancement of Science and Art in New York (B.S., architecture, 1970); received a master of arts in history and theory of architecture at the School of Comparative Studies, University of Essex, England (1972). Married to architect Nina Libeskind: 3 children. Partnership with wife, Berlin. First prize in the Berlin International Bauausstellung (IBA) urban design competition (1987); first prize in several open and invited competitions since 1993, including the Felix Nussbaum Haus (museum, 1998) in Osnabrück, Germany. Lecturer, Architectural Association, London 1975–77; head, department of architecture, Cranbrook Academy of Art, Bloomfield Hills, Michigan 1978–85; various professorships (1985–1994) at Harvard University, Cambridge, Massachusetts, University of Naples, Italy, University of Illinois, Chicago, Ohio State University, University of California, Los Angeles, University of London, Danish Academy of Art, Copenhagen, Yale University, New Haven, Connecticut, and Weisensee Academy, Berlin. Founder, director, Architecture Intermundium, Milan 1986–89; Senior Scholar, J. Paul Getty Foundation 1986–89. Elected to the German Akademie de Künste and the German Society of Architects, 1994; received the American Academy of Arts and Letters Award for Architecture, 1996. His practice, Studio Daniel Libeskind, operates in Berlin and California.

Felix Nussbaum Haus (1998), Osnabrück, Germany
© Bitter Bredt, Berlin

Selected Works

Master Plan, Groningen, Netherlands (with Fokko van der Veen), 1988
UNY Corporation Pavilion (first prize, competition), Nagoya, 1990
Garden, Polderlands, Netherlands, 1995
Bremen Philharmonic, Germany, 1998
Felix Nussbaum Haus (first prize, 1995 competition), Osnabrück, Germany, 1998
Jewish Museum (first prize, 1989 competition), Berlin Historical Museum, 1999
Imperial War Museum, Manchester, England, 2002
Danish Jewish Museum, Copenhagen, Denmark, 1996–2003
Jewish Museum of San Francisco, California, 1998–2005 (projected completion date)
Victoria and Albert Museum (spiral addition), London, 1996–2006 (projected completion date)

Selected Publications

Between Zero and Infinity: Selected Projects in Architecture, 1981
Chamber Works: Architectural Meditations on Themes from Heraclitus, 1983
Theatrum Mundi: Through the Green Membranes of Space, 1985
Daniel Libeskind—Countersign, 1992

Further Reading

For an overview of Libeskind's philosophy, see Libeskind and also Jarzombek. An abbreviated curriculum vitae is published in Papadakis 1993, and additional biographical sketches can be found in Hodge and in Johnson and Langmead.

Betsky, Aaron, *Violated Perfection: Architecture and the Fragmentation of the Modern*, New York: Rizzoli, 1990
Hodge, Daniel H., *Daniel Libeskind: An Introduction and Bibliography*, Monticello, Illinois: Vance Bibliographies, 1990
Jarzombek, Mark, "Ready-Made Traces in the Sand," *Assemblage*, 19 (December 1992)
Johnson, Donald Leslie, and Donald Langmead, *Makers of 20th Century Modern Architecture: A Bio-Critical Sourcebook* (bibliography), Westport, Connecticut: Greenwood Press, 1997
Johnson, Philip, and Mark Wigley (editors), *Deconstructivist Architecture*, New York: Museum of Modern Art, and Boston: Little Brown, 1988
Libeskind, Daniel, *Extension to the Berlin Museum with Jewish Museum Department*, edited by Kristin Feireiss, Berlin: Ernst and Sohn, 1992
Papadakis, Andreas (editor), *Theory and Experimentation: An Intellectual Extravaganza*, London: Academy Editions, 1993
Papadakis, Andreas, Catherine Cooke, and Andrew Benjamin, (editors), *Deconstruction: Omnibus Volume*, New York: Rizzoli, and London: Academy Editions, 1989

LIBRARY

The 20th century saw a remarkable transformation in library philosophy, away from the traditional understanding of the library as a treasure house that protected books from untrustworthy readers toward a new conception of the library as a building type that encouraged the encounter between readers and books. Pioneered in the United States, this new philosophy put particular emphasis on allowing readers free access to books stored on open shelves, providing children's reading rooms, and establishing branch and traveling libraries. So radical was the idea of giving readers ready access to book collections that many public libraries did so only in conjunction with architectural mechanisms aimed at controlling readers. These included turnstiles (which forced readers to file one at a time past the charging desk) and the radial arrangement of bookshelves (which enhanced the ability of a single staff member to survey several aisles of bookshelves). Because radial bookshelves were often housed in semicircular rooms that were difficult to expand, their use was discontinued in the United States by about 1910. British librarians, however, continued to support the practice at least until 1920, when several versions of the arrangement were published in the third edition of James Duff Brown's *Manual of Library Economy* (1920).

This new philosophy of service played a role in encouraging library philanthropy on an unprecedented scale, as industrialist Andrew Carnegie (1835–1919), newspaper editor John Passmore Edwards (1823–1911), and others financed public library buildings as a means of encouraging self-improvement among the working poor. Carnegie's library building program was particularly noteworthy for the number of buildings Carnegie financed directly (1,469 in the United States alone, 2,507 worldwide), for its geographic extent (including England, Ireland, Scotland, Canada, New Zealand, Australia, Fiji, Mauritius, and elsewhere), for the innovations it introduced into the planning of small-town and branch libraries, and for the library building boom that it helped fuel even in communities that did not receive Carnegie funds. The number of American public libraries more than quadrupled between 1896 and 1925, growing from 900 to 3,873.

Formulated in consultation with progressive librarians, the Carnegie ideal was a one-story building without full-height interior partitions, an arrangement that enhanced administrative efficiency by giving the librarian seated at a centrally located charging desk an unencumbered view of the bookshelves lining the perimeter walls. Readers were allowed free access to the shelves, and half the space of the building was devoted to a children's reading room. Although Carnegie recommended a simple exterior expression, many local decision makers adopted classicism in order to incorporate the library into the coordinated civic landscape advocated by the City Beautiful movement. The temple front and the triumphal arch were favorite compositional motifs, often used with a dome whose lantern lighted the circulation area and transformed it into a locus of enlightenment, both literally and figuratively. Although many of these small public libraries received additions in the 1930s (with the help of W.P.A. funds) and during the postwar period, they continued to shape the public library experience for most Americans throughout the 20th century; according to *American Libraries*, at least 744

Carnegie-financed buildings in the United States were still used as libraries in 1990.

Standardized library equipment marketed nationally helped give early 20th-century library interiors their distinctive character. Established in 1888 by Melvil Dewey (1851–1931), a leading librarian and inventor of the Dewey decimal system, the Library Bureau offered a full range of library furniture and fittings that by the turn of the century tended toward golden oak Windsor chairs and cabinetry of a simplified classical form. Snead and Company specialized in the manufacture of self-supporting iron book stacks and by 1915 had completed more than 200 book-stack installations, including those at public libraries in Washington, D.C. (1901–03, Ackerman and Ross), Denver, Colorado (1904–10, Albert Randolph Ross), and Louisville, Kentucky (1904–08, Pilcher and Tachau), as well as at Harvard's Widener Library (1912–15, Horace Trumbauer). The company also helped establish industry standards for shelf width (3 feet) and range spacing (4 feet, 6 inches on center).

In contrast to the innovative forms of smaller libraries in this period, central libraries in larger cities (and several academic libraries) tended to follow patterns set by the great public libraries of the 19th century, particularly the Bibliothèque Ste-Geneviève (1844–50, Henri Labrouste) in Paris and the Boston Public Library (1888–95, McKim, Mead and White), each of which made reference to the Renaissance *palazzo* and featured closed book stacks and a monumental reading room on an upper floor. Twentieth-century examples include the public libraries in New York (1897–1911, Carrère and Hastings), St. Louis (1907–12, Cass Gilbert), Philadelphia (1912–27, Horace Trumbauer), Detroit (1913–21, Cass Gilbert), San Francisco (1914–17, George W. Kelham), and Indianapolis (1914–17, Paul P. Cret and Zanzinger, Borie and Medary), all of which located the book stacks at the back of the building, where long, narrow windows brought daylight into the aisles.

In the interwar years, monumental classical exteriors were still the norm for central libraries in larger American cities, but these now often cloaked internal arrangements aimed at bringing readers and books closer together. One approach was to locate the book stack in the center of the building, surrounding it with reading rooms. Another was to disperse the collection, placing books in closer proximity to reading rooms, as was done in Los Angeles (1922–26, Bertram Grosvenor Goodhue). A third approach was to put the brunt of the book collection on a lower level. This approach is associated particularly with New York architect Edward L. Tilton (1861–1933), who first introduced it at the Springfield (Massachusetts) Public Library (1907–12) and later used it to provide an open plan for the main floor of large urban libraries; the Somerville (Massachusetts) Public Library (opened 1913) and the Enoch Pratt Free Library (1928–33, Tilton and Githens, consulting architects) in Baltimore, Maryland, are noteworthy examples. The Enoch Pratt building was built during the tenure of librarian Joseph L. Wheeler (1884–1970), who embraced an aggressive approach to attracting readers to the library and encouraged Tilton to emulate some of the characteristics of the department store in his library design: a facade set directly on the lot line, a sidewalk-level entrance, and large display windows. By midcentury, Wheeler was a prominent library building consultant and coauthor of *The American Public Library Building* (1941) with Tilton's former partner, architect Alfred Morton Githens.

Boston Public Library, 1888–95, by McKim, Mead and White
Photo courtesy The Bostonian Society, Old State House

In other contexts, architects took advantage of basement-level book storage to develop varied and dramatic building sections, as Alvar Aalto did at the Viipuri City Library (1927–35) in Finland. There, adult readers entered the building one level above the book storage area and climbed up another level to the main lending room, which in turn acted as a gallery that allowed the librarian's desk to overlook the main reading room and a smaller reading mezzanine; skylights brought daylighting into all these reading areas.

During the 1930s, self-supporting multitiered book stacks were reaching their greatest heights; Yale's Sterling Library (designed by James Gamble Rogers) rose to 16 tiers when it opened in 1931. At the same time, however, academic librarians began to question whether such stacks were the best mode of book storage. Prompted by pedagogical innovations, such as the seminar system that involved students in intensive library use, academic librarians were unhappy with the inflexible character of the book stacks, whose standard tier height (established by Snead and Company at seven feet, six inches) and dim lighting made them unpalatable places for reading. Angus Snead Macdonald (1883–1961), president of Snead and Company, formulated a more flexible system of library planning that employed a nine-by-nine-foot planning module (which allowed librarians to locate standardized bookshelving anywhere in the library) and an eight-foot ceiling height (which offered a compromise between shelving efficiency and reader comfort).

Although the particular dimensions of the module continued to evolve (by 1955, Macdonald advocated modules as large as 27 by 27 feet), the modular library became the norm for public and academic libraries in the decades after World War II, including among the first the Firestone Memorial Library at Princeton University (1944–48, R.B. O'Connor and Walter H. Kilham Jr.). As reading space and book storage space became integrated on each floor, the rectangular footprint of these buildings tended to grow, as did the library's dependence on air conditioning, fluorescent lighting, and flat ceilings. Although the doctrine of flexible planning offered exciting possibilities in library service, the architectural spaces that it created often were monotonous.

Particularly important to these developments was the Cooperative Committee on Library Building Plans, a loosely defined group of architects, academic librarians, and university administrators who met between 1944 and 1952 to discuss library design. In addition to Macdonald, the group included Keyes D. Metcalf (1889–1983) of Harvard University, who became an important library consultant in the 1950s and 1960s and who wrote the bible of modular library planning, *Planning Academic and Research Library Buildings* (1965). Discussions of modular library planning also took place at Library Building

Institutes, sponsored by the American Library Association, from the mid-1940s until 1967.

In the face of predictions that the computer would make the library obsolete, the last 20 years of the 20th century saw a renewed interest in library architecture, with a particular emphasis on large central public libraries that can serve a sizable audience by reaching further afield for library users while aiding in the economic redevelopment of urban centers. Several of these libraries have been the subject of national or international design competitions, including the Joensuu Library (1982–83, Helin and Siitonen Architects) in Finland, The Hague City Library (1986–95, Richard Meier and Partners), the Harold Washington Library Center (1988–91, Hammond Beeby and Babka) in Chicago, and the Vancouver Central Public Library (1992–95, Moshe Safdie and Associates with Downs Archambault and Partners). In Denver, Colorado, Michael Graves transformed and expanded the existing 1956 Central Library (Fisher and Fisher/Burnham Hoyt) with his 1995 structure located adjacent to the historic Civic Center Park.

In the last decades of the 20th century, there was also a concerted effort to make libraries delightful places to read. Architects became concerned with the provision of natural light and with the manipulation of the ceiling plane to create reading spaces that were either monumental, as at the fifth-floor reading room of the Phoenix Central Library (1989–95, bruderDWL Architects), or intimate, as in the galleries of the Vancouver Central Public Library or in the reading alcoves of the Humboldt Library (1984–88, Moore Ruble Yudell) in Berlin. Typically, these spaces are the product of functional zoning within the building, a version of the fixed-function planning that characterized prewar library design. Sometimes this zoning has been accomplished within a modular grid and square footprint, as at the Tønsberg (Norway) Public Library (1988–92, Lunde and Løvseth). More often, however, libraries of the late 20th century used irregular plans to give the various functions their own spatial articulation; notable examples of this approach include the Münster City Library (1987–93, Architekturbüro Bolles-Wilson and Partner) and the Almelo Public Library (1991–94, Mecanoo) in the Netherlands.

Equally important, there has also been a renewed appreciation for older library buildings. Late 19th-century buildings in the grand manner have been lovingly restored; readers are once again welcomed through the main doors of the Boston Public Library on Copley Square and encouraged to experience the original entry sequence: up the main stairs, past newly cleaned mural paintings, to the main reading room. More modest libraries from the early 20th century are also enjoying a renaissance, as cities such as Seattle work to revitalize the historic character of their numerous Carnegie-financed branches. At the dawn of the 21st century, library architecture is again as vital and exciting as it was at the beginning of the 20th.

ABIGAIL A. VAN SLYCK

See also **Aalto, Alvar (Finland); British Library, London; Carrère, John Mervin, and Thomas Hastings (United States); Gilbert, Cass (United States); Phoenix Public Library, Arizona; Stockholm Public Library; University Library, UNAM, Mexico City**

Further Reading

In addition to the specific sources listed below, *Library Journal* has since 1945 devoted one of its December issues to articles on library architecture.

Baumann, Charles H., *The Influence of Angus Snead Macdonald and the Snead Bookstack on Library Architecture*, Metuchen, New Jersey: Scarecrow Press, 1972

Bobinski, George S., *Carnegie Libraries: Their History and Impact on American Public Library Development*, Chicago: American Library Association, 1969

Brawne, Michael, *Library Builders*, London and Lanham, Maryland: Academy Editions, 1997

Brown, James Duff, *Manual of Library Economy*, London: Scott Greenwood, 1903; 7th edition, rewritten by R. Northwood Lock, London: Grafton, 1961

"Inviting Places," *American Libraries*, 21/4 (April 1990)

Kaser, David, *The Evolution of the American Academic Library Building*, Lanham, Maryland: Scarecrow Press, 1997

Metcalf, Keyes DeWitt, *Planning Academic and Research Library Buildings*, New York: McGraw-Hill, 1965; 2nd edition, by Philip D. Leighton and David C. Weber, Chicago: American Library Association, 1986

Oehlerts, Donald E., *Books and Blueprints: Building America's Public Libraries*, New York: Greenwood Press, 1991

Spens, Michael, *Viipuri Library, 1927–1935, Alvar Aalto*, London and New York: Academy Editions, 1994

Thompson, Anthony, *Library Buildings of Britain and Europe: An International Study, with Examples Mainly from Britain and Some from Europe and Overseas*, London: Butterworths, 1963

Van Slyck, Abigail A., *Free to All: Carnegie Libraries and American Culture, 1890–1920*, Chicago: University of Chicago Press, 1995

Wheeler, Joseph Lewis, and Alfred Morton Githens, *The American Public Library Building*, New York: Scribner, and Chicago: American Library Association, 1941

LIGHTING

Architects and lighting designers have exploited the spectacle of light through visual perception to capture emotion, recall our primal past, comfort, protect, heal, increase productivity, and expand modern culture by pushing back the night. Architectural lighting design is rapidly morphing as architecture, theater, art, cinema, and pop culture perforate a domain dominated for decades by electrical engineers. Transparent, translucent, and spectrally selective smart materials; efficient and provocative light sources modulated by sophisticated computer control; color-changing and image-producing LED systems; fiber-optic light distribution networks; and luminous thin-film surfaces are allowing architecture to be reconsidered as a luminous environment. Embracing the moods of daylight and uniquely responding to the specific physiological and aesthetic needs of building occupants, architectural illumination is becoming an integrated building ecology rather than merely technical problem solving systems.

Light and Human Response

Beyond the fact that some modicum of light is required to see—an amount quite small for general spatial movement (3 to 5 foot-candles [fc])—quite sophisticated lighting environments are required to perform the tasks common in modern society. Subsequently, the expectation for higher-quality energy-efficient systems is constantly increasing as new technologies appear and become integrated into architecture. Copious studies dating from the turn of the 20th century are well documented by the Illuminating Engineering Society of North America (IESNA) and referenced in the IESNA Handbook, demonstrating that productivity and visual acuity increase with increased illumination levels. This research provides the basis for most current building and lighting codes. The general recommended levels have varied over time in response to changing cultural conditions. In the 1950s, with advanced industrialization and cheap energy, recommended lighting levels rose to 100 fc from the 10-fc recommendations in the first decade of the century. After the oil embargo of 1975, recommendation levels were reduced to 50 fc, and daylight reemerged as a viable lighting source.

It was not until 2000 that the "Quality of the Visual Environment" chapter was officially adopted by the IESNA and included in its design handbook, significantly shifting the focus from purely practical to qualitative issues in design. Although most historical recommendations call for even illumination for visual tasks, this need has been questioned, especially for particular environments. In 1975, researcher John Flynn began groundbreaking experiments that inextricably linked light distribution with spatial qualities and judgments that he described as visual clarity, complexity, color tone, glare, private, relaxing, and pleasantness. Spatial perception relies not only on the architectonic surfaces of rooms but on the deployment of light within and on those surfaces, whether even, direct, scalloped, or grazing. A human subject's primal relationship to circadian rhythms (day–night cycles) goes well beyond the visual, affecting psychological and emotional well-being and states of mind. Recent research, for example, has demonstrated that exposure to controlled light regimes can improve seasonal affective disorder syndrome (SADS), Alzheimer's patients' quality of life, and the growth rates of premature infants. Key issues in these studies include the quality of light in terms of color spectrum (specific frequencies included in daylight) and the fact that exposure is cycled to replicate the day–night sequence. Related studies have demonstrated that nonexposure to the right frequencies of light for specified periods of time can cause degradation of physiological function, neurobehavioral performance, and sleep quality. In this case, the body does not receive specific "daytime" frequencies of light to calibrate the biological clock, raising questions about long-term daily exposure to artificial light. In a short 100 years, we have transitioned from an agrarian society linked to the diurnal cycle scanning the fields and pastures to a Postmodern, information-based global culture operating around the clock in highly specialized luminous environments.

Daylight and Architecture

Many preeminent architects of the early 20th century relied on daylight as the primary light source in their buildings. Louis Kahn's Kimbell Art Museum (Fort Worth, Texas, 1972) provides an excellent example of the integration of daylight and architecture. Kahn, along with lighting designer Richard Kelly, devised a system of vaulted ceilings and perforated stainless steel screens that softened, bounced, cooled, and filtered natural sunlight to illuminate spaces for fine art. As the daylight changes in intensity, color, and quality throughout the day and from season to season, the moods of the Kimbell's spaces are sensitively and subtlety revealed, softening the structure's modernist rectinlinearity and imbuing the architecture with life.

At the turn of the century, most buildings relied on daylight, as other artificial light sources were cumbersome, expensive, and relatively inefficient. The reliance on natural light led to significant innovations in plan organization, glazing technology, facade treatment, and window systems that could control daylight entering the building. These techniques kept spaces close to the edge of buildings, resulting in letter-shape plans (E, L, S, etc.) or courtyard schemes with open central circulation spaces. High ceilings and windows allowed daylight to penetrate deeply into the spaces, providing adequate lighting in almost all daytime conditions.

In the United States, engineered electrical lighting was incorporated into architecture when the office typology proliferated in the postwar era. Lighting design strategies favored constant illumination levels and allowed large open areas. Quantifying designs to meet these new recommended levels proved to be quite difficult given the mutability and variable nature of daylight. As electrical light sources and energy became more prolific and economical, the reliance on daylight as the primary light source diminished. The dramatic increase in energy costs from the 1975 oil embargo spurred a reconsideration of low-energy lighting systems. Buildings used approximately 30 percent of the nation's total energy, and 50 percent of the energy used in office buildings went to lighting during the daytime hours—a great potential for nationally significant energy reductions. As a result, design strategies have been developed to reestablish historic precedent lighting strategies while extending the range and control of daylight and integrating electrical systems. Windows, light shelves, clerestories, and skylights have been studied as aperture systems to admit large quantities of light, modulate heat transfer, and control glare. Building with bilateral lighting (light from two sides) is replacing the large, square floor plan of the typical speculative office building. Sophisticated monitor and control systems are being incorporated to constantly adjust electric light in response to changes in daylight.

In many European countries, the need for daylight in architecture is acknowledged by building and municipal code legislation that requires all occupied spaces to have access to daylight. Buildings in other countries, including the United States, are still being constructed with few if any windows—typically a short-view value engineering decision. This strategy relies entirely on electric light, limiting daylight access to a small percentage of perimeter spaces if at all. Effective strategies are available to integrate daylight, design, and engineering but they rely on coordinated techniques for qualifying long-term value to balance trade-offs between energy costs, glazing costs, electrical lighting costs, and the occupants' well-being.

Electric Light

Modern architecture embraced the electrical light as a technology to literally bring society out of the darkness of the industrial city. The luminous ceiling ultimately replaced the sky in office buildings around the world, providing almost antiseptic levels of illumination. Early attempts to integrate with Thomas Edison's marvelous contribution to architecture involved refitting gas and oil lamps with sources hundreds of times brighter, creating a substantial glare problem. According to architecture critic Reyner Banham, even as light sources began to be manipulated and aestheticized by designers such as Le Corbusier, "the naked and exposed bulb was always an alternative in his [Le Corbusier's] eyes," as the stark glare of the single, exposed, clear bulb illuminating the living room in the architect's Villa Cook (Boulogne-sur-Seine, France, 1926) demonstrates. As electric lamp types expanded, luminaire design became more sophisticated, and indirect light was integrated in buildings, the difficulty of glare was greatly reduced.

Electrical light sources include the glowing tungsten filaments of incandescent lamps with halogen or xenon gasses added in the bulb to improve brightness and color rendering. Significantly inefficient, producing much more heat than light, they are not economical on a large scale and are typically reserved for residential and accent lighting situations. The most common lamp is the fluorescent tube, providing moderate to good color rendering depending on the specific phosphor content. Its widespread efficiency explains the prolific use of fluorescent lighting in buildings ranging from offices to schools to hospitals. With great advances in compactness, compatibility with incandescent fixtures, and color-rendering improvements, fluorescent lights are finding new design flexibility and emerging as viable domestic alternatives for energy saving. Other gas discharge sources include metal halide, mercury vapor, and sodium vapor. Typically, these lamps are used in exterior situations with metal halide, finding applications in large spaces such as transportation terminals, sports arenas, and other medium-to-large public spaces. Mercury and sodium vapor are most commonly employed as security lighting.

Successful electric lighting design reveals the intention of the architecture by sensitively illuminating the spatial and tectonic systems with appropriate luminous technologies. It involves coordinated efforts between the architect, lighting designer, interior designer, and electrical engineer. Myriad lamp and fixture combinations proliferate on the market, and many precedent examples of building integrated lighting design exist. Without a clear understanding of how light should support and enhance the design, choosing a system can be quite difficult. Direct light at a grazing angle will reveal the texture of surfaces and provide shadows that suggest an intimate or relaxing space. Indirect light—light that is reflected into the space from a surface rather than the lamp directly—provides more evenly lit spaces with luminous surfaces that convey a sense of spaciousness. Down lighting might define spatial nodes or gathering areas within a larger open space, creating privacy in the dimmer space and spectacle in the illuminated area. These strategies represent modes of connection that link light distribution to spatial activity. As these strategies emerge, selecting appropriate technologies becomes a logical process. Meeting the criteria of local codes or IESNA guidelines provides the critical baseline level of illumination in a given space. Well-lighted spaces appeal to us by visually defining or accentuating the intentions and possibilities of the architecture.

Commercially available computer programs that use radiosity and ray-tracing algorithms provide sophisticated, photorealistic light rendering as well as quantitative calculations. Computer programs allow speculative experimentation with light sources and building surfaces that combine direct, reflected, and daylight luminance for specific geographical locations and times of day, thereby advancing the integration of daylight as a primary light source. As soon as the design is fixed, the calculations are already complete, allowing for additional experimentation within a design budget.

Emergent Technologies

Light-emitting diode (LED) lights are transitioning from the circuit board to the building as viable light source alternatives. LED lamps have life spans up to 10 years, are very small, produce very little heat, and can produce a variety of dynamic colors with a control device. Fiber-optic distribution networks allow light to be filtered and focused on a task or object while keeping the actual source in a remote location—excellent if heat or moisture is a concern or if very small size is needed. Daylight collectors have been developed in Asia to directly transmit sunlight throughout buildings via fiber-optic cables. Luminous thin film technologies can replace traditional building finishes to provide light-emitting surfaces.

Illuminated Architecture

World's fairs and international exhibitions of the early 20th century established lighting as one of many themes related to the cultural roles of architecture. Advancing from the whiteness and glare of the World Columbian Exposition in Chicago of 1893, controlled flood lighting and colored light dominated the later years. "Light Architecture" appearing in 1956 formalized modern architecture's integration of light, power, and material tectonics as part of a process that continues today. Unhindered daylight streamed into buildings during the day, internal spaces broadcast light nightly, and light radiated from illuminated edifices to redefine nocturnal urban space and the skyline of the modern city. Luminous "Jumbotron" video screens morph to shape the buildings of Times Square while commanding advertising attention and illuminate through folly and spectacle. More substantive urban gestures usually integrate multiple territories of lighting professions, including architecture, theater, interior design, art, planning, landscape, and engineering. Howard Brandston, originally a theatrical lighting designer, designed over 2500 architectural lighting projects, including the award-winning Petronas Towers in Kuala Lumpur (1996). Working with architect Cesar Pelli, the lighting design emphasizes the space between the towers as a framed gateway to Malaysia and recalls motifs of 1920s and 1930s towers in the United States such as the Empire State Building (Shreve, Harmon, and Lamb, New York City, 1931).

Sculptor and environmental artist James Turrell, known for manipulating light as an expressive substance, sculpts the Planet M Building (Hanover, Germany 2000). He combines dynamic moods of light through translucent color, intensity, and anticipation to create a stunning sense of mood and space. Turrell's project employs almost imperceptible rates of change such that one does not notice intervals of color but rather the fact that color has changed and will again—or will it? Using the latest theatrical equipment in concert with material selections and surface detailing, the scheme unifies texture, reflection, and transparency to give the floating orb substance through symphonic light.

To cite another example, New York City's famous Metropolitan Life Building, designed by Pierre LeBrun and erected in 1909, with its original gold leaf illuminated cupola, radiated day and night as an "eternal light" in the empire skyline. Replaced with aluminum in the 1960s, and finally restored in 2000, the Met Life Building's gold leaf, along with new computer-controlled color-changing diachronic filters and powerful lights suggests how contemporary applications of theater-lighting technologies can enhance the city's tradition of expressing cultural events through motifs of light and color.

Environmental lighting, first with gaslights, advanced public space in time, germinating modern culture. More recently, Crime Prevention Through Environmental Design (CPTED) identified night lighting as a leading deterrence to crime. Illuminated infrastructures of Western civilization are easily visible from space as earth's energy (transformed into photons) is beamed into the cosmos. "Dark sky," "light trespass," "light pollution," and "light nuisance" language and regulation are rapidly emerging in town meetings and municipal codes, suggesting much better control of environmental light in the future.

In his 1933 essay *In Praise of Shadows*, novelist Jun'ichiro Tanizaki laments the advancement of electric light, exiling darkness from the places we dwell. By extolling the virtues of the shadow, he challenges the "more is better" paradigm of modern lighting design. Admittedly, he would not live in the ecliptic world constructed in his narrative, which is to say that the shadow should be cultivated and enjoyed as a part of the electro-lumenescent world we live in. Inspiring lighting design responds to these currents, incorporates sustainable modes of action, and integrates with tectonic systems to advance architectural spatial occupation.

MARTIN GOLD

Further Reading

Banham, Reyner, *The Architecture of the Well Tempered Environment*, Chicago: University of Chicago Press, 1969

Brandston, Howard, "How Theatrical Lighting Influences Architectural Lighting Design," *LD+A* (1974)

Brown, G.Z., and Mark Dekay, *Sun, Wind, and Light: Architectural Design Strategies*, 2nd edition, New York: Wiley, 1985, 2001

Egan, M. David, and Victor Olgyay, *Architectural Lighting*, Boston: McGraw-Hill, 2002

Evans, Benjamin, *Daylight in Architecture*, Boston: McGraw-Hill, 1981

Fitch, James Marston, and William Bobenhausen, *American Building: The Forces that Shape It*, Boston: Houghton-Mifflin and Cambridge, Massachusetts: Riverside Press, 1949; revised edition as *American Building: The Environmental Forces that Shape It*, New York: Oxford University Press, 1999

Nuckolls, James L., *Interior Lighting for Environmental Designers*, New York: Wiley, 1983; revised as Gordon, Gary, and James L. Nuckolls, *Interior Lighting for Designers*, New York: Wiley, 1995

Millet, Marrietta S., *Light Revealing Architecture*, New York: Van Nostrand Reinhold, 1996

Neumann, Dietrich (editor), *Architecture of the Night: The Illuminated Building*, Munich and London: Prestel, 2002

Steffy, Gary, *Architectural Lighting Design*, New York: Van Nostrand Reinhold, 1990

Tanizaki, Jun'ichiro, *In'ei Raisan*, New Haven, Connecticutt: Leete's Island Books, 1977, and London: Cape, 1991; as *In Praise of Shadows*, translated by Thomas J. Harper and Edward G. Seidensticker, New Haven, Connecticut: Leete's Island Books, 1997, and London: Cape, 1991

Tomkins, Calvin, "Flying into the Light," *The New Yorker* (January 2003)

LIN, MAYA 1959–

Architect, United States

Maya Lin is renowned as the architect of the Vietnam Veterans Memorial in Washington, D.C., for which she won the design competition while an undergraduate at Yale University. Her oeuvre spans a wide range of media and venues and includes buildings, sculptures, landscape projects, and gallery installations; as a result, discussions of her work often address the tension between her identities as both architect and artist.

The Vietnam Veterans Memorial (1982) drew national attention because of the controversial nature of the design. Prominently located on the Mall in Washington, D.C., the memorial consists of two sloping, black granite retaining walls in the configuration of a "V," onto which are inscribed the names of American soldiers killed during the Vietnam war, listed in chronological order of their deaths. A path leads visitors along the base of the wall so that the viewer descends from grade level to the apex and then ascends back to grade level. One of the polished stone walls reflects the image of the Washington Monument (Robert Mills, 1884), the other the Lincoln Memorial (Henry Bacon, 1922).

The memorial's unique design drew both praise and criticism. Unlike other national monuments, the memorial was sunken into the ground instead of rising above it. Whereas critics maintained that the design dishonored the war dead and the nation itself, Lin and her supporters argued that the design's simplicity and austerity were intended to provide opportunities for private contemplation of the personal sacrifices made by American soldiers. The subject of special congressional hearings, Lin's design was ultimately built, but with the addition of an American flag and a statue of American soldiers in the near vicinity.

Today, the Vietnam Veterans Memorial receives the highest number of visitors in Washington, D.C., and has influenced the designs of other monuments, including the nearby Korean War Veterans Memorial. Since the construction of the Vietnam Veterans Memorial, Lin has designed and built several other well-known commemorative works that reflect her strong interests in minimalist geometry, natural materials, and the chronological retelling of history. In 1989 she completed the Civil Rights Memorial (Montgomery, Alabama), commemorating the American black civil rights movement. Commissioned by the Southern Poverty Law Center and located outside its offices in Montgomery, Alabama, the memorial consists of a circular black granite table 11 feet in diameter and a black granite wall 40 feet long that divides the area outside the building's entry into upper and lower plazas. Water flows up through middle of the table and out across the surface, onto which is inscribed a time line juxtaposing legislation and important events in the history of the civil rights movement. The wall is inscribed with a biblical quotation spoken by Dr. Martin Luther King Jr.: "until justice

The Wave Field, University of Michigan, North Campus, Ann Arbor (1994)
Photo © John Weise

rolls down like waters and righteousness like a mighty stream."
Similarly, *The Women's Table* (1993), Yale University, New
Haven, Connecticut is an elliptical black granite table onto
which is inscribed a spiral shaped time line depicting the history
of coeducation at Yale.

Lin's work is distinguished by her use of modern technology
as tools for viewing the natural landscape, such as aerial photography, satellite images, microscopic pictures, and views taken
from studies of fluid dynamics. Her interest in contrasting the
so-called man-made and the natural is evident in *The Wave Field*,
a tribute to an aerospace engineering student at the University
of Michigan named François-Xavier Bagnoud who died in a
helicopter accident. Located adjacent to the University of Michigan's aerospace engineering building, the piece consists of a
10,000-square-foot grassy area in the form of rows of small
waves.

Her other landscape works include *TOPO* (1991), a project
located in the median along the approach to the Charlotte Coliseum in Charlotte, North Carolina. To activate the somewhat
conventional open space, Lin collaborated with landscape architect Henry Arnold to design a configuration of 12-foot-diameter
holly bushes pruned almost perfectly spherical to appear as balls
rolling down a gentle slope while willow oaks eventually will
form arches over the median. Likewise, in her peace chapel de-

signed for Juniata College in Huntingdon, Pennsylvania, Lin
inserts a few built elements into the natural landscape: a 40-
foot-diameter circle delineated by rough-hewn stones that are
recessed into the ground and connected to a small four-foot-
diameter circle by a path.

Lin's commemorative landscape projects reinforce comparisons to those of the American sculptors and Earth or Land artists
of the 1960s, 1970s, and early 1980s. Indeed, aspects of Lin's
works recall elements of Earthworks by such artists as Mary
Miss, Robert Smithson, and Michael Heizer in her use of abstract forms and concepts, natural context and materials, and
public venues. The Native American burial mounds and Japanese Zen gardens that Lin has cited among her sources of inspiration are shared by some earth artists as well. In addition, whereas
Lin uses abstract forms commonly seen in works of environmental art, the narrative content of the Vietnam Veterans Memorial,
the Civil Rights Memorial, and *The Women's Table* creates a
resonance between the textual and the physical.

Like Richard Serra, a sculptor who gained prominence in the
late 1960s, Lin established a dialogue between sculpture and
architecture in *Groundswell* (1993), created while she was visual-
artist-in-residence at the Wexner Center for the Arts in Columbus, Ohio. Built by architect Peter Eisenman, the Wexner Center's "leftover spaces" on the building's roofs are occupied by

dreamlike landscapes of blue-green safety glass that seem to drift into the spaces like newly fallen snow. Like Serra's *Tilted Arc* (1981), a 12-foot-high, 120-foot-long curved steel sheet that subverted the intentions of the architect by interrupting pedestrian flow through Federal Plaza in lower Manhattan, *Groundswell*'s impact results from its relationship to the more rigid architectural context. Inspired by Japanese gardens, the piece is infused with landscape sensibilities and associations that act in juxtaposition with the industrial materials and as a foil to the surrounding architecture.

Although relatively few in number, Lin's buildings demonstrate her ability to design spaces that meet practical criteria of the clients' program, building code, and environmental and structural considerations. Among these is the Weber House (1993) in Williamstown, Massachusetts, and the Museum for African Art (1993) in New York. Her first design for a private residence, the Weber House features gently curved, sloping roofs made of lead-covered copper and a floor plan that is arranged around a courtyard Japanese garden, recalling Lin's fascination with natural landscape forms. The Museum of African Art is a long, narrow converted loft into which Lin reintroduces some aspects of her landscape works, such as the curving, irregular staircases and colors evocative of natural features, as well as her interests in history, narrative, and passage or circulation through space. Of her roles as both architect and artist, Lin has described the differences in the activities as analogous to the differences between "writing a novel," for which the architect-writer must make decisions about the most detailed aspects of the design, and "writing a poem," for which careful consideration must be given to each individual element because the scope of the work is smaller.

CATHERINE MOY

See also **Memorial; Museum; Vietnam Veterans Memorial, Washington, D.C.**

Biography

Born in Athens, Ohio, 5 October 1959, the daughter of Ohio University professors in literature and fine arts. Received bachelor of arts (1981) and master of architecture (1986) from Yale University. Active in independent practice in New York City since 1987. Received Honor Award of the American Institute of Architects, 1984; Henry Bacon Memorial Award, 1984; Honorary Doctorate of Fine Arts, Yale University, 1987; Presidential Design Award, 1988; inducted into International Women's Hall of Fame, 1990.

Selected Works

Vietnam Veterans Memorial, Washington, D.C., 1982
Civil Rights Memorial, Southern Poverty Law Center, Montgomery, Alabama, 1989
Juniata Peace Chapel, Huntingdon, Pennsylvania, 1989
TOPO, Charlotte Coliseum, Charlotte, North Carolina, 1991
Groundswell, Wexner Center for the Arts, The Ohio State University, Columbus, 1993
Museum for African Art, New York City, 1993
Weber House, Williamstown, Massachusetts, 1993
Women's Table, Yale University, New Haven, Connecticut, 1993
Eclipsed Time, Pennsylvania Station, New York City, 1993

The Wave Field, University of Michigan, Ann Arbor, Michigan, 1994
Asian/Pacific/American Studies Institute, New York University, New York City, 1997
A Shift in the Stream, Principal Financial Group Headquarters, Des Moines, Iowa, 1997
Ten Degrees North, Rockefeller Foundation, New York City, 1997
Bronx Community Paper Company, Bronx, New York, 1997

Further Reading

Abramson, Daniel, "Maya Lin and the 1960s: Monuments, Time Lines, and Minimalism," *Critical Inquiry*, 22/4 (1996)
Bremner, Ann (editor), *Maya Lin: Public/Private*, Columbus: Wexner Center for the Arts, Ohio State University, 1994
Maya Lin: Topologies, Winston-Salem, North Carolina: Southeastern Center for Contemporary Art, 1998
Mock, Freida Lee, and Terry Sanders, "Maya Lin: A Strong Clear Vision" (videorecording), Santa Monica, California: Sanders and Mock Productions/Ocean Releasing, and s.l.: American Film Foundation, 1995

LINCOLN CENTER, NEW YORK

Designed by Harrison and Abramovitz and others; completed 1970
New York, New York

The integration of the arts, a much sought-after goal of the modern movement, found fruition at Lincoln Center for the Performing Arts in New York City and permanent expression in its modern interpretation of classical architecture. In this major mid-Manhattan site of temple-like theaters and concert halls arranged about a monumental Beaux-Arts plan, opera, symphonic music, dance, and drama come together in white marble, the very theatricality of the composition reflecting the dramatic function of the buildings.

Modern architecture within neoclassical monumentality defines the ambiguous but ultimately acceptable design program of Lincoln Center. Like the amalgam of the arts housed within the complex, the architecture democratically wants to be all things to all people, and it fulfills this desire surprisingly well. To assess the success of this complex fairly, one must view it at night, theatrically lit, when it shines like a jewel box of illusionary beauty, as patrons stream into the floodlighted, fountained plaza after opera or theater, yellow cabs line up, and dancers exit backstage doors. This is Lincoln Center live, as it was meant to be.

Principal architects of the center were Harrison and Abramovitz, with associated architects Philip Johnson, Eero Saarinen, Gordon Bunshaft, Pietro Belluschi, and Marcel Breuer as early consultants, all modern architects and firms with close New York City ties, often to the prime movers of the project, philanthropist John D. Rockefeller III, urban planner Robert Moses, and the artistic directors of the arts organizations. Harrison and Abramovitz, for example, a very straightforward, pragmatic firm, had made their names in New York in the 1930s as one of many architects of Rockefeller Center and in the 1950s as architects in charge of the United Nations. They were insiders from the very inception of the site plan for Lincoln Center and were further commissioned for the primary anchors of the complex, Wallace Harrison for the Metropolitan Opera (1966) and Max Abramovitz for the Philharmonic Hall (1962).

View of the Lincoln Center plaza, designed by Wallace Harrison and others, New York City, (1970)
© Bill Ross/CORBIS

Philip Johnson, exponent of Mies van der Rohe and friend of dance master George Balanchine, was commissioned for the New York State Theater (1964), home of the New York City Ballet. He was then experimenting with a mode of modern classicism, seen in the tiny temple pavilion at Johnson's Connecticut home, corresponding to his theater design. Eero Saarinen was suited to the drama hall, the Vivian Beaumont Theater (1965). This theater and its accompanying treed courtyard represent one of the hidden creative strengths of the project. The more prosaic and functional programs for the Juilliard School (1969) and Library of Performing Arts (1965) were assigned to corporate architects Pietro Belluschi and Gordon Bunshaft of Skidmore, Owings and Merrill, respectively, architects experienced in large commissions with multiple-use functional parameters.

The complex history of Lincoln Center as an urban project is overshadowed by the apparent simplicity of the plan as it stands today and by the fact that most New Yorkers have little memory of a time or place before Lincoln Center moved in and lit up the neighborhood. In fact, it was once just another section of West Side high-density housing that controversial planner Robert Moses had declared a slum to make it eligible for federal urban renewal funding. Even today, the greatest failure of Lincoln Center is that its plan tends to wall the arts off from their urban environment. The project was funded via three sources:

the federal government, acting not as benefactor of the arts but as urban renewal proponent; by the arts organizations themselves; and by private patrons.

Fortunately, the time of Lincoln Center's planning and construction (1955–70) was a time of urban renaissance in the history of the city in which many things came together for the benefit of the arts: patronage, urban optimism, strong economy, excellence in American art forms, and continuity with the modernist belief that the arts really were related not only to one another but also to the basic humanity of the populace. When Lincoln Center finally opened, Mayor John Lindsay's and President John F. Kennedy's administrations were committed supporters of the arts. It is remarkable to note that at one time maestros Leonard Bernstein and George Balanchine were performing simultaneously within buildings designed by such American masters as Philip Johnson, with murals by Marc Chagall, and sculpture by Henry Moore.

Such a grand collection of artists and art forms, by nature, seemed to demand a monumental setting, and therein lies the one major aesthetic conundrum of Lincoln Center: appropriateness of form. How does one monumentalize the modern? One might see in the plan rather unsubtle contemporary references to Michelangelo's plan for the Campidoglio in Rome. Like the Renaissance plan, Lincoln Center is a three-sided, axial design arranged about a raised central ornamental plaza, open to the street via an expanse of stairs.

As in the Campidoglio, the three major anchors of the Lincoln Center plaza are basically giant boxes with only one designed facade per building, each facing inward and reflecting Michelangelo's solution of employing screens of giant orders to unify the opposing side elevations. The Metropolitan Opera, the visual focus of the plan, is ornamented with five arched bays juxtaposed with glass and intensely colorful modern murals. The colonnade of Philharmonic Hall and the piers of the New York State Theater stand perpendicular to the opera. The arches, piers, and colonnade are all the same giant scale, faced in travertine, reaching upward from the ground to the full height of the buildings in long vertical lines. Thus, the major halls are dressed up, like stage sets in which the spectators become the actors.

It would be easy to be cynical about the design of Lincoln Center, for it is neither pure classicism nor pure modernism, but it succeeds. It is simultaneously pompous and popular, decorous and democratic, pragmatic and idealistic, reflecting the personas of its originators, the time of its inception, and certainly the character of New York City itself.

LESLIE HUMM CORMIER

See also **Bunshaft, Gordon (United States); Concert Hall; Harrison, Wallace K., and Max Abramovitz (United States); Johnson, Philip (United States); Saarinen, Eero (Finland)**

Further Reading

Mayer, Martin, *Bricks, Mortar, and the Performing Arts*, New York: The Twentieth Century Fund, 1970
Young, Edgar B., *Lincoln Center: The Building of an Institution*, New York: New York University Press, 1980

LINCOLN MEMORIAL, WASHINGTON, D.C.

Designed by Henry Bacon with sculpture by Daniel Chester French and Jules Guerin; completed 1922

Like all monuments, the Lincoln Memorial (1914–22) commemorates a past; unlike most, however, it memorialized a future. The memorial, in the form of a classic Greek temple, combined Doric columns with an Ionic frieze to reference a past of Athenian democracy, rural American landscapes, and most significantly, American national reconciliation. Although its construction demonstrated the consolidation of the power of professional city planners and architects, its existence symbolized American struggles for racial equality. "This Memorial is less for Abraham Lincoln," proclaimed President Warren Harding at the Memorial Day (30 May 1922) dedication of the memorial, "than those of us to-day, and for those who follow after."

Architect Henry Bacon designed a Beaux-Arts Greek temple in which symbolic details of design, layout, decoration (paintings and writings), and sculpture created and reinforced a reflective and somber mood in the viewer. Within the context of the American appropriation of Greek architecture, the temple associated Athenian democracy with Lincoln, a suggestion made more explicit with the carving of the Declaration of Independence's claim that "all men are created equal" on the southern wall. The southern and northern walls, possibly in reference to the northern and southern pediments of the Parthenon, display the allegorical paintings *Emancipation* and *Unification* by Jules Guerin (who had illustrated Bacon's design proposal) above the Gettysburg Address and the Second Inaugural Address.

The Lincoln Memorial turned the standard Greek temple to its side and removed the triangular pediment; unlike the Parthenon, the memorial is approached on its long facade. The number of exterior Doric columns symbolizes the 36 states at the end of the Civil War. As in Greek temples, the gigantic seated sculpture of Lincoln rests on three steps, supposedly so that an attendant arrives at the sculpture on the left and more appropriate foot. Daniel Chester French's sculpture of a seated Lincoln in the rear of the middle chamber faces the Washington Monument. Originally designed to be 15 feet tall, the white Georgian marble structure was doubled in size when it became apparent that it would be dwarfed by the building. The two side chambers focus attention on the paintings and writings on the north and south walls. The attic frieze outside the memorial portrays the reunification of the nation by listing the states at the end of the Civil War in the order of their admittance to the Union.

From the western end of the National Mall in Washington, D.C., the building faces the Washington Monument and, two miles away, the Capitol at the eastern end, thus highlighting the relationship between the founder and savior of the nation and Lincoln's distance from the partisan squabbles of Congress. The Lincoln sculpture looks across the entire length of the mall toward the sculpture of General Grant seated on his horse at the foot of the Capitol.

The memorial's western location was the most contested element of its creation. It is located in what had previously been a marsh but is now a supremely well-designed landscape of boxwood and holly trees that are simply and directly spaced so as to direct attention toward the building. In the tradition of Frederick Law Olmsted, Sr., the landscape, designed in part by Frederick Law Olmsted, Jr., was intended to bring to the urban dweller a taste of the American rural past to ease the psychological stress of living and working in an industrial city. The western location, furthermore, placed the memorial in relationship with Robert E. Lee's house on the Virginia side of the Potomac to symbolize the reconciliation of North and South and the advance westward of a unified country.

Even as the memorial referenced a past, its creation demonstrated architectural methods of the future, particularly the professionalization of architecture and city planning. The World's Columbian Exposition of 1893 (specifically the urban planning exemplified in the "White City") and the American Institute of Architects (AIA) meeting in Washington, D.C., encouraged the Senate Committee on D.C. to appoint in 1901 a commission, headed by Senator McMillan of Michigan, to plan and direct the development of the National Mall area in Washington, D.C. The Lincoln Memorial was their top priority. Despite years of argument over the location and design of the memorial, the initial plan of the McMillan Commission would eventually be realized in most of its major points. One consequence of the plan was a national reconsideration of urban-planning goals and their meaning in the practice of architecture.

Lincoln Memorial, Washington, D.C. (1922)
© Historic American Buildings Survey/Library of Congress

The 1902 McMillan Plan stimulated the public and professional imagination concerning the possibilities of planning and designing a city on a very large scale. Instead of architects randomly planning and placing buildings, this plan reminded the professionals of the possibilities of creating an entire urban environment, stimulating dozens of similar plans throughout the United States in cities such as Kansas City, Harrisburg, and Denver, Colorado. Furthermore, city planning on this scale meshed with the reforms of the Progressive Era and the popularity of the City Beautiful movement from the 1890s to the 1920s to lift the spirit and productivity of the populace. The plan contributed to the growth and consolidation of the power of planning commissions in general in its influence on the commissions that later made the final decisions concerning the memorial: the Council of Fine Arts, created by Theodore Roosevelt's executive order, and the congressionally created Commission of Fine Arts.

The Commission of Fine Arts, created on 17 May 1910, consisted of Burnham and Olmsted, who served on both the McMillan Commission and the Council of Fine Arts. Added to the commission were architect Thomas Hastings; sculptor Daniel Chester French (who would later resign when he was chosen to create the statue for the memorial); the director of decoration at the World's Columbian Exposition, Francis D. Millet; architect and president of the AIA (later architect of the Supreme Court Building) Cass Gilbert; and former McMillan secretary Charles Moore. The commission had very little disagreement over the style of the monument, although there were some fantastic monuments proposed, including proposals from John Russell Pope for a pyramid and a ziggurat.

The Lincoln Memorial is the one monument on the mall that has developed its own historical significance. For example, Marian Anderson's performance there in 1939, after she was rejected from the D.A.R. Constellation Hall because she was black, still echoes in the American memory. In addition, the fact that the memorial hosted one of the most intellectually powerful moments for the definition of American democracy maintains its beloved position among American memorials: in 1964, Martin Luther King, Jr., explained his dream of a democratic America while standing on the steps of the memorial.

CHAR MILLER

See also **Memorial; Washington, D.C., United States**

Further Reading

Kohler, Sue, *The Commission of Fine Arts: A Brief History, 1910–1990*, Washington, D.C.: The Commission of Fine Arts, 1991

Lincoln Memorial: A Guide to the Lincoln Memorial, Washington, D.C.: U.S. Department of the Interior, 1986

Longstreth, Richard (editor), *The Mall in Washington, 1791–1991*, Washington D.C.: National Gallery of Art, 1991

Wilson, William, *The City Beautiful Movement*, Baltimore, Maryland: Johns Hopkins University Press, 1989

Ziolkowski, John, *Classical Influence on the Public Architecture of Washington and Paris: A Comparison of Two Capital Cities*, New York: Lang, 1988

L'INNOVATION DEPARTMENT STORE, BRUSSELS

Designed by Victor Horta; completed 1903

L'Innovation Department Store (1903), designed at the dawn of the new century by Belgian architect Baron Victor Horta (1861–1947), was one of Brussels's pioneering achievements in commercial architecture. The store, located on rue Neuve in the heart of the city's shopping district, expanded a prospering retail business operated by Bernheim Freres, a firm specializing in haberdashery and hosiery since 1897. L'Innovation's open plan and glazed exterior wall enticed consumers by making visible a plethora of merchandise, all under one roof. By commissioning Horta, the nation's leading architect, for the project, Julien Bernheim realized the commercial value of the expressive, progressive mode of Art Nouveau.

Art Nouveau (Jugendstil), the architecture and decorative arts style that dominated Europe until World War I, was a widespread popular revolt against the academicism of established historical styles, principally Beaux Arts Classicism. Horta, considered the originator of classic Art Nouveau architecture, first introduced in his Hotel Tassel (1893), had a profound respect for tradition and borrowed from such diverse sources as classicism, Rococo, and *Japonisme*. He strove, however, for a unique, contemporary expression in his designs, liberating architecture from the constraints of historicism with flowing, naturalistic details and modern-day materials, creating an overall plastic unity. Using metal and glass as natural components of his designs, Horta sought a synthesis of the structural, architectural, and ornamental.

L'Innovation, the first of several department stores designed by Horta, was an exposed iron frame structure with a double-paned glass facade, central core, and overhead skylight. Modeled after Louis-Charles Boileau's Bon Marche Department Store in Paris (1874), its open, symmetrical composition allowed for a variety of goods to be visible from many different angles both inside and out. A wide, top-lit atrium and two narrow four-story bays disposed as balconies distinguished the interior space. The store's success was linked to the amount of natural light that entered into the heart of the building, allowing views across and between floors that best presented the wares. Bold, decorative advertising signs within each department enhanced merchandizing and made shopping an exhilarating, social experience. The facade, itself a display piece, reflected the general profile of the building with its wide, sweeping arcs; high, recessed central section; and side bays that bowed outward toward the street. Fantastic organic ironwork ornament that conveyed the malleability of the material, hanging lamps reminiscent of Otto Wagner's Neumann Store (1895) in Vienna, and rhythmic, sinuous lines throughout the structure produced a harmonious, coherent unity characteristic of the evocative spirit of Art Nouveau.

Large-scale department stores proliferated in Europe and the United States in the early years of the 20th century. Meant to be grand, modern-day monuments at the core of downtown, they emerged in France in the second half of the 19th century, replacing the small, single-item shop with a bazaar-like, marketplace format. As a building type with little precedent, the utilitarian purpose of department stores made them ripe for new discoveries in mass construction. Iron's inherent ability to permit flexible planning, large glazed spans, and well-lit spaces was increasingly recognized. Horta's determination to exploit the structural potential of the latest materials in his design for L'Innovation was inspired by the writings of Eugene-Emmanuel Viollet-le-Duc (1814–1879), which he read as a young apprentice in France. In *Entretiens sur l'architecture* (1872), the neo-Gothic architect and theoretician defended manufactured materials, particularly iron, claiming they could be articulated to create organic forms suitable to present times. The most dramatic application of those principles, which deeply influenced Horta's vigorous use of iron and glass, appeared in 1889 with the Eiffel Tower.

L'Innovation was considered the finest of Horta's department stores and was well received by his contemporaries. The fusion of plan, material, and detail within the language of Art Nouveau animated architects and designers in Belgium and throughout Europe, chief among them Parisian Hector Guimard. L'Innovation Department Store was also Horta's last significant Art Nouveau achievement. Shortly after its completion, the architect abandoned his daring confrontation with the cult of historicism and reverted to what many considered a tired academicism. His reputation for inventiveness was revoked by modernist historians, only to be resurrected by Henry-Russell Hitchcock Jr., who praised his work, citing L'Innovation Department Store in particular, as a landmark of the beginning of modern architecture, comparing Horta's Art Nouveau buildings with Louis Sullivan's skyscrapers. Others, like critic Sigfried Giedion, viewed Horta's progressive designs as apt transitions to modern architecture, especially apparent in buildings that exploited vast, unsupported, illuminated spans, like L'Innovation. He noted that Horta's work foreshadowed modernism's curtain wall and its openness of structure and space. As a bridge between 19th-century eclectic classicism and 20th-century modernism, Art Nouveau's new vision of architectural space and organic detailing was admired by some of the 20th century's leading architects, among them Mies van der Rohe, Le Corbusier, Walter Gropius, and Paul Rudolph.

Regrettably, the facade and floor plan of L'Innovation Department Store were radically restructured in 1922 in an attempt to create a rationalist, contemporary department store with a solid exterior wall and partitioned interior. The original facade, with its curvilinear iron tracery and expansive windows, was considered to be one of Horta's finest; however, the store was demolished in late 1967, months after a devastating fire caused by an exploding gas cylinder claimed the lives of 322 lunchtime shoppers. As an exceptional example of the integration of merchandising and design, goods and mass-produced building materials, the demolition of L'Innovation Department Store is considered among the greatest losses of 20th-century architecture.

ANDREA FOGGLE PLOTKIN

See also **Art Nouveau (Jugendstil); Horta, Victor (Belgium)**

Further Reading

Because of the dramatic decline of his reputation, a disgruntled Horta destroyed much of his archive before his death. Few drawings and project notes remain; Horta's 1939 memoirs, compiled by Duliere (1985) in a critical, carefully researched and annotated edition, provide primary, albeit retrospective, information. It was not until the late 1960s, with the founding of the Horta Museum and restoration of several of his houses, that interest in the architect was revived. Borsi and Portoghesi wrote the first monograph on him, published in Italian and French (1970). The first English language study of Horta's complete works is their updated and revised edition (1991). Several monographs and exhibition catalogues followed, notable among them Aubry and Vandenbreeden (1996), specialists in Belgian architectural history who assess Horta's place in the history of rationalism, Art Nouveau, and modernism. Although no source exists on L'Innovation Department Store, books on Horta and Art Nouveau include discussions of his finest achievements.

Art Nouveau, Belgium, France (exhib. cat.), Houston: Institute for Fine Arts, 1976

Aubry, Francoise, and Jos Vandenbreeden (editors), *Horta: Art Nouveau to Modernism*, Ghent: Ludion Press, and New York: Harry N. Abrams, 1996

Borsi, Franco, and Paolo Portoghesi, *Victor Horta*, translated by Marie-Helene Agueros, New York: Rizzoli, and Brussels: Marc Vokar Editeur, 1991

Dernie, David, and Alastair Carew-Cox, *Victor Horta*, London: Academy Group, 1995

Duliere, Cecile (editor), *Victor Horta Memoires*, Brussels: Ministere de la Communaute Francaise de Belgique, 1985

Greenhalgh, Paul (editor), *Art Nouveau, 1980–1914*, London: V and A Publishers, and New York: Harry N. Abrams, 2000

Robert-Jones, Philippe, *Brussels: Fin de Siecle*, Koln: Benedikt Taschen Verlag, 1999

LISBON, PORTUGAL

Lisbon is situated in a particular geographic setting shaped by the hills of the Estremadura tableland and the large estuary of the Tagus River, the main symbol of Lisbon's architectural, economic, and political renewal. The ancient city is located just at the point where the Tagus joins the Atlantic Ocean: in fact, after a long journey of some 1000 kilometers, the river ends in a delta surrounded by sandbanks that link the ocean to the Mar de Pahla (Sea of Straw), a kind of tiny Mediterranean on the Atlantic coast. The river and the ocean are the main geographic elements that explain the economic and urban development of this city.

Lisbon can be considered a meeting point of various cultures. It is a place where many different architectures have always coexisted: the Baixa (downtown), the commercial space of the city, designed by right-angled boulevards in the 18th century, is perfectly connected with the irregular design of the Alfama, the medieval quarter. The Italian architect Vittorio Gregotti clearly points out that

> we can speak of structural characters in a country which, because it has strongly defended its national identity for almost one thousand years, has also been more capable than others of accepting, interpreting and elaborating both the input from distant lands gathered by great navigators, and the Arabian, Spanish, Italian influences which fol-

lowed . . . each street has two backdrops, its own narrow perspective and a distant reference point, full of sunlight: the river, the facing hill, the dome of a church, the old palaces.

For these reasons, Lisbon is a singular place, one of hills, valleys, and slopes; of buildings made of plasterwork and tiles of blue colors (the so-called *azulejos*, which decorate ancient buildings); of streets paved with glasslike stone and basalt; and with a riverfront like a frontier, a symbolic space of arrival. Probably founded by Phoenicians, the urban development of Lisbon began in 205 B.C., when the Romans structured the first town along three functional points: the castle (the hill), the civic center (the slope), and the port (the riverfront). After the Romans, the Arab occupation, the Christian reconquest, and the age of the great discoveries all contributed to the city's evolution into the 20th century, when multiple cultures and urban models coexisted.

It is evident that since the 18th century, the architectural history of Lisbon has been characterized by great urban plans that totally reoriented the city and underlined its strong relationship with the river and the sea. Even in recent years, since the end of the Salazar dictatorship (1932–74), Lisbon has undertaken a deep transformation with many new architectures, from the smallest of designs to the largest infrastructural projects. This is a clear effort to bring the city into the new millennium; the traditional architectural models have been left behind for showing a new approach to contemporary architecture. Projects such as the Competition for Ideas for the Riverside Areas (1988), the project and construction of Belém Cultural Centre (1988–92), the Strategic Plan and Lisbon Master Plan (1990–94), and the World Exposition '98 in the eastern area prove this turnaround in that people consider Lisbon a riverfront city, as it was in the past.

The first significant project was the World Exposition '98 citadel (Parque Expo), placed in the northeastern area of the city on a five-kilometer riverside stretch on the Tagus that was an abandoned industrial area. The urban conversion of this large zone was one of the main aims of Expo '98: the great new infrastructures, such as the Vasco da Gama Bridge and the new railway station, allowed its perfect integration with the heart of the city. The World Exposition focused on the theme of the oceans and celebrated the Portuguese navigator Vasco da Gama, who first discovered the sea route to India: another way to define Lisbon as a waterfront city on the Atlantic coast.

Expo '98 displayed different and brilliant ways of making symbolic architecture. A fascinating example is well represented by the high-tech railway station Gare Do Oriente, planned by Santiago Calatrava: glass and steel becomes a contemporary homage to Gothic structures. Other buildings, such as the Oceanic Pavilion (planned by P. Chermayeff of the Cambridge Seven Associates) and the Utopian Pavilion (planned by R. Cruz with Skidmore, Owings, and Merrill), are metaphorical symbols of the sea: the accurate design evokes waves, shells, and caravels.

The Oceanic Pavilion, hosting the largest aquarium in the world, is the most spectacular building of the citadel. It is situated at the quay of Doca dos Olivais, in the heart of the Expo. Four stone towers surround the huge central tank housing the marine habitat. This building displays a particular architecture made of textured stone walls and glass roof: the whole mass,

Gare Do Oriente, by Santiago Calatrava for the Lisbon World Expo '98
© Dan Delgado *d2 Arch*

rising from quiet waters, recalls a large ship. The Utopian Pavilion, too, with its particular design of an overturned caravel, evokes the vessels used in the past ages for the great discoveries. It is a multifunctional covered stadium, suited for cultural and sporting events.

However, the architectural icon of Expo '98 is represented by the austere Portuguese Pavilion, planned by Álvaro Siza with Eduardo Souto de Moura. Built in front of the dock of the Tagus, the Portuguese Pavilion shows an extraordinary and unusual space configuration: the large outside place for ceremonial functions (the pavilion is to be the future home of the country's Council of Ministers) is designed by a curved concrete veil that is suspended at either ends by steel cables. As opposed to many of the surrounding buildings, Siza chose a horizontal design, which better relates with the shore of the river.

In the western area of the city is the Belém Quarter, the ancient fortified port and a point of departure of cargo vessels. The magnificent Belém Cultural Centre (1988–93) is just situated in this significant area overlooking the Tagus, with some of Portugal's most important monuments, such as the 16th-century Monastery Dos Jeronimos. Planned by Gregotti, it is a large multifunctional citadel with an opera house, a concert hall, a museum, and a congress hall. The whole building is faced with rough limestone offset by white frames around entrances and windows. The internal spaces are a rigorous scheme that expresses a relationship with the external surrounding landmarks: the river, the large Plaça do Imperio, and the ancient monastery.

An earlier and significant intervention in the urban context of Lisbon is the Reconstruction Plan for the Chiado (1991–94) by Siza, considered one of the most remarkable urban developments currently taking place in Europe. The old Chiado is a transition zone between the Baixa, the urban area rebuilt after the earthquake of 1755, and the Bairro Alto, the most important commercial place in the city. In August 1988, a fire destroyed most part of the ancient Pombaline buildings facing the three main roads of the quarter: Rua Do Carmo, Rua Garret, and Rua Nova da Almada. The main purpose of the Restoration Plan was to preserve the historical and architectural value of this ancient district, respecting the original features of the buildings. Siza reinvents the architectural Pombaline language in a contemporary key: the facades reflect the simplicity of that age, austere and severe, with modular proportions and narrow balconies. New public walkways, once closed by gates, have now reappeared and showed small, unexpected courtyards. Furthermore, Siza's actual work on the very large Baixa-Chiado Subway Station might be considered symbolic of the renaissance of this fascinating area. Besides, even the enlargement of the National Museum of Contemporary Art, now renamed Chiado National Gallery (1994), is a clear sign of the cultural and economic renewal of this old quarter. Founded in 1911 within the walls of an 18th-century convent and a bakery, the museum now hosts a collection of contemporary art. The project was commissioned to J. M. Wilmotte. His intervention respects both existing structures but introduces a modern architectural language to enhance the exhibition spaces. New materials, such as steel, stone, and glass, perfectly coexist with the brick of the ancient walls.

Today Lisbon is a capital where contemporary architecture is increasing. The strong economic expansion is supporting different projects even for educational areas, public green spaces, and housing. Furthermore, this great waterfront city always shows its beautiful old suggestions, and "near the river, where the land is flat, it sometimes reminds of Venice with its golden sunsets shading off into the fog" (Siza).

STEFANIA ATTI

See also **Lisbon World Exposition (1998); Malagueira Quarter, Evora, Portugal; Siza Vieira, Alvaro J. M. (Portugal); Souto de Moura, Eduardo (Portugal); Tavora, Fernando (Portugal)**

Further Reading

A.A.V.V., *Lisboa Expo 98*, translated by M. Cain, Lisbon: Editorial Blau, 1996

Angelillo, Antonio, *The Reconstruction Plan of the Chiado; Conversation with Alvaro Siza*, in Casabella, N. 628 (1995)

Collovà, Roberto, *A Covered Plaza*, in Lotus, N. 99 (1998)

Gregotti, Vittorio, *The Great Theatre of the Belém Cultural Centre*, in Casabella, N. 610 (1999)

Jodidio, Philip, *Alvaro Siza*, Köln: Taschen, 1999

Nicolin, Pierluigi, *Observation on Alvaro Siza's Intervention in the Chiado*, in Lotus, N. 92 (1997)

Portas, Nuno, and Manuel Mendes, *Portogallo. Architettura, gli ultimi vent'anni*, Milan: Electa, 1995

Santos, Paulo, *Lisbon, a Guide to Recent Architecture*, London: Ellipsis, 1998

Siza, Alvaro, *Opere e progetti*, Milan, Electa, 1995

Siza, Alvaro, *Dentro la città*, Milan, Motta Architettura, 1997

LISBON WORLD EXPOSITION

Over five centuries ago, Portugal led the world in advancing the skills of shipbuilding, mapmaking, and sailing that opened the oceans and continents to Europe. In 1498, Vasco da Gama pioneered a coveted route via Africa to the Indies, crossed the Indian Ocean, and weighed anchor in Asia. Two years later, Portuguese navigators landed on the shores of the vast expanse of Brazil.

Portugal, wishing to commemorate these events, sponsored the World Exposition of 1998, an international exposition in Lisbon, its capital and historic principal port. However, in the context of the modern world, the planners desired to emphasize more than just Portugal's past accomplishments; the exhibition, therefore, also called attention to the vital modern theme of preserving the oceans and future life. Commemorating old accomplishments within a modern context and style was key to the exhibition. Architecture became the vehicle for expressing and celebrating this modernity and the future.

Expo '98 underscored the modernization of Portugal. The exposition buildings were sited on more than 800 acres of land stretching over two miles along the west bank of the estuary of the Tagus River as it enters the Atlantic Ocean. The theme of the exposition was "The Oceans, a Heritage of the Future." Rising in the eastern part of Lisbon, the exposition area rehabilitated a decrepit dock region. The new infrastructure and buildings for it comprised the first phase in a larger plan for the rehabilitation of the city. Expo '98 lasted from 22 May to 30 September, with many of the structures built to last indefinitely.

The long, rectangular grounds of the exposition created a north–south axis with entrances at each end. A wide, tree-shaded pedestrian mall traversed the western edge of the area. Between it and the riverbank lay most of the exposition buildings. Extensive riverside gardens and the pavilions of foreign nations occupied the northern half of the area. In the southern half stretched the Olivais dock, a large, rectangular marine inlet; below it, near the south entrance, were additional national pavilions. Bordering the water of the inlet were an arena, the Pavilion of Portugal, a ceremonial plaza, and water fountains. Rising from the southern edge of the inlet was a two-story "oceanarium," or ocean-water aquarium.

A short east-west axis transected the center of the exposition. It extended from the western entrance to the area at the railway and subway station stop, to the riverside. The walkway connecting these sites was dominated along the north edge by a multipurpose arena, the largest building on the site, and on the south by the upper part of the marine inlet.

Most of the buildings represented stylized nautical or marine themes. Many were white or light-colored, brilliantly contrasting with the blue of the summer sky. Among the most distinguished was the rail and subway station (Gare do Oriente), designed by Zurich-based Spanish architect Santiago Calatrava, by which the majority of visitors arrived. The platform of the Oriente terminal sheltered travelers under a high glass roof. Intertwined arched white steel trusses supported the roof, which appeared to soar with spread wings. The structure suggested both the hull of a ship and a Gothic chapel, possessing an elegance that conveyed the feeling of a provident voyage. Calatrava's terminal, a rippling complex of curves, recalled the billowing sails of a flotilla of ships.

The international pavilions—designed by Portuguese architects Alberto França Dória and António Barreiros Ferreira—in the north section were modular structures that connected the individual displays of the over 100 participating countries via patios, courtyards, and pathways.

At the northern tip of the exposition area rose the 40-story Vasco da Gama Tower, designed by Skidmore, Owings, and Merrill (United States). From the tower, which dominated the Lisbon skyline, a metal support whose profile resembled the sail of a ship curved outward. This building was the Pavilion of the European Union. A terrace at the base of the tower extended out onto the river over concrete piles. Stretching away from the tower lay extensive gardens that occupied almost a fourth of the exhibition area and displayed the plants and ecosystems encompassed in the former Portuguese empire.

The Brazilian-trained Portuguese architect Regino Cruz, together with Skidmore, Owings, and Merrill, built the central multipurpose arena, known as the Utopia Pavilion. Able to seat more than 15,000 people and occupying over 300,000 square feet, the circular building had a concrete floor from which pinewood trusses curved up, spanning almost 400 feet. The mammoth wooden arches were particularly effective, conveying a sense of encompassing warmth, and afterward it became the major arena in Lisbon.

Álvaro Siza designed the Pavilion of Portugal, the official reception area of Expo '98. Siza's elegant building, constructed

Gare Do Oriente, detail of railroad tracks
© Dan Delgado *d2 Arch*

around an interior courtyard with an open plaza for public ceremonies, demonstrated his grasp of minimalist design principles. Located along the marine inlet, the Portugal Pavilion juxtaposed the oceanarium, one of the most ingenious buildings of Expo '98.

Named the Pavilion of the Future and designed by Peter Chermayeff, the oceanarium rose from the inlet like a docked ship. Consisting of two buildings connected by pedestrian bridges, it housed a complex of tanks displaying over 20,000 types of fish, ocean flora, and fauna. The largest tank held a volume of water equal to several Olympic-size swimming pools.

Over 10 million people attended Expo '98, the only international exposition ever held in Portugal. Expo '98 was thus a singular opportunity for Portugal, a country with a long historical heritage, to reassess and express its role in the modern world and in Europe. Articulating this role through architecture, the exposition's historical themes resonated with a futuristic ambience that was framed in a landscape of dynamic interaction between structures and environment.

EDWARD A. RIEDINGER

See also **Calatrava, Santiago (Spain); Exhibition Building; Lisbon, Portugal; Siza Vieira, Alvaro J. M. (Portugal)**

Further Reading

Binney, Marcus, *Architecture of Rail: The Way Ahead*, London: Academy Editions, 1995

Lisbon Expo '98: World Exhibition Guide, Oporto: Livraria Civilização Editora, 1998

Moltenbrey, Karen, "A Tale of Two Cities—How CAD Simultaneously Transformed an Old, Run-down Section of Lisbon into a World's Fair Site and New Ultra-modern 'City within a City'," *Computer Graphics World* (1999), p. 34–43

Pavilion of the Future, 1998 Lisbon World Exposition: Official Catalogue, Lisbon: Parque Expo '98, 1998

Trigueiros, Luiz, *Lisbon World Expo '98: Projects*, Barcelona: Editorial Gustavo Gili, 1998

Utopia Pavilion . . .: 1998 Lisbon World Exposition, Lisbon: Parque Expo '98, 1998

Viagem ao século XX = A Walk through the Century, Lisbon: Parque Expo '98, 1998

LONDON

London, "the unique city" (as Steen Eiler Rasmussen titled it in his popular book first published in 1937), can never be captured in a single image but tantalizes with a succession of contradictory takes. A collection of villages, parishes, boroughs, and former suburbs, specialized as to origin and destination—the City with its financial and legal institutions, Westminster with its political bodies, Mayfair and Kensington with their residences and cultural institutions—its architectural character is as varied as its component parts, which comprise an incoherent if dynamic metropolis that developed piecemeal, largely through private initiative. London experienced no grand governmental scheme to connect the separate enclaves in a disciplined manner, and individualism has reigned architecturally and urbanistically.

It was not until 1889 that the London County Council (LCC) was established to exercise some measure of control over the 12 metropolitan boroughs; for years, the City remained resolutely outside its jurisdiction. Initially, the architectural impact of the LCC, which had its own designers, was visible chiefly in the housing estates it erected throughout London, but after World War II, it dominated construction in a number of categories. In 1965 the Greater London Council (GLC) was formed to regulate the expansion into surrounding counties; London grew from 117 to 609 square miles, and the population reached some 8 million. The GLC was dissolved in 1986 under the Thatcher government, forcing the individual boroughs to take the initiative and giving impetus to gigantic private schemes for commercial and residential development.

Queen Victoria's son, Edward VII, came to throne when Great Britain was at the height of its power and glory. A grand scale was necessary for the largest world capital of an imperial nation, and accordingly, the favored style in an era that still considered revivals indispensable was the English Baroque of the 17th and early 18th centuries. Edwardian architecture bristled with the heavy rustication, broken pediments, bold cornices, and clustered columns beloved of Christopher Wren and Nicholas Hawksmoor. Whereas Victorian buildings had achieved their size by the addition and multiplication of relatively fine-grained detail, Edwardian architecture was massive and sculptural. In many cases, Victorian polychromy via red brick dressed with pale stone was retained, though many buildings were entirely of Portland or Bath stone. Regrettably, a great deal of new construction occurred at the expense of existing buildings, especially those of the 19th century, considered stylistically outdated and spatially inadequate for perceived new urbanistic and programmatic requirements. Thus, the modestly scaled and scenographically consistent structures of the late Georgian Regent Street development fell victim to discrete huge buildings like the Piccadilly Hotel (1905–08) by R. Norman Shaw (1831–1912), the late Victorian colossus who deftly adapted to Edwardian taste.

Public and private buildings, especially government structures (Central Criminal Courts, Old Bailey, 1900–06, by Edward Mountford [1855–1908]; Lambeth Town Hall, Brixton, 1905–08, by S. Warwick and E. A. Hall; London County Council County Hall, Westminster, 1908–31, by Ralph Knott [1878–1929]), theaters (Coliseum, 1903–04, and Victoria Palace Music Hall, 1911, all by Frank Matcham [1854–1920]), and urban interventions (Admiralty Arch, 1906–11, by Aston Webb (1849–1930). The French Classical Beaux-Arts manner also made its appearance (Ritz Hotel, Piccadilly, 1903–06, by Charles Mewès [1860–1914] and Arthur Davis [1878–1851]; Selfridge's Department Store, 1907–1928, commenced by the American Francis Swales [1878–1962] and completed by Sir John Burnet [1857–1938]). Neo-Georgian formed a less extravagant, more vernacular nationalist counterpoint to neobaroque. Sir Edwin Lutyens (1869–1944), *sui generis*, looked to both traditions, manifesting his originality in his very first London building, the premises for *Country Life* magazine (1904). The heritage of the Arts and Crafts movement was still alive, particularly in domestic architecture: C. F. A. Voysey (1857–1941)

erected characteristically simple but endearing residences in Kensington, and C. R. Ashbee (1863–1942) constructed two highly original houses at 38–39 Cheyne Walk in Chelsea (1899–1904). A few buildings, like the Bishopsgate Institute (1895) and Whitechapel Art Gallery (1897–1901) by C. Harrison Townsend (1851–1928) and the Black Friar Public House, remodeled in 1903 by H. Fuller Clark, reflected the effect of the Art Nouveau.

Edwardian styles continued into the reign of George V—the first member of the House of Windsor, and king from 1910 to 1936—although surfaces were smoothed, the ornament was cut back into the wall plane rather than boldly extruding, and the attitude toward historical styles became more cavalier. Such stripped, mannerist classicism can be observed in Lutyens's first large London building, Britannic House, 1924–27. In some cases there is a fusion with Art Deco, the "other" modern style, which was gleefully welcomed in London, whereas functionalism met resistance. Thus, Broadcasting House (1932) by Val Meyers and Watson-Hart with sculpture by Eric Gill, (1882–1940) 1932, and the headquarters of the Royal Institute of British Architects (RIBA) 1934, by (George) Grey Wornum, 1888–1957, could be assigned with equal justice to the classical or Deco camp. The capital is well endowed with unequivocal Deco, both in terms of interiors (Cambridge Theatre, 1930, by Wimperis, Simpson, and Guthrie with auditorium by Serge Chermayeff [1901–1996]) as well as major buildings, such as the Daily Telegraph (1928), by Elcock and Sutcliffe with Thomas Tait (1882–1954), and the Daily Express (1932), by Sir Owen Williams (1890–1969) with Ellis, Clarke, and Atkinson, both of which employ vast swathes of gleaming glass and chrome.

In its modernistic Deco classicism, Broadway House for the London Underground, a stepped high-rise clad in Portland stone with sculptures by Gill, Jacob Epstein, and Henry Moore, resembles both Broadcasting House and the RIBA. It was designed in 1927 by Charles Holden (1875–1960), who had the good fortune—and the talent—to be chosen by Frank Pick (1878–1941), an executive at London Transport and one of the more adventurous patrons of contemporary design (he commissioned avant-garde posters and the logo still in use). Holden's Underground stations are among London's finest architectural works of the 1930s. Those for the Piccadilly Line at Arnos Grove and Acton Town (1930–33) blend functionalism with Scandinavian and Dutch influences, a combination seen throughout London. Continental architects like Gunnar Asplund of Sweden and Willem Dudok (1884–1974) of the Netherlands, who enlivened the geometrical purity and severe surfaces of the International Style through the ingenuity of their compositions and continued to employ traditional materials like brick, were more congenial to English taste than the émigrés who began to arrive from Central and Eastern Europe in the wake of totalitarian repression.

Nevertheless, their presence would eventually act as a solvent of conservatism. Although some, such as Walter Gropius, Erich Mendelsohn and Marcel Breuer, remained only briefly, others such as the Hungarian-born Ernö Goldfinger (1902–1987; houses in Willow Road, 1937–39) and Berthold Lubetkin (1901–1990) from Georgia in the Soviet Union, left a lasting legacy. The latter, in 1932, formed the Tecton Partnership with students from the Architectural Association (AA), the educational stronghold of the avant-garde. Tecton's buildings for the Regent's Park Zoo, especially the Penguin Pool (1933–34) with its cantilevered platforms, and the privately financed High Point in Highgate exuded a confident elegance that reconciled many Londoners to modernism. The nine-story cruciform Highpoint I (1935), with 60 flats, and the seven-story Highpoint II (1938), with 12 maisonettes, offered rare amenities like a basement garage, a common winter-garden, and maids' and porters' lodgings.

Lubetkin belonged to the Modern Architecture Research (MARS) Group, founded in 1933 as the British branch of CIAM. Most of the members were homegrown modernists like E. Maxwell Fry (1899–1987; Sun House, 9 Frognal Way, 1935, one of the first Corbusian villas in England) and Ove Arup (1895–1988; he established Arup and Arup in 1938 and it became the major engineering firm in the British Isles, still active as Arup Associates). The Canadian Wells Coates (1895–1958), another MARS founder, who had designed some interiors for Broadcasting House, participated in one of the most interesting experiments in London in this interwar period: the creation of "Isokon" (acronym for Isometric Unit Construction) in 1931. This firm, directed by J. Craven ("Jack") Pritchard (1899–1992), was intended to produce for busy urbanites *existenzminimum* flats and houses that would be fitted out with standardized units. All were to be designed by Coates, whose most radical achievement was the concrete-surfaced, gallery-accessed Lawn Road Service Flats (1932–33; Gropius, Breuer, and Lazlo Moholy-Nagy, all formerly connected with the Bauhaus, stayed there for various periods). Installed with built-in Isokon furniture, Lawn Road was inspired programatically by the Narkofin collective facility in Moscow and formally by the Pavilion Suisse (as was Coates's more bourgeois 10 Palace Gate apartments of 1939). Another interwar architect who deserves citation is Willliam Crabtree (1905–1991). Although he never attained the professional renown of the MARS founders, Crabtree introduced the curtain wall in his Peter Jones Department Store on Sloane Square (1936). Reminiscent of Mendelsohn's Schöcken Department Stores in Germany, Peter Jones nevertheless is an unusually well-resolved indigenous example of 1930s modernism at its most compelling.

During World War II, not only did building cease but London suffered irreparable losses of its architectural stock. The mandate after 1945 was reconstruction, especially of housing. To meet the target of 100,000 new dwellings amid postwar shortages of materials and manpower, new techniques of prefabrication were adopted, and new typologies such as the slab and the tower block joined more traditional layouts. In both material and aesthetic regards, quality at first was poor; to counter this, the LCC broadened the responsibility of the Architect's Department. Many figures that became distinguished private practitioners, such as Colin St. John Wilson (1922–) and Peter (1923–2002) and Alison (1928–1993) Smithson, gained their first practical experience there.

During the 1950s and 1960s the LCC, along with local councils, erected vast housing estates in Inner and Outer London. Many were unimaginative and shoddy, stigmatized as "Welfare State" architecture, but several, such as Alton West at Roehampton near Richmond (1955–59), were internationally hailed. A sort of Ville Radieuse made palatable through its picturesque setting and unusually careful execution, Alton West comprises five Unités d'Habitation, cunningly set against a sloping hill, and fifteen 12-story towers arranged in two groups, as well as low-rise terraces and housing for the elderly. The earlier Alton East (1952–55) takes its clues from Scandinavian public housing—the low blocks have pitched roofs and concrete walls are clad in klinker brick—and while doubtless ingratiating, is less powerful.

Private architects also worked for local councils. Denys Lasdun (1914–2001) invented a new type of public housing—the cluster block—for the Bethnal Green Council, and the Westminster City Council sponsored a competition for Churchill Gardens, Pimlico (1950–62), won by A. J. P. Powell and J. H. Moya when they were still students at the AA. It is an inner-city version of the CIAM *Siedlung*: 7- to 11-story blocks run perpendicular to the nearby river, and slabs ranging from three to five floors parallel the Thames. The estate includes a covered shopping arcade, pubs, and restaurants. Its vocabulary is reminiscent of pre–World War II modernism. The taut glazed and brick surfaces and articulation of the frame make the dwellings more open and less monolithic than one finds with customary council housing.

In a burst of postwar optimism, the Festival of Britain had been held in 1951 to showcase modern architecture as suitable for other projects besides housing and to initiate development on the South Bank of the Thames. A number of the temporary pavilions anticipated the High-Tech movement of the 1980s in their light-weight materials and novel structures. The only permanent building, the Royal Festival Hall (LCC Architects Department with Robert Matthew, J. Leslie Martin (1908–2000), and Peter Moro) is a successful fusion of English/Scandinavian empiricism with continental élan (though somewhat marred in recent years by additions and interior renovation). The interiors were beautifully crafted, and the complex interlocking spaces functioned in ways that still command admiration. The influence of Le Corbusier, consistently the favorite European pioneer among the British (Mies van der Rohe did not attain the popularity he enjoyed in the United States until much later), is discernible in the use of *pilotis* (stilts) and in the articulation of the glazed skin as separate from the structure.

But this is the Le Corbusier of the 1920s and 1930s, whereas it would be the late Le Corbusier, the man who made *béton brut* (rough concrete) a byword, who would dominate the London architectural scene, exercising a not necessarily benign influence for more than two decades. The grim concrete bunkers of Queen Elizabeth Hall and the Hayward Gallery that in 1964 joined the Festival Hall on the South Bank, designed by the LCC/GLC team, still evoke dislike and dismay. Yet the movement known as the New Brutalism, shorthand for the ubiquitous employment of rough concrete, moved far beyond imitation of Le Corbusier's postwar practice: Its essence is ethical, not stylistic (Peter and Alison Smithson, with historian Reyner Banham, coined the term). "Brutalism tries to face up to a mass-produced society, and drag a rough poetry out of the confused and powerful forces at work" (*Architectural Design*, April 1957). A leading force in Team X's revision of modernist planning orthodoxy, the Smithsons wished to balance technological innovation with humanistic concerns, reinforcing fruitful interaction and encounters between urbanites, bringing together in one ensemble the functions that had been separated out by CIAM. Their primary effect on London's architecture was polemical; they built little, and even the theory promised more than it delivered. The Smithsons's competition design for the Golden Lane estate in 1952 was never realized, but its ingenious linking of public and private space to create a community was considered exemplary. Such Brutalist concepts were in large measure realized at the concrete-and-brick Barbican Estate (1959–79), constructed over a bombed-out section of the City by Chamberlin (Peter, 1919–78), Powell (Geoffrey, 1920–), and Bon (Christof, 1921–). With its elevated streets that protect pedestrians from the traffic below, its mixture of tower blocks (the tallest residential structures in Europe at the time) and slabs, and its deft intermingling of cultural institutions (art galleries, a theatre/concert hall), exposition spaces, gardens, fountains and dwellings, the Barbican creates a discrete community within the City of London.

Amid the bulky masses of stained concrete and aggressively sculptural, shabbily detailed behemoths that disfigured the urban landscape in the 1960s and 1970s, a few promising works lived up to the post-war dreams of the Welfare State. The Alexandra Road complex (1969–79) by Neave Brown (1933–) for the London Borough of Camden Architects provides housing blocks that embrace a training center for the mentally handicapped, a school, community center, and a local park. These social buildings form the head, whereas the base has two pedestrian streets circumnavigating the park and giving access to the dwellings to either side. Although inevitably constructed of *béton brut*, the thoughtfully composed setback section offers private terraces for the inhabitants.

By 1980, Brutalism had run its course, but nirvana was not yet at hand for London. Mediocre buildings come in many different guises and materials, and rampant private development undermined much of the social agenda that had ruled the LCC/GLC. One result was the appearance for the first time on London's horizon of commercial skyscrapers. The National Westminster ("Nat West") Tower (1981) by the Swiss-born Richard Seifert (1910–2001) was the first in a regrettably continuous sequence of undistinguished tall buildings, but relief was at hand. A generation born in the 1930s was poised some 50 years later to initiate an exciting new chapter in the life of London architecture. Although each of these renewers has a recognizable personal approach to design, the contenders may be conveniently grouped under two rubrics: High-Tech exponents are faithful to their credo of using sophisticated technologies to create component-based, light, flexible, structurally expressive, future-oriented buildings unencumbered by past references. Tensile cables, prefabricated metal elements, large sheets of glass, and occasionally mesh and cloth are favored over masonry and concrete. Postmodern practitioners draw on a variety of sources and may not eschew new structural and material possibilities, but overlay these with traditional means and historical motifs, often in the interests of contextualism, a concept woefully lacking in London in the heyday of Brutalism. Whichever one's preference, both groups have revitalized London with buildings of astonishing exuberance, flair, and relevance.

Both tendencies owe something to a major British figure not mentioned heretofore, because tragically, he built little in the city he loved, the exceptions being the Clore Gallery extension to Tate Britain (1987) and the posthumous No. 1 Poultry Street. The early work of James Stirling (1926–1993) anticipated High-Tech; he was one of the first to look back to 19th-century marvels like the Crystal Palace for inspiration. Then he developed his own brand of Postmodernism, a blend of the classical and the industrial that influenced architects who had been his students at Yale University and the AA.

The AA also brought forth Archigram, whose concepts Richard Rogers (1933–) first actualized in Lloyds of London (1978–86). This striking 12-story building gleams and glows amid the congested heart of the City, its stainless steel-clad concrete structure hung with shining service ducts and pods containing lavatories and meeting rooms, its glazed elevators a source of endless fascination as they futuristically climb and ascend. Its balcony-girt atrium, traversed by escalators, adds to the excitement.

Though Rogers and Norman Foster (1935–) were briefly partners in Team 4, their work is quite different. Foster's compositions are far less complex and do not celebrate servant spaces or elevate the guts of the building; the focus is on the delicately detailed glass surfaces rather than the structure, often dematerialized. The architect's double-height offices with flats above (and a penthouse for Foster himself) on the south bank of the Thames between Albert and Battersea Bridges (1991) typifies the seemingly artless simplicity that suggests less is more.

Two other London architects of this generation who are masters of High-Tech are Michael Hopkins (1935–) and Nicholas Grimshaw (1939–). Hopkins is the author of the Mound Stand at Lord's Cricket Stand, St. John's Wood—a festive concoction of tents, guy ropes, and steel struts that make an ideal viewing pavilion. Grimshaw is perhaps the more determined of the two to use industrialized components. The Eurostar Terminal at Waterloo Station (1989–92), with its charismatic asymmetrical exterior trusses supporting a twisting glass roof, displays his grasp of intricate engineering formulae.

Postmodernism has many branches, ranging from fairly direct imitation of Palladian and Georgian buildings, advocated by Prince Charles and executed by Quinlan Terry (1937–), among others, to a neovernacular that stems from the tradition of the Picturesque, to the more successful synthesis of modern technique, often High-Tech, and historical references. Terry Farrell (1938–) is the chief exponent of the latter approach, as demonstrated in a series of monumental London buildings: Vauxhall Cross (the headquarters for Military Intelligence) on the Thames (1988–92), which has an Art Deco flavor, and the gigantic mixed use developments of Alban Gate, London Wall (1988–94), and Embankment Place at Charing Cross (1988–96). Other architects who employ this technique are John Outram (1934–; Pumping Station, Stewart Street, Blackwall, 1985–88) and Piers Gough (1946–; The Circle, Butler's Wharf, 1987–90) of Campbell, Zogolovitch, Wilkinson, and Gough (CZWG).

Another development that commenced in the 1980s was the dominance of the private sector. Whereas for decades after World War II it was the publicly funded housing estates that constituted the largest agglomerations in London, in the boom period of the Thatcher years, private commercial development, much of it in the City and eastward—especially the disused Docklands—became the largest agglomerations. Broadgate (1985–91), a virtual "City within the City," boasts pubs, restaurants, shops, gardens, public sculpture (Richard Serra, George Segal, Barry Flanagan), and even a skating rink to cheer the hours of the 25,000 office workers who inhabit its large blocks. Its 14 buildings are a mix of Postmodern Picturesque and American Corporate Modern. Phases I–IV (1984–88), were designed by Arup Associates, and for phases V–XIV (1988–91), Skidmore, Owings, and Merrill (SOM) was called in because of their experience with the rapid construction of steel-framed buildings (unusual in London up until then).

SOM is not the only major American practice to work in the capital in recent years. Earlier, John Russell Pope (1874–1937) designed the Elgin Marbles wing of the British Museum (1937–39) and the Duveen Sculpture Hall (1937) at the Tate Gallery, Millbank. In the 1980s, several Americans gained entry: Venturi, Scott Brown, and Associates designed the Sainsbury Wing of the National Gallery (1986–90), and Cesar Pelli (1926–) built one of the tallest commercial buildings in Europe at Canary Wharf in Docklands (1990–95). Canary Wharf had been planned by SOM, which constructed its own tall office building there and established a London office in 1986. Rick Mather (1937–), having studied at the AA, has his practice in London; works include renovations and a new courtyard at the Wallace Collection (2000), as well as the master plan for the South Bank (2002).

There have been times in 20th-century London when architectural design displayed a certain consistency; namely, during the Edwardian era and during the long period of postwar reconstruction lasting from 1951 through the 1970s under the dominance of the LCC and the GLC. But for much of the time, London's architecture has been extremely heterogeneous. During the first half of the century, it was conservative, and radical tendencies were few. During the middle years, it was necessarily utilitarian, with social needs coming before aesthetic experiment. During the last two decades, however, architecture in London has achieved a level of excitement and experimentation that has merited international recognition. With the Millennium funding for large architectural projects, London in the 21st century will undoubtedly witness more and more architectural triumphs.

HELEN SEARING

See also **Archigram; Art Deco; Asplund, Erik Gunnar (Sweden); Banham, Reyner (United States); Breuer, Marcel (United States); Brutalism; Foster, Norman (England); Gropius, Walter (Germany); Lasdun, Denys (England); Lubetkin and Tecton; Lutyens, Edwin (England); Mendelsohn, Erich (Germany, United States); Pope, John Russell (United States); Postmodernism; Rogers, Richard (England); Mies van der Rohe, Ludwig (Germany); Sainsbury Wing, National Gallery, London; Skidmore, Owings and Merrill; Smithson, Peter and Alison (England); Stirling, James (England); Team X (Netherlands); United Kingdom; St. John Wilson, Colin (England)**

Further Reading

Understandably, the literature about such a vast city is itself vast. Innumerable monographs on individual architects exist, and periodicals are important sources, especially *The Architectural Review, Architectural Design, AA Files, Blueprint*, and the weekly *The Architect's Journal*. Surveys of modern architecture in general and British architecture in particular include analyses of important London buildings. The books listed below concentrate on the capital.

Amery, Colin, *Four London Architects 1985–88: Chipperfield, Mather, Parry, Stanton Williams*, Cambridge, Massachusetts: MIT Press, 1987

Banham, Reyner, *The New Brutalism: Ethic or Aesthetic*, London: Architectural Press, 1966

Barker, Felix, and Peter Jackson, *A History of London in Maps*, London: Barry and Jenkins, 1991

Beattie, Ann, *A Revolution in Housing: LCC Housing Architects and Their Work*, London: Architectural Press, 1980

Benton, Charlotte, *A Different World: Emigre Architects in Britain 1928–1958*, London: RIBA Heinz Gallery, 1995

Clout, Hugh (editor), *London History Atlas*, London: Times Books, 1991

Davies, Colin, *High Tech Architecture*, New York: Rizzoli International, 1988

Esher, Lionel, *A Broken Wave: The Rebuilding of England, 1940–1980*, London: Allen Lane, 1981

Glancy, Jonathan, *New British Architecture*, London: Thames and Hudson, 1989

Glancy, Jonathan, *Bread and Circuses*, London: Verso, 2001

Greater London Council, *Home Sweet Home: Housing Designed by the London County Council and Greater London Council Architects, 1888–1975*, foreword by Kenneth Campbell, London: Academy Editions, 1976

Harwood, Elaine, and Andrew Saint, *London*, Exploring England's Heritage Series, London: Her Majesty's Stationery Office, 1991

Jackson, Alan, *The Politics of Architecture*, Toronto: University of Toronto Press, 1970

Jencks, Charles, and Andreas Papadakis (editors), *Post-Modern Triumphs in London*, London: Academy Editions, 1991

Jones, Edward, and Christopher Woodward, *A Guide to the Architecture of London*, London: Weidenfeld 1983; and Nicolson, 2nd edition, London: Weidenfeld and Nicolson, 1992. Reprinted with corrections, 1995.

Lambert, Sam (editor), *New Architecture of London: A Selection of Buildings since 1930*, London: Architectural Association, 1963

Leapman, Michael (editor), *London: The Evolution of a Great City*, London and New York: Weidenfeld and Nicholson, 1989

Maxwell, Robert, *New British Architecture*, New York: Praeger, 1973

Moffett, Noel, *The Best of British Architecture: 1980–2000*, London: E. and F. N. Spon, 1993

Murray, Peter, and Robert Maxwell, *Contemporary British Architects*, Munich and New York: Prestel, 1994

Peto, James, and Donna Loveday (editors), *Modern Britain, 1929–1939*, London: Design Museum, 1999

Powell, Kenneth (editor), *World Cities: London*, London: Academy Editions, 1993

Rasmussen, Steen Eiler, *London, the Unique City*, Cambridge, Massachusetts: MIT Press, 1974 (reprint of 1937 edition, New York: The MacMillan Co. 1937; new revised edition. London: J. Cape, 1948. Reprint of 1948 edition, Cambridge, Massachusetts: MIT Press, 1974.

Saint, Andrew, and Gillian Darley, *The Chronicles of London*, London: Weidenfeld and Nicholson, 1994

Saunders, Ann, *The Art and Architecture of London: An Illustrated Guide*, Oxford: Phaidon, 1984

Seaborne, Mike, *Photographers' London, 1839–1994*, London: Museum of London, 1995

Service, Alistair, *London 1900*, New York: Rizzoli International, 1979

Trench, Richard, and Ellis Hillman, *London under London: A Subterranean Guide*, London: John Murray, 1984

Weinreb, Ben, and Christopher Hibbert (editors), *The London Encyclopedia*, London: Macmillan, 1984; revised edition, 1995 (same publisher)

LOOS, ADOLF 1870–1933

Architect and critic, Austria

Adolf Loos's infamous denunciation of ornament helped change the course of modern architecture not because it was the first time that an architect recognized the widening gulf between decoration and structure, but because it was the first time that an architect theorized a detrimental relationship between decoration and cultural evolution. In a series of demonstrative buildings, built mostly in the Austro-Hungarian lands between the late 1890s and 1914, Loos argued that the direction of modern culture points away from the adornment of buildings. On the rear facade of the Steiner House (Vienna, 1910), Loos produced a masterpiece of austerity, a white stucco box of symmetrical windows absent of any symbolic references to the traditions of monumental architecture. For the street frontage of the Scheu House (1912), this time asymmetrically massed through staggered roof terraces, Loos similarly composed a house of severe geometric lines, plain white surfaces, and unframed windows; and, in the seminal essay "Ornament and Crime" (1908), he wrote that "the man of our own times who covers the walls with erotic images from an inner compulsion is a criminal or a degenerate . . . cultural evolution is equivalent to the removal of ornament from articles of daily use."

In the 19th century, art historians had conceived of the arts within a grand narrative that was inherently either progressive or regressive. Examples of the latter were almost exclusively the province of non-European peoples, whose arts were judged to lie on a spectrum ranging from the savage and barbaric (for example most hunter-gatherer societies) to the static (such as Egypt or China). Loos, in his essays, contrasted the most "barbaric" of artistic cultures—the baroque tools and bodies of recently studied Pacific Island cultures (the "Papuans," as he called them)—with civilized contemporary Europe. Among the latter, he stated, ornament had become an outdated fetish and wasteful social expenditure, in conflict with modern notions of propriety, efficiency, and productive labor management.

Loos found his contemporary paradise largely in England and the United States. He remarked on numerous occasions that architecture's true course of evolution led toward English values of restraint and asceticism. Between 1893 and 1896, he traveled throughout the eastern United States and experienced firsthand raw productive building forces unfettered by nostalgia for the past, the possibility of creating an architecture of the moment. On his return to Vienna, he undertook a series of articles for the influential *Neue Freie Presse* that sought to inculcate foreign ideas as models for Viennese design. These efforts eventually resulted in the creation of a short-lived, self-published journal, *Das Andere* (The Other), devoted to the introduction of Anglo-Saxon culture into Austria.

Loos criticized the backward educational methods of the major Viennese art and design schools. The truth of modern architecture could never emerge by means of historicist copying

Michaelerplatz Building (or Haus Goldman und Salatsch), Vienna (1909–11)
Photo © Mary Ann Sullivan

of decorated details; this resulted in the counterfeit architecture of Ringstrasse Vienna where entire neighborhoods appointed the elaborate sculptures and florid moldings previously reserved for the palaces of the aristocracy. Indeed, advances in industrial production had led to the widespread practice of tacking inexpensive and machine-made ornamented facades onto relatively simple buildings. Austrian cities, Loos claimed, were becoming like the Potemkin villages that Catherine the Great passed through in the poor Russian provinces, false fronts erected to cover the poverty underneath. Insofar as ornamented buildings pretended to be something that they were not, Loos regarded them as examples of the overall corruption of language, thought, and architecture in contemporary times.

If Loos condemned historicism, he also condemned the attempts of the newer generation of Viennese artists and architects to come up with a contemporary artistic and ornamental language. Although he was well acquainted with members of the Vienna Secession and the German and Austrian variants of the Art Nouveau (that is, Jugendstil and Moderne), he felt that their attempts to unify art and industry were fruitless and nostalgic. After 1900 architects such as Josef Maria Olbrich, Josef Hoffmann, and Hermann Muthesius increasingly became his adversaries. As Loos wrote in the essay "Cultural Degeneration" (1908), it was unnecessary to fabricate a contemporary style from the collective work of artists and industrialists in the manner of the German Werkbund.

Most important, one did not find the style of the times in the works of artists. As Loos described in his essay "Architecture" (1910), art and architecture have completely different aims. Art is individualistic and revolutionary; architecture is collective and conservative, based on values of purpose and comfort. Few of Loos's ideas were more controversial than this assertion that art should be excluded from everyday architectural design, in fact, from all design, with the exception of monuments and funerary shrines.

In designs for chairs and tables and for the interior of the Cafe Museum (Vienna, 1899), Loos delineated an architectural syntax of restraint and propriety. In an evolutionary sense, he sought to continue what he saw as the last sane epoch of design, the Biedermeier era of the mid-19th century, a time when middle-class design embodied values of practicality, simplicity, and clarity. This approach did not, however, exclude all historicist elements, as indicated by the Doric porticoes on the Villa Karma (Clarens, Switzerland, 1904) or the Michaelerplatz Building (Vienna, 1910). Rather, it emphasized the creation of an architecture that could fit in with both its times and its surroundings. Although the spare surfaces of the Michaelerplatz Building stand apart from its ornate historicist neighbors, its tripartite composition draws from traditional Viennese design; Loos was greatly bothered by criticism that the building was not contextual.

In Loos's buildings, beyond the jolt of seeing architecture absent of artistic screens and filters, visual interest emerges from the qualities of surfaces and the progression of interior spaces. Rooms in the Kärtner Bar (Vienna, 1907–1908), the Michaelerplatz Building, and the Knize Store (Vienna, 1913) are covered with sumptuous materials: contrasts of dark mahogany with brass and mirrors, walls of flowing marble, and deep tones of oak and cherry wood paneling. Loos's lavish revetments are the result of his idea that each material possesses its own language of form. If one material covers another, it should strive to the fullest extent to avoid any hint of replication. Loos's Raumplan (spatial plan) is present in many of his houses and even some public buildings. It embodies the idea of a series of interlocking spaces connected via staircases across the levels of a building and dismisses the separation by sectional floors (or planes) characteristic of most architecture.

In his oeuvre Loos relied heavily on the effect of shock. As one of the earliest avant-garde architects, opposed to the traditional architectural establishment as well as so-called progressive architectural movements, he was polemical and intentionally enigmatic. Throughout his life, Loos was deeply concerned with realizing the elusive qualities of the contemporary moment and thus bringing architecture closer to the design process that results in a well-cut suit. As his diverse legacy points out, however, the logic of contemporary times that Loos so avidly sought out often yielded an architectural portrait of the modern age distinguished by controversy and double entendre.

MITCHELL SCHWARZER

See also **Art Nouveau (Jugendstil); Deutscher Werkbund; Hoffmann, Josef (Austria); Muthesius, Hermann; Olbrich, Josef Maria (Austria); (Germany); Steiner House, Vienna; Vienna, Austria; Vienna Secession**

Biography

Born in Brünn, Moravia (now Brno in the Czech Republic), 10 December 1870, son of a stonecutter and sculptor. Studied at the State Technical School, Reichenberg, Bohemia, 1887–88; studied at the Dresden Polytechnik, Germany, 1890–93. Worked and traveled in the United States, 1893–96, including visits to New York, Philadelphia, St. Louis, Chicago, and the World's Columbian Exposition of 1893. Began career as an architect as assistant in the building firm of Carl Mayreder, Vienna, 1896. Published essays on architecture and design for the *Neue Freie Presse, Ver Sacrum,* and other periodicals, 1897 to 1914; founded the journal, *Das Andere* (The Other; a periodical dedicated to the introduction of Western culture to Austria), 1903–04. Active in independent architectural and interior design practice, Vienna, from late 1890s. Founded Bauschule (School of Architecture), Vienna, 1912–14. Officer of the reserve for the Austrian Army during World War I. Chief architect of the Housing Department of the City of Vienna, 1922–24. Lived in France (Paris and the Riviera), 1922–27. Returned to Vienna to continue architectural practice, 1928. Died in Kalksburg, 28 August 1933; body shifted to the main cemetery of Vienna, 1934.

Selected Works

Cafe Museum, Vienna, 1899
Villa Karma, Clarens, near Montreux, 1904
Kärtner Bar (American Bar), Vienna, 1907–08
Steiner House, Vienna, 1910
Michaelerplatz Building, Vienna, 1911
Scheu House, Vienna, 1912
Horner House, Vienna, 1912
Knize Store, Vienna, 1913
Strasser House, Vienna, 1919

Max Dvorak Mausoleum, Vienna (project), 1921
Rufer House, Vienna, 1922
Grand Hotel Babylon, Nice (project), 1923
Tristan Tzara House, Paris, 1926
Moller House, Vienna, 1928
Müller House, Prague, 1930
Austrian Werkbund Siedlung, Vienna, 1932

Selected Publications

Trotzdem 1900–1930, 1931
Ins Leere Gesprochen, 1897–1900, 1981; as *Spoken into the Void:
    Collected Essays 1897–1900*, translated by Jane O. Newman and
    John H. Smith, 1982
Die Potemkinische Stadt 1897–1933, 1983
Adolf Loos im Spiegel der Zeitgenossen, edited by Adolf Opel, 1985
"Architecture," "Ornament and Crime," and "Cultural Degeneration,"
    in *The Architecture of Adolf Loos*, translated by Wilfried Wang, with
    Rosamund Diamond and Robert Godsill, 1985
Konfrontationen, Schriften von und über Adolf Loos, edited by Adolf
    Opel, 1988

Further Reading

Amendolagine, Francesco, and Massimo Cacciari, *Oikos: da Loos a
    Wittgenstein*, Rome: Officina, 1975
Gravagnuolo, Benedetto, *Adolf Loos: teoria e opere*, Milan: Idea
    Books, 1972; as *Adolf Loos: Theory and Works*, translated by C.H.
    Evans, New York: Rizzoli, 1982
Loos, Adolf, *Adolf Loos*, edited by Heinrich Kulka, Vienna: Schroll,
    1931
Moos, Stanislaus von, "Le Corbusier and Loos," *Assemblage*, 4
    (1987)
Münz, Ludwig, and Gustav Künstler, *Der Architekt Adolf Loos*,
    Vienna: Schroll, 1964; as *Adolf Loos: Pioneer of Modern
    Architecture*, translated by Harold Meek, New York: Praeger, and
    London: Thames and Hudson, 1966
Risselada, Max (editor), *Raumplan versus Plan libre*, Delft: Delftse
    Universitaire Pers, 1987; as *Raumplan versus Plan Libre: Adolf
    Loos and Le Corbusier, 1919–1930*, New York: Rizzoli, 1988
Rogers, Ernesto, "The Reality of Adolf Loos," *Casabella continuità*
    (November 1959)
Rukschcio, Burkhardt, and Roland Schachel, *Adolf Loos: Leben und
    Werk*, Salzburg: Residenz Verlag, 1982
Schezen, Roberto, *Adolf Loos: Architecture, 1903–1932*, New York:
    Monacelli, 1996
Schwarzer, Mitchell, "Ethnologies of the Primitive in Adolf Loos's
    Writings on Ornament," *Nineteenth-Century Contexts*, 18 (fall
    1994)
Tournikiotis, Panayotis, *Loos*, Paris: Macula, 1991; as *Adolf Loos*,
    translated by Marguerite McGoldrick, New York: Princeton
    Architectural Press, 1994

LOS ANGELES, CALIFORNIA

Charles Moore explained his attraction to Los Angeles as the home of two architectural landmarks: the Gamble House and Disneyland. Although neither of these is within the boundaries of the City of Los Angeles, they both belong to Los Angeles and describe the range of fantasy and possibility discovered there in the 20th century. In a place known for suburban sprawl, it is impossible to discuss the city except as Greater Los Angeles, whose boundaries are the San Gabriel and San Fernando Valleys on the north, Orange County and Long Beach to the south, Pomona on the east, and the Pacific Ocean to the west. It is a horizontal city, interrupted by pockets of skyscrapers, a sprawling megalopolis sweeping everything in its path to the sea. It

abuts or surrounds and includes several other incorporated cities, including Pasadena, Beverly Hills, West Hollywood, Glendale, and Santa Monica. East Los Angeles conjures up a vastly different image than West Los Angeles or South Central.

Several themes run throughout the architectural development of this time and place. They include the concept of experimentation, verging on radical at times; the incorporation of the landscape, whether it was bringing the outdoors in, the indoors out, or more often, the ambiguity of the difference between the two; the unquestioned dependence on private transportation; the veneration of cheap building materials and building techniques; and a search for a usable and meaningful history, in a city known for being new and for selling the illusion of being somewhere else.

In the 20th century, Los Angeles became the city of cutting-edge architecture in the United States. It replaced Chicago, although it never developed an eponymous school. Rather, the freedom of the place encouraged several styles that shared an attitude of conscious newness.

By 1900, the City of Los Angeles was 120 years old and had been part of the United States for half a century. Its Native American and Mexican history was exchanged for a myth, the dream of a Spanish Eden as depicted by boosters, Hollywood, and health-seekers. The "Port of Iowa," as it was sometimes called, drew newcomers, including clients, architects, and sometimes developers, who were willing to take risks and experiment with new ways of living. The newly created movie industry brought people to Los Angeles who understood the creation of place and who had money to spend.

Climate was no obstacle. There were 360 days of sunshine every year. Earthquakes, fires, and mudslides challenged the benign environment, but fueled the modernist urge to bulldoze and rebuild. The vegetation was mostly all imported, but easily adapted to the environment, shaping it and giving it an exotic look. The image of the palm tree became an instantly recognizable symbol of the place. The land embraced the American assumption of the single-family home and private transportation. The backyard was perfected here, and there were more automobiles than children. It is no accident that most architectural landmarks here were residential. Public images, whether early postcards or contemporary picture books, are likely to portray streets lined with houses or an individual house with a rose garden more often than a public building or shot of downtown. Living focused on the outdoors; houses accommodated sleeping porches, outdoor dining rooms, swimming pools and backyard grills, and the beach, which was a shared backyard.

The California Building at the 1893 World's Columbian Exposition sold both the image and the dream of California. Each facade represented a different mission, and inside were displays luring tourists. Hostesses distributed fresh oranges and pamphlets that declared "Oranges for health; California for wealth." The building initiated a passion for the Mission Revival style depicting a romantic and somewhat sanitized view of history. The building itself was copied in Julia Morgan's Los Angeles Herald-Examiner Building in 1912. Parapets, bell towers, arcades, white stucco walls resembling adobe, red-tiled roofs, and arches appeared in railroad stations, schools, shops, Protestant churches, and private houses throughout the Southland and found their way across the country in the two decades preceding World War I.

Visiting that World's Fair, but more interested in the Japanese Pavilion were Frank Lloyd Wright and Charles and Henry Greene, the latter brothers on their way to California. Irving Gill worked in Louis Sullivan's Chicago office while the fair was being planned, before coming to southern California. All were intrigued by the pavilion and its flexible walls that screened space rather than enclosed it. The ethereal building was reflected in the work of all these architects when they came to Los Angeles.

Influenced by the quality of the light and the original mission buildings, Irving Gill abstracted the architectural traditions of the Spanish-Indian missions into a universal geometry. His architecture was based on four principles found in nature: the straight line of the horizon; the arch from the dome of the sky; the circle seen when a stone touches the water; and the square, symbol of power, justice, honesty and firmness. These elements translated into grand homes, women's clubs, schools, and workers' housing that all used the same principles at different scales. He experimented with new construction techniques, such as tilt-slab construction, in which the concrete walls were poured in place horizontally, cured, and lifted into place. Gill rejected traditional moldings, chair and plate rails, and gabled roofs, opting for a clean look that focused on the geometry of the space. He designed shelves with rounded corners so they would not collect dust, saving labor, especially for women. His rooms looked clean and were clean because they practically cleaned themselves through built-in vacuum cleaners and concrete floors. The houses were arranged on the site to maximize small yards, minimize maintenance, and encourage privacy, instead of centering the house in the middle of the lot with the rooms mirroring the neighbors.

Mission Revival gave way to simplicity in the Craftsman houses designed by Charles and Henry Greene. In style from the turn of the century until the 1920s, the Craftsman style emphasized nature. The Greenes opened up the interior spaces and the exterior walls with an emphasis on the landscape, natural colors, Native American fabrics, colors, and the light of the Southwest. Influenced by Shingle-style materials, Prairie-style horizontality, and Japanese flexibility and clarity of space, Greene and Greene developed the reformist ideals of the Arts and Crafts movement into an art. They attracted wealthy clients who could afford handmade houses and were willing to sleep outdoors in the winter.

The Gamble House (1908, Greene and Greene) in Pasadena is three stories tall, but appears to hug the ground because of its horizontality, overhanging roofs, and shady patios. It grows from the landscape out of the arroyo stone found there naturally, gradually mixing with clinker bricks to form a mansion disguised as a cottage. Bedrooms and the informal dining room are outdoors where the suggestion of walls and a dominant roof provide the symbolic shelter of a tree house.

The Craftsman style was democratized into thousands of middle-class homes. The bungalows among the orange groves drew inspiration and form from many sources. They were one or one-and-a-half story houses with informal and open plans, multipurpose rooms, a prominent hearth, and a variety of exterior stylings that ranged from the practical to the exotic. Built-in bookshelves and buffets saved space and lumber, and the houses featured mass-produced Mission furniture and simple stained glass.

"Bungalow fever," as it was referred to in the press, was highly contagious and quickly spread throughout the United States. Annual bungalow books were used like pattern books of earlier generations, so buyers could mix and match according to budget and taste. The houses even came prepackaged in do-it-yourself kits available from the Los Angeles–based Pacific Readi-Cut Homes, as well as dozens of other companies.

The quintessential Los Angeles home of early 20th century was period colonial revival: English Tudor, French, Moorish, and especially Spanish. Spanish colonial revival was made fashionable by the 1915 Panama-California Exposition held in San Diego to celebrate completion of the Panama Canal. These white houses decorated with red-tiled roofs and ironwork became symbols of the sun-filled lifestyle available in Los Angeles.

Spanish-Italian-Moorish buildings came to be called Mediterranean by realtors, and the name not only solved the problem of categorizing a hybrid style, but also a lifestyle to go with it, evoking blue skies and white cottages on the hillside, where one could wander barefoot and breathe fresh air. The white "adobe"-looking plaster walls shimmered in the sunlight, framed by palm trees, and front lawns, creating an exotic but familiar pattern. The front porch became a colorful tiled courtyard. Rows of two-storied white, Mexican-tiled duplexes with arched entries soon laced the city.

Frank Lloyd Wright, no fan of period revival, completed the Barnsdall House in 1921, followed by the Millard, Storer, Ennis, and Freeman Houses, in which he pursued a new system of do-it-yourself low-cost housing. All had a vaguely Mayan theme. Working with his son Lloyd Wright (who had studied landscape design with Frederick Law Olmsted and architecture with Irving Gill), Wright experimented with the common concrete block. The blocks were formed in situ using sand from the site in the aggregate. Each house had its own design for patterned blocks, which were then woven together with plain and pierced-patterned blocks to create a variety of shapes, designs, and sizes. Each block had a semicircular edge, that when placed next to the adjacent block created a full circle. As the block walls were erected, steel rods and concrete were inserted into the horizontal and vertical shafts, thus knitting together a steel-reinforced concrete wall. Any family could design, create, and build their own house at a minimal cost of both material and labor. Lloyd Wright continued to pursue this technique in the following decades, combining the patterned blocks with expanses of smooth concrete to create unique and picturesque settings. He later produced one of the most perfect of transparent organic buildings in the Wayfarer's Chapel of 1949.

Frank Lloyd Wright employed Rudolf Schindler to supervise construction of the concrete-block houses. Schindler had been born in Vienna and studied under Otto Wagner, but remained in Los Angeles for the rest of his career where he developed an oeuvre that he termed "space architecture." Encouraged by Wright that the reality of architecture is the interior space, not the exterior wall, Schindler continued his mentor's dematerialization of the wall to define space. Schindler's own house (King's Road House, 1922) included experiments in alternative living arrangements. The plan incorporated a pinwheel design for two or more families to share, with a common kitchen at the center. Each adult had his or her own studio/living space with both an indoor and an outdoor room. The roofed interior had a blank wall for privacy and a wood and glass wall overlooking the roofless exterior room edged by shrubs and different levels of plantings. The families shared labor and respected each person's alternating needs for creative space, privacy, and community.

Sharing the house with the Schindlers for a brief period were the Neutras. Richard Neutra, also born in Vienna and brought to Los Angeles by Frank Lloyd Wright, made Los Angeles his permanent home. Neutra's Lovell Health House (1927–29) epitomized and advanced the International Style along California lines. The house, built over a ravine, comprised a steel cage suspended from the roof with the open skeleton articulated on the finished exterior. Because of the mass-producible steel frame, the house could be erected quickly to Miesian precision. It was built for Dr. Philip Lovell to give form to his health principles and evidenced Neutra's own thoughts about health and survival through space. Ford headlights on the stairwell echoed the machine metaphor. Neutra continued to dematerialize walls and roofs in his unique versions of steel and glass space containers scattered throughout the city.

Californian Cliff May built on native traditions, modernizing them to merge the romance of the past with the glamour of the present in contemporary ranch houses without the ranch. They were based on the aesthetic and the plan of the early rancho and hacienda surrounding a courtyard. The house was one room deep to capture the breezes, and each room was accessed by an outdoor hallway. Having no formal training, May used what he knew worked and repeated this vernacular building thousands of times, reintroducing Los Angeles to its architectural roots. The California ranch house was exported all across the United States, including places where neither the climate nor tradition supported it.

Art moderne, specifically Art Deco, adorned Los Angeles's public face. The skyscrapers of 1920s in Los Angeles were typically encased in a hybrid of billboard neon and Cubist Modern architecture. Art Deco utilized new materials or found novel uses for traditional materials, such as glass, chrome, steel, terra-cotta, patent leather, cork, Bakelite, and Formica. Ornament, banned from European modernism as overly decadent in the early part of the century, found expression in moderne in the form of colorful chevrons, spirals, sunbursts, and abstracted and stylized animal and human forms. Los Angeles had some of the most exciting Art Deco buildings in the country, including Morgan Walls, and Clements's 1928–29 Atlantic Richfield Building; Bullocks Wilshire by Parkinson and Parkinson in 1928; and Claude Beelman's 1929 Eastern Columbia Building. They sparkled like jewels in green, blue, turquoise, and gold with beacons lighting the tops like light reflecting off diamonds.

Other buildings, such as Los Angeles's Central Library, designed by Bertram Goodhue and Carleton Winslow in 1922–26, melded Deco, Egyptian, Spanish, and Italian Renaissance to create one of the landmarks of downtown. The City Hall by John C. Austin with John and Donald Parkinson in 1926–28 mixes Deco setbacks with a Byzantine rotunda, topped by a copy of the ancient Mausoleum of Hallicarnassus. Parkinson and Parkinson's Union Station (1939) combined Art Deco with Spanish in a unique environment that bridged the two halves of the century. It was the last great railroad station built in the United States, superseded after the war by the success of air traffic. Each of these buildings has an air of set design about it. In fact, they have often been used as movie sets to represent a variety of building types.

The other half of art moderne was Streamline Moderne, also strong in the Los Angeles tradition. Streamline style popularized the horizontal speed of new modes of transportation in the 1930s, with its imagery suggested movement. The shape of that movement reflected modern transports: dirigibles, streamlined locomotives; ships, and teardrop-shaped cars. Movie theaters, such as S. Charles Lee's 1939 Academy Theatre, competed with medical offices, shops, small offices, and post offices to attract attention through swirling patterns, horizontal speed-lines, round windows, and undulating chrome railings. The best examples were the twin fleets of Wurdeman and Becket's 1938 Pan Pacific Auditorium and Robert Derrah's Coca-Cola Bottling Plant, completed in 1937. The latter resembles a ship sailing down Central Avenue with porthole windows, raised doorways, simulated rivets in the white stucco, and a captain's bridge.

After World War II, Los Angeles was again the center of postwar modernism and innovation. John Entenza, editor of *Arts and Architecture* magazine sponsored the Case Study House program to promote California architects, raise the aesthetic standards of postwar housing, and show the public that people could live in glass houses. Richard Neutra, Eero Saarinen, Charles and Ray Eames, A. Quincy Jones, Rafael Soriano, Craig Elwood, and Pierre Koenig, among others, were commissioned to build real houses for a variety of real clients that showcased

Eastern Columbia Building (1929), designed by Claude Beelman
© Robert Landau/CORBIS

the California lifestyle. Between 1945 and 1962, 24 completed projects demonstrated the possibilities for living fostered by the Los Angeles climate. All dealt with the landscape and encouraged outdoor living. Roofless dining rooms contained outdoor cooking ranges, and kitchens had interchangeable color panels made of Formica. Most had invisible room dividers, pass-throughs to the kitchen, Eames- and Saarinen-designed furnishings, and glass walls facing the backyards. The houses were typically better known by number than by name, but they were far from impersonal. Case Study House #22 by Pierre Koenig (1959), cantilevered from the hillside, was the most dramatic. With neither neighbors nor ground visible from the house, it appeared to be a glass box floating over the city.

The future was still evident in houses like Lautner's 1960 Chemosphere House, which rose up out of the canyon on a central pole, or Bruce Goff's 1984 Struckus House, a cylinder of wood and glass with overlapping op art illusions and protruding fisheye lens windows.

In the last two decades of the century, Frank Gehry dominated the city and the world with his unusual buildings of cheap materials and radically new perspectives, beginning with his own house in Santa Monica (1978). His work dealt with collisions of space, color, and form, as well as time, materials, and sometimes the neighbors. He has inspired other Los Angeles architects, including Eric Owen Moss, Steve Ehrlich, Frederick Fisher, and Morphosis, whose work can be seen throughout the area from Venice to Culver City.

Ending the century were two projects that reflected the range of 20th-century modernism: Richard Meier's sprawling Getty Center, simultaneously overlooking the Santa Monica Freeway and the Pacific Ocean, and Gehry's Disney Concert Hall downtown. Both buildings survived public discussion, protest, and success, setting precedents for the next century.

MAGGIE VALENTINE

See also **Art Deco; Art Nouveau (Jugendstil); Bungalow; Craftsman Style; Gehry, Frank (United States); Getty Center, Los Angeles; Gill, Irving (United States); Greene, Henry M. and Charles S. (United States); Lovell Health House, Los Angeles; Meier, Richard (United States); Morgan, Julia (United States); Neutra, Richard (Austria); Panama Pacific Exposition, San Francisco (1915); Schindler, Rudolph M. (Austria, United States); Williams, Paul (United States); Wright, Frank Lloyd (United States)**

Further Reading

Gleye, Paul, *The Architecture of Los Angeles*, Los Angeles: Rosebud Books, 1981

Hines, Thomas S., "Machines in the Garden: Notes toward a History of Modern Los Angeles" in *Sex, Death, and God in L.A.*, edited by David Reid, New York: Pantheon Books, 1992

McCoy, Esther, *Five California Architects*, New York: Reinhold, 1960

McWilliams, Carey, *Southern California Country: An Island on the Land*, New York: Duell Sloan and Pearce, 1946

Moore, Charles Willard, Peter Becker, and Regula Campbell, *The City Observed, Los Angeles: A Guide to Its Architecture and Landscapes*, New York: Random House, 1984

Scott, Allen John, and Edward W. Soja (editors), *The City: Los Angeles and Urban Theory at the End of the Twentieth Century*, Berkeley: University of California Press, 1996

LOVELL HEALTH HOUSE, LOS ANGELES

Designed by Richard Neutra; completed 1929

The master builders of 20th-century architecture asserted their domestic design philosophies through their groundbreaking houses. What Le Corbusier achieved with the Villa Savoye (Poissy, France, 1930), Ludwig Mies van der Rohe with the Tugendhat Villa (Brno, Czechoslovakia, 1930), Frank Lloyd Wright with Fallingwater (Bear Run, Pennsylvania, 1938), and Alvar Aalto with the Villa Mairea (Noormaku, Finland, 1939), Richard Neutra accomplished with the Lovell Health House, built in Los Angeles in 1927–29. These architects succeeded in breaking away from tradition and the eclecticism of the 19th-century bourgeois residence to design for a new 20th-century family. Changes in modern lifestyle required not only different spatial arrangements of the home but also an architectural image reflecting social and political shifts and the advancement of science and technology. Modern residential architecture became, in the hands of Le Corbusier, Adolf Loos, Mies, Neutra, and others, devoid of decoration, embellishment, or ornament. Aesthetic strength and purity lay in direct and truthful expression of structure, function, and materials.

Austrian-American Richard Joseph Neutra (1882–1970) moved to the United States in 1923. Before settling in Los Angeles, he was influenced in Vienna by the pioneering architecture of Loos, Otto Wagner, and Josef Hoffmann. With fellow friend and architect Rudolph Schindler, these men were active in Vienna along with painters Gustav Klimt and Egon Schiele, the composer Arnold Schoenberg, and the family of Sigmund Freud. Neutra worked with Erich Mendelsohn in Germany and then with the firm of William Holabird and Martin Roche in Chicago and Frank Lloyd Wright at his studio and home, Taliesin, in Spring Green, Wisconsin.

Preceding Neutra, who soldiered through World War I, his friend Schindler arrived in the United States in 1914. In 1926, Neutra and his wife Dione and infant son joined Schindler and his wife Pauline in their home on Kings Road in West Hollywood. Designed by Schindler and built in 1922, the airy, open-plan house became acclaimed as an architectural masterpiece. At the time, the Schindler house was a place for bohemian gatherings of artists, musicians, dancers, and the like. Schindler and Neutra went on to collaborate on an entry for the 1926 international design competition for the League of Nations building in Geneva, Switzerland. Their project, unfortunately, did not place in the scandal-ridden competition in which the jury rejected the nontraditional designs of modernism.

The same year, in 1926, Dr. Philip Lovell, a naturopath, and his wife Leah hired Schindler to build them a house on Newport Beach. They commissioned Schindler at the same time that Leah's sister Harriet and her husband Sam Freeman hired Wright to build their iconic textured-block home in Hollywood. The startling modernist Lovell beach house, rising on massive concrete fins, was recognized as Schindler's finest residence. However, unfortunate misunderstandings between Lovell and Schindler prompted the patron to hire Neutra, not Schindler, as the architect for his city house. This turned out to be the most important opportunity in Neutra's professional life.

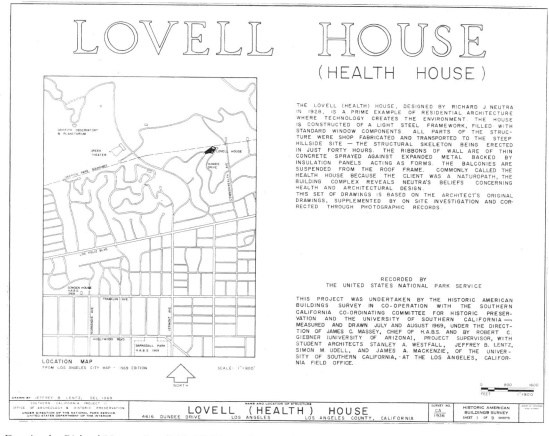

Drawing by Richard Neutra, Lovell Health House, Los Angeles
© Historic American Buildings Survey/Library of Congress

In his work as a physician, Lovell promoted drugless healing and active, healthy sexuality. His *Los Angeles Times* column, titled "Care of the Body," championed prevention, exercise, regular sunbathing, and vegetarianism. Neutra, sharing Lovell's interest in physical fitness, thus named the residence the Health House. The simple, reductive, clean lines of modernist architecture were in step with such a wholesome and essential approach to clean living.

Built on a spectacular and precariously steep site, near the city's Griffith Park, the structure was the first steel-frame house ever erected in the United States. The prefabricated steel members were designed with only one-eighth-inch tolerance. Neutra working as a contractor personally checked every one of 1000 prepunched boltholes and precut cover plates. The spreading steel skeleton of nine levels of girders was constructed in a mere 40 hours. A thin shell of concrete coated every surface (floors, partitions, and vertical enclosures) that was not made of glass. Steel cables supported the slabs and balconies from above. The suspension construction and open-web bar-steel joints, also used in a residential building for the first time, saved material. Thus, plumbing pipes and electric conduits could run freely in all directions, saving money as well. The building loomed over a swimming pool composed of a thin reinforced-concrete shell suspended within reinforced-concrete portals cutting into a slope.

The architectural expression of the Lovell Health House was derived directly from its skeletal steel frame, clad in a lightweight synthetic skin. The asymmetrical composition of dramatically suspended floors was generated by the site topography, the views to surrounding nature, and the open-plan of the house, allowing for maximum flexibility of space and circulation. The physical and visual integration of the interiors with the exterior of the house was not only an acknowledgement of modern aesthetic but also an appropriate reflection of Lovell's expansive personality and lifestyle. The progressive ideology of the client as well as the central theme of Neutra's "biorealism," linking architectural form with overall physical health and wellness, was embodied in the design of the Lovell Health House. As emphasized by Neutra in his book *Survival through Design* (1954), nothing can be further removed from the exclusively formal motivations of International Style modernism than the philosophy of the Lovell Health House. According to Neutra, "An architect who practically applies life-science to life, best learns from home design. Such activity will help him and helpfully keep him going also on all other projects that relate to human beings. All he creates is for organic human welfare" (1962).

PETER LIZON

See also **Fallingwater, Bear Run, Pennsylvania; Mies van der Rohe, Ludwig (Germany); Loos, Adolf (Austria); Mendel-**

sohn, Erich (Germany); Neutra, Richard (Austria); Schindler, Rudolph (Austria, United States); Tugendhat House, Brno, Czech Republic; Villa Mairea, Noormarkku, Finland; Villa Savoye, Poissy, France

Further Reading

Hines, Thomas S., *Richard Neutra and the Search for Modern Architecture: A Biography and History*, New York: Oxford University Press, 1982
Neutra, Richard, *Wie baut Amerika?* Stuttgart: Verlag Julius Hoffmann, 1927; reprinted München: Kraus Reprint, 1980
Neutra, Richard, *Survival through Design*, New York: Oxford University Press, 1954
Neutra, Richard, *Life and Shape*, New York: Appleton-Century-Crofts, 1962

LU YANZHI 1894–1929

Architect, China

Lu Yanzhi was one of the most significant of China's so-called first generation (*di yidai*) of architects, who received their architectural training abroad between 1915 and 1935 and returned to China to practice. Lu is renowned for two major commissions, the Sun Yat-sen Mausoleum in Nanjing and the Sun Yat-sen Memorial Hall in Guangzhou (Canton), both completed after his untimely death in 1929.

In 1911, when the Chinese Revolution overthrew the last Qing emperor, Lu entered prestigious Qinghua University to study engineering. At that time, Qinghua did not have a full-fledged program of architectural studies. However, students possessing clear aptitude in architecture, construction, or related fields, had the option of applying to academic programs in the United States under the terms of the Boxer Indemnity Fund, established in 1908 as a scholarship fund for Chinese students.

In 1914, Lu began studies in mechanical engineering at Cornell University, where he switched to architecture and graduated in 1918. He subsequently worked briefly as a draftsman at the New York City firm of Murphy and Dana, in their Oriental Department, which was beginning to design a number of commissions for China. The commissions were primarily campus plans, for Qinghua University, Yale-in-China (Changsha, Hunan), and Fudan University (Shanghai). Lu assisted with the drafting and related design tasks associated with these and other projects until 1919, when he moved to Shanghai to work in Murphy and Dana's newly established branch office. Henry Murphy, the partner who spearheaded his firm's China-based operation, was impressed with Lu's skills and hoped that he would work in Shanghai as one of the office's key architects. Lu assisted in some of the designs for Ginling College for Girls (*Ginling nuzi daxue*) in Nanjing, which was one of the most elaborate examples of what Murphy called an "adaptive Chinese Renaissance."

In 1921 Lu left Murphy's firm and began working with Chinese partners; he established the Southeastern Architectural and Engineering Company (*Dongnan jianzhu gongsi*), one of the earliest Chinese architectural firms. Most of his design work from the early 1920s remains largely unknown. In 1924 he began to collaborate with Chinese colleagues in Shanghai, including Fan Wenzhao and Zhuang Jun, on the creation of an architectural society whereby Chinese architects could discuss issues and share strategies about architectural theory and practice. The Society of Chinese Architects (*Zhongguo jianzhushi xuehui*) came to fruition in 1928.

In 1924, following the death of one of China's most important political leaders, Dr. Sun Yat-sen, the Nationalist government organized China's first major architectural competition of the 20th century; it was to design a mausoleum for the fallen leader, on a sloping knoll of Purple Hill overlooking the city of Nanjing. The competition, which attracted 40 entries from China and abroad, provided a focus for Chinese architects to test their mettle against foreign competitors, and Lu's first-prize design propelled him into the architectural vanguard. Because of its high standards of design and construction, the mausoleum (1926–31), which was completed two years after Lu's death, was widely praised by contemporaries and has become a major Chinese monument of the 20th century. Its prominence was aided by the fact that Sun Yat-sen was hailed as a revolutionary hero by the People's Republic.

Lu's concept was to reflect, within an architectural format, Sun Yat-sen's ideals regarding the combination of traditional Chinese philosophical principles with up-to-date scientific practices. To achieve this, Lu retained Chinese architectural forms, such as the temple and a traditional gateway (*pailou*), but utilized reinforced concrete as a major structural material. Visitors approached the site via a long, cypress-lined causeway, and they entered it through the *pailou*. They then ascended a long flight of steps to reach a memorial hall that, because of its glazed-tile roof and sweeping eaves, resembled a Chinese temple, but was erected using a concrete frame in-filled with brick walls and faced with Kowloon granite. The hall contained a seated statue of Dr. Sun, similar to the Lincoln Memorial in Washington, D.C. Sun Yat-sen's tomb, located behind the memorial hall and accessed through it, was (and still is) within a double-shelled concrete dome, also faced in granite. Lu designed the tomb so that the exterior form would be similar to imperial tombs found elsewhere in China. However, on the interior he used the precedents of Napoleon's Tomb in Paris and Grant's Tomb in New York, so that viewers could reflect on the central sarcophagus from behind a balustrade.

In April 1926, a month after the mausoleum's groundbreaking, Lu won a second competition memorializing Sun Yat-sen. This time the memorial was set in Guangzhou, the city where Sun had first mobilized his political forces and where Chiang Kai-shek's Nationalist government was inaugurated in 1926. Lu's concept for the Memorial Hall (*jiniantang*) was similar to that of the mausoleum in the manner in which it sought to balance Chinese architectural form with Western construction technologies. Nevertheless, it was different because of its site (within, rather than outside the city of Guangzhou), its size (210 by 240 feet in plan, 160 feet in height, and accommodating 5000 people), and its structural nature (a steel frame with reinforced-concrete walls). Voh-Kee, the company that initiated the hall's construction in April 1928, became China's foremost construction firm until 1949, when it briefly moved to Hong Kong and then became reestablished in Taiwan. After Lu's death, design supervision of the hall was assumed by Lu's friend Fan Wenzhao.

JEFFREY W. CODY

See also **China; Shanghai, China**

Biography

Born to a privileged, wealthy family in Tianjin, China, 1894. Studied in Paris until 1908; attended Qinghua University, Beijing 1911–14; degree in engineering; attended Cornell University, Ithaca, New York 1914–18; degree in mechanical engineering and architecture. Draftsman, firm of Murphy and Dana, New York 1918–19; draftsman, firm of Murphy and Dana, Shanghai 1919–21. Established Southern Architectural and Engineering Company 1921. Founding member, Society of Chinese Architects, 1928. Died in Guangzhou (Canton) 1929.

Selected Works

Sun Yat-sen Mausoleum (first prize, competition), Nanking, 1931
Sun Yat-sen Memorial Hall (first prize, competition), Canton (now Guangzhou), 1931

Selected Publication

"Memorials to Dr. Sun Yat-sen in Nanking and Canton," *Far Eastern Review* 25 (1929)

Further Reading

Chen, Mingli, "Zhongshan ling jianzhu jingtu yuan zhi shiliao jieshao" [An Introduction to the Architecture of the Zhongshan Tomb] *Chien chu shih*, 3 (1981)
Clément, Pierre, and Zhang Liang, "Lu Yanzhi," in *Dictionnaire del'Architecture du XXe Siède*, edited by Jean-Paul Midant, Paris: Hazan, 1996
Cody, Jeffrey W., *Building in China: Henry K. Murphy's "Adaptive Architecture," 1914–1935*, Hong Kong: Chinese University Press and University of Washington Press, 2001
Fan, Liang, *Wo wei zhongshan xiansheng shouling* [Regarding Mr. Zhongshan's Tomb] Nanjing: Jiangsu Guji Chubanshe, 1986
Fu, Chiao-ching, *Zhongguo gudian shiyang xin jianzhu* [New Chinese Architecture in Classical Styles], Taipei: Taipei Nantian Shusuo Faxing, 1993
Huang, Jiande, "Lu Yanzhi yu zhongshan ling" [Lu Yanzhi and the Zhonghan Tomb], *Renwu*, 5 (1986)
Liu, Fan, "Jingzhong changming bingfei Lu Yanzhi sheji zhongshan ling de yuyi" [The Design of Lu Yanzhi's Zhongshan Tomb], *Jianzhushi*, 57 (1994)
Luo, Zhewen, "Zhongshan ling," *Wen wu*, 3 (1965)
Nanjing shi dangganguan, Zhongshan lingyuan guanli chu, *Zhongshan ling dangan shiliao xuanbian* [A Compilation of Archival Information about the Zhongshan Tomb], Nanjing: Jiangsu Guji Chubanshe, 1986
Nanjing shi zhengxie wenshi ziliao weiyuanhui, *Zhongshan lingyuan shilu*, Nanjing: Nanjing Chubanshe, 1989
Rowe, Peter, and Seng Kuan, *Architectural Encounters with Essence and Form in Modern China*, Cambridge, Massachusetts: MIT Press, 2002
Wang, Shiren, "Zhongguo jindai jianzhu yu jianzhu shiqiao," *Chien chu hsüeh pao*, 4 (December 1978)

LUBETKIN AND TECTON

Architecture firm, England

Berthold Lubetkin (1901–90) and the Tecton group were among the leading practitioners of modern architecture in Great Britain in the 1930s and the years immediately following World War II. Lubetkin is credited with introducing into the United Kingdom progressive architectural ideals from the Continent. Although the firm's influence declined in the late 1950s, its reputation remained intact, having created iconic images of the International Style in England.

Lubetkin was born in Russia (Tiflis, Georgia) in 1901 and received his initial architectural training at the Vkhutemas in Moscow, a leading art and design school of the newly formed USSR. From 1920 to 1922, he studied under Constructivists Vladimir Tatlin, Alexander Rodchenko, and Alexander Vesnin, absorbing the lessons of their geometric and spatial configurations as well as their revolutionary social ideals. He left the USSR in 1922 and traveled across Europe, working briefly for Bruno Taut and Ernst May. In Paris in 1925, he assisted in the construction of Konstantin Melnikov's Soviet Pavilion for the Exhibition des Art Décoratifs and was exposed to the work of Le Corbusier. While in Paris, Lubetkin established a small practice and studied at the École des Beaux-Arts in the studio of Auguste Perret, where he learned the techniques of reinforced-concrete construction. In 1931 Lubetkin settled permanently in Great Britain, becoming an influential member of an émigré circle that eventually included Serge Chermayeff, Ernö Goldfinger, Walter Gropius, and Erich Mendelsohn. In 1932 Lubetkin established the firm of Tecton with recent graduates of the Architectural Association, including Lindsey Drake, Frances Skinner, and Anthony Chitty. Although Tecton was intended as a Soviet-style collective, Lubetkin was its principal designer, theorist, and spokesperson.

Tecton's first significant projects were buildings for the London Zoo with programs requiring specialized research into the users' behaviors and habits, which Lubetkin regarded as crucial to a committed modernist practice. In the Gorilla House (1932) and the Penguin Pool (1934), rigorous programmatic analysis (of animal occupants and human visitors) was wedded to precise formal geometry—a two-part, rotating cylinder for the apes and spiral ramps suspended above an oval pool for the birds. The abstract composition of the Penguin Pool has the dynamism of modernist sculpture and evokes the Constructivism of Lubetkin's early teachers. Structurally, the Penguin Pool is a tour de force of reinforced-concrete construction. Engineered by Ove Arup, its 46-foot-long unsupported ramps utilized the most advanced methods then available. Embraced on its completion by both the architectural avant-garde and the mainstream public, the Penguin Pool was one of the first modernist structures in Britain to receive landmark status. It was restored in 1987.

Tecton followed the critical and popular success of the zoo buildings with a series of private houses and apartments blocks, including Highpoint I and II. Highpoint I (1935) was one of the first large-scale British buildings to manifest Le Corbusier's "Five Points of Architecture." It featured all of the elements that would become clichés of the International Style but utilized them with a remarkable degree of functional clarity and compositional sophistication. Lubetkin planned the eight-story building as a double cruciform, providing ample light and ventilation to all 64 apartments. Although Highpoint I was praised by Le Corbusier himself as a vertical garden city, it fell short of Lubetkin's social ideological aspirations, quickly becoming a luxury housing complex with only a few low-rent units.

After Highpoint I, Lubetkin's use of the Le Corbusian syntax became increasingly formalist and mannered, as in Highpoint II (1938), which adjoins the original building. Here, Lubetkin utilized tiles and glazed brick as a contextual gesture and intro-

Finsbury Health Centre (1938), London
© Martin Jones/CORBIS

duced reproduction caryatids in place of *pilotis* (stilts) to support the *porte-cochère* (carriage entrance). This classical motif has been variously interpreted as an example of bricolage, or pastiche (Colin Rowe and Fred Koetter) and as a harbinger of ironic postmodernism (Charles Jencks). Inside Highpoint II, Lubetkin continued to explore Le Corbusian planning with duplex apartments and double-height living rooms. Highpoint II achieved cult status as the home of special agent Emma Peel on the 1960s television show *The Avengers*.

Besides working with Tecton, Lubetkin was a founding member of the Modern Architectural Research (MARS) Group in 1933. Aligning itself with CIAM (Congrès Internationaux d'Architecture Moderne) against the RIBA (Royal Institute of British Architects) establishment, MARS promoted the ideals of modernism in the broadest possible technical, social, and economic contexts. Eventually, Lubetkin grew dissatisfied with what he perceived as the MARS Group's unfocused social commitment, especially with the worsening political situation in Europe. In 1935, along with several Tecton members, he founded a more militant group with an explicit socialist agenda. The short-lived Architects' and Technicians' Organization (ATO) dedicated itself to housing and town-planning issues and engaged in direct, although limited, community action and political organizing. For Lubetkin, the ATO provided a forum for

his ideas on the social efficacy of architecture and offered an opportunity for promoting the social dimension of Tecton's practice, as in its Finsbury Health Centre (1938), a facility commissioned by the socialist Borough Council of Finsbury for its blight-stricken neighborhood.

As a collective firm, Tecton dissolved in 1948, although several of its members formed new partnerships, including that of Skinner, Bailey and Lubetkin. Increasingly after World War II, Lubetkin turned his attention to planning, although his attempt to design the Peterlee New Town (project, 1948–50) was ultimately unsuccessful. During the 1950s and 1960s, he designed a number of low-income residential complexes in and around London, including the 16-acre Cranbrook Estates (1955–66), an adroit composition of high-rise towers, low-rise terraces, and detached houses. By the time Lubetkin retired from practice in 1970 to devote himself to farming, his contributions to the British Modern movement had been largely forgotten. He was awarded the RIBA Gold Medal in 1982, which occasioned his return to public life as a vocal critic of Postmodernist architectural excess. The RIBA award also prompted a scholarly reappraisal of Tecton's work that established the firm's crucial role in the promotion of modernist architecture and ideology in the United Kingdom. Lubetkin died in 1990.

GABRIELLE ESPERDY

See also **Apartment Building; Arup, Ove (Great Britain); Congrès Internationaux d'Architecture Moderne (CIAM, 1927–); Constructivism; Corbusier, Le (Jeanneret, Charles-Édouard) (France); Postmodernism; Royal Institute of British Architects; Russia and Soviet Union**

Biography

Berthold Lubetkin

Born in Tiflis, Georgia, 14 December 1901; immigrated to England 1931. Educated at the Tenishevskaya Gymnasium, St. Petersburg, and Miedvendikoy Tenishevskaya, Moscow, 1910–17; studied under Kasimir Malevich, Aleksandr Rodchenko, Aleksandr Vesnin, and Vladimir Tatlin, Vkhutemas, Moscow and Svomas Petrograd (St. Petersburg) 1920–22; attended the Textile Academy, Berlin and Building School, Charlottenburg, Berlin 1922–23; studied at Warsaw Polytechnic School of Architecture 1923–25; studied at the École Spéciale d'Architecture, Paris 1925; attended the École des Beaux-Arts, Paris 1926–27; attended, École Supérieur de Béton Armée, Paris 1927; studied at the Institut d'Urbanisme, Sorbonne, Paris 1927–29. Married Margaret Church 1931 (died 1969). Reservist, Red Army, Moscow 1919–20. Worked with Bruno Taut, Berlin 1922–23, worked with Ernst May, Frankfurt 1924; assistant to El Lissitzky and David Shterenberg, Berlin 1922; architect, with Konstantin Melnikov, Soviet Pavilion, Exposition Internationale des Arts Décoratifs et Industriels Modernes, Paris 1925; architect, USSR Trades Delegation, Paris 1926–29. Private practice, Paris 1926–30; partner with Jean Ginsberg 1928–30; founder, partner, Tecton group, London 1932–48; member, editorial board, *L'architecture d'aujourd'hui*, Paris 1930–31; partner, Skinner, Bailey and Lubetkin, London 1948–52. Retired to Upper Kilcott, Gloucestershire 1952 and Clifton, Bristol 1969. Founder, member, MARS (Modern Architectural Research) Group, London 1933. Royal Gold Medal, Royal Institute of British Architects 1982. Died in Bristol, 23 October 1990.

Tecton Group

Founded in London 1932 by Berthold Lubetkin in association with: Anthony Chitty, Lindsey Drake, Michael Dugdale, Valentine Harding, Godfrey Samuel, and Francis Skinner; by 1936 only Lubetkin, Skinner, and Drake remained; Denys Lasdun joined the group in 1937; the partnership dissolved in 1948; Skinner, Bailey, and Lubetkin established a partnership, while Drake and Lasdun continued to work together.

Selected Works

Gorilla House, London Zoo, 1932
Penguin Pool, London Zoo, 1934; restored, 1987
Highpoint I Flats, Highgate, London, 1935
Berthold Lubetkin House, Whipsnade, Bedfordshire, 1936
Highpoint II Flats, Highgate, London, 1938
Finsbury Health Centre, London, 1938
Spa Green Housing Estate, Finsbury, London, 1946
Peterlee New Town Plan (project), County Durham, 1950
Cranbrook Estates, near London, 1966

Selected Publications

Opening of Finsbury Health Center, 1938
Planned A.R.P., 1939

Report to Finsbury Borough Council on Structural Protection for People against Aerial Bombardment, 1939
Spa Green Estate, 1952
La modernité, un project inachevé (with others), 1982

Further Reading

Lubetkin and Tecton have been the subject of several monographs and critical studies that have reassessed the firm's impact on the development of modern architecture in Britain.

Allan, John, *Berthold Lubetkin: Architecture and the Tradition of Progress*, London: RIBA Publications, 1992
Coe, Peter, and Malcolm Reading, *Lubetkin and Tecton: Architecture and Social Commitment*, London: Arts Council of Great Britain, 1981
Diehl, Thomas, "Theory and Principle: Berthold Lubetkin's Highpoint One and Highpoint Two," *Journal of Architectural Education*, 52/4 (May 1999)
Gold, John R., *The Experience of Modernism: Modern Architects and the Future City, 1928–1953*, London: Spon, 1997
Jordan, Robert Furneaux, "Lubetkin," *Architectural Review* (July 1955)
Reading, Malcolm, and Peter Coe, *Lubetkin and Tecton: An Architectural Study*, London: Triangle Architectural, 1992

LUTYENS, SIR EDWIN LANDSEER 1869–1944

Architect, England

Sir Edwin Landseer Lutyens was one of the most noteworthy English architects of his generation. During the first four decades of the 20th century, he designed a remarkable range of buildings, in a wide variety of styles, interpreted in an inventive and original manner. Despite his position of preeminence as a Grand Manner architect before World War II, he was above all, a domestic architect. While essentially an Edwardian, Lutyens never refused work, and as a result he was able to negotiate the architectural and social complexities of that age.

In 1885, he became a student at the Kensington School of Art, before joining the firm of Ernest George and Peto as an apprentice from late 1887 to early 1889. While there, Lutyens met Herbert Baker who would later become his colleague in New Delhi. Lutyens's early work showed a responsiveness to George's love of quality, craftsmanship, and the natural textures of brick, oak, and tile. He was also influenced by Norman Shaw and Philip Webb,

Lutyens began his independent practice with his first important commission in 1889 in Crooksbury, Surrey, with a series of houses that extended the possibilities offered by local vernacular style. The majority were built in Surrey and included Munstead Wood (1896); Godalming for Gertrude Jekyll, a garden designer who had revived the English cottage garden and who provided him with an opportunity to rise rapidly in his profession; Tigbourne Court (1899) in Surrey where he demonstrated an exceptional interpretation of the local vernacular style that highlighted texture and massing.

Lutyens built Deanery Gardens (1901) in Berkshire for Edward Hudson, the owner of *Country Life* magazine, for whom he also built an office in Covent Garden, London, which was his first project in the Grand Manner. While similar to many of Lutyens's houses of this period, Deanery Gardens' origins were the Elizabethan country house, and made it the essential embodiment of Edwardian Romanticism. The huge mullioned window, together with the massive chimneys anchoring the house to the site, are typical Arts and Crafts features, but the originality of the handling seen especially in the linking axes, evokes Frank Lloyd Wright. Lutyens's houses are carefully choreographed spaces, often arranged around a central fireplace.

By 1900, Lutyens's eclecticism became more apparent, as at Little Thakeham (1902), with its Tudor exterior and classical hall, and at Marsh Court (1904), which combined both classical and vernacular features.

Responding to contemporary preferences, Lutyens introduced a language that included neoclassical forms: mannerist features at Overstrand Hall (1901) and Homewood (1901) in Knebworth, and neoclassical forms at Papillon Hall (1904). In this instance, the eccentric butterfly plan was determined by the retention of an original house.

By 1903, Lutyens was extolling the "high game" of Palladianism; these classical preferences found their climax at Heathcote (1906) in Ilkley, Yorkshire, which invoked San Micheli. Nashdom (1908), with its whitewashed brick and contrived, understated center, heralded his neo-Georgian style, whereas The Salutation (1911) provided what is arguably the perfect essay in this genre. The "castle" style was added to his armory, most notably in Overstrand Hall and Red House (1899) in Surrey, which exploited parapets and other conceits. The enlargement of Lindisfarne (1904) on Holy Island, Northumberland, showed Lutyens's respect for the original Romantic silhouette, and Lambay Castle (1912) in Ireland involved the repair and enlargement of an old house within the confines of a huge circular rampart wall. Castle Drogo represents the most extravagant example of this work; designed in 1910, it is unlikely to be mistaken for an original castle. The subtle configuration of granite walls punctured by windows shows Lutyens's versatility.

A new mood in Britain followed the accession of Edward VII, and Lutyens was anxious to expand his practice beyond the domestic. Opportunity came with his appointment in 1912, to the Delhi Planning Commission. Despite his disagreements with fellow architect Herbert Baker, together they created one of the finest examples of 20th-century Beaux-Arts town planning. Influenced by the plan for Washington, D.C., and incorporating English garden city principles, New Delhi was centered on the Viceroy's House (1931).

As a principal architect to the Imperial War Graves Commission, Lutyens designed a series of memorials, most notably The Cenotaph (1920) in London and Thiepval (1929) in France, which rehearsed his geometric, abstracted classicism.

His later works ranged from university buildings to the design for the new Roman Catholic Cathedral in Liverpool. Commercial buildings—including Britannic House (1924), the Midland Bank Headquarters (1939) in London, and the British Embassy (1928) in Washington, D.C.—exemplify his continuation of historicist design principles from the 19th, and into the 20th century.

HILARY J. GRAINGER

See also **Arts and Crafts Movement; Baker, Herbert (England and South Africa)**

Biography

Born in London, 29 March 1869, the tenth son of a soldier turned painter. Studied architecture, Kensington School of Art (now Royal College of Art), London 1885–87; apprentice, the office of George and Peto, London 1887–89. Married Lady Emily Lytton (daughter, former viceroy of India) 1897: 5 children. Private practice, Surrey 1889; private practice, London from 1890; chief architect for the imperial capital, New Delhi, India 1912. President, Royal Academy 1938. Knighted 1918; Gold Medal, Royal Institute of British Architects 1921; Gold Medal, American Institute of Architects 1924. Died in London, 1 January 1944; funeral held in Westminster Abbey.

Selected Works

Crooksbury Lodge, Farnham, Surrey, 1890
Munstead Wood, Godalming, Surrey, 1896
Red House, Godalming, Surrey, 1899
Tigbourne Court, Witley, Surrey, 1899
Overstrand Hall, Cromer, Norfolk, 1901
Homewood, Knedworth, Herts, 1901
Deanery Gardens, Sonning, Berkshire, 1902
Blackburn House (Little Thakeham), Sussex, 1902
Lidisfarne Castle (conversion), Holy Island, Northumberland, 1903
Marsh Court, Stockbridge, Hants, 1904
Papillon Hall, Leicestershire, 1904
Heathcote, Ilkley, Yorkshire, 1906
Nashdom, Taplow, Buckinghamshire, 1908
The Salutation, Sandwich, Kent, 1911
Lambay Castle, Lambay Island, Ireland, 1912
Castle Drago, Drewsteignton, Devon, 1910–30
The Cenotaph, London, 1920
Brittanic House, Finsbury Circus, London, 1924
British Embassy, Washington, D.C., 1928
Roman Catholic Cathedral (incomplete), Liverpool, 1929–40
Viceroy's House, New Delhi, 1931
Monument to the Missing of the Somme, Thiepval, France, 1932
Midland Bank Headquarters, Poultry, London, 1939

Selected Publications

"What I Think of Architecture," *Country Life* 64 (1931)
"Tradition Speaks," *Architectural Review* 72 (1932)

Further Reading

A good deal of literature is devoted to Lutyens. Hussey's account remains one of the finest. The catalog of the Arts Council exhibition held in London in 1981 (Lutyens) provides useful essays. Brown (1996) discusses Lutyens and his patrons.

Brown, Jane, *Gardens of a Golden Afternoon: The Story of a Partnership: Edwin Lutyens and Gertrude Jekyll*, New York: Van Nostrand Reinhold and London: Allen Lane, 1982; updated edition, London and New York: Penguin, 1994
Brown, Jane, *Lutyens and the Edwardians: An English Architect and His Clients*, New York and London: Viking, 1996
Butler, A.S.G., *The Architecture of Sir Edwin Lutyens*, 3 vols., New York: Scribner, and London: Country Life, 1950
Gradidge, Roderick, *Edwin Lutyens: Architect Laureate*, London and Boston: Allen and Unwin, 1981
Hussey, Christopher, *The Life of Sir Edwin Lutyens*, New York: Scribner, and London: Country Life, 1950
Lutyens, Edwin Landseer, *Lutyens: The Work of the English Architect Sir Edwin Lutyens (1869–1944)* (exhib. cat.), London: Arts Council of Great Britain, 1981

Weaver, Lawrence, *Houses and Gardens by E.L. Lutyens*, London: Country Life, 1913; New York: Scribners, 1914; reprint, Woodbridge, Suffolk: Antique Collectors' Club, 1981

LYNCH, KEVIN 1918–84

Urban and architectural theorist
United States

Kevin Lynch was one of the leading urban theorists in the United States during the urban-renewal period whose major book, *The Image of the City*, helped establish the discipline of urban design. Lynch abandoned architecture to study engineering and biology at Rensselaer Polytechnic Institute, eventually studying city planning at the Massachusetts Institute of Technology (MIT), where he returned as a faculty member in 1948. With the assistance of Gyorgy Kepes, arts professor at MIT, Lynch focused on the visual dimension of cities, namely the perception of the form of the American metropolis. He is renowned for his urban theory and for having educated generations of city planners.

Lynch's seminal text *Image of the City* is based on interviews conducted with citizens of Boston, Jersey City, and Los Angeles about the degree of legibility of these cities' layouts. Lynch concluded that a collective mental image, a "cognitive map," would guide the citizens through their daily commutes and activities. The role of the urban designer was to make the city comprehensible to its citizens by making some of its weaker areas physically and visually more orderly and logical. *The Image of the City* instantly became one of the most popular books among practitioners and academics. The book also brought behavioral theory from psychologists such as James J. Gibson and Edward Tolman into city planning and helped outline a new discipline, that of urban design. During the 1960s, Lynch played a major role, along with Josep Lluís Sert and others at the Joint Center for Urban Studies between Harvard University and MIT, in establishing the parameters of this discipline. Urban design served as the disciplinary and professional platform from which the formal ramifications of such new development issues as downtown urban renewal, the integration of highways in the city, and new suburban development could be addressed.

The Image of the City identified five main components used by citizens to anchor their movement in the city: districts, edges, paths, nodes, and landmarks. The clearer these elements were in the city—for example, the more strongly defined a street edge was or the more clearly outlined the district was—the more clear the mental image became and the easier it was for citizens to move around and feel stable and secure in their environment. The urban image could be distinguished by the qualities of its singular elements as well as by the qualities of the general composition. Lynch proposed qualities for the individual elements, such as singularity, simplicity, and directional differentiation, and a few general principles for the total composition, relating the elements in a rather obvious manner (for example, edges defining districts and paths intersecting at nodes). The inability of Lynch to develop a more elaborate compositional strategy would eventually weaken his stance against other urban theorists, such as Colin Rowe and Léon Krier.

Lynch's other books wavered in subject matter between the study of perception of the city across time or space (*What Time Is This Place?*, 1972; *Wasting Away*, 1991; and *The View from the Road*, 1964, the last with John R. Myer and Donald Appleyard) and the study of the formal qualities of large-scale planning (*Site Planning*, 1962; *Managing the Sense of the Region*, 1976, and *A Theory of Good City Form*, 1981), the latter theme inspired by Lewis Mumford's regionalism. Lynch's work also evolves from a reliance on behavioral sciences earlier in his career to an integration of political ideas and the development of a structuralist modeling of cities in his later publications.

Lynch wrote most of his books during a period of increasing social and racial tension in American cities, but urban problems, such as racial segregation and blight, did not feature strongly in his writings. Beyond affirming a strong link between imageability and social well being, he remained vague about what constituted the link between the social and the physical. Most of the criticism of Lynch's approach focused on its behaviorist naïveté and on this ambiguous attitude toward social conditions in the city. His critics took his silence for complicity with urban-renewal politics that irreversibly changed the ethnic and social composition of urban society. Kenneth Frampton attacked the distraction from social issues that Lynch's pictorial urbanism encouraged. Manfredo Tafuri interpreted Lynch's promotion of the piecemeal development of the city as a form of complacency with laissez-faire capitalism.

Other critics, such as Roland Barthes, observed a lack of symbolic dimension in his analysis while acknowledging his attempt to establish an urban semantics. Lynch separates the structural aspects of the image from its meaning or its interpretation. His more comprehensive and later book *A Theory of Good City Form* (1981), which appeared at a time when urban theory was moving toward the semiotics of Robert Venturi and the historicism of Colin Rowe, clearly illustrates this separation. Lynch seemed to prefer the immediacy of cognition, (what might be described as a gestalt approach to perception), to linguistic models. It is collective dimension of Lynch's project that appealed to urban theorist Aldo Rossi, who shared with Lynch (directly and through the shared influence of social geographer Maurice Halbwachs) the portrayal of urban space as collective memory.

Perhaps the most relevant interpretation of Lynch's social project could be derived at a more general level from his valuation of human experience, the use of the scientific method, and the constant revision of values, ideas inspired by John Dewey. To Dewey, these constituted the preconditions of a democratic way of life to which Lynch's theories remained committed throughout his career.

HASHIM SARKIS

See also **Frampton, Kenneth (United States); Mumford, Lewis (United States); New Urbanism; Rossi, Aldo (Italy); Sert, Josep Lluís (United States); Tafuri, Manfredo (Italy); Urban Planning**

Biography

Born 7 January 1918 in Chicago. Attended Yale University and Taliesin Fellowship 1937–38; joined the U.S. Army Corps of Engineers in 1941; returned to MIT after World War II and through G.I. Bill financial support earned a bachelor's degree in city planning in 1947. Worked in North Carolina for the Greensboro Planning Commission; accepted position of assistant professor in city planning at MIT 1948; later studied urban experience while in Europe on a Ford Foundation fellowship; published *The Image of the City* in 1960, a book that would launch his career as urban theorist; published seven books on urban form and its perception between 1960 and 1984; retired from MIT in 1978 but maintained relationship with academia and became more actively involved in practice with Carr/Lynch Associates based in Cambridge, Massachusetts. Worked as consultant and participated in the planning of significant projects as the Government Center of Boston and the Rio Salado in Phoenix. Awarded the first Rexford G. Tugwell Award in planning in 1984. Died at Martha's Vineyard, 25 April 1984.

Selected Publications

The Image of the City, 1960
Site Planning, 1962
The View from the Road (with Donald Appleyard and John R. Myer), 1964
What Time Is This Place? 1972
Managing the Sense of a Region, 1976
Growing Up in Cities, 1977
A Theory of Good City Form, 1981
Wasting Away, edited Michael Southworth, 1991

Further Reading

The main reviews of Kevin Lynch's work have been featured in the body of the text above. Not much has been written about his work outside his immediate circle of influence. More recently, a renewed interest in his work has been driven by urban modeling and new urbanism.

Banerjee, Tridib, and Michael Southworth (editors), *City Sense and City Design: Writings and Projects of Kevin Lynch*, Cambridge, Massachusetts: MIT Press, 1990

Barthes, Roland, "Semiologie et urbanisme," in *L'architecture d'aujourd'hui* (1968)

Frampton, Kenneth, "America, 1960–1970: Notes on Urban Images and Theories," *Casabella* 359–60 (1971)

Sarkis, Hashim, "Space for Recognition," in *The Promise of Multiculturalism: Education and Autonomy in the 21st Century*, edited by George Katsiaficas and Teodros Kiros, New York: Routledge, 1998

Tzonis, Alexander, and Liane Lefaivre, " 'Thinking in Forms As Well As Words': Kevin Lynch and the Cognitive Theory of the City," *Design Book Review* 26 (fall 1992)

M

MACKINTOSH, CHARLES RENNIE 1868–1928

Architect, Scotland

By the end of the 19th century, the Glasgow School of Art was one of the leading art academies in Europe, and after early success in the fine arts, the late 1890s saw Glasgow's reputation in architecture and the decorative arts reach an all-time high. At the very heart of this success was a talented young architect and designer, Charles Rennie Mackintosh, whose reputation was to quickly spread beyond his native city and who, more than a century later, is still regarded as the father of "Glasgow style."

In 1884 Mackintosh was apprenticed to a local architect, John Hutchison, but in 1889 he transferred to the larger, more established city practice of Honeyman and Keppie. To complement his architectural apprenticeship, Mackintosh enrolled in evening classes at the Glasgow School of Art, where he pursued various drawing programs. Here, under the watchful eye of the headmaster, Francis Newbery, his talents flourished, and in the school's library he was able to consult the latest architecture and design journals, becoming increasingly aware of his contemporaries both at home and abroad.

Mackintosh's projects for Honeyman and Keppie during the early 1890s displayed an increased maturity. His design for the Glasgow Herald Building (1894) incorporated some cutting-edge technology, including a hydropneumatic lift and fire-resistant diatomite concrete flooring. Later at Martyrs' Public School (1895), despite a somewhat restricted brief, he was able to introduce some elaborate but controlled detailing, including the central roof trusses.

At a public lecture on architecture in 1893, Mackintosh argued that architects and designers should be given greater artistic freedom and independence. He himself began to experiment with a range of decorative forms, producing designs for furniture, metalwork, and the graphic arts (including highly stylized posters and watercolors), often in partnership with his friend and colleague at Honeyman and Keppie, Herbert MacNair, and two fellow students, Margaret and Frances MacDonald.

In 1896 Mackintosh gained his most substantial commission: to design a new building for the Glasgow School of Art. This was to be his masterwork. Significantly, the building was constructed in two distinct phases—1897–99 and 1907–09—because of a lack of money. Stylistically, the substantial delay in completion offered Mackintosh the opportunity to amend and fully integrate his original design (of 1896), which owed much to Scotland's earlier baronial tradition, with a second half to the building that looked very much to the 20th century through its use of materials and technology. Most dramatic of all the interiors was the new Library (completed in 1909), which was a complex space of timber posts and beams. Its construction owed much to traditional Japanese domestic interiors, but ultimately the building was an eclectic mix of styles and influences.

In Europe, the originality of Mackintosh's style was quickly appreciated, and in Germany, and particularly in Austria, he received acclaim and recognition for his designs. He entered an open competition to design "A House for an Art Lover," put forward in 1900 by a German design journal, *Zeitschrift fur Innendekoration*. Although he failed to win the competition, his architectural designs were judged to be of such a high standard that they were later reproduced as a portfolio of prints.

Back in Scotland at the Hill House (1904) in Helensburgh, the publisher Walter Blackie commissioned Mackintosh to design a substantial family home. In its appearance, it owed much to his House for an Art Lover designs and an earlier completed domestic commission, Windyhill (1900). Externally, the Hill House was notable for its simple and solid massed forms with little ornamentation, yet internally the rooms exuded light and space, and the use of color and decoration was carefully conceived.

Throughout his career, Mackintosh relied on just a handful of patrons and supporters. The Glasgow businesswoman Catherine Cranston proved to be one of his most influential, and her series of tearoom interiors (designed and furnished between 1896 and 1917) provided him with a virtual freedom to experiment. Responsible for their "total design," Mackintosh provided the tearooms with furniture (including the dramatic high-back chairs), light fittings, wall decorations, and even the cutlery.

Despite success in Europe and the support of clients such as Blackie and Cranston, Mackintosh's work met with considerable indifference at home, and his career soon declined. Few private clients were sufficiently sympathetic to want his "total design" of house and interior. He entered the competition to design a cathedral (1902) for the city of Liverpool, but although his design showed a Gothic quality as requested, his entry was rejected, and his design for Scotland Street School (1904) in Glasgow was to be his last public commission.

Hill House (1904), Helensburgh, Scotland
© Howard Davis/Greatbuildings.com

By 1914 Mackintosh had despaired of ever receiving the level of recognition in Glasgow that he felt he deserved. He became increasingly obstinate and incapable of compromise, and it is known that this exerted unnecessary pressures on his colleagues. In an attempt to resurrect his career, Mackintosh resigned from the practice and with his wife, Margaret MacDonald, moved to London.

This was unfortunate timing, for with the onset of World War I, all building was severely restricted. Adventurous plans for a suite of artists' studios and a theater were never built. However, after making adjustments to the exterior of a midterraced house (1916) at 78 Derngate in Northampton, the client, W.J. Bassett-Lowke, commissioned Mackintosh to redecorate a number of the building's interiors, including the Guests' Bedroom (1919). These designs show him working in a bold new style of decoration and construction, using primary colors and geometric motifs. It was an output of extraordinary vitality and originality, but it went virtually unheeded.

PETER TROWLES

See also **Glasgow School of Art, Scotland; Vienna Secession**

Biography

Born in Glasgow, Scotland, 7 June 1868. Apprenticed to architect John Hutchinson 1884–94; night classes, Glasgow School of Art 1884–88; won the prestigious Alexander Thomson Travelling Studentship (1890), which allowed him to undertake an architectural tour of Italy in 1891. Married artist Margaret MacDonald 1900. Draftsman, Honeyman and Keppie, Glasgow 1888; partner 1901–1913; with wife and Frances and Herbert MacNair, formed the artistic group The Four. Private practice as architect, textile designer, and painter from 1914. Moved to Walberswick, Suffolk 1914. 1914–15, lived in Chelsea, London designing textiles and executing small projects. Moved to Port Vendres, South of France in 1923 and took up watercolor painting. Fell ill in 1928 and returned to London. Died in London, 10 December 1928.

Selected Works

Glasgow Herald Building Tower (with John Keppie), 1894
Martyrs' Public School, Glasgow (with Keppie), 1895
Argyle Street Tearooms, Glasgow, 1897
Eastern Section, Glasgow School of Art, 1897–99
William Davidson House (Windyhill), Kilmacolm, Scotland, 1900–01
Scottish Section (destroyed), International Exhibition of Modern Decorative Art, Turin, 1902
Cathedral (competition project, unbuilt), Liverpool, 1902
Scotland Street School, Glasgow, 1904
W.W. Blackie House (Hill House), Helensburgh, Scotland, 1902–04
Redesign of Western Section, Glasgow School of Art, 1907–09
Ingram Street Tearooms, Glasgow, 1900–12
Willow Tearooms, Glasgow, 1903–17
W.J. Bassett-Lowke House, 78 Derngate, Northampton, 1916–1919

Further Reading

Barnes, H. Jefferson, *Charles Rennie Mackintosh and the Glasgow School of Art*, Glasgow: The Glasgow School of Art, 1961; 2nd edition 1979; 3rd edition 1988

Billcliffe, Roger, *Charles Rennie Mackintosh: The Complete Furniture, Furniture Drawings and Interior Designs*, London: John Murray, 1979; 2nd edition 1980; 3rd edition 1986

Brett, David, *C.R. Mackintosh: The Poetics of Workmanship*, London: Reaktion Books, 1992

Buchanan, William, et al. (editor), *Mackintosh's Masterwork*, Glasgow: Drew, and San Francisco: Chronicle Books, 1989

Cooper, Jackie, *Mackintosh Architecture: The Complete Buildings and Selected Projects*, London: Academy Editions, 1977; 2nd edition 1984; 3rd edition 1989

Crawford, Alan, *Charles Rennie Mackintosh*, New York and London: Thames and Hudson, 1995

Howarth, Thomas, *Charles Rennie Mackintosh and the Modern Movement*, London: Routledge and Kegan Paul, 1952; 2nd edition 1977; 3rd edition 1990

Kaplan, Wendy (editor), *Charles Rennie Mackintosh*, Glasgow: Glasgow Museums, and New York: Abbeville Press, 1996

Lovell, Susan (editor), *Four studies on Charles Rennie Mackintosh*, New York: New York School of Interior Design, 1996

Macaulay, James, *Glasgow School of Art: Charles Rennie Mackintosh*, London: Phaidon Press, 1993

Macaulay, James, *The Hill House: Charles Rennie Mackintosh*, London: Phaidon Press, 1994

Macleod, Robert, *Charles Rennie Mackintosh: Architect and Artist*, London: Country Life Books, 1968; 2nd edition London: Collins, 1983

Robertson, Pamela (editor), *Charles Rennie Mackintosh: The Architectural Papers*, Wendlebury, Oxfordshire: White Cockade, and Cambridge, Massachusetts: MIT Press, 1990

Robertson, Pamela (editor), *Charles Rennie Mackintosh: Architectural Sketches*, Glasgow: Hunterian Art Gallery, 1999

Steele, James, *Charles Rennie Mackintosh: Synthesis in Form*, New York: Wesley, and London: Academy Editions, 1994

MAIDAN

The term *maidan* defines a designed upon space in the urban context and has been used particularly to describe such spaces in cities of the Muslim world. An important component of several urban centers, historically the maidan was created through conscious, premeditated acts of urban design, involving not only streets, squares, and important linkages of the city but also surrounding groups of building or building ensembles within which it was sometimes contained. In this respect, the maidan differed significantly from other smaller, relatively minor, and less formal spaces created within the structure of the city through the gradual accretion and growth of urban fabric. In form and function, maidans were similar in several respects to the piazzas of medieval European cities and frequently served as independent elements of aesthetic display or as locations for community activities, such as public gatherings, processions, and parades.

The study of maidans introduces the issue of urban design in the Islamic context. The suggestion by several scholars in the past few decades that cities in the Islamic world historically were seldom planned or formally visualized before inception is somewhat extreme. Closer to the truth would be stating that while the city of Islam was seldom designed or preconceived in its totality, its most integral parts were certainly visualized and realized. These critical constructions, usually groups of monumental buildings arranged around open spaces, were controlled by strict urban bylaws and guidelines, as contained in royal decrees and endowment documents. Examining these is of enormous importance in determining what effect each such decision had on the formalization of these urban spaces. Within the major urban centers of the Islamic world, therefore, several spaces or maidans existed, some major and others relatively minor, performing varied functions as their roles changed over time.

It is a subject of debate as to where the first maidan of the Islamic world developed. Prior to the sophisticated urban environments of the Central Asian region, such as those of the Timurid capitals at Samarqand, Bukhara, and Shakrisyabz, scholars have long believed that almost no urban or civic spaces existed in Islamic cities in other parts of the world. In Central Asia, eastern Iran itself, possibly the very land that gave origin to urban spaces and public buildings appearing in combination, few cities were left sufficiently intact after the devastating onslaughts of the Mongol invasions in the first half of the 13th century. The cities of the Delhi and Deccan sultanates on the Indian subcontinent, on the other hand, while experiencing a change of several dynasties, never suffered such destruction, at least until the raids of Timur in 1398. These cities, therefore, provide us with rate instances of maidan spaces being created through calculated acts of architectural and urban design wherein specific legislative mechanisms dictated constructions on lines remarkably similar to those evolving the structure of cities in medieval Europe.

While maidans within the urban environment served a sociocultural purpose in the medieval Islamic period, their application in the modern city was limited. Rather than being seen as necessary features within the urban structure, as important places of gathering, maidans were in fact seen as wasted spaces within the precious real estate of the explanding city. By the late 19th and early 20th centuries, Islamic cities in several parts of the world, frequently struggling to survive under colonial regimes, initiated radical urban design changes. In some cases, historical urban typologies (such as maidans, courtyards, public buildings, and *chahrbagh* or the quadripartite garden), were summarily demolished in a search for a "modern" architecture that would truly represent the modern age. Influenced by the West, the city of Istanbul was transformed in this fashion during the late nineteenth and early twentieth centuries. In other instances, foreign-trained architects and urban designers were commissioned to turn historical urban centers into modern metropolises, such as Cairo undergoing Haussmann-like metamorphoses beginning in 1867. Furthermore, the reign of the automobile in several dense urban sectors began the relentless broadening of narrow streets and alleyways, breaking down the traditional contrast that had existed between the street and the maidan. During this time, urban spaces were reconfigured to modify the "old" forms for modern contexts. At Isfahan, Iran, the original Maidan-i Shah, built in the early 1600s, gained increasing popularity as a parking lot, whole the impressive Registan Square at Samarqand (Uzbekistan, Circa 15th and 16th Centuries) was the subject of major restoration between 1967–87 by the firm of Zakhidov, Krukov and Sadikov. The Registan ensemble of buildings—including the Tillya kari mosque, educational facilities (*madrasa*), and large, open public squares transformed into a venue for cultural performances for visiting tourists.

While some practitioners of modern architecture rejected historical forms in favor of novelty in form and function, others sought to bridge the Islamic past with various interpretations of regionalist and postmodern eclecticism and reworked themes along nationalist lines. Iranian architect Ali Saremi's Jolfa Residential Complex in Isfahan, Iran (1988) was intended to materially and spatially relate to surrounding city while incorporating harmonious living spaces for the inhabitants, including common courtyards and recreation areas, creating in effect, a contemporary maidan. Ten years later, Nader Ardalan sensitively combined mixed-use structures such as courtyards, arcades, retail shops, and seaside esplanade in his 1988 redesign of the Al-Sharq Waterfront project in Kuwait City, Kuwait.

In the last quarter of the 20th century, Kamran Diba (of D.A.Z. Architects, Planners and Engineers) began to reconfigure the regionalist traditions of Islamic architecture with contemporary notions of place and humanity. Designed to fuse structures such as the maidan, arcade, terrace, and landscape with the built environment, Diba's Shustar New Town redevelopment project (Shustar, Iran, 1977), Garden of Niavaran (Tehran, 1979), and Jondi-Shapour University (Ahwaz, Iran, 1975) serve as examples of how past and present architectural forms effectively commingle in modern and contemporary architecture.

MANU P. SOBTI

See also **Ardalan, Nader (Iran); Istanbul, Turkey**

Further Reading

Ashby, Thomas, and Steven Rowland Pierce, "The Piazza del Popolo: Its History and Development," *Town Planning Review* 11, no. 2 (1924)

Gaube, Heinz, *Iranian Cities*, New York: New York University Press, 1978

Hourani, Albert Habib, and Samuel Miklos Stern, editors, *The islamic City: A Colloquium*, Oxford: Cassirer, and Philadelphia: University of Pennsylvania Press, 1970

Lapidus, Ira Marvin, editor, *Middle Eastern Cities: A Symposium on Ancient, Islamic, and Contemporary Middle Eastern Urbanism*, Berkeley: University of California Press, 1969

Moughtin, Cliff, *Urban Design: Street and Square*, Oxford and Boston: Butterworth Architecture, 1992

Serjeant, Robert Bertram, and Ronald B. Lewcock, editors, *San'a': An Arabian Islamic City*, London: World of Islam Festival Trust, 1983

Zucker, Paul, *Town and Square: From the Agora to the Village Green*, New York: Columbia University Press, and Oxford: Oxford University Press, 1959

MAILLART, ROBERT 1872–1940

Engineer, Switzerland

Robert Maillart was a Swiss engineer who designed some of the most remarkable reinforced-concrete bridges ever constructed. The genius of Maillart's work resulted from his dual interests in the efficient engineering of reinforced-concrete structures as well as his highly developed visual design sensibilities.

Maillart's technical education began in 1890 at the Swiss Federal Technical Institute. Several professors had been advancing the revolutionary concept of graphic, visual analysis of structures since the middle of the 19th century, and these ideas no doubt influenced Maillart greatly. The coincidence of these ideas at the same time that reinforced concrete was being developed created a climate ripe for experimentation.

During the early years of Maillart's career, engineers were starting to develop systems of construction for reinforced concrete, which was recognized as an important new material. Because it takes the shape of its formwork, creating a monolithic, rigid structure, concrete is categorically different than steel or wood framing. Engineers who pioneered reinforced-concrete structural systems were just beginning to understand the properties of this new material. The French engineer Francois Hennebique patented the first notable system of reinforced-concrete beams, columns, and slabs in 1892. Hennebique's structural system was based on existing steel-and-wood framing systems in which the structural members are discrete units joined together.

In contrast to Hennebique's system, Maillart developed a concrete construction system in which the beams were integrated into the slab—a system similar to contemporary flat-slab construction. The columns flared out at the top as they joined the floor slab, creating a smooth transition that minimized shear stresses. Though more difficult to analyze than a traditional structural system of primary and secondary members, Maillart's innovation took advantage of the continuous, monolithic character of concrete. In lieu of mathematical engineering analysis, Maillart performed load testing on the slabs in 1908 and won a contract with this system for a warehouse in Zurich in 1910. Maillart used the same construction system in the filter building for a water treatment plant in Rorschach in 1912. In this building, flared octagonal concrete columns rise up to meet a sloping, beamless roof slab, creating a powerful interior in this utilitarian building. Maillart's Federal Granary Building (1912) in Altdorf, Switzerland, used this same beamless concrete-slab system to great effect by progressively decreasing the size of the octagonal columns beginning on the ground floor. What are stout columns on the first level become much thinner and lighter on the topmost floor.

Maillart utilized the same concept of continuity of structure in his design for the Train Shed (Chiasso, Switzerland, 1924). In this structure, a pitched concrete-slab roof connects and stiffens a series of trusses spanning 25 meters. These concrete trusses are inverted arches that are supported by splayed columns. The effect, both structurally and visually, is that the columns and trusses form a seamless, flowing whole. The remarkable form of this organic structure is a compelling example of Maillart's fusion of structural and aesthetic principles. Typical of the work of many late 19th- and early 20th-century designers who were experimenting with materials and structure, Maillart's most compelling work is found in utilitarian structures such as warehouses because these structures were not confined to a preconceived aesthetic. Bridges are one of the most interesting utilitarian structures because of the combination of technical and aesthetic challenges.

Until the late 19th century, bridge building had been dominated by the arched masonry bridge, a form used since the times of ancient Rome. In addition to iron and steel, reinforced concrete revolutionized bridge building at the turn of the century. Maillart's investigation of the structural and aesthetic possibilities of reinforced concrete is well illustrated in the series of three-hinged arch bridges he designed for three Swiss towns. The Stauffacher Bridge (1899) in Switzerland was Maillart's first significant arched reinforced-concrete bridge. Consisting of a horizontal reinforced-concrete deck slab supported by a low unreinforced-concrete arched slab, the bridge was an efficient

Salginatobel Bridge (1930), near Schiers
© Greatbuildings.com

alternative to a masonry arch bridge. Clad with stone veneer by an architect, the bridge gave no hint of its concrete structure. Maillart's next bridge (1901), crossing the Inn River at Zuoz, integrated the roadway and the supporting arch below into a large hollow box beam, effectively using the deck to stiffen the arch below. Both the edge of the roadway and the edge of the arch project beyond the connecting sides of the box beam, giving the bridge the spare elegance that Maillart pursued in his later projects. In the Tavanasa Bridge (1905), Maillart refined the concept of the box beam by removing unnecessary material from the ends of the bridge, creating both a more elegant and a more efficient form. This bridge achieves a form that is not possible with masonry construction. Maillart's Salginatobel Bridge (1930) is generally considered to be the pinnacle of his three-hinged arched bridges. The bridge integrates roadway deck and low-slung arch into a continuous box beam whose cross section decreases toward the hinge points of the arch. Spanning above a dramatic ravine, the bridge is stunning and essentially modern in character and is a rare synthesis of practical engineering and gestural form.

One of the last buildings of Maillart was the Cement Hall at the Swiss National Exhibition in 1939. This temporary pavilion was constructed by spraying concrete over reinforcing to create an amazingly thin concrete shell just six centimeters thick.

The cross section of the pavilion is largest at the center, gradually decreasing in size to the ends. Though less enduring than many of his elegant and sometimes subtle bridge designs, the Cement Hall is a dramatic statement about the structural properties and possibilities of concrete.

MARK OBERHOLZER

Selected Works

Stauffacher Bridge, Switzerland, 1899
Inn River Bridge, Zuoz, Switzerland, 1901
Tavanasa Bridge, Switzerland, 1905
Federal Granary Building, Altdorf, Switzerland, 1912
Train Shed, Chiasso, Switzerland, 1924
Salginatobel Bridge, Switzerland, 1930
Cement Hall (Project for the Swiss National Exhibition), 1939

Further Reading

Abel, John F. (editor), *Background Papers for the Second National Conference on Civil Engineering: History, Heritage, and the Humanities: Commemorating the Hundredth Anniversary of the Birth of Robert Maillart*, Princeton, New Jersey: Princeton University Press, 1972
Bill, Max, *Robert Maillart*, Zurich: Verlag für Architektur, 1949; reprint, as *Robert Maillart: Bridges and Constructions*, translated by W.P.M. Keatinge Clay, New York: Praeger, 1969

Billington, David P., *Robert Maillart's Bridges: The Art of Engineering*, Princeton, New Jersey: Princeton University Press, 1979

Billington, David P., *Robert Maillart and the Art of Reinforced Concrete*, Cambridge, Massachusetts: MIT Press, 1990

MAISON DE VERRE

Designed by Pierre Chareau; completed 1932
Paris, France

The Maison de Verre (House of Glass), designed by Pierre Chareau, ranks as one of the most extraordinary and forward-looking examples of high-modern architecture. The conception of the Maison de Verre was predicated on the standardization, mechanization, and specialization of industrial production. Chareau's use of industrial materials embodied the avant-garde spirit in architecture of the 1920s and 1930s. Its manifestation, however, depended on the individual craftsmanship and coordination of each interrelated building system. The Maison de Verre pivotally joins the tradition of craft and an ideology of modernity.

The Dalsaces, a bourgeois family connected to the intellectual community on the Left Bank of Paris, commissioned Chareau in 1928 to design a house that would accommodate the offices of Dr. Dalsace's gynecological practice, a large salon for entertaining, private spaces for the family, and servants' quarters. Bernard Bijvoët, a Dutch architect, and Louis Dalbet, a metal craftsman, assisted Chareau in the design and production of the house through its completion in 1932. The family had bought a three- story 19th-century residence in a courtyard off Rue St. Guillaume with the intention of rebuilding it. After an elderly resident on the third floor refused to move, Chareau demolished the first two floors, creating a space with masonry party walls at both sides and a masonry floor above. Within this space, Chareau inserted three new levels with the medical offices on the ground level, communal spaces on the second level (or *piano nobile*), and bedrooms on the third level. The large double-height space on the *piano nobile* became a center of Parisian intellectual activity: it doubled as a theater for musical and literary performances while displaying the Dalsaces' treasures of modern art.

Chareau supported the existing apartment above with an exposed-steel structure, allowing for an unusually open plan below. Steel had been used in industrial and commercial buildings since the mid-19th century, but it was rarely used in a residential context when left exposed. The floors were constructed of a neoteric technology: reinforced concrete. Thus, the floors could cantilever beyond their supports, further freeing the plan from the encumbrances of structure. Another innovation was casting ventilation ducts for heating and fresh air into the concrete throughout the house. To maximize the amount of natural light within the confined site, Chareau designed a continuous skin of industrial glass block. This luminous enclosure hung from the cantilevered structure like a translucent veil. During the daytime, a diffused light permeated the entire interior space. In the evening, the interior lights made the exterior of the Maison de Verre glow like a radiant jewel. In addition, exterior lights, supported on metal armatures, bathed the glass block surfaces, creating an ersatz daytime light in the interior. Chareau's appropriation of industrial materials and methods radically proclaimed modern building technologies and more subtly opined that modernity could improve the human condition.

The standardized dimension of the glass block provided Chareau with a module that organized the plan. This module of 91 centimeters, based on the width of four glass blocks, is repeated in the fixed-furniture objects that actually define the interior spaces. In the absence of walls, the fixed-furniture objects ring the periphery of the major spaces with varying levels of transparency or opacity. Each module is defined by a steel framework into which either perforated metal or wood panels are mounted, depending on their use or position in the house. Together, these objects create screens for privacy that is not integral to the structure yet is central to the house's programmatic organization. Although Chareau used materials from his industrial palette for these objects, they were crafted by Dalbet, who set up his shop on-site for the duration of the project. Paradoxically, at that time an industrial aesthetic was possible only through custom fabrication.

A theme that pervades the Maison de Verre is mechanical movement that can transform habitation of the space. For example, at the bottom of the main staircase, either perforated metal screens prevented the doctor's daytime clients from ascending the stair or the screens swung out of the way to invite the evening guests up to the grand salon on the second level. Similarly, the aluminum partition at the back of the salon slides laterally to expose an otherwise private study. This action connects the two spaces as one fluid continuum. A related preoccupation is hygiene: more than 30 plumbing fixtures are devoted to bodily ablutions. Fixtures are prominently located in the bedrooms, visible through metal screens that swing out to increase the bathing area. The Maison de Verre transforms to accommodate the diurnal cycles and rhythms of life.

Chareau undoubtedly was familiar with the work and writing of his contemporary Le Corbusier; they were both part of the Parisian avant-garde community. In his "Five Points of a New Architecture," published in 1926, Le Corbusier professes the virtues of the "free plan," liberated by a rational grid of structural *pilotis* (Stilts), the "free facade" that wraps the structure like a membrane, and the "horizontal strip window" to let more light into the body of the house. Chareau interpreted these ideas, combined them with specific responses to his confined site, and generated a unique modern object that epitomized its era. Mutual respect was returned when Le Corbusier reportedly frequented the construction site to make sketches of the Maison de Verre. Soon thereafter, Le Corbusier began to employ glass block in his designs. In the 1930s the Maison de Verre gained national and international notoriety, but subsequently it was largely neglected by the academic and architectural press. The design, which was originally heralded as an architecture for the future, in time was seen as idiosyncratic and anomalous to the modern lexicon. Not until Kenneth Frampton wrote about the Maison de Verre in the journal *Perspecta* in 1969 did Chareau's masterwork reenter the consciousness of architects worldwide. Late 20th-century High-Tech architects Richard Rogers and Renzo Piano, designers of the Pompidou Center in Paris (1977), and Jean Nouvel, architect of the Institute of the Arab World and the Cartier Center, two steel-and-glass buildings in Paris, have identified the Maison de Verre as a pivotal influence in their work.

PETER H. WIEDERSPAHN

See also **Corbusier, Le (Jeanneret, Charles-Édouard) (France); Chareau, Pierre (France); Frampton, Kenneth (United States); Glass; Nouvel, Jean (France); Piano, Renzo (Italy)**

Further Reading

Baroni, Daniele, "Pierre Chareau, Protagonist of the Modern Movement," *Ottogano* 21, no. 81 (June 1986)

Blake, Peter, "Chateau Chareau," *Interior Design* 65, no. 5 (May 1994)

Chareau, Pierre, *La maison de Verre*, edited by Yukio Futagawa, Tokyo: A.D.A. Edita, 1988

Filler, Martin, and Marc Vellay, "House of Glass, Walls of Light: A Beacon of Modernism," *House and Garden* 155, no. 2 (February 1983)

Frampton, Kenneth, "Maison de Verre," *Perspecta* 12 (1969)

Pierre Chareau: architecte, un art intérieur (exhib. cat.), Paris: Centre Georges Pompidou, 1993

Taylor, Brian Brace, *Pierre Chareau, Designer and Architect*, Cologne: Taschen, 1992

Vellay, Marc, and Kenneth Frampton, *Pierre Chareau, Architect and Craftsman, 1883–1950*, New York: Rizzoli, 1984; London: Thames and Hudson, 1985

MAKI, FUMIHIKO 1928–

Architect, Japan

A major figure in Japanese architecture since the late 1950s, Fumihiko Maki is recognized for his architectural and urban design work as well as his contributions to architectural theory. Maki's work is characterized by his critical development of the modern model, his desire to create a contemporary urban architecture and spaces of public appearance, and his attempt to fuse design concepts of the East and West. He is known for his rational approach, intelligent combination of technology with craftsmanship, and delicate details, all of which are illustrated in projects for cultural, residential, commercial, educational as well as office, convention, and sports facilities.

Maki is one of the few Japanese architects of his generation to have studied, worked, and taught in the United States and Japan. Following his architecture studies at Tokyo University, he obtained master of architecture degrees at Cranbrook Academy of Art (1953) and the Graduate School of Design at Harvard University (1954). He worked with Skidmore, Owings and Merrill in New York (1954–55) and with Josep Lluis Sert (Sert, Jackson and Associates; 1955–58) in Cambridge, Massachusetts before establishing Maki and Associates in Tokyo in 1965. Awarded a Graham Foundation Fellowship in 1958, Maki went on two extensive research trips to Southeast Asia, the Middle East, and northern and southern Europe. Impressed by the formal and spatial organization of settlements, particularly the communities along the Mediterranean coast, Maki became interested in collective forms. Impressions from this trip led to his first urban design proposal, elaborated with Masato Otaka for the redevelopment of west Shinjuku in Tokyo—conceived not as an actual plan but as an illustration of "group form." Maki further developed this concept in his *Investigations in Collective Form*, published in 1964 as one of three paradigms of collective forms. In contrast to "compositional form" and "megaform," his "group form" is a more flexible urban organization based on a human scale in which the parts and the whole are mutually interdependent and connected through various linkages.

A member of the Metabolist movement—a group of ambitious postwar Japanese architects who advocated the embrace of new technology with a concomitant belief in architecture's organic, humanist qualities—since 1959 Maki remained at the fringe of the group, concentrating on space and the relationship between solid and void and not on schemes for entire cities based on industrial technology. His attempt at an integration of architecture and urbanism brought him close to Team X (Ten), whose meeting he attended in 1960 in southern France. Projects of the 1970s, which express his idea of loosely connected and articulated parts, human scale, and transitional spaces, include the Kato Gakuen Elementary School (1972) in Numazu and the Tsukuba University Central Building (1974). The latter already features the forms of the stepped pyramid and the cross, which play a major organizing role in the Iwasaki Art Museum (1979) as well as the YKK Guest House (1982) and Maki's later works.

The project that best reflects the idea of "group form" is also his most renowned early work: the Hillside Terrace Apartment Complex in Tokyo, realized in six phases between 1969 and 1992. This residential and commercial ensemble is a rare example of a comprehensive long-term development of a large site in a Japanese city. It features a unified architectural style on an intimate human scale, with sidewalks and transitional spaces providing pedestrian access to shops and preserving privacy for the apartments on the upper levels.

Maki's preference for collaged and fragmentary composition, similar to the layered spaces of traditional Japanese architecture and gardens, is particularly evident in the facade of the Wacoal Media Center (1985). The so-called Spiral Building echoes the heterogeneous urban context of Tokyo and, like the TEPIA Building (1989), pays tribute to icons of 20th-century architecture and Cubist art in particular. The Spiral Building also illustrates the concept of phenomenological depth (*oku*): the main gallery space, surrounded by a gently sloping semicylindrical ramp, is situated at the back of the building and shielded from the street by the entrance lobby, the cafe, and gallery space. Naturally illuminated from above, it can be seen from the street entrance. An intimate relationship between the inside and the outside is created by the broad staircase that shows in the facade. It is equipped with chairs and provides a rare (nonpaying) space in Tokyo for visitors to relax and watch the street below. Maki's effort to relate to the particular environment of each place is further illustrated in his National Museum of Modern Art (1986) in Kyoto, the facade of which features an orthogonal pattern in tune with the traditional grid of the city as well as a symmetry, a reference to the surrounding neoclassical buildings.

Maki's attempt at creating a public architecture in Japan, where such a concept traditionally did not exist, is obvious in his sports and convention facilities. The expressive stainless-steel roofs of the Fujisawa Municipal Gymnasium (1984), the Tokyo Metropolitan Gymnasium (1990), and the Makuhari Convention Center (1989 and 1998) assure these buildings of a strong presence in the city. The sports complex of the Metropolitan Gymnasium at Sendagya Station forms a dynamic landscape of three major individual buildings positioned to create an overall ensemble and connected through pedestrian spaces that provide ever-changing views of the scenery, recalling Japanese strolling

Wacoal Media Center (Spiral Building), Minato Ward, Tokyo, 1985
© Toshiharu Kitajima

Biography

Born in Tokyo, 16 September 1928. Studied in Kenzo Tange's Research Laboratory 1948–52; bachelor's degree in architecture 1952; attended the Cranbrook Academy of Art, Bloomfield Hills, Michigan 1952–53, master's degree in architecture 1953; studied at the Harvard Graduate School of Design, Cambridge, Massachusetts 1953–54, master's degree in architecture 1954. Married Misao Matsumoto 1960: 2 children. Designer, Skidmore, Owings and Merrill, New York 1954–55; designer, firm of (Josep Lluis) Sert, Jackson and Associates, Cambridge 1955–58; principal, Maki and Associates, Tokyo from 1965. Assistant professor 1956–58, associate professor 1960–62, Washington University School of Architecture, St. Louis, Missouri; associate professor, Harvard Graduate School of Design 1962–65; lecturer, department of urban design 1965–79, professor of architecture 1979–89, University of Tokyo; visiting professor, Harvard Graduate School of Design 1967–68; visiting professor, University of California, Berkeley 1970–71; visiting lecturer, Columbia University, New York 1976, 1984; visiting critic, University of California, Los Angeles 1976; visiting lecturer, Technical University of Vienna 1977; visiting critic, Harvard Graduate School of Design 1978–79; Eliot Noyes Visiting Professor, Harvard University 1983. Fellow, Graham Foundation, Chicago 1958–60; honorary fellow, American Institute of Architects 1980; founder and member, Metabolist Group, Tokyo; member, Japanese Institute of Architects. Awarded Pritzker Prize 1993.

Selected Works

Hillside Terrace Apartment Complex (Phases I–VI), Tokyo, 1969–92
Kato Gakuen Elementary School, Numazu, Japan, 1972
Center for the School of Art and Physical Education, Tsukuba University, 1974
Iwasaki Art Museum, Kagoshima Prefecture, 1979
Maezawa Garden House (YKK Guest House), Kurobe, 1982
Municipal Gymnasium, Fujisawa, 1984
Wacoal Media Center (Spiral Building), Minato Ward, Tokyo, 1985
National Museum of Modern Art, Kyoto, 1986
TEPIA Science Pavilion, Minato Ward, Tokyo, 1989
Makuhari Messe Convention Center, Chiba Prefecture, 1989 and 1998
Tokyo Metropolitan Gymnasium, Shibuya Ward, Tokyo, 1990
Center for the Arts, Yerba Buena Gardens, San Francisco, 1993
Graduate School Research Center, Keio University, Shonan Fujisawa Campus, 1994
Isar Büropark, near Munich, 1995
Tokyo Church of Christ, 1995
Floating Pavilion, Groningen, 1996

Selected Publications

"Some Thoughts on Collective Form," in *Metabolism 1960* (with Otaka Masato), 1960; reprinted in *Structure in Art and in Science*, edited by Gyorgy Kepes, 1965
Investigations in Collective Form, 1964
Fumihiko Maki 1: 1965–78, 1978
"Japanese City Spaces and the Concept of 'Oku,'" *Japan Architect* (May 1979)
"Modernism at the Crossroads," *Japan Architect* (March 1983)
"The Public Dimension in Contemporary Architecture," in *New Public Architecture: Recent Projects by Fumihiko Maki and Arata Isozaki* (exhib. cat.), 1985

gardens. Maki pays close attention not only to the overall form of the buildings but also to their structure and delicate detail, which, as he points out, give architecture its rhythm and scale.

A recurring aspect in Maki's designs is his masterful use of light, a quality that is further developed in his works of the 1990s. The Graduate School Research Center (1994) at Keio University's Shonan Fujisawa Campus is characterized by its transparent entrance wall and the *brise-soleil* of perforated aluminum panels. The Tokyo Church of Christ (1995) features a *shoji*-like translucent wall of light in the main hall, separating the building from the chaotic surrounding and providing a place for spiritual reflection.

Together with Arata Isozaki, Kisho Kurokawa, and Kazuo Shinohara, Maki is one of the few Japanese architects of his generation to enjoy international success and fame. His works outside Japan include the Center for the Arts (1993) at Yerba Buena Gardens in San Francisco, the Isar Büropark (1995) near Munich, the Floating Pavilion (1996) in Groningen, and the projected Children's House in Poland. Maki has been honored with numerous prizes, including the Pritzker Architecture Prize in 1993.

CAROLA HEIN

See also **Isozaki, Arata (Japan); Japan; Kurokawa, Kisho (Japan); Kyoto, Japan; Metabolists; Shinohara, Kazuo (Japan)**

Fumihiko Maki 2: 1979–86, 1986
"City Image, Materiality," in *Fumihiko Maki: An Aesthetic of Fragmentation*, by Serge Salat and Françoise Labbé, 1988
Fragmentary Figures: The Collected Architectural Drawings of Fumihiko Maki, 1989
Fumihiko Maki 3: 1986–92, 1993
Fumihiko Maki: Buildings and Projects, 1997

Further Reading

The above-mentioned *Fumihiko Maki: Buildings and Projects* includes a text by Maki, "Notes on Collective Form," that was originally published in *Japan Architect* in 1994. It also contains essays on Maki by other authors, including those by Botond Bognar and Alex Krieger mentioned below, and gives a well-illustrated and documented overview of Maki's projects. Salat and Labbé presents Maki's work from the late 1960s to the late 1980s and includes an introductory text by Maki. Ross introduces early projects of the 1960s and 1970s in the context of Metabolism and beyond, while Munroe considers three major works of the 1980s.

Bognar, Botond, "From Group Form to Lightness," in *Fumihiko Maki: Buildings and Projects*, by Fumihiko Maki, New York: Princeton Architectural Press, 1997

Casper, Dale E., *Fumihiko Maki: Master Architect*, Monticello, Illinois: Vance Bibliographies, 1988

Friedman, Mildred (editor), *Tokyo: Form and Spirit* (exhib. cat.), Minneapolis, Minnesota: Walker Art Center, and New York: Abrams, 1986

Krieger, Alex, "(Ongoing) Investigations in Collective Form: Maki's Quarter-of-a-Century at Hillside Terrace," in *Fumihiko Maki: Buildings and Projects*, by Fumihiko Maki, New York: Princeton Architectural Press, 1997

Munroe, Alexandra (editor), *New Public Architecture: Recent Projects by Fumihiko Maki and Arata Isozaki* (exhib. cat.), New York: Japan Society, 1985

Ross, Michael Franklin, *Beyond Metabolism: The New Japanese Architecture*, New York: Architectural Record, 1978

Salat, Serge, and Françoise Labbé, *Fumihiko Maki: une poétique de la fragmentation*, Milan: Electa, 1987; as *Fumihiko Maki: An Aesthetic of Fragmentation*, New York: Rizzoli, 1988

Thorne, Martha, et al. (editors), *The Pritzker Architecture Prize: The First Twenty Years*, New York: Abrams, 1999

MALAGUEIRA HOUSING QUARTER, ÉVORA, PORTUGAL

Designed by Alvaro Siza Vieira; 1977–

Alvaro Siza Vieira's Malagueira Housing Quarter occupies the 27-hectare site of the former Quinta da Malagueira estate in Évora, Portugal, a small town of 30,000 inhabitants located in the Alentejo district 140 kilometers southeast of Lisbon. The estate initially was a privately owned farm dating from the 16th century. In April, 1974, the land was expropriated by Évora's Communist party in order to revitalize the area by creating a permanent residence for low-income workers.

The Malagueira Quarter continues Siza's long-standing commitment to social housing, beginning in 1974–75 with his work for the Serviço de Apojo Ambulatório Local (SAAL), a work group of architects and architecture students who worked with local residents' associations to reinvigorate the poor housing conditions extant throughout Portugal. Although the SAAL brigades

were disbanded in 1976, as a result of his participation, Siza received the commission to create the Malagueira master plan. The initial plan was approved in November 1977 and construction continues to this day on a site lying across a barren plain just outside of the town walls, next to an estate of middle-class homes arranged in pastel-colored, seven-story cruciform towers. The Quarter, to date, is comprised of around 1,200 low-rise, high-density houses containing one- to five-bedroom dwellings, along with several commercial and institutional buildings, including an electrical transformer room, a community center, and a supermarket.

The designs for the Malagueira houses derived from Siza's earlier SAAL-era proposal for the Boa Vontade cooperative north of Malagueira, which Siza offered to the Malagueira municipal administration for free. Later, Siza's plans were assisted and elaborated by several other architects, including Nuno Ribeiro Lopez, Eduardo Souto de Moura, and Aldalberto Dias. The results have often been compared to the "minimum existence" dwellings in Germany and Austria of the 1920s, such as the Weissenhofsiedlung in Stuttgart (1927), as well as to Adolf Loos's earlier villas in the wealthy outskirts of Vienna. A better comparison would be to the Moroccan works of ATBAT-Afrique, such as the "Nid d'Abeilles" project in Casablanca's *Carrières Centrales* (1951–53). There, as in Malagueira, modular housing was provided as a flexible frame to which a variety of different lifestyles could be accommodated.

Sharing a latitude and thus a climate with Athens, the town of Évora features a combination of classical and International Style modernism—along with a nod to a Mediterranean vernacular architecture—that both enriches and complicates its appearance. Siza chose forms that paid tribute to both traditions, and his use of white, orthogonal volumes for the principle module evokes both the purity of classical architecture and the indigenous architecture of the Alentejo. Each house is two floors high, set back from the road by an intervening patio space. The patios articulate a separation between dwellings and the street, whereas high walls provide a sense of enclosure and privacy from adjoining units. The patios also help with another problem stemming from budgetary restrictions: they control the climate within individual units, providing protection that the low-grade construction materials themselves could not.

Elsewhere Siza incorporated specific references to locally present classical architecture. A Roman-era aqueduct running near the city provided Siza with the theme of the conduit. Following this inspiration, though dictated equally by financial concerns, Siza constructed a set of elevated service ducts of concrete blocks that carries the water, electricity, gas, television, and telephone networks, with secondary pipes providing services to the individual houses. The duct is raised on slender concrete piers, and is a low-maintenance, single-scale solution to the provision of services to all of the quarter's structures, as well as one that is respectful of local history.

The resulting construction has been of a generally poor quality, mainly due to corrupt contractors and poor local skill and equipment, but Siza views this as a valuable process of discovery, preferring the results of accident to reflect the gradual process of conception and construction. The result is rigorously empirical and eclectic, bearing the marks of having been conceived against the struggles of external realities, and with all of the conflicts that true public participation entails. This honesty, pragmatism, and humility are the keystones of Siza's work.

The project remains an unfinished one, with open spaces left deliberately to eventually receive structures that will serve the community. Siza views this scheme as one that is prepared to receive changes and alterations, as compared to other, less-flexible projects that fix themselves in a historical moment without allowing for the vicissitudes of time.

Siza's Malaguiera Housing Quarter received the first ever Prince of Wales Prize in Urban Design from Harvard University in November 1988 (sharing the honor with Swedish architect Ralph Erskine's Byker Redevelopment Project in Newcastle-on-Tyne, England), chosen from among 46 nominated projects.

NOAH CHASIN

See also **Loos, Adolf (Austria); Siza Vieira, Alvaro J.M. (Portugal); Weissenhofsiedlung, Deutscher Werkbund, Stuttgart (1927)**

Further Reading

Collovà, Robert, "Cronologie: Malagueira, Évora, 1974–1999," *Lotus International* 103 (1999)

Frampton, Kenneth, "Architecture as Critical Transformation: the Work of Álvaro Siza," in *Álvaro Siza: Complete Works,* ed. Kenneth Frampton (London: Phaidon Press Limited, 2000)

Rayon, Jean-Paul, "Il quartiere Malagueira," *Casabella* 478, vol. 46 (Mar 1982)

Riso, Vincenzo, "Particolarità della forma urbana del quartiere Malagueira a Évora," *Parametro* 219 (May-June 1997)

Siza, Alvaro Vieira, "Viviendas sociales en Quinta da Malagueira," *El Croquis* 68/69 (1994)

Siza, Alvaro Vieira, "Housing in Quinta da Malagueira, Évora, Portugal," *Architecture and Urbanism* 6 [Extra Edition] (June 1989).

Alvaro Siza Vieira, "L'accumulazione degli indizi," *Casabella* 498–499, vol. 48 (Jan–Feb 1984)

MALLET-STEVENS, ROBERT 1886–1945

Architect and Film Set Designer, France

Robert Mallet-Stevens played an important role in French modernism at the beginning of the 20th century. While he practiced architecture within the mode of International Style through his collaborations with artists, sculptors, film directors, painters, and furniture designers, he also developed a unique formal language.

Mallet-Stevens was the son of a prominent art expert associated with the Paris Impressionists. In 1905 he joined the École Spéciale d'Architecture in Paris where his interest quickly turned to the work of Frank Lloyd Wright, whose organization of interior spaces he admired. The same year, his uncle Adolf Stoclet called on the Viennese architect Josef Hoffmann, a family friend, to build his main residence (the Palais Stoclet, Brussels,). Hoffmann, along with Otto Wagner and the Vienna Secessionist movement, influenced Mallet-Stevens greatly. Encouraged by Francis Jourdain, his projects for furniture and interiors were exhibited in the Salon d'Automne, access that allowed him to meet with the decorator Pierre Chareau and with the sculptors the Martel brothers, with whom he collaborated during his entire life.

In 1922, while Le Corbusier designed his master plan for a Contemporary City for Three Million Inhabitants, Mallet-Stevens was publishing an album of drawings, *Une cité moderne* that reflected the eclecticism of the Viennese Secession. (What united the Secession members was their rejection of historical realism in painting and revivalism in architecture, in favor of Jugenstil, and the proto-functionalism of Deco and Bauhaus aesthetics). *Une cité moderne* consisted of a collection of buildings, individual fragments of an urban repertoire—a police station, a town hall, a bus stop, or bridges—each type possessing an autonomous form. The project demonstrated a tendency toward eclecticism, which he would later reject.

Mallet-Stevens's most important commission came in 1923, when the Viscount de Noailles and his wife, a young French aristocrat, decided to build a splendid villa in Hyères, France. After meeting with Le Corbusier, who declined the invitation, and Ludwig Mies van der Rohe, who was not suitable for political reasons, the viscount discovered Mallet-Stevens, a Paris acquaintance who had not yet built any significant commissions. With the Villa Noailles, however, Mallet-Stevens achieved a reductive yet elegant expression of simple cubic volumes. He preferred clean facades to constructive details or ornament; smooth gray and white surfaces and large horizontal openings composed the house. The villa was later to be showcased in a Surrealist film made in 1928 by Man Ray titled *Le mystère du château de Dé* (The Mysteries of the Chateau of Die), in which the artist melded the stark forms of the villa with Stéphane Mallarmé's poem "*Un coups de dé jamais n'abolira le hasar*" ("A throw of dice will never abolish chance").

Mallet-Stevens designed numerous sets for the cinema including Marcel l'Herbier's *L'inhumaine* (The Inhuman One, 1923), a collaborative project that also included cubo-futurist painter Fernand Léger and designer René Lalique. The film was acclaimed by the *Club des Amis du Septième Art* (Friends of the Cinematographic Arts), the first avant-garde ciné-club of its kind to which Mallet-Stevens belonged. His colleagues led him to design his largest project in 1926–27, the Rue Mallet-Stevens houses in Auteuil, a street of urban mansions for the architect, artists, and his patrons. The ensemble was a series of houses ending at the border of the street, expressed through a consistent yet varied Cubist vocabulary.

After 1926, influenced in part by De Stijl aesthetics and his own shift towards reductivism, Mallet-Stevens abandoned ornamentation and continued to develop modernist pavilions for the *Exposition Internationale des Arts Décoratifs* (International Exhibition of Decorative Arts, Paris, 1925, 1937), private villas (such as the Corbusian-inspired Villa Cavroix, in Croix, France, 1932), and commercial buildings, such as the Garage Alfa-Romeo in Paris (1925). The latter reflected his passion for machines and speed shared with the Italian Futurists. At the beginning of World War II, Mallet-Stevens fled to southern France with his Jewish wife and worked on large-scale competitions in which he insisted on the value of volumetric masses. His key role in the French avant-garde was neglected until 1980, when his work was brought to light with the reconstruction of the Villa Noailles and the rediscovery of Dadaist cinema. Criticized by his peers for being too much a formalist, the architect was nevertheless a designer of great importance in the development of modern art and architecture in France in the first part of the 20th century.

MARC ITAMAR BRETLER

See also **Art Nouveau (Jugendstil); Contemporary City for Three Million Inhabitants; Corbusier, Le (Jeanneret, Charles-Édouard) (France); Hoffmann, Josef (Austria); Palais Stoclet, Brussels; Vienna Secession; Wagner, Otto (Austria)**

Biography

Born in Paris, 24 March 1886 to a Belgian family; uncle Baron Stoclet was an architect and designer. Attended the *École Spécial d'Architecture*, Paris 1903–06. Private practice, Paris from 1907; designed film sets between 1919 and 1929. Founding member, *Union des Artistes Modernes* 1929. Died in Paris, 8 February 1945, after a long illness.

Selected Works

Villa Noailles, Hyères, France, 1923
Sets for the film *L' inhumaine*, 1924
Reconstruction of the Hôtel des Roches Noires, Trouville, France, 1924
Garage Alfa-Romeo, rue Marbeuf, Paris, 1925
Mansion of Mme Collinet, Boulogne, France, 1925
Pavilion du Tourisme (with Martel Brothers), Exposition Internationale des Arts Décoratifs, 1925
Villa of M. Anger-Prouvost, Ville d'Arvay, France, 1926
Sets for *Le vertige*, 1926
Mansion of Mrs. Reiffenberg, Auteuil, Paris, 1927
Mansion of Mrs. Allatini, Auteuil, Paris, 1927
Mansion of S. and J. Martel, Auteuil, Paris, 1927
Mansion of M. Dreyfus, Auteuil, Paris, 1927
Mansion of Mallet-Stevens, Auteuil, Paris, 1927
Casino of Saint-Jean-de-Luz, France, 1928
Renovation of the Théâtre de Grasse, France, 1930
Delza shop, rue de la Paix, Paris, 1930
Bar for Les Cafés du Brésil, boulevard Haussmann and avenue Wagram, Paris, 1930
Villa of M. Cavroix, Croix, France, 1932
Villa of M. Trapenard, Sceaux, France, 1932
Fire Station, Passy, France, 1936
Pavilions, Exposition Internationale des Arts Décoratifs, 1937

Selected Publications

Une cité moderne, Paris, Jourdain, 1922
Le décor moderne au cinéma, Paris, Massin 1928
L'art cinématographique (with Boris Bibensky and A.P. Richard), volume 6, 1929
Mallet-Stevens, dix années de réalisations en architecture et décoration, foreword by Maurice Raynal, introduction by A. Sartoris (Italy), W. Dudok (Holland), E.J. Margold (Germany), M. Melnikoff (USSR), V. Bourgeois (Belgium), M. Th. Bonney (U.S.), 1930
Grande constructions, Paris, Charles Moreau, 1929

Further Reading

Banham, Reyner, *Theory and Design in the First Machine Age*, London: Architectural Press, and New York: Praeger, 1960; 2nd edition, New York: Praeger, 1967
Briolle, Cécile, Agnès Fuzibet, and Gérard Monnier, *La Villa Noailles: Rob Mallet-Stevens*, Marseilles: Parenthèses, 1990
De Stijl et l'architecture en France, Liège, Belgium: Mardaga, 1985
Deshoulières, Dominique, *Rob Mallet-Stevens, Architecte* (bilingual French-English edition), Brussels: Archives d'Architecture Moderne, 1980
Gangnet, Pierre, *Le sentiment de la nature chez Mallet-Stevens*, Paris: AMC, 1977
Moussinac, Léon, *Mallet-Stevens*, Paris: Crès, 1931
Wesley, Richard, "Gabriel Guevrekian e il giardino cubista," *Rassegna*, 8 (1981)

MANTEOLA, SÁNCHEZ GÓMEZ, SANTOS, SOLSONA, VIÑOLY

Architectural firm, Argentina

Flora Manteola, Javier Sánchez Gómez, Josefina Santos, Justo Solsona, and Rafael Viñoly constituted one of the most significant firms to practice architecture in Argentina beginning in the late 1960s. Santos and Solsona created the original studio on their graduation in 1956. Ignacio Petchersky later became an associate in 1962 and remained until he died in 1972, and Rafael Viñoly was an associate from 1966 until 1981, when he moved to the United States.

During the 1960s the firm began exploring the potential in architectural renovation. Exemplary of this exploration is their Headquarters of the Bank of Buenos Aires (1968). Converted from an existing department store, it retains its primary metal structure and expresses its original, academic, tripartite facade. The scheme yields an interior volume that is unified by an envelope of amber glass brick. It quickly gained international recognition for its transparent use of light and color and its strong volumetric articulation. The building subsequently became a prototype for the development of the institution's additional facilities. Two branch banks, in Retiro and Patricios, both in Buenos Aires and from the early 1970s, are of remarkable quality. There, the use of structural glass slabs results in translucent horizontal planes and evocative poetic forms.

In the late 1970s the group received several major commissions. Among them, the Football (soccer) Stadium in Mendoza (1978) carefully utilizes the natural topography to create the stadium's principal volume. Context is also of critical concern in the group's most acclaimed work, the competition for ATC Argentina Televisora Color (Argentinean Color TV, 1978). In preparation for the Soccer World Cup of 1978, the design, construction, and occupancy took only 18 months and constituted a new typology for the country. The design resolution was achieved by sinking a large boxlike form into the landscape to continue the scale of the surrounding area. Four cubes that house the television studios emerge from this large platform. Its perforated ceiling accommodates existing trees and provides illumination. The intent is to convey a factory of images and information. The large, one-story rooftop offers opportunities for public events and provides a whimsical playground that integrates an artificial landscape into the park, adding a river, a lake, and a ceremonial colonnaded entry.

This firm has also contributed significantly to the design of large-scale urban residential complexes. Among them are the Rioja complex (1973) in Parque Patricios, Buenos Aires, and the Piedrabuena complex (1974), designed in association with the firm of Aslan and Ezcurra. This project combined apartments with two commercial centers, a sports center, two elementary schools, and a high school. Semicircular green spaces are organized to accommodate the facilities and provide ample space to realize large-scale dwelling complexes.

The Aluar Housing Project (1975) presented several constructional and logistical problems. It is located in a remote semiarid desert, Puerto Madryn, in the province of Chubut, near the Aluar aluminum factory. The climate is harsh, dry, and subjected to constant wind. The site, however, descends toward the Atlantic Ocean, allowing for qualitative views. The program consisted of housing for the families of 800 factory workers, a primary school, a commercial center, and administrative facilities. Because of the region's severe climate, the project utilized prefabricated components to expedite construction. Parallel building units are arranged in four groups to create an in-between street offering spaces that are protected from the harsh weather. The west wall has limited small openings to minimize the wind, whereas the east side has several entrances facing the ocean.

The firm has also produced a series of significant skyscrapers that are recognized for their formal and volumetric quality. Among them is the headquarters for the Union Industrial Argentina (Argentine Industrial Association, 1976). It is located in the north quadrant of the city's historic district, known as Catalinas Norte. The 28-story office tower is a pure glass prism that offers vistas to the river. The lower level houses the auditorium and support facilities, and all service areas are expressed in well-crafted concrete. This building carefully articulates function and materials and displays a high modernist tradition through the use of the curtain wall.

The CASFPI Tower (1981) in Buenos Aires refers to Amancio Williams's use of the tower as an isolated structure, yet it is located within a traditional lot of the original Spanish grid. The CASFPI tower is linked to the urban fabric through a transparent arcade that reveals a rhythmic facade interrupted by solids and voids. The Prourban Tower (1983) is located along one of the principal access points to the city center. Its pure cylindrical shape, concrete structure, and use of glass and anodized aluminum create a feature that is unique to its urban context. The twin towers of the Alto Palermo Plaza (1997) are constructed in a residential area of Palermo. The project was executed in association with the team of Urgell, Fazio, Penedo, Salaberry, McCormack, and Minond and is considered to represent the best tradition of design and building in Argentina. The complex won recognition as a significant landmark in the city. The unique spatial effects of the interior and the buildings' iconography offer a structure that is logical, spacious, and poetic.

The firm of Manteola, Sánchez Gómez, Santos, Solsona, and Viñoly is characterized by a professional excellence, a substantial body of respected work, and a varied typological language. Their changing vocabulary can be referenced to modernists such as Pierre Chareau, Le Corbusier, Tendenza, and James Stirling.

Football (soccer) Stadium, 1976, Mendoza, Argentina
© Jose Bernardi

Internationally, their reputation began in the early 1970s through a series of glass-brick bank buildings and was reinforced later that decade by the ATC building.

Although the group's work is often seen as eclectic, their designs may be characterized by attention to program, spatial organization, and structural logic. Rather than striving for individual uniqueness, each building explores a significant archetype and develops an architectural theme.

JOSE BERNARDI

Biographies

Flora Manteola
Born in Argentina, 1936. Founding member, Manteola, Petchersky, Sánchez Gómez, Santos, Solsona, Viñoly, Buenos Aires 1964. Professor, faculty of architecture, University of Buenos Aires. Member, College of Judges of the Central Society of Architects, Buenos Aires.

Javier Sánchez Gómez
Born in Argentina, 1936. Founding member, Manteola, Petchersky, Sánchez Gómez, Santos, Solsona, Viñoly, Buenos Aires 1964. Professor, faculty of architecture, University of Buenos Aires. Member, College of Judges of the Central Society of Architects, Buenos Aires.

Josefina Santos
Born in Argentina, 1931. Founding member, Manteola, Petchersky, Sánchez Gómez, Santos, Solsona, Viñoly, Buenos Aires 1964. Member, College of Judges of the Central Society of Architects, Buenos Aires; member and advisor, Professional Council of Architecture and Urbanism, Buenos Aires.

Justos Jorge Solsona
Born in Argentina, 1931. Founding member, Manteola, Petchersky, Sánchez Gómez, Santos, Solsona, Viñoly, Buenos Aires 1964; member, Technical Qualifying Commission for the Olympic Games, Barcelona 1992. Professor, faculty of architecture, University of Buenos Aires; guest professor, École Polytechnique de Lausanne. Member, College of Judges of the Central Society of Architects, Buenos Aires.

Rafael Viñoly
Born in Argentina, 1944. Founding member, Manteola, Petchersky, Sánchez Gómez, Santos, Solsona, Viñoly, Buenos Aires 1964. Left the firm in 1981.

Firm
Partnership established in Buenos Aires 1964 as Manteola, Petchersky, Sánchez Gómez, Santos, Solsona, Viñoly. In 1971, partner Ignacio Petchersky died, and the firm became Manteola, Sánchez Gómez, Santos, Solsona, Viñoly. Partner Rafael Viñoly left the firm in 1980, and Carlos Sallaberry has since joined the partnership.

Selected Works
Headquarters, Bank of Buenos Aires, 1968
Rioja Housing Complex, Buenos Aires, 1973
Piedrabuena Housing Complex, Buenos Aires (with Aslan and Ezcurra), 1974
Football (soccer) Stadium, Mendoza, Argentina, 1978
Television Production Center, Buenos Aires (with Sadkowska, Trojtenberg, Lluma, Cano, and Grennon), 1978
Headquarters, Union Industrial Argentina, Buenos Aires, 1976
Aluar Housing Complex, Puerto Madryn, Argentina, 1975
CASFPI Tower, Buenos Aires, 1981
Prourban Tower, Buenos Aires, 1983
Towers of Alto Palermo Plaza, Buenos Aires (with Urgell, Fazio, Penedo, Salaberry, McCormack, and Minod), 1997

Further Reading

Glusberg is the most comprehensive survey of this studio's production from the late 1970s until the late 1980s; the book places architectural production within the social and cultural context of the country. The Gandelsonas article is a critical review of the Head office of the Banco de Ciudad de Buenos Airs.

"Review of the housing complex for 750 families for the industrial plant in Puerto Madryn," *Domus*, 178/588, no author
Gandelsonas, Mario, *Banco de Ciudad de Buenos Aires, Argentina: Head Office, 1968, Linears Branch, 1969, Retiro Branch, 1970*, edited and photographed by Yukio Futagawa, Tokyo: A.D.A. Edita, 1984
Glusberg, Jorge, *Breve historia de la arquitectura Argentina*, 2 vols., Buenos Aires: Editorial Claridad, 1991
"Review of Buenos Aires Color TV Production Center, Private Homes, and CASFPI Office Tower," *GA Document*, 10 (May 1984)

MARKELIUS, SVEN 1889–1972
Architect and Town Planner, Sweden

Sven Markelius was one of the most influential 20th-century architects in Sweden. Although Markelius maintained an independent practice from as early as 1910, he also held a number of influential public positions throughout his life, such as head of carpentry for the Swedish National Committee for Building Industry Standardization Design Department (1920), member of the National Board of Public Building's Research Department (1938–44), and director of the Stockholm City Planning Department (1944–54). The range of interest indicated by these positions was reflected in his work in a number of areas, including architecture, interior design, furniture and textile design, and town planning.

Markelius had the opportunity to travel extensively throughout northern Europe in the late 1920s and early 1930s, and this experience clearly influenced his views on architecture. In 1927, he was awarded a travel grant that took him to Germany, France, Belgium, and Holland. While in Germany, Markelius traveled to Dessau, where he met Walter Gropius and visited the recently completed Bauhaus buildings and the housing under construction at Dessau-Törten. Markelius also visited the Weissenhofseidlung exhibition in Stuttgart, where he was exposed to the work of Le Corbusier. His interest in the ideals of the Modern movement as they were being expressed in continental Europe was clearly reflected in his attendance at the Congrès Internationaux d'Architecture Moderne (CIAM) meetings in Frankfurt (1929) and Berlin (1931).

His travels would profoundly affect Markelius, as evidenced by the 1925 competition for the Helsingborg Concert Hall. One of the most important works of 20th-century Swedish architecture, this building represents the transition from a reliance on classical elements to the simple volumetric expression characteristic of the Modern movement, which was to become known as "functionalism" throughout Scandinavia. Markelius was initially awarded third place in the competition behind the well-established architects Lars Israel Wahlman and Ragnar Östberg. However, because the municipal authorities considered the proposals for the initial competition to be cost prohibitive, a second competition was held, and Markelius was awarded first place along with the building commission. Both the initial proposal and the subsequent winning entry by Markelius were decidedly classical; however, although the original plan and its complex entry sequence was not significantly altered, the exterior of the final building was characterized by the clearly delineated volumes, expanses of glass, and pure white walls that Markelius had encountered during his travels between the time of the initial competition and the completion of the concert hall in 1932.

Markelius played a significant role in introducing the ideals of the Modern movement to Sweden not only through his buildings but also through his lectures, articles, and participation in the influential 1930 Stockholm Exhibition. Markelius made a number of contributions, including sharing joint authorship for *acceptera*, the manifesto that accompanied the exhibition, and his built work that comprised pavilions and kiosks (Svenska Skärgårdförbundet, A.-B. Aftonbladet) and prototypes for rental apartments and private houses. A number of other important buildings date from the 1930s, including the Student's Building (1930, with Uno Århén) at the Royal College of Technology, the "collective" apartment block (1935) on Johan Ericssongatan, and the Stockholm Building Association Building (1937).

Markelius was also involved in both small- and large-scale town-planning projects including the Master Plan for the 1925 Bygge och Bo Exhibition, the Linköping Community Center (1946–53), and the Stockholm Community Center and Theatre (1945–60). As director of the Stockholm City Planning Department in 1944, Markelius strongly influenced planning in and around Stockholm. Perhaps his most significant contribution was the "new town" of Vällingby, which was envisioned as a suburban extension of the capital. As early as 1945, Markelius developed a schematic plan and a set of principles for the development of the area based on a concentrated center surrounded by a large strip of parks containing schools, day care facilities, and playgrounds.

While still serving as the director of the Stockholm City Planning Department, Markelius was appointed to the United Nations Board of Design, which was assembled in 1947 to advise on the design of the UN Headquarters in New York. This association led to the commission to design the Economic and Social Council Chamber (1951–52). Work on the UN Headquarters led to exposure beyond the borders of Sweden, and as a result Markelius was invited to serve as a guest professor at a number of American institutions, including Yale University, the Massachusetts Institute of Technology, the University of California, Berkeley, and Cornell University. After his tenure with the Stockholm City Planning Department, he went on to complete a number of commissions that included a high-rise building (1963) in Stockholm's Hötorgcity area and the Sweden House (1969).

KEVIN MITCHELL

See also **Sweden**

Biography

Born in Stockholm, 25 October 1889; educated at the Royal Institute of Technology and the Academy of Arts in Stockholm (1910–15); attained the title of architect 1913; subsequently traveled on the Continent, returning to practice in the office of Erik Lallerstedt and other leading Swedish architects (Ragnar Östberg, Ivar Tengbom, Eric Lallerstedt, and Torben Grut). Founding member of Congrès Internationaux d'Architecture Moderne (CIAM) 1928. Authored *Acceptera*, the manifesto of Swedish Functionalism (Stockholm, 1931). Member of the National Board of Public Building's Research Department 1938–44. Continued to practice up until his death in Stockholm, 27 February 1972.

Selected Works

Master plan and villas for the Bygge och Bo Exhibition, Lidingö, 1925
Student's Building at the Royal College of Technology (with Uno Århén), Stockholm, 1930
Various Buildings at the 1930 Stockholm Exhibition (First Aid Center, Private House, Rental Apartment, Pavilion for Svenska Skärgårdförbundet, A.-B. Aftonbladet Kiosk), Stockholm, 1930
Architect's private home, Nockeby, 1930
Concert Hall, Helsingborg, 1932
"Collective" apartment block on Johan Ericssongatan, Stockholm, 1935
Stockholm Building Association Building, Stockholm, 1937
Private home for Gunnar and Alva Myrdal, Stockholm, 1937
Swedish Pavilion at the New York World's Fair, 1939
Court House, Linköping, 1944
Economic and Social Council Chamber of the United Nations, UN Headquarters, New York, 1952
Linköping Community Center, 1953
Stockholm Community Center and Theatre, Stockholm, 1960
High-rise in the Hötorgcity area, Stockholm, 1963
Culture and Congress Center, Giessen, Germany, 1966
Sweden House, Stockholm, 1969

Further Reading

During the period 1920–66, a number of articles on the work of Markelius, as well as articles written by Markelius himself, appeared in the Swedish journals *Arktektur*, *Byggmästaren*, and *Arkitektur och samhälle*. A monograph dedicated to the work of Markelius has yet to appear in English; however, for a comprehensive account of his life and work in Swedish, see Rudberg, 1989.

Caldenbye, Claes and Åsa Walldén, *Kollektivhus: Sovjet och Sverige omkring 1930*, Stockholm: Statens Råd för Byggnadsforskning, 1979
Jadelius, Lars, *Folk, form och funktionalism: Om allmänt och gemensamt i offentlighetens arkitektur*, Gothenburg, Sweden: Chalmers Tekniska Högskola, 1987
Ray, Stefano, *Il contributo Svedese all'architettura contemporanea e l'opera di Sven Markelius*, Rome: Officina, 1969
Rudberg, Eva, *Sven Markelius: Arkitekt*, Stockholm: Arkitektur Förlag, 1989; as *Sven Markelius: Architect*, translated by Olof Hultin, Stockholm: Arkitektur Förlag, 1989
Sidenbladh, Göran, *Planering för Stockholm, 1923–1958*, Stockholm: LiberFörlag, 1981
Volny, Olle, *Markelius och bostadsfrågan*, Stockholm: PAN Information, 1974

MASONRY-BEARING WALL

Masonry is used to describe any number of nonmetallic and noncombustible rectangular, relatively small-unit materials, such as stone, brick, concrete block, or adobe. "Bearing" means that the material supports not only its own weight but the weight of a horizontal element as well, either a floor above or a roof. Masonry-bearing walls are certainly not a 20th-century invention since this structural system may have been the first invented by humankind. The development and proliferation of more sophisticated structural systems, however, especially the steel frame, has meant that masonry walls are just as likely to be non–load bearing as not (that is, to be installed as curtain walls or as veneer over another structural system). Of course, throughout the world the masonry-bearing wall continues to be one of the most widespread construction systems for one- and two-story buildings, especially where lumber resources are expensive and labor is cheap. Even when these economic variables are not favorable (for example, in the United States), masonry-bearing wall systems can still find popularity.

Masonry load-bearing units, either bricks or blocks, are invariably strong in compression, which means that they are best when piled one atop the next and loaded concentrically (that is, vertically at a right angle to the ground). There is a practical limit to the height of such a wall since without some form of lateral bracing, the tall and narrow wall section is unstable. In fact, the capability of a masonry-bearing wall to withstand tensile stress as a result of bending is dependent on the ability of the wall to act monolithically. Structural failure of a masonry wall usually occurs when its individual units lose their bond to one another. Thus, the most significant structural issue to be resolved is the adhesion of brick or stone to its neighbor so that the wall will act as a single unit.

Mortar is the first solution. Usually composed of a cementitious material—fine aggregate, sand, and water—mortar is the glue binding a masonry wall as well as an important component of its weatherproofing. Although mortar is an adequate adhesive under everyday conditions (such as when the wall resists the vertical force of gravity), during earthquakes mortar often fails when laterally loaded (that is, from a force other than gravity). Steel reinforcing bars or meshes making up the masonry-bearing walls are typically two wythes thick with an intervening cavity filled with grout. Steel reinforcing bars, called rebars, are placed at intervals of approximately two to four feet, while horizontal rebars are located every four to eight courses in that same grouted space between wythes. In some cases, a thin steel mesh shaped like a small ladder is placed between courses in lieu of the horizontal rebar. In either case, the reinforcing, grout, mortar, and masonry units act monolithically and, when designed and built properly, can withstand moderate earthquakes without damage. As in the case of reinforced concrete, the steel gives the masonry-bearing wall the ability to withstand tensile stress, and in many jurisdictions where earthquakes are a risk (for instance in California since the late 1970s), contractors are prohibited from building masonry walls without reinforcing. In areas where seismic activity is limited or in markets where steel is prohibitively expensive, vertical reinforcing is omitted.

The use of reinforcing steel has made bond patterns in brick little more than decoration ("bond patterning" is a technique for making wythes act monolithically). This is especially true in tall structures, where the use of stretcher courses and other brick bond patterns cannot adequately ensure stability under the extreme loads developed in tall buildings. The Denver Park Mayfair East apartments in the 1960s (Anderson and Looms), for example, stands 17 stories tall in a seismically active area. The brick-bearing wall has two wythes sandwiching a 3.75-inch grout-filled cavity with five-eighths-inch-diameter vertical rebars spaced two feet apart. The brick wythes are connected via quarter-inch steel ties embedded in the mortar at every fifth course, and the overall thickness of the bearing wall is only 11 inches. This relatively thin assembly is possible for such a tall building because the 17 floors horizontally brace the wall, preventing it from bending, buckling, and twisting. By comparison, the Monadnock Building in Chicago (1892, Burnham and Root) is 16 stories tall. Its tapered but unreinforced load-bearing wall is a staggering six feet thick at the base. Essentially, without reinforcing, compressive mass must compensate for the lack of tensile strength, which is rarely an efficient or cost-effective use of masonry-bearing walls.

The development of the steel frame, reinforced concrete, and precast concrete have in some cases made masonry-bearing walls uneconomical, but masonry offers a more human-scaled aesthetic, and in many areas masonry remains quite economical. The low-cost housing project in Vysankere, India (1983, Architect's Combine), is an example where masonry-bearing walls were used for both aesthetic and economic reasons. Local granite was quarried and set in lime mortar, and other local materials were used as well: wood for doors and Cuddapah stone for both the floor stones and the roof slabs. The unreinforced masonry was left unplastered, except for the granite lintels over the doors and windows and a lower band of red lime plaster that wrapped the housing units together. The interior face of the walls was whitewashed. The rusticated appearance of the exposed masonry was intended to impart a sense of permanence and to recall local vernacular building forms. Utilization of local materials, as well as local labor, helped make these one- and two-story housing units economical. The masonry's mass was also a key passive cooling feature.

Despite the fact that mortar requires sophisticated engineering and mixing—as does unit masonry, steel ties, rebar, grouting, and pointing—masonry-bearing walls are often perceived as a relatively low-tech construction option. In reality, the expense and technical expertise to build such walls often discourage prospective designers, builders, and clients. This has made masonry curtain walls, in-fill panels, and other non–load-bearing solutions increasingly popular, offering relatively little expense while still providing the same or similar aesthetic of solidity and permanence.

JERRY WHITE

See also **Brick; Stone**

Further Reading

Drysdale and Schneider are excellent textbook sources, while Merritt's prescriptive discussion contextualizes masonry construction with other systems. Ching and Adams is the best source for graphic information and is the best source for novices. Also useful are the proceedings from ASTM (American Society for Testing and Materials) annual conferences, published annually under varying titles.

Ambrose, James E., *Simplified Design of Masonry Structures*, New York: Wiley, 1991

Bahga, Sarbjit, Surinder Bahga, and Yashinder Bahga, *Modern Architecture in India: Post-Independence Perspective*, New Delhi: Galgotia, 1993

Ching, Francis D.K., and Cassandra Adams, *Building Construction Illustrated*, New York: Van Nostrand Reinhold, 1975; 3rd edition, New York: Wiley, 2001

Drysdale, Robert G., Ahmad A. Hamid, and Laurie R. Baker, *Masonry Structures: Behavior and Design*, Englewood Cliffs, New Jersey: Prentice Hall, 1994

Hendry, Arnold W., editor, *Reinforced and Prestressed Masonry*, Harlow, Essex: Longman Scientific and Technical, and New York: Wiley, 1991

Schneider, Robert R., *Reinforced Masonry Design*, Englewood Cliffs, New Jersey: Prentice Hall, 1980; 3rd edition, 1994

MAY, ERNST 1886–1970

Architect and Urban Planner, Germany

Ernst May was a leading architect and urban planner during the years of the Weimar Republic in Germany. He received his education in London, Darmstadt, and Munich, and worked for some years in the town-planning office of Raymond Unwin. After World War I, he was first involved in the planning of Breslau. In 1925 he was appointed *Stadtbaurat* (government building surveyor) in his native city of Frankfurt. As the head of the department of housing as well as of city planning, May succeeded in building an impressive 15,000 housing units in the space of only a few years.

May was one of the most important figures of the early years of the Congrès Internationaux d'Architecture Moderne (CIAM). He belonged to the group of founding members who met in La Sarraz in 1928, and he was responsible for the proposal to hold the second congress in Frankfurt in 1929. Frankfurt was indeed most appropriate for a discussion of the *Existenz-minimum* dwelling—the theme of the second congress. The housing units in the new settlements were designed as minimal-space apartments or houses that, thanks to their functional design and their fine equipment such as built-in kitchens and bathrooms, offered very agreeable housing for a part of the population that hitherto had been forced to live in slum conditions.

In the aftermath of the economic crisis of 1929, the financial means for the housing program in the Weimar Republic sharply diminished and May left Germany for the USSR. He became the head of one of the building brigades that was to plan the new industrial towns (including Magnitogorsk, Stseglovsk, and Tirgan) that were to become the core of the new communist society. Neither May nor the other Western architects who worked in the USSR during these years—such as Hannes Meyer and Hans Schmidt—regarded their work there as very successful given the dearth of a suitable administration, work force and construction materials. Few of the manifold plans they made were realized as the architects had foreseen, and after a few years their presence became politically embarassing for their hosts, since the official outlook on architecture and the city became disfavorable toward modern ideas.

In 1945 May returned to Germany (after a long stay in Africa), where he was further involved in the planning of new settlements, such as Neu-Altona. These settlements were far less successful than the ones he designed in Frankfurt in the 1920s. In order to reach high densities, he gave in to the pressure to build high-rises, instead of single-family homes or apartment buildings of fewer stories. The clearly demarcated urban spaces and the elegant layout of his Frankfurt settlements gave way to much larger and monotonous quarters where the organization of the traffic was ultimately the determining factor of the design.

May is thus remembered best for the exemplary housing program he set up in Frankfurt between 1925 and 1931. Every eleventh resident in the conurbation obtained a new dwelling through this program. The new settlements were all situated in a concentric ring enveloping the existing city of Frankfurt, with a large green belt separating the older parts from the new developments. May designed the overall plan for Frankfurt according to the principle of the *Trabanten-stadt* (Satellite town), May's interpretation of Ebenezer Howard and Raymond Unwin's principle of the Garden City. Unlike the English examples, however, which tend to be situated quite a distance from the existing city, May's satellites are integrated into the Frankfurt urban complex. The city of Frankfurt remains a whole, with the greenbelt acting as a complex of city parks rather than a nonurban area situated between the nucleus of the city and the *Trabanten* (Satellite).

The publication of a monthly magazine aimed at an international readership, titled *Das neue Frankfurt* (1925–31; *The New Frankfurt*), promoted the vast construction program. The name of the magazine came to stand for the whole enterprise in which May announced the emergence of a new, unified, and homogeneous metropolitan culture. May prioritized rationality and functionality. *Das neue Frankfurt* anticipated a rationally organized and conflict-free society of people with equal rights and common interests. This distant ideal and the concrete housing needs of Frankfurt combined to form the basic tenets of housing policy in the city. In this endeavor the architects of the New Frankfurt gave priority to the industrialization and good design of the construction process in the use of space. They experimented with forms of prefabrication and *Plattenbau* (panel construction); Grethe Schütte-Lihotzky developed the famous Frankfurt kitchen, which became a standard part of new housing units.

The *Siedlung* (housing development) of Römerstadt (1927–29) is the most famous and convincing example of May's city planning. The basic idea was to make good use of the qualities of the landscape; the development follows the contours of the hillside in the form of terraces, while it is related to the valley of the Nidda by viewpoints on the bastions that punctuate the retaining wall between the *Siedlung* and the valley. There is a clear hierarchy with a main street (the Hadrianstrasse), residential streets, and paths inside the blocks, a hierarchy that the architecture accentuates. The difference between the public front and the private back of the dwellings is emphasized by the neat design of the entrance section on the front, which features a canopy over the front door and a design that prevents passers-by from peering in. The blocks are no longer closed like the 19th-century type. By staggering the long straight streets at the height of the bastions, long monotonous sightlines are avoided. Römerstadt is a superb combination of organic design principles that bear the imprint of the Garden City tradition, with the sensation of simultaneity and movement created by the dynamism of a new, modern architectural idiom.

HILDE HEYNEN

See also **Congrès Internationaux d'Architecture Moderne (CIAM, 1927–); Garden City Movement; Public Housing; Urban Planning**

Biography

Born in Frankfurt am Main, Germany, 27 July 1886. Attended University College, London 1907–08; studied at the Technische Hochschule, Darmstadt, Germany 1908–10; studied under Friedrich von Thiersch and Theodor Fischer, the Technische Hochschule, Munich 1912–13. Employed in the town planning office of Raymond Unwin, London 1910–12. Served, eastern and western fronts, German Army 1914–18. Private practice, Frankfurt 1913–14; technical director, Regional Planning Authority, Breslau (now Wroclaw, Poland) 1919–21; founder, editor, *Das schlesische Heim*, Breslau 1919–25; director, Public Housing Authority, Breslau 1921–23; director, Central Office for Refugee Welfare/Distressed People's Housing, Breslau 1923–25; founder, editor, *Das neue Frankfurt* 1925–30; director of the European Town Planning Team, USSR 1930–34. Unable to return to Nazi Germany, farmed in Tanganyika, Africa 1934–37; private practice as architect and town planner, Nairobi, Kenya 1937–42; interned as an enemy alien 1942–45; resumed practice 1945–54. Head, planning department, then adviser on City Planning and Housing Techniques, Neue Heimat Housing Development Organization, Hamburg, West Germany 1954–60; founder, editor, *Neue Heimat*, Hamburg 1954–60; private practice, Hamburg from 1960. Honorary professor, Technische Hochschule, Darmstadt, West Germany 1956. Member, Akademie der Künste, Berlin; honorary president, German Association of Housing, Town, and Country Planning; honorary corresponding member, British Town Planning Institute; honorary corresponding member, Royal Institute of British Architects. Died in Hamburg, 12 September 1970.

Selected Works

Cottages, Goldschmieden-Neukirche, Germany, 1919
May House, Frankfurt, 1926
Frankfurt Redevelopment Plan, 1928–30
Römerstadt Housing Development, Frankfurt, 1929
Westhausen Housing Development, Frankfurt, 1929
Town plans for Stseglovsk, Kusnetszk, Tirgan, Magnitogorsk, Stalinsk, Nishi-Tagil, and Leninaken, USSR, 1930–34
May House, Nairobi, 1947
Aga Khan House, Oyster Bay, Dar-es-Salaam, Tanganyika, 1947
Neu-Altona Redevelopment Plan, West Germany, 1954–56
May House, Hamburg, 1970

Selected Publications

Contributions to *Das schlesische Heim* (Frankfurt), *Das neue Frankfurt*, and *Neue Heimat* (Hamburg)

Further Reading

In Germany there is an extensive scholarship on social housing during the Weimar Republic. For Ernst May and Frankfurt the most important publications are the work by Mohr and Müller, along with the catalogue published by the Deutsches Architektur Museum in 1986. Hirdina is an extensive selection of material from the magazine *Das neue Frankfurt*. The most recent publication in English discussing May's achievements in Frankfurt is a chapter in Heynen. Tafuri's article on the housing policy in the Weimar Republic remains a point of reference.

Deutsches Architektur Museum (editor), *Ernst May und das neue Frankfurt, 1925–1930*, Berlin: Ernst, 1986
Heynen, Hilde, "Das Neue Frankfurt: The Search for a Unified Culture" in *Architecture and Modernity: A Critique*, by Heynen, Cambridge, Massachusetts: MIT Press, 1999
Hirdina, Heinz (editor), *Neues Bauen neues Gestalten: Das neue Frankfurt, die neue Stadt*, Berlin: Elephanten, 1984
Mohr, Christoph and Michael Müller, *Funktionalität und Moderne: Das neue Frankfurt und seine Bauten, 1925–1933*, Cologne: Edition Fricke im Rudolf Müller Verlag, 1984
Rowe, Peter G., "Römerstadt in Frankfurt-am-Main" in *Modernity and Housing*, by Rowe, Cambridge, Massachusetts: MIT Press, 1993
Tafuri, Manfredo, "Sozialpolitik and the City in Weimar Germany" in *The Sphere and the Labyrinth: Avant-Gardes and Architecture from Piranesi to the 1970s*, by Tafuri, Cambridge, Massachusetts: MIT Press, 1987

MAYBECK, BERNARD R. 1862–1957
Architect, United States

Bernard Maybeck's architecture can best be described in terms of contradictory themes: domesticity and grandeur; innocence and sophistication; referential historical stylistic language and unprecedented form-making. His buildings were extraordinary syntheses of innovative and expressive structure, artistic form, experimental materials, and handcrafted ornament. Maybeck was among a small group of American architects schooled at the bastion of classicism, the École des Beaux-Arts in Paris, yet he is best remembered as the leading light of California regionalism that established the San Francisco Bay tradition of redwood frame and shingle-clad "simple homes." A generation of later modernists who admired Maybeck as a pioneer awarded him with the American Institute of Architects (AIA) Gold Medal, yet Maybeck himself detested the Modern style and repeatedly evidenced in his work what William Jordy once called "eclecticism . . . with a vengeance" (1972). When Maybeck brought together the monumentality of classicism and the natural setting of informal landscape, it was to create "an architecture of mood," as evidenced in his masterly Beaux-Arts project, the Palace of Fine Arts in San Francisco (1915). When the spirit of the client encouraged it, he set a New England Colonial Revival chapel amid college dormitories styled as English Tudor manor houses, and built in structural steel, stone, and concrete.

Maybeck wrote practically nothing about his work, and he was rarely published, yet his reputation and influence prompted members of the AIA, surveyed as recently as 1991, to name him among the ten most significant architects in American history. His individualistic personality and style remained open to the widest range of theoretical and practical influences on his work: from the structural expressionism of E.E. Viollet-le-Duc to the Arts and Crafts idealism of John Ruskin and William Morris, and from the constructional and ornamental concepts of Semperian cladding to contemporary Germanic theories of perception, psychology of style, empathy, and art as expression. Maybeck was a schooled architect as well as a naïve "carver of wood,". He approached the art of architecture as a painter might, using constructional materials as impasto for a picture he was composing. His painterly approach at Principia College (1931–38) created an architectonic painting full of light and shadow, color and texture, picturesque natural building, and—what he said all design comes down to—a beauty of line.

Following his study at the École des Beaux-Arts and a brief job with Carrère and Hastings who were then completing their Ponce de Leon Hotel (1888) in St. Augustine, Florida, Maybeck moved to the West in search of more fertile ground for progressive design. His contacts in San Francisco with A. Page Brown and Willis Polk established him professionally, and his association with Charles Keeler cemented his position philosophically as the leader of an emerging Bay Region Tradition of natural building. Maybeck's redwood houses in Berkeley for Keeler (1895), for himself (1892–1902, a second house in 1909), and for fellow members of the "hillside community" set a pattern of environmentally sensitive design, respect for the landscape, and employment of natural materials that influenced Julia Morgan, Henry Gutterson, and others of the Bay Region.

Among his most notable early buildings is the monumental Hearst Hall (1899, now razed) at the University of California, Berkeley, whose expressionist form is dominated by a vast range of laminated Gothic arches vaulting a single massive hall. The reception pavilion was intended as a community living room for women students at the university and was so large it was later converted to a gymnasium. Maybeck's Wyntoon (1902–03, destroyed by fire) was a baronial stone castle for Phoebe Apperson Hearst, for whom Maybeck had administered the International Competition for the Phoebe Hearst Architectural Plan for the University of California (1899). His Men's Faculty Club (1902) on the Berkeley campus referenced local mission forms while he gave the "great hall" a Nordic, rustic, male character.

At the Leon Roos House (1909) in San Francisco, Maybeck foreshadowed the more historicist stylistic language he employed in designs during the 1920s and 1930s, combining a half-timbered Tudor imagery outside and Gothic detailing inside. Here, changing ceiling heights brought a spatial drama to the open sequence from living room to dining room, and at the Bingham House (1916–17) in Montecito, California, a comparable plan with a change in floor-level created a performance stage and audience area for the client's musical soirées. At the Chick House (1914) in Oakland, California, Maybeck combined an exterior of board and batten siding, shingle cladding, and Gothic ornamental accents with an interior remarkable for its spatial flow and for the paired, floor-to-ceiling glass doors

First Church of Christ Scientist, Berkeley, California (1911)
© John Weil/GreatBuildings.com

that brought a modern openness to the living room. On a smaller scale, three houses in Berkeley suggest Maybeck's range and eccentricity: the R.H. Mathewson House (1915) was an intimate studio house with a surprisingly ample living room but no dining room; the Charles Boynton "Temple of Wings" (1912) was an open classical colonnade, more umbrella than house, for a family of Greco-philes; and the Sack House (1924) was an inexpensive replacement for his own house lost to fire. The Sack House was built out of burlap bags dipped in a frothy concrete, lighted by industrial sash, and containing a baronial concrete fireplace; the whole was an artsy-craftsy cottage nestled sensitively in the natural setting of the hillside.

Maybeck's work moved from the simpler aesthetic of his early redwood houses to the color and theatricality of his work for Earl C. Anthony in the 1920s, to the painterly imagery and craftsmanship in concrete, steel, stone, and brick for his largest and last major commission, Principia College in Elsah, Illinois. Anthony's Los Angeles house (1927–28) provided a Mediterranean-style (part Norman and part Spanish) stage set for an automobile dealer whose image of home was inspired by Hollywood. For Anthony, Maybeck built two highly imaginative Packard showrooms: a mannerist Corinthian temple for the San Francisco agency (1926) and a highly romantic medieval fortress for the Oakland agency (1928). Both were monumental frontispieces for utilitarian service and storage garages behind, but, for the showrooms, Maybeck brought forth his peculiar historicist flare. He was painting an architectural picture.

Maybeck's undisputed masterpiece was one of the most notable churches of the 20th century and a landmark of the Arts and Crafts movement: First Church of Christ, Scientist, Berkeley (1909–11). The architect crowned the auditorium with an elaborate and deep timber truss ornamented with Gothic carvings and forming a Greek cross from four Romanesque concrete piers situated in the corners. Industrial sash window-walls brought an openness to the perimeter, while two great Gothic windows with concrete tracery accented the cross axis. A gilt Venetian Gothic arcade (hiding the organ pipes) gave focus to the central axis and the readers' platform. Outside walls were clad in asbestos panels, while overhanging wood eaves and a colonnade of concrete piers supporting a trellis accented the exterior. But inside and out, the roof dominated, and, expressed as the great ornamental truss inside, it was both weighty and miraculously weightless. Both sacred and domestic in character and both expressive and sincere in intention, First Church of Christ, Scientist, Berkeley, displays Maybeck as a master builder, ornamentalist, and craftsman, but most of all as an architect of extraordinary vision.

ROBERT M. CRAIG

See also **Arts and Crafts Movement; Carrère, John Mervin, and Thomas Hastings (United States)**

Biography

Born in New York, 7 February 1862. Apprentice cabinetmaker, the firm of Pottier and Stymus, New York 1879–81; studied under Jules André at the École Nationale et Spéciale des Beaux-Arts, Paris 1882–86. Married Annie White 1890. Worked for the firm of Carrère and Hastings, New York 1886–88; partner, Russell and Maybeck, Kansas City 1888; worked for Wright and Sanders, San Francisco 1889–90; worked for A. Page Brown, San Francisco 1891–94. Private practice, Berkeley from 1894; established an office in San Francisco 1902; retired from active practice 1938. Directed the International Competition for the Phoebe Hearst Architectural Plan for the University of California 1897–99. Instructor in drawing, University of California, Berkeley 1894–97; director of architectural studies, Mark Hopkins Institute of Art, San Francisco 1895–97; instructor in architecture, and devised the first complete curriculum in architecture, University of California, Berkeley 1899–1903. Awarded Gold Medal, American Institute of Architects 1951. Died in Berkeley, 3 October 1957.

Selected Works

Keeler House, Berkeley, California, 1895
Hearst Hall (destroyed), University of California, Berkeley, 1899
Men's Faculty Club, University of California, Berkeley, 1902
Wyntoon (Phoebe Apperson Hearst Residence; destroyed by fire 1929), McCloud River, California, 1903
Bernard Maybeck House (destroyed), Berkeley, California, 1902
L.L. Roos House, San Francisco, 1909
First Church of Christ, Scientist, Berkeley, California, 1911; Sunday School Building (with Henry Gutterson), 1928
Charles Boynton House, Berkeley, California, 1912
Chick House, Oakland, California, 1914
Palace of Fine Arts, Panama Pacific International Exposition, San Francisco, 1915
R.H. Mathewson House, Berkeley, California, 1915
Bingham House, Montecito, California, 1917
Sack House (Bernard Maybeck House #3), 1924
Packard Automobile Showroom for Earl C. Anthony, San Francisco, 1926
Earl C. Anthony House, Los Angeles, 1928
Packard Automobile Showroom for Earl C. Anthony (destroyed), Oakland, California, 1928
Principia College, Elsah, Illinois, 1931–38

Selected Publications

Hillside Building (booklet), 1907
Palace of Fine Arts and Lagoon, 1915

Further Reading

The standard monographs on Maybeck are McCoy (an early introductory essay), Cardwell, who focuses on Maybeck more as architect than as artisan or artist, and Woodbridge, who publishes color photographs that are important to communicating Maybeck's artistic approach to ornament, materials, and imagery—including color chalk drawings of Maybeck's projects, both built and unbuilt. Bosley and Steele each offer studies of key buildings, while Hosmer is a guidebook to Maybeck's National Landmark campus for Principia College. Longstreth, Freudenheim and Sussman, and Winter (see Limerick) place Maybeck in the broader setting of California architecture: Longstreth offers insight on theoretical influences on Maybeck and discusses academic eclecticism; Freudenheim and Sussman define the "Bay Region Tradition" and connect Maybeck to the Arts and Crafts movement; and Winter is an anthology of California's Arts and Crafts architects (a "first generation" of nearly two dozen of Maybeck's contemporaries) as well as a second generation of regional modernists acknowledging Maybeck's influence. Jordy remains one of the most insightful discussions of Maybeck's mood imagery and expression.

Bosley, Edward R., *First Church of Christ, Scientist, Berkeley*, London: Phaidon, 1994

Cardwell, Kenneth, *Bernard Maybeck: Artisan, Architect, Artist*, Santa Barbara, California: Peregrine Smith, 1977

Freudenheim, Leslie Mandelson, and Elisabeth Sussman, *Building with Nature: Roots of the San Francisco Bay Region Tradition*, Santa Barbara, California: Peregrine Smith, 1974

Hosmer, Charles B., Jr., *Bernard Maybeck and Principia College: The Historic District*, Elsah, Illinois: Principia College, 1998

Jordy, William H., "Craftsmanship and Grandeur in an Architecture of Mood: Bernard Maybeck's Palace of Fine Arts and First Church of Christ, Scientist," in *Progressive and Academic Ideals at the Turn of the Twentieth Century*, Garden City, New York: Doubleday, 1972

Limerick, Jeffrey W., "Bernard Maybeck," in *Toward a Simpler Way of Life: The Arts and Crafts Architects of California*, edited by Robert Winter, Berkeley: University of California Press, 1997

Longstreth, Richard, *On the Edge of the World: Four Architects in San Francisco at the Turn of the Century*, New York: Architectural History Foundation, and Cambridge, Massachusetts: MIT Press, 1983

McCoy, Esther, *Five California Architects*, New York: Reinhold, 1960

Steele, James, *Faculty Club: University of California at Berkeley, Bernard Maybeck*, London: Academy Editions, 1995

Woodbridge, Sally B., *Bernard Maybeck: Visionary Architect*, New York: Abbeville Press, 1992

McKIM, MEAD AND WHITE

Architecture firm, United States

Arguably the largest architectural firm in the world at the turn of the 20th century, this highly successful New York partnership produced nearly a thousand buildings between 1870 and 1919. Almost every building type is represented—hotels, apartment houses, gentlemen's clubs, casinos, museums, libraries, universities, churches, and civic monuments. In 1874, Charles Follen McKim (1847–1909) and William Rutherford Mead (1846–1928) worked together, and in 1879 the firm was established when Stanford White (1853–1906), whom McKim had met in the office of H.H. Richardson, joined them. They employed an intelligent form of historicism that, combined with functional, coherent planning; a sophisticated manipulation of space; and a concern for excellence in materials and construction, was to shape the character of American urban architecture at a time when the city was emerging as a dominant force in American society.

Their personalities and interests were complementary. McKim was a conservative traditionalist who attended Harvard University for a year before studying at the École des Beaux-Arts in Paris. Mead had worked with the architect Russell Sturgis before pursuing an independent career in Florence. White, the son of a prominent New York literary and art critic, was an accomplished self-trained draftsman and watercolorist. The partners' respective social connections in artistic, political, business, and literary spheres provided a broad client base, including the powerful and social elite. They pioneered the concept of the large architectural office organized to address the complexities of dealing with corporate clients. Over 500 people (including Cass Gilbert, Henry Bacon, and J.M. Carrère and Thomas Hastings), spanning two generations, passed through the office, which also acted as an atelier for the Columbia University School of Architecture.

The firm rose to prominence in the 1880s, with the design of Shingle-style country houses and country clubs. The World's Columbian Exposition of 1893 in Chicago, conceived as a showcase for America's world power, was designed to be representative of American architecture. Each major building was assigned to a different designer, but all were to be classical in style and painted white. McKim, Mead and White's Agriculture Building confirmed their position as the nation's leading firm. The classical imagery of the French Beaux-Arts tradition, so admired by McKim, was combined subsequently with advanced planning to create a monumental American public architecture, exemplified by the Boston Public Library (1895), the largest of its type in the world and a reinterpretation of Henri Labrouste's Bibliotèque Sainte-Geneviève.

McKim's classical plan for Columbia University (first stage 1901, second 1930) and White's plan for the New York University campus also fall into this category. Daniel H. Burnham was later to invite McKim to serve on the Senate Park Commission to replace the District of Columbia in 1902 as a result of his plan for the university. The Rhode Island State Capitol (1904) in Providence, a white marble building, provided the model for state capitol buildings for many years. Robinson Hall (1902) for the School of Architecture at Harvard University in Cambridge, Massachusetts, was peculiarly American Beaux-Arts classical in style and followed the Harvard tradition of using red brick with light-colored trim. McKim, Mead and White were the club architects for New York City in the early 1900s, designing or altering eight of the largest men's clubs, the most prestigious being the University Club (1900) in New York. Here the firm's eclectic creativity found full embodiment. After a visit to the second-floor library in 1935, Le Corbusier is reputed to have said that he could understand how one would become a Beaux-Arts architect, detecting a "strange new firmness that is not Italian, but American." The Morgan Library (1906) in New York City, one of the firm's finest buildings, was designed for the international financier and collector and had its origins in Italian Renaissance garden buildings. Pennsylvania Station (New York City, 1910) addressed the complex functional and symbolic requirements of this building type by combining modern technology with a classical vocabulary. Invoking the Roman baths of Caracalla, it provided a symbolic gateway to the city of New York. The imagery of their Madison Square Presbyterian Church (New York City, 1906) derived from the Pantheon. Other commissions included the Knickerbocker Trust (1904), additions to the Bank of Montreal (1905) in Montreal, the patrician Southern Colonial–styled James L. Breese House (1907) in Southampton, New York, the Army War College (1908) at Fort Lesley J. McNair in Washington, D.C., and the expansion of the Metropolitan Museum (1920) in New York. Although only a small portion of McKim's design for the Brooklyn Institute of Arts and Sciences (1927) in New York was completed, it bears witness to his "great, simple and monumental style."

McKim, Mead and White's architecture fell into disfavor with the advent of international modernism, but their recent reassessment and acclaim are well deserved.

HILARY J. GRAINGER

The American Academy in Rome,
© Museum of the City of New York, from the Monograph of the Work of McKim, Mead, and
White, Vol. IV, plate 374 (1913)

See also **Burnham, Daniel (United States); Classicism; Gilbert, Cass (United States); Library; Museum**

Further Reading

McKim, Mead and White, *A Monograph of the Work of McKim, Mead, and White, 1879–1915*, 4 vols., New York: Architectural Book, 1914; new edition, 1 vol., 1981

Baldwin, Charles Crittenton, *Stanford White*, New York: Dodd Mead, 1931

Desmond, H.W. and Croly, H., "The Work of Messrs. McKim, Mead, and White," *Architectural Record* 20 (September 1906)

Granger, Alfred Hoyt, *Charles Follen McKim: A Study of His Life and Work*, Boston and New York: Houghton Mifflin, 1913; reprint, New York: AMS Press, 1972

Greenberg, Allen, *Monograph of the Work of McKim, Mead, and White, 1879–1915*, 1998

Roth, Leland M., *The Architecture of McKim, Mead, and White, 1870–1920: A Building List*, New York: Garland, 1978

Roth, Leland M., *McKim, Mead, and White, Architects*, New York: Harper and Row, 1983; London: Thames and Hudson, 1984

Sturgis, Russell, *The Works of McKim, Mead, and White*, New York: Architectural Record, 1895; reprint, New York: Da Capo, 1977

White, Samuel G., *The Houses of McKim, Mead, and White*, New York: Rizzoli, and London: Thames and Hudson, 1998

MEDGYASZAY (BENKÓ), ISTVÁN 1877–1959

Architect, Hungary

István Medgyaszay was one of the most innovative figures of early 20th-century modern architecture in Hungary. He sought to synthesize the efforts of structural rationalism and the search for national expression and was fascinated by the architectural possibilities of reinforced concrete, a new material of his time. His familiarity with the qualities of concrete goes back to his early youth, as his father founded the first cement works in Hungary around 1870. Medgyaszay started his career at a time when young architects in Hungary were concerned with the question of creating a national architectural style following the ideas of Ödön Lechner (1845–1914).

Medgyaszay was born as István Benkó, but in 1906 he changed his family name, taking on his mother's name. He simultaneously studied architecture at the Academy of Arts and engineering at the Technical University in Vienna. He was admitted to the master school of Otto Wagner (1900–03) and designed one of the most radically reduced facades of his time for a multistory department store (1902). The fine, entirely glazed iron structure was presented as an evening view illuminated by electric light. Medgyaszay absorbed the aesthetics of the Wagner school, which was based largely on Gottfried Semper's theory of style in architecture. He completed his education in Budapest, graduating at the Technical University in 1904.

During the next two years, instead of the usual grand tour in Italy, Medgyaszay took field trips to different regions of Hungary (Transylvania, Transdanubia, and northern Hungary) and studied vernacular architecture and folk art in villages. He made illustrations for the lavish book series of ethnographer Dezső Malonyai, *A magyar nép művészete* (1907; The Art of the Hungarian People). He realized his first architectural designs: two two-story brick villas (1906) for Leó Belmonte and Sándor Nagy, who were members of the life reform community in Gödöllő near Budapest. These buildings differed significantly from the contemporary architecture of villas in both their volumes and their interiors. They revealed Medgyaszay's familiarity with the vernacular house, although he made no attempt to copy or paraphrase it. Both houses were composed of simple stereometric volumes of different heights and were covered with a flat roof and a low-pitched roof; roof terraces and pergolas introduced asymmetry in their compositions. The exteriors expressed the complexity of the interior spaces, where the heights of the rooms were chosen according to their functions. It was also unusual that Medgyaszay did not hide the facades, choosing instead to show on the facade such structural parts as iron and reinforced-concrete lintels.

During 1907, Medgyaszay worked in Paris in the office of François Hennebique, a pioneer of reinforced-concrete architecture. After returning home, he designed the first theater building in Hungary with a reinforced-concrete structure (1907–08) in Veszprém. The theater was a multifunctional cultural center for a small community. Its auditorium allowed a variety of uses and could be converted to accommodate dance evenings and cinema performances. Medgyaszay believed that ornament should not be an application but rather must originate in tectonic form. Through forms, he tried to express the forces working in the elements of the concrete structure and was convinced that vernacular wood architecture could be considered a model for a structurally correct use of concrete. In 1909, the remodeling of the theater building in Sopron gave Medgyaszay the chance to develop his ideas further. The auditoriums of both theaters were covered by thin barrel vaults of precast concrete between iron beams. The inner shell of the ceiling, a light cement stucco construction on metallic lath whose function was both acoustical and decorative, was suspended from the beams of the vaults. He obtained a patent for the precast-concrete windows of the theater.

In 1908, at the eighth International Congress of Architects in Vienna, Medgyaszay delivered a paper on the artistic solution of reinforced-concrete architecture. He illustrated his lectures with details of the theater in Veszprém and noted that his intention was "to emphasize the supporting character of the elements of the construction such as pillars, beams, ribs, and consoles, contrasting them with the surface elements, which have only a separating function." The church in Rárósmulyad (1910; today Mul'a, Slovakia), which is composed of an octagonal central space and an adjoining bell tower, was a further step toward realizing this goal. The dome covering the church is a technical

tour de force: it is built of very thin prefabricated segments of reinforced concrete that were tightened together on-site with a visible belt of iron. The eight angel figures around the dome served not only as decorations but also as ballast to hold down the belt. Medgyaszay designed many modern school and apartment buildings (elementary school in Moson, 1909; apartment building on Dorottya Street, Budapest, 1914). His experience in theater design resulted in his winning competition entries for modernizing the Budapest Opera House (1912), built by Miklós Ybl in 1884, and for the National Theater (1913), which would remain unrealized.

From 1912 on Medgyaszay worked increasingly with wood. He covered the octagonal central space of the church in Ógyalla (1912; today Hurbanovo, Slovakia) with a wooden dome. During World War I, he served in the army as a military engineer and designed the pavilions for the military exhibition in Lemberg (1916; today Lviv, Ukraine). He used the opportunity to experiment with cheap materials and simple tools and realized his innovative ideas in a variety of wooden constructions. Returning to one of his favorite themes in the Wagner school, he realized his idea of a monumental tentlike wooden construction in the auditorium of the town theater (1926) in Nagykanizsa. The complex volume of the building's high-pitched roofs fits perfectly into the environment of the country town.

To study oriental architecture, Medgyaszay traveled to Egypt and Sudan (1911) and to India (1931–32). Like Lechner at the end of the 19th century, Medgyaszay attempted to introduce Asian elements into modern architecture. He designed the Sports Hotel (1927) in Mátraháza with a pagoda-like roof and the Baár-Madas High School (1929) in Budapest with clearly Indian allusions. His last significant work, the TÉBE Building (1939) in Budapest, was a mixed-function bank and residential block. The elegant, exactly cut geometric volume of the upper floors covered by polished white stone seems to float above the weightless, transparent glass box of the first two floors. Decorative motifs that were borrowed from Hungarian peasant wood carvings appear on the front bar of the balconies. Megyaszay's modern architecture in the 1930s did not sever the earlier ties to the vernacular building tradition that was considered authentic because of its capacity to resist academic conventions.

KATALIN MORAVÁNSZKY-GYÖNGY AND ÁKOS MORAVÁNSZKY

Biography

Born in Budapest, 23 August 1877. Studied under Otto Wagner at the Akademie der Bildenden Künste, Vienna 1900–03; attended the Technische Hochschule, Vienna; graduated from the Hungarian Palatine Joseph Technical University, Budapest in 1904. Independent architect, Hungary from 1904. Worked with François Hennebique, Paris 1906–07; created illustrations for *A magyar nép művészete* (The Art of the Hungarian People), by Dezső Malonyai 1907. Lecturer, 8th International Congress of Architects, Vienna 1908. Traveled Egypt 1911 and India 1931–32 to find the origins of Hungarian forms of design. Died in Budapest, 29 April 1959.

Selected Works

Department Store (unbuilt), 1902
Two Villas with Studios, Gödöllő, Hungary, 1906

Petrőfi Theater, Veszprém, Hungary, 1908
Theater Reconstruction, Sopron, Hungary, 1909
Elementary School, Moson, Hungary, 1909
Church, Rárosmulyad, Hungary (now Mul'a, Slovakia), 1910
Opera House Renovation (First prize, competition), Budapest, 1912
Church, Ögyalla, Hungary (now Hurbanovo, Slovakia), 1912
National Theater (First prize, competition; unbuilt), 1913
Dorottya Street Apartment Building, Budapest, 1914
Pavilions, Military Exhibition, Lemberg, Hungary (now Lviv, Ukraine), 1916
Auditorium, Town Theater, Nagykanizsa, Hungary, 1926
Sports Hotel, Mátraháza, Hungary, 1927
Baár-Madas High School, Budapest, 1929
TÉBE Pension Fund Building, Budapest, 1939

Selected Publication

"Über die künstlerische Lösung des Eisenbetonbaus" (On the Artistic Solution of Reinforced Concrete), in *Bericht über den VIII. Internationalen Architekten-Kongress, Wien, 1908* (Report of the 8th International Congress of Architects, 1908), 1909

Further Reading

Moravánszky, Ákos, *Competing Visions: Aesthetic Invention and Social Imagination in Central European Architecture, 1867–1918*. Cambridge, Massachusetts: MIT Press, 1998 (an analysis of Medgyaszay's major works in the context of the development of Central European architecture)

MEIER, RICHARD 1934–

Architect, United States

Consistency is a key attribute of the architecture of Richard Meier. For more than 30 years, Meier has remained unwavering in his commitment to the exploration of architectural forms and the experience of interacting with these forms. Heavily indebted to Le Corbusier's "Five Points of a New Architecture," Meier's approach to design is characterized by its complex vertical layering of spaces, its interpenetration of geometric forms (suggesting a kind of phenomenal transparency), and its proclivity for white, gridded surfaces. Although based mainly in North America, Meier became one of the late 20th century's most prolific and successful architects of civic and public buildings. He is perhaps most famous for his design for the Getty Center (1997), a complex of galleries, libraries, and offices in Los Angeles, California. This building, reminiscent in its structure and scale to a large medieval monastery, is urban in its form but isolated from the city on a series of landscaped hills. Clad externally in a mixture of travertine and white enamel panels, the Getty Center is designed to be bathed in sunlight with crisp, sharp shadows modulating its forms. Yet the origins of this approach to design may be traced in Meier's early designs for individual houses.

After working for Skidmore, Owings and Merrill and then Marcel Breuer in the late 1950s and early 1960s, Meier set up his own architectural practice in New York in 1963 and began work on a series of private residences. The first of these to be completed, the Smith House (1967) in Darien, Connecticut, is a white, seemingly abstract, geometric composition of orthogonal planes, glass walls, and exposed staircases. Meier's Hoffman House (1967) and Saltzman House (1969), both in East Hamp-

ton, New York, and the house (1971) in Old Westbury, New York, all utilize the same language of intersecting cubic, rectilinear, and cylindrical volumes. The Douglas House (1973) in Harbor Springs, Michigan, represents the culmination of this closely related sequence of designs. Spectacularly sited on a steeply sloping site that overlooks Lake Michigan, the Douglas House stands in stark contrast to its natural surroundings. With its white walls, Cubist composition, faintly nautical character, and complex vertical section, the Douglas House is the quintessential early Meier building. Meier's later houses, including the Westchester House (1986) in Westchester County, New York, the Ackerberg House (1986) in Malibu, California, the Grotta House (1989) in Harding, New Jersey, and the Rachofsky House (1996) in Dallas, Texas, are closely related to these early designs yet also show a number of subtle differences. First, these later houses possess, in section and in elevation, more complex and fine-grained compositions of forms and materials. Whereas the early houses appeared to comprise a single major volume with various geometric additions and subtractions, the later houses comprise several distinct forms that intersect. Finally, the scale and spatial disposition of these later houses tend to suggest that they are fragments of urban or public buildings and spaces rather than simply domestic structures.

A few of Meier's early houses were featured, along with the work of four other architects, in an exhibition at the Museum of Modern Art in New York in 1969. In addition to Meier, this group of five architects included Peter Eisenman, Michael Graves, Charles Gwathmey, and John Hejduk. All five were loosely connected through a common desire to extend the formal architectural languages of modernism and rationalism, particularly the geometric or purist works of Le Corbusier and Giuseppe Terragni. Known at the time as the "New York Five" or the "Whites" (because many of their buildings followed the modernist predilection for pure, white, geometric structures), they were later described by architectural critics as either neorationalists or late modernists.

Following from his success as part of the "New York Five," Meier began to complete a number of major public buildings over the following decades. Starting with the Monroe Development Center (1974) and the highly acclaimed Bronx Development Center (1977), both for the New York State Department of Mental Hygiene, Meier experimented with the repetition of forms and with prefabricated aluminum cladding. However, it was in his design for the Atheneum (1979), a cultural and visitor center in New Harmony, Indiana, that Meier finally translated the white geometric language of his houses into a major public building. The Atheneum is a striking collage of sharp, geometric forms that rests serenely on its site but makes no attempt to blend into the landscape. Externally, the Atheneum is clad in white, porcelain-enameled panels, and internally the major public spaces are lined with ramps and divided by stairs. Following the success of the Atheneum, Meier applied this same approach to the design of several influential museums in Europe and North America. The first of these, a clear relation of the Atheneum although with a more open circulation route, was the High Museum of Art (1983) in Atlanta, Georgia. This was followed by the Museum for the Decorative Arts (1985) in Frankfurt am Main, Germany, the Des Moines Art Center Addition (1984) in Des Moines, Iowa, and the Museum of Contemporary Art (1995) in Barcelona, Spain. For the Museum for the Decorative

Museum of Contemporary Art, Barcelona (1995)
Photo © Mary Ann Sullivan

Arts, Meier abstracted architectural elements from the facade of an existing historic building and repeated them on his own design. Curiously, this symbolic recognition of the historic context remains too subtle for most visitors and too contrived for many architectural critics. Meier's approach to design, like Le Corbusier's, is potentially vulnerable to criticism when working in historic urban settings. For example, although Meier's Exhibition and Assembly Building (1993) in Ulm, Germany, provides a rich and permeable boundary to the public piazza in front of Ulm Cathedral, the Museum of Modern Art in Barcelona seems strangely disconnected from its surrounding public spaces. Despite this criticism, Meier has had considerable success in several major European buildings, including the City Hall and Central Library (1995) in the Hague and the Canal + Headquarters (1992) in Paris. Both of these designs feature strong responses to the surrounding streetscape and urban fabric.

MICHAEL J. OSTWALD

See also **Corbusier, Le (Jeanneret, Charles-Édouard) (France); Getty Center, Los Angeles, California; High Museum of Art, Atlanta, Georgia; Rationalism; Skidmore, Owings and Merrill (United States)**

Biography

Born on 12 October 1934 in Newark, New Jersey and attended Cornell University c.1955–57; worked for Davis, Brody and Wisniewski, New York 1959; Skidmore, Owings and Merrill, New York, 1960; Marcel Breuer, New York 1961–63; established Richard Meier Architects in New York City in 1963. Member of the "New York Five" and Visiting Professor at the Pratt Institute, Cooper Union, Yale and Harvard. Resident Architect at the American Academy in Rome 1973; Elected to the American Academy and Institute of Arts and letters 1983; Awarded the Pritzker Prize 1984; recipient of the Royal Gold Medal by the Royal British Institute of Architects 1988.

Selected Works

Smith House, Darien, Connecticut, 1967
Bronx Development Center, The Bronx, New York, 1970
Douglas House, Harbor Springs, Michigan, 1973
The Atheneum, New Harmony, Indiana, 1979
Exhibition and Assembly Building, Ulm, Germany, 1983
High Museum of Art, Atlanta, Georgia, 1983
Museum for the Decorative Arts, Frankfurt am Main, Germany, 1985
Canal Headquarters, Paris France, 1992
Museum of Contemporary Art, Barcelona, Spain, 1995
City Hall and Central Library, the Hague, the Netherlands, 1995
Museum of Television and Radio, Beverly Hills, California, 1996
The Getty Center, Los Angeles, California, 1997
Hans Arp Museum, Rolandseck, Germany, 2000

Selected Publications

Richard Meier Architect: 1964/1984, New York: Rizzoli, 1984 (With an introduction by Joseph Rykwert)

Richard Meier Architect Volume 2: 1985/1991, New York: Rizzoli, 1991 (With essays by Kenneth Frampton and Joseph Rykwert)
Richard Meier Architect Volume 3: 1992/1999, New York: Rizzoli, 1999 (With essays by Kenneth Frampton and Joseph Rykwert)
Richard Meier Houses, London: Thames and Hudson, 1996

Further Reading

The Rizzoli three-volume set of Richard Meier's works spanning between 1984 and 1999 is the definitive reference work on Meier. Each of these three volumes contains a detailed bibliography of publications about his buildings for the relevant period as well as extracts from key writings. The introductions and essays from Joseph Rykwert and Kenneth Frampton in these volumes are among the most detailed criticisms and descriptions of Meier's works available. The 1996 Thames and Hudson volume presents a good overview of Meier's house designs.

Eisenman, Peter, Michael Graves, Charles Gwathmey, John Hejduk, and Richard Meier, *Five Architects: Eisenman/Graves/Gwathmey/Hejduk/Meier,* New York: Oxford University Press, 1975 (With introductions by Kenneth Frampton and Colin Rowe)
Klotz, Heinrich, and Waltraud Krase, *New Museums in the Federal Republic of Germany,* London: Academy, 1986
Montaner, Josep, and Jordi Oliveras, *The Museums of the Last Generation,* London: Academy, 1986

MELBOURNE, AUSTRALIA

Urban versions of the Australian suburban federation style were devised in the early part of the 20th century. Melbourne architects Ussher and Kemp (Dalswraith House, Kew, 1906) composed with elements imaginatively derived from both English and American Queen Anne sources. Their Professional Chambers (Paris-end of Collins Street, 1908) included pointed-arch windows along the street frontage. J.J. and E.J. Clark, with an Edwardian baroque repertoire, designed the Melbourne City Baths (Swanston Street, 1904; alterations and additions by Kevin Greenhatch with Gunn Williams Fender, 1980). Red brick and white stucco trim, a common fin-de-siècle medium, was eclipsed by the advent of plain unembellished surfaces. The epitome of severe classical revival was the Shrine of Remembrance by Philip Burgoyne Hudson (Hudson and Wardrop, 1934; World War II Memorial Forecourt by Ernest E. Milston, 1954) where a conjectural restoration of the tomb of King Mausolos, Halicarnassus, split a modeling of the Parthenon into two porticos.

Melbourne architects have often made imaginative compositions from many and varied sources. The former Auditorium Building (Collins Street, Melbourne, 1913), by Nahum Barnet, was inspired in program and in detail by Adler and Sullivan's 1889 Chicago building of the same name. The Renaissance palazzo tripartite division can be seen, with American Romanesque arches to the entry and vertical window bay strips, yet rendered as "blood and bandages"; the red brick with contrasting white stucco classical details also refer to contemporaneous London buildings. In Barnet's building, rows of curved projecting balconies were completed with ornate handwrought ironwork balustrades, an addition of elements that transformed the Chicago model.

Robert Haddon had Art Nouveau origins in mind for his red brick and stucco forms (Eastbourne Terrace, East Melbourne, 1901) with handwrought ironwork balcony balustrades and radiant curves. Harold Desbrowe Annear, before he committed to classicism, was a significant Arts and Crafts exponent. His Chadwick House (1903, restored by Peter Crone, 1999) was one of three Annear houses on The Eyrie, Eaglemont, set beside a steeply inclined pedestrian walk near the riverbank scenery favored by the late–19th-century Impressionist Heidelberg School *plein air* painters. Walter Butler's Mission to Seamen Building (1917) was also in Arts and Crafts style, a new amalgam of Californian Spanish Mission elements finished in rough-cast cement.

The engineer John Monash (with Bates Peebles and Smart) used Kahn bar reinforcing (patented by Albert Kahn in the United States, 1902) in the concrete-ribbed Reading Room dome in the State Library of Victoria (1911). Walter and Marion Griffin designed the stone-faced reinforced concrete Newman College (University of Melbourne, Parkville, 1918). The double-skin reinforced concrete dome and its pattern of ribbing was loosely based on a Paris patented dome construction system. The Griffins's Capitol House and Capitol Theatre (designed with Peck and Kemter, 1924) was a slip-form reinforced-concrete construction similar in method to Frank Lloyd Wright's Unity Temple (Oak Park, Illinois, 1906). Frederick Romberg's Stanhill House (1950) and Harry Seidler's Shell House (1988) concluded a long episode of innovative urban concrete construction.

The Griffins's own house, Pholiota (Magic Mushroom, 1920), was constructed out of Knitlock concrete masonry-tile construction (patented by Walter Burley Griffin and David C. Jenkins, building contractor, Melbourne, 1917). The Griffins's Knitlock system was tectonically based in the combination of French brick cavity walls with mild steel reinforcing and terra-cotta block work that Griffin used in his American houses. A number of Knitlock houses by the Griffins were built in Melbourne and Sydney. Kevin Borland, in his Rice House (1951), and Robin Boyd, with his Wood House and supermarket (1952), used a sprayed concrete system patented by the building contractors McDougall and Ireland in Melbourne (1950).

Some architectural works in Melbourne have been overtly European in inspiration. Peck and Kemter, in association with A.C. Leith and Associates (Heidelberg Municipal Offices and Town Hall, 1937), assembled brickwork blocks in the manner of Willem Dudok (Hilversum Town Hall, Netherlands, 1931). On the other hand, Keith Reid (Reid and Pearson with Stuart Calder) with his former McPherson's Pty. Ltd. Building (1937) maintained the preference of many local architects for evoking expressionistic characteristics. Erich Mendelsohn's Schocken Department Stores are exemplars in this instance. David McGlashan (McGlashan and Everist) at Heide (Bulleen, 1965), for the patrons and collectors of post-World War II contemporary art, John and Sunday Reed, designed a series of view-linked serene gallery living spaces about an intricate circulation, indicative of De Stijl principles and an appreciation of the German Pavilion, Barcelona (Mies van der Rohe, 1929). Heide is now the Museum of Modern Art in Melbourne (extensions by Andrew Andersons, 1993; rose garden pavilion by Gregory Burgess, 1991).

A curtain-wall system was created by Walter Burley Griffin for Leonard House (1922, demolished 1970), using different glass casting patterns and transparencies slotted into mild steel channels. Osborn McCutcheon (Bates, Smart and McCutcheon) developed for ICI House (East Melbourne, 1958) a curtain-walling system similar to Lever House (New York, Skidmore,

Owings and Merrill, 1952). The steel framing of ICI House was state of the art; its form, however, was closer to the precedent of the United Nations Headquarters (Wallace Harrison and Max Abramovitz, New York, 1952). The former BHP House (William Street, Yuncken Freeman, 1972) was equally structurally innovative; the diagonals of the braced steel-framed core within a braced glazed sleeve were expressed. Denton Corker Marshall (101 Collins Street, 1990), with a foyer of pale Postmodern Tuscan columns by Johnson Burgee of New York, and Daryl Jackson (with Hassell Architects, 120 Collins Street, 1991) delineated stepped skyscraper towers of vital solidity. Carey Lyon (Perrott Lyon Mathieson, Telstra Corporate Centre, Exhibition Street, 1992) and Paul Katsieris (Hassell Architects, Commonwealth Courts, 1999) have also proved that floor-level demarcations and meticulous design development can enhance office tower forms.

Roy Grounds produced a bluestone block form with a wide overhanging roof, long strip windows beneath the eaves, and a Richardsonian arched entry for the National Gallery of Victoria (St. Kilda Road, 1968; alterations and refurbishment by Mario Bellini, Milan, with Metier III, Melbourne, 1999), one of three monuments that comprise the Victorian Arts Centre. The avocado-shaped plan of the Concert Hall (1981), presented as a cylinder above ground level, and the Theatres Building (1984) were completed after Grounds's death (Suendermann Douglas McFall, decoration by set designer John Truscott). Denton Corker Marshall have provided an expressionistic airplane-wing metal and glass Melbourne Exhibition Centre beside the Yarra River (South Melbourne, 1996), and their new classicising State Museum (Exhibition Gardens, Carlton) will open in 2000. LAB Architects are completing an ensemble of crystal-patterned galleries for the arts media (Federation Square, Flinders Street) in time for the centennial of federation celebrations in 2001.

The Melbourne School was invented by Robin Boyd in 1967 to categorize some 1950s Melbourne buildings in tensile steel construction, such as the 1956 Olympic Swimming Stadium (Kevin Borland, Peter McIntyre, John and Phyllis Murphy) and the 1959 Sidney Myer Music Bowl (Yuncken Freeman Brothers Griffiths and Simpson). The school created daring forms using cavalier techniques and rejecting aesthetic rules. The steel A-framed house of Peter and Dione McIntyre (1955) and McIntyre's Snelleman house of more conventional construction (1954), but spiraling in plan down a steep slope around an existing eucalyptus tree, are examples of a number of houses of this type and approach.

Expressionism remains a favored style for a younger generation of Melbourne architects, including Norman Day (Mowbray College, Melton from 1981), Ian McDougall (Brunswick Community Health Centre, 1990), Gregory Burgess (Eltham Library, 1994), Ashton Raggatt McDougall (St. Kilda Town Hall redevelopment, 1994), Maggie Edmond and Peter Corrigan (Windsor Fire Station, 1997).

In the same adventurous spirit, with emphasis on abstract geometry, are works by Peter Elliott (Carlton Baths and Community Centre, 1989), Cocks Carmichael Whitford (Yarra Footbridge, 1989), Daryl Jackson (Melbourne Cricket Ground Great Southern Stand, 1992), Peter Crone (Trinity Grammar School Chapel, 1992), Peter Williams (Williams and Boag, Tyne Street Housing, Carlton, 1993), Allan Powell (with Pels Innes Neilson Kosloff, RMIT Building #94, 1996), Wood Marsh (Buildings

#1–5, Deakin University Burwood Campus, 1997), and Nonda Katsalidis (Nation Fender Katsalidis, Republic Tower, 1999). Denton Corker Marshall have sculpted the majestic pair of pylons astride the Henry Bolte Bridge (CityLink roadworks, 1999) together with their bright-hued and rhythmic Melbourne Gateway.

JEFF TURNBULL

See also **Arts and Crafts Movement; Australia; Sullivan, Louis (United States); Griffin, Walter Burley, and Marion Mahony Griffin (United States); Seidler, Harry (Australia); Sydney, Australia**

Further Reading

Boyd, Robin, *Victorian Modern: One Hundred and Eleven Years of Modern Architecture in Victoria, Australia*, Melbourne, Victoria: Architectural Students' Society of the Royal Victorian Institute of Architects, 1947
Boyd, Robin, "The State of Australian Architecture," *Architecture in Australia*, 56/3 (June 1967)
Goad, Philip, *Melbourne Architecture*, Sydney, New South Wales: Watermark Press, 1999

MELNIKOV, KONSTANTIN STEPANOVICH 1890–1974

Architect, Russia

Konstantin S. Melnikov was one of the most original, but also one of the most important, architects of the Soviet avant-garde. He belongs in the company of such architects as the brothers Vesnin, Ginzburg, Ladovsky, and the brothers Golosov. With the exception of the younger Leonidov, Melnikov had another characteristic in common with them: They had all received a prerevolutionary training, partly at the same institution, the Moscow School for Painting, Sculpture, and Architecture. Academically oriented, their education was strongly focused on classicism, the leading style of the day. Only after the October Revolution, influenced by avant-garde artists in the visual arts (Malevich, Lissitzky, and Tatlin), did they find their way to Modern architecture.

Early in 1917, Melnikov completed his studies with a neoclassical design for a sanatorium. Even his first independent designs, including the administrative building for the AMO automobile factory (1917) in Moscow and his work on the Alexeyev psychiatric hospital, were classicistic in conception.

Around 1920 Melnikov found his way to Modern architecture. He was attracted by the Expressionist work of the "Zhivskultparch" group, in which such architects as Ladovsky and Krinsky played a leading role. Soon Melnikov began to follow his own path, outside the mainstream of the new Soviet architecture. In the design he entered in the competition for the "The Saw," a residential complex on Serpukhovskaya Street in Moscow, he laid out the houses asymmetrically in curved lines, in blocks set back from one another, so that collective housing, family dwellings, and communal facilities are clearly and recognizably articulated. The asymmetrical composition, curved lines, and expression of building volumes are also present in his design for the competition for the Palace of Labor in the fall of 1922.

From 1923 Melnikov experienced great success as an architect of realized buildings. He received public attention, particularly for his tobacco pavilion "Makhorka" in the 1923 Agricultural Exhibition in Moscow. Traditional architects dominated that exposition, and Melnikov's pavilion was one of the exceptions. The center of gravity of his design lay in the expressive counterpoint of the volumes of the wooden building and its spatial effects. The commission had come from the traditional architect A.V. Shchusev (1873–1949). Melnikov was employed in Shchusev's Moscow studio, which was devoted to the reconstruction of the city.

Melnikov's true breakthrough came in 1924. Shchusev let him work on the glass bell over Lenin's sarcophagus for the semipermanent mausoleum and the administration building Sucharevka, which had a cafe and vending stalls. He also won the competition for the Soviet pavilion for the Exposition des Arts Décoratifs (1925) in Paris, in which Ladovsky, Ginzburg, and Fomin had also entered designs. The pavilion gave him an international reputation. The pavilion was built on a rectangular plan that was divided diagonally by a staircase. The staircase was covered with slanted awnings placed diagonally across from each other. A transparent tower was positioned near one of the entrances to draw attention to it. The pavilion was made out of glass and wood that was painted red and gray. The interior was done by Alexander Rodchenko and others. Of all the buildings at the exposition, Melnikov's pavilion, which radiated at once a certain sobriety and an expressive dynamism, was the most extensively discussed in the French and international press. Dynamism is also the dominant characteristic of the little-known design for the competition for the tower of the "Leningradskaya Pravda" (1924) in Moscow, in which three vertically arranged spaces were to revolve independently around a central axis.

At the end of his stay in Paris, Melnikov received a commission from the city of Paris for a parking garage. He completed two versions of the design, one in the form of a closed square box and the other as a rectangular space built over a bridge over the Seine and encircled by a double ramp. The inclined diagonals of the ramp gave the project an exceptional appearance of movement. Neither design was realized, but on his return to Moscow, Melnikov successfully built four parking garages.

As a result of the economic upturn of the second half of the 1920s, Melnikov was able to realize a number of projects. The clubs for workers are the most important of these. Intended for workers' leisure activities, these clubs presented a new building type, one based on a theater layout and consisting of a large hall for dramatic performances and meetings, service areas, and activity rooms. While his Constructivist colleagues attempted to create a standard type, Melnikov himself created an individual solution for each of the six clubs he built. They are built on different plans, according to the positioning of the main hall—wedge shaped, rectangular, or in the shape of a segment of a circle. Although the spatial arrangement of the plans is very different, the stereometric composition of the different volumes and the contrast of vertical and horizontal modulations are consistent throughout. The Rusakov Club, for the union of Moscow tram conductors, attracted the most attention, adding space to the hall on the street side in the form of three large bays. These spaces, which could be closed off independently, endow the building with an exceptional spatial dynamic and a highly expressive exterior.

This "expressive geometry" is particularly apparent in Melnikov's own house (1927) in Moscow. Two partially overlapping circles make up the plan, from which rise two cylinders of unequal height. The living room on the second floor and the studio on the third floor are double high, and the roof above the living room in the foremost cylinder is designed as a roof terrace. Interior spaces are highly expressive, as the round shape of the cylinders has been preserved, except on the ground floor, through the absence of separating walls. At that time, it was unusual for an architect to design his own house because the avant-garde was interested primarily in different forms of collective housing. However, Melnikov's typological solution was also unusual and bears witness to his attention for the composition of architectural space and mass. The rounded shapes return in several later projects, as in the design for the MOSPS Theater (1930–31) and the Frunze Academy (1931), both in Moscow.

Melnikov's entry for the competition for a new recreation area, known as "Green City Moscow," in 1931 is more conceptual and utopian in character. Melnikov designed the various zones of the area—woods, children's village, zoo, houses, and collective facilities—as segments of a circle. One special feature is the "sleep sanatorium," where weary workers could recuperate by means of a sleeping cure. For treatment, Melnikov invented a manipulation of light, temperature, smell, and sound.

The utopian character of this project provoked sharp criticism related, on the one hand, to changes in the cultural and political climate and the increasing repression in the USSR and, on the other, to the struggle among different architectural groups, a struggle that was fought in political terms. Melnikov did not participate in collective activities or the group polemics. He and his architecture, particularly the clubs and his own house, received a great deal of criticism for their individualism.

Melnikov had difficulty adapting to new circumstances. In his submissions for the second round of the competition for the Soviet Palace (1931) and the Ministry of Heavy Industry (1934), he continued to emphasize the symbolism of geometric forms while the cultural and political preferences of the party ran to a revaluation of traditional architecture. His designs were accused of antisocialist formalism. During the first congress of the Union of Architects in Moscow in 1937, this criticism led to Melnikov's firing as leader of the seventh Moscow City Studio, which amounted to the end of his career as an active architect. He was allowed to teach at engineering schools but was excluded from design work. After the war, he participated in competitions from time to time but without success. In the late 1960s, Melnikov was rehabilitated, and in 1972 he received the title of "Deserving Architect." He died two years later.

OTAKAR MÁCEL

Biography

Born in Petrovsko-Razumovsky, Russia, 22 July 1890. Apprenticed to a firm of heating engineers, the director of which saw his potential and put him through school; studied painting at the College of Painting, Sculpture, and Architecture, Moscow 1905–11; studied architecture, under Ilarion Ivanov-Schitz and Ivan Zholtovsky, at the College of Painting, Sculpture, and Architecture, Moscow 1912–17. Gained early professional experience under A.V. Kuznetsov and the engineer L.A. Loleit; worked with Ivan Zholtovsky and Aleksey Shchusev in the Mussoviet studio on the New Moscow Plan 1918; head of Studio No. 7, Mussoviet, Moscow 1932. Taught at the VKhUTEMAS, Moscow in a studio established by him and Ilya Golosov called the New Academy 1921–23. Discredited as an architect by the government and the First Congress of Soviet Architects 1937; had professional license revoked 1938; continued to write and design, 1938–60. Readmitted to the Union of Architects and allowed to do some teaching 1944; allowed to reassume a professional title 1953. Invited to teach at the All-Union Distance Learning Institute for Engineering and Construction, signaling the end of his professional exile 1960. Died in Moscow, 28 November 1974.

Selected Works

Main Building of AMO (now Likhachev) Automobile Works (facade), Moscow, 1917
Makhorka Pavilion (destroyed), All-Union Agriculture and Cottage Industries Exhibition, Moscow, 1923
Sarcophagus for V.I. Lenin, Red Square, Moscow, 1924
Soviet Pavilion (destroyed), Exposition des Arts Décoratifs, Paris, 1925
Rusakov Workers' Club, Moscow, 1927
Melnikov House, Moscow, 1927
Burevestnik Workers' Club, Moscow, 1929
Moscow Chamber Theater (reconstruction), 1930
Frunze Academy, Moscow, 1931
Heavy Industry Commissariat, NKTP, Moscow, 1934
Central Department Store (interior), Saratov, USSR, 1949

Selected Publications

"Arkhitekture pervoe mesto," *Stroitelstvo Movsky* 1 (1934)
"Arkhitekture osvoenie novykh materialov," *Arkhitektura SSSR* 3 (1934)
"Tvorcheskoe samochuvstvie arkhitektora," *Arkhitektura SSSR* 9 (1934)

Further Reading

Cooke, Catherine, *Russian Avant-Garde: Theories of Art, Architecture, and the City*, London: Academy Editions, 1995
Ferkai, András, *Konsztantyin Melnyikov*, Budapest: Akadémiai Kiadó, 1988
Fosso, Maria, Otakar Máčal, and Maurizio, Merriggi (editors), *Konstantin S. Mel'nikov and the Reconstruction of Moscow*, Skyra, 2000
Gerchuk, Yuri, et al., *Konstantin Mel'nikov: risunki i proekty: katalog vystavki*, Moscow: Sovetski Khudozhnik, 1989
Khan-Magomedov, S.O., *Konstantin Mel'nikov*, Moscow: Stroiizdat, 1990
Starr, S. Frederic, *Konstantin Melnikov: Solo Architect in a Mass Society*, Princeton, New Jersey: Princeton University Press, 1978
Strigalev, Anatoli, and Irina Kokkinaki (editors), *Konstantin Stepanovich Mel'nikov: arkhitektura moei zhizni tvorcheskaia kontseptsiia: tvorcheskaia praktika*, Moscow: Iskusstvo, 1985
Wortmann, Arthur (editor), *Melnikov, the Muscles of Invention*, Rotterdam: Van Hezik-Fonds 90, 1990

MEMORIAL

Long gone are the days when autocratic governments and the cult of death combined to march "great man," or military, memorials into public spaces as an uncontested staple of how society told time, took its pulse, and told its tale. By the beginning of the 20th century, memorials in the West had become as complex and cantankerous as the increasingly democratic societies creating them, fraught with debates between interest groups and civic committees, artists and architects, and government administrations. The simple and formulaic memorials to George Washington or Otto von Bismarck, requiring a prominent patch of public space and an easy subscription from public and private donors, gave way to debates over representation (artistic and multicultural), urbanism, the nature of memory, and the role that government should play in commemoration.

The monumental, classical memorials that the early 20th century inherited—triumphal arches, columns, and equestrian statues—fit easily into the City Beautiful movement and contemporary urbanism and lent a Roman grandeur to the efforts of imperialist and industrial capitalist nations to celebrate their triumphs and promote their agendas. Thus, three very different memorials—Otto Wagner's design for a monument dedicated to Emperor Franz Josef I (1917) for the Ringstrasse in Vienna, H. Van Buren Magonigle's Liberty Memorial to World War I (1926) in Kansas City, Missouri and Carlos Obregón Santacilia's Monument of the Revolution (1938) in Mexico City—all operate through conventions of scale, siting, and style, sharing more with a tradition going back to Augustan Rome than with the memorials that would be built after World War II. All use the confident visual language of classicism to represent the shakier realities of mass society and modernity.

The mechanized horrors of World War I are typically cited for altering the nature of memorialization. Nonetheless, in most of Europe, traditional memorial shafts and arches were erected after the war. In the United States, regiments of mass-produced doughboys joined their Civil War counterparts on public squares, but not without a significant protest from those utilitarians who insisted on "useful" or "living" memorials, such as community centers, parks, or public buildings, many of which were built as well. At the same time, the nascent USSR required ready-made traditions and deployed memorial strategies aimed as much at cultural invention as at amnesia (Hobsbawm and Ranger, 1983). Lenin's idea, based on Campanella's utopian City of the Sun, to erect dozens of cheap, impermanent statues of Karl Marx and other socialist heroes in order to turn the entire city into a didactic memorial to the revolution belongs to this desperate search for memory.

Where the tradition of "great man" memorials flourished under totalitarianism, democracy fielded a range of solutions. Compare the commanding monuments to Joseph Stalin that browbeat the public squares in virtually every Soviet city with the pluralistic klatch of quibbling Civil War, World Wars I and II, Korean War, and Vietnam War memorials that most American cities tolerate. Their clashing styles and scales and the gymnastic way in which they have had to avoid oncoming traffic make memorial zones some of the least welcoming sites in American cities. Their cacophony of memory already offended critics by the beginning of World War I. By World War II, with attitudes toward death and memory—not to mention representation—in flux, memorials began to take great care to sublimate claims to ultimate sacrifice into abstractions or useful services. The changing uses of memory itself were behind some of this shift, the solid, centralized memory of the ancien régime dispersed into what Pierre Nora called "Lieux de Mémoire": museums, archives, collecting, commemorations, and bald consumption.

World War II marked the end of the classical tradition in memorials. The very base of the memorial tradition—the iconic memorial—had become nearly impossible. The one prominent American example—the Marine Corps, or Iwo Jima, Memorial—tellingly derives from a widely disseminated photograph that shows the degree to which photography has complicated the nature of memory and thus the role of memorials. If the figurative tradition was under siege, so too were other underpinnings of the traditional memorial. Events themselves confounded memory. The traumatic and cataclysmic nature of much 20th-century history has pushed the boundaries of representation. Historians, critics, and theorists ask how, for example, should society represent the Holocaust (a field unto itself), the killing fields of Cambodia, El Salvador, Stalin's purges, or the bombing of Nagasaki and Hiroshima, not to mention Dresden.

In the United States after 1945, the "living memorial" finally won the day, leading to memorial halls, highways, parks, and stadiums but very few traditional memorials. Only now, 50 years after the war, is a national memorial to the so-called Good War being seriously entertained, and this long after memorials to

Korea and Vietnam found their places on national ground and in national consciousness. Living-memorial advocates fought against what they called "dead memorials," folding memory into daily life, in effect avoiding memorialization entirely. In response, Philip Johnson recommended a massive mound of dirt, bulldozed into place beside the highway: a modern memorial for the postwar commuter to contemplate at high speed.

Germany faced much trickier memorial problems. One answer has been to rebuild: faithful restoration as memorialization. The great Romanesque churches of Cologne or the old city in Nuremberg, all carefully rebuilt, stand in contrast to Egon Eiermann's Kaiser-Wilhelm-Gedächtniskirche in Berlin, a church preserved as a ruin in the midst of the commercial glitter of the Kurfürstendamm (1961). In Germany, the problem of anchoring national identity in a positive national memorial is confounded by the omnipresence of sites of ignominy. Indeed, in recent years the most heated debates on memory and memorials have taken place in Germany, giving rise to the "Countermonument," or *Gegen-Denkmal*. One of the most prominent examples is the disappearing column built by Jochen Gerz and Esther Shalev-Gerz in Hamburg (1986). Eschewing what they consider the fascist tendency of the traditional monument, the artists coated a 12-meter-high pillar with lead so that people

Russians pay homage to the memory of V.I. Lenin in front of the Kremlin, Moscow, Russia, photograph ca. 1925
© Library of Congress

could write on its surface, actively engaging in the process of memory. As writing covered the column, it was lowered into the ground in stages, freeing up more space but also suggesting both the eventual loss of memory and the willful burial of the past.

Maya Lin's Vietnam Veterans Memorial (1982) was an important bridge between traditions. Its granite wall and roll call recalls the permanent and active mourning that often goes with traditional memorials. However, as a gash or "scar" in the ground, it defies the iconic, heroic axiality and processional qualities of much commemoration and, unlike its predecessors, confronts death directly. The names run in order of death rather than alphabetically, like an epic poem (Mothersill, in Reynolds, 1996), overlaid with the mourner's own reflection in the polished stone. The double entendre on reflection makes memory emphatically shared, public; rather than merely grounding and discharging memory, as the Washington Monument does, the Vietnam Veterans Memorial absorbs and recharges it. Its pendent on the Washington Mall, the later Korean War Veterans Memorial (1995, by Cooper-Lecky, based on the designs of BL3PO), achieves a similar effect but enhances it by placing the mourner in a field of life-size soldiers on patrol.

Inevitably, memorials are inert. They express only what we bring to them, although some are easier to use or to coopt for use. A day might come when even the Vietnam Veterans Memorial fails to do "memory work," as the sentiment surrounding the Vietnam War wanes with passing generations. This is seen more dramatically with the revolutions in the former Eastern bloc, as Soviet memorials were toppled and a whole era that systematically suppressed pre-communist history found its own memorials melted down or thrown on the junk heap.

ANDREW M. SHANKEN

See also **City Beautiful Movement; Lin, Maya (United States); Lincoln Memorial, Washington, D.C.; Peace Memorial and Museum, Hiroshima; Postmodernism; Vietnam Veterans Memorial, Washington, D.C.; Wagner, Otto (Austria)**

Further Reading

Borg, Mosse, and Piehler offer standard histories of memorials. The more recent book by the art historian Boime gives sharp-eyed criticism of modern memorials in an effort to counter the dangers of the iconic tradition. Young brilliantly ranges over problems of memorialization in Germany, Poland, and in relation to the Holocaust.

Aries, Philippe, *L'homme devant la mort*, Paris: Editions du Seuil, 1977; as *The Hour of Our Death*, New York: Knopf, and London: Allen Lane, 1981
Barthes, Roland, *La chambre claire*, Paris: Cahiers du Cinema, 1980; as *Camera Lucida: Reflections on Photography*, translated by Richard Howard, New York: Hill and Wang, 1981; London: Cape, 1982
Boime, Albert, *The Unveiling of the National Icons: A Plea for Patriotic Iconoclasm in a Nationalist Era*, Cambridge and New York: Cambridge University Press, 1998
Borg, Alan, *War Memorials: From Antiquity to the Present*, London: Leo Cooper, 1990
Hobsbawm, Eric, and Terence Ranger, editors, *The Invention of Tradition*, Cambridge and New York: Cambridge University Press, 1983
Johnson, Philip C., "What Aesthetic Price Glory?" *Art News* 44, no. 9 (1945)
Lowenthal, David, *The Past Is a Foreign Country*, Cambridge and New York: Cambridge University Press, 1985
Mayo, James M., *War Memorials as Political Landscape: The American Experience and Beyond*, New York and London: Praeger, 1988
McIntyre, Colin, *Monuments of War: How to Read a War Memorial*, London: Robert Hale, 1990
Mosse, George L., *Fallen Soldiers: Reshaping the Memory of the World Wars*, New York: Oxford University Press, 1990
Nora, Pierre, editor, *Les lieux de mémoire*, 3 vols., Paris: Gallimard, 1984, 1986, 1992
Piehler, G. Kurt, *Remembering War the American Way*, Washington, D.C.: Smithsonian Institution Press, 1995
Reynolds, Donald Martin, editor, *"Remove Not the Ancient Landmark": Public Monuments and Moral Values*, New York: Gordon and Breach, 1996
Sherman, Daniel J., "Bodies and Names: The Emergence of Commemoration in Interwar France," *The American Historical Review* 103, no. 2 (April 1998)
Sontag, Susan, *On Photography*, New York: Farrar Straus and Giroux, 1977; London: Penguin, 1978
Young, James E., *The Texture of Memory: Holocaust Memorials and Meaning*, New Haven, Connecticut: Yale University Press, 1993

MEMPHIS GROUP, ITALY

Memphis was a design movement born during the winter of 1980–81 in Milan of a group of architects and designers passionately devoted to channeling a new approach to design based on an openness to innovation and on the use of creativity as a social force. One of the main protagonists of the so-called Italian new design movements in the 1980s, Memphis was part of the concerted effort to break away from the homogenization of mass markets, and it never ceased to reexamine critically the postulates of any and all established modern "isms" such as functionalism or rationalism.

Memphis's notably young designers gathered around the recognized leader and educator of the group, Ettore Sottsass, Jr. The office of *Sottsass Associati* (founded in May 1980) was a crossroad for Memphis activity, and the key members of the firm, Marco Zanini, Aldo Cibic, and Matteo Thun, were core members of Memphis as well.

Memphis developed directly from Studio Alchymia, a radical design group from the late 1970s founded by Sandro Guerriero and shortly joined by Sottsass, Alessandro Mendini and Andrea Branzi. Studio Alchymia dealt with problems of "redesigning" and researched issues of kitsch and the banal. Their disagreement manifested through their different views on the perceived necessity of the level of social engagement of the design. Although some were content with the avant-garde conceptual experimentation, Sottsass tended toward larger scale social participation, which required project realization by manufacturing prototypes and entering real industry. Sottsass's "silent secession" marked his evolution away from Alchymia's radical conceptualism into Memphis's enthusiastic all-out antirigidity.

Michele de Lucchi was the next person to leave Alchymia and join Sottsass. The realization of Memphis (whose name, first chosen in December of 1980, apparently is an allusion to a Bob Dylan song) came through the support of Renzo Brugola, a friend of Sottass's and owner of a carpentry shop, and Mario and Brunella Godani, who had a showroom available for exhibition space. The first Memphis exhibition was held 18 September 1981 in the *Arc '74* Showroom, and it became an annual event. In 1982 Memphis joined the artists collective Artemide with financial support from industrialists Fausto Celati and Ernesto Guismondi.

Although they never formulated a coherent aesthetic philosophy, they were determined to make a broad cultural and environmental impact and to instill a new movement comparable in scale and importance to the Modern movement. According to Sottsass, Memphis "was the invention of a voluminous and heavy packet of recognizable figurative intuitions; it was the invention of a very long and complicated list of possible compositions, unexpected combinations, possible chords and different chromaticisms" (Sottsass, 1988, p. 58).

Memphis rebelliously confronted and challenged the canons of good taste and tame, sterile modernism. The style manifested in all forms of art including furniture, lighting, fabrics, silverware, glassware and ceramics, industrial design, graphic arts, packaging, jewelry, and fashion but also "in complicated and vast architectural settings, in elaborate and intense design situations" (Sottsass, 1988, p. 59). Designers often melded standardized retail furniture made in industrial materials with quirky details such as frescoes of prehistoric animals for the Fiorucci Shop in Amsterdam (1981) or the stripes of warm reflected color lighting used for the Casino nightclub in Venice (1981–82). Memphis's best-known project remains a series of showrooms for the Esprit clothing manufacturer in Berlin, Frankfurt, Stuttgart (1984–85), Cologne, Dusseldorf, Zurich (1985–86), Lugano and Vienna (1987). In scope and design consistency the Memphis work encompassed the entire environment. They cultivated not only untraditional combinations of both ideas and materials, and bold experimentation with textures, colors, shapes, and styles, but also drew on the irrational, the surreal, and the exotic. Memphis baroque innovations are memorable for their application of plastic laminate, juxtaposed painted wood and metal, and spaces carpeted or tiled in wild patterns.

Memphis grew international in scale with the regional impact of contributors such as Michael Graves, Hans Hollein, Shiro Kurumata, Javier Mariscal, George Sowden, and Daniel Weil. Lesser known but significant participants in the aesthetic included Martine Bedin, Natalie du Pasquier, Terry Jones, Michele de Lucchi, Daniela Puppa, Maria Sanchez, Peter Shire, Gerard Taylor, and Masanori Umeda.

By 1987, when Memphis made its exhibition tour through American museums, its influence on the international design arena was already saturated, and the group began to dissolve. Having captured the attention of mass media from the start, Memphis managed to turn the international spotlight back to Italian design, and their own provocative production provided some inspiration and influence on the growing Postmodernism in the United States, Japan, and Europe. One of the movement's greatest contributions is that they permanently opened design and aesthetics to the rhythms of life by their acknowledgement and inclusion of popular culture and kitsch, so much so that today we talk about a recognizably flamboyant and bold "Memphis style," which encompasses the work of non-Memphis members as well.

Gordana Kostich-Lefebvre

See also **Postmodernism**

Further Reading

Radice's work should be considered a primary documentation on Memphis. Horn provides a comprehensive review of Memphis objects. The collection of essays by Sottsass and others sheds light on details and atmospheres surrounding Memphis's operations. A number of larger scale designs, installations, and architectural projects of core members are elaborated on, and the famous Memphis objects are shown in their originally intended architectural settings. Bellati positions Memphis in relation to a larger design scene, both historically and conceptually.

Bellati, Nally, *New Italian Design*, New York: Rizzoli, 1990
Horn, Richard, *Memphis—Objects, Furniture, and Patterns*, Philadelphia, Pennsylvania: Running Press, 1985; revised and expanded edition, London: Columbus, 1986
Memphis: The New Design, Stamford, Connecticut: Educational Dimensions Group, 1986, video recording
Radice, Barbara, *Memphis: Ricerche, esperienze, risultati, fallimenti e successi del nuovo design*, Milan: Electa, 1984; as *Memphis: Research, Experiences, Results, Failures, and Successes of New Design*, translated by Paul Blanchard, New York: Rizzoli, 1984; London: Thames and Hudson, 1985
Sottsass, Ettore, et al., *Sottsass Associati*, Barcelona: Gili, 1988; as *Sottsass Associati*, translated by Rodney Stringer, New York: Rizzoli, 1988

MENDELSOHN, ERICH 1887–1953

Architect, United States and Germany

Erich Mendelsohn's career showcases the evolution of modernism during the 20th century. He began by dealing with the machine age in an expressionist mode but was later forced to adapt modernism to geographic and technological circumstances different than those of Europe. He tried to develop a Hebrew version in Palestine and was able to conclude his lifework with a humanized version of modernism in his American period.

Mendelsohn was exposed to expressionism during his studies in Munich. These encounters with progressive artists led him to see artistic creation as the discharge of a personal rhythmic feeling. He believed that artists were guided by vision. Mendelsohn based his designs on the constituent elements of architecture. In his early sketches, he tried to find a personal expression for the architecture of the industrial age. The energetic forms and structures of Art Nouveau architecture influenced these designs. Through their continuous surfaces, they emphasized the dynamic conquest of space. In his forms, Mendelsohn alluded to the novel transportation vehicles for their symbolic value.

Mendelsohn abandoned expressionism quickly after World War I. He tried to build his earlier visions, particularly in the Einstein Tower (1924) in Potsdam, but was unable to find a contractor capable of producing the complicated formwork needed for the cast-concrete construction. Moreover, his political insight, which he related in his 1919 article "Das Problem einer neuen Baukunst," made Mendelsohn more pragmatic. His subsequent designs followed more closely International-style forms and surfaces. However, he never adhered to the theory that materials, structure, and function were the only requirements for good form. His buildings combined functional performance successfully with a dynamic impression of the form. He managed to formulate a personal vocabulary that has sometimes been denigrated as "Reklamearchitektur" (or commercial architecture). Mendelsohn himself aimed to develop a corporate design image for his clients through his designs. An example of this is found in the Stuttgart Schocken Store (1928), in which the masonry pattern imitates a motif found in the Schocken corporate logo. His forms were carefully composed either to create visually exciting shapes or to articulate the traffic flow of modern city streets. In the addition to the Mosse House (1923) in Berlin, exciting tensions are generated between supporting and supported parts and between open and closed, horizontal and vertical, and flat and cubical forms. In the large-scale department stores and office buildings that made him famous, he unified these contrasts into streamlined facades characterized by alternating horizontal bands. The various Schocken Department Stores and the Columbus House (1932) in Berlin were masterfully integrated into their urban context, were functionally and technologically up-to-date, and provided publicity effects through exterior and interior lighting. Emphatic staircases and other protrusions allow his buildings to be visible from oblique angles. The horizontal window bands, a Mendelsohn trademark, eliminated the need for ample interior lighting and light courts. In the Stuttgart Schocken Store, these devices allowed him to integrate the building into the radically different building contexts that faced its four sides.

In March 1933, after Hitler became German chancellor, the Mendelsohns immigrated to England. In partnership with Serge Chermayeff, he produced a few designs that continued the forms developed in his German period, thus helping bring this style to the United Kingdom. In the De-La-Warr Pavilion (1935) in Bexhill, emphatic circular staircases are added to rectangular building blocks to create highly visible accents.

Beginning in 1934, Mendelsohn received commissions in Palestine and ultimately moved to Jerusalem. There, he was intrigued by the mixture of old and new that he found in the existing local Arab tradition and the modernism brought by the Jewish immigrants. He attempted to alleviate the differences between these two contrasts by forging a Hebrew version of the International Style. While still using modernist forms, his buildings tried to accommodate themselves into the different situation. Especially in the interior layout, these houses exploit the local climate through open courtyards with pools. The houses are closed on the outside but open up inside. The exteriors were in local sandstone to integrate the buildings into the Arab traditions. His Weizmann House (1936) in Rehovot manages to combine these diverse sources masterfully and can stand on its own against the villas of Le Corbusier and Mies van der Rohe. Its main purpose is to represent, and it is situated on a promontory to provide views to Jerusalem and the Mediterranean. In the Anglo-Palestine Bank (1939) in Jerusalem, the solid exterior makes a reference to the Wailing Wall. The Hadassah Hospital (1939) in Jerusalem exploits its site on Mount Scopus to dramatic effect with cupolas, a cantilevered chapel, and vertically placed window slits.

When World War II closed in on Palestine, the Mendelsohns decided to move once more. In 1945 they settled in San Francisco. The American work consists primarily of synagogues and community centers. By providing additional spaces for educational and communal needs, Mendelsohn helped pioneer the use of synagogues during the week, not only on Sundays. His interiors were flexible to accommodate the changing numbers of worshipers on high holy days. The buildings were no longer purely modernist designs but aimed to create forms and spaces that could be grasped intuitively. In this way Mendelsohn attempted to generate a sense of community in the audience. He humanized his designs by responding to social, economic, and scientific changes. Building shapes and decoration referred to traditional Jewish symbolism, particularly to the "Temple in the Wilderness." Instead of overt stylistic references, this was essential architecture made of planar surfaces with skinlike facades. Park Synagogue (1953) in Cleveland transforms the modernist ocean-liner image into a sweeping occupation of its site; Jewish motifs make up its interior decoration.

This final creative burst shows that Mendelsohn never abandoned his visionary, progressive spirit. He influenced many younger colleagues through his teachings at the Universities of Oregon, Oklahoma, and California at Berkeley. He died on 15 September 1953 of cancer.

HANS R. MORGENTHALER

Biography

Born in Allenstein, East Prussia (now Olsztyn, Poland), 21 March 1887; emigrated to England 1933; naturalized 1938; immigrated to the United States 1941; naturalized 1946. At father's insistence, studied economics at the University of Munich 1907–08; pursued architecture at the Technische Hochschule, Berlin 1908–10; under Theodor Fischer, studied architecture at the Technische Hochschule, Munich 1910–12. Worked as an independent designer, Munich 1911–14. Served as an engineer on both fronts, German Army 1914–18; created many sketches during his service. Visited Rotterdam and Amsterdam 1920; traveled to Israel 1923; traveled to the United States 1924; toured Russia 1925–28; was invited to London by the Royal Institute of British Architects 1933; invited to Palestine 1934. Formed partnership with Serge Chermayeff, London 1933–36. Established a branch office in Jerusalem 1935; relocated practice there 1939. Moved firm to New York 1941; practiced in San Francisco, California from 1946. Taught at numerous colleges and universities 1941–46. Joined Arbeitsrat für Kunst and Novembergruppe 1918; joined Der Ring, Berlin 1925. Died in San Francisco, 15 September 1953.

Selected Works

Berliner Tageblatt Building (addition), Berlin, 1923
Einstein Tower, Potsdam, 1924
Schocken Department Store (demolished), Stuttgart, 1928
Columbus House (demolished), Berlin, 1932
De-La-Warr Pavilion, Bexhill-on-Sea, England (with Serge Chermayeff), 1935
Weizmann House, Rehovot, Palestine, 1936
Anglo-Palestine Bank, Jerusalem, 1939
Hadassah Hospital, Jerusalem, 1939
Park Synagogue, Cleveland, Ohio, 1953
Atomic Energy Commission Laboratories, Berkeley, California, 1953

Selected Publications

Amerika: Bilderbuch eines Architekten, 1926
Russland, Europa, Amerika: Ein Architektonischer Querschnitt, 1929
Neues Haus-Neue Welt, 1931
Erich Mendelsohn: Letters of an Architect, edited by Oskar Beyer, 1967

Further Reading

Mendelsohn's work has rarely found the critical acclaim it deserves. Praise by noted scholars such as Nikolaus Pevsner, Bruno Zevi, and Reyner Banham came only after his death. In the 1970s, a new generation of historians began dealing with his works. A group of them has just collaborated on a monograph that combines the latest scholarship.

Ahronov, Ram and Christina Toren, "The Lost Genius of Erich Mendelsohn," *Blueprint* 42 (November 1987)

Eckardt, Wolf von, *Eric Mendelsohn*, New York: Braziller, 1960; London; Mayflower, 1961

Der Einsteinturm in Potsdam: Architektur und Astrophysik, Berlin: Ars Nicolai, 1995

Hart, Vaughan, "Erich Mendelsohn and the Fourth Dimension," *Architectural Research Quarterly* 1 (Winter 1995)

Heinze-Mühleib, Ita, *Erich Mendelsohn: Bauten und Projekte in Palästina (1934–1941)*, Munich: Scaneg, 1986

James, Kathleen, *Erich Mendelsohn and the Architecture of German Modernism*, Cambridge and New York: Cambridge University Press, 1997

Morgenthaler, Hans R., *The Early Sketches of German Architect Erich Mendelsohn (1887–1953): No Compromise with Reality*, Lewiston, New York: Mellen Press, 1992

Nitzan-Shiftan, Alona, "Contested Zionism—Alternative Modernism: Erich Mendelsohn and the Tel Aviv Chug in Mandate Palestine," *Architectural History* 39 (1996)

Palmer, Renate, *Der Stuttgarter Schocken-Bau von Erich Mendelsohn: Die Geschichte eines Kaufhauses und seiner Architektur*, Stuttgart, Germany: Silberburg, 1995

Posener, Julius and Peter Pfankuch, *Erich Mendelsohn*, Berlin: Akademie der Künste, 1968

Posener, Julius, and Uriel Adiv, "Betrachtungen über Erich Mendelsohn: Erich Mendelsohns 'Carmelstadt,'" *Bauwelt* 79 (March 1988)

Stephan, Regina, *Studien zu Waren- und Geschäftshäusern Erich Mendelsohns in Deutschland*, Munich: Tuduv, 1992

Stephan, Regina (editor), *Erich Mendelsohn: Architekt, 1887–1953*, Ostfildern-Ruit, Germany: Hatje, 1998; as *Eric Mendelsohn: Architect, 1887–1953*, New York: Monacelli Press, 1999

Whittick, Arnold, *Eric Mendelsohn*, New York: Dodge, and London: Faber and Faber, 1940; 2nd edition, London: Leonard Hill, and New York: Dodge, 1956

Zevi, Bruno, *Erich Mendelsohn*, Bologna, Italy: Zanichelli, 1982; as *Erich Mendelsohn*, New York: Rizzoli, and London: Architectural Press, 1985

Zevi, Bruno, *Erich Mendelsohn: The Complete Works*, Basel, Switzerland, and Boston: Birkhäuser, 1999

MENIL COLLECTION, HOUSTON, TEXAS

Designed by Renzo Piano; completed 1986

The city of Houston, Texas, is home of one of North America's finest cultural oases. In the geographic area between Mandell, Mulberry, Sul Ross, and Branard Streets, four stunning museums (Menil Collection, Cy Twombly Gallery, Rothko Chapel, and Byzantine Fresco Chapel Museum) create an aura of the love for art and the beauty of modern architecture in an otherwise nondescript, partly derelict suburb. The collection, and the architectural masterpieces to house them, was made possible by the efforts of the late John de Menil (d. 1973), founder of the

oil field services company Schlumberger Ltd, and his French wife, Dominique (d. 1997).

The de Menil family started collecting art in the early 1950s with a focus on important works of the modern era, especially the Cubist School of Paris modernism and surrealist art, yet broadened soon after to include works of African tribes and the cultures of Oceania to become an expansive and eclectic collection of more than 15,000 pieces of fine art that includes art of the Paleolithic to the pre-Christian era. During the tenure of James Johnson Sweeney as director of Houston's Museum of Fine Arts (designed by Mies van der Rohe), the de Menils considered donating their impressive art collection to that museum. The need for an individual gallery within the museum led to disagreements with the Museum of Fine Arts and eventually fostered the plan to build a separate museum to present the collection to the city.

In 1981, Dominique de Menil, as president of the Menil Foundation, entrusted the Italian architect Renzo Piano of the firm Piano and Fitzgerald Architects with the design of the new museum. Piano's early design strategy of a focus on natural light had to lead to theoretical and empirical scientific research because the artwork needed to be protected against the damaging effects of ultraviolet rays, direct sunlight, and solar heat. The result is a multilayered structure for the roof of the museum, consisting of a series of 25-millimeter-thick, curved ferro-cement "leafs" that are hung from a structural, ductile iron roofing beam. Three hundred of those ferro-cement elements act as filters for light and heat, yet allow the ever-changing play of the natural light conditions to be an integral component of the exhibition experience. The roof enclosure of the 150-meter-long structure consists of a glass platform made of glass elements, slightly sloped to accommodate drainage of rainwater. The engineer Peter Rice, who worked with Piano during the design of the controversial art museum of the city of Paris, Pompidou Center, cooperated with the architects to develop the leaf and support structure of the roof. The result is an elegant and innovative museum with a successful utilization of natural light. The plan of the building distributes exhibition areas along a central inner promenade. Gallery areas, a library, shops, and processing areas are grouped into public and support areas. All exhibition rooms are on the ground-floor level of the two-story building. The second floor holds storage, research, and staff facilities (Treasure House). Only a selected number of pieces (200 to 300 pieces) of the entire collection are exhibited at the same time, which allows for optimal climatic storage of the artwork when not exhibited as well as variety. The museum has the feel of an artist's studio rather than an institution. The scale of the building echoes that of the residential neighborhood with its clapboard single-family houses. It is carefully placed: it is domestic, neither a landmark nor an antithetical statement, such as the Pompidou Center. The materials used in Houston for enclosures are taken from the context of the bungalows of the surrounding residential neighborhood: balloon frame and wood, set into a steel frame. The ferro-cement elements used inside the galleries are also used on the outside, creating a peripheral transition space, reminiscent of the verandas of the South. It is a place of quiet to enjoy the remarkable effects of the play of shadows cast by the ferro-cement leafs above on the light gray wooden facades. When the museum relies on the power and effect of natural light in the metropolis of oil, the shaded path around the museum recaptures

Menil Collection Building, Houston, Texas, designed by Renzo Piano (1986)
Photo © Mary Ann Sullivan

the value of pedestrian movement and comfort in the vertical American City. Inside the museum, enclosed tropical gardens are inserted into the exhibition zones, allowing a visual interaction between art and the lush natural environment. Plants and trees are meant to grow through the building, emphasizing a necessary true relationship between architecture and the environment.

RALPH HAMMANN

See also **Houston, Texas (United States); Museum; Piano, Renzo (Italy); Pompidou Center, Paris**

Further Reading

Buchanan, Peter, *Renzo Piano Building Workshop: Complete Works*, 3 vols., London: Phaidon Press, 1993–97; see especially vol. 2, 1995

Dini, Massimo, *Renzo Piano: Progetti e architetture, 1964–1983*, Milan: Electa, 1983; as *Renzo Piano: Projects and Buildings, 1964–1983*, New York: Electa/Rizzoli, 1984

Donin, Gianpiero (editor), *Renzo Piano: Pezzo per pezzo; Renzo Piano: Piece by Piece* (bilingual English and Italian text), Rome: Casa del Libro, 1982

The Hyatt Foundation, *The Pritzker Architecture Prize, 1998: Celebrating the 20th Anniversary of the Prize: Presented to Renzo Piano*, Los Angeles: Jensen and Walker, 1999

Menil, Dominique de, "Foreword" in *The Menil Collection: A Selection from the Paleolithic to the Modern Era*, New York, Abrams, 1987

Piano, Renzo, *Renzo Piano: Buildings and Projects, 1971–1989*, New York: Rizzoli, 1989

Piano, Renzo, *Renzo Piano: Progetti e architetture, 1987–1994*, Milan: Electa, 1994; as *Renzo Piano, 1987–1994*, translated by David Kerr, Basel, Switzerland, and Boston: Birkhäuer Verlag, 1995

METABOLISTS

The Metabolist movement emerged at the Tokyo meeting of the 1960 World Design Conference (an epilogue to the Congrès Internationaux d'Architecture Moderne [CIAM, 1927–]), with the proposal that architecture should not only embrace new technologies and the enormous scales of the postwar period, but also develop living, self-generating systems that could adapt over time. Founded by a group of ambitious young architects intent on challenging the status quo and thus establishing their own presence among the international congress of leading architects, the movement's core group included the architects Kiyonori Kikutake, Fumihiko Maki, and Kisho Kurokawa, all of whom later enjoyed enduring international reputations. In addition, another architect, Masato Otaka, the critic Noboru Kawazoe, the graphic designer Kiyoshi Awazu, and the industrial designer Kenji Ekuan were also involved in the production of the bilingual manifesto published by the group.

Although the Metabolists were a small group, Metabolism as a movement included others, especially Kenzo Tange and his assistant Takashi Asada, who nurtured the founders through a sort of late-night salon. Tange's "City for 10 Million People" (1960), to be built along a series of looped roadways stretching across Tokyo Bay, was a direct response to his proteges' work. Arata Isozaki, working for Tange during the same period, was also identified with the movement, but he took a darker view, reflected in his sketches of brutal concrete towers rising from ruins.

The original Metabolists' relative lack of professional experience was reflected in their audaciously futuristic proposals. In the group's only publication, *Metabolism 1960: The Proposals for New Urbanism*, Kikutake's sketches were particularly prominent, taking up over a third the original text; his 1958 Sky House was the only built work included. Kikutake offered up sail-shaped cities floating on ferro-cement hulls, "plug-in" housing tacked on-to soaring towers by magnets, light fixtures freely connected to electrified steel walls, and commutes by submarine or helicopter. The Metabolists are often accused of lacking the sense of improbable delight found in the slightly later Archigram's works, but Kikutake's original essay shows the same wobbly, giddy thinking. Unfortunately, his essays' English translations are clunky and difficult to comprehend, and the humor he brought to the movement was poorly recognized abroad, replaced by dry restatements of the Metabolists' positions.

Although the group established an apparently united front, the founders held a diverse set of theoretic concerns that prevented them from advancing as a movement after their debut. Maki and Otaka were not concerned with a new technological framework or production issues, but rather with understanding and incorporating traditional spatial patterns into designs for the unprecedented scale of the new city. For Kurokawa, Metabolism began as an organizing device, emphasizing structure—which allowed him to build some of its most successful buildings a decade later.

The comparisons between Archigram and the Metabolists are superficially easy, but whereas Archigram continued to publish increasingly preposterous and charming proposals throughout the 1960s, the Metabolists used their newly established reputations to snag large-scale commissions and quickly became distracted from generating additional futuristic sketches. Kikutake offered only one new scheme after the initial manifesto, whereas Maki and Otaka essentially refined their initial thesis without offering additional detail or production strategies. Only Kurokawa developed new proposals; his finest was the 1961 "Helix City." The international press tended to ignore the Metabolists' built work; in 1967, the journal *Architectural Design* titled an editorial essay "Whatever Happened to the Metabolists?" and concluded that the group was "static, if not extinct." At this point, the group's production included a number of buildings that clearly grappled with the movement's ideals, including Kikutake's Administrative building for Izumo Shrine (1963) and his odd, bellows like Miyakonojo Civic Center (1966), Otaka's Hanaizumi Agricultural Cooperative Association Center (1965),

Maki's Chiba University Auditorium (1963) and Rissho University (1967), and Kurokawa's Nitto Food Cannery (1964). Although the journal included thumbnail-sized photographs of a few built works, these were overwhelmed by the use of much larger illustrations dating from the original 1960 manifesto.

As the world withdrew its attention, the Metabolists were finding opportunities to build projects that most closely reflected their original intentions. Kurokawa produced the greatest range, from the Odakyu Drive-In Restaurant (1969) to the movement's most convincing commercial work, the Nakagin Capsule Building (1972), where shipping containers were modified for habitation and attached to core towers with only four bolts apiece. Several of Metabolism's key works from this period were for leisure facilities, a match that would seem on the surface appropriate; Kurokawa designed a lodge and a theme-based amusement complex, whereas Kikutake designed hotels for the domestic tourism industry. Although the leisure industry often most willingly embraces innovation, critics questioned the appropriateness of producing theoretic works for this market.

The 1970 Osaka Exposition appeared most in sync with a movement based on the idea of an architecture adaptable to change; many of the designers present in Metabolism's early days were involved, including Kikutake, Kurokawa, Tange, and Isozaki. Kikutake and Maki also had major commissions for the subsequent 1975 Okinawa Ocean Expo; Kikutake's Aquapolis, a remarkable pavilion floated just off shore, became a poignant symbol for the movement, unattainable and slowly rusting until it was scrapped at the end of the 20th century.

However, The Osaka Exposition came a scant three years after the 1967 Montreal Expo and suffered by comparison. Category 1 expositions are usually spaced every six years, but an exception was made because of Asian locale, a first. However, the resulting pavilions did not receive the same lavish support as at Montreal, and critics found most lacking verve. There were exceptions, especially Tange's extraordinary Festival Plaza, and the Toshiba IHP and Takara Pavilions by Kurokawa. Yet the subdued international response contributed to the Metabolist movement's collapse.

This is not to say, however, that Metabolism's adherents were persuaded that the movement's theories were irrelevant. Tange, Kikutake, and Kurokawa have each returned to their Metabolist beginnings in designs produced in the 1980s and 1990s. And many of the challenges that Metabolists took on—overcrowding, tremendous traffic congestion, and the immobility of Japanese society—remain today, yet to be adequately addressed by the professional community.

DANA BUNTROCK

See also **Congrès Internationaux d'Architecture Moderne (CIAM, 1927–); Ito, Toyo (Japan); Kurokawa, Kisho (Japan); Maki, Fumihiko (Japan); Tange, Kenzo (Japan)**

Further Reading

Banham, Reyner, *Megastructure: Urban Futures of the Recent Past*, London: Thames and Hudson, and New York: Harper and Row, 1976

Boyd, Robin, *New Directions in Japanese Architecture*, New York: Braziller, and London: Studio Vista, 1968

Jérome, Mike, "Whatever Happened to the Metabolists?" *Architectural Design* 37, no. 5 (May 1967)

Kawazoe, Noboru, "From Metabolism to Metapolis—Proposal for a City of the Future," in *Stadtstrukturen für Morgen*, by Justus Dahinden, Stuttgart: Gerd Hatje, 1971; as *Urban Structures for the Future*, translated by Gerald Onn, London: Pall Mall Press, and New York: Praeger, 1972

Kurokawa, Kisho, *Metabolism and Architecture*, Boulder, Colorado: Westview Press, 1977

Maki, Fumihiko and Masato Otaka, "Some Thoughts on Collective Form" in *Structure in Art and Science*, edited by Gryorgy Kepes, New York: Braziller, 1965

Metabolism: The Proposals for a New Urbanism, Tokyo: Bitjutu Syuppan Sha, 1960

Bilingual manifesto released by the Metabolists. The volume is very rare, but its illustrations and essays often served as the basis for subsequent discussions of the movement.

"Metabolist Kiyonori Kikutake," *Space Design*, 10: 193 (October 1980)

Nitschke, Günter, "The Metabolists of Japan," *Architectural Design* 34, no. 10 (October 1964)

Nitschke, Günter, "The Metabolists," *Architectural Design* 37, no. 5 (May 1967)

Ross, Michael Franklin, *Beyond Metabolism: The New Japanese Architecture*, New York: Architectural Records Books, 1978

Yatsuka, Hajime and Hideki Yoshimatsu, *Metaborizumu: SenKyuhyakurokujun Nendai, Nihon no Kenchiku Avan Gyarudo; Metabolism: Japan's 1960's Architectural Avante-garde*, Tokyo: Inax Shuppan, 1997

METRO STATION, PARIS

Designed by Hector Guimard; completed 1905
Paris, France

The Paris Metro (1899–1905) is one of the earliest landmarks in the evolutionary development of railway systems designed to serve commuters within a metropolis. Inaugurated concurrently with the opening of the Exposition Universelle of 1900, its series of architecturally significant station entrances were designed by French architect Hector Guimard (1867–1942). Renowned for their visual energy generated by the intricately detailed, almost calligraphic shaping of cast iron, each structure's design is intensely resonant of the Art Nouveau movement, the emerging turn-of-the-century new urban art inspired by nature. While these structures were intended to meet the pragmatic need for protected public transitional spaces between the underground railway and the surface streets, they eventually came to be regarded as urban forms in dialectic relationship with various areas of Paris.

The Metro stations' unorthodox design vocabulary, which had come to define the extant popular "style metro," was created by Hector Guimard, a celebrated exponent of Art Nouveau. It was predicated on stylized, nearly voluptuous sculptural forms inspired by magnolias, lilies, wisterias, and swaying plant life. These forms had appeared in various combinations in all entrance structures, which were constructed entirely from prefabricated modular components comprised of iron and glass, materials whose structural properties were ideally suited for the production of such delicate and curvilinear design elements. A contextual identity for each station, even under differing site conditions, was ensured by the varying of the combinations of the modules along the established design continuum. Thus, each station's design appeared to be one of a kind and without referencing the dominant 19th-century eclecticism and revivalism. However, the designs were noticeably informed by the works of Guimard's contemporary, Belgian architect Victor Horta (1861–1947), a recognized leader of the Expressionistic Art Nouveau. This was evidenced by the manner in which the aesthetic possibilities of iron and glass were exploited to achieve lightness, attenuation, and opacity of modulated structural form. Still, because of his unprecedented freedom in the manner in which he gave poetic expression to his nature-inspired industrially produced forms, Guimard had a more profound impact on the collective psyche of Parisians than Horta. Many of the Parisians believed that the design of the Metro stations represented a resolution of the contradictions that had arisen at the beginning of the industrial revolution involving the dichotomies between the crafts and industrial standardization. The stations, therefore, were seen as a tribute to the dignity of the new techniques that produced them, and in this newly defined relationship between art and technology that fused universal aesthetic and utilitarian values, many saw a symbolism of Parisian advancement toward the next millennium's modernity.

Three types of structures were constructed: simple open staircases descending from the sidewalk to the railway enclosed on three sides, covered stairs with elaborate canopies, and some complete pavilions. The Place Blanche Station, a basic open staircase entrance, elegantly exemplifies the idiosyncratic treatment of sinuous forms that are fundamental to the "style metro." The balustrades and rails, finished in green suggestive of patina on statuary bronze, are seemingly fluid as they symbiotically anchor to the white stone base at the opening's perimeter. The meeting of the sidewalk's surface and the staircase is punctuated by twin lamp standards, each terminated by bud-shaped amber-colored glass light fixtures that illuminate the signage strategically incorporated into the arch over the entrance. These features were rationally orchestrated into an integrative design statement to fully exploit not only the expressive powers of style but also its integration with structure. To achieve this, Guimard relied on E.E. Viollet-le-Duc's architectonic structural theory and his close collaboration with the Founderie de Saint-Dizier, a foundry that specialized in artistic castings.

The design parameters and aesthetics of the Metro stations had been extensively deliberated by the members of the Société Centrale des Architectes before the announcement of the design competition by the Compagnie du Metropolitain. A preference for handcrafted structures and expressions of individual creativity had prevailed over uses of standardized industrial products. Furthermore, because these entrances were to be sited in areas of international note, they were expected to aesthetically fit into such contexts. By August 1899, the winning contestants, architects Duray, Lamaresquier, and Paumier, were awarded prizes for their entries, which were exhibited in the Hotel de Ville. The jury's decision was rescinded, however, by Adrien Benard, president of the Conseil Municipal de Paris and a patron of Art Nouveau, in favor of Guimard, who was not a competition entrant. Although ambiguous aesthetic arguments had been presented to defend this decision, a more parametric and less aesthetic consideration may have also precipitated this bold action. The winning entries were characterized as shelters constructed of masonry that would have required a disproportionately larger amount of space than what was available because of site-specific

Metro Station, Paris, Designed by Hector Guimard (1905)
© GreatBuildings.com

constraints. It also stands to reason that the decision was tempered by the fact that iron was a more cost-effective material than masonry and that it was more responsive to fabrication and project delivery methods.

In 1904, after the construction of 141 station entrances, the "metro style" was rejected by the Conseil Municipal de Paris when another design in the series was proposed for the Place de l'Opéra. The design was deemed dissonant with Parisian architectural traditions and inappropriate to the vicinity of the Opéra, which was intended to become the cultural focus of Paris. An undistinguished classically styled stone balustrade design by Cassien-Bernard was implemented. Nevertheless, the 86 surviving structures that were designed by Guimard amicably complement the daily patterns of contemporary Parisian life and the urban form of the city. They are a testament to the passion that had driven the experimentation with new expressive functions for materials by freeing them of their 19th-century traditional applications and redefining their roles for 20th-century modernism. Their enduring cultural and aesthetic presence continues to crystallize out of the masses a growing number of admirers who believe that even the design of utilitarian structures cannot be reduced to exercises in the applications of generalized systems of aesthetics or quantitative analysis. Salvador Dali, the surrealist artist, for example, described the entrance structures as "divine,"

and when the Place de la Bastille Station was slated for demolition in the late 1960s, the structure was hastily acquired by the Museum of Modern Art in New York.

ATTILA LAWRENCE

See also **Art Nouveau (Jugendstil); Exposition Universelle, Paris (1900); Horta, Victor (Belgium)**

Further Reading

Fahr-Becker Sterner, Gabriele, *Jugendstil: Kunstformen zwischen Individualism und Massengesellschaft,* Cologne: DuMont Schauberg, 1975; as *Art Nouveau: An Art of Transition from Individualism to Mass Society,* translated by Frederick G. Peters and Diana S. Peters, Woodbury, New York: Barron's, 1982

Fitoussi, Brigitte, "Linea metropolitana 14, Parigi," *Domus,* 48 (February 1999)

Guimard (exhib. cat.), Paris: Éditions de la Réunion des Musées Nationaux, 1992

Selz, Peter, and Mildred Constantine (editors), *Art Nouveau: Art and Design at the Turn of the Century,* New York: Museum of Modern Art, 1959; revised edition, 1975

Sutcliffe, Anthony, *Paris: An Architectural History,* New Haven, Connecticut: Yale University Press, 1993

Thornton, Lynne, "Guimard and the Metro," *The Connoisseur,* 252 (August 1980)

METROPOLITAN FESTIVAL HALL, TOKYO

Designed by Kunio Maekawa, completed 1961
Tokyo, Japan

Kunio Maekawa (sometimes written "Mayekawa") was one of three Japanese architects closely associated with Le Corbusier's atelier, and while the three disciples were supervising the construction of Le Corbusier's National Museum of Western Art (1959) in Tokyo, Maekawa was designing the Tokyo Metropolitan Festival Hall, begun in 1957 and completed in 1961. These buildings face each other, creating a public plaza at the chief entrance to Ueno Park in Tokyo. In 1979 Maekawa completed an annex to the National Museum of Western Art, establishing the form of the complex as it stands today.

The challenge of designing a building to complement his mentor's work resulted in Maekawa's finest design, and he was able to carry out intentions sometimes difficult elsewhere, as the budget for the Tokyo Metropolitan Festival Hall was particularly generous. Commemorating the 500th anniversary of Tokyo's founding, the facilities were intended to accommodate Western musical forms unsuited to Japanese halls, especially opera. The building totals 228,560 square feet, with a fly tower extending 87 feet above grade. Within are two halls, the large hall having 2,300 seats and the small hall having 600 seats. There are also generous rehearsal and support spaces and a library with holdings on Western music. The Festival Hall unites many themes recurrent in Maekawa's work: the resolution of Western industrial techniques with traditional Japanese form; the exploitation of precast and site-cast concrete, generally left unfinished; the juxtaposition of concrete surfaces against textured, natural materials, such as stone and wood; random patterns of tiles and other materials creating an artistic effect; and the incorporation of sculptural reliefs or artworks.

In the Festival Hall, Maekawa demonstrates a rare ability to create double readings with his architectural lexicon, an effect that is difficult to perceive in photographs. This quality is seen, for example, in the weighty turned-up eaves: They both serve as a roof over the entrances and exterior space, bringing this massive building down to human scale, and read as a datum from which larger elements, such as the hall roof and fly tower, rise.

The chief designer and project architect on the building was Masato Otaka. Simultaneous with this project, Otaka wrote a discourse on Metabolism with Fumihiko Maki, eschewing the structural emphasis of other Metabolists in favor of an emphasis on space. Not surprisingly, the Festival Hall's strength is its spatial richness. Its mass is played against a fluid, horizontally compressed space that stretches beyond the delicate curtain wall of the building's envelope into the surrounding park. This space is said to be Japanese in character, but typically Western devices articulate distinct zones; steps and ramps displace the floor plane, and the ceiling rises and falls, slicing space into clearly articulated foyers. Within, the large hall is defined by canted walls that again reverse one's reading from spatial to volumetric, suggesting a smaller building at the core of the larger complex. This nested character can also be seen in the building's plan.

Maekawa feared that overreliance on industrialization was leading to degeneration in architectural design. Ironically, he is credited with advancing the use of precast concrete and the curtain wall in Japan. However, the manner in which both are used here suggests that Maekawa saw industrial materials as part of a broader palette; they are mixed with site-cast pieces of great plasticity and with a variety of randomly patterned tiles and differently colored seat fabrics. Maekawa also incorporated extensive contributions from artists. In the large hall, a playful wood relief, designed by the artist Ryokichi Mukai, is made of zelkova wood. Mukai and two other artists also designed curtains to be used in the proscenium. Masayuki Ryu contributed a relief for the lobby (no longer visible) and sculptural concrete figures in the exterior plaza and garden spaces. In the small hall, another relief by Ryu is incorporated into the site-cast concrete. This cavelike space is also enlivened by a luminous aluminum-leaf screen, apparently of Maekawa's design, as are beautifully shaped door handles and handrails. The concrete itself is frequently formed into gentle curves, angled channels, and oblique planes. The result is highly sculptural and projects a sense of craft and industry in harmony.

Although this is by far the most remarkable, Maekawa designed a number of other auditoriums and cultural facilities. The Kyoto Hall (1960) of roughly the same period is similar in execution, although it lacks the artwork and careful detailing seen in Tokyo.

In 1984 a new rehearsal space was incorporated into the Tokyo Metropolitan Festival Hall. This also allowed Maekawa to make some alterations to the interiors, most notably adding several friezes of gold tiles in random patterns. The effect is close enough to the earlier work not to be too jarring but detracts from the use of unfinished materials and bold primary colors painted elsewhere and is more typical of the era in which the building was first created. More recently, the Metropolitan Festival Hall underwent an unusually sensitive renovation. The building retains the patina appropriate to its age but has been lovingly restored.

DANA BUNTROCK

Further Reading

Very little has been published on Maekawa, and his importance in postwar Japan is little recognized abroad or even by younger Japanese. He was more concerned with making buildings that would speak for him and actually prevented one publication of collected works from reaching print. The few books available have little text and rely on sketches, drawings, and photographs.

Kunio, Maekawa, *Maekawa Kunio sakuhinshu: kenchiku no hoho* [The Collected Works of Kunio Maekawa: Method of Architecture], 2 vols., edited by Yoshihisa Miyauchi, Tokyo: Bijutsu Shuppansha, 1990
Process Architecture, 43 (January 1984) (special issue entitled "Kunio Maekawa: Sources of Modern Japanese Architecture")
Shinkenchiku (June 1961) (special issue on Tokyo Metropolitan Festival Hall)
Zairyou to Sekkei, 7/8 (1961) (special issue on Tokyo Metropolitan Festival Hall)

MEXICO

At the beginning of the 20th century, Mexican architecture was still influenced by the cultural policies of the regime of President

Porfirio Diaz. Since his ascent to power in 1876, he tried to give Mexico a modern face that could bring it to the most prominent place in the international society. The concept of reflecting Mexican modernity in the mirror of foreign nations brought severe cultural implications. The architectural education of the Mexican School of Fine Arts was given mainly by foreign professors who brought notions of the French Beaux-Arts. Therefore, the buildings produced in the first two decades of the 20th century were full of foreign elements regarding ornamentation, and this new aesthetic was the paradigm of the new progressive Mexican society, although it lacked the national elements that could give its architecture a more genuine character. The tendency grew as the most important new buildings were designed by foreign architects; the Italian Adamo Boari (d. 1928) taught in Mexico while he was working on the Post Office Building (1902) in Mexico City, on which a venetian loggia stands above a series of richly ornamented neo-Gothic windows. His most important work, the exterior of the National Theatre (1904) in Mexico City, now called the Palace of Fine Arts, is another fine example of this eclectic arrangement of architectural styles. Here, the volumetry of the building is very similar to the Garnier's Opera (1975) of Paris, but it also incorporates many organic elements that reflect an Art Nouveau influence.

Urban areas were also affected by new progressive concepts, and the creation of suburbs began, as those found in Europe. Mexico City grew very rapidly, and soon the agricultural lands that surrounded it were invaded by the rising middle and upper classes. The buildings in these new settlements were neo-Moorish, Gothic, Renaissance, and baroque. Many other styles appeared on the same street and sometimes in the same building. This exoticism can be found on the works of Emilio Dondé's (1849–1905) San Felipe Church (1900) in Mexico City, Antonio Rivas Mercado's (1853–1927) Monument for the Commemoration of the Centennial of the Declaration of Independence (1910) in Mexico City or the Guanajuato Juárez Theatre (1903), and Nicolás (1875–1964) and Federico Mariscal's (1881–1969) Police Headquarters (1906) in Mexico City, among others.

The new architecture was also determined by the use of new building techniques, one of the most important breakthroughs being the extended use of steel structures that could now provide larger spans. In most cases, they were covered with stone, but this technique was also capable of providing a new architectural language because the structural elements could remain visible, as in the Guanajuato Market (1904) by Ernesto Brunel (c.1875–c.1950) or in the Chopo Museum (1910), which was designed in Germany and brought to Mexico for its assembly.

The Mexican Revolution (1910–20) brought changes to every aspect of Mexican society and affected architectural activity as well. After a period (1919–25) during which the number of new buildings was very low, building was inspired by new ideological concepts as the influence of international exoticism began to diminish and a new nationalism emerged. The Mexican pre-Hispanic and colonial heritage was revalidated, and the ornaments on buildings began to include such motifs. The works of Manuel Amabilis (1883–1966), such as the lost Riviera Roundabout (1926) in Mexico City, with the reproduction of Mayan snakes, or the project for the Mexican Pavilion at the Seville Exposition of 1926, on which Mayan elements copied from Uxmal and Mitla were combined, are good examples. Some of the most important neo-Colonial works are those of Ignacio Marquina (1888–1981) and Manuel Torres Torrija (1872–).

Carlos Obregón Santacilia (1896–1961) was one of the prominent architects of the first half of the 20th century. He built some important examples of the neo-Colonial style but also ventured into Art Deco, creating a very interesting mix that can be seen in the Revolution Monument (1938). Although Art Deco was also an aesthetic language that was imported from Europe through the United States, it could fit into the new "revolutionary" architecture in Mexico. The exoticism that was portrayed in the Art Deco ornaments of Chicago and New York with referrals to antique cultures such as Egyptian and Babylonian could also be adapted in Mexico, as its own Aztec and Mayan tradition could supply abundant motifs to portray the desired Mexicanism. Two good examples of such buildings are the Police and Firemen Headquarters (1928) of Mexico City by Vicente Mendiola (1899–1986) with sculptures by Manuel Centurión (1883–1948) and the Fronton Mexico (1929) by Joaquin Capilla (c.1890–c.1960), both of which have pre-Hispanic decoration on their facades.

Art Deco gained importance in Mexico, as it also portrayed the use of a new material that had been scarcely used up to that time: cement. The structures that combined concrete elements with a steel structure were economical and confident, although Mexican society viewed them with reticence until the 1930s. Juan Segura (1898–1989) used it abundantly on some Art Deco buildings, such as the Ermita (1931), which also has a very innovative program in that it incorporates apartments, commercial spaces, and a cinema in a single six-story building in a very articulated manner. One of the most important examples of the new structural concepts is the so-called first Mexican skyscraper, the La Nacional Insurance Company Building (1930) in Mexico City by Manuel Ortiz Monasterio (1893–c.1960), Bernardo Calderón (c.1890–c.1960), and Luis Avila (c.1900–c.1970). The steel structure rises only 12 levels high, but it is contemporary and has the morphology of the American so-called setback mass buildings of the time.

The reformation of the revolutionary Mexican architecture was, in many cases, simply formal or ornamental, as the spatial conception of the buildings remained the same. The theoretical approach was done by José Villagran García (1901–82), mainly in his classrooms around 1930; he stated that above the social "importance" of the architecture was its social "function," as the work of an artist must always be completely identified with the people. In this way, the "modern," which seemingly had no national roots, must be combined with the "Mexican," which seemed antimodern. Combining these required relying on an architectural program that could determine the character of national problems to provide an architectural response that would be national as well. The fundamental question of the architect is, then, not aesthetic but ethical. These ideas were the platform of the Mexican School of Architecture that looked after a "modern national architecture." Examples of this functional school are works by the same Villagrán: the Sanitary Institute (1927) in Popotla and the Tuberculosis Sanatorium (1936) in Huipulco, both of which were part of an ambitious program by the Mexican government to bring health services to all Mexicans. The other natural application of the theory was in education, and the government initiated a program that built hundreds of schools in the country using the materials and techniques of every region of the country.

The Mexican School of Architecture also provided the architectural response for one of the most important social problems: popular housing. In 1932 a national contest was held to find a "worker's minimum house," and the works of Álvaro Aburto (c.1900–c.1970), Enrique Yáñez (1908–90), Juan Legarreta (1908–34), and Augusto Pérez Palacios (1909–c.1980) exemplified this new social rural architecture, in which the internal spaces were optimized but still articulated around a social area in which most of the family life occurred and with an important open space planned for particular crops. Economy and standardization were the most important considerations of this contest.

Low-income housing in the cities also occurred in multifamily housing projects, the first one being the Miguel Alemán Complex (1949) by Mario Pani (1911–93), composed of 1,080 units in an area less than 10,000 square meters with complete services, such as schools, playgrounds, sports facilities (including a swimming pool), and commercial areas. The 13-story buildings were distributed diagonally in a zigzag manner with common circulation areas and elevators and a facade of exposed brick and concrete.

Among the Mexican architects with socialist ideas, Juan O'Gorman (1905–82) was one of the most influential. Following the concepts of Le Corbusier (1887–1965) and trying to achieve the maximum efficiency with the minimum waste, O'Gorman built more than 28 schools (1932–35) in the country that remain as good examples of the Mexican functionalist architecture school. His most well known work is the studio (1930) that he built for the Mexican muralist painter Diego Rivera and his wife Frida Kahlo in San Angel. In this work, he uses some vernacular elements, such as a cactus fence and brilliant "Indian" colors, in a very simple structure with a wall of steel-framed windows. All pipes and electrical systems were exposed on the inside as an expression of the machine era of the modern world.

O'Gorman also participated in one of the most important examples of Mexico's 20th-century architecture: the University City (1946–52). All the professional schools in Mexico City had been scattered among several buildings in the downtown area for over two centuries, but the modern concept of a great campus that would concentrate all the university's activity emerged. Following this idea, a team of 150 architects led by Mario Pani and Enrique del Moral (1906–87) began work on a project that would try to solve the contradiction that had been haunting Mexican architecture the entire century: to build the environment of a modern dynamic society while still representing its history and identity. In this project, the approach was that of *integración plástica* (plastic integration), in which architecture, painting, and sculpture would be integrated into a unified work of art. The facades of the several buildings of the complex were covered with murals by such important artists as Juan O'Gorman and Diego Rivera (1886–1957) with diverse motifs, mainly from Mexico's past and present. Although University City was designed on an urban concept that was inspired by pre-Hispanic principles regarding open spaces, terracing, and scales, it also responded to the principles of modern urbanism, such as superblocks, separation of circulation systems, and zoning of activities. The result is a very interesting interpretation of the functionalist international language with the participation of a multidisciplinary array of artists very compromised with the expressionism of their national architectural language.

The same Plastic Integration movement also participated in several other buildings, such as the Communications and Transport Ministry Office (1954) by Carlos Lazo (1914–55), with paintings by Juan O'Gorman, and the General Hospital Building (1958) by Enrique Yáñez, with works by David Alfaro Siqueiros (1898–1974), among other brilliant muralists. Although this movement could achieve works of importance, it disintegrated rapidly, as different ideologies among artists prevailed. Nonetheless, it remains one of the most brilliant and original moments of Mexican architecture.

The adoption of the International Style by Mexican architects began around 1945 and sometimes is still mixed with principles of the Mexican School of Architecture, as it represented an economical way of building with open spaces and volumetric purism with no ornamentation at all. The influence of such architects as Ludwig Mies van der Rohe (1886–1969) and Walter Gropius (1883–1969) became very powerful. The building of the Latinoamericana Tower (1952) in Mexico City, a high-rise building with glass facades, marked the historic district of the city and gave way to the demolition of many historic buildings that were to be replaced by the new models. The author of the tower, Augusto H. Álvarez (1914–c.1980), was one of the most prolific of this style, and he projected several more buildings, some of the most renowned being the Mexico Valley Bank (1955) and the La Libertad Insurance Company (1959).

One building that represents an interesting approach to the International Style is the Bank of Mexico Building (1950) on the Port of Veracruz by Carlos Lazo. Here, the simple glass tower is surrounded by huge concrete pergolas and blinds that provide a bioclimatic conditioning for the office space while also providing a beautiful set of lights and shades.

On the urban level, the most important large-scale project of the second half of the 20th century was the Tlatelolco housing complex (1964) in Mexico City by Mario Pani. Here, more than 100,000 inhabitants live on a megablock that comprises all services, commercial and recreational, including several schools, health centers, specialty shops, day care centers, a cinema, a theater, and a church. The apartment buildings represent a few prototypes that are repeated, and the overall architecture follows the principles of the International Style.

Pedro Ramirez Vázquez (1919–) is one of the prominent architects of the second half of the century, his most important work being the National Museum of Anthropology (1964), in which he still uses some principles of the Plastic Integration movement, as the walls that surround the huge central patio are covered with pre-Hispanic motifs, and the open space is partially covered with an "umbrella" that raises without touching the building because it is suspended from a central column that is also a fountain. The spatial organization of the exhibit halls is articulated around this patio, each of which is unique, being adapted to the collections of the native culture that it houses. More recent works of this architect that also have great importance are the Aztec Stadium (1965) and the new Nuestra Señora de Guadalupe shrine (1975), in which the modern structure is placed next to the old 17th-century shrine and rises above it with a curved cover, under which thousands of Catholics gather daily.

An important regional movement is the Escuela Tapatia, created in Guadalajara and headed by Rafael Urzua (1905–c.1980), Ignacio Díaz Morales (1905–c.1980), and Luis Barragán (1902–88). This group of architects built some important houses in western Mexico, but Barragán grew beyond the regional level to become one of the most prominent names of 20th-century Mexican architecture. His own house (1947) in Tacubaya is considered one of his masterworks, as he could mix tradition and modernity using volumes and walls to confine the space that flows throughout the building. The use of color is one of Barragán's most important assets. He uses bright pinks, blues, and taken from the chromatic scale used in vernacular architecture but applied on solid massive surfaces that are proper of the functionalism. His language is enriched with natural elements, such as beautiful gardens or fountains. Some of his most relevant works are the Gilardi house (1976), the chapel for the Capuchines (1952), and the San Cristobal house and its riding facilities (1967), among many others.

Abraham Zabludovsky (1924–) and Teodoro González de León (1926–) are two bright architects who have worked jointly since 1965. They developed an architectural language that identifies Mexican contemporary architecture, as they use massive columns and walls made of exposed concrete with marbled chips embedded. This richly textured material has been used in buildings such as INFONAVIT (1973) in Mexico City, the Mexican Embassy (1975) at Brasilia, El Colegio de México (1975), the Pedagogic National University (1979), the Rufino Tamayo Museum (1981), and the National Auditorium (1990) in Mexico City. In all these buildings, the use of a patio that works as a transitional space between the exterior and the interior is present, as is a vast use of platforms and stairs not only as circulation elements but also as expressive elements themselves. A particularly interesting building is the Banco de México (1988), which had to be built adjacent to a beautiful 17th-century palace in the historic district of Mexico City. The solution was to transfer the volumetry of the palace (rhythm of openings, window proportion, floor levels, and cornices) to the new building, thus imitating it respectfully. These architects also have recent works of their own: González de León did a wonderful urban work (1985) at the Tomás Garrido Canabal Park in Villhermosa in which a 600-meter axis articulates a zoo, lakes, bridges, and monuments, all of which are morphologically inspired by the Mayan architecture of the region. Zabludovsky has worked on theaters in Aguascalientes (1991), Celaya (1990), Guanajuato (1991), and Dolores (1991); one of his most prominent works is the residential complex La Cantera (1992) in Coyoacan, which is an uncommon program of a series of wisely designed low-income apartments.

Since the last years of the 20th century, a group of creative artists have continued the search for Mexico's own modern architecture, including Agustín Hernández (1924–) with the use of pre-Hispanic forms in the Military Academy (1985); Ricardo Legorreta (1931–) with the massive Camino Real Hotel (1981) of Ixtapa or the great MARCO Museum (1991) in Monterrey; Francisco Serrano (1900–82), who cleverly designed different platforms for the Ibero-Americana University (1987); and Enrique Norten (1954–), who designed the round roof of the National Theatre School (1994) in Mexico City.

In a country with such a vast architectural history as Mexico, the labor of conservation and restoration is also an aspect that modern architects must resolve. The concern for preserving Mexico's cultural heritage has been achieved in many projects during the 20th century, some of the most recent being the restoration project of the 18th-century Ciudadela (1988) in Mexico City by Abraham Zabludovsky, the Image Center (1994) inside the same historic building by Isaac Broid (1952), the library (1992) inside the 17th-century Santo Domingo convent in Mexico City by Marisa Aja (1955–), and the Colegio Nacional, which completely modified a 17th-century building by González de León. All these works combine modern materials such as steel, glass, and aluminum and superimpose them on the historic building, attempting to incorporate the modern use into the old structure. This important part of Mexican architecture needs to be reinvigorated in the years to come.

ALFONSO A. SÁNCHEZ

Further Reading

Adriá, Miquel, *México 90's: Una arquitectura contemporánea: A Contemporary Architecture* (bilingual Spanish-English edition), Mexico City and Barcelona: Gili, 1996

Ambasz, Emilio, *The Architecture of Luis Barragán*, New York: Museum of Modern Art, 1976

Anda, E.X. de, *La arquitectura de la revolución Mexicana: corrientes y estilos en la década de los veinte*, [The Architecture of the Mexican Revolution: trends and styles of the twenties] Mexico City: Universidad Nacional Autónoma de México, Instituto de Investigaciones Estéticas, 1990

Attoe, W., *The Architecture of Ricardo Legorreta*, Austin: University of Texas Press, and Berlin: Ernst, 1990

Burian, Edward (editor), *Modernity and the Architecture of Mexico*, Austin: University of Texas Press, 1997

González Gortázar, Fernando, *Arquitectura Mexicana del siglo XX*, [Mexican Architecture of the 20th Century] Mexico City: Consejo Nacional para la Cultura y las Artes, 1994

Heyer, Paul, *Abraham Zabludovsky, Architect, 1979–1993*, New York: Princeton Architectural Press, 1993

Kappe, Shelly (editor), *Modern Architecture, Mexico*, Santa Monica: Southern California Institute for Architecture Press, 1981

Katzman, Israel, *La arquitectura contemporánea Mexicana: precedentes y desarrollo*, [Mexican Contemporary Architecture: Precedents and Development] Mexico City: Instituto Nacional de Antropologia e Historia, 1963

Martin Hernández, Vicente, *Arquitectura doméstica de la Ciudad de México, 1890–1925*, [Domestic Architecture of Mexico City, 1890–1925] Mexico City: Universidad Nacional Autonoma de Mexico, Escuela Nacional de Arquitectura, 1981

Noelle, Louise, and Carlos Tejeda, *Catálogo guía de arquitectura contemporánea: Ciudad de México*, [Catalog and Guide of Contemporary Architecture: Mexico City] Mexico City: Fomento Cultural Banamex, 1993

Reseña de arquitectura mexicana; Mexican Architecture Review (bilingual Spanish-English journal) (1992)

Street-Porter, Tim, *Casa Mexicana: The Architecture, Design, and Style of Mexico*, New York: Stewart Tabori and Chang, 1989

Suzuki, Makoto (editor), *Modern Mexican Architecture*, Tokyo and New York: Process Architecture, 1983

Toca, Antonio, and Aníbal Figueroa Castrejon, *México: nueva arquitectura* [Mexico: New Architecture], Mexico City: Gili, 1991; 3rd edition, 1993

Toca, Antonio (editor), *Arquitectura contemporánea en México* [Contemporary Architecture in Mexico], Azcapotzalco: Universidad Autónoma Metropolitana, and Mexico City: Gernika, 1989

Villagrán García, J. José, *Teoría de la arquitectura* [Architectural Theory], Mexico City: Instituto Nacional de Bellas Artes, 1983

MEXICO CITY, MEXICO

The unstable subsoil on which Mexico City rests has been the political, economic, and cultural epicenter of the region for centuries. Whether known as Tenochtitlán (1325–1521), the Aztec empire's majestic city on Lake Texcoco, the "muy noble y leal ciudad de México," capital of the Viceroyalty of New Spain (1521–1821), or as capital of a tentative republic whose majestic buildings by Lorenzo Rodríguez, Manuel Tolsá, and Francisco Eduardo Tresguerras housed institutions unable or unwilling to administer to citizens' needs in the 19th century, the city's architecture has served as an agent for political, social, cultural, and economic change as well as a signifier of it and has continued to do so in the 20th century.

Indeed, the city may be read as a text, revealing important insights on the nation's passage from the dictatorship of Porfirio Díaz from 1876 to 1910, through the immense pains of ten years of civil war or revolution to 1920, through the gradual consolidation of power in a new revolutionary elite and political party in the 1920s and 1930s, to efforts at modernization from the 1940s to the 1970s, to a series of economic crises and booms in the 1980s and 1990s.

A survey of the architectural history of Mexico City in the 20th century reveals the use of diverse, often discordant styles as many Mexican architects rejected what they believed to be the facile emulation of exotic architectural styles. They perceived that their revolution had afforded the nation an access to modernity and the means to achieve a uniquely Mexican identity. The capital city indicates widely varying conceptions of modernity and identity in this pluralist society. According to Mexican architect and historian Carlos Lira Vázquez, the search for modernity led to the employment of styles as diverse as the neo-colonial, California-colonial, Decó, neo-Indigenist, functionalist, nationalist, international, postmodern, and pluralist, each used for utilitarian as well as aesthetic needs.

In the first two decades following the armed phase of the Revolution of 1910, Mexican governments faced the challenges of creating legitimate institutions and refining the government's role in relation to the people in consonance with the Constitution of 1917 and re-constructing society along more egalitarian lines. The revolution had overthrown the dictatorship of Porfirio Díaz and left in its wake a devastated nation and capital. The cityscape bore witness to this devastation: pock-marked buildings along streets in the city's historic center evidenced the transit of one revolutionary army or another; massive building projects such as Adamo Boari's "Mexicanized Art-Nouveau" Teatro Nacional (1904; now the Palacio de Bellas Artes, completed in 1934) and Emile Benard's neo-classic Palacio de Poder Legislativo (1900; now the Monument to the Revolution, 1933), which Díaz intended to serve as part of the legacy of Porfirian greatness, now stood partially finished, rusting hulks on the city's profile.

The immediate tasks facing the capital's architects were numerous: to provide housing for the tens of thousands of recent migrants; to repair or build schools, health care facilities, and other government buildings; and to design commercial structures. Common to these projects was the idea of nationalism,

that architecture in service to the state could and should carry a message of identity and greatness. Apparent in such works is the lack of agreement on what should be the vehicle to convey that message. To José Vasconcelos, minister of education in the early 1920s, the neo-colonial style was the only language that could convey the Mexican identity. Hence, his department commissioned young architects, among them Carlos Obregón Santacilia, to execute works in this style; Obregón Santacilia's Escuela Benito Juárez (1924) remains one of the most eloquent examples of this style, along with commercial structures such as Antonio Torres Torija's Edificio Gaona (1922) and Rafael Goyeneche's Hotel Majestic, (1925). Together, these projects illustrate the basic strengths and weaknesses in this style: As an evocation of the colonial past, it had no peer. If one looked to the past for the source of present greatness or for inspiration, then this style was sound. Although at various times from 1917 to 1940 the government actively promoted this style as representative of national identity, it presented severe constraints. For one, the neo-colonial is primarily a horizontal style; as prices for urban land increased, developers sought projects that would bring higher returns per square meter. It was necessary to build taller, more "functional" buildings and to consider modern styles, even in the historic center of the city adjacent to distinguished 17th- and 18th-century buildings. Second, the neo-colonial is a very expensive style: Vasconcelos's school building campaign quickly exhausted his department's budget after only eight schools had been built—hardly enough to meet the city's needs. Finally, a small, yet increasingly vocal group of young architects, among them Juan O'Gorman, Juan Legarreta, and Alvaro Aburto, decried the use of the neo-colonial, given their interpretation of colonial history. To build in a colonial style, whether neo-colonial or California-colonial, signified a desire to repeat centuries of colonial oppression and a denial of the progress that the revolution promised Mexico. Architecture, they argued, must serve the interests of all the people, not merely the wealthy. Such sentiments gained in popularity in the late 1920s, and 1930s, given evidence of corruption in post-revolutionary governments as various public figures indulged in conspicuous consumption, building lavish homes in the new *colonias* of Anzures, Lomas de Chapultepec, and Hipódromo de la Condesa, among others, and embarking on what seemed to many to be piecemeal development projects of little consequence in addressing the real problems facing the city's residents.

For example, in the early 1930s, Carlos Obregón Santacilia sponsored a design competition for the development of low-cost housing for workers. The winning design for these minimalist worker's houses was submitted by Juan Legarreta; following strict functionalist dictates of economy of materials and form without ornamentation, the city erected over 300 such units at Colonias Balbuena and Plutarco Elías Calles. Yet the city needed thousands of such units; the result of this shortfall was an increase in the population density of the capital's oldest quarter, where landlords were continuing the conversion of colonial-era residences into *vecindades*, or tenements. This is not to say that no advances were made: Under President Lázaro Cárdenas's direction, the revolution moved distinctly to the left and assumed new social responsibilities. This is the context for the development of the Instituto Nacional de Cardiología by José Villagrán García (1937), the Edificio del Sindicato de Electristas by Enrique Yáñez (1938), the Hospital Militar by Luis McGregor (1940), the Edificio Guardiola by Carlos Obregón Santacilia (1938), and the Escuela Vocacional by Juan O'Gorman. Functionalism allowed for massive use of reinforced concrete in monumental structures as well as the incorporation of new materials such as aluminum and steel, affording developers and occupants of such structures flexible use of interior spaces, open floor plans, and greater illumination and ventilation. These more economical functionalist designs allowed the government to disperse scarce funding on more ambitious projects, demonstrating its commitment to social justice.

Yet, illustrating the complexity of modernization in the context of the institutionalization of the Mexican Revolution, Cárdenas also supported directives that attempted to regulate architectural styles employed in various sections of the city, allowing for the further use of the neo-colonial in structures such as the new building for the Departamento del Distrito Federal by Fernando Beltrán Puga and Federico Mariscal (1935) to maintain the stylistic integrity of the oldest section of the city.

The 1940s and 1950s witnessed further change in governmental priorities and the direction of the revolution, which greatly affected construction in the capital. Presidents actively courted foreign investment and industrialization, both serving to bring prosperity and modernity to this emerging nation. The state's promotion of industrialization brought to the capital new waves of foreign investments and new architectural developments; the post–World War II city now contained immense factories and expanded assembly plants such as those of General Motors, D.M. Nacional shopping centers, and supermarkets, whose architecture, at times uninspired, in other instances employed the most advanced construction techniques, wielded by talented engineers and architects. Furthermore, the capital gained its first true skyscraper, the glass and aluminum–clad 42-story Torre Latinoamericano, by architect Augusto H. Álvarez and engineer Adolfo Zeevaert (1948–56), built in daring proximity to colonial era structures at the corner of Avenida Madero and San Juan de Letrán (now Eje Cárdenas).

New investments brought with them demands for more labor, quickly exceeded by ever-growing migration to the capital. The failure of governmental planning initiatives to regulate urban growth was apparent in the increase in informal settlements on the city's periphery from 1940 to 1960, in which *paracaídistas* (literally, "parachutists"), or squatters, occupied marginal lands, built rudimentary shelters from found materials, and began to form communities. Governmental initiatives in the provision of social services are seen in projects such as the Edificio Central for the newly created Instituto Mexicano del Seguro Social by Carlos Obregón Santacilia (1947) and the Escuela Nacional de Maestros by Mario Pani (1945).

There is a great deal of vitality evident in the capital in those years of the "Mexican Miracle," in which the city witnessed and engendered unprecedented growth. This growth meant prosperity for some: As new colonies prospered, aspirations of grandeur found expression in the city's first condominiums, designed by Mario Pani and Salvador Ortega (1955), and sophisticated office buildings, notably Juan Sordo Madaleno's Seguros Anahuac building (1954) and Augusto H. Álvarez's Edificio Castorena (1957) firmly anchored the International Style as a central component of contemporary Mexican architecture. Use of this and the functionalist style in state architecture, as in Pani and Del Moral's Secretaría de Recursos Hidráulicos building (1950), Augusto Pérez Palacios and Raúl Cacho's Secretaría de Comunicaciones y Obras Públicas (1953), and Enrique de la Mora, Francisco López Carmona, and Félix Candela's Bolsa de Valores building (1953–56), manifested Mexico's rise out of revolutionary turmoil, and centralization of political power.

At this time, Mario Pani designed the city's first *multifamiliares* (multi-function housing projects, or "cities-within-cities," with their own markets, clinics, schools, and nurseries) in the Centro Urbano Presidente Alemán (1950) and the Centro Urbano Presidente Juárez (1952). These model housing projects for government workers, adaptations of Le Corbusian concepts, dramatically extended state responsibility for the provision of housing for its workforce. These projects later proved insufficient to meet the demands for hygienic housing for the hundreds of thousands of capital city residents lacking such. Instead, this period marked the deepening of the gap among classes in Mexico City, as wealthier individuals chose to reside in one of the new developments, such as El Pedregal de San Ángel (planned by Luis Barragán) or Ciudad Satélite (1957), with its abstract entrance towers by Matías Goeritz, providing a new context for urban life—regulated and planned.

By the close of the 1950s, the International Style, in sum, had been adopted with the same sort of enthusiasm and ambition as had functionalism a decade before. In this period, official architecture stressed monumentality, within this style representing the power that the state sought to possess, often using white marble, green flagstone, red *tezontle*, and basalt, linkages to materials traditionally employed in Mexican architecture and to the colors of the flag. The many new buildings containing great expanses of window panes, supported by aluminum frames, were further evidence of the significance of international style architecture, under the guidance of architects Enrique Yáñez, Luis Barragán, and others. The optimism inherent in this style is apparent in new construction in the city in the early 1960s, as the government reasserted the image of the state as the guarantor of development and the provider of education, health care, and housing via more monumental projects. These projects include the Centro Médico Nacional (1961) by Yáñez, José Villagrán García, and others and museums that conserve and celebrate Mexico's cultural heritage; notably the Museo de Arte Moderno (1964) and Pedro Ramírez Vázquez's magnificent Museo Nacional de Antropología (1964).

The collapse of the "miracle" is also apparent in the city's streets, as venerable viceregal and prehispanic structures witnessed new waves of student and labor protests in the mid-1960s, culminating in the massacre of students at Tlatelolco in October 1968. This slaughter severely shadowed the dynamism manifest across town, at Félix Candela's Palacio de Deportes (erected for the Olympic Games, to be held a week later). Serious economic problems were also apparent in successive governments' failures in the 1970s to provide adequate housing, educational and health care facilities for the burgeoning population.

From 1970 to the close of the 20th century, the architecture of Mexico City continued to illustrate the fundamental tensions in Mexican society, as well as its search for a national identity. Labels attached to styles were frequently misleading or value-laden: What some observers have perceived as "virtual chaos" given the diverse styles and approaches employed in various parts of this city, now the largest in the world, others label "pluralist" (Lira Vázquez, 182–85). Given the complexity and diversity of modern urban life, in living styles, entertainment, education, business and commerce, it is not surprising that a diverse design vocabulary be employed within this city—with a resulting monumental, or rational, or traditional, or plastic architecture. This pluralism in Mexican architecture signifies more an approach than a unified style: It is a rejection of the assumption that the International Style can respond to local or regional needs and ambitions. In this context are works as distinct as the plastic INFONAVIT building, in which Teodoro González de León y Abraham Zabludovsky blended the exterior into interiors smoothly, using natural elements used such as wood, large expanses of glass with textured reinforced concrete, and the architects' massive Colegio de México (1976) and the "rational" architecture, as in Ramón Torres's design for the new Lotería Nacional building (1981). "Monumental" architecture is also significant in this period. As symbols of power or status, whether religious or secular, these are grandiose works: the Basilica de Guadalupe by Pedro Ramírez Vázquez, Javier García Lascurain, José Luis Benlliure, Gabriel Chávez de la Mora, and Alejandro Schoenhofer (1976) and the Colegio Militar, inspired by prehispanic forms, by Agustín Hernández and Manuel González Rul. Further innovations in structural engineering made possible taller skyscrapers, seen in the completion of the Torre de Pémex, designed by Pedro Moctezuma Díaz Infante (1984). This structure reaffirmed the prediction made 30 years earlier by Mexico City Chronicler Salvador Novo that one day "pyramids of crystal and aluminum" would cap this august city of palaces, marking yet another conquest of this fragile soil. In sum, the city is continually remodeled and revised, reflecting the diversity and complexity of contemporary Mexican life in terms of culture, government, economy, and identity.

PATRICE OLSEN

See also **Barragán, Luis (Mexico); Candela, Felix (Mexico); Legorreta, Ricardo (Mexico); Mexico; del Moral, Enrique (Mexico); O'Gorman, Juan (Mexico); University Library, UNAM, Mexico City**

Further Reading

Born, Esther, *The New Architecture in Mexico*, New York: Architectural Record and Morrow, 1937
Bullrich, Francisco, *New Directions in Latin American Architecture*, New York: Braziller, and London: Studio Vista, 1969
Cetto, Max L., *Moderne Architektur in Mexiko*, Stuttgart: Hatje, 1961; as *Modern Architecture in Mexico*, translated by D.Q. Stephenson, New York: Praeger, and London: Tiranti, 1961
Damaz, Paul F., *Art in Latin American Architecture*, New York: Reinhold, 1963
Davis, Diane E., *Urban Leviathan: Mexico City in the Twentieth Century*, Philadelphia, Pennsylvania: Temple University Press, 1994
Franco, Jean, *La cultura moderna en América latina*, Mexico City: Editorial Grijalbo, 1985; as *The Modern Culture of Latin America: Society and the Artist*, London: Pall Mall, and New York: Praeger, 1967
Hitchcock, Henry Russell, *Latin American Architecture since 1945*, New York: Museum of Modern Art, 1955
Kandell, Jonathan, *La Capital: The Biography of Mexico City*, New York: Random House, 1988
Kappe, Shelly (editor), *Modern Architecture, Mexico*, Santa Monica, California: SCI-ARC Press, 1981
Myers, Irving Evan, *Mexico's Modern Architecture*, New York: Architectural Book, 1952
Sanford, Trent Elwood, *The Story of Architecture in Mexico*, New York: Norton, 1947
Segre, Roberto (editor), *América latina en su arquitectura*, Mexico City: Siglo Veintiuno, and Paris: Unesco, 1975; as *Latin America in Its Architecture*, translated by Edith Grossman, edited by Fernando Kusnetzoff, New York: Holmes and Meier, 1981
Smith, Clive Bamford, *Builders in the Sun: Five Mexican Architects*, New York: Architectural Book, 1967
Suzuki, Makoto (editor), *Modern Mexican Architecture/Gendai Mekishiko kenchiku* (trilingual English–Japanese–Spanish edition), Tokyo: Process Architecture, 1983
Tovar de Teresa, Guillermo, *La ciudad de los palacios: Crónica de un patrimonio perdido*, 2 vols., Mexico City: Vuelta, 1990; as *The City of Palaces: Chronicle of a Lost Heritage*, 1990
Ward, Peter M., *Mexico City: The Production and Reproduction of an Urban Environment*, Boston: G.K. Hall, and London: Belhaven, 1990

MEYER, HANNES 1889–1954

Architect, Germany

Hannes Meyer was an advocate for functionalism and social reform in modern architecture. Meyer's "scientific" rationalism and negation of aesthetics still inspire Marxian theorists today (Hays, 1992). Denied greater individual fame by his preference for collective work over personal originality ("I never design alone," he declared), Meyer's continued notoriety stems from several uncompromisingly *Neue Sachlichkeit* (New Objectivity) projects and his stormy Bauhaus directorate, when the school's endgame commenced.

Shortly after establishing his practice in Basel in 1919, Meyer built for the Swiss Co-operative Union a progressive garden housing estate, the Freidorf Seidlung at Muttenz, near Basel (1919–21). Outwardly Palladian (as seen through provincial Jura eyes), Freidorf's planning nonetheless exemplified social collectivism—particularly through its intense seriality, nascent standardization, and sectionally sophisticated communal hall.

Through the early 1920s, Basel nurtured a left-wing architectural group, the ABC, formed around the peripatetic Russian artist and designer El Lissitzky. Meyer's first avant-garde endeavor after joining ABC, the Co-op series, consisted of exhibition/performance pieces extolling collectivist virtues. His Co-op Vitrine (1925) contained arrays of 36 mass-produced items from cooperative factories as a commentary on the anonymity of the worker in the production economy; his Co-op Zimmer' (1926) was a spare indictment of bourgeois interiors; and his Co-op Theater comprised life-sized marionettes and actors miming socialist themes.

Meyer also practiced architecture with fellow ABC radical Hans Wittwer. Their uncompromisingly functionalist inventions briefly captivated the international avant-garde. The Basel Petersschule Competition entry (1927) was a stark, skylit, industrial box that stood detached within the city, furiously sprouting cantilevered playgrounds, stairs, and transparent walkways. Meyer loved formulae; calculations of illumination levels within the classrooms constituted three-quarters of the presentation.

Meyer's and Wittwer's Geneva League of Nations Competitions entry (1926–27) wrapped a brutal aggregation of functional components within the echelons of a neutral construction module. Fire stairs widened while descending the building to accommodate increasing occupant load. Although both projects bore traces of Russian Constructivist aesthetics (gratuitous masts, glass elevators, structural hysterics), the overall impression was of facts bereft of metaphysical illusion—of architecture as *sachlich* (objective, literally "thingly"). Meyer and Wittwer's extremism cast objectivity as ideological: Their rejection of formal rhetoric became, paradoxically, rhetorical.

These unrealized schemes attracted the attention of Bauhaus Director Walter Gropius. At the December 1926 opening of the Bauhaus's Dessau facility, Gropius asked Meyer to initiate the school's long-delayed pedagogical intention of launching a building department. Meyer, although hesitant over what he interpreted as an overly sectarian and aesthetic cast of the Bauhaus work, agreed. Immediately Meyer developed projects for collaborative student exercises. By 1 April 1928 Gropius resigned, naming the charismatic yet schismatic Meyer as successor. Meyer, feeling that Gropius's Werkbund mentality pandered to the aesthetic tastes of the bourgeoisie, declared his opposition to formalism in 1928 writing, "Building is only organization: social, technical, economic, psychological organization."

Meyer transformed all workshops toward production. Under his reign, income from the school's products rose. Student pay increased, allowing poorer students to attend. Meyer indirectly encouraged a growing Communist student cell.

Architectural training inexorably gained the upper hand and became increasingly scientific (solar angle studies, structural calculations, flow diagrams). Just as he was named director, Meyer, in collaboration with Bauhaus students, won a "worker's school" (the *Bundesschule*) competition from the General German Trade Unions Federation (Bernau, 1928–30). In the school, which became Meyer's major realized work, he radicalized the building's plan, creating staggered housing volumes that organized the Federation's students into "brigades." The industrial materials (reinforced concrete, brick walling, steel windows) and the expressed circulation recalled his earlier objective proposals. Another collaborative opportunity with students soon followed, the Dessau-Törten Housing Development (in Dessau, 1930). But lacking varied communal spaces, the result here verged on banal.

The remaining Bauhaus master-teachers undermined Meyer, using as a final pretext his encouragement of the Communist cell's activities during a miners' strike. Dessau's mayor summarily dismissed Meyer on 1 August 1930. Many scholars use Meyer's dismissal as a benchmark of the rising influence of Fascism in the Weimar Republic.

With several like-minded Bauhaus students, Meyer sought a proletarian culture in Russia. From 1930 to 1933, he was professor at Moscow's VASI, a newly reorganized architectural laboratory. He designed several unbuilt school projects and worked with planning groups on massive satellite towns. Factional tensions and reorganizations drove him to the newly founded Moscow Academy of Architecture during 1934–35. Stalin's imposition of Social Realism gradually ended Meyer's teaching opportunities and hopes of progressive architectural work; by 1936, even his involvement in planning became untenable.

Dejected, Meyer sought solace in native Switzerland in 1936, opening a Geneva practice. The Swiss Co-operative Union offered him another commission, the 1938–39 Mümliswil chil-

dren's convalescent home—his only realized, post-Bauhaus architectural work.

After attending several town planning congresses in Mexico, Meyer was on 1 June 1939 called to Mexico City by President Cárdenas to direct the newly founded Institute of Urbanism and Planning, which was closed due to financial difficulties by 1941. Despite a lifelong array of prestigious academic opportunities, Meyer never spent more than three years at any institution. He languished another eight years in Mexico, joining public agencies for schools and clinics, serving intermittently on governmental planning commissions, and entering competitions. His health failing, in 1949 he returned again to Switzerland and explored theoretical studies until his death.

RANDALL OTT

See also **Deutscher Werkbund; Gropius, Walter (Germany); Bauhaus; Bauhaus, Dessau**

Biography

Born 18 November 1889, in Basel, Switzerland, an architect's son. Studied building at the Gewerbeschule, Basel 1905–09; continued his training at the Berlin's School of Applied Arts 1909–12; attended classes in urban planning at the Landwirtschafts-Akademie 1909–12. Went to England 1912, where he studied the Co-operative movement and the garden cities of Letchworth, Bourneville, and Port Sunlight for a year. After military service in Switzerland (1914–16), worked for Krupps Housing Welfare; established his own practice, Basel 1919. Founded the Theater Co-op 1924 and collaborated in a wide range of Co-op activities throughout Europe; meets Hans Wittwer and begins architecture practice with him in Basel 1936; met Walter Gropius 1956 and was named his successor at Bauhaus Dessau April 1928; dismissed August 1930 for political differences. Moved to Soviet Union, 1930; 1930–36, architecture professor, VASI; 1934–35, Moscow Academy of Architecture; returned to Switzerland, 1936; moved to Mexico City 1939 to direct the Institute of Urbanism and Planning, 1939–41; returned to Lugano, Switzerland, 1949, where he died 19 July 1954.

Selected Publications

Bauen und Gesellschaft: Schriften, Briefe, Projekte, edited by Lena Meyer-Bergner, Dresden: Kunst, 1980

Selected Works

Worker's School (*Die Bundesschule*) (with Hans Wittwer), Bernau, 1920
Co-op Vitrine (project), 1925
Co-op Zimmer (project), 1926
Co-op Theater (project), 1926
Basel Petersschule Competition entry, 1927
Geneva League of Nations Competitions entry (with Hans Wittwer), 1927
Dessau-Törten Housing Development, Dessau, 1930
Mümliswil Children's Home, Mümliswil, Switzerland, 1939

Further Reading

All quotations are by Meyer are found in Schnaidt, which remains the primary, comprehensive source in English. This fully treats Meyer's

Soviet and subsequent experiences that are minimized in other sources. Much subsidiary documentation exists only in German.

Frampton, Kenneth, *Modern Architecture: A Critical History*, London: Thames and Hudson, and New York: Oxford University Press, 1980

Hays, K. Michael, *Modernism and the Posthumanist Subject: The Architecture of Hannes Meyer and Ludwig Hilberseimer*, Cambridge, Massachusetts: MIT Press, 1992

Kieren, Martin, "The Bauhaus on the Road to Production Cooperative: The Director Hannes Meyer" in *Bauhaus*, edited by Jeannine Fiedler and Peter Feierabend, Cologne: Könemann, 1999

Meyer, Hannes, *Bauen und Gesellschaft: Schriften, Briefe, Projekte*, edited by Lena Meyer-Bergner, Dresden: Kunst, 1980

Schnaidt, Claude, *Hannes Meyer: Bauten, Projekte und Schriften; Buildings, Projects, and Writings* (bilingual German-English edition), translated by D.Q. Stephenson, Teufen, Switzerland: Niggli, 1965

Wick, Rainer K. (editor), *Ist die Bauhaus-Pädagogik aktuell?* Cologne: König, 1985

Winkler, Klaus-Jürgen, *Der Architekt Hannes Meyer: Anschauungen und Werk*, Berlin: Bauwesen, and Dessau, Germany: Bauhaus, 1989

MIAMI, FLORIDA

The architectural history of Miami (incorporated 1896) is essentially a 20th-century phenomenon, based on Miami's planned identity as a tourist resort. Beginning with railroad mogul Henry M. Flagler's neo-Colonial Royal Palm Hotel (1896, demolished 1930), built as the southern terminus for his Florida East Coast Railroad, much of Miami's architecture reflects the city's ongoing efforts to attract both tourists and residents through the creation of an exotic built environment. Similarly, the lavish, ecclectic vacation homes built in the early 20th century provided influential precedents for Miami's subsequent domestic, civil, and institutional architecture.

Much of Miami's significant early 20th-century architecture may be described as Mediterranean Revival, a conflation of Venetian, Italian Renaissance, French, Spanish, and Moorish architecture. Characteristic elements include internal courtyards; large, elaborate door surrounds; arcaded loggias; arched window and door openings; low-pitched, barrel tile roofs; and pastel- or putty-colored stucco finishes. The earliest example of this sensibility is Viscaya (1917), an Italianate villa designed by F. Burrall Hoffman, Jr., and Paul Chalfin for James Deering, a founder of the International Harvester Corporation. Centered around a large arcaded courtyard fronting Biscayne Bay, Vizcaya's tripartite composition recalls that of 16th-century Veneto and Venetian villas, whereas its exterior decoration draws primarily from Italian Renaissance and Spanish baroque precedents. The elaborate formal gardens (1921), created from the surrounding mangrove and hardwood hammock, were designed by the Italian-trained landscape architect Diego Suarez and form an integral composition with the house itself. Vizcaya's influence on Miami's architecture was profound, particularly on architect Richard Kiehnel and his partner John Elliot. Their buildings in Miami include El Jardin (1918) and La Brisa (1928). Both houses exemplify the firm's signature hybrid style, in which compositional elements, such as loggias, towers, and interior court-

yards, are overlain with a neobaroque profusion of decoration derived from Italian, Spanish, and Moorish sources.

In the mid-1920s, Miami's subtropical climate and growing reputation as a resort destination fueled the city's first building boom. Motoring tourists from colder northern regions arrived in the late 1910s and after by way of the Dixie Highway. This link encouraged numerous exuberant resort hotels in Miami and other vacation destinations. Much of Miami's Mediterranean Revival architecture dates from this period, and leading exponents of this style included Walter de Garmo, architect of the Peabody Residence (1922) in Coral Gables and the Western Union Building (1925, now the Burgos Pharmacy) in Miami Beach, and the Swiss-born Maurice Fatio, who designed the Vanderbilt Mansion (1928) on Fisher Island. The best known are the New York firm of Leonard Schultze and S. Fullerton Weaver, whose works include the Roney Plaza Hotel (1926, demolished) in Miami Beach, the Miami Daily News Building (1925), and the Biltmore Hotel (1925) in Coral Gables, whose central tower was directly based on the 15th-century Giralda bell tower in Seville, Spain. The Biltmore was built to anchor the newly planned resort community of Coral Gables (1925), the creation of developer George Merrick. Together with the architects Phineas Phaist and Walter de Garmo and the artist Denman Fink, Merrick aggressively marketed the Mediterranean Revival settlement as "America's Riviera." In 1926, Merrick created zoned subdivisions or "villages" within Coral Gables, built in distinctive historicizing architectural styles, including Dutch East African, Chinese, and Colonial. Soon afterward, the inventor and enterpreneur Glen Curtiss developed two equally flamboyant planned cities in this area, the Moorish-inspired Opa-Locka (1926) and the Pueblo-style Country Club Estates (1926, now Miami Springs).

The Tropical Deco architecture that became widely popular in the 1930s reflects Miami's enthusiastic embrace of Streamline Moderne and Art Deco art and architecture. Streamline Moderne in Miami is characterized by long, sweeping curves; horizontal string courses; porthole windows; flagpoles detailed as "masts"; and pipe railings. Miami Art Deco reflects a similar but more decorative sensibility, including carved or painted door and window surrounds and friezes with abstracted organic and geometric patterns. The influence of the International Exhibition of Decorative Arts (Paris, 1925) and the Century of Progress Exhibition in Chicago (1933) is evident in a wide range of buildings built during the Great Depression and beyond, beginning with the Sears Roebuck and Company Tower (1929) by Nimmons, Carr and Wright and the Pan American Seaplane Base and Terminal (1931, now City Hall) by Delano and Aldrich.

The bright colors and abstracted tropical ornamentation of Tropical Deco characterize many of the resort hotels lining the city's "Hotel Row" in Miami Beach. Among the most prolific architects in this style were L. Murray Dixon, whose work includes the Tides (1936) and Ritz Plaza (1940) hotels, and Henry Hohauser, whose Mayfair (1936) and Governor (1939) hotels employ a remarkably diverse set of architectural and decorative Streamline and Deco forms. The influence of this style was so pervasive that even the well-known Mediterranean Revival architects Kiehnel and Elliot produced two outstanding examples of Tropical Deco, the Barclay Plaza (1935) and Carlyle (1941) hotels. The high concentration of Tropical Deco hotels in the Hotel Row area led to the placement of a one-square-mile area of Miami Beach on the National Register of Historic Places in 1979. Local adaptations to Art Deco were also evident in the work of more identifiably "Modern" architects, such as Robert Law Weed, one of the designers of the Bauhaus-influenced University of Miami campus in Coral Gables (1949, Robert Little, Robert Law Weed, and Marion Manley). Weed's streamlined, lemon-yellow General Electric Model Home (1935, now the Eastman Residence) showcased innovative new materials, such as Vitrolite, Formica, and glass block, but also included a large decorative door surround of local stone bearing unmistakably tropical motifs.

America's post–World War II economic expansion fueled Miami's second building boom, which lasted until the mid-1950s. During this period and continuing through the 1970s, Miami's architecture comprised several different sensibilities, ranging from the elaborately theatrical modernity of Morris Lapidus to the more abstracted, stripped-down "Tropical Modern" works of architects such as Rufus Nims and George Reed. Among Lapidus's most visible works are his high-rise hotels in Miami Beach, just north of the Art Deco district. These include the Fountainbleau (1954), whose monumental scale, neobaroque curves, and grand "staircase to nowhere" prompted Groucho Marx to call this hotel the "Eighth Wonder of the

World"; the Eden Roc (1955); and the Americana (1957, now the Sheraton Bal Harbour). In contrast, more rigorously modernist works, such as Rufus Nims's Otto Cohen House (1950), were characterized by an abstract, open plan and minimal exterior articulation, adapted to the subtropical climate by placing the living spaces above ground level and designing window and door openings for direct flow-through ventilation. This adaptive approach echoes that of Miami's early vernacular architecture, such as Ralph Munroe's influential Barnacle House (1891), whose open wooden frame and inventive system of louvers is ideally suited to Miami's subtropical climate. Another similarly abstract work is George F. Reed's Eig/Smith House (1963), composed of unadorned glass and wood pavilion "rooms" whose transparency and simple detailing recall Philip Johnson's Glass House (1949), minimizing the boundaries between interior space and exterior landscape. Toward the end of the following decade, Laurinda Spear and Bernardo Fort-Brescia's Spear House (1978) departed from these more traditional modernist examples through its use of load-bearing masonry, bright colors, Streamline Moderne–inspired details, and essentially urban character. The subsequent work of their firm Arquitectonica, which may be described as Miami's first Postmodern architectural firm, includes the Palace (1980), Atlantis (1982), and Im-

The Carlyle Hotel, designed by Kiehnel and Elliot
© Historical Association of Southern Florida / Miami News Collection. Photo courtesy the Historical Museum of Southern Florida

perial (1983) high-rise residential towers and is characterized by creative and often surreal juxtapositions of scale, form, and materials within an essentially modernist compositional framework.

In the late 20th century, the tropically inflected Postmodernism of Arquitectonica's work was also evident in several several large-scale urban projects, including I.M. Pei's Centrust Tower (1987, now NationsBank Tower), whose streamlined curves and atmospheric outdoor lighting system have made it one of Miami's most famous buildings. A new generation of architects, many of whom were trained or teach in Maimi, have continued the city's eclectic architectural traditions, exploring and transforming a variety of Mediterranean, Caribbean, and vernacular sources. Collectively termed "The School of Miami" by architectural historian Vincent Scully, these architects include the late Charles Barrett; Andres Duany and Elizabeth Plater-Zyberk, founders of the New Urbanism movement; Maria de la Guardia and Teofilo Victoria; Jorge Hernandez; and Jorge, Luis, and Mari Tere Trelles. Although work in this genre varies widely, it is often characterized by brightly colored load-bearing masonry construction, low-pitched roofs, abstracted classical decoration, and local vernacular adaptations, such as raised living areas, wooden verandas, and viewing platforms. As contemporary architects in Miami continue to build on and expand the historicizing foundations of its resort origins, the presence of diverse buildings suggests that the city's architectural identity remains one of stylistic eclecticism.

KRISTIN A. TRIFF

See also **Arquitectonica; Art Deco; Bauhaus; Century of Progress Exposition, Chicago (1933); Classicism; Deconstructivism; Duany and Plater-Zyberk (United States); International Exhibition of Decorative Arts, Paris (1925); Johnson, Philip (United States); Modernism; Neorationalism; New Urbanism; Pei, I.M. (United States); Postmodernism; Scully, Vincent (United States)**

Further Reading

For an expanded biography on Miami's architecture, see White. The city's architectural history is discussed in detail in Patricios and in Culot and Lejeune; that of Miami Beach is discussed in Root, who also provides a directory of Art Deco buildings. The work of individual architects is discussed in Dunlop and in Friedman. Scully documents the architectural and urbanistic projects associated with the University of Miami.

Culot, Maurice and Jean-François, Lejeune (editors), *Miami: Architecture of the Tropics*, Miami, Florida: Center of Fine Arts, and Brussels: Archives d'Architecture Moderne, 1992

Dunlop, Beth, *Miami: Trends and Traditions*, New York: Monacelli Press, 1996

Friedman, Alice T., "The Luxury of Lapidus: Glamour, Glass, and Architecture in Miami Beach," *Harvard Design Magazine* 11 (Summer 2000)

Patricios, Nicholas N., *Building Marvelous Miami*, Gainesville: University Press of Florida, 1994

Root, Keith, *Miami Beach Art Deco Guide*, Miami Beach, Florida: Miami Design Preservation League, 1987

Scully, Vincent Joseph, *Between Two Towers: The Drawings of the School of Miami*, New York: Monacelli Press, 1996

White, Anthony G., *The Architecture of Miami, Florida: A Selected Bibliography*, Monticello, Illinois: Vance Bibliographies, 1982

MIES VAN DER ROHE, LUDWIG 1886–1969

Architect, Germany and United States

Ludwig Mies van der Rohe is commonly regarded among the most select company of 20th-century architects, a distinction he shares with Frank Lloyd Wright and Le Corbusier. A leading figure in the modernist movement that flourished in Europe during the 1920s, Mies later emigrated to the United States, where his reputation and influence took on international dimensions. At least a dozen of his designs, built and unbuilt alike, are customarily numbered among the most distinguished efforts of the century.

Born Maria Ludwig Michael Mies in Aachen in 1886, he was known professionally as Ludwig Mies until about 1920, when he decided to splice his father's name with his mother's maiden name, Rohe, by adding the invented "van der." Most of his forebears were stonemasons of modest means, a station that accounts for the fact that he finished trade school at 15 and never went on to more formal training. His initial contact with building consisted of service as an apprentice on construction sites around Aachen. Relatively low-level employment at several local ateliers and architectural offices followed, with the first pronounced evidence of talent manifest in his draftsmanship, which was sufficient to suggest to friends that he apply for work at architectural firms in Berlin. This he did successfully, and by 1905, aged 19, he had made his way to the German capital.

Mies's first professional experience was served with the designer Bruno Paul, with whom he worked from 1906 until 1908. During that time, on his own, he saw to completion, in 1907, his first independent work, a private house in Potsdam-Neubabelsberg, commissioned by the philosophy professor and Friedrich Nietzsche scholar Alois Riehl. Although the design was for the most part true to the vernacular of the time, Mies added a loggia and a rampart on one side of the structure that took lively advantage of the site. The design, when published, won a fair amount of praise in the architectural press. Impressed with his young designer not only as an architect but also as a person, Riehl sponsored Mies on a trip to Italy in 1908, intending to acquaint him with the classical tradition, at the time newly popular among the cultivated classes of Germany. By 1910 a sober, relatively straitlaced manner of architecture reflective of classicism had largely replaced the freer curvilinearity of Jugendstil (the German equivalent of Art Nouveau) among Germany's architects.

In this respect, then, it is not insignificant that Mies signed on in 1908 with Peter Behrens, at the time probably the most important living German architect. Behrens was widely known for the commercial work he had done in Berlin, but he also designed residences that demonstrated the new regard for classicism as a whole and, in particular, for the work of one of Germany's most historically distinguished architects, Karl Friedrich Schinkel. While Mies worked on at least one of Behrens's factory buildings, his own proclivities led him to pay his most serious personal attention to Schinkel's classicist style, as two of his endeavors dating from the Behrens years demonstrate: a 1910–11 house for the gallery owner Hugo Perls and a major competition project (unbuilt) of 1910 that was meant as a memorial monument to the first chancellor of the united modern German Empire, Otto von Bismarck.

Despite a brief interruption of his service with Behrens that lasted from late 1909 to late 1910 (during which time he designed the Perls House and the Bismarck monument), Mies became one of his chief's most trusted assistants, and he played a substantial role in two major commissions that Behrens received in the early years of the second decade of the century: the German embassy in St. Petersburg, completed in 1912, and the unrealized design of a house near The Hague, meant as a residence-cum-art gallery for the Dutch industrialist A.G. Kroeller, whose wife, Helene Kroeller-Mueller, was the central player in the history of that commission. Behrens's project was turned down, and Mies was invited on his own to produce an alternative proposal, which the clients also rejected, in favor of a third design, by the Dutchman Hendrik Petrus Berlage. (As fate would have it, that, too, was not built.)

Although his Kroeller project failed to materialize, Mies remained proud of it, and judging from photographs of the model, which suggest a monumentality of form and an impressive interlocking of masses—as well as a nourishing influence from Schinkel—he may well have been justified in his feelings. Even so, the work was turned down a second time, under different circumstances, a development that, as matters turned out, worked eventually to Mies' favor because it forced him to face the facts of a world that he had not learned much about in the years since he worked for Behrens.

Following World War I, during which Mies served in the German armed forces, he returned to Berlin on an independent basis to find an artistic climate in the process of a nearly all-encompassing change from what he recalled of the Behrens years. The classicism he was familiar with was being rapidly replaced by a pronounced tendency toward a modernist aesthetic, free of nearly all historicist implications. That Mies was slow to embrace this newer outlook may be inferred from his decision to submit the Kroeller-Mueller project to an exhibition of younger architects staged in 1919 and supervised by another of Behrens's prewar employees, Walter Gropius, himself a determined and accomplished devotee of the modernist point of view. Mies' entry was rejected.

Even though the next two years were crucial to Mies' life and career, the records of his movements during that time are less than clear. In 1913 he had married a woman of wealth, Ada Bruhn, who bore him three daughters between 1914 and 1917. Thereafter, he and his family lived largely on her money, leaving him free to become familiar with the Berlin artistic avant-garde and to foster friendships with its more energetic members. Nonetheless (and to some extent on that very account), he and his wife separated in 1921, shortly after he had decided to change his name to the more professional-sounding Ludwig Mies van der Rohe, both moves symptomatic of the changes in the cultural life of Weimar Germany. Personal freedom was in the air, although the new modernism exerted its own form of domination, to which Mies responded brilliantly at the professional level. Between 1921 and 1924, he conceived the design of five projects that, although never built, affected not only his career but eventually the mainstream history of 20th-century architecture as well. Two of these works (1921 and 1922) were high-rise buildings notable for a striking use of open glass walls and a spareness of incident in elevations rising from plans totally remote from

classical precedent. Both works were virtually without example in the record of tall buildings either in Europe or in the United States. A third proposal, known as the Concrete Office Building (1923), was a structure composed more horizontally than vertically, with a compelling treatment of ribbon windows recessed deeply behind rows of powerful parapets. The remaining two projects were for country houses, one in concrete (1923) and the other in brick (1924). Because there was no known client for either residence, it is assumed that Mies designed them for his own satisfaction. Both reached outward from a central core, but the later of the two featured an open plan in which interior walls, true to that form so common among advanced architects of the 1920s, defined rather than enclosed space in an uncommonly free layout.

Mies showed models or drawings of several of these works in exhibitions, thus attracting to himself the attention of the Berlin art world. Moreover, he made a point of cultivating the major figures of the pan-European modernist movement, and by the middle of the decade he had assumed a place of importance in several of Berlin's professional architectural organizations. He helped to finance a journal, *G* (for "Gestaltung"), which stood for the new elementarist position and to which he contributed several manifesto-like articles.

By 1925 Mies' work had become steadfastly modernist in style, for the most part rectilinear in its contours, cubic in its massing, and open in plan whenever possible. He nonetheless retained a distinctly personal fondness for brick, a material closer to the crafts tradition than to the machine aesthetic that he claimed in his writings of the period to embrace. A unique product of this predilection was not a building so much as a monument, the Liebknecht-Luxemburg Memorial (1926), designed at the behest of a ranking German Communist, Eduard Fuchs, and made up of a set of boldly intersecting brick masses in high relief.

In the course of the decade, having developed a following within the profession not only for his creative efforts but for his administrative skills as well, Mies was named by the German Werkbund to supervise the organization and construction of a housing settlement on a hillside overlooking Stuttgart that strengthened not only his reputation but also that of what had come to be called the "neues Bauen," or "new building," a term synonymous with the lately congealed modernist style. In his new capacity, he invited a company of the leading European practitioners in the idiom, including, among others, Le Corbusier, Gropius, J.J.P. Oud, and Behrens, to contribute designs, and when the Weissenhofsiedlung, as the settlement was called, opened in 1927, it was hailed at the international level as a triumph of the new architectural outlook.

By the late 1920s, Mies was building for a variety of devoted clients, notably two officers of the Verseidag silk-weaving mills, Josef Lange and Hermann Esters, for whom he designed a pair of handsome brick houses in the Rhineland city of Krefeld, where the Verseidag factory was located. Both buildings were completed in 1930, at a time when Mies was exceptionally busy not only with other residential efforts but with commercial and urban assignments as well, including an ambitious although unbuilt proposal for the reconstitution of Berlin's Alexanderplatz. Even so, that period remains memorable mostly for two commissions that were fully realized, in the process earning him a renown that has endured to the present day: the German Pavilion (1929) at Barcelona and the Tugendhat House (1930) in Brno.

In 1928 the German government had asked Mies to design several buildings as that country's contribution to an international exposition in Barcelona, scheduled for 1929. The principal structure was a reception pavilion in which, once it was completed, Mies succeeded in bringing together virtually all he felt, all he knew, and all he had learned. The finished structure, mounted on a podium, consisted of a series of freely planned walls that shared an asymmetrically flowing space with a group of slender, precisely measured, X-sectioned, chrome-plated columns. The composition was completed by two shallow pools, the smaller one featuring a life-size sculpture of a nude woman by the German Georg Kolbe. The serene proportions of the pavilion's space were matched by some exceptionally elegant materials, most spectacularly a slab of golden onyx that acted as a backdrop for a pair of exquisitely designed chairs, visible on entry.

The chairs, since known as Barcelona Chairs, were among a number of handsome articles of furniture that Mies designed in the late 1920s and early 1930s, works that added at the time to his rapidly growing reputation. Several more classic pieces of furniture were created for the second major building of the period, the Tugendhat House, completed in Brno in 1930 for a wealthy Czech couple that spared no expense in providing Mies with the kind of budget that allowed him to indulge his taste for patrician materials. The house contained two stories, with the main living area downstairs. There the parlor, which was flanked by a dining space and a winter garden, featured a centerpiece that took the form of another wall of rich onyx. The plan was open, the fenestration notable for windows that lowered electrically into the outer walls in the manner of automobile windows, thus transforming the interior into a veranda.

Mies' fortunes changed markedly in the course of the next decade. In 1930 he accepted the directorship of the state-run Bauhaus in Dessau, where it remained until local right-wing political elements forced its closure in 1933. Shortly thereafter, he reopened it as a private school in Berlin.

His own work of the early 1930s was notable for the design of a group of houses that were opposite in plan to his earlier residences, particularly to the two country house projects of 1923 and 1924. Whereas the latter works extended from a central area outward into the landscape, the newer ones were enclosed by walled courts, hence the name they have taken on generically in the meantime. Especially noteworthy were the floor-to-ceiling glass walls through which the house interiors would have been visible—a usage he followed frequently in his later, American oeuvre. None of the court houses was ever constructed; they appear to have been done with no specific client in mind.

Indeed, relatively little of Mies' architecture of the 1930s was realized. The depression devastated Germany's economy, in large part enabling the National Socialists to take control of the government in 1933 and, under Adolf Hitler, to turn the country into a totalitarian state. Having designed the Liebknecht-Luxemburg Memorial for the Communists, Mies, who was forever more committed to his architecture than to any steadfast political position, might have worked for the Nazis had they asked him to—at least as he perceived them shortly following Hitler's accession. However, when, in 1934, the party line turned away from any substantive cordiality toward modernist

expression in the arts, Mies' years in Germany were numbered. He built next to nothing for the remainder of the 1930s. Only by mid-decade did he begin to pay attention to teaching offers that had begun to come from outside Germany.

By 1938 Mies had moved to Chicago, assuming the headship of the School of Architecture at the Armour Institute of Technology (as of 1940, the Illinois Institute of Technology [IIT]). He spent his last 30 years in the United States, a span roughly equal to that of his active career in Germany and one, moreover, in which he built more actively but went through fewer stylistic shifts.

His first major commission in the United States was a master plan for the campus of IIT, made up of buildings of his own design. Conceived in 1939–40, the plan went through a number of phases before construction began. Meanwhile, Mies' quite considerable reputation, which grew greatly in the years following World War II, earned him commissions that he carried out in a narrow assortment of building types. The relationship he struck up with the Chicago developer Herbert Greenwald led to a number of high-rise apartment buildings erected throughout the country, the most important of which were the twin towers at 860–880 North Lake Shore Drive in Chicago. There, Mies employed the floor-to-ceiling windows he had pioneered in Germany, arranging them behind a modular steel frame topped by a flat roof. He followed that recipe over and over in his American high-rises, usually hanging a curtain wall of similar form over the main frame. On account of the unornamented simplicity of Mies' American high-rises, they proved relatively inexpensive to construct, a fact that, together with his reigning position in America's eager postwar acceptance of the modernist aesthetic, exercised a huge influence on corporate-scaled architecture throughout the country in the 1950s and 1960s. By consensus, his own masterpiece in the form was the Seagram Building (1958), an office building in New York in which Mies enjoyed a lavish budget, cladding the curtain wall elegantly in bronze, lining the foyer with his favorite stone (travertine), and in a gesture notably original for its time, setting the whole structure behind a plaza on Park Avenue.

Together with his treatment of the high-rise building, the preferred form of Mies' American years was the clear-span pavilion, in which he indulged his taste for column-free interiors, insisting that such untrammeled openness—he referred to it as "universal space"—facilitated the accommodation of varying uses over the years. The concept may have been as much a rationalization as a rationale because Mies' interest in space independent of function had been an inspiration dating back to his experiments with the open plan in his buildings of the 1920s.

The clear-span pavilion was most famously realized in the architecture building of IIT, S.R. Crown Hall (1956), its roof hung from exposed plate girders; the monumental project for a Convention Hall (1954) in Chicago, its vast interior covered by a three-dimensional truss; and the Berlin National Gallery (1967), its ceiling a grid of web girders. Even so, the earliest realized example was a house, one of the few residences he produced in the United States. The Farnsworth House (1951) is quintessential American Mies. The structure consists of a floor slab connected to a roof slab by the wide-flanged columns that became an intrinsic part of his American expressive vocabulary. The resultant volume is contained within floor-to-ceiling walls of glass, the interior space kept free of all but a wood-cladded core that accommodates bathrooms, kitchen and utilities, and one freestanding cabinet.

Mies' urbanistic efforts in the United States were confined mostly to the assembly of buildings that usually featured a coupling of the types characteristic of his American years. Each was composed of several high-rise buildings sited adjacent to one low-rise, the latter more often than not a column-free pavilion. The principal examples are in Chicago, Toronto, and Montreal. The one housing settlement in his American catalog was Lafayette Park in Detroit, an endeavor in which he worked together with two of his colleagues from IIT, planner Ludwig Hilberseimer (a friend from the old Bauhaus days whom Mies had invited in 1938 to join him on the IIT faculty) and landscape architect Alfred Caldwell.

Many of Mies' signature devices in the United States were outgrowths and refinements of their counterparts in Europe. The significant differences were manifest in his approach to materials and in his underlying concept. Finding steel available in quantity in the United States, he used it often to further his belief in structure in the abstract, and the minimalism of his manner was true to the one motto he coined and followed as an expressive objective ever-more faithfully the older he grew: "Beinahe Nichts" (almost nothing).

FRANZ SCHULZE

Biography

Born Ludwig Mies in Aachen, Germany, 27 March 1886; later adopted mother's maiden name of Rohe; the son of a master stonemason; immigrated to the United States 1938; naturalized 1944. Educated in the Domschule, Aachen 1897–1900; attended Aachen Trade School 1900–02; worked at building sites with his father 1900–02. Married Ada Bruhn 1914 (separated 1921; died 1951): 3 children. Worked as a draftsman and designer in a stucco decorating firm, Aachen 1903–04. Moved to Berlin; worked briefly in the office of an architect specializing in wood structures 1905; apprenticed to architect and furniture designer Bruno Paul, Berlin 1905–07. Private architectural practice, Berlin 1907–09; assistant, with Walter Gropius and Le Corbusier, in the office of Peter Behrens, Berlin 1908–11; private practice, Berlin 1911–14 and 1919–37; financed and wrote for *G* (for "Gestaltung") magazine, Berlin 1921. Moved to Chicago 1938; private practice from 1938. Appointed director of the Bauhaus at the recommendation of Walter Gropius 1930; moved the Bauhaus from Dessau to Steglitz, Berlin to escape Nazi pressure; closed the school in 1933 following Nazi interference; director, architecture department, Armour Institute (now Illinois Institute of Technology), Chicago 1938–59. Director, architectural division, Novembergruppe, Berlin 1921–25; founder, Zhener Ring (later Der Ring), Berlin 1925; vice president, Deutscher Werkbund, Berlin 1926–32; member, Prussian Academy of Arts and Sciences 1931; Commander (with cross), German Order of Merit 1959; member, National Institute of Arts and Letters 1963; president, CIAM. Royal Gold Medal, Royal Institute of British Architects 1959; Gold Medal, American Institute of Architects 1960. Collaborated on exhibition projects with Lilly Reich; director of Werkbund exhibition Weissenhofsiedlung, Stuttgart 1927; director, Werkbund section "The

Dwelling" at the Berlin Building Exhibition 1931. Died in Chicago, 17 August 1969.

Selected Works

Riehl House, Potsdam-Neubabelsberg, Germany, 1907
Monument to Otto von Bismarck (unbuilt), 1910
Perls House, Berlin, Germany 1911
Liebknecht-Luxemburg Memorial, Berlin, Germany 1926
German Pavilion, Barcelona, 1929
Tugendhat House, Brno, Czech Republic, 1930
Illinois Institute of Technology (IIT) Campus, Chicago, 1939–56
Lake Shore Drive Apartments, Chicago, 1951
Farnsworth House, Plano, Illinois, 1951
Crown Hall, IIT Campus, Chicago, 1956
Seagram Building, New York, 1958
Berlin National Gallery, 1967

Further Reading

Neumeyer, Fritz, *Mies van der Rohe: Das kunstlose Wort*, Berlin: Siedler, 1986; as *The Artless Word: Mies van der Rohe on the Building Art*, Cambridge, Massachusetts: MIT Press, 1991
Schulze, Franz, *Mies van der Rohe: A Critical Biography*, Chicago: University of Chicago Press, 1985
Tegethoff, Wolf, *Mies van der Rohe: die Villen und Landhousprojekte*, Essen, Germany: Bacht, 1981; as *Mies van der Rohe: The Villas and Country Houses*, translated by Russell M. Stockman, edited by William Dyckes, New York: Museum of Modern Art, 1985

MINISTRY OF FOREIGN AFFAIRS, RIYADH, SAUDI ARABIA

Designed by Henning Larsen; completed 1984

The Ministry of Foreign Affairs building in Riyadh, Saudi Arabia, resulted from an invitational competition organized in 1979 by the Saudi Arabian government in association with the *Union Internationale des Architectes*. Participants were given a site occupying an entire block in the al-Namodhajiyah quarter of the city, which lies eight kilometers from the Diplomatic Quarter and two kilometers from the oldest district in Riyadh. Formulated between 1977 and 1979, the program called for offices for the Minister and his deputy; banquet hall, mosque, library, conference center, and training facilities for the diplomatic corps; 85,000 square meters of office and circulation space divided between political, social, and cultural affairs; and parking areas for over 1,000 employees and visitors.

Danish architect Henning Larsen was chosen in 1980 by a jury that included the Egyptian architect Hassan Fathy and the Minister of Foreign Affairs. Larsen's was one of 11 proposals that included the work of Ricardo Bofill (Spain), Arata Isozaki (Japan), Vedet Daloky (Turkey), Bernhard and Peter Suter (Switzerland), and Roger Taillibert (France).

Building in Saudi Arabia requires dealing with extreme climatic conditions: Riyadh is dry and hot, with temperatures that range from 20 to 47 degrees centigrade. Sand and dust carried by winds from the south in winter and the north in summer also present major challenges. As a result of these extreme conditions and the particular social structure in the Arab world that sharply delineates between the public space of the city and the private space occupied by the family, traditional buildings in

Riyadh were joined to create massive blocks and were characterized by blank facades facing the street that shielded private internal courtyards.

Larsen's proposal considered both building traditions that had developed in the region and the need for an efficient, technologically advanced building to serve the day-to-day activities and the representational functions of the Ministry. Completed in 1984, the low, compact building is based on a square in plan and is composed of three blocks that occupy the corners (the fourth corner block is left out, symbolizing the embassies abroad). The entry to the building, placed along the diagonal axis of the square, is defined by two cylindrical towers that house the auditorium and library and the exhibition hall. A large vaulted gallery leads to the central triangular-shaped court, which is defined by the three main "streets." Covered by barrel vaults, these three-story-high streets serve as the major circulation corridors. Each corner of the triangle contains an octagonally shaped domed space that is referred to as a "square." These squares occupy the center of the three blocks and provide access to the flexible open office spaces, which are interrupted by a series of internal open-air courtyards that are square in shape and divided into three types: the cross garden, the fountain garden and the water basin garden.

The interior courtyards, the thick exterior wall system, the small window openings, and the use of *mashrabiyyas* (wooden screen used to protect the privacy of the balconies in traditional houses) reveal a sensitivity to both climate and custom. The thick walls that separate interior and exterior result from a double-wall system containing an internal air cavity; this system insulates the building against the extreme temperatures and, when combined with the small windows and shading screens, provides relief from the intense sunlight characteristic of the region. In the Ministry of Foreign Affairs, as in other work by Larsen, the control and manipulation of light is a primary concern, and skylights were employed in various configurations to illuminate the spaces.

Given the significance of ornament in Islamic architecture, the lack of surface treatment in the Ministry of Foreign Affairs is noteworthy. Architects in the Arab world traditionally employed ornament to dematerialize wall surfaces and to aid in making the transition from interior to exterior. Larsen rejected ornament and relied on the solid masses of the walls to strongly define the spaces and transitional areas. In fact, the formal purity of the building is such that the clients commissioned a series of panels and other ornamental features that were installed against the wishes of the architect.

Ministry of Foreign Affairs, private courtyard with window lattices
© Aga Khan Trust for Culture

Larsen's chosen minimalism for the Ministry of Foreign Affairs reveals his affinity with the progenitors of the Modern movement. The diagrammatic clarity of the floor plan recalls the work of Louis Kahn, as does the idea of a "building within a building" that was used by Kahn to control light in the National Assembly Building in Dhaka. Although Larsen works within the modernist tradition, he nevertheless adopted principles from Mogul architecture in India and the form language of the region that resulted in the fortresslike facades. He attempted to avoid the Postmodernist tendency toward stylistic pastiche by abstracting rather than quoting the borrowed, historical forms. In this manner, Larsen's work is closer to the 1960s Italian neorationalist movement, in particular Aldo Rossi, who sought create an analogical architecture that responded to the context via elements that were abstracted from vernacular forms.

Awarded the Aga Khan Award for Architecture in 1989, The Ministry of Foreign Affairs is a significant work of 20th-century architecture that represents an attempt to mediate between the universalisms of the Modern movement and regional culture while grappling with the often-conflicting demands of function, climate, and custom in the Gulf region.

KEVIN MITCHELL

See also **Kahn, Louis (United States); Larsen, Henning (Denmark); National Assembly Building, Sher-e-Bangla Nagar, Dhaka; Riyadh, Saudi Arabia**

Further Reading

An appropriate monograph covering the work of Henning Larsen has not yet been published in English. Abel provides a lengthy discussion of the building with accompanying drawings and illustrations; the most comprehensive account of Larsen's work remains accessible only to those who read Danish (Lund).

Abel, Chris, "Riyadh Angles: Ministry of Foreign Affairs, Riyadh, Saudi Arabia," *Architectural Review* 178, no. 1061 (1985)

Davey, Peter, "Larsen in Riyadh: Foreign Ministry, Riyadh, Saudi Arabia," *Architectural Review* 173, no. 1031 (1983)

"Henning Larsen: Foreign Ministry, Riyadh, Saudi Arabia," *Architectural Design* 51, nos. 3/4 (1981)

Larsen, Henning, "Lessons from the Orient," *Diadalos* 10 (1983)

Lund, Nils-Ole, "Ministry of Foreign Affairs Building in Riyadh, Saudi Arabia, 1984," *A + U* 195, no. 12 (1986)

Lund, Nils-Ole, "Henning Larsen," *Arkitektur DK* 33, no. 2 (1989)

Lund, Nils-Ole, *Arkitekt Henning Larsen*, Copenhagen: Gyldendal, 1996

"Ministry of Foreign Affairs, Riyadh, Saudi Arabia," *Architectural Design* 186, no. 1113 (1989)

Morton, David, "Desert Buildings," *Progressive Architecture* 68, no. 5 (1987)

Petersen, Steen Estvad, "The Ministry of Foreign Affairs in Saudi Arabia," *Living Architecture* 3 (1984)

Skriver, Poul Erik, "Henning Larsens Arkitektur," *Arkitektur DK* 29, no. 7 (1985)

Steele, James, editor, *Architecture for Islamic Societies Today*, London: Academy Editions, and Berlin: Ernst, 1994

MIRALLES, ENRIC 1955–2000 AND CARME PINÓS 1954–

Architects, Spain

Enric Miralles (1955–2000) and Carme Pinós (1954–) worked together in a brief but prolific partnership from 1984 to 1989. Their reputation was established through numerous competition-winning schemes for civic projects sponsored by enlightened political leadership to stimulate the renaissance of Catalan culture following the death of Spanish dictator Francisco Franco. Although only a few of these schemes were realized, Miralles and Pinós achieved worldwide recognition for their exquisite drawings and for a modest and distinguished body of work.

Enric Miralles was born in Barcelona, where he attended the School of Architecture, receiving his professional degree in 1978 and a doctorate in 1981. He worked with Helio Piñon and Albert Viaplana from 1973 to 1985 on prize-winning competition entries and on built projects including Sants Plaza and Besos Park in Barcelona. Carme Pinós is also a native of Barcelona; she graduated from the School of Architecture in 1979. She was awarded first prize in the Rural Housing Competition of the Ministry of Public Works and Urbanism in 1982.

Completed civic projects for which the design was initiated by Miralles and Pinós include, in chronological order of commencement: La Llauna School (1994), Igualada Cemetery (1996), the pergolas of Parets des Vallés (1986), Hostalets Civic Center (1992), Morella School (1994), the Mina Quarter Civic Center (1992), Reus Rambla (1993), Huesca Sports Center (1994), the Archery Ranges (1992) and the Icaria Avenue Pergolas (1992) for the Olympic Games in Barcelona, and the Alicante Eurhythmic Sports Center (1993). In addition, a private residence, the Garau-Agustí House (1992), was completed. After the partnership ended, one or other of the newly independent offices subsequently administered the final design and construction of many of these projects.

Although the work of Miralles and Pinós clearly grew out of regional influences, including the surrealism and inventive form of Antoni Gaudí and Josep Maria Jujol, it also distills and carries forward more universally understood themes of 20th-century modernism. Like the work of Alvar Aalto, which moved away from the notion of the building as an ideal type superimposed on a tabula rasa, the formal and material language of Miralles and Pinós may be characterized as topographical, both emerging out of and amplifying the characteristics of site, program, and culture. Moving beyond the superficial contextualism of postmodernism, the work aspires to be deeply contextual, revealing intrinsic relationships between built form and landform and between nature and culture.

While exhibiting fragmented formal and spatial attributes similar to the work of the deconstructivists, Miralles and Pinós eschewed both the cynicism and theoretical focus of that movement. Maintaining a firm commitment to the inherited social idealism of modernism, their work reveals a persistent preoccupation with the architectural promenade. The designs feature dramatization of movement, expressed by elaborately articulated stairs, ramps, and circulation routes, derived in part from a strong belief in the power of architecture to stimulate communal interaction and to shape the social matrices of society. It also is derived from a focus on direct physical experience and a corresponding disavowal of the representational aspirations of architecture. A conscious awkwardness and lack of refinement that are intended to distance the work from the technical virtuosity of much late 20th-century architecture exemplifies their emphasis on the blunt physical presence of construction. This is a reflection of the influence of the late brutalist work of Le Corbusier and the subsequent generation of new brutalists, notably Alison and Peter Smithson.

Complexity is another notable characteristic of the work of Miralles and Pinós. Their buildings are open-ended and flexible entities built up of overlapping layers, each with its own internal logic. The plans, rather than being preconceived, express the aggregative order of the work by emerging from the superimposition of many layers of information. In section, a limited range of standard components is subtly inflected to create slightly varying spatial sequences like a series of freeze-frame photographs. The architects conceived structure as dynamic components in equilibrium, and they detailed buildings with multiple layers of material that create highly figured tapestries of surface pattern, light, and shadow. Critics have praised the formal and material inventiveness of Miralles and Pinós but with some reservations. Kenneth Frampton suggests that the work tends toward structural exhibitionism, and William Curtis maintains that its complexity is mannerist in its overelaboration.

Of the built work of Miralles and Pinós, the most compelling project is the Igualada Cemetery (1996), a powerful synthesis of the themes of topography, promenade, blunt physicality, and complex order. Located on an unpromising site at the edge of an industrial estate, the cemetery is a simple cut into the earth that fuses built form with the natural contours of the site. The scheme transforms the banal rock-filled gabion and precast concrete retaining-wall systems of the civil engineer into a richly expressive tectonic language. Igualada is both fresh and timeless; it arouses deep and universal emotions while at the same time being both carefully attuned to its own physical and cultural location and reflecting the particular sensibilities of its architects.

Awards for the work of Miralles and Pinós include the Fomento de les Arts Decoratives (FAD) Interior Design Prize for La Llauna School in 1987, the Barcelona Prize for the Archery Ranges in 1992, the FAD Architecture Prize for Igualada Cemetery in 1992, and the National Prize for Spanish Architecture for Morella School in 1995.

After 1989, Miralles and Pinós continued their careers separately. Pinós designed numerous schemes for sports facilities in Spain and completed the Petrer pedestrian bridge and plaza in 1999. Miralles completed projects including an industrial bridge for Camy-Nestlé in Barcelona (1990), the Social Headquarters for the Circulo de Lectores in Madrid (1992), and the Unazuki Meditation Pavilion (1993) and Takaoka Station Access Area (1993) in Japan. Beginning in 1994 until his untimely death in 2000, he worked in partnership with Benedetta Tagliabue and in 1998–99 won international competitions including the Music School in Hamburg, the new Scottish Parliament in Edinburgh, and the Instituto Universitario di Architettura in Venice.

ANNETTE W. LeCUYER

Biography

Enric Miralles

Born in Barcelona, Spain 1955. Graduated from the School of Architecture, Barcelona 1978; was a Fulbright Visiting Scholar, Columbia University, New York 1980–81. Married to Carme Pinós (divorced 1992). Collaborated with Pinon-Viaplana 1973–85. Partnership with Pinós 1984–89. Partner, Enric Miralles Benedetta Tagliabue Architects Associates, Barcelona from 1992. Professor, from 1978, chair of architecture 1996, School of Architecture, Barcelona; director, Master Class of Architecture, Stadelschule, Frankfurt from 1990; Kenzo Tange Chair, Harvard University, Cambridge, Massachusetts from 1993; John Labatou Chair, Princeton University, New Jersey 1994; lecturer, School of Architecture, University of Syracuse, New York 1996; lecturer, School of Architecture, University of Illinois, Chicago 1997; lecturer, Graduate School of Design, Harvard University 1997–98. Died 3 July 2000 in Barcelona.

Carme Pinós

Born in Barcelona, Spain 1954. Graduated from the School of Architecture, Barcelona 1979. Married to Enric Miralles (divorced 1992). Partnership with Miralles 1984–89. Part of the group of architects, led by Rem Koolhaas, working on the José Vergara C. Center in Guadalajara, Mexico since 1998. Lecturer, Columbia University, New York 1996; Plym Distinguished Professorship, School of Architecture, University of Illinois, Urbana.

Enric Miralles and Carme Pinós

Worked in partnership in Barcelona 1984–89; gained international renown for their works, especially for the Barcelona Olympics in 1992.

Selected Works

Parets des Valles, Pergolas, Barcelona, 1986
Icaria Avenue Pergolas, Barcelona, 1992
Garau-Augustí House, Barcelona, 1992
Civic Center, Hostalets, Spain, 1992
Archery Ranges, Barcelona, 1992
Mina Quarter Civic Center, La Mina, Spain, 1992
Reus Rambla, Barcelona, 1993
Eurhythmic Sports Center, Alicante, Spain, 1993
School, La Llauna, Spain, 1994
School, Morella, Spain, 1994
Sports Center, Huesca, Spain, 1994
Cemetery, Igualada, Spain, 1996

Selected Publications

Miralles

Pabellón de Baloncesto en Huesca, Basquetball Hall, 1995
Mixed Talks, edited by Benedetta Tagliabue, 1995

Further Reading

Buchanan, Peter (editor), *The Architecture of Enric Miralles and Carme Pinós*, New York: SITES/Lumen Books, 1990
Carme Pinos: Some Projects (since 1991), Barcelona: ACTAR, 1998
Curtis, William J.R., "Mental Maps and Social Landscapes: The Architecture of Miralles and Pinos," in *Miralles/Pinos, 1988–1991*, Madrid: El Croquis No. 49–50, 1991
El Croquis No. 30 (October 1987)
Frampton, Kenneth, *Studies in Tectonic Culture: The Poetics of Construction in Nineteenth- and Twentieth- Century Architecture*, Cambridge, Massachusetts: MIT Press, 1995
Miralles, Enric, *Enric Miralles, 1995*, Barcelona: El Croquis No. 72, 1995
Miralles/Pinos, 1988–1991, Madrid: El Croquis No. 49–50, 1991
Tagliabue Miralles, Benedetta (editor), *Enric Miralles: Opere e progetti*, Milan: Electa, 1996; as *Enric Miralles: Works and Projects, 1975–1995*, New York: Monacelli Press, 1996

Zabalbeascoa, Anatxu, *Igualada Cemetery: Enric Miralles and Carme Pinos*, London: Phaidon, 1996

MOBILE HOME

Increasing industrialization and advancing technology in the United States throughout the 20th century, and especially following World War II, led to many attempts to produce and market a factory-built house. The mobile home industry has contributed to the growth and expansion of industrialized housing by producing a complete unsubsidized house characterized by economy, ease of finance, and innovative techniques and materials. Among factory-built structures worldwide, the American mobile home is the most prevalent. The Mobile Homes Manufacturers Association defined the mobile home as a "movable or portable dwelling constructed at a factory to be towed on its own chassis, connected to utilities, and designed without a permanent foundation for year round living."

The history of the chassis-based house is remarkable for its rapid evolution over a short time. Physical transformation, in association with changes in use and meaning, spun off a succession of entities with different names. The "travel trailer" emerged in the mid-1920s, and its production continued until around 1940; the era of the "house trailer" spans from 1940 until 1953; the "mobile home" period lasts from the mid-1950s to the mid-1970s; and the current period begins in the mid-1970s, when the mobile home officially became "manufactured housing." Each name change signifies an effort to create a new image and public perception of the chassis-based house.

Developing from the "travel trailer," the mobile home originated in the recreational vehicle industry. Through the 1930s, travel trailers were viewed as recreational housing and were indeed highly mobile. Appealing to households with mobile lifestyles and temporary housing needs, manufacturers offered a variety of designs exploring alternative appearances and meanings in order to associatively identify this invention with accepted forms from the past as well as popular images of the future.

During World War II, the rapid development of war industries spawned dispersion and mobility of the labor force. An immediate need for housing resulted, and the travel trailer house satisfied it with a combination of mobility, affordability, and availability. Many units were used as permanent homes in single installations or in trailer parks, even as the units remained mobile. Housing shortages after World War II increased the use of such homes as year-round residences.

A newly renamed entity, the "house trailer" provided shelter that was both immediate and within economic reach of many. Families could move these units following employment or whimsy, keeping wheels, axles, and hitches obviously in place for easy transport. In recognition, however, that the interest in mobile over conventional housing was increasingly an issue of economy rather than mobility, the industry redirected its focus toward developing this industrialized housing type in comparison to other forms of factory-built housing. This shift marks the beginning of the process by which the potential mobility of the structure becomes ever more incidental in value.

The "mobile home" emerged as a distinct entity in the mid-1950s with the first production of a ten-foot-wide unit. Larger than could be pulled behind the family automobile, the mobile home soon attained lengths in excess of 30 feet. With a growing demand for longer and wider units, the industry produced an array of physical size and material variations for what remained a basic rectilinear unit set on steel travel chassis. Long, extra-long, doublewide, multilevel, foldout, pop-up, expandable, and multisection units enabled physical configuration more akin to those of site-built housing. Similarly, pitched-roof forms, interior and exterior finishes typical to conventional construction, and mobile home court site designs were adapted to make the mobile home more house like and less vehicular. The shift from the house trailer to the mobile home involved a change in attitude as well as use; the industry began to produce dwellings that happened to be mobile rather than trailers that could also serve as dwellings.

By the mid-1970s, one-fifth of all new houses were mobile homes, primarily for people seeking affordable starter housing. Manufacturers were faced with the choice to remain in the travel trailer business, to produce larger mobile homes exclusively, or to manufacture both products, essentially for different markets. In 1963, the two industries formally split, with travel trailer manufacturers identifying themselves as the recreational vehicle industry.

Mobile homes, having emerged from the recreational vehicle industry, initially were subject to little or no regulation for construction or installation. Manufacturers were either small firms turning out a few units a month or large automobile companies producing mobile homes on the side. As mobile homes became a permanent housing choice for more people, concerns about public health and safety arose. Government recognition of the importance of mobile homes in satisfying demand for affordable housing led to federal legislation regulating their construction. In 1974, Congress passed what is now known as the National Manufactured Housing Construction and Safety Standards Act, which directed the U.S. Department of Housing and Urban Development (HUD) to develop national building standards and a federal oversight program for the construction of manufactured homes. In June 1976, the Federal Manufactured Home Construction and Safety Standards became law. Known as the "HUD Code," it distinguishes manufactured housing from other forms of housing and its passage marks the end of mobile home production.

Until relatively recently—if not to the present day—mobile homes have suffered disfavor from the layperson, local and central government, the design profession, and even housing institutions. Limitations of their structural forms by transportation ordinances and the use of low-quality construction materials to maintain low market prices have led to the perception that they are less than "real" housing. As such, they do not blend well with existing built or natural environments. Design attention by the architectural profession to the mobile home concept has occurred occasionally and sporadically. Nevertheless, mobile home structures satisfy preferences for norms of ownership, detached dwelling, and private outdoor space; they have found strong market acceptance as a cost-worthy substitute for conventional construction. Recognized generally on a vernacular level by those who built and use them, mobile home structures provide a realistic option within the housing market.

CAROL J. BURNS

Further Reading

Bernhardt, Arthur D., *Building Tomorrow: The Mobile/Manufactured Housing Industry*, Cambridge, Massachusetts: MIT Press, 1980

Drury, Margaret J., *Mobile Homes: The Unrecognized Revolution in American Housing*, Ithaca, New York: Cornell University, 1967; revised edition, New York: Praeger, 1972

Kronenburg, Robert, *Houses in Motion: The Genesis, History, and Development of the Portable Building*, London: Academy Editions, 1995

Sanders, Welford, *Manufactured Housing: Regulation, Design Innovations, and Development Options*, Chicago: American Planning Association, 1998

Vermeer, Kimberly and Josephine Louie, *The Future of Manufactured Housing*, Cambridge, Massachusetts: Joint Center for Housing Studies of Harvard University, 1997

Wallis, Allan D., *Wheel Estate: The Rise and Decline of Mobile Homes*, New York: Oxford University Press, 1991

MODERNISM

What does modernism mean today when many celebrate the "end" of the project of modernity, or claim its "incompleteness"? More important, could any discussion of modernism today avoid the fact that many countries, which were peripheral to the early stages of modernization, are now formulating their own understanding of modernism in general and of modern architecture in particular?

Among other connotations, the etymology of the word "modern" suggests a manner or way of acting, a mode, but also the form or way of being. Another helpful word derived from mode is *modish*, alluding to the state of being in the latest style and fashion. To be stylish means to submit to the constant flow of transformation that is instigated by modernization. Transience is perhaps one of the most important aspects of modernity. It suggests experiencing the "now" of the present. This understanding of the word "modern" emerged in the 19th century. "By *modernite*," Charles Baudelaire wrote in 1863, "I mean the ephemeral, the fugitive, the contingent, the half of art whose other half is the eternal and the immutable" (p. 13). Before that, the term was discussed and understood differently. In the 17th century, the idea of modern was used in conjunction with ancients; most remarkable was the case of the so-called quarrel between the ancients and the moderns. This was a dispute about history and the relationship of the past to the present. Whereas some literary scholars of that century saw the past in a perfect state of values and norms, others, the moderns, questioned the validity of such a stronghold on the past. The historicity of the idea of modernity, however, is better understood when "modern" is spoused with the secularization of value and abstraction, when the authoritative role of the past is superseded and a different order of relationships among people and nature has emerged that is contingent to the flow and accumulation of capital and technological innovations.

Was the relationship between modernity and modernism transparent? In retrospect, one can agree with T.J. Clark that "modernism had truck with a modernity not yet fully in place" (Clark, 1999). It was indeed the blindness of modernity, its nihilism, and the drive for perpetual transformation that alienated modernism from its historical context. Since its inception, modernism had to confront a situation that was marked by the remnant of antiquity and even a peasant lifestyle that, again according to Clark, "resisted the disenchantment of the world." While industrialization was rapidly transforming the old order of the medieval towns of Europe, it took architects a long time to accommodate the disciplinary history of architecture to the demands of the new society and industrial materials and techniques. Some scholars, however, argue that the beginning of modernism should be pushed back to the early 18th century, when intellectual work broke with the classical discourse on art and architecture. The rupture was considered formative for the autonomy of artistic creativity, even though its horizon soon had to be modified according to the subjective and objective conditions of the rising industrial bourgeois society.

As the cultural attribute of modernity, modernism is rather a new phenomenon. It was not until modernity was questioned, after World War II, that the idea of modernism was sought to represent the totality of a movement that most architectural historians identify with the years spanning 1850 to 1945. The search for an answer to one of the fundamental questions of modern architecture, "In What Style Should We Build," framed by Henrich Hubsch, the 19th century German architect, was, in the 1940s, reduced to the idiom of the International Style. Such was the verdict of some historians and architects who channeled modernism through a speculative reading of the Zeitgeist and its presumed linear and coherent development. Historicism prevailed in Nikolaus Pevsner's *Pioneers of Modern Movement*, first published in 1936, though his many generalizations stayed intact for a couple of decades.

Beneath the unified vision of modernism depicted in the early writings of the history of modern architecture lies diverse strategies attempting to formulate an "objectivity" that shares the following concerns: first, how to reformulate a masonry based craft language with material and techniques produced by steel, concrete, and glass industries. Second, what is the future of the art of building in the metropolis where architecture had to confront the anguish unleashed by production and the consumption system of capitalism? This observation underlines the heterogeneous character of modern architecture, but more important, it suggests that architects understood modernism differently than historians or theoreticians. Still, among architects, modernism and the effect of modernization on architecture was interpreted variously: The avant-garde attempted to picture an image of architecture that formally and aesthetically was informed by a sociocultural situation that was not yet realized. For them, architecture was to play a constructive role in the realization of utopias that were mostly nurtured by the formative themes of the Enlightenment. Progress and creation of artistic work unimaginable previously were sought as basic to modernity. For the avant-garde, practicing individually or collaborating in groups, the advocacy for the autonomy of art and architecture was essential. Autonomy was sought as the passing moment of art toward its destiny: the reintegration of the work of art into the life-world. Abstraction was appropriated for its capacity in opening a space through which creative work could flourish independent of the realities of a given situation.

Futurists and the Dutch De Stijl, among other avant-garde groups, radicalized the holistic vision of the Romantic modernists, propagating a "modernist" relationship between architecture and society that today seems naïve in its understanding of the stakes involved in the nihilism perpetuated through modernization. Others pursued a rather modest agenda; these architects attempted to approach modernity through the architectural tradition of a particular region. The geographic distance separating the Scandinavian countries and America from the metropolitan centers of the Europe of the early decades of the last century produced a regionalist architecture, the best of which is exemplified in the work of Alvar Aalto and Frank Lloyd Wright. Both tendencies (the avant-garde and the others), however, shared the following convictions: that in modernity, there is no room to continue the symbolic language of classical architecture; that it is necessary to rethink the planimetric organization of architecture based on new building types and to conceive the interior spaces of the domestic architecture according to the spatial needs of modern life that was unfolding in the metropolitan centers; and finally, that technology is essential for the formation of modern architecture.

The question concerning technology is critical for understanding the different facets of modernism. Although technical reproducibility did not have the same effect on architecture as it did on visual arts (like film and painting), nevertheless, the subject's discussion could shed some light on the state of mental and technical possibilities that informed modern architecture. Before modernization of techniques, there was no understanding of technology as it is known today. A departure from a concept of fabrication in which technique is congenial to the image of the final product was instrumental for the modernization of architecture's métier. To be modern, architecture had no choice but to merge into the technological universe of capitalism. Technification of architecture meant emptying the tectonic of any import to architecture. The use of technologies invented outside of architecture's interiority (the disciplinary history of architecture), aligned design with the exigencies of technical planning. That capitalist development took away certain tasks from architecture not only is clear from architectural ideologies sought by the historical avant-garde and some sectors of the Bauhaus school but, more important, it is exemplified in the linguistic polarities differentiating, for example, Peter Behrens's AEG Turbine Factory, Berlin, 1908–09, from Adolf Meyer and Walter Gropius's design for Fagus Werk, Alfeld-an-der-Leine, Germany, 1911. These buildings demonstrate the fragmentation of the craft of building but also the struggle of architects to retain a level of symbolic meaning, aesthetically or otherwise, that was no longer attainable. It was left to some postwar architects whose work discarded the 19th century's concern for the symbolic expression of structure. Archigram of Great Britain, for one, channeled architecture's rapport with the machine through transparency of form and structure.

At the constructive level, modernism offered architecture a structural frame system, the spatial and tectonic potentialities of which varies as one moves from Le Corbusier's Villa Savoye, Poisy, France (1929–31), to Mies van der Rohe's design for the German Pavilion, World Exhibition, Barcelona (1925). These two buildings disclose different interpretations of modernism: Le Corbusier's lessons of Rome found its outlet in the Dom-ino frame, a modernist state of seeing and making in which construction "plays the role of the subconscious" (p. 87), discussed by Sigfried Giedion five years after the first publication of Le Corbusier's *Vers une Architecture* (Towards a New Architecture) in 1923. Mies instead articulated the architectonics of "exhibition

value," a concept coined by Walter Benjamin. Mies showed one way of internalizing the nihilism of modernity into architecture. In the pavilion, the suggested transparency between modernity and modernism is shattered by recollection of what Baudelaire would have called the archaic half of the art of building; the matter-of-fact quality of column, wall, and roof, but also deconstruction of the metaphysics of the interior space. If modernism succeeded in stimulating various interpretations of the new objectivity, its horizon was minimized when architecture met the city, the site where many facets of capitalism were experienced directly. This much is clear from the Reliance Building (1890–95), designed by Daniel H. Burnham and Company, Chicago, and Mies's Seagram Building (in cooperation with Philip Johnson), New York City (1958). In both cases, design strategies disclose a direct link with the institutions and techniques operating in the city. Each work also articulates a particular architectonic response to the process of accumulation of capital: from production of building as a pure sign to an attempt to renounce the mechanism of the city. To speak of the disjunction between modernity and modernism, it is enough to remember how quickly the "Chicago School" of architecture became a normative style and how soon Mies's curtain wall system was subjected to mass-reproduction and repetition to the point that postmodernists could claim, "less is bore," a satirical twist on Mies's famous dictum, "less is more."

Modernity has constantly been in conflict with its own context—that is, architecture and the city. It has also been in confrontation with any intellectual work suggesting a vision of modernism that cannot accommodate itself to the logic of modernization. If Karl Marx was correct in suggesting that in capitalism, "all that is solid melts into air," then what happens to the art of building for which durability is still one of its essential aspects? It is only through the act of construction that modernization finds the space to operate fully. The disjunction between space and time, pertinent to architecture's resistance to modernization, is addressed by the Austrian architect Adolf Loos. To him, the architect was a Roman builder who had learned Latin. In criticizing both the Deutscher Werkbund and the Vienna Secessionist groups, Loos shunned designing the style (ornament) appropriate to modern times. He also did not value technology as highly as his contemporaries did. The architect's house (*Looshaus*, Michaelplatz, Vienna, 1909–11) is an analogue to the confrontation of the culture of building with modernity. It also speaks for Loos's conviction that only tombs and monuments deserve the name architecture. The interior spaces of most of his houses too were conceived in line with the same beliefs. The idea of *Raumplan* intermingles "place" with space and time. One could suggest that for Loos, modernism was not a matter of subjective speculation; it was rather already there, in the actuality of modernization, necessitating the rethinking of architectural tradition in the matrix of human labor, money, and material, but also in making a space where "things" are reminded of their collective use-value.

In a different time and place, "things" were collected to mark the dialogue between modernism and socialism. The work of Russian Constructivists discloses a different approach to technology and abstraction. In the absence of any organized industrial institutions, and inspired in part by the ideas of Boris Arvatov and other theoreticians, most Constructivists invested in the *ur*-forms of material culture and its laden potentiality. They produced a body of work that desired to resist the reduction of the world of consumption to mere commodities. The uniform use of wooden structural elements in Aleksander Rodchenko's constructs and Konstantin Melinkov's USSR Pavilion at the International Exhibition of Decorative Arts, Paris (1925), does not mimic the rational organization of the world of technology. Here technique is derived from material, and both are perceived to be at the service of material culture. This much is clear from Vesnin brothers' Pravda Building, Moscow (1924), where the act of construction is intertwined with the realm of man–machine–communication, underlining the collective dimension of architecture. Most artists and architects associated with Constructivism assumed that they had the historical opportunity to capture the time/space dialectics of modernization and could freeze its image in a constructed place where the anticipatory potentialities of modernism could avoid ideology. Paradoxically, it was the realm of ideology that made constructivists see and interpret objects differently—different among themselves, but also different from the vision of the so-called vanguard party. That at one point the state realized its own ideological survival in the production of practical objects is clear from its adherence to an instrumental idea of "plan" that slowly diminished the aura of revolution and turned the original energy of constructivist objects into a normative praxis. Not too late, constructivists had to abandon every norm except those associated with the classical language of architecture. This was an uncanny return to the "natural" state of the object, an ideological rebuff to the crisis of the object unleashed by modernization. It also confirmed that in modernism, the ideology of plan could not contradict the instrumental logic of modernization.

If all heroes eventually die, so did the heroes of collectivism and the romantic (i.e., modern) genius. Modernization had its own heroes at stake in the United States: Mickey Mouse and other icons of the culture industry, and their landscape, Disneyland, heralded an image of modernism that was mass-produced and ready to be delivered, but more important, it opted for an economy of sign, where pure exchange value marks the difference between one representative order and another. In this no-man's-land, abstraction and relativism prevails, time is disconnected from its past and future, and everything is memory, if not the memory to become. The stand-stillness of the time, the time that celebrates the end of modernism, saturates the space of imagination too. Many contemporary scholars have called for the "death of the subject," and the "end of history."

In postmodernity, eclecticism returned to the architects' and designers' drawing board, and in search for the archaic types or formal autonomy, architecture lost its "meat." Since the post-war years, architects have moved further from modernity, regardless of how much their work is informed by the experience of modern architecture. The Team X group in the Netherlands, and Louis I. Kahn in the United States, reformulated architecture within its own phenomenal space or charged architecture with civic values, respectively. No design strategy—even those purposed by the advocates of the "greys" or the "whites"—could remain immune to the level of abstraction permeating as technology moved its realm of operation from the technical to the cultural. This development is dramatized today by the perceptual horizon opened by electronic technologies. Thus, the physical distance once governing the abstract aesthetic of early modern art and architecture has been largely neutralized by computer-generated images that have become enmeshed in every aspect of the present world.

The situation of postmodernity endorses devaluation of all values and architecture's reduction to a sign. Nevertheless, commodification and technification of architecture is not total. Although modernism was not conceivable without modernization of the various processes involved in the production of architecture, and even though skills and techniques operating in handwork were mostly discarded during the early stages of modern architecture, there still remains an artisanal residue in architecture that resists architecture's total reduction to a commodity form. In addition, many interpretations of modernism, permeating since the 1960s, suggest that history itself failed modernists. Uncertain as we enter the new millennium, one thing seems to be clear: the historical claim of the project of modernity still hovers above architects and historians like a ghost. What this means is that today, architects and historians are facing a body of work—modern architecture—that was not available to modernists. This necessitates a different approach to the immediate past: instead of total negation or affirmation of modernism, the task ahead should be to inflict the present material world by recollection of the tectonic culture of modern architecture.

GEVORK HARTOONIAN

See also **Aalto, Alvar (Finland); Abstraction; AEG Turbine Factory, Berlin; Archigram; Austria; Avant-Garde; Bauhaus; Bauhaus, Dessau; Behrens, Peter (Germany); Berlin, Germany; Burnham, Daniel (United States); Chicago (IL), United States; Chicago School; Le Corbusier (Jeanneret, Charles-Édouard) (France); Cubism; De Stijl; Deutscher Werkbund; Dom-ino Houses (1914–15); Fagus Werk, Alfeld, Germany; Farnsworth House, Plano, Illinois; Futurism; German Pavilion, Barcelona (1929); Giedion, Sigfried (Switzerland); Glass House, New Canaan, Connecticut; Gropius House, Lincoln, Massachusetts; Gropius, Walter (Germany); Hitchcock, Henry-Russell (United States); International Exhibition of Decorative Arts, Paris (1925); International Style; International Style Exhibition, New York (1932); Johnson, Philip (United States); Kahn, Louis (United States); Loos, Adolf (Austria); Melnikov, Konstantin (Russia); Mies van der Rohe, Ludwig (Germany); New York (NY), United States; Pevsner, Nikolaus (England); Postmodernism; Seagram Building, New York City; Skyscraper; Team X (Netherlands); Vienna Secession; Vesnin, Alexander, Leonid, and Viktor (Russia); Villa Savoye, Poissy, France; Wright, Frank Lloyd (United States)**

Further Reading

Arendt, Hannah, *The Human Condition*, Chicago: University of Chicago Press, 1974

Benjamin, Walter, *Selected Writings, vol. 3, 1935–1938*, Cambridge: The Beknap Press, 2002

Baudelaire, Charles, *The Painter of Modern Life and Other Essays*, translated by Jonathan Mayne, New York: Da Capo Press, 1986

Berman, Marshall, *All that is Solid Melts into Air: The Experience of Modernity*, London: Verso, 1982

Buck-Morss, Susan, *Dreamworld and Catastrophe: The Passing of Mass Utopia in East and West*, Cambridge, Massachusetts: MIT Press, 2000

Cacciari, Massimo, *Architecture and Nihilism: On the Philosophy of Modern Architecture*, New Haven, Connecticut: Yale University Press, 1993

Calinescu, Matei, *Five Faces of Modernity: Modernism, Avant-Garde, Decadence, Kitsch, Postmodernism*, Durham, North Carolina: Duke University Press, 1987

Clark, T. J., *Farewell to an Idea: Episodes from a History of Modernism*, New Haven, Connecticut: Yale University Press, 1999

Foster, Hal (editor), *The Anti-Aesthetic: Essays on Postmodern Culture*, Port Townsend, Washington: Bay Press, 1983

Frampton, Kenneth, *Labour, Work and Architecture*, New York: Phaidon Press, 2002

Frampton, Kenneth, *Modern Architecture: A Critical History*, London: Thames and Hudson, 1980

Giedion, Sigfried, *Building in France, Building in Iron, Building in Ferro-Concrete*, Santa Monica: The Getty Center for the History of Art and the Humanities, 1995

Hartoonian, Gevork, *Modernity and its Other: A Post-Script to Contemporary Architecture*, College Station: Texas A & M University Press, 1997

Hartoonian, Gevork, *Ontology of Construction: On Nihilism of Technology in Theories of Modern Architecture*, Cambridge: Cambridge University Press, 1994

Heynen, Hilde, *Architecture and Modernity*, Cambridge, Massachusetts: MIT Press, 1999

Herrmann, Wolfgang, *In What Style Should We Build: The German Debate on Architectural Style*, Santa Monica, California: The Getty Centre for the History of Art and the Humanities, 1992

Hitchcock, Henry-Russell, and Philip Johnson, *The International Style*, New York: Norton, 1966

Pevsner, Nikolaus, *Pioneers of Modern Design*, New York: Penguin Books, 1976

Tafuri, Manfredo, *Architecture and Utopia: Design and Capitalist Development*, Cambridge, Massachusetts: MIT Press, 1976

Vattimo, Gianni, *The End of Modernity*, Baltimore, Maryland: The John Hopkins University Press, 1988

Venturi, Robert, *Complexity and Contradiction in Architecture*, New York: The Museum of Modern Art, 1996

Williams, Raymond, *The Politics of Modernism*, London: Verso, 1989

MOLNÁR, FARKAS 1897–1945

Architect, Hungary

Farkas Molnár was an outstanding figure of the European avant-garde movement. After two years of graphic art studies at the Academy of Fine Arts in Budapest, he enrolled in the Architectural School of the Technical University in Budapest in 1917. Because of his involvement in leftist political actions, he had to leave Hungary after the fall of the Republic of Councils in 1920. After a study tour in Italy, he became a Bauhaus student in Weimar, Germany, in 1921. He took the graphic arts course of Johannes Itten.

In 1922, the Bauhaus published a set of lithographs by Molnár and his friend Henrik Stefán in the album *Italia 1921* (Italy 1921). Soon, he became involved in theater art and architectural design, working in Oskar Schlemmer's workshop and in Walter Gropius's architectural practice with his Hungarian friend Fred Forbát, who joined the Bauhaus before his arrival. Influenced by lectures given by Theo van Doesburg, he organized the KURI group (1922) to unite avant-garde artistic efforts in constructive art and functionalist architecture. The name of the group came from the title of its manifesto, the initials of the German words *konstruktiv* (constructive), *utilitär* (utilitarian), *rational*, and *international*. Molnár's "Red Cube" project (1923) was an early attempt to realize his ideas in architecture: a two-story family house with a flat roof, minimal footing, and flexible room connections in the interior. The house was connected to the garden by a pergola. It was planned for the housing estate *Am Horn* and was shown at the Bauhaus Exhibition in Weimar (1923). With its radical geometrical reduction, the design represented a new direction in architecture and was the starting point for Molnár's later villa projects. He experimented with mobile partitions and new possibilities of room connections in his U-Theater project (1923) as well. He published the book *Die Bühne im Bauhaus* (1925; The Stage in the Bauhaus) in collaboration with Oskar Schlemmer and László Moholy-Nagy in the series of *Bauhausbücher* (Bauhaus Books). From 1923 on, his designs and articles appeared in the publications of Hungarian avant-garde (e.g. *MA, Munka, 100%*, and *Tér és Forma*), introducing and propagating constructivist art and functionalist architecture.

In 1925, when the Bauhaus moved to Dessau, Molnár returned to Budapest and continued his studies in architecture at the Technical University, graduating in 1928. He became a leading figure of the functionalist movement in Hungary. His aesthetic views were closer to those of Le Corbusier than to those of the *Neues Bauen* in Germany. He proposed standardized, mass-produced housing with affordable minimal apartments and communal spaces based on a new social structure in which the traditional family would lose its importance. All his friends were on the political Left. They connected the goal of a new architecture with questions of political and social changes.

In 1929, Molnár participated at the Congrès Internationaux d'Architecture Moderne (CIAM), which focused on the minimum dwelling in Frankfurt. He became a member of the Comité International pour la Réalisation des Problèmes d'Architecture Contemporaine (CIRPAC) and organized the Hungarian CIAM group, whose most important members were József Fischer, Pál Ligeti, Máté Major, Fred Forbát, György Rácz, and Gábor Preisich. The group met regularly in Budapest until 1938. In the fall of 1931, the group showed the utopian KOLHÁZ project, a collective house for 800 people in the Household and Interior Design Exhibition in Budapest. In 1932, Molnár introduced his similarly utopian KOLVÁROS project, a schematic design of a collective city in the Tamás Gallery, Budapest. The social criticism of the third CIAM exhibition, "House, City, Society" (1932, Iparcsarnok, Budapest), was even more radical, confronting the existing unhealthy housing situation of poor people in Budapest with healthy social housing for low-income people, a vision of the modern architecture.

Molnár worked between 1928 and 1931 in Pál Ligeti's office, and together they realized the first modern functionalist building in Hungary, the Delej Villa at 11 Mihály Street (1929) in Budapest. Molnár's own apartment of minimal footing (52 square meters) was also in the villa. In the interior, he achieved a high grade of flexibility by sliding partitions. In furniture design, he used new materials, such as plastic or Bakelite, and exclusive materials, such as ebony. Furniture, apartment, building, city, and region design were all logical components in his systematic thinking.

From 1931 on, Molnár worked on his own, occasionally collaborating with members of the CIAM group. He built a number of private villas for middle-class intellectuals who were open to new ideas, but he never received any commission for a public building. The villa at 2/a Lejtő Street (1932) in Budapest was built for one family. It has a cubic volume enlarged by two half cylinders, the smaller of which contains the staircase and covers exactly one-fourth of one side of the building and the larger of which extends the living room on the first floor; the large roof terrace, accessible from the sleeping rooms on the second floor, covers exactly half the next side of the building. The four-story apartment house at 4/b Lotz Károly Street (1933) in Budapest has a compact volume as well as a flat roof and horizontal stripes of windows and balconies. The Molnárs' new two-story apartment was also to be found in this villa. The sliding walls were made possible a new "dynamic space connection," as László Moholy-Nagy described it. The idea of identical and connectable cells for man and woman had already appeared in the "Red Cube" project. Now the idea was elaborated in detail. The color scheme for the walls, the textiles, and the furniture was carefully planned.

Molnár frequently used his own constructivist as well as other artists' figurative decorations in the entrance areas of his villas (apartment house at Pasaréti Street, Budapest, 1936; villa at Trombitás Street, Budapest, 1936). The light elegance of the villa at 7/a Csévi köz (1935, with József Fischer) in Budapest made the most of the usual reinforced-concrete structures of Molnár's buildings. He occasionally worked with Béla Sámsondi Kiss, an inventive engineer of reinforced-concrete structures. Molnár's idea of the collective house became partly realized in the block of employee apartments for the OTI Worker Hospital (1936, with József Fischer) in Pestújhely.

In 1937 Molnár was elected the secretary of the CIAM-OST, but a year later, under growing political pressure, the CIAM group dissolved. Molnár abandoned his leftist ideas and moved in the opposite direction. The villa at 8 Mese Street (1937) in Budapest indicated that his architectural principles changed as well. He became interested in the aesthetics of Hungarian peasant architecture and started to use building forms and materials (high-pitched roof and rubble stone) that were never accepted by orthodox modernists. His last project, the Church of the Holy Land, was designed in 1938 and was between 1940–49 partly finished. It had a large oval plan and was to be covered with a concrete shell. In the interior, Molnár planned to accommodate replicas of the holy sites in Jerusalem. Molnár died when his home was hit by a bomb during the siege of Budapest in 1945.

KATALIN MORAVÁNSZKY-GYÖNGY AND ÁKOS MORAVÁNSZKY

Biography

Born in Pécs, Hungary, 21 June 1897. Attended, Fine Arts College, Budapest; studied at the Hungarian Palatine Joseph Technical University, Budapest, but did not earn a degree; studied at the Bauhaus, Weimar, Germany 1921–25; worked in the office of Walter Gropius, Weimar 1921–25; resumed studies in Budapest 1925; graduated 1928. Private practice, Budapest from 1931. President, Hungarian chapter of CIAM 1929–38; appointed Hungarian delegate to CIAM 1929; secretary, CIAM-

Ost, formed to organize the architects of eastern Europe 1937. Died in Budapest, 12 January 1945.

Selected Works

Red Cube (project), Bauhaus exhibition, Weimar, 1923
U-Theater (project), 1923
Delej Villa at 11 Mihály Street (with Pál Ligeti), Budapest, 1929
KOLVÁROS (project), 1932
Villa at 2a Lejtő Street, Budapest, 1932
Apartment House at 4b Lotz Károly Street, Budapest, 1933
Villa at 7a Csévi köz, Budapest (with József Fischer), 1935
Apartments, OTI Worker Hospital, Pestújhely, (with József Fischer), 1936
Apartment House at 7 Pasaréti Street, Budapest, 1936
Villa at Trombitás Street, Budapest, 1936
Villa at 8 Mese Street, Budapest, 1937
Hungarian Holy Land Church (unfinished), Budapest, 1940–49

Selected Publication

Die Bühne im Bauhaus (with L. Moholy-Nagy and O. Schlemmer), 1925

Further Reading

Ferkai, András, "Hungarian Architecture between the Wars," in *The Architecture of Historic Hungary*, edited by Dora Wiebenson and József Sisa, Cambridge, Massachusetts: MIT Press, 1998
Mezei, Otto, "Farkas Molnár," in *Wechsel wirkungen: Ungarische Avantgarde in der Weimarer Republik* [Interactions: Hungarian Avant-Garde in the Weimar Republic] edited by Hubertus Gassner, Marburg, Germany: Jonas, 1986
Molnár, Farkas, "A lakásépités racionalizálása" [The Rationalization of Housing], *Tér és Forma* 3 (1928)
Molnár, Farkas, *Új Épités: Molnár Farkas Munkái, 1923–1933* [Farkas Molnár's Works, 1923–1933], Budapest: Magyar Műhely Szövetség, 1933

MONEO VALLÉS, JOSÉ RAFAEL 1937–

Architect, Spain

José Rafael Moneo Vallés is one of the most influential architects in Spain today. His career has served as a model for numerous younger architects both in Spain and abroad. Moneo was known in architectural circles since the 1970s not only for his role as an architect but also for his theoretical contributions to the avant-garde publication originating in Barcelona, *Arquitecturas bis*, and his work with Peter Eisenman's Institute for Architecture and Urban Studies. He was relatively unknown outside these spheres, a condition suffered by almost all Spanish architects of that time. His name became more familiar to American audiences when he was appointed chair of Harvard's Graduate School of Design in 1985. This coincided with a period of intense activity at his "atelier" in Madrid. The acceptance of a position at Harvard reflects Moneo's deep commitment to teaching and investigation that has consistently lived alongside his love for building.

In Rafael Moneo's subtle and varied oeuvre, the importance of the site, the context, and the mission of the building all inform the resultant structure. His projects display a deep understanding of the craft of building. His apparent rejecting of "type" necessitates a careful reading of his buildings that have multiple layers of interpretation. Moneo's buildings must be understood on the basis of their elements rather than their major forms. The underlying concerns and interests are ever present, but their formal expression takes on a variety of images.

One of Moneo's first projects that gained national attention was an apartment building (1970) along the Urumea River in San Sebastian, Spain, in collaboration with the three architects of Marquet, Unzurrúnzaga, and Zulaica. There is a clever juxtaposition between the horizontal bands of windows and the vertical pull of the curved bays. The building is located on the riverbank in a prominent position. Its pitched roof and dark brick respond to the neighboring buildings.

The Bankinter building (1977), offices and banking facilities located on a main axis in Madrid, is still considered one of the architect's most outstanding works. It is sited behind an existing small palace on a difficult plot. The architect maintains a principal facade parallel to the street, almost forming a backdrop for the smaller mansion in the forefront. The irregular shape of the building fits the site neatly, and the careful use of brick and the oversize frieze panels on the upper story seem to pay homage to history and especially to the works of Louis Sullivan.

The National Museum of Roman Art (1980–85) in Mérida, Spain, launched Moneo's international reputation. Although immediately inspiring to all who enter the main exhibition space with its dramatic arches, this building has many complexities. The museum was constructed of brick, in the spirit of Roman building, and it fits within the modest scale of the city through its careful handling of the different facades. Moreover, the building is in dialogue with the still-powerful remnants of ancient Rome nearby. The exterior buttressed walls of the main hall indicate the rhythm of the arches inside. The dimensions, color, and positioning of the brick grant a sense of permanence and timelessness to the space. Elevated walkways allow the visitor to view the works on the upper level while experiencing the whole nave. The light that enters through the windows at the roofline adds to the drama of the main hall and intensifies the visitor's perception of space.

The Kursaal Cultural Center (1999) in San Sebastian, Spain, comprises two enormous glass cubes that contain performing arts facilities, cultural facilities, and the necessary support services. The extensive use of glass appears as a departure from the more traditional materials that Moneo used in the past. However, his choice is clearly understood when one witnesses the dramatic change from solid mass in daylight to glowing cubes at night. In this project, he could have continued the normal cityscape of San Sebastian right to the beach site. However, from the placement of the Kursaal Cultural Center and the formal solutions adopted, it becomes apparent that the desire was to highlight the natural attributes of the site—the beach, the river, and the sea. The simple yet bold forms employed, the emphasis on materials, and the response to the site and context all illustrate ongoing, deep concerns of the architect that are present in all his works.

Moneo was increasingly called on for international museum commissions, including the Pilar and Joan Miró Foundation (1993) in Palma de Mallorca; the Davis Museum (1993) at Wellesley College, Massachusetts; the Museums of Modern Art and Architecture (1997) in Stockholm, Sweden; and the Audrey Jones Beck Building (2000) of the Museum of Fine Arts in Houston, Texas.

Among other noteworthy projects throughout Moneo's career are the headquarters (1988) for the Prevision Española insurance company in Seville, the new Atocha Train Station (1992) in Madrid, a city hall (1998) in Murcia, and the Our Lady of the Angels Cathedral of Los Angeles (2002).

MARTHA THORNE

See also **Spain**

Biography

Born in 1937 in the village of Tudela in the Navarre region of northern Spain. Studied architecture at the Polytechnic University of Madrid; received degree in 1961. Practical experience gained in the ateliers of Spanish architect Francisco Javier Saenz de Oiza and the Danish architect Jørn Utzon before opening his own office. Spent two years as a fellow at the Spanish Academy in Rome. Taught in the 1960s in Madrid, until offered a tenured position at the School of Architecture in Barcelona.

Taught at Cooper Union (1976–77) and Princeton University (1982). Appointed Chair of Harvard's Graduate School of design in 1985, a position he fulfilled until 1990. Received numerous prizes, including the Brunner Memorial Prize of the American Academy of Arts and Letters (1993) and the Pritzker Architecture (1996).

Selected Works

Apartment building (with Marquet, Unzurrúnzaga, and Zulaica), San Sebastian, Spain, 1970
Bankinter Building, Madrid, Spain 1977
National Museum of Roman Art, Mérida, Spain, 1985
Atocha Train Station, Madrid, Spain, 1992
Pilar and Joan Miró Foundation, Palma de Mallorca, 1993
Davis Museum, Wellesley College, Massachusetts, 1993
Museums of Modern Art and Architecture, Stockholm, Sweden, 1997
Kursaal Cultural Center, San Sebastian, Spain, 1999
Audrey Jones Beck Building, Museum of Fine Arts in Houston, Texas, 2000
Our Lady of the Angels Cathedral, Los Angeles California, 2002

Selected Publications

"On Internationalism," *Casabella*, 61 (November 1997), p. 3
"On Typology," *Oppositions* 13 (Summer 1978), pp. 22–44
"The Solitude of Buildings," *Casabella* 63 (April 1999), pp. 30–31
"Third Manfredo Tafuri Lecture: Rafael Moneo: Architecture, Critics, History," *Casabella* 62 (February 1998), pp. 42–51
"Paradigmas fin de siglo: las noventa, entre la fragmentación y la compacidad" (End of the Century Paradigms, fragmentation and compactness), *Arquitectura Viva* 66 (May–June 1999), pp. 17–24, English translation, pp. 110–111

Further Reading

Frampton, Kenneth, "Rafael Moneo," *Architecture* 83 (January 1994)
Nakamura Toshio (editor), *A + U Rafael Moneo* 227 (August 1989)
"Rafael Moneo, 1986–1992," *A & V Monografías* 36 (July–August 1992)
Levene, Richard C., and Fernando Márquez Cecilia (editors), "Rafael Moneo, 1987–1994," *El Croquis* 64 (1994)
Levene, Richard C., and Fernando Márquez Cecilia (editors), "Rafael Moneo 1995–2000," *El Croquis* 98 (1999)

Moneo, Rafael, and Johan Martelius, *Modern Museum and Swedish Museum of Architecture in Stockholm*, Stockholm: Arkitektur Fårlag and Rasyer Förlag, 1998

Thorne, Martha, *Rafael Moneo, The Audrey Jones Beck Building, Museum of Fine Arts Houston*, Stuttgart: Edition Axel Menges, 2000

MONTREAL, QUEBEC

For students of 20th-century architecture, Montreal's greatest claim to fame is its heroic architectural designs of the 1960s. For international visitors, its attraction lies in its vibrant urban life and in the diversity of its premegacity districts and landmarks. Facing the harbor that was recently rehabilitated for tourism and entertainment, the old mercantile city looks very much as it did around 1910, at a time when a second downtown developed further west, around Phillips, and Dominion Squares and along east-west arteries. This area includes Boulevard René Lévesque (formerly Dorchester), a popular business address since its enlargement in the mid-1950s; St. Catherine Street, the heart of retail and mass entertainment; and Sherbrooke Street, host to cultural and educational institutions. Three upscale residential districts of great architectural significance—the Golden Square Mile, Westmount, and Outremont—occupy the southern, western, and northern slopes of Mount Royal, respectively. To the east, the French lower-middle-class district of Plateau Mont Royal offers a dense fabric of duplex or triplex flats with unique *enfilades* of individual exterior staircases.

Shaped by architects, builders, and clients born or trained in Scotland, England, France, and the United States, these districts remind tourists of Edinburgh, London, Paris, and New York City. Cosmopolitanism has been a major defining factor for this former French settlement (founded in 1642) and British colony, located 40 miles from the U.S. border, which even native-born historians have deemed a *ville d'emprunts* (a city of borrowings) (Linteau, 1992). Other historical forces have shaped Montreal's 20th-century architecture. Because of its relatively weak political status and major role as Canada's—and today specifically Quebec's—financial, transportation, and manufacturing center, commissions from entrepreneurs, rather than public buildings, have taken center stage in its growth process. The dominating influence of the Catholic clergy over the French-speaking majority until the 1960s explains why convents and eclectic parish churches are bigger and more conspicuous than in any other large North American city.

As the United States began supplanting Britain as its main economic partner, Canada was the first country to import American architectural expertise. The transformation of Montreal into a modern metropolis began with the building boom of the late 1880s, especially with two designs by New York architects: Bruce Price's Windsor Station, and Babb, Cook and Willard's eight-story New York Life Insurance Company Building. The 1890 founding of the Province of Quebec Association of Architects was mainly a reaction against this U.S. "invasion."

Around 1910 and in the 1920s, Montreal and its suburbs experienced two periods of intense building activity and demographic expansion, with the population reaching the one million mark in 1931. With the exception of Westmount and the industrial town of Maisonneuve, which implemented cohesive urban and architectural images along British and City Beautiful lines, respectively, bourgeois reformism was unable to defeat the apathy and demagoguery of local politicians, and Montreal's growth was not regulated by comprehensive planning. Nonetheless, the first three decades of the 20th century have left a rich legacy, with Anglophone architects mostly in charge of commercial work and their French-speaking colleagues taking a majority most of the public commissions, each catering to the residential, civic, educational, and religious needs of their linguistic group.

Around 1910 a distinctively North American version of Beaux-Arts classicism was exhibited in high-end commercial work by New Yorkers: McKim, Mead and White's awe-inspiring addition to the Bank of Montreal (1905) and adjacent Royal Trust Building (1912), whose tripartite composition set new standards for Canada's commercial architecture; Carrère and Hastings's Transportation Building (1912), whose T-shaped concourse anticipated the interior street network of the 1960s; and Warren and Wetmore's Ritz Carlton Hotel (1912). The same subdued and elegant style was used by local architects for major cultural institutions—in particular Edward and William Maxwell's Montreal Art Gallery (1912) and Eugène Payette's Bibliothèque Saint-Sulpice (1915). On the British side, Scottish émigré Percy Nobbs played a major role as a critic of Canadian architecture and promoter of the Garden City movement; for McGill University, he designed the Scottish Baronial Student Union Hall (1906; today McCord Museum) and Shavian Macdonald Engineering Building (1908).

In the 1920s Americanism was channeled by local designers trained in the United States, especially Ross and Macdonald, Canada's largest firm at the time. The 130-foot height limit was finally repealed. Skyscrapers ranged from the ultraclassical Sun Life headquarters (1914–18, 1923–25, and 1929–31) by Darling and Pearson of Toronto to York and Sawyer's Greco-Florentine Royal Bank and Ernest Barrott's trendy Aldred Building. Although advanced from a technical and programmatic standpoint, Montreal's architecture remained stylistically conservative. Three *diplômés* of the Paris Ecole des Beaux-Arts were among those pointing in new directions. As evidenced in his Généreux Public Baths (1926), Jean-Omer Marchand was an articulate exponent of Julien Guadet's constructive rationalism. Ernest Cormier designed Canada's first truly modern institutional building, the mammoth main pavilion of the Université de Montréal (1927, 1942) the two dates are necessary which combined baroque planning with Wright-inspired brickwork, the monumental with the picturesque, the comb-shaped superblock with the tower ideal. Along with Eaton's penthouse restaurant (1930) by French architect Jacques Carlu, Cormier's own house (1931) is Montreal's Art Deco treasure. And during the mid-1930s, although the economic depression had particularly devastating effects on Montreal's building industry, Marcel Parizeau was able to acclimate the machine aesthetic in his elegant designs for Outremont townhouses.

In the early 1940s Bauhaus design methods and social agenda were introduced at McGill University, and a municipal City Planning Department finally was created. Nonetheless, the mainstreaming of modern urbanism and architecture in Montreal occurred only in 1957 with the unveiling of two ambitious

Bank of Montreal, Winnipeg branch, designed by McKim, Mead and White (1911)
© Museum of the City of New York, from the Monograph of the Work of McKim, Mead, and
White, Vol. IV, plate 355 (1911)

projects for the downtown, Les Habitations Jeanne Mance and Place Ville-Marie. The first, a public-housing complex, was planned locally by Rother, Bland, Trudeau and designed by Greenspoon, Freedlander and Dunne, and it would remain Montreal's only radical urban renewal operation. The second, entrusted to the New York architect/developer team of I.M. Pei and William Zeckendorf, brought to fruition an air rights development project first envisioned in 1913. Its abstract cruciform tower, vast esplanade, and gallery of boutiques connected with Central Station were harbingers of a new integrated urban core suited to cold climatic conditions.

In the 1960s Montreal experienced rapid social and political modernization and a rise in its population's standard of living. Modernizing transportation infrastructures became a priority for the strong municipal government headed by Jean Drapeau. While urban highways gave rise to tremendous suburban sprawl of a particularly sorry nature, the Metro opened in 1966, with stations of varied character entrusted to major architects and artists. In Reyner Banham's (1976) words, the entire downtown rapidly became a megastructure, "unified by a subterranean network of shopping malls, pedestrian tunnels, Metro stations and parking silos, like eight kilometers of an underground root sys-

tem of which the office towers and hotels above ground were mere outgrowths." Foreign competence was called on with mixed results; while Luigi Moretti and Pierluigi Nervi's reinforced-concrete Stock Exchange Tower (1964) contributed to disfiguring Victoria Square, Mies van der Rohe's Westmount Square (1966) provided a sensitive response to increased density.

With its facade of curved precast concrete elements, the most original high-rise design was the Château Champlain Hotel (1966) by Roger d'Astous, a former apprentice of Frank Lloyd Wright. The most awesome element of the *ville souterraine* (the subterranean network of passages and shops connected to mass transportations.) was Raymond Affleck's Place Bonaventure (1968), a fortress in *béton brut* that superimposed a mega-exhibition hall, a merchandise mart, and a surprisingly intimate 400-bedroom hotel at its top. The climax of Montreal's mega-structure era was its 1967 World's Fair. "Man and His World" pointed to the future with Buckminster Fuller's geodesic U.S. Pavilion and its "multiplicity of levels, emphasis on fun or *ludique* experiences, stylish Archigram-type colors, people in complex artificial environments, visual information saturation" (Banham, 1976). Derived from his master's thesis at McGill, the fair's housing showcase was Moshe Safdie's Habitat; its staggered silhouette established a striking dialog with the harbor's grain elevators, once celebrated by Gropius and Le Corbusier. As Montreal's most widely discussed landmark, Habitat established a model for cellular prefabrication and residential design.

In the 1970s Montreal definitely had relinquished its national leadership to Toronto and began experiencing an economic and demographic slowdown from which it has yet to recover. Built for the 1976 Summer Olympics, Frenchman Roger Taillibert's stadium and the high-rise athlete housing by d'Astous were ultimate manifestations of Drapeau's *folie des grandeurs*. Influenced by contemporary European theory, a new generation of designers condemned the transformation of Montreal's public space into a "commodity" and sought to reevaluate the traditional grid determined by the old farm boundaries, in which hierarchical networks of avenues, streets, and alleys have primacy over individual buildings. Their leader was the artist/architect and Université de Montréal professor Melvin Charney. This trend for an urban architecture of fragments—mending new buildings with existing ones—was best exemplified in ARCOP's (Architect's in Co-Partnership) Maison Alcan office complex (1984). It went hand in hand with a strong involvement in preservation, spearheaded by such organizations as Heritage Montreal and DOCOMOMO (International Association For the Documentation of the Conservation of the Modern Movement) Québec, as well as adaptive reuse.

How has Montreal architecture fared? With a few exceptions, such as the Marathon Building (1991) by New York's Kohn Pederson Fox, Postmodern office buildings have been mediocre and inflated, and the best commercial designs are interiors for shops and restaurants, such as Luc Laporte's Lux (1985). Jacques Rousseau's much-publicized Maison Coloniale (1990) is a marginal experiment in an undistinguished housing market. Meanwhile, a new crop of museums, theaters, and university buildings have strengthened Montreal's cultural scene; best known are the Pointe-à-Caillère archeological museum (1992) by Romanian immigrant Dan Hanganu, and the Canadian Center for Architecture (1988) by Peter Rose, with Phyllis Lambert acting as consulting architect. These designs take their cue from the austere grey stone, which had marked Montreal before the 1880s. If the many political and economic uncertainties hanging over this metropolitan center of three million inhabitants do not augur well for another major building boom, Montreal, with the impetus provided by the Canadian Centre for Architecture, has become one of the cities in the world in which architecture, past and present, is most studied, discussed, and appreciated in professional, academic, and journalistic circles.

ISABELLE GOURNAY

Further Reading

Banham, Reyner, "Megacity Montreal," in *Megastructure: Urban Futures of the Recent Past*, by Banham, New York: Harper and Row, and London: Thames and Hudson, 1976

Bergeron, Claude, *Architecture du XXᵉ siècle au Québec*, Architecture of the XXth century on Puebec Montreal: Méridien, 1989

Charney, Melvin, "The Montrealness of Montreal," *Architectural Review* (May 1980)

Choko, Marc H., *Les grandes places publiques de Montréal*, Montreal: Méridien, 1987

Choko, Marc H., *Les habitations Jeanne-Mance*, Montreal: Saint-Martin, 1995

Communauté Urbaine de Montréal, Service de Planification du Territoire, *Répertoire d'architecture traditionnelle sur le territoire de la communauté urbaine de Montréal*, Montreal: Service, 1980–87

Couturier, Marie-Alain, *Marcel Parizeau*, Montreal: L'Arbre, 1945

Forget, Madeleine, *Les gratte-ciel de Montréal*, Montreal: Méridien, 1990

Gournay, Isabelle (editor), *Ernest Cormier et l'Universite de Montreal*, Montreal: Centre Canadien d'Architecture, 1990; as *Ernest Cormier and the Université de Montréal*, Cambridge, Massachusetts: MIT Press, 1990

Gournay, Isabelle, and France Vanlaethem (editors), *Montréal Metropolis: 1880–1930*, Toronto: Stoddart, 1998

Kalman, Harold, *A History of Canadian Architecture*, 2 vols., Toronto and New York: Oxford University Press, 1994

Linteau, Paul André, *Histoire de Montréal depuis la Confédération*, Montreal: Boréal, 1992

Marsan, Jean-Claude, *Montréal en évolution: Historique du dévélopment de l'architecture et de l'environnement Montréalais*, Montreal: Fides, 1974; 3rd edition, Laval, Quebec: Méridien, 1994; as *Montreal in Evolution: Historical Analysis of the Development of Montreal's Architecture and Urban Environment*, Montreal: McGill-Queen's University Press, 1981

Pepall, Rosalind M., *Construction d'un Musée Beaux-Arts, Montréal, 1912; Building a Beaux-Arts Museum* (bilingual French-English edition), Montreal: Montreal Museum of Fine Arts, 1986

Remillard, François, and Brian Merrett, *L'architecture de Montréal: Guide des styles et des bâtiments*, Montreal: Meridien, 1990; as *Montreal Architecture: A Guide to Styles and Buildings*, Montreal: Meridian, 1990

Wagg, Susan, *Percy Erskine Nobbs: Architecte, artiste, artisan; Percy Erskine Nobbs: Architect, Artist, Craftsman* (bilingual French-English edition), Kingston: McGill-Queen's University Press, 1982

Wagg, Susan, *Ernest Isbell Barott, architecte: Une introduction; Ernest Isbell Barott, Architect: An Introduction* (bilingual French-English edition), Montreal: Canadian Centre for Architecture, 1985

MONUMENT TO THE THIRD INTERNATIONAL

Designed by Vladimir Tatlin, 1920
Moscow, Russia

Although unrealized at full scale, the Monument to the Third International (1920), designed by Vladimir Tatlin (1885–1953), a protagonist of the Soviet avant-garde, was a notable, influential project. As a symbol of modern technology, revolution, and a utopian future, the monument was intended to signal a renewed society, based on Communist tenets, through its form and function. Tatlin's materialist construction synthesized art and architecture and explored the nature, or "culture," of materials. The architect professed that its glass and iron components would fulfill both structural and metaphoric roles and imbue the project with contemporary significance.

The Monument to the Third International was commissioned in 1919 by the Department of Fine Arts as part of Lenin's Plan for Monumental Propaganda, a division overseen partly by Tatlin. Like other artists after the October Revolution, Tatlin offered his services to the nascent state and directed his energy toward creating institutions and objects useful to the government and the proletariat. His tower, commemorating the founding of the Third International by the Bolsheviks in 1919, rejected Lenin's directive of disseminating realistic heroic statuary and instead attempted to alter the physical and social landscape. Planned as the center of world revolution, the tower was an abstract monument to an idea.

The monument's framework was a conical double spiral of iron, tilted at a 45-degree angle in accordance with the earth's axis, and was meant to rise 1300 feet over Petrograd's Neva River. Suspended in vertical alignment within the external skeletal frame were immense geometric volumes, each of glass, that coupled human activities with celestial rhythms. A ground-level cube that rotated once annually was planned for legislative assemblies. A pyramid intended for executive functions spun once a month, while a narrow cylinder, a control center for news, manifestos, and proclamations, rotated weekly. The uppermost hemispheric space, which likely revolved daily, housed an open-air screen on which news could be presented at night and a special apparatus to project a daily motto onto the clouds. The inclined spiral, bursting forth from the earth and reaching for the stars, and the cosmologically determined kinetic forms within proclaimed the dynamism and possibilities of the new age.

The symbolic and historical attributes of the spiral presumably informed Tatlin's design decisions because the employment of the motif was formal rather than structural. Traditionally a symbol of aspiration and utopianism, change, and progress, the spiral has precedent in images of the Tower of Babel, ziggurats, and church spires. The monument's cosmological elements were most likely derived from the space/time theories posited by Tatlin's friend, visionary futurist poet Velimir Khlebnikov. Although many other influences have been posited by scholars, such as the Eiffel Tower, ship masts, and the human body, the dearth of documentation has left Tatlin's intentions merely speculative.

The first of several small-scale models of the tower (which merely reflected the volumetric and spatial forms but not the constructive ideas of the final version) was 20 feet high; built of wood, wire, metal, and oil paper; and held together with 2000 hand-hewn wooden pegs. Built manually in Tatlin's Moscow studio with the help of three assistants, it was exhibited in Moscow in December 1920 at the Eighth Congress of Soviets, adorned with a red banner that pronounced, "Engineers, create new forms." As an artist/engineer, Tatlin intended both to invent new forms and to bring them to technical fruition. By conjoining art with engineering and ideology with technology and exploiting the intrinsic quality of materials, the tower became a prominent symbol of the machine age. Tatlin was pivotal to the evolution of Russian Constructivism, and the Monument to the Third International is considered the epitome of that abstract art movement. Concerned with rationally and truthfully constructing art with modern industrial materials and technologies, Constructivism stimulated the 20th-century urge to abstract and manipulate diverse materials. Tatlin's intuitive, utopian, and socially responsible approach diverged somewhat from the emphasis on pure engineering championed by the mainstream adherents of Constructivism.

The tower model was widely exhibited in the Soviet Union in the early 1920s and was re-created for the 1925 Exposition Internationale des Arts Decoratifs et Industriels Modernes in Paris, where it was awarded a gold medal. To Soviet avant-garde contemporaries, such as Alexander Rodchenko, El Lissitzky, and Konstantin Melnikov, the tower symbolized urban modernity and the potential of the machine (and art) to create a new sociocultural order. In the West, particularly in Germany at the Bauhaus and among Dadaists, the mechanistic, nonart character of the monument and its appropriateness as an emblem of the scientific and technological achievements of the modern age were lauded. Some, however, criticized it as an architecturally infeasible romanticization of the machine, and Leon Trotsky condemned it as impractical and too abstract. By the late 1920s, the ideological meaning of the monument was fractured. It came to represent not only the defeat of Soviet avant-garde art because it, along with numerous other projects, was never built, but it also signified the failed utopianism of the Socialist experiment.

The Monument to the Third International was Tatlin's most significant project. He began his career as a painter, inspired by Russian icons and folk art as well as impressionism, futurism, and Cubism, modes that swept Russia in the first decades of the 20th century. Following a 1913 visit to Picasso's studio in Paris, where he witnessed the origins of collage and assemblage, Tatlin began to explore three-dimensional construction in space. His complex, purely abstract Counter-reliefs (1913–16), assembled of various materials, signal the emergence of a preoccupation with materials, volume, and construction, ideas that reached their apex in the monument. Throughout the 1920s, Tatlin produced objects for everyday use (e.g. clothing and stoves), designed stage sets, taught numerous design courses, and attempted to fly his man-powered ornithopter *Letatlin* (1932). With the advent of socialist realism in 1932, Tatlin and his tower were virtually forgotten in the Soviet Union and the West. It was not until the 1960s that the Monument to the Third International was rediscovered. Tatlin's tower reemerged as an icon to social consciousness, utopian idealism, and artistic potential. Emblematic of its culture and representing the fusion of revolutionary art and ideology, it has become an important subject of scholarly research and public exhibition.

ANDREA FOGGLE PLOTKIN

See also **Constructivism**

Further Reading

Sources that made the postwar generation aware of Tatlin and the Russian avant-garde are Andersen and Gray. Milner's critical biography analyzes the monument's multivalent ideological program and its formal qualities, as do Elderfield and Lodder (1987). Zhadova's volume is an essential sourcebook of resources previously hidden in Soviet archives that includes illustrations, Tatlin's writings, contemporary commentary, and scholarly criticism. Lodder's (1983) social history of Constructivism suggests that Tatlin helped develop the formal language of that movement. Roman explores the tower's impact on the West while Rowell discusses Tatlin's materialist sensibility.

Andersen, Troels, *Vladimir Tatlin*, Stockholm: Moderna Museet, 1968

Elderfield, John, "The Line of Free Men: Tatlin's 'Tower' and the Age of Invention," *Studio International*, 178 (November 1969)

Gray, Camilla, *The Great Experiment: Russian Art 1863–1922*, London: Thames and Hudson, and New York: Abrams, 1962; new edition, as *The Russian Experiment in Art, 1863–1922*, New York: Abrams, 1970; London: Thames and Hudson, 1971

Lodder, Christina, *Russian Constructivism*, New Haven, Connecticut: Yale University Press, 1983

Lodder, Christina, "Tatlin's Monument to the Third International as a Symbol of Revolution," in *The Documented Image: Visions in*

Art History, edited by Gabriel P. Weisberg and Laurinda S. Dixon, Syracuse, New York: Syracuse University Press, 1987

Milner, John, *Vladimir Tatlin and the Russian Avant-Garde*, New Haven, Connecticut: Yale University Press, 1983

Roman, Gail Harrison, "Tatlin's Tower: Revolutionary Symbol and Aesthetic," in *The Avant-Garde Frontier: Russia Meets the West, 1910–1930*, edited by Gail Harrison Roman and Virginia Hagelstein Marquardt, Gainesville: University Press of Florida, 1992

Rowell, Margit, "Vladimir Tatlin: Form/Faktura," *October*, 7 (Winter 1978)

Zhadova, Larissa (editor), *Tatlin*, Budapest: Corvina, 1984; as *Tatlin*, translated by Paul Filotas, New York: Rizzoli, 1988

MOORE, CHARLES WILLARD 1925–93

Architect, United States

Along with Robert Venturi, Michael Graves, and Robert A.M. Stern, Charles W. Moore is widely considered a leading architect of the Postmodern movement. Moore's ideas and influence, however, stretch well beyond the confines of any particular movement or style and have had a significant independent influence on architectural education and practice. As a traveler, writer, teacher, lecturer, illustrator, and connoisseur, Moore saw architecture as a vehicle for enriching the everyday lives of people through memory, fantasy, sensory stimulation, and visual delight.

After earning his professional degree from the University of Michigan in 1947, Moore moved to San Francisco, where he worked in several architectural offices before accepting a teaching appointment at the University of Utah in 1950. After military service in the Korean War from 1952 to 1954, he continued his education at Princeton University, earning an M.F.A. in 1956 and a Ph.D. in 1957. During his graduate work and in the two years he stayed on at Princeton to teach, he developed valuable long-term relationships with people such as Louis Kahn, Donlyn Lyndon, and William Turnbull.

Moore's return to the Bay Area in 1959 to become an assistant professor at the University of California, Berkeley, marked the rekindling of a love affair with California that he would nurture for the rest of his life. In 1962, he helped establish the firm Moore Lyndon Turnbull Whitaker, and in 1965 that firm designed the Condominium I project in Sea Ranch, which rapidly became a hallmark of innovation in American residential design. (Moore purchased one of the condominium units himself and continued to use it as a home base for his peripatetic lifestyle for the next 30 years.) He juggled his increasing activity in professional practice with added responsibility in his academic career, serving as chairman of the Department of Architecture at Berkeley from 1962 to 1965.

Moore continued his leadership in architectural education by accepting the position of department chair and later dean of the School of Architecture at Yale University, where he served from 1965 to 1975. Although he continued work with his California practice, MLTW/Moore Turnbull, he also established a new East Coast office under the names Charles W. Moore Associates (1970—75), Moore Grover Harper (1975–78), and Centerbrook (after 1978). When he returned to California in 1975 to take a position at the University of California, Los Angeles, he similarly established new practice venues there: UCLA–Urban Innovations early on and Moore Ruble Yudell after 1976. Having made four moves back and forth between the East Coast and the West Coast, in 1984 Moore finally relocated in the middle of the country, where he became the O'Neil Ford Centennial Chair in Architecture at the University of Texas, Austin, and where he established the firms Charles W. Moore Architect in 1985 and Moore/Anderson Architects in 1991. He remained in Austin until his death in 1993.

Moore's remarkable mobility and range of associations with various universities and firms were signals of his mastery of the art of collaboration. In writing, teaching, and design, he worked productively with a very broad range of colleagues. He drew talented people to him like a magnet and had the ability to extract from them the very best they had to offer. He owed a great deal to long-term collaborators in practice, such as Donlyn Lyndon, William Turnbull, Richard Peters, Marvin Buchanan, William Grover, Robert Harper, Glenn Arbonies, Jefferson Riley, Mark Simon, Chad Floyd, Barbara Solomon, Tina Beebe, John Ruble, Buzz Yudell, Richard Dodge, Arthur Anderson, and many others. Likewise, in his teaching and writing, he worked closely with Donlyn Lyndon, Gerald Allen, Kent Bloomer, Richard Oliver, William Mitchell, Peter Zweig, Simon Atkinson, and many more. His collaboration with others, according to Moore, was like a musician playing with a jazz ensemble where "the process is informal and evolutionary enough to encourage, indeed to be dependent upon, individual expression within this communal context."

Moore's mobility, coupled with his propensity to tinker and experiment, also led him to build eight houses for himself that are among his best-known works. His homes in Orinda, California (1962); at Sea Ranch (1964); in New Haven (1967) and Essex (1973), Connecticut; and in Austin, Texas (1986) are especially poignant portraits of his architectural values. They are full of the wit, comfort, and enjoyment of living that inspired much of his work. They also took great chances, from the sunken bath and shower ("liberated from the cramped conventional bathroom" and open to view from most of the house) in Orinda to the cutout plywood towers (which he named Howard, Berengaria, and Ethel) in New Haven. The houses, Moore said, "gave eight special chances to walk the thin edge of disaster."

The houses also became treasure troves for Moore's collections. He was an inveterate traveler and seldom returned home empty-handed. He not only garnered miniatures, folk toys, books, and kitsch souvenirs from all over the world but also collected, at the same time, a rich and diverse bank of architectural images—generally documented in photographic slides but sometimes just filed away in his seemingly limitless visual memory. Moore mined those mental collections productively in his design work, which, throughout his career, drew eclectically on a startling range of fresh and diverse sources. The Sea Ranch condominiums, for example, broke new ground by forming a hybrid between the modern humanism of architects such as Alvar Aalto and the vernacular redwood barns in northern California. Kresge College (1974) at the University of California, Santa Cruz, conjoined Italian hill towns and the pop graphic character of Archigram. Moore's power came from his broad appreciation of architecture and from his belief that "the things buildings can say, be they wistful or wise or powerful or gentle or heretical or silly, have to respond to the wide range of human

Kresge College, "Triumphal Arch," U.C. Santz Cruz (1974)
Photo © Mary Ann Sullivan

feelings." His work is characterized by an accommodating adaptability rather than by fidelity to rigid formalism or a holier-thanthou doctrine. He was at his best building light dappled, energetic places full of freshness, vitality, and a love of life.

LAWRENCE W. SPECK

Biography

Born in Benton Harbor, Michigan, 31 October 1925. Attended the University of Michigan, Ann Arbor 1942–47; bachelor's degree in architecture 1947; traveled to Europe and the Near East on a University of Michigan Traveling Fellowship 1949; studied under Louis I. Kahn at Princeton University, New Jersey 1954–57; earned a master of fine arts degree 1956; earned a Ph.D. 1957. Served in the United States Army, United States, Japan, Korea 1952–54. Draftsman in the firms of Mario Corbett, Clark and Beuttler, and Joseph Alan Stein, San Francisco, California 1962. Private practice from 1962; partner, Moore Lyndon Turnbull Whitaker, Berkeley, California 1962–65; firm renamed MLTW 1965–69. Principal, Charles W. Moore Associates, Essex, Connecticut 1970–75; consultant, Urban Innovations Group, Los Angeles from 1974; partner, Moore Grover Harper, Centerbrook, Connecticut 1975–85; consultant, Cen-

terbrook Architects, Essex, Connecticut from 1975. Partner, Moore Ruble Yudell, Santa Monica, California from 1976. Principal, Charles W. Moore, Architect, Austin, Texas 1985–90; partner, Moore/Anderson Architects, Austin from 1991. Assistant professor, University of Utah, Salt Lake City 1950–52; assistant professor, Princeton University 1957–59; associate professor, 1959–65, chairman of the department of architecture, 1962–65, University of California, Berkeley; professor of architecture, 1965–76, chair of the department of architecture, 1965–69, dean of the School of Architecture, 1969–71, Yale University, New Haven, Connecticut; professor of architecture 1975–85, program head, School of Architecture, 1978–82, University of California, Los Angeles; O'Neil Ford Centennial Chair in Architecture, University of Texas, Austin from 1984; visiting professor, Harvard University Graduate School of Design, Cambridge, Massachusetts. Senior member of the Architecture Advisory Board, United States State Department's Office of Foreign Building Operations; fellow, American Institute of Architects. Gold Medal, American Institute of Architects 1991. Died in Austin, 16 December 1993.

Selected Works

Charles Moore House, Orinda, California, 1962
Charles Moore House, Sea Ranch, near San Francisco, 1964

Condominium I, Sea Ranch, 1965
Charles Moore House (renovation), New Haven, Connecticut, 1967
Church Street South Housing, New Haven, 1968
Klotz House, Westerly, Rhode Island, 1969
Charles Moore House, Essex, Connecticut, 1973
Kresge College, University of California, Santa Cruz, 1974
Piazza d'Italia, New Orleans, 1978
St. Matthew Episcopal Church, Pacific Palisades, California, 1982
Moore-Andersson Residence and Studio, Austin, Texas, 1986

Selected Publications

The Place of Houses (with G. Allen and D. Lyndon), 1974
Dimensions (with G. Allen), 1976
Body Memory and Architecture (with K.C. Bloomer), 1977
The Poetics of Gardens (with W.J. Mitchell), 1988

Further Reading

The best personal account of Charles Moore's life and career is Littlejohn. The other references focus more on his architectural work.

Allen, Gerald, *Charles Moore*, New York: Whitney Library of
    Design, 1980; London: Granada, 1981
Crosbie, Michael, *Centerbrook: Reinventing American Architecture*,
    Washington, D.C.: AIA Press, and Rockport, Massachusetts:
    Rockport, 1993
Fujii, Wayne (editor), *Charles Moore and Company*, Tokyo: A.D.A.
    Edita, 1980
Johnson, Eugene J. (editor), *Charles Moore: Buildings and Projects,
    1949–1986*, New York: Rizzoli, 1986
Keim, Kevin, *An Architectural Life: Memoirs and Memories of Charles
    W. Moore*, Boston: Little Brown, 1996
Littlejohn, David, *Architect: The Life and Work of Charles W. Moore*,
    New York: Holt Rinehart and Winston, 1984
Nakamura, Toshio (editor), *Moore Ruble Yudell, 1979–1992*, Tokyo:
    A + U, 1992
Riera Ojeda, Oscar, and Lucas H. Guerra (editors), *Moore Ruble
    Yudell: Houses and Housing*, Washington, D.C.: American
    Institute of Architects Press, 1994
The Work of Charles W. Moore, Tokyo: A + U, 1978

MORAL, ENRIQUE DEL 1906–1987

Architect, Mexico

Enrique del Moral was a leading figure in the first generation of postrevolutionary Mexican architects. Over the course of over five decades of professional practice, del Moral participated in the search for a new national identity expressed in architecture and struggled with defining a new mission for itself in the wake of the Mexican Revolution of 1910.

Del Moral began his studies in architecture in 1923 at the Academy of San Carlos in Mexico City, a school that had trained Mexican students in classical architectural theory and practice since 1785. He had witnessed the destruction of the Revolution as well as the promises embedded in the Constitution of 1917 and noted a disparity between his training in architecture and the enormous needs of a society attempting to reconstruct itself along more egalitarian lines. With classmates Juan O'Gorman, Álvaro Aburto, and Juan Legarreta, he read Le Corbusier's works and interpreted them to fit a Mexican reality. In sum, they believed urgent problems facing Mexico to be social in nature; the answer was structural.

Under the leadership of José Villagrán García, del Moral was guided toward functionalist theory, which involved intelligent use of construction methods and materials, application of advanced techniques such as reinforced-concrete foundations, the creation of forms corresponding to functions that buildings must discharge, and the imperative to construct new housing for the popular classes, hospitals, schools, and markets, among other facilities.

From 1928 to 1935, del Moral worked in the studio of Carlos Obregón Santacilia, whose works in those years encompassed diverse projects sponsored by the national government, including the massive *Monumento de la Revolución*. The functionalist movement continued to meet with considerable negative reaction from many architects throughout the early 1930s, who labeled functionalism an imperialist importation and a factor in the destruction of the city's scenery, insisting on an architecture that could convey the Mexican national spirit and a "native" Mexican architecture—which they defined as colonial-era styles, sometimes with the additions of Aztec, Mayan or Toltec elements.

In 1933 Alfonso Pallares, president of the *Sociedad de Arquitectos de México*, invited architect and engineers to participate in a historic debate at the Academy of San Carlos on the issue of national architectural styles. Discussions centered on the defense of functionalist architecture, particularly the "economical, sound and industrial architecture" that working people needed, as sustained by Juan Legarreta, Juan O'Gorman, and Álvaro Aburto, and the defense of the spiritual necessities and the production of architectural beauty by del Moral and others.

Del Moral believed it was imperative to fulfill economic needs while responding to cultural and geographic factors, employing a sense of aesthetic beauty and balance. This is clearly seen his first works, in association with Marcial Gutiérrez Camarena, such as the workers' homes in his birthplace of Irapuato (1936) or a series of houses in Colonia Chapultepec, Mexico City (1938–42). His use of native materials combined with modern construction techniques and an understanding of Mexican culture and use of interior space.

At the end of the 1940s he began to collaborate with architect Mario Pani. This prolific association culminated with the their development of the master plan for the new campus of the Universidad Nacional Autónoma de México (UNAM) and the design of the *Torre Rectoría*. Construction of this massive project on approximately six million square meters of the Pedregal of San Angel began in July 1950. Over 40 architects contributed to design of buildings in the school and administrative zones, such as those for the schools of law, medicine, architecture, and the Central Library. The *Torre Rectoría*, with its mural by David Álvaro Siqueiros depicting young people ascending to give their knowledge to the people, provides an example of unification of art and architecture. Additional works in collaboration with Pani include hotels and an airport in Acapulco (1952) and the Secretaría de Recursos Hidráulicos Building in Mexico City (1950).

Over the course of his career, del Moral designed hundreds of structures. Each manifests his dedication to aesthetics and economy. To this point, the Tejeda House (1943) and del Moral's own home (1949) illustrate in particular his attention to light and color. Similar care is apparent in large-scale projects, including his extensive work in health care facilities, such as in the Hospital General de San Luis Potosí (1946) and the Hospital de Urgencias del Centro Médico (1958), and in government buildings, such as the Tesorería del Distrito Federal (1963) and the Procuraduría General de Justicia (1969).

PATRICE OLSEN

See also **Legorreta, Ricardo (Mexico); Mexico City, Mexico; University Library, UNAM, Mexico City**

Biography

Born 20 January 1906, Irapuato, State of Guanajuato, Mexico; studied architecture at Escuela Nacional de Arquitectura, Universidad Nacional Autónoma de México, Mexico City 1923–28 under José Villagrán García; received professional certification 1928; advanced studies in philosophy in the Facultad de Filosofía y Letras from 1944 to 1946. Assistant Professor, Escuela Nacional de Arquitectura 1934–36, professor 1938–50, and director 1933–48. Professor. Universidad Iberoamericana 1959–63. Employed in the studio of Carlos Obregón Santacilia, from 1928–35; began private practice in 1935. Appointed to various governmental positions pertaining to school and hospital construction programs: Jefe del Zona del CAPFCE in Guanajuato 1944–46; member of the Comité de Construcción del Centro Médico 1945–46 and the Comisión Nacional de Hospitales. Drafted the master plan for the construction of the new campus for the Universidad Nacional Autónoma de México, 1947–52. Activities in professional associations include his participation in the CAM-SAM from 1954, serving as president of its Junta de Honor from 1972 to 1973 and from 1974 to 1975; the Academia de Artes; and the Asociación Mexicana de Críticos de Arte. Died 11 June 1987, Mexico City.

Selected Works

Ten Workers' Houses, Irapuato, Guanajuato (with Marcial Gutiérrez Camarena), 1936
Apartment building, Panuco, Colonia Cuauhtémoc, México, 1940
Tejeda House, Aída and Cedros, Tlacopac, México, 1943
Hospital General de San Luis Potosí, San Luis Potosí, 1946
Kindergarten, Colonia Buenos Aires, México, 1946
Master Plan for the Ciudad Universitaria, Universidad Nacional Autónoma de México, México (with Mario Pani), 1952
Del Moral House, Francisco Ramírez, México, 1949
Secretaría de Recursos Hidráulicos, Paseo de la Reforma, México (with Mario Pani), 1950
Torre de Rectoría, Ciudad Universitaria, México (with Mario Pani and murals by David Alfaro Siqueiros), Mexico City, 1952
Acapulco Airport, Guerrero (with Mario Pani), 1952
Emergency Hospital, Centro Médico Federal, México, 1958
Children's Hospital, Villahermosa, Tabasco, 1958
Hospital-Clinic, Tampico, Tamaulipas, 1964
Hospital-Clinic, IMSS, Ciudad Obregón, Sonora, 1968
Medical Center, Villa Olímpica, México, 1968
Procuraduría General de Justicia, México, 1969

Selected Publications

"Arquitectura en Acapulco," *Arquitectura/México* 45 (1954)
Defensa y Conservación de las Ciudades y Conjuntos Urbanos Monumentales, México, D.F.: Academia de Artes, 1980
El Estilo: La Integración Plástica, México, D.F.: Seminario de Cultura Mexicana, 1966
El Hombre y la Arquitectura, México, D.F.: UNAM, 1984

"Reflexiones sobre el Estilo," *Arquitectura/México* 69 (1960)
"Villagrán García y la Evolución de Nuestra Arquitectura," *Arquitectura/México* 55 (1953)
La Construcción de la Ciudad Universitaria del Pedregal (with Mario Pani), México, D.F.: UNAM, 1979

Further Reading

Anda, Enrique X. de, *Evolución de la arquitectura en México: Época prehispánica, virreinal, moderna y contemporánea*, Mexico City: Panorama Editorial, 1987; revised edition, as *Historia de la arquitectura mexicana*, Mexico City: G.G., 1995
Burian, Edward Rudolf (editor), *Modernity and the Architecture of Mexico*, Austin: University of Texas Press, 1997
Caso, Alejandro, "El humanismo en la obra del arquitecto Enrique del Moral," *Arquitectura y sociedad* 25 (1983)
Fernández, Justino, *Arte moderno y contemporáneo de México*, Mexico City: Universidad Nacional Autónoma de México, 1952; 2nd edition, 1994
Gómez, Lilia and Miguel Angel Quevedo, *Testimonios vivos 20 arquitectos: 1781–1981: Bicentenario de la Escuela de pintura, escultura, y arquitectura*, Mexico City: Secretaría de Educación Pública, Instituto Nacional de Bellas Artes, 1981
González Gortázar, Fernando, *La arquitectura mexicana del siglo XX*, Mexico City: Consejo Nacional para la Cultura y las Artes, 1994
Moyssén, Xavier, "La formación filosófica de Enrique del Moral," *Arquitectura y sociedad* 25 (1983)
Noelle, Louise, "Enrique del Moral," in *Arquitectos contemporáneos de México*, edited by Noelle, Mexico City: Editorial Trillas, 1989; 2nd edition, 1996
Pinoncelly, Salvador, *La obra de Enrique del Moral*, Mexico City: Universidad Nacional Autónoma de México, Facultad de Arquitectura, 1983
Toca, Antonio, *Arquitectura contemporánea en México*, Azcapotzalco, Mexico: Universidad Autónoma Metropolitana, and Mexico City: Gernika, 1989

MORETTI, LUIGI 1907–73

Architect, Italy

Luigi Moretti remains one of the most enigmatic figures of Italian modern architecture. His work falls in the cracks between art-historical categories, and his writings lack the social polemic of most of his contemporaries. Yet he exercised a profound and lasting influence on Modern and Postmodern architecture. Born in Rome, he was educated there at the University of Rome, receiving his degree in 1930. He taught at the University of Rome (mainly history courses) from 1931 to 1934.

Two conflicting opinions by recent Italian historians can explain this problem. Manfredo Tafuri and Francesco Dal Co, in their *Modern Architecture*, mention Moretti only once, stating, "Luigi Moretti (1907–74) locked himself into a formalism that was an end in itself in the so-called Sunflower house of 1950 in Rome, in the Olympic Village realized there with A. Libera, and in the Watergate Complex in Washington done in 1959–1961." On the other hand, Luciano Patetta, in his entry for the *Macmillian Encyclopedia of Architects*, said, "Probably the most successful result . . . is the Watergate . . . a work of full maturity and in full possession of expressive means."

Moretti never allied himself with either side of the heated debate about architecture of the Fascist period. When he emerged in the late 1940s and early 1950s with what were to become his major works—the Astrea and Sunflower apartment houses—he still remained aloof from contemporary polemics. However, during the Fascist period he was an ardent follower of the regime of Benito Mussolini. Even after Fascism fell and Mussolini was installed by the Germans in a puppet regime in northern Italy, Moretti joined Mussolini in the so-called Republic of Salò. For this transgression against civility, he served 18 months in prison in Milan, and during his confinement he met a developer who gave him a number of important commissions in the immediate postwar period. It has been said that Moretti never lost his love of Mussolini and Fascism. The first of these commissions was an apartment hotel (1948) in Milan, followed by the multifunctional "Transatlantico" building (1952–56), also in Milan. However, the two buildings that made Moretti's reputation and that remain his undisputed Rome masterpieces are the Casa Astrea (1949–50) and the Casa Girasole (1950–51). These two buildings are sophisticated examples of a kind of mannerist modernism. Moretti used the elements of the modernist vocabulary in a highly decorative, somewhat Expressionist way, employing thin outrigger walls and spandrels, tile decorations, travertine revetments, and glass handrails. The Casa Girasole (Sunflower House) was later published by Robert Venturi in his seminal *Complexity and Contradiction in Architecture* (1966), making the building a locus of architectural pilgrimages. Venturi

and others have asked the question, "Is this one building split, or two buildings combined?" It was both, and the gash down the middle would become a Moretti trademark.

The building was influential in the development of the *palazzina* building type, a modern equivalent of the palazzo whereby the courtyard of the typical Florentine/Roman palazzo becomes the core, and the building, a squat tower, is free on all sides. In the massing and facades of the Casa Girasole, Moretti used a shallow layering system combined with the assertive horizontality of spandrels and window blinds to establish an aggressively modern equivalent of traditional formal composition. He even hinted at a split pediment in the top profile of the building.

At the same time in the early 1950s, Moretti began publishing a magazine, *Spazio*, which lasted for only eight issues but was quite influential in establishing this new formalism in Italian modern architecture. He also published analyses of traditional buildings and spaces, including solid models of the interior spaces of baroque churches. These analyses had an important influence on Moretti's younger contemporary, the historian/theorist Bruno Zevi, and Zevi adapted Moretti's spatial and sequential analyses for his popular book *Saper vedere l'architettura* (1957; Architecture as Space).

Moretti's mature buildings include the Olympic Village housing blocks for the 1960 Olympics in Rome, an exercise in

Casa Girasole, Rome (1951)
© Thomas Schumacher

Le Corbusian Ville Radieuse urbanism and architecture. The facades of these buildings were in the Brutalist manner of concrete slabs and brick in-fill, with varying window sizes and openings. The Le Corbusian system of the "five points"—*pilotis*, ribbon window, free plan, free facade, and roof garden—was employed here to positive effect.

Rather than having any architectural significance, the Watergate complex is best known for its political significance during the Nixon era in the United States. Yet this building, a curvy array of great plasticity on the Potomac River near the Lincoln Memorial and the Kennedy Center, was one of the first multiuse buildings to be built in Washington in the post–World War II era. It, not the Kennedy Center, revitalized its neighborhood, and the building's assertive volumetrics were influential in changing a dour Washington style.

Moretti died at the time the Watergate hearings were under way in Washington.

THOMAS SCHUMACHER

Biography

Born in Rome, 2 January 1907. Studied humanities at the Istituto Romano de Merode; studied architecture at the University of Rome; graduated 1930. In private practice, Rome from 1931; founder, editor, *Spazio*, Rome 1956; contributor to *Civita delle macchine* and *L'architecture d'aujourd'hui*. Founder, Istituto Nazionale de Ricerca Matematica e Operativa per l'Urbanistica (IRMOU), Rome 1957. Academician, Accademia di San Luca, Rome 1960; honorary fellow, American Institute of Architects 1964. Died in Isola di Capraia, Italy, 14 July 1973.

Selected Works

Casa del Gioventù, Rome, 1933
Fencing Academy, Rome, 1937
Casa Albergo, Milan, 1948
Casa Astrea, Rome, 1950
Casa Girasole, Rome, 1951
Il Translantico, Milan, 1956
Olympic Village, Rome, 1960
Villa Saracena, Santa Marinella, 1963
Watergate Complex, Washington, D.C., 1964
Esso Society Headquarters, EUR, Rome, 1967
Stock Exchange Tower, Montreal (with Pier Luigi Nervi), 1969

Selected Publications

Apocalisse (with P. Pascal), 1964
"The Values of Profiles" and "Structures and Sequences of Spaces," *Oppositions*, 4 (October 1974)

Further Reading

Collins, Peter, "Stock-Exchange Tower, Montreal," *Architectural Review*, 139/832
Santuccio, Salvatore (editor), *Luigi Moretti*, Bologna, Italy: Zanichelli, 1986

MORGAN, JULIA 1872–1957

Architect, United States

When Julia Morgan was born in San Francisco in 1872, the newly emerging architecture schools in the United States had not yet graduated their first architectural student, male or female. A quarter of a century later, there were less than 400 architecture students in the nine existing U.S. architectural schools, while the 1900 census would record more than 10,000 architects in the United States. These were almost exclusively men and almost all "unschooled"; that is, they received their training through apprenticeships in established architectural offices, by experience with builders, or by the presumption of simply hanging out a shingle and declaring themselves to be qualified architects. But very few were diploma-bearing architects. In early 1902, Julia Morgan (already a graduate in engineering from the University of California, Berkeley) became the first woman in history to graduate from the École des Beaux-Arts in Paris, the best design school in the West and, since its founding in the 17th century under Louis XIV, a conservative and exclusively male academy.

Even the men who were enrolled in the new American schools of architecture at the turn of the 20th century represented a mere four percent of the practicing profession at the time. In this respect, all the would-be architects of Morgan's generation who sought formal training in schools, including those rare men who attended the Paris École, were pioneers in architectural education. To recognize this fact and also take into consideration that women were far outnumbered by men in the schools is to identify the formidable accomplishment and extraordinary significance of Morgan's professional achievement as the 20th century opened. By century's end and long after Morgan's retirement, there would be thousands of women encouraged and enabled to enter the previously restricted profession and to practice the art of building as creative architects with full credentials, thanks to the example of Morgan.

Indeed, Morgan's unassailable position as a pioneer in early 20th-century architecture, unlike that of Frank Lloyd Wright, August Perret, or others of the avant-garde of her generation, is based not on her advancing a revolutionary modern design aesthetic or on her leadership in 20th-century structural engineering and the use of new materials, but rather on her advancing a revolutionary idea: that architecture as a profession should be open to women. Nevertheless, it also is noteworthy, considering the greater notoriety of Wright and Perret as pioneer architects at the turn of the century, that Morgan was also interested in, and at the vanguard in the use of, the newly revived material of concrete. In 1903 she designed El Campanil (completed 1904), a 72-foot reinforced concrete bell tower for Mills College in Oakland, California, a building that survived the great earthquake of 1906. Morgan's campanile dates from the same year as Perret's rue Franklin concrete apartment building in Paris and three years before Wright's concrete Unity Temple in Oak Park, Illinois. By 1906 Morgan also had built a concrete library at Mills College and a reinforced concrete house in Berkeley.

Three themes inform Morgan's life's work and define her aesthetic: academic eclecticism (an outgrowth of her training in the classical tradition of the École); a respect for nature and a concern for creating a sensitive and sympathetic man-made environment that remained natural; and a love of craft, reflecting in her work the ideals of the international Arts and Crafts movement. The first theme is especially evident in such designs as the classic Hearst Memorial Gymnasium and Pool for Women (1925–26) on the University of California-Berkeley campus—a joint project with Bernard Maybeck—and her ongoing work at San Simeon for William Randolph Hearst, where she pieced together collected fragments of architectural history and decorative arts to create an enchanted hilltop castle, which is both residence and museum. The second theme is most evident at Asilomar Conference Center in Pacific Grove, California, where she built some 20 Arts and Crafts-style buildings between 1913 and 1928, their sites in a natural ocean-side setting of remarkable beauty. The Administration Building (1913), Lodge (1914–15), Chapel (1915), and Crocker Dining Hall (1918) are among the earliest Morgan works there, and Merrill Hall (1928) also is noteworthy. Finally, Morgan was part of the "Bay Region Tradition" spearheaded by Bernard Maybeck and Charles Keeler that found in natural redwood framing, structural expression, and shingle cladding an honest and environmentally sensitive approach to the building of simple homes. The Foote House (1905) in Grass Valley, California, several modest arts-and-crafts-style cottages in Berkeley, and "the Hearthstone" (1928) in a redwood grove at Dyerville Flat, California, reflect these interests. Her masterpiece in the style, however, is St. John's Presbyterian Church and Sunday School (1908–10) in Berkeley, a project contemporary with Maybeck's landmark Christian Science Church in Berkeley (1909–11).

Throughout her life Morgan developed a women's network, first finding clients among her former sorority sisters and gaining an increasing reputation internationally from her numerous commissions for Young Women's Christian Associations (YWCAs). She became a swimming-pool specialist, and while none rival either the Roman Pool (1927–32) or Neptune Pool (1935–36) at San Simeon, the 25 by 75-foot indoor pool for the Berkeley Women's City Club is remarkable. Her most formidable and best-known client, however, was William Randolph Hearst, for whom she built San Simeon (1919–42) and Wyntoon (1933–41). The latter was a complex of Gothic and fairy-tale buildings whose spirit reached from William Burges to Walt Disney. Named Bear House, Cinderella House, and Fairy House, the cottages at Wyntoon, together with "The Bend" (1935–41) and the towered, shingle-clad Bridge House (1933), form a village for the ghost of the first Wyntoon, a baronial seven-story castle that Maybeck had built in 1903 but that was claimed by fire during the winter of 1929–30.

After 44 years of practice, Morgan closed her office in 1951 and requested that the building superintendent burn her files, blueprints, and office records, believing no one besides clients (who already had their own documents and drawings) would be interested in her paper documents. Her buildings would speak eloquently for themselves. In the end, Morgan's significance beyond the 20th century quintessentially lies in a historic role that she neither sought nor acknowledged as particularly her mission. In her serving as a catalyst for revolutionary changes in the

United Presbyterian Church (now College Avenue Presbyterian Church), Oakland, California (1917)
Photo © Mary Ann Sullivan

makeup of the profession of architecture, she became one of the most influential architects in history. Rather than establishing a "Morgan" aesthetic that followers then transplanted to new fields internationally, this pioneer of 20th-century architectural education, without intention, defined her position of influence uniquely. It asserts itself long after her death, as a result of thousands of female designers who might not have produced a single building were it not for Morgan's example.

ROBERT M. CRAIG

See also **Arts and Crafts Movement; Concrete; Maybeck, Bernard R. (United States)**

Biography

Born in San Francisco, California, 20 January 1872. Graduated from the University of California, Berkeley, with a degree in engineering; was the first female graduate of the École des Beaux-Arts, Paris. In private practice, California from 1902; designed numerous facilities for the Young Women's Christian Association 1913–30; worked on projects for William Randolph Hearst intermittently 1919–41. Died in San Francisco, 2 February 1957.

Selected Works

(All works in California unless otherwise noted)

Bell Tower, Mills College, Oakland, 1904
Foote House, Grass Valley, 1905
Library, Mills College, Oakland, 1906
Cole House, Berkeley, 1906
Goddard Cottages, Berkeley, 1907
St. John's Presbyterian Church (now Julia Morgan Center for the Performing Arts), Berkeley, 1910
Asilomar Conference Center, Pacific Grove, 1913–29
Williams and Mitchell House, Berkeley, 1918
San Simeon (William Randolph Hearst House), 1919–42
Phoebe Apperson Hearst Memorial Gymnasium and Pool, University of California, Berkeley (with Bernard Maybeck), 1926
Young Women's Christian Association, Honolulu, Hawaii, 1927
Young Women's Christian Association, Salt Lake City, Utah, 1927
The Hearthstone, Dyerville, 1928
Williams House, Berkeley, 1928
Young Women's Christian Association, San Francisco, 1930
Wyntoon, McCloud River, 1933–41

Further Reading

Sara Holmes Boutelle was the major scholar on Julia Morgan, and her monograph published by Abbeville is the standard source. Longstreth's *Perspecta* article and pamphlet for the Berkeley Architectural Club were early introductions offering judicious appraisals of the work. Boutelle's essay in *Toward a Simpler Way of Life* is part of an anthology of some two dozen California "Arts and Crafts architects," including Morgan and including as well a second generation group of early modern designers acknowledging regional influence from Maybeck and his contemporaries. Wright's and Boutelle's (1981 and 1989) essays address issues of gender by considering Morgan's role as a pioneer for women in architecture. Steilberg, who worked for Morgan, presents some of her early work, and Woodbridge includes Morgan houses in her general survey of Bay area domestic design. Aidala (with Curtis photographs) is a monograph and picture book on the most popularly known of Morgan's work—her "castle" for William Randolph Hearst—and includes discussion of the architecture of the house, its collections, and surrounding grounds and pools.

Aidala, Thomas R., and Bruce Curt, *Hearst Castle, San Simeon*, New York: Hudson Hills, 1981
Boutelle, Sara Holmes, "The Woman Who Built San Simeon," *California Monthly* 86, no. 6 (April 1976)
Boutelle, Sara Holmes, "Women's Networks: Julia Morgan and Her Clients," *Heresies* 11, no. 3 (1981)
Boutelle, Sara Holmes, *Julia Morgan, Architect*, New York: Abbeville Press, 1988; revised edition, 1995
Boutelle, Sara Holmes, "An Elusive Pioneer: Tracing the Work of Julia Morgan," in *Architecture: A Place for Women*, edited by Ellen Perry Berkeley, Washington, D.C.: Smithsonian Institution Press, 1989
Boutelle, Sara Holmes, "Julia Morgan," in *Toward a Simpler Way of Life: The Arts and Crafts Architects of California*, edited by Robert Winter, Washington, D.C.: Preservation Press, 1995
Longstreth, Richard, "Julia Morgan: Some Introductory Notes," *Perspecta* 15 (1975); reprint, as *Julia Morgan, Architect*, Berkeley, California: Berkeley Architectural Heritage Association, 1977
Steilberg, Walter, "Some Examples of the Work of Julia Morgan," *The Architect and Engineer of California* 55, no. 2 (November 1918)
Woodbridge, Sally, *Bay Area Houses*, New York: Oxford University Press, 1976; new edition, Salt Lake City, Utah: Peregrine Smith, 1988
Wright, Gwendolyn, "On the Fringe of the Profession: Women in American Architecture," in *The Architect: Chapters in the History of the Profession*, edited by Spiro Kostof, New York: Oxford University Press, 1976

MORPHOSIS

The architectural firm Morphosis was founded by Thom Mayne and Jim Stafford in Santa Monica, California, in 1972. One year later, Michael Rotondi, recently graduated from the Southern California Institute of Architecture (SCI-ARC), joined the firm and worked as a partner between 1975 and 1991. Starting with modestly sized projects, the firm established a significant media presence, leading to larger and more complex urban-scaled works. Their work has consistently emphasized the tectonics of construction, formalist compositions, and saturated representations from its origin.

Recognizing the increasingly overlapping relationship between architecture and media, Morphosis maintained a strong media presence, receiving a significant number of Progressive Architecture and American Institute of Architects (AIA) awards, many for unbuilt projects. Their pursuit of the image of architecture as a projected work is an analogue of the construction process. Their published works isolate and exaggerate particular fragments of elements and spaces within the overall order. These (sometimes cryptic) layered drawings are intended to clarify the intentions of construction with extreme formalist intensity, although the intentions are often conflicting. Their absorption of artistic practice into design is most evident in their design development, primarily in the media of scaled study models (and later digital models) that transgress the disciplinary separation of sculpture and architectural representation, and it is significant that their models are often the only building arising from a project. Models and drawings supplement the partially concealed meanings and readings of their designs, privileging the fragmentary as a formalist coding of the real.

The earliest work reveals the significant influence of James Stirling's work, contextualized within the expansive sprawl of Los Angeles. Thom Mayne once stated, "I am interested in producing work with a meaning that can be understood only as absorbing and comprehending the culture for which it is made. Since culture, particularly that of the late twentieth century, is in constant flux, architecture is also perpetually in flux." The search for comprehensive order with unique localized conditions drives their buildings and representations, creating dehistoricized fragmentary assemblages that are complicated for the sake of reflecting, not resolving, culture.

The earliest small houses, renovations, and restaurants exaggerate the tectonic connections between discrete planes and sculptural forms, subordinating the constraints of program and site conditions to a larger "reflexive" agenda. In the Mexico House II (1978) and the built Venice III (1982), both in Los Angeles, the overall form mimics the typologies of the context. The interior functional spaces appear to be carved from the exterior form, selectively revealing themselves as assemblages of smaller integrated components that are organized along formalized circulation paths and vertical zoning. The remodeled Sixth Street House (1987) vertically stratifies public and private spaces upward through the existing structural shell. The enclosure often remains partial or bare, a self-conscious revelation of the process of encoding within the work and a reference to the fashions of Los Angeles culture. The internal incorporation of defunct mechanical objects into functioning structure, stairs, skylights, and a shower draw distinctly urban debris into the workings of the domestic space. This sculptural approach expresses the fragmentation of functional space, duplicated in their early commercial work, such as the Angeli Restaurant (1984) and the Kate Mantilini Restaurant (1987), both in Los Angeles. Here the architecture frames activities while self-consciously projecting into those activities. In the 72 Market Restaurant (1983) in Los Angeles, a prominent rotated building within a building in the entry appears to create a torsional dining space while secretly doubling as an earthquake-stabilizing structural device.

The Crawford House (1990), a large suburban villa, culminates the heuristic pursuit of the materializing of the art and artifice of domestic architecture from the earliest housing projects. Its repetitive linear structure becomes the foil for diverse and isolated canisters of space, often themselves assembled of discrete and separate materials. The duplication of this strategy in multiple scales within the same project anticipates an expansion beyond the domestic scale, as a type of fractal urbanism. The success of the earlier works led inevitably to projects of a larger scale, where the previous influence of urban thought could be tested in diverse programs and sites (increasingly removed from the dissipating Los Angeles topos).

The built Cedars-Sinai Comprehensive Cancer Clinic (1987) in Los Angeles adds to an existing labyrinthine hospital complex by placing the majority of the 52,000-square-foot outpatient facility underground. The design overcomes the potentially disheartening function and location by introducing a kinetic sculptural folly, generous skylighting, and optimistic detailing. The complex programming necessity of hospital spaces is concealed behind a clear hierarchy of simple circulation paths culminating in public spaces.

The competition entry for the addition to the Amerika Gedenkbibliotek (1988) in Berlin proposed a doubling of the library stack area of the 1950s icon and placed a diversity of specialized spaces on the periphery of the project to respond to diverse localized site edge conditions. A courtyard oriented toward the center of Mehringplatz pierces the linear "core" of texts, proposed to be a cathedral-like structure imposed on the scarred landscape near the Berlin Wall of the late Cold War.

The unbuilt MTV Studios (1990) is perhaps the most definitive Morphosis project. Here the interest in absorbing and reflecting the workings of popular culture literally becomes dynamic skis of images, icons, and forms clad on interiorized specular spaces. Space is structured as a "tension between objects" set obliquely to one another and framing fragments through apertures of space. The distinction between flat image and deep space has been abandoned, a procedural conclusion of the firm's earlier representational methods.

In 1991 partner Michael Rotondi, who had been director of SCI-ARC, left the firm to form ROTO Architects in Los Angeles. This split caused a period of refocusing and required rebuilding the firm during its move into larger urban and international markets. Toward the end of the 20th century, Morphosis proposed multiple urban planning schemes along the single collagist theme of a layering of objects within rotational gridded urban fabrics. The Paris "Architecture et Utopie" Competition entry (1989), the Berlin Wall Competition (1988), the Potsdamer Platz Competition (1990) in Berlin, and an urban development for a town center and educational institute submitted to the Disney media corporation (1991) in Orlando pursue the fragmentation and assemblage of parts from the earliest tectonic projects, exteriorized and projected outward without a clearly defined boundary or horizon. It is as if each urban proposal is a fragment of a larger urbanism, a globalization of their earliest Los Angeles context.

The late-20th-century adoption of computer technology in architectural design and production in the United States presented Morphosis with further opportunities to examine the place of media in the built environment. As more of their design work occurs on a screen, closer to the advances in technological media, it grows more distant from the brute facts of construction and will become the motivating tension of their future work.

THOMAS MICAL

Biographies

Thom Mayne

Born in Connecticut 1943. Graduated from the University of Southern California 1968; masters degree from the Graduate School of Design, Harvard University, Cambridge, Massachusetts 1978. Cofounder, Southern California Institute of Architecture (SCI-ARC) 1972; cofounder, with Jim Stafford, Morphosis, Santa Monica, California 1972; president, Morphosis 1977–78. Eliel Saarinen Chair, Yale University, New Haven, Connecticut 1991; Elliot Noyes Chair, Harvard University 1998; has taught at Columbia University, Berlange Institute, Holland, Bartlett School of Architecture, London, Academy of Applied Arts, Vienna, and UCLA. Rome Prize Fellowship, American Academy of Design, Rome 1997.

Michel Rotondi

Born in the United States 1949. Graduated from the Southern California Institute of Architecture (SCI-ARC) 1975. Partner, Morphosis, Santa Monica, California 1975–91; director, SCI-ARC until 1997. Founded architectural firm ROTO, Los Angeles 1991; currently president of ROTO.

Selected Works

Mexico House II, Los Angeles, 1978
Venice III, Los Angeles, 1982
72 Market Restaurant, Los Angeles, 1983
Angeli Restaurant, Los Angeles, 1984
Sixth Street House (remodeling), Los Angeles, 1987
Kate Mantilini Restaurant, Los Angeles, 1987
Comprehensive Cancer Clinic, Cedars-Sinai Hospital, Los Angeles, 1987
Crawford House, Los Angeles, 1990
MTV Studios (unbuilt), 1990

Selected Publications

Morphosis: Connected Isolation (Mayne), 1992
Tangents and Outtakes: Morphosis (Mayne), 1993
Morphosis: Buildings and Projects 1993–1997 (Mayne), 1999

Further Reading

Cook, Peter, *Morphosis: Buildings and Projects*, New York: Rizzoli, 1989
Nakamura, Toshio (editor), *Morphosis Urban Projects; Mofosisu* (bilingual English–Japanese edition), Tokyo: A + U Publishing, 1994
Weinstein, Richard, *Morphosis: Buildings and Projects, 1989–1992*, New York: Rizzoli, 1994

MOSCOW, RUSSIA

Moscow has displayed variants of every major international style in 20th-century architecture as well as some peculiar stylistic hybrids. At the beginning of the 20th century, the most decisive impact of the style moderne (the Russian equivalent of Art Nouveau) on the city's architecture occurred in the development of apartment and office buildings, whose standards of efficiency, comfort, and technological progress were suited to accommodate the growth of an increasingly prosperous professional and middle class. The distinctive aesthetic approach of the style moderne, with its emphasis on the decorative arts, also appeared in the design of the private house, primarily for the merchant elite. Fedor Shekhtel (1859–1926), Lev Kekushev (1863–1919), and William Walcot (1874–1943) were among the most prominent of the many Moscow architects that designed in the new style.

Shekhtel produced the greatest body of work in the style moderne. However, the new style's most impressive monument in Moscow is the Hotel Metropole (1899–1904), designed by Walcot with the assistance of Kekushev and other architects. There are many aspects of the Metropole that classify it as a landmark of the style moderne, including a concept of tectonics in which the structural mass is shaped without reference to illusionistic supporting elements. The facade itself contains little reference to the classical order system. The contrasts of textures and materials create a space within which the decorative arts and structural form are combined. Of particular note are the large ceramic tile panels by Mikhail Vrubel and Alexander Golovin.

The style moderne in Moscow was complemented by a variant known as the neo-Russian style, which kept the new style's emphasis on plasticity and asymmetry but allowed a greater role to decorative elements drawn from traditional folk motifs. The most notable proponents of the neo-Russian School in Moscow were the artists Viktor Vasnetsov (1848–1926) and Sergei Maliutin (1859–1937). The latter's Pertsov apartment house (1905–07) is a particularly well-preserved example of the style.

By the end of the 1900s, the style moderne had yielded to or merged with a form of neoclassical revival known in Russian as *neoklassitsizm*, which ranged from historicist designs of Ivan Zholtovskii (1867–1959) to a modernized, stripped classicism. In Moscow the most accomplished revivalist was Roman Klein (1858–1924), architect of the Museum of Fine Arts (1897–1912) and the Muir and Mirrielees department store (1906–08). Although less prolific than Klein, other architects distinguished themselves in a more modern variant of neoclassicism: Illarion Ivanov-Schitz (1865–1937), Alexander Kuznetsov (1875–1954), Boris Velikovsky (1878–1937), the Vesnin brothers, and Ivan Rerberg (1869–1932), who designed one of the first Moscow skyscrapers (the Northern Insurance Company Building, 1909–11) for the Kitai-Gorod district in the heart of Moscow's commercial center. In the same district, Ivan Kuznetsov designed a large office complex called Business Court (1912–13), which combined classicizing details with the extensive use of reinforced concrete.

After the revolution and civil war, construction gradually resumed in the mid-1920s in Moscow, which had now become the capital of the entire USSR. At first, the ideals of the avant-garde held sway in educational institutions and in cultural circles. The leading movement of the period, Constructivism, appeared in the design of state office buildings, apartment houses, and workers' clubs throughout Moscow. Notable monuments include the Izvestiia Building (1927) by Grigorii Barkhin (1880–1969), the Zuev Workers' Club (1927–29) by Ilia Golosov (1883–1945), the State Trade Agency (1925–27) in Gostorg, by Boris Velikovsky (1878–1937), the apartment house for the People's Commissariat of Finance (1928–30) in Narkomfin by Moisei Ginzburg (1892–1946) and Ignaty Milinis (1899–1974), the Commissariat of Agriculture (1929–33) by Aleksei Shchusev (1873–1949), and the Palace of Culture of the Proletarian District (1932–37) by the Vesnin brothers. Although he did not consider himself one of the Constructivists, Konstantin Melnikov (1890–1974) created a number of highly innovative works in Moscow, such as the Rusakov Club (1927–29).

With the beginning of the Stalinst era and the intensified pace of industrialization, state-sponsored architectural design in Moscow turned to more conservative stylistic approaches. Not only was architecture commanded to glorify the achievements of the new industrial power, but the very appearance of Moscow was also transformed. The earlier disputes between the "urbanists" and "deurbanists" was resolved in favor of regulated but intensive urban development, as set forth in a speech by Stalin's satrap Lazar Kaganovich at the Central Committee plenum in June 1931. As a result, Moscow developed a comprehensive city plan by Vladimir Semenov (1874–1960) and Sergei Chernyshev (1881–1963) that served as a setting for the new monumental architecture.

Moscow State University (1949–53), designed by Lev Rudnev with assistance from Pavel Abrosimov
and Alexander Khriakov
© William C. Brumfield

By the time the Moscow plan was formally adopted in 1935, measures were under way to implement a major reconstruction of the Soviet capital. The Okhotny Riad market area between the Bolshoi Theater and the Kremlin was cleared, and the former Tverskaia Street—renamed in honor of Maxim Gorky in 1932—was widened and endowed in 1936–40 with rows of buildings designed primarily by Arkady Mordvinov (1896–1964) in an eclectic style that defines the early phase of Stalinist architecture. Other major projects included the construction of Peace Prospekt as the main thoroughfare in the north of the city, the Gorky Park of Culture and Rest (1934–36) to a design by Alexander Vlasov (1900–62), and the construction of the first phases of the Moscow subway.

After World War II, Moscow's architecture achieved new levels of decorative extravagance, epitomized by the Stalinist skyscrapers. Ultimately, only seven of the towers were built (the eighth was intended for a site to the southeast of Red Square now occupied by the Hotel Rossiia). Their placement defined certain key points in the topography of the city—a role emphasized by their large spires, redolent both of medieval bell towers and of the spires of Petersburg. The role of a vertical dominant in organizing a low, seemingly chaotic array of surrounding structures had long been a feature of Russian architecture, and although not all these "tall buildings" (*vysotnye zdaniia*) were

originally designed with the spires, they obtained them in the final designs as a recognition of their symbolic and visual role in a city that would retain a largely horizontal, "communal" profile.

To the southeast of the city center, Dmitrii Chechulin (1901–81), assisted by a team of architects and engineers, erected in 1948–52 a 24-story apartment building with ramifying wings on the Kotelnicheskaia Quay at the confluence of the Iauza and Moscow Rivers. On the north of the Boulevard Ring, Aleksei Dushkin (1903–77) designed an office and apartment building at Lermontov Square (1953), and in the same area, Leonid Poliakov (1906–65) built the Hotel Leningrad (1949–53) near the Leningrad Station. The west portion of the Boulevard Ring was marked by an apartment building by Mikhail Posokhin (1910–89) and Ashot Mndoiants (1909–66) at Insurrection Square (1950–54), and at the southwest portion of the Ring stands the Ministry of Foreign Affairs and Foreign Trade (1948–53) on Smolensk Square by Vladimir Gelfreikh (1885–1967) and Mikhail Minkus (1948–53). Further to the southwest, beyond the Moscow River, is perhaps the most grotesque of the seven: the Hotel Ukraina (1950–56) by Arkadii Mordvinov.

However, the most imposing of all was the new central building of Moscow State University on Lenin (formerly Sparrow) Hills, a grandiose, symmetrical complex built in 1949–53 to a design by Lev Rudnev (1885–1956), Pavel Abrosimov (1900–61), and Alexander Khriakov (1903–76). The main architect, Rudnev, had played an important role in defining Soviet monumentalism with buildings such as the M.V. Frunze Military Academy (1932–37, in collaboration with V.O. Munts), whose rectangular mass was defined in early "totalitarian style" by an unyielding grid of square windows above a long stylobate. The new university building represents a later, flamboyant stage of totalitarian architecture and was designed as a self-contained and tightly regulated community, a melding of utopian notions of communism with the unparalleled elitism of the late Stalinist period.

The post-Stalinist period in Moscow architecture was dominated by Mikhail Posokhin, who became main architect of the city. In the 1960s Posokhin adapted the international modern style, with its glass and aluminum facades, to industrialized methods of construction in the creation of such ensembles as Kalinin Prospekt (1964–69), also known as the New Arbat, extending westward from the Kremlin and Arbat Square. Its identical towers and shopping complexes provided the capital with the facade of cosmopolitan prosperity (and its leaders with a direct highway to their dachas), but the complex wreaked incalculable and lasting damage on the original Arbat district. To the right of the bridge that takes Kalinin Prospekt over the Moscow River, Posokhin and Mndoiants interpreted modernism in more dramatic fashion in their "open-book" design for the building of the Council of Mutual Economic Assistance (1964–69), the institution through which Moscow controlled its economic

relations with the countries of the Warsaw Pact. In a similar repetitive style, a team headed by Dmitrii Chechulin (and assisted with Komsomol labor) built the gargantuan Hotel Rossiia near Red Square in 1964–69 with accommodations for 6,000 guests.

Posokhin was also entrusted with devising a new general plan for Moscow, which was accepted by the Central Committee and Council of Ministers in 1971. The city's boundary was extended to the limits of the new ring expressway (and even some areas beyond), within which were eight large zones. The outer zones contained numerous developing "microregions," designed within a system of new transportation arteries. These areas were marked above all by vast "housing massifs" with thousands of apartments. Although successful in increasing the city's usable space, the period produced only a few examples of distinctive architecture, such as the Children's Music Theater (1979) by Alexander Velikanov and V. Krasilnikov.

Although Soviet-era construction methods continue for large projects such as housing developments, post-Soviet architecture in Moscow has been influenced by Western styles and building techniques. Notable recent examples of this tendency include Moscow International Bank (1991–94), the McDonald's Corporation building (1990–93), the Sovmortrans Building (1990–95), the International Business Center of the Academy of National Economy (1992–95), the Gazprom Building (1996–97), and the International Cultural Complex (1989–2000). With a disproportionate share of the country's investment capital, Moscow and its architecture have entered a phase of rapid change

Kalinin Prospekt (also known as the New Arbat buildings, 1969), designed by Mikhail Posokhin
© William C. Brumfield

that has undoubtedly led to losses for the historic fabric of the city but that has also in many cases produced an exciting and colorful urban environment.

WILLIAM C. BRUMFIELD

Further Reading

Although there are few specialized studies of modern architecture in Moscow, the city receives primary attention in most studies of Soviet modernism. For those with a knowledge of Russian, the recently published, mammoth encyclopedia *Moskva: Entsiklopediia* has excellent coverage of the city's architecture.

Barkhin, M.G., et al. (editors), *Mastera sovetskoi arkhitektury ob arkhitekture*, 2 vols., Moscow: Iskusstvo, 1975

Brumfield, William Craft, *The Origins of Modernism in Russian Architecture*, Berkeley: University of California Press, 1991

Brumfield, William Craft, *A History of Russian Architecture*, Cambridge and New York: Cambridge University Press, 1993

Cohen, Jean Louis, *Le Corbusier et la mystique de l'URSS: Théories pour Moscou, 1928–1936*, Brussels: Mardaga, 1987; as *Le Corbusier and the Mystique of the USSR: Theories and Projects for Moscow, 1928–1936*, translated by Kenneth Hylton, Princeton, New Jersey: Princeton University Press, 1991

Cooke, Catherine, *Russian Avant-Garde Theories of Art, Architecture, and the City*, London: Academy Editions, 1995

Ikonnikov, Andrei Vladimirovich, *Arkhitektura Moskvy: XX vek* (Moscow Architecture: 20th Century), Moscow: Moskovskii Rabochii, 1984

Khan-Magomedov, Selim O., *Pioneers of Soviet Architecture: The Search for New Solutions in the 1920s and 1930s*, translated by Alexander Lieven, edited by Catherine Cooke, New York: Rizzoli, and London: Thames and Hudson, 1987

Kirichenko, Evgeniia, *Russkaia arkhitektura, 1830–1910-kh godov* (Russian Architecture, 1830–1910), Moscow: Iskusstvo, 1978

Kopp, Anatole, *Constructivist Architecture in the USSR*, London: Academy Editions, and New York: St. Martin's Press, 1985

Murrell, Kathleen Berton, *Moscow Art Nouveau*, London: Wilson, 1997

Riabushin, A.V., and N.I. Smolina, *Landmarks of Soviet Architecture, 1917–1991*, New York: Rizzoli, 1992

Shmidt, S.O., *Moskva: Entsiklopediia* (Moscow: Encyclopedia), Moscow: Bolshaia Rossiiskaia Rntsiklopediia, 1997

Starr, S. Frederick, *Melnikov: Solo Architect in a Mass Society*, Princeton, New Jersey: Princeton University Press, 1978

Zemtsov, S.M. (editor), *Zodchie Moskvy* (Architects of Moscow), 2 vols., Moscow: Moskovskii Rabochii, 1981–88

MOSQUE

The mosque, a Muslim house of worship, has and continues to function as the focal point of Muslim communities worldwide and has served as an outward and visible symbol of Islam since the seventh century.

According to Islam (submission to God's will), Allah is everywhere, and a devout Muslim does not require a defined space or structure for divine worship. The mosque, or in Arabic *masjid*, which means "a place where one prostrates oneself," is a prayer hall rather than a building enshrining a deity. Its interior is an architectural expression of *tawhid*, a doctrine of divine unity, and is usually an open unobstructed space, with no defined progressive path.

Because Mecca is considered as the center of the Islamic universe, every mosque, whether a *masjid* (district or neighborhood mosque), a *masjid i-jami* (congregational or principal mosque), or a *masjid-i juma* (Friday mosque), which is large enough to accommodate an entire adult community to assemble for Friday prayers, must have a *mihrab* (recess or niche) in the *qibla* wall indicating its direction. A place for prayer alongside this wall, a *minbar* (pulpit) for the *khutba* (oration) at Friday prayers, and a facility for the ritual ablution are the few obligatory requirements that must be met in every mosque design. The other elements, such a portal, courtyard, and even the dome and the ever-present minaret, are all optional.

The sexes have to be segregated during worship, and some mosques provide women with a special area. Women are either relegated behind a barrier such as a curtain or a screen or to a small space within the mosque such as a gallery, a mezzanine, or a separate side hall

The absence of any fixed or prescribed forms in mosque design allowed great flexibility in the architectural expression of the building and permitted each region to develop its own style and use of materials. Thus, mosque architecture reflects a great variety of styles resulting from the influence of such factors as geographical environment, available raw materials, culture, aims of the patrons, and the skills of the architect and craftsmen engaged in the building process. The earliest mosques were based on the layout of the Prophet Muhammad's house in Medina and had a *sahn* (courtyard) and a *haram* (sanctuary). Although the distinction between the outer courtyard and the prayer-hall has been kept, each region developed its own style, and in India the design of the mosque was influenced by the Hindu Temple, whereas in the eastern Mediterranean, the Byzantine church was a strong influence, as is evident in the Blue Mosque in Istanbul, Turkey (early 1600s).

The written word and floral and geometric design are the only ornamentation considered appropriate for a mosque because human representation is prohibited. Qur'anic inscription on tiled surfaces or caved in stone or stucco serve to record and transmit the word of Allah. Because the words need to be readable and not necessarily legible, they are often incorporated into the floral and geometric patterns.

Islam welds together the sacred and the secular, and through time the mosque has been viewed not only as a congregational prayer place but also as a center of social life. In addition to a prayer-hall, the mosque has provided space for education, community gatherings, and public and political functions. Until modern times when secular law was introduced to many Islamic countries, the mosque also functioned as a court of justice. In many instances, these subsidiary functions were provided with separate buildings, and the mosque served as a focal point in a complex.

Regardless of its architectural style, the mosque has served as a symbol of identity, political power, social control, justice, and piety throughout history. In the modern era, the mosque continues to reflect the values and the changes occurring in Muslim society. The 20th century, and more specifically the second half of the century, saw the mosque change not only in terms of style, material, and building technology but also in its symbolism. During this time, the mosque acquired a pan-Islamic character worldwide, that is, a design that incorporates elements that are considered recognizably Islamic without being representative of any one particular culture, and became a symbol of national

King Saud Mosque on El-Medina Road, designed by Abd al-Wahid al-Wakil (1986)
Photo courtesy Zouheir A. Hashem

independence and of declaration of Muslim presence in non-Muslim countries.

Many new Muslim independent nation-states were created out of former colonial territories in the late 1940s and the 1950s. These new political entities aspired to present themselves as both "modern" and Islamic through their new buildings and more specifically the mosques, which were viewed as monuments to independence. This led to the construction of state mosques, buildings initiated by the governments, which took over the traditional role of the king or ruler in commissioning the construction of a mosque to express nationhood, and paid for by public funds. State mosques are the embodiment of political will and national identity symbols for authority within the nations of the Islamic world and the legitimization of state regime in the eyes of the world. Therefore, their design is intended to have a clearly recognizable visual identity, which must be explicit in its regional, modern, and Islamic reference.

The architecture of mosques such as the Istiqlal Mosque in Jakarta, Indonesia (1955–84), and Masjid Sultan Salahuddin Abdul Aziz Shah Mosque Alam, Selangor, Malaysia (1988), reveal the conscious attempt to synthesize modernity and traditional form. The use of historic references serves as a reminder of a glorious past and reinforces the ideas of continuity and traditional values in Islam.

Scale is an important factor of these monumental structures; most mosques have been immense, with the capacity to accommodate from 20,000 worshippers under covered space, and up to 200,000 in the courtyard during the major Muslim festivals such as *Eid* (festival marking the end of Ramadan). They were usually conceived as complexes that incorporate multiple-use spaces and include a *madrasa* (place of study), a library, and spaces for social gatherings.

The King Saud Mosque on El-Medina Road in Jeddah, Saudi Arabia, designed by Abd al-Wahid al-Wakil (1986), features an open central courtyard for gathering with shading devices designed to circulate warm and cool air naturally through the rooftop, making the space comfortable for large groups. The King Saud Mosque boasts a novel type of dome construction that had not been realized except in architects and engineers' plans: To minimize weight (and therefore increase height), al-Wakil used hollow bricks that were load bearing in only one direction.

Unlike most of the traditional local community mosques that were integrated into the urban fabric, state mosques were treated as isolated monuments and are intended to be as visible as possible. When first planned, the Masjid Negara, in Kuala Lumpur, Malaysia (1957–65), was located at the edge of city, whereas the King Faisal Masjid, Islamabad, Pakistan (1960–86) was constructed at the foot of the Margala Hills on the main approach to the city, so that all could see it as they approached the capital.

Most of the state mosques were constructed between the 1960s and the 1980s. Afterward their need was diminished as the expression of national identity was no longer imperative, and the cost for such buildings was prohibitive.

Local authorities in Muslim nations act as branches of central government and distribute the government funds. They oversee the provision of housing, school, and hospitals and have been responsible for the construction of a large number of community mosques since the middle of the 20th century. These new mosques are either unique structures erected mostly in new urban settlements, such as the Village Mosque, Ma'ader, Algeria (1975–80), or a repeatable mosque design, such as the Housing and Development Board Mosques in Singapore or the Capital Development Authority Mosques in Pakistan.

Coinciding with the establishment of independent states in the Islamic world was a Muslim imigration to Europe as well as to North America, and the immigrant communities felt the desire to express their presence by building new mosques. Projects for Islamic centers expressing a Muslim presence in non-Muslim countries started to take shape in the 1950s.

Major mosques built in the West, like their counterparts in new independent Islamic countries, served as statements of Muslim identity. They were initiated by the influence of members of Muslim diplomatic missions and financed either by their own or other Islamic governments, most notably that of Saudi Arabia. These buildings are usually found in capitals or other cosmopolitan cities. Designs for these mosques are generally influenced by the local context and comply with the local construction regulations and planning laws, but usually include reference to regional traditions of the group that financed, designed, or acted as the project leader.

Examples of such structures are the Islamic Center, Washington, D.C. (1947–57), the London Central (Regent's Park) Mosque (1969–77), the Islamic Center and Mosque, Rome, Italy (1979–94), and the Islamic Cultural Center of New York in New York City (1987–91). These centers not only serve as places of prayer but also promote social, educational, and cultural activities for the local Muslim population. Notwithstanding the presence of Islamic centers, the immigrant Muslim communities wanted to manifest their presence in predominantly non-Muslim countries on a more local level. For those who found themselves distant from their home country, the mosque was the embodiment of their identity and became a symbol of celebration and pride.

Mosques such as the Great Mosque, Niono, Mali (1948–73), and the Yaama Mosque, Yaama, Tahoua, Niger (1962–86), rely on the community's own resources and are constructed by builders and other skilled artisans, aided by members of the community. However, some of the more recent examples, such as the Dar al-Islam Mosque, Abiquiu, New Mexico (1981), and Bait ul-Islam, Maple, Toronto, Ontario, Canada (1987–92), were designed by professional engineers and architects from outside the immediate community.

A sign of the presence of a communities that have embraced the Muslim religion are the so-called storefront mosques found in North American that signal the presence of Afro-American Muslims and the comparable situation in Indonesia, with the Chinese "shop-house" mosques in Jakarta.

Individual patrons have always played an important role in the construction of mosques. Throughout history mosques have been financed by wealthy individuals such as members of the ruling or social elite, monarchs, princes, sheiks, religious leaders, landowners or merchants, usually as an act of piety, a gesture toward their own community, or dominance. In recent times, modern patrons range from national and religious leaders to businessmen, and the buildings range from the world's largest new mosque, the Great Mosque of Hassan II, Casablanca, Morocco (1986–93), commissioned by King Hassan II of Morocco, to the more modest Bin Madiya Mosque in Deira, Dubai, United Arab Emirates (1982–90), which was donated for public use by a private patron, Majid Al Futtaim. Regardless of their size, the resulting mosques usually reflect the individual taste of the project initiator.

In recent decades mosques have also become a standard integral feature of complexes for institutions such as those dedicated to higher education, the University of Petroleum and Minerals Mosque, Dhahran, Saudi Arabia (1969–74), health care, Avicenno Military Hospital Mosque, Marrakech, Morocco (1982), as well as major providers of commercial and public transportation services such as airports and the King Khalid International Airport Mosque, Riyadh, Saudi Arabia (1974–83). These institutions recognized the need for the provision of places for collective prayer and have called for the inclusion of a prayer hall, if not a monumental mosque, in their facilities. The design of these structures is meant to signal the centrality of Islam in the institution. These religious structures are intended for the use of a select group, although the institutions anticipated that their prestige and location might eventually attract worshippers from a wider background.

Wherever Muslims went, they constructed mosques to meet the fundamental religious requirements, that is, congregational prayers five times a day. Whereas in the past the architecture of the mosque was affected by its environment, be it the climate, materials, or technology, mosques of the modern era are the product of cultural exchange and design ideas transmitted on a worldwide scale, and it is no longer possible to find buildings with what is termed "a purely regional mode," and they can no longer be grouped according to geographic areas.

Despite its appearance, as a building type, the mosque is ubiquitous and has remained immutable over time. Although styles, construction technology, and context have changed, it continues to accommodate collective acts of prayer and is a powerful symbol to both Muslims and non-Muslims alike. It is an everlasting "public affirmation of being and being seen to be Muslim" (Holod, 1997).

HAGIT HADAYA

See also **Great mosque, Niono; Great mosque of Hassan II, Casablanca**

Further Reading

Frishman (1994) provides a comprehensive architectural history of mosques around the world, whereas Holod (1997) focuses specifically on the mosques that were built in the second half of the 20th century. Humphrey (1997) and Conti (1978) look at the mosque as a religious building among sacred structures. The additional sources provide further general information on earlier and contemporary mosques and Islamic art.

Ardalan, Nader, "On Mosque Architecture," in *Architecture and Community: Building in the Islamic World Today*, edited by Renata Holod and Darl Rastorfer, Millerton, New York: Aperture, 1983

Conti, Flavio, *Splendor of the Gods*, translated by Partick Creagh, Boston: HBJ Press, 1978

Frishman, Martin and Hasan-Uddin Khan, *The Mosque: History, Architectural Development & Regional Diversity*, London: Thames and Hudson Ltd., 1994

Grabar, Oleg, *The Formation of Islamic Art*, New Haven: Yale University Press, 1973

Holod, Renata and Hasan-Uddin Khan, *The Contemporary Mosque: Architects, Clients, and Designs since the 1950s*, New York: Rizzoli, 1997 (this book was also published under the title *The Mosque of the Modern World: Architects, Patrons and Designs since the 1950*, London: Thames and Hudson, 1997)

Humphrey, Caroline and Piers Vitebsky, *Sacred Architecture*, Toronto: Little, Brown and Company, 1997

Imamuddin, Abu H., Shamim Ara Hassan, and Debashir Sarkar, "Community Mosque—A Symbol of Society," in *Regionalism in Architecture* (Proceedings of a seminar held by the Aga Khan Award for Architecture), edited by R. Powell, Singapore: Concept Media Pte. Ltd., 1985

Kuban, Dogan, *Muslim Religious Architecture*, 2 vols. Linden: Brill, 1974

Pereira, José, *Islamic Sacred Architecture: A Stylistic History*, New Delhi: Books and Books, 1994

MOSQUE OF THE GRAND NATIONAL ASSEMBLY, ANKARA, TURKEY

Designed by Behruz Çinici and Can Çinici, completed 1991

The Mosque of the Grand National Assembly, designed by Behruz Çinici (1932–) in collaboration with his son Can Çinici

(1962–), was completed in 1991. To appreciate the specificity of this mosque, it is necessary to consider its relationship to its physical surroundings, which it shares with the Grand National Assembly, and to situate it within the current debates about modernity, secularism, and religion in Turkey.

Located on a gently sloped 117.4-acre (475,000-square-meter) campus, the main building of the Grand National Assembly is based on Austrian architect Clemens Holzmeister's winning 1942 competition entry. In the years following the inauguration of the Assembly building in 1962, changes in the Turkish parliamentary system that made representatives more accountable to their respective constituencies led to an increase in the numbers and diversity of visitors and personnel, creating an eventual demand for new facilities. Husband and wife Behruz and Altug (1935–) Çinici were first commissioned to design a public relations annex with offices, meeting rooms, and food services in 1978. In 1985, in response to the growing number of people using makeshift prayer spaces throughout the complex, the Çinicis were asked to design a mosque large enough to accommodate 450 worshipers on the Assembly campus.

Strung along the central axis bisecting the roughly symmetrical site, the main Assembly building, the Public Relations Annex, and the mosque form a tripartite layout with a distinctive outdoor space in front of each structure. To the north, the solemn main entrance of the Assembly building, overlooking downtown Ankara, is reserved for formal use by representatives, cabinet members, and foreign dignitaries. Meanwhile, the large courtyard between the Assembly building and the public relations annex is bustling with personnel, various delegations, press corps, and visitors. The two wings of the Public Relations Annex form a narrow transitional corridor along the central axis leading to the base of the triangular courtyard of the mosque. Changes in geometry, scale, and soundscape highlight the significance of this transition. The remarkably quiet and secluded courtyard is bordered by the library on the southwest side and the mosque on the southeast side, both of which are modest in size. The eastern corner of the courtyard is truncated by a triangular pool, leaving a square-shaped paved area between the two buildings. A canopy runs the full length of the buildings along the courtyard, and at their intersection two superimposed square prisms highlight the apex of the triangle, the final reach of the central axis.

What is striking about this building is how the components of the conventional vocabulary of mosque architecture are reduced to an abstraction, fragmented, reconfigured, and sometimes even consciously omitted in the final design. Yet the architects maintain a dialogue with established historical precedents in each reinterpretation by invoking the users' familiarity with those compositional principles. This becomes immediately evident in the courtyard, where the canopy has replaced the typical colonnaded portico, yet the columns themselves are implied through indentations along the edge of the canopy and its projection on the ground. Similarly, the overlapping prisms at the apex and a slender cypress tree on the side stand in for the minaret that the designers chose to suggest without building it.

Of equal interest is the architects' resolve to connect with broader Islamic traditions beyond the Ottoman, as exemplified in their selective reuse of Ottoman precedents. Thus, although the site layout clearly takes after Ottoman *külliyes*, the formal articulation of individual spaces and masses hearkens back to

Facade of the glass *qibla* wall, Mosque of the Grand National Assembly
Photo by Reha Gunay © Aga Khan Award for Architecture

earlier and not necessarily Anatolian Islamic prototypes. By replacing the archetypal dome, characteristic of Ottoman mosque design, with a squat, off-centered, stepped pyramid, the architects have opted for a different geometry that deemphasizes the verticality implied by the dome and a centralized plan. More important, this design intentionally reintroduces the organizational principles of the early Islamic mosque as a simple congregational space accommodating rows of undifferentiated believers based on Mohammed's own home in Mecca. The split-level plan relegates men and women to separate areas as required; remarkably, however, the translucent plaques between the two define their boundary without severing their visual connection.

The Çinicis' experimentations with established compositional principles included the introduction of new spatial elements acknowledging Islamic liturgy. Thus, for example, the use of transparent materials to demarcate the *qibla* wall and the mihrab niche, providing a view of the sunken garden with a reflecting pool carved out of the hillside in which the mosque is ensconced, is intended as an unmistakable reference to the Islamic concept of the Paradise Garden. Moreover, the conscious omission of certain elements (such as the minaret or the colonnade), which entices each beholder to complete the picture her-

Main entrance with triangular court, Mosque of the Grand National Assembly (1991)
Photo by Reha Gunay © Aga Khan Award for Architecture

or himself, serves as a reference to the profoundly personal dimension of one's relationship with God in Islamic faith.

As evidenced by the choice of materials and scale, the building eschews monumentality and opulence. The Çinicis are experienced at using reinforced concrete for its textural, sculptural, and structural possibilities. In this building, variations in texture maximize the effects of light and shadow on both interior and exterior walls. Similarly, structural elements, such as the beams that support the stepped pyramid on the roof, also form eye-catching three-dimensional decorative patterns in the interior.

The Çinicis' project must be viewed within a long-running search for a new vocabulary in mosque design by 20th-century Turkish architects that expresses the contemporary modernist sensibilities of architectural discourse and practice in Turkey. In earlier designs, Behruz Çinici's contemporaries—such as Cengiz Bektas in his Etimesgut Mosque, Vedad Dalokay in his unbuilt Ankara Kocatepe Mosque, and later King Faisal Mosque in Islamabad—have introduced new geometries. What distinguishes the Mosque of the Grand National Assembly within this context has been the architects' decision to rework entrenched compositional principles and programmatic requirements as well. Although the contributions of the Mosque of the Grand National Assembly have been recognized internationally with the 1995 Aga Khan Award for Architecture, its reception in Turkey has been controversial. Conservative religious circles, who consider the archetypal Ottoman mosque almost as sacred as the function it houses, have attacked it for its iconoclastic design. Meanwhile, the sheer introduction of a mosque into the campus of the Grand National Assembly was denounced by secularists, who regard this to be a violation of the fundamental principles of the Republic. Whereas the Çinicis have tried to mitigate this concern by emphasizing the individual and private aspects of communion, the same cannot be said of the increasingly larger and more prominent mosques commissioned by other state agencies in the following years.

ZEYNEP KEZER

Further Reading

Çinici, Behruz, *Improvisation: Mimarlikta Dogaclama ve Behruz Çinici*, Istanbul: Boyut Kitaplari, 1999

Davidson, Cynthia, and Ismaïl Serageldin (editors), *Architecture beyond Architecture: Creativity and Social Transformations in Islamic Cultures: The 1995 Aga Khan Award for Architecture*, London: Academy Editions, 1995

Holod, Renata, and Hasan-Uddin Khan (editors), *The Contemporary Mosque: Architects, Clients, and Designs since the 1950s*, New York: Rizzoli, 1997; as *The Mosque and the Modern World: Architects, Patrons, and Designs since the 1950s*, London: Thames and Hudson, 1997

MOTEL

The motel literally grew up with the modern highway and America's growing enthusiasm for motor touring. The term "motel," formed as a combination of "motorist" and "hotel," suggests a derivational connection to the traditional hotel, but the evolution of the motel itself has more humble roots that are more directly tied to the road than the city. Along with kindred building types—the gas station and the diner—that developed into the architecture of big signs and little buildings, the motel helped to establish the unique and colorful character of the 20th-century roadscape.

The advent of the private automobile brought a new sense of freedom to travelers who could now choose their own routes, schedules, and destinations. Compared to the train, car travel was more casual and more independent. It was also more of an adventure, particularly in the early years, when roads were poor and the service infrastructure for travelers was still tied to the railroads and centered in towns and cities. Finding accommodations took travelers off the road, where they faced a choice between fleabag hotels usually located in seedy parts of town along the railroads or swanky versions in the central city with their elaborate public spaces and expensive amenities. In either case, the auto traveler faced the travails of in-town traffic, and because the hotels were more often than not oriented to streetcar lines and taxicabs, there were inadequate provisions for parking as well.

The need for cheaper and more efficient overnight lodging along the highway engendered a succession of accommodations, first in the form of tents at auto camps, followed by cabins and cottage courts. Initially at least, these were more rural than urban in character and likely to be found on the outskirts of town, where land was cheap. Cabins were rustic in appearance with few modern conveniences and most often used exclusively for seasonal trade, whereas the cottages that followed were more modern, better built, and usually designed to look like idealized little suburban houses. Both were likely to be family-owned and -operated businesses, with the manager and his family living on the premises. Many travelers were romantically attracted to these little houses with their sense of independence, privacy, and self-sufficiency, but as modern consumers, they were also demanding of a higher level of service, comfort, and security. The refinement and modernization of these early, rustic models of roadside accommodations led to the formulation of the modern motel.

The motel was a tighter and more communal organization of individual units than was found in its predecessors. In the motel format, units were characteristically gathered together in an economical party-wall arrangement under one roof and organized in a single row or, more popularly, in an L- or U-shaped plan to form an outdoor common space. Parking was directly

Howard Johnson's, Mineola, Long Island, New York (1938)
© Philip Langdon

adjacent to the rooms and sometimes accommodated in alternating carports or garages. Although the plans tended to be formulaic, the buildings were packaged in road-scale imagery designed to make them into eye-catching, architectural billboards. Motels were fashioned in every conceivable architectural style, with regional themes that promised a sense of the locale being particularly popular. Sometimes the units were shaped like Indian tepees, little replicas of the Alamo, or even airplanes and railroad cars. After World War II, designs reflected more contemporary styles of Art Deco, populuxe, and moderne that resonated well with the aesthetics of the automobile and fulfilled a hunger for the future. Highway architecture was lively, garish, and designed to catch the eye of drivers speeding by. As the form of the motel buildings settled into familiar types, design energies (and a greater slice of the budget) were invested in novel advertising signs that made one motel stand out from another. The signs themselves were elaborate, colorful works of art; usually emblazoned with neon to make them visible at night, they added a heraldic, vertical dimension to what was basically a horizontal building.

Although a rich proliferation of stylistic treatments prevailed on the outside, the rooms within were characteristically clean, efficient carbon copies of one another and full of polyester and plastic—durable materials that were part of the postwar aesthetic. Over time, the motel format was expanded on with larger lobbies, restaurants, and other amenities, such as swimming pools and playground equipment.

The evolutionary development of the motel was driven by a combination of economics and changing tastes and lifestyles. Individual entrepreneurs seeking to attract the greatest number of consumers at the lowest possible construction and maintenance cost had to balance between economics and ambience and personality. The novelty that prevailed during the earlier period of individual experimentation was significantly quieted down with the proliferation of motel chains such as Holiday Inn and Howard Johnson's, found at the interchanges of the spreading interstate highway system. Offering reliability, familiarity, and quality control, the chains standardized their designs in variants that were more often than not multistory and more hotel-like than their predecessors. Mass replication of designs and furnishings was a cost-saving measure. Except for eccentric examples, such as the Madonna Inn, a vast motel as theme park where each room is a surprise, the motel today is typically a model of familiarity and reliability. One chain's motels began to resemble another, and differences among them shifted from design differences to brand loyalties fueled by incentives that included free breakfasts, reservations services, and various discounts and premiums along with a lack of surprises.

Most of the roadside motels from the past suffered from the proliferation of the interstate highway system. Like the early roads that redirected traffic away from the railroads, the interstates have in turn redirected motor traffic away from the old roads. Individual motel owners who had consciously sought to create a unique sense-of-place experience as a part of their marketing strategies had also set themselves against the perceived uniformity of modernism. Today, these older models live precariously along little-used highways, where they have become exhibits in a living museum. The motel and hotel industries have blended into indistinguishable architectural blandness. Motel formats on the freeway are similar to those inside of towns and cities. However, few building types offer such a compelling story of their evolution. The evolution is not yet complete. As competition for the nation's leisure dollars continues unabated, new forms will likely appear that continue to wrestle with the dilemma between the familiar and the unique and between economy and a sense of place.

BRUCE C. WEBB

See also **Roadside Architecture**

Further Reading

Anderson, Warren H., *Vanishing Roadside America*, Tucson: University of Arizona Press, 1981

Belasco, Warren James, *Americans on the Road: From Autocamp to Motel, 1910–1945, Reinhold Publishing Corporation, 1955*

Jakle, John A., Keith A. Sculle, and Jefferson S. Rogers, *The Motel in America*, Baltimore: The Johns Hopkins University Press, 1996

Margolies, John, *Home Away from Home: Motels in America*, Boston: Little, Brown and Company, 1995

Marling, Karal Ann, *The Colossus of Roads: Myth and Symbol Along the American Highway*, Minneapolis: The University of Minnesota Press, 1984

MOVIE THEATER

A cultural icon of the 20th century, the movie theater borrowed, adapted, and invented forms, responding to changes in economic and social conditions. Above all, it was an expression of novelty and illusion, an environment of total escape. The American movie theater set the standard and generally remained the most exaggerated.

On 14 April 1894, the kinetoscope debuted at a New York City phonograph parlor, introducing moving pictures to the American public, combining a French invention with Yankee ingenuity. A single viewer deposited a quarter and peered down into the machine to see the flickering image. Two years later, the invention of new machinery allowed the images to be projected on a wall. When Vaudeville operators added the novelty to their programs, attendance doubled, and for the next ten years the motion picture was a staple in Vaudeville in all major American cities.

For those cities not on a Vaudeville circuit, itinerant film exhibitors would buy a movie, rent a large room and dozens of folding chairs, set up a wooden crate in the doorway to collect receipts (thus, the "box office"), and run the film until it fell apart or people stopped attending. These storefront theaters began to appear everywhere, even competing with Vaudeville in large cities. Haberdasheries were quickly remodeled, and occasionally a new building was created for the purpose of exhibition, beginning with Tally's Electric Theatre in Los Angeles in 1902. They were small, dark, shoebox-shaped buildings with a single aisle down the middle and the projector mounted in the back over the doorway. Overhead was minimal, and the buildings went up wherever there was an affordable lot. Whereas Vaudeville borrowed from the tradition and form of live theater, these were simple, nondescript, single-story wooden buildings that borrowed from circus carnival traditions—posters, sandwich boards, and spontaneous attendance. For reasons of cost, the number of seats was kept just below the legal definition of a theater, which required a license. Building code safety standards were looser as well, and fires were not uncommon.

In 1905, John Harris and Henry Davis, operating a 96-seat storefront in Pittsburgh, changed their marketing strategy. Instead of one showing a night, they ran continuous performances all day, lowering the cost of admission to five cents. The nickelodeon was born. "Nickel madness" engulfed the nation in what appeared to be a get-rich-quick scheme. The "nicks," as they came to be known, were the primary venue for exhibitors until World War I, with names such as Electric, Bijou, Liberty, or Empire outlined in bright lights in an attempt to counteract their seedy reputation.

Motion picture theaters were often named the "Opera House" in small to medium-size towns, giving an air of European legitimacy to counter the preachers' admonitions from the pulpit. Popular sheet music, such as "Take Your Girlie to the Movies, If You Can't Make Love at Home," did not help. Whereas the Hays Office attempted to clean up Hollywood from the production end, architects were commissioned to improve the exhibition end. Hollywood studios that had begun buying independent theaters to ensure a distribution outlet began to invest in the construction of new movie theaters.

In 1913, the plush 1,845-seat Regent Theatre opened in New York City, initiating the so-called movie palace. Modeled after the Doge's Palace in Venice, it was uptown both in location and in connotation. The movie palace was the big-city venue for first-run movies until World War II and set the standard for the movie theater as a distinct building type. It was a large steel-framed building with sets of balconies, studied sight lines, and asbestos curtains, containing several thousand seats and amenities such as ballrooms, marble restrooms, red carpets, chandeliers, magnificent curving stairways, gilded ornament and railings, nursery rooms, and restaurants. Theaters in the South had segregated entrances, lobbies, balconies, and facilities. The names described the environment (Majestic, Prince, Rivoli, Royal), brand names (Fox, Warner's, Loew's), or the name of the city (Chicago, Los Angeles).

The movie theater had to fit into the streetscape but be immediately recognizable as a type while distinguishing itself from the competition. The building was draped in whatever the latest fashion dictated, evolving from opulent period revival to shiny Art Deco to sleek Streamline Moderne to jazzy postwar Modern. Overscaled, lighted pylons promoted visibility and made the building appear much larger. The marquee might wrap around

Movie theater, Southside, Chicago
© Russell Lee/Farm Security Administration, Office of War Information Photograph Collection, Library of Congress

a corner or overlap across adjacent storefronts. Flashing lights and teasers spelled out the name of the theater and pointed to the box office, a separate structure, prominently placed on the sidewalk.

Both the exterior and the interior were designed and exploited to please the customer and to encourage attendance and loyalty. Banners outlined with icicles encouraged matinee attendance in the summer. Terrazzo patterns of marble chips divided by bronze bands told the customers that they were in a world of escape even before they bought their tickets. Patrons were induced to enter with seductive lines and subtle arrows that pointed toward the entry lobby.

For a quarter, patrons were treated like royalty or movie stars, beginning with the mirrored lobby. Huge plaster feathers surrounded the auditorium, encircling patrons in their plush velvet seats like feather boas. Multiple aisles and floral motifs led to a framed proscenium. There were classical paintings, statues, cherubim and seraphim, dragons, allegorical paintings on the ceiling, and organ music, usually reserved for the church. Uniformed ushers, armed with white gloves, flashlights, and caps, showed patrons to their seats. The fantasy, adventure, or romance extended from shadows on the silver screen to a physical environment when the lights came back on after the feature. The so-called atmospheric theater, introduced by John Eberson, took this approach to its ultimate expression, creating the illusion that guests were seated outdoors in velvet seats on a hillside. Plaster peacocks sat on tile roofs, and stars twinkled overhead and the moon moved across the night sky.

The U.S. Supreme Court's divestiture ruling in 1948 stating that studio ownership of production, distribution, and exhibition constituted a monopoly, combined with the advent of television, spelled change for the theater and increased the cost of operation considerably. Theaters in the 1950s offered what television could not. Cinerama, 3-D, and CinemaScope had theater owners ripping out seats and installing wider screens, new projectors, and additional speakers. Unsubsidized by production companies, the construction and operation costs, now including film rental, drove ticket prices up and services down. Exhibition was increasingly automated, culminating in the multiplex, operated from a single projection booth. The remnants are still there in references, often out of context: a pylon stabbing the sky, the marquee with its flashers and teasers, the klieg lights (even if just painted on the wall), the coming-attraction signs and posters, and the video rental employees wearing cheap cummerbunds.

MAGGIE VALENTINE

Further Reading

Hall, Ben M., *The Best Remaining Seats: The Story of the Golden Age of the Movie Palace*, New York: Bramhall House, 1961

Naylor, David, *American Picture Palaces: The Architecture of Fantasy*, New York and London: Van Nostrand Reinhold, 1981

Naylor, David, *Great American Movie Theaters*, Washington, D.C.: Preservation Press, 1987

Putnam, Michael, *Silent Screens: The Decline and Transformation of the American Movie Theater*, Baltimore, Maryland: Johns Hopkins University Press, 2000

Valentine, Maggie, *The Show Starts on the Sidewalk: An Architectural History of the Movie Theatre*, New Haven, Connecticut: Yale University Press, 1994

MUMFORD, LEWIS 1895–1990

Architecture critic, United States

Best known as a pioneering 20th-century critic of architecture, technology, and planning, Lewis Mumford served as the de facto conscience of the modern movement, urging its participants to remake the built world for the betterment of society. He was a humanist and self-styled "generalist" who wrote more than 20 books and hundreds of articles and reviews on a broad range of subjects. His writings are linked by the common theme of "utopia," or the good place, achievable through the positive deeds of the individual and the community. Partly because of his erudite yet accessible and often acerbic writing style, Mumford's influence was considerable. Professionals and laypeople alike value his criticism, even when they might disagree with his moralizing pronouncements. His writings continue to be relevant and, in many ways, prescient, as many of his fearful predictions regarding a technology's dominance of society have come to fruition.

Mumford's initial interest in architecture and planning was sparked by the writings of Patrick Geddes, the Scottish biologist turned regional planner, and of Ebenezer Howard, the originator of the Garden City. From Geddes, Mumford adopted an organic theory of civilization in which the region was identified as the natural unit of settlement. Subsequently, Mumford wedded Geddes' regionalism to Howard's Garden City to create the regional city, which Mumford believed would be the most effective means for siphoning population growth away from America's burgeoning metropolitan centers and restoring an organic balance in daily life. Toward this goal, Mumford joined with a group of progressive architects, planners, economists, and sociologists during the 1920s to form the Regional Planning Association of America. Based in New York City, the association advocated chiefly for improved and affordable working- and middle-class housing and designed and built two limited-dividend projects in the metropolitan area: Sunnyside Gardens, Queens, and Radburn, New Jersey. The latter project, designed by Clarence Stein, Henry Wright, and Frederick Lee Ackerman, was especially notable for its introduction of the residential superblock to American planning and its separation of pedestrian and automobile traffic. As a critic, Mumford promoted these projects in print as examples for architects everywhere to emulate.

Beginning in the late 1910s and continuing into the 1930s, Mumford supported himself primarily as a journalist, writing on architecture and regionalism as well as other topics for a diverse range of periodicals, including the *Dial*, the *Freeman*, the *Journal of the American Institute of Architects*, the *American Mercury*, *Commonwealth*, and the *New Republic*. At the time, the field of architectural criticism was largely free of competitors, although he was preceded by such notable figures as Montgomery Schuyler, Mariana Griswold van Rensselaer, and Herbert Croly. From the very beginning, Mumford advocated function over style in modern architecture, believing that buildings should be utilitarian in form and well suited to human need. He eschewed the historical revivalism then waning within the American profession but also what he perceived to be the ornamental excesses of the more forward-looking Art Deco movement. Among American architects, he admired the work of Claude

Bragdon, F. Barry Byrne, and especially Frank Lloyd Wright, whose organicism struck a responsive chord. Through Catherine Bauer, a colleague in the Regional Planning Association of America, Mumford came to appreciate the innovations of European modernists such as J.J.P. Oud, Ernst May, and Walter Gropius, even before seeing their work in person. Mumford was invited by Henry-Russell Hitchcock, Jr., and Philip Johnson to contribute a housing essay to the 1932 "Modern Architecture: International Style Exhibition," which they curated at the Museum of Modern Art. Although this exhibition launched the International Style in the United States, Mumford distanced himself from this movement, believing that a genuinely modern architecture would be regionally based and free to use traditional as well as modern materials.

Between 1931 and 1963 Mumford served as the *New Yorker*'s architecture critic. He inherited a column called "Sky Line," the first of its kind in a general-interest American magazine, and it became his most important and widely read forum. His early columns focused on New York City and its environs, covering subjects as grand as Rockefeller Center and as small as the corner coffee shop, with each building given the same careful scrutiny as to selection of site, expression of purpose, choice of materials, and fitness to human purpose. Following a hiatus during World War II, Mumford resumed his post but expanded the column's reach to cover such major European developments as Le Corbusier's Unité d'Habitation and the rebuilt core of Rotterdam. His lament over the neglect of New York City's Pennsylvania Railroad Station became a rallying cry for preservationists and for those alarmed by the dominance of the automobile in the United States. By the time he relinquished "Sky Line," a new generation of architecture critics, including Ada Louise Huxtable and Wolf von Eckardt, had filled the void. Mumford's best columns have been collected and republished in *From the Ground Up* (1956), *Highway and the City* (1963), and *Sidewalk Critic* (1998). His work for *Architecture* and *Architectural Record* has been collected in *Architecture as a Home for Man* (1975).

Mumford wrote few books specifically on the topics of architecture and planning, and these must be placed within the context of his other writings. His first book, *The Story of Utopias* (1922), adumbrates an intellectual blueprint for his later work. In it, he surveyed utopian schemes from Plato to the modern era and concluded with a utopian vision—largely inspired by Geddes—of organically balanced communities planted conveniently within their regions. His next four books adhered to strictly American themes, investigating what his literary colleague Van Wyck Brooks dubbed the "usable past." *Sticks and Stones* (1924), a social analysis of architecture, generated a great deal of controversy among professionals, who found Mumford's attacks on stylistic conservatism to be alternately refreshing and vitriolic. *The Golden Day* (1926), a survey of literature, and *Herman Melville* (1929), a biography of the writer, prompted Mumford to reexamine creative expression in the late 19th century. The result was *The Brown Decades* (1931), a well-received interdisciplinary study that celebrated, among others, Frederick Law Olmsted in landscape architecture, John and Washington Roebling in engineering, and Henry Hobson Richardson and Louis Sullivan in architecture. Mumford revisited Richardson's work, using Thomas Jefferson's work as a creative foil, in *The South in Architecture* (1941). Somewhat later, Mumford edited *Roots of Contemporary American Architecture* (1952), an impor-

tant collection of primary and secondary sources that posited a distinctly American pedigree for the modern movement.

Around 1930, eager to tackle weightier themes affecting Western civilization, Mumford embarked on the Renewal of Life, a four-part series that traced the parallel histories of technology, urbanism, and intellectual thought from the Middle Ages to the 20th century, ending with a plea for regionalism and individual renewal along the tenets of a secularized humanism. The first two volumes of the series, *Technics and Civilization* (1934) and *The Culture of Cities* (1938), established Mumford as a leading American intellectual and an international authority on city and regional planning. *City Development* (1945), a separate collection of his previously published essays and articles, built on this newfound reputation. The last two volumes of the Renewal of Life, *The Condition of Man* (1944) and *The Conduct of Life* (1951), focused on the less-tangible theme of the human personality and were met with a less-enthusiastic reception by both reviewers and the general public. Believing that he had not yet exhausted these themes, however, Mumford spent the greater part of the 1950s revising and expanding *The Culture of Cities* as *The City in History* (1961). His most acclaimed work and the winner of the 1962 National Book Award for Non-Fiction, *The City in History* examines human settlements from the Paleolithic cave to the 20th-century suburb. A profound pessimism characterizes the last section of the book, in which Mumford details a civilization on the brink of nuclear annihilation. *The Urban Prospect* (1968), a collection of Mumford's postwar essays on architecture, was intended by Mumford to function as a kind of appendix to *The City in History*. That humankind's destructive impulse was deeply rooted in the historical consciousness became the overriding theme of the two-volume *Myth of the Machine* (1967, 1970), in which he condemned the scientific establishment for allowing itself to become a pawn in the Cold War.

Mumford was a committed modernist who believed that 20th-century architecture should look to the future without losing sight of the lessons of the past. In his respect for history, his search for meaning, and his analysis of context in architecture, he may be seen as a harbinger of Postmodernism, even though he would have loathed the theoretical posturing and ornamental pastiches often associated with this movement. Mumford's utopian vision of moderately scaled communities filled with decent, utilitarian buildings may now be regarded as hopelessly outdated or even quaint, but his concern for the primacy of the human being still informs the best architecture everywhere.

ROBERT WOJTOWICZ

Biography

Born in Flushing, New York, 19 October 1895. Helped organize the exhibit "International Style" at the Museum of Modern Art, New York 1932. Member, Regional Planning Association of America 1923–33. Architecture critic, *New Yorker* magazine, 1931–63. Died in Amenia, New York, 26 January 1990.

Selected Publications

Elmer S. Newman's *Lewis Mumford: A Bibliography, 1914–1970* (1971) is the most comprehensive listing of Mumford's writings. Mumford's papers have been deposited in the Special Collections of Van Pelt Library at the University of Pennsylvania in Philadelphia. His drawings and his library are kept at Monmouth University, West Long Branch, New Jersey.

The Story of Utopias, 1922
Sticks and Stones: A Study of American Architecture and Civilization, 1924
The Golden Day: A Study in American Experience and Culture, 1926
Herman Melville, 1929
The Brown Decades: A Study of the Arts in America, 1865–1895, 1931
Technics and Civilization, 1934
The Culture of Cities, 1938
The South in Architecture, 1941
The Condition of Man, 1944
City Development: Studies in Disintegration and Renewal, 1945
The Conduct of Life, 1951
Art and Technics, 1952
From the Ground Up: Observations on Contemporary Architecture, Housing, Highway Building, and Civic Design, 1956
The Transformations of Man, 1956
The City in History: Its Origins, Its Transformations, and Its Prospects, 1961
The Highway and the City, 1963
The Myth of the Machine: I. Technics and Human Development, 1967
The Urban Prospect, 1968
The Myth of the Machine: II. The Pentagon of Power, 1970
Interpretations and Forecasts: 1922–1972: Studies in Literature, History, Biography, Technics, and Contemporary Society, 1973
Architecture as a Home for Man: Essays for Architectural Record, edited by Jeanne M. Davern, 1975
Findings and Keepings: Analects for an Autobiography, 1975
My Works and Days: A Personal Chronicle, 1979
Sketches from Life: The Autobiography of Lewis Mumford: The Early Years, 1982
The Lewis Mumford Reader, edited by Donald L. Miller, 1986
Sidewalk Critic: Lewis Mumford's Writings on New York, edited by Robert Wojtowicz, 1998

Further Reading

A scholarly literature on Lewis Mumford is just beginning to emerge, and it covers his contributions to architecture, planning, literary criticism, and public discourse.

Blake, Casey Nelson, *Beloved Community: The Cultural Criticism of Randolph Bourne, Van Wyck Brooks, Waldo Frank, and Lewis Mumford*, Chapel Hill: University of North Carolina Press, 1990
Hughes, Thomas Parke, and Agatha C. Hughes (editors), *Lewis Mumford: Public Intellectual*, New York: Oxford University Press, 1990
Miller, Donald L., *Lewis Mumford: A Life*, New York: Weidenfeld and Nicolson, 1989
Novak, Frank G., *The Autobiographical Writings of Lewis Mumford: A Study in Literary Audacity*, Honolulu: University of Hawaii Press, 1988
Tschachler, Heinz, *Lewis Mumford's Reception in German Translation and Criticism*, Lanham, Maryland: University Press of America, 1994
Wojtowicz, Robert, *Lewis Mumford and American Modernism: Eutopian Theories for Architecture and Urban Planning*, Cambridge and New York: Cambridge University Press, 1996

MUSEUMS

The ancient rites of giving sanctuary to the muse while bringing the muse to the people are the dual intentions of the museum. In the 20th century, these rites increasingly call forth the muses of both art and architecture. Because a museum as architecture is also judged as a work of art, a tremendous cultural and aesthetic burden falls on the designer of a museum, for the building is surely to be the largest acquisition that any art museum is likely to make, and therefore the structure becomes a major accession to the museum's collection. Thus, through the typology of the museum, bricks and stones and steel come to connoisseurship.

Because they encompass so much artistic aspiration, museums are important aesthetic touchstones, and those of the 20th century will become significant points of reference for future interpretation of the aesthetics of our era. Today, we have come to expect modern landmarks in museum design and complex building programs defining each new decade. Major European and American cities, from Paris to Los Angeles, have demonstrated their artistic commitment through museum construction, but smaller places as well, such as Nimes, Bilbao, Milwaukee, and Denver, have invested in important buildings, to the surprise and admiration of the rest of the world.

In the 20th-century explosion of museum design, architects have explored myriad manifestations of the modern, ranging from the formalized, classical geometry of Mies van der Rohe's Altes Museum (Berlin) through the vaulted light and space of Louis Kahn's Kimbell Art Museum (Fort Worth, Texas) to the curvilinear expressionism of the two Guggenheims, Frank Lloyd Wright's (New York City) and Frank Gehry's (Bilbao, Spain). Museum architecture of the late 20th century has taken many forms programmatically as well: the creation of wholly new edifices, such as Marcel Breuer's Whitney Museum of American Art (New York City); agglomerative ensembles of existing museum buildings, as in Gwathmey Seigel's Harvard University Art Museums; contemporary additions to historic museums, such as Roche Dinkoloo's Temple of Dendur at the Metropolitan Museum of Art (New York City) and Robert Venturi's Sainsbury Wing of the National Gallery (London); and adaptations of nonmuseum architecture to museum space, as at the Musee Picasso (Paris) and the Tate Gallery (London) by Jacques Herzog and Pierre de Meuron of Switzerland.

Museums must strike a subtle balance: to be stunning sites and spaces in their own right and yet to be friends to art. Works of art in themselves, they must be true to their stated mission, which is to show other art to its best advantage. Tour-de-force architectural form must not forget artistic function, and for the museum, this means to show paintings and sculpture advantageously within an inviting public arena. This is the singular challenge of museum architecture, for as always, architecture is found to be the only art form to bear the burden of function and necessity.

A small selection of truly exceptional masterpieces of modern museum architecture whose quality is based on design creativity, significance or influence of design, and appropriateness of architecture to art will underscore the significance of this building type in the 20th century. Therefore, the designs chosen are those that likely will become models defining modern museum architecture rather than the most site-specific or idiosyncratic works. Selected works are ones that demonstrate aesthetic insight, that are complementary to art, and that together begin to define the typology of the 20th-century museum. These works of late modernism will serve to explain the relationship among art, architecture, and viewer in the future, as earlier buildings, such as

Le Corbusier's Pavillon de l'esprit nouveau (1925) and Mies's German Pavilion (1929) for the Barcelona Exhibition, have defined exhibition architecture in the past. Some exemplars of 20th-century museum architecture that one can study are the Museum of Modern Art (1939) in New York, the East Building of the National Gallery (1978) in Washington, D.C., and the J. Paul Getty Museum (1997) in Los Angeles.

The Museum of Modern Art in New York City (MoMA) is the cornerstone of modern museum architecture, for it is both concretely and symbolically representative of the meaning of the modern museum. Founded in 1929, MoMA advanced the first modern architecture exhibitions in the United States as well as the first architecture and design collections and curators. Even the architectural term "International Style," in its American incarnation, was coined there by the 1932 exhibition of the same name.

The original 1939 building by Philip L. Goodwin and Edward Durell Stone, a sleek, highly polished, streamlined envelope for art within an urban setting, was well ahead of its time stylistically for America of the 1930s. Programmatically, too, MoMA was shaping the future of museum design, for now museum architecture would accommodate the hanging and viewing of works, ranging from the easel-size canvases of Cezanne to the wall-size ones of Pollock. The typology of the modern museum,

in contradiction to the weighty buildings of the Beaux-Arts, was, after MoMA, to be conceived of as a lightweight, permeable, volumetric enclosure of architecture about works of art. MoMA is currently undergoing a 21st-century expansion, a project designed by the Tokyo architect Yoshio Taniguchi (begun in 1997 with a completion date of 2005). With the many iterations of its architecture in the last decades of the 20th century, MoMA seems to be constantly in flux, although perhaps this state is fitting to the meaning of modernism.

The passage of light and views from within to without at MoMA is seamless. In a great contribution to the history of museum design, the galleries are well designed for the uninterrupted contemplation of the works, whereas the public spaces are designed to orient the viewer to the urban world outside the museum's walls.

Early in the design history of MoMA, architect Philip Johnson there created one of the most sophisticated open spaces within any city: the Abby Aldrich Rockefeller Sculpture Garden, a midcentury urban space that is truly innovative and almost romantically modern, if such a thing is possible. Here, three-dimensional works by Picasso, Rodin, Matisse, and Henry Moore are played in counterpoint to nature, the sculpture dispersed among stands of weeping beech and still water, in a Zen-like composition. Basically unchanged since its inception in

Arata Isozaki, Musuem of Contemporary Art, Los Angeles (1986)
© Donald Corner and Jenny Young/GreatBuildings.com

1953, this space is a sanctuary to modernism, where quiet contemplation of art and nature is enclosed by walls of abutting skyscrapers and townhouses and enlivened by their urbane architectural presence. Here art, architecture, nature, and city intersect.

Another of the significant museum spaces in the United States that allows space, architecture, and city to interact with art is the East Building of the National Gallery (1978), Washington, D.C., by I.M. Pei. This geometric, sculptural composition in acute angles and white marble sets the standard to which American public architecture should aspire. In a complex program that simultaneously must exhibit art, create public spaces, respond to its context (which includes the U.S. Capitol and Pennsylvania Avenue), and create a visual landmark on the National Mall, the architect has more than succeeded. Pei has gone further, designing a building that both shows art to its advantage via visually varied galleries in breathtaking interior spaces filled with the sunlight of the south and goes on to create an exterior design so elegant as to become an architectural landmark and a work of art in itself. Pei's highly creative solution is based on geometry, concretely and metaphorically. He has used the triangle, the trapezoid, the tetrahedron, and the acute angle of L'Enfant's Washington plan to dictate his plan. Within this geometric context, the complex interior glassed spaces and the contrasting smooth white marble exterior elevations together create compositional integrity.

The American National Gallery foreshadowed Pei's work for another national gallery, the French Louvre (1989). Here, again in a challenging program for a structure symbolic of a nation's artistic heritage, the architect found a solution based on geometry. Faced not only with the long historical memory of France but also with a massive site along the Seine River, including an elongated palace and enclosed courtyards, Pei wisely did not try to imitate the Louvre of history. Instead, in a multilayered juxtaposition, he designed a boldly modern glass pyramidal structure that responds to the ancient buildings. Pei's pyramid seems to comment on the French love of exoticism in art, on Napoleonic history, and on the Egyptian collections of the Louvre.

As the geometry of the pyramid is to the Louvre, the geometry of the isosceles triangle is to the National Gallery. Because geometry in architecture is eternal, Pei's pyramid and his triangle speak equally to modernism and to the antique.

The continuity of antiquity with modernism has also been explored thematically by Richard Meier in the J. Paul Getty Museum (1997) in Los Angeles. In a number of ways, this monumental project is the summation of museum architecture—even architecture in general—of the late 20th century, a kind of fin-de-siècle statement of an era. Opening with the close of the millennium and having been under construction during one of the most devastating earthquakes to hit an American city—and surviving—the Getty is a triumph of the spirit of modern architecture. Sited atop a seismically active city, it represents almost a challenge to the gods. We recall that the predecessor to Meier's Getty, the Getty Villa (1980, under renovation) in Malibu, California, is a replica of a villa in Herculaneum (and we need no reminder of the fate of that place). Perhaps it is hubris to bring art to Olympus, but this is exactly what the monumental Getty has done.

The giant edifice, floating white above the city and the Pacific, is a metaphor for the history of modern architecture and ideology. The building is rich with architectural references waiting to be read. The most apparent reference is to the Le Corbusian white machine in the garden, but the building also recalls the Bauhaus "crystalline cathedral of the arts" imagery as well as the futurist manifesto. More contemporary references are to Louis Kahn's Salk Institute and Kimball Art Museum and less directly to Wright's spiraling Guggenheim.

As a silent white train pulls the viewer up the mountain through fragrant chaparral, the city of today—its freeways and its smog—falls away below. The viewer begins to feel a strong sense of ascent to the promontory, a latter-day Athenian processional to the Acropolis. At the hilltop, the visitor must leave the white train and climb higher, via symbolic marble steps, toward the modern temple to art. Now at last, one views Meier's Getty in full, the sleek, machined, semicircular, arcing monumental entrance, leading into a dramatically void space of sun and sculpted waterways. Configured like a Mediterranean village, the limestone-faced pavilions housing the art are dispersed axially about, and cling to, the sunlit central courtyard. Although on first sight it is completely Mediterranean white, the materials—enameled metal squares and cubic cut travertine—are subtly varied and change color and contrast with the setting sun. In a subtle touch, the architect has exposed rough-cut limestone honeycombed with primitive fossils. Thus, from the most primitive geologic sources in nature—through the finely cut, unmortared stone of the ancients to the machined metals of the moderns—the materials of the museum symbolically re-create the history of art.

LESLIE HUMM CORMIER

See also **Getty Center, Los Angeles; Guggenheim Museum, Bilbao, Spain; Guggenheim Museum, New York City; High Museum of Art, Atlanta, Georgia; Holocaust Memorial Museum, Washington, D.C.; Johnson, Philip (United States); Kimbell Art Museum, Fort Worth, Texas; Museum of Modern Art, New York City; National Gallery of Art, East Building, Washington, D.C.; Peace Memorial and Museum, Hiroshima; Pei, I.M. (United States); Sainsbury Wing, National Gallery, London; Stone, Edward Durell (United States)**

Further Reading

Biasini, Émile, Jean Lebrat, Dominique Bezombeg, and Jean-Michel Vincent, *Le grand Louvre: Métamorphose d'un musée, 1981–1993*, Paris: Electa Moniteur, 1989; as *The Grand Louvre: A Museum Transfigured, 1981–1993*, translated by Charlotte Ellis and Murray Wyllie, Paris: Electa Moniteur, 1989

McLanathan, Richard (editor), *East Building, National Gallery of Art: A Profile*, Washington, D.C.: National Gallery of Art, 1978

Walsh, John, and Deborah Gribbon, *The J. Paul Getty Museum and Its Collections: A Museum for a New Century*, Los Angeles: J. Paul Getty Museum, 1997

MUSEUM OF MODERN ART, FRANKFURT, GERMANY

Designed by Hans Hollein; completed 1991

When the Darmstadt industrialist Karl Ströher died in 1977, he left not only a vast collection of exceptional American and

European artwork to the city of Frankfurt, Germany but also the dilemma of housing for these artworks. The modern collection centered on works from the 1960s including works by then-obscure artists including Carl André, Joseph Bueys, Dan Flavin, Donald Judd, Roy Lichtenstein, Walter De Maria, Claes Oldenburg, Blinky Palermo, Reiner Ruthenbeck, Franz Erhard Walther, and Andy Warhol.

Hilmar Hoffmann, chief of Frankfurt's department of culture, drew up a proposal for a new museum building and acquired for the city an irregular, triangular tract of land measuring 2,140 square meters at the intersection of Domstrasse, Braubachstrasse, and Berliner Strasse that had stood empty except for a scatter of Nissan huts since World War II. The tract was located in the ancient section of Frankfurt inside the old city walls and bordered by the cathedral Römer in the center and a Dominican monastery on the east and a Carmelite monastery on the west. City officials euphemistically put the spin on the sterile location as an arrow pointing to the east, or to the more progressive, modern part of the city, and in 1983 when an open design competition for the museum was initiated, 98 architects or firms entered. In May of that year the commission was awarded to the Viennese architect Hans Hollein.

The site perfectly complemented Hollein's architectural philosophy. The unusual requirements imposed by both the topography and purpose of the Domstrasse tract presented myriad possibilities for Hollein. As early as 1963, when Ströher was amassing his collection, Hollien was building models of utopian cities eschewing the functionalism and the narrowly controlled aesthetic of the post-Bauhaus period. Hollein sought to return to the joy of building and rediscover not only the practical aspects of the craft, but also the interpretation of meaning in construction. To Hollein and his fellow enthusiasts, Peter Cook, Dennis Crompton, Kisho Kurokawa, Isozaki Arata and others, architecture was not a shell showcasing the activity within, but an interactive, philosophical statement that transformed building and function into a whole.

Hollein's design was immediately dubbed *Tortenstuck* (Slice of Cake) because of the atypical physical features of the existing site. He built a Postmodern construction reminiscent of both the flatiron of the past century and a mighty ocean liner, cresting into the cityscape of Frankfurt. Hollein managed to integrate the building with the traditional architecture surrounding the museum, despite its challenging geography. He accomplished this primarily through the use of conventional materials such as glass, gray-blue stucco, and red sandstone to echo the buildings of the neighborhood.

Although the competition was decided in 1983, construction did not begin on the museum until June, four years later. During that time, plans were made for the inclusion of an exhibition space of 4,150 square meters, which incorporate an area with natural lighting of 1,472 square meters. In addition, a 714-square-meter administration area housing the museum's library was planned as well as a 519-square-meter area for workshops and conservation. The museum opened to the public 6 June 1991 and won a special commendation from the European Museum Awards in 1994.

The building may be viewed as an example of artwork equal to the premier collection of modern and contemporary art it houses. The entrance to the building is not in the expected center of any of the three sides but is located at the corner end of

Museum of Modern Art, Frankfurt (1991)
Photo © Rudolf Nagel

Domstrasse and Braubachstrasse. The thrust of the main-floor gallery reveals an interior structure that rises the entire three stories to the sectional skylit gallery that occupies much of the roof area. The central spine of stairs cuts through the length of the building connecting each of the 40 exhibition rooms. In addition, each room is also linked to the next by asymmetrical passages. Each exhibition area is informed by lighting, perspective, and ambiance. Hollein creates a sense of anticipation as the visitor wanders throughout the structure in a nonregimented manner, creating interaction not only with the artworks but also with the building itself.

Perhaps the most ingenious component of the Frankfurt Museum of Modern Art is Hollein's treatment of the roof. Although he has reserved areas in the narrow east point of the building for purposes requiring darkened environments, the uppermost skylights—created by a network of tempered glass—suffuse the space with brilliant but mediated daylight. In addition to this, Hollein has a virtual city in miniature housing the infrastructure of air-conditioning and technical transformers. Cased in copper, oxidized into luminous greens and bronze, the technical structures combine with the tempered glass like a reliquary reminiscent of the surrounding monastic architecture.

The Frankfurt Museum of Modern Art defies reference to both past stylistic developments as well as contemporary ones.

In this building, Hollein has succeeded in producing in his words an absolute architecture, an expression not just of the intellect but also of the spirit.

ALLISON HOUSTON SAULS

See also **Frankfurt, Germany; Hollein, Hans (Austria); Museum**

Further Reading

Ammann, Joseph, and Jean-Christophe Rykwert, "Hans Hollein: Museum of Modern Art, Frankfurt/Main," *Domus* 731 (1991)

"El collage arquitectónico: Museo de arte moderno en Frankfurt" [Architectonic Collage: Museum of Modern Art in Frankfurt], *A&V* 18 (1989)

Crüwell, Konstanze, "Kunst Kommt von Künstler: Jean-Christophe Ammann und das neue Museum für Moderne Kunst," [Art from the Artist: Jean-Christophe Ammann and the New Museum of Modern Art], *Kunst und Antiquitaten* 6 (1991)

Doubilet, Susan, "Hewn from the City Block," *Progressive Architecture* 10 (1991)

"Francfort: Musée d'Art Moderne," "Frankfurt: Museum of Modern Art," *Architecture Intérieure Créé* 246 (1991)

"Hans Hollein: Museum for Modern Art, Frankfurt am Main, Germany, Design: 1982–83, 1985–90; Construction: 1987–91," *GA Document* 31 (1991)

Kalusche, Bernd, and Wolf Christian Setzepfandt, *Architecturfuher Frankfurt am Main*, Berlin: Reimer, 1992

Klotz, Heinrich (editor), *Jahrbuch fur Architektur 1984 das neue Frankfurt 2*, [1984 Yearbook of new Frankfurt Architecture], Braunschweig, Germany, and Wiesbaden, Germany: Vieweg, 1984

Kuhrt, Mark, "Museum für Moderne Kunst in Frankfurt am Main" [Museum of Modern Art in Frankfurt am Main], *Baumeister* 8 (1991)

MacAuley, Michael, "It's the Taste That Counts," *Building Design* 1040 (1991)

"Le mostre: Hans Hollein a Francoforte" [Extended overlap: Hans Hollein in Frankfurt], *L'Archittetura, Cronache e Storia*, 435/1 (1992)

Museum Architecture in Frankfurt, 1980–1990 (exhib. cat.), Munich and New York: Prestel, 1990

"The Museum of Modern Art [project], Frankfurt am Main, West Germany, design, 1983," *GA Document* 18 (1987)

Pagliari, Francesco, "Una sfida urbana." [An Urban Challenge], *L'Arca* 65 (1992)

"Projet de musée d'art moderne à Francfort-sur-le-Main" [Museum of Modern Art Project in Frankfurt am Main], *L'Architecture d'Aujourd'hui* 228 (1983)

"Triangle de la modernité" [Modern Triangle], *Connaissance des Arts* 473–474 (1991)

Weis, Klaus Dieter, "Auftritt für Kunst." [Art Rises], *DBZ* 7 (1991)

MUSEUM OF MODERN ART, NEW YORK

The Museum of Modern Art in New York City was the first museum in the world dedicated to modern art. Founded in 1929 as the private initiative of a small group of wealthy, advance-minded collectors, its goal was to create an environment for the public presentation of works of modern art at a time when the major artistic institutions in New York scorned the new style. Initially located in rental space on the 12th floor of the Heckscher Building at 730 Fifth Avenue, the museum soon began to consider construction of a permanent home. George Howe and William Lescaze, still engaged in the design of the PSFS Building in Philadelphia and recently in partnership, were invited to prepare schemes for a hypothetical midblock site. Over the next year and a half, they prepared six schemes, including one of daringly stacked Constructivist-style boxes, but plans were put on hold when in 1932 the museum moved to a brownstone at 11 West 53rd Street donated by John D. Rockefeller, Jr. It was not until after the dissolution of the Howe–Lescaze partnership and the acquisition of further brownstones that the museum again began to consider construction of a permanent site along 53rd Street.

Selection of the architect was, however, a delicate matter. As the arbiter of taste in modernism, a role the museum claimed for itself, the architect and the nature of the building were necessarily significant. Alfred H. Barr, Jr., the first director, argued in favor of Ludwig Mies van der Rohe, Walter Gropius, or J.J.P. Oud. When Oud and Gropius pulled out, he endorsed Mies van der Rohe, who was invited to New York in 1937. However, Barr was overruled by Abby Aldrich (Mrs. John) Rockefeller and other building committee members who favored Philip L. Goodwin, a traditionalist architect who had a taste for modern art, excellent family connections, and money. Under pressure from Barr, the committee agreed that the young Edward Durell Stone, then working for the architect Wallace Harrison at Rockefeller Center, would assist Goodwin in an attempt to give the design a more up-to-date appearance. Barr resigned from the building committee in protest.

The Goodwin-Stone building, now largely submerged in a sea of restorations and improvements, was a disappointment to modernists. Although the exterior lines were simplified and boxlike, the overall effect was modernized Art Deco, with a curving canopy that reached out over the sidewalk and was echoed by a curved information booth inside and by the stepped-back roof terrace. The galleries were defined on the facade by white Thermolux, the exterior walls were treated in marble, and two stories of offices were shielded by gridded windows. At first glance at least, the facade seemed to express modernist design principles in which distinct interior functions received distinctive exterior treatments, yet the reality was illusion, for the facade elements were merely hung off the floor slabs. Contemporary critics such as Talbot Hamlin lamented the fact that the result was "pure facade pictorial architecture," no different from "old fashioned buildings with a colossal order." The sculpture garden at the rear of the building was designed by Barr and curator of architecture John McAndrew and has been called "the first attempt to building a sculpture garden according to modernist principles" (Benes).

Significant renovations by Philip Johnson began after World War II and, ironically, reflect a return to the architectural style of Mies van der Rohe, the architect originally preferred by Barr. Though the Grace Rainey Rogers Annex (1951), the result of the purchase and destruction of yet another brownstone along 53rd Street, was in the words of its architect, "just a sliver," the use of decorative mullions expressed the underlying steel skeleton, much like Mies's contemporary projects in Chicago. Johnson also added a facade to the Whitney Museum of American Art (1954) on 54th Street (which backed onto the museum's Sculpture Garden) and built two further wings to the museum—

the East Wing and the Garden Wing (1964), recalling Mies van der Rohe. With the addition of a reconfigured lobby (also 1964) and the elimination of the curving sidewalk canopy, much of the Art Deco character of the original structure was now eliminated.

In the Abby Aldrich Rockefeller Sculpture Garden (1953), which replaced that of Barr and McAndrew, Johnson made what was most acclaimed space. The surface of the garden was paved, and two offset, shallow-water channels were laid into the ground, bridged by identical stone slabs. A series of tree groups were disposed around a central piazza-like space. As a whole, the garden recalled Mies's garden court designs from Germany and from the Barcelona Pavilion as well as the newly popular Japanese garden.

In 1979–84, Cesar Pelli added a glass circulation stack to house escalators facing the Sculpture Garden as well as a rental tower, Museum Towers, at the west end of the block. Fiercely criticized at the time, the additions were made in a period of economic crisis for the museum and represented its attempt to transform itself into an international center of modern art.

In 1997, a new in-fill expansion lot was added to the museum with the purchase of the Dorset Hotel (on 54th Street). The competition aroused much interest. Two megamuseums, Richard Meier's Getty Center in Los Angeles and Frank Gehry's Guggenheim, Bilbao, had just opened, and it was thought that

the Museum of Modern Art competition might have the same *éclat*. Though the complex process of selection was much debated, the results were both strangely predictable and totally surprising. In the end, the museum passed over the most-noted contemporary architects and selected Yoshio Taniguchi, a Japanese architect virtually unknown in North America and Europe. Taniguchi's renovation, now under way, will reorient the entrance to the museum and provide for a more varied series of paths through the galleries as well as providing a high-modernist connection to the museum's variegated modernistic past. In 1999, the museum merged with P.S. 1, the Contemporary Gallery in Long Island City.

Though the architecture built of the museum has been insufficiently bold, the museum has maintained its standing and increased its reputation through exhibitions, symposia, and lectures. In 1932, the museum was the site of "Modern Architecture—International Exhibition," organized by Philip Johnson and Henry-Russell Hitchcock, which heralded the new modern style and defined its characteristics. Fiercely debated, the exhibition served a catalytic function in bringing issues about modern architecture to the fore. Indeed, the museum has often served an educational role, informing visitors about the advantages of new design or the new housing. In the 1970s, the museum even took up what seemed to be antimodernist positions,

Museum of Modern Art, New York City (1939 facade by Philip Goodwin and Edward Durell Stone)
© Lawrence A. Martin/GreatBuildings.com

as in the exhibition organized by curator Arthur Drexler on the French École des Beaux-Arts (1975–76) and the Deconstructivist Architecture exhibition (1988). Under Terence Riley (appointed 1995), the museum has been the site of important exhibitions on key figures of modernism (Alvar Aalto and Mies van der Rohe) as well as the site for discussions of issues in contemporary architecture.

NICHOLAS ADAMS

See also **Art Deco; Hamlin, Talbot (United States); International Style Exhibition, New York (1932); Johnson, Philip (United States); Mies van der Rohe, Ludwig (Germany); Museum; Stone, Edward Durell (United States)**

Further Reading

Beneš, Mirka, "A Modern Classic: The Abby Aldrich Rockefeller Sculpture Garden," in *Philip Johnson and the Museum of Modern Art* Elderfield, John (editor) pp. 104–151.
Elderfield, John (editor), *Philip Johnson and the Museum of Modern Art*, New York: Museum of Modern Art, 1998
Hamlin, Talbot F., "Modern Display of Works of Art," *Pencil Points* 20 (September 1939); reprinted in *New York 1930: Architecture and Urbanism Between the Two World Wars*, edited by Robert A. M. Stern, Gregory Gilmartin, and Thomas Hellins, New York: Rizzoli, 1987
Kantor, Sybil Gordon, *Alfred H. Barr, Jr. and the Intellectual Origins of the Museum of Modern Art*, Cambridge: MIT Press, 2002
Lynes, Russell, *Good Old Modern: An Intimate Portrait of the Museum of Modern Art*, New York: Atheneum, 1973
Stern, Robert A.M., *George Howe: Toward a Modern American Architecture*, New Haven, Connecticut: Yale University Press, 1975
Stern, Robert A.M., Gregory Gilmartin, and Thomas Mellins, *New York 1930: Architecture and Urbanism Between the Two Wars*, New York: Rizzoli, 1987

MUTHESIUS, HERMANN 1861–1927

Architect, Germany

Hermann Muthesius is one of several influential architects born during the 1860s whose written and built works shaped the architectural culture of Germany before World War I. Working at the crossroads of the architecture and government policy professions, Muthesius enjoyed an unusually prolific career as an architect, writer, diplomatic attaché, civil servant, and reformer of Prussian arts-and-crafts education.

Seeking to enhance German architectural culture while boosting the nation's competitiveness, Muthesius exercised a formative influence on Germany's approach to 20th-century architecture, the applied arts, and the application of design to industry. Working in Japan, Germany, and England between 1888 and 1903, Muthesius became known for reinterpreting the principles of the British Arts and Crafts movement in light of contemporary German economic, cultural, and technological conditions. Assigned to report to his government on English cultural, economic, and technical affairs from the German Embassy in London between 1896 and 1903, he authored countless articles, reports, and such well-known books as *Style-Architecture and Building-Art*, and his landmark three-volume study, *The English House*. In dozens of buildings and more than 100 articles

and books published before World War I, Muthesius was responsible for design theories and policy formulations which, in combination with the leadership of the politician Friedrich Naumann and the craftsman-entrepreneur Karl Schmidt, would lay the basis for the Deutscher Werkbund in 1907.

Muthesius was perhaps most influential in the realm of design theory. Building on writings from the 1890s by the art historian Richard Streiter and the cultural critic Ferdinand Avenarius, he was the first to disseminate widely the principle of rational, objective, or realist design, known as *Neue Sachlichkeit* (New Objectivity). Muthesius succeeded at institutionalizing this and such related ideas as fitness of form to functional purpose, workshop-based instruction, and the centrality of the machine to modern design in dozens of Prussian applied arts and building trades schools.

Developed simultaneously in his writings, government work, and in houses that bridged traditional Germanic forms and rational, practical planning, these principles went on to have a formative influence on the Werkbund. In a speech delivered in honor of being appointed Chair of Applied Arts at the newly opened Berlin Commercial College in January 1907, entitled "The Significance of the Applied Arts," Muthesius provoked a split between so-called "traditional" crafts practitioners and those artists, architects, and crafts manufacturers interested in exploring new relationships between tradition, the possibilities of machine-influenced design, and more competitive modes of integrated, artist-driven production. The resulting "Muthesius case," as the eight-month public controversy over Muthesius's divisive speech was dubbed, provoked the formation of the Deutscher Werkbund in October of 1907 as a private, national association of progressive producers and designers. Comprised of architects, artists, craftsmen, and manufacturing and business leaders, the Werkbund sought to influence producers, consumers, and markets. Its extremely diverse membership sought to strengthen German culture and national competitiveness through improvements in the quality of German products, factories, and the designed environment generally.

Muthesius earned his architectural reputation through the refinement of a modified suburban "country house" type known as the *Landhaus*. Designing the *Landhaus* as a paradigmatic modern dwelling for the accomplished, professional suburban elite, Muthesius eliminated the characteristic raised plinth of the traditional aristocratic villa and settled the *Landhaus* directly onto its site. Providing highly rational and individualized day-lit rooms in accordance with the free planning principles of the Arts and Crafts movement, the architect emphasized the provision of direct access to light, air, and "outdoor rooms" that extended domestic spaces onto terraces in favorable weather and further to geometrically planned gardens beyond. Reflecting German conditions following World War I, Muthesius wrote numerous popular books on the design of middle-class houses as well as modest yet efficient dwellings for workers in publications that ran into several editions.

The buildings for which Muthesius is best known include the Freudenberg House in Berlin-Nikolassee (1908, built adjacent to the Muthesius House of 1906), the de Burlet House and the Mohrbutter House in Berlin-Schlachtensee (1911 and 1913), workers' housing and single-family dwellings at Hellerau Garden City (1910), the Cramer House in Berlin-Dahlem (1912), and the Silk Factory of Michels & Co. (1912). Best remembered as a pragmatist whose passions lay at the intersection of architectural practice, policy making, and writing, Muthesius achieved his reputation in ways other than through great formal innovations or radical new buildings. Nevertheless, his clear formulations and tireless campaign to tie changes in early 20th-century German architecture and design to technological, political, social, and economic developments guaranteed that the architect's ideas would exercise a formative impact on much of Germany's subsequent 20th-century architectural culture.

JOHN V. MACIUIKA

See also **Arts and Crafts Movement; Deutscher Werkbund; Werkbund Exhibition, Cologne (1914)**

Biography

Born in Gross-Neuhausen in the Grand Duchy of Saxony-Weimar-Eisenach, 20 April 1861. Completed apprenticeship in masonry with his father, a master mason and contractor; earned an architecture degree, Royal Technical University in Berlin (Charlottenburg) in 1887; worked for the firm of Ende and Böckmann in Tokyo, Japan 1887–91; returned to Germany in 1891 after a four-month journey through China, Siam, India, and Egypt; passed state architectural examinations in 1893. Designed buildings for Prussian Ministry of Public Works (1893–96); guest edited its journal, the *Central Newspaper for Building Administration (Centralblatt der Bauverwaltung)*. October 1896–June 1903 stationed at the German Embassy in London as a Prussian technical reporter and cultural attaché; returned to the Prussian Ministry of Commerce and Trade in Berlin to reform the state applied arts, crafts, and trades school system (1903–26); opened private architectural practice (1904–27). Helped found Deutscher Werkbund in 1907; served as Werkbund vice president in 1912. Died in Berlin, 26 October 1927.

Selected Works

Muthesius House, Berlin-Nikolassee, 1906
Freudenberg House, Berlin-Nikolassee, 1908
Workers' housing and single-family dwellings, Hellerau Garden City, 1910
De Burlet House, Berlin-Schlachtensee, 1911
Cramer House, Berlin-Dahlem, 1912
Silk Factory, Michels & Co., Nowawes-bei-Potsdam, Germany, 1912
Mohrbutter House, Berlin-Schlachtensee, 1913

Selected Publications

Stilarchitektur und Baukunst: Wandlungen der Architektur im XIX.: Jahrhundert und ihr heutiger Standpunkt, Mülheim-Ruhr, Germany: Verlag von K. Schimmelpfeng, 1902; reprinted as *Style-Architecture and Building-Art: Transformations of Architecture in the Nineteenth Century and Its Present Condition*, translated and introduced by Stanford Anderson, Santa Monica, California: Getty Center for the History of Art and the Humanities, 1994

Das englische haus: Entwicklung, Bedingungen, Anlage, Aufbau, Einrichtung und Innenraum, 3 vols., Berlin: Wasmuth, 1904–05; as *The English House*, edited and introduced by Dennis Sharp, translated by Janet Seligman, New York: Rizzoli, 1979
Landhaus und Garten: Beispiele neuzeitlicher Landhäuser nebst Grundrissen, Innenräumen und Gärten [Country House and Garden: Examples of Recent Country Houses with Plans, Interiors, and Gardens], Munich: Bruckmann, 1907

Further Reading

Hermann Muthesius, 1861–1927 (exhib. cat.), London: Architectural Association, 1979
Hubrich, Hans-Joachim, *Hermann Muthesius: Die Schriften zu Architektur, Kunstgewerbe, Industrie in der "Neuen Bewegung,"* [Hermann Muthesius: The Writings on Architecture, applied arts, and Industry in the "New Movement"], Berlin: Mann, 1980
Maciuika, John Vincent, "Art in the Age of Government Intervention: Hermann Muthesius, *Sachlichkeit*, and the State, 1897–1907," *German Studies Review*, 21/2 (May 1998)
Maciuika, John Vincent, "Hermann Muthesius and the Reform of German Architecture, Arts, and Crafts, 1890–1914," Ph.D. diss., University of California at Berkeley, 1998
Maciuika, John Vincent, *Before the Bauhaus: Architecture, Politics, and the German State, 1890–1919*, Cambridge: Cambridge University Press, (in press)
Posener, Julius, *Berlin auf dem Wege zu einer neuen architektur: Das zeitalter Wilhelms II.* [Before on the Path to a New Architecture: The Age of Wilhelm II] Munich: Prestel, 1979

N

NATIONAL ART SCHOOLS, HAVANA, CUBA

On 1 January 1959, a new period in Cuban history commenced with Fidel Castro's revolutionary ousting of the dictatorship of Fulgencio Batista (1952–58), initiating a process of radical political transformations that would culminate with the integration of the country with a socialist system from 1961 onward. The new government attributed particular significance to architecture, manifest in three works built in Havana that symbolize the epoch of the Revolution (1959–65): the Neighborhood Center of La Habana del Este, the "José Antonio Echeverría" University Campus, and the National School of Art.

With the exodus of the high bourgeoisie, the mansions, golf courses, and country clubs that once dotted the outskirts of the capital were abandoned. Castro decided to turn this site into a center for artistic education for approximately 3000 scholarship students who were coming to Cuba from other third world countries. In 1961 he assigned a team of young architects the construction of the ENA (National School of Art). The architects included Ricardo Porro of Camagüey, who designed the schools of Visual Arts and Modern Dance; Vittorio Garatti of Milan architect for the schools of Music and Ballet; and Roberto Gottardi of Venice, who designed the school of Dramatic Arts. The buildings were to be finished in the course of the year to open by 1962. However, because of differences among the directors of the teaching centers, the project for an impressive "City of the Arts" on the urban periphery was finally limited to a series of independent buildings placed along the border of the golf course. Despite the autonomy of architectural syntax used by each of the three designers, some common norms were established. Porro, Garatti, and Gottardi each sought to relate the buildings to the natural surroundings with minimal alterations; to create open, organic compositions based on the organization of interrelated "pavilions"; to clearly separate the various school functions (administration, library, classrooms, refectories, rehearsal spaces, workshops, main auditorium); and to define interior common spaces. The various National Art Schools were also designed to achieve natural ventilation and climatic conditioning through filter and latticework. All three structures were built of brick and constructed with Catalan vaults because of the scarcity of steel and cement, brought about by North American governmental embargoes.

The symbolic nature of architecture greatly influenced the artistic vanguard in Cuba. Regionalist expressionism was employed to signify the cultural traditions of the Hispanic colonial past and of the African cultural heritage, transcribed into contemporary language. Whereas the European socialist countries experienced a post-Stalinist dogmatism that led to a schematic functionalism, the National Art Schools represented the search for a national identity alongside the innovative and critical trends of the architecture in capitalist countries. Porro identified himself with the Afro-Cuban tradition, filtered through surrealism and Le Corbusier's rational Brutalism. In contrast, Garatti and Gottardi incorporated Italian neorealism and the reclamation of historical memory in works that echoed Frank Lloyd Wright, Carlo Scarpa, and Ernesto Rogers. Porro conveys two different messages through the Schools for Visual Arts and Modern Dance. In the first, he freely organizes two systems of vaulted enclosures—the painting and sculpture workshops—around a central court, united by a freely drawn curvilinear gallery that allows circulation under the shade of continuous vaults. The brick domes evoke the cylindrical shapes of African huts, whereas the persistent sinuosity of the corridors echoes the organicism of the tropical landscape. The Modern Dance school, in contrast, comprises a monumental, angular central court with rough, white brick surfaces. In Garatti's Ballet building, he submerges the cupolas of the dance hall in a massive, hollow space where galleries freely follow the natural curves of the site. In the Music school, the rehearsal halls and classrooms are built along a sinuous, 300-meter-long ribbon that links an ancient *ceiba* (a sacred tree) with the Quibú river. Finally Gottardi, in the Dramatic Arts building, effects a system of vaulted spaces with irregular perimeters whose compositional freedom recalls medieval Italian cities.

The complexity of the projects, the sophistication of the construction, compounded by the material difficulties during a convulsive phase of Cuban history extended the completion of the National Art Schools indefinitely. At the Havana celebration of the VII Congress of Architects of the UIA (1963), only Porro's two schools had been completed. Moreover, internal questioning around the National Art Schools began, namely from critics who argued that the project represented an excessive investment in

National Art School, School of Visual Arts, Havana
© Robertyo Segre

light of the widespread architectural poverty that already existed throughout the country. In 1965 the project was halted by the government. The Ballet, Music, and Dramatic Arts buildings were left unfinished. Subsequent deterioration and vandalism turned them, according to critic Gerardo Mosquera, into an abandoned ruin in the middle of the jungle, thereby constituting the first postmodern ruin in Cuba. In the 1980s, a young generation of Cuban architects sought to restore the Schools of Art, but they received a meager governmental response. Today, the extant buildings constitute an example of passionate creativity in the search for new social and cultural values in a peripheral country that aspired to become independent of the inexorable tutelage of the metropolitan centers.

ROBERTO SEGRE

See also **Brick; Brutalism; Catalan (Guastavino) Vaults; Constructivism; Contextualism; Expressionism; International Style; Masonry Bearing Wall; Portoghesi, Paolo (Italy); Postmodernism; Regionalism; Scarpa, Carlo (Italy); School; Wright, Frank Lloyd (United States)**

Further Reading

Baroni Sergio, "Rapporto dall'Avana," *Zodiac, Rivista Internazionale di Architettura* (1992)
Barré, François, and Isabelle Cazés, *Ricardo Porro*, Paris: Institut Français d'Architecture, Pandora Editions, 1991
Bullrich, Francisco, *Nuevos caminos de la arquitectura latinoamericana*, Barcelona: Blume, 1969
Gutiérrez, Ramón, *Arquitectura y urbanismo en Iberoamérica*, Madrid: Ediciones Cátedra, 1983
Loomis, John A., *Revolution of Forms. Cuba's Forgotten Art Schools*, New York: Princeton Architectural Press, 1999
Porro, Ricardo, *Ricardo Porro Architekt*, St. Veit/Glan: Ritter Klagenfurt, 1994
Porro, Ricardo, "Porro por Porro. Obra construída," *Arquitectura Cuba* (1998)
Rodríguez, Eduardo Luis, *La Habana. Arquitectura del siglo XX*, Pictures by Pepe Navarro, Barcelona: Blume, 1998
Segre, Roberto, *Cuba. Architettura della Rivoluzione*, Padua: Marsilio, 1970
Segre, Roberto, *Arquitectura y urbanismo de la Revolución cubana*, Havana: Editorial Pueblo y Educación, 1995
Segre, Roberto, "Tres décadas de arquitectura cubana: la herencia histórica y el mito de lo nuevo," *Revolución y Cultura* (1994)

NATIONAL ASSEMBLY BUILDING, SHER-E-BANGLANAGAR, DHAKA

Designed by Louis Kahn; completed 1974–83

Designed by Louis Kahn as the capitol of east Pakistan, the Sher-e-Banglanagar complex was commissioned in 1962 and eventually completed in 1974 (the year of Kahn's death) to be the capitol of the newly formed country of Bangladesh, although work on the assembly building itself continued through 1983.

The National Assembly complex is organized with a civic sector in the north, followed by the secretarial sector, and eventually the assembly sector to the south. The citadel of institutions with the secretariat and a citadel of assembly face each other on the north–south axis. The Assembly Building itself constitutes the formal and political focus of this complex and is surrounded by a lake that the residential quarters for ministers and members of the assembly also face; the approach from the north is emphasized by a sweeping axis up a brick plinth that epitomizes an acropolis. Kahn chose brick for most of the buildings, but the importance of the central assembly building was emphasized by contrast. Instead of brick, it is built of rough-shuttered, poured-in-place concrete, the walls being inset with bands of white marble at regular intervals. Arranged in three concentric rings, the octagonal assembly building is organized around an internal street that encircles the building and extends to its full height. This provides light and air and emphasizes space dramatically through light and shadow. At the core, the central chamber that houses the assembly is a 300-seat, 30-meter-high, domed amphitheater flanked by the library. The outer layer is composed

of various office spaces that surround the circulation ring. In each of the cardinal directions there is a distinct feature—the garden entrance hall to the north, a cafeteria and recreational space to the east, the ministerial lounge to the west, and a prayer hall above the entrance to the south.

The Assembly Building evinces many characteristics that one finds in Kahn's later work: the served inner focus that houses the parliament chamber itself and the service spaces in the outer ring that consist of offices and social spaces, a great interest in the play of light and shadow—especially evident in the handling of internal street and more so in the columns of light in the prayer hall, the contrasts of mass and void, and the complex juxtaposition of forms to satisfy secular institutional and more transcendental spiritual requirements. An important aspect that Kahn was trying to incorporate was the celebration of democracy. The concept of the acropolis or the citadel derives partially from this idea. In another sense this symbolism is achieved through a centralized focus that is equally expressed and visible in all directions.

Attention has been drawn to influences from other architectures in Kahn's designs. Among them are references to Mughal mausoleum gardens—especially in the formal qualities and spatial organization of the octagonal plan, the transformations of

National Assembly Building (1983), designed by Louis Kahn
© Aga Khan Trust for Culture

shapes, the two-tiered articulation of the facade with openings that allow for deep shadows, the scale of the monumental building, and the reflecting pool. The contrasting use of materials recalls the Taj Mahal and especially Humayun's tomb in the dynamics of the red-brick buildings surrounding the assembly building itself and the treatment of the latter, which uses the contrasting concrete and marble strips. The fortress-like qualities are reminiscent of the forts of Rajasthan, Delhi, and Agra. In addition to these eastern associations, there are references to western influences such as Roman monumentality and engineering, the spatial organization of Renaissance churches, Beaux Arts planning, classicism, and the work of other architects from Louis-Etienne Boullée to Le Corbusier. Qualities from all these different sources are present in Kahn's architecture and in the assembly building in a very refined manner.

Architectural critics, historians, and the public have described Kahn's work in Dhaka as iconic, monumental, symbolic, transcendental, and a white elephant. His masterful juxtaposition of geometries and forms can be read as an expression of regionalism and humanism. As a recipient of the Aga Khan award for architecture in its fourth cycle (1987–89), this building can in various ways be seen to emulate all these qualities and more. There has been some feeling about this building being foreign and not "Bangladeshi" in character. Nevertheless, quite a contrary opinion was evident in the Aga Khan jury report, which emphasized that the building "while universal in its sources of forms, aesthetics, and technologies, could be in no other place" and, in fact, praised it for having "assimilated both the vernacular and monumental archetypes of the region, and abstracted and transformed, to a degree of utter purity, lasting architectural ideas from many eras and civilizations."

For many, the national assembly building is especially fascinating to study because it seems as emblematic of the future; it has often been referred to as symbolic of Bangladesh's independence and an iconic beginning of a new architecture in the region.

AARATI KANEKAR

See also **Concrete; Dhaka, Bangladesh; Kahn, Louis (United States); Ministry of Foreign Affairs, Riyadh, Saudi Arabia**

Further Reading

Ashraf, Kazi K., "Louis I. Kahn, National Capital of Bangladesh, Dhaka, Bangladesh, 1962–83," *Global Architecture* 72 (1994)

Brownlee, David Bruce, and David Gilson De Long, *Louis I. Kahn: In the Realm of Architecture*, New York: Rizzoli, and Los Angeles: Museum of Contemporary Art, 1991

Giurgola, Romaldo, and Jaimini Mehta, *Louis I. Kahn*, Boulder, Colorado: Westview Press, 1975

Ksiazek, Sarah, "Architectural Culture in the Fifties: Louis Kahn and the National Assembly Complex in Dhaka," *JSAH*, 52/4 (December 1993)

Langford, Fred, "Concrete in Dacca," *Mimar* 6 (October/December 1982)

Taylor, Brian Brace, "National Assembly Hall, Dacca," *Mimar* 6 (October/December 1982)

Vallebuona, Renzo, "Louis Khan in Wonderland," *Daidalos* 61 (September 1996)

NATIONAL FARMERS' BANK

Designed by Louis Sullivan; completed 1908
Owatonna, Minnesota

The National Farmers' Bank in Owatonna, Minnesota, is the earliest and most notable of eight innovative bank buildings that Louis Sullivan designed between 1906 and 1920 for small farming communities in the upper Midwest. By closely uniting function, structure, and artistic form in these designs, Sullivan clearly illustrated the basic tenets expressed in his writings on organic architecture. At the same time, he introduced a uniquely American solution for a particular building type: the modern, rural bank.

Like many small-town financial institutions of the late 19th century, the National Farmers' Bank was originally located in a corner storefront. In 1906, when this facility was deemed no longer suitable, the bank's board of directors, led by Vice President Carl Bennett, appropriated one-sixth of the bank's total assets for the construction of a new building. Bennett firmly believed that the new building should not only serve the local residents but also celebrate the bank's central role in the prosperity of the surrounding agricultural community. Firmly rejecting the prevailing trend of adapting classical temple forms for bank buildings, he searched for an architecture that would more appropriately represent his progressive financial institution while also meeting its functional needs. Bennett's quest ended with his discovery of the work and ideas of Louis Sullivan, most likely through an essay by the architect in *Craftsman* magazine.

Sullivan first visited Bennett in Owatonna during the fall of 1906. Immediately upon returning to his Chicago office, he and his longtime chief draftsman, George Grant Elmslie, went to work on the bank's design. Appealing to Bennett's musical background, Sullivan wrote to the banker that he was attempting to create "a color symphony" for the bank that reflected the "many shades of the strings and the woodwinds and the brass."

The resulting design, often referred to as a "jewel box," was well received by Bennett and his fellow bankers. In the design, Sullivan successfully unified simple, geometric massing with rich, colorful detailing. The variegated red-brick exterior walls of the square banking hall were highlighted by a massive semicircular window on each of the two street facades. These large arched voids recall the grand portal of Sullivan's Transportation Building at the World's Columbian Exposition of 1893 or the arcuated features of the Richardsonian Romanesque popular throughout the Midwest. Divided by vertical steel mullions symbolically representing the bars of a teller's wicket, the windows project a sense of security to those entrusting their savings inside. The building's heavy cornice and small, deep, square window openings in the ashlar stone base contribute to this expression of strength and financial protection.

The boldness of the exterior massing gives way to delicate detailing as one approaches the bank. The upper part of each facade is framed by a band of identical "Teco green," terra-cotta relief panels of seed pods, swirling leaves, and stretched geometric forms characteristic of Sullivan's organic ornament. Large brown cartouches, comprised of similar geometric and vegetative elements, fill the upper corners of the banding. The small windows at street level provide a human scale to the monumental facades.

Like the exterior, the interior of the bank is simple in its basic geometric form yet intricate in its details. On entering the grand banking hall, after passing under a low, deep lintel, one becomes engulfed in Sullivan's color symphony of predominantly green and gold tones: the colors of money. On sunny days, the hall is bathed in greenish-tinged light shining through the opalescent glass panes of the great arched windows and through a large skylight above. Opposite the windows are two

Interior, National Farmers Bank of Owatonna, Steele County, Minnesota, by Louis Sullivan (1908)
© Historic American Buildings Survey/Library of Congress

large semicircular murals by Oscar Gross depicting a pastoral scene and a harvest in recognition of the agricultural base of the local economy. Outlining the basic geometric elements are elaborate bands of colorful stenciling and terracotta panels. The upper space of the banking hall is dominated by four massive green cast-iron electroliers with large spiraling tendrils that appear to grow out of the ceiling.

According to Bennett, the basic interior layout of the building was composed prior to Sullivan's involvement in the design process. The bank's desire for a democratic office plan that avoided an obvious hierarchy of spaces was in keeping with Sullivan's ideas for an American architecture. Small office spaces lined the lower level of the banking hall. The president's office located on one side of the entrance was balanced by the farmers' exchange room located on the other side. Instead of hiding the vault, as was typical at the time, it was placed in full view of patrons, immediately behind the teller's enclosure and on axis with the main entrance.

The main hall has undergone four major remodelings, each of which was carried out to better meet the evolving needs of the bank. During the first remodeling in 1940, interior brick partition walls and the teller counters and wickets were replaced by freestanding counters to create an open plan. Later remodelings, including one carried out under the direction of Harwell Hamilton Harris in 1956, strove to bring back some of the

original character of Sullivan's design that had been lost in the earlier alterations. A 1997 remodeling incorporated an alley and an adjacent two-story wing that was part of Sullivan's original design. Norwest Bank, the occupant, took great care to ensure that the new spaces complemented Sullivan's bank design.

From the start, the National Farmers' Bank was well publicized in both architectural and financial journals. The commission led to a small but important resurgence of Sullivan's fading career. It also contributed to a wave of civic and commercial buildings constructed in small midwestern towns by other members of the Prairie School, including Purcell and Elmslie, Claude and Stark, and William Steele—designers who shared Sullivan's belief that organic design principles could produce an architecture appropriate for the American Midwest.

LISA D. SCHRENK

See also **Prairie School; Sullivan, Louis (United States)**

Further Reading

Andrew, David S., *Louis Sullivan and the Polemics of Modern Architecture: The Present against the Past*, Urbana: University of Illinois Press, 1985
Bennett, Carl K., "A Bank Built for Farmers: Louis Sullivan Designs a Building which Marks a New Epoch in American Architecture," *The Craftsman*, 15 (November 1908)

De Wit, Wim (editor), *Louis Sullivan: The Function of Ornament*, New York: Norton, 1986

Frazier, Nancy, *Louis Sullivan and the Chicago School*, New York: Crescent Books, 1991

Manieri-Elia, Mario, *Louis Henry Sullivan, 1856–1924*, Milan: Electa, 1995; as *Louis Henry Sullivan*, New York: Princeton Architectural Press, 1996

Menocal, Narciso G., *Architecture as Nature: The Transcendentalist Idea of Louis Sullivan*, Madison: University of Wisconsin Press, 1981

Millett, Larry, *The Curve of the Arch: The Story of Louis Sullivan's Owatonna Bank*, St. Paul, Minnesota: Minnesota Historical Society Press, 1985

Prairie School Architecture in Minnesota, Iowa, Wisconsin (exhib. cat.), St. Paul, Minnesota: Minnesota Museum of Art, 1982

Sprague, Paul E., "The National Farmers' Bank, Owatonna, Minnesota," *Prairie School Review*, 4 (1967)

Sullivan, Louis H., *National Farmers' Bank, Owatonna, Minnesota, 1907–08; Merchants' National Bank, Grinnell, Iowa, 1914; Farmers' and Merchants' Union Bank, Columbus, Wisconsin, 1919*, Tokyo: A.D.A. Edita, 1979

"Sullivan's Owatonna Bank," *Northwest Architect*, 22 (July–August 1958)

Twombly, Robert C., *Louis Sullivan: His Life and Work*, New York: Viking, and Chicago: University of Chicago Press, 1986

Warn, Robert R., "Bennett and Sullivan, Client and Creator," *Prairie School Review*, 10 (1973)

Weingarden, Lauren S., *Louis H. Sullivan: The Banks*, Cambridge, Massachusetts: MIT Press, 1987

NATIONAL GALLERY OF ART, EAST BUILDING, WASHINGTON, D.C.

Designed by I.M. Pei; completed 1978

The National Gallery of Art, East Building, opened in 1978, was a gift from Andrew Mellon's son, Paul Mellon, and his late sister, Alisa Bruce Mellon, and the Andrew W. Mellon Foundation. The National Gallery of Art, West Building, opened in 1941 was designed by John Russell Pope, a gift from Andrew W. Mellon to the United States of America.

The site for the East Building, bordered by the Mall and Pennsylvania Avenue and facing the Capitol to the east, is prominent and significant within the urban framework of Washington. Site restrictions included building setbacks along the streets, different building height limits along the Mall and Pennsylvania Avenue, and entry only from Fourth Street. The building design needed to relate directly to the existing, neoclassical West Building. The program required a variety of flexible galleries for temporary and 20th-century exhibitions and a Center for Advanced Study in the Visual Arts totaling 450,000 square feet of floor area.

The East Building's architect, I.M. Pei, resolved these restrictions and requirements with a brilliant design concept. He divided the trapezoidal site into an isosceles triangle for the museum and a right triangle for the study center with a gap in between. The museum element has its entrance facade on Fourth Street, on axis with the West Building, and its primary facade along Pennsylvania Avenue. The study center facades face the Capitol and the Mall with its entry in the gap on Fourth Street. The 20-degree angle of Pennsylvania Avenue yielded the triangular grid and spatial module for the building plans.

This resulted in a knifelike edge of marble, 70 feet high, at the entry to the study center. A concourse below a plaza physically connects the old and new buildings. The spatial concept for the museum component is based on an isosceles-triangle-shaped atrium surrounded by galleries with towers at the three corners. The study center has a right-triangle-shaped atrium surrounded by six levels of libraries, offices, and study spaces. The spatial sequence from open plaza to recessed porch to low lobby to expansive atrium is dramatic and dynamic. Circulation suffuses the museum atrium with a grand staircase and escalator leading to bridges that cross the space at each level. Entry to the study center is also afforded from the museum atrium, whose tetrahedron skylight bridges the gap between the two primary building components.

J. Carter Brown, director of the National Gallery, was concerned with flexibility in the galleries and the experience of a visitor. The architect provided a variety of gallery shapes, such as trapezoids, triangles, parallelograms, and hexagons, some with adjustable walls and ceilings. The spatial configuration of the museum enables visitors to personalize their experience visiting one gallery at a time. In between, they return to the atrium for orientation, repose, relaxation, and socialization.

The builder, Charles H. Tompkins Company, produced an extremely high level of construction craftsmanship. The finished surfaces of the cast-in-place concrete structure, infused with marble dust, were formed using furniture-quality fir. The exterior cladding is of Tennessee marble from the same quarry utilized for the West Building, placed in the same-size pieces and same color gradation, from brown at the bottom to pink at the top. This marble is also utilized in triangular pieces for floor paving. The 16,000-square-foot museum atrium is covered by a tetrahedron steel structure supporting skylights with integral tubular filters. Tempered glass railings with chrome handrails line the bridges and balconies.

Brown wanted the building to be a work of art in its own right but also to exhibit specific works of art commissioned for this building. The most notable is the gigantic untitled aluminum mobile by Alexander Calder, his last work. Its red and black shapes undulate slowly around the atrium guided by the building's air supply system. At the entry porch is a large bronze sculpture by Henry Moore called *Knife Edge Mirror Two Piece*.

The East Building demonstrated unequivocally that modern architecture could strongly contribute to a neoclassical context, albeit through different stylistic expression. This is due to the clear geometric relationship to the site and the axial relationship to the West Building. The two buildings share an affinity because of the common marble exterior; they are also equally epic befitting the scale of monumental Washington. This was the mature expression of Pei's vision of modern architecture and one of his finest works.

The two buildings also relate well to each other through similar spatial concepts, for example, a grand entrance leading directly to a dramatic central space that leads to a variety of galleries. The difference is that the circulation in the West Building is in discrete halls, whereas in the East Building it is all in the central space. Another difference is that many of the West Building galleries have natural light and are fixed in size and shape. The orthogonal spaces of the West Building symbolize an era of static cultural values, whereas the angular spaces of the

National Gallery of Art, East Building, designed by I.M. Pei (1978)
© Michael Bednar

East Building reflect the dynamic circumstances of contemporary life.

When President Jimmy Carter opened the East Building in 1978, he stated that it symbolized the connection between art and public life in the United States. The design makes the museum available to the public through its welcoming openness; the movement from mall to plaza to porch to lobby to atrium is an effortless transition. Moreover, some of the art is in the atrium, enabling visitors to freely mingle with it. The museum and its exhibits are not placed on a pedestal or an easel. This accessibility is accomplished mainly through the dramatic triangular atrium that turns pedestrian circulation into choreographed movement where every visitor is a public dancer. In this way, the design relates to the earlier Guggenheim Museum in New York by Frank Lloyd Wright with its circular atrium and spiral ramp.

The architectural critics at the time gave the East Building design mixed reviews. Everyone applauded the contextual resolution and constructional mastery, but the most common criticism was the spatial dissociation between the galleries and the atrium and the awkward exterior massing. The art and cultural critics were much more sanguine in their views. The public, however, voted with its feet and embraced the building with great enthusiasm, with more than a million visiting the building in the first

two months. It is best known as a provocative work of architecture that engages the senses of the visitor and provides a memorable museum experience.

MICHAEL J. BEDNAR

See also **Museum; Pei, I.M. (United States)**

Further Reading

Cannell, Michael T., *I.M. Pei: Mandarin of Modernism*, New York: Carol Southern Books, 1995
Canty, Donald, "Building as Event," *AIA Journal* (Mid-May 1979)
Marlin, William, "Mr. Pei Goes to Washington," *Architectural Record* (August 1978)
McLanathan, Richard B., *National Gallery of Art, East Building*, Washington, DC: National Gallery, 1978
Wiseman, Carter, *I.M. Pei: A Profile in American Architecture*, New York: Abrams, 1990

NAVARRO BALDEWEG, JUAN 1939–

Architect, Spain

Juan Navarro Baldeweg is considered one of the most talented architects practicing in Spain today. His buildings can be characterized as serene, elegant, refined compositions. Born in the northern Spanish city of Santander, his first artistic studies were begun in 1959 in the field of engraving at the School of Fine Arts in Madrid. He continued studying architecture at the Polytechnic University of Madrid, receiving his doctorate in 1969. He received a special research grant for the Center for Advanced Visual Studies at the Massachusetts Institute of Technology. On his return to Spain, the first public recognition was granted in the artistic field through exhibitions of his installations. His architectural reputation was established by his entries to competitions. In 1979, he won first prize in the international Shinkenchiku Competition and in 1982 placed first in a major competition for his ideas for the restructuring of a large area of Madrid. Many of his public buildings are also the result of important competitions.

Navarro Baldeweg currently has his own architectural practice in Madrid and combines architecture, painting, and academic pursuits. He has been professor at the School of Architecture of the University of Madrid since 1977 and has held visiting professorships at Princeton University, Yale University, and the University of Pennsylvania.

Navarro Baldeweg has stated that architecture is made in two rooms or two chambers. One exists only in the mind of the architect, and that is where the principal work is realized. This conviction distances Navarro Baldeweg from his contemporaries, who state that architecture is the resolution of situations imposed by reality. On the one hand, his work is very personal. His investigation into the field of painting was carried a step further in his architecture. On the other hand, his architecture is the most truly universal, celebrating what connects the inhabitant and building with a wider world. The constant in the architecture of Navarro Baldeweg is an exploration of natural phenomena as a participant influencing and informing the built environment: rain, light, gravity, or wind. His architecture celebrates the natural phenomena and heightens the user's perception of it.

Navarro Baldeweg's first built work, House of Rain (1982), located in a village in the northern province of Santander, Spain, is represented in an early drawing totally surrounded by rain. The house looks out over a valley. The material configuration is structured as simple layering: stone connecting it to the ground, glass for light and views, and the zinc roof. From inside the house, one can always see out. During the rain, the exterior materials change, intensifying their appearance.

The Hydraulic Museum of the Segura River Mills, completed in 1988 in Murcia, incorporates the remains of an 18th-century mill with the new construction on its riverside site. The new addition for a museum, cafeteria, and library is clad in a smooth stone often devoid of windows and rather free in form, in contrast to the punctuated, strictly ordered former building. A new rooftop terrace on top of the old building connects the river and the city. The light that penetrates through the multistory well creates an axis of light that changes in intensity and quality with the passage of time. The dome above a small theater in the building seems to hover there as the light filters through from above.

The 1985 competition for the Castilla-León Congress Center in Salamanca resulted in one of the architect's most significant works to date. Completed in 1992, the Center comprises two parts: a main building housing the auditoriums, and a smaller volume for exhibitions and seminar rooms. The architect often seeks to create points of equilibrium in his buildings through contrasts. The main building is basically a solid cube, whereas the smaller building forms a contrast by using more glass. The two are connected at the lower level. The main building is really architecture within architecture. A giant concrete dome covers the main hall. However, the light entering through the top and all around the sides makes it seem to float. Reality and perception are forced in opposite directions, as are ideas of gravity and ingravity.

The winning competition scheme for the Extremadura Government Offices at Mérida (1995) is a large building, meant to be seen as part of the cityscape from across the river. It is stretched horizontally, maintaining a height similar to its urban context. However, the scale of the facade toward the river is broken down through the creation of courtyards. These recessed bays, which reflect the different departments of the regional government, establish light as a theme of this building. Daylight enters the offices but is mitigated on the west through the use of metal *brises-soleil*.

In 1997, Navarro Baldeweg completed his first commission in the United States—an addition to the Department of Music at Princeton University. It was also the first time that Princeton employed a foreign architect to build on its campus. The new building is an understated neighbor to some of the nearby buildings. The building contributes to its surroundings, enhancing voids and creating spaces. The brick and concrete building locates the main entrance toward the network of pedestrian pathways that cross the campus. The atrium entrance lobby embodies the contextual characteristics of the street. As one passes through the building toward the back garden, a more domestic or private character is created. Light, which enters through the large overhead skylights, flows into the atrium and library. The lower-level rehearsal room is also partially enclosed with glass to allow light to enter.

Other noteworthy works of the architect include a cultural center outside Madrid; a courthouse (1995) in Mahon, Menorca; and the new Museum and Visitors Center (2000) at the Altamira Caves site in northern Spain.

MARTHA THORNE

See also **Spain**

Selected Publications

Juan Navarro Baldeweg, 1999
Juan Navarro Baldeweg: Opere e progetti, 1990; new edition, 1996

Further Reading

Buchanan, Peter, "Gravitational Pull," *Architecture: AIA Journal* 86, no. 10 (October 1997)
Cohn, David, "Projects: The Mahon Courthouse, Minorca, Spain," *Architectural Record* 187, no. 5 (1999)
Levence, Richard C., and Fernando Márquez (editors), *El Croquis* (1992) (special issue on Juan Navarro Baldeweg)
Fiz, Simón Marchan, *Juan Navarro Baldeweg: Arquitectura piezas y pintura*, Santander, Spain: Fundación Marcelino Botin, 1997
Lupano, Mario (editor), *Juan Navarro Baldeweg: Il ritorno della luce*, Milan: Motta, 1996

NEO-RATIONALISM

Much more than being yet another style in the second half of the 20th century, Neo-Rationalism developed from within Postmodern architecture. It was already taking shape at the beginning of the 1960s but found integrated expression in the 1970s and 1980s. Its chief representatives, Aldo Rossi and Leon Krier—who became known as Neo-Rationalists—associated their name with the urban planning critique of Modernism and the pursuit of a rational austerity in the principles of composition and the morphology of architecture. The *Architettura razionale* and *Rational Architecture* exhibitions that were held in 1973 and 1975, respectively, at the Milan Triennale and in London, as well as various publications that followed, helped to publicize this trend. Behind the unity of the term, however, various approaches associated with the thought and work of its more important representatives can be recognized: there is an Italian school (the *Tendenza*), in which the names of Aldo Rossi (1931–97) and Giorgio Grassi (1935–) predominate; a Belgian school with individual extensions into France and Britain and the name of Leon Krier (1946–) in a leading position; and a German, a Swiss, and a Spanish school.

Neo-Rationalism was an architectural formalization based on reason, classification, and a will to overcome individuality by establishing a rigid language of architectural types and its own body of rules. The Neo-Rationalists invoked an interpretation of architecture's autonomy that made reference to eternal principles and lasting values as those that are formulated only by man's reason. To provide a foundation for their approach, Rossi and Grassi went back to two periods when Rationalism was in great favor: to the 18th century and the French theory of architecture, with references to M.A. Laugier (1713–69), C.N. Ledoux (1736–1806), and J.N.L. Durand (1760–1834), on the one hand, and on the other, to the early decades of the 20th century and the minimalist aesthetic of architecture, with references to Adolf Loos (1870–1933) or Ludwig Hilberseimer (1885–1967). Their theoretical elaboration was marked by a return to the rationalism of the Classical on the eve of the Industrial Revolution in the form that the classical took in the period of strict Modernism and in the form it acquired during the 1930s in the Soviet Union, Germany, and Italy under the domination of communism and fascism. At the same time, Leon Krier cultivated the idea of a return to the logic and the forms of traditional building activity; that is, to the innate and archetypal rationalism of ordinary builders, which contrasted the repetition of the familiar with the pursuit of novelty.

In Neo-Rationalism, certain set forms (archetypes) are recognized that permeate the whole of architecture and develop autonomously and self-reflexively, whereas function is more variable and dependant on the complexity and fluidity of society. Consequently, to a very large degree function follows form rather than the other way around. The theoretical underpinning of this approach is grounded in typology and makes clear reference to the classificatory approach to architectural forms in the late 18th and early 19th centuries. Rob Krier (1938–) has devoted a large part of his theoretical work to the study of urban planning and architectural typology. Leon Krier has recognized diachronic archetypes even in the form of the ziggurat and has resorted to them to design the contemporary European city. Aldo Rossi designed his architecture with the help of typology, only he

has charged his own archetypes with emotional memories and indirect symbolisms. Rows of arches, factory chimneys, pyramidal or conical roofs, oblong glass-roofed arcades, purely geometrical solids, and square windows with cruciform divisions co-exist with modes of organizing space that refer to the typology of typical buildings of the early 19th century, such as hospitals and prisons.

In contrast to the urban planning principles of Modernism, which supported the functional construction of large-scale buildings on boundless green areas, the Neo-Rationalists have brought back the logic and the scale of the street, the square, and the block that were a characteristic of historic European cities from the Middle Ages and the Renaissance to the 20th century.

It is difficult to understand the thought of the Neo-Rationalists without taking into account associated architectural work. For example, Rossi often designed experimentally, but his architecture went beyond the confines of paper and was transformed into reality first of all in Italy and later throughout the world. The Modena cemetery (1984) and the housing block at Gallaratese, Milan (1973), sum up his fundamentally austere Classicism. Equally imposing is the austerity of the Student housing at Chieti (1980) by Giorgio Grassi and Antonio Monestiroli (1940–); the Public Library in Groningen (1992) by Giorgio Grassi; the school at Ikastola in the Basque country, Spain (1978), by Miguel Garay (1936–) and José-Ignacio Linazasoro (1947–); and the Ritterstrasse housing in Berlin (1980) by Rob Krier. The typological and morphological discipline of these projects recalls a sense of the public in architecture, which is the central theme of Neo-Rationalism.

The revitalized reading and interpretation of urban space undertaken by the Neo-Rationalists has contributed to a new approach to the relationships between architecture and urban planning as well as to a more substantive understanding of the fundamental values of urbanism. More particularly, the recognition of the continuity and significance of the fabric of streets and squares and a recognition of the structural role of the contrasting of ordinary (private) and distinctive (public) architectural forms have served as the basis for an urban approach to contemporary megalopolises that predominated in the late 20th century.

PANAYOTIS TOURNIKIOTIS

See also **Postmodernism; Rossi, Aldo (Italy)**

Further Reading

Architecture rationnelle: La reconstruction de la ville européenne = Rational Architecture: The Reconstruction of the European City, Brussels: Archives d'Architecture Moderne, 1978

Grassi, Giorgio, *Architettura, lingua morta = Architecture, dead language*, Milan: Electa, and New York: Rizzoli, 1988

Krier, Rob, *Architectural Composition*, London: Academy Editions and New York: Rizzoli, 1988

Krier, Leon, *Architecture: Choice or Fate*, Windsor: Andreas Papadakis, 1998

Porphyrios, Demetri (editor), *Building & Rational Architecture*, London: Architectural Design, 1984

Rossi, Aldo (editor), *Architettura razionale*, Milano: F. Angeli, 1973

Rossi, Aldo, *The Architecture of the City*, translated by Diane Ghirardo and Joan Ockman, Cambridge, Massachusetts: MIT Press, 1982

Ungers, Oswald Mathias, *Architettura come tema = Architecture as Theme*, Milan: Electa and New York: Rizzoli, 1982

NERVI, PIER LUIGI 1891–1979

Engineer and architect, Italy

Pier Luigi Nervi was one of the great engineers of the 20th century who applied his engineering innovations to the design of buildings. From the 1930s to the 1960s, he built a variety of public building types in Italy and around the world, ranging from airport hangars to skyscrapers to stadiums. In many of his designs, Nervi made novel use of modern materials, especially concrete, to create his trademark style. He opened his first office in 1920, called Nervi and Nebbiosi, in Rome and practiced his craft for almost 50 years. In 1932, the name of the practice was changed to Nervi and Bartoli. Believing architecture and engineering to be interrelated, Nervi designed his structures with an eye to knowing laws of nature, materials, and construction.

Important buildings by Nervi begin with the Municipal Stadium of Florence (1932), with a grandstand constructed of dramatic cantilevered reinforced-concrete beams and a helectical concrete staircase. Immediately, Nervi displayed his virtuoso skill in the manipulation of concrete structures, molding them into dynamic configurations that always retain their structural purpose and integrity. "An architect is a builder, not an artist," he said in his Norton Lectures delivered in 1961–62 at Harvard University. The beauty and dynamism of the forms come from their structural capacities and necessities, not from an applied aesthetic. A good structural solution has an inherent aesthetic force; thus, aesthetic theories were not necessary in architecture. The building is conceived as a structural organism, exploiting the qualities of the materials with which it is built. In the case of Nervi's public works, the materials are mainly steel and reinforced concrete.

Between 1935 and 1955, Nervi built a series of airplane hangars, exhibition halls, and stadiums with long-span concrete roof structures, ribbed reinforced-concrete trusses, and assembled precast-concrete components. With his particular understanding of concrete's potential for an expressive combination of strength and beauty, Nervi utilized two important concrete construction methods in his buildings, both of which have continued to define the structural limits of concrete. Nervi's buildings, like others of concrete, use reinforced concrete that is cast in place or from prefabricated forms, creating carefully engineered structures that this architect and theorist imbued with an enduring sense of simplicity and power. In this way, some believe, Nervi rivals Mies van der Rohe as a pioneer in the adaptation of building

Palazetto dello Sport, Rome (1957)
© GreatBuildings.com

materials and technology in the 20th century. Nervi's most compelling structures include the Turin Exhibition Hall, with a vaulted roof and a perimetric roof system of precast beams in a material called "ferro-cement." Ferro-cement combines reinforced concrete and several layers of fine steel mesh sprayed with cement mortar. This malleable material provides strength and elasticity as a building material and enabled Nervi to sculpt his dynamic structures. Whereas the structural necessities of the building create its aesthetic, the "structural architecture" of Nervi is based on the combination of structural analysis, static systems, and tension and compression in materials. Other factors in the design of his buildings are economic efficiency (as in the low-cost production of steel and concrete), the technology of the construction, and the functional requirements of the building.

All these factors were optimized by Nervi in a series of important buildings realized between 1955 and 1961. Nervi included these designs in a book called *New Structures* in 1963. These structures include the UNESCO Headquarters (1958, in collaboration with Marcel Breuer and others) in Paris, the Pirelli Building (1959, in collaboration with Giò Ponti and others) in Milan, and the three sports stadiums built in Rome for the Olympic Games in 1961: the Palazetto dello Sport (Small Sports Palace, 1957), the Palazzo dello Sport (Large Sports Palace, 1958), and the Flaminio Stadium (1958). The Palazzo per Lavoro (1961, Worker's Palace) in Turin has mushroom columns and floor slabs with ribs following isostatic lines of bending movements, which were also applied to the Gatti Wool Factory (1951) in Rome. Nervi's Port Authority Station (1962) at George Washington Bridge in New York City is characterized by triangulated roof trusses. The Nathaniel Leverone Field House (1962) at Dartmouth College in Hanover, New Hampshire, features a vaulted construction. The Cathedral of Saint Mary (1971) in San Francisco features a roof made from large cement slabs in the form of a cross. The Aula delle udienze pontificie (Papal Audience Hall, 1971) in Vatican City in Rome is constructed in elastic structural forms sculpted in white cement.

Nervi expressed his ideas about architecture in several books and articles, including *Arte o scienza del costruire* (1945; *The Art and Science of Construction*), *Costruire correttamente* (1954; *To Construct Correctly*), *Structures* (1956), and *Aesthetics and Technology in Building* (1961–62; The Charles Eliot Norton Lectures, Harvard University). For many architectural historians, Nervi joins Frank Lloyd Wright for his profound grasp of the meaning of materials and their intricate relationship with nature and methods of construction, and both were fearless experimenters. In 1962, Nervi received honorary degrees from Dartmouth College and Harvard University. Contemporary with Kenzo Tange, Nervi was the architectural craftsman par excellence of the 20th century, making use of the structural capabilities and malleability of steel and precast concrete to create large-scale urban projects that answer the demands of modern functions and make optimum use of modern technologies. All of Nervi's buildings are intricate structures of grace and elegance born from an insightful understanding of the structural capabilities of materials and a rigorous adherence to the role of the architect as servicing the functional needs of a society. He was awarded a Gold Medal by the Royal Institute of British Architects, the American Institute of Architects, and the Academi d'Architecture.

JOHN HENDRIX

Biography

Born in Sondrio, Italy, 21 June 1891. Graduated with a degree in engineering from the University of Bologna 1913. Married Irene Calosin 1924: 3 children. Served in the Italian Army 1915–18. Engineer with the Society for Cement Construction, Bologna 1913–15 and 1918–23. In private practice, Rome from 1923; partner, Nervi and Nebbiosi 1923–32; president, Nervi and Bartolia from 1932–60; partner with sons Antonio, Mario, and Vittorio, Studio Nervi from 1960; consultant engineer, UNESCO, Paris 1952. Professor of the technique of construction, faculty of architecture, University of Rome 1947–61. Honorary member, American Institute of Architects 1956; honorary member, National Institute of Arts and Letters 1957; foreign member, Royal Academy of Fine Arts, Stockholm 1957; corresponding member, Academia Nacional de Ciencias Exactas Fisicas y Naturales, Buenos Aires 1959; corresponding member, Bayerischen Akademie der Schönen Künste, Munich 1960; member, Accademia di San Luca, Rome 1960; honorary member, American Academy of Arts and Sciences 1960; member, Royal Institute of Dutch Engineers 1964; member, Akademie der Künste, Berlin 1964; member, Institut des Beaux-Arts, Paris 1973; foreign member, Institut de France, Paris 1973. Gold Medal, Royal Institute of British Architects 1960; Gold Medal, American Institute of Architects 1964. Died in Rome, 9 January 1979.

Selected Works

Municipal Stadium of Florence, 1932
Turin Exhibition Hall, Turin, 1949
Gatti Wool Factory, Rome, 1951
Palazetto dello Sport, Rome, 1957
Palazzo dello Sport, Rome, 1958
Flaminio Stadium, Rome, 1958
UNESCO Headquarters, Paris (with Marcel Breuer), 1958
Pirelli Building, Milan (with Giò Ponti), 1959
Palazzo per Lavoro, Turin, 1961
Port Authority Terminal, New York City, 1962
Nathaniel Leverone Field House, Dartmouth College, Hanover, New Hampshire, 1962
Cathedral of St. Mary, San Francisco, 1971
Aula delle udienze pontificie, Città del Vaticano, Rome, 1971

Selected Publications

Arte o scienza del costruire, 1945
Costruire correttamente, 1954
Structures, 1956
New Structures, translated by Giuseppe Nicoletti, 1963
Aesthetics and Technology in Building (The Charles Eliot Norton Lectures 1961–62), translated by Robert Einaudi, 1965

Further Reading

Desideri, Paolo, *Pier Luigi Nervi*, Bologna: Zanichelli, 1979
Huxtable, Ada Louise, *Pier Luigi Nervi*, New York: Braziller, and London: Mayflower, 1960
Pica, Agnoldomenico, *Pier Luigi Nervi*, Rome: Editalia, 1969
Nervi, Pier Luigi, *The Works of Pier Luigi Nervi*, translated by Ernest Priefert, New York: Praeger, and London: Architectural Press, 1957

NETHERLANDS

During the 20th century, the Netherlands experienced an architectural blossoming unknown in its history. The opening and concluding decades brought forth buildings that attained world renown for their formal inventiveness, fine execution, and social resonance. Even during the 50-year fallow period that commenced in the late 1930s, individual contributions maintained the spark of ingenuity and commitment to excellence that would reignite on a much larger scale in the mid-1980s, when the economy exploded and the geographic range of notable buildings expanded.

Although Dutch architecture often reflects international currents, it displays some distinctive features derived from special topographical and historical conditions. The land is predominantly flat, which means that it tends to be organized along Cartesian principles. The straight line predominates, although the curve and the polygon have occasionally provided alternative layouts in cities and suburbs. Throughout much of its history, Dutch architecture has been modest in scale; typically, grandeur has been shunned and size tamed by intricate and varied details. The discomfort with the grandiose stems in part from the fact that housing is the overwhelmingly dominant building type in the world's most densely populated nation. The dwelling, whether the single-family house or publicly funded apartment, has always been a preoccupation, and in that realm, intimacy is a cherished characteristic.

Because much of the country has first to be won and then protected from the sea, an unusual degree of cooperation is required, and regulations to foster collaboration are mandated. Nevertheless, despite the smallness of their country, the Dutch have a penchant for ideological divergence, although this in turn has been complemented by a tendency for individuals to forge alliances to disseminate their beliefs. In architecture, this can be seen in the consistent formation of small, usually short-lived polemical factions, often congregated in a given city and invariably mounting exhibitions and publishing tendentious manifestoes and periodicals. Groups such as the Amsterdam School, De Stijl, "Opbouw" in Rotterdam and "De 8" and "Groep 32" in Amsterdam, plus the later "Forum" group of Structuralists, have shaped Dutch architecture in profound ways.

If an idealist strain persists, practical objectives cannot be ignored in a country where every particle of the man-made environment is cultivated. Standardization in the interests of cost-effectiveness and rapid production is an ever-burning issue, along with ingenious attempts to temper its propensity toward monotony. Another significant and enduring trait that relates to practicality is the long tradition of recycling. Commissions often involve the metamorphosis of an existing shell for new uses; some of the most interesting dwellings to have been created since the 1970s are inserted into former warehouses.

Although the Dutch are often typecast as stolid, frugal, and businesslike (*zakelijk*), a generous quotient of playfulness invigorates their environment, demonstrated in the historic canal houses, which may conform in plan and elevation but are enlivened by unique and whimsical details. In the 20th century, this quality is on view in the ludic imagery of the Amsterdam School; in the witty metaphors of Forum architects such as Aldo van Eyck, Herman Hertzberger, and Piet Blom; and in the provocative inversions of firms like the Office for Metropolitan Architecture (OMA), Mecanoo, MVRDV (Winy Maas, Jacob van Rijs, and Nathalie de Vries), and Neutelings Riedijk (Jan Neutelings). A complementary characteristic is a fondness for polychromy; brick has been manufactured in many hues and textures, laid in novel patterns, and employed, together with tile and stone, in contrasting colors, to charming effect. Since the 1980s, plastered, clapboarded, metallic, and polymer surfaces and details, similarly multihued and multitextured, have become popular; the completely monochromatic building, even when fashioned of concrete, finds little favor in this nation where skies are often overcast. A further source of unity is the preference for the employment of geometric systems of proportion to generate harmony.

The individualism that lurks behind the generic, and sometimes borders on the idiosyncratic, may relate to a fundamental aversion to classicism and to the compositional methods of the Ecole des Beaux Arts. Nevertheless, a brake on too extreme a degree of heterogeneity has been the numerous rules and regulations imposed by government, especially after the passage in 1901 of the National Housing Act. Frequently revised and continually expanded, government policy, operating at both the national and municipal level, manipulates through financing projects with public funds no less than direct legal action. Recently, the tediousness and utilitarian expediency characteristic of architecture during the post–World War II era and its long aftermath have been mitigated by the recognition that formal inventiveness and atypical solutions tailored to local situations contribute to social as well as aesthetic satisfaction. This attitude has been abetted by a new government policy giving architects more autonomy and by a wealthy economy that has supported experimental design and construction.

These general observations should serve as guide to the brief chronological survey of 20th-century Dutch buildings that follows. The turn of the century set the stage for renewal. From 1890 to 1905 the fundamental contrasts that would be recapitulated throughout the century were adumbrated—the fancifully libidinous versus the soberly Calvinistic. In the 1890s these contrasts are seen in the two currents related to Art Nouveau, one indebted to the dominant Franco-Belgian interpretation propagating the curvilinear and the symbolically laden, with The Hague as the center and H.P. Mutters (1884–1954) the chief architect, and the other representing a peculiarly Dutch variant dubbed *Nieuwe Kunst*, whose avatars concentrated on sturdy, rectilinear construction and disciplined organic forms through geometric stylization. They were also motivated by ethical considerations, seeking to create a beautiful and moral environment for a more egalitarian society.

The fin-de-siècle initiated an architectural flowering that lasted until the 1930s and was similarly rife with contradictions and collisions. The one figure that seems to have provided inspiration of varying kinds to almost every subsequent movement was Hendrik P. Berlage. Although there were common points of reference, including Berlage himself, especially his advocacy of geometric systems, the Amsterdam School and De Stijl, which next took center stage, display contrasts comparable to those between the two variants of Art Nouveau. Some architects moved from one mode of expression to the other. Two works in The Hague, stemming from the office of Jan Buijs (1889–1961) and J.B. Lürsen (1894–1995), illustrate this path: the Rudolf Steiner Clinic (1926–28), predictably paying homage

Apartments, Mercatorplein, Amsterdam, Hendrik P. Berlage, 1927
© GreatBuildings.com

to the Goetheanum and therefore kin to productions of the Amsterdam School, and the multipurpose headquarters (office, dental clinic, shops) of the cooperative society, De Volharding (1927–28), indebted to De Stijl for its composition. Russian Constructivism is another source because the crystalline enclosure incorporates advertising: at night, De Volharding is a glowing signboard of interpenetrating volumes "decorated" with words and slogans.

Jan Buijs offered not a synthesis but alternative approaches, whereas some sought to blend the best of both worlds. The chief exponents of a merger are Willem Dudok (1884–1974) and S. J. Bouwma (1899–1959). Dudok, municipal architect of Hilversum, forged an enduring personal legacy in the town where he planned numerous neighborhoods and executed 19 schools, municipal housing and offices, public baths, and the monumental Hilversum Town Hall (1924–30). Contrasting vertical and horizontal envelopes of yellow Roman brick accented with glazed tile, stone, and glass are slotted together; dramatic cantilevers hover over the pool and gardens that are incorporated into the ensemble. Bouwma, less renowned, also deserves attention as a spectacular combiner of the two idioms. Employed by the Public Works Department of the northeastern city of Groningen, Bouma, at first influenced exclusively by the Amsterdam School, increasingly applied cubistic strategies. Interlocking curved and

rectilinear volumes and beautifully shaped windows and stairs executed in wood, metal, tile, and stained glass, draw attention to his Public Works building (1929) and numerous schools, which testify to the assimilation during the 1920s throughout the length and breadth of the Netherlands of metropolitan aesthetic movements.

Groningen offers yet another surprise: the first example of Dutch Functionalism (*Nieuwe Bouwen*): the Polytechnic School (1922–23) by J.G. Wiebenga (1886–1964) and L.C. van der Vlugt (1894–1936). The ribbon windows that run the length of the entire facade are an innovation made possible via the concrete frame devised by Wiebenga, at the time director of the school. Although few buildings that truly belong to this movement were produced in the Netherlands, those executed are among the most poetic examples in the International Style canon. Several exponents of the *Nieuwe Bouwen* joined the Congrès Internationaux d'Architecture Moderne (CIAM) and Cor van Eesteren, its president from 1930–47, made the ideals of that group common currency in the Netherlands. The separation of functions and the use of open-row housing shaped the new extensions in Dutch cities until the 1970s and beyond.

By 1930, the economic turndown had put paid to the extravagances of the Amsterdam School, and former De Stijl members had accepted the strictures of the *Nieuwe Bouwen*, with its predominantly left-wing sympathies. The opposition, conservative both politically and architecturally, was motivated by religious or nationalist considerations to maintain traditional forms and materials as symbolic of eternal Dutch values (though they also admired Scandinavian Romanticism). They equated Functionalism with materialism and godlessness. Echewing classicism per se, they nonetheless adopted symmetry in their ordered compositions. The Roman Catholic Delft School, led by the converts M.J. Granpré Molière (1883–1972) and A.J. Kropholler (1881–1973), sought truth and beauty in the harmonious relation between form and technique. In addition to designing low-rise, pitched-roof housing for the "little people"—farmers and the devout working class—the Delft School excelled in churches and town halls, where their affection for ritual and divinely ordained hierarchy could be expressed. Representative examples include the town hall in Waalwijk, (Kropholler, 1929–31) and the Seminary Church in Haaren (Granpré-Molière, 1938–39), both in the predominantly Catholic southeast. Conservatives also obtained important cultural commissions such as the Boymans Museum in Rotterdam (1928–35) and the Van Abbe Museum in Enschede (1933–35), the former by A.J. van der Steur (1893–1953) and the latter by Kropholler.

Several former Functionalists became disillusioned in the later 1930s; although not making a common cause with the conservatives, they nevertheless came to disapprove of the apparent lack of symbolic content in the *Nieuwe Bouwen* and sought to moderate its mechanistic and minimalist thrust. Sybold van Ravesteyn (1889–1983) skillfully retained the sophistication of modernism while alleviating its dourness through art deco detailing (generally not much in evidence in the Netherlands) and complex shapes deriving from an admiration for the Baroque; for example, the office building "Holland van 1859" (1937–39) and the addition to the Kunstmin Theatre (1938–40), both in Dordrecht. Most members of *Groep 32*, having fervently embraced the ideas of *De 8* in 1938, withdrew and proselytized for a more consciously aesthetic and less ephemeral approach without adopting the Delft School's traditionalism. By this time, lingering economic depression, the rise of fascism, the gathering war clouds, and for the Netherlands, eventual Nazi occupation, resulted in conditions that were hardly conducive to construction of any sort.

After the war, *Groep 32* went on the offensive by repudiating the CIAM-dominated planning practice during the reconstruction. The most potent challenge to CIAM came from within its ranks. J.B. Bakema (1914–81), with Van Eyck, helped form Team X and used *Forum* to protest against CIAMs technocratic rigidity and doctrinaire separation of functions—work, dwelling, recreation, tied together by transit—in favor of making the built environment more responsive to specific human needs, including those of productive and emotionally satisfying personal encounters, maximized through delivering an agglomeration of small units rather than a featureless mass. An example of what this meant in practice is Herztberger's Centraal Beheer in Apeldoorn (1967–72). The modular concrete frame produces a grid of spaces that may be configured by the occupants as private or communal offices and mutual meeting places. Although most Structuralists (a name associated with the Forum group that found inspiration in anthropology rather than the

mechanistic dictates of CIAM) use cubic modules, some introduce rhomboids and pyramids: Piet Blom (experimental housing, De Kasbah [1969–73], in Hengelo; "pole dwellings" [1975] in Helmond), Onno Greiner (Silveren Schor youth center [1962–67] in Arnemuiden), and Frank van Klingeren (community center 't Karregat [1970–73] in Eindhoven). Nevertheless, all emphasize the domestically scaled modular unit and typically offer possibilities for growth and change.

If during the 1960s and 1970s the international professional press focused on the Structuralists, their output could not compete with that of large firms who were complicit in dismantling many historic centers. An ominous development was the replacement of small-scale housing stock by gigantic government and commercial complexes. Although affordable housing never ceased production, increasingly it was relegated to vast settlements beyond the urban core, served by megalomanic rapid transit systems and highways that were devouring the land. H.A. Maaskant, a respected figure from his *Nieuwe Bouwen* days, became a vocal apologist for bigness and did his share to transform the skyline with obtrusively huge ensembles sculpted from monochromatic concrete, such as his Brasilia-like ensemble for the Province of North Brabant (1963–71) in Hertogenbosch. Hertzberger, too, eventually participated in this un-Dutch *folie de grandeur* (Ministry of Social Affairs, 1973–79, The Hague), as did the numerous firms who produced behemoths gigantic in height and breadth for bureaucracies such as the postal service (Headquarters PTT, Groningen, 1985–90, by F.J. van Gool), and municipalities (Town Hall in Apeldoorn, 1985–90, which includes a parking garage and commercial and cultural spaces, by H.J.M. Ruijssenaars).

Nevertheless, in the late 1970s a renewed appreciation for the *Nieuwe Bouwen* surfaced to counter both Structuralism and Brutalism (which appeared in the Netherlands after its heyday in Britain and the United States) and reprises of the modestly scaled, white Functionalist projects and buildings of the 1920s and early 1930s appeared (Row housing, Amsterdam [1978–83] by Arne van Herk [b. 1944–], and Cees Nagelkerke [1944], an updated version of Oud's project for dwellings on the Strandboulevard of 1917). The battle cry became "Modernism without Dogma," and it did seem that a revival, without the moral imperatives that putatively animated the Functionalism of the prewar period, was underway.

However, soon thereafter such approaches were challenged by Rem Koolhaas, the first Dutch winner of the Pritzker Prize (2000) and founder of the firm OMA (Office of Metropolitan Architecture). Koolhaas's cosmopolitan background sets him apart from many of his contemporaries. A confrontational and controversial figure who arouses both admiration and hostility, he has set the agenda for much of the theory and practice of the 1990s in his native country and abroad. His critique of the historic smallness of Dutch architecture has been heeded with a vengeance, and his exploration of the effect of global economic forces has been revelatory for many architects—and clients.

During most of the century, Dutch architecture has mainly been a matter for professionals and government regulators; only the Amsterdam School garnered popular attention. But that dramatically changed in the last two decades of the 20th century. As architectural practice became theoretically more sophisticated, treating design as a more open and fluid process that increasingly takes into account changes wrought by the information age and the possibilities offered by electronic media, and as buildings became stylistically more diverse, exuberant, and sometimes downright outrageous, a cadre of articulate younger architects attained the celebrity of pop stars, and comment and criticism moved from the elite journals to the lay press. Dutch architects began to win prestigious commissions from abroad, in part because they embarked on research and explorations that were global in character and implication.

To an important degree, this situation was fostered by the government, which created a number of institutes and prizes. The Nederlands Architectuurinstitut/NAi, incorporating a Documentation Center, bookstore, and cafe along with exhibition halls, opened in 1993 in an extravagant new building in Rotterdam, subject of an invited competition of 1987. The winner was Jo Coenen, who set the tripartite composition of transparent, translucent, and opaque volumes over an ornamental pool. The Berlage Institute, founded in 1990, fosters architectural research and grants Master's degrees to students from all over the world. The Netherlands Architectural Fund was established to subsidize architecture centers, in numerous towns throughout the country, that disseminate information and give guided tours of notable local buildings.

In 1900, the Netherlands, isolated architecturally for two and a half centuries, began to claim architectural attention fitfully but surely and became an inspiration for all those interested in renewal, consolidation, and social responsibility in architecture as interpreted by this small but morally authoritative nation. As it moves into new millennium, with its great prosperity and growing and well-educated population, which requires new buildings of various purposes that public and private bodies are eager to supply, and its wealth of design talent, which now includes foreign practitioners, the Netherlands definitively is on the cutting edge and has become the international mecca for architecture's future potential and realization.

HELEN SEARING

See also **Amsterdam, Netherlands; Amsterdam School; Art Nouveau; Berlage, Hendrik Petrus (Netherlands); Brutalism; De Stijl; Dudok, Willem (Netherlands); Duiker, Johannes (Netherlands); van Eyck, Aldo (Netherlands); Hertzberger, Herman (Netherlands); Hilversum Town Hall, Netherlands; Koolhaas, Rem (Netherlands); Oud, J.J.P. (Netherlands); Rietveld, Gerrit (Netherlands); Rotterdam, Netherlands; Structuralism; Team X (Netherlands)**

Further Reading

From the late 1960s, when the Dutch as well as foreigners (especially the Italians) began to rediscover Dutch modern architecture, there developed (in contrast to the previous paucity) an enormous bibliography, initially in Dutch—and Italian—but increasingly bilingual (English–Dutch). The government (national, provincial, and municipal) issues pamphlets on cities and regions describing city planning efforts and buildings, historical and new, and there are a number of firms that specialize in architecture and urbanism, such as SUN (Sociaalistische Uitgeverij Nederland), which became i10, the Dutch Architectural Institute (NAi: Nederlands Architectuur Instituut, previously the Documentatiecentrum voor de Bouwkunst), which published a definitive series of catalogues in connection with museum exhibitions; in addition, the remarkable bookstore in Amsterdam, *Architectura et Natura*, has been the pilgrimage for architecture enthusiasts for 50 years and, since 1990, has been publisher of its own volumes, including those for ARCAM. There is an annual *Architecture in the Netherlands Yearbook* (recently edited by Hans van Dijk).

Barbieri, S. Umberto (editor), *Architectuur en Planning, Nederland: 1940–1980*, Rotterdam: i10, 1983

Barbieri, S. Umberto, and Leen van Duin (editors), *Honderd jaar Nederlandse architectuur, 1901–2000*, Nijegem: SUN, 1999

Bergvelt, Ellinoor, Frans van Burkom, and Karin Gaillard, *From Neo-Renaissance to Post-Modernism: A Hundred and Twenty-Five years of Dutch Interiors*, Rotterdam: 010, 1996

Buch, Joseph, *A Century of Architecture in the Netherlands: 1880–1990*, Rotterdam: NAi, 1993

Casciato, Maristella, Franco Panzini, and Sergio Polano, *Architectuur en volkshuisvesting, Nederland: 1870–1940*, Nijmegen: SUN, 1980; translation of original Italian publication, *Funzione e Senso: Architettura, Casa, Città, 1870–1940*, Milan: Electa, 1980

Crimson (Wouter Vanstiphout and Cassandra Wilkins), Michael Speaks, and Gerard Hadders, *Mart Stam's Trousers: Stories from Behind the Scenes of Dutch Moral Modernism*, Rotterdam: 010/ Crimson, 1999

Derwig, Jan, and Erik Mattie, *Functionalism in the Netherlands*. Amsterdam: Architectura et Natura, 1995

Dijk, Hans van, *20th-Century Architecture in the Netherlands*, Rotterdam: 010 Publishers, 1999.

Fanelli, Guido, *Architettura moderna in Olanda*, Florence: Marchi & Bertolli, 1968; as *Moderne architectuur in Nederland, 1900–1940*, revised edition in Dutch, with English summary and translation by Wim de Wit, The Hague: Staatsuitgeverij, 1978

Fanelli, Guido, *Architettura, Edilizia, Urbanistica Olanda 1917– 1940*, Florence: Papafava, 1978

Grinberg, Donald, *Housing in the Netherlands, 1900–1940*, Rotterdam: Nijgh-Wolters-Noordhoff Universitaire, 1977

Groenendijk, Paul, and Piet Vollaard, *Guide to Modern Architecture in the Netherlands*, Rotterdam: i10, 1st edition, 1987, 2nd revised edition, 1997

Ibelings, Hans, *Americanism: Dutch Architecture and the Transatlantic Model*, Rotterdam: NAi, 1997

Ibelings, Hans, *20th Century Architecture in the Netherlands*, Rotterdam: NAi, 1996

Ibelings, Hans, *The Modern Fifties and Sixties: The Spreading of Contemporary Architecture over the Netherlands*, Rotterdam: NAi, 1996

Kraayvanger, H.M. (editor), *Nederland bouwt in baksteen, 1800– 1940* (exhib. cat.), Rotterdam: Boymans Museum, 1941

Langmead, Donald, *Dutch Modernism: Architectural Resources in the England Language*, Westport, CT: Greenwood Press, 1996.

Loosma, Bart, *Super Dutch: New Architecture in the Netherlands*, London: Thames and Hudson, 2000

Lüchinger, Arnold, *Structuralism in Architecture and Urban Planning*, Stuttgart: Karl Krämer, 1981

Mieras, J.P., *Na-oorlogse bouwkunst in Nederland*, Amsterdam: Kosmos, 1954

Mieras, J.P., and F.R. Yerbury, *Dutch Architecture of the 20th Century*, New York: Charles Scribner's Sons, 1926

Molema, Jan, *The New Movement in the Netherlands 1924–1936*, Rotterdam: i10, 1996

Strasser, Emil E., *Neuere Holländische Baukunst*, Mönchen-Gladbach: Führer Verlage, 1926.

Woud, Auke van der, *The Art of Building, from Classicism to Modernity; The Dutch Architectural Debate, 1840–1990*, Burlington, VT: Ashgate, 2000.

Yerbury, Frank, *Modern Dutch Buildings*, New York: Charles Scribner, 1931.

NEUE STAATSGALERIE, STUTTGART

Designed by James Stirling, Michael Wilford, and
Associates; completed 1984

One of the most energetic examples of the museum as cultural
center constructed during the second half of the 20th century,
the Neue Staatsgalerie in Stuttgart, designed by James Stirling,
Michael Wilford, and Associates, is regarded as the culmination
of Stirling's practice. Reflecting the complex program of extending the existing Italianate State Gallery (1838–43) of Baden-
Württemburg in northwest Germany, to which it is linked by
a bridge at the second story, with permanent and temporary
exhibition galleries for 20th-century art and including a chamber
theatre, music school, café, the Bauhaus theatre archive, library,
and administrative offices, the Neue Staatsgalerie resembles a
terraced village that has sympathetically incorporated older adjoining structures into its precincts.

Stirling and Wilford (partners since 1965) embarked in the
mid-1970s on a more inclusive approach to design that would
embrace a wider range of past precedent, both typological and
urbanistic, while continuing to incorporate the formal and technical innovations of the Modern movement. This odyssey commenced in two competition designs for German museums that
obliged Stirling to weave the new building into the fabric of the
existing cities damaged both by war and by careless postwar
development. The mixture of modernist and historical references, the employment of the rotunda form, and the distribution
of the composition into distinct parts that link the new structure
with existing ones, manifest in the two unsuccessful entries of
1975 for the North Rhine Westphalia Museum, Dusseldorf, and
the Wallraf-Richartz Gallery, Cologne, would be majestically
realized in the controversial premiated proposal for Stuttgart.

The firm was one of four foreign and nine German firms
invited to enter the competition of 1977, as an earlier one in
1974, won by Behnisch, Kammerer, and Belz, was aborted. The
monumentality of Stirling's composition and its evocation of
such primal 19th-century institutions as Karl Friedrich Schinkel's Altes Museum in Berlin (1823–30) brought accusations of
totalitarianism and megalomania from such disappointed German contenders as Frei Otto and third-prize winner Günther
Behnisch. However, international opinion overwhelmingly can-
onized Stirling's solution as democratic and populist, and he
received a number of major museum commissions thereafter.

The building was to serve the city beyond the creation of an
ensemble for cultural activities by knitting the upper and lower
town together. Stirling's brilliant solution was a pedestrian ramp

Neue Staatsgalerie, Stuttgart, 1977–84
© Donald Corner and Jenny Young/GreatBuildings.com

that could be negotiated without entering the museum and terraces and plastic forms that restored an urban presence along the six-lane motorway that had replaced the street in front of the original U-shaped institution. Above the garage that constitutes the pedestal of this small acropolis, the main platform is reached from the parking area or the sidewalk through a metal and glass pavilion, a sort of Laugerian "primitive hut" as dreamed by Ludwig Mies van der Rohe. There is no closed facade as one would have in a proper classical building but, rather, a series of incidents, including an irregularly curved glass and steel wall that boldly contrasts with the masonry-covered walls (broad travertine bands alternating with narrower ones of local sandstone) and the cavetto cornice that lines the inner "U" of the museum proper, which is the only symmetrical element in the plan. The Neue Staatsgalerie is entered via two revolving doors (the restaurant can be accessed directly from the terrace) that lead into the fluid spaces of the ground floor. There, the irregularly shaped exhibition areas are lit artificially and subdivided by mushroom-shaped columns of concrete with the form-work left visible, a device used by Stirling's occasional hero, Le Corbusier. Another resolutely 20th-century touch is the glazed elevator shaft where the machinery that governs the rising and falling cab is left visible and the elevator itself becomes a kinetic sculpture, a strategy employed by Russian Constructivists, whose work had fascinated Stirling since he designed, with his former partner James Gowan, the engineering labs at Leicester University.

At the upper level, Stirling rejected the amorphous flexible spaces in vogue at the time in favor of a formal sequence of conventional rooms arranged enfilade within the "U" that surrounds the central rotunda. This story, given over entirely to exhibition space, is top-lighted to accord with the approved practice that after the late 1960s restored natural light to museums (a practice pioneered by Louis Kahn and Alvar Aalto). The elaborate mechanisms required to control zenithal-entering light are concealed by a flat ceiling of translucent panes set in a green-painted metal grid, a contemporary touch that contrasts with the light fixtures hidden in fragments of cornice and the doors topped by stylized Neo-Greek pediments. The organization and detailing of the main floor thus departs from the aggressively 20th-century character of the ground level to establish a dialogue between old and new totally fitting the museum enterprise.

The same symbolic dualism pervades the exterior. At the rear, two exhaust funnels in green and blue cheekily evoke the Pompidou Center, a distinctly alternative home for contemporary art. Because Stuttgart is famed as the site of the Weissenhof-siedlung, the Deutsche Werkbund's housing exhibition of 1927, Stirling could not resist allusions to its plastered facades and especially to Le Corbusier's double house with its long narrow windows and *pilotis* (stilts), which he used on the administration wing. However, the strip windows cutting the flat plane of the wall are mocked by the square openings above, which are framed in stone, and by the ferrovitreous temple front over the revolving door of the entrance. Similarly, the Kammertheater is both traditional (stone-clad first story with arched openings) and modernist (stuccoed second level), and the ubiquitous square windows, in single and quadruple format, speak of the late 1960s (works by Robert Venturi, Aldo Rossi, and Michael Graves). Stirling also plays this double game on himself when he deconstructs a portion of the adjacent street wall to demonstrate that it is not bearing but merely cladding over the concrete frame. The re-

moved blocks of stone rest like a Richard Long sculpture in front of the "excavation"; some Stuttgart residents find it an unhappy reminder of wartime devastation. Controversial as well, but absolutely characteristic, is the clash between the well-mannered stone and stucco surfaces and the metal detailing—sash bars and tubular railings—painted in day-glow colors of fluorescent pink and acid green as well as the less hallucinatory primaries (red, blue, and yellow). The colors are coded to function: green always signals metal sash bars, and orange-red revolving doors.

The rotunda recalls not only the very different work of Swedish architect Gunnar Asplund, who like Stirling attempted to reconcile classicism and modernism, but also one of the defining elements of the first public museums. However, at Stuttgart the rotunda is open and overgrown by plants, a feature that together with the indeterminate facade suggests Stirling's ambivalence toward the Enlightenment positivism manifest in the original institution and his acknowledgement of the museum's difficult trajectory between the competing claims of the past and the contemporary. Stirling has created a stunning building, contextual in every sense of the word, that also is consummately appropriate to its manifold purposes.

HELEN SEARING

See also **Abteiberg Municipal Museum, Mönchengladbach, Germany; Asplund, Erik Gunnar (Sweden); Graves, Robert (United States); Museum; Stirling, James (England); Venturi, Robert (United States)**

Further Reading

Arnell, Peter, and Ted Bickford (editors), *James Stirling: Buildings and Projects; James Stirling Michael Wilford and Associates*, New York: Rizzoli, 1984

Colquhoun, Alan, "Democratic Monument," *The Architectural Review* 1054 (December 1984)

Dal Co, Francesco, and Tom Muirhead, *I musei di James Stirling, Michael Wilford and Associates*, Milan: Electa, 1990

Girouard, Mark, *Big Jim: The Life and Work of James Stirling*, London: Chatto and Windus, 1998

Medini, Alessandro, "Neue Staatsgalerie," *Domus* 651 (June 1984)

Rodiek, Thorsten, *James Stirling: Die Neue Staatsgalerie*, Stuttgart: Gerd Hatje, 1984

Sudjic, Deyan, *Norman Foster, Richard Rogers, James Stirling: New Directions in British Architecture*, London: Thames and Hudson, 1986

Werner, Frank, "The New Acropolis of Stuttgart: The Neue Staatsgalerie," *Lotus International* 43 (1984)

NEUTRA, RICHARD 1892–1970

Architect, Austria and United States

More than three decades after his death, Richard Neutra remains among the most celebrated of the founders of modern architecture who managed to capture the spirit of modernism in a powerful and memorable way, and several of his works have become icons of twentieth-century architecture.

Born and reared in Vienna around the turn of the century, Neutra very early on demonstrated the facility for exquisite draftsmanship that would mark his later drawings. In 1911 he enrolled in architecture department of the Vienna Technical University. His professors at the Technical University included Rudolf Salinger, Karl Mayreder, and Max Fabiani. In addition, Neutra was drawn to the teachings and ideas of Otto Wagner and Adolf Loos, and he regularly attended Loos's private lectures and tours of Vienna's architecture.

The outbreak of World War I interrupted his education, and Neutra, who served for a time as an artillery officer in the Balkans, was unable to complete his training until 1918. He subsequently worked briefly for Erich Mendelsohn and others in Berlin before immigrating, in 1923, to the United States. He settled first in Chicago, finding employment with the venerable firm of Holabird and Roche, but, ever restless, he soon accepted a position with one his early heroes, Frank Lloyd Wright, at Taliesin. By 1925, Neutra was in Los Angeles, where he established a partnership with his Viennese friend and former classmate, Rudolph Schindler.

Neutra's early designs, such as his visionary project for "Rush City Reformed" (1923–30), show the imprint not only of the ideas of Wright, Wagner, and Loos but also of the flowing lines and curvilinear forms of Mendelsohn and Antonio Sant'Elia and the other Italian futurists. By 1927, he had begun to develop a more elemental design language based on simple post and lintel constructions of steel or wood, wrapped with thin wall planes, ribbon windows, and flat overhanging roofs. This new style reached its apotheosis in his design for the Lovell Health House in Los Angeles (1927–29), now widely regarded as one of the signal contributions to the Modern movement.

In the Lovell House, the lyrical qualities of Neutra's spare frame structures derived as much from their honest and direct use of modern materials—metal, concrete, and glass—as from their undisguised, almost classical composition. Enthralled with these new industrial building products, Neutra explored the possibilities of prefabrication and tectonic austerity, transforming his faith in a technological modernity into a distinctive design vocabulary.

In contrast to many of his contemporaries, Neutra demonstrated a particularly strong interest in meeting the needs and wishes of those for whom he built. He sometimes observed his clients for days, or even weeks, in an effort to discern which type of layout would best suit their lifestyles and habits. Throughout his career, he was also attentive to the siting and landscaping of his buildings—a sensitivity he had learned from Frank Lloyd Wright. Neutra's designs, however, although strongly rooted in their contexts, retain a more abstract quality: They appear less part of the natural landscape than artificial objects in the landscape, an approach later adopted by many of the younger Californian architects.

During the 1930s and 1940s, Neutra's architecture became compact and controlled while retaining the elemental vocabulary of the Lovell House. The repetition of his distinguishing mannerisms, such as his use of parapets, spandrels, or spider legs,

Lovell Health House interior (1928–29), Los Angeles, California. Designed by Richard Neutra.
Photo © Roberto Schezen / Esto. All rights reserved.

evoke an impression of strong uniformity in his designs despite manifest differences in their planning and composition. This uniformity was further reinforced by Neutra's preoccupation with the single-family house, which constituted the mainstay of his practice for much of his career. Indeed, he preferred these houses to the commissions for large-scale buildings he began to receive after World War II. Many of his later works, produced in collaboration with Robert Alexander, lack the complexity and visual potency of his best designs, betraying an inability to transfer his concepts to large scale.

Among Neutra's important mature designs, however, was the house he designed in Palm Springs, California, for Edward Kaufmann (1947), which has become one of the most widely reproduced buildings in the history of modernism. It is notable not only for its splendid realization of the principles of openness and transparency that were so central for Neutra but also for the introduction of natural materials—stone rubble and wood—that became emblematic of his late domestic designs and of the California Modern in general.

Neutra's role as begetter of modernism extended beyond his work as an architect. He was also a tireless advocate for his own work and the cause of the new architecture. Over the course of his career, he wrote numerous articles and several books that brought his work and ideas about modernism to worldwide attention.

CHRISTOPHER LONG

See also **Holabird, William, and Martin Roche (United States); Loos, Adolf (Austria); Lovell Health House, Los Angeles; Mendelsohn, Erich (Germany, United States); Wagner, Otto (Austria)**

Selected Works

Rudolf-Mosse Press Building (Berliner Tageblatt), Berlin, 1923
Lovell Health House, Los Angeles, 1929
V.D.L.-Research House, Los Angeles, 1933
Villa von Josef von Sternberg, San Fernando Valley, 1935
Kaufman House, Palm Springs, California, 1947
Elkay Apartments, Los Angeles, 1948
Miramar Chapel, La Jolla, 1957
Lincoln Memorial Museum, Gettysburg, Pennsylvania (with Robert Alexander), 1963
Psychiatric Children's Clinic, University of Southern California, Los Angeles (with Robert Alexander), 1963
Cultural Centre, Reno, Nevada, 1965

Selected Publications

Wie baut Amerika? (How does America build?), 1927
Survival Through Design, 1954
Building With Nature, 1971

Further Reading

Drexler, Arthur, and Thomas S. Hines, *The Architecture of Richard Neutra: From International Style to California Modern* (exhib. cat.), New York: Museum of Modern Art, 1982
Hines, Thomas S., *Richard Neutra and the Search for Modern Architecture: A Biography and History*, New York: Oxford University Press, 1982; Berkeley: University of California Press, 1994
Lamprecht, Barbara Mac, *Neutra—Complete Works*, Cologne, Germany: Taschen, 2000
McCoy, Esther, *Richard Neutra*, New York: Braziller, 1960
McCoy, Esther, *Vienna to Los Angeles: Two Journeys*, Santa Monica, California: Arts and Architecture Press, 1979
Neutra Richard Joseph, *Buildings and Projects; Bauten und Projekte; Réalisations et Projects* (trilingual English–French–German edition), 3 vols., edited by Willy Boesiger, New York: Praeger, 1959–66
Neutra, Richard Joseph, Rupert Spade, and Yukio Futagawa, *Richard Neutra*, London: Thames and Hudson, 1971
Sack, Manfred, *Richard Neutra: mit einem Essay von Dion Neutra, Erinnerungen an meine Zeit mit Richard Neutra; Richard Neutra: With an Essay by Dion Neutra, Memories of my Years with Richard Neutra* (bilingual German–English edition), Zürich: Verlag für Architektur, 1992; 2nd edition, Zürich: Artemis, 1994
Zevi, Bruno, *Richard Neutra*, in Architetti del movimento moderno, vol. 10, Milan: Il Balcone, 1954

NEW DELHI, INDIA

At his Delhi coronation ceremony in 1911, King George V of Great Britain made a surprise announcement—the transfer of the Indian capital from Calcutta (the seat of British power for over a century) to Delhi. The British had been considering a more central administrative capital as early as 1857, when revolts throughout northern India shook their control. Delhi's strategic north-central location, where the ancient Grand Trunk Road and the navigable Yamuna River come together, made it a logical choice. The fact that it was cooler and less polluted than Calcutta certainly helped as well. The site had been home to at least a dozen different cities over the previous three millennia and served as capital for over six centuries during the rule of the Hindu Rajputs, the Delhi Sultanates, and the Moguls.

After the announcement, the Delhi Town Planning Committee was immediately established, whereas the selection of principal architect was a more contentious affair. British architect Edwin Lutyens (1869–1944) was awarded the prestigious project of design of the imperial city, more for his political connections than for his professional experience. The British viceroy had preferred architect Herbert Baker (1862–1946), who was asked to collaborate.

At the time, half of the native population of 233,000 lived in the crowded city of Shahjahanabad (founded in 1648 by the Mogul emperor Shah Jahan), in an area of about four square kilometers. The Committee searched for a location at a respectable distance from the Indian city but close enough that they would be able to make their presence felt. They ultimately selected a site on Raisina Hill some 5 kilometers southwest of the native city, between a high ridge and the Yamuna River. The new city would accommodate over 50,000 residents on an area of 26 square kilometers and would have provisions for future expansion.

The team of Lutyens and Baker organized the layout of the city in the tradition of the City Beautiful, a stylistic movement with roots in 19th-century France. The style was then becoming fashionable for large civic projects throughout the world and was particularly popular in colonial capitals because it conveys with ease a sense of both dominance and exclusivity, two important constructs to maintain when controlling alien regions. The plan for New Delhi incorporated all the basic tenets of City Beautiful design, including large-scale Beaux-Arts architectural elements, grand boulevards, and an abundance of gardens, parks, fountains, and sculpture.

The apex of Raisina Hill was blasted to create an artificial plateau above the old city. Atop this plateau were located the most important buildings of the British Raj: the Viceroy's House (1929, now *Rashtrapati Bhavan*) and the Secretariat Blocks (1928). Despite its solid horizontal massing (measuring 189 by 158 meters), the Viceroy's House appears monumental, given its hilltop location and a dome that rises 35 meters above the ground. Designed by Lutyens, the Viceroy's House contains several grand halls and courtyards, including the famous circular throne room under the dome for the Viceroy and his wife (presently Durbar Hall, used for ceremonial occasions). The gardens on the west side of the Viceroy's House were laid out in the Mogul tradition of four-squares with watercourses and fountains. The Secretariat Blocks, designed by Baker, are identical oblong classical structures on the east side of the Viceroy's House and today house the offices of the various government ministries. The Viceroy's court and the courts of the two secretariat blocks create a grand urban space known as the Government Court. This space is further defined by the Jaipur Column (1931), gift of the Maharaja of Jaipur, and the Dominion Columns (1931), gifts from the other great dominions within the British Empire.

From this commanding acropolis, the team laid out the processional avenue Kingsway (presently *Rajpath*) running between the Secretariat Blocks and east for 3 kilometers; it was lined by canals and fountains for its entire length. At the terminus Lutyens designed the monumental All-India War Memorial Arch, popularly called India Gate (1931), which, located at the center of five radiating axes, recalls Paris's *Arc de Triomphe*. The Palladian-style India Gate is 43 meters high and commemorates the Indian and British soldiers who died in three wars, including World War I. Facing it is a sandstone canopy that originally contained a statue of George V sculpted after his death in 1936; the statue has since been relocated to a more peripheral location.

The Kingsway was intersected by perpendicular axes and by grand diagonal boulevards radiating out from these axes to form a hexagonal network. The overall effect was reminiscent of L'Enfant's plan for Washington, for which Lutyens especially had expressed great admiration. The intersecting nodes of this network contained plazas and important buildings, such as the two churches designed by Henry Alexander Medd: the Cathedral Church of Redemption (1931, the main Anglican church for the British officials) and the Italianate Roman Catholic Church of the Sacred Heart (1934). The boulevards themselves were lined with bungalows, residences derived from the indigenous architecture of Bengal (*bungalow* is, in fact, an English corruption of the word *bangla*, meaning "from Bengal"). A typical bungalow was a single-storied horizontal structure with covered verandahs and a high ceiling to keep the interior shaded and cool. The bungalows originally housed British officials and today are home to ministers and other high bureaucrats in the Indian government.

Other prominent buildings of New Delhi include Connaught Place (1934), designed by Robert Tor Russell and named after the king's uncle, the Duke of Connaught. North of Lutyens' and Baker's central plan, this two-story shopping arcade with Palladian arches and stuccoed colonnades is arranged radially in two rings about a central lawn. Russell also designed the Commander-in-Chief's House (1930) south of the Viceroy's

House, later the home of Prime Minister Nehru and today a museum.

Lutyens wished to use a purely classical European idiom for the entire design; he was especially open in his aversion to Hindu and Mogul architecture and his disdain for stylistic admixtures. Baker was more open to integrating Indian and European elements. For political reasons, however, Lutyens used Indian motifs in his final designs for many of the buildings; these include the *chajja* (stone cornice), *chattri* (rooftop cupola) and other decorative detailing. Some critics argue that the use of Indian motifs can hardly qualify as being a true synthesis of traditions, whereas others testify to the harmonious effect created by the mixture.

The British ruled India for only 16 years after the completion of New Delhi, until Independence in 1947. In that time, and in the over 50 years since independence, New Delhi has expanded into new territory in every direction beyond the relatively small City Beautiful envisioned by Lutyens and Baker. The city's population is now estimated at 12 million people; this unprecedented growth is primarily a result of migration first from western Punjab after partition with Pakistan in 1947 and more recently from the entire country. In the process, it has expanded to incorporate *Shahjahanabad* (now called Old Delhi) and other older cities and villages around it. Lutyens' and Baker's colonial architecture and British urban planning (characterized by low-lying buildings in garden settings with tree-lined avenues) remain mostly intact in what is now called Central Delhi, with some stylistically mixed and high-rise in-fill. The remainder of the city is more diverse in terms of both economic level and style; modern New Delhi encompasses everything from the slum to the gated community, and styles as diverse as European classical, Islamic, Modern, and Postmodern, blended with vernacular traditions from an entire subcontinent.

MANISH CHALANA

See also **Baker, Herbert (England and South Africa); India; Lutyens, Edwin (England); Plan of New Delhi**

Further Reading

Hall, Peter Geoffrey, *Cities of Tomorrow: An Intellectual History of Urban Planning and Design in the Twentieth Century*, Oxford, UK and New York: Blackwell, 1988
Irving, Robert Grant, *Indian Summer: Lutyens, Baker, and Imperial Delhi*, New Haven: Yale University Press, 1981

NEW TOWNS MOVEMENT

It is largely accepted that two major design trends influenced the shape of the built environment in the 20th century: the new towns movement and the modern movement in architecture. Many reform movements emerged in response to the rapid industrialization of the 19th century, which had left cities in a poor state of overcrowding and social strife. For Lewis Mumford, the arrival of the new towns, which offered a recipe for social reform as well as environmental change, was as important as the invention of the airplane.

Ebenezer Howard, who introduced the idea of garden cities in 1898, argued for a marriage between town and country to create places that had the advantages of both and the disadvantages of neither. In Britain the two garden cities of Letchworth (1903–04) and Welwyn (1919–20) were developed, to be followed by a generation of new towns after World War II. The postwar new towns were planned and developed as an alternative both to city overgrowth and congestion and to intensified suburbanization.

The approach to, and principles used in the design of, the new towns changed over the period of their development, in line with the wider changes in society. Although each new town was a specific case, it is possible to arrive at a typology of design approaches in four main stages. The first stage is that of isolated, small towns with limited mobility and a radial, dispersed pattern of form. The second is a more compact urban entity that, under the influence of the automobile, finds a linear form. The third is a synthesis of these two opposites, and the fourth is the introduction of an open matrix of roads to which urban fabric is freely adapted.

In the first stage, the aim was to create a healthy and relaxed environment as opposed to the overcrowded city and its potential conflict of social classes. The design brief was to create a small settlement whose inhabitants, with their supposedly simple and predictable activity patterns, were expected to form well-integrated communities.

In the first generation of the new towns, such as in Stevenage, Crawley, and Hemel Hempstead, the influence of garden cities is visible. The town consists of separate, relatively independent neighborhood units of low density brought together around a town center. It is possible to walk to the shopping center or the workplace in a few minutes. The industrial zone is often concentrated in central locations served by railways and major roads, which also serve the town center. The town center is designed on the pattern of a market square. One- or two-story cottages flank winding roads and cul-de-sacs. Each neighborhood unit, formed of one or more superblocks, has enough population to support a primary school located at its center for easy and safe access, and the community center is not far away. Greenery fills the space between neighborhood units. Social integration is to be achieved through clustering people and places and serving them through a number of centers.

An increase in the target population of the new towns leads to the design of larger towns set in a regional context and linked with a demand for increased mobility and a critique of idealizing social integration at the neighborhood level. The increase in scale caused changes in transportation: from slow patterns of movement to higher mobility and from relying on walking and cycling to public transport and private automobile.

In response to the demand for "urbanity," as opposed to the suburban character of the first stage, a compact, linear form was adopted. All the inhabitants lived within walking distance of a concentrated linear center that included covered shopping streets with multilevel vehicular and pedestrian access. Separate neighborhoods were eliminated, density was increased, buildings became taller, and the industrial zone spread across the town. Only one new town, Cumbernauld, was developed at this stage.

The third stage of the evolution of new town design combined the first two stages. In what is known as the second generation of new towns, such as in Runcorn, Redditch, and Irvine, a town is formed of separate residential units of certain size connected to one another by a public transport route around whose stopping points local facilities are concentrated. Each unit

shows a radial scheme based on walking distance. A number of units are grouped together in a linear form around a public transport route as the generator of urban form. A network of roads encompasses these component parts of the town structure, connecting them to one another.

In the wealthier and more mobile society of the 1960s, the problem was not simply providing minimum acceptable standards but also striving for a better quality of life that included more freedom of choice and flexibility. The design approaches had to be adapted to the new circumstances or else be regarded as outdated or paternalistic prescriptions belonging to previous ages, especially at a time when before a scheme could be operated, its rationale was subject to change.

In the fourth stage of the evolution of new town design (for example, Washington), these ideas are reflected in the complete dominance of the private automobile over the town structure. The grid network as a large, flexible infrastructure is the characteristic of the last new town, Milton Keynes. In the course of change, the private automobile shifts the local center from the heart of the residential area to its boundaries to make it accessible from the road network.

Nearly all these transformations in 30 years of new town design show the increased importance of movement and mobility, which was also at the heart of the modern movement. They also show a continuous search for some form of social interaction through design, as reflected in the use of cul-de-sacs and cluster housing, despite heavy criticism against their systematic use as a means of social engineering. Superblocks, abundant green spaces and green belts, and functional segregation of access are other constant features, although considerable change in detail is traceable. Despite their failure in meeting their social agenda, such as halting the growth of cities and suburban sprawl or attracting a cross section of the population, new towns continue as viable towns. Apart from the four towns in Northern Ireland, the 28 new towns created nearly half a million jobs and added more than a million people to the original population of the designated areas. They inspire current debate and practice in Britain and the United States, where new settlements and New Urbanism are seen as a form of sustainable urban expansion.

ALI MADANIPOUR

See also **Garden City Movement; Mumford, Lewis (United States); New Urbanism**

NEW URBANISM

New Urbanism is a planning reform movement that evolved in the United States during the early 1990s from a marriage between two radical critiques of modernist planning and urban design: traditional neighborhood development (TND) and transit-oriented development (TOD). The movement aims to change the ways in which people understand and build towns and cities, opposing modernist concepts of separated single-use zoning areas, buildings isolated in open space, and an environment dominated by the automobile. Instead, the main organizing principles involve the creation of compact, defined urban neighborhoods comprising a compatible mixture of uses and housing types; a network of connected streets with sidewalks and street trees to facilitate convenient and safe movement throughout neighborhoods for all modes of transportation; the primacy of the pedestrian over the automobile; the integration of parks and public spaces into each neighborhood; and the placement of important civic buildings on key sites to create a strong and memorable vision as well as appearance.

The movement has provided a new paradigm for suburban development and refocused interest on existing urban areas. During the late 1990s, the ideals and principles of New Urbanism melded with the upsurge of professional and public interest in "smart growth," or "sustainable development," as an antidote to suburban sprawl and a way of managing urban growth into more environmentally responsible patterns. The title "New Urbanism" comes from a desire to counteract the faults of a sprawling *suburban* model of city development by a coherent *urban* form, with the adjective "New" added to distinguish the ideals from the old and now discredited urbanism of Le Corbusier, Walter Gropius, and other pioneers of Modernism.

Traditional neighborhood development (also known as neo-traditional development or neotraditional planning) is the term used to describe the planning and urban design of new developments that specifically take their forms from the structure and layout of "pre-automobile" neighborhoods. These are primarily streetcar suburbs and commuter rail suburbs around larger cities dating from the early decades of the 20th century and, at a smaller scale, traditional American small towns of the same period. The planning concepts and physical attributes of such places, with their human scale and lively mix of uses, are considered to be as appropriate now as they were when originally developed, 60 to 100 years ago.

The original proponents of TND were the Miami-based firm of DPZ and Company, founded by the husband-and-wife team of Andres Duany and Elizabeth Plater-Zyberk. Their best-known developments include the new communities of Seaside (1981, Walton County, Florida, 80 acres) and Kentlands (1988, Gaithersburg, Maryland, 356 acres).

The plan of Seaside features a range of traditional urban forms laid out on the site in a series of grids overlaid with diagonal axes focusing on the town center and providing key locations for monumental buildings. The streets are designed as narrow pedestrian "rooms" along which cars can move at slow speed and that often terminate at a public building or public space. Garages are accessed from the rear by means of narrow planted alleyways.

Duany and Plater-Zyberk acknowledge the impact of Léon Krier and his neorationalist ideas derived from the European city on the planning of Seaside. Krier was a consultant during the design process and has remained an important contributor to New Urbanist theory. During the 1970s in Europe, Krier was a leading advocate in the Movement for the Reconstruction of the European City, whose major themes included the preservation of historic centers; the use of historic urban types and urban patterns such as the street, square, and neighborhood (*quartier* in Krier's lexicon) as the basis for new city development; and the reconstruction of single-use residential "bedroom suburbs" into articulate mixed-use neighborhoods. Although the specific European urban morphologies and typologies were transformed by their travel across the Atlantic during the following decade, these underlying theoretical principles became founding concepts for TND in the 1980s and New Urbanist theory in the 1990s.

The parallel strand of TOD embodies many similar and complementary ideas but evolved specifically from the concept of the "pedestrian pocket," a place organized primarily around the needs of the pedestrian, and developed with an urban form that made it possible for public transit—usually light rail—to meet many individual mobility needs. Pedestrian pockets were developed in theoretical studies on the West Coast primarily by Peter Calthorpe in conjunction with Douglas Kelbaugh and others. The best-known built development following these ideas is Calthorpe's plan for Laguna West (1990, Sacramento County, California), although the execution of the master plan by others falls short of Calthorpe's original vision and intentions. The 1,033-acre development comprises 3,300 housing units, 66 acres of lakes, 55 acres of parks, and a town square for a future transit stop surrounded by a town hall, community center, offices, shops, and apartments.

The City of San Diego adopted Calthorpe's transit-oriented development principles in an official city ordinance in 1992, and New Urbanist ideas have had considerable influence in California on the design and planning of new projects. Calthorpe's reconstruction of a 16-acre derelict mall in Mountain View, California, into a mixed-use neighborhood (1996) exemplifies this trend.

Transit-oriented development extended the same planning and urban design ideas found in TND into a regional context by connecting development along fixed transit corridors, utilizing mainly light rail or commuter rail technology. Each transit stop catalyzed a neighborhood planned for a mixture of higher-density uses within a five- or ten-minute walking radius (one-quarter to one-half mile) laid out around pedestrian-friendly streets, squares, and parks.

Beginning as isolated developments during the 1980s, TNDs and TODs became far more common during the 1990s, largely because of the avid proselytizing of the ideas around the nation by Duany, Plater-Zyberk, Calthorpe, and others. These two movements coalesced in the formation of the Congress for the New Urbanism (CNU) in 1993, which has held annual congresses every year since then. The basic tenets of the movement were defined in the Charter of the New Urbanism, which was ratified at the CNU's fourth congress in Charleston in 1996.

Although it stands for principles that are often in direct contradiction to those of modernist architecture and planning, the CNU models itself on the Congrès Internationaux d'Architecture Moderne (CIAM), seeking to become the primary organization for town-planning theory and practice in the postmodern period, as was CIAM during the heyday of modernism. Its adopted Charter of the New Urbanism consciously recalls the Charter of Athens produced at the fourth congress of CIAM in 1933: whereas the older document set forth the ideals of the modernist city, the new charter establishes guiding principles and paradigms for postmodern urbanism.

The charter is organized into four sections: (1) an untitled preface of general statements; (2) the Region—Metropolis, City, and Town; (3) the Neighborhood, District, and Corridor; and (4) the Block, the Street, and the Building. The document first emphasizes coherent urban design and planning at a regional scale, promoting the renewed urbanity of existing areas and the increased urbanity of new development. This focused urbanism is balanced by a concern for the environmentally sustainable relationship between any metropolis and its agrarian hinterland

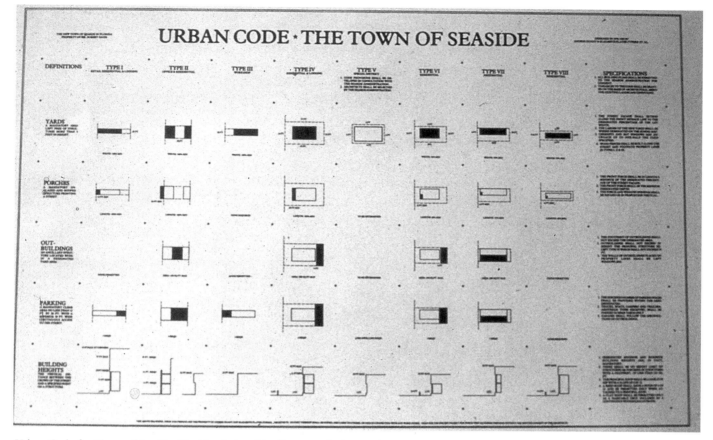

Urban Code for Town of Seaside, Florida, designed by Duany and Plater-Zyberk
© Duany/Plater-Zyberk

and natural landscapes. The subsequent sections spell out the movement's concerns for the reconstruction of American cities at a variety of scales, utilizing many of the concepts articulated previously by Krier and his fellow neorationalists in their manifesto for the reconstruction of the European city and adapting them to American practice.

Although Krier was a major influence on the development of New Urbanism, his was by no means the only European influence. Ebenezer Howard's Garden City reform movement of the turn of the 20th century, with its emphasis on well-planned, self-contained new towns served by transit and defined by large tracts of productive countryside, was also an important contributor to New Urbanist theory. The British architect and planner Raymond Unwin, with his brother-in-law Barry Parker, gave tangible form to Howard's Garden City ideals in the English new town of Letchworth (begun 1903) and Hampstead Garden Suburb in north London (begun 1907, developed in collaboration with Sir Edwin Lutyens). Unwin's book *Town Planning in Practice* (1909) spread his planning and urban design ideas through Europe and the United States early in the 20th century, and the volume's republication (1994) has revived the relevance of the work to postmodern urban designers.

A theoretical backbone of Unwin's treatise was the work of Austrian teacher and designer Camillo Sitte, whose book *City*

Planning According to Artistic Principles (originally published in German in 1889) set out principles regarding the artful composition of public space. Sitte's work looked back to medieval, Renaissance, and baroque Europe in its analysis of human-scaled public space, but in an empirical and experiential rather than a rationalist or typological manner.

In the United States, apart from the extensive vernacular tradition of small-town and suburban design from the late 19th century to the 1930s, the lineage of New Urbanist influences includes the Beaux-Arts traditions of the City Beautiful movement, the Arts and Crafts movement, the work of F.L. Olmsted and his successors, the innovative town plans of John Nolen, and Clarence Perry's work in 1929 to define the ideal neighborhood unit.

More recently, Werner Hegemann and Elbert Peets's republished work from the 1920s, *The American Vitruvius* (1988), became a seminal text for traditional neighborhood design in the 1990s, summarizing the work of Sitte and European garden cities as well as codifying Beaux-Arts and City Beautiful concepts for American use.

The rediscovery of these older works that were banished by the doctrines of modernist urban design and planning illustrates a developing trend toward regionalism, historicism, contextualism, and the vernacular that is traceable from the early 1960s.

In Britain, this was evident in the Townscape movement and especially in the work of Gordon Cullen, whose book *Townscape* (1961) became a seminal work about pedestrian-scaled urban environments based on traditional elements of streets and squares. From the 1970s on, this approach to urbanism gave rise to neotraditional developments in Britain under the rubric "neovernacular design." This trend was formalized with the publication of the official County of Essex *Design Guide for Residential Areas* (1973), a visual codebook that established the principles of good (i.e., traditional) urban design that new developments were expected to follow.

In France this neotraditional direction was presaged in 1966 by the idiosyncratic development of "Provincial Urbanism" by Jacques Riboud at La Verrière-Maurepas in St. Quentin-en-Yvelines outside Paris. Seven years later, in southern France, Françoise Spoerry expanded on this use of traditional and picturesque urban forms in his resort development at Port Grimaud (1973) and later hill-town developments at nearby Gassin.

Both European neotraditional townscape and the neorationalist approach to city design emphasized the art of relationships between buildings and the importance of well-defined public space. This view of the human-scaled city found its American counterpart in the work of Paul Goodman, Kevin Lynch, and Jane Jacobs during the early 1960s. Lynch's seminal work *Image of the City* (1960) introduced the powerful idea of making the city "legible" to the user through the coding and manipulation of simplified urban elements, such as districts, paths, edges, nodes, and landmarks. Jacobs, in her powerful indictment of modernist city planning, *The Death and Life of American Cities* (1961), refocused attention on the street as the basic building block of neighborhood and community and lambasted modernist ideas of urban renewal as being too large scale, too abstract, and devoid of human scale and feeling.

The emphasis on contextualism and respect for the older patterns of the city is also evident in works of Colin Rowe and Fred Koetter (*Collage City* [1978]) and Christopher Alexander (*Pattern Language* [1977] and *A New Theory of Urban Design* [1987]). These books focused designers' attention on, among other things, bringing back streets and squares as the public living rooms of the city, thereby reversing the destruction of the street by modernist theory and practice.

During the late 1980s and 1990s, in parallel to New Urbanism, a new interest in "urban villages" developed. In Britain, under the impetus of HRH Prince Charles and his planning adviser Léon Krier, this work focused on the creation of sustainable mixed-use urban developments as the incremental building blocks of urban expansion and redevelopment, creating high-quality but affordable urban living while preserving the economic and environmental resources of the countryside. One tangible result of this initiative was the new village of Poundbury, outside Dorchester, designed by Léon Krier in 1988, the first phase of which (1997) is complete. Similar concepts are evident in the contemporaneous German new town of Potsdam-Drewitz, by Léon Krier's elder brother, Rob Krier.

Preserving the rural landscape is also the main concern of American planners such as Randall Arendt, whose book *Rural by Design* (1994) sets out planning principles for residential subdivision development that conserve as much as possible of the appearance and ecology of natural landscapes under development.

Outside Chicago, in Grayslake, Illinois, developers recruited award-winning residential architects to design vernacular-style houses around restored wetlands and prairies in a conservation community called Prairie Crossing. Calthorpe's TOD ideas were rejected by city officials, demonstrating the difficulties that many New Urbanist planners still face.

New Urbanists and like-minded designers in the United States face a major obstacle in implementing their ideas: most aspects of this traditionally based urbanism are illegal under conventional American zoning ordinances. These ordinances, developed in the decades after World War II, provide the framework of detailed regulations that have implemented the modernist and suburbanized view of the city, categorized by low-density single-use developments separated out across the landscape. The solution adopted by New Urbanist designers has been to rewrite development codes on the basis of models of traditional urbanism and to persuade municipalities to implement these as parallel or substitute zoning regulations.

Planners, local government officials, citizens, and some developers have shown great interest in New Urbanist design, particularly those in areas that are experiencing growth-related conflicts. Many see New Urbanism as an approach that enables a community's growth to be channeled into a physical form that is more compatible with the scale of existing neighborhoods, discourages excessive automobile use, is less costly to service, and uses less land and natural resources.

However, New Urbanism continues to meet resistance to its implementation, and not simply because of antiquated regulations. The highly integrated development strategy inherent to New Urbanism requires a more holistic approach to community building than the real estate and development industries are currently structured to deliver. These industries are highly segmented by land use category (e.g., single-family housing, multi-family housing, retail, office, and industrial), and each category has its own practices, markets, trade associations, and financing sources that are somewhat resistant to change. From within these sectors, New Urbanism is often perceived as a threat to current profitable practices.

Other critics of New Urbanism, particularly academics in American schools of architecture, often relabel it "New *Sub*urbanism" and criticize it for being nothing more than better-designed sprawl. New Urbanists defend themselves by pointing out that the CNU charter argues explicitly for "the restoration of existing urban centers and towns within coherent metropolitan regions, the reconfiguration of sprawling suburbs into communities of real neighborhoods and diverse districts, the conservation of natural environments, and the preservation of our built legacy," that is, an integrated approach to city building that gives full weight to redevelopment of existing urban areas. Unfortunately, many of the current social, political, and economic realities in the United States prioritize development at the metropolitan periphery, and only during the late 1990s have development opportunities in the inner city provided a clear forum for New Urbanist ideas.

Despite opposition from these various quarters, New Urbanism remains at the heart of the American debate regarding the future of its cities and suburbs. By its emphasis on human-scaled community design based on traditional models, New Urbanism has established itself as one of the central themes of postmodern urban theory and practice.

DAVID WALTERS

See also **Athens Charter (1943); City Beautiful Movement; Congrès Internationaux d'Architecture Moderne (CIAM, 1927-); Corbusier, Le (Jeanneret, Charles-Édouard) (France); Duany and Plater-Zyberk (United States); Gropius, Walter (Germany); Krier, Léon (Luxembourg); Suburban Planning; Urban Planning**

Further Reading

Aldous, Tony, *Urban Villages: A Concept of Creating Mixed-Use Urban Developments on a Sustainable Scale*, London: Urban Villages Group, 1992; 2nd edition, London: Urban Villages Forum, 1997

Alexander, Christopher, *A New Theory of Urban Design*, New York and Oxford: Oxford University Press, 1987

Alexander, Christopher, Sara Ishikawa, and Murray Silverstein, *Pattern Language: Towns, Buildings, Construction*, New York: Oxford University Press, 1977

Arendt, Randall, *Rural by Design: Maintaining Small Town Character*, Chicago: American Planning Association Planners Press, 1994

Barnett, Jonathan, *The Fractured Metropolis: Improving the New City, Restoring the Old City, Reshaping the Region*, New York: Harper Collins, 1995

Calthorpe, Peter, *The Next American Metropolis: Ecology, Community, and the American Dream*, New York: Princeton Architectural Press, 1993

Collins, George R., and Christiane Crasemann Collins, *Camillo Sitte and the Birth of Modern City Planning*, New York: Random House, and London: Phaidon, 1965; revised edition, New York: Rizzoli, 1986

Cullen, Gordon, *Townscape*, London: Architectural Press, and New York: Reinhold, 1961; new edition, as *The Concise Townscape*, London: Butterworth Architecture, 1990

Design Guide for Residential Areas, Chelmsford: Essex County Council, 1973; new edition, as *The Essex Design Guide for Residential and Mixed Use Areas*, Essex: Essex Planning Officers Association, 1997

Duany, Andres, et al., *Towns and Town-Making Principles*, New York: Rizzoli, 1991; 2nd edition, 1992

Duany, Andres, et al., *The Lexicon of the New Urbanism*, Miami: DPZ, 1999

Hegemann, Werner, and Elbert Peets, *The American Vitruvius: An Architect's Handbook of Civic Art*, New York: Architectural Book, 1922; reprint, New York: Princeton Architectural Press, and Braunschweig, Germany: Friedrich Vieweg, 1988

Jacobs, Jane, *The Death and Life of Great American Cities*, New York: Random House, 1961; London: Jonathan Cape, 1962

Katz, Peter, *The New Urbanism: Toward an Architecture of Community*, New York: McGraw-Hill, 1994

Kelbaugh, Douglas (editor), *The Pedestrian Pocket Book: A New Suburban Design Strategy*, New York: Princeton Architectural Press, 1989

Kelbaugh, Douglas, *Common Place: Toward Neighborhood and Regional Design*, Seattle: University of Washington Press, 1997

Krier, Léon, *Houses, Palaces, Cities*, London: Architectural Design Edition, 1984

Kunstler, James Howard, *Home from Nowhere: Remaking Our Everyday World for the 21st Century*, New York: Simon and Schuster, 1996

Leccese, Michael, and Kathleen McCormick (editors), *Charter of the New Urbanism*, New York: McGraw-Hill, 2000

Lynch, Kevin, *The Image of the City*, Cambridge, Massachusetts: MIT Press, 1960

Rowe, Colin, and Fred Koetter, *Collage City*, Cambridge, Massachusetts: MIT Press, 1978; London: MIT Press, 1979

Sitte, Camillo, *Die Städte-Bau nach seinen künstlerischen Grundsätzen*, Vienna: Graeser, 1889; as *City Planning according to Artistic Principles*, translated by George R. Collins and Christiane Crasemann Collins, New York: Random House, and London: Phaidon, 1965

NEW YORK (NEW YORK), UNITED STATES

Aesthetically, New York is generally considered the preeminent city of the 20th century. As the 18th century was the century of the London terrace and square, and the 19th that of the Parisian boulevards and Beaux Arts, the 20th century belongs to the skyscraper, the subway, and the grid. For New York, crucible of American indigenous ideals and imported European style, has achieved in the modern era the stature of international urban icon.

Manhattan Island

One cannot think of the architecture of New York City without the associations of skyscraper and skyline. Here on a skinny island, skyscrapers seem to grow out of the stony soil. The natural conditions of Manhattan Island are fertile ground for skyscrapers, for the city is built on a rocky outcropping of Manhattan schist, geologically strong enough to support high buildings. Poets including Walt Whitman have described it as "an island sixteen miles long, solid-founded" ("Mannahatta," 1860).

Physical constraints of the island site are also creators of form for the city. The actual twenty-two and a half square miles of Manhattan are highly circumscribed, surrounded on all sides by fast-moving rivers and a deep harbor, pushing the city's economic development while simultaneously limiting its physical expansion. Long piers once were once thrown out from the island's shores, expanding the city into its waterways. The city grew further horizontally, crossing its waterways into neighboring cities and counties, and eventually annexing them. For the urban core of Manhattan, however, the only way to go was up, and the city reached ever skyward.

In the modern era, New York has become the symbolic emblem of American ideals, the skyscraping architectural triumph of America. The city's national symbolism has been noted by many—for good and for bad. In the fall of 2001, a piece of the Manhattan skyline was obliterated in a violent terrorist act. Two of the tallest buildings in history, the twin towers of the World Trade Center (Minoru Yamasaki and Associates, 1973), with occupants and other innocent victims, were destroyed on 11 September, 2001. Manhattan, however, is built on rock and American urban ideals, and thus New York City endures.

The Boroughs and the New York Metropolitan Area

New York, in the broad sense, is an agglomerative environment with a population of eight million composed of five counties or boroughs: Manhattan, Brooklyn, Queens, the Bronx, and Staten Island—counties with populations each larger than most American cities. The New York metropolitan region further expands into vast leafy suburbs from Long Island to the east and Westchester to the north to northern New Jersey and to shoreline Connecticut. In the narrower definition of New York, as in common parlance, New York City is Manhattan Island.

Certain features of the boroughs individually, though, may of some interest to the reader—especially the boroughs' unique open spaces, (open space being in short supply in Manhattan), and their linkages to Manhattan, particularly their bridges. For example, the creators of Manhattan's Central Park in the heart of Manhattan (Frederick Law Olmsted and Calvert Vaux, 1860), later designed Brooklyn's Prospect Park (1874). The New York Botanical Gardens (Vaux and Parsons, 1895), with its graceful glass conservatory, can be found in the Bronx. Queens' Flushing Meadows Park still exhibits reminders of its history as the futuristic site of the 1939 and 1964 World's Fairs.

The Brooklyn Bridge (John and Washington Roebling, 1883), to Manhattan, is justly famed for both its engineering and its monumental Egyptoid aesthetic. Also of architectural note are the baroque Queensboro Bridge (Palmer and Hornbostol, 1909) across the East River and the sweeping cables of the George Washington Bridge (Cass Gilbert, 1931) crossing the Hudson River. The old-fashioned Staten Island Ferry offers the most stunning approach to the pinnacled skyscrapers of the lower Manhattan skyline. It sails through New York Harbor blithely past the Statue of Liberty.

Modern Architecture in New York, 20th Century

In the earliest part of the 20th century, the architecture of New York was influenced by European styles, first by the Beaux-Arts and then by Art Nouveau (Jugenstil) and the decorative arts. Later in the century, however, New York began throw off its foreign-designed cloak and to assert itself architecturally, creating a modern architectural language that is, in many respects, unique to the city. This was the city's first modern urban architecture that was truly architectonic, based on form, upward thrust, and massing, as dictated by the setback skyscraper zoning law (1916). By mid-century however, European influence again returned to Manhattan—this time via the entry of émigré architects fleeing artistic and intellectual oppression.

The modern architecture of New York City can therefore be classified into five major periods: the Beaux-Arts, the Deco Skyscraper, Manhattan Modern, the International Style, and Alternative Modernism. Though these classifications can only begin to define the myriad forms of the city that comprise New York's distinctively urbane modernity, this article will briefly define and examine examples of each style chosen not only for their architectural presence but also for their public accessibility to the reader.

Beaux-Arts Architecture in New York, 1900–20s

Although the Beaux-Arts looked back to classical Rome for its facades and elevations, it was truly a modern movement in its approach to plan and function. Through this style, New York was able to weave the gravity of ancient forms and facades into its modern functional fabric. Significant public urban monuments were designed in the early part of the 20th century by Beaux-Arts–trained architects and their large firms. Important commissions such as the New York Public Library (Carrere and Hastings, 1911), the Metropolitan Museum of Art (Richard Morris Hunt, 1902), and Columbia University (McKim, Mead, and White, 1897) are lasting examples of the style.

New York City skyline, 2001
Photo © Robert M. Byrne

Columbia University, on the upper west side, is perhaps the clearest example of the melding of the symbolic antique cloth of the Beaux-Arts with modern plan and intent. Here Charles McKim's Pantheon-like Low Library (1897) overlooks a classically arranged campus in a highly functional and urban setting. The ponderous domed facade, its giant orders, and ranges of ascending stone steps remind the modern student that all knowledge, even the ground-breaking modern thought of the contemporary university, represents a continuity with the past.

McKim's ability to integrate historical symbol with modern function was even more strongly felt in Pennsylvania Station (1910), a much-lamented landmark of steel and glass configured in classical form (demolished, 1962). Fortunately as New York has gained a renewed appreciation for the Beaux-Arts, old Penn Station is now scheduled to be replaced by another McKim, Mead, and White building across the street, substituting their decommissioned classical General Post Office (1913) for the lost train station. Further, New York has recently witnessed a renaissance of restoration in two other classical monuments, the New York Public Library and Grand Central Station (Reed and Stem and Warren and Wetmore, 1913). Thus, the Beaux-Arts remains a living and vital part of today's city.

Art Deco Skyscrapers, 1920s–30s

During the teens, through the 1920s, and onto the era of the 1939 World's Fair, the visual historicism of the Beaux-Arts gave way to the futurism of the fair. A new look in New York was apparent, as architecture now changed from a decorative dress of classicism into one of organic and zigzagging ornament. New York architecture continued to be quite ornamental throughout the 1920s, although, in contrast to the freestanding classical orders, deco ornament is usually suppressed into the facade's frontal plane. By the 1930s, New York moved toward a new integration of the basic cube and grid pattern of Manhattan with a stylized decorative motif.

Though this style was not generally applied to public monuments, other than the World's Fair, perhaps being considered too frivolous, excellent examples of deco modernism can be found from midtown and north, on the entrance facades and rising stories of commercial skyscrapers and residential buildings alike.

One of the most attractive and accessible deco facades is found on the Chanin building (Sloan and Robertson, 1929) near Grand Central Station, where flat-patterned carved ornament, reminiscent of Louis Sullivan, rings the building's walls. The Chanin construction firm and other commercial rather than architectural firms spread the deco style along Central Park West in the chain of striking entrances to high-rise apartment towers that form the western architectural backdrop of Central Park today, including examples such as the Majestic and the San Remo Apartments. Continuing further north in Manhattan, one finds the unique Masters Apartments and Museum (Harvey Corbett, rendered by Hugh Ferriss, 1929) along Riverside Drive. This building subtly transforms from dark brick to light as it rises upward in an unusual coloristic display, which is less clear today. The Masters, fusing ornament and color with form, may be read as a transitional work, moving early modernism from

the deco verve of applied ornament into a more restrained modernism to come.

The epitome of art deco modernism and the crowning pinnacle (1048 feet) of the deco skyscraper is without question the Chrysler Building (William Van Alen, 1930), a fully integrated spire shining in steel, sleek and dynamic as the automobiles it symbolizes for the modern age. Its mid-town setting, its beautiful presence on the skyline, and its urbane interiors set the Chrysler Building forever apart from all deco structures. It is without peer, even in the city that defined the concept of the deco skyscraper.

Manhattan Modern, 1930s–40s

"Manhattan Modern" is the first truly architectonic, rather than decorative, movement in modern New York architecture, designed exclusively by American architects. This is the indigenous American modernism of tall, spare, attenuated structures of polished granite, steel, and glass, conceived on the principles of Sullivan's treatise, "The Tall Office Building Artistically Considered."

For it is here in New York that Sullivan's ideal of the skyscraper as "it is lofty" is best illustrated. Loftiness is certainly the defining characteristic of New York, and Sullivan's aesthetic approach dovetailed well with New York's 1916 zoning law, which obligated tall buildings to set back as they rose from the street. The fortunate resulting massing of the New York skyline thus came to point upward in a collection of closely sited, skyscraping pinnacles.

The finest examples of the formal aesthetics of Manhattan Modern may be found in the Empire State Building (Shreve, Lamb and Harmon, 1931), as an individual pinnacle; and in Rockefeller Center (The Associated Architects: Reinhard and Hofmeister; Corbett, Harrison, and McMurray; Raymond Hood, Godley, and Fouilhoux, 1932–40), an urban agglomeration of buildings and space.

Just as the Chrysler building is the perfection of deco skyscraper, the Empire State Building is the perfect Manhattan Modern composition. From the day it opened, the Empire State Building was notable for its height (1250 feet), its function and efficiency, its feat· of speedy construction, and its stylistic simplicity and aesthetic spareness. Symbolic of the city itself, the composition of the Empire State Building exhibits a synthesis of restraint and power that creates a lasting iconic design.

The other great exponent of Modernism is an ensemble of tall buildings tightly dispersed about a midtown plaza of benches under clipped trees, of banners and monumental deco sculpture: Rockefeller Center. Created during the Depression as a public–private pedestrian urban place, Rockefeller Center proves that skyscrapers need not affront human scale in the city. Somewhat analogous to the meaning of Central Park, the open space of Rockefeller Center, protected space amid a series of stone skyscrapers, here provides a welcome Fifth Avenue counterpoint for the pedestrian within the relentless city grid.

The International Style, 1950s–70s

The International Style in mid-century turned the great stone face of modernism to glass. The 20th century is bisected by the arrival of the European modernists, including Mies van der Rohe, Walter Gropius, and Marcel Breuer, and their International Style. The transparent shining glass slabs of Park Avenue, in particular, are the legacy of the émigré movement of modernism.

The earliest inklings of the International Style in New York, however, were American, based on European aesthetics, including the New School for Social Research (Joseph Urban, 1930) and the original modern home of the Museum of Modern Art (Philip Goodwin and Edward Durell Stone, 1939).

The high point of the style in New York is certainly the Park Avenue duo of the Seagram Building (Mies van der Rohe with Philip Johnson, 1958) and Lever House (Gordon Bunshaft of Skidmore, Owings, and Merrill, 1951). The sleek, dark bronze, steel, and glass slab of the Seagram rises out of its opposition, an open cube of space, creating a dialectic of architectural space with object as significant as that dynamic in classical architecture. Lever House takes a more constructivist approach to space and object, with an ice-blue glass tower rising asymmetrically from its base. Thus, these two buildings are of interest not only as perfected exemplars of classical International Style, itself, but also for their daring spatial massing.

Both the Seagram and the Lever took advantage of the midcentury changes in the set-back zoning laws that had dictated the pinnacle form of the earlier Manhattan modern. New zoning now allowed buildings to rise straight upward in exchange for creating open plaza space at street level. Though here experiments breaking the New York City grid have provided interesting effects of solid–void relationships, in the case of their neighbor, building outside the grid was disastrous for the city. As the Pan Am Building (Emery Roth and Sons, Pietro Belluschi, and Walter Gropius, 1963) illustrates, a skyscraper set atop the Beaux-Arts landmark Grand Central Terminal in the middle of Park Avenue, breaking the flow of the avenue, casts shadows and exhibits a basic disregard for the urban fabric. At least this problematical building has served to promote serious questions on the idea of urban context.

The United Nations (Wallace Harrison of Harrison, Abramovitz, and Harris, with Oscar Niemeyer and Sven Markelius, 1947–53), sited along the East River on land donated by the Rockefeller family, by contrast, created its own urban context. A powerful and symbolically significant skyscraper, appropriately "international" in style, the United Nations complex is based on a Le Corbusier design. The open site affords the New York International Style a viewing of the thin green glass and white stone building, very rare in the canyons of Manhattan, for the United Nations Secretariat slab (544 feet) may be seen unobstructed from the Queensboro Bridge, while crossing the East River, in all its shining symbolic optimism. Especially while lit at night, it seems to stand as a beacon calling a global community together. Appropriate to its function of bringing together disparate nations, the United Nations tower is also an ensemble of highly varied forms. The inverted bowl shapes and sweeping curves of the General Assembly chambers point toward late romantic variations on the modern.

Alternative Modernism in New York, 1960s–80s

The endurance of modernism in Manhattan, through adaptation and alternative forms, is exemplified by variations on the style in the last decades of the 20th century. Successful examples include the Ford Foundation Building with its glass-enclosed atrium (Kevin Roche, John Dinkeloo and Associates, 1967), the CitiCorp Center with its simple but daring slanted roofline (Hugh Stubbins and Associates, 1978), and the quite recent return to the pure International Style geometry of the cube and the sphere in the millennial Rose Center for Earth and Space, American Museum of Natural History (Polcheck and Partners, 2000).

Alternative modernism, or perhaps modernisms, in New York have always been exemplified best by museums, for by nature, museums will be daring in their artistic choices. Certainly the public has long been enthralled by that most obvious New York landmark by the most famous American architect, Frank Lloyd Wright's Guggenheim Museum (1959). A romantic, spiraling, shell-like sculpture, the Guggenheim sits on Fifth Avenue overlooking Central Park. Its location and relation to the urban environment must give us pause as we think of the architecture of New York. For although the building is certainly masterly, it defies its place within the order of the city grid and thus does not speak to its environment.

By contrast, the Whitney Museum of American Art (Marcel Breuer, 1960), a hulking Brutalist, abstract composition overhanging Madison Avenue, comments on its city. The concrete sculptural quality of this work, although accepting its containment within the grid, still makes itself a powerful urban testament to its turbulent times.

New Architecture in New York, 2001 into the Future

Times are turbulent again today in the city of the new millennium, not from internal urban unrest but from causes far away. New York has always been an architectural bellwether for America, and thus the nation watches intently as Manhattan, perpetually constructing, now ponders re-construction. Major architectural decisions await, as the city re-envisions itself. Of one thing we can be certain though: out of rubble and hope, the future of the American city will rise again, literally, from the ashes.

LESLIE HUMM CORMIER

See also **Art Deco; Bunshaft, Gordon (United States); Chrysler Building, New York City; Empire State Building, New York City; Grand Central Station, New York City; Guggenheim Museum, New York City; International Style; Lever House, New York City; Lincoln Center, New York City; McKim, Mead, and White (United States); Museum of Modern Art, New York City; Rockefeller Center, New York City; Seagram Building, New York City; Skyscraper; United Nations Headquarters, New York City; Woolworth Building, New York City; World Trade Center, New York City**

Further Reading

Huxtable, Ada Louise, *The Architecture of New York: A History and Guide*, Garden City, New York: Anchor Books, 1964

Reynolds, Donald Martin, *Manhattan Architecture*, New York: Prentice Hall, 1988; London: Bloomsbury, 1989

Robinson, Cervin, and Rosemarie Haag Bletter, *Skyscraper Style: Art Deco, New York*, Oxford and New York: Oxford University Press, 1975

Stern, Robert A.M., Thomas Mellins, and David Fishman, *New York 1960: Architecture and Urbanism between the Second World War and the Bicentennial*, New York: Monacelli Press, 1995

White, Norval, and Elliot Willensky (editors), *A.I.A. Guide to New York City*, New York: American Institute of Architects, 1967; 4th edition, New York: Random House, and London: Hi Marketing, 2000

NEW YORK WORLD'S FAIR (1939)

The New York World's Fair of 1939–40 was, to many commentators, the last true world exposition in a long line stretching back to the Crystal Palace Exhibition of 1851. The fair arrived at a critical historical juncture at the end of the Great Depression and on the eve of World War II. Although the architecture and planning of the fair were rooted in the struggles of the 1930s between Beaux Arts classicism and modernism, behind the streamlined facades the theme and exhibits presaged the consumer culture of the 1950s. Under the guiding theme of "Building the World of Tomorrow," exhibits inside the modern classical buildings heralded an American society with a renewed faith in the private sector and the power of consumption, supported by government subsidies of automobility, domesticity, and suburbanization.

The New York Fair, as originally conceived, was ostensibly a 150th-anniversary celebration of George Washington's inauguration and the ratification of the Constitution, but it quickly adopted other agendas. The idea of a fair in New York began in 1934 as the brainchild of an obscure civil engineer named Joseph F. Shadgen of Queens, New York. Through a distant relative of Franklin Roosevelt, Shadgen brought the idea to George McAneny, president of Title Guarantee and Trust and the Regional Plan Association, who joined forces with Percy Straus, president of R.H. Macy's, to form a committee under the auspices of the Regional Plan Association in 1935. From the onset, progressive planning and consumerism were wed in the planning of the fair. McAneny's committee would become the World's Fair Corporation, adding New York City's "official greeter," Grover A. Whalen, as president in 1936.

Although there is some evidence of an initial struggle, Robert Moses, the infamous czar of city planning in New York City, showed little interest in controlling the management or content of the fair. However, he fought hard and effectively to locate the fair on the site of the old Corona Ash Dump in Queens. Author F. Scott Fitzgerald had called the site "a valley of ashes— a fantastic farm where ashes grow like wheat into ridges and hills and grotesque gardens," but Moses saw something else. In an interview in 1936, Moses crowed that long after the 1939 fair was gone, he would have a cleared, leveled, and landscaped site for the largest urban park in his domain, a linchpin in his system of parkways leading from the city to the future suburbs of Long Island.

The evolution of the fair's theme, "Building the City of Tomorrow," reflects the transformation of progressive ideas about planning and society during the 1930s from a preoccupation with science and production to a celebration of consumption and abundance. Early in 1936, the Theme Committee of the Board of Design, consisting of industrial designer Walter Dorwin Teague and former president of the American Institute of Architects Robert Kohn, settled on the theme of "Building the World of Tomorrow," specifically, "a happier way of American living through the Interdependence of Man and the Building of a Better World of Tomorrow with the Tools of Today." Under pressure from the fair's organizers and retail sponsors, the more idealistic rhetoric of the theme became in reality a focus on future progress through images of abundance. As the planned buildings filled with commercial exhibitors, space reserved for the theme-driven "focal exhibits" designed by the Board of Design quickly gave way to exhibition space for retailers.

The physical arrangement of the fair drew sharp criticism from planners and commentators expecting a modernist plan in the manner of Le Corbusier or Ludwig Mies van der Rohe. Where Chicago's Century of Progress Exposition (1933) had permitted pavilions to stand alone in a modernist free plan, the New York Fair plan, designed by consultant William Orr Ludlow and architectural delineator Hugh Ferriss, followed a rigid classical scheme that many saw as a refutation of the fair's futurist theme. At its heart, just off Moses's Grand Central Parkway, rose the "Theme Center": Wallace K. Harrison and J. André Fouilhoux's Trylon and Perisphere. Radiating eastward from the Theme Center, broad avenues divided the fair into four pie-shaped slices. The main axis led east from the Trylon along the Constitution Mall, past statues by Paul Manship, through a statue of George Washington to the Lagoon of Nations (home for the foreign pavilions), terminating at the Court of Peace and the United States Pavilion. To the northeast, the Avenue of Patriots led to the Community Interests Zone, containing a prototypical Town of Tomorrow. The Avenue of Pioneers led southeast to the Food Zone and Court of States. North of the Theme Center sat Communications. To the immediate south was Production and Distribution, and beyond them the Amusement Zone sprawled along the shore of Fountain Lake. Across the Grand Central parkway to the west lay the Transportation Zone, including the popular Ford and GM Pavilions.

The architecture of the fair has been variously described as "Modern Classicism," a synthesis (often incomplete and less than successful) of modernist forms and Beaux-Arts logic that had emerged in the 1930s; Depression Moderne; or Streamline Modern. The common theme is the identification of a style or styles that sought to stand apart from both classicism and European modernism. The dominance of the various "moderne" styles at the expense of what many considered a more honest "modernism" was, in part, the result of the preponderance of industrial designers, such as Teague, Raymond Loewy, Henry Dreyfus, and Gilbert Rhode, on the Board of Design. The consensus of contemporary critics was that the Fair Corporation's architecture represented a "confused" and "pompous" modernism, while they singled out the works of a few, such as William Lescaze and George Howe, as well as Harrison and Fouilhoux, for praise.

Harrison and Fouilhoux's Trylon and Perisphere expressed an abstract modernism that met with critical approval, even as many found the buildings' meaning obscure. The Perisphere, a 180-foot-diameter sphere, lay at the focus of the fair's radiating avenues, attached to the 610-foot-high pyramidal Trylon by a 65-foot spiral bridge, or Helicline. The Trylon and Perisphere were composed of a steel structure covered in gypsum board

New York World's Fair, Court of Peace, Federal Building, Italian building, New York World's Fair
and League of Nations
© Underwood & Underwood/CORBIS

painted white, producing an effect of pure abstraction. Although the architects never identified their specific inspirations, the most compelling precedents come from the Romantic Classical work of enlightenment architects Claude Nicholas Ledoux and Etienne-Louis Boulee, specifically Boulee's famous unbuilt (and unbuildable) project for a Cenotaph for Newton (1784).

Entering the Theme Center's Perisphere, audiences looked down from peripheral galleries onto Henry Dreyfus's "Democracity," an enormous diorama of a city circa 2039. Centerton, the central city for 250,000 white-collar workers, was surrounded by satellite suburbs for 1.5 million residents. "Pleasantvilles" were dormitory suburbs, and "Millvilles" were light industrial developments. Visitors saw a five-and-a-half-minute show portraying a 24-hour day with light and sound effects—a 1930s virtual reality show.

The Fair Corporation's buildings provided focal exhibits for each zone. To provide stylistic coherence, the Fair-built buildings followed the Design Committee's exact aesthetic specifications. Long expanses of windowless wall, colonnades, abstract domes, and exedra characterized these structures. A complex system of color coding determined the hue of each building, from bright white at the Theme Center through pale hues to darker hues at the "Rainbow Avenue" on the periphery. The

larger Fair-built pavilions would manifest function through form. The Marine Transpiration Building is perhaps the most famous of the Fair-built buildings in the mode of such "speaking architecture." Framing the entrance were two enormous ships' prows.

If consistency was the byword of the Fair Corporation's buildings, then eclecticism characterized the houses of the Town of Tomorrow. Although the Fair Corporation designed the suburban cul-de-sac around which they were arranged, the houses of the Town of Tomorrow were each designed by individual architects chosen by their corporate sponsors. Promoting innovations in comfort and convenience, the homes themselves were notable for their traditionalism and historical familiarity including the Home Insurance Company's "Fire-Safe House," and the Johns-Manville "Triple Insulated House." Two exceptions deserve mention: the Douglas Fir Plywood Association's "House of Plywood," designed by A. Lawrence Kocher, celebrated the properties of plywood in a vaguely modernist scheme that included strip windows and an asymmetrical plan and a free facade stripped of historical allusion. The "Pittsburgh House of Glass," designed by Landefeld and Hatch, comes closest to the International Style domestic paradigm, with a free plan, great expanses of glass, and a free-flowing connection between inside and outside that draws heavily on European examples and presages Philip Johnson's Glass House (1949).

Perhaps the most intriguing and significant architecture occurred around the Lagoon of Nations. Among the international luminaries participating were Michele Busori-Vice of Italy; Boris Iofan of the Soviet Union; Belgians Victor Bourgeois, Leo Stijnen, and Henry van der Velde; Sven Markelius of Sweden; Oscar Niemeyer of Brazil; and famed Finns Alvar Aalto and Aino Marsio-Aalto. Fifty-eight foreign nations participated in the fair, 21 building their own pavilions around the Hall of Nations, which framed the Lagoon. The Italian and Soviet Pavilions were among the most memorable for their hyperbolic modern classicism. Each focused on a monumental elevated statue—Italy's on a replica of the seated female "Roma" from the Capitoline Hill and the Soviets' on a Russian youth holding aloft a five-pointed star. Both pavilions used stripped classical colonnades and blocky massing to provide a base for these figural symbols of people and nation. Lewis Mumford encapsulated the common response to Busori-Vice's monumental pile with typical mordancy, writing that "the Italian Building is funny almost to the point of pathos."

Iofan and Alabean's Soviet Pavilion fared a bit better. Like it or not, critics agreed that it was among the most-talked-about buildings at the fair. A stainless-steel Socialist Realist youth stood atop a marble-and-porphyry pylon exceeded in height only by the Trylon itself. The pavilion wrapped around the base in a horseshoe, housing exhibition halls celebrating the industrial advances and social harmony in the Soviet Union. Although the use of monumental stripped modern classicism in both the Italian and the Soviet Pavilion seems to support the long-standing association of the style with totalitarianism, it must be noted that Howard Cheney's United States Pavilion rivaled the Italian and Soviet Pavilions in its use of stripped classical motifs and surpassed both in scale.

More modest works in the International Style would exercise greater influence among later architects. Oscar Niemeyer and Lúcio Costa's Brazil Pavilion heralded the late modernism and Brutalism of Le Corbusier and others in its use of concrete *brise-soleil* and ramps. Alvar Aalto and Aino Marsio-Aalto's Finnish exhibit has achieved iconic status in the academy as the paradigm for regionalist modernism. The Swedish Pavilion, by Sven Markelius, was a collection of open wooden canopies supported by lithe columns, tapered at top and bottom, all surrounding a garden.

Although the international pavilions hold special appeal for historians, it was the commercial pavilions that drove the fair and attracted popular attention. Advertising and architecture collided in buildings designed to sell products. Skidmore and Owings produced a radio tube–shaped building for RCA and a Wonder Bread wrapper facade for Continental Baking. Perhaps the most un-self-conscious celebration of design in the service of consumption was Ely Jacques Kahn and Walter Dorwin Teague's National Cash Register building, a nondescript shed with a hypertrophic cash register sitting on its top. Beyond celebrating the almighty dollar, the numbers on the register tallied the daily attendance.

Pride of place, just across Robert Moses's Grand Central Parkway from the Theme Center, was reserved for the automobile pavilions. Designed by industrial modernist Albert Kahn, the GM and Ford Pavilions would become two of the most popular attractions. The Ford building included a one-and-a-half-mile "Road of Tomorrow," a miniature version of a modern highway (right next to the real thing, built by master builder Moses), including a full-size replica of a cloverleaf ramp, where visitors could test-drive new Fords. Perhaps even more significant than the more passive entertainments, the Ford exhibit put viewers literally in the driver's seat toward the automotive future.

However, the most popular exhibit was GM's "Highways and Horizons" Pavilion, dominated by Norman Bel Geddes's "Futurama." Entering the architect Albert Kahn's pavilion on two serpentine "on-ramps" and passing through a dramatic rent in the curving facade, most visitors would go straight to Geddes's $6.5 million, 36,000-square-foot model of the American landscape in 1960. The exhibit drew an estimated 25 million viewers over two years, with up to 28,000 people per day lining up to see it. As an industrial designer, Geddes was not bound by the conventions of city planners, architects, or policymakers and thus could synthesize a popular vision of the future that borrowed opportunistically from a variety of fields.

Not surprisingly, the automobile held pride of place in Geddes's vision of the future. Where 1920s planners might have placed modest parkways, railroads, or even canals, the "City of 1960" ran eight-lane motorways, a cross-continental system of highways serving as the means for radical decentralization. Although most of the population lived in the countryside, large cities with 1500-foot-high skyscrapers housed the corporate, white-collar labor force and service activities. Most significant, at the end of the ride, visitors found themselves outside in a full-size "intersection of tomorrow," based on Geddes's model and filled with GM cars. The roads and stores of the city of 1960 would be full of 1939 GM products. The fair would be dismantled in 1940, but the vision of automobility, consumption, and domesticity sold by "the world of tomorrow" would be a lasting legacy.

ANDREW MEYERS

See also **Century of Progress Exposition, Chicago (1933); Costa, Lúcio (Brazil); Exhibition Building; Ferriss, Hugh (United States); Kahn, Albert (United States); New York (New York), United States; Niemeyer, Oscar (Brazil)**

Further Reading

Bletter, Rosemarie Haag, et al., *Remembering the Future: The New York World's Fair from 1939 to 1964*, New York: Rizzoli, 1989

Cusker, Joseph P., et al., *Dawn of a New Day: The New York World's Fair, 1939/40*, Flushing, New York: Queens Museum, and New York: New York University Press, 1980

Federal Writers' Project, *New York City Guide: A Comprehensive Guide to the Five Boroughs of the Metropolis: Manhattan, Brooklyn, the Bronx, Queens, and Richmond*, New York: Random House, and London: Constable, 1939

Rydell, Robert W., *World of Fairs: The Century-of-Progress Expositions*, Chicago: University of Chicago Press, 1993

Rydell, Robert W., John E. Findling, and Kimberly D. Pelle, *Fair America: World's Fairs in the United States*, Washington, D.C.: Smithsonian Institution Press, 2000

Stern, Robert A.M., Gregory Gilmartin, and Thomas Mellins, *New York 1930: Architecture and Urbanism between the Two World Wars*, New York: Rizzoli, 1987

NEW ZEALAND

New Zealand architecture of the 20th century has reflected the country's strong cultural ties with Europe and the United States on the one hand and a romantic wish for national identity on the other. Influences from international metropolitan centers were taken up in turn as they emerged and were disseminated through architectural journals and books. New Zealand architects, always acutely aware of the country's geographic isolation and small scale, also traveled widely and brought direct experience of international precedents to bear on their own work at home. The concern for a local architecture became strong at midcentury as a reaction to the centennial in 1940 of the establishment of British rule and the relative isolation experienced during the war years. This localism was played out most self-consciously in small, timber houses. Their designs reflected both the adoption of modernist principles and a wish to establish identity through links to a putative local pioneer tradition from the early days of European settlement. Architecture in New Zealand has consequently focused on the small house as its most important achievement, to the neglect of the urban realm.

In the first part of the century, architecture in New Zealand was overtly derived from American and British models. The best work of William Gray Young, one of the most successful architects of the prewar years, reflects his interest in English Georgian architecture, as in the Wellesley Club (1925) in Wellington. However, his most notable public work, the Wellington Railway Station (1937), is influenced by American precedents. The work of the distinguished practice Gummer & Ford also has a mix of American and British themes. William Gummer spent periods in the offices of both Edwin Lutyens and Daniel Burnham before returning to practice in New Zealand in 1913. Principal works are the Auckland Railway Station (1930), the Dominion Museum (1936) in Wellington, and the State Insurance building (1941) in Wellington.

After World War I, suburbs in the towns expanded quickly. Popular housing since the 1880s had followed American precedents; the Californian bungalow style became dominant in the 1920s in part under the influence of Hollywood movies. However, the popularity of this type can be attributed not only to the ongoing New Zealand enthusiasm for American popular culture but also to the flexibility of domestic organization it entailed. Economic depression the following decade caused a massive downturn in building activity, although after the major earthquake of 1931, the towns of Napier and Hastings were rebuilt in a modest but consistent Art Deco style. The earthquake also led to an ongoing interest in improving the seismic performance of building stock in the country.

In the years following 1937, the government built tens of thousands of conservatively designed "state houses." However, this housing program also included experiments with high-rise slabs—notably Dixon Street Flats (1942) in Wellington—designed in a much more contemporary style under the guidance of Gordon Wilson. Modern explorations increased after the arrival of several Central European refugee architects in the late 1930s. Most notable was Ernst Plischke, who had worked for Ely Kahn in New York in the late 1920s and designed important buildings at the Vienna Werkbundsiedlung (1930–32) and for the Government Employment Office (1930–31) at Leising, Vienna. Before returning to Vienna in 1963, Plischke undertook town-planning work for the New Zealand government and designed private houses, such as the Sutch house (1956) and, with Cedric Firth, the Massey House office block (1957), both in Wellington.

In 1947, Plischke published *Design and Living*, one of a number of postwar initiatives to promote modern architecture in New Zealand. Others included the foundation in 1946 of the Architectural Centre in Wellington and the Architectural Group in Auckland. The Architectural Centre evolved into a still-extant lobby organization, and in the 1950s the Architectural Group developed a domestic architecture based on local timber building construction coupled with modernist economy of plan and structure. Its experiments with the small, single-family house were the most rigorous of the period and are now the most locally revered. The Group's 1946 manifesto, *On the Necessity for Architecture*, called for an architecture specific to New Zealand.

By 1960, a number of architects were employing a language of concrete-block walls left unrendered, concrete frames, and roofs with complex timber structures. An early achievement in this idiom is the Futuna Chapel (1960) in Karori by John Scott, also influenced by Maori building traditions. However, the most successful devotees of this Brutalist mode, the Christchurch architects Peter Beaven and Warren & Mahoney, were still looking to Scandinavia and to England. As well as restrained domestic work, these architects were responsible for a number of innovative institutional buildings: the Lyttelton Road Tunnel Authority Building (1965) by Beaven and Christchurch College (1966) and Christchurch Town Hall (1972), both by Warren & Mahoney.

During the 1960s and 1970s, there was expansion in office and industrial building, but quality was uneven. In the 1960s, in reaction to the lack of character in emerging urban and suburban environments, Wellington architects Ian Athfield and Roger Walker began to make intricately scaled buildings that extended the vernacular references of earlier New Zealand domestic work but no longer framed them in modernist terms. The village-like qualities of their work offered a challenge to the social isolation of the dormitory suburb and the functional separations of modern town planning. Athfield has continued to develop material and social complexity in the work of his increasingly prominent practice (Wellington Public Library, 1992, and Palmerston North Public Library, 1997).

Economic reform from the mid-1980s has generated wealth for an entrepreneurial Auckland business class. Its members have commissioned adventurous and often indulgent houses from architects such as Marshall Cook, David Mitchell, Pete Bossley, Pip Cheshire, and Noel Lane. They have worked under a range of international influences: Cook seems to have been heavily influenced by Charles Moore, for example, whereas Cheshire's most accomplished building to date, the Congreve house (1994), apparently reflects a careful study of Mario Botta and other Ticino architects. In response to this eclecticism, the firm of Architectus Bowes Clifford Thompson has retrieved the consistent structural and constructional rigor of the immediate postwar years (Mathematics and Statistics and Computer Science Building, University of Canterbury, Christchurch, 1998), and Rewi Thompson has developed an approach based in material directness and aspects of Maori culture.

PAUL WALKER

Further Reading

Clark, Justine, and Paul Walker, *Looking for the Local: Architecture and the New Zealand Modern*, Wellington: Victoria University Press, 2000

Mitchell, David, and Gillian Chaplin, *The Elegant Shed: New Zealand Architecture Since 1945*, Auckland: Oxford University Press, 1984

Shaw, Peter, *New Zealand Architecture from Polynesian Beginnings till 1990*, Auckland: Hodder & Stoughton, 1991

Toomath, William, *Built in New Zealand: the Houses We Live In*, Auckland: HarperCollins, 1996

NIEMEYER, OSCAR 1907–

Architect, Brazil

Oscar Ribeiro de Almeida de Niemeyer Soares, (b. Rio de Janeiro, 1907–) is Brazil's most celebrated architect, known internationally for his designs and writings. His leftist politics support an architectural philosophy with a strong moral agenda dedicated to social change. Many of Niemeyer's commissions have been for progressive clients seeking to use architecture as a transformative medium.

Niemeyer studied at the Escola Nacional das Belas-Artes in Rio de Janeiro with architects, Lúcio Costa and Gregori Warchavchik, who introduced him to works by European modernists. Costa encouraged Niemeyer to seek a personal expression rooted in his own national traditions, tempering modern technology and theory with a respect for Brazil's complex culture and landscape. As a draftsman in Costa's office, Niemeyer participated on team headed by Costa that designed the headquarters of the Ministry of Education and Public Health in Rio (1936–43). Le Corbusier's initial participation as a consultant greatly affected Niemeyer, who, in developing Le Corbusier's project, significantly shaped and executed scheme. By advocating reinforced concrete for the building, Le Corbusier further influenced Niemeyer and other Brazilian designers.

Niemeyer's key role in the Ministry design soon led to other noteworthy commissions. His Obra do Berço (1937), a philanthropic daycare and maternity center in Rio displayed his adaptation of Le Corbusian forms to local climatic conditions. This composition anticipated his design with Lúcio Costa for the Brazilian Pavilion at the 1939 New York World's Fair. The central ramp curved dramatically through a rectangular façade screened by brises-soleil and supported on pilotis. In response, critics proclaimed Costa and Niemeyer formgivers of a new Brazilian modernism.

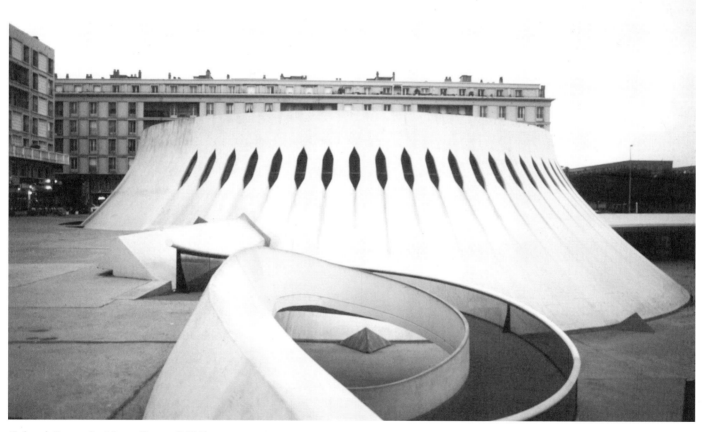

Cultural Center, Le Havre, France (1982)
Photo © Mary Ann Sullivan

The sensuous asymmetry of the Brazilian pavilion emerged fully at Pampulha, a suburban resort complex (1942–43) near Belo Horizonte. Niemeyer's lakeside Casino linked a rectangular gambling hall on pilotis to an ovoid nightclub pavilion. At the Casa do Baile, a crescent shaped restaurant encircled an open dance space connected to a circular stage via a sinuous pergola. This commission introduced Niemeyer to his most important client, President Juscelino Kubitschek, then, mayor of Belo Horizonte and, subsequently, founder of Brasilia.

While such innovative spaces for social ritual addressed the urban elite of Belo Horizonte, they prefigured more social inclusive works while compelling Niemeyer to think in terms of comprehensive planning. The latter proved essential to Niemeyer's participation on the international team designing the United Nations Headquarters (New York, 1947). Evolving from a hybrid of schemes by Le Corbusier and Niemeyer, the Headquarters design recalls the Ministry of Education while anticipating Niemeyer's work of the 1950s and 1960s.

In helping Kubitschek realize his dream of a modern centralized capital, Niemeyer directed a vast, politically sensitive project. Niemeyer's designs complemented Lúcio Costa's Pilot Plan (1956). Resembling an airplane, the plan disposes key government agencies along a monumental east-west axis with commercial and residential functions relegated to north-south "wings." Niemeyer's palatial ministry buildings, faced with grand arcades or tapered pilotis, frame Costa's monumental axis. At its head, anchoring the Plaza of the Three Powers, the National Congress complex strikingly articulates its functions. Meeting chambers for the Senate and Deputies rise from a long low platform as a shallow dome and a low swelling bowl, with twin office towers behind. While bestowing social and political symbolism upon such monumental plastic shapes, Niemeyer creates the effect of sculpture on a Cartesian plane, one paralleled by the presence of the city itself on Brazil's Planalto. Critics subsequently attacked Brasilia's inhumane scale, noting its elitist zoning and citing and citing the failure of Niemeyer's abstract forms as symbols.

Despite such criticism, Niemeyer has arrived at a distinctive individual style. In the biomorphic shapes of his most original designs the architect reveals his engagement with the beauty of Brazil's landscape and the human form. The undulating parabolic vaults of the church of São Francisco de Assis (Pampulha, 1943) clearly synthesize Le Corbusian and Baroque colonial forms. Yet, in mature works such as his Metropolitan Cathedral for Brasilia (1958–60) Niemeyer achieves a more delicate personal statement. From a distance, skeletal concrete ribs serve as a metaphor for a crown of thorns. Approached via a subterranean ramp through a low entrance, the space of the sanctuary opens dramatically overhead, with light filtering through blue, green and frosted white glass, creating a nearly submarine effect, and evoking a state of reverence.

Insisting "architecture is not important, life is important," Niemeyer reiterates his commitment to socially responsible design through works celebrating political or cultural allegiances, such as the Communist Party Headquarters (Paris, 1967–80) and the Memorial da America Latina (São Paolo, 1989). Expressed through architecture, Niemeyer's aims are ultimately humanistic, grounded in a respect for nature but relying on technology to achieve them.

Oscar Niemeyer has written extensively on his works and ideas in monographs and, since 1955, in his journal, Módulo.

Niemeyer's work has been covered extensively in architectural journals and books in multiple languages. His archive, the Fundação Oscar Niemeyer, in Rio de Janeiro, contains important correspondence, photographs and drawings documenting his work.

See also **Ricardo Burle-Marx, Roberto (Brazil); (CIAM, 1927–); Corbusier, Le (Jeanneret, Charles-Édouard) (France); Costa, Lúcio (Brazil)**

Selected Works

Obra do Berço, Rio de Janeiro, 1937
Brazilian Pavilion, New York World's Fair (with Lucio Costa), 1939
Pampulha buildings, Belo Horizonte, Brazil, 1943
Church of St. Francis of Assisi, Pampulha, 1943
Metropolitan Cathedral, Brasilia, 1960
Communist Party (PCF) Headquarters, Paris, 1980
Cultural Centre, Le Havre, France, 1982
Samba Stadium, Rio de Janeiro, 1984
Memorial da America Latina, São Paolo, 1989
Museu de Arte Contemporânea, Niterói, Brazil, 1996

Selected Publications

Como se faz arquitetura, Petropolis: Vozes, 1986
Meu sósia e eu, Rio de Janeiro: Editoria Revan, 1992
Minha experiencia em Brasília, Rio de Janeiro: Vitoria, 1961
Museu de Arte Contemporânea de Niterói, Rio de Janeiro: Editoria Revan, 1997
Niemeyer, Paris: Alphabet, 1975, 1977
Quase memorias: viagens, tempos de entusiasmo e revolta—1961–1966, Rio de Janeiro, Civilização Brasileira, 1968
Textes et dessins pour Brasilia, Paris: Editions Forces Vives, 1965

Further Reading

Bruand, Yves, *Arquitetura Contemporânea no Brasil*, translated from the French by Ana M. Goldberger, São Paolo, Brasil: Editoria Perspectiva, 1981
Bullrich, Francisco, *New Directions in Latin American Architecture*, New York: Reinhold, 1969
Evenson, Norma, *Two Brazilian capitals; architecture and urbanism in Rio de Janeiro and Brasilia*, New Haven: Yale University Press, 1973.
Goodwin, Philip, and G.E. Kidder Smith, *Brazil builds; architecture new and old, 1652–1942*, New York: The Museum of Modern Art, 1943
Goodwin, Philip, Oscar Niemeyer, and Juscelino Kubitschek, *Pampulha*, Rio de Janeiro, Brasil: Imprensa Nacional, 1944.
Harris, Elizabeth Davis, "Le Corbusier and the Headquarters of the Brazilian Ministry of Education and Health, 1936–1945," Ph.D. diss. University of Chicago, 1984
Hyatt Foundation, *The Pritzker Architecture Prize 1988: presented to Gordon Bunshaft and Oscar Niemeyer*, Los Angeles: The Foundation, 1988
Katinsky, Julio Roberto, *Brasília em tres tempos: a arquitetura de Oscar Niemeyer na capital*, Rio de Janeiro: Editora Revan, 1991
Mindlin, Henrique, *Modern Architecture in Brazil*, New York: Reinhold, 1956
Papadaki, Stamo, *The work of Oscar Niemeyer*, New York: Reinhold, 1950
Papadaki, Stamo, *Oscar Niemeyer: works in progress*, New York: Reinhold, 1956
Santos, Cecília Rodrigues dos (et al), *Le Corbusier e o Brasil*, São Paolo: Tessela, Projecto Editoria, 1987
Spade, Rupert, and Yukio Futagawa, *Oscar Niemeyer, Masters of modern architecture*, London: Thames and Hudson, 1971

Underwood, David, *Oscar Niemeyer and the Architecture of Brazil,* New York: Rizzoli, 1994

Underwood, David, *Oscar Niemeyer and Brazilian Free-Form Modernism,* New York: George Braziller, Inc., 1994

Published Interviews

Dialogo pre-socratico com Claudio M. Valentinetti, Sao Paolo, Instituto Lina Bo E.P.M. Bardi, 1998

Niemeyer par lui-meme: l'architecte de Brasília parle a Edouard Bailby, Paris: Balland, 1993

Niemeyer, Oscar, and Henri Raillard, *Les courbes du temps: memoires,* Paris: Gallimard, 1999

Niemeyer, Oscar, Josep Maria Botey, and Dalmau Miquel, *Oscar Niemeyer,* Barcelona: Fundacio Caixa Barcelona: Generalitat de Catalunya, Departament de Politica Territorial i Obres Publiques: Collegi d'Arquitectes de Catalunya, 1990

NITZCHKE, OSCAR 1900–1991

Architect, France

Although he built little and seldom appears in standard histories of modern architecture, Oscar Nitzchke was much admired among avant-garde architects. During 50 years in practice in France and the United States, Nitzchke produced consistently innovative designs that remain surprisingly fresh. As an influential professor of design at Yale University School of Architecture (1938–48), he invited a series of progressive European artists and architects for visiting lectures and studios and helped establish a graduate program in urban planning. Nitzchke owed his appointment to Wallace K. Harrison, whom he met in Paris. Dividing his time between New Haven, Connecticut, and New York, Nitzchke also worked for Harrison and Abramovitz (1938–54), where he contributed to some of the firm's most inventive buildings.

Although Nitzchke's training combined apprenticeship and formal academic study, his sensibilities were distinctly modern. Unhappy with the conservatism of the Ecoles des Beaux Arts in Geneva, Switzerland (1917–20), and in Paris (1921–27), he sought progressive architects as mentors. Abandoning the staid Atêlier Laloux-Lemarequier (1920), Nitzchke and other students asked Le Corbusier to create an alternative atêlier. He referred them instead to Auguste Perret, who founded the Atêlier du Palais de Bois. Perret taught Nitzchke (1923–27) to articulate structural form with a clarity that would typify his later work. By working for Le Corbusier and the Perret brothers, Nitzchke further refined his abilities. Friendships with avant-garde artists (Pablo Picasso, Fernand Léger, Amedée Ozenfant, Alexander Calder, and Man Ray) opened a world of experimental approaches to design in a wide range of media from which Nitzchke continuously drew inspiration.

Early projects suggest the direction of Nitzchke's later work in their articulation of form and materials and in their marked legibility of functions. His interest in prefabricated housing originated in the Maisons Métalliques (1929), a collaboration with former Perret students, Adrien Brelet and André Le Donné, for a competition sponsored by the Forges de Strasbourg. Perret's influence emerged clearly in the frank expression of the external corrugated copper and steel cladding, which made no attempt to imitate traditional materials, as earlier prefabricated metal buildings had. Their first-place design was displayed in a proto-type that drew considerable interest, but only 520 houses were constructed. Nitzchke drew from this project in subsequent research for prefabricated housing for Harrison and Nelson Rockefeller's I.B.E.C. Corporation in the 1940s and 1950s. In his detailing of the cellular aluminum skin of the Alcoa Building (Harrison and Abramovitz, Pittsburgh, 1949–53), Nitzchke's prior experiments elided perfectly with Alcoa's demands that its main product be conspicuously deployed in its new headquarters.

Nitzchke's openness to technology and willingness to draw from vernacular sources emerged in his application of electrical signs on his buildings. His Pavilion de la Musique (1922) study for the International Exhibition of Decorative Arts, Paris (1925), assumed the form of an oversized gramophone with inscriptions on the main block. Evolving from the Enlightenment tradition of architecture parlante, the Pavilion anticipated by several decades the bold expressiveness of pop art. The pronounced legibility of this work prefigured the Maison de la Publicité (1934–36), his best-known project. Commissioned by an advertising executive for a narrow site on the Champs-Elyssées, the Maison hosted a variety of functions including offices, café, newsreel cinema, interior courtyard, and luxury apartments. The building included 12 levels, with circulation relegated to a peripheral volume separated by a curving wall of glass block. Here, the sophisticated disposition of functions and innovative use of materials ably synthesized Le Corbusier's and Perret's formal vocabularies.

Yet Nitzchke's treatment of the facade, as a giant metallic frame supporting a panoply of changing electric signs and cinematic projections, offered fresh solutions to a novel problem. Periodic installations of colored neon exploited the latest developments in commercial outdoor lighting while recalling such earlier Constructivist projects as the Vesnins's 1924 Pravda tower. It also anticipated the megastructural framework of the Pompidou Center (Piano and Rogers, 1977). The prominent signage in this project drew praise from Post-modernist architects and critics who rediscovered Nitzchke's early work in the 1970s. Because the client mysteriously disappeared, the project, like many of Nitzchke's most brilliant schemes, remained unexecuted.

In Paris, collaborating with the American architect Paul Nelson, Nitzchke prepared a diverse series of designs. Their 1937 Palais de la Découverte (with Paul Jourdain) offered a monumental complex for the exploration of the sciences for the Jardin des Plantes. Combining such functions as planetarium, auditoria, and flexible spaces for exhibits grouped by discipline, the Palais assumed a series of concentric forms on two levels, radiating out from a central conical great hall. Critics praised the flexibility in the floor plans, but construction was prevented by World War II. Nitzchke realized further innovations in exhibition design in the African Habitat at the Bronx Zoo (New York, Harrison and Abramovitz, 1939), where he provided a series of clear tubes from which visitors could observe animals freely roaming in their native habitat.

After 1954, Nitzchke worked for a series of other New York firms, occasionally serving as a design critic at Columbia University, and executing small jobs like the Addo-X business machines display room (1956–57, with Hans Lindblom) and the Martha Jackson Gallery (1957–58). Despite becoming deaf in 1951, Nitzchke continued to develop imaginative projects for competitions such as San Salvador Cathedral (1953–54), with soaring concrete shell vaults. In 1970, he retired to Paris, preparing drawings for exhibitions of his work, and lived with his family until his death in 1991.

LINDA PHIPPS

See also **Harrison, Wallace K., and Max Abramovitz (United States); International Exhibition of Decorative Arts, Paris (1925); Perret, Auguste (France); Pompidou Center, Paris**

Biography

Born in 1900, Altoona, Germany, died in 1991, Paris, France.

Further Reading

Cahiers d'Art recorded some of Nitzchke's most significant early projects, including the Maison de la Publicité. Nitzchke's former colleague, George Dudley, of the Harrison and Abramovitz office, and his son, Gus Dudley, helped organize a retrospective exhibition of Nitzchke's work at the Cooper Union in 1985. The catalogue of this exhibition constitutes the most comprehensive scholarly source on the architect. Edited by Gus Dudley, it includes essays by Joseph Abram, Isabelle Gournay, Kenneth Frampton, John Hedjuk, and George Dudley.

Abram, Joseph, "Oscar Nitzchké, notre contemporain (obituary)," *L'Architecture d'Aujourd'hui* (April 1991)
"Addo-X showroom designed by H. Lindblom and O. Nitzchke," *Interiors* 117 (November 1957)
"Cathedral in steel and concrete for San Salvador: O. Nitzchke, architect," *Interiors*, 117 (December 1957)
Dudley, Gus (editor), *Oscar Nitzchke: Architect*, New York: Irwin S. Chanin School of Architecture of the Cooper Union 1985
Morey, Colette, "Design Genius: Colette Morey de Morand remembers Oscar Nitzchke," *Building Design*, 1027 (March 1991)
"Museum of Science designed for flexibility and extensibility, P. Nelson, O. Nitzchke and F.P. Jourdain, architects," *Architectural Record*, 85 (February 1939)
"Oscar Nitzchké: La Maison de la Publicité, Paris 1935," *AMC* (Architecture/Mouvement/Continuité) (December 1984)
"Projet d'un palais de la decouverte, 1937; P. Nelson, O. Nitzchke and F.P. Jourdain, architectes," *Cahiers d'Art*, 15/3–4 (1940)
Zervos, Christian, "Architecture et publicité; projet d'un immeuble publicitaire par O. Nitzchke," *Cahiers d'Art*, 11/6–7

NORBERG-SCHULZ, CHRISTIAN 1926–2000

Architecture historian and critic, Norway

The historian Christian Norberg-Schulz is a solitary figure who began by studying the cultural and formal roots of Western architecture and then went on to explore more deeply the concept of genius loci, or spirit of place. In his later years he concentrated on Scandinavian themes because he felt that the northern Scandinavian peoples had preserved a particularly strong connection with nature.

Norberg-Schulz's earliest comprehensive theoretical statement is presented in *Intentions in Architecture* (1963), based on the phenomenological premise that considered human perception as a transformative rather than a passive exercise. In perceiving objects, we change the phenomena by changing our attitude.

Founded by Edmund Husserl at the beginning of the 20th century, phenomenology distinguishes sharply between perceptual properties on the one hand and abstract properties on the other. Following Egon Brunswik, Norberg-Schulz replaced "attitude" with "intention." To deal with the active character of perception, he introduced the concept of *schema* and its plural, *schemata*, which he defined as "habits of perception." These acquire the character of "quasi-object" as the important platforms from which we build relatively stable mental representations of external reality.

Although he regarded modernism as the only true tradition, Norberg-Schulz considered that modern architecture suffered from an inner contradiction because it continued to rely on static classical ideas, such as proportion and balance. In practice, however, modern architecture, with its "free plan," demanded flexibility above all else, and this did not admit any classical balancing of the parts. The challenge, accordingly, was to unify the "organic" and the "technological" tendencies. Norberg-Schulz further emphasized that every building must "express its character" through the formulation of distinct and recognizable types in such a way that they constitute a hierarchy corresponding to the task-structure.

Norberg-Schulz's argument was anticipated in a joint essay by Tobias Faber and Jørn Utzon in 1947. He came into contact with Utzon through Arne Korsmo. Utzon's architecture closely approximates the organic ideal advocated by Norberg-Schulz in the Sydney Opera House and other of the architect's works.

Norberg-Schulz's phenomenological theory of architecture as presented in *Intentions in Architecture* was later widened and expanded to include topography and landscape in such works as *Existence, Space and Architecture* (1971), which traversed much the same theory using simplified language and with a broader set of historical references. *Genius Loci* (1979) examined the role of landscape in urban and architectural place making in defining how humans may create places that better serve the complexities and contradictions of contemporary life.

As a historian who attached so much significance to perception, Norberg-Schulz believed that baroque architecture, with its integration of space, painting, sculpture, and decoration in a total work, presented a unique challenge. He pursued this topic in a series of triumphant monographs: *Kilian Ignaz, Dientzenhofer e il barocco boemo* (1968; Kilian Ignaz Dientzenhofer and the Bohemian Baroque), *Baroque Architecture* (1971), and *Late Baroque and Rococo Architecture* (1974).

In 1980, in Venice, Norberg-Schulz advocated his phenenological approach, which he defined as "the study of the nature of what is given." He based his understanding on what can be inferred from the philosophical thinking of Martin Heidegger (1889–1976) and Maurice Merleau-Ponty (1907–61). It was the philosophy of Heidegger especially that was of primary importance in Norberg-Schulz's development of a theory of architecture. The aim was to help man find a better way of life by offering him access to meanings already inherent in the world and based on a poetic perception. Significantly, Norberg/Schulz called for *stabilis loci* as being particularly important, as he felt that there was a loss of place as a "general fact" that threatened a "total loss of content." The only way out of this dilemma was, in his words, "a rediscovery of the world." To make this happen, man must again become aware of his environment as a concretely given "here." In *Nightlands: Nordic Building* (1996), Norberg-

Schulz seeks to do precisely this for the northern Scandinavian countries by examining what Nordic building truly is by contrasting it with its counterpart: the classical architecture of the south.

The significance of Norberg-Schulz's thinking and ideals is exemplified by architects such as Utzon in Denmark, Alvar Aalto and Reima Peitilä in Finland, and Korsmo and Fehn in Norway. In Scandinavia and elsewhere in the 1980s, he acted as a counterweight against a pluralist-cum-Postmodernist eclecticism almost wholly severed from a sense of regional identity and locality that refused to recognize the need for organic linkages as they existed in the past between architecture and its setting, history, and culture. In countries such as Australia, where European settlers encountered strange and unprecedented types of landscapes, Norberg-Schulz's phenomenological approach supplied an invaluable theoretical perspective for interpreting and evaluating such Australian pioneer architects as Glenn Murcutt, Richard Le Plastrier, and Gregory Burgess.

Norberg-Schulz wrote mostly in English, and his texts were translated by his wife, Anna Maria, into Italian and then into Spanish and French editions from the English. Further translations appeared in German and other European and Asiatic languages.

PHILIP DREW

Biography

Born in Oslo, 23 May 1926. Completed diploma in architecture at the Eidgenössische Technische Hochschule in Zurich under Sigfried Giedion 1949, then returned to Norway; helped to start PAGON (the Norwegian section of CIAM) in 1950 with Arne Korsmo, and a year later assisted Korsmo in building up the study of design at the Norwegian College of Art Craft and Design in Oslo; Fulbright scholar at Harvard University 1952–53, studying with Walter Gropius and visiting Mies van der Rohe in Chicago at the Illinois Institute of Technology; formed partnership with Korsmo 1951–56; with Korsmo completed a house for three families at Vettlkollen, Oslo, 1955, comprising Miesian glass cubes with open interiors mounted on a common timber deck; collaborated with several other noted Norwegian architects during this time; studied architectural history and building technology with Pier Luigi Nervi in Rome 1956–58; member of Group 5 (with Sverre Fehn, Geir Grung, Håkon Mjelva, and Odd Østbye); completed doctoral degree at the Polytechnic in Trondheim 1964; appointed professor at the School of Architecture in Oslo 1966, later becoming its dean (1984–86); member of the organizing committee of the first International Exhibition of Architecture at the 1980 Venice Biennale directed by Paolo Portoghesi. Died 2000.

Selected Publications

Michelangelo som arkitekt, 1958
Intentions in Architecture, 1963
Kilian Ignaz, Dientzenhofer e il barocco boemo (Kilian Ignaz Dientzenhofer and the Bohemian Baroque), 1968
Baroque Architecture, 1971
Existence, Space and Architecture, 1971
Late Baroque and Rococo Architecture, 1974
Significato nell'architettura occidentale, 1974; as *Meaning in Western Architecture*, 1975; revised edition, 1980

Alla ricera dell'architettura perduta: le opere di Paolo Portoghesi, Vittorio Gigliotti, 1959–1975; as *On the Search for Lost Architecture: The Works of Paolo Portoghesi, Vittorio Gigliotti, 1959–1975*, 1975
Mellem jord og himmel; as *Between Earth and Sky*, 1978
Genius loci: paesaggio, ambiente, architettura, translated by Ana Maria De Dominicis, 1979; as *Genius Loci: Towards a Phenomenology of Architecture*, 1979
Bauhaus, Dessau, 1980
Louis I. Kahn, idea e immagine, 1980
"Jørn Utzon: Sydney Opera House 1957–73," *Global Architecture* 54 (1981)
"Church at Bagsværd," *Global Architecture* 61 (1982)
The Concept of Dwelling: On the Way to Figurative Architecture, 1985
Casa Behrens: Darmstadt, 1980; 2nd edition, 1986
The Functionalist Arne Korsmo, 1986
Modern Norwegian Architecture, 1986
Architecture, Meaning and Place, 1988
New World Architecture, 1988
Roots of Modern Architecture, edited by Yukio Futagawa, 1988
Scandinavia: architettura, gli ultimi vent'anni, 1990
Minnesjord, 1991
Balthasar Neumann, Abteikirche Neresheim, 1993
Nightlands: Nordic Building, translated by Thomas McQuillan, 1996
Stedkunst, 1996
Sverre Fehn: Works, Projects, Writings, 1949–1996 (with Gennaro Postiglione), 1997

Further Reading

Bugge, Gunnar, *Stav of laft i Norge*, Oslo: Buggekunst, 1969
Futagawa, Yukio (editor), *Ricardo Bofill: Taller de Arquitectura*, New York: Rizzoli, 1985

NORTEN, ENRIQUE 1954–

Architect, Mexico

Karl Marx once wrote that humankind sets itself the tasks that it can solve. These tasks, however, are part of a particular historical paradigm in which the material conditions are already present for their solutions or are, at least, in their formative stages. The history of Mexican modern architecture is the paradigm through which Enrique Norten's work operates and responds. Within this logic, it is insufficient to describe the work of Norten as being representative of a tension of postmodern globalization. Equally inadequate would be to ascribe to it a character derived solely from the metropolitan condition of Mexico City, the geographic center of his practice. Although historians have been quick to judge the work as foreign to Mexican sensibilities and to say that, using Marx's own logic, it offers solutions that are not present in Mexico's material conditions of production, we can see it as inheritor of the legacies of Mexico's historical avant-garde. It would be best, therefore, to position Norten as a figure in a long historical lineage that comprises the history of modern architecture in Mexico.

Like his immediate architectural forefathers, Juan O'Gorman and the radical functionalists, Norten's work uses the most contemporary materials—in his case, stainless steel, concrete, and glass—to reconceptualize our understanding of these within the context and the needs of contemporary Mexico. Surely it would be easy to ascribe to them as foreign, but the tradition of modern forms and sensibilities is deeply rooted and is part of the Mexican landscape. What Norten has done is to make them do things that they had not done before. He was using them, in other words, not as signifiers of a new modernity to the exterior world but rather as referents of a new self-identity. Although critics lament the loss of a Mexican architecture—a loss founded on some mythical and highly ideological construction of history and style—the development of Norten's work shows an active relation with the tradition of syncretism, experimentation, alternate space making, and legibility. These, historically, have been part of the modus operandi of architects and builders since the time of the colony. Norten's work, therefore, poignantly shifts architectural production from purely formal and stylistic references to the conceptual explorations of these traditions.

Norten is, himself, a result of modern syncretism: trained at the Universidad Iberoamericana in Mexico City and at Cornell University in Ithaca, New York. His work is part of a collaborative effort of the firm that he founded in 1985 (TEN Arquitectos: Taller de Enrique Norten), which was joined by Bernardo Gómez-Pimienta in 1987. Norten's teaching, much like his practice, is not limited to Mexico, as he has also taught throughout the United States.

Norten's early work, such as the Lighting Center (1988–89) in Mexico City and Houses N and R (1989–90) in Valle de Bravo, expresses an active investigation into the materiality of architecture. Both buildings express not only the craft tradition of brick construction but also a reconfiguration of traditional architectural elements through the introduction of industrialized materials. As with the historical avant-garde, these new materials, however, are mediated equally by the hand of the craftsman. Perforated sheet metal, for example, was painstakingly punched by hand, reminding us of the obsession of craft in William Morris's work. In Houses N and R, we find the result of morphological explorations of the home as mediated by the telluric agency of the place. The pitched, tiled roof clearly references vernacular forms. The open, double-height interiors and the reliance on industrial materials express, in contrast, the elimination of forms needed in this geographic place. Instead of reproducing the typology of the courtyard common to Valle de Bravo, for example, Norten chose to reflect what that typology does through an exploration of how the materials themselves can render and express what traditional form has maintained for centuries. The same can be said of the Brasil Street Workers Housing (1991–92), which adheres to some of the social concerns of the radical Mexican functionalists about the role of architecture and ornament. This building resolves a traditional typological requirement for a *vecindad* (an internalized and autonomous neighborhood) through the disposition of the housing block, circulation system, and courtyard, while ornament is explicitly abolished and the materials and forms are left to speak for themselves. In addition, the project itself solves a concern that has been at the forefront of Mexican modern architecture since the revolution: housing for the urban proletariat.

The work of the Alliance Française (1990–92), Moda en Casa (1991–93), and Insurgentes Theater (1993–95) reflects a long tradition of experimentation with known forms and stylistic traditions. In the same way that Alberti's *Four Books on Architecture* was interpreted in the Spanish colony or Le Corbusier's *Vers une architecture* was read as a manifesto for a revolutionary architecture in the 1920s and 1930s, these works show a keen understanding and incorporation of a contemporary stylistic vocabu-

lary. Here, the formal language of Norman Foster, Rem Koolhaas, and other contemporary architects is competently presented and reproduced using a craft tradition that would appear to be antithetical to its forms. These projects would become building blocks for some of Norten's later work insofar as they explore tectonic expression, materiality, and craft.

His later work illustrates an additive process of forms, materials, and spaces. Paradigmatic of this are the National School Theater (1993–94) and the TELEVISA Services Building, (1993–95), all in Mexico City; House LE (1994–95); and the Addams Hall and Fine Arts Building (1999–) at the University of Pennsylvania. Although they conform to the concerns outlined previously, this new work—of which part is located or proposed outside of Mexico—could be described as a spatial inversion of its predecessors. In it, the shift is rendered from the objects in space of his earlier work (which create clearly defined spatial boundaries) to the objects within spaces of his later work (which create internalized formal and spatial relations within sometimes ambiguous boundaries). This transformation could also be understood as a shift from clearly tectonic expressions to a messy stereotomic manifestation—messy because the concerns of structural expression are in tension with the volume of the architectural objects and because these volumes are rendered primarily as thin surfaces in tension around a seemingly exaggerated structural frame. We could ascribe to this work the volumetric qualities of pre-Hispanic forms as they sit on the landscape. However, their forms, materials, and structures develop new formal relationships with the interior, where, while appearing to close off from the exterior, they generate new spatial interrelationships with the interior.

LUIS E. CARRANZA

See also **Corbusier, Le (Jeanneret, Charles-Édouard) (France); Mexico; Mexico City, Mexico; O'Gorman, Juan (Mexico)**

Biography

Born in Mexico City, 1954. Graduated from the Universidad Iberoamericana 1978; received a master's degree in architecture from Cornell University 1980. Co-director, Albin and Norten Architects, Mexico City 1981–85; director of TEN Arquitectos, Mexico City from 1986; principal, Taller de Enrique Norten, Mexico City; technical coordinator for the José Vergara C. Center project in Guadalajara, Mexico, from 1998; cofounder and member of editorial board, *Arquitectura*. Taught at institutions in the United States and Mexico, including Sci-Arc, Rice University, and the Pratt Institute; O'Neil Ford Chair in Architecture, University of Texas, Austin 1996; Emil Lorch Professor of Architecture and Urban Planning, University of Michigan.

Selected Works

Lighting Center, Mexico City, 1989
House N, Valle de Bravo, Mexico, 1990
House R, Valle de Bravo, Mexico, 1990
Brasil Street Workers Housing, Mexico City, 1992
Alliance Français, Mexico City, 1992
Moda en Casa, Mexico City, 1993
National School Theater, Mexico City, 1994
Insurgentes Theater, Mexico City, 1995

TELEVISA Services Building, Mexico City, 1995

House LE, 1995

Addams Hall and Fine Arts Building, University of Pennsylvania, Philadelphia, 1999

Parking Garage, School of Engineering, Princeton University, Princeton, New Jersey, 2000

Selected Publication

The Work of TEN Arquitectos, 1997

Further Reading

Adriá, Miquel, *Mexico 90's: una arquitectura contemporanea*, Mexico City and Barcelona: Gili, 1996

TEN Arquitectos: Enrique Norten, Bernardo Gómez-Pimienta, New York: Monacelli Press, 1998

TEN Arquitectos: Taller de Enrique Norten Arquitectos, S.C., Barcelona: Gili, 1995

NORWAY

Twentieth-century architecture in Norway is characterized by a search for a cultural, historical, and aesthetic identity, primarily as the result of the country's independence from the Swedish union in 1905. Thus, Norwegian architects at the turn of the 20th century sought more national traditions, as displayed in the other arts.

A Norwegian architect who tried to create a national architectural style at the beginning of the 20th century was Arnstein Arneberg. Arneberg joined forces with the Norwegian architect Magnus Poulsson in building farmers' houses that used gables and turfed roofs. Arenberg's house at Madserud Allé 38 (1924) is an example of this regional style, with its red exterior wood paneling and with its half-hipped roof. Arneberg and Poulsson were educated in Sweden, a country also in quest of a national identity that could be represented in a national architectural style. Arneberg returned to Norway from Sweden in 1906, with Poulsson arriving four years later; they went on to develop a postwar romantic style in town houses as well as for large public buildings. Their design for the competition for the City Hall (Radhus) in Christiania (Oslo) in 1915–17 was a culmination of this idea. However, it was not built until 1930, and thus, new ideas were included in the final design.

However, after World War I, the works of Arneberg and Poulsson would be criticized for their "Norwegian-ness" and their superficial ornamentation. A rejection of historical styles and monumentality ensued. Although not created as such, these older styles were thought of as expressions of power and repression. Classicism—with its emphasis on universal architectural forms—came to the forefront at this time. Architects attempted to create an objective architecture that would replace Norwegian architects' preoccupation with national romanticism. Many of these architects had been trained at the new Norwegian Institute of Technology, which had opened in 1910, with its first graduates in 1914.

Gudolf Blakstad and Dunker's winning neoclassical project for the New Theatre in Oslo (1919), which displayed an ordered plan and exterior symmetry, was the first to be shown in the new periodical *Byggekunst*, which was first published that same year. Following this competition, neoclassicism's major propo-

nent, Herman Munthe-Kaas, would herald this new style in the same journal. A large portion of buildings from 1920 to 1925 appeared in this new, restrained classical style. During this time, Blakstad and Munthe-Kaas won the competition and had built the new city hall in Haugesund (1924–31), also based on neoclassical principles.

Two of Norway's leading exponents of national romanticism, Arneberg and Poulsson, tried to adapt to Neoclassicism, but without complete success. In 1924 and 1925, the Norwegian painters Henrik Sørensen and Erik Werenskiold began to attack neoclassicism in architecture as being foreign. There was to be no middle ground reached between the two schools of national romanticism and classicism; instead, architects turned toward modern functionalism.

Modern architecture flourished in Norway between the world wars. Especially during the 1930s, some Norwegian architects became concerned with creating an international architecture based on global sameness. Such formal expressions as white building volumes, flat roofs, strip windows, free plan, and minimal detailing made their way into the language of Norwegian architecture.

Le Corbusier's Pavillon de l'Esprit Nouveau was praised in 1925 by Edvard Heiberg as a new form created from a functional aesthetic. Lars Backer adopted the new architecture of functionalism, declaring it to be the new objective architecture in which form follows function. In 1927, Johan Ellefsen, in an article entitled "What is Modern Architecture?" claimed that functionalism creates forms that contain both national and local characteristics. He rejected any use of historical styles and advocated in the manner of Le Corbusier the consideration of landscape, climate, materials, and construction.

Backer's first project, the Skansen Restaurant in Oslo (1927), was the first modernist building in Norway. Here he introduced the continuous window band, the flat roof, clear skeleton construction, free plan, and continuous glass sections. An amalgamation of other architectural precedents—such as the work of Le Corbusier, Frank Lloyd Wright, and the German expressionist architect Erich Mendelsohn—Backer's restaurant also contains horizontal and vertical elements of De Stijl architecture.

Ideas on modern architecture also entered the Norwegian architectural discipline through a study tour to Holland in 1928 and also through a 1930 manifesto of Nordic functionalism. This manifesto was written in conjunction with the 1930 Stockholm exhibition displaying architecture and utilitarian objects. This exhibition, with Gunnar Asplund as the featured architect, influenced many Norwegian as well as Swedish architects. Munthe-Kaas, the Norwegian architect, became the Norwegian delegate to the Congrès Internationaux d'Architecture Moderne (CIAM) and had direct contact with international ideas on architecture. In 1932, he made a study tour of ten European countries and reported his findings in *Byggekunst* in the following year.

Ove Bang, who opened his architectural practice in Oslo in 1930, also helped lay the foundation for modern architecture in Norway. His Villa Ditlev-Simonsen (1937) and the worker's association (Samfunnshuset) in Oslo (1939) combine modernist structure with the traditional material of wood. This Norwegian interpretation of modernism contained architectural elements with a sense for nature and humanism that would be further incorporated in Norwegian architecture during the postwar years.

Villa Busk, Bamble, Norway (1990), designed by Sverre Fehn
© Richard Dargavel

After World War II, the architectural historian Siegfried Giedion brought to the forefront the need for a modernist architecture that considered the local essence of place, often cited as the "new regionalism." According to Giedion, Alvar Aalto's work exemplified such an architectural language. Many Norwegian architects, including Knut Knutsen, responded to Aalto's organic functionalism. Knutsen, like other Norwegian architects after World War II, attacked international modernist architecture, claiming that it threatened Norwegian identity. Knutsen's approach is exemplified in his design of the Portør house (1948), in which he abandons modernist rectilinearity for the organic shape of the landscape that in turn, influences, the house's plan.

In contrast to Knutsen, Arne Korsmo, an early proponent of functionalism, emerged as the leading proponent of International Style architecture during this time. In 1949, he traveled to the United States to study the works of Frank Lloyd Wright, Ludwig Mies van der Rohe, Walter Gropius, and other modernists. Korsmo became fascinated with Gropius's teaching methods, and he introduced these to Norway at the Arts and Crafts school in Oslo. His own house in Oslo (1952–55), with free plan and modernist structure, combines the saturated colors of traditional Norwegian farm interiors. Korsmo's architecture did not bring nature into a more regional articulation of elements, as in Knutsen's work, which gained a wider acceptance in Norway.

Korsmo became inspired by Gropius's ideas of solving tasks by collaboration and led to the founding of the Norwegian group within CIAM named PAGON (Progressive Architects' Group Oslo Norway). Members included Korsmo, Sverre Fehn, Geir Grung, Odd Østbye, P.A.M. Melbye, Håkon Mjelva, Robert Esdaile, and Christian Norberg-Schulz. This group took part in numerous architectural competitions during the 1950s.

The dissolution of CIAM in 1956 triggered the beginning of the crisis in modern architecture. The free plan of modern architecture used in an urban context brought an end to traditional urban spaces such as the street and the square, with the result of a loss of place. This loss of place created by late modernism was also discussed in Kevin Lynch's book *The Image of the City* (1960). To counteract this sense of loss, Norwegian architects began to create a strong identity in the building itself through expressionistic experiments. Eero Saarinen's TWA air terminal in New York (1962) and his United States Embassy in Oslo (1955–59) emphasized a sculptural quality to architecture. Both buildings reflect the expressionistic tendencies that soon would develop in Norwegian architecture.

Expressionistic experiments in Norwegian architecture continued, but other architects still developed ideas that followed Knutsen's organic functionalism and Korsmo's modern idiom. Eliassen and Lambertz-Nilssen carried Knutsen's ideas farther, as seen in their the Aust-Agder Central Hospital (Arendal) and Telemark Central Hospital (Skien) and in the 1970s with Sandefjord's Civic Center (1969–75). Korsmo's student Fehn carried his ideas into a regional and individualized architecture, as did Kjell Lund and Nils Slaatto.

One of Fehn's earlier works, the Norwegian Pavilion at the Brussels World's Fair in 1958, shows the use of the structural clarity of Mies van der Rohe along with the use of traditional Norwegian materials. In his Archbishopric Museum in Hamar (1979), Fehn inserts into ruins of the medieval bishop's quarters a modernist form. In this project, he combines wood and concrete in an interest for the tectonic. His Glacier Museum in Fjærland (1991) also displays the same qualities and translates the local landscape into the architectural design and form. Fehn has become a major influence in Norwegian architecture with his incorporation of the ideas introduced by Korsmo concerning the poetry of architecture and using past architectural forms within a modernist language.

Significant shifts in Postmodernism also appeared in Norwegian architecture, often filtered through the writings of American architect Robert Venturi, who promoted an architecture that reflected the complexity of life by incorporating memories of identity and historic architectural forms in a new context. Architect Jan Digerud, who was educated in the United States, brought Venturi's ideas to Norway in an article in Byggekunst titled "An Inclusive Architecture." Digerud eventually joined with Jon Lundberg to create the firm Jan and Jon; they designed five one-family houses as well as a cottage near Risør illustrating these Postmodern tendencies.

Venturi's and Louis Kahn's ideas also inspired Are Telje, Fredrik A.S. Torp, Knut Aasen, Arne Henriksen, Harald Hille, Thomas Thiis-Evensen, and the group 4B. Throughout the 1970s, 1980s, and 1990s, Postmodernist architecture developed alongside works produced by Korsmo's and Knutsen's followers.

Most recently, during the 1990s, Norwegian architects began to develop a sense of place within building practices by integrating ideas of sustainability and tectonics. One work that is a response to climate is Jarmund's and Vigsnæs's Offices for the Governor of Svalbard (1997–98). Svalbard, located in the Arctic, has severe winters with little light, harsh wind, and large amounts of snowfall. The west face of the building resembles the windbreakers seen across the mountainous roads of Norway, which give protection from harsh winds, indicative of the winter climate. Jarmund and Vigsnæs apply tectonics in a metaphorical and functional manner giving a sense of place to the building. Bjerk's and Bjørge's Samelandssenteret (Sami Center, 1998–2000) in Karasjok—the Norwegian capital of the Sami people—also responds to the harsh environment and cultural identity of northern Norway. The center, used for cultural, commercial, and political activity, combines, to a certain extent, symbols of the Sami culture. One of the structures is reminiscent of the traditional dwellings of the Sami and uses exposed timber, and a few window frames use the national colors of red, yellow, and blue.

Sustainable design is beginning to infiltrate the Norwegian landscape. In the Steiner School in Stavanger, designed by Arbeidsgruppen HUS, there is a focus on healthy materials. The architects used low-emission materials. They have also treated the wood with traditional beeswax lacquers. With a predominantly cold and wet climate, this building has walls that breathe to avoid condensation. The wall comprises an outer permeable layer of buckskin, a cavity, cladding of timber or board, then insulation and plasterboard as the inner finish.

REBECCA DALVESCO

See also **Aalto, Alvar (Finland); Fehn, Sverre (Norway); Giedion, Sigfried (Switzerland); Glacier Museum, Fjaerland Fjord, Norway; Norberg-Schulz, Christian (Norway); Sustainability and Sustainable Architecture; Venturi, Robert (United States)**

Further Reading

Battistoni, Jan, "Norvegia: Architettura e tradizione," *Casabella* 209 (January/February 1956)

Davey, Peter, "Norwegian Reflections," *Byggekunst* nos. 4–5 (1986)

Davey, Peter, "Human and Ecological Dimensions Never Forgotten," *Norsk Samtidarkitektur Byggekunst* nos. 1–2 (1996)

Ellefsen, Johan, "What is Modern Architecture," *Byggekunst* 9 (1927)

Grønvold, Ulf, "Summer House: Portør Cottage," *Architectural Review* 200, no. 1194 (August 1996)

Holan, Jerri, *Norwegian Wood: A Tradition of Building*, New York: Rizzoli, 1990

Kavli, Guthorm, *Norwegian Architecture: Past and Present*, Oslo: Dreyers and London: Batsford, 1958

Lund, Nils-Ole, "Arne Korsmo og den Norske Funktionalisme," *Byggekunst* no. 1 (1966)

Lund, Nils-Ole, "To Norske Arkitekten: Arne Korsmo og Knut Knutsen," *Arkitekten* 76, no. 22 (December 1974)

Maine, Anna, "Midnight Sun-Dance: Civic Center, Karasjo," *Architectural Review* 200, no. 1194 (August 1996)

Miles, Henry, "Horizon, Artefact, Nature: Private House, Bamble, Sverre Fehn," *Architectural Review* 200, no. 1194 (August 1996)

Miles, Henry, "Love in a Cold Climate: School, Stavanger," *Architectural Review* 200, no. 1194 (August 1996)

Norberg-Schulz, Christian, *Modern Norwegian Architecture*, Oslo: Norwegian University Press, 1986

Overgaard, Ole, "Ut av Romantikken, 1916–1926," *Byggekunst* nos. 5–6 (1956)

Thiis-Evensen, Thomas, "Recent Trends in Norwegian Architecture: Towards a Diversity on a Human Scale," *A+ U* 120, no. 9 (September 1980)

Thiis-Evensen, Thomas, "An Experience in Norwegian Architecture," *A+ U* 171, no. 12 (December 1984)

Torp, Niels A., "Asker Stasjon," *Byggekunst* no. 6 (1999)

Vigsnæs, Håkon, "Administrasjonsbygg for Sysselmannen på Svalbard," *Byggekunst* no. 6 (1998)

NOTRE DAME, LE RAINCY, FRANCE

Designed by Auguste Perret; completed 1923

A number of churches were built in France in the period between the two world wars, especially in the north, where they replaced those destroyed in the devastated areas, but some were to serve the new suburbs of the big cities. The earliest and most technically innovative of these was undoubtedly Notre Dame (1923) at Le Raincy, near Paris. Intended as a war memorial to the soldiers who fell at the Battle of the Ourcq—one of the most dramatic and tragic battles of World War I—the church established its French architect Auguste Perret (1874–1954) as the leading exponent of reinforced-concrete construction.

Designed in collaboration with Perret's brother Gustave, the structure demonstrates the way in which a modern material such as reinforced concrete could be used to reinterpret traditional ecclesiastical typologies while maintaining a visual connection with established forms. It marked a departure from, and yet a logical culmination of, Perret's pre–World War I work. The limitations of a small budget were turned to advantage by the architects in their bold, frank use of reinforced concrete. The church has a traditional rectangular plan with a 138-foot tower dominating the center of the west end. Notre Dame forms a prototype for their design for Ste. Thérèse at Montmagny (1925). The roof has a flat segmental vault in the center with a series of transverse segmental vaults at the sides creating the reminiscence of bays. Above the plinth, which is about seven feet high, the outer walls are almost entirely composed of prefabricated components forming geometric latticed windows, allowing the light to filter into the interior. These combine with the nave, aisles, and slim columns carrying shallow, segmental "barrel" vaults to create a light and graceful interior. This luminosity is suggestive of a 20th-century reinterpretation of the 13th-century spirit of Ste. Chapelle, freed from historical reference. Traditional principles, both classical and Gothic, are invoked, and yet the building denies adherence to either. In this respect, it could be contrasted with the church of St. Anthony (1926) in Basle by Karl Moser, who also worked with a modern reinforced-concrete structure but who was reluctant to dispense with traditional elements, such as deep classical coffering in its vaults, deriving from an earlier constructional system.

The stepped-up concrete steeple of Notre Dame is of almost Gothic power, although the whole spirit of the building is clearly classical. The motif of the long, plain, slender columns of the interior is repeated in the tower, which is in three stages. Its character is very largely determined by the slender, rodlike columns. A long window forms a panel in the first stage and a ventilator in the second, and the termination consists of three vertical concrete rods and decorative fret panels formed to buttress the slender tower.

The design of the church, especially the treatment of the columns, has proved very disturbing to many traditionalists who assert that it is primarily engineering. Perhaps such concerns stem from the misapplication of the principles of brick-and-stone construction to reinforced concrete construction. A. Trystan Edwards criticized the design of the tower, believing it to be so strangely composed that it appeared "to suffer from a mechanical instability." He contended that the lack of vertical punctuation and of terminal features for the long, straight concrete ribs gave rise to the idea that the stages are capable of sliding downward in telescopic fashion. Traditionalists looking at the tower are apt to judge it by towers where walls play a supportive structural role, whereas here they are screens on a framed construction. The vertical ribs criticized by Edwards are the uprights of the frame, and they are given more prominence than the horizontal members because vertical emphasis was desired. The architects were clearly anxious to achieve a pleasing proportional sequence in the three stages of the tower. Their church of St. Thérèse at Montmagny follows the same principles of design and construction, although it varies in many details. The same geometric latticework is used for the windows; indeed, the same molds were employed as in the church at Le Raincy. The first two stages of the tower are similar, but the terminating stage is much simpler and finishes with a pyramid and a cone. Perret was later to design the church of St. Joseph (1952), which occupied a site in the plaza at Le Havre (1956), the master plan for the reconstruction of which stands as Perret's most important postwar commission.

HILARY GRAINGER

See also **Church; Perret, Auguste (France); Reinforced Concrete**

Further Reading

Collins (1959) provides the most comprehensive consideration of Perret's work in reinforced concrete.

Ache, Jean-Baptiste (editor), *Perret* (exhib. cat.), Paris: 1959

Champigneulle, Bernard, *Perret*, Paris: Arts et Métiers Graphiques, 1959

Collins, Peter, *Concrete: The Vision of a New Architecture: A Study of Auguste Perret and His Precursors*, London: Faber and Faber, and New York: Horizon Press, 1959

Jamot, Paul, *A.-G. Perret et l'architecture du béton armé*, Paris and Geneva: Vanoest, 1927

Perret, Auguste, *A. and G. Perret: 24 Phototypies*, Paris: Librairie de France, 1928

Perret, Auguste, *Contribution à une théorie de l'architecture*, Paris: Cercle d'Études Architecturales Chez A. Wahl, 1952

Rogers, Ernesto Nathan, *Auguste Perret*, Milan: Il Balcone, 1955

Notre Dame, Le Raincy, designed by Auguste Perret
© Donald Corner and Jenny Young/GreatBuildings.com

NOUVEL, JEAN 1945–

Architect, France

Beginning in 1970 and over the next 24 years, Jean Nouvel formed four different partnerships with other French architects eventually taking the name Architectures Jean Nouvel in 1994. Nouvel began to acquire international recognition for his work in the 1980s, culminating in the critically acclaimed Cartier museum (Paris, 1994).

The Cartier Foundation for Contemporary Art (1994) in Paris is representative of the perceptual illusions that are the crux of Nouvel's architecture. The layered glass walls, partly framing and sandwiching the existing trees (including one planted by the writer Chateaubriand in 1823), create ambiguous perceptions of the building's volume and mass. As one walks or drives along Boulevard Raspail, the glass face, with its changing reflections and refractions, appears to alternately materialize and vanish. The "Parisian jewel," as it has been called, is often photographed under different lighting conditions, as if to call attention to the building's primary existence as a light prism.

The glass-walled exhibition spaces are well suited for the iconoclastic artwork for which the Cartier is known. Issey Miyake's 1998 exhibition "Making Things" particularly captured the ambiguity that is characteristic of the architecture. Similar to Nouvel's work, the Japanese designer's clothes are simultaneously insubstantial and solid, the perceived mass of the object differing from its physical reality by virtue of its texture or shape and its interaction with the human body. A later example of Nouvel's use of light and glass to generate illusory spaces is the Friedrichstrasse department store (1996) in Berlin. While the parti for the Cartier Foundation building was planar and in its facade, here it is centrifugal and in its core. Interior cones of curved, partly reflective silvered glass provide a kaleidoscopic view of the spaces surrounding the center void. The lobby of the Lyons Opera House (1993) is yet another example of his mastery of the architecture of illusion. Nouvel created a ghostly, ethereal space by surrounding one's descent and ascent on escalators with dimly lit black curved shiny surfaces.

Contemporary art has had a marked influence on Nouvel's architecture. The Chocolate Factory (1990) in Blois, clad in black and sitting on a grass lawn, is reminiscent of the work of minimalist and environmental sculptor Richard Serra. Also Dan Graham's work, specifically the use of alternately reflective and transparent surfaces and the incorporation of landscape elements to create fragmented views through layers of glass (much as the Chateaubriand cedar functions at the Cartier Center), has had a decisive and acknowledged influence on the architect.

Cartier Foundation for Contemporary Art, Paris (1994)
© Maria Sieira

The commission that catapulted him onto the international scene was the Institut du Monde Arabe (Arab World Institute) that he won in 1981 with several other French architects in the first competition of President François Mitterand's ambitious new architecture agenda. The building was a critical success, and at the time of its completion in 1987 it was hailed as the best high-tech building since the Pompidou Center. In the context of his later work, however, it is more significant as an early example of spatial illusions, reflection, and refraction, in which, as the architect himself has observed, it is sometimes difficult to ascertain whether a wall is 5 or 50 feet away. The south facade is a skin of light-sensitive metal diaphragms. These open and close like camera apertures, embedding modern technology in a mosaic of Arabic patterns. By alluding to past and present, the facade acquires the illusion of permanence typically associated with monuments, yet it is light as air: a reflected sunset or sunrise vaporizes the wall, transforming the metal layer behind the glass into a shimmering lacy curtain.

Nouvel's architecture reconfigures the curtain wall, whether glass and aluminum or stainless steel, into an image-making device, and hence his facades are akin to screens. He alludes to modern technology in an effort to make architecture that reflects contemporary society. He sometimes uses forms and materials that make portions of his buildings and sites resemble boats, trains, or even airport runways, as in the Onyx Center (1988). Superimposed and offset grids or views through perforated metal to a brighter space allude to the pixilated and striated nature of computer and television screens. Sometimes he screen prints onto the glazing, as in the holographic scenes on Euralille's shopping center (1995) in Lille, France, or the text that wraps the Cartier Factory (1993).

Although his work may differ greatly from such postmodernists as the Spanish-born Ricardo Boffil, whose historicist approach Nouvel has openly criticized, it exhibits some affinities with the United States firm Venturi, Scott Brown and Associates, namely, in the use of signage and graphics as architectural components and in the reconfiguration of vernacular elements into a new language, such as the wood shutters of the Hotel des Thermes (1992) in Dax, or the hotel in Bouliac, both in Southwest France, where he was born. In addition, elements of architectural representation often inform his buildings, as in the Belfort Theater (1984), in which a severed wall is patterned with the striping of a section drawing, or in the high-rise project for La Défense (1989), in which he emphasizes the perspectival diminished visibility of a 100-meter tower as viewed from the ground by gradating materials and colors from black to grays to white, so that the "Endless Tower" disappears into the often overcast Parisian sky.

Nouvel has transformed the picture window of modern architecture into an image screen. He uses the same glass curtain walls with which Gropius built literal transparency but toward phenomenal ends, in the service of space that constantly reconfigures itself as the light changes. Although Nouvel's work demonstrates dexterity with new building technology, it is the construction of spatial illusions that makes his architecture. In this regard, he rightly claims Mies van der Rohe as his artistic father, another master of glass and light whose precisely detailed physical structures were only the means to more ethereal architectural ends.

MARIA SIEIRA

See also **Bofill, Ricardo (Spain); Curtain Wall System; Glass; Gropius, Walter (Germany); Mies van der Rohe, Ludwig (Germany); Venturi, Robert (United States)**

Biography

Born in Fumel, Lot et Garonne, France, 12 August 1945. Studied architecture at the École des Beaux-Arts, Paris 1966–71. Private practice, Paris 1971–88; partnership with engineer Emmanuel Cattani from 1988; founder and director of art, *Biennale d'Architecture* 1980; co-founder, MARS 1976; co-founder, Syndicat de l'Architecture 1979; vice president, Institut Français d'Architcture, Paris 1991. Chevalier des Arts et Lettres 1983; F.A.I.A. honorary fellow, AIA Chicago 1993; honorary fellow, RIBA (Royal Institute of British Architects) 1995.

Selected Works

Theater Restoration, Belfort, 1984
Institut du Monde Arabe (First prize, competition), Paris (with The Architectural Studio, Gilbert Lézénè, and Pierre Soria), 1987
Nemausus Housing Development I, Nîmes (with Jean-Marc Ibos), 1987
Centre Culturel "Onyx," Saint-Herblain (with Myrto Vitart), 1988
Hôtel Saint-James, Bouliac-Bourdeau, France, 1989
La Tour Sans Fin (project), La Défense, Paris (with Emmanuel Cattani), 1989
Usine Poulaine Headquarters, Blois (with Cattani), 1990
Hôtel des Thermes et Thalassothérapie, Dax, France (with Cattani), 1992
Opera House Extension, Lyon (with Cattani), 1993
Cartier-Façade Interdica, Fribourg, Switzerland (with Cattani), 1993
Fondation Cartier, Paris (with Cattani), 1994
Euralille Shopping Center, Lille, 1995
Friedrichstrasse Department Store, Berlin, 1996

Selected Publications

"The Meeting Line," *Architectural Design* (July/August 1991)
"On Designing," *Domus* (October 1992)
"Nouvel Cuisine," *RIBA Journal* (January 1993)
"Art Nouvel—Shop, Berlin, Germany," *The Architectural Review*, 200 (September 1996)

Further Reading

Bergold, Barry, "New Challenges for Nouvel," *Progressive Architecture*, 70/8 (1989)
Boissière, Olivier, *Jean Nouvel*, Paris: Pierre Terrail, 1996; revised and bilingual English and German edition, Boston and Basel: Birkhauser, 1996
Dixon, John, "Theatrical Revival," *Progressive Architecture*, 66 (1985)
Goulet, Patrice, *Jean Nouvel*, Paris: Electa Moniteur, 1987
Loriers, Marie Christine, "Through the Looking Glass," *Progressive Architecture*, 69/5 (1988)
McGuire, Penny, "Art Nouvel," *Architectural Review*, 200 (1996)
Morgan, Conway Lloyd, *Jean Nouvel: The Elements of Architecture*, New York: Universe, and London: Thames and Hudson, 1998.
Shortt, Barbara, "Parisian Jewel," *Architecture*, 83/9 (September 1994)
Zaera, Alejandro, *Jean Nouvel 1987–1998*, Madrid: El Croquis 65/66, 1995.

O

OFFICE BUILDING

No other building type serves as a more reliable indicator of the complex and interwoven economic, political, cultural, and regional changes reflected by architecture than structures designed and built to house the functions of commercial, cultural, or government administration. At the turn of the 20th century, strong economic development in the two major industrial growth sectors in the United States, livestock and meat processing and the steel industry, created a new extraordinary demand for office space in metropolitan centers. Chicago and New York exemplified a trend to accommodate administrative functions away from the actual places of production. A new building type was born.

Form, technology, construction methods, and the organizational system of the office work environment significantly changed in the next 100 years. At the beginning of the 20th century, office building architects and clients still needed the stylistic assurance of the classical template for the new building type. The early office building designs by the firms of Holabird and Roche, D.H. Burnham and Company, and later Adler and Sullivan in Chicago; Cass Gilbert, Sloan and Robertson; and McKim, Mead and White in New York resembled mostly Italian Renaissance palaces or the French nobility's city residences in the style of Second Empire buildings. Examples include the Flatiron Building (1902) by Daniel Burnham and the F.W. Woolworth Building (1911) by Cass Gilbert in New York City.

Despite its neoclassical appearance, the building type was technologically the most advanced architectural expression of its time. The new technique to carry the load of a building was no longer by use of massive walls but rather by a system of vertical steel columns and horizontal beams, a wind-braced steel frame and its fireproofing, organized in a rational grid. This was the result of cooperation among client, architect, and the steel industry. Using the technique of the steel frame meant decreasing the obstructing traditional walls, increasing the usable office space per floor. Important technological progress in other areas, such as in mechanical building systems for vertical circulation (such as the 1852 invention of the safety elevator, a mechanism for a lifting platform by Elisha Otis in New York), ventilation, and artificial lighting, freed the new building type from limitations of heights and depth of the floor plan. With the Larkin Building (1904, demolished 1950) in Buffalo, New York, Frank Lloyd Wright opened a dramatic new path by introducing new tectonic and technological elements such as curtain walls, steel furniture, and air conditioning. The discourse among architects and investors between "classical" and "modern" expression of the new building type continued well into the 1920s, finding its climax during the quarrels about the international competition for the new office building of the *Chicago Tribune* in 1922. The winning design, which celebrated an office building in a Gothic Revival style, succeeded over entries including a design by German architect and then director of the Bauhaus, Walter Gropius. The jury and the general public were not yet willing to accept his design based on a sensible balance of expression derived from the rationality of the structural grid system. This discussion continued, enriched by events such as the Exposition des Arts Décoratifs in Paris in the 1920s, which recharged the formal catalog of architects, especially in the United States, with decorative elements. The Chrysler Building (1930) by William Van Alen in New York City is an example of a highly developed Art Deco style. With the immigration of the majority of the leading proponents of the Bauhaus, such as Gropius and Ludwig Mies van der Rohe, to the United States, the avant-garde philosophy of the use of material and production techniques finally altered the course of the formal expression of the building type. The face of the office building changed from historicism to congruence between structure and expression as the International Style emerged.

Advances in material technology, mainly in the areas of glass, stainless steel, and aluminum in the years after World War II, led to the curtain-wall office buildings of the International Style and their domination of city centers around the world. Examples are the Lever House (New York, 1952) by Gordon Bunshaft, Skidmore, Owings and Merrill; the Seagram Building (New York, 1958) by Mies van der Rohe and Philip Johnson; and the Citicorp Center (New York, 1978) by Hugh Stubbins. Higher energy costs in Europe drove the expression of a "pure" International Style, with the reduction of the office facade to a glass-and-metal-frame skin, to change to highly developed multi-layered systems. Outside louvers, blinds, and balconies reduced energy consumption by reducing solar heat gain and also allowing for easy access and maintenance.

The internal spatial organization of the office between 1945 and the present has been a combination of open-plan (German, *Bürolandschaft*) and cellular offices. In European countries, different organizational patterns, labor laws, and building codes generated a hybrid office plan (Swedish, *Combi-Offices*), resulting in different building forms. The Central Beheer Administration Building (1967–72) by Hermann Hertzberger in Apeldoorn, the Netherlands, is an example. Despite changes in office work and technological advances of electronic media and information processing, extensive office building development will most surely continue. In the last decade, an increase in the upward building trend in the cosmopolitan areas of Southeast Asia serve as a way to recoup for the high cost of urban land. Never before has the race for the tallest office building created interesting designs in both a structural and an aesthetic sense. Office buildings such as the 1,483-foot Petronas Towers (1998) by Cesar Pelli in Kuala Lumpur, Malaysia; the 1,379-foot Jin Mao Building (1998) by Skidmore, Owings and Merrill in Shanghai, China; Hongkong and Shanghai Bank (Norman Foster and Partners, 1986), and the World Financial Center (2000) by Kohn Pederson Fox in Shanghai have long left behind the once-admired wonders of office design, such as the Sears Tower (1976) by Bruce Graham (Skidmore, Owings and Merrill) in Chicago, the Empire State Building (1931), and the World Trade Center (1977) by Minoru Yamasaki in New York City. Late 20th-century European and Asian tendencies in office building design show an increased concern for energy efficiency and bioclimatic considerations as promising design primers for sustainable architecture.

RALPH HAMMANN

See also **Bunshaft, Gordon (United States); Chicago (IL), United States; Chrysler Building, New York; Empire State Building, New York; Flatiron Building, New York; Gilbert, Cass (United States); Glass; Hertzberger, Herman (the Netherlands); Holabird, William, and Martin Roche (United States); International Exhibition of Decorative Arts, Paris (1925); Larkin Building, Buffalo, New York; McKim, Mead and White (United States); Pelli, Cesar (Argentina, United States); Petronas Towers, Kuala Lumpur; Seagram Building, New York; Sears Tower, Chicago; Skidmore, Owings and Merrill (United States); World Trade Center, New York; Yamasaki, Minoru (United States)**

Further Reading

Condit, Carl W., *The Rise of the Skyscraper*, Chicago: University of Chicago Press, 1952; revised edition, as *The Chicago School of Architecture: A History of Commercial and Public Buildings in the Chicago Area, 1875–1925*, 1964

Daniels, Klaus, *Technologie des ökologischen bauens: Grundlagen und massnahmen, beispiele und ideen*, Basel and Boston: Birkhauser, 1995; as *The Technology of Ecological Building: Basic Principles and Measures, Examples, and Ideas*, Boston and Basel: Birhhäuser, 1997

Frampton, Kenneth, *Modern Architecture: A Critical History*, New York: Oxford University Press, and London: Thames and Hudson, 1980; 3rd edition, revised and enlarged, London: Thames and Hudson, 1992; New York: Thames and Hudson, 1997

Giedion, Sigfried, *Space, Time, and Architecture*, Cambridge, Massachusetts: Harvard University Press, and London: H. Milford, Oxford University Press, 1941; 5th edition, revised and enlarged, Cambridge, Massachusetts: Harvard University Press, 1967

Goldberger, Paul, *The Skyscraper*, New York: Knopf, 1981; London: Allen Lane, 1982

Hitchcock, Henry Russell and P. Johnson, *The International Style: Architecture Since 1922*, New York: Norton, 1932; as *The International Style*, London and New York: Norton, 1995

Slessor, Catherine, *Eco-Tech: Sustainable Architecture and High Technology*, London and New York: Thames and Hudson, 1997

Yeang, Ken, *The Green Skyscraper: The Basis for Designing Sustainable Intensive Buildings*, Munich and New York: Prestel, 1999

Hongkong and Shanghai Bank, designed by Norman Foster and Partners (1986)
© Howard Davis/GreatBuildings.com

O'GORMAN, JUAN 1905–82

Architect, Mexico

The architectural career of the Mexican architect and painter Juan O'Gorman can be roughly divided into two phases: his early functionalist phase and his later organic phase. Separating the two is a pivotal understanding of the role of architecture that, for some time, prompted him to abandon architecture to focus exclusively on painting.

O'Gorman began his studies in 1922 at the Architecture School of the National University, where he studied under, among others, Guillermo Zárraga and José Luis Cuevas. During this time, he worked in the offices of his professors, Carlos Obregón Santacilia and José Villagrán García. These two architects were involved in important architectural investigations: the first was building the Centro Escolar Benito Juarez (1923–25), which explored the possibilities of reinforced-concrete construction on neo-Colonialist forms, and the second was building the Granja Sanitaria (1925), which became one of the earliest explorations into functionalism in Mexico. Also influential was the publication and arrival in Mexico of Le Corbusier's *Vers une architecture*, which he read as a manifesto for a rationalist functionalism of the engineer and a call for a self-referential, autonomous architecture.

O'Gorman's earliest works conformed to these concerns, as demonstrated by two of his early works: the House-Studio (1930) for the painter Diego Rivera and his work for the Department of Public Education in 1932. The House-Studio was a simple volume with a sawtoothed roof and exposed industrial materials. Expressive of O'Gorman's functionalism, it attempted to solve practical necessities rather than to address aesthetic interests. These concerns would materialize in his designs for the Department of Public Education, where, under the auspices of the socialist-minded Secretary of Education Narciso Bassols, O'Gorman would build and renovate a total of 53 public schools. These school buildings were unornamented and constructed in concrete, were efficiently planned on a 3-meter grid, and used standardized and mass-produced architectural elements and fixtures. For both Bassols and O'Gorman, these schools responded to the lack of adequate teaching facilities in a direct, efficient, and economical way while providing the students an education in economy and efficiency.

During this time, O'Gorman also participated in the founding of the School of Construction Technicians (1932), which was to teach students how to produce rational buildings while avoiding aesthetic issues associated with architecture. It was the founding of this school, however, that initiated a series of debates, under the auspices of the Society of Mexican Architects, about the direction that architecture should take in Mexico. This conference, known as the "Talks about Architecture" (1933), expressed the culmination of two intellectual assertions regarding architecture in Mexico. On one hand, the "Functionalist" line was advocated by a group of young socialist-minded architects headed by O'Gorman and Juan Legarreta; on the other hand, the "Academic" line was a reactionary position waged by the professional architectural establishment. The primary intent of these debates was to clarify the role of architecture in postrevolutionary Mexico and, subsequently, the role of functionalism within that definition. In his presentation, O'Gorman attacked the architectural establishment for trying to establish its hegemony over architecture by limiting it to spiritual and aesthetic considerations that, for him, served only to reproduce their capital. Instead, he called for an architecture that was honest to its time and to its function and construction and that, because of its efficiency, allowed a greater of number of buildings to be constructed and thus solve the needs of a larger population.

By 1936, however, O'Gorman had become fully disillusioned with functionalist architecture, forcing him to abandon it completely for painting, a passion from his childhood. Traditional historiography has not clarified this sudden change but rather has limited its interpretation of it either to an interest in pursuing Frank Lloyd Wright's organic architecture or to his distaste of the business of architectural practice. O'Gorman's writings at the time, however, point to a disillusionment due to a clear understanding of the ideological aspects that structured functionalist architectural production and its inevitable social failure. In "Capitalist Architecture and Socialist Architecture," published in the 1935–36 issue of *Edificación* (the journal of the School of Construction Technicians), O'Gorman defined functionalist architecture as a means through which the bourgeoisie reproduced their power and capital while pretending to address the concerns of the population. Specifically, functionalist architecture allowed its users to conform to the new realities of standardization, industrialization, and mass production that were central to capitalist reproduction of its conditions of production and thus its power. In functionalist architecture, its own autonomy prevented it not only from reflecting bourgeois class interests (as O'Gorman had believed at the beginning of his career) but also, dialectically, from being used for political and social change.

On his brief return to architecture, O'Gorman adopted Wright's theories on organic architecture, reflecting his interest, on the one hand, in the importance of a telluric agency and, on the other, in exploring the communicative qualities of architecture. Two buildings from this period are indicative of these concerns. O'Gorman's House (1949) in the Pedregal region of Mexico City—an area known for its volcanic rock landscape—formally incorporated itself into the site and used its materials in its construction. On its exterior, O'Gorman decorated its walls with sculptures and mosaics made with colored rocks. This was the same method that he, along with Gustavo Saavedra and Juan Martínez Velasco, would employ for the decoration of the National Library (1952) for the National University in Mexico. The library stack (a windowless vertical mass) is separated from the reading rooms (a double-height and functionally organized horizontal mass) through its formal relations and its exterior treatment. The volume of the library stack is covered in colored mosaics that were intended to be didactic in nature, although O'Gorman later acknowledged their failure in communicating a clear message.

LUIS E. CARRANZA

See also **Corbusier, Le (Jeanneret, Charles-Édouard) (France); Mexico; Mexico City, Mexico; Norten, Enrique (Mexico); Wright, Frank Lloyd (United States)**

Biography

Born in Mexico City, 6 July 1905; father was the painter Cecil O'Gorman. Studied under José Villagrán García and Guillermo Zárraga at the School of Architecture, University of Mexico, Mexico City 1922–26; degree in architecture 1926; apprenticed to Carlos Obregón Santacilia 1927; studied painting with Antonio Ruiz, Diego Rivera, and Frida Kahlo. Worked in the architectural offices of José Villagrán García, Carlos Tarditi, and Carlos Contreros, Mexico City 1927–29; chief draftsman, the office of Carlos Obregón Santacilia 1929–32; chief architect for the Ministry of Education, Mexico City 1932–34. Withdrew from architectural practice for ideological reasons 1934–48;

co-founder and professor, Escuela Superior de Ingenieros y Arquitectos, Instituto Nacional Politécnico, Mexico City 1932–48; founder, Workers' Housing Study Group, Mexico City 1936. Returned to architectural practice 1948. Member, National College of Architects of Mexico 1956; member, Bolivarian Society of Architects, Caracas 1967; member, Academy of Arts, Mexico City 1971. Died, by suicide, Mexico City, 18 January 1982.

Selected Works

Diego Rivera House and Studio, Mexico City, 1930
Juan O'Gorman House I, San Angel, Mexico City, 1930
Tomás O'Gorman House, San Angel, Mexico City, 1931
28 Primary Schools throughout Mexico for the Ministry of
    Education, 1932–34
Technical School, Mexico City, 1934
Castellaños House, Mexico City, 1934
Electricians' Union Building, Mexico City, 1936
National Library, State University of Mexico, Mexico City (with
    Gustavo Saavedra and Juan Martínez Velasco), 1952
Juan O'Gorman House II (destroyed), San Angel, Mexico City,
    1956

Selected Publications

El arte útil y el arte artístico, 1932
*Autobiografía, antología, juicios criticos y documentación exhaustiva
sobre su obra*, 1973

Further Reading

Aja, Marisol, "Juan O'Gorman" in *Apuntes para la historia y crítica
    del la arquitectura mexicana del siglo XX, 1900–1980*, edited by
    Alexandrina Escudero, volume 2, Mexico City: Secretariá de
    Educación Pública, 1982
Born, Esther, *The New Architecture in Mexico*, New York:
    Architectural Record, 1937
Burian, Edward R., "The Architecture of Juan O'Gorman:
    Dichotomy and Drift" in *Modernity and the Architecture of
    Mexico*, edited by Burian, Austin: University of Texas Press, 1997
Carranza, Luis E., "Paradigms of the Avant-Garde: Mexican Modern
    Architecture, 1920–1940" (Ph.D. dissertation), Harvard
    University, 1998 (see chapter titled "Against a New Architecture:
    Juan O'Gorman and the Disillusionment of Modernism")
O'Gorman, Juan, *Juan O'Gorman: autobiografía, antología, juicios
    críticos, y documentación exhaustiva sobre su obra*, edited by
    Antonio Luna Arroyo, Mexico City: Cuadernos Populares de
    Pintura Mexicana Moderna, 1973
Rodríguez Prampolini, Ida, *Juan O'Gorman: architecto y pintor*,
    Mexico City: Universidad Nacional Autonoma de Mexico, 1982
Rodríguez Prampolini, Ida (editor), *La palabra de Juan O'Gorman
    (selección de textos)*, Mexico City: Coordinación de Extensión
    Universitaria, Dirección General de Difusión Cultural, Unidad
    Editorial/UNAM, Instituto de Investigaciones Estéticas, 1983
Smith, Clive Bamford, *Builders in the Sun: Five Mexican Architects*,
    New York: Architectural Book, 1967

O'HARE INTERNATIONAL AIRPORT, CHICAGO

In the second half of the 20th century, Chicago's O'Hare International Airport was the largest and busiest facility of its kind in the world. Remarkable for its seamless integration of transportation infrastructure and architectural expression, O'Hare served as an international model for modern airport planning and design as well as an example of a modern architecture nearly completely conditioned by technology. An architectural ensemble at the scale of a small city, the scope and complexity of O'Hare's planning provided an unprecedented opportunity for the testing of modernist principles by generations of Chicago architects and engineers.

In the years following World War II, Ralph Burke and Associates began preliminary planning on what would become O'Hare. Although construction began in 1949, O'Hare's development accelerated following the election of Mayor Richard J. Daley in 1955. By 1957, following Burke's death, the Chicago architectural firm of Naess and Murphy (later C.F. Murphy Associates) was retained to prepare plans for the jet-age expansion of O'Hare. The 1958 plan described three pairs of parallel runways that remain in use today. The facility profited from a number of breakthroughs in airport design and planning first implemented by C.F. Murphy and Associates at O'Hare as well as from the adaptation of many precedents from other facilities internationally. Among these was the development of a two-tier split-level roadway system bringing enplaning passengers to the upper level and deplaning passengers to the lower level of the two-story terminal buildings. The extensive system of Y finger concourses extending from the terminal buildings was augmented with the addition of mechanically telescoping gangways connecting passengers and crew from gate to plane on the same level. The basic premises of the 1958 C.F. Murphy plan, its organization of multiple infrastructures, its innovation of a dual-level entry and exit roadway, and its use of mechanical telescoping jetways have all served the facility admirably over the course of its nearly continuous expansion and renovation. The airport's still-serviceable planning was derived from the near-direct extrusion of its complex programmatic organization, and its architectural expression was unified though the application of an International Style enclosure system of steel and glass over a structural frame of reinforced concrete.

By the time of its official dedication ceremonies in 1963, O'Hare was the busiest airport in the world, serving 13.5 million passengers per year, a volume of traffic exceeding even the most optimistic growth projections by nearly 20 years. The completion of the Northwest (later Kennedy) Expressway in 1960 and the introduction of a Chicago Transit Authority (CTA) train/bus connection from the city to O'Hare fueled this extraordinary growth. The entire facility continues to be served by a remarkable transparent utility building that houses massive pumps, furnaces, and refrigeration equipment in a steel-and-glass box. Intended as an image of the airport's modern aspirations and faith in the image of technology, the bowels of the airport are served up to arriving and departing passengers—well lit and prominently visible from plane, train, or automobile.

In 1963 the American Institute of Architects recognized C.F. Murphy Associates for their work at O'Hare, and subsequent work at the site has consistently garnered awards and critical acclaim. More recent work at the site, as well as the passing of time, has reflected favorably on the initial site planning and architectural design decisions taken at O'Hare, even as growth has occasionally threatened to overwhelm the facility.

In 1971 construction was completed on a new air traffic control tower of slip-formed concrete construction designed by I.M. Pei Associates with Landrum and Brown Architects. In

United Airlines Terminal, O'Hare International Airport, designed by Helmut Jahn (1988)
© Donald Corner and Jenny Young/GreatBuildings.com

1973 construction was completed on a new airport hotel and parking garage at the center of the terminal complex, designed by C.F. Murphy Associates.

In 1981, a consortium of firms, including the reorganized Murphy/Jahn (formerly C.F. Murphy Associates), Envirodyne Engineers, Schal Associates, and Landrum and Brown, completed plans for further expansion at O'Hare, including the addition of domestic and international gates. This plan further specified the construction of several long-awaited transportation infrastructures, including the completion of the CTA train connection to the city, a highway connection to the Northwest Tollway, and the construction of an intra-airport transit train, or ATS, system.

In 1988 construction was completed on a new domestic terminal building for United Airlines, designed by Murphy/Jahn. The United terminal appropriated the original terminal's International Style vocabulary of a glass-and-steel enclosure for use as a structural frame but featured a Postmodern arched section and other architectural devices as references to the extruded halls of 19th-century train sheds and gallery buildings. Five years later, construction was completed on a new international terminal designed by Chicago architects Perkins and Will in collaboration with Heard and Associates as well as Consoer, Townsend, and Associates.

Although the ongoing expansion of the world's busiest airport through the addition of buildings of such high quality and architectural merit has been an extraordinary accomplishment, the more important contribution of O'Hare is to be found in its integration of multiple infrastructural systems and their expression in architectural terms. By this measure, O'Hare ranks as one of the world's most significant sites for the development and testing of the principles of modern planning applied at the scale, complexity, and indeterminacy of the city itself.

CHARLES WALDHEIM

See also **Airport and Aviation Building; Jahn, Helmut (United States); Perkins and Will (United States)**

Further Reading

Bouman, Mark, "Cities of the Plane: Airports in the Networked City" in *Building for Air Travel*, edited by John Zukowsky, Chicago: Art Institute of Chicago, and Munich and New York: Prestel, 1996

Brodherson, David, "All Airports Lead to Chicago: Airport Planning and Design in a Midwest Metropolis" in *Chicago Architecture and Design, 1923–1993*, edited by John Zukowsky, Chicago: Art Institute of Chicago, and Munich: Prestel, 1993

Brodherson, David, "An Airport in Every City: The History of American Airport Design" in *Building for Air Travel*, edited by

John Zukowsky, Chicago: Art Institute of Chicago, and Munich and New York: Prestel, 1996

Bruegmann, Robert, "Airport City" in *Building for Air Travel*, edited by John Zukowsky, Chicago: Art Institute of Chicago, and Munich and New York: Prestel, 1996

Kirchherr, Eugene, "The Changing Pattern of Airport Land Use in the Chicago Region, 1941–1975," *Bulletin of the Illinois Geographical Society*, 25 (Spring 1983)

OLBRICH, JOSEPH MARIA 1867–1908

Architect, Austria

Joseph Maria Olbrich was among the foremost representatives of the small group of turn-of-the century reformers in Central Europe who sought to forge a new style liberated from the constraints of late 19th-century historic revivalism. During the early years of the century, his works in Austria and Germany won wide acclaim from contemporary critics, and later historians have generally regarded him as one of the early pioneers of modern architecture and design. Yet, despite the seminal role he played in the architectural experiments of the early years of the century, Olbrich's position with regard to both the uses of past forms and the formation of a new, modern architectonic language is complex and ambiguous.

Upon graduating from Vienna Staatsgewerbeschule (State Trades School), Olbrich returned to Troppau to work for a local builder, but in 1890 he entered the Academy of Fine Arts in Vienna, where he was a student of Carl von Hasenauer, one of the preeminent architects of the city's famed Ringstrasse. A brilliant draftsman, Olbrich won numerous prizes, including the school's prestigious Rome Prize, which allowed him to undertake an extended trip through Italy and North Africa. In 1894, after completing his studies, he was offered a position in the office of Otto Wagner, who had succeeded von Hasenauer at the academy. He soon became Wagner's chief assistant, working principally on the *Stadtbahn* (city railway) project, and by 1896 his work for Wagner began to manifest the transition from late historicism to the new florid Jugendstil language.

Olbrich's attempt to find an alternative to historicism, however, is most strikingly evident is his first independent work, an exhibition hall for the Vienna Secession (1897–98). The design, inspired partly by a sketch by Gustav Klimt, featured a large perforated dome of gilded metal laurel leaves set on four squat pylons and high battered stucco walls with incised vegetal forms framing the entrance and the corners. The building's unconventional exterior, however, concealed the innovative character of its interior that centered on a large, flexible exhibition gallery. Lighted by four skylights and three north windows, the entire space had only six permanent stanchions; secondary walls could be positioned or removed at will, allowing the gallery to be reconfigured for each new show.

Although the Secession provoked a storm of indignation from the Viennese public, who mockingly referred to it as the "Mahdi's Tomb" and the "Golden Cabbage," it brought Olbrich international accolades and an invitation, in 1899, from Ernst Ludwig, the grand duke of Hesse, to join the artists' colony he was establishing in Mathildenhöhe Park in Darmstadt. Olbrich found kindred spirits among the new colony's painters, sculptors, and designers (which included Peter Behrens), and Lud-

wig's patronage provided him the freedom to pursue his ideas; eventually, except for Behrens's house, he would design all the buildings at the colony, including the artists' residences and studios, and a variety of permanent and temporary exhibition buildings.

Olbrich's early designs on the Mathildenhöhe represented a continuation of the free mixing of historical forms—often from quite disparate epochs—and Jugendstil decorative elements that had been a hallmark of his later Viennese works. The Ernst Ludwig Haus (1899–1901), designed to be a communal studio and exhibition hall for the colony's first public exhibition, "*Ein Dokument deutscher Kunst*" ("A Document of German Art"), in 1901, offered an eclectic blending of stripped classicism and geometric ornament, suggesting an updating of Wagner's own formal inflections. However, for many of the colony's houses, including his own house of 1901, Olbrich employed traditional German folk elements and picturesque massing and composition, to which he added Jugendstil accents. This style, although widely influential at the time, drew strong condemnation for its expensive, overabundant ornamentation and its seeming detachment from everyday life.

Olbrich's arrogance and his privileged position with Ludwig aroused resentment among the other artists, and a number left the colony after 1901. Undeterred by the criticisms and defections, Olbrich continued to experiment with a welter of new ideas, but his later works show a gradual shift toward an emphasis on simple rectilinear forms and a pared-down classicism. This new attitude is discernible already in the *Hochzeitsturm* (Wedding Tower, 1905–08), designed to commemorate the grand duke's marriage, which became the dominant motif of the assemblage of buildings crowning the Mathildenhöhe and an often-reproduced icon of the early Modern movement. Olbrich's move toward classicism, however, became even more conspicuous in a series of buildings he designed outside Darmstadt after 1906, including the Villa Feinhals (1909) in Cologne and his last project, the Tietz Department Store (1906–09) in Düsseldorf.

After his death, Olbrich was lauded as one of the leaders of the effort to create a modern architecture in Germany, and although he was later sometimes criticized for his "overconcentration on decorative aims" (Giedion, 1967), he has nonetheless found a secure place in the modernist pantheon. However, although Olbrich investigated the possibilities of a new architectonic language, he never wholly abandoned the idea that history could provide useful and meaningful forms and ideas. Indeed, much like Wagner, Olbrich sought to reconcile the new and old, to shape a contemporary style while still maintaining a link to the past. In that sense, Olbrich's approach was profoundly different from the later radical functionalists, who attempted to devise an architecture devoid of historical precedent and aesthetic aspiration.

CHRISTOPHER LONG

See also **Art Nouveau (Jugendstil); Austria; Behrens, Peter (Germany); Darmstadt, Germany; Hoffmann, Josef (Austria); Vienna Secession; Wagner, Otto (Austria)**

Biography

Born in Troppau, Silesia (now Opava, Czech Republic), 22 December 1867. Studied in the building department under Camillo

Secession Building, Karlsplatz, front facade, designed by Josef Maria Olbrich (1898)
Photo © Mary Ann Sullivan

Sitte, Staatsgewerbeschule, Vienna 1881–86; apprentice to a builder, Troppau 1886–90; attended the Akademie der Bildenden Künste, Vienna 1890–93; traveled to Italy and North Africa 1893–94. Assistant to Otto Wagner, Vienna 1894–98. In private practice, Vienna from 1898. Founding member, Vienna Secession 1897. Died in Düsseldorf, 8 August 1908.

Selected Works

Max Friedmann House (First prize, competition), Hinterbrühl, Austria, 1898
Secession Building, Vienna, 1898
Hermann Bahr House, Vienna, 1900
Ernst Ludwig House, Darmstadt, 1901
Joseph Maria Olbrich House, Darmstadt, 1901
Wedding Tower and Exhibition Building, Darmstadt, 1908
Tietz Department Store, Düsseldorf, 1909
Joseph Feinhals House, Cologne, 1909

Selected Publications

Ideen, 1900
Architektur von Professor Joseph Maria Olbrich, 3 vols., 1901–04

Further Reading

Clark, Robert Judson, "Joseph Maria Olbrich and Vienna" (Ph.D. dissertation), Princeton University, 1973

Giedion, Sigfried, *Space, Time, and Architecture: The Growth of a New Tradition*, Cambridge, Massachusetts: Harvard University Press, and London: Oxford University Press, 1941; 5th edition, revised and enlarged, Cambridge, Massachusetts: Harvard University Press, 1967
Krimmel, Bernd (editor), *Ein Dokument deutscher Kunst: Darmstadt, 1901–1976*, 5 vols., Darmstadt, Germany: Roether, 1976
Krimmel, Bernd (editor), *Joseph M. Olbrich, 1867–1908*, Darmstadt, Germany: Mathildenhöhe, 1983
Latham, Ian, *Joseph Maria Olbrich*, London: Academy, and New York: Rizzoli, 1980
Lux, Joseph August, *Joseph M. Olbrich*, Berlin: Wasmuth, 1919
Schreyl, Karl Heinz, Kristin Klosterman, and Gerhard Bott (editors), *Joseph Maria Olbrich, 1867–1908: Das Werk des Architekten*, Darmstadt, Germany: Hessisches Landesmuseum, 1967
Sperlich, Hans-Günther, *Versuch über Joseph Maria Olbrich*, Darmstadt, Germany: Liebig, 1965
Veronesi, Giula, *Joseph Maria Olbrich*, Milan: Balcone, 1948

OLIVETTI FACTORY, BUENOS AIRES

Designed by Marco Zanuso; completed 1954

In 1954 Marco Zanuso was commissioned by Ariano Olivetti to design a factory to manufacture typewriters and calculators on a 123,000-square-meter triangular site in Merlo, on the periphery of Buenos Aires. Zanuso at the time was primarily known as an industrial designer who designed products for numerous Italian companies including Olivetti and who had been editor of the architectural publications *Domus* and *Casabella*. His products were exhibited at the Low-Cost Furniture show at the Museum of Modern Art in 1948, and his well-known chairs include the Atropus Chair and the Lady Chair.

The Buenos Aires Olivetti project was his first large-scale building and was used as a way to begin his architectural practice in earnest. It also allowed for him to further explore the issues of building as product and structure as service, transforming the concept of the "machine for living" to a "machine for working" and initiating Zanuso's investigation of the transference between industrial design and architecture from the small component to the larger complex building. This exemplified his treatment of a building as a large-scaled machine. The project also allowed him to pursue ideas of relating the buildings to the open landscape, creating a harmony between the civic and the natural. Viewed as an industrial product, the building elements became the points of design innovation.

In following the research of the Olivetti production team, the building was required to contain light industrial processing under a 25,000-meter-square roof in a closed production sequence but with a structure that would allow for expandability at each side for the company's future growth. Zanuso chose a repeatable module of 18 by 12 meters to develop the building on the vast site with a grand axis for central interior distribution. The plan of the building consisted of the main entrance that led to a classroom, a dining room, and an infirmary and changing rooms opposite the administrative and technical offices, which opened onto the main manufacturing floor. Beyond was the L-shaped central assembly room connected to the plant and maintenance room at the periphery of the site. The zones between the work areas and leisure areas were separated to create a transition point as a place of social interaction. This could be seen in the microcosm of the factory as the place of consumption versus that of production. There was little division between the head offices and the plant, so the space had a potential flexibility. A heat and electric plant was built separately from the main facility, and outside the complex, Olivetti built housing for the workers.

The one-story factory had few but very dominant and innovative design concepts. One was the tubular hollow concrete girder system containing the air conditioning and air circulation. Four-pronged lightweight and highly articulated concrete columns equally spaced apart supported the hollow ovoid shaped girders, which in turn supported the roof structure. Between the columns, glazed walls rose to the height of the shed and were set back from the roof line, creating a much needed brise-soleil. The sheds opened to interior courtyards that separated the assembly from the main hall.

The concrete construction technique was new with steel cables twisted in spirals as a helical metal cage around which the concrete was poured and stabilized by this internal system. Other columns were prefabricated and brought to the site. The columns kept the ground open with many distribution points for power and energy, and they created a vertical union between the transmission elements underground and from the central heating plant that passed along the side of the structural system

and the length of the hollow columns. Inside the hollow girder, air exchanges and technical cables created a coordinated system between structure, physical plant, and architectural details.

The main thrust of the building was the mechanical system invented by Zanuso, who described the building as a living organism, with the life-support elements distributed through hollow beams that are also structural. This guided the articulation of the air flow spaces and those protected zones, emphasizing differences between production and rest. The unique air conditioning systems for the microclimate transformed the building into a machine or technical box integrated into the building design. The system was made of two parts: one was fitted out in a body shop in sheet metal and the casing was built in a metal and varnished. This long-beam system became the standard system for all the Olivetti projects in Argentina. The technical elements became architectonic forms that influenced the early concepts of a "high-tech" architecture, where the pieces of the buildings are functional not only as systems of support but as the internal plant, electrical systems, and organs of the building. The flexibility proved itself later, as partitions could be moved to change the space, and it was eventually adapted by a cigarette factory that could use the space without major alternations.

Zanuso treated the project as a large-scale industrial habitable object that emphasized his crossover between industrial designer and architect that was a key topic at the time, especially in Italy. This linked the mental process for creating highly functional industrial buildings to that of creating the industrial object.

NINA RAPPAPORT

Further Reading

Burkhardt, Francois, *Marco Zanuso*, Motta Editor, 1999
Guiducci, Roberto, "Casabella continuita," *Di Marco Zanuso a Buenos Aires*, 229 (1959)

OLYMPIC GAMES SPORTS ARENA, TOKYO 1964

Designed by Kenzo Tange and others; completed 1964

Kenzo Tange, together with Yoshikatsu Tsuboi, structural engineer, and Uichi Inoue, mechanical engineer, designed Japan's national gymnasium for the 18th Olympic Games. The construction began in 1963 and was completed in time for the Olympics of the fall of 1964. It consists of two arenas. The main arena, seating about 15,000 spectators, was for swimming competitions and is convertible for ice-skating or floor activities when concrete slabs are slid over the pools. The smaller arena of about 4,000 seats was initially for wrestling, and other possible activities including basketball. A low, linear block of building with administrative offices and restaurants runs between the two arenas as if to mediate their strong and independent forms.

The two arenas employ tensile structure in which cables bear the load of the roofs. This structural system allows an expansive interior space devoid of load-bearing columns or walls. This type of structure had been carried out in other countries, including the exhibition hall (1953) in Raleigh, North Carolina, by Matthew Nowicki; the Philips Pavilion (1958) at the World's Fair in Brussels, by Le Corbusier; and the Yale University hockey rink (1958) in New Haven, Connecticut, by Eero Saarinen.

Tange's design is a mature application of this system, realizing not only the largest spans ever but also a form convincing and even reflective of Japanese tradition and spirit.

The main arena's primary structural elements are two main steel cables, each of which is made of 37 ropes to achieve a high-tension capability. These cables are anchored to the two concrete blocks on the ground level at the two ends of the building. The two tall concrete posts carry the cables to about 27.5 meters from the ground. The specially designed steel pieces were placed in these concrete posts in order to allow the main cables to turn in both axial and oblique directions. The subordinate cables, each of which is connected to a main cable at one end and anchored to the reinforced-concrete stands at the other, carry the weight of the roof. Steel ring joints allow flexible connection between the main and subordinate cables. The result is geometry of rotational symmetry along the axis line between the two posts and the two anchor blocks. The smaller arena, in comparison, is in a spiral shape with the cables radiating from its single post. In both buildings, visually dominant from outside as well as inside are the sweeping curves of this suspension structure. Particularly notable in this regard is the main arena's interior illumination. The two main cables, pulled apart by the weight of the side roofs, create an almond-shaped void, which was then turned into the source of both natural and artificial light. It gives a sense of axis to the interior space, which coincides with the direction of the swimming lanes. The result is a successful synthesis of structural system, formal order, and the use of space.

Tange's prior and concurrent contemplative quests on architecture are reflected on his arena design, particularly in regard to the role of Japanese building traditions within modern building. The successful realization of this quest placed Tange's work in the critical position against the modernists' banner of mere functionalism. Tange had previously been involved in what was called "The Debate on Tradition" (*Dento Ronso*) with other architects and critics, writing magazine articles and designing, for example, the Kagawa Prefecture Government Office. In the latter building, the posts and beams of traditional wooden structure were replicated in form in concrete construction. At the time of the stadium design, Tange was coauthoring a book on Ise, Japan's Shito Shrine. In the case of Olympic Stadium, Tange's efforts were not so much to imitate traditional buildings' forms but to create, using the most progressive building technology, a communicative space that allows the users, both athletes and spectators, to have an exhilarating experience. For Tange, this was the kind of symbolism appropriate to contemporary society.

The complex is laid along a north-south orientation that parallels the main axis of the Meiji Shrine nearby. The rooftop of the low, linear building between the two arenas serves as the multilevel pedestrian passages from nearby train stations. As a result, the spectators enter the gymnasium from the upper level and descend to their seats looking down to the event floor as well as looking up to the sweeping ceiling. The singularity of the interior space, with no columns or walls to interrupt the vision, allows the sense of unity among the spectators as well as the sense of empathy between the athletes and spectators.

Tokyo Olympic Stadium played the decisive role in placing Tange's work on the international stage. He had already been recognized as one of Japan's top architects when he designed Hiroshima Peace Hall (1949) and Kagawa Prefecture Govern-

ment Office Building (1955–58). He had held the prestigious position of a professor of architecture at the University of Tokyo. Engaging the international audience for the Olympic games, Tange's stadium brought opportunities for his works to be publicized widely in the international scenes. The Olympic Committee awarded an Olympic Diploma of Merit to Tange, the first architect to receive this honor. The Royal Institute of British Architects awarded its Gold Medal in 1965, and the American Institute of Architects Gold Medal followed in 1966, both of which were based primarily on the stadium design. Tange's career was to be further elaborated in the coming decades, his quests were to continue in a number of topics, and celebrated records of honors were to continue, including the Pritzker Architecture Prize of 1987. Yet this stadium design continues to be at one of the culmination points of Tange's opus and of 20th-century architecture at large.

UMIKO HANDA

Further Reading

Tange, Kenzo, "From Architecture to Urban Design," *Japan Architect* (May 1967)
Tange, Kenzo, "Recollection: Architect Kenzo Tange 6," *Japan Architect* (September 1985)
Tange, Kenzo, and Noboru Kawazoe, *Ise: Nihon kenchiku no genkei*, Tokyo: Asahi Shinbunsha, 1962; as *Ise: Prototype of Japanese Architecture*, Cambridge, Massachusetts: MIT Press, 1965
Tange, Kenzo, and Noboru Kawazoe, *Gijutsu to Ningen* (Technology and Man), Tokyo: Bijutsu Shuppansha, 1968
Tange, Kenzo, and Udo Kultermann, *Kenzo Tange, 1946–1969: Architecture and Urban Design; Architektur und Städtebau; Architecture et urbanisme* (trilingual English-German-French edition), Zurich: Verlag für Architektur Artemis, New York: Praeger, and London: Pall Mall Press, 1970

OPEN-AIR SCHOOL, THE NETHERLANDS

Designed by Johannes (Jan) Duiker; completed 1930
Amsterdam, the Netherlands

The Open-Air School (*openluchtschool*) in Amsterdam, the Netherlands, was designed and constructed between 1927–30. Conceptualized by Johannes (Jan) Duiker (1890–1935), it was a response to the necessity of providing a healthier and more therapeutic educational alternative for feeble children.

Developed during the new movement known as functionalism, it was a marriage between the dichotomous rational and spiritual philosophies or *esprit nouveau,* while retaining its functionality. This movement decried the importance of hygiene with designs that were spacious and allowed the most possible light and air.

After graduating from Delft University of Technology, Duiker worked in the office of his former professor, Henri Evers, architect of the Rotterdam City Hall, along with fellow student and future partner, Bernhard Bijvoet. Duiker's burgeoning career was initially influenced by Evers, Hendrik Petrus Berlage (1856–1934) and the Amsterdam School, and the American architect, Frank Lloyd Wright (1867–1959); and later affected by the developing International Style and the *Nieuwe Bouwen* movement. Because influence to Duiker's evolving career can be attributed to a cacophony of individuals and the era's incipient movements, including the De Stijl, he essentially developed his own design philosophy and aesthetic that employed the use of new building materials and methods in the integration of architecture and science.

This functionalist idiom became stronger and more expressive as his style developed. The dissonance between simplistic and complex avant-garde architecture created by his quest for an ideal structural form was influential enough to have inspired Ludwig Mies van der Rohe's (1886–1969) Tuberculosis Sanatorium at Paimio (1929–33). Sadly, between his limited design repertoire, due to his early death at age 45, and the demolition of much of his built architecture, his life, career, and legacy have become increasingly obscure, slowly deteriorating the recognition of his prominence in the Dutch modern movement. Fortunately, the work that garnered him the earliest and greatest visibility, the Zonnestraal Sanatorium (1926–31) in Hilversum, was auspiciously restored and is still extant.

Following the success of the Zonnestraal Sanatorium, the Open-Air School was designed to also reflect Duiker's propensity for natural and therapeutic architecture. The non-residential Open-Air School in Amsterdam began conceptually with Jan Duiker and Bernard Bijvoet on 12 May 1927. This proposal gave Duiker, without Bijvoet, the commission for an *openluchtschool voor het gezonde kind* (open-air school for the healthy child) and has become known as one of his most characteristic and significant buildings.

The first design concept was a cruciform-shaped plan, the main axis rising three stories. With the exact location not yet defined and the layout not optimally designed, it was soon modified. The original proposed site was one block to the east of its present location, was one-half the size, and was sited amid parkland fronting Cliostraat. Project subsidies were unavailable and as a result, the parkland concept was abandoned. After a zoning modification, a revised design presented the modern freestanding structure in the central courtyard of a perimeter block, bounded by Rubens Straat, Anthonie V. Duckstraat, Quinten Massus Straat, and Cliostraat, as it is today.

Five other variants were developed for the school as well as four proposals for the gateway entrance block. Some of the most significant changes within these proposals led to the creation of the extant structure. First, in contrast to its immediate surroundings, the building was rotated 45 degrees, creating a diagonal juxtaposition to the linear and perpendicular forms of the perimeter block. Second, the concrete structural elements were moved from the building's corners to the center of each quadrant edge, producing an open, cantilevered corner and creating a delicate floating appearance that allowed for attenuated window and door frames and large expanses of glass. Finally, a reduction in

Open-Air School, school complex facade (1930), Amersterdam, Netherlands. Designed by Jan Duiker (1930)
Photo © Elisabeth A. Bakker-Johnson

the number of outdoor classrooms as well as their locations were also modified. Influenced by Wright's "beyond the building," detailed design approach, Duiker also designed special study tables that complemented the architecture.

Like an island of modernism surrounded by a sea of Dutch vernacular, the Open-Air School is the antithesis of its environs. Its slender concrete skeleton with large expanses of glass are in sharp contrast to the adjacent solid dark brick residential masses, producing an open and free educational environment true to its name.

In floor plan, the overall four-story cube can be divided into four quadrants surrounding a central core stair tower. The east and west quadrants house the classrooms; the north is a void, and the south-facing quadrant contains the open-air terraces, essentially a hybrid between the solid and void. Attached to the east quadrant stands a one-story gymnasium. The building's location in the northern end of the courtyard allows the most available sunlight onto the south-facing open-air terraces.

The portal, or entrance into the courtyard, consists of a column-supported narrow passage connecting flanking spaces, the largest to the east being a three-story concrete, steel, and glass unit with small-railed balconies. This gateway closes the void created by the two ends of the circumscriptive perimeter block. Access is currently restricted by a chain-link fence, but it was once open and inviting.

Critics have consistently lamented the school's obscured location as well as the contrast between its open air, free design intent and its restricted, urban reality. Because of its close proximity to the neighboring residences, there is a marked lack of privacy for both assemblages. Also, it is felt that later alterations, albeit small, have destroyed the overall sculptural quality of the complex.

Nevertheless, the functional modern aesthetic of simple elegant design and lightweight construction creates an ethereal educational atmosphere with the freedom of light, air, and space maximized, remaining true to its original intent. Although the school's site may be ill suited, the Zonnestraal Sanatorium and the Open-Air School cultivated Duiker's design philosophy, where he subsequently produced other architecturally significant structures including Nirwana Flats in The Hague and the Scheveningen School. This series of outstanding examples would ultimately lead to the Cineac News Theater (Amsterdam), Magazijn Winter (Amsterdam), and the Gooiland Hotel (Hilversum). Still functionally extant, the Open-Air School is a significant modernist example and a transitional, while symbolic structure in Duiker's individual career and limited design repertoire.

ELISABETH A. BAKKER JOHNSON

See also **Berlage, Hedrick Petrus (Netherlands); Duiker, Johannes (Netherlands); Modernism; Wright, Frank Lloyd (United States); Zonnestraal Sanatorium, Hilversum**

Further Reading

A fairly comprehensive, albeit brief, history of Duiker and his architectural accomplishments can be found in Molema (1989). Derwig (1995), Ibelings (1995), and Overy (1991) offer insight into the stylistic developments of the period.

Derwig, Jan, *Functionalisme in Nederland* (*Functionalism in the Netherlands*), Amsterdam: Architectura & Natura, 1995
Ibelings, Hans, *20th Century Architecture in the Netherlands,* Rotterdam: Netherlands Architecture Institute, 1995
Leuthäuser, Gabriele and Peter Gössel, *Funktionale architektur, 1925–1940* (*Functional Architecture: The International Style, 1925–1940*), translated by John Bannister and Karen Williams, Köln: B. Taschen, 1990
Molema, Jan, *Jan Duiker: Obras y proyectos* (*Jan Duiker: Works and Projects*). Rotterdam: Uitgeverij 010, 1989
Molema, Jan and Peter Bak, *Jan Gerko Wiebenga: apostel van het Nieuwe Bouwen* (*Jan Gerko Wiebenga: An Apostle of the New Buildings Movement*), Rotterdam: Uitgeverij 010, 1987
Overy, Paul, *De Stijl,* New York: Thames and Hudson, 1991

ORDINANCES: DESIGN

The incorporation of design codes and guidelines into ordinances covering urban redevelopment has a long history. Their purpose, whether used by a public agency or a private developer, has generally been to ensure the build-out of a master development plan at a consistent level of quality and detail. An important secondary use has been to control the appearance of new development in relation to the historic urban fabric of an area.

In Paris, for example, during the reign of Louis XIV, building regulations required that all new buildings respect the street alignment and specified details such as the solid-to-void ratio of building facades, the continuity of eaves lines from one building to the next, and the depth of courtyards in the building plans (Nan Ellin, *Postmodern Urbanism*, revised edition, 1999). Whereas this level of aesthetic control has remained common to varying degrees across several European countries, American urban development has historically been far less constricted.

In the United States, the powers of government to control private development have been much more limited than in European countries and have rarely extended beyond the zoning of land according to use. Issues of design have been restricted to specifying the placement of buildings in relation to parking, landscape requirements, and so on.

One of the earliest American examples of design affecting zoning ordinances dates from 1916 in New York. These regulations followed German models in constraining the bulk of skyscrapers rising directly from the line of the street by limiting their height and mandating setbacks at specific levels above ground level in order to ease the overshadowing of public streets and adjacent buildings. The architectural illustrator Hugh Ferris rendered these ordinances into three-dimensional forms in his famous series of drawings titled "Zoning Envelopes: First through Fourth Stages," first published in *The New York Times* in 1922. This zoning law was not replaced until 1961, when new ordinances were enacted on the basis of different design ideas.

The 1961 New York ordinance was based on the modernist design concept of the tower surrounded by open space. Models for this new ordinance—buildings such as the Seagram Building (1958) by Mies van der Rohe and Philip Johnson—were simple vertical boxes positioned well back from the street with an intervening plaza. Residential ordinances in the city followed the same pattern, and these regulations became a prototype for similar ordinances in cities across the United States.

These codes virtually eliminated the traditional idea of the street as a linear public space defined by the walls of buildings, and not until the 1980s did cities such as New York, Pittsburgh, and San Francisco lead a revisionist trend in urban design, bringing back requirements for streets and plazas defined by continuous "street walls" of building facades.

Typical of these new zoning codes during the 1980s and 1990s have been a proliferation of "urban design guidelines" attached to, or parallel with, zoning categories. Such guidelines spell out criteria that developers and their architects are obliged to follow in developing their designs. These criteria include street width and building height, volumetric massing, percentages and arrangements of glazed areas in building facades, entrances and storefronts at sidewalk level, and landscaping provisions to streets and sidewalks.

This approach to regulating the urban environment would not be possible without the rise, dating from the late 1960s, of the new discipline of "urban design." Specifically designed to fill the gap between architecture and planning, urban design extends the two dimensions of planning—zoning areas on a map—into three-dimensional form and space. Urban design is concerned primarily with the spaces between buildings and the relationships of buildings to the urban infrastructure of space, transportation, and utilities.

One of the most innovative attempts to code the urban environment was developed in the 1960s by the English urban designer Gordon Cullen. Under the title "Notation," Cullen developed the "HAMS Code" (Humanity, Artifacts, Mood, and Space), in which he used a system of symbols and numeric values both to record the content and quality of an existing urban setting and then to orchestrate future urban development by means of a notational system that he likened to a musical score. In this analogy, the urban designer became the conductor, and individual architects for individual projects played the role of musicians, interpreting their parts of the melody within the overall arrangement. This approach has overtones of Camillo Sitte's view, expressed in his 1889 book *City Planning According to Artistic Principles*, that architects "should compose the city like a Beethoven symphony." (Sitte's work was reprinted in full with detailed commentary by George R. Collins and Christiane Crasemann Collins in *Camillo Sitte and the Birth of Modern City Planning*, 1965; revised edition, 1986.)

Although unsuccessful in terms of wide acceptance, Cullen's method of coding towns and cities informed his own influential work. His bias toward the reinterpretation of traditional urban forms and spaces—what he referred to as "Townscape"—boosted the rise of neotraditional planning practices during the following decades. The influential design code manual *A Design Guide for Residential Areas*, prepared for the County Council of Essex in England by Melvin Dunbar and others (1973), is a direct descendant of Cullen's work and is a model for many similar ordinances in England.

Ordinances in the United States during the post–World War II period that governed suburban development mandated the classification of buildings by single-use categories (residential, retail, office, and so on) and the separation in open space of these buildings, set back from streets and surrounded by private parking.

However, just as the design ordinances for central cities were being revised in the 1980s to incorporate traditional concepts of defined urban spaces, urban designers began to examine suburban environments from similar viewpoints, seeking to ameliorate the bland appearance and environmental degradation of suburban areas.

In the United States, the 1980s and 1990s saw the rise of "neotraditional" design under the rubrics of Traditional Neighborhood Development, Transit-Oriented Development, and later New Urbanism. This approach to the design and planning of towns and cities formed a radical critique of conventional planning and zoning, reorganizing sprawling suburbs into coherent urban neighborhoods in a more environmentally sensitive manner.

However, one of the main obstacles faced by New Urbanist architects and planners to the implementation of their ideas is the fact that most aspects of this traditionally based urbanism are illegal under most American zoning ordinances developed after World War II. The solution of these designers has been to rewrite development ordinances on the basis of models of traditional urban design and to implement these as parallel or substitute zoning regulations.

Simplified graphic diagrams and dimensions deal explicitly with the scale, massing, and placement of buildings; the organization of parking; and the design of streets, parks, and squares. This coding of development in easy-to-understand pictorial formats was first developed by Andres Duany and Elizabeth Plater-Zyberk in their design for the new town of Seaside (1981). The "Seaside Code" has provided a model for similar design-based ordinances across the United States.

In privately controlled developments, these private codes can specify detail in terms of architectural style, materials, and construction (e.g. Seaside and Celebration [1995], the latter a new town near Orlando, Florida, financed by the Disney Corporation). However, in normal suburban contexts, where municipal zoning controls development, state laws usually restrict the ability of municipalities to control this level of detail, and during the 1990s much work focused on marrying the concepts and practices of the New Urbanist design codes with the full complexity of public zoning ordinances for towns and cities.

This has led to the development of "parallel codes," by which a set of New Urbanist ordinances is established as the preferred option for development but that leaves the old sprawl-producing regulations in place as a matter of political expediency, and, more radically, to the creation of full zoning ordinances based on undiluted New Urbanist design principles. One accessible example of both types of municipal codes can be found in the three contiguous North Carolina towns of Davidson, Cornelius, and Huntersville, an area of 100 square miles where New Urbanist zoning ordinances were enacted in 1995 and 1996.

Such ordinances indicate a change from conventional zoning, which has been predicated on building use as the main criterion for organizing urban development. Instead, these design-based codes operate on the principle that buildings and spaces outlast their original uses and that regulations should be based on good design criteria rather than transient activities. Accordingly, the creators of such new regulations analyze examples of successful urbanism, either from history or from detailed design studies, and then encode these models into three-dimensional envelopes of urban form and public space that become the vocabulary for building towns and cities. A range of uses is then allowed within these various typologies, with the emphasis on mixing compatible uses rather than separating them.

DAVID WALTERS

Further Reading

The primary sources for design ordinances are the codes themselves. The most famous codes in America are the ordinances for the private new towns of Seaside and Celebration, in Florida. Other ordinances noted exemplify the various types of regulatory documents typically in use in North American practice.

Barnett, Jonathan, *The Fractured Metropolis: Improving the New City, Restoring the Old City, Reshaping the Region*, New York: Harper Collins, 1995

Burgess, Warren, et al., *The Third Ward Plan*, Charlotte, North Carolina: Charlotte/Mecklenburg Planning Commission, 1997

Calthorpe Associates, *Transit-Oriented Development Design Guidelines*, San Diego, California: City of San Diego, 1992

Cullen, Gordon, "Notation 1–4," *The Architects Journal (Supplements)* (31 May 1967, 12 July 1967, 23 August 1967, 27 September 1967)

Design Guide for Residential Areas, Chelmsford: Essex County Council, 1973; new edition, as *The Essex Design Guide for Residential and Mixed Use Areas,* Essex: Essex Planning Officers Association, 1997

Duany, Andres and Elizabeth Plater-Zyberk, "Urban Code: The Town of Seaside" in *Seaside: Making a Town in America*, edited by David Mohney and Keller Easterling, New York: Princeton Architectural Press, and London: Phaidon, 1991

Duany, Andres and Elizabeth Plater-Zyberk, "Codes" in *Towns and Town-Making Principles*, edited by Alex Kreiger and William Lennertz, New York: Rizzoli, 1991; 2nd edition, 1992

Hammond, Ann and David Walters, *Town of Huntersville Zoning Ordinance*, Huntersville, North Carolina: Town of Huntersville, 1996

Keane, Timothy and David Walters, *The Davidson Land Plan*, Davidson, North Carolina: Town of Davidson, 1995

Leich, Jean Ferriss, *Architectural Visions: The Drawings of Hugh Ferriss*, New York: Whitney Library of Design, 1980

Marshall, Macklin (editor), *Making Choices: Alternative Development Standards*, Toronto: Ontario Bookstore, 1995

ORDINANCES: ZONING

Zoning ordinances govern the function and form of land and the structures on that land and are part of a more encompassing system of regulations concerning the built environment that include subdivision controls, building codes, deeds, and housing occupancy codes, among many others. Unlike these other regulations, which apply uniformly throughout a city, zoning orders land into districts (zones) and assigns to each permitted uses (e.g. industrial, commercial, or residential) while detailing restrictions and other conditions (e.g. regarding height, bulk, density, size, and setback requirements).

This brief article covers the United States, where zoning is a far more local matter than in Europe, where it must conform more often to plans developed at higher levels of government.

Although legislated land use regulations in the United States go back to the time of the colonists in the early 17th century, the foundations for modern land use controls are nuisance cases from the 1800s, when the courts upheld restrictions on the uses of land deemed to threaten public health, safety, or morals. The actions were reactive rather than preventive and were oriented to the elimination of negative arrangements rather than to the establishment of positive ones.

In the late 19th century, the development of land use regulations was stimulated by several factors. First, there was a need for planning health and other basic public services for urban populations whose numbers were growing because of an unprecedented influx of immigrants. Further impetus came from technological factors—for example, the introduction of electric trolleys (promoting streetcar suburbs) as well as steel-frame construction and elevators (leading to high-density urban centers). At the turn of the century, sponsors of zoning included the Progressive reform movement, concerned with imposing restraints on undesirable urban development, as well as powerful real estate and business interests concerned with preserving property values and maximizing profits.

In 1916 New York City was the first to adopt a comprehensive zoning ordinance. It applied only to new development and thus did not address problems arising from existing conditions. Herbert Hoover's Advisory Committee on Building Codes and Zoning drafted the Standard State Zoning Enabling Act, published in 1924, which quickly became the model for similar legislation in many states. The annals of U.S. zoning history are replete with court cases documenting challenges to a local government's authority to exercise police power in the control of land uses. In 1926 the U.S. Supreme Court upheld the constitutionality of zoning in the case of *Village of Euclid, Ohio, v. Ambler Reality Co.* This milestone decision became an important reference point in comprehensive land use regulation for decades to come. By 1929 60 percent of the U.S. urban population lived in areas governed by zoning ordinances.

Although ostensibly targeting physical aspects of the environment, zoning has also been a frequent instrument in discriminatory practices aimed at preventing unwanted population groups from residing in particular neighborhoods. Certain zoning ordinances require minimum lot sizes for residential development, specify minimum house sizes, prohibit mobile homes or multifamily buildings, or impose unusually high subdivision standards. Intentionally or otherwise, such ordinances drive up the cost of housing and thus keep out low-income households, among whom racial and ethnic minorities are overrepresented. Known as exclusionary zoning, this practice is most common in affluent, suburban communities. Critics have decried it as a form of discrimination and a cause of reduced housing affordability and concentrated poverty in inner-city areas. They have challenged it in legislative and litigative actions. In this connection, the series of *Mount Laurel* cases, argued in the New Jersey Supreme Court (1975–86), became a landmark, establishing the doctrine that a municipality's land use regulations had to offer a "realistic opportunity for the construction of its fair share of the prospective and future regional need for low and moderate income housing." This doctrine was also adopted in other states (Arizona, California, and Oregon) but has been difficult to enforce. Exclusionary zoning is subject to federal law only if it violates the Fair Housing Act or the Fourteenth Amendment to the U.S. Constitution. In this regard, the U.S. Supreme Court has held that the equal protection clause does not apply to income (i.e. zoning that excludes the poor is not illegal) and that in the case of minorities it must be shown that discriminating purpose was a motivating factor. However, in cases brought under the Fair Housing Act, lower federal courts have held that discriminatory effect is enough.

Inclusionary zoning ordinances are meant to promote the provision of low-cost housing by allowing residential developers a higher density in return (so-called incentive zoning) or as a mandatory set-aside. Another technique is zoning for mobile homes, which are becoming more important as a source of affordable housing. Local governments may also target nonresidential developers, for example, in the form of a linkage program that makes permits for commercial building contingent on a specified funding percentage for low-cost housing.

Zoning is a tool of, but not a substitute for, planning. Zoning ordinances for local districts are intendedly developed within the context of a comprehensive plan for a larger region. However, zoning decisions frequently are politically motivated by desires to produce tax revenues, to exclude unwanted uses or population groups (the Not-In-My-Back-Yard [NIMBY] syndrome), and to preserve the status quo. The resulting configuration of commercial, industrial, residential, and other land uses often reflects the balance of power among competing local jurisdictions rather than what is best for the region as a whole.

WILLEM VAN VLIET

Further Reading

Cullingworth, J.B., *The Political Culture of Planning: American Land Use Planning in Comparative Perspective*, New York: Routledge, 1993

Haar, Charles Monroe and Jerold S. Kayden (editors), *Zoning and the American Dream: Promises Still to Keep*, Chicago: Planners Press, 1989

Mallach, Alan, *Inclusionary Housing Programs: Policies and Practices*, New Brunswick, New Jersey: Center for Urban Policy Research, 1984

Mandelker, Daniel R. and Roger A. Cunningham, *Planning and Control of Land Development: Cases and Materials*, Charlottesville, Virginia: Michie, 1990; 4th edition, 1995

Sies, Mary Corbin and Christopher Silver (editors), *Planning the Twentieth-Century American City*, Baltimore, Maryland: Johns Hopkins University Press, 1996

ORNAMENT

Ornamentation is a critical element in architecture demonstrating significant choices and intentions of the architect, including the selection of specific materials, the decision to include or exclude applied decoration, and the expression of symbolic meaning. During the 20th century, the significance of ornament in architecture was carefully considered by architects who experimented with, rejected, or created new forms and decoration to express attitudes toward or reactions against the incredible cultural and technological changes taking place in the world around them. The ideas introduced by Owen Jones (1809–74) in the middle of the 19th century, linking culture and architecture and advocating the use of ornament to enhance structure and evoke a new contemporary style, were repeated by some and rejected and fiercely debated by others.

Before the turn of the century, designers continued the historicism, eclecticism, and Beaux-Arts classicism of their predecessors, selecting conventional decorative elements to imbue a building with a particular character and associations. The ability of ornament to communicate specific values and stimulate expected emotional responses was clearly understood. As a result,

designers interested in producing a new style reflective of a changing world rejected the motifs of the past and experimented with new types of embellishment expressing acceptance of technological advances and the latest thinking. Art Nouveau (Jugendstijl) represents one of the earliest experiments, substituting new forms inspired by nature for traditional motifs. European designers, including Victor Horta, Hector Guimard, and Henry van de Velde, demonstrated the structural possibilities of iron and glass by developing thin, plantlike stalks with wispy whiplash curves to replace the staunch columns and solid lintels of masonry construction.

Exhibitions and the increase in architectural publications promoted a widespread interest in this novel style, and designers throughout the Western world became aware of the possibilities of creating additional styles and a new aesthetic through changes in form, materials, and decoration. This realization stimulated strong reactions and further experimentation. In an article titled "Ornament and Crime," the architect Adolf Loos condemned the use of ornamentation as wasteful, debased, and uncivilized. At the same time, Frank Lloyd Wright argued for simplified ornament adapted to machine production to achieve items of simple good taste for modern living. Examples of new styles introduced early in the century include a development in Holland, known as De Stijl (1918), and an international style nicknamed Art Deco, derived from abbreviating the title of the *Exposition Internationale des Arts Décoratifs et Industriels Modernes* (Paris, 1925). De Stijl displayed the direct influence of Cubism, introducing a vocabulary of forms including geometric shapes, orthogonal grids, and intersecting planes dynamically arranged in solids and voids and intersecting with continuous space. Traditional ornament was eliminated, replaced by simple elements painted in the primary colors or in black, white, and gray and finished to appear machine produced. Art Deco continued the celebration of mechanization with stylized, geometricized patterns fabricated in exotic woods and expensive metals. At the same time, designers in the Deutsche Werkbund and later in the Bauhaus focused on the production of everyday objects made from modern materials and industrialized components, such as ship railings and steel tubing, to elevate and enhance the design of mass-produced objects.

When Henry-Russell Hitchcock and Philip Johnson codified the Modern movement in the text accompanying the 1932 exhibition at the Museum of Modern Art in New York, they explained that one of the tenets of the International Style was the avoidance of applied decoration. Sophisticated architects, such as Ludwig Mies van der Rohe, understood the importance of ornamentation to enhance design and recognized the difference between elements used for decoration and those components necessary to produce designs of eloquence and expressiveness. As a result, he used exquisite materials, pure forms and proportions, and walls of clear glass to reveal the beauty of nature and achieve a level of refinement and modern elegance. At the same time, Mies and other modernists emphasized the expression of structure and highlighted the industrial components of construction. The most obvious example is Mies' attachment of I beams on the exterior of the Lake Shore Drive Apartments (1948) in Chicago. Following World War II, Ray and Charles Eames and other designers used standardized parts in their Case Study Houses in California in an attempt to produce both affordable and contemporary design; however, most architects and the general populace continued to prefer traditional design and ornament, both classical and vernacular.

Before World War II, another international phenomenon is observable in the influence of modernism on buildings with classically inspired ornament. Ironically, this phenomenon appeared in the symbolic structures erected to proclaim and serve the Fascist governments of Italy and Germany and the stripped-down classicism expressing economy and a modern aesthetic in the thousands of government buildings constructed and financed during the New Deal in the United States.

Reactions against the Modern movement began in the 1950s and 1960s with architects such as Louis Kahn continuing to use modern materials but shifting the focus of design to an increased emphasis on form, space, and light. In the works of Eero Saarinen, Jørn Utzon, and Kenzo Tange, the increased attention to form resulted in buildings seen as sculptural or ornamental objects in the landscape.

Robert Venturi joined the critique of the Modern movement by parodying Mies' dictum that "less is more" with his phrase "less is a bore." In *Complexity and Contradiction* (1966), Venturi praised architecture of earlier periods and promoted the importance of context, color, texture, and especially ornament in architecture. Venturi sanctioned a plurality of styles to bring back the visual vibrancy and life of earlier cities and to allow buildings to communicate with the public. As a result, architects, including Robert Stern, Charles Moore, and Charles Jencks, began to rely on ornament to introduce a new language of architecture and dialogue with the public. At times, their overscaled architectural elements contained witticisms and at other times irony, instigating confusion for a public and profession unaccustomed to ornament and uneducated in the original meanings of the elements being used. Consequently, "enlightened" Postmodernism did not receive universal acceptance, but it did initiate a new awareness of the importance of our built environment and a pluralistic diversity in design.

Subsequent developments have continued to respond to the function and visibility of ornament as a critical design component. For example, in deconstructivist and poststructuralist architecture, the assemblages of materials and shapes in the work of Peter Eisenman, Rem Koolhaas, and Eric Owen Moss are more ornamental than functional and are introduced for critique and aesthetic rather than as a display of new construction methods or new principles of structure. This is also true in the work of Frank Gehry, who does not espouse poststructuralism but produces assemblages of unconventional components and materials used in new ways, such as his specification of titanium for the surface covering of the Guggenheim Museum (1997) in Bilbao, Spain. New technology, materials, and methods of construction are expressed ornamentally in the High-Tech works of Norman Foster, Richard Rogers, Will Bruder, and others. At the same time, Postmodernism's acceptance of previous ideas and styles has prompted a renewed emphasis on classicism, allowing designers, including Quinlan Terry and Demetri Porphyrios, to continue the vocabulary and ornamentation of conventional architecture. Minimalist architects, such as Tadao Ando, Antoine Predock, and the late Luis Barragán, recognize that the avoidance of applied ornament can still make a powerful statement, and their works achieve a level of serenity and sublimity unusual in the overstimulated atmosphere of the late 20th century.

Today, a plurality of polemics and styles coexist, with no dominant position on the role of ornament and meaning in architecture established. A review of the century's built works, however, reveals the critical significance of ornament in both enhancing and articulating the form and expression of contemporary structure and ideas.

CAROL A. HRVOL FLORES

See also **Art Deco; Art Nouveau (Jugendstil); Barragán, Luis (Mexico); De Stijl; Deutscher Werkbund; Eisenman, Peter (United States); Foster, Norman (England); Guggenheim Museum, Bilbao, Horta, Victor (Belgium); International Exhibition of Decorative Arts, Paris (1925); International Style; International Style Exhibition, New York (1932); Kahn, Louis (United States); Koolhaas, Rem (Netherlands); Loos, Adolf (Austria); Mies van der Rohe, Ludwig (Germany); Symbolism; van de Velde, Henri (Belgium); Vienna Secession**

Further Reading

Fernie, Eric (editor), *Art History and Its Methods: A Critical Anthology*, London: Phaidon Press, 1995

Castel Beranger, Paris, front entry with wrought iron gate, designed by Hector Guimard (*c.*1890)
© Donna M. Matthews/GreatBuildings.com

Jameson, Fredric, *Postmodernism; or, The Cultural Logic of Late Capitalism*, Durham, North Carolina: Duke University Press, and London: Verso, 1991

Nesbitt, Kate (editor), *Theorizing a New Agenda for Architecture: An Anthology of Architectural Theory, 1965–1995*, New York: Princeton Architectural Press, 1996

Rose, Margaret, *The Post-Modern and the Post-Industrial*, Cambridge and New York: Cambridge University Press, 1991

Steele, James, *Architecture Today*, London: Phaidon Press, 1997

Wigley, Mark, *The Architecture of Deconstruction: Derrida's Haunt*, Cambridge, Massachusetts: MIT Press, 1993

OTTO, FREI 1925–

Architect, Germany

Frei Otto's contribution is much greater than his act of bringing the tent into the 20th century and making it part of the current architectural vocabulary would suggest. Not only did he highlight minimal lightweight structures in architecture as a liberating force and bridge to natural or organic form, but his formulation of membrane and cable-net surface and convertible structures, as well as lattice grid shells, led to the realization that they could be used to advance an adaptable and flexible approach to building. This had the additional property of optimizing the consumption of energy and materials while being more responsive to changing human requirements. He sought to apply economical lightweight solutions on a large scale to solve environmental and microclimatic adaptation in harsh regions in simple, ingenious ways.

In place of the artist–architect who creates from his imagination, Otto substituted automatic iterative processes to produce a series of structures from which he selected the fittest. Coincidentally, they were often the most beautiful. This is encapsulated in his operational phrase "form finding," a procedure whereby he classified structural shapes into systems and then chose one from among the many that best fit the task.

From 1931 to 1943, Otto attended Schadow School at Zehlendorf, Berlin, as a trainee mason. In World War II, he served as a fighter pilot in the German air force, an experience that unquestionably conditioned him to think in terms of lightweight solutions in architecture. At the end of a period of compulsory labor service, Otto studied architecture at the Technical University in Berlin under Freese, Bickenbach, and Jobst. Soon after this, he founded a studio at Zehlendorf (1952–58). Its activities were later transferred to Stuttgart, where Otto established his new Institute for Lightweight Structures. Otto worked closely with Peter Stroymeyer, a German tent manufacturer who, from the early years, served as both a client and a source of practical advice on tent fabrication techniques and design.

Historically, European urban tents were fabricated with a simple predetermined geometry; consequently, there was no need for architects or engineers to adopt a form-finding procedure. Otto broke with tent tradition and brought the tent into the 20th century by introducing more complex surface shapes that demanded a more sophisticated approach in determining their true shape. This happened in the 1950s, when the static analysis of complex surface structures was only beginning. Otto employed models to define and test the behavior of his shapes. Before the mid-1960s, his textile pavilions were made up of primary anticlastic saddle shapes arranged additively, often in repetitive symmetrical compositions.

The small Bundesgarten textile pavilions are among Otto's most elegant early constructions, both for their beauty and for their simplicity. The best are the riverside shelter and dance pavilion at Cologne (1957) and the small star pavilions at Hamburg (1963). These modest tent shelters integrated aesthetics with construction and display an unusual purity of conception that was rarely equaled in the later, larger, more technically elaborate structures that followed.

The German Pavilion of the Federal German Republic at Expo '67 (Montreal) represented a significant departure, being many times larger and having a picturesque combination of low funnel-shaped anchor points and eye-shaped cable-loop high points attached to masts in a deliberately asymmetrical configuration, suggesting the up-and-down physical terrain of Germany.

The restaurant pavilions at the Swiss National Exhibition at Lausanne (1964) introduced cable nets for the first time to strengthen and support a membrane. Prior to this, all Otto's roofs were fabricated from cotton canvas with modest spans of 20 to 30 meters. The Lausanne restaurant pavilions marked a new technical stage in modern tensile roofs, when they could be said to have come of age in their introduction of a new cable-net technology.

Otto's next great opportunity came after he was appointed roof design consultant by Gunter Behnisch, who won the competition for the main stadium and indoor arenas for the Munich Olympics (1972), with a scheme inspired by the Montreal German Pavilion. The Olympic roofs realized an entirely new scale for this type of structure, which stimulated the development of purely mathematical computer-based procedures to determine their exact dimensions, shape, and behavior in parallel with elaborate modeling techniques that allowed the new mathematical procedures to be cross-checked.

Otto's versatility and restless creativity led him to explore new types of systems and applications that exploited such unrecognized properties of tents as their flexibility and economical use of material to achieve new goals of adaptability and responsiveness to changing human and environmental needs. His convertible or retractable roofs are an instance of this. These roofs had a variable geometry that allowed them to be mechanically extended or retracted—in effect, they were converted into self-erecting and self-striking tents. A number of such convertible roofs were erected over swimming pools and sporting facilities in Germany, France, and elsewhere, but none proved so sculpturally captivating or appropriate, in contrast with the historical ruin that it covers, as the Open-Air Theater at Bad Hersfeld, Hessen (1968).

Following completion of the Munich Olympic roofs, Otto received a variety of commissions, including the delightful umbrella roofs at Cologne (1971); the roofs of the Conference Centre at Mecca, Saudi Arabia (1974); the timber-grid-shell Multi-Purpose Hall and Restaurant at Mannheim (1975); a sports complex and stadium at King Abdul Aziz University, Jeddah (1975–78); an aviary for Munich (1980); and the Diplomatic Club at Riyadh (1985).

Less active in the 1980s, Otto created a series of production pavilions for a German furniture manufacturer (1988) based on his IL test structure at Vaihingen, a series of inverted bowls for his German pavilion at the Seville Expo (1992), and a remarka-

Olympic Stadium, north concourse, Munich, Germany (1971)
© GreatBuildings.com

ble Gothic roof cover for the old shell of St. Nikolai Church, Hamburg (1988).

After 1972 Otto focused increasingly on the study and interpretation of biological structures, at the same time pursuing and extending his research into grid shells and other topics.

Otto must be ranked with Felix Candela, Richard Buckminster Fuller, and Pier Luigi Nervi as a structural innovator. He was responsible for bringing the tent into line with 20th-century structural and materials technologies and thereby creating a new range of flexible building types. He is less an architect in the conventional sense and much more an innovator and experimenter who worked in collaboration with other architects and structural researchers. His most unique creation was his Institute for Lightweight Structures at Vaihingen, which depended so much on his personal vision that it could not be continued without him. Because he was interested in minimal structures, Otto was driven to explore minimal lightweight structures in nature to further his objectives.

PHILIP DREW

Biography

Born in Siegmar, Saxony, 31 May 1925. Attended the Technische Universität, Berlin; degree in engineering 1952; doctorate in engineering 1954. Served in the German Air Force 1943–45; Prisoner of War, France 1945–47; prison camp architect, Depot 501, Chartres, France 1946–47. Private practice, Zehlendorf, Berlin 1952–58; adviser to L. Stromeyer and Company, Constance, West Germany 1953–74; founder, Development Center for Lightweight Construction, Berlin 1957; established architecture studio in Zehlendorf 1958–68; studio in Warmbronn, West Germany from 1968. Professor, director, Institute for Lightweight Structures, University of Stuttgart 1964–91; visiting professor, Washington University, St. Louis, Missouri 1958; visiting professor, Yale University, New Haven, Connecticut 1960; visiting professor, Massachusetts Institute of Technology and Harvard University, Cambridge 1962; visiting professor, University of Maracaibo, Venezuela 1962; visiting professor, National Institute of Design, Ahmedabad, India 1966; visiting professor, Ulm, West Germany 1969; visiting professor, International Summer Academy, Salzburg, Austria 1971. Honorary fellow, American Institute of Architects 1968; member, Akademie der Künste, Berlin 1970; honorary fellow, Royal Institute of British Architects 1982; member, Academia di Archaeologica, Lettere et Belle Arti, Naples 1983; member, Académie d'Architecture, Paris 1983; member, International Academy of Architecture, Sophia, Bulgaria 1987. Aga Khan Award for Architecture, with Rolf Gutbrod 1980.

Selected Works

Bundesgartenschau, dance floor tent, entrance canopy, and tent
 shelters, Cologne, 1957
Bundesgartenschau, undulating tent, membrane structure hall, and
 star hall, Hamburg, 1963
Snow and Rocks Restaurant Pavilion, Swiss National Exhibition,
 Lausanne, 1964
German Pavilion, Expo '67, Montreal, Canada (with Gutbrod and
 Leonhardt), 1967
Open-Air Theater with Retractable Roof, Bad Hersfeld, Germany
 (with Romberg and Bubner), 1968
Mobile Umbrella Roofs for Music Pavilion, Cologne, 1971
Olympic Stadium, Arenas, and Roofs, Munich (with Behnisch,
 Leonhardt, and Bubner), 1972
Hotel and Conference Center, Mecca, Saudi Arabia (with Arup and
 Gutbrod), 1974
Multi-Purpose Hall and Restaurant, Mannheim, Germany, 1975
Sports Hall, King Abdul Aziz University, Jeddah, Saudi Arabia (with
 Gutbrod, Henning, Arup, and Happold), 1978
Great Aviary, Hellabrunn, Germany (with Gribl and Happold),
 1980
Diplomatic Club, Riyadh, Saudi Arabia (with Omrania and
 Happold), 1985
Production Pavilions, Wilkhahn Furniture Factory, Bad Münder,
 Germany, 1988
Roof Cover, St. Nikolai Church, Hamburg, 1988
German Pavilion, Seville Exposition, 1992

Selected Publications

Das hängende Dach: Gestalt und Struktur, 1954
Zugbeanspruchte Konstruktionen (coeditor with R. Trostel and F.K.
 Schleyer), 2 vols., 1962, 1966; as *Tensile Structures: Design,
 Structure, and Calculation of Buildings of Cables, Nets, and
 Membranes*, translated by D. Ben-Yaakov and T. Pelz, 2 vols.,
 1967, 1969
IL-Publications (editor), 25 vols., 1969–85
Natürliche Konstuktionen (with others), 1982
Schriften und Reden, 1951–1983, edited by B. Burkhardt, 1984
*Gestaltwerdung: Zur Formentstehung in Natur, Technik, und
 Baukunst*, 1988

Further Reading

Frei Otto's principal publications in German are available in English
translations. His early reports from Entwicklungstätte für den Leichtbau
(EL) at Berlin-Zehlendorf, which commenced in January 1958, are
not generally available. The later IL-Publication series (see Selected
Publications) in 25 volumes that began publication in 1969 provides
valuable detailed technical reports of the form finding and modeling
procedures, as well as reporting presentations at colloquiums, at the
Instituts für leichte Flächentragwerke (IL), at the Universität Stuttgart,
at its site at Stuttgart-Vaihingen.

Doumato, Lamia, *Frei Otto's Tensile Structures: A Selected
 Bibliography*, Monticello, Illinois: Vance Bibliographies, 1979
Drew, Philip, *Frei Otto: Form und Konstruktion*, Stuttgart, Germany:
 Hatje, 1976; as *Frei Otto: Form and Structure*, London: Crosby
 Lockwood Staples, and Boulder, Colorado: Westview Press, 1976
Glaeser, Ludwig, *The Work of Frei Otto*, New York: Museum of
 Modern Art, 1972
Roland, Conrad, *Frei Otto—Spannweiten: Ideen und Versuche zum
 Leichtbau*, Berlin: Ullstein, 1965; as *Frei Otto: Tension Structures*,
 translated by C.V. Amerongen, London: Longman, and New
 York: Praeger, 1970
Schanz, Sabine, *Frei Otto, Bodo Rasch: Gestalt finden: auf dem Weg
 zu einer Baukunst des Minimalen: der Werkbund zeigt Frei Otto,
 Frei Otto zeigt Bodo Rasch: Ausstellung in der Villa Stuck,
 München, anlässlich der Preisverleihung des Deutschen Werkbundes
 Bayern 1992 an Frei Otto und Bodo Rasch*, Stuttgart, Germany:
 Axel Menges, 1995; as *Frei Otto, Bodo Rasch: Finding Form:
 Towards an Architecture of the Minimal: The Werkbund Shows
 Frei Otto, Frei Otto Shows Bodo Rasch: Exhibition in the Villa
 Stuck, Munich, on the Occasion of the Qward of the 1992
 Deutscher Werkbund Bayern Prize to Frei Otto and Bodo Rasch*,
 Stuttgart, Germany: Axel Menges, 1995
Teague, Edward H., *Frei Otto: A Bibliography and Building List*,
 Monticello, Illinois: Vance Bibliographies, 1985

OUD, J.J.P. 1890–1963

Architect, the Netherlands

In the 1930s, architecture critics on both sides of the Atlantic
were hailing the apostles of the International Style: Le Corbusier,
Walter Gropius, Mies van der Rohe, and the Dutchman J.J.P.
Oud. There is no question that Oud was an important figure
in modern architecture, yet in a 57-year career he undertook
only 90 projects, less than half of which were realized. Just five
were outside the Netherlands, and only one of those was built.

Oud began his studies in 1903 at the Quellinus School of
Decorative Arts in Amsterdam. Three years later, he designed
his first building: a house for a relative in his native Purmerend.
In 1907, under pressure from his father, he began to study architecture, finding work as a draftsman in the office of Joseph
Cuypers and Jan Stuijt. In May 1908 he left them to enroll at
the National School for Drawing Education, where in 1910 he
was awarded the Structural and Mechanical Engineering Drafting Diploma; he augmented his studies with various courses at
the Delft Institute of Technology. In 1912 Oud worked briefly
in the Munich office of Theodor Fischer (who was then engaged
in public housing and urban redevelopment) and attended Fischer's lectures at the Munich Polytechnic.

Oud returned to Holland enthusiastic about an architecture
based on new construction and materials, but his practice in
Purmerend produced only a few vernacular buildings: the Voor-
uit Laborers' Association premises (1911), the Schinkel Cinema
(1912), and a house (1912) in Aalsmeer. In 1913 Oud moved
to Leiden, but he found little work until, in 1915–16, he designed the Leiderdorp housing estate with Willem Marinus
Dudok.

In 1916 Oud met the painter-critic Theo van Doesburg and,
together with architects Jan Wils and Bart van der Leck and
expatriate Hungarian painter Vilmos Huszár, founded the De
Sphinx art club. Soon, joined by philosopher Anthony Kok and
painter Piet Mondrian, they formed the loose-knit group of
avant-garde artists known as De Stijl. For varying periods over
the next decade, others came and went. Membership seems to
have consisted of writing for the polemical journal *De Stijl*, edited by van Doesburg; between 1918 and 1920, Oud published
seven pieces. However, he did not sign De Stijl's November
1918 manifesto, finally withdrawing from the group in 1921
because, like all the rest, he fell out with van Doesburg.

Meanwhile, they collaborated on several projects, including
the Allegonda villa (1917) at Katwijk aan Zee and the De Vonk
holiday house (1917) at Noordwijkerhout. Van Doesburg's role

was limited to color schemes and stained-glass windows. The association ended in 1919, when Oud disagreed about colors for a public housing scheme. Oud also expounded on Frank Lloyd Wright's work for De Stijl as well as the European architectural community. Unlike his De Stijl colleagues Wils and Robert van 't Hoff, he was interested more in Wright's technology than in his philosophy. Oud had known about Wright since 1912, but his work showed none of the American's influence until some unrealized projects—concrete low-income houses (1918) and industrial buildings (1918–19) for his father's Purmerend distillery—echoed Wrightian forms. Although Oud thought that Wright's architecture was "flawless," he accurately predicted widespread, ill-informed imitation.

In 1918 Oud became the Rotterdam municipality's chief housing architect. His bland schemes in the Spangen (1919–20) and Tusschendijken (1920–23) districts of Rotterdam led observers to conclude that he was a socially concerned architect. He later denied that motive, stating that he simply sought "a good and agreeable form for [the housing] . . . as exact and as clear as the form of a good car." Those words point to a change of path. Oud read Le Corbusier's *Vers Une Architecture* (1923) soon after it was published, and his subsequent work demonstrates its immediate effect. His worker's row houses (1924–27)—brick disguised as concrete—in Hoek van Holland

and his "dwelling Fords" (1925–29) in Rotterdam's Kiefhoek are stuccoed white cubes. Neither scheme hinted at Wright or De Stijl. Indeed, Oud's only references to the latter can be found in the Rotterdam Witte Dorp site office (1923) and the Café De Unie facade (1925), both in Rotterdam.

Oud's reputation as a modernist was established in 1927 by a "model dwelling"—another row of white boxes—for the Stuttgart Weissenhofsiedlung exhibition. Thereafter, largely through his frenetic self-publicity, he was applauded in Europe and especially in America as a leader of what Henry-Russell Hitchcock and Philip Johnson dubbed the International Style. Johnson later asserted that Oud inspired him to become an architect. He commissioned the Hollander to design a house (1931) for his parents, but it was never built.

After about 1928, Oud's anxiety about fame, combined with his workload, plunged him into depression for several years. He accepted few commissions, and fewer were realized—notably, a church (1928–29) at Kiefhoek and some furniture after 1931. Public housing proposed for Blijdorp, Rotterdam, in 1931 remained unbuilt. The breakdown interrupted his career for almost a decade and changed his destiny.

Oud's career limped through the 1930s. In 1933 he resigned his post to concentrate on private practice. Three years later, he was offered a Harvard professorship but declined it, and Gropius

Netherlands Exhibition Hall, main entrance from west (1969)
© GreatBuildings.com

was appointed. Only some interiors of the liner Nieuwe Amsterdam (1937) and a new headquarters (1938–42) for the Shell Company in The Hague were realized. For the Shell building, Oud chose again to embrace ornament, and when his former American devotees saw photographs of it after World War II, they immediately consigned him to the scrap heap, accusing him of compromising modernist principles.

Oud's last major project, a National Congress Center in The Hague, begun in 1956, was unfinished at his death. Nothing distinguishes it as his or even as Holland's. His slender oeuvre reveals him as a seeker after architectural truth in the Dutch vernacular and in the work of Wright and, because he was eager for recognition, in the anonymous, austere forms of Western European objectivity. Perhaps in the Shell building, he found it in being true to himself.

DONALD LANGMEAD

See also **Amsterdam Netherlands; Corbusier, Le (Jeanneret, Charles-Édouard) (France); De Stijl; Doesburg, Theo van (the Netherlands); the Netherlands; Rotterdam, the Netherlands; Weissenhofsiedlung, Deutscher Werkbund (Stuttgart 1927)**

Selected Publications

Building and Teamwork, Rotterdam: privately published, 1951
Mein Weg in "De Stijl," The Hague: Nijgh en Van Ditmar, 1958
Holländische Achitektur, Munich: Langen, 1926; as *Hollandse Architectuur*, translated into German from the Dutch, Nijmegen, The Netherlands: Socialistiese Uitgeverj Nijmegen, 1983

Further Reading

Barbieri, Umberto, *J.J.P. Oud*, Bologna: Zanechelli, 1986
Langmead, Donald, *J.J.P. Oud and the International Style: A Bio-bibliography*, Westport, Connecticut: Greenwood, 1999
Oud, Hans, *J.J.P. Oud: Architekt, 1890–1963*, The Hague: Nijgh en Van Ditmar, 1984
Taverne Ed and Dolf Broekhuizen, *Het shell-gebouw van J.J.P. Oud: Ontwerp en receptie; Oud's Shell Building: Design and Reception* (bilingual Dutch–English edition), Rotterdam: NAI Uitgevers, 1995

OUR LADY OF PEACE BASILICA

Designed by Pierre Fakhoury; completed 1989
Yamoussoukro, Ivory Coast

Our Lady of Peace Basilica in Yamoussoukro, Ivory Coast, was designed by the Lebanese-Ivorian-French architect Pierre Fakhoury for the late President Houphouët-Boigny, who donated the edifice as a personal gift to the Roman Catholic Church on 9 and 10 September 1990. With an appraised price tag of U.S.$150 to $300 million (15 percent of the Ivory Coast national budget in 1987), this personal gift to Pope John Paul II holds a unique position in the history of architecture. Built in three years (1986–89), it is taller than St. Peter's dome in Rome, which can fit within it. Unlike its contemporary, the Hassan II Mosque, which could not be seen from a distance in the center of Casablanca, Our Lady of Peace Basilica could be seen from the center of the town of Yamoussoukro. The visibility of its 300-ton silver dome from a long distance encourages a curious spatial interaction between a pedestrian and the monument.

The fact that out of an estimated total national population of 12.91 million only about 10 percent are Catholics makes it difficult to justify a Roman Catholic church on the scale of Our Lady of Peace Basilica at Yamoussoukro. When the national population data are broken down according to religious preferences, the scale of the project raises issues of social justice and power dynamics between Catholics and Christians of other denominations as well as among Moslems and people who believe in other religions. For example, 27.5 percent of the total population of the country is Christian, 40 percent is Moslem, 17 percent is ancestor worshipers, and the remaining 16 percent might believe in nothing or in other religions.

Francois Mathey (1990), chief conservator of the Ivorine Museum of Fine Arts, suggests that what one experiences at Yamoussoukro is an illusion that "Rome . . . is no longer in Rome, but Rome is in Yamoussoukro"—that the basilica is designed to convince people that places like Rome can be replicated in Africa. The basilica is partially obscured from view until one goes through a modest one-story building whose explicit symmetry, through the treatment of its roof, cornice, and edges, forecasts the classicism of the main edifice that lies beyond. Moreover, the scale of Our Lady of Peace Basilica becomes clearer as one ascends the steps leading to the parvis. The cloister of Doric columns dwarfs the individual as one ascends the steps, and the bases of the columns are at eye level. It is a humbling experience as one realizes how small one is compared to the ivory trunks—the columns—of the edifice. Once one reaches the parvis, the structure exhibits itself in component parts that together form a unified whole. The cruciform floor plan resembles others, such as St. Peter's in Rome, but with a circle similar to the Roman Pantheon inscribed inside it. Whereas the cross forms the surrounding parvis, the circle forms the interior of the shrine. The crucifix form of the balcony and its cuffed ceilings read very well. The gigantic shiny Doric columns read both individually and collectively in harmony as they hold the floor of the balcony above, and the flutes of the shafts emphasize the muscles and strength of each column. An ambulatory skylight goes around the main chapel and separates the balcony from the tambour, creating a transition space between the parvis and the chapel. The transition space is further highlighted by a layer of marble that screens the vitrail drum of the shrine at the top, acting both as a protective shield for the vitrail and as a transitional demarcation from the parvis. The articulation of the parvis culminates on the rectangular and linear stained-glass bays that enclose the shrine, especially the enormous doors. The floor of the parvis makes its own statement like any other part of the edifice; it is a cross that spreads out to the four major cardinal points and is lavishly decorated with ivory-white, ochre, and brown marbles on which one sees one's reflection while standing.

The treatment of the floor of the parvis with ivory-white, brown, and ochre marbles is extended to the esplanade to create a sense of continuity of the spaces. A careful observation of the southern facade of the edifice shows six major segments that constitute the superstructure of the basilica in four basic colors: (1) a crucifix platform (a white, solid base) that is raised above the surrounding fields by layers of steps, (2) a cloister of majestic ivory-colored Doric columns that give volume and shade to the platform, (3) an ivory-colored terrace that forms the frieze and the porticoes of the edifice following the crucifix plan, (4) an ivory-colored tambour that is braced with pairs of Corinthian columns, (5) a silver dome with double-spaced oculi on its panels, and (6) a golden copular that is surmounted with a golden cross. This is the fundamental facade of the edifice, except for the northern facade, which has an elaborate esplanade that is defined by the peristyle. Here, the oblong peristyle spreads its arms out as one walks toward it.

The canopy located in the center of the basilica is the first structure one sees when entering the shrine. It has four polished bronze and brass spiraling treelike columns, topped with a light and dark blue chandelier with center and edges trimmed by brilliantly elongated strings of crystals. Here is the cynosure. The chandelier seats under a throne of God. Next is the dome, which rises more than 60 meters with a diameter of 90 meters and undoubtedly is the largest dome in the world. Architect Pierre Fakhoury produced a drawing that shows how the dome of St. Peter's Basilica in Rome could fit comfortably inside the dome of Our Lady of Peace Basilica. It is made primarily of laminated aluminum panels that are installed on a frame of galvanized steel. It is also crowned by a waterproof vitrail at its pinnacle, on which is seated a 38-meter-high stainless-steel golden lantern. Altogether, the dome weighs 320 tons. The glistening burgundy-colored African iroko-wood pews follow the circular form of the internal floor plan, and here, unlike the hall of the mosques whose interiors are to be open and free of furniture for prayers, the pews are wooden gems, delightfully made to reflect the extravagance of the entire project. Next are the vitrails: there is no building on the face of the earth that can boast of such an amount of luxuriously done stained glass as in Our Lady of Peace Basilica, each one finished to narrate a biblical passage. There are 12 rectangular bays of vitrail, 21 meters high by 11 meters wide, and 12 cylindrical bays, 28 meters high by 11 meters wide. In the ambulatory balcony are 12 bays of Apostle windows, 13 meters high by 8 meters wide. The largest of the windows is the Holy Spirit window, 40 meters wide, resulting in a total stained-glass surface area of 7400 square meters. Each window is luxuriantly colored to mimic the African vegetation, especially the palms. As one wanders around the balcony, the giant Corinthian pilasters (a total of 48) that delineate the Apostles window bays read very well. More important, the tinted air from the surrounding glistening variegated vitrail that encloses the shrine makes the interior look like a giant jewelry box. Moreover, one obtains a perspective of the rotunda and its cylindrical pews, especially the drum of the base of the balcony, which is carried by 12 hybridized Ionic columns. A series of 12 ornately cuffed barrel vaults are held by four Doric columns each. Twelve giant Ionic columns contain elevators to whisk people to the balcony. It is indeed a "*merveilleux* (marvelous)" spectacle, as Francois Mathey (1990) has suggested, but the basilica has received mixed reviews from the worldwide press because it was built in a country that was suffering severe economic problems. Some Catholic priests protested the building of the edifice. One priest began a hunger strike when the pope went to consecrate it, confirming the fact that the edifice divided opinions along religious, class, ethnic, and political affiliations.

NAMDI ELLEH

Further Reading

Basilica of Our Lady of Peace, Yamoussoukro: Basilique Notre-Dame de la Paix, B.P. Yamoussoukro, Côte d'Ivoire, 1990

Fakhoury, Pierre, *La Basilique Notre-Dame de la Paix, Yamoussoukro*, Liege: Mardaga, 1990

Mathey, Francois, "Preface" in *La Basilique Notre-Dame de la Paix, Yamoussoukro*, Liege: Mardaga, 1990